Foundations of Bilingual Education and Bilingualism

BILINGUAL EDUCATION & BILINGUALISM

Series Editors: **Nancy H. Hornberger** *(University of Pennsylvania, USA)*
and **Wayne E. Wright** *(Purdue University, USA)*

Bilingual Education and Bilingualism is an international, multidisciplinary series publishing research on the philosophy, politics, policy, provision and practice of language planning, Indigenous and minority language education, multilingualism, multiculturalism, biliteracy, bilingualism and bilingual education. The series aims to mirror current debates and discussions. New proposals for single-authored, multiple-authored, or edited books in the series are warmly welcomed, in any of the following categories or others authors may propose: overview or introductory texts; course readers or general reference texts; focus books on particular multilingual education program types; school-based case studies; national case studies; collected cases with a clear programmatic or conceptual theme; and professional education manuals.

All books in this series are externally peer-reviewed.

Full details of all the books in this series and of all our other publications can be found on https://www.multilingual-matters.com, or by writing to Multilingual Matters, St Nicholas House, 31–34 High Street, Bristol, BS1 2AW, UK.

BILINGUAL EDUCATION & BILINGUALISM: 150

Foundations of Bilingual Education and Bilingualism

8th Edition

Wayne E. Wright and Colin Baker

MULTILINGUAL MATTERS
Bristol • Jackson

DOI https://doi.org/10.21832/WRIGHT0543
Library of Congress Cataloging in Publication Data
A catalog record for this book is available from the Library of Congress.
Names: Wright, Wayne E., author. | Baker, Colin, author.
Title: Foundations of Bilingual Education and Bilingualism / Wayne E. Wright and Colin Baker.
Description: 8th edition. | Bristol; Jackson: Multilingual Matters, [2025] | Series: Bilingual Education & Bilingualism: 150 | Includes bibliographical references and index. | Summary: "The eighth edition of this bestselling textbook has been revised and updated to provide a comprehensive and accessible introduction to bilingualism and bilingual education in an everchanging world. Written in a compact and clear style, the book covers all the crucial issues in bilingualism at individual, group and societal levels" – Provided by publisher.
Identifiers: LCCN 2024055895 (print) | LCCN 2024055896 (ebook) | ISBN 9781836680543 (hardback) | ISBN 9781836680536 (paperback) | ISBN 9781836680567 (pdf) | ISBN 9781836680550 (epub)
Subjects: LCSH: Education, Bilingual. | Education, Bilingual – Great Britain. | Bilingualism. | Bilingualism – Great Britain.
Classification: LCC LC3715 .B35 2025 (print) | LCC LC3715 (ebook) | DDC 370.117/5 – dc23/eng/20241227
LC record available at https://lccn.loc.gov/2024055895
LC ebook record available at https://lccn.loc.gov/2024055896

British Library Cataloguing in Publication Data
A catalogue entry for this book is available from the British Library.

ISBN-13: 978-1-83668-054-3 (hbk)
ISBN-13: 978-1-83668-053-6 (pbk)

Multilingual Matters
UK: St Nicholas House, 31–34 High Street, Bristol, BS1 2AW, UK.
USA: Ingram, Jackson, TN, USA.
Authorised Representative: Easy Access System Europe – Mustamäe tee 50, 10621 Tallinn, Estonia gpsr.requests@easproject.com.

Website: https://www.multilingual-matters.com
Bluesky: https://bsky.app/profile/multi-ling-mat.bsky.social
X: Multi_Ling_Mat
Facebook: https://www.facebook.com/multilingualmatters
Blog: https://www.channelviewpublications.wordpress.com

Copyright © 2025 Wayne E. Wright and Colin Baker.

All rights reserved. No part of this work may be reproduced in any form or by any means without permission in writing from the publisher.

The policy of Multilingual Matters/Channel View Publications is to use papers that are natural, renewable and recyclable products, made from wood grown in sustainable forests. In the manufacturing process of our books, and to further support our policy, preference is given to printers that have FSC and PEFC Chain of Custody certification. The FSC and/or PEFC logos will appear on those books where full certification has been granted to the printer concerned.

Typeset in Sabon and Frutiger by R. J. Footring Ltd, Derby
Printed and bound in the UK by Short Run Press Ltd

Contents

Acknowledgments — vii
Introduction — ix

1. Bilingualism and Multilingualism: Definitions and Distinctions — 1
2. The Measurement of Bilingualism — 21
3. Languages in Society — 47
4. Language Endangerment and Revitalization — 77
5. The Early Development of Bilingualism — 100
6. The Later Development of Bilingualism — 126
7. Bilingualism, Cognition and the Brain (updated by Becky H. Huang) — 151
8. Theories of Bilingualism and the Curriculum — 177
9. Historical Introduction to Bilingual Education in the United States — 190
10. Types of Education for Bilingual Students — 219
11. Education for Bilingualism and Biliteracy — 237
12. The Effectiveness of Bilingual Education — 270
13. Effective Schools and Classrooms for Bilingual Students — 303
14. Literacy, Biliteracy and Multiliteracies for Bilingual and Multilingual Students — 338
15. Support and Assessment of Special Needs and Exceptional Bilingual Students — 366
16. Deaf-Signing People, Bilingualism/Multilingualism and Bilingual Education (by Jean F. Andrews and Stephen M. Nover) — 390
17. Bilingualism and Bilingual Education as a Problem, Right and Resource — 428
18. Bilingualism and Bilingual Education: Ideology, Identity and Empowerment — 449
19. Bilingualism in the Modern World — 465

Glossary — 491
Bibliography — 505
Index — 570

Acknowledgments

The first edition commenced in the early 1990s, when Colin Baker was asked by the founder of Multilingual Matters, Mike Grover, to 'consider writing *the* textbook on bilingual education'. The Multilingual Matters team, past and present, have continually encouraged and facilitated the eight editions: in particular Ken Hall, Marjukka Grover, Tommi Grover, Anna Roderick, Sarah Williams, Ellie Robertson, Laura Jordan, Flo McClelland, Rose Stuart, Rosie McEwan and Stanzi Collier-Qureshy.

Tommi Grover, as Managing Director of Multilingual Matters, was instrumental in bringing in Wayne E. Wright as coauthor with Colin starting with the sixth edition. Tommi's enthusiastic support for this book and the collaboration has been inspirational and instrumental.

Anna Roderick, as Editorial Director and Commissioning Editor, worked closely with us in the compilation and production of this eighth edition. Completion could not have occurred without her enthusiasm for this project and her expertise.

Multilingual Matters perceptively appointed Emeritus Professor Ofelia García (The Graduate Center, City University of New York) as Academic Consultant when this project began in the early 1990s. She has consistently provided wise and judicious advice over many editions. Much gratitude is owed to Ofelia, who helped to shape this book from its beginnings to this edition. *Muchas gracias*.

In the previous seven editions, the following scholars were thanked for their support, reviews, advice and expertise: Panos Athanasopoulos, Hugo Baetens Beardsmore, Claudine Brohy, Jasone Cenoz, Tony Cline, Sarah Compton, Jim Crawford, Jim Cummins, Margaret Deuchar, Jean-Marc Dewaele, Nancy Dorian, Viv Edwards, Peter Garrett, Alsu Gilmetdinova, Tamar Gollan, Nancy Hornberger, Annick De Houwer, Meirion Prys Jones, Sylvia Prys Jones, Juliet Langman, Sharon Lapkin, Christer Laurén, Hilaire Lemoine, Gwyn Lewis, Gigi Luk, Kate Mahoney, Karita Mard, Stephen May, Terri McCarty, Aneta Pavlenko, Trevor Payne, Peter Sayer, Bernard Spolsky, Merrill Swain, Ruth Swanwick, Terry Wiley, Cen Williams, Iolo Wyn Williams, Li Wei, Phil Hiver, Nicholas Subtirelu, Katie Bernstein, Bedrettin Yazan, Anne Margaret Smith, Amy Heineke, Ilana Umansky, Gabrielle Jones, Jennifer Leeman, Greg Poarch, Maite T. Sánchez, Sara Brennan and Rachel O'Neill. Colin Baker also expressed his sincere gratitude to the person who joined as coauthor starting with the sixth edition – Wayne E. Wright.

For this eighth edition, various scholars gave expert advice on improvements and needed developments. We wish to offer our great thanks to the reviewers appointed by Multilingual Matters for their constructive, perceptive and expert analysis and advice on draft chapters: Amanda Kibler, Mary Linn, Luis Poza, Sunny Park-Johnson and Taewoong Kim.

We also wish to express our deep gratitude to Ralph Footring for his outstanding work reformatting, editing, proofreading and typesetting this eighth edition and the previous seventh edition.

Particular and special thanks go to three scholars who joined the seventh edition and again on the eighth edition to lead updates on two key chapters: Becky H. Huang (The Ohio State University) for her excellent revision and thoroughly updated Chapter 7, on bilingualism and the brain, and to Jean Andrews (Lamar University) and Stephen Nover (Gallaudet University), who have provided a brand new and updated Chapter 16, on Deaf bilingual education. It has been a great pleasure to work with these outstanding scholars.

We also owe a debt of gratitude to Purdue University student Michael Sopat Wright for his help with updating and reformatting the bibliography for this eighth edition. We also thank other former students who provided much assistance on the previous edition, including Matthew Kraft and Yeng Yang (University of Texas at San Antonio) and Alsu Gilmetdinova, Sungae Kim, Chen Li, Woongsik Choi and Amanda Shie (Purdue University). The Department of Bicultural–Bilingual Studies at the University of Texas at San Antonio and the Department of Curriculum and Instruction at Purdue University graciously provided funding for these outstanding students, as well as prior support for Wayne through a faculty development leave, course releases and funding for travel to academic conferences, research sites and the Library of Congress.

From Colin: Working on bilingualism has been inspired by my Welsh wife, Anwen, and our three bilingual children (Sara, Rhodri and Arwel). For over 40 years, they have taught me the gifts of bilingualism that go beyond language. Seven greatly loved grandchildren (Ioan Tomos, Joseff Rhys, Lily Enfys, Brenig Iorwerth, Steffan Tomos, Lleucu Gwen and Jac Emyr) allow me to observe and celebrate with them the thrilling experiences of simultaneous bilingualism from birth. *Diolch yn fawr iawn am bopeth*.

From Wayne: I had the privilege of growing up in an English-speaking home with a love for language learning. My parents studied Chinese, Hebrew and Greek. Between myself and my five siblings are varying levels of intermediate to advanced proficiency in Spanish, Chinese, Korean, Khmer (Cambodian), Modern Yucatec Mayan and even Ancient Maya Hieroglyphs. My life as a bilingual continues to be inspired by my dear wife of 30+ years, Phal Mao – a native of Cambodia – and our children, Jeffery Sovan, Michael Sopat and Catherine Sophaline. In addition to Khmer as a language of our home, my wife and children have added further to our linguistic diversity with formal and informal study of Chinese, Khmer, Spanish and French. I've gained much by observing and talking with them about their bilingual and multilingual experiences. សូមអរគុណ!

From Colin & Wayne: The help and support given to us by those mentioned above have been extremely generous and received with great gratitude. However, the responsibility is ours for all that is not perfect.

Colin Baker and Wayne E. Wright

Permissions

Every attempt has been made to contact copyright holders and gain permissions where needed. If there are any omissions, we will be pleased to correct them in the next edition.

Introduction

This eighth edition of *Foundations* is intended as a comprehensive and modern introduction to bilingual education, bilingualism and multilingualism (as bilingualism often includes multilingualism). Written from a multidisciplinary perspective, the book covers a wide range of topics: individual and societal concepts in minority and majority languages; childhood developmental perspectives; general bilingual and multilingual education issues; bilingual and multilingual classrooms; and political and ideological perspectives. Bilingualism and multilingualism relate to, for example, the use of two or more communication systems, identity and personality, globalization and assimilation, thinking and reading, education and employment, politics and culture. All of these, and more, are encapsulated in this book.

In compiling eight editions, increasingly tough decisions have been made as to what to include and exclude, what to present in detail and what to summarize, what assumptions to explore and what to take 'as read'. We have been asked: 'Why don't you put Chapter X earlier?' We agree, everything should be earlier. Other frequently asked questions are 'Why don't you expand on Y?', 'Why don't you leave out Z because it is irrelevant to me?', 'Why can't we have an edition just for our region?' and 'Why isn't a chapter in an earlier edition still included?' What follows are some explanations.

An attempt is made to balance the psychological and the sociological; macro and micro education issues; and the linguistic and the socio-political, with discussion at individual and societal levels. An attempt is also made to be inclusive of major international concerns in bilingualism, multilingualism, and bilingual and multilingual education, based on research evidence and theory. Faced with the many social and political challenges that surround bilinguals and multilinguals, students will find in this book an attempt to analyze constructively those problems and recognize the positive values and virtues of a future multilingual world.

This book starts with definitional, sociological and psychological issues that are essential to understanding bilingual/multilingual children and bilingual/multilingual education. Later discussions of bilingual/multilingual education and classrooms are built on that foundation. However, the book is more than a cross-disciplinary foundation with a series of education layers built on top. Within the boundaries of clarity in writing style and structuring, explicit interconnections are made between chapters.

In writing the book, a constant challenge has been 'From whose perspective?' There are majority language mainstream viewpoints, relatively advantaged minoritized language viewpoints and various disadvantaged minoritized language viewpoints. There are left-wing and right-wing politics, activist and constructivist ideas, debates about globalization, immigration, Europeanization, regionalism and preserving grassroots. The book attempts to represent a variety of viewpoints and beliefs. Where possible, multiple perspectives are shared. Readers and reviewers (including on social media) have kindly pointed out some of the hidden and implicit assumptions made, and kindly provided alternative viewpoints that we have tried to represent faithfully in the text. Where there are conclusions and dominating perspectives, we are responsible.

Another issue has concerned generalization and contextualization. The book is written for an international audience to reflect ideas that transcend national boundaries. The book attempts to locate issues of international generalizability. Unfortunately, space limits discussion of a variety of regional and national language situations. There are many other writings mentioned in the chapters that will provide necessary contextualization. Where particular situations have been discussed (e.g. US debates), it is often because of the thoroughness of documentation, plenty of research evidence and the depth of analysis in the surrounding literature.

In an attempt to make the contents of this book relevant to a variety of contexts and regions, various chapters focus on integrating theories. From one individual research study, it is usually impossible to generalize. A study from Europe may say little about North America. Results on six-year-olds may say nothing about 16- or 60-year-olds. Research on middle-class children speaking French and English in a bilingual school may say little or nothing about children from a lower social class in a bilingual environment where a second language is likely to replace the first language. From a mass of research, but occasionally despite a paucity of research, a theoretical framework will attempt to outline the crucial parameters and processes. Thus, a theoretical framework on a particular area of bilingualism may attempt to do one or more of the following: attempt to explain phenomena; integrate a diversity of (apparently contradictory) findings; locate the key parameters and interactions operating; be able to predict outcomes and patterns of bilingual behavior; be capable of testing for falsification or refinement; express the various conditions that will allow the theory to be appropriate in a variety of contexts.

However, in providing a relatively comprehensive synthesis of bilingualism, multilingualism, and bilingual and multilingual education, the danger lies in suggesting that there is a systematic coherence to the subject. While some teachers and many students want 'recipes' and clear assertions, the current state of our knowledge and understanding rarely provides that clarity. The book therefore attempts to represent contested positions, varied viewpoints and the limitations of research and theory.

New to the Eighth Edition

What are the specific changes in the eight edition? There are many. First, each and every chapter has been updated, and additional revisions have been made based on external expert reviews. Second, to keep up with the latest research, current developments in policy and practice, and recent trends in the field, we have added over 500 new citations and removed many older ones. Third, all demographic and other statistical information has been fully updated with the latest figures available at the time of writing. Fourth, Chapter 16, 'Deaf-Signing People, Bilingualism/Multilingualism and Bilingual Education', has been expanded. Fifth, given the book's growing length with each subsequent edition, we made a deliberate effort to shorten the text by removing some sections and condensing or rewriting others to preserve the most salient points. These cuts made space for many new sections, tables, figures and text boxes.

Sixth, and importantly, there are several new and/or more thoroughly covered topics, including, for example: multilingualism; plurilingualism; multilingual education; national, local, family and individual language policy; dynamic bilingualism; multimodal communication; codeswitching; translanguaging; translanguaging pedagogy; biliteracy; multiliteracies; transdisciplinary approaches to second language acquisition; raciolinguistics; anti-racist education; language and power; language variation; language attitudes; language revival and revitalization; translanguaging among Deaf **signing** students; dynamic assessment; bilingual assessment; gifted and talented education; special education; language proficiency standards; the hybrid, constructed, complex and fluid nature of identity; the gentrification of bilingual education; bilingualism and economic inequalities and advantages; language learning and technology; mobile apps and social media; technology enhanced language proficiency assessments; artificial intelligence (AI); recent developments in and limitations of brain imaging research; and multilingualism on the internet and in information technology.

Important policy developments in the US context are covered, including the Every Student Succeeds Act (ESSA), the Seal of Biliteracy, the Science of Reading (structured literacy), response to intervention, and state consortia for shared English language proficiency standards and assessments (WIDA, ELPA21) and for alternative assessments for disabled students (Dynamic Learning Maps), the US Census, Proposition 58 (California), the LOOK Act (Massachusetts), Arizona Senate Bill 1014 and the Native American Languages Preservation Act. Attention has also been given to expanded discussion of the Common European Framework of Reference and its use across Europe and around the world. Efforts have also been made to update and diversify the global examples of research, policy and practice, with a particular focus on adding examples outside of Europe and North America.

Seventh, several new bolded keywords and their corresponding entries have been added to the book's comprehensive glossary. Eighth, the end-of-chapter resources have been updated and revised, including many recent books as suggested further reading, web resources, discussion questions and study activities. All website links were accessed and checked prior to publication.

Ninth, readers familiar with the previous editions will no doubt have noticed a change in the order of authors. Colin Baker wrote the ground-breaking first edition of this book in 1993, and provided thorough updates as the sole author of *Foundations* through the 5th edition published in 2011. As noted above, Colin extended the honor to Wayne E. Wright to join him as the coauthor of the sixth and seventh editions, and Colin remained actively engaged in the revisions and updates of these two prior editions. With his advancing age, Colin was insistent that Wayne be listed as first author on this eighth edition and on subsequent editions. While substantial revisions have been made across the last three editions, Wayne wishes to stress that the majority of the text continues to contain Colin's original writing and continues to reflect Colin's comprehensive knowledge, experience, insights and vision for this book.

Finally, it is important to acknowledge that the world is changing. We are continuing to recover from the global Covid-19 pandemic which began in the spring of 2020 just as the seventh edition of this book was going to press. We are still discovering the many ways the pandemic disrupted the lives of all people and of educational systems around the world. There is evidence now of a particularly harmful impact on immigrants, language minorities and on Black, Indigenous and other peoples of color. The pandemic laid bare many issues of inequity in schooling, employment, income, internet and technology access, access to health care and other needed services. The impact of the pandemic has been acknowledged and addressed in some of the chapters, but much is still unknown and it will be many years before we fully understand the impact of Covid-19 on bilingual and multilingual students, schools and communities.

Also, the global pandemic of systemic racism was brought to the fore in late spring 2020 following the murder of George Floyd and growing attention to many other unarmed Black men, women and children who died at the hand of police officers and others, which led to protests across the United States and in cities around the world. These movements reminded all that Black Lives Matter and brought renewed attention to the larger underlying issue of systemic racism that deeply impacts the lives of African-Americans and other people of color. This period also saw increased incidents of violence and discrimination against Asian Americans and Pacific Islanders (AAPIs), leading to a grassroots movement calling for the stop of AAPI hate. These movements led to much soul searching and calls for change, including within educational institutions.

These movements were followed by backlash from some corners of the political world through 'anti-wokeness' campaigns targeting what some politicians and their allies believed were inappropriate diversity programs in K-12 schools, institutions of higher education, government initiatives and even private companies. These campaigns have been successful in ending certain programs in some states, and even in banning particular books from classroom, school and community public libraries. Increasingly harsh anti-immigrant rhetoric was prominent during the 2024 US Presidential campaign. As this eighth edition goes to press, we acknowledge the immense suffering of people around the globe due to war, civil and political unrest and violence, and extreme changes in weather.

Nonetheless, this book continues to be grounded in the critical reality of linguistic, cultural, ethnic and racial diversity within multilingual communities around the world, and emphasizes the many benefits of bilingualism and multilingualism and of bilingual and multilingual education. Readers will find in these pages greater attention to issues of race in language and education. We acknowledge these additions may be insufficient, but hope they will contribute to important discussions among readers willing to reflect and effect much-needed changes.

In short, the eighth edition has been systematically revised and updated.

Chapter Organization

At the beginning of the book (Chapter 1) there is a needed introduction to the language used in discussing bilingualism and multilingualism. Not only are important terms introduced, but also key concepts, distinctions and debates which underpin later chapters are presented. There are important dualisms and paradoxes throughout the study of bilingualism and multilingualism: for example, the individual bilingual person as different from groups and societies where bilinguals live; the linguistic view compared with the sociocultural and sociopolitical view; language skills and language competences; codeswitching and translanguaging. Chapters 1 to 8 present foundational issues that precede and influence discussions about bilingual and multilingual education. Before we can sensibly talk about bilingual and multilingual education, we need to tackle questions such as:

- Who are bilinguals and multilinguals?
- How does bilingual and multilingual education fit into minoritized language maintenance, language decline and language revival?
- How does a child become bilingual or trilingual?
- What roles do the home and the neighborhood play in developing bilingualism and multilingualism?
- Does bilingualism have a positive or negative effect on thinking?
- What do we know about bilingualism in the brain?

Chapters 9 to 16 focus on the many aspects of bilingual and multilingual education. They commence with a broad discussion of different types of education programs for bilingual and multilingual students, followed by an examination of the effectiveness of those types. After a focus on systems of bilingual education, the book proceeds to examine bilingual classrooms, multiliteracies and biliteracy, and key bilingual education strategies. The underlying questions are:

- Which forms of bilingual education are more successful?
- What are the aims and outcomes of different types of bilingual education?
- What are the essential features and approaches of a classroom fostering bilingualism?
- What are the key problems and issues of bilingual classrooms?
- Why are Deaf signing people an important group to study both as bilinguals and in terms of bilingual education?

Chapters 17 and 18 are central to understanding bilingualism, multilingualism and bilingual education. They consider the political and cultural dimensions that surround bilingualism in society (and bilingual education in particular). Different views of the overall value and purpose of bilingualism and multilingualism join together many of the threads of the book. The finale of the book (Chapter 19) takes a look at the present and future, with themes of multilingualism and the internet, artificial intelligence, employment, mass media, economy and tourism.

Thus the concluding issues of the book include:

- Why are there different viewpoints about language minorities and bilingual education?
- Why do some people prefer the assimilation of language minorities and others prefer linguistic diversity?
- How do bilingualism and multilingualism relate to particular employment, economic, technological and leisure developments in the modern world?

End-of-Chapter Resources

All of these resources have been updated for this eighth edition.

- **Suggested Further Reading** refers readers who wish to delve deeper into the topics covered in the chapter to recent books.

- **On the Web** directs interested readers to relevant websites, videos, articles, broadcasts, images and other online resources.
- **Discussion Questions** are to engage students in meaningful discussions in small groups, in online forums, or for self-study on chapter topics.
- **Study Activities** (updated) are designed for students wishing to extend their learning by engaging in various practical activities. Such activities are flexible and adaptable. Instructors and students will be able to vary them according to local circumstances.

Finale

To end the beginning. Over eight editions, the book has become a major introduction to bilingual education and bilingualism. It has been studied by thousands of students in many countries of the world. This eighth edition provides a comprehensive update based on the international partnership of two expert scholars. We hope you will read and learn, but also become interested and inspired, enthused and excited by topics that are of increasing importance in a rapidly changing world.

CHAPTER 1

Bilingualism and Multilingualism: Definitions and Distinctions

Introduction

Terminology
Some Dimensions of Bilingualism and Multilingualism

An Individual's Use of Two or More Languages
Language Choice

Bilingual and Multilingual Ability
The Four Language Skills
Degrees of Bilingualism

The Monolingual View of Bilingualism

The Holistic View of Bilingualism

Language Proficiency
Communicative Competence

Conclusion

CHAPTER 1

Bilingualism and Multilingualism: Definitions and Distinctions

Introduction

Since a bicycle has two wheels and binoculars are for two eyes, it would seem that **bilingualism** is simply about two languages. Likewise, **multilingualism** seems simply to be about two or more languages. While bilingualism and multilingualism are different, for the sake of brevity multilingualism will be combined under bilingualism where there is similarity, and distinctions will be made only as necessary.

The aim of this chapter is to show that the ownership of two or more languages is not so simple as having two wheels on a bicycle. Is someone bilingual if they are fluent in one language but less than fluent in their other language? Is someone bilingual if they rarely or never use one of their languages? Is someone multilingual if they have memorized a handful of words and phrases in other languages? Such questions need addressing before other topics in this book can be discussed.

To understand the answers to these questions, it is valuable to make an initial distinction between bilingualism and multilingualism as an individual characteristic, and bilingualism and multilingualism in a social group, community, region or country. Bilingualism and multilingualism can be examined as the possession of the individual. Various themes in this book start with bilingualism as experienced by individual people. For example, a discussion of whether or not bilingualism affects thinking requires research on **monolingual**, bilingual and multilingual individuals.

From sociology, **sociolinguistics**, politics, geography, education and social psychology comes a 'group' perspective. Bilinguals and multilinguals are usually found in groups. Thus, linguists study how the vocabulary and language use of multilingual groups change across time. Geographers plot the density of minoritized language speakers in a country. Educationalists examine bilingual and multilingual educational policy and provision for particular language groups. Such groups may be located in a particular region (e.g. Basques in Spain) or may be scattered across communities (e.g. Arabic-, Chinese- and Spanish-speakers in the United States).

The initial distinction is therefore between bilingualism (and multilingualism) as an individual possession and as a group possession. This is usually termed **individual bilingualism** and **societal bilingualism**. Like most distinctions, there are important links between the two parts. For example, the attitudes of individuals towards a particular minoritized language may affect **language maintenance**, language restoration and downward **language shift** or **language death** in society.

In order to understand the term 'bilingualism', some important distinctions at the individual level are discussed in this chapter. We consider terminology, the ways individuals use two more languages, bilingual and multilingual ability, degrees of bilingualism, monolingual versus holistic views of bilingualism, and communicative competence as a way of conceptualizing language proficiency. An introduction to bilingualism and multilingualism as a group possession (societal bilingualism or pluralingualism) is provided in Chapters 3 and 4.

Terminology

If a person is asked whether they speak two or more languages, the question is ambiguous. A person may be able to speak two languages but may tend to speak only one language in practice. Alternatively, the individual may regularly speak two languages, but competence in one language may be much stronger. Another person may use one language for conversation and one or two others for writing and reading. Yet another may mix their languages in creative ways when communicating with others. An essential distinction is therefore between **language ability** and language *use*. This is sometimes referred to as the difference between degree and function.

Before discussing the nature of language use and abilities, an awareness of often-used terms and distinctions is needed. For example, apart from 'language ability' there are **language achievement, language competence, language performance, language proficiency** and **language skills**. Do they all refer to the same thing, or are there subtle distinctions between the terms? To add to the problem, different authors and researchers sometimes tend to adopt their own specific meanings and distinctions.

Some Dimensions of Bilingualism and Multilingualism

(1) *Ability*. Some bilinguals actively speak and write in both languages (**productive bilingualism** or competence) while others are more **passive bilinguals** and have **receptive bilingualism** (ability to understand or read). For some, an ability in two or more languages is well developed. Others may be moving through the early stages of acquiring a second language as **emergent bilinguals**. Ability is thus on a dimension or continuum, with dominance and development varied across speakers.
(2) *Use*. The **domains** (**contexts**) where each language is acquired and used are varied (e.g. home, school, work, street, phone, online). An individual's different languages may be used for different purposes. For example, one language may be used at home and another in school.
(3) *Balance*. Rarely are bilinguals and multilinguals equal in their ability or use of their two or more languages. Often one language is dominant, and this can change over time.
(4) *Age*. When children learn two languages from birth, this is often called **simultaneous bilingualism**, infant bilingualism or bilingual first language acquisition. If a child learns a second language after about three years of age, the term **sequential bilingualism** (or consecutive bilingualism) tends to be used. Chapters 5 and 6 consider age issues in detail.
(5) *Development*. **Incipient bilinguals** have one well developed language while the other is in the early stages of development. When a second language is developing, this is **ascendant bilingualism**; in contrast, **recessive bilingualism** is when one language is decreasing, resulting in temporary or permanent **language attrition**.
(6) *Culture*. Individuals with two or more languages typically become more or less **bicultural** or **multicultural**. It is possible for someone (e.g. a world language major)

to have high proficiency in two languages but be relatively **monocultural**. A process of **acculturation** accompanies language learning when immigrants and refugees, for example, learn the majority language of the host country. Bicultural competence tends to relate to knowledge of language cultures; feelings and attitudes towards those two cultures; behaving in culturally appropriate ways; awareness and empathy; and having the confidence to express biculturalism (Grosjean, 2019). **Culture**, however, is dynamic; a bilingual's biculturalism is likely to be an ever-shifting hybrid mix of their two cultures, into what some scholars refer to as the 'third space' (Bhabha, 2004).

(7) **Contexts**. Some live in bilingual and multilingual **endogenous communities** that use more than one language on an everyday basis. Others live in more monolingual and monocultural regions and network with other speakers of their languages by phone, email, text messages, video chats, social media or travel for in-person visits. Where there is an absence of a second language community, the context is exogenous (e.g. Russian bilinguals in the United States). Some contexts may be subtractive, where the politics of a country favors the replacement of the home language by the majority language (e.g. Korean being replaced by Japanese in Japan). This particularly occurs among immigrants and refugees in the United States, the United Kingdom and elsewhere. Other contexts are additive, such that a person learns a second language at no cost to their first language, as occurs in **elite** (or **prestigious**) **bilingualism**.

(8) **Choice**. **Elective bilingualism** is a characteristic of individuals who choose to learn a language, for example in the classroom. Elective bilinguals typically come from majority language groups (e.g. English-speaking North Americans who learn French or Arabic; Chinese-speakers in China who learn English). They add an additional language without losing their first language. **Circumstantial bilinguals** learn another language to function effectively because of their circumstances (e.g. as immigrants or refugees). Their first language is insufficient to meet their educational, political and employment requirements, and the communicative needs of the society in which they reside. Circumstantial bilinguals are groups of individuals who must become bilingual to operate in the majority language society that surrounds them. Consequently, their first language is in danger of being replaced by the second language – a subtractive context. The difference between elective and circumstantial bilingualism is important because it immediately locates differences of prestige and status, politics and power among bilinguals.

An Individual's Use of Two or More Languages

Grosjean (2012: 4) proposes a definition of bilingualism that places emphasis on the regular use of languages rather than fluency: 'bilinguals are those who use two or more languages (or dialects) in their everyday lives'. Valdés (2015: 38) offers a similar definition but with a focus on ability to function: 'Bilingual/multilingual individuals … are able to function (i.e. speak, understand, read, or write) even to a very limited degree in more than one language'. Mohanty (2019: 17) defines multilingualism from a communicative point of view: 'the ability of communities or persons to meet the communicative requirements of themselves and their society in normal daily life in two or more languages in their interactions with the speakers of any of these languages'. Kalaja and Melo-Pfeifer (2019: 1) emphasize that 'multilingualism is lived or subjectively experienced', and thus it is important 'to figure out how multilinguals themselves feel about becoming or being multilinguals, or what the different languages and their use might mean to them personally' (Kalaja & Melo-Pfeifer, 2019: 3).

Language use cannot be divorced from its context, nor from the effects of the interactions of different combinations of people in a conversation. Language is not produced in a vacuum; it is enacted in changing dramas. As in the theatre, props, scenery and stage change, so does our use of two or more languages. Communication includes not only the structure of language (e.g. grammar, vocabulary) but also who is saying what, to whom, in which circumstances. One person may have limited linguistic skills but, in certain situations, be successful in communication. Another person may have relative linguistic mastery but, through undeveloped social skills or being in a strange circumstance, be relatively unsuccessful in communication. The social environment where two or more languages function is crucial to understanding bilingual and multilingual usage. Therefore, this section considers the use and function of an individual's languages.

An individual's use of their bilingual ability (**functional bilingualism**) moves into language production across a wide range of everyday contexts and events. Functional bilingualism concerns when, where and with whom people use their two languages. Table 1.1 provides examples of the different targets (people) and contexts (often called domains) where functional bilingualism is enacted in different role relationships.

Table 1.1 Examples of language targets and contexts

Examples of language targets	Examples of language contexts (domains)
Nuclear family	Shopping
Extended family	Visual and auditory media (e.g. TV, radio, videos)
Work colleagues	Printed media (e.g. newspapers, magazines, books)
Friends	Cinema, nightclubs, restaurants, cafés, theaters, concerts
Acquaintances	Work
Neighbors	Correspondence, telephone, official communication
Religious leaders	Clubs, society, organizations, sporting activities
Teachers	Leisure and hobbies
Principals, other leaders	Religious meetings
Bureaucrats	Schools, universities, government agencies
Complete strangers	Internet, information and communications technology (e.g. email,
Local community	texting, video chatting, social media)

Language Choice

Not all bilinguals have regular opportunities to use their languages. In a largely monolingual community there may be little choice about language use from day to day. However, in communities where two or more languages are widely spoken, bilinguals may use their languages on a daily or frequent basis. When bilinguals use both their languages, there is often language choice. If the other person is known to the bilingual as a family member, friend or colleague, a relationship has usually been established through one language. If both are bilingual, they have the option of changing to the other language (e.g. to include others in the conversation) or to use a mix of both languages as they communicate.

If the other person is not known, a bilingual may quickly pick up clues as to which language to use. Clues such as dress, appearance, age, accent and command of a language may suggest which language is appropriate. In multilingual areas of Canada, the United States and other communities around the world, employees dealing with the general public may glance at a person's name on their records to help them decide which language to use.

An individual's attitudes and preferences will influence their choice of language. In a minority/majority language situation, older people may prefer to speak the minoritized language. Teenagers from the **1.5 generation** or second generation, for example, may reject the minoritized language in favor of the majority language because of its higher status and more fashionable image. A comment from a trilingual Chinese-Cambodian refugee high school student who arrived in the United States at a young age illustrates how perceptions about language and **identity** may affect language choice: in describing her language preference, she said, 'English has all the words to describe how I feel'.

In situations where the native language is perceived to be under threat, some bilinguals may seek to avoid speaking the majority or **dominant language** to assert and reinforce the status of the other language. For example, French-Canadians in Québec sometimes refuse to speak English in shops and offices to emphasize the status of French.

Mohanty (2019) observes that language choice for multilingual individuals depends on a host of complex sociolinguistic, political and cultural conditions. He gives the example of the Phulbani District in India, where Kui-speaking Kond tribal members make up the majority of speakers in some areas while non-tribal members in the district speak Odia. Kui and Odia are the main languages spoken within their respective language communities. However, both languages are freely used in the weekly markets and other public domains, along with Hindi, Telugu and borrowed English words (e.g. table, car, school, cinema) in codemixed forms of the languages. Mohanty also gives the example of Indian civil servants, who are often required to learn the majority language of the state to which they are assigned. The civil servants choose to learn the language for a specific purpose and benefit (e.g. to do their job and get paid) but may not personally identify with it. Likewise, Mohanty notes that in many non-English-speaking multilingual societies 'there is a growing group of people with formal education and varying degrees of functional competence in English, mostly for professional use; not all of them identify with the language or have a sense of pride in it' (Mohanty, 2019: 17).

Sayer's (2012) ethnographic work in Oaxaca, Mexico, demonstrates the ambiguities and tensions surrounding language choice as experienced by local (Mexican) English teachers. For example, one teacher explained her hesitancy to help translate for a foreigner struggling to communicate with a pharmacist in terms of a fear of being viewed as a 'show-off' by other Mexican customers. Another teacher described a conflict he had with a guy at a football pitch. During the confrontation (in Spanish), one of the guy's friends came over and said in English 'Hey, take it easy! What's the problem?' The teacher viewed the sudden interjection in English as this guy looking down on him, showing off, 'putting on airs' because he had lived in 'el norte' (the north, i.e. the USA), demonstrating what he called a 'pocho attitude'. The teacher, who was well educated and who had also spent time in the United States, refused to respond to 'pocho guy' in English (despite the urging of friends) because he didn't want to 'drop down to his level'.

Some minoritized languages are mostly confined to a private and domestic role. This happens when a minoritized language has historically been disparaged and deprived of status. In western Brittany in France, for example, many people use the Breton language only in the family and with close friends. They can be offended if addressed by a stranger in Breton, believing that such a stranger is implying they are uneducated and cannot speak French.

An individual may also switch languages, either deliberately or subconsciously, to accommodate the perceived preference of the other participant in the conversation. A language switch may be made because one language is regarded as the more prestigious or more appropriate for the other person. To gain acceptance or status, a person may deliberately and consciously use the majority language. Alternatively, a person may use a minoritized language as a form of affiliation or belonging to a group.

Bilingual and Multilingual Ability

The Four Language Skills

Edwards (2013: 14–15) suggests that 'language repertoire expansion is not a particularly rare feat' and asserts that 'all normally intelligent people can at least become functional in another language'. However, if we confine the question 'Are you bilingual?' to ability in two languages, the issue becomes 'What particular language ability?' There are four basic language domains, abilities or skills: listening, speaking, reading and writing. As Table 1.2 illustrates, these four abilities fit into two dimensions: receptive or productive skills, and oracy or literacy.

Table 1.2 The four basic language skills

	Oracy	Literacy
Receptive skills	Listening	Reading
Productive skills	Speaking	Writing

WIDA (2020), a consortium of US states sharing common English language proficiency standards and assessment, conceptualizes these four basic language skills as modes of communication, with listening and reading as *interpretive* modes of

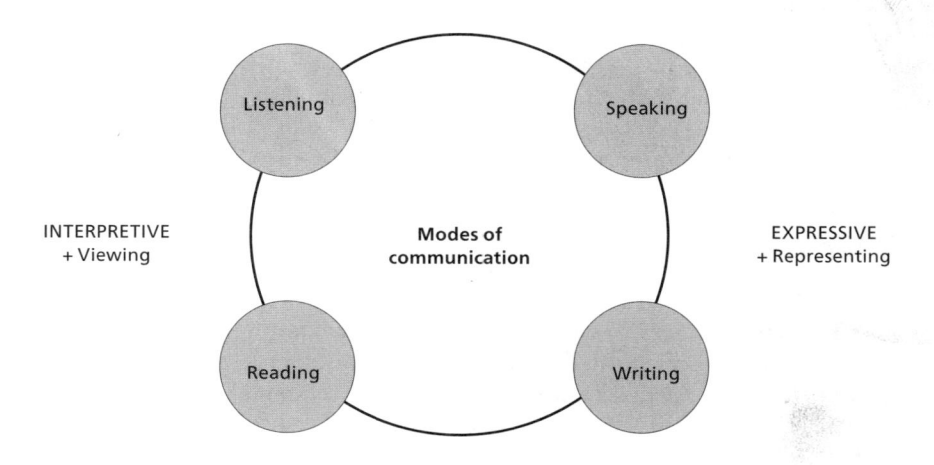

Figure 1.1 Modes of communication (adapted from WIDA, 2020)

communication, and speaking and writing as *expressive* modes of communication. Within a framework of multimodal communication, WIDA broadens the traditional four language skills by adding *viewing* and *representing* as forms of interpretive and expressive modes of communication, respectively (Figure 1.1). Viewing includes the consumption of multimodal materials such as images and videos, while representing includes the production of a visual product that incorporates a combination of print, sound (including speech), images and/or video (Rubin *et al.*, 2022).

Table 1.2 and Figure 1.1 suggest avoiding a simple classification of who is, or is not, bilingual. Some speak a language but do not read or write it. Some listen and read in a language with understanding (passive bilingualism) but do not speak or write it. Some understand a spoken language but do not themselves speak it (receptive bilinguals). To classify people as either bilinguals or monolinguals is thus too simplistic. Or, to return to the opening analogy, the two wheels of bilingualism exist in different sizes and styles. García (2009a) suggests that a more accurate depiction of the complex and dynamic nature of bilingualism is a moon buggy with an intricate wheel system capable of moving in multiple directions across varied terrains. The four basic language skills do not exist in black and white terms. Between black and white are not only many shades of gray: there also exist a wide variety of colors. Each language skill can be more or less developed. Reading ability can range from simple and basic to fluent and accomplished. Someone may listen with understanding in one context (e.g. in shops) but not in another context (e.g. an academic lecture). Many bilingual and multilingual individuals in African and Asian nations speak home languages with no writing systems but may be literate in a standardized variety of a regional, national or international language. And some of these individuals may use the orthography of a national or international language to approximate the sounds of their unwritten home languages so that they can communicate via text messages.

These examples show that the four skills (plus viewing and representing) can be further refined into sub-scales and dimensions. There are skills within skills, such as pronunciation, extent of vocabulary, correctness of grammar, the ability to convey exact meanings in different situations, and variations in style and modalities. However, these skills tend to be viewed from an academic or classroom perspective. Using a language on the street or on social media requires a greater focus on social competence with language (e.g. the idioms and 'lingo' of the street or online community).

The range and types of sub-skills that can be measured are large and debated. Language abilities such as speaking or reading can be divided into increasingly microscopic parts. What in practice is tested and measured to portray an individual's bilingual performance is considered later in the book. What has emerged so far is that a person's ability in two or more languages is multidimensional and will tend to evade simple categorization.

Degrees of Bilingualism

So far, it has been suggested that deciding who is or is not bilingual or multilingual is difficult. Simple categorization is arbitrary and requires a value judgment about the minimum competence needed to achieve a label of 'bilingual'. Therefore, a classic definition of bilingualism such as 'the native-like control of two or more languages' (Bloomfield, 1933) appears too extreme ('native-like'). The definition is also ambiguous; what is meant by 'control' and who forms the 'native' reference group?

At the other extreme is **incipient bilingualism**, which allows people with minimal competence in a second language to squeeze into the bilingual category (Diebold, 1964). Tourists with a few phrases and business people with a few greetings in a second language could be incipient bilinguals. Almost every adult in the world knows a few words in another language. The danger of being too exclusive is not overcome by being too inclusive.

Valdés (2003) suggests that one possibility is to view bilinguals as existing on a continuum, as illustrated in Figure 1.2, where A and B are the two languages. The first letter is the stronger language, and font sizes and case suggest different levels of proficiency in each.

Language A	A 'bilingual' individual's proficiency	Language B
Monolingual in A	A$_b$ A$_b$ Ab Ab Ab AB BA Ba Ba Ba B$_a$ B$_a$	Monolingual in B

Figure 1.2 Bilingual language proficiency continuum

Key: The first letter (A or B) is the stronger language, and font sizes and case (upper and lower) suggest an individual's different levels of proficiency.

However, as Grosjean and Li (2013: 12) point out, 'Bilinguals usually acquire and use their languages for different purposes, in different domains of life, with different people. Different aspects of life often require different languages'. They call these different uses of a bilingual's languages for different functions the 'complementarity principle'. Thus, a bilingual's 'stronger' language may vary depending on the context (e.g. at home, at school, at work, at church, in an online community). Consider, for example, a Latina graduate student in a US university who works as a bilingual teacher and who is active in a Spanish-speaking church. She may feel more competent in English when discussing educational theories, feel competent in both languages when teaching children, and feel more competent in Spanish when discussing and practicing her religion. Thus, a complex but more accurate view of one person's bilingual's proficiency is shown in Figure 1.3.

	Language A	A 'bilingual' individual's proficiency may vary in different contexts	Language B
Context 1	Monolingual	A$_b$ A$_b$ Ab Ab Ab AB BA Ba Ba Ba B$_a$ B$_a$	Monolingual
Context 2	Monolingual	A$_b$ A$_b$ Ab Ab Ab AB BA Ba Ba Ba B$_a$ B$_a$	Monolingual
Context 3	Monolingual	A$_b$ A$_b$ Ab Ab Ab AB BA Ba Ba Ba B$_a$ B$_a$	Monolingual
Context 4	Monolingual	A$_b$ A$_b$ Ab Ab Ab AB BA Ba Ba Ba B$_a$ B$_a$	Monolingual
Etc...			

Figure 1.3 A more complex continuum of an individual's bilingual language proficiency, by context

Key: The first letter (A or B) is the stronger language, and font sizes and case (upper and lower) suggest different levels of proficiency according to changing contexts.

If all of these contexts were broken down by proficiencies across each of the four basic language skills (i.e. listening, speaking, reading and writing), an even more complex, multifaceted representation of bilingualism would emerge. And then consider the additional layers of complexity for multilinguals who use three or more languages across various contexts and domains.

Who is or is not categorized as a bilingual or multilingual will depend on the purpose of the categorization. At different times governments, for example, may wish to include or exclude **language minorities**. Where an **indigenous language** exists (e.g. Irish in Ireland), a government may wish to maximize its count of bilinguals. A high count may indicate government success in **language planning**. In comparison, in a suppressive, **assimilationist** approach, immigrant minoritized languages and bilinguals may be minimized.

There is danger in making arbitrary cut-off points about who is bilingual or not along the competence dimensions. Differences in classification will continue to exist among different authors. One alternative is to move away from the multicolored canvas of proficiency levels to a portrait of the everyday use of the two languages by individuals. The literature on bilingualism, however, frequently spotlights one particular group of bilinguals whose competences in both languages are well developed (i.e. those at AB or BA on the continuum in Figures 1.2 and 1.3). Someone who is approximately equally fluent in two languages across various contexts and domains has been termed an equilingual or ambilingual or, more commonly, a balanced bilingual.

Balanced bilingualism is mostly used as an idealized concept. Rarely is anyone equally competent in two or more languages across all their domains. As the complementarity principle asserts, most bilinguals will use their languages for different purposes and with different people. Balanced bilingualism is also a problematic concept for other reasons. The balance may exist at a low level of competence in the two languages that are nevertheless approximately equal in proficiency. Or, they may have well developed languages but in non-standard varieties that are less valued by the broader society. Or, they may equally draw upon two well developed languages that they frequently mix in creative and effective communicative ways. While these cases are within the literal interpretation of 'balanced bilingual', they are not the sense employed by many researchers on bilingualism.

The implicit idea of balanced bilingualism has often been of 'appropriate' competence in the standard variety of both languages, typically in academic contexts. Thus, a student who can fully understand the delivery of the curriculum in school in either language and effectively participate in classroom activities in either language would be an example of a balanced bilingual.

Given its rarity, is 'balanced bilingualism' of use as a term? While it has limitations of definition and measurement, it has proved to be of value in research and theory (see Chapter 7). However, categorizing individuals into such groups raises the issue of comparisons. Who is judged 'normal', proficient, skilled, fluent or competent? Who judges? Based on what criteria? The danger is in using monolinguals as the point of reference, as considered in the next section of this chapter.

An argument advanced by several scholars (e.g. Grosjean & Li, 2013) is that there are two contrasting views of individual bilinguals. First, there is a monolingual (or fractional) view of bilinguals, which evaluates the bilingual as 'two monolinguals in one person'. The second, holistic (or multi-competence) view argues that the bilingual is not the sum of two complete or incomplete monolinguals, but that he or she has a unique linguistic profile. We now consider these views in more detail.

The Monolingual View of Bilingualism

Despite the fact that between half and two-thirds of the world's population is bilingual to some degree, a monolingual view (or **monoglossic perspective**) of bilingualism takes **monolingualism** as the norm. Thus monolingual English-speakers in countries such as the United States and England may consider bilinguals to be an oddity or inferior. Valdés (2015: 39) explains:

> Embedded with the **discourse** of monolingualism are strong beliefs about (a) the dangers of early bilingualism, (b) the negative effects of 'unbalanced' bilingualism on individuals, and (c) the expectation that the 'true' or 'real' bilingualism will be identical to native speakers in both their languages.

The construct of monolingualism is often taken for granted, unquestioned and assumed to be perfectly normal. Gramling (2016), however, argues that monolingualism itself is a social invention, and traces the history of its development, including its correspondence with the development of nation states. Nevertheless, the ideologies surrounding the invention of monolingualism lead many teachers, administrators and politicians to treat the two languages of a bilingual as separate distinct systems, as if students are two monolinguals in one. Such a view leads to overly simplistic notions of languages simply being added or subtracted from the mind of the bilingual. The monolingual view is closely associated with the **language-as-a-problem orientation**, leading to education programs that either restrict the use of the home language or use it only temporarily, to transition students as quickly as possible to the dominant school language (Hornberger, 2017; Ruiz, 1984). Even in some stronger forms of bilingual education, a monolingual view leads to an insistence on the strict separation of the students' languages by time, day or subject (see Chapter 10).

One expectation from this fractional viewpoint is for bilinguals to show a proficiency comparable to that of a monolingual in both languages. If that proficiency does not exist in both languages, especially in the majority language, then bilinguals may be denigrated and classified as inferior. This perceived lack of proficiency is often determined by standardized language proficiency tests in English or other languages spoken by the students, in which their scores are compared with those of monolingual speakers. This results in misleading and deficit-oriented labels to describe students. One label from the 1970s describes such students as **semilinguals** (or double semilinguals), suggesting students lack vocabulary, grammar knowledge and ability to express themselves fully in either language. MacSwan *et al.* (2002) documented a common practice in many US schools of labeling **Latinx** immigrant children as both 'non-English speaking' and 'non-Spanish-speaking', based on the results of language proficiency tests, and of referring to such students as 'non-nons'. More recently, the label 'long-term English language learner' (LTELL) has been commonly used across the United States to describe students classified as English language learners for five or more years (Menken & Kleyn, 2010; Olsen, 2010). These labels evoking the construct of 'semilingualism' from a monolingual view of bilingualism are unfair and are more politically and often racially motivated than accurate or commonplace (Flores, 2020b; Flores *et al.*, 2015; García *et al.*, 2022).

A number of scholars have pointed out the major problems with 'semilingualism' and its associated terms (Cushing, 2022; Edelsky *et al.*, 1983; García *et al.*, 2022; MacSwan, 2000; MacSwan & Rolstad, 2003; MacSwan *et al.*, 2002; Menken & Kleyn, 2010; Wiley, 2005; Wiley & Rolstad, 2014). First, these terms have disparaging and belittling overtones that invoke expectations of underachievement and failure. Second, if languages are relatively undeveloped, the origins may not be in bilingualism *per se*, but in the economic, political and social conditions that create such underdevelopment. Third, as noted above, most bilinguals use their languages for different purposes in different contexts. Thus, a person may be competent in some domains but not in others. Fourth, the educational tests used to assess language proficiencies measure only standard varieties of languages and typically measure only a small, unrepresentative sample of a person's daily language behavior (see Chapter 2). Finally, these terms often serve to misrepresent and marginalize the language practices of language minoritized communities of color (Flores, 2019). For example, Flores *et al.* (2015: 129) interviewed Latinx New York high school students officially classified as LTELLs who strongly disagreed with the school's classification of their language proficiency:

Candido: We already know English and all that stuff.
Claudia: For most of us, it's like our first language, I mean our main language.
Yamile: 'Cuz they think we don't know much English, but we do. Just 'cuz we know another language.

Flores *et al.* (2015: 130) argue that these 'are not students lacking language, but (emergent) bilinguals with a repertoire that allows them to maneuver multiple languages and contexts in ways that are complex and dynamic'. Flores and Rosa (2015) argue the use of such terminology marginalizes the language practices of language minoritized students and thus represent raciolinguistic ideologies. **Raciolinguistics** considers ideologies surrounding language, race and power, and how they are related and intersect (Cushing, 2022; Flores & Rosa, 2023; Rosa, 2019). The focus on race is important, given that bilinguals and multilinguals within a given society are often racialized minorities, and language often shapes our ideas about race (Alim *et al.*, 2016). Flores and Rosa (2015: 167) describe how the language practices of racialized minorities are constantly judged by the 'white gaze and the white listening subject'. Cushing (2022: 245) asserts that 'a raciolinguistic perspective rejects that any speech can be "limited" or "broken" and instead relocates critical attention towards the limited and broken hearing practices of the white listening subject'. As Ortega (2019: 31) explains:

> Raciolinguistics offers a lens through which to understand that it is deep social inequities, not language per se, that shape whose multilingualism is accepted and praised and supported, whose multilingualism is feared as a problem to be remedied or even eradicated, and whose multilingualism remains invisible.

These criticisms do not detract from the fact that people do differ in their language abilities. This may not be the result of being bilingual or multilingual. Economic and social factors or educational provision may, for example, lead to differences in individual linguistic repertoires. Rather than highlight an apparent 'deficit' in language development, the more equitable and positive approach is to emphasize that, under the right conditions, students are capable of developing high levels of competence in a standardized named language variety. Instead of concentrating negatively on a 'language deficit', a better approach is to locate the causes in, for example, the type of language tests used, material deprivation, or the type and quality of schooling, and not in language itself (see Chapters 9, 15 and 17). Second language users are not deficient communicators. They need to be seen as legitimate speakers of a language in their own right.

Students in the process of developing proficiency in a new language may be more accurately viewed as emergent bilinguals (García, 2009a). 'Emergent bilinguals' is a wide-ranging term accenting future language development towards fuller bilingualism. The term is preferred by many to labels such as **English language learner** (**ELL**) and the deficit-oriented label **limited English proficient** (**LEP**) students, because these labels do not acknowledge the students' other language(s). While 'emergent bilinguals' suggests a more holistic view of bilinguals, there is no obvious end-point when 'emergent' finishes. Some use 'advanced bilinguals' to address this limitation (e.g. Smith & de Oliveira, 2019). **Multilingual learners** has gained popularity as a far more general and inclusive term which emphasizes that students anywhere in the process of developing one or more new languages or dialects are indeed multilingual. Wright (2025) notes the shortcomings of each label with concern that more recent labels, while more inclusive, lack precision in identifying students who may be legally entitled to bilingual or other education models tailored to their linguistic and academic development strengths and needs. Kanno *et al.* (2024: 1) warn that debates about which label to use can draw attention away from the political and educational systems 'that position and frame linguistically minoritized students in a deficit light in the first place'.

The Holistic View of Bilingualism

Those who take a holistic or **heteroglossic perspective** view bilingualism as the norm, and treat the languages of a bilingual as interconnected and coexisting, or as making up a single linguistic system (García & Li Wei, 2014). Hopewell and Escamilla (2015: 39) explain:

> Holistic understandings of bilingualism are grounded in the idea that what is known and understood in one language contributes to what is known and understood in the other, and that all languages contribute to a single and universally accessible linguistic and cognitive system.

García (2009a) introduced the term **dynamic bilingualism** to focus on the ways bilinguals draw on the range of features associated with socially constructed named languages within their linguistic repertoire in complex and dynamic ways as they communicate with others and engage in collaborative tasks. As explained by García and Li Wei (2014: 13–14):

> Unlike the view of two separate systems that are added (or even interdependent), a dynamic conceptualization of bilingualism goes beyond the notion of two autonomous languages, of a first language (L1) and a second language (L2), and of **additive** or **subtractive bilingualism**. Instead, dynamic bilingualism suggests that the language practices of bilinguals are complex and interrelated; they do not emerge in a linear way or function separately since there is only one linguistic system.

García (2009a) extended Welsh educator Cen Williams's (1994) concept of **translanguaging** to describe the natural ways bilinguals use their languages in their everyday lives as they make sense of their bilingual worlds. In contrast to 'monolingual view' practices that insist on strict separation of languages in the classroom, a holistic dynamic view of bilingualism calls for the use of translanguaging as a pedagogical tool for teaching and learning (see Chapter 13).

The languages of bilinguals may also be viewed positively as multicompetences (Grosjean & Li, 2013). Grosjean (2008) uses an analogy from the world of athletics, and asks whether we can fairly judge a sprinter or a high-jumper against a hurdler. The sprinter and high-jumper concentrate on one event and may excel in it. The hurdler concentrates on two different skills, trying to combine a high standard in both. With only a few exceptions, the hurdler will be unable to sprint as fast as the sprinter, or jump as high as the high-jumper. This is not to say that the hurdler is a worse athlete than the other two. Any judgment of who is the best athlete makes little sense. This analogy suggests that comparing the language proficiency of a monolingual with a multilingual's proficiency is similarly unjust.

There is sometimes a political reality that deters the blossoming of a holistic view of the bilingual. In Australia, much of Canada, the United States and the United Kingdom, the dominant English-speaking monolingual politicians and administrators tend not to accept a different approach or standard of **assessment** (one for monolinguals, another for bilinguals). There is also the issue of preparation for the employment market. In countries like Wales, where first-language Welsh-speaking children compete in a largely English-language job market against monolingual English-speakers, the dominant view is that they should be given the same English assessments at school.

Yet a bilingual is a complete linguistic entity, an integrated whole. Levels of proficiency in a language may depend on in which contexts (e.g. street and home) and how often that language is used. We turn next to considerations of language proficiency.

Language Proficiency

So far, this chapter has centered on the variety of language abilities and the danger of categorization using a small or biased selection of language sub-skills. One issue has been whether a wide variety of sub-skills can be reduced to a small number of important dimensions. Oller and Perkins (1980) have suggested that there exists a single factor of **global language proficiency**. This view is associated with attempts to quantitatively measure language proficiency through standardized tests. It has led to the view of a singular **academic language proficiency** essential for success in the classroom.

The idea of a single factor of global language proficiency is contentious, as the evidence indicates that there are both global and specific aspects of language proficiencies. Most (but not all) language tests narrowly focus on language use in academic contexts (see Chapter 2). Such tests leave qualitative differences between people unexplored. Out-of-school communicative profiles of people are relatively ignored.

This narrow view of a singular form of 'academic language proficiency' led to the proposal that there is a conceptually distinct category of conversational competence (Cummins, 2000b). This includes the ability to hold a simple conversation in the shop, on the street or on the playground. This dichotomy suggests that conversational language competence may be acquired fairly quickly (in two to three years), but it is not enough to cope with classroom instruction. Academically related language competence in a second language may take from five to eight years or longer to acquire. This divide between 'conversational' and 'academic' language proficiency has been called a false dichotomy and a misrepresentation of the complex nature of language acquisition and proficiency (Flores, 2019; Wiley & Rolstad, 2014). This debate is considered in detail in Chapter 8.

Table 1.3 Communicative competence

Competences	Description
Grammatical competence	Is concerned with sentence-level grammatical forms, the ability to recognize the lexical, morphological, syntactic and phonological features of a language and to make use of these features to interpret and form words and sentences
Discourse competence	Is concerned with the interconnectedness of a series of utterances, written words and/or phrases to form a text, a meaningful whole. Includes both bottom-up and top-down text processing and concerns with text coherence and cohesion
Sociocultural/pragmatic competence	An understanding of the social context in which language is used: the roles and relationships of the participants, the information they share and the function of the interaction
Strategic competence	The coping strategies used in unfamiliar contexts, with constraints due to imperfect knowledge of rules or limiting factors in their application, such as fatigue or distraction
Metalinguistic competence	Knowledge of linguistic/grammatical concepts and functions, and the ability to use linguistic terminology to describe and discuss them

Communicative Competence

The language theories of the 1960s tended to center on language skills and components. The skills comprise listening, speaking, reading and writing, and the components of knowledge comprise grammar, vocabulary, **phonology** and graphology. These earlier models did not indicate how skills and knowledge were integrated. For example, how does listening differ from speaking? How does reading differ from writing? Earlier models fail to probe the competence of other people in a conversation. In a conversation, there is negotiation of meaning between two or more people. Real communication involves anticipating a listener's response, understandings and misunderstandings, sometimes clarifying one's own language to ensure joint understanding, plus the influence of different degrees of status and power between people.

Earlier models tended to be purely linguistic and to ignore the social contexts where language is used. A more sociolinguistic approach examines actual content and context of communication, called 'speech acts' or the 'ethnography of communication'. This approach includes looking at the rules of dual language use among bilinguals, their shared knowledge in conversation, and the culturally, socially and politically determined language norms and values of bilingual speech events.

Various holistic models of language competence have been developed. One of the most widely accepted is **communicative competence**. This view of language proficiency was first proposed by Hymes (1972) in direct contrast to Chomsky's cognitive theory of language, with its narrow focuses on the ability of native-speakers to produce grammatically correct sentences. Hymes, a leading founder of sociolinguistics, argued that language proficiency considerations must include the types of knowledge speakers need to communicate competently with others in a given **speech community** (Richards & Rodgers, 2014). These foundational notions of competence have been the subject of recent critique from a raciolinguistic perpective. Flores and Rosa (2023) argue that both Chomsky's construct of linguistic competence and Hymes's construct of communicative competence reproduce raciolinguistic ideologies by framing the language practices and modes of communication of racialized populations as deficient when compared with idealized (racially unmarked) white majority linguistic norms.

Canale and Swain (1980) further developed Hymes's construct by identifying and describing four dimensions of communicative competence: grammatical, discourse, sociocultural and **strategic competence**. Richards and Rodgers (2014) note that the many attempts to refine and add dimensions to the notion of communicative competence since it was introduced are evidence of its usefulness. Communicative competence provides the foundation for the **communicative language teaching** (**CLT**) approach prevalent today and has been influential on other widely used communicative frameworks, including the standards for foreign language learning of the American Council on the Teaching of Foreign Languages (ACTFL), the Common European Framework of Reference for Languages and the Canadian Language Benchmarks (Duff, 2014). Table 1.3 provides a description of the various dimensions of communicative competence, drawn from Savignon (2001: 17–18) and the Stanford Center for Assessment, Learning, and Equity (2016: 2).

Note that this model of communicative competence is inclusive of the types of linguistic knowledge reflected in earlier models of language proficiency (i.e. grammatical and discourse competence), but here the emphasis is on the use of these skills for meaningful communication within the social context, hence the integration with sociocultural/pragmatic competence. This competence is sensitive to the context where language is used, ensuring that language is appropriate to the person or the situation. This may entail sensitivity to differences in local dialect, sensitivity to differences in **register** (e.g. the register of boardroom, baseball, bar and bedroom). Sociocultural competence may also refer to sensitivity to speaking in a native-like or natural way. This will include cultural variations in grammar and vocabulary (e.g. Black English). Another part of sociocultural competence is the ability to interpret cultural references and figures of speech. Sometimes, to understand a particular conversation, one needs cultural understanding of a specific language. A Welsh figure of speech such as 'to go round the Orme' (meaning 'to be long-winded') is fully understandable only within local northern Welsh cultural idioms. Similarly, students new to English may find western cultural idioms such as 'piece of cake' (meaning 'a simple or easy task to do') confusing, even when they know the meaning of each word. Sociocultural competence also includes the kind of knowledge needed in greeting people and leave-taking, in expressing feelings and persuading, matters of politeness in a particular context, the style and formality of language, and even body language (e.g. smiles, eye contact) and the use of silence.

Another important issue within the social context is how speakers cope communicatively in less familiar contexts when confronted with unfamiliar vocabulary or expressions or when they need to express an idea for which they lack the precise vocabulary or structures. Strategic competence addresses strategies learners may use to compensate for gaps in their knowledge, such as requesting their interlocutors to repeat or speak more slowly, or asking for clarification. Learners may paraphrase where unknown words and structures would otherwise be required (e.g. substituting 'long soft chair' for the unknown word 'sofa'). **Metalinguistic competence** (or **awareness**) provides students with the terminology they need to reflect on and talk about their language learning and use.

The holistic view of language proficiency reflected in the construct of communicative competence has led to attempts to create language proficiency assessments that measure communicative ability (Purpura, 2017). The emphasis has therefore moved over time from the linguistic to the communicative, to interactional competence and the adaptivity of a person in using two or more languages. Since competence in a language is viewed as an integral part of language performance and not abstracted from it, measuring language competence cannot just use pencil-and-paper or computer-based tests, but also needs to investigate the language of genuine communication. Instead of tests that are artificial and stilted (e.g. language dictation tests), communicative performance **testing** involves creative, unpredictable, contextualized conversation. However, predicting 'real world' performance from such tests, and the 'one-sidedness' that ignores the reality that conversations are jointly constructed and negotiated, remains problematic. This suggests that it will be difficult to measure communicative proficiency in an unbiased, comprehensive, valid and reliable way.

Discussions of language competence often move to questions about the extent to which we can measure a bilingual's performance in their two languages. How can we portray when, where and with whom people use their languages? What are the problems and dangers in measuring bilinguals? These questions provide the themes for the next chapter.

Conclusion

Defining exactly who is or is not bilingual or multilingual is essentially elusive and may ultimately be impossible. Some categorization, however, is often necessary and helpful to make sense of the world. Therefore, categorizations and approximations may be required. Simple, narrow definitions such as 'native-like control of two languages' (Bloomfield, 1933) offer little help as they are intrinsically arbitrary and ambiguous. Overly broad definitions that include anyone who can utter a few words or phrases in another language are also of little use.

A more helpful approach may be to locate important distinctions and dimensions surrounding the terms 'bilingualism' and 'multilingualism' that help to refine our thinking. The fundamental distinction is between bilingual ability and bilingual usage. Some bilinguals may be fluent in two languages but rarely use both. Others may be much less fluent but use their languages regularly in different contexts. Bilinguals frequently translanguage, drawing from their linguistic repertoire in creative and effective ways to communicate with other bilinguals. Many other patterns are possible. Languages are not static. Bilingualism is dynamic. Students growing up with or learning two or more languages are 'emergent bilinguals' or 'multilingual learners'.

Profiling a person's use of two or more languages raises questions about when, where and with whom. This highlights the importance of considering domain or context. As individuals move from one situation to another, so may the languages being used, in terms of type (e.g. Spanish, English or translanguaging), content (e.g. vocabulary) and style. Over time and place, an individual's languages are never static but ever changing and evolving.

In terms of ability in two or more languages, the four basic domains are listening, speaking, reading and writing. It is possible to fragment each of these proficiency domains into more detailed dimensions (e.g. pronunciation, vocabulary, grammar, meaning and style). These dimensions can themselves be further dissected and divided. Creating a multidimensional, elaborate structure of bilingual or multilingual proficiency may make for sensitivity and precision. However, ease of conceptualization and brevity require simplicity rather than complexity. Therefore, simple categorization is the paradoxical partner of complex amplification. This chapter has considered problematic categories, such as balanced bilingualism, semilingualism, linguistic competence, long-term English language learners, and monolingual (one-factor) views of language ability. These categories have received some depth of discussion and critical response in the research literature. As will be revealed in later chapters, these categories also relate to central research on bilingualism and bilingual education. This chapter has considered theories of the structure of language competence. In particular, the focus has been on linking a linguistic view of language competence with a social communicative competence view. Language can be decomposed into its linguistic constituents (e.g. grammar, vocabulary). It is also important to consider language as a means of making relationships and communicating information. This important dualism will follow us through the book: ability and use; the linguistic and the social; competence and communication.

Key Points in This Chapter

- There is a difference between bilingualism/multilingualism as an individual possession and as two or more languages operating within a group, community, region or country.
- At an individual level, there is a distinction between a person's ability in two or more languages and their use of those languages.
- Bilinguals and multilinguals typically use their languages with different people, in different contexts and for different purposes.
- Language domains are listening, speaking, reading and writing.
- Balanced bilinguals, with equal and strong competence in their two languages, are rare.
- Dynamic bilingualism focuses on the ways bilinguals draw on their linguistic repertoire in complex and dynamic ways as they communicate with others.
- The monolingual view of bilingualism sees bilinguals as two monolinguals inside one person.
- The holistic view of bilingualism sees bilinguals as a complete linguistic entity, an integrated whole.
- Translanguaging describes the natural ways bilinguals use their languages in their everyday lives as they make sense of their bilingual worlds.
- Raciolinguistics considers the intersections of race, language and power.
- Language competence includes not only linguistic competence (e.g. vocabulary, grammar) but also competence in different social and cultural situations with different people.

Suggested Further Reading

- Cushing, I. (2022) *Standards, Stigma, Surveillance: Raciolinguistic Ideologies and England's Schools* Palgrave Macmillan.
- Flores, N. (2024) *Becoming the System: A Raciolinguistic Genealogy of Bilingual Education in the Post-Civil Rights Era*. Oxford University Press.
- Grosjean, F. (2021)*: Life as a Bilingual: Knowing and Using Two or More Languages*. Cambridge University Press.
- Kalaja, P. and Melo-Pfeifer, S. (eds) (2025) *Visualising Language Students and Teachers as Multilinguals: Advancing Social Justice in Education*. Multilingual Matters.
- Otcu-Grillman, B. and Borjian, M. (eds) (2022) *Remaking Multilingualism: A Translanguaging Approach*. Multilingual Matters.

On the Web

- *International Journal of Bilingual Education and Bilingualism*
  https://www.tandfonline.com/toc/rbeb20/current
- *International Mother Language Day*
  https://www.un.org/en/observances/mother-language-day
- *International Multilingual Research Journal*
  https://www.tandfonline.com/loi/hmrj20
- *Journal of Multilingual and Multicultural Development*
  https://www.tandfonline.com/toc/rmmm20/current
- Multilingualism – United Nations
  https://www.un.org/sg/en/multilingualism/index.shtml

Discussion Questions

(1) Do you consider yourself and/or people known to you to be bilingual or multilingual? Would you describe yourself, or someone known to you, as 'balanced' in ability and use of two or more languages or somewhere else along the continuum represented in Figure 1.2? Which language or languages do you think in? Does this change in different contexts, as represented in Figure 1.3? In which language or languages do you dream, count numbers, pray and think aloud?

(2) What are the differences between taking a monolingual versus a holistic view of bilingualism? Discuss some of the common beliefs or practices in your local area regarding bilingualism and which view they seem most closely aligned with.

(3) View the YouTube video 'One Semester of Spanish – Love Song' (https://youtu.be/ngRq82c8Baw?si=clG0So1T6syZrSYF). Would you argue that Mike is bilingual? Discuss why or why not, based on the various criteria for bilingualism described in this chapter. How would you also describe Mike's understanding/portrayal of Hispanic culture?

Study Activities

(1) This activity can be based on self-reflection or you may wish to interview someone who is bilingual or multilingual. Make a table or diagram to illustrate how one person's bilingual or multilingual ability and language usage have changed and developed since birth. Write down how different contexts have affected that change and development. The diagram or table should illustrate the life history of someone's languages, indicating changes over time and over different contexts.

(2) In a school with which you are most familiar, find out how students are labeled and categorized in terms of their languages. Who applies what labels? Which students are seen positively and negatively? Do labels have consequences? Is there interest in the language competences and language use of multilingual students?

(3) Explore the linguistic diversity of an area of the United States using the 'explore' tool from the US Census Bureau (https://data.census.gov/cedsci/). On the front page, enter a US county, city, town or zip code into the search bar. Click on relevant results such as 'ACS demographic and housing estimates', 'Total population', 'Language spoken at home', 'Limited English speaking households' and 'Characteristics of people by language spoken at home' (you may need to click on 'view all' links or select the 'Populations and People' topic from the left side bar, then select 'Language Spoken at Home'). Report on your findings and discuss what these demographics reveal about the linguistic diversity of the community.

CHAPTER 2

The Measurement of Bilingualism

Introduction

Ambiguity of Language Assessment Terminology

Purposes and Uses of the Measurement of Bilinguals
Measuring Languages in a Population
Selection
Summative, Formative and Dynamic Assessments
Norm- and Criterion-Referenced Language Tests

Communicative Language Testing

English Language Proficiency Testing for College Admission

Common European Framework of Reference

Examples of the Measurement of Bilingualism in Research
Language Background Scales
Language Balance and Language Dominance Measures
Self-rating of Proficiency
Limitations in Measuring Language

A Political View of Language Testing

Bilingual Assessment and Testing

Language Censuses
Languages in the United States Census and the American Community Survey
Limitations of Language Censuses

Conclusion

CHAPTER 2
The Measurement of Bilingualism

Introduction

The topic of measuring bilingualism and multilingualism both elaborates and illuminates the previous discussion about definitions, dimensions and distinctions. Problems of defining bilinguals are illustrated by the measurement and categorization of such individuals and groups. This chapter clarifies the different reasons for measuring bilinguals and multilinguals. This occurs not only in education but also in society (e.g. censuses). Illustrations are then given of such measurement as well as ways of profiling the **language ability** and use of individuals and language groups. It is important to develop a critical awareness of language measurement, both of the internal limitations of measurement and of the politics surrounding language **testing**.

It is customary to try to categorize in simple terms the complexity of individual differences in **bilingualism** (e.g. 'he's fluent in French', 'she lacks proficiency in English' or 'I can understand a little Japanese'). We attempt to make sense of our world by continual classification. People are constantly compared and contrasted (e.g. language, race, ethnicity, gender, religion, education level, socioeconomic status). Yet the simplification of categorization often hides the complexity of individuality. Individual differences are reduced to similarities (e.g. 'Spanish-speakers', 'English language learners', 'multilingual learners', 'heritage learners', 'level 2 students'). Yet over-complexity can be unwelcome and confusing. The measurement of bilinguals attempts to locate similarities, order and pattern.

Ambiguity of Language Assessment Terminology

The **terminology** associated with language tests and **assessments** is often confusing and ambiguous. **Language skills** tend to refer to highly specific, observable, measurable, clearly definable components such as pronunciation, spelling or handwriting. **Language competence** is a broad and general term, used particularly to describe an underlying system of an inner, mental representation of language, something latent rather than overt. **Language performance** becomes the outward evidence for language competence. By observing general language comprehension and production, language competence may be inferred. Language ability and **language proficiency** tend to be used more as umbrella terms and therefore somewhat ambiguously. For some, language ability is a general, latent disposition, a determinant of eventual language success. For others, it tends to be used as an outcome, similar to but less specific than language skills, providing an indication of current language level. Similarly, language proficiency is sometimes used synonymously with language competence; at other times as a specific, measurable outcome from language testing. However, both language proficiency and language ability are distinct from **language achievement** (attainment), which is usually seen as the outcome of formal instruction. Language proficiency and language ability are, in contrast, viewed as the product of a variety of mechanisms: formal learning, informal non-contrived language acquisition (e.g. on the street) and individual characteristics such as 'intelligence'.

These terms represent different language-related constructs that can potentially be measured. To avoid ambiguity, these constructs need to be well defined by those who attempt to measure them. Ambiguity leads to lack of **validity** and **reliability** in testing, and decreases 'fitness for purpose'. Validity refers to the accuracy of a test in measuring what it purports to measure; reliability refers to the consistency with which a test measures whatever it is measuring (Popham, 2025). Precise definitions are needed to ensure the validity and reliability of language-related measurements (Mahoney, 2024).

Purposes and Uses of the Measurement of Bilinguals

The measurement of **bilinguals** can take place for a variety of purposes and uses and with different methods and instruments (Mahoney, 2024). It is valuable to differentiate between overlapping aims and understand the uses of different types of testing instruments.

Measuring Languages in a Population

One purpose of measurement may be to determine the distributions of people in a given population. An example is the use of a census questionnaire (instrument) requesting information about ability or usage in two or more languages (e.g. in the United States, Canada, Ireland). Such census data estimates the size and distribution of bilinguals in a particular area. For example, the California Department of Education conducts an annual survey to determine the number of speakers of over 125 specific languages among over 5.8 million pre-K-12 students. However, schools report over 12,000 speakers of other non-English languages, suggesting there could be many other languages. Linguists map the proportion and geographic location of regional and minoritized language groups. For example, linguists associated with Ethnologue attempt to document details on over 7,000 languages around the world (https://www.ethnologue.com).

Selection

Bilinguals can be distinguished as a 'separate' group for selection purposes. For example, a school may wish to allocate children to classes, sets, streams, groups or tracks based on their bilingual proficiency or language background. Bilinguals may be assessed for placement in bilingual, **sheltered content instruction**, CLIL (content and language integrated instruction), mainstream or **special education** classes (see Chapter 15). A different example is measuring bilinguals at the outset of research. An investigation may require the initial formation of two or more groups (e.g. 'balanced' bilinguals, 'partial' bilinguals and **monolinguals**).

Summative, Formative and Dynamic Assessments

Language assessments may be used for summative or formative purposes, particularly in classrooms and schools (Gottlieb, 2024; Phakiti & Leung, 2024). **Summative assessment** means 'totaling up' to indicate the destination a student has reached in their language-learning journey, for example at the end of a semester or a school year. When measuring the current performance level of a student, a wide variety of language proficiency and achievement tests are available (e.g. reading comprehension, vocabulary). Such tests may be used in schools to measure the four basic language skills. In multilingual contexts, particularly in schools with bilingual programs, emphasis is often on measuring proficiency in both the majority language and the minoritized languages (i.e. those used for instruction).

A test or assessment instrument that gives feedback (and feed-forward) during learning, and aids further development, is a **formative assessment**. In England, formative assessment is commonly referred to as 'assessment for learning' (AfL) (Leung et al., 2021). An example would be an assessment of a student's oral presentation or evaluation of a student's writing. The results are used to determine the student's strengths as well as to plan subsequent lessons focused on areas of needed improvement. MacDonald et al. (2015: xi–xii) make a distinction between *formative assessment* and *assessment for formative purposes*: traditionally, *formative assessment* is understood to occur 'in the midst of instruction and compares students' ongoing progress to possible trajectories of learning' and thus 'can help identify the most productive next steps of instruction'; in contrast, *assessment for formative purposes* 'is a much broader category of tools and processes that could be used to shape instruction over time'.

Summative and informative assessments are more effective when they are interconnected (Phakiti & Leung, 2024). Thus, any type of language assessment could be a formative assessment if the results are used to analyze and shape language instructional practices. For example, a student may be profiled on a precise breakdown of language skills to provide facilitative feedback to the teacher that directly leads to action. If the test reveals areas where a child's language needs developing, there can be immediate intervention.

Leung et al. (2021) describe the development of the English as an Additional Language (EAL) Assessment Framework for use in schools in England and internationally, which features rating scales for the four basic language skills across five bands of English proficiency (Band A, 'New to English', to Band E, 'Fluent') that teachers can use for daily formative assessments and for more formal summative assessments. Gottlieb (2024) provides a comprehensive model of assessment *as, for* and *of* learning for multilingual learners. In the United States the WIDA and the English Language Proficiency Assessment for the 21st Century (ELPA21) are state assessment consortia with shared formative and summative assessments.

The concept of **dynamic assessment** goes beyond static notions of formative and summative assessment by incorporating interactive teaching into the assessment process (Alsaadi, 2021; Kushki & Nassaji, 2024). As described by Poehner et al. (2017: 244), in dynamic assessment:

> a teacher or assessor, referred to as a mediator, engages cooperatively with learners and intervenes when difficulties arise and their performance breaks down. Through a process of mediation, which is qualitatively different from corrective feedback, a diagnosis of learner development emerges that includes abilities that are fully formed, as indicated by learner independent performance, and abilities that are still emerging, determined by learner responsiveness during the mediating process.

Kushki and Nassaji (2024: 2), for example, describe the use of dynamic assessment (DA) for second language (L2) reading assessments:

> DA involves assessing learning within the interactive moments between teachers and learners. In these interactions, teachers continuously evaluate their students' understanding of specific content and offer feedback accordingly. As such, DA adjusts feedback according to the individual learner's knowledge and utilizes their responses to the feedback, painting a detailed picture of their reading abilities and developing appropriate instructional interventions. By its very nature, not only does DA provide feedback, but it also feeds forward into the whole process of teaching and assessing. The insights gained from DA are particularly crucial given the current operational constraints of standardized tests in accurately capturing learners' proficiency across the diverse skills and subskills that constitute reading.

Mahoney (2024) recommends an assessment decision-making process called PUMI – Purpose, Use, Method, Instrument – that teachers, administrators and policymakers should follow to best inform the design, use and interpretation of summative, formative and dynamic assessments for bilingual children.

Norm- and Criterion-Referenced Language Tests

Measurements of bilinguals may also be used for purposes of comparison or determining level of mastery. Language proficiency tests may be classified as norm-referenced or criterion-referenced. Standardized **norm-referenced tests** essentially compare one individual with others; examples include IQ tests and college placement exams (e.g. SAT). A norm-referenced test of reading ability, for instance, may enable the teacher to compare one student with a national or regional average (norm). The student can then be placed in an ordered list with descriptors such as 'the top 16%', '32nd percentile', 'above average' or 'bottom quartile'. However, when norm-referenced tests compare bilinguals with monolinguals, the results may misrepresent the linguistic abilities of bilingual students (Mahoney, 2024) (see Chapter 1).

In contrast, **criterion-referenced tests** move away from comparing one student with another. The test results show what a student can and cannot do on a precise breakdown of language skills. Thus, rather than a score providing a comparison with other students (e.g. 16th percentile), criterion reference scores indicate the percentage of mastery (87% correct answers) and whether or not the student met or exceeded a cut-off score. In the case of standards-based academic achievement tests, a student's individual score may be reported as meeting, exceeding or failing to meet the standards. Detailed score reports can indicate which test items or concepts students did well on and which are in need of further development.

While criterion-referenced tests may seem more fair for bilinguals in theory, in practice they can be used to create comparisons between children (e.g. monolingual native speakers and bilinguals), between groups of children and between schools. Behind every criterion lurks a norm. The norm is usually the point of departure for setting criteria such as the standards the test is designed to measure and the cut-off scores that determine 'passing'. An advantage of criterion-referenced language tests is that they may facilitate feedback on student learning needs to the teacher that directly leads to intervention. Thus, they may be used as assessments for formative purposes (see Box 2.1).

> **Box 2.1** Criterion-referenced language tests
>
> **Criterion-referenced language tests** should provide direct feedback in the following areas:
>
> - teaching decisions (e.g. diagnosis of curriculum areas not mastered by an individual student);
> - reporting and discussing achievement with students;
> - reporting and discussing achievement with parents;
> - recognizing children in need of special support and the type of curriculum support they need;
> - identifying children for accelerated learning.

Regardless of whether a test is norm- or criterion-referenced, the sub-components of language proficiency are not easily definable or measurable. Apart from language skills, there are the qualitative aspects of language that are not simply reducible for testing (e.g. the emotive, status and poetic functions of languages). There is growing recognition that a single test cannot provide an accurate measure of a bilingual's proficiency. To get an accurate picture, multiple measures of students' language proficiency and growth are needed through a school year (Boals *et al.*, 2015; Gottlieb, 2024). Classroom assessment plans should include a combination of summative and formative assessments and alternative assessments such as checklists, informal and formal observations, and portfolios of students' work (Wright, 2025).

Communicative Language Testing

In attempting to assess a bilingual's competence in two languages, there is a danger of believing that a simple paper-and-pencil multiple-choice test will provide a faithful estimation of everyday language life. Reducing everyday language competence to tests of specific skills is like measuring Michelangelo's art solely by its range of colors. A particular emphasis in language testing is on **communicative competence** (see Chapter 1). While tests of spelling, grammar, written comprehension and reading abound, the importance of using languages in everyday settings is reflected in current testing preferences. Communicative competence assessment is based on genuine communication with various participants. Sometimes such conversation moves in unpredictable directions and makes sense only within a particular social context. An alternative is to see how bilinguals perform in both languages in a range of real communicative situations: in a shop, at home, at work and during leisure activity. This though is time-consuming and may be biased by the presence of the researcher. Thus, a test that measures purposeful communication across sufficient contexts without tester effects is improbable. For some, the answer is simply not to test. For others, a best approximation is accepted. Communicative language tests therefore tend to measure the more limited notion of performance rather than the wider idea of competence.

English Language Proficiency Testing for College Admission

Two major language proficiency tests – the Test of English as a Foreign Language (**TOEFL**) launched in 1964, and the International English Language Testing System (**IELTS**) launched in 1989 – have been used for decades to determine if students have sufficient English language proficiency to communicate competently in the context of an English-medium university classroom. Most universities in Australia, Canada, New Zealand, the United Kingdom and the United States accept one or both of these tests. While minimum acceptable scores vary by university or degree programs, a common admissions requirement is that international students from non-English-dominant countries obtain a score of 6.5 or higher on the IELTS, or 79 or higher on the internet-based version of the TOEFL (iBT).

Table 2.1 outlines each of the four sections of the TOEFL (iBT). Note that the tasks attempt to replicate the ways students may need to use and understand English in the classroom. For example, on the listening section the student may listen to a short excerpt of a lecture on the greenhouse effect; for the speaking section, the student may be asked to describe some places in their country they would recommend to a friend from another country to visit.

Table 2.1 TOEFL iBT test sections

Section	Time limit	Questions	Tasks
Reading	57–72 min	30–40 questions	Read three or four passages from academic texts and answer questions
Listening	41–57 min	28–39 questions	Listen to lectures, classroom discussions and conversations, then answer questions
Speaking	17 min	4 tasks	Express an opinion on a familiar topic; speak based on reading and listening tasks
Writing	50 min	2 tasks	Write essay responses based on reading and listening tasks; support an opinion in writing

Source: https://www.ets.org/toefl/test-takers/ibt/about/content.

The IELTS features similar questions and tasks, but also includes an oral interview in the speaking section. A candidate answers basic questions for 11–14 minutes about topics such as: where you live, clothes, travel, family, free time and shopping. Questions on shopping, for instance, might be:

- Do you like shopping? Why or why not?
- What kind of things do you like to buy?
- When do people in your area usually do their shopping?
- What are some of the advantages and disadvantages of large shops?

Candidates receive a 'band score' on a scale from 1 to 9, with allocation based on a rigorous and detailed system of performance descriptors (shown in Box 2.2).

Interview procedures such as those used on the IELTS may not reflect authentic everyday situations and use, and thus pose concerns regarding validity. Does genuine communication take place between strangers in a contrived, artificial context? Is the language repertoire of a person truly elicited? Is 'interview language' representative of a person's everyday language? Can we generalize from oral communicative tests based on a single type of test, given on a single occasion, based on a test interview which is not a typical daily event? To what extent are language abilities comprehensively sampled in an interview? There are doubts about whether such interview procedures can validly imitate and investigate real communicative competence. In addition, the tester is an influence on the outcome and not neutral. The conversation is constructed by both

> **Box 2.2** International English Language Testing System (IELTS) scale
>
> **Band 9: Expert User**
> The test taker has fully operational command of the language. Their use of English is appropriate, accurate and fluent, and shows complete understanding.
>
> **Band 8: Very Good User**
> The test taker has fully operational command of the language with only occasional unsystematic inaccuracies and inappropriate usage. They may misunderstand some things in unfamiliar situations. They handle complex and detailed argumentation well.
>
> **Band 7: Good User**
> The test taker has operational command of the language, though with occasional inaccuracies, inappropriate usage and misunderstandings in some situations. They generally handle complex language well and understand detailed reasoning.
>
> **Band 6: Competent User**
> The test taker has an effective command of the language despite some inaccuracies, inappropriate usage and misunderstandings. They can use and understand fairly complex language, particularly in familiar situations.
>
> **Band 5: Modest User**
> The test taker has a partial command of the language and copes with overall meaning in most situations, although they are likely to make many mistakes. They should be able to handle basic communication in their own field.
>
> **Band 4: Limited User**
> The test taker's basic competence is limited to familiar situations. They frequently show problems in understanding and expression. They are not able to use complex language.
>
> **Band 3: Extremely Limited User**
> The test taker conveys and understands only general meaning in very familiar situations. There are frequent breakdowns in communication.
>
> **Band 2: Intermittent User**
> The test taker has great difficulty understanding spoken and written English.
>
> **Band 1: Non-User**
> The test taker has no ability to use the language except a few isolated words.
>
> Source: https://ielts.org/take-a-test/your-results/ielts-scoring-in-detail

tester and tested (assessor and student). Performance and achievement are the result of a social event and not just an individual's competence. It is a joint performance. Thus the issue of 'whose performance' suggests that the result is about the assessor as well as the assessed. At the same time, these types of interviews are a compromise between artificial pencil-and-paper tests and the impracticality of the detailed observation of individuals across many **domains**.

The **Duolingo English Test** (DET) is a recent alternative language proficiency test for higher education admissions that began rapidly gaining acceptance by universities around the world during the global Covid-19 pandemic (Wagner, 2020). The main appeal of the DET is that students can take the test at any time, from anywhere, online, rather than having to schedule an appointment at a designated and approved testing center (many of which were closed or had limited access during the pandemic). The test is also less expensive and much shorter (about an hour) due to computer adaptive

> **Box 2.3** Examples of items from the Duolingo English Test (DET)
>
> **Reading**
> - *C-Test* – Complete a text by completing the 'damaged' words in a paragraph.
> - *Yes/no vocabulary test* – Read words and pseudo-words and select real English words among them.
> - *Interactive reading* – Engage with a text by sequentially performing a series of tasks tapping different sub-constructs of reading.
> - *Vocabulary in context* – Fill in the blank in a sentence by reconstructing a 'damaged' word.
>
> **Writing**
> - *Extended writing* – Respond to five writing prompts that require extended responses: three picture description tasks and two independent tasks based on a written prompt.
> - *Interactive listening summarization* – Write a summary of the conversation you had in the 'Interactive listening' task.
> - *Interactive writing* – Respond to a writing task in two stages with a follow-up prompt based on the themes discussed in the initial response.
>
> **Listening**
> - *Dictation* – Listen to a spoken sentence or short passage and then transcribe it.
> - *Yes/no vocabulary test (audio-based)* – Listen to words and pseudo-words and select real English words among them.
> - *Interactive listening* – Participate in a situationally driven conversation in a university setting; each interlocutor's turn is presented in an audio format.
>
> **Speaking**
> - *Elicited imitation (read-aloud)* – Record yourself speaking a written sentence.
> - *Extended speaking* – Respond to five speaking prompts: one picture description task and four independent speaking tasks, with written and aural prompts.
>
> Source: Kostromitina (2024: 3–4)

testing (CAT), which adjusts the level of difficulty during the test based on the student's prior answers. Another advantage is that the results are returned in days rather than weeks. Concerns have been raised about the lack of evidence of the validity of the DET for college admission purposes, as well as about test security and other issues (Wagner, 2020). Duolingo reported many improvements have been made since 2020, and that as of fall 2024, some 5,000 universities around the world accept the DET (Kostromitina, 2024). A technical manual provides reports on the evidence of validity, reliability and fairness for the DET (Cardwell *et al.*, 2024). The DET has a scoring scale of 10–160, with scores above 115 generally indicating sufficient English proficiency for college admissions. Many of the test items are quite different from the types of item found on the TOEFL and IETLS (see Box 2.3).

Common European Framework of Reference

A more holistic communicative competence framework for language assessment is the **Common European Framework of Reference (CEFR)** developed by the Council of Europe (2001, 2020a) and available in 40 languages. As described in the CEFR *Companion Volume* (Council of Europe, 2020a: 11):

> The CEFR is intended to promote quality **plurilingual education,** facilitate greater social mobility and stimulate reflection and exchange between language professionals

Table 2.2 Common European Framework of Reference (CEFR) – global scale, common reference levels

Proficient user	C2	Can understand with ease virtually everything heard or read. Can summarise information from different spoken and written sources, reconstructing arguments and accounts in a coherent presentation. Can express him/herself spontaneously, very fluently and precisely, differentiating finer shades of meaning even in more complex situations
	C1	Can understand a wide range of demanding, longer texts, and recognise implicit meaning. Can express him/herself fluently and spontaneously without much obvious searching for expressions. Can use language flexibly and effectively for social, academic and professional purposes. Can produce clear, well-structured, detailed text on complex subjects, showing controlled use of organisational patterns, connectors and cohesive devices
Independent user	B2	Can understand the main ideas of complex text on both concrete and abstract topics, including technical discussions in his/her field of specialisation. Can interact with a degree of fluency and spontaneity that makes regular interaction with native speakers quite possible without strain for either party. Can produce clear, detailed text on a wide range of subjects and explain a viewpoint on a topical issue giving the advantages and disadvantages of various options
	B1	Can understand the main points of clear standard input on familiar matters regularly encountered in work, school, leisure, etc. Can deal with most situations likely to arise whilst travelling in an area where the language is spoken. Can produce simple connected text on topics which are familiar or of personal interest. Can describe experiences and events, dreams, hopes and ambitions and briefly give reasons and explanations for opinions and plans
Basic user	A2	Can understand sentences and frequently used expressions related to areas of most immediate relevance (e.g. very basic personal and family information, shopping, local geography, employment). Can communicate in simple and routine tasks requiring a simple and direct exchange of information on familiar and routine matters. Can describe in simple terms aspects of his/her background, immediate environment and matters in areas of immediate need
	A1	Can understand and use familiar everyday expressions and very basic phrases aimed at the satisfaction of needs of a concrete type. Can introduce him/herself and others and can ask and answer questions about personal details such as where he/she lives, people he/she knows and things he/she has. Can interact in a simple way provided the other person talks slowly and clearly and is prepared to help

Source: https://www.coe.int/en/web/common-european-framework-reference-languages/table-1-cefr-3.3-common-reference-levels-global-scale

for curriculum development and in teacher education. Furthermore the CEFR provides a metalanguage for discussing the complexity of language proficiency for all citizens in a multilingual and intercultural Europe, and for education policy makers to reflect on learning objectives and outcomes that should be coherent and transparent. It has never been the intention that the CEFR should be used to justify a gate-keeping function of assessment instruments.

The CEFR defines levels of proficiency that allow assessment of learners' progress irrespective of age, language or region. The framework identifies three levels of language users – (A) basic, (B) independent and (C) proficient – with two levels of proficiency for each (i.e. A1, A2, B1, B2, C1, C2). Global descriptions of each level are shown in Table 2.2. The CEFR was designed to provide a common basis for the development of language course syllabi, curriculum guidelines, exams, language textbooks and other language learning resources across Europe. However, the CEFR has moved beyond Europe and is used in language programs around the world. The Council of Europe has developed additional CEFR scales, including a self-assessment grid (available in 32 languages), qualitative aspects of spoken language use (with focus on range, accuracy, fluency, interaction and coherence) and reference level descriptors designed to provide more detailed content specifications descriptions for textbook and syllabus developers.

The Council of Europe (2020b) has also developed the **European Language Portfolio** to complement certificates and diplomas based on the CEFR. The portfolio has three components:

- a language passport, which presents a regularly updated overview of the owner's linguistic profile;
- a language biography, which helps the owner to reflect on his/her language learning and language use, focusing on goal setting and self-assessment, learning strategies, the intercultural dimension of language learning, and plurilingualism (the ability to communicate in two or more languages at any level of proficiency);
- a dossier in which the owner collects samples of work that reflect the language proficiency he/she has achieved and his/her intercultural experience (the dossier may also be used to organize work in progress) (Council of Europe, 2020b: 1).

A great danger lies in viewing languages only within an academic context. The classroom is one language domain where language minoritized students from different cultural contexts may not reveal their wealth of language talents. Thus, academic testing is often more suited to elective bilinguals, whereas **circumstantial bilinguals** require their language abilities and uses to be portrayed across out-of-school domains so as to be fully representative.

Leung (2022) contends that the recent research on English as a lingua franca (ELF) and translanguaging has raised questions about the validity of the CEFR's underlying construct of communicative competence, given it represents a monolingually framed view of language proficiency with an idealized notion of a 'native speaker' as the reference point. This is related to the critique of communicative competence from a raciolinguistics perspective as discussed in Chapter 1, which highlights that the 'native speaker' model represents idealized (racially unmarked) white majority linguistic norms (Flores & Rosa, 2023). Leung (2022: 58) argues that 'proficiency itself does not have an independent existence outside an educational or training scheme or an assessment framework', and that 'the whole notion of language proficiency is very much an artefact created by language education professionals'. He notes that English is widely used among speakers of other languages without the presence of any 'native English speaker', for a wide variety of purposes across the education, business, scientific and government sectors. Leung notes this suggests that, in real life, the 'native speaker model is not necessarily being adhered to' (2022: 67). Furthermore, he argues the reality is that many of these speakers are 'translanguaging in their everyday communication practices' (2022: 69) and, thus, 'the validity of any monolingually framed notion of language proficiency has to be questioned, particularly in relation to additional/second language education' (2022: 70).

In light of these concerns, Leung welcomes some of the revisions and additions introduced in the 2020 *Companion Volume* of the CEFR (Council of Europe, 2020a). This includes expanding the notion of 'plurilingual mediation', which attempts to 'embrace contingency, dynamic fluidity and multilingualism in interactional language use as part of language proficiency' (Leung, 2022: 70). Byram *et al.* (2023: 3) explain that plurilingualism 'is a concept which describes how people possess language and languages' and 'means that languages and varieties of languages – such as dialect variations – are all "one," are all integrated into one entity, and can work together rather than in competition' as a singular 'competence' or 'repertoire'. As described in the CEFR *Companion Volume* (Council of Europe, 2020a: 30), individuals draw on their plurilingual repertoire in flexible ways:

- to switch from one language or dialect (or variety) to another;
- to express oneself in one language (or dialect or variety) and understand a person speaking another;
- to call upon the knowledge of a number of languages (or dialects or varieties) to make sense of a text;
- to recognize words from a common international store in a new guise;
- to mediate between individuals with no common language (or dialect or variety), even with only a slight knowledge oneself;
- to bring the whole of one's linguistic equipment into play, experimenting with alternative forms of expression;
- to exploit paralinguistics (mime, gesture, facial expression, etc.).

The *Companion Volume* (2020a: 116) offers a scale for **plurilingual** mediation (using the same A1–C2 scale as the CEFR itself) titled 'Acting as an intermediary in informal situations (with friends and colleagues)'. For example, at level A1, an individual:

Can communicate (in Language B) other people's personal details and very simple, predictable information (in Language A), provided other people help with formulation.

At level B1 an individual:

Can communicate (in Language B) the main sense of what is said (in Language A) on subjects of personal interest, while following important politeness conventions, provided the interlocutors articulate clearly and they can ask for clarification and pause to plan how to express things.

At level C1 an individual:

Can communicate fluently (in Language B) the sense of what is said (in Language A) on a wide range of subjects of personal, academic and professional interest, conveying significant information clearly and concisely as well as explaining cultural references.

Leung (2022: 74) welcomes this scale of plural mediation as an attempt in the right direction of reconceptualizing language proficiency away from 'native speaker' norms. However, he contends 'the assigning of levels for mediation activities seems arbitrary'. Noting that much work is still needed, Leung (2022: 76) concludes:

We should embrace the possibility that some aspects of language use in some contexts may not lend themselves to scripted description and categoric evaluation (e.g. pragmatic moves). Some aspects of language proficiency may be beyond static description. The shifting intellectual sensibilities have opened up an opportunity for us to re-think what counts as language proficiency in additional/second language education in contemporary contexts.

To collect *realistic* and *representative* communicative competence data, we need to know how situations (domains) relate to one another. We also need to know the sample of language performance that relates adequately to all-round language competence.

Examples of the Measurement of Bilingualism in Research

A full inventory of bilingual measurement devices and techniques would be immense and is not provided (for a comprehensive survey of this area, see Li Wei & Moyer, 2008; Winke & Brunfaut, 2020). The examples given below help to make some essential points and tend to exemplify some of the styles most often used in research on bilinguals.

Language Background Scales

Language background or **functional bilingualism** scales are self-rated. They endeavor to measure actual use of two languages as opposed to proficiency. An example for bilingual Spanish–English schoolchildren is presented in Figure 2.1 (adapted from Baker, 1992). The scale in Figure 2.1 may be helpful for teachers in the process of identifying English language learners, or determining students' language dominance. However, it has limitations besides the problems of ambiguity and 'social desirability' considered later. It is not exhaustive of targets (people) or of domains (contexts). Language activity with uncles and aunts, dance clubs, correspondence, organizations, social media, hobbies and travel are not included, for example. The choice of items included in such a scale is somewhere between an all-inclusive scale and a more narrow sample of major domains.

At first glance, it may appear that the more inclusive a scale is, the better. There is a problem though, as illustrated by the following example. A person who says she speaks Spanish to her father (mostly working abroad), her grandparents (seen twice a year) and her friends (but tends to be a loner), reads Spanish books and magazines (only occasionally), attends church services in Spanish (marriages and funerals only) but spends most of her time with an English-speaking mother and in an English-speaking school, might gain a fairly high 'Spanish' score. This example suggests that the 'to whom' question is insufficient. Frequency of usage in such contexts and with certain targets needs adding. To accompany 'to whom' and 'where', 'how often' and 'why' questions are necessary. Also, such scales do not indicate networking or status and power in relationships, which are important in **language shift** and language attitudes.

Language Balance and Language Dominance Measures

Various tests have been devised to gauge the relative dominance or balance of a bilingual's two languages (Grosjean & Li, 2013). This is not without controversy. A dynamic view of bilingualism challenges traditional notions of language dominance, which view the languages of a bilingual as separate. Such language dominance measures have been used in both research and in US education. Because instruction for US language minoritized children may take place in the child's **dominant language**, some measure of language dominance is needed. This may be through, for example, English and Spanish language proficiency tests. These are not without problems, as will be discussed later. Some examples of the types of tasks and test items used to determine language dominance are given below.

- *Vocabulary knowledge.* A simple picture identification is used to determine the extent of vocabulary known in both languages. The language with the highest number of correct responses is assumed to be dominant.

Here are some questions about the language in which you talk to different people, and the language in which certain people speak to you. There are no right or wrong answers. Leave an empty space if a question is inappropriate.

	Almost always in Spanish	In Spanish more than English	In Spanish and English about equally	In English more often than Spanish	Almost always in English
In which language do YOU speak to the following people?					
Father					
Mother					
Brother/sisters					
Friends in the classroom					
Friends on the playground					
Friends outside school					
Teachers					
Neighbors					
Grandparents					
Other relatives					
In which language do the following people speak TO YOU?					
Father					
Mother					
Brother/sisters					
Friends in the classroom					
Friends on the playground					
Friends outside school					
Teachers					
Neighbors					
Grandparents					
Other relatives					
Which language do YOU use for the following?					
Speaking on the telephone					
Text messaging					
Using the computer/internet					
Watching TV/DVDs/videos					
Listening to radio					
Listening to music					
Reading newspapers/comics/magazines					
Reading books					
Shopping					
Playing sports					
Participating in clubs/ societies					
Working/earning money					
Attending religious services					
Other leisure activities					

Figure 2.1 Language Background Scale

- *Speed of reaction in a word association task.* This seeks to measure whether a bilingual can give an association to stimulus words more quickly in one language than the other. The language with the fastest responses is assumed to be dominant.
- *Quantity of reactions to a word association task.* Bilinguals are measured for the number of associations given within one minute when a stimulus word (e.g. 'color') is presented. The language with the highest number of associations is assumed to be dominant.
- *Detection of words using both languages.* Words in both languages are extracted from a nonsense word such as DANSONODEND. This requires languages that use the same alphabet, and it can be difficult to create as the letters must be equally representative of both languages. The language with the largest number of extracted words is assumed to be dominant.
- *Time taken to read.* The language a bilingual can read the fastest is assumed to be dominant.

In seeking to determine the dominant language, it must be remembered that dominance is different from competence. A multilingual person may be competent in two or more languages while being dominant in one. Also, some cultures do not value speed of reaction, preferring accuracy. Thus there may be a cultural bias in the use of such tests. Another major problem with such balance and dominance tests lies in the representativeness of the measure of language proficiency and performance. In this respect, such tests would appear to tap only a small part of a much larger and more complex whole (language ability or language use). The tests cover a small sample of the language sub-skills that might be tested. Dominance will vary by domain and across time, being a constantly changing personal characteristic. It is possible to be approximately equally proficient in two languages, yet one may be dominant. Speed of processing may provide evidence about balance but not about dominance in actual language use, either in different sociocultural contexts or over time. These point to issues of lack of construct validity in many measures used to test for dominant language.

Self-rating of Proficiency

A simple means of determining language balance and dominance is to ask students to assess their own language strengths and weaknesses. A simple example to illustrate self-rating of language proficiency appears in Figure 2.2.

Can you understand:	English?	Spanish?	Can you speak:	English?	Spanish?
Yes – fluently	☐	☐	Yes – fluently	☐	☐
Yes – fairly well	☐	☐	Yes – fairly well	☐	☐
Yes – some	☐	☐	Yes – some	☐	☐
Yes – just a little	☐	☐	Yes – just a little	☐	☐
No – not now	☐	☐	No – not now	☐	☐
Can you read:			**Can you write:**		
Yes – fluently	☐	☐	Yes – fluently	☐	☐
Yes – fairly well	☐	☐	Yes – fairly well	☐	☐
Yes – some	☐	☐	Yes – some	☐	☐
Yes – just a little	☐	☐	Yes – just a little	☐	☐
No – not now	☐	☐	No – not now	☐	☐

Figure 2.2 Self-Rating of Bilingual Language Proficiency (English/Spanish)

Limitations in Measuring Language

Self-assessments, such as the example in Figure 2.2, may cover the basic four language abilities across two languages (e.g. Spanish and English). The answers are possibly too broad (e.g. there are many gradations possible in between each of the answers). Also, this self-assessment does not account for **translanguaging** or multimodalities. Apart from these issues, there are many other limitations frequently encountered that may introduce validity and other problems when attempting to measure language competence. These may be listed as follows:

(1) *Ambiguity.* Words such as 'speak', 'understand', 'read' and 'write' include a wide variety of levels of proficiency. The range is from an absolute beginner to Bloomfield's (1933) maximum notion of 'native-like control of two languages'. Tests also often contain only a small, unrepresentative sample of the totality of language proficiencies.

(2) *Context.* A bilingual may be able to understand a language in one context (e.g. a shop) and not in another context (e.g. an academic lecture). Proficiency and usage will vary with changing environments.

(3) *Social desirability/subjectivity.* Respondents may consciously or subconsciously give a 'halo' version of themselves. Self-ratings are vulnerable to exaggeration or understatement. People may say they are fluent in a second language (when in reality they are not) for **identity**, self-esteem or status reasons. Others may indicate they do not speak a language when they actually can, for example in a low-prestige minoritized language environment where the introduction of the second language may replace the first language. Questions about proficiency can be interpreted as about personal attitudes and identity and not just language.

(4) *Acquiescent response.* There is a slight tendency for respondents to answer questions 'Yes' rather than 'No'. It appears preferable to be positive rather than negative. This extends to a slight preference for 'Agree' rather than 'Disagree'.

(5) *Self-awareness.* A self-rating depends on accuracy of knowledge about oneself. For one person, the frame of reference may be other neighborhood children who are not so fluent. When compared with children in another community, apparent fluency may be less. What is competent in one environment may seem less competent in another. The age, nature and location of the reference group may cause self-assessment to be not strictly comparable across a representative sample of people.

(6) *Point of reference.* There is a danger in using monolingual proficiency and performance as the point of comparison (see Chapter 1).

(7) *Objectivity.* Another danger is raising language measurement to the level of objective scientific measurement, with its accompanying mystique. More 'natural' forms of non-standardized language sampling may be given lower status, as too subjective (e.g. recording natural conversation), as they rarely carry the mystique of 'objective' standardized educational and psychological (psychometric) measurement, even though they may provide more authentic samples of language.

(8) *Narrow sampling of dimensions of language.* Language measurement may unwittingly be perceived as something tangible and concrete (as when measuring height and weight). Rather, language tests mostly contain a specification of language skills that is open to interpretation and debate.

(9) ***Insensitivity to change.*** It is essential to produce measurement instruments that are reliable (i.e. individuals attain consistent scores over weeks or months; consistent for individuals in different contexts). However, the paradox is that such measurement instruments may be insensitive to changes within individuals (e.g. changes in home life, mental health, access to supplemental learning opportunities) and contexts (e.g. change in curriculum, policies, programs). Test results and testing instruments need an expiration date and to be revised and updated as needed.

(10) ***Labeling.*** Test scores are apt to create labels for individuals (e.g. someone is seen as being an underperformer) which create expectations (e.g. of further underachievement) that may lead to a self-fulfilling prophecy. Consequential validity (Popham, 2025) requires careful consideration of the harmful consequences that may stem from testing, such as labeling.

A Political View of Language Testing

Language testing is not a neutral activity. For example, language tests are sometimes introduced to achieve curriculum change. Indeed, there is almost no more powerful route to educational policy control or curriculum change than tests that virtually force the teacher to 'teach to the test'.

Centrally or locally imposed language tests define what skills are to be accented (e.g. communicative competence or literacy) and what languages are to be promoted (e.g. the majority language at the expense of minoritized languages). Language tests can include or exclude, marginalize or motivate, stagnate or innovate. Behind language tests are often agendas, motives, **ideology** and politics. For example, language proficiency tests in national languages are often used to determine the eligibility of immigrants for citizenship (Frost & McNamara, 2018). A language testing policy is typically an operationalized language policy (Menken, 2017).

Language testing relates to cultural, social, political, educational and ideological agendas that shape the lives of all students and teachers. Such language tests are deeply embedded in cultural, educational and political debates, where different ideologies are in contest. Critical language testing examines the uses and consequences of tests in education and society and thus views test-takers as political subjects in a political context (Shohamy, 2017). An example is the high-stakes language assessment of K-12 emergent bilingual students in the United States (see Chapter 9) and the use of English proficiency exams (e.g. TOEFL, IELTS) as a gate-keeping mechanism for which international students are allowed to enter universities in Australia, Canada, the United States and the United Kingdom.

Critical language testing asks questions about whose formal and hidden agendas tests relate to, and what sort of political and educational policies are delivered through tests. Critical language testing argues that language testers must ask themselves what sort of vision of society language tests create and for what vision of society tests are used. For example, are language tests intended to fulfill pre-defined curricular or proficiency objectives, or are there hidden aims, maneuvers or manipulations?

Critical language testing asks questions about whose knowledge the tests are based on. What is the intended or assumed status of that knowledge (e.g. 'truth' or something that can be negotiated and challenged)? What is the meaning and use of language test scores, and to what degree are they prescriptive, final and absolute, or to what extent are they open to discussion and interpretation?

Critical language testing thus widens the field of language testing by relating it to political and social debates. As Shohamy and Menken (2015: 254–255) argue:

> In most societies, tests have been constructed as symbols of success, achievement and mobility, and reinforced by dominant social and educational institutions as major criteria of worth, quality, and value. Tests, then, have been associated with standards and merit, and, in the context of immigration, are markers of productivity in the workplace, citizenship, and academic achievement in school. Tests are accepted as objective measures, which serve to enforce conformity and ensure the continuity of various declared agendas of policy makers. Governments and other central authorities use tests to impose their policies and agendas, knowing that those who are affected by such tests will change their behavior, given their fear of failure and its associated high stakes consequences; accordingly, they are eager to succeed.

Shohamy and Menken (2015) also note the power of language tests to privilege certain language practices, raise the status of tested (usually dominant) languages, and suppress non-tested languages in school and society.

Bilingual Assessment and Testing

A major limitation of monolingual tests is that they fail to capture the full linguistic repertoire of bilinguals, nor do they allow bilinguals to draw on this repertoire to fully demonstrate their knowledge and skills. As Valdés and Figueroa (1994: 87) argue:

> When a bilingual individual confronts a monolingual test, developed by monolingual individuals, and standardized and normed on a monolingual population, both the test taker and the test are asked to do something they cannot. The bilingual test taker cannot perform like a monolingual. The monolingual test can't 'measure' in the other language.

Monolingual forms of testing and assessment treat bilinguals as two monolinguals in one, as if their two languages are isolated and disconnected. However, as we saw in Chapter 1, bilinguals actually use their languages in complex, dynamic and flexible ways. Thus, there is a need for bilingual assessment policies and practices that enable students to show what they know and can do (Shohamy, 2017). For example, a selected response test could display questions and answers in both of a student's languages, allowing the student to answer either one, or consult one while determining the answer in the other. Open-ended constructed response items could allow students to respond in one or both languages. Shohamy (2011) gives an example of a bilingual student who accurately used both English and Hebrew to complete a recipe-writing task, and provides other empirical evidence suggesting the potential of such multilingual assessment practices to provide a more valid measure of students' knowledge and skills.

Solís et al. (2024) document the efficacy of translanguaging by teacher candidates in teaching and assessing mathematics, and Bravo et al. (2022) provide a classroom observation tool for assessing mathematics in English and Spanish. However, research in this area is just beginning and there are many questions to answer and issues to resolve (Lopez et al., 2017; Lopez, 2024; Mosquda et al., 2022). Nonetheless, by accepting multilingualism as the norm, researchers and assessment experts are now beginning to explore dynamic assessments that allow bilinguals to demonstrate their knowledge and skills using their entire linguistic repertoire.

Language Censuses

The Belgian census of 1846 was one of the first national censuses to ask language questions. Other countries were soon to follow Belgium's lead: Switzerland in 1850, Ireland in 1851, Hungary in 1857, Italy in 1861, Canada in 1871, Austria and Finland in 1880, India and Scotland in 1881, the United States in 1890, Wales in 1891 and Russia in 1897 (Ó Gliasáin, 1996). Many countries now include language questions in a census. Such censuses are often perceived by governments as providing relatively accurate measures of the number of language-speakers in local communities, regions and countries. However, as Leeman (2019: 114) argues, 'censuses are inherently political' and a 'symbolic imagining of the nation'. She notes that the inclusion and phrasing of specific language questions 'can embody very different orientations toward individual and societal multilingualism, and can be tied to very different language policies' (Leeman, 2019: 131).

Languages in the United States Census and the American Community Survey

The United States Census was instituted at the beginning of the United States political system, in Article 1, Section 2, of the Constitution, which stated that political representation in the House of Representatives was to be based on a population census. The census has been taken every 10 years since 1790, when Secretary of State Thomas Jefferson supervised the first. A question on race was included in that first census. Questions on race and ethnicity were revised in subsequent censuses to reflect changing demographics, understandings and views. A question on Hispanic origin was introduced in 1970 and on 'ancestry' in 1980 (Macías, 2000). Further changes to race and ethnicity questions were planned for the 2020 Census following several years of testing to more accurately capture 'multiethnic America'. Despite this substantial effort, the first Trump administration refused to approve these changes (Jurjevich, 2019). Changes were ultimately made in 2024 under the Biden administration, which combined race and ethnicity into a single question (i.e. 'What is your race and/or ethnicity?') and will allow respondents to select 'all that apply' from a list of racial/ethnic categories (Svitek, 2024). The changes also include the addition of 'Hispanic or Latino' and 'Middle Eastern and North African' (MENA) categories. Respondents can write in any of their ethnicities that are not listed.

The first Trump administration did, however, fight for the addition of a citizenship question. This proved to be highly controversial over concerns that it was politically motivated, would create fear among immigrant and minoritized communities, and thus lead to lower levels of participation and less accurate counts of the population. Legal battles ensued and ultimately the proposal was blocked by the US Supreme Court in 2019 (Wines, 2019). However, while unable to change the Census itself, Trump issued a memorandum in July 2020 directing the Secretary of the US Department of Commerce to exclude unauthorized immigrants from the numbers used to divide up seats in Congress among the states. It was unclear whether the President had the authority to make this decision and unlikely that the US Census Bureau could actually produce such a count. Legal battles ensued to block it. These political moves greatly complicated the implementation of the 2020 US Census, which was already facing difficulties due to the Covid-19 pandemic (Wang, 2020). Trump's memorandum was rendered moot the following year under the Biden administration, though some members of Congress continue to push for same types of exclusions.

The first time a question was asked about 'languages spoken at home' on the US Census was in 1890. Since then, census data has helped states and localities 'benchmark' and measure progress in meeting their objectives and legislatively mandated targets. Thus, a census does not just provide information. It also can assist or invoke political action (e.g. the 1910 US Census spurring the Americanization campaign). For example, the current language questions were first added in 1980 in response to federal legislation mandating data to best determine educational program needs for language minoritized children (Leeman, 2019).

In 2005, the Census Bureau began administering the annual American Community Survey (ACS) in addition to the decennial census to collect population data more frequently. The language questions were moved to the annual ACS and are no longer included in the Census.

Three examples are given below of language questions from the United States, the first from the 1910 Census, the second from the 2000 Census and the third from the 2022 ACS. These examples illustrate how census questions are constructed in a way that does not always give accurate and comprehensive information about use of languages, and also reveals implicit official and politicized attitudes towards the use and maintenance of minoritized languages.

The United States Census of 1910

In the 1910 United States Census, advice was given to enumerators when asking respondents about the **mother tongue** of members of the household. The extracts in Box 2.4 illustrate notions from a bygone era.

> **Box 2.4** Extracts from 'Advice to Enumerators' in the United States 1910 Census
>
> '127. The question of mother tongue should not be asked of any person born in the United States'
> '133. Column 17. Whether able to speak English; or, if not, give language spoken. This question applies to all persons age 10 and over. If such a person is able to speak English, write English [on the form]. If he is not able to speak English – and in such cases only – write the language which he does speak, as French, German, Italian.'

Note that:

- The question of mother tongue did not apply for those born in the United States. This indicates an assumption that all those born in the United States would be able to speak English, and that the maintenance of minoritized languages or bilingualism in English and a minoritized language was not considered.
- A person's ability in languages other than English was ignored if they were able to speak English.
- Ability in a **heritage language** was counted only if a person was unable to speak English.
- The language of children aged under 10 years was ignored.

The United States Census of 2000

Starting in January 2000 with visits to very remote areas and in March 2000 with postal delivery, Census 2000 questionnaires were made available in six languages – English, Spanish, Chinese, Tagalog, Vietnamese and Korean. Language Assistance Guides were produced in 49 languages other than English. Two questionnaires or forms were used. A short form was sent to about five in six of all households in the United States,

> **Box 2.5** Language question on the 2000 US Census
>
> (a) Does this person speak a language other than English at home?
>   ☐ Yes
>   ☐ No *Skip to 12*
>
> (b) What is this language? *(For example: Korean, Italian, Spanish, Vietnamese)*
>
> (c) How well does this person speak English?
>   ☐ Very well
>   ☐ Well
>   ☐ Not well
>   ☐ Not at all

requesting information on individual household members (e.g. gender, race, Hispanic origin, home ownership and age). The long form was sent to about one in six of all US households. The longer form included the same questions as the short form, with additional questions about ancestry, residence five years ago (migration), income, education and home languages. Thus, the language data was based on a sample of one in six households. Statistical procedures were used to generalize to the entire US population. The language question on the 2000 Census long form was phrased as shown in Box 2.5.

This question is more comprehensive than the 1910 language question. It asks about the use of a minoritized language in the home irrespective of command of English. It also asks a more searching question about the level of ability in English, which is the dominant question. However, note the lack of questions about proficiency in non-English languages spoken at home, lack of attention to use of non-English languages outside of the home and the assumption that there can be only one other language. Leeman (2019: 131) argues that these questions reveal a 'US monolingual ideology that is interested in non-English languages only to the extent that they threaten English'.

The American Community Survey (ACS, 2022)

In 2005 the US Census Bureau moved the language questions from the decennial census long form to the annual American Community Survey (ACS). The wording of the language question remained the same (US Census Bureau, 2015a). The ACS is sent to one in 38 households (US Census Bureau, 2015b). Thus, the annual administration of the ACS provides much more timely data about language. However, the smaller sample size means estimates are less accurate, particularly for smaller language minoritized populations.

The 2022 ACS, using five-year estimates, reported that out of the total US population aged five and over (312.1 million), there were 67.9 million people (21.7%) who spoke a language other than English at home. Of these, 41.4 million (61%) spoke Spanish, 11.7 million (17%) spoke another Indo-European language, 11 million (16%) spoke an Asian or Pacific Island language and 3.7 million (5%) spoke other languages. The majority of these individuals (62.1%) spoke English 'very well' and thus were bilingual or multilingual.

In 2015 the US Census Bureau identified 384 languages spoken in the United States through the ACS, which represented 'the most detailed language list used in any Census or survey in the world' (Gambino, 2018: 4). Nonetheless, the Bureau recognized that this list was insufficient to accurately capture the linguistic diversity of the country. In 2016, Census researchers undertook a major effort to analyze and assign a language code to every unique language reported on a US Census or ACS survey between 1980 and 2015. The result was an updated list of 1,334 language codes, more accurately representing languages spoken in the United States (Gambino, 2018).

The 2022 ACS (five-year estimates) reported that the 10 languages other than English with the largest numbers of speakers (five years or older) were:

(1) Spanish (41,434,050);
(2) Chinese (including Mandarin, Cantonese) (3,486,356);
(3) Tagalog (1,728,450);
(4) Vietnamese (1,537,182);
(5) Arabic (1,341,739);
(6) French (including Cajun) (1,214,884);
(7) Korean (1,091,912);
(8) Russian (987,364);
(9) Portuguese (911,501);
(10) Hindi (882,803).

Of indigenous languages, Diné bizaad (Navajo) had 157,026 speakers, and there were 178,695 speakers of other Native North American languages.

The 2000 US Census and the 2022 ACS showed a substantial increase since the 1980 US Census in the number and percentage of residents aged five years and over speaking a language other than English at home (see Table 2.3).

Table 2.3 Number of US speakers of languages other than English

Year	Number speaking a language other than English	Proportion of US population
US Census 1980	23.1 million	11.0%
US Census 1990	31.8 million	13.8%
US Census 2000	46.9 million	17.9%
America Community Survey 2022*	67.9 million	21.7%

*5-year estimate

Limitations of Language Censuses

Language census data has limitations, even when there is a long tradition of census compilation.

- Census questions about home language, mother tongue and first language are often ambiguous. In the 2011 Canadian census, one of the four language questions was 'Can this person speak English or French well enough to conduct a conversation?' The phrase 'speak well enough' may be interpreted in different ways. What one person considers 'well enough' may be at a different level of fluency to another. Another Canadian census question asks 'What is the language this person first learned at home in childhood and still understands?' The terms 'first learned' and 'still understands' are also subject to interpretation. This question also poses challenges for simultaneous bilinguals who learned two languages at home in childhood at the same time. The question suggests there can be only one that was learned 'first'.

> **Box 2.6** Language use surveys
>
> Language use surveys may be helpful for language policy and planning purposes. The language background of a language group needs to include many different contextual dimensions. Listed below are some of the contexts that need to be included in such a language use or language census survey. The examples are from the European Commission (2012a):
>
> - Geographical (areal) extent of the language; number and density of users.
> - Legal status of language; use of the language in bureaucracy; effect of local and central government on the language.
> - Recent and past immigration and emigration affecting the language.
> - Use of the language by parents with their children and between siblings; use of the language in new and existing marriages.
> - Use of language in elementary and secondary education, vocational, technical, adult, continuing and higher education; language learning classes.
> - Literacy and biliteracy of the language group.
> - Unemployment in the language group. Types of employment in the language group (e.g. socio-economic status).
> - Cultural vitality of the language group; institutions dedicated to supporting the language and culture.
> - Attitudes of speakers and non-speakers to the language. Optimism or pessimism surrounding the language.

- Sometimes census questions do not distinguish between language use and language ability (see Chapter 1). Thus the question 'Do you speak English?' does not specify whether the question is about everyday language use, ability to speak the language irrespective of regular use, or both use and ability. This points to the need for a broader focus on language use in such surveys (see Box 2.6).
- Questions on census forms do not usually include the four basic language skills: listening, speaking, reading and writing. Thus typically only oracy is measured, not literacy.
- Questions about contexts or domains of language use (e.g. home, school, religion, street, shopping) are rarely asked. Therefore, a response is very generalized across many domains and is insensitive to where languages are used.
- Census data may rapidly become out of date when factors such as migration, social upheaval, war or a high birth rate mean that the language situation is rapidly changing.
- Language questions can be politically inflammatory. For example, in the 1846 Belgian census the language question simply asked what language is usually spoken by respondents. Subsequent censuses restricted choices to knowledge of official languages only. This provoked contention and controversy. Combined with other political controversies, in 1961 the majority of parliamentarians in Belgium decided to suspend the language censuses, to avoid further dispute.
- Not all censuses include questions on language. Some censuses ask about ethnic groups, which may not correspond to language groups. This occurred in the 2001 census in England, where there was no language question and only a question on ethnic origins. The 2011 census in England included questions on ethnic group, 'main language' and English proficiency so as to respond to such criticism.
- Conversely, a language question in a census may be treated by respondents as referring to identity. For example, in Ireland, a non-Irish-speaker may wish to be seen as Irish and therefore positively answer the Irish language question. Thus a

census language question may be interpreted as an attitude question. People from a particular ethnic group may feel they ought to say that they speak the indigenous or heritage language even if they do not. Alternatively, if a minoritized language is disparaged and of low status, a speaker of that language may claim not to speak it.
- Censuses do not usually cover all of the population of a country despite considerable efforts to be inclusive. Some of the population may refuse to respond through the mail system, or to answer census personnel calling at their dwelling. Some recent immigrants may be fearful of the census. For example, the 1980 US Census is suspected to have substantially undercounted the Cambodian refugee population. When native Cambodian American census-takers made home visits to those who failed to return the census form (sent in English), many were accused of collecting information to send to the oppressive political regime back in Cambodia. Other people are out of reach or difficult to track down. Itinerants, illegal immigrants and the homeless, for example, may be missed by the census.

Conclusion

Just as dimensions and categorizations can never capture the full nature of bilingualism, so measurement usually fails to capture fully various conceptual dimensions and categorizations. Just as the statistics of a football or an ice hockey game do not convey the richness of the event, so language tests and measurements are unlikely to fully represent an idea or theoretical concept. Complex and rich descriptions are the indispensable partner of measurement and testing. The stark statistics of the football or ice hockey game and a colorful commentary are complementary, not incompatible. There are many language background scales to measure language usage and even more tests to measure language proficiency. The latter include norm-referenced and criterion-referenced language tests, self-rating scales and language dominance tests. Suitable for both first and second languages, sometimes based on theoretical principles, sometimes eclectic, such tests tend to relate directly to the process of teaching and learning. Bilingual assessments hold the potential to provide more valid measures of bilinguals' knowledge and skills. The assessment and testing of bilinguals in school will be addressed more fully in Chapter 15.

Key Points in This Chapter

- Bilinguals are measured for both their proficiency and their use of languages.
- Examples include census surveys of languages in a population, selection for different classes in school according to language ability, and assessment of competence following second language learning.
- Language background scales attempt to measure a person's use of their languages in different domains and in different relationships.
- Language balance and dominance measures attempt to gauge the relative strength of each language of a bilingual.

> - Communicative language testing attempts to measure a person's use of language in authentic situations.
> - Criterion-referenced language tests seek to provide a profile of language sub-skills, whereas norm-referenced tests compare a person with other people.
> - 'Critical language testing' examines whose knowledge the tests are based on, and for what political purposes the tests will be used. It regards test-takers as political subjects in a political context.
> - Bilingual assessments have the potential to enable bilinguals to demonstrate their knowledge and skills by drawing on the full range of their linguistic repertoires.
> - Language censuses are used in many countries to measure the extent and density of speakers of different languages. There are problems with terms used, validity of the questions and reliability of the answers.

Suggested Further Reading

- Byram, M., Fleming, M. and Sheils, J. (eds) (2023) *Quality and Equity in Education: A Practical Guide to the Council of Europe Vision of Education for Plurilingual, Intercultural and Democratic Citizenship*. Multilingual Matters.
- De Angelis, G. (2021) *Multilingual Testing and Assessment*. Multilingual Matters.
- Gottlieb, M. (2024) *Assessing Multilingual Learners: Bridges to Empowerment* (3rd edn). Corwin.
- Little, D. and Figueras, N. (eds) (2022) *Reflecting on the Common European Framework of Reference for Languages and its Companion Volume*. Multilingual Matters.
- Mahoney, K. (2024) *The Assessment of Multilingual Learners: Supporting English Language Learners* (2nd edn). Multilingual Matters.

On the Web

- Modern Language Association Language Map
  https://www.mla.org/map_main
- Explore Census Data (access to US Census and American Community Survey data)
  https://data.census.gov/
- Ethnologue – Languages of the World
  https://www.ethnologue.com
- European Charter for Regional or Minority Languages
  https://www.coe.int/en/web/european-charter-regional-or-minority-languages
- Common European Framework of Reference for Languages (CEFR)
  https://www.coe.int/en/web/common-european-framework-reference-languages
- WIDA Consortium
  https://wida.wisc.edu/

Discussion Questions

(1) Why is the measurement of bilinguals so challenging? Describe any experiences you have had with language proficiency tests or assessments. What was challenging

about these measures and how accurately did they reflect your perceived level of proficiency?
(2) Complete the Language Background Scale (Figure 2.1), the Self-Rating of Bilingual Language Proficiency (Figure 2.2) or the Common European Framework of Reference (CEFR) self-assessment (https://www.coe.int/en/web/portfolio/self-assessment-grid). Compare and discuss your background and ratings with other members of the class. Specify the criteria you used to determine your responses.
(3) Listen to the sample listening task item for the TOEFL at https://www.ets.org/toefl/test-takers/ibt/about/content/listening and/or take the Duolingo English Test (DET) practice test at https://englishtest.duolingo.com/register. How realistic and representative do you feel these tasks are in terms of the communicative competence needed for success in university classrooms?

Study Activities

(1) Find out what tests local school(s) use to measure language achievement in the majority and other languages. These may be listening, speaking, reading, writing or language development tests. Find out whether these are norm-referenced or criterion-referenced tests and if they are used for summative or formative purposes. How fair are these to multilingual learners?
(2) Gather detailed information about one country's language census (e.g. United States, Canada, East Africa, Wales, Ireland, Scotland (Gaelic), Australia, India, Bolivia, Venezuela, Caucasus region, etc.). What were the major findings? What problems are there in the wording of the question(s)? What other limitations do you find in the survey?
(3) Obtain and analyze a standardized language proficiency test or sample test (e.g. TOEFL, IELTS, DET, Pearson Test of English, BEST Plus, BEST Literacy, WMLS-R, IPT, WIDA Access 2.0, ELPA21, CELDT, TELPAS, LAS Links, Peabody Picture Vocabulary Test). Assess strengths and weaknesses of the test when used with multilingual learners in the classroom (e.g. selection, placement, formative and summative judgments).

CHAPTER 3
Languages in Society

Introduction

From Diglossia to Transglossia

From Additive and Subtractive to Recursive and Dynamic Bilingualism

Language Shift and Language Maintenance

Language Decline and Death

Language Revival

Language Conflict

Language and Nationalism

Social Varieties of Language

English as a Global Language
The Spread of English
The Future of English

Critical Post-Structuralist Sociolinguistics

Conclusion

CHAPTER 3
Languages in Society

Introduction

Bilinguals are present in every country of the world, in every social class and in all age groups. Numerically, bilinguals and multilinguals are in the majority: it is estimated that they constitute between half and two-thirds of the world's population (Grosjean, 2012). The United Nations Educational, Scientific and Cultural Organization (UNESCO) declares, 'In today's world, multilingual contexts are the norm rather than the exception' (Giannini, 2024: 1). As Romaine (2013: 448) observes, 'there are over 30 times as many languages as there are countries' and, thus, 'bilingualism and multilingualism are present in practically every country in the world, whether officially recognized or not'. The bilingual population of the world is growing as internationalism is spreading in trade and travel, communications and mass media, immigration and an interlinked global economy. Globalization and interculturalism are both the cause and an effect of bilingualism and multilingualism.

Bilingual and multilingual individuals do not exist as separate islands. Rather, people who speak two or more languages usually exist in networks, communities and sometimes in regions. People who speak a minoritized language or variety within a majority language **context** may be said to form a **speech community** where members interact and communicate based on shared norms, values and communicative practices (Morgan, 2014). **Bilingualism** at the individual level is half the story. The other essential half is to analyze how groups of language speakers behave and change. Such an examination focuses on movements and developments in language use across decades. Such change in a minoritized language is often downwards. A **language minority** is rarely stable in its size, strength or safety. Therefore, examining the politics and power situation in which minoritized languages are situated becomes important (see Chapters 17 and 18).

This chapter focuses on the idea that there is no language without a language community. Since language communities do not usually exist in isolation from other communities, it becomes important to examine the contact between different language communities. The rapid growth of access to information (e.g. via the internet) and international travel has meant that language communities are rarely if ever stable. Some languages become stronger (e.g. English); other languages decline, even die. Some languages thought to be dead may be revived (e.g. Manx Gaelic in the Isle of Man). This chapter therefore seeks to examine language communities, language contact, language change and language conflict. This will reveal that decisions about bilingual education are part of a much wider whole. That is, bilingual education can be properly understood only by examining the circumstances of language communities in which such education occurs.

This chapter takes a sociolinguistic perspective. **Sociolinguistics** is the study of language in relation to social groups, social class, ethnicity, race and other interpersonal factors in communication. The chapter examines central sociolinguistic concepts such as **diglossia, transglossia, language shift, language maintenance, language death,** language variation and **language spread,** including the rise of global English in bilingualism and **multilingualism,** and concludes with the shift towards critical post-structuralist sociolinguistics.

From Diglossia to Transglossia

The term **bilingualism** is typically used to describe the two languages of an individual. When the focus changes to two languages in society, the term often used is **diglossia** (Ferguson, 1959). Terms such as 'triglossia', 'multiglossia' or 'polyglossia' are used to describe societal contexts with three or more languages. 'Diglossia' is derived from the Greek word for having two languages. In practice, a language community may use one language in certain situations and for certain functions, and the other language in different circumstances and for different functions. For example, a language community may use a minoritized language in the home, for religious purposes and in social activity, but use the majority language at work, in education and with mass media. This is not universal, and some language communities use two or more languages for the same purpose (e.g. in bilingual education).

Ferguson (1959) first described diglossia in terms of two varieties of the same language (dialects). Fishman (1980) extended the idea of diglossia to two languages existing side by side within a geographical area. Ferguson's original description distinguishes between a higher-status language (called H) and a lower-status one (called L). This distinction can reflect the difference between a majority (H) and minority (L) language within a country. H and L languages or varieties may be used for different purposes, as illustrated in Table 3.1, which illustrates how the minority language is more likely to be used in informal personal situations and the majority language used more in formal official communication contexts. It is sometimes embarrassing or belittling for a speaker to use the 'low' variety of language in a situation where the 'high' variety is the norm. For example, at a graduation ceremony at a rural high school

Table 3.1 Diglossia

Context	Majority language (H)	Minority language (L)
1. The home and family		✓
2. Schooling	✓	
3. Mass media, internet sites	✓	
4. Business and commerce	✓	
5. Social and cultural activity in the community		✓
6. Email, texting, social media		✓
7. Correspondence with government departments	✓	
8. Religious activity		✓

deep in southern Thailand, students giggled with delight and teachers squirmed in embarrassment as the student speaker slipped from Standard Thai (H) into the local southern dialect of Pak Thai (L).

The distinction between majority and minority languages is possibly more about the status and power of languages than about the languages as language varieties. Table 3.1 suggests that different language situations usually make one language more prestigious than the other. The majority language will often be perceived as the more eminent, elegant and educative language. It is usually seen as the door to both educational and economic success. With concern that labels such as H and L suggest that L languages and varieties are inferior, Fishman (1991) updated his diglossia model to describe Xish and Yish functions, where X represents a threatened (minority) language and Y represents an unthreatened or less threatened (majority) language.

The concept of diglossia has been examined alongside the concept of **individual bilingualism**. Fishman (1980) combines the terms bilingualism and diglossia to portray four language situations where bilingualism and diglossia may exist with or without each other, as shown in Table 3.2. The first situation is a language community containing both diglossia and bilingualism. In such a community, almost everyone will be able to use both the majority and the minoritized language. The majority language is used for one set of functions, the minoritized language for a (more or less) separate set of functions. In Paraguay, for example, most people speak both Spanish and Guaraní, but mainly use Spanish for official purposes and Guaraní for more **identity** functions (García, 2009a).

Table 3.2 Diglossia and bilingualism

		Diglossia +	Diglossia −
Individual bilingualism	+	1. Both diglossia and bilingualism	3. Bilingualism without diglossia
	−	2. Diglossia without bilingualism	4. Neither bilingualism nor diglossia

The second situation is diglossia without bilingualism. In such a context there will be two languages within a particular geographical area. One group of inhabitants will speak one language, another group a different language. This tends to be a theoretical case with few strong examples. Historically, in a colonial situation, a ruling power group might speak the 'high' language, while the larger, less powerful group speak only the 'low' language. For example, English (e.g. in India) or French (e.g. in Haiti and Vietnam) was spoken by the ruling elite in colonial countries where the local languages were spoken by the masses.

The third situation is bilingualism without diglossia. In this situation, most people will be bilingual and will not restrict one language to a specific set of purposes. Either language may be used for almost any function. Or, as in the case of the United States, many people are bilingual due to immigration, but there are few societal supports to develop, maintain, promote or protect immigrant languages. Fishman regards such communities as unstable and likely to change. Where bilingualism exists without diglossia, the prediction is that the majority language will become even more powerful and extend its use. The other language may decrease in its functions and decay in status and usage. Fishman (2013) laments the historical track record of the United States in squandering, destroying and neglecting non-English languages.

The fourth situation is where there is neither bilingualism nor diglossia. One example is where a linguistically diverse society has been forcibly changed to a relatively **monolingual** society. In Cuba and the Dominican Republic, the native languages have been exterminated. In Japan, efforts by the Meiji government to create a common Japanese language resulted in the near extinction of the languages of indigenous Ainu and Ryukyu people (Tomozawa & Majima, 2015). A different example would be a small speech community using its minoritized language for all functions and insisting on having no relationship with the neighboring majority language.

Fishman believes that keeping up with the prestige and power of a worldwide language such as English is impossible and impractical. If a minoritized language attempts to take over (or share) the functions of the majority language, it is doomed to fail, as the majority language will be too powerful, too high status and impossible to defeat. He argues that minoritized language survival requires each language to have its own separate set of functions and space, without threatening the other. Otherwise, minoritized language shift and death may occur. Fishman in particular argues that trying to reclaim all functions for the minoritized language sets the wrong goal for that language. Instead, **intergenerational transmission** of the minoritized language must be safeguarded in the home and community primarily through self-supporting operations, rather than complete reliance on public or other outside sources. As Fishman (2013: 475) argues:

> Without such self-supported, self-protected and self-initiated islands of demographically concentrated local non-English language-and-culture transmission, particularly given the social mobility, modernization, and urban interaction so typical of American life, non-English mother tongues lack 'safe houses' or 'safe harbors' wherein the young can be socialized according to the languages, values, and traditions of sidestream cultures. They also increasingly lack a protected intimate space for adults and old folks during their after-work and out-of-work lives.

However, family language reproduction does not exist in a vacuum. Parents and children are influenced by the status and prestige of a language in society (e.g. its use in institutions and government). If high-status functions operate in the majority language, the message to parents and children is about the power of the majority language rather than the minoritized language. Thus, increasing the functions of a minoritized language is also about sending the right signals to parents and teachers.

Fishman's model of diglossia and bilingualism has helped (and continues to help) guide many valuable studies of **societal bilingualism**. Yet scholars are increasingly finding that linguistic realities in many countries often do not neatly conform to the model (Jaspers, 2017). Language shift and maintenance may vary by domain and even vary within some domains depending on different sites and situations, role relationships and topics of conversation. Bilingualism without diglossia is predicted to lead to the decay of the minoritized language. In Wales, however, Welsh has been increasingly available in hitherto English language **domains** (e.g. in education, television and pop music), thus giving bilinguals a choice of language. It is believed in Wales that allowing separate functions for Welsh will relegate the language to low status and subordinate uses only.

Stable diglossia in a globalized language world is becoming less likely, as the discussion of World Englishes later in this chapter will illustrate. García (2009a) notes other concerns: diglossia accepts situations of **domination** as normal, takes language arrangements to be consensual and fails to consider underlying conflicts. Furthermore, rather than compartmentalization of languages as suggested in diglossic situations, the reality is an overlapping and intermeshing use of languages. Some scholars have called such situations 'leaky diglossia'.

Given this coexistence and interplay between languages, García (2009a: 79) suggests 'transglossia might be a better term to describe societal bilingualism in a globalized world: a stable, and yet dynamic, communicative network with many languages in functional inter-relationship, instead of being assigned separate functions'. For example, the Puerto Rican community of East Harlem in the United States where Spanish and English are used concurrently within the same domains reveals a more fluid use of two or more languages. Individuals translanguage in a way that maximizes efficiency of communication and reflects multiple identities. Thus, transglossia and other alternative concepts (e.g. critical diglossia, lifestyle diglossia, heteroglossia) call attention to the agency of multilingual speakers 'and to the existence of a whole range of hybrid linguistic practices that a diglossic approach usually would dismiss as undesirable leakage' (García, 2009a: 190).

Growing ease of travel, faster communication, increased social and vocational mobility, urbanization and the global economy result in more contact between language communities, thus leading to greater transglossia. Changes in the fate and fortune of a minoritized language occur because the purposes of the two languages tend to change across generations. Neither a minoritized language community, nor the uses that community makes of its minoritized language, can be permanently compartmentalized. The geographical and personal boundaries that separate one language from another are never permanent. These boundaries are conceptualized as territorial and personality principles.

The territorial principle occurs when language rights or laws apply to a specific region. Keeping boundaries between the languages and compartmentalizing their use in society are regarded by many language planners as important for the minoritized language to survive. For example, in Belgium there are three designated regions where Flemish-, French- and German-speakers have language rights inside their regions, but not outside those regions. In contrast, the 'personality principle' applies when official recognition of the language is given wherever speakers travel in a country (Williams, 2013). For example, in Canada, Francophones have the theoretical right to use French wherever they travel across Canada (although most areas outside Québec do not have French language service provision).

An attempted merging of the territorial and personality principles when applied to language rights has been termed the 'asymmetrical principle' or 'asymmetrical bilingualism'. As conceived by its Canadian advocates (e.g. in Québec), the principle gives full rights to minoritized language speakers and fewer rights to the speakers of a majority language. This is a form of positive discrimination, seeking to discriminate in favor of those who are usually discriminated against. The argument is that the minoritized language can survive only if it is given protection and preferential treatment. Some of the functions of a minoritized language will be regulated, so as to preserve that language. This may result in enforcement and 'language policing' rather than (or as well as) winning hearts and minds through education and persuasion. We return to the underlying question of individual and minoritized group language rights in Chapter 17.

An argument for the maintenance and revitalization of **indigenous languages** is often based on their historic existence within a defined geographical boundary, for example Basque in the Basque Country (Spain), Quechua in the Andes (South

America), Dong in Guizhou (China) or Bunong in Mondulkiri (Cambodia). Language rights for indigenous languages may be enshrined in national laws. But what status do immigrant languages have when they cannot claim either territorial or personality rights? Geographical arguments for an indigenous language can have unfortunate implications for immigrant language minorities. Do languages belong to regions and territories and not to the speakers of those languages wherever they may be found? Do immigrant languages in countries such as Australia, Canada, Germany, Korea, Thailand, the United Kingdom and the United States not 'belong', as they are not indigenous languages? Do such immigrant languages belong only in the home country (e.g. Korean in Korea, Turkish in Turkey or Somali in Somalia)? In Europe, there are many national (or autochthonous) languages that are seeking preservation status in the European Union, but almost no status is accorded to the immigrant languages of Europe (e.g. the various Asian languages, such as Panjabi, Urdu, Bengali, Vietnamese, Korean, Hindi and Gujarati).

In language communities, the functions and boundaries of the two languages will both affect and be reflected in bilingual education policy and practice. In diglossic and transglossic situations, how are the majority and minoritized languages used in the different stages of schooling, from kindergarten to university? If the minoritized language is used in school, in which curriculum areas does it function? Is the minoritized language used just for oral communication or is **biliteracy** a goal of the curriculum? Are science, technology and computing taught in the majority or the minoritized language? Is the minoritized language allowed just for a year or two in the elementary school, with the majority language taking over thereafter? Are the minority and majority languages rigidly separated in the curriculum, or is **translanguaging** allowed and used as a pedagogical tool? Or does the school deliberately exclude the minoritized language as a medium for classroom learning? The purposes and functions of each language in diglossic or transglossic situations are both symbolized and enacted in the school situation (see Chapter 10).

From Additive and Subtractive to Recursive and Dynamic Bilingualism

This chapter has indicated the potential importance of different functions for the minority and majority language. Various models attempt to describe the functions and relationships between languages in a bilingual context. In the 20th century, bilingualism was viewed as being either additive or subtractive (Lambert, 1974). In the 21st century, new models describe bilingualism as recursive or dynamic (García, 2009a).

In an **additive bilingualism** context, the addition of a second language and culture is unlikely to replace or displace the first language and culture. For example, students in China and Korea learning English will remain proficient in Chinese and Korean respectively. They do not lose their native language, but gain another language and some of its attendant culture. The 'value added' benefits may be not only linguistic and cultural, but social, economic and cognitive as well.

When the second language and culture are acquired with pressure to replace or demote the first language, **subtractive bilingualism** may occur. Students who immigrate to countries such as Australia, England and the United States are required to learn English and conform to the dominant culture, just as immigrants in Japan are under immense pressure to learn Japanese and assimilate to Japanese culture as quickly as possible. This may lead to a less positive self-concept, loss of cultural or ethnic identity, with possible alienation or marginalization. For example, an immigrant may experience pressure to use the **dominant language** and feel embarrassment in using the home language. When the second language is prestigious and powerful, used in mainstream education and in the job market, and when the minoritized language is perceived as being of low status and value, the latter may be threatened. In many cases subtractive bilingualism is less about students losing proficiency in their home languages, and more about students lacking opportunities to develop their oral proficiency or develop literacy skills in their home languages due to schooling being exclusively in the dominant language, such as English-medium instruction in the United States.

In the 21st century, new understandings of bilingualism require additional constructs. For example, in cases of **language revitalization** efforts to reverse the effects of linguistic discrimination and suppression (e.g. Māori in Aotearoa/New Zealand, Hawaiian in Hawaii, Diné bizaad (Navajo) in the four corners region of the United States), or in programs targeting heritage-speakers (e.g. Vietnamese for Vietnamese-Americans) who are dominant English-speakers due primarily to English-medium schooling, students are not starting from the beginning of the language-acquisition process simply 'to add a new language'. Such students have some knowledge and proficiency of these languages due to exposure in the home and in their communities. García introduced the term **recursive bilingualism** to describe the ways a speaker 'reaches back to the bits and pieces of an ancestral language as it is reconstituted for new functions and as it gains momentum to thrust itself forward towards the future' (García, 2009a: 53).

García also introduced the construct of **dynamic bilingualism** to reflect the complex bilingual competence often needed to communicate in the 21st century due to increasing migration, transnationalism and globalization. Rejecting the simple linear nature of additive and subtractive bilingual models above, she argues:

> With language interaction taking place on different planes including multimodalities, that is, different modes of language (visuals as well as print, sound as well as text, and so on) as well as multilingualism, it is possible for individuals to engage in multiple complex communicative acts that do not in any way respond to the linear models of bilingualism. (García, 2009a: 54)

The dynamic, simultaneous existence of different languages in communication makes for a close inter-relationship between languages, which is more than additive. Dynamic bilingualism reflects the translanguaging practices of bilinguals as they draw on all of their linguistic resources to communicate and learn (García & Li Wei, 2014).

Such dynamic use of linguistic resources and multimodalities is evident in the way many Cambodians in Cambodia interact with each other and with Cambodians living in countries around the world via social media. A typical Facebook post, for example (see Figure 3.1), may include a text in either Khmer or English, or a mixture of both. The post may be accompanied by a photo, a video, an article, or an image combined with text, which may be in one or a mixture of the two languages. Likewise, comments on the post from friends may be in Khmer, English or both, may incorporate emojis, and may include images, photos, videos, memes or links across the two languages. Some Cambodians will even use the English alphabet to write Khmer phonetically (as in Oun's comment in Figure 3.1), because they do not have access to Khmer fonts, because they do not know how to write using the Khmer script, or simply because they find it faster to write it that way. This dynamic use of translanguaging and multimodalities is used

Figure 3.1 A Facebook example of dynamic bilingualism in social media

by many other bilinguals in various languages across social media for meaningful and effective communication (see e.g. Stæhr, 2017). The dynamic, hybrid, overlapping and simultaneous use of different languages and modalities reflects transcultural identities and multilingualism in an increasingly globalized world of communication. García and Li Wei (2015) argue that a dynamic bilingualism lens has the potential to transform structures and practices of bilingual education (see Chapters 10 and 11).

Language Shift and Language Maintenance

With changes of season and weather come growth and death, blossoming and weakening. Minoritized language communities are similarly in a constant state of change. Such language shift may be fast or slow, upwards or downwards, but never absent.

Language shift refers to a reduction in the number of speakers of a language, a decreasing saturation of language-speakers in the population, a loss in **language proficiency** or a decreasing use of that language in different domains. Without intervention, the ultimate outcome of language shift is language dormancy or **language death**, although a language could be revived from recordings (oral and written). Language maintenance usually refers to relative language stability in the number and distribution of its speakers, its proficient usage by children and adults, and its retention in specific domains (e.g. home, school, religion). **Language spread** concerns an increase – numerically, geographically or functionally – in language users, networks and use.

However, there is a danger in the ways these terms are used because they are ambiguous and may refer to the numerical size of the language minority, their saturation in a region, their proficiency in the language or the use of the language in different domains. In addition, terms such as 'language death' and 'extinct languages' suggest a negative, pessimistic and irreversible situation. Instead, language revivalists prefer to talk about sleeping or dormant languages, because if there is a record of that language and a community is motivated to resurrect it, then language reversal is possible (Leonard, 2008). Such is the case with Klallam, a dormant language being learned by some Native American students in Washington through recordings of deceased ancestors (Kaminksy, 2014). Zuckerman and Monaghan (2012) refer to such extinct languages as 'sleeping beauties'.

A variety of factors create language shift. For example, out-migration from a region may be vital to secure employment, a higher salary or promotion. In-migration can be forced (e.g. capture and enslavement) or voluntary (e.g. guest workers). Sometimes this movement of minoritized language groups occurs within a particular geographical area. Within a country, marriage may also cause a shift in bilingualism. For example, a bilingual person from a minoritized language community may marry a majority language monolingual. The result may be majority language monolingual children. Increasing industrialization, urbanization and globalization have led to increased movement of labor. With the growth of mass communications, information technology and tourism, and the increasing ease of travel by road, sea and air, minoritized languages seem more at risk. Bilingual education, or its absence, will also be a factor in the ebb and flow of minority and majority languages. Table 3.3 provides a relatively comprehensive list of factors that may encourage language maintenance or loss. This list essentially refers to immigrants rather than indigenous minorities, but many factors are common to both groups. What is missing from this list is the power dimension.

This initial consideration of important factors in language shift has shown that such shifts are particularly related to economic and social change, to politics and power, to the availability of local social communication networks between minoritized language speakers, and to the legislative and institutional support supplied for a minoritized language. While such factors help clarify what affects language shift, the relative importance of these factors is debated and still unclear.

There are various approaches to establishing the causes of language shift, such as considerations of political, economic, psychological (e.g. at the individual or home level) and sociolinguistic factors. A list of the relative importance of these factors is simplistic because the factors interact and intermingle in a complicated equation. Such a list does not distinguish the more important factors in language shift. Nor does it reveal the processes and mechanisms of language shift. It is thus difficult to predict which minoritized languages are more or less likely to decline, and which languages are more or less likely to be revived.

Table 3.3 Language maintenance and language loss

Factors encouraging language maintenance	Factors encouraging language loss
A. Political, social and demographic factors	
1. Large number of speakers living closely together	1. Small numbers of speakers, well dispersed
2. Recent and/or continuing in-migration	2. Long and stable residence
3. Close proximity to the homeland and ease of travel to homeland	3. Homeland remote or inaccessible
4. Preference to return to homeland with many actually returning	4. Low rate of return to homeland and/or little intention to return and/or impossible to return
5. Homeland language community intact	5. Homeland language community decaying in vitality
6. Stability in occupation	6. Occupational shift, especially from rural to urban areas
7. Employment available where home language is spoken daily	7. Employment requires use of the majority language
8. Low social and economic mobility in main occupations	8. High social economic mobility in main occupations
9. Low level of education to restrict social and economic mobility, but educated and articulate community leaders are loyal to their language community	9. High levels of education giving social and economic mobility. Potential community leaders are alienated from their language community by education
10. Ethnic group identity rather than identity with majority language community via nativism, racism and ethnic discrimination	10. Ethnic identity is denied to achieve social and vocational mobility; this is forced by nativism, racism and ethnic discrimination
B. Cultural factors	
1. Mother-tongue institutions (e.g. schools, community organizations, mass media, leisure activities)	1. Lack of mother-tongue institutions
2. Cultural and religious ceremonies in the home language	2. Cultural and religious activity in the majority language
3. Ethnic identity strongly tied to home language	3. Ethnic identity defined by factors other than language
4. Nationalistic aspirations as a language group	4. Few nationalistic aspirations
5. Mother tongue is the homeland national language	5. Mother tongue not the only homeland national language, or mother tongue spans several nations
6. Emotional attachment to mother tongue giving self-identity and ethnicity	6. Self-identity derived from factors other than shared home language
7. Emphasis on family ties and community cohesion	7. Low emphasis on family and community ties. High emphasis on individual achievement
8. Emphasis on education in mother-tongue schools to enhance ethnic awareness	8. Emphasis on education in majority language
9. Low emphasis on education if in majority language	9. Acceptance of majority language
10. Culture unlike majority language	10. Culture and religion similar to those of the majority language
C. Linguistic factors	
1. Mother tongue is standardized and exists in a written form	1. Mother tongue is non-standard and/or not in written form
2. Use of an alphabet which makes printing and literacy relatively easy	2. Use of writing system which is expensive to reproduce and relatively difficult to learn
3. Home language has international status	3. Home language of little or no international importance
4. Home language literacy used in community and with homeland	4. Literacy (or aliteracy) in the home language
5. Flexibility in the development of the home language (e.g. limited use of new of new terms from the majority language)	5. No tolerance of new terms from majority language; or too much tolerance of loan words leading to mixing and eventual language loss

Source: Adapted from Conklin and Lourie (1983)

A frequent, if generalized, scenario for immigrants observed in the United States is a three-generation shift to English. The first generation (grandparents) maintain their native language even if they gain some proficiency in English. The second generation (children) – born in the United States but raised in a home where the non-English language is spoken – typically become bilingual, though most often are more dominant in English. The third generation (grandchildren) are typically monolingual English-speakers.

However, this 'three-generation shift' is not the only possible pattern. Some groups, such as the Pennsylvania Dutch (Amish), historically avoided a three- or four-generation shift by retaining boundaries between them and the outside world. Other examples of language maintenance beyond the third generation include Yiddish-speaking Ultra-Orthodox Jews; French-speakers in northern Vermont, New Hampshire and Maine; and Spanish-speakers in small rural communities along the United States–Mexico border (Fishman, 2013). In recent immigrant groups, however, language shift may occur by the second generation, especially in cases where younger members of the first generation – the **1.5 generation** – start school at a young age with few opportunities to develop or maintain their native language (Wright, 2014a).

Among Panjabi, Italian, Gaelic and Welsh communities in Britain, there are occasional fourth-generation individuals who wish to revive the language of their ethnic origins. For some, **assimilation** into the majority language and culture does not give self-fulfillment. Rather, such revivalists seek a return to their roots by recovering the language and culture of their ethnic heritage. In Europe, with increasing pressure towards a European identity, language minoritized members seem increasingly aware of the benefits of a more distinctive and intimate local identity. The pressure to become part of a larger whole seems to result in a counterbalancing need to have secure roots within a smaller, more domestic community. A local language is valuable in this more particular identity. Bilingualism provides the means to be both international and local.

Language Decline and Death

Another way of identifying the causes of language shift is to examine a dying language within a particular region. In a classic study, Gal (1979) studied the replacement of Hungarian by German in the town of Oberwart in eastern Austria. After 400 years of relatively stable Hungarian–German bilingualism, economic, social and family life became more based on the German language. By focusing on intervening processes, Gal showed how social changes such as industrialization and urbanization change social networks, relationships between people and patterns in language use in communities. As new environments arise with new speakers, languages take on new forms, new meanings and create new patterns of social interaction. This suggests that social networks may play a more important role than communities in language shift.

Another celebrated study is a detailed case study by Dorian (1981) on the decline of Gaelic in east Sutherland, a region in the north-east highlands of Scotland. Historically, English and Gaelic coexisted, with English generally perceived as the high-status 'civilized' language and Gaelic the 'savage' language of lower prestige. The last two groups in the region to speak Gaelic were the 'crofters' (small land farmers) and the fishing community. Surrounded by English-speaking communities, these fisher-people originally spoke only Gaelic and later became bilingual in English and Gaelic. When the fishing industry began to decline, the boundaries between the Gaelic-speakers and the English-speakers began to crumble. The fisher-folk began to find other jobs, intermarriage replaced in-group marriage and 'outsiders' migrated to the east Sutherland area. Over time, the community gave up its fishing identity and the Gaelic language tended to decline with it. In the 20th century, a three-generation shift from monolingual Gaelic grandparents to monolingual English grandchildren was apparent.

Violent metaphoric labels such as 'language murder', 'language suicide' and 'linguicide' (linguistic genocide) are often used to draw attention to ways that dominant languages oppress minoritized languages, or that some linguistic groups purposely abandon their native languages. Davis (2017) warns that such rhetoric can falsely attribute blame to the speakers of the languages, rather than to social, political, economic and other factors. Thomason (2015: 68) also urges caution:

> It seems to me that these terms are overblown.... The death of any language is a sad event for a speech community.... But using labels of violence tends to distract attention from the real and complex sociolinguistic issues surrounding language death. A term like 'suicide' appears to blame the victim, the speech community that is losing its heritage language; the term 'murder' suggests that dominant-language speakers are actively killing the language as opposed to creating – often without intending any such result – conditions under which a minoritized speech community finds it impossible to maintain its own language.

While Thomason's point is well taken, the histories of the Native American languages of Canada and the United States, and particularly the histories of the African languages of those who were enslaved, provide strong evidence of extreme linguistic oppression deliberately designed to eradicate native tongues. In many cases, actual physical (and psychological) violence was used on individuals to enforce oppressive anti-native-language policies (Wiley & Wright, 2004). The Truth and Reconciliation Commission of Canada (2015) documented the negative impacts of the century-long Canadian Indian residential school system, which sought to eradicate indigenous languages and cultures. The Commission concluded in its final report that the school system amounted to cultural genocide, with long-lasting impacts on survivors and their families. As in the US Indian schools, thousands of indigenous children literally died while attending the residential schools.

When minoritized language speakers become bilingual and prefer the majority language, the outcome for the minoritized language may be decline, even death. Yet, where people are determined to keep a language alive, it may be impossible to destroy it. Language activists, pressure groups, affirmative action and language conservationists may fight for the survival of the threatened language. In Puerto Rico, failed English-only instruction policies were followed by instruction policies aimed at the bilingualization of the island. Nonetheless, factors such as nationalism, political uncertainty and the relationship between language and identity have led to resistance, keeping the majority of the island's population functionally monolingual in Spanish.

Language shift often reflects a pragmatic desire for social and vocational mobility, an improved standard of living and a personal cost–benefit analysis (Edwards, 2012). There may be a gap between the rhetoric of language preservation and harsh reality. This is illustrated in a story from Spolsky's early work among Native Americans:

> A Navajo student of mine once put the problem quite starkly: if I have to choose, she said, between living in a hogan a mile from the nearest water where my son will grow

up speaking Navajo or moving to a house in the city with indoor plumbing where he will speak English with the neighbors, I'll pick English and a bathroom! (Spolsky, 1989: 451)

However, where there are oppressed language minorities who are forced to live in segregated societies, there is often little choice of where to live and work. In the above quote, the Diné (Navajo) mother may have had the choice. In actuality, many language minorities have little or no real choice. Mass urbanization often results when impoverished families in under-developed and under-resourced rural and remote areas feel that moving to a large city where more jobs are available is necessary for survival; by way of example, see Smith (2021) for the case of planned urbanization in China. Such economic drivers of displacement and migration can have an enormous impact on language shift (Angouri *et al.*, 2023; Canagarajah, 2017; Monsen & Steien, 2022).

Language shift and the erosion of minoritized languages have been related to the growth of a few powerful majority languages, such as English, Spanish, Arabic, Mandarin and Hindi/Urdu. For some, bilingualism is threatened by such growth. Engman and King (2017: 205) observe that 'awareness of language endangerment only becomes widespread when language loss has progressed to the point at which action is urgent in the community'.

The chapter continues with the more positive and optimistic possibilities of language resurrection, using the example of Manx Gaelic. This example particularly reveals the major part that education can play in the fast decline of a minoritized language and in its slow resurrection.

Language Revival

Manx Gaelic is a Celtic language, closely related to the Gaelic spoken in Scotland and Irish in Ireland. It is spoken on the Isle of Man, a small island set between Ireland and England. In a survey in 1874, close to 50% of the island's population were found to speak Manx Gaelic, numbering around 12,350 speakers. However, the 1872 Education Act banned Manx Gaelic in schools. If Manx was spoken by a child in school, a whipping could result. While not the only cause of language decline, banishment from schools triggered a fast shift to English. A language expelled from education sends a message to parents: the language is becoming obsolete, with no employment or economic value. The language transmission of Manx Gaelic in the home no longer prepared children for school, employment or a social life.

By 1931, the Isle of Man Census showed only 531 speakers of Manx remaining. In 1974, Edward (Ted) Maddrell died, regarded as the last native speaker of Manx Gaelic (Abley, 2005). Thereafter, the word among international linguists was that Manx was dead. In the 1981 Decennial Census on the Isle of Man, a language question was symbolically eradicated.

However, there remained a few second language speakers of Manx. Even at the lowest point (the 1961 Census), there were 165 recorded second language speakers (0.3% of the population), thus making revival possible. By the 1991 Census, an increase to 643 speakers had occurred, and the 2011 Census counted 1,823 speakers out of a population of 84,497 (2.2%) (Economic Affairs Division, 2012). Remarkably, new native speakers began to appear in 2001, having been spoken to in Manx Gaelic by their fluent second language parents from birth. Manx Gaelic is being slowly resurrected. In 2021, the Isle of Man Census reported the number of Manx Gaelic speakers to be 2,223 (Statistics Isle of Man Cabinet Office, 2022). The Manx Gaelic revival continues, inspired by the dedication of a number of language enthusiasts. This revival is particularly driven by the desire for an Isle of Man identity that is separate and different from only having a general British identity. A Manx language immersion education program is successfully operating, called Bunscoill Ghaelgagh. There are second language Manx Gaelic classes in Isle of Man elementary and high schools (Ó hIfearnáin, 2015).

The main point of this illustration is that a language can decline very rapidly by its ban from all schools and its non-transmission in the home. The revival of a language via schooling is very slow. A language can be cut down within a few decades, but takes much time to grow from small seedlings, and even longer to spread. The revival in education does not only start with young children; it needs *a priori* the training and availability of teachers who can operate in the revived language. Teachers thus join crusading parents, language activists and language planners as the human foundation of language salvage and salvation.

Apart from the societal and speech community levels of analysis of language change, there is the individual person level in revival. Teachers and their students are important individuals in such revitalization efforts. This point is strongly made by McCarty (2013: xx): 'When we speak of language loss and revitalization, we should be ever mindful of the living, breathing children, families and communities those abstractions reference'.

Language Conflict

Contact between ethnic groups with differing languages does not always occur in a peaceful and harmonious fashion. There are sometimes tensions, rivalries and disputes. Such disputes do not always lead to conflict, although, as in the cases of Indonesia, Ethiopia, Rwanda, Bosnia, Serbia and the Middle East, ethnic conflicts do develop. At the extreme, there can be 'linguistic cleansing'. Inter-ethnic conflict and civil war can involve attempts to impose the language of the ascendant group. As an instrument of social control, languages can be a component in social conflict. For example, a monolingual and centralized bureaucracy may believe that multilingualism is like Babel: when there is linguistic diversity, there is a state of chaos, with resulting effects on law and order, economy and efficiency. **Monolingualism** is seen as a stable condition, multilingualism as linguistic imperfection leading to problems and conflicts (see Chapter 17).

When languages enter such conflicts between groups, language tends to become a marker or a symbol of the identities in the conflict, rather than the real source of the conflict, which is often racial, ethnic, religious, economic or cultural. When there are struggles for power and dominance between groups in society, language is often the surface feature or focal point of deeper-seated conflicts. For example, in the United States, conflicts about the place accorded to immigrant languages in bilingual education hide deeper concerns about political dominance, status, defense of economic and social position, as well as concerns about immigration, cultural integration, nationalism and an American identity. Thus language minorities may, on the surface, appear as a threat to national unity, with language acting as a symbol of the threat. Underneath, the conflict is more about economic and political advantage, political power and ethnic or national solidarity, and not least about identity (see Chapter 18).

The source of a conflict is often rooted in political and economic power differences, and issues about rights and privileges (Roche, 2022). Social and economic disadvantages often underlie language conflicts. Language is usually a secondary sign of the primary or fundamental causes of conflict. Nevertheless, politicians and administrators often seize upon language as if it were the cause, and sometimes as if it were the remedy. Underlying causes are thus ignored or avoided. In essence, conflicts cannot occur between languages, only between the speakers of those languages. Thus, while language oppression is real, the idea of language conflict can often be a misnomer.

Language and Nationalism

Nations are divided along socially constructed international borders that have real political, social, cultural and linguistic consequences, particularly for those living in the 'borderlands' (Valdés, 2017). Nationalism concerns a consciousness of belonging to a perceived separate people, located in a defined territory, bounded by a belief in having a common culture and history, with common institutions and the desire to achieve or maintain political autonomy. Thus 'borderlands' also exist in the metaphorical sense. Language helps create that consciousness and has been an important symbol of national identity. Nationalism is often said to have emerged after the French Revolution and became a major determinant of political policy and change throughout much of the 19th and 20th centuries.

Yet, particularly in the latter half of the 20th century, many minoritized ethnic groups became concerned about their own identity, including the desire to maintain their languages and cultures and to achieve a measure of political self-determination. The maintenance of regional ethnic identities, however, is often seen by many as contrary to the unity of the nation. Thus, attempts have been made by governments to eradicate minoritized languages and emphasize the majority language by means of education and compulsory use of that language in public and official life. In recent decades, the rise of cosmopolitan multilingual cities has posed a challenge to this view of nationalism. Cities such as Brussels, London, Montréal, New York and Phnom Penh contain multinational and transitional peoples, with a multitude of languages, identities and cultures.

The concept of a supra-ethnic nation state has been perceived as a necessity in many African and Asian countries in the post-colonial era. For example, Indonesia, Kenya, Nigeria, Papua New Guinea and Tanzania consist of many local ethnic groups. Hence, the maintenance of supra-ethnic unity has been regarded as vital for economic and technological development. One practical outcome of this is the need for a majority language for international relations, official life and education, with local vernaculars being used in the home and neighborhood. This shows that the concept of a nation does not inevitably mean cultural assimilation and the eradication of local languages.

Nationalism often has negative connotations due to its association with 20th-century fascism in Germany, Italy and Spain. Extreme nationalistic views overlap with forms of racism and language imperialism. Racist nationalism maintains that some 'races' and languages are superior to others. Afrikaner nationalism in South Africa was traditionally based on the myth of the White man's superiority. The racist ideology of Nazis and neo-Nazis represents an extreme form of nationalism based on the myth of racial purity. This is also evident in contemporary Britain, where, for example, some extreme right-wing groups express their nationalism with explicit racism and hatred of languages other than English.

The basis of US nationalism also relates to recent support for the increased dominance of English over immigrant languages. US nationalism cannot be based on historical territory, given the massive immigration into the country. There is no long, shared history, and no overall religious dimension that unites people in nationhood. While political feeling, for example against communism and terrorism, has been used as a means of trying to create nationalist unity, US nationalism is instead based around dimensions such as political freedom, emancipation, social and economic mobility, individual freedoms and liberties, individual enterprise, economic advantage, the superiority of the US military, world political and economic power, and the English language. US nationalism is thus based in modernity rather than history, on a shared economic and political aspiration rather than on long ownership of territory, and is based on self-determination and strong patriotism. Such a basis for US nationalism has strong implications for language policy, including policies favoring the replacement of immigrant and indigenous languages by English.

Language is often viewed as the pre-eminent badge of a loyalty that expresses a sense of belonging to a national group (e.g. English in the United States). Language becomes a symbol of the independence of a separate nation and of a separate people. The Basques define their boundaries and separatism by who speaks, and who does not speak, the Basque language. Language comes to represent an attitude to independence and separation. Thus the Québécois in Canada make French a symbol of their drive for more independence from Canada.

Nevertheless, language is not essential to either nationalism or ethnicity. Concerns about loyalty, self-determination and political independence do not necessarily require a separate language. African nationalism is not based on language. Given the many different languages and dialects in Africa, language is clearly not a common denominator in African self-determination, membership or loyalty, nor in the desire for self-determination and political independence from Europe. In countries such as Pakistan, it is religion that tends to be the cement and symbol of loyalty, rather than language. Thus language is a valuable but not essential condition for nationalism to survive and thrive.

Bilingualism and multilingualism are often seen as obstacles to nationalism. Given that a minoritized language is always in danger of being swamped by a majority language, bilingualism can also be seen as an unstable state, a halfway house for people who are moving from the minoritized language to the majority language. However, bilingualism and multilingualism can be supported by nationalism, particularly in areas where there are a variety of ethnic groups, and where a group is in a numerical minority but uses a majority language as its mother tongue.

Political changes throughout the world are changing the concept of nationhood. In China, with 55 officially recognized ethnic minority groups, Feng and Adamson (2015: 488) note that 'the promotion of English into the classrooms dominated by minoritized groups has further amplified the complexity' of the nation's linguistic situation. There are tensions in the desire to promote trilingualism in regional languages and English while upholding Mandarin as a national language. As one concerned policy-maker urged, 'we must put Chinese at the center and focus our attention on promoting Chinese national consciousness and identity' (Feng & Adamson, 2015: 489). In Europe, with the growth of the European Union and the drive towards Europeanization, a sense of a more European identity rather than a purely national identity has begun (e.g. Irish,

Slovenian). In the world of the internet, the global economy and ease of transport between countries, the growth of economic and political interdependence in the world, new forms of loyalty and identity are beginning to occur. Thus supranationalism is beginning to have effects on language.

In the 21st century, new demographic patterns of migration have altered the nature of language minoritized communities in European nations and beyond (Canagarajah, 2017; Monsen & Steien, 2022). Traditional patterns involved large influxes from a relatively small number of countries (e.g. former colonies, bordering countries, impoverished countries, sites of armed conflict). Today, however, rapidly growing diversity in these nations is often made up of smaller groups from a much wider variety of countries. The term **superdiversity** has been refined by sociologist Steven Vertovec (2007, 2017) to describe these complex and new patterns. Using Britain as an example, Vertovec describes the country's superdiversity as 'distinguished by a dynamic interplay of variables among an increased number of new, small and scattered, multiple-origin, transnationally connected, socioeconomically differentiated and legally stratified immigrants who have arrived over the last decade' (Vertovec, 2007: 1024). Superdiversity also describes diversity within individual immigrant and ethnic minoritized groups – diversity within diversity, or 'the diversification of diversity' (Vertovek, 2017). Blommaert (2013) credits two connected forces in the development of superdiversity – the end of the Cold War opening up new migration possibilities, and the internet, particularly Web 2.0 technologies in the late 1990s, which offer 'a vast and unparalleled expansion of the means for exchanging long-distance information and for developing and maintaining translocal ties' (Blommaert, 2013: 5).

Creese and Blackledge (2018: xxii) explain that 'superdiversity describes people coming into contact or proximity as a result of (*inter alia*) migration, invasion, colonisation, slavery, religious mission, persecution, trade, conflict, famine, drought, war, urbanisation, economic aspiration, family reunion, global commerce, and technological advances'. Spotti and Blommaert (2017: 170) note:

> New objects such as Internet memes or mobile phone texting codes, as well as identity repertoires and transnational communication taking place through the means of social media channels offer both descriptive as well as theoretical challenges [in traditional sociolinguistic research] because such complex multimodal objects defy standard assumptions of language, channel, meaning, and uptake.

Thus, sociolinguists are just beginning to explore the ways this new superdiversity 'becomes the site of negotiations over linguistic resources', not just among the newly arrived, but also among established ethnic minoritized communities (Creese & Blackledge, 2010a: 550) and how it is changing the linguistic landscape (Gorter & Cenoz, 2024; Malinowski & Tufi, 2020).

An embracing of superdiversity, and the move towards supranationalism may have a positive effect on bilingualism and multilingualism (Arnaut *et al.*, 2017). The drive to share a wider identity (e.g. to be European or part of the global village) may lead to a reaction among individuals. To belong to a supranational group may initially require local loyalty, a rootedness in local group cohesion, a sense of belonging to a community first of all, and before being able psychologically to identify with large supranational groups. Thus bilingualism in the majority and the minoritized language may become important in gaining a feeling of rootedness locally, as well as belonging to an increasingly larger identity.

Social Varieties of Language

In addition to different languages in a society, there is much variation within given named languages. Speakers of a given named language (e.g. English) can often pinpoint another speaker's country of origin (e.g. the United States), or even a particular region within a specific country (e.g. New York), based on how they talk. This may include slight to significant differences in pronunciation (accent), vocabulary and grammar. The study of language variation considers different varieties or dialects of language. A language variety refers to the language of a particular speech community or social group. When a language variety becomes recognizable and different enough, it may be considered a separate dialect (e.g. Appalachian English, the Shanghai dialect of Chinese). However, there is much disagreement and inconsistency in distinguishing different languages, varieties and dialects (see Chapter 4).

Language ideologies are ideas and feelings individuals may have about language that typically lead to evaluations about the ways people speak and use language (Valdés, 2017) (see Chapter 18). A standard language ideology often results in discrimination by privileging a standard variety of a language over non-standard varieties (Lippi-Green, 2012). In the United States, for example, African-American English is a legitimate yet highly stigmatized variety of English (Baker-Bell, 2020a; Wolfram, 2020). Controversy erupted in 1996 when the Oakland Unified School District proposed an Ebonics program designed to recognize and value the variety of English spoken by many African-American students while helping them master Standard American English (Ramirez et al., 2005). Baker-Bell (2020b) documents continuing 'anti-Black linguistic racism' in English language arts classrooms in the United States and calls for an anti-racist Black language pedagogy. Baker-Bell's work highlights how language ideologies are often grounded in and intertwined with the racist views individuals may have of other people. **Raciolinguistics** considers the relations of ideologies at the intersection of language, race and power (Cushing, 2022; Flores, 2024; Rosa, 2019).

Immigrant students lumped together as 'Arabic-speakers' use many different varieties of Arabic, some of which are not even mutually intelligible. Many 'mother tongue' bilingual programs in the United States and around the world focus on a standard variety of a language which may in fact be very different from the varieties students actually speak at home (Henderson & Sayer, 2020; Weber & Horner, 2018). Puerto Rican students, for example, may find their variety of Spanish marginalized in bilingual programs where the teacher and other students are predominantly from Mexico. Some well-meaning school districts recruit bilingual teachers from Spain who end up teaching standard Castilian Spanish, which is quite foreign to their students born in the United States, Mexico and Central America.

These issues speak to the need for educators to develop critical language awareness (Fairclough, 2013) or critical dialect awareness, that is, the ability to analyze language differences critically, be aware of how varieties and dialects are valued differently, understand aspects of language and power, and plan appropriate programs and instruction accordingly. García (2017b: 269) builds on early notions of language awareness by calling for multilingual critical language awareness, which includes, for example: (1) 'awareness of plurilingualism and merits for democratic citizenship'; (2) 'awareness of histories of colonial and imperialistic oppression'; and (3) 'awareness that language is socially created, and thus socially changeable'. Curricular programs can also be provided to help students and teachers develop multilingual critical language awareness

(Carter *et al.*, 2020; Cenoz *et al.*, 2017). Language variation is central to considerations of the use and spread of English around the world.

English as a Global Language

The spread of English throughout the world is sometimes viewed favorably as a homogenizing, positive characteristic of globalization. Others see such spread unfavorably, often driven by ideologies of neoliberalism, and leading to the loss of small minoritized languages to colonization and to **linguistic imperialism**. These are ideological positions to which need adding the perspectives of individuals who speak different forms of native and international English, plus a recognition of the increasing varieties of World Englishes. As this term reveals, English is more than one language. Standardized forms of English include Standard American English, Standard British English and Standard Australia English, but these are just three of many standard and non-standard varieties of English. Englishes have local and international dimensions, are ever-changing and complex. They interact with cultural heritage and popular culture, technology and travel, identity and belonging to imagined communities. Englishes are powerful and pervasive, yet many varieties are related to inequality of access and assimilation of immigrants, empowering some and disempowering others.

World Englishes reveal that the situation of English and its relation to bilingualism are not uniform throughout the world but vary according to a multitude of factors, including the local political situation, other languages spoken in the country, inter-ethnic relations and cultural attitudes (Nelson *et al.*, 2020). Tupas (2015) uses the term 'unequal Englishes' to emphasize that non-standard varieties of English are rarely treated equally within society. In the last decade, there has been a growing emphasis on the inclusion of a standardized variety of English in the curriculum in many countries of the world. This is partly based on English-dominant economic, financial and political associations with the language. However, there can also be the paradoxical resurgence of localism and the vernacular language as a subtle resistance to English (Tollefson & Tsui, 2018; Tupas & Rani, 2015).

Kachru (2005, 2020) conceptualized World Englishes as three concentric circles: the inner circle, the outer circle and the expanding circle (for a review of critiques, see Bolton, 2020). In the inner circle are countries where English is the first language of the majority of the population. In the outer circle are countries where English is spoken widely as a second language and enjoys official status. In the expanding circle are countries where English has no official status but may be used, for example, in business and multinational communications. Kachru's circles largely correspond to, respectively, ENL (English as a native language), **ESL (English as a second language)**, and EFL (English as a foreign language). The world pre-eminence of English lies in that it is a first, second and foreign language and is found across the globe in all three categories. These three categories will now be considered more fully in turn.

(1) *Inner-circle countries*. English is the first language and often the only language of the majority of the population. In the United States, Australia, Canada, the United Kingdom, Ireland and New Zealand, the majority of the population are monolingual English-speakers. Historically, however, the spread of English in the wake of political and economic expansion has led to the decline and sometimes death of indigenous languages in all these countries.

(2) **Outer-circle countries**. English coexists as a second language in bilingual or multilingual contexts. In former British colonies, English has often remained the official language or at least one of the official languages. English is still used widely in official contexts and education (e.g. in South Africa and India). English is not spoken as a first or home language by the majority of the population. It may be spoken only by an exclusive social elite and only in certain contexts (e.g. official and formal contexts).

(3) *Expanding-circle countries*. English is a foreign language, may have no official status and may not be spoken at all by the majority of the population (e.g. in Cambodia, China, Japan, Mozambique, Thailand, Malaysia and Slovenia). In these countries, however, English is acknowledged as an important and prestigious language, and people may be exposed to it in particular domains. There may be considerable emphasis on the teaching of English as a foreign language in schools and also in business and industry. English language films may be shown with subtitles on television and in the cinema, and English language pop songs may be widespread. Many English words may have been adopted by the indigenous language, and English may be used widely in advertising to suggest power, popularity and prestige.

Attempting to force countries into one of these circles or categories, however, is increasingly difficult and may be insensitive to a variety of differences. Tupas and Rani express concern that the concentric circles model makes an ideological claim about the ownership of English:

> No one has the exclusive rights to the language; anyone who speaks it has the right to own it. The norms of use are multilingual norms and the strategies to teach English are also multilingual in nature. The English language is deeply embedded in the multilingual and multicultural lives of its speakers – so who are the native speakers of English today? To insist that those who can be called native speakers are only those who come from Inner Circle countries, especially the United States and the United Kingdom (where users of English are typically described as 'native speakers'), is to disenfranchise the majority of English speakers today. (Tupas & Rani, 2015: 1)

Furthermore, the concentric circles model suggests a one-way flow from the inner circle to the outer and expanding circles. However, the global cultural flows of culture and knowledge, including language, are complex and 'new technologies and communications are enabling immense and complex flows of people, signs, sounds, images across multiple borders in multiple directions' (Pennycook, 2013: 593). For example, the global hip hop movement may have roots in African-American rap music, but it flows through many countries and is influenced by, and hybridized with, local languages and cultures (see, e.g. Lin, 2015).

The Spread of English

The spread of English, like that of other prestigious languages throughout time, has come about in a variety of ways, including political domination, the subordination of vernacular languages, trade, colonization, emigration, education, religion, mass media, technology and social media (Salomone, 2024). Through such channels, the English language has penetrated to the furthest reaches of the globe. However, the influence of each of these factors, and the level of intent in domination or market-led change, is much contested (see e.g. Phillipson & Skutnabb-Kangas, 2013).

According to SIL International's Ethnologue (www.ethnologue.com), approximately 380 million people in the world speak English as a first language and an even greater number, 1.14 billion, speak it as a second language (Eberhard *et al.*, 2024). Estimates by the British Council (Patel *et al.*, 2023) are even higher, reporting 388.2 million English first language speakers and 1.93 billion second language speakers of English (basing these estimates on Crystal, 2018). It also estimates that worldwide, 31% of the population speaks English and 41% has been exposed to English. However, these and other estimates are often contentious, with criteria for inclusion as a second language speaker or learner (see Chapter 1) being highly variable.

Numbers of speakers is less important when considering the spread of English than the prestigious domains and functions into which English has spread and often dominates. The international prestige of English and English-speaking nations and the popularity of Anglo-American culture has given the English language associations of status, power and wealth. Access to English means access to valued forms of knowledge and access to affluent and prestigious social and vocational positions. As a global language, English has dominated many prestigious domains and functions: international communication, science, technology, medicine, computers, research, books, periodicals, transnational business, tourism, trade, shipping, aviation, advertising, diplomacy, international organizations, mass media, entertainment, news agencies, the internet, politics, youth culture and sport.

At the end of the 1990s, it was estimated that 80% of the information on the internet was stored in English, though in hindsight that estimate was likely exaggerated (Crystal, 2006). While English remains the single most commonly used language online, a 12-year study by UNESCO estimated that the proportion of English content had decreased to about 45% by 2005 (Pimienta *et al.*, 2009). A 2015 estimate suggested that 55.5% of web content is in English, followed at a far distance by Russian, German, Japanese, Spanish, French and Chinese, each accounting for around 3–6% (Wood, 2015). In 2017, CSA Research, a market research firm focused on global language services markets, reported that English-speakers' share of the online audience fell to 20% as ease of internet access increased around the globe (Sargent, 2017). However, this figure likely does not appear to account for second language speakers of English. Thus, a 2009 UNESCO estimate of native and second language English-speakers making up 55% of internet users may be more accurate (Pimienta *et al.*, 2009). In 2020 the Miniwats Marketing Group estimated that English first-language speakers make up only about a quarter (25.9%) of internet users (as cited in Patel *et al.*, 2023).

At the time of this writing, W3Techs (https://wtechs.com/technologies/overview/content_language), which provides daily updates, reported that English is used in slightly less than half of websites (49.7%). The languages with the next highest figures – Spanish and German – account for only 5.9% and 5.4% respectively of content languages for websites. Thus, over 150 other languages account for a little more than half of websites, revealing the increasing multilingual nature of the internet. The multimodal content of social media sites such as YouTube, Facebook, X (Twitter), TikTok, Instagram, Pinterest and many others generated by users around the world is truly multilingual.

The Future of English

Figure 3.2 provides estimates from Graddol (2006) of the number of past and future native (L1) speakers of English and other major languages. While acknowledging that

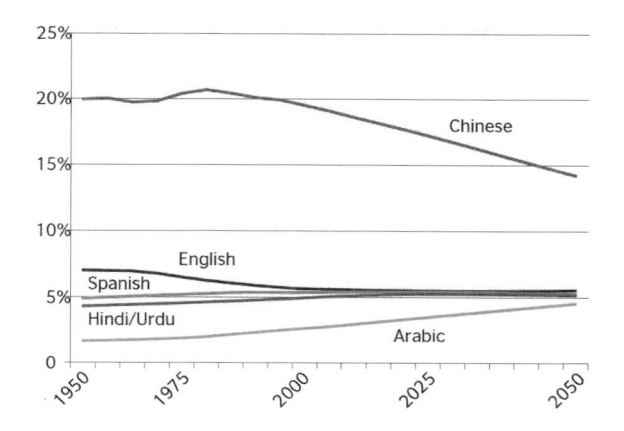

Figure 3.2 Trends in native-speaker numbers for the world's largest languages, expressed as the proportion of the global population. Source: Graddol (2006: 60)

estimating these figures is 'surprisingly difficult', Graddol nonetheless concludes that the second rank of English in native-speaker rankings is declining, with the emergence of similar numbers of native speakers of Spanish, Hindi/Urdu and Arabic.

Recent data from Ethnologue suggests Graddol's prediction is on track. In terms of the numbers of L1 speakers, Spanish is number 2, with approximately 486 million L1 speakers, and English is number 3, with approximately 380 million L1 speakers. However, when the number of second language (L2) users is considered, English is ranked as the most commonly spoken language in the world, followed closely by Mandarin Chinese. Table 3.4 shows the top 10 world languages when both L1 and L2 users are combined.

Table 3.4 Total numbers of users (L1 and L2) of the top 10 world languages, 2024

Language	Total number of users
English	1,515,000,000
Mandarin Chinese	1,140,000,000
Hindi	608,800,000
Spanish	559,500,000
French	332,500,000
Standard Arabic	311,600,000
Bengali	278,200,000
Portuguese	263,800,000
Russian	255,400,000
Urdu	237,900,000

Note: Numbers rounded to the nearest million.
Source: Eberhard *et al.* (2024), https://www.ethnologue.com/guides/ethnologue200

The advantages and disadvantages of English are much debated by scholars (e.g. Crystal, 2012; Mohanty, 2019; Phillipson, 2018). On one side there are those who regard English as valuable for international and intercultural communication, the *de facto* global language, a relatively neutral vehicle for communication that gives access to quality higher education. A 2023 British Council publication on the future of English (Patel *et al.*, 2023: 328) analyzes and extends the 2006 report by Gradol and provides several projected future trends for the next decade, including the following:

- Online language English language learning will be a major growth area.
- English-medium instruction will continue to be widely employed in higher education, but the teaching of English as a subject will continue to be the main way English is taught in basic education.
- Native-speaker norms will continue to be used as a standard, but efforts to identify alternative ways of assessing English as a global language will accelerate.
- The paradigm shift away from EFL will continue with pedagogies that emphasize global English and multilingual realities gaining more ground.
- English will continue as the dominant lingua franca, despite the economic power of several non-Anglophone countries.
- The importance of multilingualism will lead to concerted efforts to promote additional language learning in Anglophone countries to enhance international trade and participate in global dialogue.

A developing country that encourages the learning and use of English in trade and business may facilitate economic and employment opportunities. However, as these trends and data above suggest, English is not alone in this scenario, with Spanish, Mandarin Chinese and Arabic, for example, also having growing prestigious economic and employment associations.

In 2004, China began actively promoting Chinese language learning by establishing non-profit Confucius Institutes and classrooms all over the world. At the beginning of 2020, this included 135 in Asia, 61 in Africa, 142 in the Americas, 187 in Europe and 20 in Oceania. Such promotion by one national government of its language in another country may be viewed with suspicion. In 2018 the US Congress restricted federal funding to schools with a Confucious Institute and in 2020 the first Trump administration directed the US Department of State to designate Confucius Institutes as a foreign mission of the People's Republic of China amid accusations that the Institutes were propaganda machines on US college campuses and in K-12 classrooms (Pompeo, 2020). Thus, US schools and universities were highly pressured to break ties and close their Confucius Institutes (US Department of State, 2020). The US Government Accountability Office (2023) reported that nearly all of the Confucius Institutes in the US have since been closed. It also found that some institutions were able to draw on other sources of funding to continue Chinese language instruction (including US federal funding and government funding from Taiwan), while many others ended their programs.

Many people on all continents have been willing to learn and accept English as a universal utilitarian language. Such learners have been willing to embrace English, not for Anglo-American **enculturation**, but as an international language that facilitates trade and commerce, and international and multinational communication. English is regarded by such learners as a means of communication to an economic or political (rather than a cultural or social) end. In such situations, the stigma of a colonializing English is being replaced by a positive attitude about the multinational functionality of English amidst globalization (Bhatia, 2020; Boun & Duran, 2024; Van Horn, 2020). However, 'long shadows' of inequality and divisiveness, class divides and subordination remain (Tupas, 2015).

The growth of English in China is an example of the rapid spread of English as a universal language (Graddol, 2013). Feng and Adamson (2015) attribute this growth to China's open-door policy, which views English as key to modernization, along with other important factors such as membership in the World Trade Organization in 2001, the 2008 Olympic Games in Beijing and the 2010 World Expo in Shanghai, all of which have led to high levels of enthusiasm for English competence. Hundreds of millions of people in China are learning English – a number far greater than the total US population (Hong & Pawan, 2014). Since 2001, English has been a compulsory subject in grades 3 and higher in Chinese schools, and universities are expected to provide 5–10% of undergraduate instruction in English or another foreign language.

On the other side there is a critical perspective that sees English as part of linguistic imperialism, dominance by the United States and other English-speaking countries, a means of reproducing structural, cultural, educational and economic inequalities, maintaining capitalist economic advantages and control, and oppressing weak minoritized languages and their peoples (Phillipson, 2018). Gandhi (1927), for example, accused English of being an intoxicating language, denationalizing a country such as India, and encouraging mental slavery to Anglo forms of thinking and culture. He argued that English had been used in some multilingual societies to internally colonize and to preserve the power of ruling elites. English has imposed linguistic uniformity that is culturally, intellectually, spiritually and emotionally restricting. Other languages are then portrayed as confining, ethnocentric, divisive, alienating and anti-nationalistic. Asserting the dominance of English can become a means by which power elites justify exclusion and sustain inequality.

The relationship between Islam and English is a topic of ongoing concern as a result of issues such as 9/11 and the global 'War on Terror' (Karmani & Pennycook, 2005). Rahman (2005) claims that there are three Islamic responses to English: acceptance of English and assimilation into Anglophone culture; rejection and resistance based on religion and preferred identity and values; and pragmatic utilization so as to share power and knowledge, raise wealth and social status, and 'learn the language of your enemy'. While there may sometimes be a clash of cultural values and a polarizing conflict between Islam and western Anglophone culture, this is not necessarily the preferred position of Islam. Mohd-Asraf (2005) suggests that the Qur'an invokes many Muslims proselytizing by the learning of other languages and the gaining of wisdom from other cultures through their languages. She argues the learning of English is not in conflict with Islamic values; so long as a child is socialized thoroughly into Islamic religion, identity, culture and the Muslim way of life, then bilingualism and biculturalism have additive effects that are enabling rather than conflicting. Bolander and Sultana (2019: 162) describe the 'ordinariness of English amongst Muslim communities in South and Central Asia' and through their ethnographic work found 'that religion is co-constructed and emergent in, across, and through English and other languages and semiotic resources'.

Yet it is not the language that is dominating, but the people who use it. A language such as English is not intrinsically dominating. No language is more suited to oppression, domination, westernization, secularization or imperialism than another. It is the speakers of that language who are the oppressors and dominators. Whether English is empowering or divisive, it is those who, for example, impose, teach, learn and use it that make it so. The danger is that language is made the symbolic scapegoat for political and economic domination, which are, in fact, the consequences of people and politics.

There are major concerns over English as a language of former colonial powers and the need for efforts to promote national and regional languages (Phillipson, 2018). Others stress this should not prevent us from acknowledging that English gives access to personal status, modernization (e.g. technology, science), the global economy and international communication. Dörnyei *et al*. (2006), for example, suggest that English provides the lingua franca in a world that is getting smaller, providing the means of direct communication (e.g. face-to-face, phone, texting, email, videoconferencing, social media) between people of different languages, cultures and economies. Thus students are often very motivated to learn English. Nevertheless, the advantages for individuals in the globalization of English need to be understood against the elitism and hegemony that have often been attached to English. For example, Bhatia and Ritchie (2013: 854) cite an 1835 colonial education document by Lord Macaulay in India that set out his vision of elite English education to create 'a class of persons, Indian in blood and colour, but English in taste, in opinions, in morals and intellect'.

For some, the spread of English has been connected to the decline and death of many indigenous languages (e.g. Phillipson & Skutnabb-Kangas, 2013). The dissemination of Anglo-American culture is claimed to have caused the weakening and eradication of local, indigenous cultures. Such a widespread use of English means that Anglo culture, Anglo institutions and Anglo ways of thinking and communicating are spreading. English then tends to displace the functions of other languages and even to displace the languages themselves. For example, in technology, communications and entertainment, English has become the dominant language in some countries. It can take over some of the internal functions of other languages in a country (e.g. in business, mass media) and become the means of the external link in, for example, politics, commerce, science, tourism and entertainment.

Where English has rapidly spread, the danger is that it does not encourage bilingualism but, rather, a shift towards English as the preferred language, especially in schools. English has sometimes become an official language or a national language, for instance in Singapore, India and Kenya, and local vernaculars may be viewed as substandard. Advanced schooling, for example in Kenya, has often required English to be the principal language in the classroom. The use of vernaculars in the classroom will then be seen as of lower status, for the poor or less socially and economically mobile peoples.

There are exceptions to the growth of English around the world. Where a country has a 'great tradition', the place of English may be restricted to particular modern and separate functions. For example, in Arabic and Islamic countries, and in some Asian countries such as Malaysia, the strong promotion of religion or nationalism may help restrain English from infiltrating a variety of domains. Yet in other countries, such as Singapore and India, English has been adopted as a unifier between different regions and as a common language. In India, there are 15 languages that have constitutionally guaranteed status, with English and Hindi being the main languages of communication between different regions.

When there are reactions against English as a colonizing language, the arguments tend to take on different dimensions: that English creates anti-nationalism and is likely to destroy native cultures; that English will introduce materialism and values that may destroy the religion of the people (e.g. Islam, Hinduism, Buddhism); that a people learning English will be rootless, in a state of flux and transition; that decadent western values such as sexual permissiveness, drug use and lack of respect for elders will be transmitted by the language; that English will bring divisions in the country, in the community and in families, separating those who speak the native languages and those who prefer to move towards English; that there will be alienation from traditional culture, heritage values and beliefs, plus a lack of individual and unique identity.

The predictions in Figure 3.2 suggest that the rise of English globally may have peaked and may fade in the future. With current changes in internationalism, the global economy, global companies, technology, telecommunications and religion, the international information and knowledge economy may move the world away from monolingual English operations to one where languages such as Spanish, Arabic and Mandarin Chinese may grow in use. The rising major economies of India, China, Brazil and Russia are already indicating that varieties of World Englishes rather than the standardized varieties of 'native' English will be the prestigious varieties of the future. In this world, bilinguals and multilinguals will be of more economic value than monolinguals.

Critical Post-Structuralist Sociolinguistics

Spotti and Blommaert (2017: 172) declare that 'the study of language and society has moved from the study of bilingualism to the study of multilingual languaging', that is, the ways bilingual and multilingual people actually use their languages in daily practice. García *et al.* (2017a, 2017b) recognize the important role sociolinguistics has played in supporting language diversity and in working with language-minoritized communities to resist societal inequities and to seek social justice. However, they contend that much sociolinguistic scholarship, from its positivist modernist roots, actually reinforces the inequalities it aims to critique by ignoring the root causes. They argue that new and more robust understandings of the complex inter-relationships between language inequalities and other forms of social inequality require a reframing through an emerging *critical post-structuralist sociolinguistics*. Their specific concern is the way that traditional positivist modernist sociolinguistics uncritically accepts language varieties as bounded entities that can be objectively named, defined, assigned to specific bounded speech communities, managed through policies and programs, and mastered as additional languages. They also contend that these traditional approaches tended to view relationships between linguistic differentiation and other forms of social differentiation as relatively straightforward processes, and that sociolinguistic research typically neglected the investigation of the historical roots of contemporary language ideological processes. Thus, many sociolinguists offered solutions that failed to address the root causes of linguistic inequalities.

In contrast, critical post-structuralist sociolinguistics calls into question many of the foundational concepts of sociolinguistics by analyzing how language shapes relations of power (Foucault, 1978). Thus, the emphasis is on studying 'language practices in inter-relationship to the *socio-historical, political, and economic conditioning* that produce them' (García *et al.*, 2017a: 5, emphasis in original). To promote critical post-structuralist sociolinguistics, García *et al.* (2017b) offer the following 11 principles:

(1) All understandings of language are ideological.
(2) It is necessary to historicize contemporary language ideological processes (e.g. impact of colonization on local languages).

(3) It is necessary to situate contemporary language ideological processes within the contemporary world order (e.g. impact of nationalism, globalization, neoliberalism, migration, social inequalities, etc.).
(4) Linguistic differentiation is produced within daily social interactions that are shaped by larger sociopolitical processes (e.g. understanding the ways listeners and speakers take up, negotiate or resist language practices and registers perceived to be different from their own speech community).
(5) Linguistic differentiation occurs in relation to other forms of social differentiation (e.g. race, ethnicity, gender, social class, religion).
(6) Speakers use language as a way of producing particular identities (e.g. doctors, teachers, hip hop artists).
(7) It is necessary to shift the unit of analysis beyond language towards the multimodal nature of communication (e.g. gestures, facial expressions, emojis, audio, video, illustrations, photos, hyperlinks, memes).
(8) There is a need to shift from discussions of languages towards a discussion of languaging (e.g. ways bilingual students translanguage for learning and authentic communication).
(9) Sociolinguistics must be aware of the institutional constraints of language users (e.g. English-only schooling).
(10) A major goal is to open up spaces for the legitimization of new subjectivities.
(11) Sociolinguists must work in solidarity with others to effectively advocate for language-minoritized communities (e.g. anthropologists, sociologists, social geographers, cultural studies scholars).

García *et al*. (2017b) acknowledge that these principles are not completely new and build on previous sociolinguistic work, including work highlighted in this chapter. But they suggest that these principles are the beginning of a conversation to help the field of sociolinguistics take a more critical turn in the 21st century.

Conclusion

This chapter has focused on languages at the group, social and community level. Majority and minoritized languages are frequently in contact, sometimes in conflict. The relationship between two languages tends to shift constantly as a consequence of a variety of changeable cultural, economic, linguistic, social, demographic and political factors.

Indigenous languages are located in a defined territory and will claim the territorial principle for their preservation. Immigrant language minorities may lay claim to the personality principle, their language group having unifying ethnic characteristics and identity. But the future of languages goes wider and deeper. The history of nationalism and the modern role of global English suggest that the fate of languages relates to wider social, economic and political issues. The future of the world's languages, and the future of English as the international language, is not only about the behavior of individuals but also about the economic, social and symbolic values attached to different languages, about institutional support, about power and not least about regional and global politics.

Key Points in This Chapter

- Diglossia has traditionally been used to describe and analyze two languages existing together in a society in a relatively stable arrangement through different uses attached to each language.
- Transglossia considers the coexistence and interplay between languages as bilinguals translanguage in ways that challenge traditional views of diglossia.
- The territorial principle is a claim to the right to a language within a geographical area, while the personality principle is a claim to the right to use a language based on an individual's ownership of a language that belongs to them wherever they travel within their country.
- There are a variety of factors that may contribute to language maintenance or language loss.
- Minoritized languages may decline by a three-generation shift: L1 monolingual grandparents, bilingual children, to L2 monolingual grandchildren. Languages may decline more rapidly in some recent immigrant communities.
- Language revitalization is slow and challenging, but possible, and often starts with a few enthusiasts.
- Language has been a key symbol of national identity and seen as a badge of loyalty.
- There is not a single language called English but, rather, a wide variety of World Englishes.
- The English language has spread rapidly, mostly as a second and foreign language.
- There are more second language speakers of English than native speakers.
- The advantages and disadvantages of English as an international language are much contested, as are its effects on the future of indigenous and minoritized languages.
- Bilingualism and multilingualism in English and another language or languages is globally increasing.
- Critical post-structuralist sociolinguistics calls into question many of the foundational concepts of sociolinguistics through analyses of how language shapes relationships of power.

Suggested Further Reading

- Boun, S. and Duran, C.S. (eds) (2024) *English Education in Southeast Asian Contexts: Policy, Practice, and Identity*. Lexington Books/Rowman & Littlefield.
- Gorter, D. and Cenoz, J. (2024) *A Panorama of Linguistic Landscape Studies*. Multilingual Matters.

- Horner, K. and Dailey-O'Cain, J. (eds) (2020) *Multilingualism, (Im)mobilities and Spaces of Belonging*. Multilingual Matters.
- Nelson, C.L., Proshina, Z.G. and Davis, D.R. (2020) *The Handbook of World Englishes* (2nd edn). Wiley Blackwell.
- Saiegh-Haddad, E., Laks, L. and McBride, C. (eds) (2022) *Handbook of Literacy in Diglossia and in Dialectal Contexts: Psycholinguistic, Neurolinguistic, and Educational Perspectives*. Springer.
- Salomone, R. (2022) *The Rise of English: Global Politics and the Power of Language*. Oxford University Press.

On the Web

- A day in the life of the Bunscoill Ghaelgagh (video of Manx language revitalization school)
  https://youtu.be/6rUEZ8A-678
- 25 maps that explain the English language
  http://www.vox.com/2015/3/3/8053521/25-maps-that-explain-english
- David Crystal – World Englishes (video)
  https://youtu.be/2_q9b9YqGRY
- Rosemary Salomone – How English became the world's common language (video)
  https://youtu.be/x8UCs9_vJjs?si=X97iC-GfXWNG90Ph

Discussion Questions

(1) Using Table 3.2, discuss which label best describes the relationship between individual bilingualism and diglossia in your community or within your larger society. Would transglossia be a more accurate description? Why or why not?

(2) Read and listen to the audio clips from the National Public Radio story 'Living in two worlds, but with just one language' at https://tinyurl.com/o74s9rt. How does O'Brien's experience relate to the three-generation shift? What factors contributed to this shift? How has this shift impacted O'Brien?

(3) What do you see as the future of English as a global language? Do you agree with the predictions shown in Figure 3.2? Why is it important to think of English in the plural, Englishes, particularly now that second language speakers outnumber native speakers of English?

Study Activities

(1) Using the list of factors in Table 3.3, conduct a study on a minoritized language in your community to determine if there is likely to be maintenance or loss of the language over the next 10 years.

(2) Explore online social media platforms (Facebook, YouTube, Bluesky, X (Twitter), TikTok, Instagram, Pinterest, etc.) to find and analyze examples of dynamic bilingualism.

(3) Interview individuals from immigrant language minoritized families in your community. Is the 'three-generation shift' evident in some or most of those families? What have been the changes in language use and status since immigration in those families? What reasons do the families give for language change? What factors seem to aid language preservation?

CHAPTER 4

Language Endangerment and Revitalization

Introduction

Language Endangerment

Language Policies

Language Planning

Language Revitalization

A Theory of Language Reversal
Steps in Reversing Language Shift
Limits and Critics
Digital Tools for Language Revitalization

Conclusion

CHAPTER 4

Language Endangerment and Revitalization

Introduction

How would you feel if you were the last speaker of your language? Chief Marie Smith Jones, the last speaker of the Alaskan Eyak language, gave her answer: 'I don't know why it's me, why I'm the one. I tell you, it hurts. It really hurts' (Nettle & Romaine, 2000: 14). Richard Littlebear (1999), a Native American Cheyenne citizen, tells of his meeting with Chief Marie Smith Jones. 'I felt that I was sitting in the presence of a whole universe of knowledge that could be gone in one last breath. That's how fragile that linguistic universe seemed.' She died, age 89, on January 21, 2008, at her home in Anchorage. Her name in Eyak was Udach' Kuqax*a'a'ch', meaning 'a sound that calls people from afar'. Amadeo García García became the last remaining speaker of Taushiro – once spoken by thousands in the Amazon – when his brother died from dengue fever. His brother's final words in Taurshiro were 'I am dying'. With limited Spanish proficiency, Amaedo lamented to a missionary with him when his brother died, 'it's over for us now' (Casey, 2017).

To be told that a loved one is dying or dead is one of the most unpleasant experiences in life. To talk about a dead language or a dying language sounds academic and without much sentiment. Yet languages have no existence without people. A language typically dies with the last speaker of that language, or lies dormant, awaiting future revival, if possible. For humanity, that is a great loss. It is like an encyclopedia formed from that language and culture being buried. Five examples of language endangerment and revival will illustrate.

(1) In Cameroon in 1994/95, a researcher, Bruce Connell, visited the last speaker of Kasabe (or Luo). In 1996, he returned to research that moribund language. He was too late. The last speaker of Kasabe had died on November 5, 1995, taking the language and culture with him (Crystal, 2014). Simply stated, on November 4, 1995, Kasabe existed. On November 5, it was dead.
(2) In June 2013, Grizelda Kristina, the last speaker of the ancient Baltic language of Livonian, died at the age of 103. Born and raised in a fishing village on the northern coast of Latvia, Grizelda's village and dozens of other Livonian villages were devastated by Nazis and later by the Soviets. She fled Latvia in 1944 to escape the war, and settled in Canada, where she remained until her death (Berlin, 2013).
(3) On February 4, 2014, Hazel M. Sampson died at the age of 103 in Port Angeles, Washington. She was the last native speaker of Klallam, a language targeted for elimination by the US government along with all other Native American languages since the 1800s. A reversal in federal policy under the Native American Languages

Act of 1990/92 provided funding for Klallam (Kaminksy, 2014) but this support was too little too late to save the language from extinction. However, revitalization efforts using recordings of Sampson and other deceased tribal elders are being used for Klallam as a second language in a few local schools.

(4) There have been no fluent first-language speakers of the Native American language Myaamia (Miami) since 1962. However, thanks to documentation of the language before it went dormant, Myaamia is 'awakening' as members of the tribe are making an effort to learn and use the language. The Myaamia Center at the University of Miami in Ohio was established in 2001 in partnership with the Miami tribe to conduct research, education programs and outreach activities that promote Myaamia language, culture, knowledge and values.

(5) A significant decline in the number of speakers of the indigenous te reo Māori language in New Zealand in the 1940s led to a language revival movement by the Māori in the late 20th century. Language nest programs (Kōhanga reo) for infants and preschoolers, K-12 language programs, national policy initiatives and other activities have slowed the decline and increased the number of native speakers. New Zealand's Māori Language Act of 1987 gave official status to the language and established the Māori Language Commission. A 2019 government language revitalization strategy (Maihi Karauna Māori) established a goal to increase the number of teo reo Māori speakers to 1 million by 2040.

Figure 4.1 illustrates the historical trends in the number of languages in the world since 1500, and leads to a consideration of how many will survive in the future.

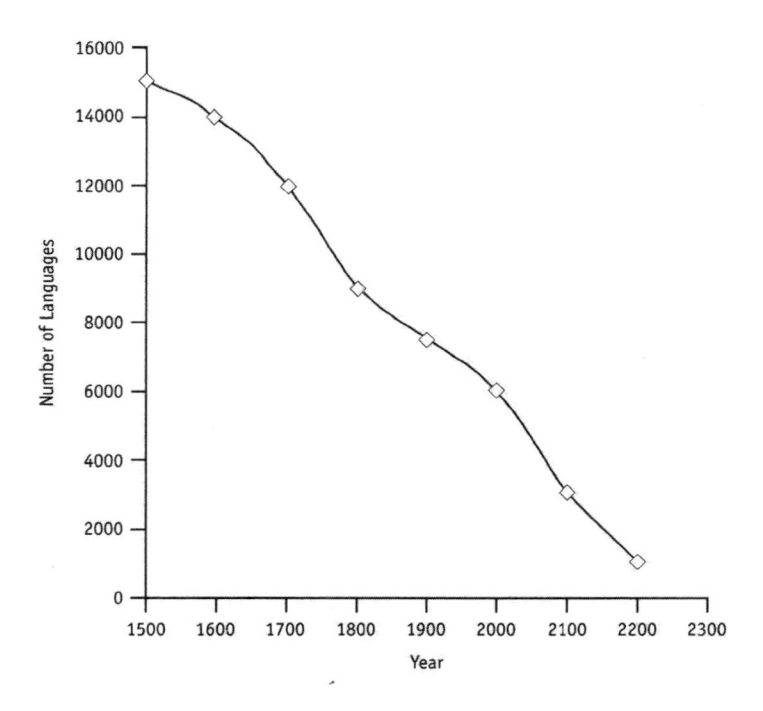

Figure 4.1 Approximate number of languages in the world, 1500–2200 (after Graddol, 2006: 60)

Language Endangerment

Language shift, endangerment and 'death' are phenomena that have existed as long as languages themselves. Well known historical examples of major language decline include Latin and Ancient Greek. However, scholarly attention to issues of language endangerment began in earnest in the 20th century. There is no exact agreement as to the number of living languages in the world today. The 27th edition of SIL International's Ethnologue (www.ethnologue.com) lists a total of 7164 living languages distributed across the globe, as shown in Table 4.1 (Eberhard *et al.*, 2024). However, the Ethnologue list is a synthesis of approximately 40,000 distinct names SIL International has identified to account for 'all the language names, alternate names, dialect names, and alternate dialect names that appear in the language entries' (Moore, 2017: 228).

There is also a lack of agreement about the exact number of languages that will 'die' (become dormant), though most experts acknowledge that many languages are in trouble. UNESCO's *Atlas of the World's Languages in Danger* (Moseley, 2010) claimed that 43% of the world languages are at various stages of endangerment (see Figure 4.2). Thomason (2015) suggests most experts agree that about half of the world's languages will be extinct by the end of the 21st century.

Table 4.1 Distribution of languages in the world, by region

Area	Number of languages	Percent
Africa	2,169	30.3%
Americas	1,070	14.9%
Asia	2,310	32.2%
Europe	294	4.1%
Pacific	1,321	18.4%

Source: Eberhard *et al.* (2024), https://www.ethnologue.com/statistics

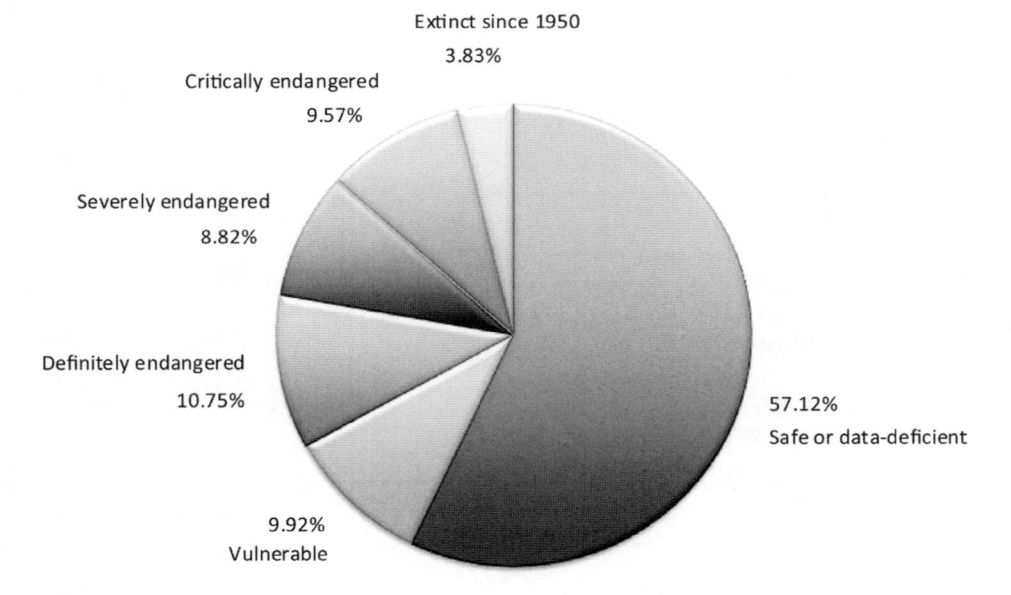

Figure 4.2 Overview of the vitality of the world's languages. Source: Moseley (2010)

The estimates in Figure 4.2 are based on UNESCO's Language Vitality and Endangerment Framework of six categories (Moseley, 2010), defined as follows:

- *Safe*. Language is spoken by all generations; **intergenerational transmission** is uninterrupted.
- *Vulnerable*. Most children speak the language, but it may be restricted to certain **domains** (e.g. home).
- *Definitely endangered*. Children no longer learn the language as **mother tongue** in the home.
- *Severely endangered*. Language is spoken by grandparents and older generations; while the parents' generation may understand it, they do not speak it to children or among themselves.
- *Critically endangered*. The youngest speakers are grandparents and older, and they speak the language partially and infrequently.
- *Extinct*. There are no speakers left.

Variations in estimates are due to the fact that languages are dynamic, variable and constantly changing (Eberhard et al., 2024). It is difficult to identify separate, distinct languages, given that languages are constructed socially and often are politically rather than linguistically defined (Makoni & Pennycook, 2007). Boundaries between languages and their different varieties and dialects are blurred and overlapping. There are also problems of gathering reliable, valid and comprehensive information about languages in large expanses such as Africa, South America and parts of Asia. Moore (2017) outlines the challenges and pitfalls of linguistic enumeration and argues that we need to move away from named countable languages and instead focus on the linguistic resources speakers deploy in actual contexts. Drawing on notions of **superdiversity** and the ways in which languages and speech practices evolve and change in multilingual contexts, he goes so far as to ask 'what if (socio-)linguistic diversity is actually increasing, not decreasing, around the world, albeit taking forms that the discourse of endangered languages cannot countenance?' (Moore, 2017: 237).

Of the estimated 7164 languages in the world today, it is predicted that most will not survive. Ethnologue declares that about 42% of languages (3045) are now endangered, many with fewer than 1000 remaining speakers (Eberhard et al., 2024). As defined in Ethnologue, a language is 'stable' when children continue to learn and use the language within their community. 'Institutional' languages are higher than 'stable' as they are used by governments, taught in schools, used in mass media and other domains, and may be common second languages. A language becomes 'endangered' when a more dominant language begins to be taught and spoken more to children in the community. Figure 4.3 provides Ethnologue's current estimate of the percentage of institutional, stable and endangered languages.

Earlier work by UNESCO estimated that 596 languages are vulnerable, 695 are definitely endangered, 529 are severely endangered, 574 are critically endangered and 230 have become extinct (Moseley, 2010). Thomason (2015) suggests a language 'dies' (becomes dormant) every three months or so. She notes variations in estimates of the demise of current living languages, with optimists arguing that 50% of languages will become extinct by 2100, while pessimists suggest a figure closer to 90%. Thus, as few as 700 languages (10%) may survive. There are consequently enthusiastic conservation measures in progress. If approximately 90% of the world's languages are vulnerable, **language planning** measures to maintain linguistic and cultural diversity are urgently required.

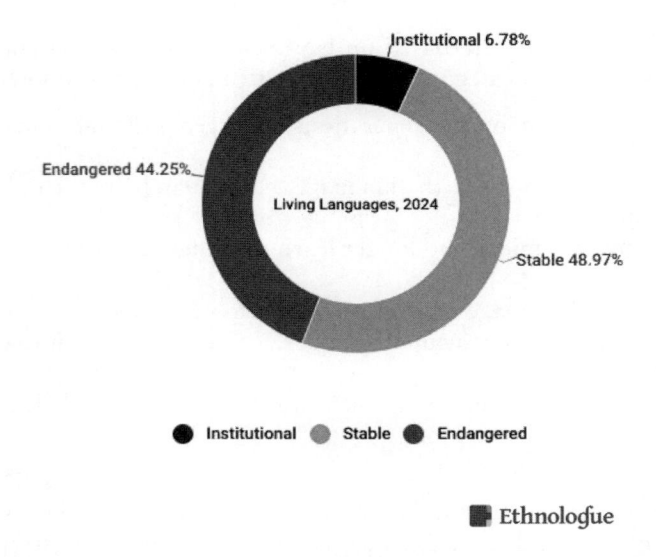

Figure 4.3 Percent of institutional, stable and endangered living languages. Source: Eberhard *et al.* (2024); https://www.ethnologue.com/insights/how-many-languages-endangered/

Thomason (2015: 19–35) identifies six causes of language endangerment:

(1) **Conquest**. The conquerors' language replaces the language(s) of the conquered.
(2) **Economic pressures**. Employment (or perception that employment) requires proficiency in the majority language.
(3) **Melting pots**. A nation state with a strong **ideology** towards linguistic and cultural assimilation places pressure on immigrants and indigenous groups to abandon their native languages and cultures.
(4) **Language politics**. Nation states establish (formal and informal) language policies designed to restrict or suppress uses of minoritized languages.
(5) **Attitudes**. The way minoritized speakers feel about their language, its value and its usefulness (due to internal and external societal pressures).
(6) **Loss of linguistic diversity via standardization**. Most endangered languages have no standardized form. Selection of a single variety for standardization for use in written communication and in schools may lead to further endangerment and ultimate loss of other varieties of the language.

These causes are not necessarily independent of one another. They often overlap in complicit ways that lead to **language loss**, particularly of smaller languages associated with less powerful groups.

Crystal (2014) provides five basic arguments why retaining language diversity is essential and why language planning is needed:

(1) **Diversity is essential**. The concept of an ecosystem is that all living organisms, plants, animals, bacteria and humans survive and prosper through a network of complex and delicate relationships. Damaging one of the elements in the ecosystem will result in unforeseen consequences for the whole of the system. Cultural diversity and biological diversity may be inseparable. For example, where forests are decimated, so are the homelands of the linguistic minoritized groups living there. Where

biodiversity and rich ecosystems exist, so do linguistic and cultural diversity. Evolution has been aided by genetic diversity, with species genetically adapting in order to survive in different environments. Diversity contains the potential for adaptation. Uniformity can endanger a species by providing inflexibility and inadaptability. The range of cross-fertilization becomes less as languages and cultures die and the testimony of human intellectual achievement is lessened. In the language of ecology, the strongest ecosystems are those that are the most diverse. Thus, diversity is directly related to stability; variety is important for long-term survival.

(2) ***Languages express identity***. Identity concerns the shared characteristics of members of a group, community or region. **Identity** helps provide the security and status of a shared existence. Sometimes identity is via dress, religious beliefs, rituals, but language is almost always present in identity formation and identity display. Language is an index, symbol and marker of identity (see Chapter 18).

(3) ***Languages are repositories of history***. Languages provide a link to the past, a means to reach an archive of knowledge, ideas and beliefs from our heritage. 'Every language is a living museum, a monument to every culture it has been vehicle to' (Nettle & Romaine, 2000: 14). The range, richness and wealth of cultures, homelands and histories are lost when a language becomes dormant. This limits the choice of 'pasts' to preserve, and the value of life past and present. It is analogous to humanity losing a whole library, built over years. The Sicilian poet Ignazio Buttitta (1972) expressed it thus:

> Shackle a people, strip them bare, cover their mouths: they are still free. Deprive them of work, their passports, food and sleep: they are still rich. A people are poor and enslaved when they are robbed of the language inherited from their parents: it is lost forever.

Batibo (2005), in discussing the potential demise of many of Africa's 2000 languages, provides the example of medicine. If African languages die, so will centuries of knowledge of the powers of natural medicines: 'some of the traditional medicines used by some of these communities have proved to be effective in treating complex diseases such as cancer, asthma, leprosy and tuberculosis, as well as chronic cases of STD, bilharzia and anaemia' (Batibo, 2005: 41). The stored knowledge and understandings in oral languages (without literacies) may die with that language. Written text may store accumulated meanings after language death, although translations will often lose a degree of stored insight and nuance.

(4) ***Languages contribute to the sum of present human knowledge***. Inside each language is a vision of the past, present and future. When a language dies, its vision of the world dies with it. Language not only transmits visions of the past but also expressions of social relationships, individual friendships as well as community knowledge, a wealth of organizing experiences, plus ideas about art, craft, science, poetry, song, life, death and language itself. A language contains a way of thinking and being, acting and doing. Different languages contain different understandings of people as individuals and communities, different values and ways of expressing the purpose of life, different visions of past humanity, present priorities and our future existence. When a language dies (or becomes dormant), so does a considerable amount of the culture, identity and knowledge that has been passed down from generation to generation through and within that language (e.g. local land management, lake and sea technology, plant cultivation, animal husbandry, etc.).

> **Box 4.1 Avoiding language death**
>
> Crystal (2014) suggests that there are a number of ways to avoid language death. While the solutions will be different for languages at different stages of survival and revitalization, he suggests that an endangered language will progress if its speakers:
>
> - increase their prestige within the dominant community;
> - increase their wealth relative to the dominant community;
> - have access to a stable economic base;
> - increase their legitimate power in the eyes of the dominant community;
> - increase the number of domains in which their language is used;
> - have a critical mass in communities and regions;
> - have a strong presence in the educational system;
> - have a literacy in that language;
> - make use of electronic technology;
> - have a strong sense of ethnic identity;
> - have internal and external recognition as a group with a unique unity;
> - resist the influence of the dominant culture or are protected and formally recognized by that dominant culture.

(5) *Languages are interesting in themselves.* Language itself is important, each language having different sounds, grammar and vocabulary that reveal something different about linguistic organization and structure. The more languages there are to study, the more our understanding of the beauty of language grows.

An additional argument is simply that using and learning one's own language is a basic human right, as emphasized in the Universal Declaration of Linguistic Rights (UNESCO, 1996) and the US Native American Languages Act of 1990.

Crystal (2014) suggests that there are a number of ways language death can be avoided, as outlined in Box 4.1.

Language Policies

The solution to avoiding languages becoming dormant involves language policy, with interventions to stop or reverse the decline of a language (Spolsky, 2021). This is also termed **language revitalization**. Some majority languages, particularly English, have expanded considerably during the last century. Many minoritized languages are in danger of extinction and therefore need extra care and protection. Intervention by language planning is essential to avoid such trends.

In contrast, a language policymaker who is concerned only about majority languages will regard protecting rare languages as expensive and unnecessary, and will wish to standardize the variety of language in the country. In the United States, for example, many politicians prefer **monolingualism** and the assimilation of minoritized language communities to standard American English and its perceived associated culture. Many policymakers may have an evolutionist attitude towards languages. That is, following Darwin's idea of the survival of the fittest, if a weaker language fails to adapt to the modern world, it deserves to 'die'. A different way of expressing this is in terms of a free, *laissez-faire* language economy. Languages must survive on their own merits without the support of language planning.

There are criticisms of this evolutionary or *laissez-faire* viewpoint:

> **Box 4.2** The ecology of language
>
> Hornberger (2006: 280) succinctly expresses three themes of an **ecology of language** perspective: 'The first theme is that languages, like living species, evolve, grow, change, live, and die in relation to other languages – a language evolution theme. Second, languages interact with the environment (socio-political, economic, cultural, educational, historical, demographic, etc.) – the language environment theme. A third theme is the notion that some languages, like some species and environments, may be endangered and that the ecology movement is about not only studying and describing those potential losses, but also counteracting them; this I call the language endangerment theme.'
>
> Hult (2013: 1) explains that 'the ecology of language is a conceptual orientation to critical thinking about multilingualism that calls upon researchers to focus on relationships among languages, on relationships among social contexts of language, on relationships among individual speakers and their languages, and on inter-relationships among these three dimensions'.

(1) Survival of the fittest is too simplistic a view of evolution. It accents only the negative side of evolution – killing, exploitation and suppression – while ignoring positive aspects like cooperation and symbiosis.
(2) Political and economic policies are human-made reasons why languages 'die'. It is possible to analyze and determine what causes language shift rather than simply believing language shift occurs by accident. Social and political factors, and not just 'evolution', are at work in language loss. Power, prejudice, discrimination, marginalization and subordination are some of the causes of language decline and death (e.g. Native American languages in North America). Language loss is thus not 'evolutionary' but determined by politicians, policymakers and peoples (May, 2011).
(3) Evolutionists who argue for an economic, cost–benefit approach to languages, with the **domination** of a few majority languages for international communication, hold a narrow view of the function of languages. Languages are not purely for economic communication. They are also concerned with human culture, human heritage, identity and social relationships, and the value of a garden full of different languages rather than the one variety.
(4) Those who advocate monolingualism often feel that their particular culture and perspectives are the only legitimate or modern varieties – others are inferior and less worth preserving. Rather than constant competition, a more positive and accurate view of evolution is interdependence, that is, cooperation for mutually beneficial outcomes.

Language Planning

If the world's languages are to be retained, then immediate policy interventions and impactful strategies are needed. **Language planning**, sometimes called language management or language engineering, refers to 'deliberate efforts to influence the behavior of others with respect to the acquisition, structure, or functional allocation of their language codes' (Cooper, 1989: 45). Wiley (2015: 166) notes that Cooper's definition helped move language planning away from a narrow view of solving language 'problems'. He also notes that Cooper's use of the word *influence* 'suggests that planning is not always official or even explicit as influence often functions as a dimension of ideological control, wherein compliance can be obtained through the "manufacture of consent" rather than by coercion'.

Traditionally, language planning involves three interdependent and integrated processes (Wiley, 2015): **acquisition planning** (creating language spread by increasing the number of speakers and uses); **status planning** (e.g. raising the status of a language within society across as many institutions as possible); and **corpus planning** (e.g. modernizing terminology, standardization of grammar and spelling). We consider each below in more detail.

(1) *Acquisition planning* is the bedrock of language planning. In the past, acquisition planning focused on the acquisition of a language in school. It is now also particularly concerned with language reproduction in the family. The intergenerational transmission of a language – parents passing their language(s) onto their children – and language learning in bilingual education are essential but insufficient foundations for language survival and maintenance. In all minoritized languages, there are families who use the majority language (e.g. English) with their children, perhaps under the belief that this will lead to economic, employment or educational advantages. Or perhaps the majority language has such high prestige in the neighborhood that parents feel the minoritized language has associations of poverty or powerlessness. Such attitudes can have an immediate effect on the fate of a language. This lack of family language reproduction is a principal and direct cause of language shift. In this scenario, a minoritized language can die within two or three generations unless bilingual education can produce language-speakers who then find everyday purposes (e.g. economic, social, religious) for that language.

Language acquisition planning is therefore partly about encouraging parents to raise their children bilingually. Morris and Jones (2008) note grassroots interventions to persuade parents to use a minoritized language with their very young children in the Basque country, Wales, Ireland and Sweden. They portray a scheme whereby midwives, nurses and health workers provide expectant mothers and new parents with information about the many benefits of bilingualism. This intervention attempts to lead new parents to make a deliberate and rational choice about the languages of the home, choice in pre-school education and later bilingual education. They also indicate the strong influence of the mass media in a child's **language socialization**. Siblings also have a powerful effect on the development of a minoritized language in the home.

Where there is a shortfall in **language maintenance** in families, education becomes the principal means of producing more language speakers. Hornberger and De Korne (2018: 94) argue 'while schools alone cannot change the global conditions of language endangerment ... there are undeniable impacts that education can have on the vitality of endangered languages and the well-being of endangered language speakers'. School-based language revitalization approaches include language classes, bilingual education programs (including immersion programs, small immersion schools and language nests) and adult education programs (Hinton, 2018). For example, the Fairbanks Native Association, with support of a federal grant from the US Department of Education, established a dual language Denaakk'e Head Start pre-school program for Athabascan children aged three to five years in Fairbanks, Alaska. After a few years in the program, children could use a range of common Danaakk'e vocabulary words, such as animal names, clothing and food items, and could understand phrases for typical classroom routines. The program is seeking ways to increase opportunities for parents and families to learn Denaakk'e, and creating e-books and websites with audio recordings so children can use the language in more than just the context of the school (David & Sundberg, 2019).

(2) ***Status planning*** is political by nature, attempting to gain more recognition, functions and capacity for a language. By maintaining use in particular **domains** (contexts), and sometimes spreading into new language domains, a language may be secured and revitalized, for instance through its official use in courts of law, local (regional) and central government, education, mass media and as many public, private and voluntary institutions as possible. Through laws, rights (see Chapter 17) and constitutions, but also by persuasion and precedent, status planning attempts to conserve, revitalize or spread a language. For example, there are well established bilingual or multilingual parliaments (legislatures) in the Basque Country, Canada, Catalonia, Ireland, Scotland, Singapore, South Africa, Switzerland and Wales. Such parliaments give the minoritized language(s) prestige and value. Special attention is often given to modernization to ensure that the language is used in modern, influential spheres such as in television, radio, movies, advertising, newspapers and magazines, computers, smartphones and other mobile devices, the internet and in popular culture domains such as rap, reggae and hip-hop music (Moriarty, 2015b).

Status planning is found in a variety of policies: political movements seeking recognition or official status for a language (both minoritized languages like Māori and Welsh, and majority languages like English in the United States), as well as religious and nationalist movements seeking revitalization of a language, such as Hebrew in Israel. However, while individuals may be influenced by such changes in status of a language, these actions are not guaranteed to maintain a language. To influence language change, status planning has to affect everyday usage in the home and street, family and work relationships, and not just official usage. Thus, opportunity planning for daily use of the minoritized language is essential. Demand has to precede and follow supply. Also, people's choices about language may be governed by their perceptions of the 'market', and be neither easily influenced nor rational (as is supposed by rational interventions in language planning).

(3) ***Corpus planning*** is a typical part of language planning both where languages are precarious and where they are resurgent. Many endangered languages are spoken but lack writing systems, and/or their use has traditionally been almost entirely in oral domains. Thus, corpus planning may be deemed necessary to undertake orthographic development to provide an endangered language with a writing system (Cahill, 2018). However, such efforts to provide a standardized writing system for use in bilingual education and other language revitalization education programs may actually result in an artificial, idealized form based on just one variety of the language, and may further endanger authentic traditional varieties of the language. Weber and Horner (2018) argue this was the case with efforts surrounding the Breton language in France. In Cambodia, attempts to address the concern of privileging one variety over another in the creation of an orthography for the indigenous Tampuen language are handled in part through a Tampuen Language Committee that consists of speakers representing different varieties. This committee reviews and approves books and other materials created for use in bilingual education programs.

A common process for all languages, majority and minority, is to modernize vocabulary. Science and information communications technology (ICT) are just two examples where standardized terminology is created and spread. An alternative is the increasing use of 'loan words'. Schools, books and magazines, television, movies, radio, the internet and social media all help to standardize a language, and hence new concepts need an agreed term. The Catalans, Basques, Welsh and Irish are examples of language groups that formally engage in corpus planning through centrally funded initiatives. Another example is provided by France, which, since the establishment of the Académie Française, has tried to maintain the purity of French and halt the influence of English. When corpus planning is about purity and normalization there is a danger that power and status will go to those who claim to speak a purer language, and a lower status will be ascribed to those who speak non-standard varieties and dialects.

In Wales, it has been found useful to consider also a fourth category: usage or opportunity language planning (see Box 4.3). This refers to top-down and bottom-up language planning interventions that directly seek to increase the integrative use of the Welsh language and its attendant culture in areas such as leisure, sport and technology, to foster social networking through Welsh, and to increase the instrumental use of the Welsh language in the economy, for example in the workplace, employment and education (Baker, 2008). McCarty (2018) shows that efforts to revitalize Native American Indigenous languages in the United States can successfully include grassroots language planning, through community involvement, parent–community links, asserting the link between language and ancestral land, 'master speakers' mentoring apprentice language learners, revitalization immersion programs and heritage language schooling (see also Coronel-Molina & McCarty, 2016; McCarty et al., 2019).

However, such planning is interconnected. What happens inside the family is affected by government policies, and vice versa. The spreading of a language into more high-status domains is both a cause and an effect of increased intergenerational transmission of a language (e.g. the use of a minoritized language for employment).

It is possible to plan for the status, corpus and acquisition of a language and yet not affect the daily language usage of ordinary people. To be effective in achieving its goals, language planning has to impact on individual language life. Languages decline when speakers drop in number and their daily usage diminishes. Therefore, language planning has to relate to everyday language life as enacted in homes, streets, schools, communities, workplaces and leisure activities. In Wales, such planning involves interventions in the economy so that minoritized language speakers can function in Welsh in employment (Williams, 2014; Özerk & Williams, 2023). A Welsh saying declares 'No local economy, no community; no community, no language'. Such planning also

---

Box 4.3 Language planning: The strategy in Wales

Acquisition
1. Family language reproduction
2. Bilingual education – pre-school to university
3. Adult language learning

Status – societal
1. Institutionalization (e.g. use in local and national government and organizations)
2. Modernity (e.g. use on television, internet)

Corpus
1. Linguistic standardization (e.g. by dictionaries, school, television)
2. Public vernacular (Clear or Plain Welsh)

Usage/opportunity – individual
1. Economic, workplace (instrumental)
2. Culture, leisure, sports, social, religious, social networks (integrative)

involves targeting key local cultural, leisure, social and community institutions where minoritized language speakers will use their language and form relationships and networks using that language. Planning also needs to empower local communities directly, enabling everyday language life to be enacted through a minoritized language. Opportunities for 'teenagers and twenties' to use their minoritized language is particularly crucial, as they are the next generation of parents and hence the fate of a minoritized language partly rests on their shoulders.

However, even the most advanced and dynamic language planning may not be enough to save a threatened minoritized language. Such planning can attempt to persuade parents and speakers; it cannot control. It is nearly impossible to plan for a less dominant role for English or control its spread across domains and dominions. Language planning also has to be part of wider economic, social and political processes and policymaking, sensitive to regional and area differences and traditions.

Cooper (1989: 98) provides a classic scheme for understanding language planning by asking a series of key questions:

- *Which actors* (e.g. elites, influential people, counter-elites, non-elite policy implementers)?
- *Attempt to influence which behaviors* (e.g. the purposes or functions for which the language is to be used)?
- *Of which people* (e.g. of which individuals or organizations)?
- *For what ends* (e.g. overt, language-related behaviors, or latent, non-language-related behaviors, the satisfaction of interests)?
- *Under what conditions* (e.g. political, economic, social, demographic, ecological, cultural)?
- *By what means* (e.g. authority, force, promotion, persuasion)?
- *Through what decision-making processes and means?*
- *With what effect or outcome?*

This relatively comprehensive set of questions indicates that language planning may be generated by different groups. For example, poets, linguists, lexicographers, missionaries, soldiers as well as administrators, legislators and politicians may become involved in language planning. Cooper argues, however, that language planning is more likely to succeed when it is embraced or promoted by elite groups or counter-elites. Such elites tend to work primarily from their own self-interests. Language planning is thus often motivated by efforts to secure or reinforce the interests of particular people. Makoni and Makoni (2015: 552), reflecting on many tensions and conflicts in the policy sphere that have arisen between different language institutions in South Africa, concluded that sometimes 'too many cooks spoil the broth'. However, language planning may positively affect the masses by adding to their self-identity, self-esteem and social connectedness and giving increased economic and employment opportunities.

Language planning is rarely a high priority for governments. First, there is often piecemeal political pragmatism rather than planning. The revival of Hebrew is often quoted as one triumphant and successful example of language planning. Yet the rapid advance of Hebrew in Israel appears to have occurred by improvisation and diverse ventures rather than by carefully structured, systematic and sequenced language planning (Weber & Horner, 2018).

Second, political and economic decisions usually govern language decisions. Language decisions are typically relatively minor concerns of governments, whose pervading interests are more frequently about power and purse. Language is usually an outcome of other decisions rather than a determinant of social, political or economic policies. Yet, as the European Commission has increasingly stressed, the need for **bilingualism** and **multilingualism** in Europe relates to European cultural and economic development, and to stability and equality in society. Bilingualism is one part of interconnected politics anywhere in the world.

Third, language planning depends on winning hearts and minds (e.g. of parents). Top-down government language planning cannot control: it merely attempts to influence. Therefore, bottom-up language planning is also needed. As Williams (2014: 268) reflects on many years of Welsh language revitalization efforts:

> If the Welsh example of language revitalization teaches us anything, it is that stubborn collective action by the community must be stimulated before government language policy responds in a reactive manner, but having so responded, that community engagement must also be maintained, for fear of losing direction and long-term momentum.

Teachers play a major role as language policymakers and planners in their classrooms and schools (Menken & García, 2010). Teachers are authoritative role models who can influence both language assimilation (e.g. when they use only one majority language in the classroom) or language sustainability (e.g. when they use the minoritized language in the classroom). When top-down language policy and planning enter the classroom door, it is up to the teacher to understand, negotiate and implement the policy. Thus, teachers often control language norms and what constitutes educated speech, and thereby allow bilingualism or monolingualism to flourish.

Status, corpus, acquisition and usage language planning cannot focus exclusively on the minoritized language but must also address bilingualism. Minoritized language monolingualism is usually impracticable and unfavorable to individuals (e.g. for employment). Where minoritized languages exist, there is usually the need to be bilingual, if not multilingual. A monolingualism approach to a minoritized language and culture may be tantamount to language death. Thus, language planning centered on bilingualism may be key to a minoritized language's survival.

Language Revitalization

According to Williams (2014), language revitalization is an attempt to counter the factors and trends that lead to the decline in the learning and use of a language. He describes language revitalization as a 'sometimes mysterious, often idiosyncratic process which always involves struggle, sacrifice, and tension' and ultimately is 'a conscious effort to change ideas, values, attitudes, and behaviors' (Williams, 2014: 242). McCarty (2018: 363) notes that language revitalization is a 'passionate, political, and deeply personal' process for those involved at the grassroots level.

We need a historical and sociological perspective to help explain patterns of interaction that relate to language revitalization (Hinton *et al.*, 2022). Williams (2000) suggests there are often five historical stages in minoritized language revitalization: (1) idealism (e.g. to construct a vision of language revival); (2) protest (e.g. to mobilize people to change the use or status of a minoritized language); (3) legitimacy (e.g. to attain language rights for the minoritized language, in order to secure its survival and enhance its status); (4) institutionalization (e.g. to secure the presence of the language in key agencies of the state, such as public administration, law, education, employment and commercial activity); and (5) parallelism (e.g. to extend the minoritized language to as many social domains as possible, such as sport, media, entertainment, public services, private industry). Williams (2014) also identified four pillars of language revitalization: (1) language policy and socio-legal developments; (2) formal education; (3) the family; and (4) community life.

Language revitalization is possible even for dormant languages that have not been spoken for generations (Rehg & Campbell, 2018). Examples of such language 'regenesis', 'resurrection' and 'reclamation' among Indigenous languages in North America include Wôpanâak and Myaamia (Miami) (Leonard, 2008, 2017; McCarty, 2019; see Chapter 3 for the example of Manx Gaelic in the United Kingdom). Due to the potential for revival, many scholars and revivalists prefer to speak of dormant or 'sleeping languages', or what Ghil'ad Zuckerman calls 'sleeping beauties' (Zuckerman & Monaghan, 2012). Indeed, there are growing critiques of metaphors of 'death' and 'extinction' among language revitalization scholars. Perley (2012: 133) notes that use of these metaphors 'not only frame discourses of language endangerment, but they also influence actions and interventions'.

The overall aim of language revitalization is the cultivation of new speakers (O'Rourke & Walsh, 2018). McCarty (2018) describes the 'new speaker movement' as a new paradigm, because it recognizes that a revived language may not look exactly like the (perceived) original language. New speakers will unlikely attain proficiency across a wide range of linguistic **registers** and **domains**. Furthermore, with often limited documentation of the original language, a major challenge is determining what constitutes authentic language uses and 'native' competence. McCarty argues that the language ideologies and practices of new speakers of revitalized languages force us 'to rethink static labels such as second language (L2) learner and native speaker' (McCarty, 2018: 361). She further notes the need to 'recognize the diversity and complexity of what it means to revitalize a language, the historical and embeddedness of who and what counts as a speaker (and a language), and the ways in which these understandings can be used to support individuals and communities' in revitalization efforts (McCarty, 2018: 363).

The *Report on the Status of B.C. First Nations Languages* (Gessner et al., 2022) embraces this concept of new speakers when reporting on language revitalization efforts in the Canadian province of British Columbia. For each Indigenous language, the report makes a distinction between three types of speaker, acknowledging there is subjectivity in these definitions (Gessner et al., 2022: 12):

(1) *fluent speakers* 'can speak and understand their language to the degree that they self-identify or are identified by fellow community members as having the ability to converse and understand the language with no use of English' (even if they consider themselves less fluent than their grandparents);
(2) *semi-speakers* (including silent speakers) 'can speak and understand their language to some degree' or 'understand the language but haven't yet begun speaking again';
(3) *non-speakers* 'don't speak or understand the language yet'.

The report also tracks the number of active language learners, defined as 'anyone in process of learning a First Nations language by participating in any type of language learning method, program or class' (Gessner et al., 2022: 13). Active learners overlap with and are reported as the percentage of the total of fluent, semi- and non-speakers. Thus, as shown in the example in Figure 4.4, out of a total of 3564 members of the

Tsilhqot'in

Tsilhqot'in is spoken in central interior B.C.

Total # of B.C. communities	# of communities reported to us	Population reported to us	Number of language learners
6	5	3,564	430

Language is learned in:

Language nests	Head Start programs	Other ECE programs
2	3	0

First Nations schools	Public schools	Adult community programs	University courses
2	4	3	Yes

FLUENT SPEAKERS 13.2% SEMI-SPEAKERS 10.8% ACTIVE LEARNERS 12.1%

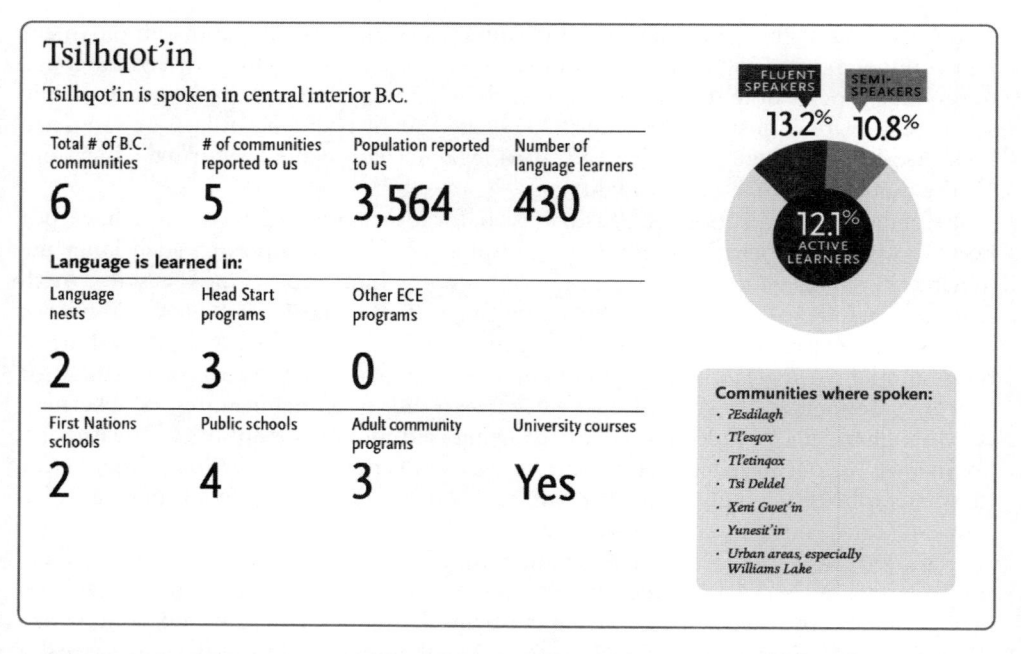

Communities where spoken:
- ʔEsdilagh
- Tl'esqox
- Tl'etinqox
- Tsi Deldel
- Xeni Gwet'in
- Yunesit'in
- Urban areas, especially Williams Lake

Figure 4.4 Number of speakers of Tsilhqot'in, from the *Report on the Status of B.C. First Nations Languages* (Gessner et al., 2022: 45)

Tsilhqot'in First Nation, 13.2% are fluent speakers, 10.8% are semi-speakers and 12.1% are active learners. The unmarked section of the pie chart on the right of Figure 4.4 represents the percentage of non-speakers. This report represents a more positive and beneficial method of tracking progress in language revitalization efforts, capturing new speakers and active learners in ways that previous methods could not.

We must also recognize that within a language ecology, the revival of one language can lead to the decline of other languages within the same area. For example, Weber and Horner (2018) note that revitalization efforts for Hebrew in Israel were harmful to Arabic and other Jewish languages, such as Yiddish and Ladino. Shohamy (2008) analyzed historical documents from the Hebrew revitalization period and found that not only were the policies often subtractive of linguistic diversity, but also violated the basic human rights of many individuals. As she describes it, 'the goal of reviving Hebrew was so important that all means were justified, no questions asked' (Shohamy, 2008: 215). In Canada, Europe, Cambodia and other countries, efforts to revitalize many of the indigenous languages have not been matched by an interest in preserving the languages of immigrants.

A Theory of Language Reversal

In the early 1990s, Joshua Fishman began refining his major theories grounded in his many years of research and reflection regarding the reversal of language shift (see Fishman, 2001; and for collections of Fishman's writings see García *et al.*, 2006;

Hornberger & Pütz, 2006). Fishman sought to answer the question 'what are the priorities in planning language shift?' For example, what is the point of pouring money into mass media and bilingual bureaucracy when use of the minoritized language in the home, family, neighborhood and face-to-face community is lacking? Is it like blowing air into a punctured balloon?

Fishman's underlying philosophy is to achieve social justice and to support cultural pluralism and cultural self-determination. The destruction of minoritized languages is the destruction of intimacy, family and community, often involving oppression of the weak by the strong. Thus, Fishman argues for greater sociocultural self-sufficiency, self-help, self-regulation and initiative among linguistic communities. He also argues that language reversal derives not just from a societal philosophy but also from personal motivations. Human values, feelings, loyalties and basic life philosophies are present in the complex reasons for language change. Minoritized languages and cultures, in the desire for their a healthy existence, may be sometimes irrational or super-rational. This is similar to religion, love, art and music, where there are personal elements that transcend conscious rationality and go beyond self-interest in power and money.

Steps in Reversing Language Shift

Fishman (1991) began by systematically publishing on his eight-level Graded Intergenerational Disruption Scale (GIDS) in the early 1990s as an aid to understanding language planning and attempted language reversal from an international perspective. The GIDS has been reprinted many times, including in a 2013 publication by Fishman himself less than two years before he passed away at age 88 (Fishman, 2013). Thus, Fishman's GIDS is a highly influential scale that has guided language revitalization around the world for over two decades.

An important amplification and modification of Fishman's scale was introduced by Lewis and Simons (2010) as the Expanded GIDS (EGIDS), with 13 levels, as shown in Table 4.2. Levels 1–8 correspond to Fishman's (1991) original scale, though with some rephrasing for greater clarity. Lewis and Simons (2010) added level 0, combined Fishman's original levels 4a and 4b, expanded his levels 6 and 8 to levels 6a and 6b, 8a and 8b respectively, and added levels 9 and 10. These changes integrate language vitality frameworks from both UNESCO and Ethnologue. A benefit of the EGIDS is the ability to include languages which no longer have active speakers.

Just as the Richter Scale measures intensity of earthquakes, EGIDS provides a guide to how far a minoritized language is threatened and disrupted in international terms. The higher the score on the scale, the more a language is threatened by a dominant majority language. The idea of stages is that it is little good attempting later stages if earlier stages are not at least partly achieved. Various foundations are needed before building the upper levels. The value of the EGIDS is that it prioritizes major actions for reversing language decline or for revitalizing languages that are dormant or extinct.

Lewis and Simon (2010: 117) also added a separate subset of Revitalization EGIDS levels, as shown in Table 4.3, to provide a more positive perspective on language revitalization instead of language loss. These modifications of level descriptions at the lower end of the scale 'reflect the upward trend of language use as the community moves from one less robust level of language vitality to a stronger one' because of language revitalization efforts or naturally occurring language spread (Lewis & Simon, 2010: 117).

Table 4.2 Expanded Graded Intergenerational Disruption Scale (EGIDS) (adapted from Fishman, 1991)

Level	Label	Description	UNESCO
0	International	The language is used internationally for a broad range of functions	Safe
1	National	The language is used in education, work, mass media, government at the nationwide level	Safe
2	Regional	The language is used for local and regional mass media and governmental services	Safe
3	Trade	The language is used for local and regional work by both insiders and outsiders	Safe
4	Educational	Literacy in the language is being transmitted through a system of public education	Safe
5	Written	The language is used orally by all generations and is effectively used in written form in parts of the community	Safe
6a	Vigorous	The language is used orally by all generations and is being learned by children as their first language	Safe
6b	Threatened	The language is used orally by all generations but only some of the child-bearing generation are transmitting it to their children	Vulnerable
7	Shifting	The child-bearing generation knows the language well enough to use it among themselves but none are transmitting it to their children	Definitely endangered
8a	Moribund	The only remaining active speakers of the language are members of the grandparent generation	Severely endangered
8b	Nearly Extinct	The only remaining speakers of the language are members of the grandparent generation or older who have little opportunity to use the language	Critically Endangered
9	Dormant	The language serves as a reminder of heritage identity for an ethnic community. No one has more than symbolic proficiency	Extinct
10	Extinct	No one retains a sense of ethnic identity associated with the language, even for symbolic purposes	Extinct

Source: Lewis and Simons (2010: 110)

Table 4.3 Revitalization EGIDS Levels

Level	Label	Description
6a	Vigorous	The language is used orally by all generations and is being learned at home by all children as their first language
6b	Re-established	Some members of a third generation of children are acquiring the language in the home with the result that an unbroken chain of intergenerational transmission has been re-established among all living generations
7	Revitalized	A second generation of children are acquiring the language from their parents who also acquired the language in the home. Language transmission takes place in home and community
8a	Reawakened	Children are acquiring the language in community and some home settings and are increasingly able to use the language orally for some day-to-day communicative needs
8b	Reintroduced	Adults of the parent generation are reconstructing and reintroducing their language for everyday social interaction
9	Rediscovered	Adults are rediscovering their language for symbolic and identificational purposes

Source: Lewis and Simons (2010: 117)

Limits and Critics

While Fishman (1991, 2013) was careful to point out that one stage is not necessarily dependent on a previous stage, there are priorities. The more advanced stages cannot usually be secured unless the fundamental stages are either first built or repaired. The danger is in advancing on all fronts. Attempting to win individual battles without having a strategy for the whole war does not champion success. Changing the language of road signs and tax forms and gaining minoritized language presence on television are battles that have been fought and won in some minoritized language regions. For Fishman, however, it is reproduction of informal and intimate spoken language across generations that is the ultimate pivot of language shift.

Fishman (2013) was particularly guarded about how much bilingual education can achieve in reversing language shift. There is sometimes the belief that, where families do not transmit the minoritized language, the school is there to do it instead. Where parents do not bring up their children in the minoritized language, the school is expected to be the substitute parent. A school can initiate second language acquisition in the minoritized language. However, not all students will continue to use the school-learnt language throughout life, including in parenting their children. Even when a child successfully learns minoritized language oracy and literacy skills in school, unless there is considerable support in the community and the economy outside school, that language may wither.

For that language to survive inside the individual, there needs to be before-school, out-of-school and after-school support and reward systems for using the minoritized language, embedded in the family–neighborhood–community experience, and in the economics of the family. Unless this happens, it is much less likely that bilingually educated children will pass on the minoritized language to the next generation. Thus, for Fishman, each stage needs examining for how it can be used to feed into level 6 – the inter-generational transmission of the minoritized language.

The EGIDS levels must be seen as overlapping and interacting. In language revival, it is not the case of going one step or level at a time. The myriad factors in language reversal link together in complex patterns. A language at level 2 may still be securing elements of previous levels. A language at level 6 may be engaged in long-term planning to secure higher levels.

Language settings vary so much that the scale cannot be indiscriminately applied to each. For example, different communities and different geographical areas may be at different levels within the same nation. Also, the use of the minoritized language in business and the local economy may vary considerably from rural to urban areas, social class to social class, and according to closeness of access to airports, roads, railways and sea links. Some minoritized language groups may aspire to just an oral rather than a literate transmission of language to succeeding generations. For other groups, reaching the highest EGIDS level may be difficult and more of a long-term aim, for example the language being used in higher education. There may not be the financial basis for developing mass media or any political will for minoritized language higher education.

Spolsky (2004: 215) suggests that the danger of Fishman's scale is that it 'puts too much emphasis on language and language management, and so distracts attention from the social and economic factors which are likely to be the major sources of changes in language shift'. Hornberger and King (2001) also argue that reversing language shift does not indicate the economic processes and interventions that are so important for language revival. For parents to raise their children in the minoritized language, for schools to have a strong reason for content teaching through the language, economic and employment incentives and rewards are crucial, but not sufficient in themselves.

Integrative motives and cultural sentiment may not be enough to persuade parents, educators and students to use the minoritized language. The economic base of the language community can be a vital safeguard to the maintenance of a threatened language. The state, and not just the local language community, is thus important (e.g. in economic regeneration of a language minoritized area). Material dimensions of success (individual and societal) and economic advancement have grown in importance in a consumerist society. Because these areas are often controlled by majority language groups, a power struggle becomes vital.

Digital Tools for Language Revitalization

Internet technology and other digital tools for language revitalization were mentioned briefly in the discussion above, but require deeper consideration. Thomason (2015) notes that modern efforts are heavily dependent on the internet. Revitalization websites exist for many endangered languages. Social media, video-streaming, blogs, wikis, smartphones, tablets and other mobile devices, talking digital dictionaries, machine translation and artificial intelligence open up new domains for the use of endangered languages, especially among the 'digital native' youth, who rely on digital tools for much of their verbal and textual communications. However, Thomason also outlines several concerns and other issues that need to be considered in language revitalization efforts in the digital age:

(1) *Informed consent*. The ease of making language data widely available online raises complications with treating members of the **speech community** with respect and obtaining their informed consent. Some in the community may object to having their voices, or the voices of their deceased ancestors, online and available to the general public.
(2) *Intellectual property rights*. Language communities should have the right to decide whether their languages are included for use in software packages such as Microsoft products or Google Translate.
(3) *Digital divide*. The majority of endangered languages are unlikely to cross the digital divide because many speakers do not have access to expensive digital tools or the internet. Those who do have access may lack the requisite knowledge to create websites or use their languages on existing sites, and thus resort to using a dominant societal language.
(4) *Forms of writing*. While official websites established for endangered languages may use a standardized variety of the language, the written language in social media, especially by the youth, is typically very informal. However, such informality tends to foster language use among the youth.

Nonetheless, Thomason notes there have been many successful initiatives to establish a digital presence for endangered languages. For example, revitalization efforts for the Native American language Northern Pomo – spoken in northern California for thousands of years – include a website (https://northernpomolanguagetools.com) that features a range of digital language tools, and mobile apps for both iOS and Android devices. Perhaps as the cost for digital tools comes down, as free or at least affordable access to the internet expands around the world, and as social media sites become ever more accommodating of linguistic diversity, language revitalization activists and digital-native youth will find it increasingly easier and quite natural to use their languages online for fun, meaningful and authentic communication.

Artificial intelligence (AI) technologies such as large language models and machine learning also have strong potential to aid in language documentation and revitalization. For example, Miyagawa (2024) describes the development of bidirectional neural machine translation between the endangered Ainu language and Japanese as a groundbreaking approach to language preservation. Wang (2024) notes the potential for AI to accelerate endangered language documentation efforts and ways AI-infused pedagogy could also revolutionize the teaching and learning of endangered languages. He argues that 'as the digital age continues to evolve, merging AI's capabilities with traditional linguistic approaches holds the promise of a more inclusive and comprehensive strategy to rejuvenate and preserve the world's rich linguistic tapestry' (2024: 123).

Conclusion

This chapter commenced with the current concerns about the future of the world's estimated 7164 languages, many of which are dying. Forecasts of wide-scale language decline and death are met with calls to retain language diversity. Such retention of the world's languages requires the intervention of language planning. Such language planning requires a reproduction and production line among the young, via families and schools. For parents and schools to be motivated to pass on minoritized languages, there must be reasons: instrumental and integrative, economic, employment, social and cultural, sometimes religious. The fate of minoritized languages requires an understanding of how two or more languages interact in society.

Language planning is aided by conceptual frameworks regarding **language vitality**, revitalization and language reversal. Language reversal sometimes means that such language groups shift to insignificance, even death. At other times, they attempt to spread and not just survive. One argument for the survival of languages has been that as languages die, so does part of the totality of human history and culture. However, language revival efforts may be undertaken to awaken dormant or 'sleeping' languages. A theory of language revitalization is also about the realities of everyday futures for children.

Key Points in This Chapter

> - The languages of the world are rapidly declining in number, with predictions of 50–90% of the world's languages dying or near death in the next century. The world's language and cultural diversity is thus endangered.
> - Language planning is needed for language maintenance, revitalization and reversing language shift. Language planning includes acquisition planning (e.g. home and education), status planning (e.g. in key institutions) and corpus planning (e.g. standardization and modernization).

- Language revitalization efforts are affected by a range of factors, including intergenerational language transmission, number and proportion of speakers, shifts in domains of language use, attitudes towards the language, and availability of and responses to materials, new domains and media.
- The EGIDS model of reversing language shift has 13 levels that reflect different conditions in the health of a language and steps needed to revive a language.
- The transmission of a minoritized language in the family is an essential foundation for the rebuilding of that language.
- So-called 'dead' languages may be better thought of as dormant or sleeping, and can be revived or 'awakened' when there is record of the language and a community that identifies with it.
- Digital technology and artificial intelligence hold great promise but also introduce new challenges in language revitalization.

Suggested Further Reading

Adamou, E. (2024) *Endangered Languages*. MIT Press.

Derhemi, E. and Moseley, C. (eds) (2023) *Endangered Languages in the 21st Century*. Routledge.

Hinton, L., Huss, L. and Roche, G. (eds) (2022) *The Routledge Handbook of Language Revitalization*. Routledge.

Linn, M.S. and Dayán-Fernández, A. (eds) (2024) *Agency in the Peripheries of Language Revitalisation: Examining European Practices on the Ground*. Multilingual Matters.

Olko, J. and Sallabank, J. (eds) (2021) *Revitalizing Endangered Languages: A Practical Guide*. Cambridge University Press.

On the Web

American Indian Language Development Institute
https://aildi.arizona.edu

Canadian Indigenous Languages and Literacy Development Institute
https://www.ualberta.ca/canadian-indigenous-languages-and-literacy-development-institute

Endangered Languages Project
https://www.endangeredlanguages.com

Foundation for Endangered Languages
https://www.ogmios.org/home.htm

Institute on Collaborative Language Research (CoLang)
https://www.colanginstitute.org

National Breath of Life Archival Institute for Indigenous Languages
https://mc.miamioh.edu/nbol

Northwest Indian Language Institute (NWILI)
https://nili.uoregon.edu

Discussion Questions

(1) Watch the following video about Amadeo García García, the last speaker of Taushiro, whose story was told at the beginning of this chapter – https://www.nytimes.com/2017/12/26/world/americas/peru-amazon-the-end.html. Why should we care when a language dies? Of the arguments for language diversity offered by Crystal, which do you find the most compelling?

(2) What are the three major types of language planning? How are they interlinked, and why is each needed to preserve or revitalize a threatened language?

(3) View the following video about Eliezer Ben-Yehuda, a key activist in the revitalization of Hebrew – https://youtu.be/pgjq8uqQ79E. Discuss the issues of language planning and language revitalization described in this chapter that are evident in Ben-Yehuda's efforts.

Study Activities

(1) Using the Ethnologue website (https://www.ethnologue.com) or the Native Land Digital Map (https://native-land.ca), identify and map an endangered language within your local region or country. Drawing on library, internet and/or original source materials (i.e. interviews with local speakers), create a multimedia presentation about the language, its stage on the EGIDS scales (Tables 4.2 and 4.3) and what revitalization efforts are currently taking place, or could be taking place to preserve the language.

(2) Search on the internet for information on one revived language (e.g. Manx Gaelic in the Isle of Man, Hawaiian, Hebrew, Basque, Catalan, Welsh, Myaamia (Miami)). What is the recent history of the language in numbers and use across domains? What revival efforts have been made? What interventions have been particularly successful?

(3) Choose an immigrant language in your community. Using Thomason's (2015) framework of six factors leading to language endangerment, and Crystal's solutions for avoiding language death (Box 4.1), interview some youths from the community to evaluate the degree to which their immigrant language may be endangered.

CHAPTER 5

The Early Development of Bilingualism

Introduction

Childhood Bilingualism

The Simultaneous Acquisition of Bilingualism and Multilingualism
Differentiation Between Two Languages in the Infant
Language Choices of Parents

Approaches to Early Childhood Bilingualism
The One-Parent One-Language Approach
Home Language Is Different from the Language Outside the Home
The Mixed Language Approach
Delayed Introduction of the Second Language
Limitations

Case Studies of Early Bilingualism
One-Parent Families and Bilingualism

Trilingualism/Multilingualism

Codeswitching and Translanguaging
Codeswitching
Translanguaging
The Context of Codeswitching and Translanguaging
The Purposes and Uses of Codeswitching and Translanguaging

Children as Language Interpreters and Brokers

Conclusion

CHAPTER 5

The Early Development of Bilingualism

Introduction

This chapter looks at the various ways in which young children become bilingual and multilingual. There are various routes to **bilingualism** and **multilingualism**, some from birth, others much later (see Chapter 6). Such bilingual routes include: acquiring two or more languages early on in the home; acquiring additional languages in the street, in the wider community, in the nursery school, elementary school or high school; and, after childhood, learning additional languages in adult language classes and courses or by informal interaction with others. This chapter outlines different major routes to becoming bilingual early in childhood and examines some of the central issues involved in this more informal aspect of language development.

As the previous chapters of this book have illustrated, a discussion of bilingualism and multilingualism has to include psychological, linguistic, social and educational factors. Later in the book, it will be shown that political factors are also crucial in understanding bilingualism and bilingual education. While psychologists and linguists have studied the development of children's two languages, it is valuable to examine simultaneously the social and political **context** in which children acquire their languages. Early bilingual development in the home, for example, does not take place in isolation. It occurs within a community, country and **culture**, which means that the home is surrounded by expectations, pressures and politics.

For example, being a member of an immigrant community, an elite group, a majority or a minoritized language group are important societal or 'macro' influences in the acquisition of bilingualism. Consider the different life experiences of middle- and upper-class privileged bilinguals (e.g. children of diplomats, expatriates learning two prestigious languages), majority language children living in minoritized language communities and minoritized language children living in majority language communities (e.g. immigrants, refugees, Native Americans). In each of these groups, societal pressures and family language planning may be supportive or conflicting, affecting choices, access and language outcomes. There are also 'micro' environments such as the street, crèche, nursery, school, local community and the extended family that similarly foster bilingualism. Such contexts tend to make dual language use by a child a constantly shifting rather than a stable phenomenon.

The variety of individual differences and social contexts makes simple generalizations about the development of bilingualism difficult and risky. The chapter therefore commences with a basic typology of the development of childhood bilingualism. Note that while the discussion below makes many references to *parents*, *mothers* and *fathers* – reflective of the fact that much of the research has been conducted in more 'traditional' families – it is important to acknowledge that many bilingual and multilingual children are raised in single-parent homes, or by two parents of the same gender, or by guardians who may or may not be blood relatives or adoptive parents, and in many other 'non-traditional' family arrangements.

Childhood Bilingualism

It is estimated that more children worldwide grow up to become bilinguals or multilinguals rather than **monolinguals**. Grosjean (2014), for example, suggests that 'probably half or slightly more than half of the world's population is bilingual'. Some children become bilinguals almost effortlessly from birth. Others learn a language in school or as adults. An initial distinction is between simultaneous and sequential childhood bilingualism. Simultaneous childhood bilingualism refers to a child acquiring two languages at the same time from birth, sometimes called infant bilingualism, bilingual language acquisition and bilingual first language acquisition (De Houwer, 2017a). For example, some two-parent families attempt a one-parent one-language (OPOL) approach (Quay & Chevalier, 2019), where one parent speaks one language to the child and the other parent speaks a different language. An example of sequential childhood bilingualism is when a child learns one language in the home, then goes to a nursery or elementary school and learns a second language.

In contrast, second language classes for children and adults usually foster bilingualism through direct instruction (see Chapter 6). This has led to attempts to distinguish between informal language acquisition and more formal language learning. However, the boundary between acquisition and learning is not distinct. Informal language acquisition can occur, for example, in a second language classroom. Thus, the boundary between naturally becoming bilingual and being taught to become bilingual is imprecise. The profile of bilinguals constantly changes, because their need for and use of each of their languages can vary greatly over time, depending on such factors as context, purpose, the formality of the situation and whom they wish or need to interact with (Serratrice, 2013). The term **dynamic bilingualism** captures this ever-changing nature of language use by emergent bilinguals (García, 2009a).

The Simultaneous Acquisition of Bilingualism and Multilingualism

Families, members of the public and politicians sometimes buy into the false belief that acquiring two languages from birth is detrimental to a child's language growth. On the contrary, babies appear biologically ready to acquire, store and differentiate two or more languages from birth onwards (Serratrice, 2013). Infant bilingualism is normal and natural, with evidence that it is typically beneficial in many ways: cognitively (see Chapter 7), culturally (see Chapter 18), communicatively (see Chapter 1), for higher curriculum achievement (see Chapters 11 and 12) and to increase the chances of employment and promotion (see Chapter 19).

To acquire two languages from birth, babies need to be able: (1) to differentiate between the two languages and (2) to store the two languages for both understanding (input) and speaking (output). Research suggests infants have these capacities, making infant bilingualism very viable (De Houwer, 2017a).

As early as eight months, but more often around a bilingual child's first birthday, they may utter their first words in both languages. While the growth in the two languages may be uneven due to differential experience in them, the vocabulary of such bilingual children tends to show a similar number of meanings. Studies of early bilinguals 'that compare the total number of meanings (or conceptual vocabulary) that bilingual children expressed with monolingual children's total number of meanings found no differences between the two groups' (De Houwer, 2009: 229). Early bilinguals may even have an advantage compared with monolinguals in that they learn new words and labels for concepts at a faster pace (De Houwer, 2017a, 2021). This may be due to their need to understand people referring to the same thing in two languages.

Differentiation Between Two Languages in the Infant

Infants show discrimination between the two languages very early. Memory for language sounds even operates in the fetal stage, such that the processes of bilingual acquisition appear to start before birth. There is also immediate sound discrimination: the beginning of 'breaking the code'. There appears to be an immediate **receptive language** differentiation in the newborn, particularly in intonation (De Houwer, 2017a, 2021). A study of newborn infants in Sweden and the United States found evidence that soon after birth, babies respond to the familiar native language they heard in the womb differently from unfamiliar non-native languages (Moon *et al*., 2013). Another study found that newborn babies born to bilingual Tagalog–English mothers could discriminate between, and showed preferences for, the two languages equally (Byers-Heinlein *et al*., 2010). This was in contrast to the control group of babies born to English-speaking Canadian mothers who showed a strong preference for English. Other research has shown that infants in the babbling stage (around 10–12 months of age) exposed to two languages from birth have a tendency to babble in their stronger language and demonstrate language-specific babbling features of each language (Maneva & Genesee, 2002). Garcia-Sierra *et al*. (2011) found that the brains of infants raised in bilingual Spanish–English homes demonstrate a longer period of being open and flexible to different languages than infants raised in monolingual households, whose brains typically narrowed to their sole language by the end of their first year.

Research has shown that by age two, bilingual children know which language to speak to whom and in what situation (De Houwer, 2017a, 2021; Serratrice, 2013). They are able to use 'appropriate language matching' when talking to others, and can even rapidly and accurately accommodate the monolingualism or bilingualism of a stranger and talk in the appropriate language (Quay & Chevalier, 2019). Bilingual children tend to produce less mixed language utterances when addressing monolinguals, and produce more mixed utterances when addressing bilinguals (see below) (Comeau *et al*., 2003). Thus, the ability to use the appropriate language with a particular person occurs very early. A variety of factors affect a child's language choice as they grow older: exposure to two languages in different social contexts, the attitudes of parents to the two languages and to mixing the languages, the **language competences** and metalinguistic abilities of the child, personality, peer interaction, exposure to different forms of language education, as well as sociolinguistic influences such as the norms, values and beliefs of the community.

Language Choices of Parents

When parents can potentially use more than one language with their children, there is language choice in raising their children. This choice has been referred to as 'private language planning' (Piller, 2001) and more recently as 'family language policy' (Curdt-Christiansen, 2018; King *et al.*, 2008; Wright & Higgins, 2022). Where parents have the ability to speak both languages to their children, there may be a latent understanding or sometimes a conscious strategy about which language to use with the child from birth onwards. However, many couples do not make a conscious decision about which language(s) to use in the home (Piller, 2002). Such language choice may derive from a habit formed from the first interaction between the couple, compensation (e.g. using one's native language in return for not living in the homeland) and **identity** (projecting a desired self-image). Parents' attitudes towards languages, their preferred identity and an overall cost–benefit analysis are additionally influential in their choices. Also important is the belief that they 'can exercise some sort of control over their children's linguistic functioning' (De Houwer, 1999: 83). Lanza and Lexander (2019) note the influential role of digital family language practices in and around media (e.g. text messaging, email, video chat and other digital tools). Other influences include the extended family and friends. Language choice may change depending on where a family currently resides. For example, a transnational bilingual Japanese–English family is more likely to use more Japanese at home while living in Japan but more English while living in Australia. Similarly, a bilingual Spanish–English family living in Nogales along the Mexican border in southern Arizona may find their use of Spanish at home decline if they move further north, to Phoenix or Flagstaff.

Children have their own independent thoughts and actions (agency), which can be a powerful influence on their language learning and use. Thus their own preferences, attitudes and individual personalities can be highly influential (Lanza & Lexander, 2019). Nguyen (2022) refers to such independence as 'individual language policy'. Fogle (2013: 196–197) argues that 'Family language policy is not simply the result of parental ideologies and strategies, but rather a dynamic process in which children play an active role of influencing code choice and shaping family language ideologies'. Sibling interactions are also a major determinant of language choice and shape language interactions in the family (Quay & Chevalier, 2019). Multilingual extended families may have increased choices of language. Grandparents, aunts and uncles, cousins and caregivers can all affect which language a child speaks with whom, when and where. Transnational travel to visit extended family in countries of origin where a home language is dominant may create further opportunities for children's language choices (De Houwer, 2017b; Kwon, 2022). Ability to return frequently to a family's country of origin, however, may depend on a number of factors, such as geographical distance, family finances, political stability and legal status, and need for or ability to obtain travel documents (e.g. passports, visas).

Some bilingual parents choose to use just one of their languages with the child. For varied reasons, a mother and father, for example, may use just Arabic or only English with the child. A different approach, as noted earlier, is a one-parent one-language policy. For example, the mother may speak Arabic to the child and the father may speak English. Very few families obtain an equal balance between the two languages. A different circumstance is when both bilingual parents speak the minoritized language to their children, leaving the child to learn the majority language outside the home. Quay and Chevalier (2019) note that keeping a majority language out of the home increases the proportion of exposure to the minoritized language, thus making multilingualism for children more likely. De Houwer (1999) identified several possible patterns in bilingual dual-parent families, based on the extent to which each parent uses each language when addressing their children (none, sometimes, half the time, mainly and only).

Parents make language choices by conscious, subconscious and spontaneous decisions that are both general and local/specific (Festman *et al.*, 2017). Choice of family languages relates to desired language, cultural and gender identity. Child agency and language use patterns also impact the language behaviors of their parents and other family members. Thus, the societal contexts in which the family is placed affect language choices. Such choices may be relatively stable across time, but there are also choices that reflect a local, particular event (e.g. when a stranger enters the house everyone changes to the majority language). Thus, strategies and choices are often pragmatically flexible in family language situations, as visitors and contexts change.

Emotions affect language choice and strategies. Parents are often multilingual in their language interactions with their children to convey the emotions of praise and discipline, love and instructions. Pavlenko (2004: 200) observed, 'Many [parents] draw on multiple linguistic repertoires, uttering "I love you" in one language, endearments in another, and "Go clean your room!" in yet another'.

Bilingualism in childhood is also influenced by factors outside of families and the home. Parents who have recently immigrated may speak their native language(s) in the home, but the children (especially teenagers) speak to each other in the language of the street, school and television. Playing with neighborhood children, making friends in and out of school with majority language speakers and use of the mass media may help create bilingualism in the child. An alternative scenario is when the grandparents and other relatives use a different language with the child than the home language. For example, Chinese-American children may speak English at school and at home with their parents and siblings, but acquire at least a passive understanding of Chinese through regular visits to extended family members or with live-in grandparents (Rampton & Charalambous, 2012). This was illustrated, for example, in the popular US comedy television series *Fresh off the Boat* featuring a Taiwanese-American family. The grandmother spoke only Chinese, but carried on conversations with her grandchildren, who responded in English. However, De Houwer (2015) warns that such 'dual-lingual conversations' may lead to children not speaking the **heritage language**.

Approaches to Early Childhood Bilingualism

Broad approaches to early childhood bilingualism may be considered based on the language or languages spoken by parents to their children and the language of the community. Not all children fit neatly into such approaches. For example, the most typical input pattern a bilingual child experiences is a combination of hearing some people speaking only one language plus hearing other people speaking both languages on a regular basis (De Houwer, 2017a). In contrast, there are many reasons why a parent may use their non-native language to address their child. For example, parents who have learnt Basque as a second language sometimes speak Basque to their children so that it becomes their first language.

Many people grow up with several languages from an early age, and many others replace their first learned language by another language and no longer use, or want to use, the first language learned. Some parents are encouraged by misinformed professionals (e.g. pediatricians, clinicians, and educators) to stop speaking their 'native' language to their children. Others do not speak their 'native' language to their children because the other parent would not understand.

There will also be an uneven distribution in the use of two or more languages, and that tends to change over time as family, social and educational circumstances as well as language use opportunities vary. A bilingual child rarely or never has an equal balance in two-language experience. Hence, **balanced bilingualism** (see Chapter 1) is more of a myth than a reality.

The One-Parent One-Language Approach

The one-parent one-language (OPOL) approach, as described earlier, is commonly viewed as a successful strategy in two-parent families. An example would be the mother speaks only English and the father speaks only Dutch (the community language) to their child. However, it tends to imply incorrectly that it is only the parents who influence language acquisition. Community influences are also important (e.g. preschool, extended family, mass media, social media). An example is when children are raised in multilingual cities (e.g. Brussels, New York, Sydney) and the diverse language experience may add much variation to this strategy. As De Houwer (2007) found in research on 1899 families in Flanders, Belgium, the OPOL strategy does not provide a necessary nor a sufficient context for the growth of bilingualism in children. The success rate in her families was 75%. Also, the OPOL approach is much more difficult than it sounds, and can be physically and emotionally taxing on families (Barron-Hauwaert, 2004). It assumes the child interacts equally with both parents – an unlikely scenario if one parent works outside the home and the other is the primary caregiver. Furthermore, the fact that it requires such constant conscious effort suggests that it grinds against the dynamic nature of bilingualism and the ways bilinguals naturally use their languages in daily life (García, 2017a).

Home Language Is Different from the Language Outside the Home

There is much variation within this category in terms of parental first language, neighborhood, language of schooling and other factors. What is central is that the child acquires one language in the home and another outside the home. Both parents use the same language in the home and the child acquires a different language formally or informally outside the home. One parent may be using their second language. For example, the father is a native English-speaker but uses fluent Korean with his child, while the mother speaks her native language, Korean, but the community language is English. The parents' language may or may not be the same as that of the local neighborhood. If it is different, then the child may, for example, acquire the second language at school. One further variation can produce multilingualism. If each parent speaks a different language to the child from birth, the child may gain a third language outside the home, thus leading to trilingualism. For example, the mother speaks German, the father speaks Italian and the community language is English.

The Mixed Language Approach

One or both parents speak both languages to the child. Translanguaging (see below) is acceptable in the home and the neighborhood. The child will typically translanguage with other bilinguals but not with monolinguals. However, some **domains** (e.g. school) may expect strict separation of languages. The community may have a **dominant language** or not. For example, the mother and father may speak Maltese and English, and more widely the community languages are also Maltese and English.

Delayed Introduction of the Second Language

Where the neighborhood, community and school language is a higher-status and dominant language, a few parents may delay exposure to that language. For example, parents may exclusively speak Farsi in the home until the child is two or three years of age, then add English. The tactic is to ensure a strong foundation in a heritage language before the dominant language outside the home becomes pervasive.

Limitations

One main limitation of this category system is that most approaches are concerned with 'prestigious bilingualism', where there is a relatively stable additive bilingual environment and a family commitment to bilingualism. In communities where **assimilation** is politically dominant (see Chapter 18), childhood bilingualism can be much less stable. Piller (2001) also suggests that, of the four approaches listed above, approaches 1 and 2 have come to be regarded as successful strategies, and that approaches 3 and 4 are more negatively evaluated. However, this masks a social class difference. Approach 1 is associated particularly with 'elite' and middle-class families. Approaches 2, 3 and 4 are often found among economically disadvantaged heritage language groups, immigrants and working-class families.

Note that the above approaches do not account for languages spoken by siblings or others who may be living in the home (e.g. nannies, maids or other domestic workers – see e.g. Lorente, 2018), or other major linguistic influences in the home such as books, mass media, the internet, social media and video games. Fukuda (2017), in her study of trilingual Japanese–Catalan–Spanish families in Catalonia, found that the OPOL strategy worked best for parents with just one child. Slavkov (2017), surveying 170 school-aged children from multilingual families in Canada, found that 79% of the children watched television and played video games exclusively in English. Also, there are agencies other than the family that can play a major role in early childhood bilingualism. Before the age of three, the language experience with neighbors, friends, crèche and the nursery school may be a particularly important part of becoming bilingual. This chapter continues by focusing on the relatively well documented routes to childhood bilingualism.

Case Studies of Early Bilingualism

Some of the earliest research on bilingualism concerns detailed case studies of children becoming bilingual. For example, Ronjat (1913) described a case of the mother speaking German and the father speaking French in a French community. This case study introduced the OPOL concept. Of the case studies of children growing up bilingually since then, one of the most detailed is by Leopold (1970/1939–49). In his classic studies of his daughter Hildegard from 1939 to 1949, Leopold spoke only German and his wife spoke only English to Hildegard at home in the United States.

Leopold was a phonetician by training and made a comprehensive record of the development of Hildegard's speech, which he published in four books.

One important aspect of Leopold's studies is the shifting balance of the two languages in childhood. When Hildegard went to Germany, her German became stronger. When back in the United States and attending school, Hildegard's English became the dominant language. Many bilingual situations are changeable, where, at an individual level (and not just at a societal level), the languages shift in dominance. Hildegard, for example, was reluctant to speak German during her mid-teens, with German as the weaker language. Leopold's second daughter, Karla, understood German but spoke very little German to her father. In childhood, Karla was a passive bilingual. Yet at the age of 19, Karla visited Germany, where she was able to change from receptive German to productive German, and managed to converse relatively fluently.

A more recent longitudinal study of bilingual first language acquisition is by Taura and Taura (2012), who documented the linguistic and narrative development of a Japanese–English bilingual girl for 14 years from early childhood (age 4 years 9 months) to late adolescence (19 years 1 month). The girl, referred to as 'M', grew up in Japan with an English-speaking mother and a Japanese-speaking father. She received most of her education in Japan except for kindergarten and grade 6, which she received during extended stays in Australia. M attended a bilingual secondary school in Japan for grades 7–12, where half the subjects were taught in English and half in Japanese. Despite the typological distance between English and Japanese, and despite far less exposure to English than Japanese during her lifespan, the researchers found that with just a few exceptions, M's English language development was 'similar or identical to that of a monolingual [English speaker] in core linguistic areas' (Taura & Taura, 2012: 475). However, they acknowledged that it was difficult to tell if M's English proficiency would have been the same without the time she spent living and attending school in Australia. Nonetheless, like Hildegard in Leopold's study, M experienced some notable shifts in her language balance at various points during her childhood and adolescent years.

Other recent examples of shifting bilingualism in childhood are also found in shorter-term case studies: by Paing (2018), who describes the challenges of heritage language maintenance among Burmese immigrant families in New York; by Velázquez (2019), who studied Spanish language maintenance and loss among first-generation **Latinx** families in the US Midwest; by Tsushima and Guardado (2019), who focus on the struggles of Japanese mothers in raising their children through the Japanese language in the multilingual context of Montreal, Canada; by Kiaer (2023), who documents the development of her own two daughters' multilingual and multimodal communication in their Korean–English home in the UK; and by Park-Johnson (2024), who documents the development of four Korean–English bilingual children in two Korean American families in the United States. In Japan, Yamamoto (2002: 545) reported that many parents testify that 'in spite of their full-fledged care, their children have not developed active bilingual abilities'. De Houwer (2003) found that among 2250 bilingual families, one in five children reared bilingually do not use one of those languages. Rumbaut (2009) declared the United States a 'language graveyard' given the prevalent lack of home language proficiency among the over 5000 young adult children of immigrants in his longitudinal national study. But as Quay and Chevalier (2019: 214) argue, 'passive bi/trilingual children have the potential for active multilingualism later in life'. Thus, passive competence can rapidly change to productive language competence by a major increase in input and a need to speak that language, for example when visiting monolingual grandparents, traveling to a home/ancestral country or obtaining a job requiring bilingual skills.

There are other case studies showing different approaches to raising children bilingually. Two of these have already been mentioned: each parent speaking a different language to the child (OPOL); and parents speaking a minoritized language to the child, who acquires a second language in the community or extended family. A third approach, which may be more common, occurs where both parents (and the community) are bilingual and use both their languages with the children. This is quite common across Spanish bilingual communities in the United States and other English-speaking countries (Fuller, 2013; Potowski & Rothman, 2011). A similar pattern is found among Spanish-speaking families in the official Dutch-speaking region of Flanders in Belgium (De Houwer, 2007). Parental dual use of languages can still lead to a child communicating effectively in two languages, especially as the child learns that the two languages have relatively distinct forms and uses.

A classic example of parents using both languages with their first-born is by Deuchar and Quay (2000). Here is a simplified profile of such dual language use with Deuchar's daughter (from the age of 10 months to 2 years and 3 months):

- *Mother.* Born in United Kingdom, native speaker of English, learnt fluent Spanish in adulthood.
- *Father.* Born in Cuba, later lived in Panama and then the United Kingdom. Native speaker of Spanish; began learning English at high school and became fluent in English.
- *Language spoken to daughter by mother.* English up to age one, then Spanish. Spanish used by the mother when talking to the father; English when in the company of English-speakers (e.g. crèche) or in a specific context (e.g. university campus).
- *Language spoken to daughter by father.* Spanish except when English-speaker present, in which case English.
- *Language spoken to daughter by maternal grandmother/ caregivers/ crèche.* English.
- *Community.* English.
- *Trips abroad.* Spanish.

What is significant in this case study is that the daughter experienced her parents speaking both languages, with the context providing the rule-bound behavior. Both parents were fluent and effective role models in both languages, although each parent was a native speaker of one language and a learner of the other. The switching between English and Spanish was not random but governed by the situation. Siblings, members of the extended family, caregivers, crèche, pre-schooling, friends of the family and many varying contexts (e.g. religious, geographical mobility) often have an additional language effect (Barron-Hauwaert, 2011). Parents may be able to plan language use when together as a nuclear family, but once other people enter family life, parental control is limited, andthis is especially true of the child's language experience outside the home.

The development of a child's bilingualism is affected by both local (e.g. street, school) and regional contexts. Quay and Chevalier (2019: 273) warn that 'early successful multilingualism before children enter school and society is no guarantee of later multilingualism when family-external influences on communication and language learning become more prevalent'. They emphasize the importance of bilingual education programs in this effort. For example, Newcomer (2020) studied a group of

Latinx high school students who credited their elementary school's bilingual program for helping them develop and maintain their bilingualism. These students were fortunate to be in a high school that valued their bilingualism. Other local contexts may be less supportive. Chang (2004), for example, found that children in Taiwan who attain high levels of English proficiency, if they are perceived as becoming too 'Americanized', can be socially rejected for not being Chinese enough.

One-Parent Families and Bilingualism

Most case studies of bilingual children have been based on two-parent families. Books dealing with raising children bilingually tend to assume the presence of two parents in the family home. By accident rather than design, this implies that a one-parent family has little or no chance of raising a child bilingually. This is not true. Two examples will illustrate this.

(1) A second language is often acquired outside the home. In parts of Africa, children acquire one language at home or in the neighborhood and another language (or even two or three) at school or in inter-ethnic communication in urban areas (see e.g. Chimbutane, 2011). Children in immigrant US communities may acquire Spanish, for example, in the home and neighborhood, and learn English at school. A single parent who speaks French but resides in the United States may decide to make French the family language so that the children have the opportunity to become bilingual. In cases like these, the absence of a father or mother does not necessarily hinder a child's bilingual development.

(2) In some cases, the maintenance of a family's bilingualism may be challenged by the absence of a parent. In cases where one parent speaks the dominant language of the community to the children, and the other parent uses a minoritized language with them, the death or departure of the second parent may mean that the family becomes monolingual. However, if the remaining parent is committed to the maintenance of the family's bilingualism, it can be accomplished in various ways.

The disruption of a family by death or divorce is typically traumatic for both parents and children. At times of great mental and emotional stress, when many practical difficulties and changes have to be faced, bilingualism may seem low on the list of priorities. However, single-parent families are often adept at meeting challenges and may look for ways of maintaining a child's bilingualism without causing further disruption to the child's life. In addition, where a child has undergone such stress, it may be wise to avoid, if possible, the added trauma of losing a language, a culture and an intrinsic part of the child's identity. Trauma-informed practices adopted by teachers can help mitigate the impacts of such trauma on bilingual and multilingual students (Schepers *et al.*, 2022, 2023). In one of the few studies comparing dual- and single-parent multilingual families, De Houwer (2004) found no differences in heritage language transmission.

Trilingualism/Multilingualism

Many people are multilingual, speaking three or more languages. For example, some Swedish people are fluent in Swedish, German and English. Many individuals in the African and Indian continents speak a local, regional and national or international language. In the Republic of Zaire, children may learn a local **vernacular** at home, a regional language such as Lingala or Kikongo in the community or at school, and French as they proceed through schooling. Early trilingualism, when a child is exposed to three languages from birth, is rarer than trilingualism achieved through schooling (e.g. two languages learnt at school).

Examples of trilingual schooling are found in the Basque Country (Basque, Spanish, English) (Cenoz, 2009), Catalonia (Catalan, Spanish, English) (Muñoz, 2000), Finland (Finnish, Swedish, English) (Björklund & Suni, 2000), Friesland (Frisian, Dutch, English) (Ytsma, 2000) and Romania (Romanian, Hungarian, English) (Iatcu, 2000). **Trilingual education** is common throughout South Asia (Panda & Mohanty, 2015), Hong Kong (Wang & Kirkpatrick, 2019) and Mainland China (Feng & Adamson, 2015), with instruction in a regional and national language, plus English as an international language. Some trilingual programs may also be found in the United States, where elementary dual language schools (e.g. English–Spanish) may add instruction in a third language (e.g. Chinese) when students move into the upper grades (Wright & Chan, 2019). A particular challenge in these settings, however, is maintaining an appropriate balance between powerful international and national languages and the local and regional languages. Trilingual education is returned to in Chapter 11.

One route to multilingualism is parents speaking two different languages to their children at home and then the children then take their education through a third language. Another route is parents speaking one language at home (e.g. Chinese) but enrolling their children in a dual language bilingual education program in two other languages (e.g. English and French in Canada, or English and Spanish in the United States). For example, Park (2024) documents the active participation of K'nyaw (Karen) refugees from Burma in a Korean–English dual language bilingual education program in the United States. Alternatively, children may pick up a third language from their grandparents, caregivers, visitors, playmates or the mass media. The majority language of the community is likely to influence the relative strengths of the three languages. The relative proficiency in each of the three languages may change over time. Stable trilingualism seems less likely than stable bilingualism. Three languages can be acquired simultaneously or consecutively, with a wealth of individual and societal variables interacting with such acquisition. Hence, simple conclusions about the development of trilingualism become difficult. However, **metalinguistic awareness** (see Chapter 7) seems to be a typical outcome of trilingualism (Wang, 2019).

There are a small but growing number of case studies of the development of multilingual children (for a review see Quay & Chevalier, 2019). Wang (2008, 2011, 2015) provides a most comprehensive, detailed and thorough study as both an academic and as a mother. Her 11-year observation of her two sons acquiring French (their father's language), Chinese (Putonghua – their mother's language) and English (in the context of the United States) involved careful observation on a daily basis with audio and video recordings. This remarkable study is refreshingly holistic, including linguistic and sociolinguistic perspectives, while at the same time revealing considerable parental insight and wisdom. Wang details the complexities, challenges and achievements of a decade of development, not only of three languages but also of related identity, personality and literacy.

Quay (2001) studied a boy raised in German (spoken by the father to the child and the language used between mother and father) and English (used by the mother when addressing the child). Both parents were fluent in Japanese, which was the language of the local community (e.g. where their son attended daycare). There was a change in language exposure over the first two years, for example due to visits abroad and changes in the father's work schedule (see Table 5.1). Such changes are quite common for early trilinguals and bilinguals.

Table 5.1 Language exposure of the trilingual child in the case study by Quay (2001)

Age of child	% English heard	% German heard	% Japanese heard
Birth to 11 months	70%	30%	0%
11 months to 1:0 year	50%	20%	30%
1:0 to 1:5 years	43%	23%	34%
1:5 to 1:6 years	45%	10%	45%

Table 5.1 shows that this child was less exposed to German than English. At 1:3 it was not apparent that he understood much German. Yet after two weeks in Germany at 1:3, the mother reported that he 'shocked us with how much he understood in German when spoken to by the extended family' (Quay, 2001: 174). This is a common experience for families: understanding (and speaking) a second or third language quickly grows once there is sufficient exposure and incentive. However, Quay also shows that the child was an emergent trilingual rather than an active trilingual. This child preferred to speak Japanese to his parents as he had more lexical resources in Japanese, and his parents understood and accepted his Japanese utterances. He tended to be a passive trilingual, understanding English and German, but speaking Japanese.

A set of case studies by Dewaele (2000, 2002, 2007) and colleagues (Festman *et al.*, 2017) provides a longitudinal view of Livia, who was raised in Dutch by her mother, in French by her father (OPOL), with English acquired in her London neighborhood. The mother and father used Dutch when speaking together, making Dutch the dominant language of the family. English quickly became her 'default language' when meeting new children in London. From 0:5 to 2:6 Livia learnt Urdu from a childminder, thus becoming quadrilingual at an early age. By 1:2 she could comprehend about 150 French, Dutch, Urdu and English words. Multiword utterances in Dutch and French appeared at 2:2. Awareness of her languages (metalinguistic awareness – see Chapter 7) came before her second birthday. Her parents reported, 'If she doesn't get the cookie she ordered in one language, she codeswitches to the other, just to make sure we understand her request' (Festman *et al.*, 2017: 5).

By five years of age, status and acceptance by peers had become important. Livia's father reported that she 'does not want me to speak French to her at school and addresses me … in English, or whispers French in my ear' (Dewaele, 2002: 547). She wanted to avoid standing out from her peers, even in multi-ethnic London. In later childhood, Livia remained fluent in three languages; nonetheless, Dewaele (2007: 69) noted 'she goes to an English school, is surrounded by English-speaking friends, watches English films, reads English books, hence the logical and inevitable dominance of English. It is her social language and also her "inner" language'. Livia was allowed to respond in English when her OPOL parents talked to her in another language (although the quote from Livia below suggests that the perception of parents and child may differ). 'By insisting too much on using our languages, we feared we could create the opposite effect, namely a complete refusal to use the languages at all' (Dewaele, 2007: 70). Dewaele concluded that, by the age of 10, becoming trilingual from birth was not hard to achieve for Livia, but the difficulty predominantly existed in the maintenance and development of all three languages.

At the age of 16, Livia wrote:

> It frequently amazes people that I speak three languages, but to me it is not special, definitely not an achievement. If anything, it is my parents' achievement, for making sure I always spoke in French/Dutch to them and stuck to the one parent/one language rule. If not properly enforced, I would have lost the ability to speak either or both of the two, especially as I became most proficient in English.... When asked if my multilingualism does not somehow have a negative effect on me, I answer (forgive me for lack of modesty) that I have consistently achieved top grades in both French and English at school, attaining the highest mark in the year in my English GCSE exam last year. Psychologically, of course, some might argue that speaking three languages is affecting my mental balance and I may someday become a psychopathic killer. Not to worry, I have always been happy, and it seems to me, at least, that I don't have any mental problems, or any issues in fact. If I did, I highly doubt they would spring from my multilingualism. (Festman *et al.*, 2017: 25)

In 2019, Livia graduated with a bachelor's degree in French and linguistics from the University of Oxford. Dewaele concludes that Livia's case shows that:

> It is perfectly possible for a child to grow up with multiple languages, and that there was no lack of brain capacity to absorb these four languages simultaneously in her first years. It also shows that the early multilingualism was not linked to any delay in rate of acquisition of English, French nor Dutch. (Festman *et al.*, 2017: 31)

Research on trilingualism reveals that 'bilingualism does not hinder the acquisition of an additional language and, to the contrary, in most cases bilingualism favors the acquisition of a third language' (Cenoz & Genesee, 1998: 20). Cenoz (2003: 82) suggests that 'studies on the effect of bilingualism on third language acquisition tend to confirm the advantages of bilinguals over monolinguals in language learning'. The cognitive advantages of bilingualism such as a wider linguistic repertoire, enhanced learning strategies, cognitive flexibility and metalinguistic awareness (see Chapter 7) and the development of enhanced linguistic processing strategies may help explain this positive effect of bilingualism on acquiring a third language (Cenoz, 2009).

Clyne *et al.* (2004) found multiple positive social, cultural and cognitive advantages of multilingualism. Bilinguals were found to be effective and enduring language learners whose bilingualism is a language apprenticeship for learning additional languages. They concluded that 'acquiring a third language at school boosts students' confidence in their bilingualism and makes them appreciate their home language more, in some cases even leading to a desire to maintain their heritage language in the future and pass it on to the next generation' (Clyne *et al.*, 2004: 49). They also found that acquisition of a third language awakens and deepens interest in other languages, cultures and countries, creating more **multicultural** and global citizens.

Codeswitching and Translanguaging

One issue frequently raised by parents and teachers of bilingual children of differing ages is about one language being mixed with another. Terms such as Hinglish, Singlish, Spanglish, Tex-Mex and Wenglish (respectively for Hindi–English, Singaporean English mixed with other languages of the country, Spanish–English, Texan Mexican Spanish–English and Welsh–English) are used – sometimes in a derogatory fashion – to describe what may have become natural practices within a bilingual community.

Codeswitching

Various terms have been used to describe switches between languages in conversation. The terms **codemixing** and **codeswitching** are often used interchangeably. While some scholars make clear distinctions between them in the context of their specific studies, for example restricting codeswitching to mixing within a sentence (De Houwer, 2019), the broader field does not make a sharp distinction (MacSwan, 2020). Here we will simply use the term codeswitching to refer to any switches between languages that occur within or across sentences during the same conversation or **discourse**.

Very few bilinguals keep their two languages completely separate, and the ways in which they mix them are complex and varied. Grosjean and Li (2013) distinguish between the 'monolingual mode', when bilinguals use one of their languages with monolingual speakers of that language, and the 'bilingual mode', when bilinguals are in the company of other bilinguals and have the option of switching languages. Even in the monolingual mode, bilinguals occasionally switch their languages inter-sententially.

Here are a few examples of types of codeswitches:

- switching a single word within an utterance or sentence (Spanish/English)
  Leo un magazine [I read a magazine];

- switching within a sentence (English/Spanish)
  Please go to the mercado and buy some leche y queso. [Please go the store and buy some milk and cheese];

- switching from one sentence to the next (English/Welsh)
  Come to the table. Bwyd yn barod. [Food is ready].

Many scholars study codeswitching from a linguistic perspective (e.g. 'where in a sentence can a speaker change languages?'). Some seminal and recent examples include MacSwan (2013, 2014, 2020, 2022a, 2022b), MacSwan and Faltis (2020), Muysken (2000), Myers-Scotton (1997), Poplack and Meechan (1998), Stavans and Porat (2019) and Toribio (2004). One main language (called the matrix language) provides the grammatical rules that govern how something is said when there is codeswitching (Myers-Scotton, 2002). Codeswitching thus involves a rule-bound (e.g. concerning word order or verb endings) use of the 'other' language, as such language insertions will fit those matrix language rules.

In contrast, **language interference** is a term that was once used to refer to when people learning a second language mix their languages due to lack of vocabulary and grammar knowledge in the target language. Many bilinguals regard 'language interference' as a negative and pejorative term that comes from a monolingual perspective, perpetuating a deficit view that there is a problem when a bilingual speaks. A child may move between languages to convey thoughts and ideas in the most personally efficient manner. The child may also realize that the listener understands such switching. As MacSwan (2020: 28) asserts, drawing on decades of codeswitching research:

> Researchers' concerns with the underlying structure of codeswitching – or the use of *grammar of codeswitching* – have labored to reveal the specific mechanisms at work in defining the structure of language mixing itself, and showing in the course of doing so that the underlying grammar of codeswitching gives evidence of a rich and complex system of rules, every bit as impressive as the rules of monolingual grammar.

Codeswitching research has been instrumental in challenging deficit views of bilingualism to reveal instead the rich language practices of bilingual and multilingual students (MacSwan, 2022b; MacSwan & Faltis, 2020; MacSwan & Rolstad, 2024). At the turn of the 21st century, it has been joined by consideration of translanguaging, initially in schools and later in families and in society as a whole.

Translanguaging

The term **translanguaging** has become highly popular in usage across different disciplines. Colin Baker and colleagues document the origin of the term (Baker, 2019; Lewis *et al.*, 2012). It was originally coined in Welsh as *trawsieithu* in the late 1980s by Cen Williams (1994) to describe the planned and systematic use of two languages inside the same lesson in a classroom. Cen requested an English translation from Colin, who ultimately suggested *translanguaging*. Colin first reported Cen's ideas and the term *translanguaging* in the third edition (2001) of this book, *Foundations of Bilingual Education and Bilingualism*.

Williams stated in a 2002 Welsh education committee document titled *Extending Bilingualism in the Education System* that 'translanguaging simply means (i) receiving information in one language and (ii) using or applying it another'. He noted this is 'a skill that happens naturally in everyday life' and advocated for translanguaging to be developed in Welsh schools so that pupils could 'fully utilize their bilingual capability'. Ofelia García (2009a) popularized and expanded upon the original notion of translanguaging in her influential book *Bilingual Education in the 21st Century*, where she first described translanguaging as the 'multiple discursive practices in which bilinguals engage in order to make sense of their bilingual worlds' (García, 2009a: 45). Translanguaging has since been adopted and adapted by a large number of scholars and educators around the world, researching its use in classrooms, schools, families, religious institutions, community-based organizations, workplaces and other formal and informal societal contexts.

As a relatively new concept, the meaning and use of translanguaging are still developing (Moore *et al.*, 2020) and being debated (MacSwan & Rolstad, 2024; Wiley, 2020). To offer additional clarity, Otheguy *et al.* (2015: 281) defined translanguaging as 'the deployment of a speaker's full linguistic repertoire without regard for watchful adherence to the socially and politically defined boundaries of named (and usually national and state) languages'. Lin and He (2017: 229) describe how the concept of translanguaging 'has been further developed to refer to a scaffolding strategy, a pedagogical approach and a framework that enlightens 21st-century bilingual education'. MacSwan (2020) suggests that current views of translanguaging revolve around three components: (1) a conceptual framework that affirms a holistic view of bilingualism, (2) a pedagogical approach that rejects the strict separation of (named) languages, and (3) a perspective on bilingual grammar that questions the existence of discrete languages.

Translanguaging is different from and goes well beyond the more linguistic idea of codeswitching (Otheguy *et al.*, 2015, 2019). Quay and Chevalier (2019: 215) explain that translanguaging may encompass the linguistic behaviors of codeswitching but 'differs from it by moving away from attention to the traditional concept of language as a solid systemic unit to the use of a multilingual speaker's full linguistic repertoire beyond the socially and politically defined boundaries of named languages'. Translanguaging also goes beyond the mixed use of (named) languages within or across sentences produced by an individual bilingual, to also account for phenomena such as a conversation between two bilinguals where one speaks in Arabic and the other speaks in English (described above as a dual-lingual conversation), or students reading a text in English and then discussing it in Spanish (i.e. Cen Williams's original pedagogic concept of translanguaging). Translanguaging can account for other flexible linguistic uses, such as a teacher previewing a lesson in Spanish before it is taught in English, students discussing and creating outlines of their stories in Korean before writing them in English, or bilinguals posting comments in English in response to a YouTube video in Vietnamese. These are just a few translanguaging practices that are outside the purview of codeswitching.

There is academic debate about whether codeswitching is tied to 'outdated' understandings of language (García *et al.*, 2021). This debate is over the third component of current views of translanguaging as identified my MacSwan (2020) above, and thus is centered around theoretical arguments on underlying linguistic structure and bilingual grammar (Cummins, 2022; MacSwan, 2017, 2020, 2022a, 2022b; Otheguy *et al.*, 2015, 2019). MacSwan and Rolstad (2024) trace the history of the development of translanguaging theory and distinguish early from late translanguaging theory. Cummins (2022) makes a similar distinction, referring to early and late translanguaging theory as 'crosslinguistic translanguaging theory' and 'unitary translanguaging theory' respectively. MacSwan and Rolstad (2024) note that early translanguaging theory was grounded in and built upon decades of empirical codeswitching research (Auer, 2022; Bhatt & Bolonyai, 2022; Faltis, 2020; MacSwan, 2017, 2020, 2022a, 2022b; MacSwan & Rolstad, 2024; Stavans & Porat, 2019). However, late translanguaging theory has been attached to a postmodernist approach of deconstructivism (Makoni & Pennycook, 2007) which rejects the very existence of different languages, at least at the individual cognitive level and thus rejects codeswitching as outdated and 'abyssal' thinking (García *et al.*, 2021; Otheguy *et al.*, 2015, 2019). MacSwan and Rolstad (2024: 1) contend that 'late translanguaging theory is at odds with empirical research and holds negative consequences for pluralist language ideologies and civil rights advocacy'. Cummins (2022) contends this late or unitary translanguaging theory may also prevent effective bilingual pedagogical practices such as teaching for transfer across languages.

As these theoretical debates continue, there is nonetheless rich and ongoing empirical research on both codeswitching and translanguaging which is complementary, which further builds our understanding of bilingualism and which has important implications for bilingual and multilingual education. Mendoza (2023), for example, contends that the rejection of codeswitching in late translanguaging theory and the denial of the psycholinguistic reality of distinct (named) languages prevents high-level analyses of the ways bilinguals and multilinguals creatively draw on their full linguistic repertoire for learning and identity construction. Mendoza drew on both codeswitching and translanguaging in her study of multilingual high school classrooms in Hawaii. Thus, using both terms currently remains important.

Translanguaging recognizes that the languages we use integrate, change and adapt to new learning and new situations, with effects on identity and experiences. We combine all our language resources to unlock meaning and share our understandings with others. Translanguaging in bi/multilingual communication is thus fluid and dynamic, sometimes messy and inventive, making and conveying meaning as best as possible (García, 2009a). 'Trans' suggests continual movement across and between socially named languages, but also suggests that such translanguaging is transformative in thinking and speaking, in identity and interpersonal relationships (García & Li Wei, 2014).

While codeswitching research tends to focus more on the 'code' (i.e. the mixed language utterances produced by a bilingual speaker) and translanguaging research tends to focus more on the ways bilingual speakers draw on their various linguistic resources in their daily lives, there is overlap. García (in an interview with Grosjean) acknowledged that from an external social perspective, the behavior of codeswitching and translanguaging may look the same, 'but seen from the internal perspective of the bilingual speaker, translanguaging behavior is clearly different' because it 'legitimizes the fluid language practices with which bilinguals operate' and also 'posits that bilinguals have a much more complex and expanded repertoire than monolinguals' (Grosjean, 2016: 1). However, as noted above, codeswitching research has likewise helped to legitimize the language practices of bilinguals and has sought to detail the complex but rule-governed nature of mixed language use.

Faltis (2020: 57) argues that 'the commonalities [of codeswitching and translanguaging], in terms of what each contributes to promoting bilingualism, far outweigh their theoretical differences'. Wiley (2020: 273) cautions about the bandwagon effect, 'which can lead to falling into the trap of presuming that a new label represents a fundamental break with all things in the past'. While acknowledging the importance of academic critique to move the field forward with new insights and understandings, Wiley (2020: 279) concludes 'let us not forget the implications of our theories and critiques for communities of practice. Both the extensive literature on codeswitching and the emerging literature on translanguaging have much to contribute to those communities'. In this spirit, our discussion in this section will consider the natural ways bilinguals make use of codeswitching in their translanguaging practices, and also ways in which translanguaging practices extend beyond traditional notions of codeswitching (see Chapter 13 for further discussion of translanguaging).

Box 5.1 Language borrowing

The term **language borrowing** refers to foreign loan words or phrases that have become an integral and permanent part of the recipient language. Examples are 'le weekend' from English into French and 'der computer' from English into German. All languages borrow words or phrases from other languages with which they come into contact. Words commonly used by English-speakers such as 'patio', 'croissant' and 'jaguar' are loan words from Spanish, French and Portuguese, respectively. Loan words may start out as frequently occurring codeswitches, though it is often difficult to distinguish between them. It may be more accurate to think of them as forming a continuum.

The Context of Codeswitching and Translanguaging

Children's codeswitching and translanguaging are influenced by the language model provided by parents and significant others in the family, school and community. If parents use both languages regularly, then their children may imitate this. If, on the other hand, parents discourage mixing languages (e.g. by clear language separation), then less codeswitching may occur. What is culturally appropriate, the norm of the community, and what is valued by parents and others will have an important influence, as may the extent of the child's repertoire in each language.

Codeswitching and translanguaging may also be less acceptable for political, social or cultural reasons. If a power conflict exists between different ethnic groups, then language may be perceived as a prime marker of a separate identity and codeswitching may seem disloyal. Some monolinguals have negative attitudes to codeswitching and translanguaging, believing that it shows a communication deficit, or a lack of mastery of both languages. Some monolinguals and bilinguals are language purists who strongly believe that codeswitching is a corruption of both languages. When scholar Ilan Stavans (2003) published a Spanglish dictionary, translated a portion of *Don Quixote* into Spanglish, taught a university course about Spanglish and undertook other activities in defense of Spanglish, he reported receiving hostile messages and even death threats from individuals in the United States, Spain, Mexico, Colombia and Argentina (Stavans, 2014). But Stavans (2014: 2) noted he was also 'showered with great applause' and held up by many as a 'folk hero' and 'a subversive intellectual undermining the status quo'. Codeswitching is thus not always acceptable, including to some bilingual speakers themselves. Some bilinguals adopt a more monolingual approach and attempt to keep their languages separate. Bilinguals themselves may be defensive or apologetic about their codeswitching if they have internalized negative societal views that falsely attribute it to laziness or sloppy language.

Some **bilingual education** programs (and multilingual ones) (e.g. dual language education; see Chapter 11) attempt a relatively strict separation of the teaching and use of two or more languages in the classroom. However, translanguaging can be a valuable thinking tool, including in the classroom. It does not happen at random. There is typically purpose and logic in changing languages, as will be shown below. It is using the full language resources that are available to a bilingual, usually knowing that the listener fully understands the dual language or multilingual communication.

If codeswitching is highly prevalent in a language group, it is sometimes regarded as a sign that the minoritized language is about to disappear. Such codeswitching may be seen by some as a halfway house in a societal shift from the minoritized language to the dominant majority language. Identifying the matrix (main, dominant) language that provides the rules for codeswitching becomes a key indicator of the health of a minoritized language. For example, if the matrix language is Diné bizaad (Navajo) and there are English insertions, this may indicate the future of Diné bizaad will be positive. However, if the grammatical frame is English, this may indicate the future of Diné bizaad is negative.

Familiarity, projected status, the ethos of the context and the perceived linguistic skills of the listeners affect the nature and process of codeswitching and translanguaging (Martin-Jones, 2000). Thus, codeswitching and translanguaging are not just linguistic; they indicate important social and power relationships. A variety of factors may affect the extent to which children and adults switch between their languages. The perceived status of the listeners, familiarity with those persons, atmosphere of the setting and perceived linguistic skills of the listeners are examples of variables that may foster or prevent codeswitching and translanguaging. Such factors operate as young as two years of age.

The Purposes and Uses of Codeswitching and Translanguaging

The following mostly derives from the research on codeswitching. However, given the overlap between codeswitching and translanguaging, much of the text also appears to relate to translanguaging. Codeswitches and translanguaging have a variety of purposes and aims. Translanguaging will vary according to who is in the conversation, what the topic is and in what kind of context the conversation occurs. The languages used may be negotiated and may change with the topic of conversation. Also, social, economic, political, identity and symbolic factors can influence translanguaging. For example, competition between language groups, the relationships between the language majority and **language minority**, the norms of the community and inter-group relations in a community may have a major effect on the use of translanguaging.

Fifteen overlapping purposes of codeswitching and translanguaging will now be considered:

(1) *Emphasis*. Codeswitches may be used to emphasize a particular point in a conversation. If one word or phrase needs stressing or is central in a sentence, a switch may be made (e.g. English/Welsh: 'get out of the mud, *hogyn drwg*!' [bad boy]).

(2) *Efficiency*. Sometimes it is simply quicker or easier to express a word or idea in one language versus another. For example, the Khmer word for television is also four syllables (/tou-ro-tos-aa/), but many Khmer speakers simply use the two-syllable English abbreviation *TV*, which flows easily in Khmer phonology. The English word *video* has essentially become a loan word in the Khmer language with a Khmer pronunciation given this single word is more efficient (and precise) than the full Khmer phrase need to convey the same concept.

(3) *Substitution*. If a person does not know a word or a phrase in a language, that person may substitute a word in another language. As Genesee (2006: 53) suggests, 'bilingual children might be compelled to draw on the resources of their more proficient language in order to express themselves fully when using their less well-developed language'. This lexical gap often happens because bilinguals use different languages in different domains of their lives. A bilingual may translanguage when talking at home about school or work, because the associated technical terms may only be known and used in one language. Substitutions, however, are not necessarily due to lexical gaps. The substituted word or phrase may be strategically selected or subconsciously used because it carries more of a precise or intended meaning than the 'equivalent' in the other language would convey.

(4) *Concepts without equivalences*. Words or phrases in two languages may not correspond exactly and the bilingual may switch to one language to express a concept that has no equivalent in the culture of the other language. For example, a French–English bilingual living in Britain may use words like 'pub' or 'bingo hall' when speaking French, because there are no exact French equivalents. Likewise, in Cambodian university courses on education, words and phrases such as 'child-centered instruction', 'active learning' and even 'codeswitching' and 'translanguaging' may be used in English during lectures presented in Khmer as standardized equivalents of these terms have not yet been coined in Khmer or widely adopted.

(5) *Problem solving*. Children sometimes move between their languages to help think through a problem. Having tried a problem in one language, they may use their other language(s) to rephrase and rethink. For example, different associations of words in another language, moving to or from the pedagogic language by teachers, or using the counting system in another language, may help problem solve. This is part of the origins of the term 'translanguaging'.

(6) *Reinforcement*. Codeswitching may be used to reinforce a request. For example, a French language teacher may repeat a command to accent and underline it (e.g. '*Taisez-vous les enfants*! Be quiet, children!'). An Arabic-speaking mother in New York may use English with her children for short commands like 'Stop it! Don't do that!' and then switch back to Arabic (or vice versa).

(7) *Clarification*. Repetition of a phrase or passage in another language may also be used to clarify a point. Some teachers in classrooms introduce a concept in one language and then explain or clarify it in another language, finding that it adds reinforcement and completeness of understanding.

(8) *Identity*. Codeswitching and translanguaging may be used to express identity, shorten social distance and communicate friendship or family bonding. For example, moving from the common majority language to the minoritized language which both the listener and speaker understand well may communicate friendship and common identity. Similarly, a person may deliberately use codeswitching to indicate the need to be accepted by a peer group. Someone with a rudimentary knowledge of a language may inject words of that new language into sentences to indicate a desire to identify and affiliate. The use of the listener's stronger language in part of the conversation may indicate deference, wanting to belong or to be accepted.

(9) *Reported speech*. In relating a conversation held previously, the person may report the conversation in the language or languages used. For example, two people may be speaking Spanish together. When one reports a previous conversation with an English monolingual, that conversation is reported authentically – for example, in English – as it occurred. For instance, a son might say to his mother, '*Mi maestro me dijo* [My teacher told me], "you can't go to the fieldtrip until your parents sign the form"'.

(10) *Interjections*. Codeswitching and translanguaging are sometimes used as a way of interjecting into a conversation. A person attempting to break into a conversation may introduce a different language. Interrupting a conversation may be signaled by changing language.

(11) *Ease tension and/or inject humor.* Codeswitching and translanguaging may be used to ease tension and inject humor into a conversation. If discussions are becoming tense in a committee, the use of a second language may signal a change in the 'tune being played'. Just as in an orchestra, different instruments may be brought in during a composition to signal a change of mood and pace, so a switch in language may indicate a need to change mood within the conversation. A professor in Cambodia who mostly taught his graduate courses in English described switching to Khmer as a way of 'waking up' students who were drifting off.

(12) *Change of attitude or relationship.* Codeswitching and translanguaging often relate to a change of attitude or relationship. For example, when two people meet, they may use the common majority language (e.g. Swahili or English in Kenya). As the conversation proceeds and roles, status and ethnic identity are revealed, a change to a regional language may indicate that boundaries are being broken down. A switch signals that there is less social distance, with expressions of solidarity and growing rapport indicated by the switch. Conversely, a change from a minoritized language or dialect to a majority language may indicate the speaker's wish to elevate their own status, create distance between themselves and the listener, or establish a more formal, business relationship. A Vietnamese American customer at a department store might notice the cashier is also Vietnamese and strike up a friendly conversation in Vietnamese, then ask for a discount. The cashier may switch the conversation back to English to say 'Sorry, can't do that'.

(13) *Exclusion*. Codeswitching and translanguaging can also be used to exclude people from a conversation. For example, when traveling on the metro (subway, underground) in an English-speaking city, two people speaking English may switch to

their minoritized language to talk about private matters, thus preventing other passengers from eavesdropping. Bilingual parents may use one language together to exclude their monolingual children from a private discussion. However, monolinguals sometimes feel threatened and excluded by such codeswitching, even when that is usually not the intention of the speakers.

(14) *Change in topic*. In some bilingual situations, translanguaging occurs regularly when certain topics are introduced. For example, English might be used to discuss the local sports team (e.g. 'Go Spurs go!') while Spanish is used to discuss a recent episode of a popular *telenovela* (Spanish soap opera). Bilinguals may use English when discussing financial matters with American currency but the home language when discussing currency used in the home country (e.g. '*Mi abuela en Guatemala wants me to send her 100 quetzales*' [My grandmother in Guatemala wants me to send her 100 quetzals]). However, 'Spanglish' terms for American coins and currency are commonly used in the southwest United States, such as *daime* (dime), *cuara* (quarter) and *dolar* (dollar). Thus, codeswitching does not just involve clean switches between two languages but also involves the creation of new terms in the mixing.

(15) **Imitation**. In some contexts, children are simply copying the codeswitching and translanguaging practices of the peers and adults around them. If a daughter in England frequently hears her French-speaking father say 'Let's go to le boulangerie [the bakery]', chances are she will start saying it that way too. When children are emulating adults, they may be identifying with higher-status and more powerful people in their lives.

In addition, García (2017a: 261) identifies five purposes for translanguaging pedagogies that have been documented in classroom studies: (1) translanguaging to assist and motivate learning, deepen meaning, understandings and knowledge; (2) translanguaging for greater metalinguistic awareness and linguistic consciousness, including critical sociolinguistic consciousness; (3) translanguaging to affirm bilingual identities; (4) translanguaging for greater social interaction and communication, including home–school cooperation; and (5) translanguaging for empowerment.

The chapter concludes by examining a topic related to translanguaging: children acting as interpreters for their parents and others.

Children as Language Interpreters and Brokers

In language minoritized families, children sometimes act as interpreters (or **language brokers**) for their parents and others (Guo, 2014). Immigrant parents may have little or no competence in the majority language. Therefore, their children act as interpreters in a variety of contexts (as do hearing children with deaf parents). Language brokering goes beyond translation. Rather than just transmit information, children act as cultural mediators, often ensuring the messages are socially and culturally translated, as in the following example:

Father to daughter (in Italian): *Digli che è un imbecille!* [Tell him he is an idiot!]
Daughter to trader: My father won't accept your offer.

Valdés (2003) argues that young immigrants' ability to use their bilingual skills to mediate for their families both linguistically and culturally in this manner is evidence of 'giftedness' that is rarely recognized by schools. This is extended by Orellana (2009), who studied immigrant children in Los Angeles and Chicago to explore how they translated and acted as language and culture brokers at home and school, but also in the community and across institutions. Using two or more languages, children 'work' to shoulder the responsibility for some quite complicated verbal exchanges for non-English-speaking adults. She also shows how such children's sociocultural learning and development are shaped by acting as translators.

Language minoritized students can be important language brokers between the home and the school. Also, when there are visitors to the house, such as sellers and traders, religious persuasionists and local officials, a parent may call a child to the door to help translate what is being said. Similarly, at stores, hospitals, medical and dentist offices, motor vehicle and social security offices, schools and many other places where parents visit, the child may be taken to help interpret and mediate interculturally. Interpretation may be needed in more informal places: on the street, when a parent is phoned, watching the television or listening to the radio, reading a note from school, reading a local newspaper or working on the computer.

Pressure is placed on children in language brokering: linguistic, emotional, social and attitudinal pressure. First, children may find an exact translation difficult to achieve, as their language is still developing. Words often have multiple meanings, making interpretation far from simple or straightforward. Second, children may be hearing information (e.g. medical troubles, financial problems, marital issues, arguments and conflicts) that should be the preserve of adults. Third, children may be expected to be adult-like when interpreting and child-like at all other times; to mix with adults when interpreting and 'be seen and not heard' with adults on other occasions. Fourth, there can be stress, fear and uncertainty for the child in providing an accurate and diplomatic interpretation. Fifth, seeing their parents in an inferior position may lead children to feel embarrassed and develop negative feelings towards their home language. Children may quickly realize when language brokering that the language of power, prestige and purse is the majority language. Sixth, bilinguals are not necessarily good interpreters. Interpretation assumes an identical vocabulary in both languages. Since bilinguals tend to use their two languages in different places with different people, an identical **lexicon** may not be present. Also, proficiency in two or more languages is not enough. Some reflection on language such as an awareness of the linguistic nature of the message may also be required (i.e. metalinguistic awareness).

Despite these pressures, language brokering may also result in positive outcomes for children and their families, such as the following:

(1) *Self-esteem*. Children earn parental praise and status within the family, leading to gains in self-esteem.
(2) *Maturity*. Children quickly learn adult information, learn to act with authority and trust, and take on great responsibility, leading to greater maturity.
(3) *Unity*. Children and parents learn to trust and rely on each other, leading to greater feelings of family unity.
(4) *Empowerment*. Children learn to take initiative such as answering questions on their own rather than relaying the question to their parents, leading to a greater sense of personal **empowerment**. But this can also lead to a shift of power from parents to children, and may cause parental feelings of inadequacy, frustration or resentment.
(5) *Metalinguistic awareness*. Children learn to address the problems and possibilities

of translation of words, figures of speech and ideas, leading to greater gains in metalinguistic awareness.
(6) *Empathy*. Children learn to negotiate between two different social and cultural worlds while trying to understand both, leading to greater feelings of empathy.

Conclusion

This chapter has discussed bilingual development in early childhood through themes of differentiating between languages. Parental influence starts at the fetal stage and language difference is apparent at the babbling stage. Children aged two or three years raised in two languages from birth will know what language to speak, to whom. There are several potential pathways to bilingualism in early childhood. The one-parent one-language approach is a well documented but does not guarantee success. Some parents use two languages with their children. Some bilingual children are raised in one language but become bilingual early via influences outside the home. One-parent families can be as successful as nuclear and extended families. However, **language loss** can occur when political contexts are particularly unfavorable to minoritized **language maintenance**. Other families succeed in raising trilingual children, although it is not usual for a person to become equally proficient in all three languages.

Codeswitching and translanguaging are frequent behaviors among bilinguals, with a variety of valuable purposes and benefits. Interpreting is a similarly frequent expectation of bilinguals – including young children in immigrant families.

Key Points in This Chapter

- Children are born ready to become bilinguals, trilinguals, multilinguals.
- There is a difference between simultaneous (acquiring two languages together) and sequential (acquiring one language later than the other) childhood bilingualism.
- Dual language acquisition starts at the fetal stage, extends into babbling and can be operating successfully at two or three years of age.
- Young children learn to differentiate between two languages.
- Early studies of bilingual children revealed that if each parent speaks a different language to the child, dual language competence can occur, although the balance shifts throughout an individual's language history.
- The one-parent one-language approach to bilingualism in a family is well documented but not always successful. Many other routes can be successful, including where both parents speak both languages to the child.
- Trilingualism and multilingualism can be successfully achieved in young children, although proficiency across the languages may not be equal.
- Bilinguals tend to have an advantage in learning a new third language.

> - Codeswitching refers to any switches between languages that occur within or across sentences during the same conversation or discourse.
> - Translanguaging is the deployment of a speaker's full linguistic repertoire without regard to the socially and politically defined boundaries of named languages.
> - Translanguaging encompasses but goes beyond the linguistic behaviors described as codeswitching. Despite theoretical debates over their compatibility, both remain important concepts.
> - Codeswitching and translanguaging are typical in bilinguals and have many valuable purposes in relationships and relaying messages, as well as expressing roles, norms and values.
> - Codeswitching and translanguaging vary according to who is in the conversation, what the topic is and in what kind of context the conversation occurs.
> - Children may act as language and culture brokers for parents when their proficiency in the majority language is ahead of their parents'. This has many advantages and disadvantages for the child.

Suggested Further Reading

- De Houwer, A. (2021) *Bilingual Development in Childhood*. Cambridge University Press.
- Hayes, D. (2022) *Early Language Learning in Context: A Critical Socioeducational Perspective*. Multilingual Matters.
- Kiaer, J. (2023) *Multimodal Communication in Young Multilingual Children: Learning Beyond Words*. Multilingual Matters.
- Nguyen, T.T.T. (2022) *Individual Language Policy: Bilingual Youth in Vietnam*. Multilingual Matters.
- Park-Johnson, S.K. (2024) *Korean–English Bilingualism in Early Childhood: A Longitudinal Investigation of Development*. Multilingual Matters.

On the Web

- Meet Bella the 4 year old polyglot – *Little Big Shots Australia* (video)
  https://youtu.be/25U0GQAcJRw
- Bilingual Monkeys: Ideas and inspiration for raising bilingual kids (without going bananas)
  https://bilingualmonkeys.com
- National Public Radio – These students speak perfect Spanglish – And now they're learning to own it
  https://www.npr.org/2019/11/29/775035698/these-students-speak-perfect-spanglish-and-now-theyre-learning-to-own-it
- Multilingual Parenting
  https://multilingualparenting.com

Discussion Questions

(1) How easy or difficult do you think it would be to raise children bilingually? If you were to raise a bilingual child, which approach or approaches mentioned in this chapter would you use? If you were raised bilingually, or have or are currently raising a bilingual child, share what strategies seem to be effective.
(2) If you are bilingual, consider your own use of translanguaging. How frequently do you translanguage? For what purposes? In which contexts? If you are not bilingual, what translanguaging practices have you observed among bilingual school children or other bilinguals around you?
(3) What are the pros and cons of bilingual children acting as interpreters? What are some situations where the use of children to interpret may be more or less appropriate?

Study Activities

(1) Conduct a case study of a child's bilingual (or trilingual) development. Using this chapter and specific research studies of children's bilingual development, prepare a list of questions appropriate to ask the child and their parents during an interview to identify if there were particular stages of their development. Share the findings in a written report and/or class presentation.
(2) Review the YouTube Video "'Translanguaging is what bilinguals and multilinguals do": A primer for teachers' featuring trangslanguaging scholar Ryan Pontier and produced by Education Week – https://youtu.be/u53ARlXR0sw?si=IGghIqRGaF8hYe1t. Then observe and record samples of codeswitching and translanguaging inside or outside of a classroom. Try to determine the different purposes of the translanguaging. Ask the people in your sample how conscious they are of translanguaging. What are their explanations for translanguaging? What particular purposes for translanguaging did they give? If in a classroom setting, how effective was the translanguaging in support of teaching and learning?
(3) Review the post on the *Psychology Today* blog by Cara Goodwin on raising bilingual children (https://www.psychologytoday.com/us/blog/parenting-translator/202209/raising-bilingual-children). Select one of the myths she identifies, and analyze her answer. Do you agree? Is there anything else you would add, or experiences you could share? Write your own response to dispel the myth. Identify and address any other myths you could add to her list.

CHAPTER 6

The Later Development of Bilingualism

Introduction

Reasons for Second Language Learning
Societal Reasons
Individual Reasons

Formal Second Language Learning

The Age Factor
Language Loss in Children

Individual Differences: Attitudes and Motivation

Identity and Second Language Acquisition
Social Identity and Second Language Learning
Constructing Meaning in Second Language Learning
Language and Power
Multiple Identities and Second Language Acquisition
Imagined Communities
A Transdisciplinary Framework for Second Language Acquisition

Conclusion

CHAPTER 6

The Later Development of Bilingualism

Introduction

Sequential acquisition of **bilingualism** refers to the situation where a child or adult acquires a first language and later becomes proficient in the second language and sometimes further languages. The sequential acquisition of bilingualism takes us into the field of second language acquisition. Such acquisition may be through formal or informal means: informally through street, nursery school and community, or formally through school, adult classes and language courses. There is no single 'best' route by which learners, young or old, become competent in a second language. There are a variety of informal and formal educational means of acquiring proficiency in a second language.

Many children become competent bilinguals through the process of **simultaneous bilingualism**. The track record of bilingualism achieved through sequential routes (e.g. world or 'foreign' language learning) is not always positive (see Box 6.1). In the

---

Box 6.1 America's world language deficit

The online journal *The Conversation* features an article by Kathleen Stein-Smith (2019) lamenting that 'foreign' language classes in the United States are becoming more scarce. Stein-Smith notes the importance and value of language learning:

> Of all the skills that a person could have in today's globalized world, few serve individuals – and the larger society – as well as knowing how to speak another language. People who speak another language score higher on tests and think more creatively, have access to a wider variety of jobs, and can more fully enjoy and participate in other cultures or converse with people from diverse backgrounds. Knowledge of foreign languages is also vital to America's national security and diplomacy. (Stein-Smith, 2019: 1)

Nonetheless, she found many instances that point to America's growing world language deficit:

- The US Government Accountability Office found that nearly one in four Foreign Service officers do not meet the language proficiency requirements that they should meet to do their jobs.
- The Modern Language Association found that colleges lost 651 foreign language programs from 2013 to 2016 – dramatically more than the number of programs lost between 2009 and 2013.
- Only 20% of K-12 students study a foreign language.
- Only 7.5% of college students are enrolled in a foreign language course – and that percentage has been steadily declining in recent years.
- Only 58% of middle schools and 25% of elementary schools offered a foreign language in 2008.
- For the 2016–17 school year, 44 states and Washington, DC, had a shortage of qualified foreign language instructors at the K-12 level.

United States and United Kingdom, despite extensive world language learning in school (and extensive research on second language acquisition), only a small proportion of children learning a world language become fluent or even functionally bilingual. Even among US college students who major in common world languages, the average student reaches only a limited working proficiency in the language (Brown & Brown, 2015). There are various common reasons for such failure: the emphasis on grammar, reading and writing rather than on developing authentic **communicative competence**; having a low aptitude to learn a second language; a lack of motivation and interest; and a lack of opportunity to practice second language skills. Another popular explanation is attempting to learn a language too late, that is, believing that it is easier to learn a language when someone is younger rather than older. The issue of age in learning a language is considered later in this chapter.

In certain European countries (e.g. the Netherlands, Luxembourg, Slovenia, Sweden, Belgium) and eastern countries (e.g. Israel, Singapore), world language learning has been more successful. Such international comparisons highlight the need to bring political, social, cultural and economic factors into discussions of second language learning (Atkinson, 2011). No language learner or language instruction is an island. Surrounding the shores of the individual psychology of effective second language acquisition lie the seas of social, cultural and political **context**. Any map of **sequential bilingualism** needs to include all these features.

Reasons for Second Language Learning

The various overlapping reasons why second or third languages are taught can be clustered under two headings: societal and individual. Such purposes may clash. For example, national politics may insist on the teaching of a national language for unity and social cohesion, while individuals may prefer instruction through the regional language. Basque separatists in Spain and eastern Europeans rejecting Russian as the language of communism are two examples of difference between societal and individual wishes. Some reasons are for learning a language, others for teaching a language, and there may be variance between the two.

Societal Reasons

For language minoritized children, the aim of second language instruction may be **assimilationist** and subtractive. For example, the teaching of **English as a second language** in the United States and the United Kingdom often aims at rapidly assimilating minoritized language groups into mainstream society. Assimilationist **ideology** (see Chapter 18) tends to work for the dominance of the second language, even the repression of the home, minoritized language. In contrast, children are sometimes taught minoritized languages in order to preserve or restore a language that is being or has been lost (see Chapter 4). A different societal reason for second language acquisition is to reduce conflict and obtain increased harmony between language groups through bilingualism. In Canada, French-speaking children learning English and English-speaking children learning French may help parents and politicians produce a more integrated Canadian society.

The assimilationist, preservationist and harmony viewpoints all argue for the importance of a second language for careers, access to further and higher education, access to information and communications technology and for travel. However, it is important to distinguish whether the second language is intended to replace a student's first language or is to be added to their linguistic repertoire.

While teachers may not have the power to change the basic societal aims and reasons for second language teaching, understanding the role they play in such teaching is important. Second language teaching does not exist in a political vacuum. Nor is language teaching a neutral, value-free activity. Even within an assimilationist system, teachers have some degree of influence and power as policymakers within their own classrooms and schools (Menken & García, 2010) and can help create an environment that values and encourages bilingualism (de Jong, 2011; Wright, 2025).

Second and third language learning is often encouraged for economic and trade reasons. In tourist areas, learning additional languages such English, Chinese, Spanish, French and Japanese is valuable for those working in hotels, shops, cafes and restaurants, and other tourist attractions. Given notions such as globalization, common markets, open access to trade, the free market economy and the importance of international trade to developing nations, facility with languages is seen as opening doors to economic activity. Selling to the Japanese, for example, may be quite difficult through English or German. Speaking Japanese and having a sympathetic understanding of Japanese **culture**, manners, values and thinking may be the essential foundation for successful economic activity (see Chapter 19).

There is a growing realization that speaking world languages is important in increasingly competitive international trade, even for long-range economic self-interest. For example, an effort by the city of San Antonio in Texas to engage in trade with a Chinese company was nearly derailed over a misunderstanding about the 'sweaters' the company hoped would be big sellers in this hot southwest city. The deal was saved thanks to a competent Chinese-American translator who was able to explain that in Chinese 'sweaters' is simply a generic word for all knitted garments. Translation jobs in the United States tend to be filled by foreign-born individuals because there are relatively few US students and adults – including heritage speakers – who are proficient enough in the second languages required for such posts.

Second and third language learning is also encouraged for its potential value in interaction across continents. For many mainland Europeans, for example, to speak two, three or four languages is not uncommon. Such language facility enables time to be spent in neighboring European countries or in North, Central or South America. In Europe, traveling across frontiers is becoming more common, encouraging a person to acquire a repertoire of languages. However, English is growing as a 'common denominator' language, not only in Europe but internationally. Therefore, the learning of English as a second or foreign language has grown considerably (see Chapter 3).

Languages provide access to information and hence power. Whether the information is in academic journals, on the internet, on satellite television or in international news media, a repertoire of languages gives wider access to social, cultural, political, economic and educational information. For the business person and the bureaucrat, for the scholar and the sports person, access to multilingual international information opens doors to new knowledge, new skills and new understanding.

Language learning is also ideally a means of promoting intercultural understanding and peace. Such ideals have become more focused following a new wave of terrorism across the world, but interact uncomfortably with defense and intelligence needs. For example, following the September 11, 2001 terrorist attacks in New York, the lack of world **language proficiency** in US intelligence was much criticized (Brecht & Ingold,

2002). Since 9/11, it has become more apparent that English cannot be the only language of international diplomacy or the lens through which to view the world. Languages identify, symbolize and embody their cultures. The creation of coalitions, friendships and peace requires the use of languages other than English. The healing of longstanding wounds requires bridges to be built through the languages of old opponents and recent rivals. Yet, in contrast, the more basic need is often to search out intelligence, which requires ground operatives, interpreters and translators. A supply line of both operatives and translators is possible not only via language learning in school and at college, but also via heritage language speakers (e.g. Arabic, Farsi, Pashto). In contrast, however, current US ideology tends to prefer the **assimilation** of heritage language speakers by the sole use of English at school (Gándara & Hopkins, 2010). Shortages of staff with world language expertise hinder US military, law enforcement, intelligence, counter-terrorism and diplomatic efforts. Brecht and Ingold (2002: 1) indicate that a reservoir of language talent is typically ignored:

> There exists, however, a largely untapped reservoir of linguistic competence in this country, namely heritage language speakers – the millions of indigenous, immigrant, and refugee individuals who are proficient in English and also have skills in other languages that are developed at home, in schools, in their countries of origin, or in language programs provided by their communities in the United States.

Unfortunately, in the United States there is a great divide between national language needs and federal education policies which seek to assimilate **language minoritized students** and squander their linguistic skills, which are critically needed by the country (Wright, 2010). Some initiatives in the United States to address shortages in the areas of critical-needs languages include the National Security Education Program, STARTALK and the National Heritage Language Resource Center.

Individual Reasons

There are many reasons why the individual child or adult can benefit from being taught a second or third language. Gallagher-Brett (2005) identified 700 reasons within the academic literature for learning a second language.

One reason is cultural awareness. To break down national, ethnic and language stereotypes, second language learning may encourage intercultural sensitivity and awareness. This is seen as important as the world becomes more of a global village, with more sharing of experience and mutual understanding. Cultural awareness in the classroom may be achieved at one level by discussing ethnic variations in eating and drinking, rituals of birth, death and marriage, and religious practices. Such activity widens human understanding and attempts to encourage sensitivity towards other cultures and creeds. While cultural awareness may be conveyed in the first language, the inseparability of culture and language means that such awareness may best be achieved through simultaneous language learning.

A second 'individual' reason for second language teaching has traditionally been cognitive development. The learning of world languages is of general educational and academic value. Just as history and geography, physics and chemistry, mathematics and music have traditionally been taught to increase intellectual fitness and stamina, so modern language learning has been defended as a way of sharpening the mind and developing the intellect. Given the memorization, analysis (e.g. of grammar and sentence structure) and the need to negotiate in communication, language learning has been regarded as a valuable academic activity in itself.

A third reason for an individual to acquire a language is to gain social, emotional and moral development, self-awareness, self-confidence and social and ethical values. Such affective goals include the possibility of **incipient bilinguals** being able to create more effective relationships with target language speakers. Bilinguals can potentially build social bridges with those who speak the second language. Self-confidence and enhanced self-esteem may result from being able to operate socially or vocationally with those who speak the second or third language. The addition of a second language skill can boost an individual's self-confidence as a learner, a linguist and a cultural broker. An old Czech saying is 'learn a new language and get a new soul'.

A fourth 'individual' reason for acquiring a language is careers and employment. For language minoritized and language majority children, being able to speak a second or third or fourth language may mean avoiding unemployment, opening up possibilities of a wider variety of careers or gaining promotion in a career (see Chapter 19). Potential individual careers include becoming translators and interpreters, working in tourism, buying and selling goods and services, exchanging information with local, regional, national and international organizations, migrating across national frontiers to find work, gaining promotion in neighboring countries and becoming part of an international team or company, as well as working from home or from the local village and using multilingual telecommunications to spread a product (e.g. US and UK call centers that are located in India).

Box 6.2 Eurobarometer language survey

The European Commission (2024) Eurobarometer language survey of nearly 27,000 people across 27 European Union (EU) countries reports the following selected findings.

- Overall, EU citizens have positive attitudes towards multilingualism and value linguistic diversity:
    - 76% of Europeans think improving language skills should be a policy priority;
    - 86% think everyone should speak at least one other language than their mother tongue;
    - 84% think regional and minority languages should be protected.

- Foreign language proficiency:
    - four out of five of young Europeans (15–24 years old) can have a conversation in a foreign language (a 5% increase from 2012);
    - 31% of Europeans proficient in a foreign language use it on a daily basis (an 8% increase from 2012);
    - 47% Europeans can speak English (a 5% increase from 2012), making it the most popular foreign language. They also consider it as very important for personal development.

- Young people report they increase their language proficiency by using the internet and social media.

- When watching foreign-language films, the majority of Europeans (53%) and in particular youth (65%) now prefer subtitles to dubbed content.

- When thinking about the main benefits of learning a new language, Europeans include:
    - job opportunities (51%);
    - the ability to understand people from other cultures (45%);
    - getting a better job in the country where they live (42%);
    - using it on holidays abroad (42%);
    - using it at the workplace and on business trips (40%).

Bourdieu (1991) argued that language learning takes place in the competitive and political dynamics of society. Inequality, dominance and social hierarchization shape language learning, in that the individual engaged in such learning is also negotiating their social worth and wealth. Languages operate in a marketplace, since languages have different currency values (linguistic capital). The ability to 'command the listener' is unequal for different speakers, owing to the power relations between them (e.g. a minoritized language person learning English). Norton (2013) has applied this perspective to language learning, suggesting that such learners invest in additional languages to enrich their social, cultural and economic capital, as well as their symbolic and material resources. It is an investment that may yield a return (e.g. a Canadian immigrant learning English; employment and promotion for being a multilingual; evolving a multiple **identity**) or not (e.g. marginalization by the target language community).

Formal Second Language Learning

Where a second language is not acquired in the community, the school has been the major institution expected to produce second language learning (for both **elective** and **circumstantial bilinguals** but for different reasons – see Chapter 1). Through second language and world language lessons, via language laboratories and computer-assisted language learning, drill and practice routines, immersion classes, drama and dance, the initial stages of moving from **monolingualism** to bilingualism may occur.

The routes to bilingualism are not solely in early childhood and in formal education. Voluntary **heritage language** classes, complementary schools and supplementary schools sometimes exist for school-age children. When the school does not support immigrant languages, reproduction of those languages in the family may not be enough for **language maintenance**. Therefore, local community groups have developed extra schooling for their children. In England, Canada and the United States, for example, evening and weekend classes, Saturday schools and vacation schools are organized by various communities for children to learn the heritage language of their parents and grandparents. Children of first-, second-, third- or fourth-generation immigrants may have learnt English as their first language or shifted to English as their **dominant language**. If parents have chosen to speak English to their children, even if their own first language is not English, the heritage language may be learnt in voluntary classes. Where English is the dominant language of the community and the only language of the school, such voluntary heritage language classes may be important in children attaining bilingualism rather than moving towards majority language monolingualism (Wiley *et al.*, 2014).

Such voluntary provision may be for religious, cultural, social, integrative and ethnic minority vitality reasons. Thus the providers are often religious institutions such as synagogues, mosques, temples and Orthodox churches. Jewish families attending a local synagogue are often enthusiastic for Hebrew to be taught to their children so that they might maintain a Jewish identity and for religious observance. Muslims have often been keen for Qur'anic Arabic to be transmitted for worship in the mosque, just as gurdwaras have been instrumental in the acquisition of Panjabi. The Roman Catholic Church has also promoted the community language teaching of Polish, Ukrainian and Lithuanian.

In Canada, the United States and the United Kingdom there are thousands of heritage and community language classes (or complementary schools) in at least 60 languages, including Spanish, French, German, Japanese, Czech, Chinese (Mandarin and Cantonese), Arabic, Hebrew, Khmer, Vietnamese, Finnish, Italian, Portuguese, Greek, Turkish, Urdu, Hindi, Gujarati, Panjabi and Bengali, just to name a few. In the case of some European languages, high commissions and embassies in London have often lent support. In other communities across the United States and United Kingdom, particularly among Asians, the providers are groups of enthusiastic parents and local community organizations who rent premises such as schools and halls to teach a heritage language. Foreign governments sometimes provide financial or material assistance to promote the teaching of their national languages to heritage speakers (and others); Germany provides such assistance through the Goethe-Institut, France through the Académie Française and China through the Confucius Institutes. However, direct support from foreign governments may sometimes be viewed with suspicion and subject to restrictions by the host country (see Chapter 3).

Such heritage language schools also have broad educational, literacy and identity outcomes for their children, and play an important role in community cohesion and the heralding of bilingualism as an advantage rather than as a deficit. Parents are often volunteer teachers. There is typically a focus on literacy, a large age range of students in the same class and some use of English as well as the heritage language. Community-based heritage language schools typically face a wide range of challenges, however, in providing quality and consistent language education and in keeping students motivated to attend and reach high levels of proficiency (Lee & Wright, 2014).

Apart from voluntary classes for children (e.g. Saturday schools), another well traveled route to developing bilingualism and **multilingualism** is adult education. This takes varying forms in different geographical areas and online contexts:

(1) *Evening classes* (sometimes called night schools or classes). A second or world language is taught on a once- or twice-weekly basis for a period ranging from several weeks to several years. Such classes have often traditionally aimed to secure for the student formal qualifications in the language (e.g. passing exams in a second majority language) or proficiency in the majority language. One example is 'English as a second language' classes established for immigrants in Australia, Canada, the United States and the United Kingdom. A more recent focus has been **communicative competence** in a heritage language (e.g. Hebrew, Basque, Welsh).
(2) *Immersion programs*. Many adults may choose an intensive short-term immersion program. For example, in the United States the Wisconsin Intensive Summer Language Institutes provide two months of intensive instruction for college students and professionals (including heritage learners) in over 30 less commonly taught languages, including South Asian languages, Southeast Asian languages, Central Eurasian languages, Middle Eastern and Mediterranean languages, and Brazilian Portuguese. Popular Spanish immersion programs are held regularly in countries such as Costa Rica, Mexico, Peru and Spain, with similar in-country immersion programs for other languages.
(3) *Ulpan courses*. Perhaps the most notable example of a mass movement of adult language learning has been the case of Hebrew in Israel. After the establishment of the State of Israel in 1948, the steady flow of immigration into Israel became a flood. Emergency measures were needed to teach Hebrew in a short time to large numbers of people as a living, spoken language. The idea of creating an intensive Hebrew language course was born, called an Ulpan (Raijman, 2012). The word 'Ulpan' is derived from an Aramaic root meaning 'custom, training, instruction, law'. There

were originally about 25 students in a class and they met for six hours each day apart from the Sabbath. From the beginning, the emphasis was on equipping the learners for everyday communication in the spoken language. Cultural activities such as singing and field trips were part of the course. Over the years, different kinds of Ulpanim have been established in Israel. Like their Israeli counterparts, the Basque and Welsh Ulpanim vary in intensity from five days a week to two mornings or two evenings a week (Baker & Jones, 1998; Newcombe, 2007). Some vocational courses are held for teachers, hospital workers, administrators and workers in industry. Other courses have a bias towards the needs of particular groups, such as parents. As in Israel, the emphasis is on developing competence in the spoken language.

(4) *Distance learning and online methods.* A variety of media-based courses for learning a second language are often available to adults. Radio and television series, books, DVDs, CDs, computer programs (computer-assisted language learning), correspondence courses, podcasts, websites, YouTube videos, social media and paid and free online courses including MOOCs (massive online organized courses) are all well tried or emerging approaches in second language acquisition. Even a site like Netflix and YouTube can be turned into language-learning opportunities through the webb-browser extension Language Reactor, which provides highlighted and clickable subtitles for selected movies, series and other videos in both target and home languages (see https://languagereactor.com). Evaluation studies of the relative effectiveness of these different approaches tend to be lacking.

(5) *Mobile apps.* Mobile language learning apps such as Duolingo, Babbel and Busuu have grown in popularity. Long-time producers of distance and computer-based programs have moved into the mobile app space, including Pimsleur and Rossetta Stone. Apps are available for the learning of dozens of different languages.

(6) *Artificial intelligence.* Large language models, machine learning, machine translation, speech recognition, text-to-speech and other AI technologies are poised to revolutionize language learning. For example, many online language-earning sites and mobile apps now incorporate chat-bots; learners can interact via text or voice with these human-like agents in the new language, risk free. Chat-bots can adjust to the learner's current proficiency level and provide real-time corrective feedback.

In early childhood, becoming bilingual is often a subconscious event, as natural as learning to walk or to ride a bicycle. In a school situation, a child is not usually the one who has made a decision about the language(s) of the classroom. Second language acquisition at school is often required by teachers and a local or national educational policy. For migrant workers, refugees and immigrants, adult language learning may be essential for work and adaptation to new institutions and bureaucracy. However, for other adults, second language acquisition is more voluntary, more open to choice. This raises the issue of whether it is preferable to learn a new language as a child or as an adult.

The Age Factor

A much-debated theme in second language acquisition is the relationship of age at learning a second language and success in gaining language proficiency. One argument is that the lower the age at which a second language is learnt, the greater is the long-term proficiency in that language. This is the basis of the **critical period hypothesis,** which suggests younger children have biological cognitive advantages for language learning that close as they enter adolescence and adulthood. Others argue that older children and young adults have some advantages that may help them learn a language more efficiently and quickly than young children. For example, a 14-year-old learning Spanish as a second language has superior intellectual processing skills to the five-year-old learning Spanish. Therefore, it is thought that less time is required in the teenage years to learn a second language than in the younger years owing to older children's cognitive superiority. However, the use of two or more languages changes across the years, so exact comparisons are difficult.

Reviews of this area are provided by Birdsong (2006), Cenoz (2009), Marinova-Todd *et al.* (2000) and Singleton and Ryan (2004). Their analyses may be briefly summarized as follows:

- Younger second language learners are neither globally more nor less efficient and successful than older learners in second language acquisition. There are many factors that intervene. Simple statements about age and language learning are simplistic and untenable.
- People who learn a second language in childhood tend to achieve higher levels of proficiency than those who begin after childhood. This difference found between younger and older learners reflects typical outcomes rather than potential. Thus, a finding favoring the young does not contradict the idea that someone can become proficient in learning a second language after childhood. This may be related to social contexts in which language is acquired and maintained or lost (e.g. kindergarten), as well as to the psychology of individual learning (e.g. motivation, opportunity). While older learners tend in practice not to master a second language as well as young learners, 'age differences reflect differences in the situation of learning rather than in the capacity to learn' (Marinova-Todd *et al.*, 2000: 9).
- In formal classroom language learning, older learners tend initially to learn quicker than younger ones. However, the length of exposure (e.g. the number of years of second language instruction) is an important factor in second language success. Those children who begin to learn a second language in the elementary school and continue throughout schooling tend to show higher proficiency than those who start to learn the second language later in their schooling. In absolute rather than comparative terms, this still includes the possibility of late learners becoming highly proficient, particularly when they are strongly motivated or have strong needs (e.g. immigrants, missionaries) or excellent opportunities (e.g. extensive immersion across many months). Adults can learn to a native-like level of competence in a second language.
- There is some research on and much public discussion about the large numbers of high school students and adults who fail to learn a second language (Marinova-Todd *et al.*, 2000). In comparison, there is a lack of research on adults who are successful learners of second and third languages. The concentration of research on language learning success among younger children is in danger or perpetuating a 'younger is better' belief about age and language learning.
- In the United States, federal and state education policies place immense pressure on schools and teachers to help immigrant children to learn English as soon as possible (see Chapter 9).

Proponents of the critical period hypothesis claim that the optimal time to learn a language is from three to seven years of age and, because of supposed biological constraints, such learning should occur before the onset of puberty. However, more recent research drawing on a large data-set of over 669,000 native and non-native English-speakers suggests that the critical period (for grammar learning) extends up to age 17 (Hartshorne *et al.*, 2018).

In a review of this area, Kenji Hakuta (2001: 11–12) argues that:

> The evidence for a critical period for second language acquisition is scanty, especially when analyzed in terms of its key assumptions. There is no empirically definable end point, there are no qualitative differences between child and adult learners, and there are large environmental effects on the outcomes.... The view of a biologically constrained and specialized language acquisition device that is turned off at puberty is not correct.

A review by Singleton and Muñoz likewise found little support for a critical period:

> Postulating a critical period for language acquisition is fraught with problems.... There is no consensus regarding the duration and scope of such a critical period, and the evidence presented in support of the notion of a critical period is far from conclusive. (Singleton & Muñoz, 2011: 419)

Singleton and Muñoz provide a musical comparison to illustrate: 'The fact that children who start to play the violin early tend to reach higher levels of attainment than adult beginners does not lead us to conclude that there is a "critical period" for violin playing' (Singleton & Muñoz, 2011: 419). Similarly, Marinova-Todd *et al.* (2000: 28) conclude that 'age does influence language learning, but primarily because it is associated with social, psychological, educational and other factors that can affect L2 proficiency, not because of any critical period that limits the possibility of language learning by adults'.

A 'weaker' version of the critical period hypothesis suggests that there may be an age-related advantage for younger learners in the area of **phonology**. In other words, older learners, including those who are highly successful in attaining proficiency in a second language, may nonetheless retain a slight foreign-sounding accent, whereas younger learners are more likely to gain a second language with no discernible accent.

Huang (2014) suggests that the larger debate over the critical period hypothesis is drawing attention away from needed scholarship to better understand age effects in second language learning. She argues for a framework of multiple critical/sensitive periods given that different **domains** of linguistic dimensions such as grammar, morpho-syntax, phonology (including prosody) and spatial **semantics** may have different timelines in terms of age advantages. Her own research with Mandarin-speaking immigrants to the United States, for example, found the 'age of learning' variable had a stronger impact on speech production than on grammar. Furthermore, her synthesis on the age effect in formal instruction contexts (i.e. world language learning contexts) reveals potential limited benefits in the phonology dimension but not other dimensions (Huang, 2015). Taken together, the research findings suggest that the strength of the age effect varies across linguistic domains and interacts with language input and exposure.

Debates over the critical periods of language learning aside, there are clearly advantageous periods. Early childhood and elementary and secondary school days seem to be two such. How successful are adults in becoming bilingual? There is a distinction between answering this question in an absolute and a relative manner. The 'absolute' answer simply is that adults do learn a second language to varying degrees of fluency. Some fall by the wayside, others reach a basic, simple level of communication, and others become operationally bilingual. In Israel, Wales and the Basque country, the adult route to bilingualism has many success stories.

The 'relative' answer involves comparing children and adults of varying ages. In this sense, the question becomes 'Who is more likely to become proficient in a second language, children or adults?' Chiswick and Miller (2008) plot immigration into the United States against English-speaking proficiency using data from the 2000 US Census. Their graphs suggest that children before the age of 11 have a much better chance of becoming fluent in English than those who immigrate at high school age. After the age of 16, the probability of becoming proficient in English declines fairly linearly over the next 40 years (i.e. age 16 to 55+).

From 1950s Israeli census data, it is possible to examine whether more older or younger adults become functional in Hebrew. For example, do young immigrants become more or less functional in Hebrew as a second language compared with older immigrants? The results follow a clear pattern (Bachi, 1955). As Figure 6.1 illustrates, the extent of the everyday use of Hebrew varies with age at immigration. The younger the child, the more likely he or she will use Hebrew. Between 30 and 40 years of age, a notable drop occurs. Is this due to a loss of learning ability, less exposure to Hebrew, less motivation or decreasing social pressure? From age 40 onwards, the likelihood of being functional in Hebrew falls again. Similar research in the United States has shown a fairly linear decline in language attainment among immigrants from age 5 to 50 according to age of arrival (Birdsong, 2006).

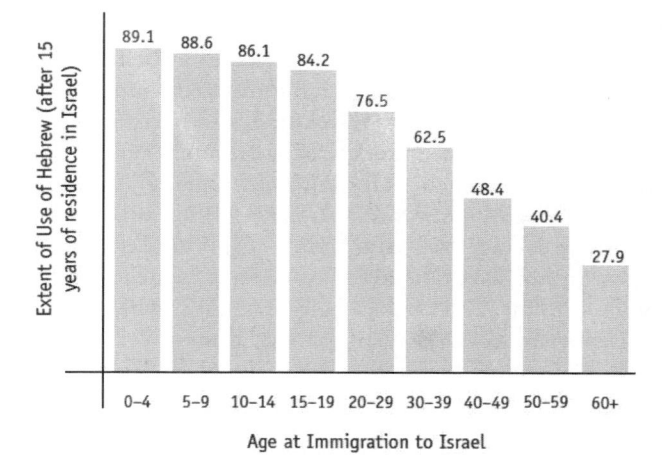

Figure 6.1 Extent of use of Hebrew (after 15 years of residence in Israel) by age at immigration. Adapted from Bachi (1955)

Language Loss in Children

Apart from children learning a second or third language, it is important to mention that **language loss** occurs in bilingual and multilingual children and adults. Language minoritized children and young adults are at risk of losing their minoritized language, even when very young. With a higher-status majority language ever present on the screen, in the street, at school and in shops, children and adults quickly learn which language has prestige, power and preference. They soon understand that there are differences in language, behavior, ethnicity and culture, and some children, particularly teenagers, may come to perceive their minoritized language and culture as undesirable. Students quickly perceive what helps them belong in mainstream society.

Birdsong (2006) has reviewed the considerable research on the typical decline in second language attainment with increasing age among adults and the less native-likeness found in the later learner. He suggests that there are complex biological, cognitive, experiential, linguistic and affective dimensions of L2 learning and processing involved. For example, associative memory and 'incremental learning elements of language learning' decline with age, as does the working memory and processing speed. Other variables include the amount of time spent in contact with second language speakers, the relative use of the first and second language in everyday activities, the amount of formal education in the second language, motivation to learn a language, integration with the second language culture, language aptitude, imitative language ability, metalinguistic awareness, and learning styles and strategies.

Language loss in children is a particular reality in the United States. Research by Fillmore (1991), Hakuta and d'Andrea (1992), Valdés (2004), Wright (2004), Wright and Chan (2021) and others indicates that the dominance of English in US society places considerable pressure on language minoritized students not only to acquire English at a young age but also to replace their minoritized language with English. Early exposure to English (e.g. in the home) can also lead to a shift to English and the potential loss of home languages. In such subtractive situations, the ideal of early bilingualism meets a challenge owing to a societal ethos that frequently does not favor bilingualism.

This suggest that the minoritized language needs care and consideration, support, and status, as well as much usage in the young child to support early bilingualism. Minoritized language development needs particular nurturing in political situations where another language is ever dominant. For example, when English is introduced very early and dominantly into a US language minoritized child's life, the minoritized language may be insufficiently stable and developed, and may therefore be replaced by the majority language. A loss of the minoritized language may have social, emotional, cognitive and educational consequences for the child.

Latinx students in the United States who lack proficiency in Spanish have been given an insulting mock label – 'no sabo kids' – a grammatically incorrect way of saying 'I don't know' in Spanish. The derogatory term is meant to instill shame and unfairly places blame on Latinx kids (or their parents) for their 'failure' to develop Spanish fluency. A report by NBC News (Flores & Brown, 2023) describes how such blame ignores the policy contexts and systematic linguistic discrimination in schools and society that limited the opportunities for the 'no sabo kids' to attain Spanish proficiency. The NBC report also describes how the 'no sabo kids' are pushing back on Spanish-proficiency shaming with memes and videos on TikTok and other social media with millions of views under the hashtags of #nosabo and #nosabokid, where they assert that their Latinx identity is separate from their proficiency in Spanish. Later chapters (e.g. Chapters 17 and 18) will further consider the linkage between language and identity.

As Fillmore argued in her classic article 'When learning a second language means losing the first':

> What is lost is no less than the means by which parents socialize their children: When parents are unable to talk to their children, they cannot easily convey to them their values, beliefs, understandings, or wisdom about how to cope with their experiences. (Fillmore, 1991: 343)

These and other consequences of losing one's language are listed in Box 6.3.

Box 6.3 Consequences of first language loss

- Children are unable to communicate effectively with parents.
- Parents have difficulty passing on their values, beliefs, understandings and wisdom.
- Conflicts arise between children and parents because of a communication breakdown.
- Children lose respect for their parents.
- Children experience difficulty, embarrassment and shame when trying to communicate with older relatives and community members.
- Children face humiliation and shame if they return to their (or their parents') home country and cannot effectively communicate.
- Children become ashamed of their home language and culture and struggle with identity issues.
- Students have fewer job opportunities than they would have had, had they maintained their home language.
- The society as a whole loses needed linguistic resources to fulfill the language demands of national and international institutions, organizations and agencies.

Source: Wright (2025: 29)

The immigrant, refugee and asylum-seeker context and its effect on family language patterns is under-researched, with most of the studies on early childhood bilingualism being done with middle-class, majority language and geographically stable families. Tannenbaum and Howie (2002) argue that immigration often potentially means loss of the extended family and significant people, a loss of familiarity, family cohesion, family 'atmosphere' and secure attachment. Uprooting may affect not only the act of parenting but also the cultural and linguistic development of young children and the language patterns of the immigrant family. Tannenbaum and Howie's research on Chinese immigrant families in Australia suggests that family relations affect language maintenance or loss. Families that are more cohesive, more positive in relationships and with secure attachment patterns tend to foster language maintenance in young immigrant children.

The dialogue that takes place between parents and children is an important contributor to the child's cognitive development. As children interact with parents, they are introduced to new features of language. When the child loses the home language, the parent can no longer offer this language education to the child in that language. Important cognitive **scaffolding** is dismantled. Thus, minoritized language loss is an issue not just of geographical regions and language communities but also for individual children. Family **language planning** is needed to initiate, establish and maintain childhood bilingualism (Macalister & Mirvahedi, 2017).

Individual Differences: Attitudes and Motivation

A popular explanation for success or failure to learn a second language is attitudes and motivation (Al-Hoorie & MacIntyre, 2020; Takahashi, 2023). Some level of motivation is needed for students to initiate learning a new language. Motivation becomes even more important to sustain the long process towards attaining a sufficient level of communicative competence in that new language. Lamb *et al.* (2019: 4–5) note the challenges that necessitate high levels of motivation:

> Language development … involves the deployment of the four skills, with their own sub-skills and strategies, which in turn rely on the acquisition of pragmatic, sociolinguistic, textual, and grammatical knowledge that is difficult for teachers to convey even when linguists have managed to accurately describe it. Language skills … need extensive practice in communicative contexts of use, for which monolingual classrooms are often poor substitutes. The result is that even for highly achievement-oriented, goal-driven language learners, progress can be frustratingly slow, and can easily lead to a downward spiral of negative learning experiences, reduced effort and fewer rewards.

What, then, are the motives for learning a second language? Are the motives economic, cultural, social, vocational, integrative or for self-esteem and self-enhancement? Reasons for learning a second (minority or majority) language tend to fall into two major groups, according to the type of motivation:

- Group 1: *A wish to identify with or join another language group* (**integrative motivation**). Some learners want to affiliate with a different language community. They wish to join in and identify with the minority or majority language's cultural activities, and consequently find their roots or form friendships.
- Group 2: *Learning a language for useful purposes* (**instrumental motivation**). The second reason is utilitarian in nature. Learners may acquire a second language to find a job and earn money, further career prospects, pass exams, help fulfill the demands of their job, or assist their children in bilingual schooling.

Considerable research on this area has been conducted by R.C. Gardner and associates, beginning in the 1950s (for reviews, see Al-Hoorie & MacIntyre, 2020; Gardner, 2019). Gardner (2010) argued that integrative and instrumental attitudes are independent of 'intelligence' and aptitude. Integrative motivation may be particularly strong in an additive bilingual environment. Gardner's socio-educational model of motivation and language acquisition sees motivation impacted by the educational and cultural context, and impacting language use in formal and informal contexts with a range of linguistic and non-linguistic outcomes. These usages and outcomes are simultaneously impacted by and interact with students' actual ability in the language. Dörnyei (2020) suggests that integrative motivation is rather an ambiguous and enigmatic concept that has recently been expanded to include integration with the global community among some of those learning English as an international language. Principles of complex dynamic systems may also be needed to better understand the shifting nature of motivation in individual learners and classrooms (Dörnyei, 2020; Hiver & Papi, 2019).

Much of the research in this area, but not all, links integrative motivation rather than instrumental motivation with the greater likelihood of achieving proficiency in the second language. Gardner and Lambert (1972) originally considered that integrative motivation was more powerful in language learning than instrumental motivation. The reason was that integrative motivation concerns personal relationships that may be long lasting. On the other hand, instrumental motivation may be purely self-oriented and short term. When employment has been obtained or financial gain has accrued, instrumental motivation may wane. An integrative motive was thought to be more sustained than an instrumental motive, owing to the relative endurance of personal relationships.

A problem with integrative motivation is: with whom does the language learner wish to integrate? If an adult is learning Diné bizaad (Navajo), then the target community is obvious. But what of a student in China learning English? Is the target group English-speakers in China, the United States, England, New Zealand or Kenya? Given that English has become the predominant international language, then with whom do those learning 'international English' wish to integrate? Is it the global English-speaking community? Can integrative motivation be towards a global community? Or is this really instrumental motivation?

Dörnyei (2019) suggests that integrative motivation can be explained by the 'ideal self-concept' rather than the need for integration with a target reference group. Dörnyei's 'L2 motivational self-system' model is 'based on the premise that the way in which people imagine themselves in the future plays an important role in energizing them in the present' (Dörnyei, 2019: 47). Thus, the motivation to learn international English may be the attraction of becoming (and being seen as) a second language speaker of global English, even of having the mutual intelligibility of a global or world citizen.

Pavlenko (2002) provides a critique of these socio-psychological studies. In a post-structuralist approach, language attitudes are partly replaced by language ideologies, which are seen as more socially and culturally derived, ever developing and not static, and capable of being criticized and changed. Language attitudes are part of larger societal ideologies and processes that can be examined for bias, racism, discrimination and oppression (Rosa & Burdick, 2017). Pavlenko suggests that motivation research tends (1) to be reductionist and static in its approach; (2) to lack insights into the social and political origins of attitudes; (3) to assume that cause–effect is stable and in one direction, whereas social contexts and attitudes/motivation constantly shape and influence each other; (4) to lack recognition that individual differences are socially constructed with variations across communities and cultures; and (5) to relate to wholesome, agreeable contexts whereas, 'in reality, no amount of motivation can counteract racism and discrimination, just as no amount of positive attitude can substitute for access to linguistic resources such as educational establishments' (Pavlenko, 2002: 281).

Dörnyei (2020) acknowledges there are several fundamental challenges related to motivation research and practice, including how motivation is conceptualized (e.g. a learner trait or a process?), understanding the dynamics of motivation, and how motivation can be applied and measured in classroom settings. Looking towards the future, Dörnyei identifies three 'frontiers' of research on language learning and motivation: (1) unconscious motivation, (2) the relationship between vision and motivation and (3) long-term motivation and persistence. Another research frontier is related to motivational influences associated with digital technologies and language learning (Henry & Lamb, 2019). Teachers are still left with the question 'How can I motivate learners?' What interventions and strategies are possible to motivate language learners? Box 6.4 provides some suggestions.

> **Box 6.4 Strategies for motivating students**
>
> Research has suggested many overlapping and interacting strategies teachers can use to motivate students in the language learning classroom. The following are just a few suggestions from Dörnyei (2001):
>
> - Include a sociocultural component in the syllabus (e.g. television programs, inviting native speakers).
> - Promote student contact with second language speakers (e.g. exchange programs, pen pals, trips).
> - Promote favorable self-perceptions of competence in the second language (e.g. highlighting what students can do rather than what they cannot do, students not worrying about making mistakes).
> - Encourage students to set attainable sub-goals for themselves (e.g. by a personal learning plan).
> - Make the syllabus relevant (e.g. based on a student 'needs analysis').
> - Increase the attractiveness of course content (e.g. use of more authentic materials, audio-visual aids, multimedia technology).
> - Match the difficulty of the students' language learning tasks with students' abilities.
> - Use motivating feedback, give feedback that is informative and not over-react to errors.
> - Minimize any detrimental effects of assessment on intrinsic motivation by focusing on improvement and progress, avoiding comparison of one student with another.
> - Use cooperative learning techniques by plenty of group work where the evaluation of success is appropriate to the group rather than a focus on individual success.

Identity and Second Language Acquisition

All the world's a stage,
And all the men and women merely players;
They have their exits and their entrances;
And one man in his time plays many parts.
(William Shakespeare, *As You Like It*, Act 2, Scene VII)

This drama metaphor suggests that we are like actors. We play different roles that vary according to the scenery, the audience, our fellow actors and the expected lines of the play. As scenery, co-actors, audience and the play change, so do our many identities in life's drama. We construct our identities, yet they are also created and confined by other players, situations and the unfolding play. Second language acquisition is such a play and it relates to identity formation.

Social Identity and Second Language Learning

While psychometric tests attempt to profile us as individuals (e.g. extrovert, creative, IQ of 110), we are also simultaneously members of different groups (e.g. as a woman, young parent, teacher, Muslim, Democrat, Californian, bilingual). Such membership helps form our social identity. Our multiple social identities are thus created dynamically by us, by our interactions and negotiations with other group actors, the expectations of each group and the varying social environments in which we play a part. Second language acquisition is affected by and affects our membership of groups (e.g. majority and minoritized language networks and groups). Acquiring a second language is not just about gaining vocabulary, grammar and pronunciation. When we use a second language, it is a social event with particular others. It is also often about joining a social group (e.g. a target language community or networks) and finding an accepted voice. Bourdieu (1991) argued that finding such an accepted voice is about the value given to people who are speaking (e.g. a newly learnt language). A speaker wants to be understood but there is also a social dimension to this: being believed, respected and valued as a speaker.

This has been extended by Norton (2013, 2020) with her concept of 'investment'. Language learners may be aware of the social, political, economic, power and status value (or not) of investing in second language learning. If successful, they may acquire more symbolic, social, identity and material resources, which can increase their cultural capital and social power. For example, learners might not be very motivated to learn a language, but may invest in that language if they are then seen as more employable or politically as of higher social status.

A learners' active evaluation of their investment may lead them to either continue learning an additional language formally in a class or to drop out (Kim, 2022). In a study of a group of recent immigrants from Mexico in an urban community-based adult ESL class in the US Southwest, Kim (2022: 122) found that the students' decision to drop out were based on *superación* (self-actualization) as they evaluated their investment in the class on the constructs of capital, identity and ideology:

> It seems they asked the following questions: 'Does this teacher/class help me gain economic capital (income, promotion), cultural capital (knowledge, educational credential) and social capital (network with people in power)? Does this teacher/class help me to better position myself with English-speaking conversation sites? Does this teacher/class respect my ideological background and help me stand up with equal access to mainstream ideology?' Under the term superación, it seems that the students simultaneously and in multilayered ways evaluate their teacher and class. When these expectations are met, it seems that they want to stay or vice versa.

Language learning is partly about becoming socialized through interaction with other language speakers in particular social contexts. Classrooms, in this perspective, have major limitations. They tend not to provide spontaneous interaction. Outside the classroom, target language speakers may be reluctant or refuse to interact with learners (e.g. too low a level of conversation, or because of gender, race, ethnicity, heritage language, social class, age, sexuality or creed). Opportunities for participation in the second language may be rare – a limitation of bilingual education that often produces competent bilinguals who use only one language outside the school. Authentic language situations may be restricted by target language speakers 'gate-keeping', or suitable opportunities not being available for new speakers to internalize the 'voices' of target language speakers. A sense of vulnerability and powerlessness may decrease a learner's investment in language learning (Norton, 2013; Kim, 2022).

Second language learners become socialized by and through language into new areas of knowledge, understandings and cultural practices. The learner of Chinese as a second language acquires not only new vocabulary but also new ideas, expectations, relationships, knowledge, values and ideologies. That is, when a second language is acquired, there is a parallel inculcation into a culture, a possible change in identity and a socialization into the life that surrounds that second language (Bayley & Langman, 2011; Duff, 2010).

Constructing Meaning in Second Language Learning

While each language has shared sounds, signs and symbols, there are often different and sometimes contested meanings and values within each language.

'When I use a word,' Humpty Dumpty said, in rather a scornful tone, 'it means just what I choose it to mean – neither more nor less.' (Carroll, 1872)

Words don't have fixed or ideal meanings.

Humpty Dumpty apart, words are constructed by people in dialogue with others to find shared or contested meanings. Such **discourse** takes place in changing situations (contexts) with differences of power and status between people affecting whose meaning is ascendant or dominant, and with such meanings being open to change, even conflict. For example, there is no correct or true definition of a 'bilingual' or of 'bilingual education'. Meanings of these terms vary across people, time and place, with dominance at any one time being about who has status, prestige and power. Meaning and the importance of an utterance are thus determined in part by the status and value attributed to the speaker of the second language.

Language and Power

Interacting in a second language both uses and shapes our identity, and this relationship needs to be understood in terms of differential power and prestige between people and language groups. In this post-structuralist tradition, learning a second language is not just about language: it is also about who we are, what we want to become and what we are allowed to become (e.g. by first language speakers).

In all language contexts, there are underlying dimensions of control and influence, **domination** and subordination (see Chapter 18). Gaining belief, respect and social value from dialogue with others is not straightforward as there is unequal dominance, status and power in relationships. There may be sensitive listeners, empathic conversationalists in the target language community and much faith in second language learning. However, many immigrants have experiences of obstruction, ridicule or rejection when using the majority language. Thus power relationships and social structures in the target language community are an important component in the extent to which a second language learner (including those exiting from bilingual education) will be accepted as a speaker of that language. Opportunities for practicing and participating in that new language, access to the usual utterances of native speakers, acceptance of errors when using that language and acceptance as 'non-native speakers' by the target community will affect a learner's acceptance, identity and language life.

Drawing on the seminal work of Foucault (1978, 1980), Rojo (2017: 77–78) notes shifts in our understanding of the relationship between power and language within a post-structural framework:

- 'Power is not concentrated in a single place, such as the state apparatus, but is, instead, ubiquitous and at once visible and invisible, present and hidden.'
- 'Power is not always exercised in a single direction, with some people on one side and some on the other, [thus] it will be difficult to ascertain who holds power in a precise sense.'
- 'Power is repressive and/or destructive, but productive as well, since it produces knowledge (about the individual, illness, penalties, languages, etc.) and action (such as resistance).'
- 'Power reaches into the very grain of individuals, touches their bodies and inserts itself into their actions and attitudes, their discourses, learning processes and everyday lives.'
- 'Whenever there is a power relation, there is a possibility of resistance.'

Rojo (2017) argues that these new conceptualizations of power will (1) compel us to re-examine the relationships between language and power, (2) help us understand who exercises power, in what spheres and by what means, (3) help us identify and analyze the technologies of power, and (4) help students resist existing forms of power.

Multiple Identities and Second Language Acquisition

The identity of second language learners has sometimes been seen as relatively stable, essential to a coherent 'core' in an individual's psyche. Just like IQ and personality traits, identity was seen as fairly fixed. A contemporary view is that identity is multiple, complex, context contingent, varied, overlapping, sometimes fragmented and even contradictory across different contexts. Our identities constantly develop and change, across time and across situations. We are made and remade in our conversations across time, place and person. Acquiring a second language may, for example, change our identity from a 'refugee' to a 'New Yorker'. Since not all languages are equal in power and status, learning a prestigious language may (or may not) lead to employment, social mobility, new friends and access to good-quality education. Learning a minoritized language may also affect identity, for example increasing the chances of acceptance into a local community. Acquiring a language affects individual identity, but this interacts with other dimensions (e.g. gender, socioeconomic class, race, ethnicity, creed) that mediate the outcomes of such acquisition (Pavlenko, 2002). The success of language learning may be affected by the wealth or restriction of opportunities for identity development in new networks (e.g. acceptance, rejection).

Identity conflict may sometimes occur, for example when a person's preferred self-identity (e.g. as Latinx) is different from other people's attempts to label that person (e.g. as an American). This is sometimes found in the case of immigrants, where second language learners of a majority language are regarded as incompetent workers or uneducated parents or social oddities. They may find resistance from majority language speakers to their having a new identity via second language acquisition, with subsequent effects on the extent of second language acquisition and reconstruction of identities. Surrounding ideologies may work against the best of language acquisition intentions. Or language minoritized speakers may resist the symbolic domination of them as a people that is attempted by majority language power and politics.

Kim (2016) documented the case of a North Korean defector to South Korea who went through a dramatic identity transformation while learning English. Having grown up in North Korea and having been taught that English was the language of the enemy, the defector was appalled by the amount of English present in South Korea, including in the signage of the linguistic landscape. She originally resisted learning English as it challenged the core of her identity. However, she eventually yielded to the need for English learning and, over time, she became 'an active learner who found English learning valuable and meaningful'; finally, she became 'a visionary who aimed to care about those in need, particularly English-learning needs' (Kim, 2016: 3). Thus, 'during the identity-transformation process, the defector constantly negotiated her identities in response to multiple social factors' (Kim, 2016: 3).

Language learning may change how we think of ourselves, how others see us and, importantly, (in turn) how we then confirm their expectations in our behavior. Acquiring a second language goes beyond linguistic competence to having the potential to be heard in that language, the means to address an audience in that language on chosen stages and to mix with other actors using that language. Language learning is not just a cognitive activity operating in the mind, but is also about becoming part of a new language community and developing multiple identities (see Chapter 18).

An important component in being accepted as a speaker is our other identities (e.g. gender, race, religion), which interact with being a second language learner. A second language learner's identity is multiple and goes well beyond language to gender, social class, ethnicity, sexuality, age, creed, lifestyle, networks and many other constantly changing scenarios. Sometimes, despite achieving linguistic proficiency in a second language, access to a language community is difficult, as other dimensions of identity bar easy (or any) access and entry.

Imagined Communities

Language learning, negotiating meanings and identity come together in the concept of 'imagined communities' (Norton & Pavlenko, 2019). As described by Kanno and Norton (2003: 241), 'imagined communities refers to groups of people, not immediately tangible and accessible, with whom we connect through the power of imagination'. For example, when students in second language classrooms are learning French in the United States, they commence as beginners. The teacher is introducing them to the language practices of a community of French-speakers. What language practices? What is the 'imagined community' for such learners? Or are such communities 'imagined' for them in a controlled manner? Desirable imaginings may motivate learners; less desirable and low-status imaginings may demotivate learners; hidden or controlled imaginings from outside may remove understanding and alienate. For example, one second language learner imagines obtaining well paid employment, while another imagines returning to the land of her ancestors and extended family.

Some further examples from research demonstrate the powerfulness of 'imagined communities'. Dagenais (2003) found that parents with Asian-background children attending **immersion bilingual education** in Canada were investing in that education to prepare their children for imagined multilingual, transnational, multiple communities of the future. In Japan, Kanno (2003) found that schools have visions of 'imagined communities' for which they are preparing their students: the least privileged children for impoverished bilingual communities; the most privileged children for elite international bilingualism. Pavlenko (2003) found that teaching TESOL students about bilingualism and second language acquisition opened up new imagined communities for them, as bilingual or multilingual multi-competent speakers. The low expectation of becoming two competent **monolinguals** in one person and belonging to two separate imagined communities was replaced by feeling part of an imagined community of worthy multilingual speakers. Seals (2020) describes the imagined community of a more European-oriented (as opposed to Russian-oriented) Ukraine following the Orange Revolution in 2004, where many Ukrainians invested in shifting their language practices from Russian to Ukrainian to reassert their Ukrainian identity. The war between Russian and Ukraine which began in early 2022 may be further driving an investment in Ukrainian language learning and use (Sterzuk & Sarkar, 2024).

A Transdisciplinary Framework for Second Language Acquisition

In recognition that a growing body of theories and research across different disciplines have identified a variety of factors that impact the acquisition of a second (or additional) language, a group of scholars gathered in the Douglas Fir room at the conference of the American Association for Applied Linguistics and began discussions that what would eventually lead to the development of a transdisciplinary framework for second language acquisition. Their multifaceted framework, published under the name Douglas Fir Group (2016), reflects the multilingual realities of the 21st century and the influence of globalization, technologization and mobility on language learning and teaching. As shown in Figure 6.2, it considers three levels – the micro, meso and macro – of mutually dependent influences. It begins with L2 learning at the micro-level, involving both cognitive and social processes, including 'engaging with others in specific multilingual contexts of action and interaction, resulting in recurring contexts of use that contribute to the development of multilingual repertoires' (2016: 24). Those interactions take place in sociocultural contexts at the meso-level, where issues of power and agency influence learners' investment and social identities. These meso-level contexts are influenced by large-scale societal macro-level ideologies (beliefs and values) 'that both shape and are shaped by sociocultural institutions and communities of the meso level' (Douglas Fir Group, 2016: 24).

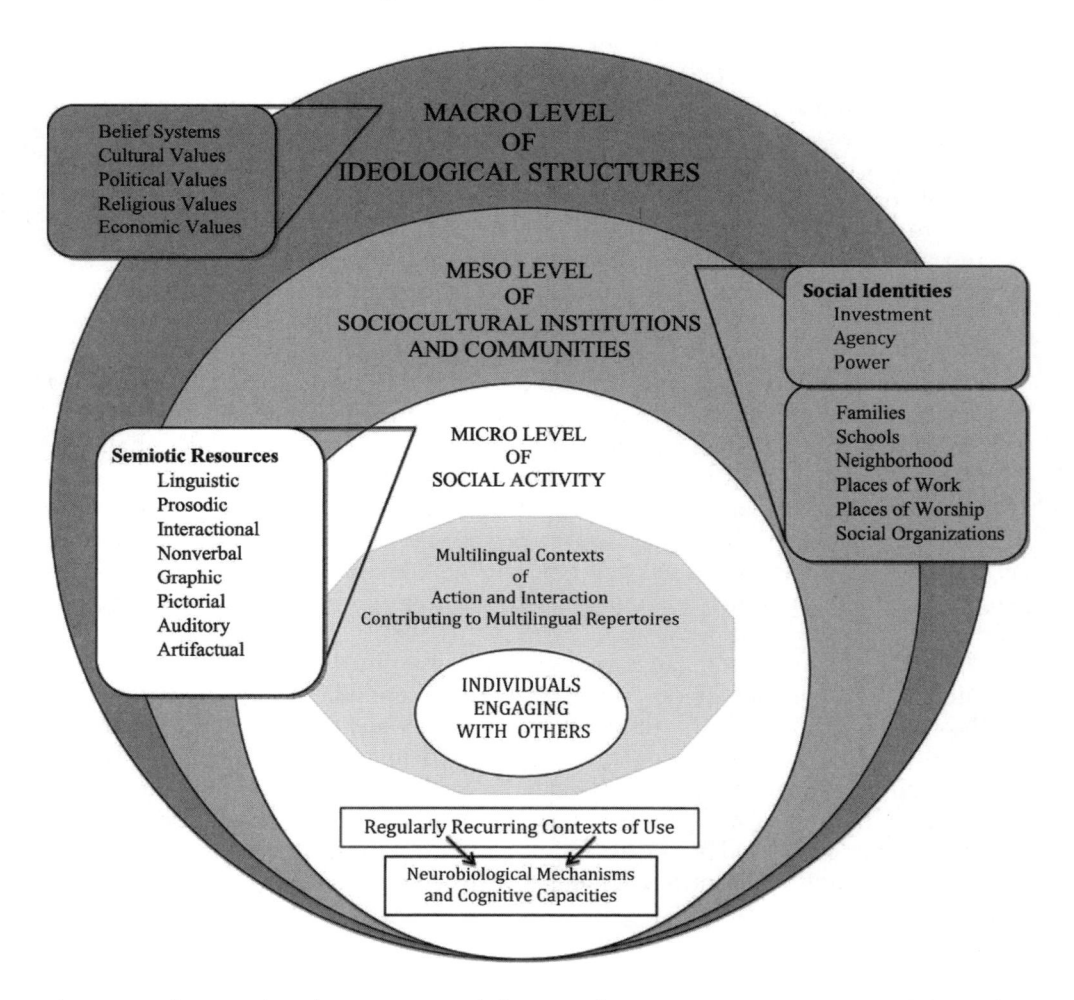

Figure 6.2 The Transdisciplinary Framework for Second Language Acquisition in a multilingual world. *Source:* Douglas Fir Group (2016: 25).

One of the goals of the Douglas Fir Group (2016: 25) in presenting this complex, multilayered and multifaceted framework 'is to expand the perspectives of researchers and teachers of L2 learners with regard to learners' diverse multilingual repertoires of meaning-making resources and identities' and thus enable students to participate 'in a wide range of social, cognitive, and emotional activities, networks, and forms of communication and learning in their multilingual lifeworld'.

Conclusion

There are both societal and individual reasons for a person learning a second language later in life. This mirrors the opening chapters of this book, which portrayed bilinguals as individuals and as groups, and as communities. Once societal reasons are present, then politics is not far away. Such reasons are varied, even paradoxical: assimilation but also harmony between different language communities; trade and profit but also intercultural understanding; security and defense yet also diplomacy. Individual reasons for language learning are not separate from societal reasons. Languages for career enhancement and employment have become more important motives as international trade and globalism have risen. Schools and communities influence language learning, in that societal and individual reasons interconnect and merge.

Sequential bilingualism occurs through a variety of routes, with school a major source of formal learning. Such schools may be state-funded and mainstream, with long histories of language teaching. There are also many schools run by religious organizations, language communities and embassies that teach languages after school or at weekends, for example. For adults, language learning can be by classes at work and for leisure, self-study or an intensive Ulpan experience. The vehicles of voluntary classes and adult courses provide the opportunity for a second or world language to be learnt and developed. Also, playing in the street and using mass media and internet technology can be informal means to bilingualism and multilingualism.

Such 'later' routes to bilingualism and multilingualism allow individuals of all ages to become bilingual and multilingual. While younger learners tend to achieve higher levels of proficiency, older learners tend to learn faster. While there may be no critical periods for language learning, there are times when there will be greater opportunities (e.g. in school) and varying levels and types of motivation. Surrounding societal ideologies (e.g. for immigrants) and individual differences may interact to make language learning more or less successful.

There are outcomes from language learning that go further than bilingualism and multilingualism. For immigrants, this may relate to assimilation or integration into the host society. For students, this may mean employment and career progression. For adults, it may mean moving closer to desired imagined communities. For all these groups, language learning affects identity. Such learners are socialized into new meanings and values as well as new language. They enter into new relationships that involve different status and power, acceptance or rejection. Learning a language means changes to our multiple identities. Language learning is so much more than learning a language.

Key Points in This Chapter

➢ Reasons for second language learning include ideological (e.g. assimilation), international (e.g. trade, peace) and individual (e.g. cultural awareness, employment) reasons.

➢ Formal world language instruction, voluntary language learning classes, community classes, Saturday schools, classes in the mosque, synagogue, temple or church, immersion programs and Ulpan adult language learning schemes are routes to sequential bilingualism and minority language maintenance for individuals.

➢ While there are no critical periods of language learning, there are advantageous periods. Early childhood and school days are two advantageous of these. Many successful adult second language learners show that increasing age is not a disadvantage.

➢ Individuals differ in their language learning histories because of societal and personal factors.

➢ Among immigrants, language loss is often present, as assimilation can be a dominant influence. Among individuals, integrative and instrumental motives are regarded as influencing success.

➢ Second language learning affects social identity. Language learning is partly about socialization into a new group. We learn the meaning, values and power relationships of a new group, and change our multiple identities.

➢ The Douglas Fir Group's Transdisciplinary Framework for Second Language Acquisition reveals the complex, multilayered and multifaceted nature of learning a new language in a multilingual world.

Suggested Further Reading

- Dörnyei, Z. (2020) *Innovations and Challenges in Language Learning Motivation*. Routledge.
- Hajar, A. and Manan, A. (eds) (2024) *Multilingual Selves and Motivations for Learning Languages other than English in Asian Contexts*. Multilingual Matters.
- Kim, T. (2022) *Understanding Success and Failure in Adult ESL: Superación vs Dropout of Adult English Learners in the US*. Multilingual Matters.
- Machowska-Kosciak, M. (2020) *The Multilingual Adolescent Experience: Small Stories of Integration and Socialization by Polish Families In Ireland*. Multilingual Matters.
- Takahashi, C. (2023) *Motivation to Learn Multiple Languages in Japan: A Longitudinal Perspective*. Multilingual Matters.

On the Web

- American Council on the Teaching of Foreign Languages
  https://www.actfl.org
- National Heritage Language Resource Center
  https://www.nhlrc.ucla.edu/nhlrc/home
- National Security Education Program
  https://www.nsepnet.org

Discussion Questions

(1) Consider your own or others' successes and failures with learning a new language. What role did motivation play and what was the nature of this motivation? How can motivation and investment change over time?
(2) While there may not be a critical period for language learning, there are advantageous periods. What are some advantages for younger learners? What are some advantages for older learners?
(3) What software, mobile apps, artificial intelligence tools or other digital technologies have you used for language learning? How effective were they in your efforts to learn a new language?

Study Activities

(1) Visit a school where students are learning a new language. By interviewing the teachers and observing classroom sessions, describe the overt and latent reasons for second (or third) language acquisition. Ask the teachers and the students their purposes in learning the language. If there are differences in aim between teachers and students, examine whether you think these can be made compatible or are in conflict.
(2) Use the Transdisciplinary Framework for Second Language Acquisition in Figure 6.2 to reflect on your own efforts or successes in learning a new language. List the various factors, contexts and ideologies at the micro-, meso- and macro-levels you believe may have influenced and impacted your language learning progress.
(3) Listen to the Freakonomics Radio (podcast) program 'Is learning a foreign language really worth it?' (https://freakonomics.com/podcast/is-learning-a-foreign-language-really-worth-it/). What is the economic value of learning a foreign language, according to these economists? What language or language(s) seemed to have the highest return on investment (ROI)? In what ways is ROI too narrow a view on the 'value' of learning a new language?

CHAPTER 7

Bilingualism, Cognition and the Brain

Updated by Becky H. Huang

Introduction

Bilingualism and 'Intelligence'
The Period of Detrimental Effects
The Period of Neutral Effects
The Period of Additive Effects

Bilingualism and Metalinguistic Awareness
Initial Research
Recent Research

Bilingualism and Divergent/Creative Thinking

Bilingualism and the Brain

Age Effects

Implications and Explanations

Bilingualism and Communicative Sensitivity

Thinking Implications of Speaking Specific Languages

Limitations of the Findings

Conclusion

CHAPTER 7
Bilingualism, Cognition and the Brain

Updated by Becky H. Huang

Introduction

There is one piece of advice that parents sometimes receive from well meaning teachers, doctors, speech therapists, school psychologists and other professionals: *Don't raise your child bilingually or problems will result*. Predicted problems include **bilingualism** as a burden on the brain, mental confusion, slowing down of the acquisition of the majority language, **identity** conflicts, split loyalties, alienation and even schizophrenia. The population of the world is estimated to be approximately 8.1 billion (US Census Bureau, 2024) and if more than half are bilingual (Grosjean, 2010a), then do 4 billion bilinguals in the world share these problems? Clearly not. Yet prejudice about the problems of bilingualism has been widespread, particularly in English-speaking regions.

Parents and teachers are sometimes still advised by professionals to use only one language with individual children. However, in the last decade or so such prejudiced and unfounded advice has decreased. Better advice, based on a wealth of research, is slowly spreading. Yet historically, anti-bilingualism has frequently predominated. For example, when Welsh children persisted in speaking two languages in school, having their mouths washed with soap and water and being beaten with a cane for speaking Welsh were once common. A quotation from a professor at Cambridge University in 1890 portrays this historical (and hysterical) deficit viewpoint:

> If it were possible for a child to live in two languages at once equally well, so much the worse. His intellectual and spiritual growth would not thereby be doubled, but halved. Unity of mind and character would have great difficulty in asserting itself in such circumstances. (Laurie, 1890: 15)

Such anxieties about bilingualism and thinking remain among some members of the public. The anxiety that two languages may have a negative effect on an individual's thinking skills tends to be expressed in two different ways. First, some tend to believe that the more someone learns and uses a second language, the less skill a person will have in their first language. Rather like weighing scales or a balance, the more one increases, the more the other decreases. Second, concern is sometimes expressed that the ability to speak two languages may be at the cost of efficiency in thinking. The intuitive belief is sometimes that two languages residing inside the thinking quarters will mean less room to store other areas of learning. By comparison, the **monolingual** is pictured as having one language in residence and therefore maximal storage space for other information.

Does the ownership of two languages interfere with efficient thinking? Do monolinguals have more effective thinking quarters? Is a bilingual less intelligent than a monolingual because of a dual language system? This chapter examines these typically negatively phrased questions and evaluates the evidence on bilingualism and cognition. Cognition is defined as the internal processing involved in language, memory, perception and thought (Eysenck *et al.*, 1994). The specific topics covered in this chapter, which include **intelligence, intelligence quotient (IQ), metalinguistic awareness, executive function, communicative sensitivity** and **divergent (or creative) thinking**, have been the focus of bilingualism research.

We start by considering the relationship between intelligence and bilingualism. 'Intelligence' has been a major concept in psychology and sometimes related to bilingualism. It is also a term often used by members of the public in phrasing questions about bilingualism. We provide an overview of the historical timeline of bilingual research, and discuss the shift of perspectives on and attitudes towards bilingualism. The chapter then considers recent research that focuses on a wider sample of the products and processes of a bilingual's cognition. Do bilinguals and monolinguals differ in thinking styles? Are there differences in the processing of information? Does owning two languages create differences in thinking about language? These types of question are examined in this chapter.

Bilingualism and 'Intelligence'

The Period of Detrimental Effects

From the early 19th century to approximately the 1960s, the dominant belief among academics was that bilingualism had a detrimental effect on thinking. The early research on bilingualism and cognition tended to confirm this negative viewpoint, finding that monolinguals were superior to bilinguals on mental tests. Research up to the 1960s looked at this issue through one concept – 'intelligence'. A typical piece of research gave bilinguals and monolinguals an 'intelligence test'. When bilinguals and monolinguals were compared on their intelligence quotient (IQ) scores, particularly on verbal IQ, the usual result was that bilinguals were behind monolinguals. An example of this early research is by a Welsh researcher, Saer (1923). He gathered a sample of 1400 children aged 7 to 14 from bilingual and monolingual backgrounds. A 10-point difference in IQ was found between bilinguals and monolingual English-speakers from the rural areas of Wales. Saer concluded that bilinguals were mentally confused and at a disadvantage in thinking compared with monolinguals. Further research by Saer suggested that university student monolinguals were superior to bilinguals: 'The difference in mental ability as revealed by intelligence tests is of a permanent nature since it persists in students throughout their university career' (Saer, 1924: 53).

While it is possible that situations exist where bilinguals may perform on such tests at a lower level than monolinguals, the early research that pointed to detrimental effects had a series of weaknesses that tend to invalidate the research in terms of individual studies and cumulatively across studies. These limitations are as follows.

Defining and Measuring Intelligence

The construct of 'intelligence' and the use of intelligence tests are controversial and hotly debated (Gardner, 2011). One part of the controversy lies in the problems of defining and measuring intelligence. The underlying questions are: What is intelligence and who is intelligent? A thief who cracks a bank vault? A famous football coach? Someone poor who becomes a billionaire? Don Juan? Are there different types of intelligence – social intelligence, musical intelligence, military intelligence, marketing intelligence, monitoring intelligence, political intelligence? Are all or indeed any of these forms of intelligence measurable by a simple IQ test that requires a single, acceptable, correct solution to each question? IQ tests tend to relate to a middle-class, White, Western view of intelligence (Henrich *et al.*, 2010).

A challenge to the construct of a single intelligence quotient is Gardner's (2011) **multiple intelligences** theory, which includes eight distinct types of intelligence – logical-mathematical, verbal-linguistic, visual-spatial, musical-rhythmical, bodily-kinesthetic, naturalist, interpersonal, and intrapersonal – in addition to one speculated type (existentialist). Gardner argues that IQ tests tend to focus narrowly on logical-mathematical and verbal-linguistic intelligence. A further recent interest is in emotional intelligence, both as a personality trait and as a component in performance (Goleman, 2006). Emotional intelligence may have facets related to bilingualism and multiculturalism, such as adaptability, perception and communication of feelings, relationship skills, self-esteem, social competence and empathy (Pavlenko, 2014).

A subjective value judgment is required about what constitutes intelligent behavior, as well as about the kind of person regarded as of more worth. This stance may affect how language minorities are seen. A simple view of intelligence can enable language majorities to justify social inequalities impacting ethnic or linguistic minorities as a natural consequence of their 'lack of intelligence'. In a challenge to these simplistic views of IQ, Sternberg (2002) points out that so-called 'intelligent' individuals often do incredibly stupid and foolish things. Dweck (2006) sidesteps issues of defining intelligence and instead focuses on how an individual's behavior may be impacted by their own implicit theories – or 'mindsets' – about intelligence. Dweck contrasts students who believe intelligence cannot be changed (the **'fixed' mindset**) against those who believe intelligence can increase with hard work and persistence (a **'growth' mindset**). She argues that when parents, teachers and others praise students for their intelligence (e.g. 'You got an A on your vocabulary quiz. *You are so smart!*'), students may internalize a fixed mindset that may actually impede their academic growth. Alternatively, students can be praised on their effort and progress in ways that help them develop a **growth mindset** (e.g. 'You studied hard and got an A on your vocabulary quiz. *Great work!*'). The growth mindset theory and its related interventions have garnered substantial attention from researchers, educators, parents, funding agencies and media. However, a recent systematic review and meta-analysis study by Macnamara and Burgoyne (2023) identified major shortcomings in the design, analysis and reporting of empirical studies that claimed positive effects of growth mindset interventions on academic achievement. The authors concluded that these issues, along with potential publication bias, may have contributed to the overly positive results reported.

Language of Testing

Another problem is the language of the IQ test. Standards established by the American Education Research Association, American Psychological Association and

National Council on Measurement in Education (2014) call for bilinguals to be tested in their stronger language or in both languages. In the early research, however, many verbal IQ tests were administered in English only (Hakuta, 1986). This tended to be to the disadvantage of bilinguals, in that they were tested in their weaker language and thus underperformed on the IQ test. Even **testing** bilinguals in their stronger language may be less than fair. Tests that cater holistically and sensitively for the dual language capabilities of bilinguals may be preferable (Guzman-Orth *et al.*, 2019) (see also Chapter 2 for issues related to bilingual assessments).

Analysis

The early research tended to use simple averages when comparing monolingual and bilingual groups. Statistical tests were often not performed to see whether the differences between the average scores were real or due to chance factors. Thus, for example, when Jones (1966) re-analyzed Saer's (1923) research, he found that there was no statistically significant difference between the monolingual and bilingual groups.

Classification

As has been shown in Chapter 1, the classification of people into bilingual and monolingual groups is fraught with difficulty and too simplistic. We need to ask what **language competences** are being used for classification (Grosjean, 2012). Are all four basic language abilities (i.e. listening, speaking, reading, writing) being used? What is the degree of fluency in each language? Were bilinguals classified by their use of languages (**functional bilingualism**) or by their ability in language? As Chapter 1 revealed, who is or is not bilingual is a complex issue. The earlier research on bilingualism and cognition tended to regard classification as non-problematic. This means that the research results are simplistic and ambiguous, having classified bilinguals in an imprecise manner.

Generalizability

Another problem concerns sampling and the generalizability of research results to the population of bilinguals. With all research, the findings should be restricted to the population that the sample exactly represents. In particular, research using a non-random sample of a population, merely a convenience sample, should theoretically have no generalization beyond that sample. Thus, research on 11-year-olds cannot be generalized to other age groups. Findings in the United States cannot be generalized to the rest of the world. The early research studies on bilingualism and cognition tended to have small samples, making generalization dangerous. Much of the recent research on bilingualism and cognition is also based on convenience samples, particularly undergraduate students from Western, educated, industrialized, rich and democratic (WEIRD) societies (Henrich *et al.*, 2010), limiting the generalizability of the results.

Context

The language and cultural environment of the research sample needs to be considered. This relates to the notion of subtractive and additive environments (see Chapter 3). Negative, detrimental cognitive findings may be more associated with minoritized language groups in subtractive environments. Subtractive environments are where the child's first language is in danger of being replaced by a more prestigious second language. For example, children from immigrant families who speak a home language other than English in certain parts of the United States or United Kingdom would be considered to be living in a linguistically subtractive environment. Where bilingualism has high prestige in an additive environment, a different pattern of results may be more likely. Also, IQ and similar tests are presented as context-free circumstances. In reality, 'intelligent' responses will be affected by the particular context in which a task is completed (Gordon, 1997). 'Intelligent' responses are relative to situations (e.g. car-driving, money-making, musical composition, classroom learning).

Matched Groups

The final problem is particularly important. To compare a group of bilingual children with monolinguals on IQ, or on any other measure of cognitive ability, requires that the two groups be equal in all other respects. The only difference between the two groups should be in their bilingualism and **monolingualism**. If such control does not occur, then the results of the research may be due to the other factor(s) on which the groups differ, rather than their language backgrounds. Take the example of a monolingual group being mostly of higher socioeconomic status and the bilingual group being mostly of a lower socioeconomic status. A result (e.g. showing monolinguals to be ahead of bilinguals) may be due to social class rather than, or as well as, bilingualism. The great majority of research on bilingualism and 'intelligence' failed to match the groups on other factors that might explain the results. It is necessary to match the groups on variables such as socioeconomic and cultural class, gender, age, type of school attended and urban/rural and subtractive/additive environments. However, as Laine and Lehtonen (2018) noted, exact equivalency of groups is impossible. Bilingual children are never exactly the same as monolinguals and there could be other background variables, some of which unknown, that influence the results. Therefore, cognitive differences between bilinguals and monolinguals may have explanations other than language.

Summary

The period when research accented detrimental effects lasted from approximately the 1920s to the 1960s. While the dominant conclusion was that bilinguals were inferior to monolinguals, particularly on verbal IQ, these early studies share many serious methodological weaknesses. Singly and cumulatively, the early research on bilingualism and IQ has so many limitations and methodological flaws that its conclusion of detrimental effects cannot be accepted.

Modern research suggests that bilinguals have a few potential cognitive disadvantages when compared with monolinguals. There are studies that identified differences favoring monolinguals in language-specific processing. For example, Bialystok *et al.* (2008) showed that a monolingual's semantic fluency is a little faster than a bilingual's semantic fluency, as bilinguals need to ensure the correct word is chosen from their two languages. Bilinguals also appear slower in picture naming (Fu *et al.*, 2017; Nicoladis & Smithson, 2018; Sullivan *et al.*, 2018), less able to identify a word through noise (Rogers *et al.*, 2006) and disadvantaged in producing some tongue-twisters (Li *et al.*, 2017). They are more likely to report a 'tip of the tongue' state, that is, being unable to retrieve a word immediately (Gollan & Acenas, 2004). This is possibly because they use some words in each language less often (Li *et al.*, 2017) and there is interference from words from the other language (Costa, 2005), particularly when those words are false **cognates** (share the same sound but have different meaning in the two languages – for example, Welsh *glas* means 'blue' but sounds the same as the English word 'glass'). Also, bilingual children initially possess a smaller vocabulary in each of their languages than their monolingual peers (Bialystok *et al.*, 2022; Ehl *et al.*, 2019). However, research comparing bilingual children's 'conceptual vocabulary' (i.e. the combined vocabulary size in both of their languages minus the overlapping words) with that of monolinguals shows no reliable differences between the two groups (Bialystok *et al.*, 2022; Ehl *et al.*, 2019).

However, none of these studies suggests that bilinguals have a mental overload, process inefficiently or have weaknesses compared with monolinguals in everyday thinking. In areas such as speed of reaction in retrieving words, a difference of milliseconds is of little or no importance in everyday functioning. In any case, word frequency (i.e. how often words are used in everyday language production) rather than bilingualism *per se* seems to be the important factor in how quickly humans are able to access and retrieve words. According to Gollan *et al.* (2008), bilinguals by definition use each language less often than monolinguals. By implication, bilinguals use words in each language less frequently than monolinguals, and decreased use may lead to slightly weaker lexical access. An alternative, or supplemental, view is that the slower lexical access may be induced by the cognitive control bilinguals need to exert to inhibit the co-activated words from the non-target language (Sullivan *et al.*, 2018). Given the complexity involved in lexical retrieval, it is likely that both lower frequency and cognitive control play a role.

The Period of Neutral Effects

A series of studies reported no difference between bilinguals and monolinguals in IQ. For example, early research in the United States by Pintner and Arsenian (1937) found a zero correlation (no relationship) between verbal (and non-verbal) IQ and Yiddish–English bilingualism/monolingualism. While the number of studies with a 'no difference' conclusion is small, the period of neutral effects is important because it highlighted the inadequacies of the early research that found detrimental effects. An example is the research by Jones (1959) in Wales. With a sample of 2500 children aged 10 and 11, Jones initially found that bilinguals were inferior to monolinguals on IQ. A re-analysis, however, showed that this conclusion was invalid. After taking into account the varying socioeconomic class of bilinguals and monolinguals, Jones concluded that monolinguals and bilinguals did not differ significantly in non-verbal IQ so long as parental occupation was taken into account. He also concluded that socioeconomic class largely accounted for previous research that had reported the inferiority of bilinguals on non-verbal IQ. Therefore, his conclusion was that bilingualism is not necessarily a source of intellectual disadvantage.

While the period of neutral effects overlaps chronologically with the detrimental and additive periods, there was a period when (in Wales, for example) such neutral effects were taught and publicized. Such a 'neutral' conclusion was historically important as it gave a boost to parents who wished to support bilingualism in the home and in the school. As a transitional period, it both helped to question a fashionable belief of bilingualism as a source of cerebral confusion and became a herald for the modern and current 'additive effects' period.

The Period of Additive Effects

A major turning point in the history of the study of the relationship between bilingualism and cognition was reached in Canadian research by Peal and Lambert

(1962). This research broke new territory in three respects, each setting the pattern for future research. First, the research overcame many of the methodological deficiencies of the period of detrimental effects. Second, the research found evidence that bilingualism need not have detrimental or even neutral consequences. Rather, there is the possibility that bilingualism leads to cognitive advantages over monolingualism. Peal and Lambert's (1962) finding has been widely quoted to support bilingual policies in various educational contexts. The political implication of the study was that bilingualism within a country was not a source of national intellectual inferiority. Third, the research by Peal and Lambert, while using IQ tests, moved research towards a broader look at cognition (e.g. thinking styles and strategies). Other areas of mental activity apart from IQ were placed firmly on the agenda for research into bilingualism and cognitive functioning.

Peal and Lambert (1962) studied 110 middle-class, 10-year-old children from French schools in Montréal, Canada, after narrowing down an initial sample of 364. The children were divided into balanced bilinguals and monolinguals, matched by socioeconomic status. Bilinguals outperformed monolinguals on 15 of 18 IQ measures, with no significant difference on the remaining three. The study concluded that bilingualism enhances mental flexibility, abstract thinking, concept formation and verbal IQ due to the enriched bilingual and **bicultural** environment and positive language **transfer**. These results provided the stimulus for further research and debate.

The study by Peal and Lambert (1962), while being pivotal in research on bilingualism and cognitive functioning, has four basic methodological weaknesses that need to be briefly considered before accepting the research at its face value. First, the results concern 110 children 10 years of age and of middle-class, Montréal extraction. This is not a sample that can be generalized to the population of bilinguals either in Canada or throughout the world. This is particularly true since the 110 children were selected from an original sample of 364. It remains unknown how the other 254 children performed across the broad range of tests.

Second, children in the bilingual group were 'balanced' bilinguals (see Chapter 1). While the term 'bilingual' includes balanced bilinguals, there are many other groups of children 'less balanced'. We cannot assume that the results from this study apply to such 'less balanced' bilinguals.

The third problem with Peal and Lambert's (1962) research is the chicken and egg problem. Which comes first? Is it bilingualism that enhances IQ? Or does a higher IQ increase the chances of becoming bilingual? When research suggests that IQ and bilingualism are positively related, we cannot conclude the order of cause and effect. The relationship may also be such that one is both the cause and the effect of the other. Research by Diaz (1985) suggests that, if there is a particular direction in the relationship, it is more likely to be bilingualism positively affecting 'intelligence', rather than 'intelligence' affecting bilingualism.

The fourth problem concerns socioeconomic status. While Peal and Lambert (1962) tried to match their bilingual and monolingual groups on socioeconomic class, they did not control for all the differences in a child's home environment. Socioeconomic class is only a simple and very partial measure of a child's home and environmental background. This is true of monolingual children. It is even more so with children who are bilingual/bicultural; there may be an even more complicated home and family background with regard to sociocultural factors.

In the following example, notice how the sociocultural element is very different, yet the socioeconomic class is the same. Take two **Latinx** children of the same age and gender living on the same street in New York. Their fathers both have the same job – taxi drivers. One family regularly attends church services in Spanish and belongs to a Latinx organization with cultural activities in Spanish. This taxi driver and his wife send their children to a Spanish–English dual language school. The child is bilingual. In the second family, the child speaks English only. The parents have no interest in sending their children to a dual language school. Neither does the family attend a church or another organization where Spanish is spoken and valued. Their Latin-American roots are neither discussed nor appreciated. While the families are matched on socioeconomic status, the sociocultural differences between them are considerable. In this example, the first child is bilingual and the second child is monolingual, with the bilingual child having a higher IQ. The child's bilingualism may not be the only explanation of a higher IQ. Rather, the alternative or additional explanation may be in the different social and cultural environments of these children. Thus, with Peal and Lambert's (1962) study, socioeconomic class may have been controlled, but not sociocultural class.

This completes the examination of Peal and Lambert's (1962) historically important and pivotal study. Since their research, the dominant approach to bilingualism and cognitive functioning has moved away from IQ testing to a range of thinking styles, strategies and skills. Studies since the 1960s mostly confirm Peal and Lambert's positive findings.

A related area of research concerns the mental representation of a bilingual's two languages and the processing emanating from such representation (Fricke et al., 2019). A principal issue has been the extent to which a bilingual's two languages function independently or interdependently. The early research attempted to show that early bilinguals (compound bilinguals) were more likely to show interconnections and inter-relatedness in their two languages than late (coordinate) bilinguals. In the 1960s, Kolers (1963) redefined the issue in terms of memory storage. A **separate storage hypothesis** stated that bilinguals have two independent language storage and retrieval systems, with the only channel of communication being a translation process between the two separate systems. A **shared storage hypothesis** stated that the two languages are kept in a single memory store but with two different language input channels and two different language output channels. Evidence exists for both independence and interdependence (Heredia & Brown, 2013; Ng & Wicha, 2013). Recent theories and research have therefore emphasized both the separate and connected aspects of bilinguals' mental representations by integrating the topic with general cognitive processing theories. For example, Bialystok (2017) suggests that the lexical representations for each language are separately stored by a bilingual, while the conceptual representations are shared. This is further considered in the next chapter. However, there is general agreement that (1) both languages are active even when just one of them is being used, and (2) that even if there are shared conceptual representations and both languages are active in bilinguals, functionally the languages are independent (e.g. when speaking, reading, writing).

Bilingualism and Metalinguistic Awareness

Initial Research

The research on bilingualism and divergent thinking suggests that bilinguals may have some advantage over matched monolinguals. For many bilingual children, the size of their total vocabulary across both languages, including the overlapping words, is likely to be greater than that of a monolingual child in a single language (Montanari *et al.*, 2018). Does a larger overall vocabulary allow a bilingual to be more free and open, more flexible and original, particularly in meanings attached to words? Is a bilingual person less bound by words, more elastic in thinking because they own two languages? Leopold's (1970/1939–49) famous case study (see Chapter 5) of the German–English development of his daughter, Hildegard, from 1939 to 1949 noted the looseness of the link between word and meaning – an effect apparently due to bilingualism. Favorite stories were not repeated with stereotyped wording; vocabulary substitutions were made freely in memorized songs and rhymes. Word sound and word meaning were separated. Hildegard is a single case. What has research revealed about samples of bilinguals?

Ianco-Worrall (1972) tested the idea of sound and meaning separation on 30 Afrikaans–English bilinguals aged four to nine. The bilingual group was matched with monolinguals on IQ, age, sex, school grade and social class. In the first experiment, a typical question was: 'I have three words: CAP, CAN and HAT. Which is more like CAP: CAN or HAT?' A child who says that CAN is more like CAP would appear to be making a choice determined by the *sound* of the word. That is, CAP and CAN have two out of three letters in common. A child who chooses HAT would appear to be making a choice based on the meaning of the word. That is, HAT and CAP refer to similar objects. Ianco-Worrall showed that four- to six-year-old bilinguals tended to respond to word meaning, monolinguals more to the sound of the word. However, by seven years of age, both groups' answers were governed by the meaning of the word. Ianco-Worrall concluded that bilinguals 'reach a stage of semantic development, as measured by our test, some two–three years earlier than their monolingual peers' (Ianco-Worrall, 1972: 1398).

In a further experiment, Ianco-Worrall (1972) asked the following type of question: 'Suppose you were making up names for things, could you call a cow "dog" and a dog "cow"?' Bilinguals mostly felt that names could be interchangeable. Monolinguals, in comparison, more often said that names for objects such as cow and dog could not be interchanged. Another way of describing this is to say that monolinguals tend to be bound by words and bilinguals tend to believe that language is more arbitrary. For bilinguals, names and objects are separate. This seems to be a result of owning two languages, giving the bilingual child awareness of the free, non-fixed relationship between objects and their labels.

Other early research in this area, for example by Ben-Zeev (1977b), suggested that the ability of bilinguals to analyze and inspect their languages stems from the need to avoid 'interference' between the two languages. That is, the process of separating two languages and avoiding **codemixing** may give bilinguals superiority over monolinguals through an increased analytical orientation to language. One of Ben-Zeev's tests, called the Symbol Substitution Test, asked children to substitute one word for another in a sentence. For example, they had to use the word 'macaroni' instead of 'I' in a sentence. Thus, 'I am warm' becomes 'Macaroni am warm'. Respondents have to ignore word meaning, avoid framing a correct sentence and evade the interference of word substitution in order to respond to the task correctly. Bilinguals in Ben-Zeev's study were superior on this kind of test, not only with regard to meaning but also with regard to sentence construction. Therefore bilinguals appear to be more flexible and analytical in language skills.

Recent Research

Much of the older research on bilingualism and cognitive functioning concentrated on cognitive style (e.g. divergent and creative thinking). The focus of research tended to be on the person and on the product. It attempted to locate dimensions of thinking where bilinguals perform better than monolinguals. The recent trend has been to look at the process of thinking rather than the products of thinking, working within the information-processing, memorization and language-processing approaches in psychology (e.g. De Bot & Houtzager, 2018). In particular, much of the recent research effort has been devoted to investigating the effect of bilingualism on two cognitive **domains**: non-verbal executive functioning and metalinguistic awareness (Bialystok, 2018). Non-verbal executive functioning refers to a set of inter-related processes in the brain, particularly the frontal lobe (Bialystok, 2018; Warmington *et al.*, 2019). The executive control system is generally believed to consist of three components: inhibition, updating (or working memory) and shifting (or cognitive flexibility). However, there is still debate over the specific number and nature of these components. Executive function skills help individuals plan, focus attention and manage multiple tasks effectively. These cognitive processes are fundamental for decision-making, self-control, and problem-solving, which are critical for cognitive development and successful functioning in daily life.

On the other hand, metalinguistic awareness may loosely be defined as thinking about and reflecting upon the nature and functions of language (for more precise definitions and differences see Bialystok, 2001a). Metalinguistic awareness includes a collection of abilities, such as print awareness, morphological awareness, grammatical awareness and phonological awareness. They are distinct from language proficiency but are crucial to academic achievement and the acquisition of literacy (Eviatar *et al.*, 2018; Huang, 2019). An example of metalinguistic knowledge is second language learners who do not have to relearn the fundamentals of language structure. They already have that metalinguistic knowledge from first language acquisition: many studies have shown that the metalinguistic knowledge can **transfer** cross-linguistically from bilinguals' first to their second or even third languages (Huang, 2018; Kuo *et al.*, 2017; Woll, 2018).

Not all such studies are 'favorable' to bilinguals (Adesope *et al.*, 2010; Goldsmith *et al.*, 2023; Lowe *et al.*, 2021; Paap, 2023). For example, Goldsmith *et al.* (2023) found no differences in executive function, specifically conventional and sequential congruency measures, between monolingual and bilingual children when controlling for the influence of confounding variables such as age, socioeconomic status and general cognitive ability. Some studies have also shown that bilinguals are slower in learning low-frequency words, such as irregular past tense forms, and slower also in their access and retrieval of vocabulary (Nicoladis & Smithson, 2018; Sullivan *et al.*, 2018). However, despite these potential disadvantages, bilinguals may be equally as good at problem solving and getting correct mathematical solutions (Bialystok, 2001a). Research also shows that bilingual children are able to solve problems that contain misleading cues earlier than monolingual children. Bialystok and Martin (2004) asked children to group a set of stimuli by one common feature (e.g. color) and then to regroup them by another common feature (e.g. their shape). In order to complete the task successfully in the second round, children needed to be able to attend to the new relevant feature while ignoring the previously relevant feature. The study showed that bilingual children were able to complete the task successfully at an earlier age than monolingual children.

There is another limitation to research on bilinguals and cognition. Is the research about bilingualism, or is it really about cognition (or both)? Research on memorization, language recall, reaction times and processing times tends to use bilinguals to help describe and explain the larger issues surrounding cognitive processing and language processing. Comparisons with monolinguals aim to aid psychological understanding of cognitive processes rather than explain the nature of bilinguals *per se*. Pavlenko (2000) provides a review that is critical of research in this area but places understanding the bilingual at the forefront.

As mentioned above, research that has focused on bilinguals has particularly studied the **metalinguistic awareness** of bilingual children. Early research suggested a relationship favoring bilinguals in terms of increased metalinguistic awareness (for a review, see Bialystok *et al.*, 2014a). It appeared that bilingual children develop a more analytical orientation to language through organizing their two language systems. To illustrate, in research that directly examined bilingualism and metalinguistic awareness, Bialystok *et al.* (2014a) found that bilingual children were superior to monolingual children on measures of the cognitive control of linguistic processes. Bialystok (1987) conducted three studies each involving children aged five to nine. In the experiments, children were asked to judge or correct sentences for their syntactic acceptability irrespective of meaningfulness. Sentences could be meaningfully grammatical (e.g. Why is the dog barking so loudly?); meaningful but not grammatical (e.g. Why the dog is barking so loudly?); anomalous and grammatical (e.g. Why is the cat barking so loudly?); or anomalous and ungrammatical (e.g. Why the cat is barking so loudly?). The children were asked to focus on whether a given sentence was grammatically correct or not. It did not matter whether the sentence was silly or anomalous. Bialystok found that bilingual children in all three studies consistently judged grammaticality more accurately than did monolingual children at all the ages tested.

Kuo *et al.* (2017) compared the development of **morphological awareness**, one specific aspect of metalinguistic awareness, between three groups of fourth-grader children with comparable socioeconomic background and non-verbal IQ. The three groups were (1) monolingual English-speaking children in English-only class, (2) native Spanish-speaker children in a Spanish–English dual language immersion class and (3) native English-speaker children in the same dual language class. The English-only class included only English-speaking students, and the language of instruction was English. The Spanish–English dual language program consisted of both native English-speakers and native Spanish-speakers, and the instruction was in both Spanish and English. All child participants completed measures of vocabulary and morphological awareness in both Spanish and English. Results from the Spanish measures showed that English-speaking children in dual language class performed comparably with their Spanish-speaking peers in morphologically complex words and in awareness of derivational morphology. Compared to their English-speaking peers in the English-only class, English-speaking children in the dual language class also performed better on English measures of vocabulary that involved cognates and morphologically complex words. Taken together, the findings suggested that bilingual experience can positively shape children's metalinguistic development through cross-language transfer.

A conclusion based on an overview of research can be summarized as follows. A bilingual does not have across-the-board metalinguistic advantages or universally superior metalinguistic abilities. Relatively balanced bilinguals have increased metalinguistic abilities, particularly in those tasks that require selective attention to information (e.g. when there is competing or misleading information). Such selective attention relates to two components: (1) bilinguals' enhanced analysis of their knowledge of language and (2) their greater control of attention in internal language processing.

Bilingualism and Divergent/Creative Thinking

One problem with IQ tests is that they restrict children to finding the one correct answer to each question. This is often termed convergent thinking. Children have to converge onto the sole acceptable answer. An alternative style is **divergent thinking**. A child regarded as a diverger is more creative, imaginative, elastic, open-ended and free in thinking. Instead of finding the one correct answer, divergent thinkers prefer to provide a variety of answers, all of which can be valid.

Divergent (or creative) thinking is investigated by asking questions such as: How many uses can you think of for a brick? How many interesting and unusual uses can you think of for tin cans? On this kind of question, the student has to diverge and find as many answers as possible. For example, on the 'uses of a brick' question, a convergent thinker would tend to produce a few rather obvious answers to the question: to build a house, to build a barbecue, to build a wall. The divergent thinker will tend to produce not only many different answers but also some that may be fairly original: for blocking up a rabbit hole, for propping up a wobbly table, as a foot wiper, breaking a window, making a bird bath.

In the North American tradition, it is more usual to talk about 'creative' than about 'divergent' thinking (for a review see Simonton, 2008). Torrance (1974) analyzes answers to the 'uses of an object' test (e.g. unusual uses of cardboard boxes or tin cans) using four categories. This test may be adapted to any language and culturally appropriate use of objects. Also, there are figural tests where a person is given a sheet of 40 circles or 40 squares and asked to draw pictures using these individual circles or squares, and subsequently place a label underneath. A person's fluency score in creative thinking is the number of different acceptable answers that are given. A flexibility score is the number of different categories (listed in the test manual) into which answers can be placed. Originality is measured by reference to the test manual, which gives scores of 0, 1 or 2 for the originality (statistical infrequency) of each response. 'Elaboration' refers to the extent of the extra detail that a person gives beyond the basic use of an object.

The underlying hypothesis concerning creative thinking and bilingualism is that the ownership of two or more languages may increase fluency, flexibility, originality and elaboration in thinking. Bilinguals will have two or more words for a single object or idea. For example, in Welsh, the word *ysgol* not only means a school but also a ladder. Thus, having the word *ysgol* in Welsh and 'school' in English may provide the bilingual with added associations – the idea of the school as a ladder (with the steps representing grades). Similarly, having words for folk dancing or square dancing in different languages may give a wider variety of associations than having a label in just one language. Research has compared bilinguals and monolinguals on a variety of measures of divergent thinking (Adesope *et al.*, 2010; Kharkhurin, 2015). The research is international and cross-cultural: from Ireland, Malaysia, Russia and elsewhere in

Eastern Europe, Canada, Singapore, Mexico, New Zealand and the United States, sampling bilinguals who use English plus Chinese, Bahasa Melayu, Tamil, Polish, German, Greek, Hebrew, Māori, Russian, Spanish, French, Ukrainian, Yorubo, Welsh, Italian or Kannada. Most studies have been conducted with children but there has been some recent work with college students (Kharkhurin, 2018). The research findings largely suggest that bilinguals are superior to monolinguals on tests of divergent thinking.

To illustrate, Cummins (1977) found that relatively balanced bilinguals were superior to 'matched' non-balanced bilinguals on the fluency and flexibility scales of verbal divergence, and marginally on originality. The 'matched' monolingual group obtained similar scores to the balanced bilingual group on verbal fluency and flexibility but scored substantially higher than the non-balanced group. On originality, monolinguals scored at a similar level to the non-balanced bilinguals and substantially lower than the balanced group. Probably because of the small numbers involved, the results did not quite attain conventional levels of statistical significance. The differences found between matched groups of balanced bilinguals and non-balanced bilinguals suggests that bilingualism and superior divergent thinking skills are not simply related. Thus Cummins proposed that the difference between balanced and non-balanced bilinguals can be explained by a threshold. Once children have obtained a certain level of competence in their second language, positive cognitive consequences can result. However, competence in a second language below a certain threshold level may fail to give any cognitive benefits. This is the basic notion of the controversial **threshold theory**, which is examined further in Chapter 8. Cummins's argument has been supported by other empirical studies (for reviews see Ricciardelli, 1992; Kharkhurin, 2018).

However, some care must be taken in reaching too firm a conclusion. For example, Kharkhurin (2009, 2018) argued that bilingualism enhances the ability to activate a multitude of unrelated concepts, but not the ability to *generate* novel ideas. Furthermore, most studies have been conducted in a laboratory setting, and so it remains unknown whether bilinguals are also superior to monolinguals in their real-life creative accomplishments. A recent well-powered, pre-registered study by Booton *et al.* (2021) actually found no evidence for a positive effect of bilingualism on divergent thinking.

Nonetheless, Kharkhurin (2018: 44) asserts that 'altogether, the empirical findings suggest that bilingual development may facilitate an individual's creative thinking'. The term 'creativity' is defined in different ways. As Kharkhurin (2018) suggests, the traditional definition of creativity as novelty and utility is a Western perception. Laurén (1991) revealed different interpretations by psychologists (e.g. cognitive flexibility, fluency, originality and elaboration; tolerance of ambiguity); by linguists (e.g. the ability to create new meanings in different contexts); child development researchers (e.g. transforming the language input of parents and teachers); and creative writing proponents.

Bilingualism and the Brain

Just as members of the public ask basic questions about 'intelligence' and bilingualism, so questions often arise about bilinguals' brains. Neuroscientific/neurolinguistics research on bilingualism frequently asks inter-related questions such as: How are multiple languages represented and controlled in the brain? And what are the consequences and implications of experience with multiple languages? The expectation has been that images of relevant areas of the brain would help us answer these questions. Advances in neuroimaging have led to bilinguals being studied by (1) electroencephalography (EEG) and event-related potentials (ERPs), (2) magneto-encephalography (MEG), (3) positron emission tomography (PET) and (4) functional magnetic resonance imaging (fMRI).

Basically, each approach takes a snapshot of the brain to try to show, when we are thinking, which part is doing what. EEG is able to tell us precisely *when* things are happening in the brain during thinking or perceiving external stimuli, by capturing the signals in the brain. It also captures electric signals associated with a particular event, which are known as an event-related potentials (ERPs). We know, for example, that it takes about 400 milliseconds for the brain to register the semantic anomaly in the sentence 'I like my coffee with cream and dog'. Whereas EEG captures the brain's electric signals, MEG captures the magnetic fields. Compared with EEG/ERP, MEG provides more precise data on the origins of the signals as well as both temporal and spatial information. However, MEG requires the participants to wear a helmet and stay in a fixed position in a special room. On the other hand, fMRI and PET techniques generally tell us *where* things are happening in the brain, by measuring changes in blood flow in certain areas while the research participant performs a task (when an area of the brain is working hard, more blood flows into that area). fMRI provides high-quality, high-resolution whole-brain images. However, it requires the participants to lie in a narrow tube of a machine with their head confined in a coil. Participants also need to wear headphones to cancel the loud noise of the machine, and the magnetic field can be potentially dangerous for participants with metal implants.

The past two decades have witnessed an explosion in bilingualism research that utilizes these neuroimaging techniques, in particular fMRI (Gold *et al.*, 2013). To understand how multiple languages are represented and organized in the brain, neurolinguistics researchers examine lateralization (Vaid, 2018). In the majority of right-handed adults, the left hemisphere of the brain is dominant for language processing (Vaid, 2018). The question has naturally arisen as to whether bilinguals are different from monolinguals in this left lateralization. Using a quantitative procedure called meta-analysis to review previous research in this area, Hull and Vaid (2007) found that the left hemisphere dominates language processing for monolinguals while bilateral involvement is pronounced in early fluent bilinguals compared with late fluent bilinguals. Thus bilinguals appear to be less left lateralized than monolinguals, and the degree of lateralization among bilinguals varies as a function of their age at exposure to the second language. However, the are no differences in lateralization between bilinguals' L1 and L2.

Another recent area of such research on bilinguals is how their two languages are stored and used in the brain. For example, if someone learns two languages from birth, are those languages stored differently in the brain from someone who learns a second language at school or in adult life? The effect of age of learning on language and cognition outcomes, commonly known as the **critical period hypothesis**, has been a topic of heated debate in psycholinguistics/neurolinguistics research communities (Bialystok & Kroll, 2018; Birdsong, 2018; Hartshorne *et al.*, 2018; Mayberry & Kluender, 2018). One much publicized piece of neurolinguistics research by Mechelli *et al.* (2004) suggested that learning a second language increases the density of gray matter. When comparing 25 monolinguals, 25 early bilinguals and 33 late bilinguals, gray matter density was greater in bilinguals than monolinguals, with early bilinguals having increased density compared with late bilinguals. Thus, such density of gray matter 'increases with second language proficiency but decreases as the age of acquisition increases', such that 'the structure of the brain is altered by the experience of acquiring a second language' (Mechelli *et al.*, 2004: 757). Moreover, the region of the brain where this increase in gray matter was observed is activated during vocabulary acquisition in both monolinguals and bilinguals, but yields enlargements in slightly different areas, depending on the specific languages of the bilingual (Green *et al.*, 2007). However, the implications of such early findings for everyday thinking and performance are not clear.

In a more recent brain imaging study, Gullifer *et al.* (2018) tested 27 French–English bilinguals who reported French as their first language (L1) and English as their second language (L2) and daily use of both languages. Their age of acquisition (AoA) for L2 ranged from birth to 13 years, and they also varied in the proportion of L1 and L2 use. All participants completed a behavioral task of executive control. The researchers also collected data on participants' seed-based resting-state functional connectivity, a technique that assessed the influence of language experience on brain organization. Results from the study showed that, controlling for language use, early L2 AoA correlated with stronger connectivity between left and right prefrontal regions and connectivity was greater for bilinguals with an early than for those with a late L2 AoA. These results suggest that early L2 AoA could help bilinguals resolve interference in executive control tasks, such as the Simon task, thus leading to a greater bilingual advantage.

However, as argued by Bialystok *et al.* (2018), we are only just beginning to understand the neural architecture underlying language and cognition in bilinguals. Snapshots of the brain can give a visible representation of thinking but do not reveal the complex operation of the mind. The correspondence between these images of the brain and thought processes and the relationship between brain and cognition need further investigation for us to make meaningful conclusions. De Bot (2008) offers a critical overview and concludes that neuroimaging has failed so far to provide any real breakthrough in our understanding of the multilingual brain. The reasons for this are many. The main one seems to be that the majority of studies are carried out by neuroscientists who have only recently developed an interest in **multilingualism** research. As such, these researchers tend to ignore or not to measure adequately several important variables that have been shown to affect multilingual processing and that multilingualism specialists routinely take into account. These variables include age of second language acquisition, level of proficiency, language contact and use, motivation to learn the language, language aptitude, and attitudes towards the L1 and L2. As a result, it is not possible to draw any firm conclusions regarding the functional organization in the brain of the multilingual's languages.

In addition, multilinguals typically exhibit larger individual variation in their patterns of brain activity than monolinguals, by virtue of the fact that they may still be in the process of learning. Some neuroimaging studies treat this variation as unwanted noise and ignore it, whereas in many cases it is in this variation that the real information about language processing in the brain may lie (for specific examples see De Bot, 2008). Nevertheless, there has been a surge in neuroimaging research on bilingualism/multilingualism in the decade and more since De Bot's publication (see e.g. work by Jubin Abutalebi, Ellen Bialystok, Jason Rothman, Christos Pliatsikas, Teresa Bajo and Eleonora Rossi). Neuroimaging techniques have opened up new research possibilities with the potential to better understand the multilingual brain. Some researchers are beginning to use more sophisticated research methodologies, such as collecting longitudinal imaging data and combining neuroimaging techniques with behavioral data such as language proficiency in advanced statistical models (see e.g. Gullifer *et al.*, 2018).

Age Effects

Are these metalinguistic advantages of balanced bilinguals temporary and located with certain younger children (e.g. those already embarked on the initial stages of reading)? Do they give a child an initial advantage that soon disappears with growing cognitive competence? Are the effects in any way permanent? Are these early benefits for bilinguals cumulative and additive?

Older bilingual adults may have some advantages as measured by cognitive behavioral tasks (e.g. Alladi *et al.*, 2021; Calvo *et al.*, 2023; Keijzer & Schmid, 2016). Bialystok and her colleagues provide evidence across a series of studies that bilingualism helps lessen some of the negative cognitive effects of aging in adults. Older bilingual adults have been shown to outperform their monolingual peers on cognitive tasks that assess executive functioning, such as the Simon task (e.g. Bialystok *et al.*, 2004) and the Stroop task (Bialystok *et al.*, 2008). These tasks require the participants to attend to target information when presented with conflicting or misleading distraction. For example, Bialystok *et al.* (2008) used the Stroop task with younger and older bilingual and monolingual individuals. Participants have to name the color of the ink that a color word is written in (e.g. name the ink that the word 'green' is written in). In congruent trials, the color of the ink is the same as the color word (e.g. the word 'green' is written in green ink) but in incongruent trials the color of the ink conflicts with the color word (e.g. the word 'green' is written in red ink). Typically, participants are slower to respond in the incongruent condition than in the congruent condition. Bialystok *et al.* found that this switching cost between the congruent and incongruent trials was smaller in both younger and older bilinguals than in their age-matched monolingual counterparts. However, other studies that used similar cognitive tasks which measure executive function but with verbal stimuli actually found a disadvantage for bilinguals. Bilinguals performed better on tasks using non-verbal stimuli but worse than their monolingual peers on tasks using verbal stimuli (Anderson *et al.*, 2017).

The Simon and Stroop effects are similar to advantages found in bilingual children (discussed previously) and young adults, who appear to be superior in selective attention to problems, inhibition of attention to misleading information, and switching quickly between competing alternatives. From these experiments, such inhibitory control appears to last a lifetime (Bialystok *et al.*, 2004). This advantage may be due to bilinguals using one language while both their languages are constantly active (Marian & Spivey, 2003).

Since abilities that depend on executive cognitive control show a decline in efficiency with aging, researchers argued that bilingualism may also provide a partial defense against the normal decline in cognitive control associated with aging. Although many studies have demonstrated that older bilingual adults (e.g. age 60 and above in these experiments) fare better than their monolingual peers in preserving memory (Bialystok *et al.*, 2014a), delaying the signs of dementia (Bialystok *et al.*, 2007) or the onset of symptoms of Alzheimer's disease (Bialystok *et al.*, 2012, 2014b), some have failed to replicate the positive benefits of bilingualism on aging (Bialystok *et al.*, 2018). In light of the conflicting results from behavioral studies comparing monolingual and bilingual older adults, Bialystok *et al.* (2018) concluded that brain imaging data are needed to resolve the controversy.

It is worth noting that a recent systematic review by Carthery-Goulart *et al.* (2023) investigated how the linguistic distance between the languages spoken by bilinguals might influence the cognitive reserve that helps protect against cognitive decline and dementia, focusing on older adults. The results suggest that older bilingual adults who speak more linguistically distant language pairs show improved performance in tasks that require monitoring, a cognitive process related to attention and cognitive control. However, language distance did not significantly affect other cognitive domains such as inhibition, working memory or shifting.

Implications and Explanations

Bilinguals appear to understand the symbolic representation of words in print earlier than monolinguals, as they see words printed in two separate ways. In turn, this may facilitate earlier acquisition of reading. Such metalinguistic awareness is regarded as a key factor in the development of reading in young children (Huang, 2019). This hints that bilinguals may be ready slightly earlier than monolinguals to learn to read. In a review of this area, Bialystok (2007) analyzes the effects that early bilingualism has on children's early literacy development, but urges caution. Three areas of early literacy development are analyzed: experience with stories and book reading, concepts of print, and phonological awareness. These three areas cover the social, cognitive and linguistic aspects of literacy learning. Bialystok argues that each of these three areas of competence will have a different link to bilingualism.

However, there are many intervening variables that make simple statements currently impossible. The child's experience and level of proficiency in each language, the relationship between the two languages and the type of writing systems employed by each language are examples of intervening factors that alter the nature of the bilingual experience. For example, the L1–L2 pairings of bilinguals play a role in determining the metalinguistic advantage. For bilinguals to develop a specific type of metalinguistic skill, it may be necessary for both of the bilingual's two languages to include that same language feature or to share a similar writing system (Adesope *et al.*, 2010). Cross-linguistic studies that have compared children's development of phonological awareness have revealed an important role of a shared writing script and phonological system (Bialystok *et al.*, 2005; Verhoeven, 2017) and recent studies using neuroimaging techniques supported such findings with neurolinguistic evidence (Verhoeven *et al.*, 2019). Bialystok *et al.* (2005) compared the early literacy skills of four groups of first-graders: a monolingual English-speaking group, and three groups of bilinguals from different L1–L2 pairings (Hebrew–English, Chinese–English and Spanish–English). All children were learning to read in English and the bilinguals were also learning to read in another language. The results showed a bilingual advantage in phonological awareness for Spanish–English and Hebrew–English bilinguals, whose L1 and L2 both have alphabetic writing systems, but not for Chinese–English bilinguals, whose L1 uses a logographic writing system. However, a bilingual advantage in non-word decoding tasks was observed for all three bilingual groups relative to the monolingual group.

Apart from literacy, Hartanto *et al.* (2018) examined the relationship between bilingualism and mathematical achievement in pre-schoolers, kindergarteners and first-grade students using two large, independent datasets in the United States. Critical covariates such as age, race/ethnicity, socioeconomic status and children's language proficiency in English were controlled in the analyses. Results from the study showed strong and positive relationships between bilingualism and mathematical achievements as measured by teacher-rated mathematical reasoning, emergent numeracy skills and test scores on standardized mathematical assessments. The authors attributed the bilingual advantage in mathematical achievements to these children's stronger executive functions.

Researchers have provided refinement of the reasons for differences between bilinguals and monolinguals on cognitive processes. Carlisle *et al*. (1999) found that the degree of bilingualism constrains or enhances metalinguistic performance. Those in the early stages of bilingualism do not share the benefits until sufficient vocabulary development has occurred in both languages. Cross-linguistic studies on bilingual advantage (Verhoeven, 2017) also showed that metalinguistic benefits are more apparent in bilinguals whose languages have similar sound structures or writing systems (e.g. Spanish–English bilinguals) than in bilinguals whose languages use distinctly different sound structures or writing systems (e.g. Chinese–English bilinguals), suggesting that enhanced metalinguistic awareness may not necessarily be a product of bilingualism *per se*, but rather of speaking specific combinations of languages with similar features.

Bilingualism and Communicative Sensitivity

Social preferences based on primary categories such as gender, race and age have long been documented in the literature for both adults (Stangor *et al*., 1992) and children (Kowalski & Lo, 2001). Since spoken language provides information about individuals' ethnicity, regional membership and social class, researchers have argued that spoken language may also function as an additional social category that guides individual preferences (Dautel & Kinzler, 2018; DeJesus *et al*., 2018). In particular, research on bilingualism has shown that bilinguals appear to have increased sensitivity to the social nature and communicative functions of language, that is, **communicative sensitivity**. In Ben-Zeev's seminal research (1977a) on the comparative performance of bilingual and monolingual children on Piagetian tests, she found that bilinguals were more responsive to hints and clues given in the experimental situation. That is, bilinguals seemed more sensitive in an experimental situation, and corrected their errors faster, compared with monolinguals. Ben-Zeev's research gave the first clue that bilinguals may have cognitive advantages regarding communicative sensitivity. Because bilinguals need to be aware of which language to speak in which situation, they need to constantly monitor the appropriate language in which to respond or in which to initiate a conversation (e.g. on the telephone, in a shop, speaking to a superior). Not only do bilinguals often attempt to avoid interference between their two languages, they also have to pick up clues and cues as to when to switch languages. The literature suggests that this may lead to bilinguals' advantage in communicative sensitivity.

Wermelinger *et al*. (2017) compared three groups of 2½-year-old toddlers in a communicative task to examine the enhanced communicative abilities afforded by bilingualism. The three groups were (1) non-German bilinguals who had one parent speaking Swiss German and the other parent speaking a different non-German language (e.g. French), (2) German bilinguals who had one parent speaking Standard German and the other Swiss German and (3) monolinguals who had both parents speaking

Swiss German at home. The experimenter and the child engaged in a communication repair task in which they put shoes on to a stuffed animal. The experimenter elicited references to a missing shoe and also appeared to misunderstand the child's reference in order to elicit the child's repair behavior. The results revealed that non-German bilinguals exhibited higher communicative abilities than both German bilingual and monolingual peers. They not only informed the experimenter of the missing shoe at a higher frequency but also repaired their utterances when the experimenter pretended to misunderstand them. Wermelinger *et al.* argued that bilinguals' daily unique experience with communication difficulties and failures stimulates their communicative skills. More recent research has found a similar advantage among bilingual children in perspective-taking (Fan *et al.*, 2015) and in integrating multiple cues to understand speakers' intent (Yow & Markman, 2011, 2015). Researchers have also discovered that bilingual infants, compared with their monolingual peers, are better able to exploit audiovisual speech cues because of the need to process two languages and to keep them apart (Pons *et al.*, 2015; Sebastián-Gallés *et al.*, 2012). In addition to the bilingual advantage in cognitive and social tasks, a recent study examining how children process information about the talker also found a bilingual advantage (Levi, 2018). In this study, monolingual English-speaking children and bilingual children between the ages of 6 and 12 completed tasks that required them to discriminate and identify the voices of unfamiliar speakers in English. Bilingual children outperformed their monolingual peers across tasks, showing higher ability in talker-voice processing, which is a social aspect of speech perception.

Taken together, these results imply that bilingual children may be more sensitive than monolingual children in a social situation that requires careful communication. This links with sociolinguistic and **communicative competence** (see Chapter 1) and suggests a heightened social awareness among bilinguals of verbal and non-verbal message cues and clues in communication. More research is needed to define precisely the characteristics and the extent of the sensitivity to communication that bilinguals may share. Research in this area is important because it connects cognition with interpersonal relationships. It moves from questions about bilinguals' cognitive skills to their social skills.

Thinking Implications of Speaking Specific Languages

Is it the case that different languages, or combinations of languages, influence the thinking of individuals? The Whorf hypothesis (Whorf, 1956) holds that speakers of different languages perceive the world through the lens of their native language, and speakers' perceptions and information processing may vary as a function of the differences in the linguistic features across languages (Bylund & Athanasopoulos, 2017; Ünal & Papafragou, 2020). Recent research has focused on individuals who view the world through the lens of more than one language. This new line of research focuses on the thinking processes rather than the thinking abilities of the bilingual. The targeted thinking processes include both perceptual (e.g. color and objects) and conceptual domains (e.g. numbers, spatial frames of reference), as well as the predictors of differences in those processes between L1 and L2 speakers, including age of L2 acquisition (Kousaie *et al.*, 2017), L2 use and proficiency (Bylund & Athanasopoulos, 2014a) and L2 proficiency (Pavlenko & Malt, 2011) (for a detailed overview see Bylund & Athanasopoulos, 2014b).

To illustrate, some researchers have focused on categorization of objects and substances in noun class and classifier languages (Papafragou, 2017). Noun class languages like English distinguish between count and mass nouns grammatically. Count nouns refer to discrete entities that are marked for number (e.g. candle – candles). In classifier languages like Japanese or Chinese, there is no count/mass distinction. Nouns in these languages refer to substances and are accompanied by numeral classifiers (e.g. one long thin wax [=candle]). Speakers of the two types of languages were shown to perform differently on a similarity judgment task that required participants to match objects based on their common shape or material. Speakers of English favored shape and speakers of Japanese favored material, presumably because noun class languages draw speakers' attention to discreteness of entities and classifier languages to material (Lucy & Gaskins, 2001). Japanese–English bilinguals were influenced by the level of proficiency in the L2 and their length of stay in the United Kingdom when making their judgments (Athanasopoulos, 2007). Those bilinguals with advanced proficiency and/or longer length of stay were beginning to resemble speakers of their L2 English in favoring shape over material in similarity judgments.

Other studies have also shown shifts in mental representation of bilinguals in different perceptual domains such as time (Casasanto & Boroditsky, 2008, but cf. Yang *et al.*, 2022), motion events (Bylund & Athanasopoulos, 2015; Wang & Wei, 2021), grammatical gender (for a review see Samuel *et al.*, 2019) and frame of reference for talking about locations and directions (Li & Abarbanell, 2018). What is particularly interesting is that different factors appear to affect the degree of cognitive restructuring observed. So for domains like grammatical number and gender, it seems that proficiency achieved in the L2 is the most important factor, while factors such as length of stay and frequency of language use appear to affect color cognition. Boroditsky (2001) found that the degree to which time representations changed in Chinese–English bilinguals depended on the age at which they had started to acquire English, while the study by Boroditsky *et al.* (2002) found that bilinguals shifted their behavioral responses toward the language in which they received task instructions. The application of the Whorfian hypothesis to bilingualism has the potential to reveal invaluable information about how the bilingual mind views the world as a result of speaking specific languages; yet research is still at a very early stage, and the precise role of specific linguistic and sociocultural factors, as well as the extent of the effects in different perceptual domains, remains elusive for the time being (for detailed discussions see Bylund & Athanasopoulos, 2014a; Pavlenko, 2014).

Cross-linguistic differences have also been identified in how languages employ grammatical devices to encode emotions (Martinovic & Altarriba, 2013). For example, in English, emotions are relayed through adjectives as emotional states, while in Russian the tendency is to convey emotions more via verbs as actions and processes, with, for example, more attention to body language. Pavlenko and Driagina (2007) found that advanced American learners of Russian use the copula verbs *byt* ('be') and *stanovit'sia* ('become') with emotion adjectives in contexts where Russian monolinguals use emotion verbs. These patterns suggest that in discussing emotions in Russian, these learners transfer the L1 concept of emotions as states into their L2 and have not yet internalized the representation of emotions as processes. Evidence of internalization comes from a study by Panayiotou (2007), who found that Greek–English bilinguals internalized the notion of 'frustration' from English and codeswitched to refer to it when speaking Greek. For example: '*Imoun polla frustrated me tin katastasi*' ('I was very *frustrated* with the situation') (Panayiotou, 2006: 8). Using a sorting task,

Stepanova Sachs and Coley (2006) found that Russian–English bilinguals grouped situations eliciting jealousy and ones eliciting envy together as similar, whereas Russian monolinguals sorted the two types of situations separately. This suggests a certain degree of restructuring of emotion perception in bilinguals. Pavlenko (2011) discusses similar research that shows that bilinguals may have access to different conceptual representations, experience different imagery and index more varied **discourses** and identities than monolinguals.

Limitations of the Findings

In their meta-analysis of the cognitive advantages of bilingualism, Adesope *et al.* (2010) reviewed 63 empirical studies and found that bilingualism is associated with several cognitive benefits. Those include increased working memory, attentional control, metalinguistic awareness, and abstract and symbolic representations. A recent study by Peristeri *et al.* (2021) also found an advantages for bilingual children with autism spectrum disorder over their age- and IQ-matched monolingual peers in a 'theory of mind' task that measured children's ability to understand other's beliefs. The research reviewed in this chapter converges with the meta-analysis and suggests cognitive advantages of bilinguals. However, the research on bilingual advantages mostly focuses on balanced bilinguals, who are a subgroup of all bilinguals. MacNab (1979) argued that (balanced) bilinguals are a special, idiosyncratic group in society. Because they have learned a second language and are often bicultural, bilinguals are different in major ways from monolinguals. For example, parents who want their children to be bicultural/bilingual may encourage creative thinking in their children and foster metalinguistic skills. They may also want to accelerate their children's language skills and thus give higher priority to the development of languages within their children than monolingual parents do. While this does not detract from the possibility that bilinguals do share some cognitive advantages, it does suggest a need to consider non-language factors (e.g. the immigrant experience, political pressures, subtractive and additive contexts) before attributing the cognitive advantages to bilingualism.

We also need to ask which types of children share the benefits of bilingualism. This concerns whether children of all socioeconomic backgrounds and cognitive skills share the cognitive advantages of bilingualism (Naeem *et al.*, 2018; Valian, 2015; for an up-to-date review of bilingual advantage see Poarch & Krott, 2019). Many bilingualism studies either did not report socioeconomic information or included bilingual children of a higher socioeconomic status than the monolingual group (Adesope *et al.*, 2010). Those that controlled for socioeconomic backgrounds of the monolingual and bilingual/multilingual groups (Dunabeitia *et al.*, 2014; Gathercole *et al.*, 2014; Poarch, 2018; Poarch & Bialystok, 2015; Poarch & Van Hell, 2012) or included children from backgrounds of lower socioeconomic status (Vivas *et al.*, 2017) yielded mixed results. Thomas-Sunesson *et al.* (2018) found a cognitive advantage on executive control among young Spanish–English bilingual children from low socioeconomic backgrounds in the United States. However, the study also showed that children's degrees of bilingualism and proficiency modified the cognitive advantage – those with balanced proficiency performed better than their bilingual peers with lower language proficiency (see also Poarch & Bialystok, 2015; Poarch & Van Hell, 2012). On the other hand, Cheatham *et al.* (2012) reviewed comparison studies that investigated the impact of bilingualism for bilingual students with disabilities. The researchers concluded that a bilingual cognitive advantage may be shared by bilingual children with below-average cognitive skills (or with cognitive impairments) and is not limited to bilingual children with average and above average cognitive skills. Taken together, these results call for further research on the mediating/moderating roles of socioeconomic backgrounds, language proficiency and developmental disorders in the investigations of bilingual advantages.

In addition, researchers have found that levels of education, exercise and music training, among other cognitively enriching activities, can also improve cognitive functioning, and these factors should have been controlled in studies that compared monolinguals and bilinguals to examine bilingual cognitive advantages (Valian, 2015). When reviewing all research, we also need to consider the hopes and the ideologies of the researcher (confirmation bias) as well as the bias of journal editors to publish only positive results (publication bias) (de Bruin *et al.*, 2015, but cf. Leivada, 2023, who reanalyzed de Bruin *et al.*'s data and refuted the claims about a strong publication bias favoring positive results supporting bilingual advantages). A recent meta-analysis study by Yurtsever *et al.* (2023) found evidence in support of bilinguals outperforming monolinguals on executive function tasks independent of task, publication bias, publication year, and sample size. However, when reviewing bilingual advantage research, it is still worth asking whether researchers' assumptions or perspectives have inadvertently influenced their findings and interpretations, and whether recent studies might reflect a bias toward reporting positive rather than neutral or negative results regarding bilingualism and cognitive functioning.

As Pavlenko (2005) argues, the dominant research on bilingualism and cognition is about the implications of bilingualism for individual cognition. This assumes that such cognitive effects of bilingualism are universal. However, neither behavioral nor neuroscience data have provided unequivocal evidence for a universal bilingual advantage in cognition (Bialystok *et al.*, 2018; Paap *et al.*, 2015, 2016; Paap, 2022). The current consensus in the research community is that a bilingual cognitive advantage exists for selective components of cognitive functioning, and may be restricted to specific circumstances of bilingualism (Valian, 2015). To specify and determine the mechanism, future research that addresses the above-mentioned methodological issues is clearly needed.

Conclusion

This chapter has reviewed the view from the 1920s to the 1960s that bilingualism leads to lower intelligence. Recent research has shown this to be a misconception. The narrow view of intelligence contained in IQ tests and severe flaws in the design of early research cast doubts on this negative link.

Rather, the need is to specify the **language ability** levels of bilinguals (see Chapter 1) and to ensure like is compared with like. Since 1960, the indication has been that a more positive relationship between bilingualism and cognitive functioning can be expected, particularly in 'balanced' bilinguals.

A review of research on cognitive functioning and bilingualism suggests that two extreme conclusions may both be untenable. To conclude that bilingualism gives undoubted cognitive advantage fails to consider the various failures of replication studies and limitations of research in this area (Nichols *et al.*, 2020; Paap, 2022; Paap *et al.*, 2015, 2016). It also fails to recognize the potential disadvantages of bilinguals compared with monolinguals. However, to conclude that all the research is invalid fails to acknowledge that the judgment of the clear majority of researchers tends to be that there are many positive links between bilingualism and cognitive functioning (Valian, 2015), with bilinguals having some distinct cognitive as well as social-communicative advantages over monolinguals. Such advantages are not just individual, but societal and global: 'those who envision a future world speaking only one tongue ... hold a misguided ideal and would do the evolution of the human mind the greatest disservice' (Whorf, 1956: 244).

Key Points in This Chapter

- Historically, bilinguals were regarded as having a lower IQ than monolinguals because IQ tests were lacking in cultural and linguistic validity.
- The idea of 'intelligence' as a singular fixed construct has been challenged by more recent theories of multiple intelligences, emotional intelligence and mindsets.
- Research on the relationship between intelligence and bilingualism has moved from a period of investigating 'detrimental effects' to a current focus on the additive effects given by bilingualism.
- The ownership of two languages does not interfere with efficient thinking. On the contrary, bilinguals who have two well developed languages tend to share cognitive advantages.
- Bilinguals have advantages on certain thinking dimensions, particularly in divergent thinking, creativity, early metalinguistic awareness and communicative sensitivity. There are likely to be many other cognitive skills on which there are no real differences between bilinguals and monolinguals.
- Research on the metalinguistic advantages of bilinguals is strong and suggests bilinguals are aware of their languages at an early age, separating form from meaning, and having reading readiness earlier than monolinguals.
- Research on the language-specific cognitive consequences of bilingualism shows that bilinguals may have a unique perspective of the world, dissimilar to that of monolinguals of either language.
- Recent neurological studies suggest that bilingualism may help fend off the decline of cognitive function in late adulthood, and delays the onset of aging and diseases such as dementia and Alzheimer's disease.

Suggested Further Reading

📖 Brennan, J.R. (2022) *Language and the Brain: A Slim Guide to Neurolinguistics*. Oxford University Press.
📖 Costa, A. (2020) *The Bilingual Brain: And What It Tells Us About the Science of Language*. Penguin Books.

- Grosjean, F. (2021) *Life as a Bilingual: Knowing and Using Two or More Languages.* Cambridge University Press.
- Jiang, N. (2023) *The Study of Bilingual Language Processing.* Oxford University Press.
- Luk, G., Anderson, J. and Grundy, J.G. (eds) (2023) *Understanding Language and Cognition Through Bilingualism: In Honor of Ellen Bialystok.* John Benjamins.
- Marian, V. (2023) *The Power of Language: How the Codes We Use to Think, Speak, and Live Transform Our Minds.* Dutton/Penguin Random House.
- Paap, K. (2022) *The Bilingual Advantage in Executive Functioning Hypothesis: How the Debate Provides Insight into Psychology's Replication Crisis.* Routledge.
- Schwieter, J.W. and Festman, J. (2023) *The Cognitive Neuroscience of Bilingualism.* Cambridge University Press.

On the Web

- François Grosjean's bilingualism website
  https://www.francoisgrosjean.ch/index.html
- Human Abilities in Bilingual Language Acquisition Laboratory's blog
  https://2languages2worlds.wordpress.com
- Ellen Bialystok's Lifespan Cognition and Development Laboratory
  https://lcad.lab.yorku.ca/research-projects
- Max Planck Institute for Psycholinguistics
  https://www.mpi.nl
- Judith F. Kroll, Bilingualism, Mind, and Brain Laboratory
  https://bilingualismmindbrain.com/lab-members/judith-f-kroll
- Multilingual Children's Association
  http://www.multilingualchildren.org/faq.html

Discussion Questions

(1) Why is it difficult to measure intelligence in general, and for bilinguals in particular? As the majority of IQ tests include a verbal intelligence component, how can we make sure that the test results are not confounded with bilinguals' language proficiency? Describe any experience you have had with IQ tests and discuss ways to improve their validity.

(2) If you speak more than one language, compare your languages in terms of (a) the expressions of time, (b) grammatical gender, (c) emotional terms and (d) other significant differences. Do these cross-linguistic differences affect your thinking when you switch from one language to another? Compare and discuss these cross-linguistic differences and their role in thinking.

(3) Review carefully the text on age of acquisition (a.k.a. the critical period hypothesis) in the 'Bilingualism and the Brain' section of this chapter. Discuss how the age of learning influences cognitive abilities and brain plasticity. In your response, compare the potential cognitive and neurological benefits experienced by early versus late bilinguals.

Study Activities

(1) Find one or more examples of an IQ test (e.g. Wechsler Adult Intelligence Scale for adults, Wechsler Intelligence Scale for Children, Woodcock–Johnson Tests of Cognitive Abilities). Examine the content of the test and identify any items that you think may be unfair to bilinguals in your region. Examine both the language and the cultural content of the IQ test.

(2) Using one of the tests or experiments mentioned in this chapter, select a student (or a group of students) and give them that test or experimental task. For example, ask them how many uses they can think of for a brick or for a cardboard box. Compare the answers of those who are more and less bilingual and see if there are differences in the quality and quantity of answers.

(3) Watch the Youtube video about bilingualism and the brain at https://www.youtube.com/watch?v=WSUj3PRvzzg. Answer the following discussion questions:
- According to the video, how does being bilingual benefit the brain?
- Why is learning a new language considered more beneficial for building cognitive reserve than the acquisition of other new skills?
- What did the study at Great Ormond Street reveal about the brain activity of early bilingual children compared with monolingual children?
- How does bilingualism affect perspective-taking abilities in individuals, as discussed in the video?

CHAPTER 8
Theories of Bilingualism and the Curriculum

Introduction

Early Theories

Criticisms

Current Views and Practices

Language Proficiency Standards

Conclusion

CHAPTER 8

Theories of Bilingualism and the Curriculum

Introduction

This chapter considers the historical development of ideas about **bilingualism** and the ways they have influenced the language learning curriculum for bilingual students. These theories began emerging in the 1970s and 1980s to provide justifications for the growing number of bilingual programs. This corresponded with increasing support and funding for bilingual education in the United States (see Chapter 9). These theories led to curriculum innovations, not only for teaching strategy and learning activities, but also for assessment. However, earlier theories led to some misunderstandings about language and contributed to an oversimplification of the complex nature of bilingualism and the multifaceted processes of second language learning. Nonetheless, scholarly debates and critiques of these theories helped move the field forward with new understandings that have informed current views of bilingualism and language learning. Thus, this chapter also considers more recent theories and understandings of these issues and the ways that they are informing current instructional and assessment strategies, including language proficiency standards.

Early Theories

The previous chapter noted that initial research into bilingualism and cognitive functioning often found bilinguals to be inferior to **monolinguals**. This connects with an outdated and naïve theory of bilingualism that represents the two languages as existing together in balance, as on a balance scale: as proficiency in one language increases on one side of the scale, the proficiency of the language on the other side of the scale decreases. A similar negative picture portrays the monolingual as having one well filled balloon, while the bilingual is pictured as having two less filled or half-filled balloons. As the second language balloon is pumped higher (e.g. English in the United States), the first language balloon (e.g. Spanish) diminishes in size, leading to confusion, frustration and failure. These depictions falsely suggest the brain has room for only one fully developed language.

This idea was challenged in the early 1980s by Cummins (1981a, 1981b), who labeled this false view the **separate underlying proficiency** (SUP) model of bilingualism. The SUP model conceives of the two languages as operating separately, without **transfer** and with a restricted amount of 'room' for languages. To counter the SUP model, Cummins (1981a, 1981b) proposed the **common underlying proficiency** (CUP) model of bilingualism. The CUP model was typically represented metaphorically in the form of an iceberg with two peaks above the water surface, thus appearing to be two separate icebergs. These peaks represent the first and second language of a bilingual. This illustration suggested that two languages may be visibly different in outward production, but underneath the surface the two icebergs are actually one. Thus, the two languages of a bilingual do not function separately. Both operate through the same central processing system. The CUP model was helpful to teachers and is consistent with current views that a bilingual is not two monolinguals in one (Grosjean & Li, 2013; MacSwan, 2020; Otheguy *et al.*, 2019). Nevertheless, the CUP model was an oversimplification of the complexities of the bilingual brain. It does not sum up the findings from research on cognitive functioning and bilingualism, nor does it reflect recent research on the brain and bilingualism (see Chapter 7).

As shown in Chapter 7, many studies have found cognitive advantages in individuals with well developed proficiency in two or more languages (see e.g. Bialystok *et al.*, 2012; Grosjean & Li, 2013; Li, 2013). Studies such as these raised questions about the relationship between bilingualism and **cognition**, and the extent to which one needed to be bilingual in order to attain these cognitive advantages. The **threshold theory**, first postulated by Cummins (1976) and Toukomaa and Skutnabb-Kangas (1977), suggested that the research on cognition and bilingualism is best explained by the idea of two thresholds. Each threshold is a level of **language competence** that has consequences for a child. The first threshold is a level for a child to reach to avoid the 'negative' consequences of bilingualism. The second threshold is a level required to experience the possible cognitive benefits of bilingualism. Thus, according to the theory, when a child has age-appropriate ability in both their languages, they may have cognitive advantages over monolinguals (for a review see Cummins, 2000b).

Proponents of the threshold theory believed it helps explain why minoritized language children taught through a second language (e.g. immigrants in the United States, the United Kingdom, Canada and Australia) sometimes fail to develop sufficient competence in their second language (e.g. English) and fail to benefit from 'weak' forms of bilingual education (see Chapter 10). Their low level of proficiency in English, for example, limits their ability to cope with the curriculum. Therefore, **dual language programs** that allow a child to operate in their more developed home language can result in superior performance compared with submersion and **transitional bilingual education** (see Chapter 10).

One problem with the threshold theory, however, is in precisely defining the level and nature of **language proficiency** a child must obtain in order, first, to avoid the negative effects of bilingualism and, second, to obtain the advantages of bilingualism. What language skills need to be developed to what point so as to reach a higher threshold? Indeed, the danger may be in constructing artificial 'critical stages' or levels, when transition is in fact gradual and smooth. Furthermore, the threshold theory does not account for the dynamic nature of bilingualism, and is related to the discredited construct of semilingualism, which suggested potential 'negative' cognitive consequences of bilingualism (see Chapter 1). It thus fails to understand the more complex, interactive nature of language and thinking (see Chapter 7).

From the threshold theory, Cummins developed a succession of more refined theories of bilingualism. The linguistic developmental interdependence hypothesis suggests that a child's second language competence is partly dependent on the level of competence already achieved in the first language (Cummins, 2000a). Thus, the more developed the first language, the easier it will be to develop the second language.

Alongside this, a distinction developed between surface fluency and the more evolved language skills required to benefit from the education process (Cummins, 1984).

In the late 1970s, Cummins (1979) suggested that everyday 'conversational language' could be acquired in two years while the more complex language abilities needed to cope with the school curriculum could take five to seven years (or more) to develop. This led to his naming of, and distinction between, the constructs of basic interpersonal communicative skills (BICS) and cognitive academic language proficiency (CALP). It was typically explained to teachers and others that BICS refers to highly contextualized conversational skills, such as the language children speak on the playground ('playground language'). In contrast, as teachers were told, CALP refers to language use in context-reduced academic subjects of the classroom, including reading and writing ('classroom language' or 'academic language'). For over three decades, the BICS/CALP distinction was highly influential in guiding policy, programs and instruction for bilingual students. It helped teachers develop some sensitivity about students' language proficiency and the need to provide linguistic support. The distinction also helped educators recognize why bilingual students who 'sounded' proficient in English nonetheless struggled with the literacy and academic demands of English language instruction in mainstream classrooms.

To elaborate the distinction, Cummins (1981a, 1981b) proposed a model of two intersecting continua – context (from embedded to reduced) and cognitive demand (from undemanding to demanding) – forming four quadrants. **Context** refers to the amount of contextual support available to a student (e.g. body language, gestures, pointing, visual support, intonation, facial expressions, etc.), suggesting that in context-reduced communication there are fewer cues to the meaning. The cognitive continuum refers to the level of the cognitive demand required in the communication; cognitively demanding communication may occur in a classroom where much information at a challenging level needs processing quickly. Many teachers found the four quadrants to be a helpful tool in creating cognitively challenging but contextually supported lessons and activities, thus maximizing the language and literacy development of their bilingual students (Cummins, 2017a: 81). In other words, the four quadrants helped teachers consider the linguistic and cognitive demand of various classroom tasks and learning experiences and the kinds of **scaffolding** that would be needed to help students successfully participate and complete these tasks.

Criticisms

The original problems with the BICS/CALP distinction were not fully resolved in the elaborated four-quadrants model, and use of the distinction remained common in schools, teacher education programs and research. A number of scholars, however, have been critical of the work as an oversimplification of the complex and dynamic nature of second language learning and a misrepresentation of bilingual proficiency (Edelsky, 2006; Edelsky *et al.*, 1983; Flores, 2020a, 2020b, 2024; Flores & Rosa, 2015; Frederickson & Cline, 2015; MacSwan & Rolstad, 2003; Martin-Jones & Romaine, 1986; Martínez & Mejía, 2020; Moore & Schleppegrell, 2020; Rivera, 1984; Rosa & Burdick, 2017; Seltzer, 2019; Valdés, 2017; Valdés *et al.*, 2015; Wiley, 2005; Wiley & Rolstad, 2014). Responses to his critics can be found in Cummins (2000a, 2000b, 2003, 2017a, 2021). The criticisms can be briefly summarized as follows:

(1) The BICS/CALP distinction may be intuitive. However, a bilingual's language competences are evolving, dynamic, interacting and intricate. They are not simple dichotomies, easily compartmentalized and static (see Chapter 1).
(2) It was assumed that students first developed BICS followed by CALP. However, the order is not absolute. For example, older newcomer students who studied English as an international language in their home country often could read and write well in English but initially struggled with oral communication skills. This challenges the underlying theoretical underpinnings of the distinction.
(3) Oral language and interpersonal communication are not necessarily less cognitively demanding than so-called 'academic language'. Careful logic, metaphor and other abstract aspects of language occur in face-to-face communication and not just in written language. Consider, for example, the cognitive differences (if any) between having an oral discussion about the results of a science experiment and writing a journal entry about the favorite part of a story. Also consider the number of 'higher-order thinking processes' typically associated with CALP that students may use on the playground as they organize a soccer match (e.g. analyzing, synthesizing, comparing, evaluating, etc.).
(4) The relationship between language development and cognitive development is not unequivocal or simple. The early theory was essentially individual and psychological. Cognition, language acquisition, bilingualism, bilingual education and academic success exist in a relationship that is influenced by various other factors: social, cultural, economic, political, community, motivation, power relations, teacher expectations and home factors. Each and all of these variables help explain bilingualism as an individual and societal phenomenon. Cummins (2000a, 2017a, 2021) has addressed these issues in further theoretical formulations.
(5) The dichotomy between context-embedded and context-reduced communication is misleading because everything a student does is embedded in some sort of context – the context of the school, of the classroom, of the unit or lesson, of what was taught/practiced the day before, of the particular activity or task at hand, and so on. Thus, all communication is embedded in some kind of context. Also, what is cognitively demanding and the amount of scaffolding needed can vary widely from student to student, and can depend on the topic or nature of the learning activity. This makes the placement of instructional activities within the four quadrants problematic.
(6) School-based 'academic language' does not represent universal higher-order cognitive skills nor all forms of literacy practice. Different sociocultural contexts have different expectations and perceived patterns of appropriateness in language and thinking such that a school is only one specific context for 'higher-order' language production.
(7) From a **raciolinguistics** perspective, the false dichotomous framing of 'academic' versus 'non-academic' language disproportionately impacts racialized students by characterizing their home language practices as deficient and in need of remediation, and fails to recognize and value the rich linguistic repertoires students bring to school.
(8) Finally, as the previous chapter has considered, there is a new wave of research on bilingual brains and developing research on bilingualism and cognition. This will in turn be related to the curriculum, with implications for teaching and learning by bilinguals. For example, such research points to the value of bilingualism from an early age, suggesting that bilingual education should begin earlier rather than later.

However, much credit can be given to Jim Cummins, whose ideas and theories have helped guide bilingual education policies and programs, and have helped **English as a second language** (ESL), bilingual and other classroom teachers pay closer attention to students' language proficiency and to think about ways to modify and scaffold their instruction. His ongoing scholarship and advocacy continue to inspire educators, transform schools and promote educational equity for bilingual students (see e.g. Isola & Cummins, 2020; Cummins, 2021, 2022). His early theories – and the debates about them – have led to new understandings and ideas about bilingualism, cognition and language learning and teaching.

Current Views and Practices

After 30 years of influence on research and practice in the education field, researchers and educators are moving away from the oversimplified and problematic concepts and constructs of the early theories and on to more sophisticated ways of viewing the dynamic nature of bilingualism (as described in Chapter 1), the language development of bilingual students (as described in Chapters 5 and 6) and new understandings of bilingualism and cognition (as described in Chapter 7). Issues, however, remain. For example, while the term 'CALP' is used less frequently, the construct lives on as many educators, policymakers and researchers now focus on 'academic language' or 'academic English'. This continues to perpetuate the problematic view that there is a singular type of English proficiency that is a prerequisite for academic success in all content areas.

The problematic construct of 'academic language' has now moved into the realm of language majority education and even into teacher preparation. For example, in the United States the many state standards feature language standards designed to ensure *all* students – not just those classified as English language learners (ELLs) – learn and use 'academic language'. Teacher certification in the United States through the Education Teacher Preparation Assessment (EdTPA) requires all teacher candidates to demonstrate their own ability to use 'academic language', as well as their ability to teach it to all students. As the term has moved into the mainstream, some scholars are declaring that 'there are no native speakers of academic language', suggesting that even monolingual English-speakers must learn 'academic English' to be successful in school (Fillmore, 2013). Despite its broadening and widespread usage, there is no clear and agreed-upon definition of what exactly 'academic language' is (Jensen & Thompson, 2020; Valdés, 2017; Valdés *et al.*, 2015). Wiley and Rolstad (2014) reject the idea that 'the ability to use academic English is a prerequisite for understanding academic content'. They argue:

> One sees the persistence of the idea that language itself is the gateway to greater cognitive development, and that the language of the literate somehow contributes special qualities which permit access and insight into academic disciplines which other forms of language do not allow…. Proficiency in academic language cannot be associated with universal cognitive thresholds; rather, literacy and academic success is associated with one's ability to accept the norms, practices, and expectations of school. It is simply not the case that literacy and academic language involve higher order cognition, while other domains in which we use specialized language do not. (Wiley & Rolstad, 2014: 51)

Wiley and Rolstad emphasize that, instead, the focus must be to 'engage students in interesting, challenging work which can then lead to the expansion of students' linguistic repertoires and their development of literacy, rather than the other way around' (Wiley & Rolstad, 2014: 51). MacSwan and Rolstad (2003) introduced the term **second language instructional competence** (SLIC) and suggested that the amount of SLIC needed to complete an academic task depends on the linguistic demand of that task. Thus, for example, an academic task such as discussing and giving examples of the five senses would have a lower linguistic demand than the academic task of reading a science text about how the five senses are inter-related and then writing a summary. Moore and Schleppegrell (2020) suggest use of the term 'disciplinary language' to draw attention to the different linguistic resources required for engagement with academic tasks in different subject areas.

From a raciolinguistics perspective, Flores (2020a, 2024) has proposed 'language architecture' as an alternative non-dichotomous framing of language. This framing 'takes as its point of entry the assumption that racialized students can already engage the types of complex linguistic practices desired by state standards but that their knowledge is being misrecognized because of the pervasiveness of raciolinguistic ideologies' (Flores, 2020a: 22). Under such framing, bilingual students engage in critical inquiry about their language use to become 'language architects' as they apply their new knowledge 'to design language in their own terms and for their own purposes' (Flores, 2016: 2). Flores argues that this approach shifts the deficit view to a positive view of language-minoritized students as 'gifted sociolinguists'. Seltzer (2019) provides a vivid example of this shift in her work helping New York high school students take a critical translingual approach to talk and write about their own language.

Jensen and Thompson (2020: 3–5), while acknowledging the differing perspectives and debates over academic language as described above, identify points of agreement. Based on these points of agreement, they offer four principles for ensuring equity when teachers are attempting to help their students develop 'academic language', however it may be defined and conceptualized in their particular institutions:

Principle 1: Understand how language is more than just vocabulary.
Principle 2: Recognize academic features in students' everyday talk.
Principle 3: Develop awareness of language and its contexts of use with students.
Principle 4: Foster critical language awareness.

Language Proficiency Standards

These current views of language learning and bilingualism are beginning to be reflected in the curriculum and put into practice through various language proficiency standards. The English language proficiency standards established by Teachers of English to Speakers of Other Languages (TESOL) in the first decade of the 2000s moved away from the ideas that conversational language is non-academic and reserved for the playground and also rejected the idea that all language use in the classroom is academic (TESOL, 2006). Furthermore, the TESOL standards moved away from the idea of a singular type of English language proficiency (e.g. CALP) that students either have or don't, that they must possess to achieve academically. Rather, the TESOL standards recognized that students communicate for social, intercultural and instructional purposes in a variety of contexts within the school setting. In addition, the

TESOL standards recognize that language use to 'communicate information, ideas, and concepts' is different across various content areas. Thus, TESOL has separate standards for the language of (1) language arts, (2) mathematics, (3) science and (4) social studies.

In the United States, the majority of states have joined the WIDA Consortium to share common English language proficiency standards, which are nearly identical to the TESOL standards. The WIDA Consortium (2012) 'amplified' the standards by developing materials and resources to help teachers put the standards into meaningful practice. The 2020 edition of the *WIDA English Language Development Standards Framework* 'added new and expanded resources to address updates in policy, theory and practice', with 'a commitment to drive equity for multilingual learners in curriculum, instruction, and assessment' (WIDA Consortium, 2020: 9).

A smaller group of states have joined the English Language Proficiency Assessment for the 21st Century (ELPA21) Consortium. Independent (non-consortium) states such as California and New York have established their own language development standards. Rather than taking a deficit view of what students cannot do because of limited skills in English, the **WIDA**, **ELPA21** and individual state standards focus on describing what students *can do* at each level of English proficiency. Thus, these standards represent a 'can do' philosophy. Through proficiency-level descriptors and other resources, teachers are given specific examples of academic tasks that students are capable of accomplishing across different levels of English language proficiency and grade levels, with proper scaffolding and support. Thus, the standards show that even students at the beginning levels of English proficiency are capable of academic work. More importantly, the standards help teachers identify the linguistic demands of a particular academic task (e.g. 'describe the life cycle of a plant'), determine what might be reasonable to expect of students at each level of English proficiency, and identify the scaffolding and support that students need to meet these expectations.

As an example, Table 8.1 shows the performance indicators for grades 2 and 3 from the English Language Proficiency (ELP) standards of the Council of Chief State School Officers (CCSSO, 2014), which are used by states in the ELPA21 Consortium.

Table 8.1 Example of proficiency-level descriptors from the CCSSO English Language Proficiency Standards (CCSO, 2014: 14)

By the end of each English language proficiency level, an ELL can...				
Level 1	Level 2	Level 3	Level 4	Level 5
use a very limited set of strategies to:	use an emerging set of strategies to:	use a developing set of strategies to:	use an increasing range of strategies to:	use a wide range of strategies to:
• identify a few key words and phrases from read-alouds, simple written texts and oral presentations	• identify some key words and phrases • identify the main topic or message/lesson from read-alouds, simple written texts and oral presentations	• identify the main topic or message • answer questions • retell some key details from read-alouds, simple written texts and oral presentations	• determine the main idea or message • identify or answer questions about some key details that support the main idea/message • retell a variety of stories from read-alouds, written texts and oral presentations	• determine the main idea or message • tell how key details support the main idea • retell a variety of stories from read-alouds, written texts and oral communications

The indicators are in connection with ELP Standard 1, 'An ELL can construct meaning from oral presentations and literary and informational text through grade appropriate listening, reading, and viewing'. Note that the task and expectations are modified based on students' English language proficiency. Nonetheless, students at all proficiency levels are expected to be able to engage in grade-appropriate academic tasks related to constructing meaning from texts and oral presentations.

WIDA's proficiency-level descriptors are organized in grade-level bands and aligned with content-area standards (i.e. language arts, mathematics, science and social studies) and more general communication for social and instructional purposes, with a focus on interpretive (listening, reading, viewing) and expressive (speaking, writing, representing) modes of communication. They address language use across different dimensions (i.e. **discourse**, sentence and word/phrase level), specific language functions and language expectations which make explicit the types of things students need to do with language in order to meet grade-level content standard expectations.

WIDA has established 10 guiding principles that inform their work (see Box 8.1). These principles provide a nice overview of the more current understandings of language development. Note that WIDA uses 'multilingual learners' broadly to refer 'to all children and youth who are, or have been, consistently exposed to multiple languages' and to 'students who speak varieties of English or indigenous languages' (WIDA Consortium, 2012: 1).

Box 8.1 WIDA guiding principles of language development

These updated Guiding Principles of Language Development and Learning exemplify WIDA's overarching and ever-present Can Do Philosophy.

1. Multilingual learners' languages and cultures are valuable resources to be leveraged for schooling and classroom life; leveraging these assets and challenging biases help develop multilingual learners' independence and encourage their agency in learning
2. Multilingual learners' development of multiple languages enhances their knowledge and cultural bases, their intellectual capacities, and their flexibility in language use
3. Multilingual learners' language development and learning occur over time through meaningful engagement in activities that are valued in their homes, schools and communities
4. Multilingual learners' language, social-emotional, and cognitive development are inter-related processes that contribute to their success in school and beyond
5. Multilingual learners use and develop language when opportunities for learning take into account their individual experiences, characteristics, abilities, and levels of language proficiency
6. Multilingual learners use and develop language through activities which intentionally integrate multiple modalities, including oral, written, visual, and kinesthetic modes of communication
7. Multilingual learners use and develop language to interpret and access information, ideas, and concepts from a variety of sources, including real-life objects, models, representations, and multimodal texts
8. Multilingual learners draw on their metacognitive, metalinguistic, and metacultural awareness to develop effectiveness in language use
9. Multilingual learners use their full linguistic repertoire, including translanguaging practices, to enrich their language development and learning
10. Multilingual learners use and develop language to interpret and present different perspectives, build awareness of relationships, and affirm their identities

© 2019 The Board of Regents of the University of Wisconsin System, on behalf of WIDA
Note: For the original document in multiple languages, an illustrated version the guiding principles, and academic references informing each principle, see https://wida.wisc.edu and search 'guiding principles' in the search bar.

Along with this new direction is a growing recognition that students can do highly 'academic' work in 'less than perfect English', through **translanguaging** (Corral & Sayer, 2024; Fu *et al.*, 2019; García, 2020; García & Li Wei, 2015; Henderson & Sayer, 2020; MacSwan, 2022a; Mendoza, 2023; Tian & King, 2023). In a study of a middle-school social studies classroom with linguistically diverse students, Bunch (2014) made an important observation as he focused on how students drew on a wide range of their linguistic resources as they engaged in academic tasks. As students worked in small groups to discuss and generate their ideas, their English was less than perfect and would fall into what teachers typically call 'conversational' or 'informal' language. However, as students prepared their presentation materials and presented their work to the class, their language use was more formal. Bunch calls this difference the *language of ideas* versus the *language of display*. He also found that the students were aware of the different **registers** and made strategic use of them for different purposes and audiences. Moore and Schleppegrell (2020), in their work with Arabic-speaking ELLs in upper elementary school grades, found that students were capable of critically analyzing ways authors present evidence in written science texts, offer their own points of views in oral science presentations and challenge each other's arguments. They argue that the students' disciplinary language practices, their engagement in critical language awareness and their ability to bring their own voices to learning 'transcends a generic understanding of academic language' (Moore & Schleppegrell, 2020: 99). Corral and Sayer (2024: 158), in their study of elementary school emergent bilingual students in Texas and Mexico, found that translanguaging pedagogy 'can transform the talk-for-learning in the classroom and create a *corriente* or flow of ideas that is more free and less constrained than traditional classroom interaction patterns'.

These language proficiency standards and ways of understanding students' language development and ability to use their emerging English and bilingual proficiency to engage in academic work have moved the field forward in a new and positive direction. Rather than taking a deficit view of what an individual student can't do because 'he only has BICS', the focus now shifts to 'What are the linguistic demands of this academic task, and what modifications and types of scaffolding would be needed to help students at different levels of English proficiency accomplish this task?' The performance indicators also form the basis for effective classroom assessments, providing teachers with a clear road map of where a student is at and what types of instruction can push them up to the 'next level' of English proficiency.

However, these standards are limited. Note that they focus only on the English language development of bilingual students. Also, they may create the impression that language development is linear, as students progress up through neatly defined stages. WIDA's guiding principles (Box 8.1) make it clear that it views students as multilingual learners. WIDA has also developed Spanish language proficiency standards and tools (called Marco DALE) to guide practice and assessment in bilingual classrooms. This is certainly very important and, as indicated above, space has opened up for translanguaging as students draw upon all of their linguistic resources. However, the existence of separate English and Spanish standards (and the absence of similar standards for other languages) demonstrates that we still need models to better understand bilingual development. One development in this area is Literacy Squared – a model that emphasizes the simultaneous development of literacy in two languages (Escamilla *et al.*, 2013). It also provides tools for planning and observing bilingual instruction and for evaluating the writing development of emergent bilinguals across their two languages (see Chapter 14).

Conclusion

Early and now discredited ideas of two languages within an individual are represented by two pictures: first, two languages as a balance; second, two languages operating as two separate balloons in the head. Such misconceptions were replaced by pictures such as the dual iceberg, illustrating a common underlying proficiency with easy **transfer** of concepts and knowledge between languages. Early theories of bilingualism and the curriculum suggested a dichotomous distinction between social and **academic language proficiency**, later elaborated into four quadrants emphasizing levels of context and cognitive demand. These early theories guided much policy and practice for bilingual students and drew attention to the need to consider students' language proficiency and to provide appropriate scaffolding. Several scholars became critical of these early theories, arguing they were oversimplified and misleading. Current understandings of language, language learning and the dynamic nature of bilingualism are moving the field toward standards and practices that recognize external factors that impact students' language learning. The focus is now on what students can do – even at beginning levels of English proficiency – to engage in academic tasks. We now recognize that language use varies across different content areas and recognize that students have a wide range of linguistic resources to draw on as they engage in academic work. New curricular and pedagogical models are developing that better reflect these current understandings.

Key Points in This Chapter

- The concept of the two languages acting like a balance in the brains of a bilingual is incorrect.
- The common underlying proficiency (CUP) model suggests that languages operate from the same central operating system.
- On average, English oral proficiency takes three to five years to develop, while English proficiency needed for academic success can take four to seven years. A variety of factors impact the amount of time it takes for students to reach 'proficiency' in English.
- Early theories suggested that bilingual students must reach a certain threshold of proficiency to attain the cognitive benefits of bilingualism, made a distinction between everyday context-embedded conversational language and decontextualized academic language, and argued that cognitive academic language proficiency is a prerequisite for academic success in school.
- These early theories have been highly criticized by a number of scholars as misleading and an oversimplification of the nature of language, the dynamic nature of bilingualism, and language learning.
- Current understandings of language emphasize that there is no single 'academic language' that students must attain in order to achieve academic success.

> - Alternatives to the problematic and ill-defined construct of 'academic language' include disciplinary language, second language instructional competence and language architecture.
> - English language proficiency standards (e.g. TESOL, WIDA, CCSSO and those of individual US states) now recognize that students use language for social, intercultural and academic purposes in school settings and that language use differs across various content areas.
> - With proper scaffolding and support, there is much that students can do at each level of English proficiency to engage in academic tasks.
> - Students are aware of different registers and make strategic use of their linguistic repertoires as they engage in the language of ideas and the language display.

Suggested Further Reading

- Cummins, J. (2021) *Rethinking the Education of Multilingual Learners: A Critical Analysis of Theoretical Concepts*. Multilingual Matters.
- MacSwan, J. (ed.) (2022) *Multilingual Perspectives on Translanguaging*. Multilingual Matters.
- Mendoza, A. (2023) *Translanguaging and English as a Lingua Franca in the Plurilingual Classroom*. Multilingual Matters.
- Tian, Z. and King, N. (eds) (2023) *Developing Translanguaging Repertoires in Critical Teacher Education*. De Gruyter Mouton.
- WIDA (2020) *WIDA English Language Development Standards Framework, 2020 Edition: Kindergarten – Grade 12*. Board of Regents of the University of Wisconsin System.

On the Web

- New York State Bilingual Common Core Initiative
  https://www.engageny.org/resource/new-york-state-bilingual-common-core-initiative
- TESOL Standards
  https://www.tesol.org/professional-development/publications-and-research/research-and-standards/standards/
- WIDA Consortium
  https://wida.wisc.edu
- The ELPA21 Assessment System
  https://www.elpa21.org/
- Stanford University Graduate School of Education, Center to Support Excellence in Teaching, Integrated language and content fundamentals for educators of multilingual students
  https://ul.stanford.edu

Discussion Questions

(1) Why do you think the balance and balloon pictures of bilingualism and cognition were held so intuitively by many people? Discuss how these theories, along with the contrasting dual iceberg picture, compare with the findings of cognitive research about bilingualism and the brain as presented in Chapter 7.
(2) Why is the construct of 'academic language' problematic? In what ways have you seen students use less than perfect English to successfully accomplish academic tasks?
(3) Some have argued that teachers need only the simple past theories of language because sophisticated and competing language, bilingualism and language learning theories are too complex to inform practice. How does such an argument view teachers? In what ways do you find the current understandings of language, bilingualism and language learning helpful in moving the field forward with more effective instructional practices?

Study Activities

(1) Observe a classroom with bilingual children. Make a 10-minute audio recording of the discourse between the teacher and various students, and/or between students themselves. Use the concepts and ideas of this chapter to describe and discuss the language used.
(2) Download and review some of the proficiency-level descriptors from WIDA, CCSSO or from an independent non-consortium state like California or New York. Describe how these descriptors provide evidence that students at the beginning levels of English proficiency are capable of using their developing language(s) to engage in grade-level academic tasks.
(3) Choose a grade-level academic task that you would want students to complete as part of a lesson plan. Using the English Proficiency Standards and associated resources from WIDA, CCSSO or independent non-consortium states as a guide, create a plan for how students at each level of English proficiency would engage in this task, including the scaffolds or supports students would need to complete the task.

CHAPTER 9

Historical Introduction to Bilingual Education in the United States

Introduction

A Short History of Bilingual Education in the United States
Before the 20th Century
The Earlier 20th Century
The Later 20th Century
Legislation and Lawsuits
Title VII Bilingual Education Act
Passages and Repeals of 'English for the Children' State Voter Initiatives
No Child Left Behind
Race to the Top
Common Core State Standards
ESEA Flexibility
Seal of Biliteracy
Every Student Succeeds Act
Other Federal Developments

Current Statistics

Explanations of Underachievement in Bilinguals

Conclusion

CHAPTER 9
Historical Introduction to Bilingual Education in the United States

Introduction

One of the illusions about **bilingual education** is that it is a recent phenomenon. The 20th century saw bilingual education blossom in publications and practice. The first books on bilingual education were by Sissons (1917) on Canada and Aucamp (1926) on South Africa. In the United States it may appear that bilingual education was born in the 1960s. The US dual language school approach is typically dated from 1963 (see Chapter 11). The Canadian bilingual education movement is often charted from an experimental kindergarten class set up in St Lambert, Montréal, in 1965. Earlier than that, bilingual education in Ireland is sometimes presented as a child of the Irish Free State of 1922. The story of bilingual education in Wales often starts in 1939, with the establishment of the first Welsh-medium elementary school. Coyle (2007) suggests that bilingual education was established in Europe in the 19th century, for example in Luxembourg in 1843, with **trilingual education** in 1913. But bilingual education started well before the 20th century.

The illusion of bilingual education as a modern phenomenon is dangerous on two counts. First, it fails to recognize that bilingual education has existed in one form or another for 5000 years or more (Mackey, 1978; Ostler, 2005). **Bilingualism** and **multilingualism** are 'a very early characteristic of human societies, and monolingualism a limitation induced by some forms of social change, cultural and ethnocentric developments' (Lewis, 1977: 22). Gramling (2016) argues that **monolingualism** was a sociopolitical invention. Second, there is a danger in isolating current bilingual education from its historical roots. In many countries (e.g. the United States, Canada, England and Sweden), bilingual education must be linked to the historical context of immigration as well as political movements such as civil rights, equality of educational opportunity, affirmative action and integrationist or **assimilationist** policies.

Bilingual education relates to debates about the fundamental purposes and aims of education in general: for individuals, communities, regions and nations. At its most basic definition, bilingual education may refer to where some, most or all the education is through two languages. However, as will be discussed in Chapter 10, bilingual education is a simplistic label for a complex phenomenon. Bilingual education is also just one component inside a wider social, economic, educational, cultural and political framework. The political context of bilingual education is considered in Chapters 17 and 18. The early history of bilingual education in the United States is first considered, with a particular emphasis on the dynamic and ever-developing nature of bilingual education policy. More recent history and current practice are contextualized within the broader context of US policies and programs for students classified as English language learners (ELLs) and other multilingual learners.

A Short History of Bilingual Education in the United States

In the United States, bilingual education has been determined partly by federal government, partly by state government, partly by litigation, partly by local initiatives and partly by individuals. There has been neither total centralization nor full devolution to states in bilingual education. While states engage in much planning and policymaking, the federal government has exerted a powerful influence through funding, legislation and law. Bilingual education in the United States has moved through constant changes in the perspectives of politicians, administrators and educationalists that indicate underlying shifts in **ideology**, preference and practice.

Before the 20th Century

Long before European immigrants arrived in the United States, the land contained many Native American **indigenous languages**, for example Tsalagi (Cherokee), Hopílavayi (Hopi), Kanien'kéha (Mohawk), Diné bizaad (Navajo) and Anishinaabemowin (Ojibwe). When the Italian, German, Dutch, French, Polish, Czech, Irish, Welsh and other immigrant groups arrived, there were already more than 300 indigenous languages in the United States. The indigenous languages were not immediately colonized. Often led by Jesuits and Franciscans, the Catholic Church sometimes taught through Spanish (also French and English) but often through a native language. Other missionaries (e.g. Dutch Reform, German Moravian) also instrumentally used indigenous languages to secure conversion to Christianity and for teaching (McCarty, 2004).

Immigrants brought with them a wide variety of languages and initially there was linguistic tolerance (McCarty, 2004). In the 18th and 19th centuries in the United States, up until World War I, linguistic diversity was often accepted and the presence of different languages was frequently encouraged through religion, newspapers in different languages and in both private and public schools.

There were exceptions to the acceptance of language diversity in this early period. An example is Benjamin Franklin's anti-German stance in the 1750s, despite the fact that he published the nation's first German-language newspaper in 1732. Other examples include the Californian legislature mandating English-only instruction in 1855 and the ruthless native-language suppression policies of the Bureau of Indian Affairs in the 1880s (Crawford, 2004).

The concepts of 'bilingualism' and 'language minorities' were not part of a major national consciousness about language in the 18th and 19th centuries. A high-profile and much-debated US language policy is a more recent phenomenon. However, there were early, pioneering public and private examples of bilingual education in the United States, such as the German–English schools in the mid-19th century (Wiley, 1998). Set up by German communities in Ohio, Pennsylvania, Missouri, Minnesota, North and South Dakota, Wisconsin and Texas, bilingual as well as **monolingual** German education was accepted. This was not just a 19th-century phenomenon, as German-speaking

Americans started schools using their **mother tongue** as early as 1694 in Philadelphia (Crawford, 2004). Also, Dutch, Danish, Norwegian, Swedish, Hungarian, Italian, Polish, Spanish, French, Russian and Czech were among the languages of instruction within ethnic-based and other schools in the 1800s and early 1900s (Kloss, 1998).

This openness to immigrant languages in the latter half of the 19th century was partly motivated by competition for students between public and private schools. Other factors such as benevolent (or uninterested) school administrators, the isolation of schools in rural areas and ethnic homogeneity within an area also enabled a permissive attitude to mother-tongue and bilingual education before World War I.

In most large cities in the latter half of the 19th century, English monolingual education was the dominant pattern. However, in cities such as Cincinnati, Baltimore, Denver and San Francisco, **dual language bilingual education** was present. In some schools in Cincinnati, for example, half the day was spent learning through German and in the other half the curriculum was delivered through English.

The Earlier 20th Century

At the turn of the 20th century, Italian and Jewish immigrants were mostly placed in English-medium mainstream schools. However, bilingual education was permitted. For example, some Polish immigrants in Chicago attended Catholic schools where a small amount of teaching was through the mother tongue. So long as policy was within the jurisdiction of local towns and districts, the language of instruction did not become an issue.

In the first two decades of the 20th century, a change in attitude to bilingualism and bilingual education occurred in the United States. A variety of factors are linked to this change and a subsequent restriction of bilingual education.

- The number of immigrants increased dramatically around the turn of the 20th century. Classrooms in many public schools were filled with immigrants. This gave rise to fear of new foreigners and a call for the integration, harmonization and **assimilation** of immigrants. Immigrants' lack of English language and English literacy was a source of social, political and economic concern. A demand for Americanization was made, with competence in English becoming associated with loyalty to the United States. The Nationality Act of 1906 required immigrants to speak English to become naturalized Americans. The call for child literacy in English rather than child labor, socialization into a unified America rather than ethnic separation, along with increased centralized control, led to a belief in a common language for compulsory schooling.
- In 1919, the Americanization Department of the United States Bureau of Education adopted a resolution recommending that all private and public education in each state be conducted in the English language. By 1923, 34 states had decreed that English must be the sole language of instruction in all elementary schools, public and private.
- A major influence on bilingual education came with the entry of the United States into World War I in 1917. Anti-German feelings in the United States spread, with a consequent extra pressure for English monolingualism and an assimilationist policy achieved through monolingual education (Wiley, 1998). The German language was portrayed as a threat to the unity of Americanization. Linguistic diversity was replaced by linguistic intolerance. Schools became the tool for the socialization,

assimilation and integration of diverse languages and **cultures**. Becoming an American meant the elimination of languages and cultures other than English from schools. An interest in learning foreign languages declined.

This period was not totally restrictive (Wiley, 2013a). In 1923, the US Supreme Court declared that a Nebraska state law prohibiting the teaching of foreign languages to children in private language classes was unconstitutional under the Fourteenth Amendment (no state shall 'deprive any person of life, liberty, or property, without due process of law; nor deny to any person within its jurisdiction the equal protection of the laws'). This case, known as *Meyer v. Nebraska*, concerned a teacher at a private elementary school facing a charge for teaching a Bible story in German to 10-year-old children outside of regular school hours. The original Nebraska ruling was that such mother-tongue teaching cultivated ideas and attachments that were foreign to the best interests of the United States. The US Supreme Court, in overturning the Nebraska ruling, found that proficiency in a foreign language was 'not injurious to the health, morals, or understanding of the ordinary child'. A similar case, *Farrington v. Tokushige*, reached the US Supreme Court in 1927; the court ruled that attempts by Hawaiian education authorities to put restrictions on after-school community-based Japanese and Chinese **heritage language** programs was unconstitutional (Del Valle, 2003).

These Supreme Court findings did not, in essence, support bilingualism or bilingual education. Rather, the court upheld the right of state governments to dictate the language of instruction in schools, but declared that states cannot prevent private language instruction outside of the regular school system. The Court observed in *Meyer v. Nebraska* that the desire of a state legislature to foster a homogeneous people was 'easy to appreciate'.

The Later 20th Century

In 1957, the Russians launched their Sputnik satellite into space. For US politicians and the public, a period of soul-searching led to debates about the quality of education, scientific creativity and competence to compete in an increasingly international world. Doubts arose about the hitherto over-riding concern with English as the melting-pot language, and a new consciousness was aroused about the need for foreign language instruction. In 1958, the National Defense Education Act was passed, promoting foreign language learning in elementary schools, high schools and universities. This, in turn, helped to create a slightly more soul-searching attitude to languages other than English spoken among ethnic groups in the United States.

In the 1960s, various other factors allowed a few opportunities to bring back bilingual education, albeit in a disparate, semi-isolated manner. This needs to be understood in the wider perspective of the civil rights movement, the struggle for the rights of African-Americans and the call to establish general equality of opportunity (and equality of educational opportunity) for all people, irrespective of race, color or creed. The 1964 Civil Rights Act prohibited discrimination on the basis of color, race or national origin, and led to the establishment of the Office of Civil Rights. This Act symbolized a less negative attitude to ethnic groups and possibilities for increased tolerance of ethnic languages, at least at the federal level.

The restoration of bilingual education in the United States in the second half of the 20th century is often regarded as starting in 1963, in one school in Florida. In that year,

Cuban exiles established the first modern dual language school (Coral Way Elementary School) in Dade County in South Florida (Coady, 2020). Believing they were in exile only for a short period, the educated, middle-class Cubans set up this Spanish–English bilingual school. The need to maintain their mother tongue of Spanish was aided by (1) highly trained professional teachers being ready to work in such schools, (2) the Cubans' plight as victims of a harsh Communist state and (3) their expected temporary stay in the United States. Their unquestioned loyalty to US policies and democratic politics gained sympathy for the Cubans. Bilingual education in Dade County received both political support and funding. While Coral Way gained the most attention, there were other bilingual programs in the United States during this period. In the mid-1960s the National Education Association (NEA) held a meeting and issued a subsequent report on the dire educational needs of Mexican-American students, and called for legislation supporting bilingual education (National Education Association, 1966). To make its case, the Association conducted a survey documenting innovative school programs making use of Spanish in Texas (El Paso and Laredo), New Mexico (Albuquerque and Pecos), California (Merced), Colorado (Pueblo) and Arizona (Tucson). While the re-establishment of bilingual schools in the United States has benefited from the example and success of Coral Way and other schools, an understanding of bilingual education in the United States requires a grasp of legislation and lawsuits.

Legislation and Lawsuits

In 1967, one year after the NEA report, Texas Senator Ralph Yarborough introduced a **Bilingual Education Act** as an amendment of the 1965 Elementary and Secondary Education Act (ESEA). The legislation was originally conceptualized to help mother-tongue Spanish-speakers who were seen as failing in the school system, but ultimately was expanded to include all students for whom English was not their native language. Enacted in 1968 as Title VII of the ESEA, the Bilingual Education Act (BEA) indicated that bilingual education programs were to be seen as part of federal educational policy (Moore, 2021; Wiese & Garcia, 2001). It authorized the use of federal funds for the education of speakers of languages other than English. It also undermined the English-only legislation still in place in many states. The 1968 BEA allocated funds for such minoritized language speakers while they shifted to working through English in the classroom. After 1968, the BEA was re-authorized as part of the ESEA in 1974, 1978, 1984, 1988 and 1994 (for details see San Miguel, 2004).

A landmark in US bilingual education was *Lau v. Nichols*. A court case was brought on behalf of Chinese-speaking students against the San Francisco School District in 1970 (Morita-Mullaney, 2024b). The case concerned whether or not non-English-speaking students received equal educational opportunities when instructed in a language they could not understand (Wiley, 2013a). The failure to provide a program that adequately addressed the students' linguistic needs was alleged to violate both the equal protection clause of the 14th Amendment and Title VI of the Civil Rights Act of 1964. The case was rejected by the federal district court and a court of appeals but was accepted by the US Supreme Court in 1974. The verdict outlawed English mainstreaming (often called '**submersion**') programs for students who were not yet proficient in English. The US Supreme Court ruled that 'There is no equality of treatment merely by providing students with the same facilities, textbooks, teachers, and curriculum; for students who do not understand English are effectively foreclosed from any meaningful education'.

Following the ruling, the Office of Civil Rights issued a set of guidelines for school districts called the **Lau remedies**. These remedies acknowledged that students not proficient in English need help. Such remedies included classes in **English as a second language**, English tutoring and some form of bilingual education. The Lau remedies created some expansion in the use of minoritized languages in schools. However, the accent nationally was still on a temporary, transitional use of the home language for **English language learners**.

The *Lau* case is symbolic of the dynamic and continuing contest to establish language rights in the United States, particularly through testing the law in the courtroom. However, the kind of bilingual education needed to achieve equality of educational opportunity for **language minoritized students** was not defined. Although the right to equal opportunity for language minorities was asserted, the means of achieving that right was not declared. Nevertheless, during this era there was a modest growth in developmental maintenance bilingual education (see Chapters 10 and 11) and ethnic community mother-tongue schools (Fishman, 2006).

From the 1980s, there were moves against an emergence of a strong version of bilingual education in the United States, particularly found in the rise of pressure groups such as English First and US English that sought to establish English monolingualism and cultural assimilation (consideration of such political movements is found in Chapter 18). For several decades in the United States, bilingual education has been contentious, as will be illustrated by examining legislative changes during this period. However, as will be noted below, the United States appears to be entering a period of more general acceptance for some forms of bilingual education.

Title VII Bilingual Education Act

We return to the 1968 Title VII Bilingual Education Act. This provided a compensatory 'poverty program' for the educationally disadvantaged among language minorities. The original version lacked a definition of bilingual education and did not require schools to use a child's home language other than English. However, it did allow a few schools to bring students' home languages into the classroom rather than exclude them. In the 1974 ESEA re-authorization, Title VII provided clearer definitions of bilingual education and required schools receiving grants to include teaching in a student's home language so as to allow the child to progress effectively through the educational system (Wiese & Garcia, 2001). Effective progress in student achievement could occur via the home language or via English. However, this gave rise to fierce debates about how much a student's home language should be used in school. Some argued that it was essential to develop a child's speaking and literacy skills in their home language before English was introduced in a major way. Others argued that educational equality of opportunity could best be realized by teaching English as early as possible and assimilating language minoritized children into mainstream culture. The 1974 re-authorization stressed **transitional bilingual education** (see Chapter 10) over maintenance bilingual education programs and did not allow **dual language programs** (see Chapter 11).

In 1978, the US Congress again re-authorized the ESEA. The 1978 version lifted the restrictions on dual language programs under Title VII, but the political climate still favored transitional bilingual education in which the home language was to be used only to the extent necessary for a child to achieve competence in the English language. The 1984 and 1988 re-authorizations of the ESEA allowed support for more developmental and maintenance program models under Title VII, but also increasing percentages of Title VII funds were made available specifically for alternative programs where only English was used (Wiese & Garcia, 2001).

The Reagan administration was generally hostile to bilingual education. In the *New York Times* on March 3, 1981, President Reagan is quoted as saying that 'It is absolutely wrong and against the American concept to have a bilingual education program that is now openly, admittedly, dedicated to preserving their native language and never getting them adequate in English so they can go out into the job market'. Reagan believed that preservation of the native language meant neglect of English language acquisition. Bilingual education programs were seen as serving to neglect English **language competence** in students. Reagan dismissed bilingual education in favor of mainstreaming/submersion and transitional programs.

The Lau remedies were weakened by the Reagan administration to give local politicians more flexibility to create their own policies. Further changes in the rights to bilingual education in the United States are listed in Table 9.1 below (p. 210). This reveals that legislation and litigation mostly led to 'weak' forms of bilingual education (e.g. transitional bilingual education). During the presidencies of both Reagan and George H.W. Bush, the accent was more on mainstreaming/submersion and transitional bilingual education. The right to early education through a minoritized language failed to blossom in those years (Crawford, 2004).

In the early 1990s, the election of Bill Clinton as President brought some hope, as he 'had campaigned in support of bilingual education and promised to strengthen it' (San Miguel, 2004: 79). In 1994, the 103rd Congress undertook a major reform of education through legislation entitled Goals 2000: Educate America Act. The ESEA was re-authorized in 1994 as the Improving America's Schools Act (IASA). This extensive reform included an acknowledgment that students for whom English was a second language ('limited English proficient' or LEP students) should be expected to achieve high academic standards. The legislation aimed to provide children with an enriched educational program, improving instructional strategies and making the curriculum more challenging. Title VII strengthened the state role by requiring state educational authorities to review Title VII appropriations and provide additional funds for specific groups such as immigrants (Wiese & Garcia, 2001). Thus, the 1994 re-authorization continued limited federal support for bilingual education programs. The issue about bilingual education moved partly from being narrowly focused on the language of instruction to a broader range of questions being asked about the quality and standards of education for **language minoritized students**. The Clinton administration tended to a more 'language as a resource' stance (see Chapter 18) but also tended to lessen federal influence on bilingual education (Crawford, 2004).

Opponents of bilingual education in the United States do not generally oppose foreign language programs for English-speakers. Such programs are regarded as important in educating students for the global economy and are seen to be of value for US economic prosperity. The National Education Goals Panel (1999) called for a substantial increase in the percentage of students who are competent in more than one language. The 1994 revisions to Title VII of the ESEA meant that proficient bilingualism became a desirable goal when it brought economic benefits to individuals and particularly to the nation. Hence the revisions resulted in funding for a larger number of dual language programs.

However, the 1994 re-authorization of Title VII came under attack from both politicians and the US press. Congress considered legislation to repeal the law and eliminate its funding. While this did not succeed, it nevertheless pointed to many politicians and much of the mass media being against bilingual education. Title VII appropriations were reduced by 38% between 1994 and 1996, and a proportion of Title VII funds were reserved for English-only approaches. This led to cuts in bilingual programs and in teacher training, and reduced the budgets for research, evaluation and support.

Passages and Repeals of 'English for the Children' State Voter Initiatives

Between 1978 and 2000, the number of English language learners (ELLs) in California rose from approximately 250,000 to 1.4 million, with significant populations of speakers of Spanish, Vietnamese, Hmong, Cantonese, Tagalog, Khmer, Korean, Armenian, Mandarin, Russian, Ukrainian, Serbo-Croatian, Urdu, Hindi, Punjabi and other languages. With a multilingual population, California had become a state where bilingual education had blossomed.

In early 1996, the *Los Angeles Times* gave extensive coverage to the political activism of a small group of Spanish-speaking parents pulling their children out of the Ninth Street Elementary School. Ron Unz, a Silicon Valley businessman, saw this as his political opportunity after his failed attempts to get elected to political office. Based on a personal philosophy of assimilation, he criticized bilingual education and made false and misleading claims about the supposed educational ineffectiveness of bilingual schools in California (Ovando, 2003). The press added heat to the debate with mostly one-sided, personality-based, controversy-cultivating reports (Crawford, 2004).

California's **Proposition 227** – the 'English for the Children' initiative – was presented in 1998 as an effort to improve English language instruction for children who needed to learn English for economic and employment opportunities. It aimed to outlaw bilingual education in that state. 'Therefore', said the text of Proposition 227, 'it is resolved that: all children in California public schools shall be taught English as rapidly and effectively as possible' and such children 'shall be taught English by being taught in English'. Bilingual education programs were greatly restricted and required ambiguous waiver provisions of the law to be met; sheltered (or structured) English-immersion programs were put in their place (Crawford, 2004; Quezada *et al.*, 1999/2000).

Proposition 227 was approved by voters on June 2, 1998, by a margin of 61% to 39%. Analysis of the voting and subsequent surveys found that many Latinx were clearly against the Proposition; nevertheless, bilingual education had become virtually illegal. With the sweet scent of victory in California, Unz proceeded elsewhere across the United States with successful **'English for the Children' initiatives** in Arizona (**Proposition 203**, passed by a 63% vote in 2000) and Massachusetts (**Question 2**, passed by a 68% vote in 2002). In these two states the waiver provisions were more stringent, parental choices were more severely limited and penalties for non-compliance increased, including the threat of personal lawsuits. However, Unz was soundly defeated in Colorado (44% vote) in 2002 thanks to a politically savvy campaign supported by a billionaire businesswoman, Pat Stryker, whose daughter was in a dual language program (Escamilla *et al.*, 2003; for a critical view of the campaign see Crawford, 2004).

Despite provision for parental waivers, the number of students in Californian bilingual education programs fell from 498,879 in 1997 to 167,163 in 2000 (Valdés *et al.*, 2006) and to around 141,000 (9% of ELLs) in 2002 (Crawford, 2004). There were also substantial reductions in bilingual programs in Massachusetts (de Jong *et al.*, 2005) and near elimination in Arizona (Wright & Choi, 2006). Wiley and Wright (2004) indicate variations in the extent to which parents were informed of their right to waivers from English-only programs, and the continuation of some quality bilingual programs.

There is little evidence that Proposition 227 led to faster English language learning or higher rates of academic achievement (Bali, 2001; Crawford, 2004; Gándara et al., 2000; Parrish et al., 2002; Rumberger et al., 2003; Thompson et al., 2002; Valdés, 2006; Wiley & Wright, 2004; Wright, 2004). A five-year evaluation of the effects of the implementation of Proposition 227, commissioned by the state of California, concluded that there was no evidence to support the argument that the English-only programs mandated by Proposition 227 were superior to bilingual education models (American Institutes for Research & WestEd, 2006). Research in Arizona similarly found that there was no evidence that Proposition 203 had resulted in higher academic achievement (Wright & Pu, 2005) or greater increases in English proficiency among ELL students (Mahoney et al., 2005; Moore, 2014). In fact, by 2018 less than half of Arizona ELL students were graduating from high school – a rate 30% below the general student population in the state (*Language Magazine*, 2020).

Despite the passage of the 'English for the Children' initiatives, bilingual programs continued in California, Arizona and Massachusetts and other states. Loopholes, waiver provisions and various degrees of interpretations and implementation of the law by different state superintendents of public instruction enabled many existing bilingual programs to survive or even expand, and many new ones to be established. Bilingual education survived because, when properly implemented, it works, and because many parents want their children to be bilingual. It is important to note that many of the surviving and new programs have been dual language immersion programs, which are particularly popular among language majority parents and thus attract greater political support.

Recognition of the failure of English-only instruction to improve education for ELL students, the growing popularity of dual immersion programs and greater societal recognition of the value of multilingualism in the 21st century have resulted in efforts to overturn the restrictions on bilingual education. In 2014 California Senator Ricardo Lara drafted Senate Bill 1174 to give Californians the opportunity to repeal Proposition 227. The approved bill was placed on the November 2016 ballot as **Proposition 58** under the title 'English Proficiency. Multilingual Education'. The official voter guide indicated that the Proposition 'Preserves the requirement that public schools ensure students be proficient in English' but also 'authorizes schools districts to establish dual language immersion programs for both native and non-native English speakers'. Other points indicated parental and community input on language acquisition programs and the rights of parents to 'select an available language acquisition program that best suits their child'. Proposition 58 passed on November 8, 2016, by a wide margin, with 72% voter approval. Less than two years later, the California State Department of Education (2018) unveiled a plan titled *Global California 2030*, which outlines ambitious goals for 'the path to a multilingual California', including increasing the number of dual immersion schools from 407 (2017 school year) to 1,600 by 2030.

In Massachusetts, Question 2 was repealed on November 22, 2017, when the governor signed Bill H.4032, 'An Act relative to language opportunity for our kids (LOOK)' (Massachusetts Language Opportunity Coalition, 2017). Under the **LOOK Act**, Massachusetts school districts now have the flexibility to provide bilingual education programs (Massachusetts Department of Elementary and Secondary Education, 2018).

In Arizona, bipartisan efforts began in 2019 to repeal Proposition 203 (*Language Magazine*, 2020). While these efforts failed to place a measure on the November 2020 ballot, the Arizona legislature did pass Senate Bill (SB) 1014 in 2019 which loosened some of the restrictions of Proposition 203 on bilingual education and removed Arizona's prior mandates of a rigid four-hour structured English immersion (SEI) model for students classified as ELLs (Williams, 2023). SB 1014 gave school districts much greater flexibility in offering more innovative instruction models that are supported by research, including dual language bilingual education (DLBE) programs. Despite the broad bipartisan support from state leaders, including the Governor, the State Board of Education, the Attorney General and members of state legislature, stark opposition has been mounted by the Arizona's Superintendent of Public Instruction, Tom Horne, who was elected in November 2022. Horne had previously served two terms in the same office, from 2003 to 2011, during which time he made strict enforcement of Proposition 203 and 'ending bilingual education' his top priorities. To date, his legal efforts to force school districts to end their DLBE programs have failed, with courts finding that he lacks the authority to mandate such program closures given that that power rests with the State Board of Education. The courts also found that Horne lacks the legal standing to bring lawsuits against the targeted school districts (Gomez, 2024). He is now attempting to recruit private citizens with the legal standing to file lawsuits against the school districts, with his spouse acting as their lawyer (Fischer, 2024). In the meantime, Arizona's DLBE programs continue to operate under the affordances of SB 1014 with full support of the State Board of Education and other state political leaders.

Box 9.1 Defending and promoting bilingual education

The attempted outlawing of bilingual education in California, Arizona and Massachusetts, and the recent successes and current efforts to repeal such legislation, indicate important considerations in its defense and promotion.

- There is a need to disseminate research findings on bilingual education, not just to teachers but also to parents and the public. The public image of bilingual education needs to be based on fact rather than fiction, on evidence rather than on prejudice.
- Bilingual education is not simply about provision, practice and pedagogy but is unavoidably about politics. To survive and thrive, bilingual education needs to demonstrate it works for the national interest in helping students attain proficiency in English and in producing the bilingual citizens any country needs.
- Secure evidence is needed, not just from individual case studies, studies of outstanding schools or examples of effective practice. In a culture of high-stakes testing, standards and accountability, raising the achievement of all students in all schools is needed. Bilingual education needs to provide evidence for high standards, high achievements and those outputs and outcomes of schooling that parents, the public and politicians regard as important. This includes helping children acquire a thorough competence in English and another language. Such outcomes go beyond language to other curriculum areas (e.g. mathematics, science), affective outcomes (e.g. self-esteem) and employment and vocational success.

Evidence is not enough. There is a propaganda battle that goes beyond the dissemination of research. The media (e.g. newspapers, magazines, television, online news sites) are influential and can be utilized to support bilingual education. McQuillan and Tse (1996) found that in the period 1984–94, 82% of research studies reported favorably on the effectiveness of bilingual education. However, only 45% of newspaper articles in the United States took a similarly favorable position on bilingual education. Less than half of all newspaper articles made any mention of research findings, while nearly a third of such articles relied on personal or anecdotal accounts. This implies that research findings need to become more accessible as well as being disseminated through influential mass media channels. Promotion and marketing of research and reviews may be necessary in such a politicized climate, targeted at policymakers and politicians, parents and the press. The alternative is that prejudice and ignorance will be dominant.

No Child Left Behind

No Child Left Behind (NCLB) was approved on December 13, 2001, by an overwhelming vote of 381 to 41 in the House of Representatives. President George W. Bush signed it into law on January 8, 2002. It re-authorized the ESEA and remained in effect for over a decade – several years past its expected re-authorization date. NCLB was radical in its requirements for the treatment of students classified as ELLs. The Title VII Bilingual Education Act was eliminated; ELL issues were addressed under Title III, 'Language Instruction for Limited English Proficient and Immigrant Students'.

NCLB's use of the term **limited English proficient (LEP)** brought back a deficit view of students, focusing on what they lack (English) rather than on focusing on who they are (multilingual learners) and what they are actively doing (learning English and other languages). 'Bilingual' as a term was silenced. For example, the Office of Bilingual Education and Language Minority Affairs was renamed the Office of English Language Acquisition. NCLB had a narrow focus on **English language development**.

States were required to ensure students are taught by 'highly qualified teachers'; however, no criteria were outlined for teachers of ELL-classified students. Also, NCLB eliminated the direct encouragement of and specific funding for bilingual education (with the exception of some program support for Indian, native Hawaiian and native Alaskan education). Bilingual programs were still allowed, but it was up to each state to determine what program models would be eligible for federal funding. NCLB only required that supported approaches be 'scientifically based'. However, as Wiley and Wright (2004) found in the case of Arizona, the Superintendent of Public Instruction at the time touted a single highly flawed study by Guzman (2002) as 'scientific' evidence that bilingual education is ineffective. The following chapters carefully examine the scientific research. Suffice to say at this point that the research evidence supports 'strong' forms of bilingual education. These forms appear, paradoxically, to have been discouraged by NCLB.

NCLB held states, districts, schools and teachers accountable for the academic performance and English language development of 'LEP' students. The requirements included the following: (1) establish academic standards for content areas and English language development; (2) assess LEP students annually on their progress in learning English and attaining proficiency; (3) test all students annually in grades 3–8 and high school on their attainment of reading and mathematics standards (plus science at selected grade levels); (4) ensure that students in different subgroups (race/ethnicity, **special education** and LEP) make adequate yearly progress (AYP) toward the ultimate goal of 100% of students passing state standards-based tests by 2014; (5) ensure that LEP students make AYP in learning English and attaining English proficiency; and (6) implement a system of increasingly severe sanctions for schools and/or districts with subgroups of students who fail to make AYP two or more years in a row.

Originally, NCLB did not allow the exclusion of newcomer ELL students from state tests. After much protest from states, two allowances were added for students who have been in the country less than one year: (1) they could be excluded from the state reading test and (2) they were required to take the state math test but their scores could be excluded from school-wide AYP calculations (Wright, 2005a). NCLB also called for ELLs to be tested in a valid and reliable manner using 'reasonable' accommodations. Unfortunately, these were not specified in the law, and research on **testing accommodations** (see Chapter 15) for ELL students remains sparse and insufficient to inform practice (Francis *et al.*, 2006; Rivera & Collum, 2006; Wright, 2025; Yang, 2020).

While bilingual education programs still qualified for funding if states allowed it, the federal legislation functioned in a manner that encouraged English-only instruction due to its heavy influence of high-stakes assessment (see Chapter 15). There is almost no more powerful way to transform a curriculum than via compulsory and focused large-scale standardized testing. Despite limited allowances for **testing** in languages other than English for the first few years if 'practicable', most states provided exams only in English, and even in those states with non-English tests the vast majority of ELL-classified students took state exams in English.

Such testing placed pressure on teachers to ensure the rapid learning of test-driven content-area and English language skills to avoid sanctions. Each state was required to establish a timeline with gradually increasing annual goals (pass rates) to ensure AYP toward the mandate of 100% pass rates by 2014. Schools that did not meet annual performance targets for each subgroup were labeled 'failing schools'. Such subgroups included major ethnic groups and 'LEP' students.

Where there is assessment failure, then the blame is likely to be placed (often unfairly) on the school and on the teacher (and not the system, e.g. lack of support for a child's bilingualism). Underachievement on tests is therefore seen as an education management problem, not a societal issue (see Chapter 15). A narrow focus on preparing students for **high-stakes testing** may lead to higher test scores; this is different from actually improving the quality of teaching and learning (Menken, 2017). Wiley and Wright (2004) noted several negative outcomes: increased drop-out rates, less time for curriculum areas other than mathematics and English, failure to rectify human and material resource inequalities between schools, measurement of an unstable and inconsistently defined LEP subgroup producing inaccurate results, and the loss of fluent bilingual teachers and native-speaker aides as insufficiently qualified.

The ESEA was due for re-authorization in 2007. However, the US Congress failed to take any action on the federal education law until 2015 (see below). This left the requirements of NCLB in place for an additional eight years, despite growing dissatisfaction and wide bipartisan recognition of the law's flaws, unrealistic expectations and failures.

Race to the Top

Barack Obama was elected 44th President of the United States in November 2008. During the presidential election campaign, education took a backseat in the debate over other major national issues. Nonetheless, Obama occasionally acknowledged problems with NCLB and its heavy emphasis on testing, and the need for education reform. He also spoke in favor of bilingual education. Given the failure of Congress to re-authorize the ESEA, Obama began his own initiatives for major educational reform through his American Recovery and Reinvestment Act (ARRA) of 2009, designed to help the country recover from economic crisis. The Recovery Act included over $44 billion in stimulus funding for education, as Obama believed that improving education was central to rebuilding the US economy. Over $10 billion was reserved for Title I schools, and funds were used to raise standards, improve teacher quality and turn around struggling schools.

In July 2009 President Obama announced a new program as part of the Recovery Act called Race to the Top (RTTT), with $4.3 billion in competitive grants for states to pursue education reform. The administration outlined four general requirements for states to qualify for stimulus funding and RTTT grants: (1) adopt internationally benchmarked standards that prepare students for success in college and the workplace ('college and career readiness standards') and high-quality assessments that are valid and reliable for all students, including ELLs and students with disabilities; (2) recruit, develop, reward and retain effective teachers and principals; (3) increase transparency by building data systems that measure student success and inform teachers and principals how they can improve their practices; and (4) support effective intervention strategies to turn around the lowest-performing schools. Advocates for ELLs were disheartened that these reforms still centered on high-stakes testing, and were especially alarmed at requirements that teacher evaluations be tied directly to student test performance. Ultimately, 11 states plus the District of Columbia were awarded RTTT grants. More importantly, RTTT set the national agenda for further reforms and relief from NCLB mandates, as will be seen below.

Common Core State Standards

Soon after the Obama administration began its education reform efforts, a major state-led initiative emerged to develop college and career readiness standards in English language arts and math that would be shared across participating states. The development of the Common Core State Standards (CCSS) was completed in 2010 through the leadership of the National Governors Association and the Council of Chief State School Officers (CCSSO). By 2016, a total of 42 states, the District of Columbia, four territories and the Department of Defense Education Activity (DoDEA) had adopted the standards. Two state consortia were formed to develop 'next-generation' computer-based exams to measure the CCSS – the Partnership for Assessment of Readiness for College and Careers (PARCC) and the Smarter Balanced Assessment Consortium. Common Core states were free to join one of these testing consortia or to develop their own state assessments to measure the CCSS. These new Common Core standards and assessments still met the mandates for NCLB, but also made states eligible for RTTT and other federal initiatives (see below).

The period of rapid and widespread adoption of the Common Core was followed by a substantial political backlash. Many educators and ELL advocates were concerned about the continuing focus on accountability through high-stakes testing. Neither PARCC nor the Smarter Balanced Assessment Consortium developed exams in Spanish or other languages, raising concerns that teachers would be under pressure to prepare ELL students for English-only exams, further discouraging bilingual education programs. However, most of the backlash against the Common Core came from conservatives. They viewed it as pseudo-national standards and testing and thus an intrusion on state rights. While the Common Core was technically a voluntary 'state-led' initiative, it was neatly aligned with the Obama administration's reform agenda. The US Department of Education provided grants to PARCC and the Smarter Balanced Assessment Consortium to develop its assessments, and other reform efforts encouraged the adoption of the Common Core (see below). Some critics took to calling the Common Core 'Obama Core'. By 2020 most states had withdrawn from the Common Core and from the two testing consortia. However, much of the content of the original Common Core standards have been incorporated in each state's language arts and mathematics standards.

ESEA Flexibility

The Obama administration made an unprecedented move in 2011 to offer states waivers from some of the accountability mandates of NCLB under a program called

ESEA Flexibility. This move stemmed from: (1) the continuing failure of Congress to re-authorize the ESEA, (2) a growing number of states, districts and schools failing to meet increasingly unrealistic AYP targets, (3) an unattainable mandate for 100% test pass rates just a few years away and (4) few defenders of NCLB remaining. To qualify, states were required to create their own alternative testing and accountability plans aligned with key principles reflective of the administration's RTTT program: (1) adopt college and career readiness standards for all students; (2) adopt **English language proficiency** (ELP) standards that correspond to the college- and career-readiness standards; (3) adopt 'next-generation' assessments to measure these standards; and (4) develop a rigorous administrator and teacher evaluation system, including the requirement to consider student test scores as part of the evaluation (US Department of Education, 2012). ESEA Flexibility proved to be very popular and by 2015 nearly all states had approved plans.

To meet these principles, states had the option of adopting the CCSS or developing their own college- and career-readiness standards. Those that adopted the Common Core had the option of joining the PARCC or Smarter Balanced Assessment consortia or developing their own assessments. States also had the option of developing their own ELP standards and assessments, or join WIDA, a state consortium with shared ELP standards and assessments that met the federal criteria (see https://wida.wisc.edu). As of 2024, 37 states, plus the District of Columbia, the US Virgin Islands and the Northern Mariana Islands, and schools associated with two federal agencies (Bureau of Indian Affairs and the Department of Defense Education Activity) had joined WIDA. Seven states belong to smaller state consortia called English Proficiency Assessment for the 21st Century (ELPA21) (see https://www.elpa21.org). Six states remain independent and use their own ELP standards and assessments.

A major concern was that many state plans eliminated tracking the achievement of ELLs as a separate subgroup and simply lumped them along with other 'at-risk' students into one large 'super-subgroup'. States would then require schools to focus on students within the lowest quartile of performance on state achievement tests. Morita-Mullaney and Singh (2019) call the ESEA flexibility waivers a 'language blind' policy, given that the unique linguistic and academic needs of ELLs would be buried within the super-subgroup. Also, the language needs of ELLs in the other three quartiles would potentially be ignored. However, ESEA Flexibility did not waive Title III requirements that held districts and states accountable for increases in and attainment of English proficiency.

Seal of Biliteracy

A concurrent but separate initiative from the above education reform efforts began in California in 2011. Under the leadership of the nonprofit advocacy group Californians Together, legislation was passed to recognize the bilingual skills of graduating high school seniors with a **Seal of Biliteracy** attached to their high school diploma (Olsen, 2020). By 2017, 46,952 California students had earned the Seal (California State Department of Education, 2018). The Seal of Biliteracy quickly went national, including support from the National Association for Bilingual Education (NABE) and the American Council of Teachers of Foreign Languages (ACTFL). As described on the initiative's website:

> The Seal of Biliteracy is an award given by a school, school district, county office of education or state in recognition of students who have studied and attained proficiency

in two or more languages by high school graduation. The Seal of Biliteracy takes the form of a gold seal that appears on the transcript or diploma of the graduating senior and is a statement of accomplishment for future employers and for college admissions. In addition to the Seal of Biliteracy that marks attainment of high level mastery of two or more languages, schools and districts are also instituting Bilingual Pathway Awards, recognizing significant steps towards developing biliteracy along a student's trajectory from preschool into high school. (https://sealofbiliteracy.org/faq)

By 2024, all 50 states plus the District of Columbia had approved a State Seal.

While requirements and types of Seals may vary across states, districts and schools, in general, (former) ELL students can demonstrate their bilingual skills by reaching the proficiency level on state English language proficiency exams and by passing their state's English language arts exam (Davin, 2020; Heineke, 2020). Native English-speakers and **heritage language** speakers can demonstrate their proficiency through completion of advanced levels of heritage language and world languages courses and/or by predetermined scores on language proficiency tests, such as Advanced Placement (AP) exams in world languages.

The Seal of Biliteracy marks an important move away from the restrictions on bilingual education under the 'English for the Children' initiatives, the elimination of the Title VII Bilingual Education Act and the lack of recognition and value of bilingualism under NCLB. However, there is some concern moving forward as the Seal of Biliteracy gains in popularity (Heineke & Davin, 2020). Some fear that Seals will overwhelmingly be awarded to and benefit affluent native English-speakers who attain marginal skills in a second language, rather than lower-income current and former ELLs who develop higher levels of bilingualism and far greater use of two or more languages in their daily lives (Valdés, 2020). Another concern is to what degree the Seals will be taken seriously beyond being a simple symbolic gesture. Finally, and most important, what will states actually do to help students develop and/or maintain bilingualism and biliteracy? This is a particularly important concern for ELL-classified students, as most school programs are subtractive in nature: students enter school as emergent bilinguals but typically graduate as dominant English-speakers with weakened oral language skills and little to no literacy skills in their home languages (Fillmore, 1991; Wright, 2004; Wright & Boun, 2011). Some states, such as Indiana, have tied Seal of Biliteracy legislation to legislation supporting the launch of new dual language programs. However, in Indiana and other states such as Utah, many dual language programs are mostly serving English-speaking students rather than ELLs and heritage language students (Freire *et al.*, 2017; Sung & Tsai, 2019).

Every Student Succeeds Act

Eight years after the ESEA was due for re-authorization in 2007, the US Congress finally approved bipartisan legislation for a new version of the federal education law. The **Every Student Succeeds Act** (**ESSA**) was signed into law by President Barack Obama on December 10, 2015, thus bringing NCLB to an end. This new version of the ESEA reflects some recognition of the failures of NCLB, including its unrealistic achievement expectations and over-reliance on high-stakes standardized tests as the sole measure of student achievement. The testing regimen outlined in **Title I** remains the same, including annual testing of English language arts and mathematics in grades 3–8 and high school. However, reflective of the ESEA Flexibility program, states were given greater flexibility for goal setting and how they will intervene in low-performing schools. States now consider factors other than test scores in their school accountability program. This has opened space for a student's level of English proficiency to be considered when setting achievement targets and in interpreting their test scores, and for other measures of students' opportunities to learn to be considered. There are now opportunities to consider a student's growth over time, rather than just meeting set passing scores.

States are required, however, to track the progress of separate subgroups of students – including ELLs – rather than lump students together in a single super-subgroup. This addressed a major concern of the ESEA Flexibility program, as noted above, and helps ensure that the unique language and academic needs of ELL-classified students are not overlooked. ELL-classified students are required to take state ELA and math exams regardless of how long they have been in the United States. However, states have some flexibility in how ELL test scores are included in school accountability ratings (see Box 9.2).

Box 9.2 Inclusion of ELLs in state testing and accountability programs under ESSA

Under ESSA, ELLs are required to take state reading/English language arts (ELA) and math tests, regardless of how long they have been in the United States. States have two options for including ELL test scores in school accountability ratings:

Option A
ELLs' test scores count towards a school's rating only after they have been in the United States for one year

Option B
First year in the United States
- Test scores must be reported to the public
- Test scores won't count towards a school's rating

Second year in the United States
- States must incorporate ELL scores for both reading/ELA and math, using some measure of growth

Third year in the United States
- ELL scores incorporated just like those of any other students

---

The requirements for English language proficiency standards and assessments and the expectations for ELL-classified students to make progress in learning and ultimately attaining English proficiency remain the same. However, these requirements were moved from **Title III** to be included alongside the academic achievement testing and accountability requirements of Title I. This change marks a further departure from a separate section of the law focused on ELL-classified students; but inclusion under the accountability requirements of Title I helps elevate the focus on the language needs of ELL-classified students. As in NCLB, there will be some allowances for testing students in their home language.

In a major reversal of a key policy priority of the Obama administration, ESSA removed requirements that teacher evaluations be tied to student test scores. This change may help relieve pressure on teachers who were being held accountable for ELL test scores of questionable **validity**. And in another direct challenge to the Obama administration's perceived ties to the Common Core, ESSA explicitly forbids the US Secretary of Education from forcing or encouraging states to adopt any set of standards. Nonetheless, states' option to adopt the Common Core standards or join one of the assessment consortia remain unchanged (though most states ultimately chose to withdraw). The option to join English language proficiency standards and assessment consortia (e.g. WIDA, ELPA21) also remains unaffected (nearly all states have continued their memberships).

Donald J. Trump became the 45th President of the United States in January 2017 as the implementation of ESSA was just getting started. ESSA had a slow roll-out and was never fully implemented during the four years of the first Trump administration (2017–2021). The US Department of Education took about three years to engage in negotiated rule-making, to formulate and issue guidelines for states and districts on how to implement these new requirements, and to review and approve each state's ESSA plan. Education reform through accountability based on the results of large-scale standardized tests remains the centerpiece of the federal education law, and ELL-classified students are still required to take and ultimately pass these exams. A two-year exclusion of ELL test scores from school accountability ratings is likely to be insufficient. However, the greater flexibility afforded to states to design their own accountability systems opened up the possibility for more realistic expectations for ELL-classified students, more attention to their linguistic needs and the potential for greater support for bilingual education programs.

The Migration Policy Institute (MPI) conducted a thorough analysis of all approved state ESSA plans and raised the concern that these plans 'offer often-scattered information that creates a fractured and incomplete picture of English learner (EL) education. As a result, EL education policies remain disjointed and inaccessible to local education officials, teachers, and education advocates, within and across states' (Villegas & Pompa, 2020: 1). The MPI found, for example, that state plans provided little guidance on what to do about ELL-classified students who fail to attain English language proficiency (ELP) within the set timeline. Of greater concern is the finding that 'the long-term goals that states established for ELs in their plans – both for academic achievement and ELP – are generally symbolic and do not carry any weight in accountability systems in most states'. Also, it found that the complexity of the state's accountability frameworks can make it difficult to understand 'how and to what extent the EL subgroup's performance counts toward overall school accountability ratings'. Other issues and ambiguities in the state ESSA plan make it 'impossible to say with certainty what the ELP indicator is measuring' (Villegas & Pompa, 2020: 2). The MPI acknowledges, however, that it is too early to tell what the impact of these policies will be.

Full implementation of ESSA was just getting underway when it experienced a major disruption in the spring of 2020 due to the global coronavirus disease (Covid-19) pandemic. Schools across the United States (like those around the world) were forced to shut down and suddenly shift to online instruction (see Box 9.3). The US Department of Education relieved states of the ESSA-mandated testing requirements. Thus, assessment scores and other data were not available for school accountability purposes. Full implementation of ESSA began toward the end of the Biden administration, but it remains to be seen the degree to which individual state accountability programs are fair and beneficial for ELLs, and the degree to which they value and promote bilingualism.

It should be noted that during the first Trump administration, despite the President's anti-immigration rhetoric and controversy over his appointment of Betsy DeVos as the US Secretary of Education, Trump himself showed little direct interest in education policy. Likewise, Secretary DeVos appeared to have paid little attention to ELL student issues and did not interfere with the continuing ESSA activities and programs of the

> **Box 9.3** Impact of Covid-19 on bilingual education and students
>
> Bilingual education, along with the entire education enterprise in the United States and around the world, experienced substantial disruptions due to the global Covid-19 pandemic. Nearly all US schools shut down and shifted immediately to online or other distance forms of education through the end of the school year in spring 2020. The pandemic had worsened in the United States by the time schools began the 2020/2021 academic year. Lack of federal and state leadership left local school leaders scrambling for solutions, with many continuing to offer online and distance options. While all students were negatively impacted, there is growing recognition that the negative impact on ELL-classified students has been even greater (Sayer & Braun, 2020). The pandemic laid bare the inequalities of the United States, with poor and racialized minority communities suffering from higher infection and death rates. The provision of bilingual education and other language programs and supports for ELL-classified students in online formats proved challenging and was complicated by the fact that many students in urban and rural areas lacked access to needed technology and adequate wifi services to participate in online instruction (Mitchell, 2020). Other distance options typically consisted of teachers preparing large homework packets for families to pick up from the school each week. Even when schools returned to mostly in-person instruction, masking, social-distancing and other Covid-related protocols restricted the types of student and teacher interactions that are important for language learning and success in bilingual classrooms (Li *et al.*, 2023; Renn *et al.*, 2024). The pandemic also disrupted the preparation and practicum experiences of bilingual and other language education teachers (England *et al.*, 2023; Pu & Wright, 2022; Renn *et al.*, 2024).
>
> The challenges left most students, parents, teachers and administrators stressed and frustrated. It may be several years before we fully understand the overall impact of the pandemic on students in general, and on bilingual students in particular. However, the history of bilingual education has demonstrated its resilience. The pandemic brought attention to the need for new policies and initiatives to address gross educational inequalities and unequal access to technology and wifi, and for better models of bilingual family engagement. Technological and instructional innovations gained by dedicated bilingual teachers during the pandemic continue to be implemented in bilingual classrooms, to the benefit students.

Office of English Language Acquisition (OELA), which began under the Obama administration. The staff and appointed OELA directors were supportive of bilingual education, issued ESSA implementation guidelines to states that highlighted the strong research base for bilingual programs and have awarded grants to universities which include a focus on dual language programs, bilingual teacher training and research. At one point, the first Trump administration made plans to consolidate the various offices of the Department of Education which would have eliminated OELA and potentially many of these programs. However, the administration backed off these plans, given the strong opposition of members of Congress and language advocacy groups. The first Trump administration had also proposed major budget cuts to the Department of Education, but these were opposed by members of Congress and were not enacted. However, immigration and visa restrictions, justified by the first Trump administration in the context of the global pandemic, led to some challenges for districts that recruit and rely on bilingual teachers from outside the United States (Koran, 2020).

Joe Biden became the 46th President of the United States on January 20, 2021. He appointed Miguel Cardona as the US Secretary of Education. Cardona was a former ELL, had a master's degree in bilingual education (and a doctorate in education) and had a long career in public education as an elementary school teacher, principal, district administrator and State Commissioner of Education (Connecticut). Secretary Cardona was a strong advocate for ELLs and bilingual education. In November 2023 he launched an initiative for the US Department of Education titled 'Being Bilingual is a Superpower', which mainly served as a symbolic umbrella to highlight ongoing and new initiatives connected to promoting bilingual and multilingual education, including grant programs, guidelines, tool kits, webinars, technical assistance and other resources in English and additional languages.

Donald Trump returned to the White House as the 47th President of the United States on January 20, 2025. During the presidential campaign, despite Trump's anti-immigrant rhetoric, critiques of diversity initiatives and general threats to shut down the US Department of Education, overall little attention was given to education. As of this writing, it is unclear what the education priorities will be of the second Trump administration, or what may be the impact on federal policies and programs for bilingual students classified as ELLs. ESSA was due for re-authorization in 2021, but it remains unclear if or when the US Congress will make re-authorization of the federal education law a priority.

Other Federal Developments

In November 2019, the Congressional Caucus on America's Languages was established, jointly led by a Republican, Don Young of Alaska, and a Democrat, David Price of North Carolina, with support from the Joint National Committee for Languages (JNCL). The Caucus aims to set a national agenda to increase the study of world languages, improve education for ELLs and Native Americans, and address the shortage of bilingual and biliterate citizens in the United States, who are needed to help ensure the nation's economic and national security (see https://www.languagepolicy.org/americaslanguages). The Caucus helped push the re-authorization of the Esther Martinez Native American Languages Preservation Act, which President Trump signed into law in December 2019. This grant program (originally passed in 2006) provides federal funding to empower Native communities to establish immersion programs to revitalize Native languages and improve Native economies. In 2023, Representative Raúl Grijalva from Arizona (re)introduced HR 3607, the Supporting Young Language Learners' Access to Bilingual Education (SYLLABLE) Act, in the House of Representatives. Previous attempts to pass this bill dated back to 2020. The bill is designed to provide a small number of federal grants to help school districts establish high-quality pre-K-5 dual language immersion programs, particularly in low-income communities. Another proposed bill coming forward with support of the Caucus, the Biliteracy Education Seal and Teaching (BEST) Act (H.R. 7007, S.3595), was (re)introduced at the beginning of 2024; it would provide support for Seal of Biliteracy implementation and student loan relief for dual language teachers. In fall 2024, these proposals were stuck at the committee level, but their introduction marks an important turning point in terms of growing support for bilingual education.

Table 9.1 provides a timeline and overview of important legislation, acts of litigation and initiatives that impact or have implications for bilingual education.

Current Statistics

The estimated number of ELLs in the United States is 5,263,596, making up 10.6% of all pre-kindergarten to grade 12 students in 2021 (National Center for Education Statistics, 2024a). These latest figures mark an increase of 2.5 percentage points from 2000, when 3.8 million ELLs made up 8.1% of the total student population. The numbers and percentages of US public school students participating in programs for ELLs over the period 2011–2021 are given in Table 9.2. Note that these official figures

Table 9.1 US legislation, litigation and initiatives impacting bilingual education

Year	Legislation/litigation/initiative	Implications
1906	Nationality Act	First legislation requiring immigrants to speak English to become naturalized
1925	*Meyer v. Nebraska* ruling by the US Supreme Court	The ruling outlawed, as an unconstitutional infringement of individual liberties, arbitrary restrictions on the teaching of languages other than English outside of regular school hours
1950	Amendments to the Nationality Act	English literacy required for naturalization
1954	*Brown v. Board of Education*	Segregated education based on race made unconstitutional
1958	National Defense Education Act	The first federal legislation to promote foreign language learning
1965	Immigration and Naturalization Act	The Act eliminated racial criteria for admission, expanding immigration especially from Asia and Latin America. The Act also emphasized the goal of 'family unification' over occupational skills. This encouraged increased immigration by Mexicans in particular
1965	Elementary and Secondary Education Act (ESEA)	First federal K-12 education law. An outgrowth of the civil rights movement. Federal funds specifically granted to meet the needs of 'educationally deprived children'
1968	Title VII, Bilingual Education Act, an amendment to Elementary and Secondary Education Act (ESEA)	Provided competitive grants to establish bilingual programs for students who did not speak English and who were economically poor
1974	*Lau v. Nichols* ruling by the US Supreme Court	Established that language programs for language minorities not proficient in English were necessary to provide equal educational opportunities
1974	Re-authorization of ESEA and the Title VII Bilingual Education Act	Native language instruction was required for the first time as a condition for receiving bilingual education grants. Bilingual education was defined as transitional (transitional bilingual education – TBE). Grants could support native language instruction only to the extent necessary to allow a child to achieve competence in the English language. Funding was thus restricted to TBE; maintenance and dual language programs were ineligible for funding
1975	Lau remedies	Issued by the Office of Civil Rights following the *Lau v. Nichols* decision. Provided guidelines on schools' obligations to 'limited English speaking' students. This required the provision of bilingual education in districts where the civil rights of such students had been violated
1976	*Keyes v. School District No. 1*, Denver, Colorado	Established bilingual education as compatible with desegregation
1978	Re-authorization of ESEA and the Title VII Bilingual Education Act	Restriction of dual language programs lifted. The term 'limited English proficient' (LEP) introduced, replacing LES (limited English speaking)
1980	Lau regulations	The Carter administration attempted to formalize the Lau remedies, requiring bilingual instruction for 'LEP' students where feasible. The Reagan administration subsequently withdrew the proposal, leaving uncertainty about schools' obligation in this area
1983	US English Movement	An organization advocating that English be declared the official language of the United States, and opposing the use of languages other than English in government and education. Sparked national debates about the dominant place of English in law, society and education
1984	Re-authorization of ESEA and the Title VII Bilingual Education Act	While most funding was reserved for TBE, monies for maintenance programs were once again permitted. However, for the first time funds were made available for 'special alternative' instructional (English-only) programs
1988	Re-authorization of ESEA and the Title VII Bilingual Education Act	Same as in 1984, but an increase up to 25% of funding given for English-only special alternative instructional programs (SAIPs)
1994	Improving America's Schools Act (IASA) – re-authorization of ESEA and the Title VII Bilingual Education Act	Full bilingual proficiency recognized as a lawful educational goal. Funded dual language programs that included English-speakers and programs to support Native American languages. The quota for funding SAIPs was lifted. The new law sought to bring 'LEP' students into mainstream school reform efforts, making it more difficult for their particular needs to be ignored in policymaking
1998	Proposition 227 passed in California	The 'English for the Children' initiative imposed severe restrictions on bilingual education for English-learners in California and mandated structured English immersion. Most bilingual programs dismantled

2000	Proposition 203 passed in Arizona	The 'English for the Children' initiative imposed severe restrictions on bilingual education for English-learners in Arizona and mandated structured English immersion. Criterion for waivers made more stringent and penalties for noncompliance added. Most bilingual programs dismantled
2002	Question 2 passed in Massachusetts	The 'English for the Children' initiative imposed severe restrictions on bilingual education for English-learners in Massachusetts and mandated structured English immersion. Many bilingual programs were dismantled, but blanket waivers were subsequently given by the state to dual language programs
2002	Amendment 31 defeated in Colorado	The 'English for the Children' initiative is rejected by Colorado's votes. Unz abandons efforts to take the initiative to other states
2002	No Child Left Behind (NCLB) Act – re-authorization of the ESEA; the Title VII Bilingual Education Act is repealed and replaced by Title III	Approved by Congress on December 8, 2001, and signed into law by President George W. Bush in January 2002, NCLB replaced IASA. The Bilingual Education Act is eliminated and replaced by Title III, 'Language Instruction for Limited English Proficient and Immigrant Students'. Bilingual education allowed but not valued or encouraged. Mandates for accountability through high-stakes testing in content areas and English proficiency, and the threat of sanctions associated with failures to make adequate yearly progress encourage a move toward more English-only programs
2006	Esther Martinez Native American Languages Preservation Act (HR 4766)	Named in honor of Esther Martinez, a leading advocate for the revitalization and preservation of the Pueblo Indian language of Tewa. This program authorizes federal funding for new programs focusing on preventing the loss of tribal heritage and culture
2009	Race to the Top	An initiative of President Barack Obama to provide $4.3 billion in competitive grants for states to pursue education reform. Included a focus on the development of college and career-readiness standards
2010	Common Core State Standards (CCSS) initiative	A state-led initiative to develop shared college and career-readiness standards in English language arts and math. States also had the option of joining one of two consortia developing tests to measure the CCSS – PARCC and Smarter Balanced
2011	Seal of Biliteracy	California becomes the first state to offer bilingual students an opportunity to earn a Seal of Biliteracy on their high school diploma. Most states have since adopted the Seal
2011	ESEA Flexibility	An initiative of the Obama administration to offer states waivers from key accountability provisions of NCLB and to propose their own accountability system meeting the administration's guidelines. This included the requirement to develop or adopt college- and career-readiness standards and assessments and corresponding English-language proficiency standards and assessments
2015	Every Student Succeeds Act (ESSA) – re-authorization of the ESEA	Signed into law by President Barack Obama on December 10, 2015, ESSA replaced NCLB. Accountability through testing of content and English language proficiency was still in place, but states were afforded greater flexibility to set achievement goals and to use multiple measures to assess students
2016	Proposition 58 passed in California	The 'English Proficiency. Multilingual Education' ballot initiative; repealed Proposition 227 in California
2017	LOOK Act passed in Massachusetts	Bill H.4032, 'An Act relative to language opportunity for our kids (LOOK)', repeals Question 2 in Massachusetts
2019	Congressional Caucus on America's Languages established	A bipartisan group of members of Congress focused on setting a national strategy to address the nation's economic and national security by increasing the number of bilingual and biliterate citizens through programs for world languages, ELLs and Native Americans
2019	Re-authorization of the Esther Martinez Native American Languages Preservation Act (HR 912, S 256)	Re-authorizes this grant program through 2024 (originally passed in 2006), which provides federal funding to empower Native communities to establish immersion programs to revitalize Native languages and improve Native economies
2019	Arizona Senate Bill 1014	Loosened restrictions of Proposition 203 on bilingual education and removed Arizona's prior mandates of a rigid four-hour structured English immersion (SEI) model for students classified as English language learners. Grants school districts greater flexibility in offering more innovative instruction models that are supported by research, including some forms of bilingual education
2022	Native American Languages Resource Center Act	Further aligns the resources provided by the Department of Education with the policies set forth in the Native American Languages Act through establishment of a program within the Department of Education to support one or more Native American language resource centers

Table 9.2 Numbers and percentages of US public school students participating in programs for English language learners, fall 2011 to fall 2021

Year	Number of ELL students	Percentage of total student population
2011	4,635,185	9.4%
2012	4,850,293	9.7%
2013	4,929,989	9.9%
2014	4,813,693	9.6%
2015	4,854,285	9.6%
2016	4,949,423	9.8%
2017	5,010,505	9.9%
2018	5,024,177	9.9%
2019	5,115,887	10.1%
2020	4,963,388	10.1%
2021	5,263,596	10.6%

Source: National Center for Educational Statistics (2024a)
Note: NCES states, 'Caution should be used when comparing 2020 and 2021 estimates to those of other years due to the impact that the coronavirus pandemic had on reporting Title III data'

Table 9.3 Top languages spoken by ELLs in the United States (fall 2021 school year)

Language	Reported number of ELL speakers	Percentage of ELL students
Spanish	4,023,289	76.44%
Arabic	130,917	2.46%
English*	116,771	2.46%
Chinese**	95,584	1.91%
Vietnamese	75,070	1.27%
Portuguese	50,205	0.59%
Russian	39,403	0.52%
Haitian, Haitian Creole	31,122	0.40%
Hmong	30,181	0.39%
Urdu	26,567	0.37%
Korean	24,270	0.25%
French	23,648	0.21%
Swahili	21,833	0.19%
Somali	19,367	0.16%
Tagalog	19,319	

*NCES explains: Examples of situations in which English might be reported as an English Learner's home language include students who live in multilingual households and students adopted from countries who speak English at home but also have been raised speaking another language
**Includes Mandarin, Cantonese, and other Chinese languages
Source: National Center for Educational Statistics (2024b)

were released by the National Center for Educational Statistics in 2024, but only go up to 2021 due to the time it takes to collect and report prior years' data. Note also that these numbers exclude ELLs who attend private schools, who are being home schooled and ELLs who may have been unidentified. Thus, the total number of ELLs is likely much higher than reported here.

According to the National Center for Education Statistics (2024a), in 2021 ELLs made up 20.2% of the total student population in Texas, 18.9% in California and between 10% to 13% in 10 other states (Alaska, Colorado, Delaware, Hawaii, Illinois,

Maryland, Massachusetts, Nevada, Rhode Island and Washington), the District of Columbia and in the schools administered by the Bureau of Indian Education. Table 9.3 shows the top languages spoken by ELLs in the United States. Note how these are languages spoken in North, Central and South America, Europe, Asia, Africa and the Middle East, thus demonstrating the great diversity of the US ELL population.

Explanations of Underachievement in Bilinguals

In the United States (and in other countries with high immigration) language minorities are frequently found to underachieve – as measured by large-scale achievement tests – or to have high drop-out rates. According to reports published on the official website for the National Assessment of Education Progress (NAEP), also known as 'The Nation's Report Card' (https://nationsreportcard.gov), on the 2022 NAEP, ELLs scored significantly lower than non-ELLs. For reading, the gap in scores between ELLs and non-ELLs was 32 points in grade 4 and 39 points in grade 8. For math the gap in scores was 23 points in grade 4 and 36 points in grade 8. The Office of English Language Acquisition (2023) reported that the high school graduation rate for ELLs in 2019-2020 was 71%, while the national average was 86%.

Why do many language minoritized children appear to underachieve? Explanations are likely to be multiple, complex, about associations that are not necessarily causal, and may include the following: majority language competence, socioeconomic background, poverty and material home conditions, racism, gender, school attendance, parental encouragement and assistance (e.g. with homework), peer influence and the quality of teachers and school. Eight of the most typical explanations are considered below.

(1) *Bilingualism*. Bilingualism itself is sometimes viewed as a cause of cognitive confusion. The explanation given is a picture of the bilingual brain with two engines working at half throttle, while the monolingual has one well tuned engine at full throttle. As detailed in Chapter 8, such explanations are based on misunderstandings of how languages are stored and work in the brain and ignore the cognitive advantages that may be related to bilingualism.

(2) *Insufficient exposure to English*. Obviously, the less proficient students are in the language of a test, the less likely they will do well on it, even if they know a great deal about the tested content. 'Insufficient exposure to English' is often used as an excuse to eliminate bilingual education programs under the view that students should receive instruction in the same language as the test. This explanation falsely equates English language exposure with English language proficiency, and also fails to note the advantages of bilingual education for English language learning and academic achievement. Bilingual education, when effectively implemented, is not the cause of lack of English proficiency and underachievement; rather, it is the cure (Baker & Lewis, 2015). The research support for bilingual education is detailed in Chapter 12.

(3) *Mismatch between home and school*. The language, literacy practices and culture of most classrooms in the United States more closely match those of monolingual English-speakers from the middle and upper classes. Thus, linguistic and racialized minorities are placed at a disadvantage. A common 'solution' is an expectation that the child and family adjust to mainstream language and

culture practices to ensure their child's success in school. This reflects a majority viewpoint that is assimilationist, imperialist and even oppressive, and driven by raciolinguistic ideologies. For example, some teachers, educational psychologists and speech therapists may advise language minoritized parents to speak to their children only in English at home. Parent education programs may attempt to train language minoritized parents how to talk, read and interact with their children like middle-class White parents. The alternative view is that the school system should be flexible enough to value, incorporate, and sustain home languages and cultures. A mismatch between home and school can be positively addressed by 'strong' forms of bilingual education (see Chapter 11). Parent engagement programs can involve parents as partners in their child's education (Arias, 2015), recognizing and building upon rather than attempting to replace parents' **funds of knowledge** (González et al., 2005). The mismatch can become a merger. Instead of assimilation, an additive outcome is then probable: bilingualism, biliteracy and biculturalism.

(4) *Socioeconomic factors*. The correlations between students' socioeconomic status and level of academic achievement are consistently strong. However, correlation does not equal causation. Socioeconomic status does not explain why different language minorities of similar socioeconomic status may perform differently at school. Some have attempted to attribute student underachievement to a 'culture of poverty'; however, such explanations are grounded in a deficit view that 'blames the victim'. Also, underachievement cannot be simply related to one cause. Rather, the focus should be on seeking to understand the causes and impact of structural inequalities, economic deprivation, material circumstances and living conditions, as well as psychological and social features such as **identity**, self-esteem, racial prejudice and discrimination. Solutions can then focus on ways schools can help address these inequalities. For example, if underemployment means parents cannot afford to buy books, and if good public libraries are not accessible to students in their local neighborhoods, then schools can focus on developing well stocked school and classroom libraries, and increase students' opportunities to take out books – including multicultural and multilingual books – for use at home. Thus, instead of socioeconomic factors being static explanations or political criticism, actions must result to change and enhance. After the elucidation of cause must come transformation.

(5) *Type of instructional model*. Academic achievement may depend on the types of program models that exist in the schools students attend. Does the school offer ESL, sheltered content-area instruction or bilingual education programs? Or are bilingual students thrown into submersion mainstream classrooms and left to 'sink or swim'? There are often different outcomes for **language minoritized students** in 'strong' compared with 'weak' and 'non' forms of bilingual education (see Chapters 10 and 11). The same child will tend to attain more if placed in programs that use the home language as a medium of instruction rather than in programs that seek to replace the home language as quickly as possible. Therefore, when underachievement occurs, the system of schooling needs scrutiny. A system that suppresses the home language is likely to be part of the explanation of individual and ethnic group underachievement where such problems exist.

(6) *Quality of education*. Even if a school offers 'strong' forms of bilingual education, the models themselves may not make a difference if they are not implemented correctly. Also, the language of instruction is just one of many factors that need to be

considered in the quality of education. Chapter 13 considers some of the attributes that need examining to establish the quality of education for language minoritized children (e.g. the supply, ethnic origins and bilingualism of teachers, the commitment of teachers to bilingual education, the balance of language minoritized and language majority students in the classroom, the use and sequencing of the two languages across the curriculum over different grades, reward systems for enriching the minoritized language and culture, appropriate curriculum resources and the engagement of parents).

(7) *Interrupted schooling.* Many immigrant and refugee bilingual students experience interruptions in their formal education (Lukes, 2015). In the United States, the term 'students with interrupted formal education' (SIFE) is commonly used to describe such students. Access to schools in the home country may have been limited, or they may be been prevented from attending school for long periods of time due to war, civil unrest or oppression (Cohan & Honigsfeld, 2017). Schools are often unavailable or limited in refugee camps and refugee students typically lack access to schools in temporary host countries. Transnational students frequently travel back and forth between their current and their 'home' countries (e.g. United States and Mexico) during the school year (Kwon, 2022). Economic necessities sometimes require older students to leave school temporarily to work one or more jobs to help support the family. Complicated enrollment procedures (forms, immunizations, testing) can sometimes lead to months of delays for newcomer students to start school. Such interruptions lead to missed opportunities to learn, further compound challenges of learning and learning through a new language and make it even more difficult for catch up with grade-level peers. Chang-Bacon (2021) notes that due to Covid-19, all US students may now be considered as SIFE.

(8) *Racism and discrimination.* Many bilingual children are students of color who face discrimination based on their physical appearance and/or linguistic practices. This overlaps with many of the areas above. Systemic discrimination typically results in education, program models and curricular materials that are monoglossic and focused on quick assimilation. Racialized bilingual students may face racism and discrimination at a personal level, which can also have a severe impact on their opportunities to learn and succeed in school. Even strong forms of bilingual education (see Chapters 10 and 11) can become 'gentrified', wherein the program shifts to cater more to the needs of students from the dominant racial and linguistic group over the needs of the racialized and linguistic minority students (Delavan *et al.*, 2024).

(9) *Real learning difficulties.* Bilingual children are susceptible to the same types of disabilities and cognitive deficit disorders that can impact any children, and may require some form of special education. However, it is critical to make a distinction between real and apparent learning difficulties. Too often, bilingual children – including speakers of non-standard varieties of the majority language – are labeled as having learning difficulties that are attributed to their bilingualism. Language and learning challenges that are a normal part of second language development may be misinterpreted as speech impediments or cognitive difficulties. Other perceptions of apparent learning problems may be much less in the child and much more in the school or in the education system. In the 'sink or swim' mainstreaming approach, 'sinking' can be attributed to an unsympathetic system and to insensitive teaching methods rather than individual learning problems. Tests, assessments and procedures used to identify students for special education must distinguish

between real, genuine individual learning difficulties and problems that are related to language learning or caused by factors outside the individual. These issues will be addressed in Chapter 15.

Conclusion

There are three conclusions to be drawn. First, the history of bilingual education in the United States shows that there is constant change, a constant movement in ideas and ideology. One conclusion is that change will always occur in bilingual education policy and provision. Nothing is static. While there will be periods when bilingual education is criticized, forbidden and rejected, there will be reactions, with the more positive, accepting periods ahead. Uncertainty and constant change provide occasional opportunities for bilingual education to progress.

Second, the conclusion must not be that bilingual education moves in only one direction: from more positive 'golden' times to being dismissed and rejected. The history of bilingual education in the Basque Country and Wales follows a different sequence from that in the United States. In these countries, bilingual education has moved from being dismissed and suppressed to a period of considerable expansion. From a time when Basque and Welsh were banned in the classroom, there is currently a widespread acceptance and provision of bilingual education in these countries (Özerk & Williams, 2023).

Third, a current international issue is the underachievement of many language minoritized students. The blame for this is easily but wrongly attributed to bilingualism or to insufficient experience in learning a majority language. Instead, the achievement gap is often related to failing to use a child's ability and achievements that are available in their home language. Sometimes the achievement gap is blamed on language, when the real roots are situated in the relatively impoverished economic, social and educational environments that immigrants, for example, experience. For such students, bilingual education utilizing the home language becomes the cure and not the cause of underachievement.

Key Points in This Chapter

> Bilingual education has a history spanning 5000 or more years.
> Bilingual education in the United States has a rapidly changing history, impacted directly or indirectly by a wide range of legislation, litigation and state and federal initiatives.
> 'English for the Children' voter initiatives in California, Arizona and Massachusetts did not live up to their promise of faster English language learning and higher academic achievement. They failed to fully eliminate bilingual education programs, and have now been repealed in California and Massachusetts, and restrictions in Arizona have been loosened.

> - The Seal of Biliteracy has been adopted in all states. It affords graduating high school seniors recognition and value of their bilingual skills.
> - The shift of federal education policy from NCLB to ESSA continues a focus on education reform through testing and accountability, but states are afforded more flexibility with potential for more reasonable expectations for ELLs and a greater focus on their language and academic needs. Nonetheless, there are problems in most state plans, and it is too early to tell the extent to which ELL students may benefit from these changes.
> - Underachievement in school is typically unfairly blamed on bilingualism. Lack of exposure to the majority language and a mismatch between the languages of home and school are often cited as causes of underachievement.
> - The real causes of underachievement tend to lie in relative social and economic deprivation and exclusion, a school which rejects the home language and culture of the child, and occasionally real learning difficulties.

Suggested Further Reading

- Coady, M. (2020) *The Coral Way Bilingual Program*. Multilingual Matters.
- Delavan, M.G., Freire, J.A. and Menken, K. (eds) (2024) *Overcoming the Gentrification of Dual Language, Bilingual and Immersion Education: Solution-Oriented Research and Stakeholder Resources for Real Integration*. Multilingual Matters.
- Heineke, A.J. and Davin, K.J. (eds) (2020) *The Seal of Biliteracy: Case Studies and Considerations for Policy Implementation*. Information Age Publishing.
- Moore, S.C.K. (2021) *A History of Bilingual Education in the US: Examining the Politics of Language Policymaking*. Multilingual Matters.
- Morita-Mullaney, T. (2024) *Lau v. Nichols and Chinese American Language Rights: The Sunrise and Sunset of Bilingual Education*. Multilingual Matters.

On the Web

- National Association for Bilingual Education
  https://www.nabe.org
- Office of English Language Acquisition, US Department of Education
  https://www2.ed.gov/about/offices/list/oela/index.html
- National Clearinghouse of English Language Acquisition
  https://ncela.ed.gov
- Center for Applied Linguistics
  https://www.cal.org
- James Crawford's Language policy website and emporium
  https://www.languagepolicy.net/index.html

Discussion Questions

(1) Choose three of the items from the historical timeline in Table 9.1 and discuss why and how these have impacted bilingual education.
(2) There have been direct attempts to eliminate bilingual education (e.g. the 'English for the Children' initiatives), the Title VII Bilingual Education Act was eliminated in 2002 and under NCLB there was a lack of federal funding and encouragement for bilingual education. Nevertheless, bilingual education remains alive and well in the United States, and former restrictions are now being reversed. Why do you think bilingual education has been able to survive and regain popularity?
(3) What recent policy changes and initiatives may support or restrict bilingual education going into the future?

Study Activities

(1) Visit one or more schools and ask about the history of the bilingual education program or other language programs within that school. What have been the aims of the school with regard to languages? Have these aims changed over the last 10 or 20 years? How do the teachers perceive the first and second language of children being ignored or used over the last decade or more? Are there issues about the 'achievement gap' in the school? If so, what explanations do teachers give for underachievement?
(2) Choose one of the more recent initiatives or policies discussed in the chapter to explore further. Conduct an internet search to find news articles, reports, videos, social media postings and research articles to learn of the historical and more recent developments and how they are impacting language minoritized students and bilingual education.
(3) Visit the website of the National Clearinghouse for English Language Acquisition. Read one or more of the fact sheets (https://ncela.ed.gov/resources/oela-resources/factsheets). Prepare a short presentation based on these fact sheets and discuss the implications for bilingual education.

CHAPTER 10
Types of Education for Bilingual Students

Introduction

A Typology of Program Models for Bilingual Students

Monolingual Forms of Education
Mainstreaming/Submersion Education
Mainstreaming with Pull-Out or Push-In Classes
Sheltered/Structured Immersion

Weak Forms of Bilingual Education
Transitional Bilingual Education
Mainstream Education with World Language Teaching
Separatist Education

Exclusion and Interruptions

Conclusion

CHAPTER 10

Types of Education for Bilingual Students

Introduction

At its most basic definition, **bilingual education** may refer to programs where some, most or all the education is through two languages. However, bilingual education is a simplistic label for a complex phenomenon. A program should not be called 'bilingual education' simply because it serves students who are bilingual. Thus, at the outset, a distinction is needed between education that uses and promotes two languages versus relatively **monolingual** education in a second language, typically for **language minoritized** children. This is a difference between (1) a classroom where formal instruction fosters **bilingualism** and (2) a classroom where bilingual children are present but bilingualism is not promoted in the curriculum. 'Bilingual education' has been misleadingly used to refer to both situations, leaving the term ambiguous and unclear. This chapter aids understanding of programs for bilingual students by distinguishing between monolingual forms of education and weak and strong forms of bilingual education. Monolingual programs provide formal instruction only in the majority language. Weak forms of bilingual education may make some use of two languages in formal instruction but generally do not aim for bilingualism. Strong forms of bilingual education aim for bilingualism and biliteracy. In this chapter we discuss monolingual forms and weak forms of bilingual education. Strong forms of bilingual education are the focus of Chapter 11.

The aims of different forms of bilingual education can vary greatly (Wright & Baker, 2017; Wright & Choi, 2024). Baker (2010a) suggests that bilingual education has four major contemporary perspectives: (1) as part of **language planning** (see Chapter 4), (2) as politics (see Chapter 17), (3) as economics and cost-efficiency (see Chapters 18 and 19) and as pedagogy (see Chapter 13). Thus, bilingual education is not just about education. There are sociocultural, political and economic issues ever present in the debate over the provision of bilingual education, particularly politics.

One distinction in the aims of bilingual education is that between transitional and maintenance types. **Transitional bilingual education** is a weak form of bilingual education because it aims to shift the child quickly from the home minoritized language to the dominant, majority language. Social and cultural assimilation into the language majority is the underlying aim. Maintenance bilingual education is a strong form of bilingual education because it attempts to foster the minoritized language in the child, as well as the associated **culture** and **identity** (e.g. Irish language education). This is sometimes referred to as **enrichment bilingual education** for language minoritized children. (The term is also used for language majority children who are adding a second language in school.) Enrichment bilingual education aims to extend the individual and group use of minoritized languages, leading to cultural pluralism and linguistic diversity.

A Typology of Program Models for Bilingual Students

A typology of program models for bilingual students helps illustrate the varying aims of monolingual education and weak and strong forms of bilingual education, as presented in Table 10.1. Ten types of language education are portrayed. Many international examples of these different types can be found in García (2009b), Skutnabb-Kangas and Heugh (2013) and Wright et al. (2015). The 10 different types of program have multitudinous sub-varieties, as Mackey's (1970) 90 varieties of bilingual

Table 10.1 Typology of program models for bilingual students

Type of Program	Typical type of child	Language of the classroom	Societal and educational aim	Aim in language outcome
Monolingual forms of education				
Mainstreaming/submersion	Language minority	Majority language	Assimilation	Monolingualism
Mainstreaming/submersion with pull-out or push-in majority language instruction support	Language minority	Majority language	Assimilation	Monolingualism
Sheltered/**structured** **immersion**	Language minority	Majority language	Assimilation	Monolingualism
Weak forms of bilingual education				
Transitional	Language minority	Moves from minority to majority language	Assimilation/ subtractive	Relative monolingualism
Mainstreaming with world language teaching	Language majority	Majority language with L2/WL lessons	Limited enrichment	Limited bilingualism
Separatist	Language minority	Minority language (out of choice)	Detachment/ autonomy	Limited bilingualism
Strong forms of bilingual education				
Immersion	Language majority	Bilingual with initial emphasis on L2	Pluralism and enrichment	Bilingualism and biliteracy
Maintenance/heritage language	Language minority	Bilingual with emphasis on L1	Maintenance, pluralism and enrichment	Bilingualism and biliteracy
Two-way/dual language	Mixed language minority and majority	Minority and majority	Maintenance, pluralism and enrichment	Bilingualism and biliteracy
Mainstream bilingual	Language majority	Two majority languages	Maintenance and enrichment	Bilingualism and biliteracy

Notes: L2 = second language, L1 = first language, WL = world language. This table is based on discussions with Ofelia García. She provides an in-depth discussion of models in García (2009a)

education indicate. Even more variety is achieved by including multilingual education (Cenoz, 2009).

One of the intrinsic limitations of typologies is that not all real-life examples will fit easily into the classification. For example, elite 'finishing schools' in Switzerland, and classrooms in Wales where first language Welsh-speakers are taught alongside 'immersion' first language English-speakers make classification overly simplistic, although necessary for discussion and understanding (de Mejía, 2002). This is well illustrated by Bartlett and García (2011) in their case study of Gregorio Luperón High School in New York. The school is a hybrid of maintenance (heritage) bilingual education and transitional bilingual education. It also moves away from a focus on individual second language learners of English to a social process involving the identity of an entire **speech community** of Dominican students. Spanish is given a high status and bilingualism is the norm. At the same time, there is a rigorous academic preparation in English. Such a school does not fit easily into a typology.

The whole notion of a 'program model' has been challenged as problematic out of concern that models represent a **monolingual/monoglossic perspective** in which the languages of bilingual students are treated as two separate distinct systems, as if students are two monolinguals in one and placed in programs where languages are simply subtracted or added (Flores & Baetens Beardsmore, 2015; García, 2009a). In contrast, a multilingual/**heteroglossic perspective** views the languages of bilinguals as dynamic and coexisting. Such a perspective opens up space to engage with optimal classroom translanguaging practices that maximize growth and gains for individual students, as well as positive outcomes for schools in an accountability era (Cenoz & Gorter, 2021; García & Li Wei, 2014; Juvonen & Källkvist, 2021a; Kenfield, 2021; Menken & Sánchez, 2019; Tian & King, 2023). We thus may be witnessing a shift from effective *models* to effective *practices*, although the latter are built upon the former, and space can be made within existing program models for multilingual/heteroglossic perspectives and effective **translanguaging** practices. Some effective practices may be similar across models, making pedagogic decisions more universally informed rather than just from within a model.

Typologies have value for conceptual clarity, and for comparisons across countries and **contexts**, but they have limitations: (1) models suggest static systems whereas bilingual schools and classrooms constantly develop and evolve; (2) there are wide and numerous variations within a model; (3) models address 'inputs' and 'outputs' of the education system, but rarely address classroom processes; (4) models do not explain the successes or failures or the relative effectiveness of different types of bilingual education; (5) models are non-theoretical, reductionist, essentialist and, compared with complex individual schools, tend to simplify unsympathetically; (6) models are often relevant to one context (e.g. Canada) and cannot be exported or imported without the traditions and ideologies of a new context being considered; (7) the models derive from the Global North, particularly North America and Europe, with Global South traditions weakly represented (Benson, 2009; Heugh & Skutnabb-Kangas, 2010); and (8) models are not typically part of the way that policymakers, administrators and particularly teachers talk about bilingual education.

Baker (2008) suggests that it is increasingly more valuable to profile the key dimensions and issues along which bilingual schools vary, such as the language profile of children and balance of languages, use and allocation of languages in the classroom, the language profile of staff in the school, learning resources, staff development and parental inclusion. Cenoz's (2009) proposal that there are 'continua of multilingual education' draws on insights from Hornberger's (2008) continua of biliteracy (see Chapter 14). The continua of multilingual education framework considers the sociolinguistic context, including the school context, teacher, language of instruction, the school subject and the linguistic distance between the home language and the school language. It also considers macro factors such as the speakers, their status, the media and the linguistic landscape, as well as micro factors such as the students' parents, siblings, peers and neighborhood. These dimensions interact in dynamic ways. Cenoz's model illustrates the complex realities that challenge simplistic typologies. To assist educators in decision making within the complex realities of multilingual schools, de Jong (2011: 170, 178) outlines four principles to be considered when designing programs and instruction:

(1) *Striving for educational equity*. Engage in practices that reflect respect, non-discrimination and fairness for all students.
(2) *Affirming identities*. Respect students' linguistic and cultural identities and validate their cultural experiences in school policies and classroom practices.
(3) *Promoting **additive bilingualism***. Build on students' existing linguistic repertoires and create opportunities for using, developing, displaying and engaging in multiple languages.
(4) *Structuring for integration*. Look at how a school's various components (students, parents, teachers, as well as programs and activities) connect, relate and interact with each other and how these relations reflect equal status among those involved.

While the typology in Table 10.1 is about programs in K-12 schools, bilingual education can be cradle to grave, including pre-school education, further education, higher education and lifelong learning. A growing interest is in bilingual education at the university level (Boun & Wright, 2021; Hibbert & van der Walt, 2014; Kenfield, 2021; Mazak & Carroll, 2017; Palfreyman & van der Walt, 2017; Rubio-Alcalá & Coyle, 2021; van der Walt, 2015). This is particularly concerned with including minoritized languages as a medium for teaching, dual language approaches to lectures (e.g. use of translation, translanguaging), the identity of multilingual students at university, and progression from bilingual schooling to university.

Having acknowledged these challenges and complexities, we now briefly consider each of the broad types of monolingual forms of education and weak forms of bilingual education program models in this chapter; strong forms of bilingual education are considered in Chapter 11.

Monolingual Forms of Education

Monolingual forms of education for bilingual students provide formal instruction only in the majority language. There is no attempt to develop or maintain the students' home languages. However, while the aim is **monolingualism**, some support may be provided in the home language by a bilingual paraprofessional or by a teacher who is bilingual or who can at least speak a few words and phrases in the languages of their students. Teachers may also make allowances for students to draw on all of their linguistic resources by engaging in translanguaging pedagogies, even if they themselves cannot speak their students' languages (García *et al.*, 2016). For example, teachers could facilitate opportunities for bilingual students to work together in small groups and translanguage as they engage in academic tasks; for students with some home language literacy skills, teachers could provide bilingual books and materials for use in the classroom and at home, or encourage students to take notes or draft outlines of writing assignments in their home language before producing a final draft in the majority language (Wright, 2025). These temporary supports, while helpful, are mainly designed to facilitate mastery of the majority language. Monolingual forms of education are clearly assimilationist oriented and most often result in students who can speak only one language.

Mainstreaming/Submersion Education

Submersion describes education for language minoritized children who are placed in mainstream education. However, no school calls itself a submersion school. 'Mainstreaming' is the more common label. Submersion contains the idea of 'sink or swim'; a language minoritized student is thrown into the deep end of a pool and expected to learn to swim as quickly as possible without the help of floats or special swimming lessons. The language of the pool will be the majority language (e.g. English in the United States) and not the home language of the child (e.g. Arabic, Chinese, Spanish). The language minoritized student will be taught all day in the majority language, often alongside fluent speakers of the majority language. Both teachers and students will be expected to use only the majority language in the classroom, not the home language. There is no provision of specialized instruction in the majority language (e.g. **English as a second language**) or attempt to modify the curriculum and instruction to make it more comprehensible (e.g. **sheltered instruction**). The teacher does not have any specialized training or certifications for providing such instruction or support. Thus, language minoritized students will sink, struggle or swim.

The basic aim of such mainstreaming is the **assimilation** of language minoritized speakers, particularly where there has been immigration (e.g. the United States, the United Kingdom, Japan, Korea). Also, where **indigenous language** minorities are perceived as 'outside' the common good, mainstreaming becomes a tool of integration. Considerable variations in student **language ability** in a mainstream classroom can create challenges in teaching and class management for the teacher. If the classroom contains students who range from fluent majority language speakers to those who can understand little classroom talk, the task of the teacher may be onerous. It is unreasonable to assume that children will quickly and effortlessly acquire the majority language necessary to cope in the curriculum (see Chapter 8).

Alongside problems of language, there may be problems of social and emotional adjustment for mainstreamed language minoritized children. Wright (2004) documented the experiences of former students who began school in the United States as newcomer refugees with little to no proficiency in English and were placed in submersion classrooms:

> Many had difficulty initially just understanding what was being said in class. Bo, describing his first year, laughed and said, 'I just sat there'. Ken remembers being very bored in 2nd and 3rd grade because he simply could not understand what was being said. Mony described her frustration of wanting to participate in class discussions, but was afraid that she might say something wrong, or that the other students would laugh at her English. Ken never raised his hand for the same reason. Even if the teacher called on him, he would not respond.... Ken recalls his kindergarten class: 'I could tell the

difference between an apple and an orange, but I couldn't say the words right. Some of those kids, they could spell it too. They just spelled the word apple, but I couldn't. I just struggled to say the word. I guess they were just smarter than me.' (Wright, 2004: 14)

It is not just the child's home language that is deprecated in submersion education. The **identity** of the child, the parents, grandparents, the home, community, religion and culture appear to be deprecated, discredited and disparaged. It is not only the students' language that is denied. Submersion also denies or denounces what they hold most sacred: self-esteem, identity, relationships, roots, religion and sometimes race. One of the former refugee students in Wright's study recalled denying his ability to read and write in his native Khmer language to a paraprofessional at his school:

By now, I was very ashamed, because people would say 'go back to your country' and all this. I didn't want anything to do with that. I want to fit in. I was embarrassed about being Khmer, by knowing how to read and write. That's when I said, I'm not going to write anymore, people will see me writing that stuff. You get a lot of these kinds of pressures. (Wright, 2004: 16)

Learning through an undeveloped language in mainstreaming is stressful. Listening to a new language demands high concentration. It is tiring, with a constant pressure to think about the form of the language and less time to think about curriculum content. A child has to take in information from different curriculum areas and learn a language at the same time. Stress, lack of self-confidence, 'opting-out', disaffection and alienation may occur.

Submersion mainstream education was declared illegal by the US Supreme Court in the landmark 1974 case *Lau v. Nichols* (see Chapter 9). In writing the Court's opinion, Justice William Douglass declared: 'There is no equality of treatment merely by providing students with the same facilities, textbooks, teachers, and curriculum; for students are who do not understand English are effectively foreclosed from any meaningful education'. Thus, US schools are required to do *something* to address the language and content-area learning needs of **English language learners (ELLs)**, as will be reflected in the other types of programs discussed below and in Chapter 11.

Mainstreaming with Pull-Out or Push-In Classes

Mainstream education may take a step beyond submersion with the provision of 'withdrawal' or 'pull-out' classes to teach the majority language. Language minoritized children in mainstream schools may be withdrawn for 'compensatory' lessons in the majority language – for example, English as a second language (ESL) or English as an additional language (EAL) pull-out programs in the United States and United Kingdom. Most ESL programs aim to develop English language skills (grammar, vocabulary and communication) for communication and academic purposes. Some programs may also teach **content-based ESL**, focusing on the vocabulary and language structures students will encounter during actual content-area instruction in their mainstream classrooms. Others may go as far as substituting for and 'sheltering' the English language arts instruction students would ordinarily receive in their regular classroom. The hope is that such pull-out programs provide a way to help language minoritized children cope in their mainstream classrooms. The more English they learn from their **pull-out ESL** teacher, the more they can understand and participate in their regular mainstream classroom. This is preferable to giving no English language support. In the United States such ESL support is therefore valuable, giving students not only English language learning provision but also the chance to build self-esteem and acquire the sole language of instruction. In short, pull-out ESL is far better than nothing (Wright, 2008).

However, 'withdrawn' children may fall behind on curriculum content delivered to others while they are out of the classroom. There may also be a stigma around absence and extraction, and feelings of alienation. A student may be seen by peers as 'remedial', 'disabled' or 'backward in English' (Ovando & Combs, 2017). Wright documented the feelings of one such former student reflecting on what it was like being pulled out of her mainstream classroom for ESL instruction: 'The other kids wouldn't say anything, but I would feel lost. Here I go again. Why do I have to do this? I felt so dumb. I felt like I'm dumb' (Wright, 2025: 124).

Pull-out ESL classes tend to be frequent in the United States but, as Wright notes, they have been highly criticized as the least effective model:

> The problems are many. First and perhaps most important, students miss out on instruction in their regular classrooms when they are pulled out. Second, pull-out ESL may lead some mainstream classroom teachers to view that the ELLs are mainly the responsibility of the ESL teacher. Third, many students feel stigmatized about being pulled out day after day in front of their English-only peers.... And finally, ESL instruction provided by the pull-out teacher typically is not coordinated with what the students are learning in their regular classrooms, largely because ESL teachers generally pull out students from several different classrooms, making it very difficult to coordinate with every teacher. Furthermore, pull-out teachers sometimes find mainstream teachers are unwilling to collaborate. (Wright, 2025: 124)

Wright (2025) also notes pull-out ESL is more expensive because it requires the hiring of additional teachers beyond the regular classroom teachers, and also creates challenges finding appropriate space for the pull-out teacher in typically overcrowded schools. Thus students may receive their ESL instruction in the hallway, the cafeteria, the basement, the auditorium stage or even in converted broom closets or storage rooms in the back of other teachers' classrooms. Such accommodations can send students implicit messages about the value of ESL instruction and how the school values them (and their ESL teacher).

Alternatively, 'push-in' ESL is where the ESL teacher comes into the mainstream classroom to provide ESL instruction (e.g. in the back of the room) and/or to provide instructional support during the regular teacher's instruction. In the best-case scenario, there is co-teaching (or complementary teaching), where the ESL and classroom teacher plan and deliver linguistically appropriate classrooms lessons together. Dove and Honigsfeld (2018) argue this is a far more effective arrangement, and provide several co-teaching models for effective collaboration of ESL and mainstream classroom teachers as they plan, teach, assess and reflect together on the progress of their ELL students (see also Lachance & Honigsfeld, 2023). However, such planning takes time, administrative support and a commitment from both teachers. When these factors are absent from a push-in model, the ESL teachers can become 'overpaid pointers' who simply lurk around the desks of ELL students, quietly pointing to things in the students' books or on their worksheets while the mainstream classroom teacher lectures on and on.

Sheltered/Structured Immersion

A more effective alternative to submersion with pull-out is when classroom teachers are trained and licensed to provide majority language instruction and to modify their curriculum and content-area instruction for students who are not yet proficient in the majority language. In the United States, such arrangements are called structured or **sheltered English immersion (SEI)** programs. In some states such as New York, SEI classrooms may simply be referred to as 'self-contained ESL' classrooms. In California and other states, sheltered instruction is called **specially designed academic instruction in English (SDAIE)**. Rather than a separate ESL teacher pulling students out or pushing herself into the classroom, the students receive ESL and sheltered content-area instruction directly from their regular classroom teacher. Various models of integrated English language development (ELD) aim to integrate language and sheltered content-area instruction.

The argument for an SEI program instead of a bilingual program is often pragmatic. In a class of 20 or more children, there may be many different home languages. For example, in London there are over 300 immigrant languages. In many US school districts with high ELL enrollments, over 100 different languages may be spoken (Seilstad, 2021). With such superdiversity, many schools claim that bilingual education is impossible, and SEI is the most practical approach. However, in many such diverse schools, there may still be a sufficient number of speakers of the same language to offer a bilingual program. In Texas and a few other states, bilingual education is required when there are at least 20 ELLs at the same grade level who speak the same language.

In **sheltered English** content-area instruction, content is taught in English, but the academic instruction is specially designed to make it comprehensible for ELLs, commensurate with their level of English proficiency (Echevarría & Graves, 2011). The teaching is also designed to facilitate students' **English language development** and thus helps supplement (but should not supplant) the teacher's ESL instruction (Wright, 2025). Sheltered instruction may feature simplified vocabulary, purpose-made materials and a variety of instructional strategies to make input comprehensible and language use interactive (e.g. cooperative learning, use of non-verbal communication, visual aids, demonstrations, hands-on experience and frequent checks for understanding).

One commonly used model of SEI was developed by Echevarría *et al.* (2023), who present a model of 30 specific components and strategies for effective sheltered instruction called the **Sheltered Instruction Observation Protocol (SIOP)**. The SIOP provides a tool for planning, observing and evaluating a teacher's implementation of sheltered instruction that teaches content material to ELLs. In immersion, dual immersion and other bilingual programs geared towards native English-speakers learning a minoritized language such as Spanish, sheltered Spanish content-area instruction is provided. For example, the Center for Applied Linguistics has extended the SIOP model to TWIOP (Two-Way Immersion Observation Protocol), which adds cultural objectives to a well defined and elaborate instructional approach (Howard *et al.*, 2006). Another popular model of sheltered instruction in the United States is called Guided Language Acquisition Design (GLAD), which is less structured than the SIOP model and features five broad components of instruction (Salgado & Olague, 2020).

SEI programs are designed for ELLs, though in practice many SEI classrooms contain a mix of ELL and English-proficient students. While some home language and translanguaging strategies can and should be used in an SEI classroom, such use is quick and temporary; students' home languages are not developed or used for instruction (Wright, 2025). In the United States and the United Kingdom, bilingual paraprofessionals or 'English as an additional language' (EAL) support staff are found in some primary (elementary) and secondary schools to aid the transition (Baker, 2012). Such bilingual support staff provide individual support, translate where needed, team-teach with the class teacher and may occasionally manage the whole class for bilingual storytelling sessions. However, some classroom teachers may feel use of a language other than English is inappropriate or embarrassing, or may feel uncomfortable not knowing everything that is being said, and therefore mostly use English. Regardless of such bilingual support, SEI has a linguistic aim of monolingualism in the majority language.

In both majority language and minoritized language contexts, there are sometimes transitional 'newcomer centers' using an SEI-type model. For example, in the United States recent immigrants and refugees may be placed in a newcomer program, particularly if they arrive as older secondary school students (Short & Boyson, 2012). In Welsh language regions of Wales, English-speakers will sometimes be placed in 'latecomer (newcomer) centers' so as to learn Welsh rapidly before moving to bilingual elementary or high mainstream schools (Brentnall et al., 2009). Such centers offer a 'shock-absorber' transitional experience, culturally, educationally and linguistically. In a sheltered, welcoming and supportive environment, newcomers can adjust to a new language, receive an orientation to the new society, adapt to a new culture over one or two semesters, or one to two years. A student with low-level literacy skills may stay in such a center for longer.

SEI may involve temporary segregation from first language English-speakers for one or more years until students reach sufficient proficiency for placement in a mainstream classroom. Faltis (1993: 146) notes that there can nonetheless be some positive features to temporary segregation: (1) greater opportunity for participation among students (they may be less inhibited because of no competition or comparisons with first language speakers of English); (2) greater sensitivity among teachers to the linguistic, cultural and educational needs of a homogeneous group of students; and (3) a collective identity among students in a similar situation. However, such language segregation removes proficient-speaker role models of the new language; may produce social isolation with overtones of stigmatization and reinforce negative stereotypes; may encourage the labeling of segregated students as linguistically and educationally inferior, deprived and in need of remedial attention; and may generate inequality in treatment (e.g. in curriculum materials and the lack of relevant training of teachers).

On the other hand, when SEI classrooms contain a mix of both language majority and language minoritized students, teachers may focus more attention on the native speakers and those with higher levels of English proficiency. Many teachers do not understand the differences and the relationship between ESL and **sheltered content instruction**, and mistakenly believe the latter is sufficient for both. A particular challenge in the United States is that many teachers believe that SEI is 'just good teaching' and thus that modifications specific to ELLs are not really needed (de Jong & Harper, 2005). This means that, in practice, SEI classrooms may actually be no different from mainstream submersion. In Arizona, following the passage of **Proposition 203** mandating SEI instruction (see Chapter 9), Wright (2014b) found that the state's initial enforcement of SEI simply meant making sure ELLs were taught only in English. When such ill-defined SEI instruction proved to be insufficient, the state established a rigid four-hour SEI model that focused on isolated grammar and vocabulary instruction devoid of academic content (Lillie & Moore, 2014). This model was widely criticized by ELL experts and advocates as lacking any grounding in second language acquisition research and what we know about effective second language teaching and learning (Lillie & Markos, 2014). The model also prevented ELLs from having full access to the academic curriculum and even prevented high school ELLs from obtaining the credits they needed to graduate. Arizona ultimately conceded the failure of this model and passed legislation (SB 1014) in 2019 which granted schools and districts greater flexibility in provided SEI instruction. But the Arizona case illustrates how SEI can vary widely in terms of program design and effectiveness (Moore, 2014, 2021).

SEI – when implemented properly – will potentially provide students with much greater opportunities for majority language development and academic content learning than submersion with pull-out or pull-in, or submersion alone. However, all three are forms of monolingual education for bilinguals and are **assimilationist**. These forms neglect students' bilingual development and fail to build on students' strengths in existing and emergent linguistic repertoires. A classic intensive two-year study by Valdés (2001) focused on Latinx students in US schools. Her findings provide an exemplification of the paradox of English language learning policies enacted in such US schools that can deny access to the language and knowledge that could empower immigrant children. She showed that, separately and cumulatively, complex interacting classroom factors frequently work against a student's English language development, achievement, employment, citizen rights and opportunities and self-esteem. Such factors include: impoverished second language interactions owing to a teacher–student ratio of over 1:30, passive learning and 'tight discipline' strategies, mixed **language competence** classes working to a low common denominator, subject matter kept simplistic as the second language is insufficiently developed, and teachers' concerns with 'flawed language' forms rather than communication. Valdés engages multi-level explanations: 'Placing blame is not simple. Structures of dominance in society interact with educational structures and educational ideologies as well as with teachers' expectations and with students' perspectives about options and opportunities' (Valdés, 2001: 4).

Weak Forms of Bilingual Education

Weak forms of bilingual education may make use of two languages in formal instruction, but generally do not aim for bilingualism. Instruction of the home language and/or instruction through the home language may be limited to a few years or less of schooling. At best, weak forms may result in limited levels of bilingualism. At worst, they result in relative monolingualism in the dominant societal language.

Transitional Bilingual Education

Far preferable to monolingual forms of education are programs that provide at least some instruction through students' home languages. In the United States and other parts of the world, the most common form of bilingual education is transitional bilingual education (TBE). In the United States this was the most frequently supported model under the Title VII **Bilingual Education Act** (see Chapter 9). The aim of transitional bilingual education is, nonetheless, assimilationist. It differs from monolingual forms of education in that language minoritized students are temporarily allowed to use their home language. Such students are taught through their home language for just a few years or until they are thought to be proficient enough in the majority language to cope in mainstream education. Thus, transitional education is a brief, temporary swim in one pool until the child is perceived as capable of moving to the mainstream pool. The aim is to increase use of the majority language in the classroom while proportionately decreasing the use of the home language in the classroom.

An educational rationale is based on perceived language, social and economic priorities: children need to function in the majority language in society. The argument is that if competence in the majority language is not quickly established, such children may fall behind their majority language peers. Thus, arguments about equality of opportunity and maximizing student performance are used to justify such transitional programs. The extent to which such justifications are valid or invalid is considered in Chapter 12.

In the United States, TBE programs typically begin in kindergarten and seek to fully transition students to all English instruction by the end of third grade. In many schools, however, TBE programs may last only one to two years. Some TBE programs are for older students (e.g. middle and high schools) who have received education through their native language, immigrated and require a transition to mainstream classes.

Scholars such as Ovando and Combs (2018) and García and Kleifgen (2018) criticize the TBE model for being remedial, compensatory and segregated, perpetuating the status quo by separating language minoritized students from the mainstream and thus reproducing differences in power and progress for those with lower class status.

While majority language monolingualism is the aim of TBE, teachers or their assistants need to be bilingual. The temporary home language 'swim' requires, for example, a Spanish-speaking teacher, who may be more sensitive and successful in teaching English to Spanish-speaking children than English-only teachers. The former can switch from one language to another and be more sympathetic to the language of the children. Nonetheless, a bilingual teacher can become the unwitting promoter of transition from one language to another and of assimilation into the majority culture. However, bilingual teachers – especially native-speakers who share the same cultural background as their students – may alternatively recognize the needs and wishes of their own communities. Thus they may continue to push the rapid transition to English in TBE but also try to preserve Spanish in the children, becoming allies of the community and not just allies of politicians and bureaucrats.

Similarly, in schools with transitional programs, there can be a hidden message in the staffing. People with power and prestige – the principals, assistant principals, counselors and the majority of the school's teachers – are often English monolinguals (Menken & Solarza, 2015). The people with the least power and status are cooks, lunch monitors, custodians, office staff and paraprofessionals who speak a minoritized language such as Spanish. The language of formal announcements is English; the language used by those who serve may be Spanish.

The transitional model is found not just in the United States. Where there is a majority language and much immigration, education is often expected to provide a linguistic and cultural transition (Wright *et al.*, 2015). Also, in developing countries such as Cambodia, transitional models have been successful in extending educational opportunities to indigenous ethnic minorities who do not speak the national languages (Wright & Boun, 2015; Wright *et al.*, 2022). In such cases as the latter, the notion of TBE as a 'weak form' may be called somewhat into question. In this case of Cambodia, Wright and Boun (2015) described several empowering features of the establishment of so-called 'weak' TBE programs, including: (1) the development of orthographies of previously oral-only languages, (2) the recognition and valuing of the language by the national government as a medium of instruction in state schools, (3) access to education in villages where previously schools were linguistically or physically inaccessible, (4) the rise in the status of the language through the publication of high-quality books and instructional materials, (5) opportunities for village leaders and members to oversee the school through community school boards, (6) employment opportunities for community members as bilingual teachers, (7) a 'foot-in-the-door' strategy of establishing a transitional bilingual model that can later be extended to a stronger developmental model and (8) an increase in ethnic minorities attending and graduating from high school, thus leading to an educated class that can better advocate for their communities.

Mainstream Education with World Language Teaching

In the United States, Australia, Canada and parts of Europe, most language majority school children receive their education through their home language. For example, children whose parents are English-speaking monolinguals attend school where English is the sole teaching medium. However, there is often some learning of other languages. Traditionally the term 'foreign language' is used. However, the term 'world languages' is now preferred, to emphasize that in our interconnected global world other languages are not so 'foreign' and may even be spoken widely locally and nationally (e.g. French in Canada, Spanish in the United States).

In Wales and elsewhere, world languages are sometimes informally called a 'drip-feed' language program. The term 'drip-feed' highlights the kind of language element in mainstream schooling. Second (foreign) language lessons of around half an hour per day may constitute the sole 'other' language diet. Drip-feeding Arabic, French, German, Chinese Mandarin (Putonghua), Japanese or Spanish makes the language a subject in the curriculum similar to science and mathematics. This is distinct from teaching through the medium of a second language, where curriculum content is the main focus rather than language learning (the latter is sometimes called embedding or content instruction).

In England and the United States, world language study is minimal. In England, Wales and Northern Ireland, 'language stopped being compulsory at key stage four (years 10 and 11) in 2004', leading to significant declines in the number of students taking a foreign language for the General Certificate of Secondary Education (GCSE) (Stollhans, 2024). The Commission on Language Learning (2017) estimated that only about 20% of US K-12 students were enrolled in foreign/world language courses. Most US students take only two years of world language courses in high school. Thus, relatively few world language students become competent in that second language. Where children receive a short second language lesson per day for between 5 and 12 years, few become functionally fluent in the second language.

However, there are increasing demands by **heritage language** students for opportunities to develop their languages at school (Wiley et al., 2014). **Heritage language education** will be discussed further in Chapter 11. In our increasingly globalized world, the distinctions between bilingual education, world language and heritage language are harder to discern. For example, as García noted, there is growing interaction 'between Spanish as a global language on the one hand, and Spanish as the minoritized language of US Latinos' (García, 2008: 31). In the United States, Spanish is taught as a world language, a heritage language, in **dual language bilingual education** programs and as part of global language teaching.

The Canadians found that after 12 years of French drip-feed language teaching, many English-background students were not fluent enough to communicate in French with French Canadians. Similarly in the United Kingdom, five years of French or German or Spanish in secondary school (age 11 to 16) results in only a few sufficiently competent to use that second language. For the great majority, the second language quickly shrivels and dies. Mainstream education rarely produces functionally bilingual children. A limited knowledge of a world language tends to be the typical outcome for most language majority students.

This is not the only outcome of second and world language teaching. The learning of English in, for example, Scandinavia and Slovenia, and in many countries in Asia and Africa does not fit this pattern, with many learners becoming proficient in English as a second or third language. When personal motivation and the status of a language are high, and when economic and vocational circumstances encourage the acquisition of a trading language, then world language teaching may be more successful. Learning a world language at elementary school has become increasingly favored in mainland Europe. The learning of English as an international language has increased in schools throughout the world (Salomone, 2024).

Separatist Education

A narrower view of language minoritized education would be to choose to foster monolingualism in the minoritized language in an area where another language is dominant. The aims are minoritized language monolingualism and monoculturalism in a context where such choice is possible. Such 'minoritized language only' education is relatively rare. The language minoritized group aims to detach itself from the language majority to pursue an independent existence. As a way of trying to protect a minoritized language from being overrun by the language majority, or for political, religious or cultural reasons, separatist minoritized language education may be promoted. This type of education may be organized by the language community for its survival and for self-protection.

It is unlikely that a school would formally state its aims in a linguistic separatist fashion. Rather, in the implicit functioning of isolationist religious schools and the political rhetoric of extreme language activists, the 'separatist' idea of such schools exists. Small in number, the importance of this category is that it highlights that language minoritized education is capable of moving from the goal of pluralism to separatism. In times of globalization, such separatism disconnects and withdraws children from the wider world.

Exclusion and Interruptions

Before concluding, it must be acknowledged that many language minoritized students are excluded – in part or in whole – from a meaningful education. In Cambodia, for example, prior to policies promoting multilingual **mother tongue** education programs, thousands of indigenous ethnic minoritized children in remote areas of the northeastern provinces had little to no access to even a basic education (Wright & Boun, 2015). In many cases, there simply were no schools in the village or surrounding area for children to attend. In some villages, schools were available but students did not attend because they could not understand the teacher or the curriculum taught only in the national language (Wright & Boun, 2016; Wright et al., 2022).

Many oppressed ethnic minoritized groups are denied access to national schools in their home countries. Wars and refugee crises may prevent children from attending school for several months or years. Civil unrest, drug violence and government corruption (e.g. demanding bribes for 'free' public education) may also prevent some children from attending school. In the United States, immigrant and refugee students who have experienced such exclusions are officially referred to as 'students with interrupted formal education' (SIFE) (Herrera, 2022). Lukes (2015) provides a detailed account of the interruptions in schooling experienced by many Latinx youth in the United States. Even within the United States and other 'developed' countries, there are extreme cases where language minorities have been completely denied access to schooling. In 2016 the Associated Press reported:

> In at least 35 districts in 14 states hundreds of unaccompanied minors from El Salvador, Guatemala, and Honduras have been discouraged from enrolling in schools, or pressured into what advocates and attorneys argue are separate but unequal alternative programs – essentially an academic dead end, and one that can violate federal law. (Burke & Sainz, 2016: 1)

Even worse, during the first Trump administration hundreds of migrant children were detained in Customs and Border Protection facilities in Texas along the Mexican border, where they were not only denied access to schools but were kept in deplorable conditions. The *New York Times* reported that in an overcrowded border station in Clint, Texas, the children had no opportunities to bathe and had no access to toothbrushes, toothpaste or soap (Dickerson, 2019).

More often, it is subtle forms of exclusion that prevent full access to education. In the context of immigration debates in the United States, Wiley (2013b) describes the process of constructing 'illegal children' (even in cases where children of immigrants are US-born citizens) and how this dehumanizing discourse is an assault on the educational rights of language minoritized children. Lillie (2016) describes the experiences of high school English language learner students in Arizona who were prevented from taking core academic courses needed to graduate because of the state's then mandated four-hour English language development (ELD) model. Ramanathan (2013) refers to these and other practices that prevent immigrants from fully participating in society as citizens of their adopted nation as a form a (dis)citizenship.

Excluding linguistic minoritized students from schooling is a violation of the basic rights of children (Skutnabb-Kangas, 2015) and is against the law in most countries (and individual US states) where constitutions guarantee children's access to education (Wright, 2019). Educational practices that prevent students from obtaining credits needed to graduate from high school must also be challenged. For immigrant students with limited or interrupted formal education, traditional program models of bilingual education alone may not be sufficient to fully address the students' linguistic and academic needs, and may require creative solutions tailored to the needs of individual students.

Conclusion

The typology of program models for bilingual students introduced in this chapter reveals important differences between monolingual, weak and strong forms of education for bilingual students. Monolingual forms are clearly assimilationist oriented and most often result in students who can speak only one language. However, this chapter has also revealed that weak forms of bilingual education are also often assimilationist and at best lead to limited levels of bilingualism.

Having considered some of the history of bilingual education and 'weak' types of such education, the next chapter moves onto 'strong' forms of bilingual education, where bilingualism and biliteracy are part of the aims. What can then be examined (in Chapter 12) is the relative success and effectiveness of these different forms of 'weak' and 'strong' bilingual education.

Key Points in This Chapter

- Monolingual forms of education for bilinguals promote assimilation and aim for monolingualism in the majority language.
- Submersion mainstream education programs provide no linguistic or academic support for language minoritized students. In the United States such instruction was declared illegal by the US Supreme Court in *Lau v. Nichols*.
- Some support can be provided for language minoritized students in mainstream classrooms through pull-out or push-in instruction designed to help students gain proficiency in the majority language.
- In sheltered (structured) English immersion (SEI) programs, the classroom teacher provides ESL and sheltered content-area instruction in English. Support using the home language and translanguaging strategies may also be provided.
- The basic aim of 'weak' forms of bilingual education is assimilation of language minorities rather than maintenance of their home languages and cultural pluralism.
- Transitional bilingual education allows a student temporary use of their home language for content learning. The basic aim remains assimilation and not bilingualism or biliteracy.
- Some students are completely or partially excluded from access to education. This is a violation of children's rights in most places.
- Immigrant students with interrupted formal education (SIFE) may require additional assistance tailored to their linguistic and academic needs, beyond placement in a traditional (bilingual) program model.
- World language programs for majority language students rarely result in students becoming proficient bilinguals.

Suggested Further Reading

- Herrera, L.J.P. (ed.) (2022) *English and Students with Limited or Interrupted Formal Education: Global Perspectives on Teacher Preparation and Classroom Practices*. Springer.
- Kenfield, Y.H. (2021) *Enacting and Envisioning Decolonial Forces while Sustaining Indigenous Language: Bilingual College Students in the Andes*. Multilingual Matters.
- Rubio-Alcalá, F.D. and Coyle, D. (eds) (2021) *Developing and Evaluating Quality Bilingual Practices in Higher Education*. Multilingual Matters.
- Seilstad, B.D. (2021) *Educating Adolescent Newcomers in the Superdiverse Midwest: Multilingual Students in English-centric Contexts*. Multilingual Matters.
- Wright, W.E. (2025) *Foundations for Teaching English Language Learners: Research, Theory, Policy, and Practice* (4th edn). Brookes Publishing.

On the Web

- Video – Becoming bilingual: first steps (sheltered English immersion classroom in El Paso, Texas) https://youtu.be/fHgSnEOOvro
- Video – How multilingual education helped Cambodia boost indigenous student enrolment https://www.youtube.com/watch?v=MNcxNKbWNv8
- Video – Multilingual education in Cambodia: A bridge for ethnic children at school https://youtu.be/-bX0Y-Zn8JE
- National Association for Bilingual Education https://www.nabe.org
- American Council of Teachers of Foreign Languages https://www.actfl.org

Discussion Questions

(1) Share your experiences participating in or observing any of the program types described in this chapter. How effective did you find this program to be in helping (or not helping) students become bilingual?

(2) The presence of many different languages in a school is often used as an excuse for not providing a bilingual program, even when there are large numbers of speakers of the same language (e.g. Spanish). The argument may be 'we can't do a bilingual program for our Chinese-, Burmese-, Somali- or Arabic-speakers, so we shouldn't do one for our Spanish-speakers'. How would you respond to such an argument?

(3) In the United States and other countries, many language minoritized students start school bilingual but end school monolingual or with very limited bilingual skills. At the same time, students are expected to study a world language in high school for a couple of years. What are the problems with such a system that fails to produce bilingual students?

Study Activities

(1) Observe and report on one program designed for bilingual students. Based on Table 10.1, what would you call that program? Note the nature and amount of use

of the two languages in the program for different content areas or different parts of the day. How would you describe the program's societal, educational and language aims?
(2) Teachers of sheltered/structure English immersion (SEI) are supposed to provide their own ESL and sheltered content-area instruction within their classroom. However, some programs are SEI in name only, and differ little from mainstream submersion. Observe and report on an SEI classroom, noting what, if anything, differentiates the classroom from a mainstream classroom in ways that are beneficial to the language and academic development of the students.
(3) Interview a teacher of one of the program types described in this chapter. Ask about the educational, societal and linguistic aims of the program. How do they compare to those listed in Table 10.1?

CHAPTER 11

Education for Bilingualism and Biliteracy

Introduction

Dual Language Bilingual Education
Origins and Development
Dual Language Schools and Peace

Heritage Language Education
Indigenous Education in the United States

Immersion Bilingual Education
Types of Immersion Bilingual Education

Bilingual and Multilingual Education in Majority Languages
Content and Language Integrated Learning (CLIL)
International Schools
European Schools Movement
Other European Examples of Multilingual Education

Conclusion

CHAPTER 11

Education for Bilingualism and Biliteracy

Introduction

The two previous chapters respectively provided a historical background to bilingual education and an introduction to 'weak' forms of bilingual education. This chapter examines the 'strong' forms of bilingual education introduced in the typology outlined in Chapter 10. Both US and international models are examined.

Strong forms of bilingual education have **bilingualism, biliteracy** and biculturalism as intended outcomes. Some schools aim for **multilingualism, multiliteracies** and multiculturalism. This chapter particularly examines (1) **dual language bilingual education**, (2) **heritage language** bilingual education, (3) **immersion bilingual education** and mainstream bilingual education through two or more majority languages. Each of these models is well established, favorably evaluated and flourishing.

Dual Language Bilingual Education

Dual language bilingual education (DLBE) includes both two-way and one-way programs. In traditional two-way DLBE programs in the United States, approximately equal numbers of **language minoritized** and **language majority students** are in the same classroom and both languages are used for instruction. For example, approximately half the children may be from Spanish-speaking homes, the other half from English **monolingual** homes, and they work together in the classroom. Since both languages are used for learning, the aim is to produce relatively balanced bilinguals. Biliteracy is as much an aim as full bilingualism (see Chapter 14). Other terms used to describe two-way DLBE programs include two-way immersion and two-way bilingual education.

In one-way DLBE programs, all students are from the same language background. In cases where all the students are language minoritized speakers, the program is essentially a **developmental bilingual education** program (e.g. Spanish-speaking students in the United States learning in Spanish and English). In cases where all the students are language majority speakers, the program is essentially a world language immersion program (e.g. English-speaking students in the United States learning in Chinese and English).

The growth of DLBE programs has been considerable. The oldest publicly funded school program, at Coral Way Elementary School, dating back to 1963 in Dade County, Florida, was developed by a US Cuban community (Coady, 2020). The US Center for Applied Linguistics (CAL) maintains a national database of two-way bilingual

Table 11.1 Languages used in US dual language schools (2019–2020)

Language	No. of states with dual language schools	Language	No. of states with dual language schools
Spanish	30	Armenian	1
Chinese/Mandarin	15	ASL	1
French	9	Cantonese	1
German	5	Greek	1
Japanese	5	Hawaiian	1
Korean	5	Ilokano	1
Native American languages	5	Italian	1
Arabic	4	Nepali	1
Hmong	3	Polish	1
Portuguese	3	Somali	1
Russian	3	Swahili	1
Vietnamese	3	Urdu	1
Haitian	2	Yiddish	1
Hebrew	2		

Source: Office of English Language Acquisition (2023c). Based on state self-reported data. The actual number is likely to be higher. There may be more than one partner language in use per state. Illinois, Florida, and Utah did not report the partner languages in its dual language programs.

immersion schools and had over 886 programs listed in 2020 (see https://www.cal.org/twi/directory/index.html). The list does not appear to have been updated at the time of this writing. For example, the Dual Language Training Institute associated with the Gómez and Gómez dual language enrichment model claimed in 2020 that over 700 schools across 11 states had adopted this particular model alone (see https://www.dltigomez.com/). However, this number includes both one-way and two-way models. According to Palmer *et al.* (2015), the Gómez and Gómez two-way DLBE model does not meet CAL's criterion for inclusion because, according to the program design, English-speaking students in pre-K to grade 1 receive less than 50% of instruction through Spanish. Data from the US Department of Education for the 2019–2020 school year revealed dual language programs in 33 different languages (see Table 11.1) across 37 states (Office of English Language Acquisition, 2023c). With states such as Utah (Sung, 2024; Sung & Tsai, 2019), New York (García & Kleyn, 2016), Indiana (Chestnut & Dimitrieska, 2018), New Mexico, Delaware, Georgia, North Carolina, Washington and others passing legislation or undertaking other activities to promote one-way and two-way immersion programs, the actual number of various forms of dual language programs is likely in the thousands (Arias & Markos, 2018) and will continue to grow, especially with restrictions on bilingual education removed or loosened in California, Massachusetts and Arizona.

Traditional US two-way dual language programs tend to share the following features:

- A non-English language (i.e. a minoritized language) is used for at least 50% of instruction, which lasts for up to six years or more.

- In each period of instruction, only one language is normally used. Instruction must be adjusted to the student's language level, but must also be challenging, empowering and enabling. Language is learned primarily through content.
- Both English-speakers and non-English-speakers are present in approximately balanced numbers and integrated for most content instruction.

A language balance among students close to 50%–50% is attempted because if one language becomes dominant, the aim of bilingualism and biliteracy may be at risk. The reality of such schools is often different, with an imbalance towards larger numbers of **language minoritized students** being more common.

Where there is a serious imbalance in the two languages among students, one language may become dominant (e.g. Spanish-speaking children having to switch to English to work cooperatively). Alternatively, one language group may become marginalized, for example Spanish-speakers being excluded from English-speaking groups. Segregation rather than integration may occur. In the creation of a dual language school or classroom, careful student selection decisions have to be made to ensure a social language balance that goes beyond a balance of numbers. Differences in minority and majority language status, and power relations between English and other languages, make language balance decisions crucial in such a school. Thus, numerical balance and attempts to designate specific times, subjects or spaces for one language or the other do not necessarily lead to language balance.

A study of third-grade two-way dual immersion classrooms in Texas by Henderson and Palmer (2020) found that much English was spoken by the students and even the teacher during times and in spaces specified for Spanish. There was also some Spanish use by students during English-designated instructional time. While students had some agency in their hybrid language practices, Henderson and Palmer found the presence of a powerful overarching dominant language **ideology** of English superiority.

When an imbalance does exist, it may be preferable to have more language minoritized children. Where there is a preponderance of language majority children, the tendency is for language minoritized children to switch to the higher-status, majority language. In most language **contexts**, the majority language is well represented outside school (e.g. in the media and for employment). Therefore, the dominance of the majority language outside school can be complemented by a corresponding weighting toward the minoritized language in school (in both student enrollment and curriculum delivery). However, if the school enrolls a particularly large number of language minoritized children, the prestige of the school can sometimes suffer because of societal **raciolinguistic** ideologies (see Chapter 1). Also, dual language schools aim to develop both languages to full fluency, so both languages need to be able to grow to all individuals' optimal potential.

In dual language magnet schools in the United States, students may be drawn from a wide geographical area. A good reputation and perceived effectiveness of the program are crucial. The growing popularity of dual language programs is attracting more and more language majority students. It is important to ensure that the interests, values and voices of language minoritized parents are not pushed out by more vocal and powerful language majority parents. This has become a growing concern among bilingual education scholars, who have coined this problem the 'gentrification' of dual language education (Delavan *et al.*, 2024). Community backing and community involvement in the school are also important to initial and long-term success (Kleyn *et al.*, 2024). The development of dual language bilingual schools may preferably start with the creation of a dual language kindergarten class. As the kindergarten students move through the grades, a new dual language class is created each year.

Apart from elementary dual language bilingual schools, there is also dual language secondary education in the United States and, with different names, in many other countries of the world (e.g. Wales, Spain, India). A dual language bilingual school may be a whole school in itself; alternatively, there may be a dual language strand within a 'mainstream' school, with one or two dual language classrooms in each grade.

The following are major goals of dual language programs (Arias & Markos, 2018; Howard et al., 2018):

- *Bilingualism* – high levels of proficiency in students' first and a second language.
- *Biliteracy* – reading and writing at grade level in both languages.
- *Academic achievement* – academic achievement at, or above, grade level (e.g. mathematics, science, social studies).
- *Sociocultural competence* – positive intercultural (**multicultural**) attitudes and behaviors. Communities and society benefit from having citizens who are bilingual and biliterate, who are positive toward people of different cultural backgrounds and who can meet national needs for **language competence** and a more peaceful coexistence with peoples of other nations.

Cervantes-Soon et al. (2017) call for an additional goal – critical consciousness – to address issues of inequalities in dual language programs that may disadvantage marginalized English language learner, immigrant and transnational students (see also Freire et al., 2024).

The aim of dual language bilingual schools is thus not simply to produce bilingual and biliterate children. Such schools enhance inter-group communicative competence and cultural awareness. The integration of native speakers of two different languages (e.g. Spanish and English) provides authentic, meaningful communication between children from the two different language groups, both of whom are 'native speakers'. Such schools produce children who, in terms of inter-group relations, are likely to be more tolerant, respectful, sensitive and equalized in status. Genuine cross-cultural friendships may develop, and issues of stereotyping and discrimination may be diminished (Arias & Markos, 2018).

To gain status and to flourish, dual language schools need to show success throughout the curriculum (Lindholm-Leary & Genesee, 2014). On high-stakes state **testing**, on attainment compared with other schools in the locality, and in specialisms (e.g. music, sport, science), dual language bilingual schools should strive to show relative success. A narrow focus on proficiency in two languages would be insufficient to attract parents and students to enroll.

Dual language schools also aim to promote the competences students will need to enter the global jobs market. Students graduating in Spanish and English, for example, should be well placed to operate in international markets, transnational businesses and global operations (e.g. national defense), as these two languages are spoken across different continents and in many countries outside the United States (see Chapter 19). However, this has drawn some criticism. For example, it may be that native English-speakers who become fluent in Spanish may benefit most. It may be that this reduces **Latinxs'** natural advantage as bilinguals in such employment (Valdés, 1997, 2020).

The mission of dual language bilingual schools may also be couched in terms such as 'equality of educational opportunity for children from different language backgrounds', 'child-centered education building on the child's existing language competence', 'a positive self-image for each child', 'a community dedicated to the integration of all its children', 'enrichment not compensatory education', 'a family-like experience to produce multicultural children' and 'supporting bilingual proficiency'. The mission of all dual language schools (compared with mainstreaming) is to produce bilingual, biliterate and multicultural children (Freire *et al.*, 2024). Language minoritized students are expected to become literate in a standardized variety of their home language as well as in the majority language. At the same time, majority language students should make 'age-relevant' progress in their first language and in all content areas of the curriculum. To achieve these aims, a variety of practices are implemented in dual language bilingual schools:

(1) The two languages of the school (e.g. Spanish and English, or Mandarin and English) are given equal status in the school. Both languages are used as a medium of instruction, with an integration of language and content learning. Mathematics, science and social studies, for example, may be taught in both languages. However, care has to be taken not to be repetitive and not to teach the same content in both languages.
(2) The school ethos will be bilingual. Such an ethos is created by classroom and corridor displays, notice boards, school web pages, school social media, curriculum resources, cultural events, lunchtime and extracurricular activities using both languages in a relatively balanced way. Announcements across the school address system will be bilingual. Letters to parents will also be in two languages. While student-to-student talk is difficult to influence or manipulate, the school environment aims to be transparently bilingual.
(3) Language arts instruction is provided in both languages. Here, aspects of spelling, grammar, metaphors and communicative skills may be directly taught. Biliteracy is as much an aim as full bilingualism. Literacy will be acquired in both languages either simultaneously or with an initial emphasis on minoritized language literacy (see Chapter 14).
(4) Most staff in dual language classrooms are bilingual. The exception is some co-teaching models that pair a bilingual teacher with a monolingual (English) teacher. Some teachers use both languages on different occasions with their students. In school-wide programs, bilingual paraprofessionals, secretaries, custodial staff and/or parents volunteers complement classroom instruction by also being bilingual. Language minoritized parents can be valuable 'teacher auxiliaries' in the classroom. For example, when a wide variety of Spanish-speaking cultures from many regions are brought into the classroom, parents and grandparents may describe and provide the most authentic stories, dances, recipes, folklore and festivals (see Chapter 14). This underlines the importance of the many and varied cultures of language minoritized speakers being shared in the classroom to create an additive bilingual and multicultural environment.
(5) The dual language bilingual program needs to be longer rather than shorter: two or three grades is insufficient; a minimum of five years, or extending as far as possible through the grades, is more effective (see Chapter 8). Elementary school programs can feed into middle school and high school dual language programs. A child's longer experience of a dual language bilingual program is important to ensure a fuller and deeper development of language skills, and biliteracy in particular. Students in such longitudinal programs should be able to easily earn their

state's Seal of Biliteracy upon graduation from high school (Heineke *et al.*, 2024). However, where a US dual language bilingual program exists across more years, there is a tendency for the curriculum to be increasingly taught in English; this can undermine the goals of the program.

These practices and more are addressed by the Center for Applied Linguistics (CAL), which has established a set of 25 guiding principles for dual language education across seven strands: (1) program structure, (2) curriculum, (3) instruction, (4) assessment and accountability, (5) staff quality and professional development, (6) family and community, and (7) support and resources (Howard *et al.*, 2018). CAL provides a set of self-assessment rubrics for educators to use to determine the extent to which their dual language programs adhere to these principles. Guilamo (2022) provides an overarching framework for bilingual educators and researchers to assess the effectiveness of dual language bilingual education programs.

A longstanding but recently questioned practice in dual language bilingual schools is language separation and compartmentalization. In each period of instruction, only one language is used. Language boundaries are established in terms of time, curriculum content and teaching. The growing debate over this practice will be discussed below.

A decision is made about when to teach through each language. One common practice is for each language to be used on alternate days or weeks. For example, Spanish is used one day, English the next, in a strict sequence. Another common practice is to alternate languages in the morning and afternoon (e.g. Spanish in the morning, English in the afternoon). Teachers typically signal the expected language of use through signs on the doors and walls, or even by wearing colored tags or necklaces (e.g. red for Spanish, blue for English). Alternatively, different lessons may use different languages with a regular change-over to ensure both languages are used in all curricular areas. For example, Spanish may be used to teach mathematics on Monday and Wednesday and Friday; English to teach mathematics on Tuesday and Thursday. During the next week, the languages are reversed, with mathematics taught in Spanish on Tuesday and Thursday. There are other possibilities. The division of time may be in alternate days, weeks or even half semesters. In some programs, rather than a single bilingual teacher providing instruction in both languages, a co-teaching model is used, with one teacher for Spanish and another for English. The essential element is a careful distribution of time to achieve bilingual and biliterate students.

The model used, the names that such models are given, the composition of language minoritized and majority students, and the amount of time spent learning through each language vary greatly across states and schools (Boyle *et al.*, 2015; Wright & Choi, 2024). The two main models in the United States are 50:50 and 90:10. In the 90:10 model, 90% of instruction is in the minoritized language in the kindergarten and first grade, with 10% to develop English oral **language proficiency** and pre-literacy skills (see Figure 11.1). Variations are possible where the minoritized language will be given more time than the majority language (80:20, 75:25, 60:40), especially in the first two or three years. Over the remaining elementary grades this ratio gradually changes to 50:50 (e.g. by the fourth to sixth grade).

The Gómez and Gómez dual language enrichment model (Gómez *et al.*, 2005) is unique in that it allocates different languages for different content areas. That is, it divides languages by subject and not time (although, overall, English and Spanish are approximately equally used). Mathematics is taught through the English language, science and social studies through Spanish. This model also does not require a balance

An example of language allocation in dual language models

	Grades K–1	Grades 2–3	Grades 4–6
50:50 dual language model – Spanish instruction	50	50	50
50:50 dual language model – English instruction	50	50	50
90:10 dual language model – English instruction	10	20	50
90:10 dual language model – Spanish instruction	90	80	50

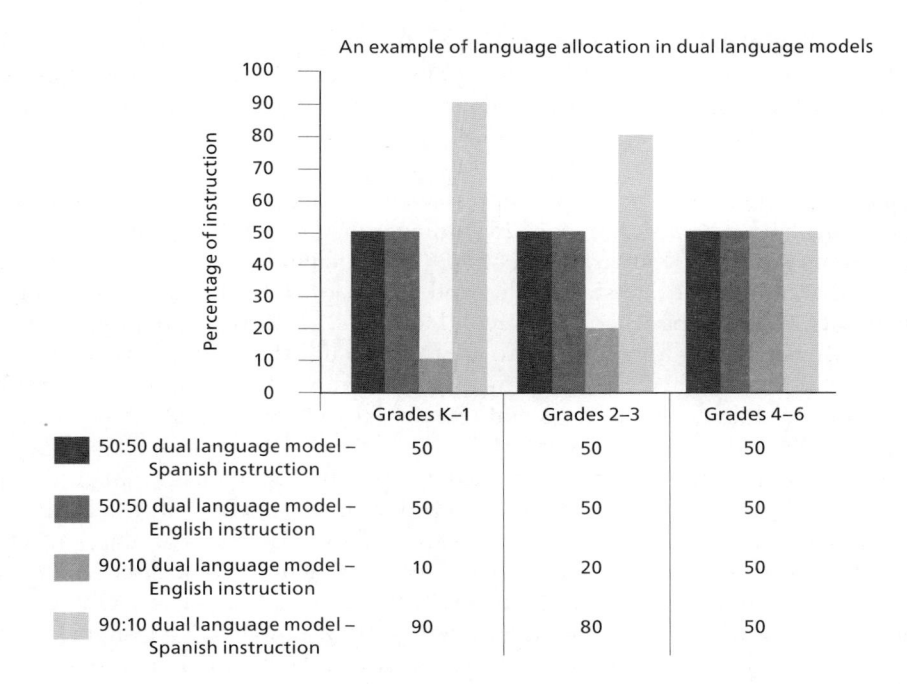

Figure 11.1 Language allocation in 50:50 and 90:10 dual language bilingual education models

of dominant English- and Spanish-speakers, and thus is particularly popular in schools with large Latinx populations such as those along the Texas–Mexico border, where it was first developed. Usage of this model has expanded rapidly across 11 states, but is restricted to schools that have agreements with the Dual Language Training Institute (https://www.dltigomez.com), which requires strict fidelity to the model. However, in a study of the implementation of the model in a central Texas school district, Palmer *et al*. (2015: 453) found that 'the primarily top-down implementation appears to have mixed results when confronted with the realities of different school contexts and educator language ideologies'.

Whatever the division of time or subject, instruction in most dual language bilingual programs attempts to keep boundaries between the languages. However, both languages will, in reality, likely be mixed in the classroom (e.g. in private conversations, in group work, in further explanations by a teacher and in internal use of the dominant language) (Henderson & Sayer, 2020). Use of languages by children, especially when young, is not usually consciously controlled. **Translanguaging**, or drawing upon one's entire linguistic repertoire (e.g. moving easily between Spanish and English), often has both communication value (see Chapter 5) and pedagogic value (see Chapter 13). Translanguaging can be as natural as smiling. In classrooms, however, the degree to which strict separation is practiced or enforced can vary widely (Henderson & Palmer, 2020).

Translanguaging occurs naturally in a bilingual classroom where children spontaneously and pragmatically draw upon all of their language practices to communicate (Sánchez & García, 2022). For many bilingual children, and some bilingual teachers, it is cognitively, linguistically and operationally sensible to use both of their languages together. It maximizes both linguistic and cognitive resources, and helps achievement and progress (Sánchez, 2024). Thus, dual language education that insists on strict boundaries and compartmentalization between languages may be based on an outdated conception of language acquisition (see Chapter 8). Insistence on strict language separation may be unnecessary and even counterproductive. For example, when a student does not understand curriculum content or instructions, a teacher may naturally move into the child's stronger/other language to explain, allowing the student to learn the content most efficiently along with the new language related to it. Some researchers remain concerned, however, that students in this context will come to realize that they do not need to learn to understand their second or weaker language, because the teacher or peers will translate for them (Fortune & Tedick, 2019). This is a concern especially in two-way or one-way world language immersion contexts in which majority language speakers are present or predominant. Another danger is that lack of protected time to focus on the minoritized language may lead to fewer opportunities for students to develop proficiency in the language.

One danger in language separation is when the allocation of languages is by content – for instance, the majority language is used for science and technology and the minoritized language is used for social studies. In this example, the majority language becomes aligned with modern technology and science, while the minoritized language becomes associated with tradition and culture. This may affect the status of the language in the eyes of the child, parents and society. The relationship of each school language to employment prospects, economic advantage and power also needs to be considered. The caution issued by Valdés (1997) many years ago and reissued more recently (Valdés, 2018) about the power relations between, for example, Spanish- and English-speakers in dual language schools continues to be of great importance, especially where programs contain White middle-class English speakers and low-income Spanish-speakers (Delavan *et al.*, 2024). Opportunities for both groups to reach high levels of achievement are important. Otherwise, native Spanish-speakers may be exploited as a language resource, and English-speakers become the bilinguals with high achievement and the economic/employment advantages of bilingualism and biliteracy (Cervantes-Soon *et al.*, 2017).

Other issues about dual language bilingual education programs need to be considered. Will both language groups gain high competence in a second language? Or, for example, will the teacher need to spend too much time on developing Spanish in English-speakers, with consequent effects on the language or academic development of Spanish-speakers? The opposite could also occur. Will the English language receive preferential treatment in instruction as English is the status language in society and legislation? For example, Palmer *et al.* (2016) observed that the language of high-stakes state tests became the dominant language of instruction, despite program models being officially 50:50. Thus, for students taking the tests in Spanish, instruction was predominantly in Spanish, while for students taking the tests in English, instruction was predominantly in English. The pressure associated with raising test scores transformed the dual language program into more of a monolingual education program. Hinton also observed this phenomenon in a high-poverty, overwhelmingly Latinx (over 90%) school district, where many programs for ELLs were what he called 'bilingual-in-name-only classrooms' (Hinton, 2015: 265).

Dual language bilingual education is not just about a more or less desirable form of education with educational and dual language effectiveness as its *raison d'être*. The underlying politics of dual language education need also to be understood. Salaberry (2009: 193) shows that such schools are instruments of social engineering, 'aiming to develop a more coherent and demographically representative new mainstream civic identity'. Such dual language education is the antithesis of **assimilation**. Instead, it may provide children with a cosmopolitan, integrated, multilingual, pluralistic ideology.

As dual language bilingual education has grown in popularity, new issues are emerging. For example, in many schools in the United States, the English-speakers may include African-American students who at home speak the non-standard (and often stigmatized) dialect of African-American Vernacular English (Baker-Bell, 2020a, 2020b; Bauer et al., 2018; Dobbs & Bauer, 2024) (see Chapter 13). However, in some schools African-American students may be discriminated against by being systematically excluded from DLBE classrooms over fears they will be 'poor' models of English for the minoritized language students (Wall et al., 2022). Such discriminatory practices ignore the long history African-American student involvement in bilingual education programs, including in Chinese–English bilingual programs in San Francisco following the US Supreme court ruling in the landmark *Lau v. Nichols* (1974) case (Morita-Mullaney, 2024b). Some DLBE programs include students with home languages other than English and the target language (e.g. speakers of Asian and Arabic languages in Spanish–English programs; Spanish-speaking students in Chinese or Korean dual language programs, etc.) (Martínez et al., 2017; Morita-Mullaney, 2024a; Wright & Choi, 2024). There may also be speakers of indigenous Mayan languages in Spanish–English DLBE classrooms. An increasing number of exceptional students with special needs are also being placed in dual language programs (see Chapter 15). As the student population becomes more multilingual and multicultural beyond the binary bilingual/bicultural bounds of a traditional dual language classrooms, new models and ways of addressing the academic, linguistic and cultural needs of all dual language program students will be needed.

Origins and Development

Modern dual language bilingual education programs in the United States date from 1963 in Dade County, Florida, and were developed by the US Cuban community in that area (Coady, 2020). In September 1963, the Coral Way Elementary School started a bilingual program that embraced both Spanish- and English-speaking students. During the 1960s, another 14 such bilingual schools were set up in Dade County. This is related to the fact that many Cubans expected to return to Cuba, believing the Castro regime would not survive. Local people supported the maintenance of Spanish among the 'soon-to-leave' Cubans. Local English-speaking children from middle-class families were enrolled in the school. This reflected a wish among majority language parents for more foreign language instruction, driven by Russia's initial triumph over the United States in the space race following the launch of Sputnik in 1958. Since that era, there has been a steady rise in the number of dual language bilingual education programs across the United States (Palmer et al., 2015).

Another early example of a dual language bilingual school – documented in an ethnographic account by Freeman (1998) – is the James F. Oyster Bilingual Elementary School in Washington, DC (now called the Oyster-Adams Bilingual School). The school's two-way Spanish–English program commenced in 1971. The initiative was taken by the local community (by parents and local politicians) to produce a school that crossed language, cultural, ethnic and social class lines. Parents were active in the running of the school. Freeman reported an ethnic mix of students (from kindergarten to sixth grade) of around 60% Hispanic, 20% White; 15% Black and 5% Asian and other language minorities. Approximately two in every five children came from low-income families (e.g. they were eligible for the free-lunch program under federal guidelines). The school remains diverse and the program continues to be in high demand, so much so that a lottery system has been established for the admission of out-of-boundary students.

Strong equality dimensions pervade the curriculum (ethnic, multicultural, linguistic, social class), with the contributions of different children encouraged and respected. The notion of language equality permeates the ethos of the school (Freeman, 1998, 2004), as reflected in the school's mission statement:

> We believe that ALL students regardless of race, class, gender or circumstance can achieve bilingually at high levels. We hold high expectations for our students, our colleagues and ourselves.... Oyster-Adams Bilingual School is an inclusive community of learners dedicated to academic excellence and creativity that develops globally responsible leaders who are bilingual and bi-literate in Spanish and English.... Our motto: Be Bilingual. Embrace Diversity. Achieve Excellence.

Kleyn *et al.* (2024) provide a recent example of the lesson learned from the development of the dual language bilingual school, Dos Puentes Elementary School, in New York City. Kleyn and Hunt (2024: 13), as co-founder and founding principal, describe the four Dos Puentes pillars that represent the bilingual school's philosophy and collaborative commitments:

(1) *bilingüismo, bilteracidad, y multiculturalismo,*
(2) *las familias son* partners, leaders, and advocates,
(3) *investigaciones* and hands-on learning, and
(4) partnerships with universities organizations, *y la communidad*

Dual Language Schools and Peace

In several countries around the world, dual language bilingual education attempts to effect social, cultural, economic or political change, particularly in strengthening the weak, empowering the powerless, and working for peace and humanity in the midst of conflict, racism and terror. As Lo Bianco (2016: 1) explains, 'the term peacebuilding is generally understood to involve a range of measures to reduce the risk of lapse or relapse into conflict by addressing causes and consequences of conflict'. In his research on peacebuilding efforts in Malaysia, Myanmar and Thailand, Lo Bianco (2016: 2) found that 'some aspects of language are present in many conflicts, some kinds of conflict involve many aspects of language, and some conflicts are only about language'. Lo Bianco (2019) provides details about these types of conflicts in the deep south of Thailand between the Thai and Patani Malay language. He argues that 'addressing language issues in non-reductive ways can be a component of general conflict reduction strategy' (Lo Bianco, 2019: 295).

Two particular examples – Macedonia and Israel – demonstrate the potential of dual language schools as a measure for addressing such language aspects of conflict resolution and peacebuilding efforts. The role of dual language schools in bringing peace in Macedonia is well illustrated by Tankersley (2001) in her article aptly entitled

'Bombs or bilingual programmes?' Contextualized within the ethnic conflict in the Balkans at the end of the last century, she examines a Macedonian–Albanian dual language program. The program demonstrated success in aiding community rebuilding after the war and the growth of cross-ethnic friendships. The research shows the potential for bilingual education programs to develop students' respect for different languages and cultures, and to help to resolve ethnic conflict. However, since the Macedonian language was connected with greater power and prestige, obtaining an equal balance of languages in the classroom was complex.

Dual language Arabic–Hebrew (Palestinian–Jewish) bilingual programs in Israel that aim to break down barriers of mistrust and build peace are portrayed by Bekerman, who has studied such bilingual schools since 1998. She explains:

> The schools … aspire to offer a new educational option to two groups of Israelis – Palestinian Arabs and Jews – who have been in conflict with each other for the past 100 years. The goal of this initiative is to create egalitarian bilingual multicultural environments that will facilitate the growth of Israeli youth who can acknowledge and respect 'others' while maintaining loyalty to their respective cultural traditions. The hope is that Hebrew and Arabic will be used equally in these environments and that the historical narrative and heritage of each group will be recognized. (Bekerman, 2016: ix)

Each of the dual language bilingual schools has Arab and Jewish co-principals and each classroom is co-taught by Jewish and Arab teachers. Schools attempt to keep equal numbers of Arab and Jewish pupils in each class. Students are instructed in and through both Hebrew and Arabic. They learn to cherish both languages and cultures and build mutual understanding, tolerance and respect. Such schools provide a showcase to reveal that Jews and Arabs can study, work and seek to live together in peace, forgiveness and reconciliation (Amara *et al.*, 2009).

Peace schools are inevitably part of a wider society, such that equality of languages and resoluteness of purpose and mission can be difficult to maintain (Amara *et al.*, 2009). Arabic has less power and cultural capital than Hebrew in Israel. Many Arabs speak Hebrew, while most Israeli Jews do not know much Arabic. As Cummins (2000a) has argued, bilingual education cannot reconstruct power and status differences in society. Such schools cannot be islands, and 'bottom-up' rather than 'top-down' initiatives are not always easy to sustain in such contexts. Parents also have other dreams, such as English language fluency, high educational achievement and social mobility for their children. That makes language and political ideology just one component of a complex whole. Yet such initiatives symbolize that bilingual education can include a vision that goes beyond languages, beyond a troubled past, and work toward a better present and future. Through dialogue and reconciliation, social change may be achieved.

Heritage Language Education

Heritage language education refers to a wide variety of in-school and out-of-school programs that give students an opportunity to develop higher levels of proficiency in their home or heritage languages. Cushing-Leubner (2020: 304) reminds us that 'the realities of heritage language education cannot be separated from the political and ideological contexts in which certain languages are supported, demanded, removed, or replaced through state-sanctioned mechanisms, particularly language policies of schooling'. Thus, heritage language education is ultimately intertwined with issues of language rights. Some heritage language programs provide only a few hours of heritage language instruction, as an add-on to the regular curriculum. Such programs are weak forms of bilingual education because they are unlikely to lead to high levels of proficiency in the heritage language. However, heritage language programs may be considered a strong form of bilingual education when the home or heritage language of language minoritized children is used as a **medium of instruction** with the goal of full bilingualism. In addition, a strong form of heritage language bilingual education requires adequate resources, sufficient instructional time focused on developing the heritage language, and proper training and professional development for the teachers. The *Handbook of Heritage, Community, and Native American Languages in the United States* (Wiley et al., 2014) provides examples of education through, or more often partly through, the medium of: American Sign Language, Arabic, Chinese, Filipino, French, German, Hindi, Italian, Japanese, Khmer, Korean, Portuguese, Russian, Spanish and Yiddish, in addition to Native American languages, including Diné bizaad (Navajo), Pueblo languages, Myaamia (Miami), Hawaiian and Warm Springs languages. Heritage language programs are also found for indigenous speakers in many countries, including Mexico, Canada, Australia, Japan, the United Kingdom, Peru and India, as well as South American, African, European, Middle Eastern and post-Soviet countries (see Wright et al., 2015). The native language is protected and cultivated alongside development in the majority language.

In New Zealand, the Māori language has been promoted in schools with indications of positive outcomes in achievement and expansion (Hill & May, 2014). The full immersion pre-school programs (called Te Kohanga Reo – language nests) were first established in 1982 and have become internationally famous for their early language success with Māori speakers. An early start to bilingual education can create a 'domino effect', producing a demand for bilingual education beyond pre-school to elementary, secondary and higher education, helping to legitimize the minoritized language, and transforming its power and status. A similar promotion of Aboriginal languages occurs in heritage language education in Australia (Nicholls, 2005).

In Ireland, Irish-medium (Gaeilge-medium) education is sometimes available for children from Irish language backgrounds (Harris & Cummins, 2013). Irish-medium youth work provides an important complement to formal education by providing social opportunities for Irish students to speak Gaeilge outside of school (Roibeaird, 2024). In China, there are 55 ethnic minority groups, plus the Han, who are in a majority (92% of the 1.2 billion population). Since 1979, minoritized language education has been provided for over 20 minority groups, partly as a way of improving ethnic minority relationships with the central government (Feng & Adamson, 2015). Similar movements are reported in Papua New Guinea and elsewhere across Oceania (Lo Bianco, 2015) and for Native Americans (McCarty, 2017).

In its more inclusive usage, heritage language education is found (1) in schools and classes for established and recent *immigrant* language groups and (2) in community-based language initiatives (Wiley, 2014a, 2014b). For example, in the early 1980s in the United States, Joshua Fishman located 6553 heritage language schools (mostly private) and had an impression that there might be 1000 more he had not located (Fishman, 2014). These schools were using 145 different **mother tongues** of various communities, and focused on students who appeared to have lost or were losing their 'native' language. Such schools may receive some support from community organizations, foreign governments or religious institutions (churches, mosques, temples, synagogues). Some community-based organizations foster after-school programs, Saturday schools, weekend schools and religion-based programs. These supplemental schools have grown, especially among the Chinese and Korean communities (Lee, 2014). Such efforts are grassroots-based and therefore often have much vibrancy and an enthusiasm to succeed.

Heritage language schools have hitherto lacked documentation. However, in the United States, the Coalition of Community-Based Heritage Language Schools has begun an effort to document heritage language schools through an online survey (https://www.heritagelanguageschools.org). By 2023, the Coalition had documented over 860 US schools offering 57 languages across 41 states. Seven of these have been in existence for over 80 years, the oldest for 142 years. The Consortium for Language Teaching and Learning attempted to document the number of US heritage language programs in 2017 and identified 878 programs for 49 languages (https://webapp.cal.org/ConsortiumDB/Default.aspx). Compared with the thousands of heritage language programs Fishman was able to identify in the 1980s, these recent efforts to document heritage language programs are likely just scratching the surface.

Day schools are typically fee-paying, private establishments. Hence the students tend to come from middle-class and more affluent working-class backgrounds. For example, there are over 1000 Jewish day schools in the United States (Rosenbaum, 2022), including over 350 in New York alone, most of which provide some instruction in Hebrew or Yiddish (Avni & Menken, 2013; Peltz & Kliger, 2013). There are also about 133 Jewish schools in the United Kingdom (Horup *et al.*, 2021). In contrast, non-religious day schools organized by ethnic groups have tended to become more English-focused. For example, many Greek schools in New York are now teaching in English, with Greek taught as a second language each day of the week. Hantzopoulos (2013) identified 11 Greek Orthodox parochial day schools (operating under the Direct Archdiocesan District), with 39 teachers of the modern Greek language. However, Hantzopoulos noted that most Greek children learnt Greek language (and culture) at church-sponsored afternoon schools or Saturday schools.

In Canada, heritage language education refers to programs in languages other than the official languages of English and French (Duff, 2008). The Canadian Multicultural Education Act (1988) encourages – but does not provide any federal funding support for – ethnic groups to preserve their languages and cultures through heritage language instruction (Ricento, 2015a). Some support is available from the provinces and territories but, as Ricento (2015a: 467) notes, there is considerable variability in 'the amount of funding they provide for heritage language teaching, the languages offered, and the grades in which classes are offered'. Wright and Chan (2019) note a few examples of programs available in different Canadian provinces, including the Mandarin–English program in British Columbia, the American Sign Language–English, Arabic–English, Mandarin–English, German–English and Hebrew–English programs in Alberta, the Ukrainian–English program in Saskatchewan, and the Ukrainian–English, German–English, Hebrew–English and Cree–English bilingual education programs in Manitoba.

The term 'heritage language' is used broadly for indigenous and immigrant languages, and can also include colonial languages (e.g. German in Pennsylvania) and non-standard dialects such as African-American Vernacular English in the United States (Baker-Bell, 2020a, 2020b; Ramirez *et al.*, 2005). Valdés (2014) and Wiley (2014b) examine the definitional issues of 'heritage language' in terms of educational programs, community and the language itself. In the United States, the term encompasses those raised in a non-English language home who understand and may speak a language other than English. However, heritage language education programs will teach (and typically teach through) a heritage language, and not just include heritage language children. Such a program may include other native language children as well.

A 'heritage language' may also be called a 'native language', 'ethnic language', 'minority language', 'ancestral language', 'aboriginal language' or, in French, *langues d'origine*'. A danger of the term 'heritage' is that it points to the past and not to the future, to traditions rather than the contemporary (Wiley, 2014b). Partly for this reason, the UK and Australian term tends to be 'community language'. The term 'international languages' is increasingly used in Canada (Ricento, 2015a). Thus, the heritage language may or may not be an **indigenous language**. Both Diné bizaad (Navajo) and Spanish can be perceived as heritage languages in the United States, depending on an individual's perception of what constitutes his or her heritage language.

Heritage language programs in the United States and elsewhere vary in structure and content. The strongest forms are similar to **bilingual immersion programs**, or may resemble a 90:10 model of dual language education. In weaker forms, the heritage language is simply taught as a subject. For example, at the primary school level, instruction in the heritage language may be provided for just a few hours a week, as a separate subject. At the secondary level, heritage language classes often take the form of traditional world language courses, but carry designations such as 'Spanish for Spanish-speakers' or 'Arabic for heritage speakers'. Heritage language students may take these courses to fulfill world language credits needed for graduation and college admissions. In many cases, heritage language classes are school-sponsored informal after-school classes that do not carry any credits. However, such courses can lay the foundation for a heritage language course that can later be incorporated as an official credit-bearing class – a strategy that can be effective for less commonly taught languages (see Chik & Wright, 2017). Most heritage language programs, however, are community-based programs that vary widely in terms of size, organization, support, consistency and effectiveness (Lee & Wright, 2014).

Some of the likely features of strong, school-based heritage language programs are as follows:

- Most but not necessarily all of the children will come from language minoritized homes. At the same time, the minoritized language may be the majority language of a local community. In certain areas of the United States, ethnic minority groups (e.g. Chin, Chinese, Cubans, Hmong, Karen, Mexicans, Puerto Ricans, Somalians, Vietnamese) are in a majority in their neighborhood or community. In Gwynedd (Wales, UK) where the minoritized language (Welsh) is sometimes the common language of the community, heritage language programs are prevalent (Williams, 2003). The Welsh-speaking children are typically joined in these programs by a varying number and balance of majority language children.
- Parents will often have the choice of sending their children to mainstream schools or to heritage language programs. Ukrainian, Hebrew and Kanien'kéha (Mohawk) heritage language programs in Canada, and Hmong charter schools in Minnesota and California, for example, have given parents freedom of choice in selecting schools.
- The language minoritized student's home language will often be used for approximately half or more of the curriculum time. The Ukrainian programs in Manitoba have allotted half the time to Ukrainian, half to English. Mathematics and science,

> **Box 11.1 Ten certainties about multilingual education policy and practice**
>
> From a wealth of experiences of indigenous forms of bilingual and multilingual education, Hornberger has expressed a 'deep conviction that multilingual education constitutes a wide and welcoming educational doorway toward peaceful coexistence of peoples and especially restoration and empowerment of those who have been historically oppressed' (Hornberger, 2009: 197). She expresses this in terms of 10 certainties about multilingual education policy and practice:
>
> 1. National multilingual language education policy opens up ideological and implementational spaces for multilingual education.
> 2. Local actors may open up – or close down – opportunities for multilingual education as they implement, interpret and perhaps resist policy initiatives.
> 3. Ecological language policies take into account the power relations among languages and promote multilingual uses in all societal domains.
> 4. Models of multilingual education establish linguistic and sociocultural histories and goals in a particular context.
> 5. Language status planning and language corpus planning go hand in hand.
> 6. Communicative modalities encompass more than written and spoken language.
> 7. Classroom practices can foster transfer of language and literacy development along receptive–productive, oral–written and L1–L2 dimensions and across modalities.
> 8. Multilingual education activates voices for reclaiming the local.
> 9. Multilingual education affords choices for reaffirming our own.
> 10. Multilingual education opens spaces for revitalizing the indigenous experience.

for example, have been taught in English, music, art and social studies in Ukrainian. There is a tendency to teach technological scientific studies through the majority language. Other models use the student's home language for between 50% to almost 100% of curriculum time. Changes across grades usually move from much early use of the student's home language to approximately equal use of the two languages (e.g. by grade 6).

- In the later stages of elementary schooling, increasing attention may be given to majority language development, ensuring that full bilingualism occurs.
- Heritage language schools are mostly elementary. This need not be the case. In Wales, for example, such schools are available to the end of secondary education and the heritage language can be used as a medium of vocational and academic study at college and university (Baker & Jones, 2000). Another example is a Hawaiian heritage language program that operates from kindergarten through to grade 12, with additional opportunities for Hawaiian-medium instruction through graduate school (Wilson, 2014). In the US some HL classes may only available in high schools as world language classes modified for heritage speakers (e.g. Vietnamese-for-Vietnamese speakers) (Chik & Wright, 2017).

Two-way dual language bilingual schools differ from heritage language (developmental maintenance) schools in aiming for more of a balance of majority and minoritized language children. Heritage language education is more concerned with preservation of the ethnic language and culture and, in many cases, has a large preponderance of language minoritized children. The type of school possible in a neighborhood is often determined by the demographic and sociolinguistic character of the school population (e.g. the size of one or more language minoritized groups, the presence of recent or more established immigrants, and the numbers of majority language speakers).

Indigenous Education in the United States

An important example of heritage language bilingual education is provision for indigenous American Indians, Alaskan Natives and Native Hawaiians. Hawaiian now shares official language status with English in Hawaii and is used in some schools for content teaching (Wilson, 2014). Lee and McCarty (2015) note that in 2012 there were 556 federally recognized tribes and 617 reservations and Alaska Native villages. Approximately 300 or more American Indian languages were once spoken in the United States (McCarty, 2017). The number is quickly declining. According to McCarty (2014), there are currently 169 Native American languages, with approximately 397,000 speakers among 6.7 million self-identified American Indian, Alaska Native, Native Hawaiian and other Pacific Islander peoples. As few as 20 of those languages are likely to survive – for example, Diné bizaad (Navajo), Ojibwemowin (Ojibwe), Dakhód'iapi (Dakota), Chahta anumpa (Choctaw), Naishan and N'dee biyát'i (Plains and Western Apache), Tsalagi Gawonihisdi (Cherokee), O'odham ha-ñe'okĭ (Tohono O'odham) and Yugtun (Yup'ik) – because only about 20 are spoken in the home by younger generations. Such language transmission in the family is highly important for language survival (Fishman, 2001). All of California's 50 or more Native American Indian languages may be dying, as they are spoken only by small numbers of elders.

A history of American Indian education is a record of attempts to eradicate their heritage languages and cultures (Reyhner & Eder, 2004). Forced assimilation has been prevalent for over 100 years, symbolized in phrases from the Commissioner of Indian Affairs, John D.C. Atkins, in his 1887 annual report to the Bureau of Indian Affairs:

> Teaching an Indian youth in his own barbarous dialect is a positive detriment to him ... and the first step toward civilization, toward teaching the Indians the mischief and folly of ... their barbarous practices, is to teach them the English language. (Atkins, 1887: 23)

Children were removed from their tribes and sent to distant boarding schools. Stories abound of children being kidnapped from their homes and taken on horseback to boarding schools, many of which were located at former military forts. Such children were given an English-only curriculum, as well as military-style discipline, with resulting physical and psychological scars (Spring, 2021). There was severe punishment (e.g. use of belts and hoses) for speaking their native language and a manual labor system that required them to work half days in kitchens and boiler rooms to minimize school costs. Many children died at the boarding schools. Canada's century-long Indian residential school system (1874–1977) was declared as amounting to a cultural genocide by the Truth and Reconciliation Commission of Canada (2015). As part of the reconciliation effort, Canada passed the Indigenous Languages Act in 2019 with funding to help indigenous peoples reclaim, revitalize, strengthen and maintain indigenous languages. In the 1970s, the US Congress approved the Indian Education Act (1972) and the Indian Self-Determination and Educational Assistance Act (1975). In 1990, with the passage of the Native American Languages Act (authorized for funding in 1992), then in 2006, with the passage of the Native American Languages Preservation Act (with additional funding provided in 2008), and with the passage of the Esther Martinez Native American Languages Program in 2006 and re-authorization in 2019 (see Chapter 9), and most recently with the passage of the 2022 Native American Languages Resource Center Act, further efforts have been made to preserve, protect and promote the rights and freedoms of Native Americans to use and develop their own indigenous languages. The US Department of Education provides funding through competitive grants for the Native American and Alaska Native Children in School Program. However, such funding may be sufficient to support only a limited number of programs.

An example of a Native American **language maintenance** program is the Rock Point Community School in Arizona, which was established in the mid-1930s and has been famous since the early 1970s for its role in maintaining the Diné bizaad (Navajo) language (Holm & Holm, 1990). Rock Point is a reservation-interior community on the middle reaches of Chinle Wash in northern Arizona. Enrolling 99% Diné (Navajo) children, the languages used in this bilingual education program, which covers kindergarten to grade 12, are Diné bizaad and English. The three program aims are defined as: (1) students to become proficient speakers, readers and writers of the Diné bizaad and English languages; (2) students to acquire cultural knowledge of at least two cultures (Diné bizaad and Anglo-American); (3) students to develop critical thinking skills in Diné bizaad and English. In kindergarten to grade 5, Diné bizaad is used for 50% of class time, in grade 6 for 25% and in grades 7–12 for 15% of total class time. In kindergarten to grade 5, reading, language arts, math, science, social studies and health are taught through both Diné bizaad and English, with separation of languages by differing blocks of time. In grades 6–12, teaching through Diné bizaad occurs for literacy, social science, electives and science (one semester in grade 6), with teaching in English for reading, language arts, math, science, social studies, health, home economics and physical education.

The language of initial reading in instruction for Diné bizaad-speakers is Diné bizaad and for English-speakers it is English. All program teachers are proficient in both languages. Over 90% of the teaching staff are members of the Diné (Navajo) ethnic group and provide bilingual role models. A similar Diné bizaad case study of Rough Rock is effectively portrayed in words and pictures by McCarty (2002) and of Fort Defiance by Arviso and Holm (2001). Lee and McCarty note, however, that despite these successes, 'by the mid-1980s, a shift to English was becoming more apparent across the Navajo Nation' and thus 'the goals of Navajo education have increasingly turned to revitalization' (Lee & McCarty, 2015: 413; see also Chapter 4). This was apparent during a visit to the K-12 To'Hajiilee Community school in New Mexico in 2023, which aims to 'integrate the Navajo language and culture for quality academic achievement'. During the visit it was readily apparent that the Navajo students, teachers and administrators were English dominant, and that the school's Diné bizaad instruction was focused on keeping the language alive and connected to the student's Navajo culture. For example, the school's culinary arts class for high school students was taught bilingually, with targeted Diné vocabulary and community knowledge integrated into lessons involving cooking traditional Navajo dishes using locally sourced ingredients.

Master–apprentice language learning programs have been developed by the Advocates for Indigenous California Language Survival (AICLS) organization (Hinton, 2017). They pair someone fluent in a native and threatened Californian language with someone who is often of child-bearing age with a commitment to learn that language and transmit it to others. The apprentice is expected to avoid using English and use just the native language (and gestures) for communication (immersion). Authentic, everyday situations are used so that the language learned relates to real-life contexts such as housework, preparing food and family life. The master and apprentice typically spend between 10 and 20 hours per week together over a three-year program. At the end, the apprentice typically emerges with full conversational fluency. Such apprentices then go on to teach the language to others, in a cascade fashion, some becoming teachers in schools who can pass on the native language in an educational setting (Hinton, 2017). Lee and McCarty (2015) describe efforts among the Pueblo communities of New Mexico to establish language nest immersion programs, summer language programs for children and youth, and language activities in Head Start and local elementary schools. In 2012 the Keres Children's Learning Center opened for pre-school children aged three to six with Cochiti Keres-medium instruction designed to 'educate the whole Pueblo child' (Lee & McCarty, 2015: 415).

These interventions show that bilingual education can be successful in raising language awareness, raising standards of education and preserving the indigenous languages of the United States. Such bilingual education gives a sense of **identity** and pride in their origins to American Indian children, preserving not just their languages but also their rich cultures. This reflects the growing US awareness of historical, brutal assimilation and the current need to preserve the deep repository of history, customs, values, religions and oral traditions that belong to Native Americans but which can be valuably shared far beyond the reservations, to enrich all people.

Yet language rights and bilingual education programs do not guarantee language maintenance for American Indians. Parents have sometimes made choices against language maintenance, often based on their own indoctrination that 'White and English is best' (McCarty, 2002). Also, it is dangerous to expect too much from heritage language education in saving a language and culture (see Chapter 4). Nevertheless, this form of education can produce new speakers and ensure deeper language and cultural roots for native speakers. Without these kinds of initiatives, a minoritized language can quickly die. When schools do nothing, it is not only the minoritized language that is not being produced in children. Such a policy also signals the low value, economic worthlessness and stigmatization of a language, affecting the decisions of both parents and students, and not least the fate of the language.

Indigenous and other forms of heritage language schooling are a language and culture supply line that creates potential. But supply is dependent on demand. Also, potential has to be turned into everyday language usage, outside the school and for the life span. Parents and students expect bilingual education to have purpose and value beyond schooling. It needs to lead to economic enhancement and employment, social and cultural opportunities, or heritage language education can create a fine product without much future use.

Immersion Bilingual Education

When applied to language, 'immersion' was first used to describe intensive language programs for US troops about to go abroad in World War II. In the 1960s, 'immersion education' was coined in Canada to describe a new form of bilingual education. Genesee (2015) provides a thorough overview of the factors, forces, mechanisms and counterweights that shaped the development of immersion education in Canada. Immersion bilingual education derives from a Canadian educational experiment in the Montréal suburb of St Lambert, starting in 1965 (Lambert & Tucker, 1972). However, Rebuffot (1993) suggests that École Cedar Park in West Island Québec (started in 1958) and the Toronto French school (dating from 1962) were already in existence. A few English-speaking, middle-class parents persuaded school district administrators in

St Lambert to set up a French immersion kindergarten class of 26 children. The stated aims were for students: (1) to become competent to speak, read and write in French; (2) to reach normal achievement levels throughout the curriculum, including the English language; and (3) to appreciate the traditions and culture of French-speaking Canadians as well as English-speaking Canadians. In short, the aims were for children to become bilingual and **bicultural** without loss of achievement. The economic and employment advantages to be gained from bilingualism, biliteracy and biculturalism may also have been motivations (see Chapter 19).

It is important to clarify that the bilingual immersion model originating from Canada is a strong form of bilingual education that differs substantially from the monolingual form of education called structured English immersion in the United States (see Chapter 10). Table 11.2 contrasts these two models and makes clear that bilingual immersion programs are designed to help majority language speakers become bilingual and biliterate.

Table 11.2 Differences between Canadian immersion and US structured English immersion approaches

	Bilingual immersion (Canada)	Structured English immersion (United States)
Includes home language instruction	Yes	No
Bilingualism as an outcome	Yes	No
Biliteracy as an outcome	Yes	No
Cultural diversity promoted	Yes	Unlikely
Teacher operates bilingually	Likely	No
Bilingual (certified) teacher	Likely	No
Home language of the student	Majority	Minority
Underlying ideology	Pluralism	Assimilation

Types of Immersion Bilingual Education

Immersion education is an umbrella term. Within the concept of immersion experience are various programs (in Canada and countries such as Finland, Spain, Ireland and the United States) differing in terms of the following respects:

- *Age at which a child commences the experience.* This may be at the kindergarten or infant stage (early immersion), at 9–10 years old (delayed or middle immersion) or at the secondary level (late immersion).
- *Amount of time spent in immersion.* Total immersion usually commences with 100% immersion in the second language, reducing after two or three years to 80% for the next three or four years, finishing junior schooling with approximately 50% immersion in the second language. Partial immersion provides close to 50% immersion in the second language throughout infant and junior schooling.

Early total immersion has been the most popular entry-level program in Canada, followed by late and then middle immersion. Figure 11.2 illustrates several possibilities, with many other variations around these.

The St Lambert experiment was a success. Evaluations suggested that the educational aims were met. Attitudes and achievement were not hindered by the immersion experience. Tucker and d'Anglejan (1972: 19) summarized the outcomes as follows:

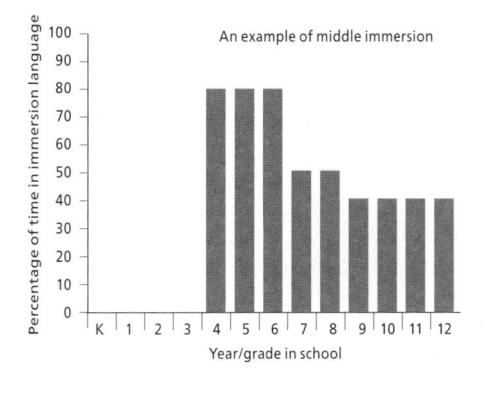

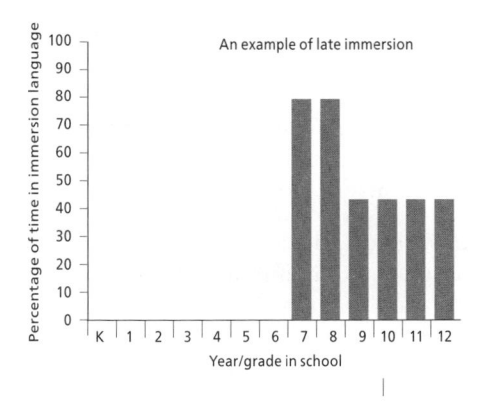

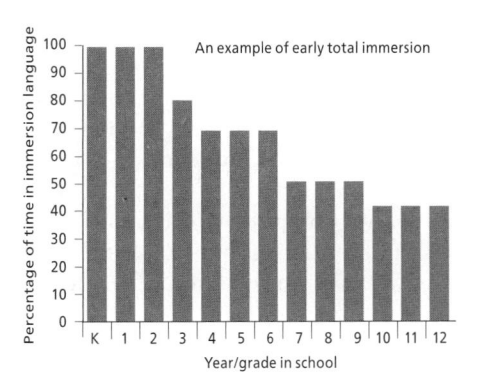

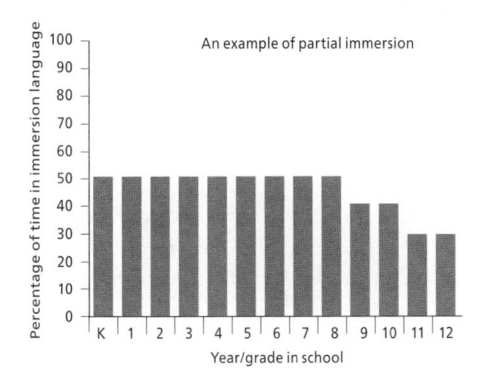

Figure 11.2 Examples of bilingual immersion programs

The experimental students appear to be able to read, write, speak, understand, and use English as well as youngsters instructed in English in the conventional manner. In addition and at no cost they can also read, write, speak and understand French in a way that English students who follow a traditional program of French as a second language never do.

Since 1965, immersion bilingual education has spread rapidly in Canada and in parts of Europe. In 2021, there were about 700,000 Canadian children (16.9% of the total school population) enrolled in French immersion schools – more than double the enrollment of 261,447 in 1998 (Statistics Canada, 2024). Statistics Canada (2024: 1) also reported the following French immersion highlights for 2021:

- Outside Quebec, 1.6 million adults and children whose mother tongue is not French were in or had been in French immersion at the elementary or secondary level in an English-language school in Canada.
- In municipalities outside Quebec, where at least 30% of adults knew French, approximately half of school-aged children whose mother tongue is not French were in or had been in French immersion.
- Outside Quebec, close to half (47.0%) of school-aged children whose mother

tongue is not French and who were in or had been in French immersion had an immigrant background. Nearly one in five had a mother tongue other than English or French, such as Mandarin, Punjabi or Arabic.
- Outside Quebec, nearly two-thirds (65.7%) of bilingual English–French young adults aged 18 to 24 whose mother tongue is not French had been in French immersion for at least one year during their childhood.

Immersion education, as well as language reproduction in the home, has been a key to develop and maintaining Canada's English–French bilingualism, even among its growing immigrant population.

From one school started in 1965, immersion education spread rapidly in Canada. What are the essential features of this swift educational growth?

(1) Immersion in Canada aims at bilingualism in two prestigious and official majority languages (French and English). This equates to an additive bilingual situation. Such a situation is different from 'structured or sheltered immersion' of children from language minoritized backgrounds in the majority language (e.g. Spanish-speakers in the United States 'immersed' in English). Use of the term 'immersion' in a subtractive, **assimilationist** situation is best avoided. **Submersion** is a more appropriate term.

(2) Immersion bilingual education has been optional, not compulsory. Parents choose to send their children to these schools. The cultural and economic convictions of parents plus the commitment of the teachers may aid the motivation of students. Immersion thrives on conviction, not on conformity.

(3) Children in early immersion are often allowed to use their home language for up to one and a half years for classroom communication. There is no compulsion to speak the second (school) language in the playground or dining hall. The child's home language is appreciated and not belittled.

(4) The teachers are competent bilinguals. They initially appear to the children as monolingual French-speakers who can somehow also understand (but not speak) English.

(5) Classroom language communication aims to be meaningful, authentic and relevant to the child's needs, not contrived, tightly controlled or repetitive. The content of the curriculum becomes the focus for the language. Perpetual insistence on correct communication is avoided. Learning a second language in early immersion becomes incidental and subconscious, similar to the way a first language is acquired. Emphasis is placed on understanding before speaking. Later on, formal instruction (e.g. French grammar) may be given.

(6) The students start immersion education with a similar lack of experience of the second language. Most are monolingual in English. Students commencing schooling with relatively homogeneous language skills not only simplifies the teacher's task, it also means that students' self-esteem and classroom motivation are not at risk because other students are linguistically more expert.

(7) Students in immersion education experience the same curriculum as mainstream 'core' students.

(8) Immersion is not simply an educational initiative: there is also a societal, political and sometimes economic rationale.

Societal, political and economic rationales differ from country to country. In Canada, immersion matches a French/English dual language history and differentiates

Canada from its larger neighbor, the United States. In the United States, some bilingual immersion programs focus on helping revive or preserve threatened indigenous languages, such as Diné bizaad (Navajo), Ōlelo Hawai'i (Hawaiian) and Yugtun (Yup'ik). However, most immersion programs are advocated more from a foreign language perspective, that is, serving language majority (English-speaking) middle- and upper-class parents who wish their children to become bilingual in languages such as Spanish, Japanese and Chinese. In Wales and Ireland, bilingual immersion is partly about establishing a Celtic identity separate from England (Jones & Martin-Jones, 2004). Unification of a country with varying languages, economic advantage in global trade, international communications and increasing peace, harmony and integration may also be elements of a wider rationale than education.

As with all forms of bilingual education, there are challenges, issues and questions with bilingual immersion (Tedick *et al.*, 2011). For example:

(1) Why do some language majority students not achieve native-like language proficiency in speaking and writing the second language, even after 12 or 13 years of immersion schooling?
(2) What kinds of students do not share in the achievement advantages of immersion education? How much do students with a variety of language and learning difficulties (see Chapter 15) achieve in immersion? What are the outcomes for children who have dyslexia, autism, Asperger's syndrome or Down's syndrome, for example? What about ethnically diverse students who are long-term or recent immigrants whose home language is neither the majority language nor the minoritized language of the immersion program?
(3) What are the social and cultural benefits, possibly long term, for immersion students (e.g. increased tolerance of diversity and difference)?
(4) What is the optimal initial training for immersion teachers, and continued professional development, as teachers are such an important part of the equation in immersion education?
(5) What are the economic and financial advantages of immersion education, at both an individual and a societal level?

Immersion schooling occurs internationally: Australia, the Basque Country, Catalonia, Colombia, Finland, Hong Kong, Hungary, Ireland, Japan, New Zealand, Scotland, Singapore, South Africa, Switzerland and Wales, for example. With over 1000 research studies, immersion bilingual education has a track record of unusual success and growth (see Johnstone, 2002, for an overview of the international research; see also Chapter 12). It has influenced bilingual education throughout the world, with variations to suit regional and national contexts. For example, the Finnish implementation of immersion derived not from parents but from a politically active women's group at Vaasa (Finland), which quickly gained political credibility for integrating Swedish- and Finnish-speaking children. It also gained high academic credibility from the research of Laurén and his team at the University of Vaasa (de Mejía, 2002; Laurén, 1994). The Finnish implementation is also noted for: evolving into incorporating third and fourth languages (e.g. English and German) to produce fluent multilinguals; and providing high-quality teacher preparation courses (including by distance learning) that include immersion teaching methodology.

In Catalonia, research indicates not only that Spanish-speaking children who follow an immersion program become fluent in Catalan, but also that their Spanish

> **Box 11.2** Core and variable features of bilingual immersion programs
>
> Swain and Johnson (1997) and Swain and Lapkin (2005) provide a list of the core features and variable features of bilingual immersion programs, to include contexts where children are learning through French as their third language (e.g. immigrants).
>
> *Core features*
> - The immersion language is the medium of instruction.
> - The immersion curriculum is the same as the local first language curriculum.
> - The school supports development in all the child's languages.
> - Additive bilingualism occurs.
> - Exposure to the immersion language is largely confined to the classroom.
> - Students enter with similar (limited or nonexistent) levels of proficiency in the immersion language.
> - All the teachers are bilingual.
> - The classroom culture recognizes the cultures of the diverse language communities to which the students belong, including immigrant communities.
>
> *Variable features*
> - The grade level at which immersion is introduced.
> - The extent of immersion, full or partial.
> - The ratio given to the first and second language in content-based teaching at different grade levels.
> - Whether there is continuity from elementary to secondary education, and occasionally from secondary to further and higher education – e.g. University of the Basque Country (Cenoz & Etxague, 2013), University of Barcelona, University of Ottawa, University of Helsinki, University of Fribourg, Aberystwyth and Bangor Universities in Wales; Stellenbosch University) (see van der Walt, 2013).
> - The amount of language support given to students moving from their first to their second language, including the training that teachers need so as to give bridging support.
> - The amount of resources that are available in the first and second language and the teacher training to use these. The commitment of teachers and students, administrators and politicians to immersion.
> - The attitudes of students, particularly towards the second language culture.
> - The status of the second language.
> - What counts as success in an immersion program.

does not suffer. Throughout the curriculum, Catalan immersion children 'perform as well and sometimes better than their Hispanophone peers who do not [follow an immersion program]' (Artigal, 1993: 40–41). Similarly, research studies in the Basque Country show that the model B immersion program (50% Basque and 50% Spanish) has successful outcomes in bilingual proficiency (Cenoz, 2009).

Immersion bilingual education differs from two-way dual language schools in the language backgrounds of the students. Immersion schools usually contain only language majority children learning much or part of the curriculum through a second language (e.g. English-speaking children learning through the medium of French in Canadian schools). Two-way dual language bilingual schools aim to contain a balanced mixture of children from two (or more) different language backgrounds (e.g. from Spanish-speaking and English-speaking homes in the United States).

Bilingual and Multilingual Education in Majority Languages

Bilingual education in majority languages (mainstream bilingual education) comprises the joint use of two (or more) majority languages in a school. The aims of these schools usually include bilingualism or multilingualism, biliteracy and **cultural** pluralism (de Mejía, 2002). Such schools exist in societies where much of the population is already bilingual or multilingual (e.g. Singapore, Luxembourg) or where there are significant numbers of natives or expatriates wanting to become bilingual (e.g. learning through English and Japanese in Japan). Asian examples of bilingual education in majority languages include Arabic–English, Bahasa Melayu–English, Mandarin Chinese (Putonghua)–English and Japanese–English. In Africa and India there are also schools where a 'majority' regional language and an international language coexist as teaching media in a school. Bilingualism in that regional language and an international language (e.g. French, English) is the aim and outcome of formal education. Generally, these schools will contain majority language children, but with variations in the language heterogeneity/homogeneity of the classes.

In the Asian examples, a country (e.g. Brunei, Taiwan) or a region may have one dominant indigenous language with a desire to introduce a second international language (especially English) into the school (see, e.g. Boun & Duran, 2024 on English in the ASEAN region). The international language will be used as a medium of instruction alongside the native language. The aim is for fully bilingual and biliterate students through an **enrichment bilingual education** program. For example, the *Dwibahasa* (two-language) school system in Brunei operates through Standard Malay and English (Haji-Othman, 2024; Jones, 2012). However, many students in Brunei speak indigenous languages, and Malay-speakers in Brunei speak a national variety – Brunei Malay – that differs from the Standard Malay taught in the schools. Thus, as Jones has observed, 'children starting school in Brunei have never had the benefit of studying in their mother tongue' (Jones, 2015: 536–537). In Hong Kong, many primary schools aim for multilingualism in Cantonese, Putonghua and English, and biliteracy in Chinese and English. However, there is a lack of uniform approach or a clear method for implementation (Wang & Kirkpatrick, 2019). In Nigeria, bilingual education is present in English and one of the national languages of Nigeria (Hausa, Ibo or Yoruba), particularly at the secondary school level, though implementation varies widely in different regions of the country (Igboanusi & Peter, 2015). In Singapore, English plus Mandarin, Malay or Tamil (the four official languages of the country) create bilingual education (Lee & Wu, 2024; Silver & Bokhorst-Heng, 2016).

Content and Language Integrated Learning (CLIL)

Bilingual education in majority languages means that some curriculum content is learnt through a student's second language. In Europe, this is called **content and language integrated learning (CLIL)** (Coyle & Meyer, 2021; Coyle *et al.*, 2023; Nikula *et al.*, 2016). CLIL blossomed in many European countries, building partly on the evidence-based success of Canadian immersion and US dual language bilingual education (Mehisto, 2012). Now it has expanded beyond Europe to many countries around the world (Ballinger *et al.*, 2024; Chap & Wright, 2025). Launched in 1995/1996, CLIL is a generic term and 'was originally introduced to bind together diverse dual-focused educational practices with explicit attention given to both content and language' (Marsh, 2008: 243). While definitions vary, Coyle *et al.* (2010: 1) describe it as 'a dual-focused educational approach in which an additional language is used for the learning and teaching of both content and language'. Cenoz *et al.* (2014) argue that CLIL is better understood as an umbrella term and cite a need for a taxonomy of different forms of CLIL to bring about greater conceptual clarity that may better guide research and practice.

For example, CLIL may involve Dutch-speaking secondary school students in the Netherlands learning content areas such as sciences, humanities and/or arts through the medium of English (or occasionally German), while at the same time developing proficiency in Dutch (De Graff & van Wilgenburg, 2015). Some 10–50% of the curriculum may be taught through another language. While there are many variations in CLIL, the additional language is typically taught as a subject in itself and not just as a vehicle for transmitting content. Yet the emphasis is very much on education and not just on language: 'the major concern is about *education*, not about becoming bilingual or multilingual, and that multiple language proficiency is the "added value" which can be obtained at no cost to other skills and knowledge, if properly designed' (Baetens Beardsmore, cited in García, 2009a: 211, original emphasis).

CLIL has some similarities with **content-based instruction** (**CBI**) in the United States, including sheltered content-area instruction, in that the focus is on learning a new language through the medium of content-area instruction in that language (Ballinger *et al.*, 2024). However, CBI and **sheltered content instruction** in the United States are forms of monolingual and assimilationist education focused on helping language minoritized students attain proficiency in English (see Chapter 10). In contrast, CLIL is a form of bilingual education focused on helping language majority students attain proficiency in an additional language. Nevertheless, CLIL might benefit from using similar strategies and techniques as used in sheltered content instruction to help make content-area instruction in a second language more comprehensible.

Educators and advocates provide a strong rationale for CLIL (Ball *et al.*, 2016; Coyle & Meyer, 2021; Coyle *et al.*, 2023; Ożóg & Marsh, 2009), including psychological benefits (Talbot *et al.*, 2021). First, learning a language may be quicker when it is via an integration of language and content, and much slower if just learnt as a language. Second, CLIL ensures a student gains language competence in academic domains and not just in social communication. Third, such an integration of language and content is efficient. Two outcomes can be achieved at the same time: learning a language and subject- matter learning. Fourth, CLIL provides a communicative approach to second language teaching that emphasizes meaningful and authentic communication. The purpose of using language is to interpret, express and negotiate meaning. Thus, integrating the second language and content provides a purpose for using that second language, reflecting real curriculum needs and purposeful learning for success in the curriculum. Constructivist theory also stresses that learning best takes place in a holistic sense with the parts making a unified whole in a meaningful way.

CLIL is used in over 30 European countries and many other countries around the world, with variations in terms of, for example, intensity, starting age, duration and amount of explicit language teaching (Cenoz *et al.*, 2014). As yet, CLIL practice has advanced without the same research evidence as is available for Canadian immersion and US dual language schools. Cenoz *et al.* (2014: 257) note that 'there are challenges to carrying out research on CLIL because of the diversity of CLIL program formats and the lack of a standardized CLIL framework'. Nonetheless, the growing research attention to various forms of CLIL attests to its growing success, strength and sustainability (Chap & Wright, 2025; Coyle *et al.*, 2023; Sylvén, 2019).

CLIL cannot be understood from a purely linguistic or educational perspective. As with all forms of bilingual education, there is a political ideology underneath. CLIL was developed in the context of the European Union's vision of a multilingual Europe in which people can function in two or three or more languages. With increased trade between European countries, there has been an increased demand for multilingual employees (e.g. speaking English and other European national languages). CLIL is about helping to create Europeanization, a multilingual and global economy, and transnational workers. Similar neoliberal forces have helped spread CLIL approaches to countries beyond Europe.

International Schools

It is estimated that there are over 14,450 English-medium international schools across nearly every country of the world (https://www.iscresearch.com). Mainly for affluent expatriates, parents pay fees for mostly private, selective, independent education but there are also scholarships and bursaries. Children in these schools often have parents in the diplomatic service, in multinational organizations or in international businesses who are geographically and vocationally mobile. Other children in an international school come from the locality, typically with affluent parents who want their children to have an English-medium education in a school that meets international standards. The schools tend to follow a US, Canadian, UK, Australian or Singaporean curriculum, with some inclusion of local traditions. The teachers are from various countries, usually with a plentiful supply of US-, Australian-, British- and Canadian-trained staff. Many international schools have an International Baccalaureate (IB) program, which focuses on preparing children for US or UK examinations and for future attendance in universities in Europe and North America. The official language policy of the International Baccalaureate Organization (2014: 1) declares that it is 'committed to supporting multilingualism as fundamental to increasing intercultural understanding and international-mindedness, and is equally committed to extending access to an IB education for students from a variety of cultural and linguistic backgrounds'. Each IB program is encouraged to establish its own local language policy, though a review of language policies and programs at selected IB programs by the Center for Applied Linguistics found that implementation varies widely (Fee *et al.*, 2014).

International schools that have English as the sole medium of transmitting the curriculum cannot be included under the heading of 'bilingual education in majority languages'. Such schools may become bilingual when a national or international language is incorporated in the curriculum (Carder *et al.*, 2018). The degree to which a school is bilingual may vary by students. An English-medium school is a monolingual form of education for native English-speakers, but may serve as a form of English immersion education for international and local students from other language backgrounds. Thus, a key question is the extent to which the school provides opportunities to help students (1) to develop and maintain proficiency and literacy in their native languages and (2) to develop proficiency and literacy in additional languages. For example, does the school provide instruction for international students in the national language(s) of the country where the school is located?

Carder (2013: 276) argues that international schools provide an ideal setting for developing bilingualism, biliteracy and cultural pluralism:

> International students are living in an 'international space'. Much of their life will be lived in an 'international' arena: the parents(s) probably work in an international organization where English is likely to be the medium. Their friends will be international school students, and they may be viewed by those not in this milieu as being an elite; elite children, however, may well require as much understanding and attention to their linguistic, emotional and related profiles as any other children. In fact the model most applicable for such students is that of pluralism and multiculturalism;

in international schools an assimilationist model is not appropriate as there are no political pressures for assimilation; there is no nation-state to assimilate to, nor political measures to treat immigrants circumspectly. Therefore, a model can be provided that promotes enrichment in each student's mother tongue while encouraging students to gain biliteracy with English; international schools provide a unique opportunity for a truly multicultural and multilingual teaching program.

While many international schools provide some instruction in languages other than English, practices vary widely. Sometimes second language instruction (for up to 12 years) is only for language learning and not to transmit curriculum content. In other schools, the second language is used as a medium to teach part of the curriculum. Some schools aim for multilingual education by enabling their students to acquire third and fourth languages. Generally, the languages of international schools are majority languages with international prestige. Minoritized languages are rarely taught in these schools. In some cases, international schools may even be subtractive. For example, in Cambodia some local children of the affluent attend English-only international schools where they have no opportunities to learn how to read and write or develop their oral language skills in Khmer – the national language. Despite the high status and growing use of English in Cambodia, this nonetheless places these students at a considerable disadvantage. The government now requires most private English-medium (and other foreign-language-medium) schools in the country to also provide the Khmer curriculum for Cambodian students. However, the use of traditional teaching methods and approaches for the Khmer curriculum is often less engaging than the international curriculum, such that students' Khmer language and literacy development may lag far behind their English language development.

European Schools Movement

Another European example of multilingual education in majority languages is the European Schools movement. The first European School opened in Luxembourg in 1953 followed by the European School, Brussels (ESB1) in 1958. Today, the European Schools are a network of 13 schools serving over 27,500 students across six countries – Belgium, the Netherlands, Germany, Italy, Spain and Luxembourg (https://www.eursc.eu/en). The United Kingdom's European School (Culham) was closed in 2017.

European Schools are organized in language sections so that students can receive much of their education in their native language. Most students (often the children of European civil servants) begin primary school in their first language. However, there is a need to integrate those students who do not have their own language section as, for example, they speak a majority language (e.g. Lithuanian, Slovenian) or a minoritized language that is not part of the curriculum (Leaton *et al.*, 2018).

Three *langues véhiculaires* have a special status: French, German and English. Students choose to learn one of these when they enter the first year of primary school. History, geography and economics are typically taken in the student's second language from the third year of high school onwards. The third language may also be a potential language of instruction (Cenoz & Gorter, 2015). Students are linguistically mixed to avoid stereotypes and prejudices, and to build a supranational European identity.

The outcome of such schooling tends to be functionally bilingual and often multilingual students with a sense of European multiculturalism and European identity. Leaton *et al.* (2018: 49) observed that 'graduates are not only proficient in their L1, but have achieved a sufficient degree of fluency in an L2 to have successfully studied content subjects such as history through their L2 and sometimes their L3'. These authors also provide a detailed critique of European Schools.

Integration and harmonization of students from different nationalities is facilitated in part through collaborative group project lessons called 'European Hours'. These lessons provide students and teachers with opportunities to communicate in different languages while exploring cultural subjects through fun and creative activities.

A major difference between the European Schools movement and bilingual immersion programs is that the second language is taught as a subject before being used as a medium of instruction. The second language also continues to be taught as a subject (language learning), leading to a high level of grammatical accuracy. Research by Housen (2002) suggests multiple positive program outcomes from the European Schools model. He found that L2 proficiency is close to native-speaker levels by the end of secondary schooling at no cost to either L1 proficiency or academic achievement. Pupils also gain high levels of proficiency in a third, and sometimes fourth, language, becoming multilinguals. However, bilingualism, biliteracy and multiculturalism are not only due to the effects of schooling. The parents may also be bilingual or multilingual, and the children are more likely to come from literacy-oriented, middle-class, affluent homes, with a positive view of bilingualism.

Other European Examples of Multilingual Education

In Europe, many other schools use two or more prestigious languages in the curriculum (Björklund & Björklund, 2023; Cenoz & Gorter, 2015). In the Basque Country, bilingual schools have successfully provided content teaching in Basque and Spanish. The increasing interest of parents in English language learning led to English instruction starting at kindergarten or in grade 3 for about three hours per week (Zalbide & Cenoz, 2008). **Trilingual education** has been evaluated with positive outcomes in terms of multilingualism and educational achievement (Jessner, 2008). The European Commission promotes a policy of 'mother tongue plus two' languages through early second and foreign language instruction. However, as Cenoz and Gorter (2015: 474) have observed, 'it is often the case that students acquire very limited competence in languages other than English unless they are speakers of minoritized languages who also learn the state language'.

In Luxembourg, children who speak Luxembourgish (Lëtzebuergesch) after birth become trilingual (Luxembourgish, French and German) through schooling. As explained by Weber (2014: 149):

> Luxembourgish has increasingly become the main language used in preschool education. Then, in the first years of primary school, all children go through a German-language literacy programme.... French is introduced in the second year of primary school and becomes a full subject from the third year onwards. Most other subjects continue to be taught through the medium of German throughout primary school (with the exception of sports, music, and arts where Luxembourgish is specified as the medium of instruction).

Most students have a working knowledge of three languages by the conclusion of schooling. However, Weber (2014) notes that the rigidity of this model assumes Luxembourgish is the 'mother tongue' of students, fails to recognize the varieties of

German and French spoken by the students at home, and fails to address the linguistic needs of immigrant students who speak other mother tongues.

Switzerland has four national languages (German, French, Italian and Romansh), although, contrary to popular expectation, 'the majority of Swiss citizens are not multilingual' (Grin *et al.*, 2003: 86). Each of the 26 Swiss cantons has control over language, culture and education, without central rule. English is on the increase as a student-favored language. Central guidelines favor children becoming trilingual. Brohy (2005) portrays the many and varied optional and compulsory models of bilingual and trilingual education in Switzerland. She argues that the optional or compulsory component of such bilingual education has political rather than pedagogic justifications.

Conclusion

Support for bilingual education tends to circle around eight interacting advantages of bilingual education that are claimed for students:

(1) Bilingual education typically enables a student to attain higher levels of competence in the two languages. This potentially enables children to engage in wider communication across generations, employment, regions and cultural groups.
(2) Bilingual education ideally develops a broader **enculturation**, a more sensitive view of different creeds and cultures. Bilingual education will usually deepen an engagement with the cultures associated with the languages, fostering a sympathetic understanding of differences.
(3) Strong forms of bilingual education frequently lead to biliteracy (see Chapter 14). Accessing literacy practices in two or more languages adds more functions to a language (e.g. using it in employment), widens the choice of literature for enjoyment, gives more opportunities for understanding different perspectives and viewpoints, and leads to a deeper understanding of history and heritage, traditions and territory.
(4) Research on dual language schools, Canadian bilingual immersion education and heritage language education suggests that classroom achievement is increased through content learning via dual language curriculum strategies. This is considered in the next chapter.
(5) Research suggests that children with two well developed languages share cognitive benefits (see Chapter 7).
(6) Children's self-esteem may be raised through bilingual education for minoritized language students. The opposite occurs when a child's home language is replaced by the majority language. Then, the child, the parents and relatives, and not least the child's community, may appear as inadequate and disparaged by the school system. When the home language is used in school, children may feel themselves, their home, family and community to be accepted, thus maintaining or elevating their self-esteem.
(7) Bilingual education can aid the establishment of a more secure identity at a local, regional and national level. Welsh, Māori or Native American identities may be enhanced by the heritage language and culture being celebrated and honored in the classroom. Developing a Korean–American, Bengali–British or Greek–Australian identity can be greatly aided by 'strong' forms of bilingual education, and challenged or even negated by 'weak' forms.

(8) In an increasing number of regions (e.g. Catalonia, Scandinavia) there are economic advantages in having experienced bilingual (or trilingual) education. Being bilingual can be important to secure employment in many public services (see Chapter 19), particularly when there is a customer interface requiring effortless switching between two or more languages. To secure a job as a teacher, to work in the mass media, to work in local government and increasingly in the civil service in countries such as Canada, Wales and the Basque Country, bilingualism has become important. Thus, bilingual education is increasingly seen as delivering more marketable employees than monolingual education.

To this list may be added the potential societal, ethnic group or community benefits of bilingual education, such as: continuity of heritage, cultural transmission, cultural vitality, empowered and informed citizenship, increased school and state achievement standards, social and economic inclusion, socialization, social relationships and networking, ethnic identity, ethnic group self-determination and distinctiveness. There are also societal benefits, which have already been alluded to and which will be considered fully in Chapter 17.

At the same time, bilingual education does not guarantee effective learning. The language policy, provision and practices of the school are but components alongside many others that enable children to succeed. These other components also need to be effective for strong forms of bilingual education to prosper. They include, for example: high-quality and well trained teachers; good-quality learning resources, especially in the minoritized language; and support from stakeholders, be they politicians, policymakers, practitioners or parents and the local community. Strong forms of bilingual education raise the probability of higher learning achievement by children. They do not assure it. This will be considered in the next chapter.

Having summarized various types of bilingual education in this and the previous chapter, the natural question to ask is whether one type is more effective than another. Is it better for Spanish-speaking children in the United States to be placed in mainstream, transitional, developmental maintenance or dual language schooling? For a monolingual English-speaker, is it detrimental to enter immersion schooling compared with mainstream schooling? Such questions will be examined in the next chapter, in particular in the light of 'effectiveness' research.

Key Points in This Chapter

> - Varieties of bilingual education include different forms of strong bilingual education, where the use of both languages in the curriculum is fostered.
> - Strong forms of bilingual education aim for students to become bilingual, biliterate and bicultural, and sometimes multilingual, multicultural and with multiliteracies.
> - Immersion, heritage language and dual language education are the most well known forms of strong bilingual education.
> - Dual language bilingual education is growing in popularity in the United States. Two-way programs mix majority and minoritized language students.

- In heritage language programs, the development or revitalization of home (or ancestral) languages and cultures is a key aim.
- Immersion bilingual education started in Canada and has spread to many countries of the world.
- Immersion bilingual education enables majority language children to learn through a second language.
- Content and language integrated learning (CLIL) began as a European form of bilingual education and refers to a variety of approaches in which an additional language is used for the learning and teaching of both content and language.
- Content teaching can occur through two or more majority languages, as in the European Schools movement.
- The varieties of strong bilingual education differ in the amount of time given to the minority and majority languages in the classroom but full bilingualism and biliteracy are expected as outcomes.

Suggested Further Reading

Ballinger, S., Fielding, R. and Tedick, D.J. (eds) (2024) *Teacher Development for Content-Based Language Education: International Perspectives*. Multilingual Matters.

Coyle, D., Meyer, O. and Staschen-Dielman, S. (eds) (2023) *A Deeper Learning Companion for CLIL: Putting Pluraliteracies into Practice*. Cambridge University Press.

Freire, J.A., Alfaro, C. and de Jong, E. (2024) *The Handbook of Dual Language Bilingual Education*. Routledge.

Kibler, A.K., Walqui, A., Bunch, G.C. and Faltis, C.J. (eds) (2024) *Equity in Multilingual Schools and Communities: Celebrating the Contributions of Guadalupe Valdés*. Multilingual Matters.

Kleyn, T., Hunt, V., Jaar, A., Madrigal, R. and Villegas, C. (eds) (2024) *Lessons from a Dual Language Bilingual School: Celebrando una década de Dos Puentes Elementary*. Multilingual Matters.

On the Web

Coalition of Community-Based Heritage Language Schools
https://www.heritagelanguageschools.org

Video – Making dual-language immersion work (Claremont Immersion School in the United States)
https://youtu.be/j1UlcByWXNQ

Office of the Secretary-General of the European Schools

The OfficeEuropean SchoolsAccredited European Schools
https://www.eursc.eu/en

Video – Six videos demonstrating CLIL used in classes from primary schools and vocational colleges
https://youtu.be/dFuCrxRobh0

Video – German Trilingual International School Yaounde (Cameroon)
https://youtu.be/QONRa1IZELo?si=gytNnhYCEY2WKUSw

Discussion Questions

(1) Share your experiences participating in or observing any of the strong forms of bilingual education described in this chapter. How successful was this program in producing bilingual, biliterate and bicultural students? To what do you attribute this success (or lack thereof)?
(2) Dual language bilingual education is growing in popularity, particularly among language majority parents who want their children to become bilingual. The presence of language majority students and the strong support of their parents have helped to move bilingual education away from remedial to enrichment forms of education. However, there is a concern about the 'gentrification' of dual language bilingual education, namely that language majority students, their language (e.g. English) and their parents are more empowered than the language minoritized students, their language and their families. Why might this be? What can be done to help ensure a true balance in dual language programs?
(3) There is often confusion between Canadian (bilingual) immersion and US structured (English) immersion, and about the differences between content-based instruction (CBI) or sheltered instruction (SI) in the United States and content and language integrated learning (CLIL), which began in Europe. What are the differences? Why are these strong forms of bilingual education in Canada and Europe, but monolingual (English) forms of education in the United States? How can content-based instruction approaches be transformed into bilingual models for the United States?

Study Activities

(1) Observe and report on a dual language bilingual education classroom. Note the nature and amount of use of the two languages in the program for different content areas or different parts of the day. How much mixing or translanguaging is happening?
(2) Interview a teacher of one of the strong forms of bilingual education described in this chapter. Ask about the educational, societal and linguistic aims of the program. How does that compare to the type of program as listed in Table 10.1?
(3) Explore the map and database of US community-based heritage language programs that is being built by the Coalition of Community-Based Heritage Language Schools (https://heritagelanguageschools.org/coalition/schoolmap). What do these reveal about language diversity in the United States? Contribute to these databases by adding programs you may be aware of that are not currently included.

CHAPTER 12

The Effectiveness of Bilingual Education

Introduction

Key Themes in School and Classroom Effectiveness

The Effectiveness of Bilingual Education: The United States Debate
Early Research
21st Century Research
Public Opinion Polls and the Effectiveness of Bilingual Education
Expert Overviews of the Effectiveness of Bilingual Education

The Effectiveness of Dual Language Bilingual Education

The Effectiveness of Immersion Bilingual Education
Second Language Learning
First Language Learning
Other Curriculum Areas
Attitudes and Social Adjustment
Problems and Limitations

The Effectiveness of Heritage Language Education

Aims, Scope and Limitations of Research
Methodological and Theoretical Issues
The Sample of Children
Interacting Factors
Measures of Success
Quantitative and Qualitative Methods of Research
The Researchers

Conclusion

CHAPTER 12

The Effectiveness of Bilingual Education

Introduction

Having considered various types of **bilingual education** in the last two chapters, this chapter turns to considering research on the major types of bilingual education. Is there a 'best model'? How effective are these major models for different types of children? What are the successes and limitations of different models? From very early research in the 1920s in Wales (Saer, 1923) and Malherbe's (1946) evaluation of bilingual education in South Africa, there have been many evaluations of bilingual projects, programs and interventions.

In the history of research on bilingual education, it is possible to find support for most of the different forms of bilingual education by selecting and emphasizing a particular study. Consider, for example, three early studies conducted between 1978 and 1980 in the United States. Dannoff *et al.* (1978) found mainstreaming to be superior to **transitional bilingual education**, McConnell (1980) found transitional bilingual education to be better than mainstreaming, while Matthews (1979) found no difference between the two. However, major reviews of past research and more recent comprehensive longitudinal studies provide evidence of the benefits of bilingual education. This chapter gives an overview of both the major historical and more recent research on the effectiveness of bilingual education, and the varying results that relate to particular political and educational contexts.

Key Themes in School and Classroom Effectiveness

The effectiveness of bilingual education can be addressed from different perspectives. First, there is the effectiveness at the level of the individual child. Within the same bilingual classroom, children may respond and perform differently. Second, there is effectiveness at the classroom level. Within the same school and type of bilingual education program, classrooms may vary considerably, for example because of the teacher and instructional style. Third, effectiveness is often analyzed at the school level. What makes some schools more effective than others, even within the same type of bilingual education program and with similar student characteristics? Fourth, beyond the school level there can be aggregations of schools in different types of program (e.g. transitional compared with **heritage language** programs) or in different geographical regions. It is possible to look at effective bilingual education at each and all four of these levels, and at the inter-relationships between them. For example, at the individual level we need to know how bilingual education can be most effective for children of different levels of ability, background and learning needs. How do children with specific language learning needs (e.g. those with dyslexia or language delay) fare in bilingual education? At the classroom level, we need to know what teaching methods and classroom characteristics create optimally effective bilingual education. At the school level, the characteristics of staffing, the range of language abilities and the language composition of the school all affect 'whether, where, when and how' bilingual education is successful. At all these levels, there are frequently issues about human, material and physical resources. The demands are for an adequate supply of well trained bilingual teachers, curriculum materials in all content areas, buildings and facilities in order for success to be maximized.

Apart from individual classroom and school characteristics, the effectiveness of bilingual education is influenced by the social, economic, political and cultural context of such education. Chapters 17 and 18 explore how political and ideological differences impact on bilingual education. The willingness of teachers to involve parents, and good relationships between the school and its community, may be important in effective bilingual education. Also, the local economics of schooling play an important part. In countries like the United States, where the funding of schools is based on a local tax, then 'per student' expenditure in more affluent areas will be considerably greater than in less affluent areas. For example, many US **language minoritized students** are in economically poor urban and rural school districts with considerably less per-pupil expenditures than those in more wealthy suburbs. It is more difficult to advance the effectiveness of bilingual education with very limited financial and material resources. It is also important in research on the effectiveness of bilingual education to examine a wide variety of outcomes from such education. Such outcomes may derive from **high-stakes testing**, measures of basic skills (e.g. oracy, literacy, numeracy, information and computer literacy), or the broadest range of curriculum areas (e.g. science and technology, humanities, mathematics, languages, arts, physical, practical and theoretical pursuits, skills as well as knowledge). Non-academic outcomes such as school attendance, attitudes, self-concept, self-esteem, tolerance, anti-racism, social and emotional adjustment, employment and moral development are also important to include in an assessment of effectiveness. For example, evidence suggests students who experienced bilingual education were significantly less likely to drop out of school (Crawford & Krashen, 2007).

Effective bilingual education is not a simple or automatic consequence of using a child's home language in school. Various home and parental, community, teacher, school, stakeholder and society effects may act and interact to make bilingual education more or less effective. Any effectiveness equation is complex, variable across regions and politics, multivariate, and often contested.

The Effectiveness of Bilingual Education: The United States Debate

This section centers on the US debate about the effectiveness of bilingual education. After a substantial number of individual research studies on bilingual education had accumulated in the United States, various reviews and overviews appeared. A reviewer will assemble as many individual studies as possible and attempt to find a systematic pattern and an orderliness in the findings. Is there a consensus in the findings? Is it possible to make some generalizations about the effectiveness of different forms of bilingual education? Rarely, if ever, will all the individual research studies agree. Therefore, the reviewer's task is to detect reasons for variations. For example, different age groups, different socioeconomic class backgrounds, varying types of measurement device, different experimental designs and varying research methodologies may explain variations in results.

Early Research

The initial reviews of bilingual education effectiveness were published in the late 1970s. Zappert and Cruz (1977), Troike (1978) and Dulay and Burt (1978, 1979) each concluded that bilingual education in the United States effectively promoted **bilingualism** with language minoritized children and was preferable to **monolingual** English programs. From the late 1970s to the end of the 20th century, many more individual studies and reviews emerged (e.g. August & Hakuta, 1997; Dutcher & Tucker, 1996).

While in the 1960s and 1970s bilingual education slowly evolved in the United States, from the late 1970s to the present politicians have not tended to favor such evolution (see Chapter 9). One branch of political opinion in the United States sees bilingual education as failing to foster integration and producing underachievement. Such opinion regards bilingual education as leading to both a lack of proficiency in English and to social and economic divisions in society along language lines. Minoritized language groups are sometimes portrayed as using bilingual education for political and economic self-interest, even separatism.

In this political context, the federal government commissioned a major review of bilingual education in the early 1980s. For this review, Baker and de Kanter (1983) focused on just two narrow questions: (1) Does transitional bilingual education lead to better performance in English? (2) Does transitional bilingual education lead to better performance in non-language subject areas? Only English language proficiency and achievement in academic areas were regarded as the desirable outcomes of schooling. Other outcomes such as self-esteem, employment, preservation of home languages, the value of different **cultures**, moral development, **identity**, social adjustment and personality development were not considered. They located 300 studies of bilingual education from North America and the rest of the bilingual world, rejected 261 studies as irrelevant or for being of poor quality and contentiously used just 39 studies. Canadian French immersion (a bilingual program for majority language speakers) was incorrectly classified as the same as US structured English immersion (a non-bilingual program for minoritized language speakers), thus skewing the findings. The conclusion of their review is that no particular education program should be legislated for or preferred by the US federal government. The review therefore came out in support of English-only and transitional bilingual education. **Assimilation** and integration appeared to be the social and political preference behind the conclusions.

There was considerable criticism of the Baker and de Kanter (1983) review (e.g. American Psychological Association, 1982; Rolstad *et al.*, 2005a; Willig, 1981). The main criticisms may be summarized as follows: a narrow range of outcome measures was considered, although this is often the fault of the original research rather than the review; focusing on transitional bilingual education implicitly valued assimilation and integration and devalued aims such as the preservation of a child's home language and culture; and the criteria used for selecting only 39 out of 300 studies were narrow and rigidly applied. The approach of Baker and de Kanter (1983) was narrative integration. This is essentially a subjective and unsystematic process, and the methods of procedure tend to be variable from reviewer to reviewer.

A comparison of the review by Baker and de Kanter with the earlier reviews by Zappert and Cruz (1977), Troike (1978) and Dulay and Burt (1978, 1979) shows that reviews of almost the same studies can result in differing conclusions. That is, different reviewers use the same research reports to support contrary conclusions. An alternative and more systematic approach is to use meta-analysis. The technique mathematically examines the amount of effect of differences in the research studies. For example, how much difference is there in outcome between transitional and **immersion bilingual education**? Typically, a larger number of studies can be included in a meta-analysis than in other types of reviews because the varying quality of evaluation studies can be allowed for statistically.

Willig (1985) adopted a statistical meta-analysis approach to review 23 of the studies included in the Baker and de Kanter (1983) review. These 23 concerned US bilingual education evaluations and excluded Canadian immersion education evaluations. Willig (1985) concluded that bilingual education programs were consistently superior in various outcomes. Small to moderate advantages were found for bilingual education students in reading, **language skills**, mathematics and overall achievement when the tests were in the students' second language (English). Similar advantages were found for these curriculum areas and for writing, listening, social studies and self-concept when non-English-language tests were used. A criticism of Willig's (1985) meta-analysis is that she included only 23 studies. An international review of the bilingual educational effectiveness studies could have included many more, and provided more generalizable conclusions. Further criticisms of Willig are given by August and Hakuta (1997) and Baker (1987).

An eight-year, Congressionally mandated longitudinal study of bilingual education in the United States compared structured English 'immersion', early-exit and late-exit bilingual education programs (Ramirez, 1992; Ramirez et al., 1991). The term 'immersion' is not used in the original Canadian sense – English **submersion** or mainstreaming is more accurate. Over 2300 Spanish-speaking students from 554 kindergarten to sixth-grade classrooms in New York, New Jersey, Florida, Texas and California were studied. As a generalization, the outcomes were different for the three types of bilingual education. By the end of the third grade, mathematics, language and English reading skills were not particularly different between the three programs. By the sixth grade, late-exit transitional bilingual education students were performing at a higher level in mathematics, English language and English reading than students on other programs. Parental involvement appeared to be greatest in the late-exit transitional programs.

One important conclusion reached by the authors was that Spanish-speaking students 'can be provided with substantial amounts of primary language instruction without impeding their acquisition of English language and reading skills' (Ramirez et al., 1991: 39). When language minoritized students are given instruction in their home language, this does not interfere with or delay their acquisition of English language skills but helps them to 'catch up' with their English-speaking peers in English language arts and mathematics. The data suggest that by grade 6, students provided with English-only instruction may actually fall further behind their English-speaking peers. Data also document that learning a second language will take six or more years. The results also showed little difference between early-exit and the English immersion (submersion) students. Opponents of bilingual education have used this result to argue for the relative administrative ease and less expensive mainstreaming (submersion) of language minoritized students (e.g. Baker, 1992).

A series of reviews and criticisms of the Ramirez *et al.* (1991) research followed (e.g. Baker, 1992; Cazden, 1992; Dolson & Mayer, 1992; Meyer & Fienberg, 1992; Rossell, 1992; Thomas, 1992; US Department of Education, 1992). These critiques emphasized the following:

- The benefits of strong forms of bilingual education programs were not considered (e.g. two-way bilingual education; heritage language education). This means that the statements about bilingual education were based on an incomplete range of possibilities. Mainstream classrooms with English second language (ESL) pull-out (withdrawal) classes – widely implemented in the United States – were also not included in the study.
- The range of variables used to measure 'success' was narrow.
- The considerable differences that exist within bilingual education programs (let alone differing types of bilingual education programs) make comparisons and conclusions most difficult. Also, the complexity of organization within a school, its ethos and varying classroom practices make watertight categorization of schools into bilingual education programs formidable (Willig & Ramirez, 1993).
- The design of the study was ill-suited to answer key policy questions. More clarity in the aims and goals of bilingual education in the United States is needed before research can be appropriately focused.
- There was a lack of data to support the long-term benefits of late-exit transitional programs over other programs.

Near the close of the 20th century, Rossell and Baker (1996) reviewed 75 studies they regarded as methodologically acceptable. They concluded that there was no evidence that bilingual programs were superior to English-only options. Greene (1998) re-analyzed the Rossell and Baker (1996) studies using meta-analysis (echoing Willig's re-analysis of Baker and de Kanter). Greene indicated that classification of 'weak' forms of bilingual education into transitional bilingual education (TBE), ESL and developmental maintenance was fraught with difficulty. What was called TBE in one district could be ESL in the next. Crucially, Greene controlled for background characteristics between 'treatment' and control groups (e.g. socioeconomic class, parents' level of education); on that basis a third of the 75 research studies were ruled out of the analysis. Others were excluded because they lacked legitimate control groups; some studies were unpublished or unavailable, some duplicated reporting of the same program and some were not actually evaluations of bilingual education. From the 11 remaining studies, it was found that the use of native language instruction helps achievement in English. That is, use of the home language in school tends to relate to higher achievement than English-only instruction. The numerical 'effect size' of home language programs on English reading, mathematics and a non-English language were almost an exact mirror of Willig's (1985) findings, although only four studies were in common.

21st Century Research

Research on the effectiveness of bilingual education in the United States continues in the 21st century with renewed interest, especially given the debates surrounding the political restrictions on bilingual programs (e.g. California's **Proposition 227**, Massachusetts' **Question 2** and Arizona's **Proposition 203**) and their subsequent reversals (e.g. **Proposition 58** in California, the **LOOK Act** in Massachusetts) or scale-back of restrictions (e.g. SB 1014 in Arizona) and the de-emphasis of bilingual education in federal education policy (e.g. NCLB and ESSA) as described in Chapter 9. A meta-analysis by Rolstad *et al.* (2005a), which included 17 studies conducted after Willig's (1985) study, also found that 'bilingual education is consistently superior to all-English approaches' (Rolstad *et al.*, 2005a: 572). Rolstad *et al.* (2005b) also conducted a separate meta-analysis with four post-Willig evaluation studies focused on Arizona, and once again found a positive effective for bilingual education over English-only instruction in that state. They concluded that 'the evaluation literature has been remarkably clear in demonstrating that bilingual education is not only as effective as English-only alternatives, but that it tends to be *more effective*' (Rolstad *et al.*, 2005b: 62, original emphasis). A meta-analysis by Slavin and Cheung (2005) included 17 studies that focused narrowly on the language of reading instruction for English language learners (ELLs). They found that 'existing evidence favors bilingual approaches, especially paired bilingual strategies that teach reading in the native language and English at different times each day' (Slavin & Cheung, 2005: 247). McField and McField (2014) conducted a 'meta-analysis of meta-analyses', including the major studies discussed above. Taking an innovative approach, the researchers extracted from the studies included in the previous meta-analyses, but with attention not just to *research* quality (as done in the previous meta-analyses) but also to *program* quality (e.g. weak, strong, or undefined bilingual education programs). Consistent with the prior meta-analyses, they found bilingual education to have positive outcomes when compared with English-only programs. However, by considering both research and program quality, McField and McField found an even larger effect for strong forms of bilingual education – nearly double the size of that of weak forms of bilingual education.

Public Opinion Polls and the Effectiveness of Bilingual Education

Apart from effectiveness studies, bilingual education research includes public opinion surveys. The amount of parental and public support that exists for different forms of bilingual education is important in participative democratic societies, as bilingual education is both an educational and a political key topic. The opinion of teachers is also important to survey, particularly when these differ from parents' viewpoints. Krashen (1999) provides a wide-ranging review of US public opinion polls regarding bilingual education. In polls that attempted to ask a representative sample of people, approximately two-thirds of the public were in favor of bilingual education. However, considerable differences in public opinion polls occur because questions differ considerably. How bilingual education is defined differs widely. Leading questions that hint at the preferred or desirable answer, and the ambiguity of what respondents perceive as bilingual education, clearly have an effect on results. When questions are phrased so that bilingual education includes proficiency in both languages, then generally there is a consensus support for bilingual education.

Expert Overviews of the Effectiveness of Bilingual Education

While public opinion surveys are infrequent, expert opinion is more likely to be privately or publicly sought. The US Committee on Education and Labor asked the General Accounting Office (1987) – now called the Government Accountability Office

(GAO) – to conduct a study on whether or not the research evidence on bilingual education supported the current government preference for assimilationist, transitional bilingual education. The GAO therefore decided to conduct a survey of experts on bilingual education. Ten experts were assembled, mostly professors of education, selected from prestigious institutions throughout the United States. Eight out of 10 favored using the native or heritage language in the classroom. They believed that progress in the native language aided children in learning English because it strengthened literacy skills that easily transferred to operating in the second language. On the learning of other subjects in the curriculum, six experts supported the use of heritage languages in such teaching. However, it was suggested that learning English is important in making academic progress.

Another high-profile review in 1997 was by an expert panel of the US National Research Council – the Committee on Developing a Research Agenda on the Education of limited English proficient and bilingual students. It declared that: (1) all children in the United States should be educated to be become fully functional in the English language; (2) the expectations of, and academic opportunities given to, such students must equal those of other students; and (3) 'in an increasingly global economic and political world, proficiency in language other than English and an understanding of different cultures are valuable in their own right, and should be among the major goals for schools' (August & Hakuta, 1997: 17). But this expert panel concluded that the effectiveness debate over various English and bilingual models was too simple and polarized. All programs could be effective, depending on the demographics, needs, interests, goals and resources of the school and local community. Theory-based research and interventions which predicted the effects of components on the 'growth' of children in different environments were needed.

As Crawford (2004) argues, being even-handed, wanting to depoliticize the issue and injecting scientific detachment into research is an academic vision that has little or no impact on journalists and politicians. The 487-page National Research Council review was seized on by both opponents and proponents of bilingual education as justification of their quite different positions. The report thus became a tool used by opposing political groups to support their position.

In 2006 there were major reviews conducted by two groups of experts of the scientific research literature on language and literacy instruction for ELL-classified students. One review was conducted by the Center for Research on Education, Diversity, and Excellence (CREDE) (Genesee *et al.*, 2006) and the other by the National Literacy Panel (NLP) on Language Minority Children and Youth (August & Shanahan, 2006). Both studies received support from the US Department of Education's Institute for Education Science. The findings outlined in the CREDE and NLP reports highlight what is currently known – and what is not known – about language and literacy development for ELL-classified students. While these panels of experts were not charged with nor attempted to compare program models, both reports include conclusions in strong support of bilingual education. One of the major conclusions of the CREDE report is that the 'use of home language for beginning-level ELLs contributes to academic development'. Major findings in the NLP report include the following:

- Home language literacy skills plus good English oral language skills are strongly associated with good English reading comprehension skills.
- Oral proficiency and literacy in the first language is an advantage for literacy development in English.

- Home language experiences can have a positive impact on literacy achievement.
- Students with literacy skills in their home language can **transfer** many of these skills to English writing.

Bilingual education programs are designed to facilitate this kind of oral language, literacy and academic development in the home languages of ELLs, and help students transfer their knowledge and skills from the home language to English.

The most recent extensive expert review of the research literature was conducted in 2017 by the National Academies of Sciences, Engineering, and Medicine in a report titled *Promoting the Educational Success of Children and Youth Learning English: Promising Futures* (Takanishi & Le Menestrel, 2017). The findings are consistent with the reviews by CREDE and NLP described above. Conclusion 7-1 from the National Academies report declares:

> Syntheses of evaluation studies that compare outcomes for ELs instructed in English-only programs with outcomes for ELs instructed bilingually find either that there is no difference in outcomes measured in English or that ELs in bilingual programs outperform ELs instructed only in English. Two recent studies that followed students for sufficient time to gauge longer-term effects of language of instruction on EL outcomes find benefits for bilingual compared with English-only approaches. (Takanishi & Le Menestrel, 2017: 7)

The Civil Rights Project of the University of California released a report in 2023 titled *Bilingual Education and America's Future: Evidence and Pathways*, which includes a brief literature review synthesizing the findings of research on bilingual education, in terms not only of academic benefits but also of broader educational and societal benefits. The authors (Porter *et al.*, 2023: 17) conclude from this synthesis:

> There is strong evidence that bilingual education provides immediate benefits to students by boosting academic growth, supporting multilingual development, and creating learning environments that promote positive identity development. A less robust, yet growing number of studies indicate that bilingual education supports students' longer-term outcomes, including core content access, postsecondary enrollment, and eventual earnings and well-being. Ultimately, the benefits of bilingual education translate to wider social benefits.

This chapter now examines recent reviews and major research on dual language, immersion and heritage language education. Each of these three models has a relatively large collection of literature, allowing some overview of findings. In comparison, there are relatively few sufficiently rigorous evaluations of other types of bilingual education such as content and language integrated learning (CLIL) (see e.g. Nikula *et al.*, 2016), preventing consideration here.

The Effectiveness of Dual Language Bilingual Education

Many overviews and evaluations of the effectiveness of two-way immersion models of **dual language bilingual education** (DLBE) indicate relative success (Alvear, 2019; Cazabon *et al.*, 1993; Howard *et al.*, 2004; Krashen, 2004a; Lindholm, 1991; Lindholm & Aclan, 1991; Lindholm-Leary, 1994, 2001; Lindholm-Leary & Borsato,

2006; Lindholm-Leary & Genesee, 2010, 2014; Morita-Mullaney *et al.*, 2021; Steele *et al.*, 2017; Thomas & Collier, 1995, 2002b; Thomas *et al.*, 1993; Umansky & Reardon, 2014; Umansky *et al.*, 2016; Valentino & Reardon, 2015). While bilingual education is an international phenomenon, given the political debates surrounding bilingual education, and requirements for evaluations of federally funded programs, much of this research has taken place in the United States. This research typically compares DLBE to other forms of bilingual education and to monolingual forms of education for language minoritized students. As Lindholm-Leary and Genesee (2014: 172) summarize:

> Over three decades of research in the U.S. indicates that minority language students in two-way [dual language] and DBE [**developmental bilingual education**] programs acquire English speaking, listening, reading and writing skills as well and as quickly as their minority language peers in mainstream programs.... Minority language students in TWI [two-way immersion] programs achieve at similar or higher levels than their peers in mainstream English-only programs; this includes achievement in mathematics, science, social studies, and other content areas.

Many individual studies have small sample sizes, are short term rather than longitudinal, inadequately control variables such as social class and initial language differences, and ignore variations in design and program (Krashen, 2004a). Students in dual language education are not a random selection of the population of students. They are self-selecting. Hence, it is difficult to know if the successes of dual language schools are due to the program, the characteristics of the students, or both these, or other factors, such as the quality of the teachers.

One of the first rigorous and comprehensive evaluations of dual language schools was by Lindholm-Leary (2001). With wide-ranging and well documented data from 18 schools, she analyzed teacher attitudes and characteristics, teacher talk, parental involvement and satisfaction, as well as student outcomes (with a sample of 4854 students) in different program types, including transitional bilingual education, English-only, the 90:10 dual language model and the 50:50 dual language model. The measured outcomes included Spanish and English **language proficiency**, academic achievement and attitudes of the students. Socioeconomic background and other student characteristics were taken into account in reporting results. Among a wealth of findings, Lindholm-Leary found the following:

- Students who had 10% or 20% of their instruction in English scored as well on English proficiency as those in English-only programs and as well as those in 50:50 dual language (DL) programs.
- Spanish proficiency was higher in 90:10 than in 50:50 DL programs. Students tended to develop higher levels of bilingual proficiency in the 90:10 than the 50:50 DL program.
- For Spanish-speaking students, no difference in English language proficiency was found between the 90:10 and 50:50 DL programs. However, DL students outperformed transitional bilingual education (TBE) students in English by grade 6.
- Students in both the 90:10 and 50:50 DL programs were performing about 10 points higher in reading achievement than the Californian state average for English-speaking students educated in English-only programs.
- Higher levels of bilingual proficiency were associated with higher levels of reading achievement.

- On mathematics tests, DL students performed on average 10 points higher on Californian norms for English-speaking students educated only in English. There was a lack of difference in the scores of 90:10 and 50:50 DL students.
- DL students tended to have very positive attitudes towards their DL programs, teachers, classroom environment and the learning process.

Lindholm-Leary (2001) concluded that DL programs are effective in promoting high levels of language proficiency, academic achievement and positive attitudes to learning in students. In contrast, English language learners educated in mainstream classes tend to lack the English academic language skills needed to understand content well even after 10 years of English instruction (Lindholm-Leary & Genesee, 2010). Also, parents and teachers involved in such DL programs are both enthusiastic and recommend the expansion of such programs to raise the achievements of other majority and minoritized language children.

Thomas and Collier (2002b) compared the performance of dual language students with those in other programs. Their data spans from 1982 to 2001 and includes around 700,000 language minoritized students from school districts around the United States. Their conclusion is that two-way bilingual education at the elementary school level is the optimal program for the long-term academic success of language minoritized students. Such students maintain their first language skills and cognitive/academic development while developing in a second language. In such a model, students acquire deep academic proficiency and cognitive understanding through their first language to compete successfully with native speakers of the second language.

> 90–10 and 50–50 one-way and two-way developmental bilingual education (DBE) programs (or dual language, bilingual immersion) are the only programs we have found to date that assist students to fully reach the 50th percentile in both L1 and L2 in all subjects and to maintain that level of high achievement or reach even higher levels through the end of schooling. The fewest drop-outs come from these programs. (Thomas & Collier, 2002b: 333)

Thomas and Collier (1995, 1997, 2002a, 2002b) produce a growth pattern of language minority English **language achievement** in different types of bilingual education programs. Major findings include the following:

- In kindergarten through to grade 2, there is little difference between language minoritized children in ESL 'pull-out', transitional and two-way (dual language) programs. On an 'English language achievement' scale of 0–100 (with 50 as the average performance of native English-speakers), language minoritized children score around the 20 mark.
- ESL 'pull-out' children initially (grades 1 and 2) progress faster in English language achievement than children in transitional and **dual language programs**. This might be expected, as they have more intensive English-medium activity.
- By grade 6, students in dual language programs and late-exit transitional programs are ahead on English **language performance** compared with early-exit and ESL pull-out students. Dual language and late-exit transitional students' achievements in English language tests are close to those of native English-speakers (i.e. around the 50th percentile). Early-exit and ESL pull-out students tend to perform around the 30th percentile on such tests.

- By grade 11, the order of performance in the English language is:
  - two-way bilingual education (*highest performance*);
  - late-exit transitional bilingual education;
  - early-exit transitional bilingual education;
  - ESL pull-out programs (*lowest performance*).
- By grade 11, two-way bilingual education students are performing above the average levels of native English-speakers on English language tests. On the 'English language achievement' scale of 0–100, two-way bilingual education students average around 60, late-exit students about the same as native English-speakers at around 50, early-exit students around 30 to 40, and ESL pull-out students around 20.

Subsequent work by Thomas and Collier extended and corroborated these earlier findings (Collier & Thomas, 2009, 2017; Thomas & Collier, 2012). This includes extensive work in collaboration with the North Carolina Department of Education to research the effectiveness of the state's dual language programs. While their North Carolina longitudinal studies have not yet been fully published, Thomas and Collier (2012; Collier & Thomas, 2017) describe their preliminary findings from comparisons of DL students and non-DL students across grades 3 to 8 in 2009. In each grade level, DL students scored higher in end-of-grade exams in reading and mathematics than non-DL students. These findings held true in separate analyses of different types of DL and non-DL students: Whites, African-Americans, ELLs, language minoritized students fluent in English (mostly **Latinxs**) and students from low socioeconomic backgrounds. Advantages were also found for **special education** students in DL programs. Thomas and Collier note that 'by the middle school years and sometimes sooner, two-way dual language students, regardless of subgroup, are often at least one grade level ahead of their comparison group' (Thomas & Collier, 2012: 72).

In a brief executive summary of the third year of their study prepared for the North Carolina Department of Public Instruction, Thomas and Collier (2015) noted that they continued to find overall higher reading and math scores for DL students, regardless of ethnicity, socioeconomic, ELL or special education status. Among other brief finding statements, they made special note of the achievement of African-American DL students:

> In Reading, low-SES African American students attending dual language classes are scoring at least one grade higher than their low-SES African American peers not in dual language as early as 4th grade. Furthermore, in Math, low-SES African American dual language students are more than two grades ahead of low-SES African American non-dual language students as early as 5th grade. (Thomas & Collier, 2015: 3)

In a brief overview article published by the California Association of Bilingual Education in its *Multilingual Educator* magazine, Collier and Thomas (2020: 4) draw on their research findings to argue that 'dual language works for everyone'. They mention the success for African-American students as noted above, and then conclude:

> In our North Carolina research, DL students with learning disabilities, autism, and other categories of special need scored significantly higher than their peers with special needs not in DL. It does not harm these students to study through two languages – they benefit! Native English Speakers, new immigrants, English Learners, Latinos, Asians, indigenous groups, students of low socioeconomic status – all students thrive in DL enrichment classes.

Criticisms of Thomas and Collier's methodology and growth trajectories of language minority English language achievement in different types of bilingual education programs include the following:

- Their aggregation is based on selective individual research studies and well implemented and mature programs.
- Little information is presented on how the growth trajectories were determined.
- The effects of student geographical mobility (e.g. leaving a district) are not clear and may produce biased results (e.g. when such students are excluded from longitudinal data).
- Few details are provided about the hundreds of thousands of language minoritized students on which the growth trajectories are based and which date from early the 1980s to the early 2000s.
- The only peer-reviewed publication of their work with North Carolina is a 2017 publication in the *Annual Review of Applied Linguistics* (Collier & Thomas, 2017). However, this is a review article which summarizes findings across their 32 years of research and includes only general statements of their previously reported findings from North Carolina.

Beginning in the mid-2010s, other scholars began undertaking sophisticated longitudinal studies in school districts willing to share their data. Umansky and Reardon (2014) and Umansky *et al.* (2016) analyzed 12 years of data (2000–12) from a large urban California school district with four types of ELL programs: English immersion, transitional bilingual education, maintenance bilingual education and dual language bilingual education. In this diverse school district, the bilingual programs served speakers of Spanish, Cantonese, Mandarin, Filipino and Korean. Only ELLs who began schooling in the district in kindergarten during the time frame of the study – about 40,000 students – were eligible for inclusion. Students in the four programs were compared on three outcomes: attainment of English proficiency, reclassification (from ELL to **fluent English proficient**), and academic performance and growth. The 2014 study focused only on the ELLs in the Spanish-speaking Latinx population, while the 2016 study included all ELL students. The findings of both studies are roughly similar. Thus, we will focus here on the findings from the more inclusive 2016 study.

In terms of English acquisition, Umansky *et al.* (2016) found that, regardless of program type, over 90% were proficient by seventh grade. However, ELLs in the two-language programs (i.e. transitional, maintenance and dual language) took slightly longer to become proficient in English. While rates were nearly identical by the fifth grade (about 80%) there were slight differences in seventh grade, with more students in maintenance bilingual (95%) and dual immersion (94%) reaching proficiency in comparison with students in English immersion and transitional bilingual (both at 92%). Reclassification rates were also very similar across program models by grade 7; however, rates were highest for students in transitional bilingual (92%), followed by English immersion (88%), maintenance bilingual (87%) and dual immersion (86%). These results are illustrated in Figure 12.1.

There were also variations in terms of academic achievement and growth across the four program types. Taking a short view, by second grade, students in transitional bilingual had the highest English language arts (ELA) and mathematics scores, while students in dual language had the lowest scores. However, taking the long view of the ELA scores, by seventh grade, students in dual language surpassed students in English immersion and maintenance bilingual, and attained scores that were essentially the

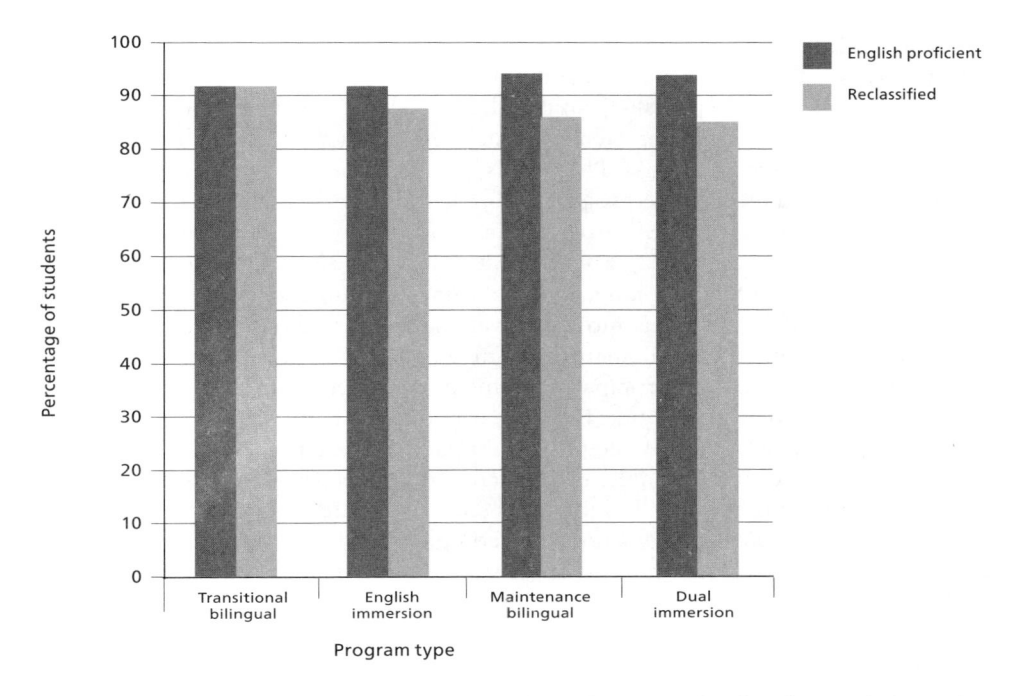

Figure 12.1 Percentage of students attaining English proficiency and reclassification by seventh grade, by program type. Adapted from Umansky et al. (2016)

same as students in transitional bilingual. Results on the math test were much different. Students in all programs tended to have slower growth rates than average students in the state, and by sixth grade the scores of students in transitional bilingual were slightly higher than those in the other three programs (which had roughly similar scores).

In a similar longitudinal study, Valentino and Reardon (2015) followed the academic achievement of 13,750 ELLs from 2001 to 2010 in kindergarten through grade 8 across four programs models: English immersion, transitional bilingual, developmental bilingual and dual immersion. They describe the setting as a 'large urban school district' with a sizable ELL population (Valentino & Reardon, 2015: 618) but do not indicate the city or state. The ELL population was predominantly Latinx (33%) and Chinese (45%). They found that ELA test scores of ELLs in the three bilingual programs increased at least as fast, if not faster than, those of ELL students in English immersion programs. For math, the growth of ELL test scores was as fast or faster in the transitional and developmental bilingual programs, while ELLs in the dual immersion program had math scores that increased more slowly than those in English immersion. Also they found that the Latinx ELLs in bilingual programs performed better longitudinally in both ELA and math than the Chinese ELLs. Of significance to the Valentino and Reardon (2015) study is that the school district used a complex algorithm and lottery system to assign students to programs, after accounting for parental preference, but their data focused on students who were not placed in the programs of parental first choice. This allowed for the removal of parental 'selection bias' and thus had 'a somewhat stronger causal warrant' than prior studies (Valentino & Reardon, 2015: 617).

In the Midwest state of Indiana, the number of ELLs and bilingual education programs is small but rapidly growing. In this 'new destination' state, Morita-Mullaney *et al.* (2021) followed 26 Spanish-speaking ELLs in a dual language school from grades 3 to 6, comparing their academic achievement with 136 of their Spanish-speaking ELL peers in ESL programs across 11 schools in the same district. They found that students in the dual language program scored significantly higher on the state ELA exam than students in the ESL program, but had mixed results on the math exams. Morita-Mullaney *et al.* (2022) also provide one of the few empirical quantitative studies on students' Spanish language proficiency within dual language (50/50 and 90/10 models) and ESL program models. Given the Indiana school districts they worked with lacked data on students' Spanish language development, Morita-Mullaney and her research team assessed participating elementary students using a Spanish-language proficiency assessment (LAS Links Español) over one academic year. While the findings in general provide evidence of the positive impact of the DLBE on students' Spanish proficiency, the findings were quite mixed across domains (speaking, listening, reading and writing) given differences in individual student characteristics, teachers, program models and time. The authors note the complexity of measuring and comparing Spanish proficiency across program models and highlight the need for more research and for longitudinal data.

In contrast with Thomas and Collier, the longitudinal studies described above do not find a clear superiority of dual language education across all measures. Nonetheless, their findings do suggest that bilingual programs generally benefit ELLs as much as, or more than, English immersion programs across academic, English proficiency and reclassification outcomes by the time they reach middle school. Another important finding is that 'the speed with which students are reclassified is not necessarily a good indicator of how well students progress linguistically or academically' (Umansky & Reardon, 2014: 908). Based on these findings, Umansky *et al.* (2016: 16) urge schools and districts (1) to 'invest in high-quality two-language programs', (2) to 'choose among two-language programs based on community and stakeholder voice', (3) to 'opt for slow and steady – ... ELLs can succeed in all three areas, but need time to do so' and (4) to 'take the long view' – tracking students for only a couple of years on a single outcome (e.g. reclassification rates) can paint a misleading picture.

Umansky and Reardon (2014) acknowledge a number of limitations of their study. First, program implementation can vary widely and little is known about the pedagogy and practices in the actual classrooms. Second, there appears to be some barriers to reclassification even after English proficiency is attained, but it is unknown what these barriers are. The authors hypothesize these may be more political or programmatic than linguistic or academic (e.g. waiting until the natural end of a program to reclassify). Third, it is unknown what happens with students after they reclassify. We do not know if they excel or continue to struggle linguistically and academically. And finally, while the authors used a sophisticated statistical design and went to great lengths to control for a number of factors, they acknowledge 'this study does not provide as strong a causal warrant as would a randomized experiment or rigorous quasi-experimental design' (Umansky & Reardon, 2014: 907). Randomized experiments of this scope and magnitude are rarely feasible (see below).

Valentino and Reardon (2015) acknowledge similar and other limitations in their study, including the fact that the school district was somewhat unique and the achievement measures were only in English. They warn: 'Our estimates are not identified sharply enough; the sample is not generalizable enough; and the mechanisms driving these patterns are not clear enough to warrant strong policy recommendations' (Valentino & Reardon, 2015: 634). In addition to these author-identified limitations, another limitation is their focus on ELLs who began school in kindergarten and most likely were born in the United States. Thus we do not know how effective any of these programs may be for foreign-born and late-arrival ELLs, or ELLs with interrupted formal education such as refugee students. Given the limitations, the authors caution that their results may differ from findings in other school districts and states.

A study by Alvear (2019) of a dual language program in a large urban Texas school did account for student outcomes in both English and Spanish. Alvear tracked a cohort of Latinx ELL students from kindergarten to grade 5, across English immersion, transitional bilingual, developmental bilingual and dual language (DL, two-way bilingual immersion). She found that by grade 5, students in the dual language program had the highest English reading performance. Students in the transitional bilingual program and the DL program had similar Spanish reading growth. Students in the developmental bilingual program 'had significantly slower growth than transitional students' (Alvear, 2019: 477). While students in all bilingual programs saw improvements in their Spanish reading, the author acknowledges the surprise that the most additive (i.e. stronger) forms of bilingual education – developmental and DL – did not lead to greater Spanish reading growth. Alvear suggests this may have to do with variations in local implementation of these models and the limited time span for analysis. As other studies have shown, it is important to track students' progress beyond grade 5 to measure the full impact of various program models.

An important study by Steele *et al.* (2017) claims to be the first to come close to using randomized control trials in a study of the effectiveness of dual language bilingual education. In the Portland (Oregon) public schools, the researchers tracked the progress of seven cohorts of students in the district's dual language (DL) immersion programs in Spanish, Japanese, Mandarin Chinese and Russian, since 2004, across 11 elementary schools, four middle schools and five high schools. The Russian and all but one Spanish DL program followed a two-way immersion model, while the Chinese and Japanese programs followed a one-way model serving predominantly native English-speakers.

Because demand for the program is so high, the district uses a lottery system to allocate places. By comparing a sample of students selected through the lottery ($n = 864$) with those students who entered the lottery but were not selected ($n = 1082$), Steele *et al.* (2017) are able to claim students were randomly selected into the program. Findings show that students (both native English-speakers and native speakers of the partner languages) randomly assigned to the DL programs outperform their peers on state reading 'by about seven months of learning in Grade 5 and nine months of learning in Grade 8' (Steele *et al.*, 2017: 302s). No statistically significant differences were found for math and science scores, but also no detriment. The authors note this is significant given that DL students received 25–100% of their math and science instruction in the partner language. The native speakers of the partner languages in the DL programs (i.e. those most likely to be ELLs) were found to benefit 'to the same extent, if not modestly (and insignificantly) more than native English DL students' (Steele *et al.*, 2017: 300s). The authors also found that native speakers of the target language in the DL programs were slightly more likely to reclassify as 'proficient English-speaker' sooner than those in English immersion programs.

While Steele *et al.* (2017) may be the most rigorous study of the effectiveness of DL programs to date, the authors acknowledge limitations. As with the other longitudinal studies above, there was no observation of actual classrooms, thus findings cannot account for variations in quality of instruction, teacher quality, fidelity to the DL models and the effects of peer attributes such as motivation. Even with the lottery random assignment, these are still children with parents who were sufficiently motivated to apply for the DL programs. As the authors note, 'our research design cannot fully disentangle the effects of dual language instruction from other possible mechanisms' (Steele *et al.*, 2017: 302s). An additional limitation is that the authors lumped ELL students in with the larger 'native speakers of the target language' group, thus making it difficult to know how ELLs compare to non-ELLs. Nonetheless, the authors conclude the robust findings have much to offer policymakers and educators: 'A program that yields improved reading in English, improved long-term exit rates from EL status, and no apparent detriment to mathematics and science skills – all while promoting proficiency in two languages – seems difficult to criticize' (Steele *et al.*, 2017: 303s).

The Effectiveness of Immersion Bilingual Education

Majority language speakers may learn a minoritized language through immersion bilingual education (see Chapter 11). There are six decades of international research and reviews of immersion bilingual education; these paint a relatively uniform picture of success. Major works in the 1980s include reviews by Swain and Lapkin (1982) and the California State Department of Education (1984) and studies by Genesee (1983, 1984, 1987). Research and reviews in the 1990s corroborate and build on these earlier findings, including work by Arnau (1997), de Courcy (2002), Genesee (1992), Hickey (1997), Laurén (1994) and Swain and her colleagues (Johnson & Swain, 1994, 1997; Swain, 1997; Swain & Johnson, 1997; Swain & Lapkin, 1991). International research on bilingual immersion continues in the 21st century (e.g. Bérubé *et al.*, 2022; Bourgoin & Dicks, 2019; Davis *et al.*, 2019; Johnstone, 2002; Nicolay & Poncelet, 2015; Purić *et al.*, 2017; Swain & Lapkin, 2005, 2008; Tedick, 2014). The research highlights four major sets of outcomes of immersion bilingual education, which will now be considered.

Second Language Learning

It is easy to predict that immersion students will surpass those in mainstream (core) programs given 'drip-feed' second language (e.g. French in Canada) lessons for 30 minutes a day. Most students in early total immersion programs approach native-like performance in **receptive language** skills (listening and reading) in the second language at around 11 years of age. Such levels are not so well attained in the **productive language** skills of speaking and writing (Swain & Johnson, 1997).

The reviews confirm that immersion students mostly succeed in gaining competence in two languages (Johnstone, 2002) although many students do not achieve native-like abilities in speaking and writing. However, as Chapter 1 revealed, bilingual ability is not the same as being functionally bilingual. One of the limitations of immersion bilingual education is that, for some students, the second language can become a school-only phenomenon. Outside the school walls, immersion students tend not to use the second language any more than 'drip feed' students (Swain & Johnson, 1997). Lack of spontaneous or contrived opportunity to use the second language actively and purposefully may partly be the explanation (other explanations will be considered later). Ideally, immersion programs not only create bilinguals but also widen students' cultural horizons and sensitize them to second language culture and values.

First Language Learning

If immersion bilingual education provides the route to near-native fluency in a second language, is it at the cost of attainment in the first language? Does bilingualism result in lesser achievement in the first language compared with 'mainstream' students? Like a balance, as one goes up, does the other go down?

For three or four years of early total immersion, students tend not to progress in the first language to the same extent as monolingual students in mainstream classes. This first language development relates more to school language measured by tests rather than **vernacular** first language. Reading, spelling and punctuation, for example, are not as developed, albeit the lag is only temporary. Since such children are usually not given first language instruction for one, two or three years after starting school, these results are to be expected. However, the initial pattern does not last. After approximately six years of schooling, early total immersion children have typically caught up with their monolingual peers in first language skills. Indeed, when occasional differences in first language achievement between immersion and mainstream children have been identified by research, they tend to be in favor of immersion students (Johnstone, 2002; Swain & Lapkin, 1982, 1991), thus linking with the possible cognitive advantages of bilingualism described in Chapter 7.

Early partial immersion students tend to lag behind for three or four years in their first language skills. Their performance is little different from that of total early immersion students, which is surprising since early partial immersion education has more first language content. By the end of elementary schooling, partial early immersion children typically catch up with mainstream peers in first language attainment. Unlike early total immersion students, partial immersion children do not tend to surpass mainstream comparison groups in first language achievement. Similarly, late immersion has no detrimental effect on first language skills (Genesee, 1983).

The evidence suggests that immersion children learn a second language at no cost to their first language. Rather than acting like a weighing balance, early total immersion, in particular, seems more analogous to cooking. The ingredients, when mixed and baked, react together in additive ways. The product becomes more than the sum of its parts.

Other Curriculum Areas

If immersion education results in children becoming bilingual, the question is whether this is at the cost of achievement in other curriculum areas. Compared with children in mainstream education, how do immersion children progress in curriculum areas such as mathematics and science, history and geography? The reviews of research suggest that early total immersion students generally perform as well in these subjects as do mainstream children. That is, achievement in the curriculum is typically not adversely affected by early total immersion bilingual education.

The evaluations of early partial immersion education are not quite so positive. When children in early partial immersion learn mathematics and science through the medium of a second language, they tend to lag behind comparable mainstream children, at least initially. The results for late immersion are similar. The important factor appears to be whether second language skills are sufficiently developed to cope with fairly complex curriculum material. Johnson and Swain (1994) argue that there is a gap in second language proficiency that needs bridging when students move from learning a language as a subject to learning through that second language. The more demanding the curriculum area, the higher is the level of learning expected; and the later the switch to learning through a second language, the more important it is to provide 'bridging' programs. Such bridging programs ease the discrepancy between second language proficiency and the language proficiency required to understand the curriculum. A bridging program may require a language teacher and a content teacher (e.g. of mathematics) to operate together.

The overall results suggest that bilingual education by an immersion experience need not have negative effects on curriculum performance, particularly in early total immersion programs. Indeed, most children gain a second language without cost to their performance in the curriculum (Johnstone, 2002). However, the key factor seems to be whether students have sufficient second language instructional competence (MacSwan & Rolstad, 2003) or disciplinary language knowledge (Moore & Schleppegrell, 2020) in order to work in the curriculum in their second language (see Chapter 8).

There is also some evidence to suggest that immersion programs are suitable for almost all children, including those in the lower ability ranges. De Courcy *et al.* (2002) found that, in Australia, such children were successful in immersion education (e.g. in mathematics). Indeed, in immersion classes they appear to fare better, partly due to 'the attention to language the teachers need to have' (de Courcy *et al.*, 2002: 117). This parallels Bruck's (1978, 1982) research in Canada, where 'language impaired' children were not found to suffer but to gain some second language proficiency from the immersion experience. Canadian research also suggests that there are no adverse effects from immersion on 'below average IQ students' compared with such students in a monolingual program. Rather, some degree of bilingualism is attained (Genesee, 1992). De Courcy *et al.* (2002: 125) found that:

> The research identified in the literature review and our own data leads us to conclude that children from diverse backgrounds should not be forced out of immersion programmes, as they would do no better in the English mainstream, but would lose the benefit of learning an additional language, at a cost to their self-esteem.

Attitudes and Social Adjustment

Apart from performance throughout the curriculum, evaluations of immersion education have examined whether immersion has positive or negative effects on students' motivation, attitude and study skills. The most positive results in this area have been found with early total immersion students. Parents of such students tend to express satisfaction with their offsprings' learning as well as their personal and social behavior (e.g. Hickey, 1997, in Ireland). Early immersion students also tend to have more positive attitudes toward themselves, their education and, in Canada, to French Canadians (in comparison, for example, with late immersion students). However, the danger here lies in attributing the positive attitudes to schooling. The cause may alternatively be parental values and beliefs, home culture and environment. This is further discussed in the next section.

Problems and Limitations

Over the years, various scholars and educators have highlighted potential problems and limitations in immersion education (Dagenais, 2003; de Courcy, 2002; Hammerly,

1988; Heller, 2003; Netten & Germain, 2004; Swain & Lapkin, 2008). In the Canadian context in particular, these concerns include the following:

- Canadian immersion students do not always gain grammatical accuracy or competence in all dimensions in their French comparable to native speakers. This may be due to the limited nature of communication between students and teachers in the social environment of the classroom and a greater instructional focus on content and curriculum achievement.
- Graduates of Canadian immersion programs may not make much use of French after leaving school. This partly reflects opportunity, partly a lack of confidence in their competence in speaking French and partly a preference for English use.
- There is difficulty in pinpointing the crucial interacting factors that create an effective immersion experience. There are, for example, intervening variables such as teacher preparation, teaching techniques, student motivation, parental attitudes, curricular choices and classroom management. Also, there are debates over what is more important – the intensity of language learning (i.e. number of hours of study per day) or length of time learning the language (i.e. number of years of language instruction).
- Immersion programs can have effects on mainstream schools such as a redistribution of classroom teachers and leaders, a change in the linguistic and ability profile of mainstream classes, and discrepancies in class size, with increasing numbers of mixed-aged classes.
- Canadian immersion schools provide Anglophones with the linguistic and cultural capital for increased social and economic mobility and for political power. Hence, immersion education may produce conflict with the minority Francophone community (e.g. in Ontario) rather than the harmonious unity and 'bridge building' that bilingualism aims to achieve in Canadian society.

Box 12.1 Cautions in generalizing from Canadian immersion education

If immersion education is thought worthy of generalizing from Canada to other countries, there are certain conditions that need to be kept in mind:

- *Conviction*. Immersion bilingual education as practiced in Canada is optional. The convictions of teachers and parents and of the children themselves affect the ethos of the school and the motivation and achievement of the children. Immersion education will work best when there is conviction and not enforced conformity.
- *Homogeneity*. Immersion education in Canada typically starts with children who are at a similar level in their language skills. Such a homogeneous grouping of children may make the language classroom more efficient. Outside of Canada, adjustments may be needed when such homogeneity is not realistic or even desirable.
- *Respect*. The Canadian immersion experience ensures that there is respect for the child's home language and culture. Parents are generally seen as partners in the immersion movement and some dialogue has existed with administrators, teachers and researchers.
- *Commitment*. Immersion teachers in Canada tend to be committed to immersion education. Research suggests that teacher commitment to, and enthusiasm for, bilingual education is of high importance in student achievement.
- *Ideologies*. Behind Canadian immersion education is a political, social and cultural ideology aimed at creating a different kind of society. By promoting bilingualism in English-speakers, immersion education in Canada may support French language communities, increase the opportunities for Francophones outside Québec and help promote bilingualism in the public and private sectors. However, immersion education is seen as a Trojan horse of further English assimilation by some Francophones while giving Anglophone children with bilingual abilities an advantage in the jobs market.

- Research has concentrated more on the outcomes of immersion education and less on the immersion learning processes from the students' perspectives.
- There is a danger in generalizing from the successful Canadian experience to elsewhere in the world (see Box 12.1). In Canada, immersion concerns two major high-status international languages: French and English. In many countries where bilingualism is present or fostered, the situation is different. Often the context is one of a majority and a minoritized language (or languages) coexisting.

The more educators are aware of and acknowledge these problems and limitations, the better they can attempt to address them.

The Effectiveness of Heritage Language Education

Reviews and evaluations of heritage language education programs span four decades and multiple countries. As described in Chapter 11, heritage language can take various forms and thus may overlap with other models of bilingual education. Reviews focused on Canada include those by the Canadian Education Association (1991), Cummins (1983, 1993), Cummins and Danesi (1990), Duff (2008) and Nagy (2021). Reviews focused on heritage language programs for Indigenous (e.g. American Indian, Hawaiian) and immigrant communities in the United States include work by Bhalla *et al.* (2021), Brinton (2008), Carreira (2021), Demmert (2001), Kagan *et al.* (2017), Lee and Wright (2014), Lee and Chen-Wu (2021), McCarty (2002, 2017, 2018, 2019), McCarty and Baker (2024); Peyton *et al.* (2001), Wiley *et al.* (2014) and Wright and Chan (2021). While these evaluations are from the Global North, there is a growing literature from the Global South (e.g. Benson, 2014, 2019a, 2019b; Benson & Wong, 2019; Heugh & Skutnabb-Kangas, 2010; Heugh *et al.*, 2007; Lipski, 2021; Mohanty *et al.*, 2009; Windle *et al.*, 2020; Wright *et al.*, 2022) and literature that is international in coverage (e.g. Dutcher & Tucker, 1996; Kagan *et al.*, 2017; Montrul & Polinsky, 2021). Apart from looking at individual international educational interventions, the reviews also look at the pattern that can be found in the results of evaluations of heritage language education, thus attempting to derive international generalizations.

The results of such evaluations suggest that heritage language programs can be effective in four different ways. First, the students develop and maintain their home languages. Second, they tend to perform as well as or better academically than comparable mainstream children. Third, studies suggest that when children are placed in heritage language education their attitudes are particularly positive. When the home language is used in school, there is the possibility that a child's sense of identity, self-esteem and self-concept will be enhanced. In comparison, a language minoritized child who is mainstreamed is vulnerable to a loss of self-esteem and status. The home language and culture may seem disparaged. The school system and the teachers may seem latently or manifestly to be rejecting the child's home language and values. This may affect the child's motivation and interest in schoolwork and thereby performance. A student whose skills are recognized and encouraged may feel encouraged and motivated; a student whose skills are ignored may feel discouraged and rejected. Hence, intra-family communication may improve in terms of language, cultural identity and bonding. The fourth finding of heritage language evaluations is perhaps the most unexpected. Even with less instructional time devoted to English, when **testing** children's English language performance (or whatever the second language is for that child), they are likely to perform at least as well as children in mainstream education. The explanation seems to lie in self-esteem being enhanced, language and intellectual skills being better promoted by education in the home language, and the transfer of such skills into second language (majority language) areas.

While evaluations of heritage language education are positive, not all Canadians are agreed on the issue. For some, **empowerment** of heritage language groups (i.e. non-English and French) is perceived as a major societal challenge – a challenge to existing power and political arrangements. Official Canadian policy has been supportive of multiculturalism, especially of the two 'solitudes' – French language and English language cultures (Nagy, 2021; Wright & Chan, 2019). Extending multiculturalism to other 'heritage' languages has been more contentious. Lukewarm support for heritage language communities tends to stop short if public monies are to be used to support heritage language education. The anxieties of sections of public opinion and of government include: the disruption of mainstream schools (e.g. falling rolls), problems of staffing, minimal communication between heritage language teachers and mainstream teachers, segregation of school communities, the financial costs of the absorption of immigrants into a bilingual education system, loss of time for core curriculum subjects, social tensions and effects on the integration and stability of Canadian society. Such anxieties have grown with the increased levels of immigration into Canada. Owing to low birth rates and an aging population in Canada, the population has been increased by government immigration policies. Hence language diversity in Canada has increased. In Toronto and Vancouver, for example, more than half the school population comes from a non-English-speaking background.

An important extra perspective comes from a World Bank report in the mid-1990s which included an economic analysis of heritage language and other forms of bilingual education (Dutcher & Tucker, 1996). The report examined international evidence from Haiti, Nigeria, the Philippines, Guatemala, Canada, New Zealand, the United States (Diné bizaad (Navajo)), Fiji, the Solomon Islands, Vanuatu and Western Samoa. It found that bilingual education is not an expensive option and has similar costs to mainstream programs. However, the most important conclusion was that strong forms of bilingual education create cost savings for the education system and for society. For example, such bilingual education provides higher levels of achievement in fewer years of study. Student progress is faster, and higher achievement benefits society by less unemployment and a more skilled workforce.

Where there are weak forms of bilingual education, or language minoritized children are mainstreamed, there may be costs to a national economy owing to slower rates of progress at school, lower levels of final achievement and sometimes the need for special or compensatory education. Higher drop-out rates mean lower potential for the employment market, and the economy suffers with a lower level of skills among the workforce and higher unemployment rates. In economic terms, students need to gain productive characteristics through education and early use of the native language. For example, Dutcher (2004) describes a World Bank cost-effectiveness study on Guatemala that found that bilingual education was an economically prudent policy (see World Bank, 1997). Repetition and drop-out rates were decreased through a bilingual education intervention program, and standards of achievement rose (including in Spanish). It was estimated that the education cost savings due to bilingual education were $5.6 million per year, while cost benefits were in the order of $33.8 million per year. Also, individual earnings rose by approximately 50%. In Guatemala, a strong form of bilingual education made economic sense as it produced a more skilled, highly trained and employable workforce. Weak forms of bilingual education, in comparison, tend to have higher drop-out rates and lower levels of achievement, and thus have less chance of serving and stimulating the economy through a skilled workforce.

Aims, Scope and Limitations of Research

So far in this chapter, we have examined research on specific models of bilingual education (dual language, heritage language, immersion). Underneath, irrespective of which model is being discussed, is politics. Bilingual education is, and will continue to be, a political issue. For some, pluralism, biculturalism and **multilingualism** are desirable outcomes. For others, the assimilation of minoritized languages and the integration of minorities within the overall society are the important outputs. This suggests that a definitive statement on whether bilingual education is more or less successful than, for example, mainstream education is impossible owing to the variety of underlying values and beliefs that different interest groups have with respect to education and the future society they envisage.

It may appear that the research reviews highlighted in this chapter can directly inform policymaking. In reality, there are hundreds of variables that affect program outcomes, such that research cannot, by itself, directly advise policy, provision and practice. Within the complex nature of educational settings, data or 'facts' become relevant for policy purposes only in the context of a coherent theory. It is the theory rather than the individual research findings that permits the generation of predictions about program outcomes under different conditions. That is, research should commence from theoretical propositions, testing, refining and sometimes refuting those propositions. When theory is firmly supported by research and if it accounts for findings from a variety of contexts, theory will explicitly inform policymaking.

However, policymakers rarely base their decisions solely on theory or research. The reason is that the researcher–policymaker relationship is not one of 'truth speaking to power' or of 'science providing evidence-based decisions'. That is too simplistic. Policy in bilingual education is shaped by myriad influences other than research and theory (e.g. political **ideology**, attractiveness to voters, pragmatism, economics, conflicting interests and various stakeholders).

For example, Utah's enthusiastic embrace of dual language immersion began when Utah State Senator Howard Stephenson visited China and was deeply impressed with the English proficiency and academic skills of the Chinese university students he met (Utah Senate, 2016). Concerned that Chinese students were better prepared for the global market than American students, he championed DL legislation in the state. He was also key in encouraging other conservative states such as Indiana to adopt similar legislation. Thus, Utah's influential DL programs, which are primarily one-way programs serving non-heritage and non-ELL students, were driven by the political ideology of neoliberalism rather than by academic research (Sung & Tsai, 2019).

When research and theory do have an influence, they can inform policy and be a part of the shaping of that policy. Their effects will be partial and modest, and be part of a continuous shared search for worthwhile education. In the case of Utah, for example, research was cited to justify its policy and practice once the political decision was made to support DL programs. Critical research is helping to open up more two-way programs in Utah that serve more ELLs and heritage speakers (see e.g. Freire *et al.*, 2017). Thus, 'interest convergence' may generate opportunities for researchers and policymakers to work together to extend and improve policy and practice to the benefit of all students. While research cannot provide evidence-based policy, it can provide evidence-informed policy. No research on bilingual education is perfect or totally objective. This section now provides the critical lens to assess such research.

Methodological and Theoretical Issues

In the United States, under No Child Left Behind (NCLB), education programs were expected to be grounded in 'scientifically based research'. In experimental research studies, an intervention, treatment or innovation is introduced (e.g. teaching children bilingually) and the effects are then studied. Under the current Every Student Succeeds Act (ESSA), there has been a shift from a narrow focus on 'scientifically based research' to a broader view of 'evidenced-based interventions'. This evidence, of course, is generally drawn from experimental studies, but evidence from other forms of research is also valued. Many research methods and approaches are used within the education field. As will be discussed below, the highest tier of evidence under ESSA calls for experimental studies using randomized controlled trails (RCTs). Study participants are randomly assigned to one of two groups: the treatment group (i.e. those who receive the treatment) and the control group (i.e. those who do not receive the treatment). RCTs are considered the 'gold standard' and are important in medical research studies such as trials to determine if a new drug is effective. In the context of an idealized bilingual education study, for example, half the students would be randomly assigned to a well designed dual language classroom (the treatment group) and the other half to a typical English sheltered immersion or mainstream classroom (the control group).

In reality, meeting this gold standard is problematic. To date, only the Steele *et al.* (2017) study described earlier in this chapter has come close to adopting an RCT model. However, random assignment was a result of the school district's lottery system to address demand for the program and did not originate as part of the research design. The randomized students were only a sample of the larger population of students in the program and in the control group. Even in this case, randomization occurred only among students with highly engaged parents who had actively sought enrollments for their children in the program. True randomization would be free of parental demand.

Baker and Lewis (2015: 119) argue that RCTs 'are normally pragmatically unachievable and ethically undesirable in education'. They explain:

> [RCTs tend only] to work in a laboratory setting which can be reduced to single components and controls, whereas schools and classrooms have complex multi-causality, are ever dynamic and fluid, evolving and ever-changing, some unpredictable and inconsistent. The gold standard is thus not usually possible in bilingual education effectiveness research. A randomized controlled trial is still dependent on local conditions and is situated within a particular time. Students, teachers, and instructional styles cannot be reduced to isolated variables and manipulated as if they were seeds in agricultural experimental research.... The search for the Holy Grail of a perfect piece of research on bilingual education is not elusive. It is unattainable. (Baker & Lewis, 2015: 119)

Furthermore, Lortie-Forgues and Inglis (2019), in a review of RCTs commissioned by the Education Endowment Foundation in the United Kingdom, and by the National Center for Educational Evaluation and Regional Assistance in the United States, found that these large-scale RCTs in education typically report a small effect size and relatively large confidence intervals. Thus, they argue the results of these studies are often 'uninformative'. In other words, the findings not conclusive enough to effectively guide policy and practice.

Nevertheless, the US push for 'scientifically based research' led to the establishment of the What Works Clearinghouse (WWC) in 2002 as an initiative of the Institute of Education Sciences (IES) at the US Department of Education (DOE). ESSA sets out four tiers of evidence (on interventions) with direct reference to the WWC criteria (REL Midwest, 2019: 1):

- Tier 1, *Strong evidence*. Well designed and implemented experimental study. Meets WWC standards without reservation.
- Tier 2, *Moderate evidence*. Well designed and implemented quasi-experimental study. Meets WWC standards with reservations.
- Tier 3, *Promising evidence*. Well designed and implemented correlational study, statistically controls for selection bias.
- Tier 4, *Demonstrates a rationale*. Well defined logical model based on rigorous research.

The goal of the WWC is to provide educators with information needed to make evidence-based decisions. The WWC prioritizes experimental studies using RCTs (Tier 1), though quasi-experimental designs and other well designed quantitative studies may partially meet the Clearinghouse's rigorous requirements of evidence of effectiveness. A quasi-experimental design (Tier 2) lacks randomized assignment to control and treatment groups, but still attempts to establish a causal relationship between the treatment and the results (e.g. bilingual instruction leads to higher test scores). A correlation study (Tier 3) can indicate a strong relationship between two factors (e.g. bilingual instruction and higher test scores), but correlation does not equal causation because many other factors may be at play (e.g. level of funding, class size, access to needed instructional materials, socioeconomic status of the students, teacher quality). Tier 4 opens space for other types of research, including ethnographic and other forms of qualitative studies. These may be based on extensive classroom observations; interviews with educators, students, parents and others; and analyses of documents such as lesson plans, student work, curricular materials and policies. We shall return to the issue of quantitative and qualitative research later in this chapter.

Over 11,000 studies have been reviewed by the WWC, but very few meet the high evidence standards of Tier 1 or even the criteria for 'moderate evidence' of Tier 2. This is especially true of the studies included in the English language learner section. The IES and DOE now require recipients of their research and professional development grants to include evaluation studies that attempt to meet these high standards. These requirements have greatly narrowed the range of potential research projects and programs eligible for federal funding.

Baker and Lewis (2015: 119) argue that imperfect research studies – including those that do not meet the WWC standards – still have important value:

> Research is valuable when it is well replicated, cumulative across time, place and person, and when the limitations of individual research are honestly and openly stated. That individual pieces of research on bilingual education are imperfect also means that reviews and overviews are essential. One piece of research can never be final, conclusive, or definite. It is the accumulation of research across time, place and person that allows trends to be located, generalizations to be attempted, and policymakers presented with a synopsis of well-replicated and evidenced-informed conclusions, even if they are temporary, transient, and to be further tested.

The Sample of Children

The results of one study are limited to that sample of children at the time of the study. If there is some form of probability sampling (e.g. a random sample of a defined population is chosen), then these results may generalize to that specific population. Such sampling rarely occurs in evaluations of bilingual education. Instead, most studies are small scale and utilize convenient or purposive sampling. As noted above, it is usually ethically questionable and practically impossible to allocate children randomly to experimental and control groups that contain perfect mirrors of a large population of schoolchildren. Generalization of results from one group to another is rarely valid because bilingual students vary widely in terms of home languages, length of time in the target country or school, number of years learning the new language, socio-economic status, parents' level of education, prior schooling and many other factors.

Interacting Factors

Various factors other than the sample of children may influence the effectiveness of bilingual education. Parental engagement is one, and another is likely to be the enthusiasm and commitment of teachers to the education program. The level of resource support (e.g. books, curriculum guidelines, computers, science equipment) may also produce variable outcomes. In contrast, policymakers deal in general scenarios and trends and prefer a broad-brush canvas.

There can be as much variation in outcomes inside a particular bilingual education program (e.g. achievement in different curriculum areas) as between different types of program (e.g. transitional, immersion or heritage language). The crucial point is this: the language policy and language practice in schooling are only two elements among many that make a school more or less successful. A recipe for success is unlikely to result from one ingredient (e.g. the language of the classroom). A great variety of factors act and interact to determine whether bilingual education is successful or not. It makes more sense to consider the wide variety of conditions which make bilingual education more or less successful. Bilingual education, whatever the type or model, is no guarantee of effective schooling. Particular models of bilingual education interact with a host of student, teacher, curriculum and contextual variables in complex ways to influence student outcomes. Also, attempts to compare different types of program models can be difficult because programs are often not labeled accurately (e.g. a **sheltered English immersion** program might be labeled 'bilingual' simply because it serves bilingual children) and there is often great variability in how specific programs (e.g. dual language, heritage language) are actually structured and put into practice at the classroom level.

Measures of Success

In bilingual education investigations, a range of measurement problems need to be addressed. The following are just four important issues to consider:

(1) Measuring something like language proficiency is more elusive than portrayed due to problems such as definition, ambiguity, **validity** and **reliability** (see Chapters 1 and 2).
(2) Measuring constructs such as academic achievement in reading and math is also plagued with problems of definitions, ambiguity, validity and reliability,

particularly when testing students in a language in which they are not yet proficient. These challenges are acknowledged in the standards for educational testing issued jointly by the American Education Research Association, American Psychological Association and National Council on Measurement in Education (2014). Attempts are made to address these issues through the use of testing accommodations (see Chapter 15).

(3) Timing of the measurement is key. If intended outcomes (e.g. English vocabulary knowledge) are measured too soon, the wrong conclusion may be drawn about the effectiveness of the bilingual program. If the intended outcome is measured too late, causality may wrongly be attributed to a bilingual program after a range of other factors (e.g. parental, peer and out-of-school experiences) have entered into the equation to affect the outcome.

(4) An important question in any research study is: what tests or other sources of evidence are used to determine whether a form of bilingual education is successful? Should the sole outcomes be competence in one or two languages, or performance across the whole curriculum? Measures of success in bilingual education tend to focus narrowly on language proficiency, literacy and math. What of important outcomes such as personality and identity development, social and emotional adjustment, self-esteem, integration into society, cultural and ethnic participation, anti-racism, moral development and employment? These are rarely included as measurements of successful outcomes. These questions suggest that there will be debates and disputes over what are the valuable outcomes of schooling. Research on the effectiveness of bilingual education has varied in the choice of measures of outcome. Such a choice reflects a particular emphasis, ideology or conviction. It is not a neutral or value-free judgment.

Quantitative and Qualitative Methods of Research

There is continuous debate regarding the appropriate research methods to be used when studying bilingual education. As noted above, only quantitative studies are viewed under US federal education policy as sufficient to provide some level of evidence (promising, moderate, or strong). At best, qualitative research may be sufficient only to 'demonstrate a rationale' for a particular intervention or approach.

There is tension between quantitative research studies, which attempt to analyze 'objective' measures such as test scores, and qualitative research, which seeks a deeper understanding of a phenomenon through observations, interviews and analysis of artifacts (e.g. policy documents, school memos, teacher lesson plans, student classwork). Chosen methods are often ostensibly related to the research questions asked (Hult & Johnson, 2015). If the question is on the effectiveness of a particular bilingual program model in helping students gain high levels of proficiency in both English and Spanish, then English and Spanish language test scores from the beginning and end of the school year could be collected from hundreds of students in similar programs across a school, district, state or even the nation. The researchers would not even need to visit the classrooms or meet the students to answer such a question. However, if the research question is how a bilingual program helps students to attain high levels of bilingualism, then a researcher needs to spend time in the classroom to observe instruction, talk to students and teachers, and review program documents, lesson plans and curricular materials.

Mixed-methods studies are often used. For example, a large-scale survey of bilingual teachers can provide a broad overview of teacher's attitudes and beliefs, which can then be explored in greater depth through observations and focus group interviews with representative samples of teachers. A wide variety of both quantitative and qualitative research methods and approaches are needed to investigate various aspects of bilingual education to inform policy and practice.

Nevertheless, as noted above, in the US context only certain experimental studies that meet the highest standards of rigor (e.g. randomized control trials) are considered acceptable for providing strong evidence of 'what works'. Such a narrow view is akin to suggesting that a play can be judged only by objective measures using an applause meter. The following illustrate some of the limitations of such experimental research:

- Findings on a program with a new approach to bilingual children may exaggerate its effectiveness (novelty effect). There may be extra enthusiasm and motivation to succeed (and better materials) in a new approach. A comparison of new and old can be unfair as the effect is temporary.
- Being in an experiment can change schools' or teachers' behavior (this is the Hawthorne effect). Being 'under the spotlight' can make a difference (positive or negative) to the customary performance of teachers and students.
- It is impossible to match teachers, so differential gains may be due to teachers rather than a particular model of bilingual education. Even when (unusually) the same teachers are used in different models, their motivation may be different in each, thus not controlling this important and influential variable.
- An intervention found to be effective through experimental research in one context (e.g. among middle-class **language majority students** in an urban French immersion class) cannot necessarily be generalized to another context (e.g. a sheltered English immersion class in a low socioeconomic rural community along the Arizona–Mexico border).
- An experiment measures success on a very narrow range of outcomes.
- There is a distinction between program effectiveness (e.g. attaining learning outcomes) and effects (i.e. any consequence, intended or not).
- An experiment does not investigate process (e.g. how a teacher interprets and operates within a program). Fidelity of implementation of a 'treatment' can vary widely. In other words, within a given program or intervention, teachers interpret and adapt in the light of their own experience and the type of students to be instructed, so that the process can vary considerably across classrooms within the same program.
- Experimental studies are assumed to be 'objective'. Yet the decisions about what variables to include and exclude in a model (e.g. test scores, English proficiency level, parents' level of education) and decisions about where to collect data, from what types of students, and how to interpret the findings are all highly subjective decisions.
- Random assignment of students to different types of program is unethical. Parental choice is taken away. Assigning students randomly to a program known to be inferior (e.g. English submersion) deprives them of a quality education.
- An experiment is a 'black box' model of research. It can be run by researchers without ever visiting a school. They need to send pre-tests and post-tests to the school and then analyze the returned results. There is no guarantee all were administered in a standardized way. In contrast, engaging in the processes of classrooms

is called a 'glass box' model of research, whereby the detail of classroom activity is open to view. Experiments take snapshots. A glass box model (e.g. observation) takes a film.
- Attention is focused on program aggregation and averages. Outstanding individual schools that may be atypical are lost in an overall result. Outliers – those at the highest and lowest ends – are often removed from the sample for being 'atypical'. Yet an in-depth (qualitative) study of these outliers could potentially result in important discoveries.
- The assumption is that there is an objective scientific truth, experimentally demonstrable that allows a trustworthy prediction of outcomes. This can sometimes be linked to the desire to impose uniformity and political control. Instead, educational outcomes will always be debated and contested, being changeable across time and ideology.

The Researchers

Research on bilingual education is rarely neutral. No educational research can be totally value-free, neutral or objective. The questions asked, the methodological tools chosen, decisions in analysis and manner of reporting usually reveal ideological and political preferences. Many researchers will be supporters of bilingual education, ethnic diversity, anti-racism, minoritized language rights and **cultural pluralism**. Such supporters may be convinced of the correctness of their beliefs. This is definitely not to argue that all evaluation research on bilingual education is invalid. Rather, it cannot be assumed that results are not affected by researchers, their beliefs, opinions and preferences.

There is a fine line between research and advocacy, which some attempt not to cross; others cross it very quickly. However, this is not to suggest that researchers are relieved of their responsibility to give back to the communities they research by ensuring their research is used in ways that are beneficial to these communities. Indeed, research on the effectiveness of bilingual education can and should inform practice in building effective bilingual education programs (see Box 12.2).

Conclusion

This chapter has examined the development of studies that have investigated whether bilingual education is more or less effective than monolingual education. It has also examined studies that look at the relative effectiveness of different forms of bilingual education. The initial studies examined individual programs and schools. A wide variety of different outcomes and conclusions resulted. The evaluations of dual language, immersion bilingual education and heritage language education tend to favor strong forms of bilingual education. Such studies indicate that strong forms of bilingual education not only result in bilingualism and biliteracy but also tend to heighten achievement across the curriculum. That is, strong forms of bilingual education tend to raise the standards and performance of children. However, these results do not stop at individual achievement. In societal terms, there are benefits for the economy from strong forms of bilingual education.

The chapter has revealed a paradox. US research on bilingual education has clearly shown advantages for bilingual approaches and has tended to find that stronger forms

> **Box 12.2 Building bilingual education systems**
>
> Peeter Mehisto and Fred Genesee (2015) are co-editors of the ground-breaking book *Building Bilingual Education Systems: Forces, Mechanisms and Counterweights*. In the concluding chapter, Mehisto has developed a relatively comprehensive overview of bilingual and multilingual education. He suggests that such language education can be globally analyzed using a conceptual prism of forces, mechanisms and counterweights.
>
> Mehisto provides an overarching table of 35 forces, 52 mechanisms and 14 dimensions of counterweights. By addressing the needs of a variety of stakeholders (e.g. politicians, providers, practitioners, parents), the framework is extensive and far-reaching. While elements will vary across countries, contexts and creeds, the lists are nevertheless wide-ranging and quite inclusive. To give a brief flavor:
>
> - Forces belong to the ideational realm, but lead to action and affect people and decisions. For example, a force can be a belief in and a commitment to bilingual education, or concerns about justice and injustice, social cohesion and national unity.
> - Mechanisms, in contrast, are material and tangible (e.g. teacher education, leadership initiatives, learning resources, budgets).
> - Counterweights consider the inherent tensions of bilingual education and the balancing needed between the different interests of stakeholders. One such dimension is seeking stability and the status quo compared with a need for change and development. Another dimension can be the positive tension between 'top-down' implementation compared with grassroots initiatives and allowing for more local autonomy in the gradual evolution of bilingual education.
>
> In addition, the book's Appendix provides valuable tools for planning, implementing and evaluating bilingual and multilingual education. These tools include:
>
> - National and regional planning considerations for bi-/trilingual education. The checklist includes: identifying and working with stakeholders, key considerations for government officials, public issues, needs for learning resources, the selection and training of teachers, principals and other school staff, professional development of staff, financing, curriculum decisions, 'good pedagogy', student assessment and high-stakes assessment, extracurricular activities, libraries, managing risks, research and working with disadvantaged students.
> - A bilingual education continuum provides a list of factors fostering but also undermining the meaningful learning of the curriculum, alongside a list of effective and ineffective pedagogical practices in bilingual and multilingual education (e.g. ample and detailed language scaffolding, psychologically safe environment for students to experiment with content and language, authentic materials).
>
> In particular, results-based management frameworks are offered as planning tools for establishing a bilingual program. In the book itself, over 50 outputs (short-term results) from one of these frameworks are provided in Chapter 4. The results-based management frameworks provide an overview of the investments made in establishing both an early and late bilingual education program in Estonia (regarded as one of the most systematically designed bilingual education programs in Europe and, indeed, the world). The frameworks also include success indicators and a selection of program development activities.

with more years of bilingual instruction are more effective than weaker forms with fewer years of instruction. Yet during periods when federal support for bilingual education is offered, it tends mainly to support weaker, transitional forms that last only a few years at the most. Politics has proved stronger than research, selectively using the evidence, and marching on regardless. Bilingual education, as practiced in the United States, has tended to be more about politics than pedagogy, 'mythodology' more than effective methodology, and prejudice rather than preferable practice.

However, another conclusion is that simple questions give simplistic answers. We cannot expect a simple answer to the question of whether or not bilingual education is more (or less) effective than mainstream education. The question itself needs to be more refined. It needs to look at the conditions under which different forms of bilingual education become more or less successful. This means departing from simple studies and simple results and proceeding to broad investigations that include a wide variety of conditions and situations. The effectiveness of bilingual education needs to consider children, teachers, the community, the school itself and the type of program. One particular factor cannot be isolated from another. Children have a wide variety of characteristics which also need investigation. Children cannot be isolated from the characteristics of the classroom within which they work. Within the classroom there are a variety of factors that may make for effective education. Outside the classroom the different attributes of schools may, in their turn, interact with children and their classrooms to make education for language minoritized children more or less effective. Outside the school is the important role played by the family and the community. The social, cultural and political environment in which a school works will affect the education of language minoritized children at all levels.

The key issue becomes: what are the optimal conditions for children who are either bilingual or becoming bilingual, or who wish to be bilingual? The chapters that follow address this issue.

Key Points in This Chapter

- Immersion, heritage language and dual language bilingual education generally promote both first and second languages for academic purposes with no lowering of performance elsewhere in the curriculum and typically increased achievement.
- Research generally supports strong forms of bilingual education, where a student's home language is cultivated by the school. Weak forms of bilingual education (where the student's minoritized language is quickly replaced for educational purposes by a majority language) tend to show less effectiveness.
- Strong forms of bilingual education can be an economically valuable policy. Repetition and drop-out rates are decreased, and a more skilled, highly trained and employable workforce is produced.
- Individual studies, meta-analyses, expert reviews and public opinion polls do not demonstrate an agreed belief in the effectiveness of bilingual education. This is explained partly by the varying political aims of those who either support or oppose bilingual education.
- Experts fail to agree about the value of bilingual education because their political beliefs differ. Reliance on tested theory is one answer to differing opinions.

Suggested Further Reading

Coyle, D. and Meyer, O. (2021) *Beyond CLIL: Pluriliteracies Teaching for Deeper Learning*. Cambridge University Press.

Gazzola, M., Gobbo, F., Johnson, D.C. and de León, J.A. (2023) *Epistemological and Theoretical Foundations in Language Policy and Planning*. Palgrave Macmillan.

Juvonen, P. and Källkvist, M. (eds) (2021) *Pedagogical Translanguaging: Theoretical, Methodological and Empirical Perspectives*. Multilingual Matters.

Wernicke, M., Hammer, S., Hansen, A. and Schroedler, T. (eds) (2021) *Preparing Teachers to Work with Multilingual Learners*. Multilingual Matters.

Windle, J.A., de Jesus, D. and Bartlett, L. (eds) (2020) *The Dynamics of Language and Inequality in Education: Social and Symbolic Boundaries in the Global South*. Multilingual Matters.

On the Web

- What Works Clearinghouse – English Learners (Institute of Education Sciences)
  https://ies.ed.gov/ncee/WWC/Search/Products?Topic=7
- The benefits of a bilingual education (video TedX talk by seventh-grade student Madison Bonaventura)
  https://youtu.be/eVg2BC038kc
- Dual language education of New Mexico
  https://www.dlenm.org/
- National Association for Bilingual Education
  http://www.nabe.org
- Video – Are bilingual education programs effective and how do we know? (interview with Peeter Mehisto and Fred Genesee)
  https://youtu.be/emzegJOxlCw
- Thomas and Collier Research
  https://www.thomasandcollier.com

Discussion Questions

(1) Why is it difficult to conduct research comparing English-only programs and various types of bilingual education program to determine which is the most effective? And why must we be careful generalizing the findings of a single study conducted in a school or district to other schools and districts across the state, nation or around the world?

(2) Randomized control trials (RCTs) are considered the 'gold standard' in research. Many scholars, however, argue that use of RCTs in bilingual education effectiveness research (and in education in general) is impractical and unethical. Do you agree? Why or why not?

(3) Despite the political debates surrounding bilingual education and the lack of 'perfect' research studies, what have been the consistent overall findings of four decades of research about the effectiveness of bilingual education? Why do you think that, despite this evidence, debates over bilingual education continue?

Study Activities

(1) Locate and review a recent research article on the effectiveness of a particular bilingual education program. Identify the strengths and limitations of the study, and the extent to which findings can be generalized to other contexts.

(2) Design a research proposal for comparing two or more program types (e.g. sheltered English immersion and dual language immersion) at a local school to determine which program is most effective. Determine what data you will collect, how you will collect it and how you will analyze it. Discuss the challenges and limitations you may have in conducting this study.
(3) Interview teachers of various bilingual (and non-bilingual) program types. Ask the teachers, 'Is your program effective?' 'How do you know?'

CHAPTER 13

Effective Schools and Classrooms for Bilingual Students

Introduction

Home Language Development at School
Securing the Minoritized Language
Codeswitching in the Classroom
Pedagogical Translanguaging
Sociocultural and Cross-cultural Competence

Monolingual Schools and Classes
Majority Language Development in Monolingual Schools
Teachers and Bilingual Support Assistants
Scaffolding Language

Language Teaching and Learning in Bilingual Immersion Classrooms
Main Classroom Features of Bilingual Immersion Classrooms
Language Strategies in Bilingual Immersion Classrooms

Key Topics in Effective Bilingual Schools
Intake of Students and Language Balance
Shared Vision, Mission and Goals Among Staff
Staffing
Teacher Professional Development and Training
Leadership
Curriculum
Supportive Ethos and Environment
Anti-racist Education
High Expectations
Individualization
Parents

Conclusion

CHAPTER 13

Effective Schools and Classrooms for Bilingual Students

Introduction

The aim of this chapter is to outline some of the foundational elements of effective and successful bilingual schools and classrooms for their students. When a school adopts a particular model (e.g. **submersion**/mainstreaming, bilingual immersion, **dual language bilingual education, heritage language education**), there is an implementation that entails interpretation, adjustments and compromises to meet local traditions and realities. The idealized model is translated from academic and administrative concepts into the intricate actualities of local school and classroom life.

Schools and classrooms are highly complex organizations. They are sites where there are a multitude of actions and reactions, inputs and processes, variable and changing environments, and differing local, regional and national expected learning outcomes, targets and outputs. The formula for success is never simple, partly as success is diversely defined and understood, and partly as perceived effectiveness varies across person, administration, region and time. Also, the mixture of factors affecting effectiveness is so complex that simple recipes are impossible. Effectiveness inevitably goes far beyond language medium and language outcomes, to embrace the full education of a student. Ultimately, effectiveness is about what is deemed best for the child and society, and not just for the future of a language. However, there is sufficient international research, grounded wisdom and accumulated expertise to make it possible to suggest key factors that need discussion and interpretation in relation to effective bilingual schools and classrooms. This chapter attempts to provide a menu for that dialogue.

Two introductory points. First, it is important to repeat the distinction between teaching a language and teaching through a language. Language acquisition in bilingual immersion, heritage and dual language bilingual programs is mostly through a second language being used as a medium of instruction (see Chapter 11). In the United States, this is sometimes called **content-based instruction**. In Europe, it is increasingly referred to as **content and language integrated learning** (CLIL). This chapter is about such an approach, and not about teaching a language for its own sake, as in second language lessons.

Second, close to the idea of two or more languages being used for instruction is the concept of **language across the curriculum**. In all content areas, students learn skills, knowledge, understanding, concepts and attitudes mostly through language. Thus, every curriculum area develops **language competence**. All subject areas, from music to mathematics, science to sport, contribute to the growth of a child's language or languages. At the same time, achievement in a particular curriculum area is partly dependent on proficiency in the language of that area. Obtaining fluency in the language of chemistry, psychology or mathematics, for example, is important to understanding that subject.

The chapter now proceeds to consider those classroom **contexts** where the home language of students is developed. We first consider the importance of and issues related to home language development in schools. Next we discuss the challenges bilingual students may face in monolingual schools, and ways such schools can still provide **scaffolding** and bilingual supports. We then turn to the specific context of bilingual immersion and the features and strategies used in these classrooms. Before we conclude, we consider a range of key topics for effective bilingual schools in general.

Home Language Development at School

For **language minoritized** bilingual children, the school is usually an essential agent in developing the home (or first) language. When a child enters kindergarten or elementary school, home language development needs to be formally addressed, irrespective of whether or not that child has age-appropriate competence in the home language. While home language development throughout schooling is important for majority and minoritized language children, the minority context gives extra reasons for careful nurturance of a minoritized language, otherwise the majority language may become dominant even to the detriment of the minoritized language.

Two quotes from a historically influential report by UNESCO (1953) entitled *The Use of Vernacular Languages in Education* provide the basis for the development of the home language in school:

> It is axiomatic that the best medium for teaching a child is his mother tongue. Psychologically, it is the system of meaningful signs that in his mind works automatically for expression and understanding. Sociologically, it is a means of identification among the members of the community to which he belongs. Educationally, he learns more quickly through it than through an unfamiliar linguistic medium. (UNESCO, 1953: 11)

> It is important that every effort should be made to provide education in the mother tongue.... On educational grounds we recommend that the use of the mother tongue be extended to as late a stage in education as possible. In particular, pupils should begin their schooling through the medium of the mother tongue, because they understand it best and because to begin their school life in the mother tongue will make the break between home and school as small as possible. (UNESCO, 1953: 47–48)

Millions of school-age children of lesser-used languages live in non-industrialized countries of the world. Many never go to school. Others drop out early. The remaining children often struggle to learn through a majority language they hardly understand. As described in UNESCO's (2007: iii) *Advocacy Kit for Promoting Multilingual Education*:

> The true panorama of languages found in a nation's population is rarely reflected in their educational systems, and large numbers of learners are confronted with either a foreign medium of instruction or a language that is different from their mother tongue.... It is an obvious yet not generally recognized truism that learning in a

new language that is not one's own provides a double set of challenges: not only of learning a new language but also of learning new knowledge contained in that language.

Dutcher (2004) observed that the effects of instruction only in the majority language on students not yet proficient in the language can leave students feeling culturally devalued, confused, inferior and less competent in their academic abilities. The negative effects can be long term. Therefore, use of the **mother tongue** in education is important for children's transition from home to school, achievement, self-esteem and, not least, for learning the majority language (see Box 13.1 and Chapter 8).

Box 13.1 If you don't understand, how can you learn?

In recognition of International Mother Language Day (February 21), UNESCO (2016) issued a Global Education Monitoring Report entitled *If You Don't Understand, How Can You Learn?* The report noted that 'as much as 40% of the global population does not have access to education in a language they speak or understand' (p. 1). The following are UNESCO's recommendations for policy and program changes to ensure the needs of linguistic minority students are being met (p. 9):

- **Teach children in a language they understand**. At least six years of mother-tongue education should be provided in ethnically diverse communities to ensure those speaking a different language from the medium of instruction do not fall behind. Bilingual or multilingual education programs should be offered to ease the transition to the teaching of the official languages.
- **Train teachers to teach in more than one language**. To fully support the implementation of bilingual/multilingual education programs based on the mother tongue, teachers should receive pre-service and ongoing teacher education to teach in more than one language.
- **Recruit diverse teachers**. Policymakers need to focus their attention on hiring and training teachers from linguistic and ethnic minorities, to serve in the schools of their own communities.
- **Provide inclusive teaching materials**. Curricula need to address issues of inclusion to enhance the chances of students from marginalized backgrounds are able to learn effectively. Textbooks should be provided in a language children understand. Classroom-based assessment tools can help teachers identify, monitor and support learners at risk of low achievement.
- **Provide culturally appropriate school-readiness programs**. Locally recruited bilingual teaching assistants can support ethnic minority children from isolated communities as they make the transition into primary school, including by providing additional instruction for them after they have enrolled.

When some minoritized language children start school, teachers do not always believe they are 'fluent' in their mother tongue. For example, a teacher may consider that the child speaks a non-standard dialect of Spanish that needs developing into a standard variety. Or a US teacher may hear a child speak a 'non-standard' variety of English (e.g. African-American Vernacular English) and therefore wrongly deduce that a child's home language is underdeveloped (Baker-Bell, 2020a, 2020b; Lee-James & Washington, 2018). In such cases, securing the minority (and majority) language can become a valuable classroom aim.

Securing the Minoritized Language

Special attention needs to be paid to the continuous evolution and progression of the minoritized language in bilingual schools. This is due to the typically lower status of the minoritized language, the Anglophone nature of much mass media and the dominance of 'common denominator' majority languages outside the school. Such bilingual schools can considerably develop the minoritized language learnt at home so that it has more uses and potentially can be used in more domains (e.g. reading, writing, preparation for employment). The child's use of the home language is raised to a much higher level of complexity, communication, competence and confidence. The school will widen vocabulary, deepen meanings, teach conventional **syntax** and help with the standardization of the minoritized language (e.g. new **terminology** in information technology). The school also gives the minoritized language status, esteem and market value to its students.

To preserve and reproduce the minoritized language in the young, a strong form of bilingual education needs to include a 'home language' program with explicit language development aims and goals (see Chapters 10 and 11). Such a program may involve lessons devoted to that language (e.g. Spanish language arts in the United States). It may also valuably involve a strategy for home language development across the curriculum through content-based language approaches. Where children take lessons (e.g. social studies, science) through the medium of their home language, language development in those curriculum areas can be overtly planned and fostered. A child's home language develops when it is cultivated, encouraged and promoted in a purposeful way in many or all curriculum areas. Such content areas shape the language that is learnt, although **language proficiency** may constrain or liberate the content that can be learnt.

The learning methodologies and teaching strategies used to support language minoritized children in school are also important. Mainstream classrooms often assume a homogeneous student population, with similar linguistic and cultural characteristics, and deliver a standardized 'transmission' or 'banking' curriculum with individual competitiveness symbolized in regular standardized norm-referenced high-stakes tests (see Chapter 2).

In contrast, language minoritized students may thrive in an atmosphere where linguistic and cultural diversity is assumed, sharing a **multicultural** and **anti-racist** curriculum with multiple perspectives and linguistic equality of opportunity. Supportive and non-threatening cooperative learning techniques that stress teamwork, interdependence, social interaction and partnership have been successfully used with culturally and linguistically diverse students (Echevarria *et al.*, 2023). For example, groups of around four students can work together to complete a given task, especially in classes that are numerically large. Active learning, the amalgamation of language and content, and the integration of linguistically diverse students can be engineered in such cooperative learning (Ovando & Combs, 2018).

For such children, Cummins (2000a) argues for a 'transformative pedagogy' that sees knowledge as fluid and not fixed, collaboratively constructed rather than memorized, where the sharing of experiences affirms students' **identity**, but essentially also involves critical inquiry to understand power, inequality, justice, and local social and economic realities (see the critical literacy approach in Chapter 14).

The benefits inherent in a well developed home (minority) language spread to the learning of an additional language(s). First language literacy, in particular, enables relative ease of learning (and learning through) a second language by the **transfer** of knowledge, **language abilities** (e.g. literacy strategies, communication skills) and learning processes (see Chapters 8, 11, 12 and 14).

Codeswitching in the Classroom

As discussed in Chapter 5, there is academic debate surrounding the terms **codeswitching** and **translanguaging**. Many agree there is overlap, with the former seen as part of the latter. Much of the academic debate surrounds different perspectives on the underlying bilingual grammar and existence of discrete languages (Cummins, 2022; MacSwan, 2020, 2022b; May, 2022; Otheguy *et al.*, 2015, 2019).

Chapter 5 provides the history of the newer concept of translanguaging and considers ways it is similar to, yet far different from codeswitching. We will not revisit the history or the debate in this chapter, but we will consider the ways that both codeswitching and translanguaging provide a holistic view of bilingualism with implications for pedagogical practices. Given the long empirical research tradition on codeswitching in the classroom, this will be considered first. Then, we will discuss the more recent exploration of **translanguaging pedagogy** (Cenoz & Gorter, 2021; Juvonen & Källkvist, 2021a).

Codeswitching is a common phenomenon in many bilingual classrooms (Auer, 2022; Bhatt & Bolonyai, 2022; Faltis, 2020, 2022; MacSwan, 2020, 2022b). Research in Hong Kong classrooms, for example, has shown that the patterns of codeswitching are highly ordered and patterned (e.g. using Cantonese to explain or interpret English key terms) and also have pedagogic, political and social functions, such as increased communication of meaning, decreasing distance, saving face and emphasis (Lin, 2006). Boun and Wright (2021) document similar purposes of codeswitching in Cambodia in a graduate education program where the official medium of instruction was English. In countries such as Malawi in Africa, codeswitching is a resource particularly when there are multiple languages (16 in Malawi). It allows a child to understand areas such as mathematics in their home language while learning the national language of Chichewa (Chitera, 2009).

Martin-Jones (2000) surveyed three decades of research on such interactions between students, and between students and teachers. She observed that bilingual classroom talk is best understood within the context and traditions of that school and class. Such situations provide clues and cues for expected and allowable patterns of talk. For example, codeswitching by the teacher may be used to signal the start of a lesson or a transition in the lesson, to specify an interaction with a particular student, or to move from teaching content to classroom management. Children also initiate codeswitching in the classroom, and have an influence on a teacher's use of two or more languages, and particularly the languages used in small-group work and conversations with other students.

The student's choice of 'which language to use and when' tends to be reasonably regular and patterned and will reflect (1) the teacher 's declared preference and management of languages, (2) a student's (and peer group's) proficiency or choice or (3) a negotiation between teacher and child. A teacher's language choice tends to be more child-centered in the early years of schooling, for example when explanations, clarifications and checks on understanding are needed with young children (e.g. language minoritized children in mainstream, language majority classes).

Facilitating understanding by moving between two or more languages tends to underlie much classroom codeswitching and translanguaging. Such bilingual language use in classrooms varies among teachers, schools and countries in terms of its prohibition, discouragement, allowance or encouragement (Paulsrud *et al.*, 2021). Even when there is discouragement, students may privately move from the teacher's language to their own preferred language, for example to help each other understand. Thus, there is often a difference between formal policy and the informal practice of codeswitching, with 'center stage' and 'back stage' choices (Boun & Wright, 2021; Chan, 2016).

Research has examined the patterns of language choice and codeswitching in classrooms (e.g. Barnard & McLellan, 2014). Behind such patterns are often traditions and histories of dual or multiple language use, latent and stated pedagogies from different models of bilingual education (e.g. immersion, dual language) and the pressures of regional or national politics. There is also the typical preference of a teacher to do whatever it takes to help students learn, which includes codeswitching and translanguaging even when it is discouraged by policymakers or administrators. For example, Moschkovich (2020) documents how codeswitching provided resources for students' participation in math instruction.

The use of two languages in the classroom is also about which language is relatively valued or privileged, how use of two languages is synchronized and sequenced, negotiated and changed, and how meanings and understandings are constructed. Such bilingual talk occurs in the classroom, yet can often *only* be understood and explained beyond the school through the lens of community, economic, historic and especially political contexts. For example, there is a tendency in classrooms for minoritized language children, even when very young, to move toward the majority high-status language. The research of Oller and Eilers (2002) in Miami found that regardless of school type (e.g. dual language education), and regardless of age, students from Spanish language homes spoke predominantly in English. Even in the first semester of kindergarten, the Miami Spanish-speaking children seemed to be aware that English was the prestigious language and used English for conversations. Jaffe (2007) has shown that the distribution of Corsican and French in the bilingual classrooms in Corsica aims to achieve balance in parity between the two languages, yet Corsican is privileged as the language of discovery and learning. Thus codeswitching in the classroom has to be understood within a particular political context, the history of two languages within a region, values, expectations and intentions. It is this wider contextual consideration that has become one major strand of considerations about translanguaging, and this is now discussed.

Pedagogical Translanguaging

As noted in Chapter 5, Cen Williams (1994, 1996) coined the original concept of *trawsiethu* in Welsh in the late 1980s, later translated by Colin Baker into English as *translanguaging* (Baker, 2019), which he introduced to the world in the third edition of this book (Baker, 2001). Williams was among the first researchers to suggest that there are pedagogical strategies that develop both languages successfully and also result in effective content learning. In particular, he found translanguaging to work well in high schools in Wales. Since 1994, the concept of translanguaging has captured the imagination of those who believe that teachers and particularly students naturally draw on their entire linguistic repertoire to maximize learning. We have recently become emancipated from strict language separation ideas to concepts about **bilingualism** that are holistic rather than fractional (see Chapter 1), less compartmentalized than **diglossia** with separate functions for two languages (see Chapter 3), with codeswitching in early childhood language acquisition more customary than strict OPOL-type strategies (see Chapter 5), and less concerned with language separation in the classroom than strategic language integration (Baker, 2010b).

Separating languages in the bilingual classroom by subject or topic, teacher or time (half days, whole days) continues to be fashionable. Palmer (2020) notes that dual language programs often use a color-coding system – blue for English, red for Spanish – to designate which language is allowed during a particular time or lesson. Some programs go as far as labeling the kids blue or red based on their 'native' language.

Palmer argues we need to view the kids as purple, that is, see them as bilinguals – a mixture of red and blue – and that there is a need to push back on requirements for the strict separation of languages in bilingual programs. This reflects the growing acceptance of the idea that children pragmatically use both of their languages in order to maximize understanding and performance in any lesson (García & Li Wei, 2015). Translanguaging is the process of making meaning, shaping experiences, understandings and knowledge through the use of two languages (García *et al.*, 2016; García & Kleyn, 2016). Pedagogical translanguaging describes teachers' intentional and planned use of their students' multilingual resources during language and content subject instruction in the classroom (Juvonen & Källkvist, 2021b). Cenoz and Gorter (2021: iii) assert that 'pedagogical translanguaging is learner centered and endorses the support and development of all the languages used by learners' and that it 'fosters the development of metalinguistic awareness by softening the boundaries between languages while learning languages and content'.

In Cen Williams's (1994, 1996) original pedagogical use of 'translanguaging', the input (reading and/or listening) tends to be in one language and the output (speaking and/or writing) in the other language, and this is systematically varied by the teacher, although students themselves can often initiate use of translanguaging (Lewis *et al.*, 2013). For instance, a science worksheet in English is read by students. The teacher then initiates a discussion on the subject matter in Spanish, switching to English to highlight particular science terms. The students then complete their written work in Spanish. In the next lesson, the roles of the languages are reversed. In this example, the students need to understand the work to use the information successfully in another language.

Ofelia García (2009a) has helped expand the notion of translanguaging beyond its original pedagogical notions. She observes that translanguaging is a very typical way in which bilinguals engage their bilingual worlds not only inside school but throughout their everyday life. It is hybrid language use that is systematic, strategic and sense-making for speaker and listener. 'Bilinguals translanguage to include and facilitate communication with others, but also to construct deeper understandings and make sense of their bilingual worlds' (García, 2009a: 45). It expresses the idea that there are no clear-cut boundaries between the languages of bilinguals, but functional integration. It is dynamic bilingualism with the interconnected use of the two languages being used to negotiate meaning and situations (Creese & Blackledge, 2010b). This expanded view and understanding of children's dynamic bilingualism has further informed translanguaging as a pedagogical practice (Cenoz & Gorter, 2021; García *et al.*, 2016; Juvonen & Källkvist, 2021b).

Teachers can maximize learning by encouraging children to use their languages, for instance in collaborative writing, task-based conversations with other children, use of resources and not least when working electronically (e.g. on the internet) (García & Li Wei, 2015). For example, Tigert *et al.* (2020) describe the pedagogical power of translanguaging in peer reading interactions of bilingual elementary school students and Gort (2020) describes how young bilingual pre-school children effectively draw on their linguistic repertoire in creative and effective ways when engaged in story-retelling tasks. Wedin (2021) documents the effective use of translanguaging pedagogy in an upper-secondary mathematics classroom in Sweden. Kirsch and Mortini (2023) conducted a longitudinal study of translanguaging among three-year-old multilingual students and their teachers in a Luxembourg pre-school designed to help the children develop proficiency in Luxembourgish. They document several classroom exchanges where the teachers and students 'orchestrated' and moved fluidly across their complex linguistic resources, including one exchange between a teacher and her students inclusive of four different languages (Luxembourgish, Portuguese, French and Cape Verdean Creole) as they looked through a picture book together.

García (2009a) suggests that bilingual children regularly use both their languages for learning, even when this is surreptitious. She suggests that linguistically integrated group work is increasingly prevalent in many bilingual classrooms. This suggests a movement away from the compartmentalization of languages and a requirement for clear boundaries of language use, and toward strategic translanguaging that maximizes students' language repertoires, preferences and practices. 'Translanguaging is indeed a powerful mechanism to construct understandings, to include others, and to mediate understandings across language groups' (García, 2009a: 307). García *et al.* (2016) make a distinction between translanguaging *stance*, *design* and *shifts*. Translanguaging *stance* refers to the teacher's attitudes toward the students' multilingualism and their personal views on the use of their languages in the classroom for teaching and learning. Translanguaging *design* refers to the teacher's planned strategic uses of translanguaging in lessons and learning activities. Translanguaging *shifts* refer to the more spontaneous moves the teacher may make during lessons or other times in the classroom, drawing on the students' and his or her own linguistic repertoires in response to students' questions, language use and interactions.

Translanguaging has four potential advantages (Baker, 2003a). First, it may promote a deeper and fuller understanding of the subject matter. Given that pre-existing knowledge is a foundation for further learning and there is ease of cross-linguistic transfer, translanguaging builds understanding in a most efficient way. It is possible, in a **monolingual** teaching situation, for students to answer questions or write an essay about a subject without fully understanding it. Whole sentences or paragraphs can be copied or adapted out of a textbook or cut and pasted from the internet without real understanding or any attempt to process for meaning. It is less easy to do this with translanguaging. To read and discuss a topic in one language, and then to write about it in another language, means that the subject matter has to be processed and 'digested'. This fits into a sociocultural theory of learning (Lantolf, 2011; Swain *et al.*, 2015).

Sociocultural theory provides reasons why a classroom should not operate solely through a second language, even in an immersion situation. A child who is speaking and writing is not just involved in language development. Speaking and writing mediate learning. Speaking and writing, irrespective of using a first, second or third language, is how we learn. When a student cannot cope with processing in their second or third language (e.g. early on in an immersion classroom), then they naturally turn to their first (home) language for thinking, to find answers and to be cognitively successful. In this sense, telling children to work through a second language on a problem they cannot cope with in that language is asking the child to fail.

The home language is often the best resource that the child has in order to respond to a classroom task, including in private speech and retrieving from memory. Requiring a child to work only in a second or third language is reducing their thinking power. When curriculum content is cognitively very demanding, then using the first language (as well as a second language) may both achieve success and enhance second language development. This includes developing strategies to manage a task, scaffolding, externalizing in speech and working through a task with others (Gibbons, 2015).

The second potential advantage of translanguaging is that it may help students develop oral communication and literacy in their weaker language. Students may otherwise attempt the main part of the work in their stronger language and then undertake less challenging related tasks in their weaker language. Translanguaging attempts to develop language skills in both languages for academic purposes, leading to a fuller bilingualism and biliteracy.

Third, the dual use of languages can facilitate home–school cooperation. If a child can communicate to a minoritized language parent in their usual medium, the parent can support the child in their schoolwork. This overlaps with a common complaint from some parents when their children are operating bilingually in school: that the child is being educated in a language that the parent does not understand. The claim is then made that the parent is less able help the child with their homework or discuss their schoolwork with them. The idea of translanguaging is that movement from one language to another involves much more than translation of words. The reprocessing of content may lead to deeper understanding and learning. If so, what the child has learned through one language in school can be expanded, extended and intensified through discussion with the parent in the other language. What appears to be a potential weakness between school and home may become a strength in learning.

Fourth, the integration of fluent English-speakers and English language learners (e.g. in US schools) of various levels of attainment is helped by translanguaging. If English language learners are integrated with proficient English-speakers, and if sensitive and strategic use is made of both languages in class, then learners can develop their second language ability concurrently with content learning. In Cen Williams's (1994, 1996) original conceptualization, translanguaging is important because it strongly develops a student's minoritized language, whether it be their first or second language.

There are potential problems in the complexity of managing, allocating and organizing such a use of two languages. A threatened language, for example, may need protected space and dedicated time in the classroom. Otherwise, the higher-status majority language will increasingly dominate. For example, Potowski (2019: 15), while supportive of translanguaging as a 'sensible and socially just idea', nonetheless expresses the following concern:

> My work and that of others has shown that English 'leaks in' to spaces where Spanish is supposed to be used, much like how kudzu chokes out all other plants around it by growing so quickly that it blocks the sun. An outcome of this can be that Spanish proficiency is not as strong as we might expect after nine years of dual immersion (Potowski, 2007). And if Spanish isn't developed, there will be nothing for students to 'trans-'.

However, even in those spaces reserved for a minoritized language, translanguaging may still be used by a child in making meaning and in speaking and writing. Tian and Lau (2023) documented a similar concern in a third-grade Mandarin one-way dual immersion program for English-speaking students in the United States. The teacher was initially skeptical and concerned about how translanguaging would impact the limited amount of classroom time she had to help develop her students' proficiency in Mandarin, particularly when students had few opportunities to use the language outside of the classroom. Tian and Lau describe the tensions as the researcher (Tian) and the classroom teacher 'wrestled' and 'negotiated' their way into a shared understanding of what translanguaging design and shifts should look like in this particular context (see also Wright *et al.*, 2023). In contrast, Wright observed Mandarin language lessons for elementary school students taught in a Cambodian international school where the teacher skillfully engaged in translanguaging shifts to draw on the students' linguistic resources in Khmer and English to help them learn new vocabulary in Mandarin. In observations of two-way Spanish–English dual language elementary school classrooms in the US state of Indiana, Wright *et al.* (2023) found that the bilingual teachers had developed a positive translanguaging stance but rarely engaged in explicit translanguaging design. Of greater concern, they found that the teachers' translanguaging shifts tended to happen more often during Spanish instruction time to benefit the English-dominant students, and far less often during English instruction time, for the benefit of their Spanish-dominant students. Thus, while translanguaging can be powerful and transformative for linguistic minoritized students, it is also subject to unequal power relations and 'gentrification'. Faltis (2024) warns against this hegemonic power of English.

These and many other examples documented in the research literature illustrate that: (1) there is no one-size-fits-all model of pedagogical translanguaging that is appropriate and effective for all classroom contexts, and (2) translanguaging and the strategic allocation of language in learning in the classroom as directed by the teacher needs care and consideration.

For some bilingual educators, translanguaging may not be seen as valuable in a classroom when a child is in the early stages of learning a language. For input and output to occur in both languages requires those languages to be reasonably well developed, or at least emerging strongly. This will vary according to different curriculum areas, with some areas requiring less technical and complex language and therefore being more suitable for translanguaging at an earlier time. For example, translanguaging in an area of the curriculum where there is more jargon, more abstract language and greater complexity may not be appropriate, particularly for those who are still beginning to develop their second language. For other educators, however, using a child's perspective, translanguaging may have a valuable different role in early learning. It may help them scaffold. The teacher then needs to understand that the active use of the child's entire language repertoire in learning means that they will increasingly integrate the developing language into their own holistic repertoire. With those students further along the bilingual continuum, translanguaging is potentially more transforming in learning, and not just a scaffold.

Another issue is that while the teacher may favor translanguaging, students may prefer using their stronger language or the one which has the higher status. In dual language bilingual programs, for example, students may mirror language prestige by moving from Spanish to English even in Spanish-medium lessons (Henderson & Palmer, 2015, 2020). Thus, translanguaging may be naturally used by children; or it may be engineered by the teacher (Henderson & Palmer, 2020). Yet sometimes students may prefer one language rather than two.

One value of the idea is that each teacher plans the strategic use of two languages, thinks consciously about the allocation of two languages in the classroom, reflects and reviews what is happening, and attempts to cognitively stimulate students by a 'language provocative' and 'language diversified' lesson. In many language education classrooms, the home language has often been ignored, even forbidden (see Chapter 9). Indeed, many 20th-century language teaching methods either banned or minimized the use of home languages in teaching a second language.

It is often more efficient to use the first language in a second language classroom, to convey content, to explain grammar, to provide a shortcut for giving instructions and explanations, to build on rather than denying existing understanding, to interlink home and school languages, to increase learning, and to create more authentic and natural situations that reflect the world outside the classroom (Cook, 2001; Wright, 2025). This suggests that the strict separation of languages belongs to the 20th century, while the 21st century will see the deliberate and systematic use of both languages in the classroom. For example, a PowerPoint slide may present both languages on the screen, using the same content but using a different font or different color, arranged systematically so that students can easily understand using one language or both (Welsh Language Board, 2001). Translanguaging in a mainstream classroom with Deaf students occurs when those students follow a talk through sign and others through hearing, and when a video presentation allows some students to listen and others to read the subtitles (see Chapter 16).

Sociocultural and Cross-cultural Competence

Developing sociocultural or cross-cultural competence and appropriate cross-cultural attitudes and behaviors is an essential component of bilingual education (Feinauer *et al.*, 2024; González *et al.*, 2024). Strong forms of bilingual education generally have this as an outcome, although occasionally **heritage language education** will concentrate on the minoritized language culture. It is possible to become bilingual and not develop cross-cultural or multicultural competence. While developing heritage cultural awareness alongside home language teaching is an important element in minoritized language education, developing intercultural competence is also important (Valdiviezo & Nieto, 2015).

Classroom activities to foster cross-cultural competence can include: enacting social conventions; the presentation of cultural rituals and traditions using authentic visual and written materials; discussing cultural variations (e.g. the colorful kaleidoscope of Latin American dances, festivals, customs and traditions); identifying the varying experiences and perspectives of the particular language variety (e.g. of French Canadians, of the French majority in France, of bilinguals in France [e.g. Bretons, Provencal]); and classroom visits by native speakers of the language for question-and-answer sessions. It is important for bilingual classrooms to go beyond the surface-level features of cultures (e.g. food, holidays, dance, traditional costumes, etc.) to deeper understandings of how culture frames one's understanding of and interactions with the world, how culture is dynamic, and the complex and ever-shifting relationships between language, identity and culture – especially as experienced by bilingual students (Valdiviezo & Nieto, 2015).

In Wales, developing a cultural awareness about the country is contained in the Cwricwlwm Cymreig (the Welsh Cultural Curriculum), which endeavors to reflect the whole range of historical, social, economic, cultural, political, communication, technical and environmental influences that have shaped contemporary Wales. This involves giving students a sense of place, distinctiveness and heritage, of belonging to the local and wider community with its own traditions, a strong Welsh identity, access to the literature of Wales, differences and traditions in the use of the Welsh and English languages in Wales, and the distinctive nature of Welsh music, arts, crafts, technology, religious beliefs and practices (ESTYN, 2001). Such activity is directly related to students' experiences, contexts and interests, and is therefore seen as important and relevant. Homework can involve active discovery and personal research. Fieldwork, visits and extracurricular activities may be integral to such an approach. It uses teachers' local knowledge, enabling teachers to be creative and original, hopefully firing their enthusiasm.

There can also be an emphasis on developing heritage cultural awareness in mathematics, science and technology, and not just in humanities and aesthetic areas. For example, in Wales, students study the Welsh mathematician William Jones (1675–1749), who first used the pi symbol (π) in a mathematical sense, and Robert Recorde, who in the 16th century devised the equals symbol (=). In science, children discuss local soil samples and how they connect with local farming and agriculture; coal and slate mining, which have been important to the Welsh economy; local small industries; local environmentalism and sustainability; and working from home via computer and communication networks. Some of this involves cross-curricular activity. Al-Gasem (2015) describes an ethno-mathematics curriculum in San Antonio, Texas, which raised interest in mathematics among Latina youth and instilled in them cultural pride as they studied the way the ancient Mayans and Aztecs understood and made use of math in their daily lives.

It is sometimes argued that a minoritized language must be fostered to preserve the attendant culture. The opposite is also possible. The attendant culture must be fostered in the classroom to preserve the minoritized language. While separation of culture and language is false, minoritized language culture can be weakly or strongly represented in the classroom and in the whole ethos of the school. Such culture may be incidentally taught with little intent or rationale. Alternatively, such culture may be consciously included in language teaching and the overall physical and psychological environment of the school. This is particularly valuable in encouraging participation by children in their heritage language culture. Language skills in the minoritized language are no guarantee of continued use of that language into teens and adulthood. **Enculturation** therefore becomes essential if that language is to be useful and used.

Not all language minoritized children are allowed to develop their home language at school. Many such students are mainstreamed, where all content teaching is through the majority language. The chapter now considers this context.

Monolingual Schools and Classes

Unfortunately, too few bilingual students are afforded the opportunity to develop their home language more fully at school. This section considers the particular challenges bilingual students face in monolingual schools, but also considers ways such schools can still provide bilingual support and other forms of scaffolding.

Majority Language Development in Monolingual Schools

When language minoritized children are placed in mainstream schools, the emphasis is on securing proficiency in the second (majority) language (e.g. English in the United States). This section examines the issue of how long this takes, and then how scaffolding is important to ensure a sensitive and sympathetic transition into the second language. If a student is required to work through a second language in school to complete academic tasks, a sufficient level of language proficiency is required to meet the language demands of those tasks, and this proficiency has to be developed throughout schooling. It is difficult for second language students to develop proficiency levels in their second language to compete with native speakers. One reason is that native speakers are not static and waiting for non-native speakers to catch up. During the school years, native speakers' first language development continues at a rapid rate, such that the goal of proficiency equal to a native speaker is a moving target for the language learner. Thomas and Collier found that such students in mainstreaming or transitional forms of education 'must make fifteen months of progress for each ten months of progress that the native-English speaker is making each year of school, and they must do this for six consecutive years to eventually reach the 50th percentile – a dramatic accomplishment!' (Thomas & Collier, 2002a: 19–20).

In the United States, estimates vary on how quickly **English language learners** (ELLs) can reach a level of English proficiency to work successfully in a mainstream classroom. The National Academies of Sciences, Engineering, and Medicine concluded from its research synthesis that 'it can take from 5 to 7 years for students to learn the English necessary for participation in a school's curriculum without further linguistic support' (Takanishi & Le Menestrel, 2017: 5). Progress at the beginning is rapid but is slower from middle to higher levels of oral language proficiency. As higher levels of oral proficiency develop, reading achievement and academic uses of language both increase (August & Shanahan, 2008). ELL students with well developed English oral skills achieve greater success in English literacy than those with less well developed skills. However, if a minoritized language student has literacy skills in their first language, these transfer relatively easily to reading in English (see Chapter 14). A review of the research by Genesee *et al.* (2006) also indicates that oral proficiency increases with: (1) use of English outside school (which increases with proficiency), (2) friendships with proficient English-speakers (which also increase with proficiency) and (3) paired work with proficient speakers, so long as the task is well designed.

Collier's (1995) longitudinal study suggests that, in US schools where all the instruction is given through the second language (mainstream schooling), second language speakers of English with no schooling in their first language take between 7 and 10 years or more to reach the language proficiency of native English-speaking peers. Some never reach native levels of language proficiency. Where students have had two or three years of first language schooling in their home country before emigrating to the United States, they take between five and seven years to attain English proficiency. Collier found this pattern among different home language groups, different ethnic groups and different socioeconomic groups of students.

In a longitudinal study by Umansky *et al.* (2016) on ELLs who began schooling in the United States in kindergarten, over 80% were considered to be proficient in English by grade 5, and more than 90% were proficient by grade 7. This is consistent with prior estimates of five to seven years to attain English proficiency (Crawford & Krashen, 2007).

Decisions about when students are ready for mainstream instruction in the majority language are also highly political. In Arizona, for example, some state education leaders have resisted federal pressures to increase school funding for ELLs (Moore, 2014). Within this context, Arizona made changes to the way ELLs were identified and also lowered the test cut-off scores used to classify ELLs as proficient in English. These changes resulted in far fewer ELLs being identified, and also exited large numbers of students from ELL programs more quickly. In 2015, researchers from WestEd raised concerns when they found that over 90% of the Arizona's ELLs were reclassified as proficient in English within six school years (Haas *et al.*, 2015). They also found that only 18% of ELL high school students graduated within four years – the lowest in the nation. Upon investigation, the Office of Civil Rights (of the US Department of

Education) and the US Department of Justice found that Arizona's practices were in violation of ELL students' civil rights, resulting in both under-identification and premature exiting of tens of thousands of ELLs from language assistance programs (Mitchell, 2016). Resolution agreements between Arizona and the federal government signed in 2016 required the state to provide or restore language-support services for the affected ELL students.

The most significant variable in becoming proficient in the second language is often the amount of formal schooling students have received in their first language. There is strong development through the first language of academic-cognitive thinking skills. Thinking abilities, literacy development, concept formation, subject knowledge and learning strategies developed in the first language transfer to the second. As students expand their vocabulary and literacy skills in their first language, they can increasingly demonstrate the knowledge that they have gained in the second language.

Teachers and Bilingual Support Assistants

In many mainstream schools where there are bilingual students, there is a frequent shortfall of teachers who are either trained to work with such children or who come from the same language communities, or both of these (Mitchell, 2018). This is a worldwide experience. In the early 2000s in the United States it was estimated that between 2 and 3.5 million new teachers were required for bilingual and ESL education (Menken & Barron, 2002). This shortage is far from being rectified. For example, the state of Indiana began serious efforts only in 2016 to encourage – but not require – teachers of ELLs to obtain additional training and licensure in 'teaching English as an Additional Language' (Morita-Mullaney, 2016). In 2020, Indiana established a requirement that all teachers of ELLs must complete at least one ELL methods university course – an improvement, but still insufficient to ensure teachers are well prepared to provide effective instruction for their ELL students. Indiana and many other US states still lack bilingual teacher licensure and education programs. Leider *et al.* (2021) found that in 2021, only 24 US states offered a bilingual education teacher credential and that requirements for general teacher training and certification for working with ELL-classified students varied widely in terms of what teachers were required to complete (from none to all) and in terms of the amount of training required (e.g. a single course, passing of an exam, a certificate program, an add-on license program, or a full teacher credential program).

One solution to a lack of suitable bilingual teachers has been to hire bilingual teaching assistants who work, especially in the early grades, under the guidance of the mainstream teacher and typically can speak the home language of some, most or all of the bilingual students. In the United Kingdom, such support workers help the very young, newly arrived and slower learners, often working with small groups (European Commission, 2015). They may translate, interpret or create classroom materials (e.g. dual language texts) and sometimes assist the mainstream teacher in **assessment**. The assistant may also be the link between teacher and home, enabling parents to collaborate in their children's education.

At its best, this creates a bilingual resource that enables the student to learn in their home (and stronger) language while they are acquiring a majority language such as English. This discussion will be extended in terms of scaffolding (see the next section). In the UK and US experience, however, there are a few challenges to using bilingual teaching assistants properly. One danger is that the bilingual assistant uses English rather than the home language because English is the dominant and prestige language of a mainstream school. Another danger is that the mother tongue is used by the bilingual assistant mainly for discipline and control but not for content learning, sending the wrong message about language use and functions. Conversely, in teacher-centered and lecture-dominant classrooms, the bilingual assistant may not be able to provide much help beyond looking over the students' shoulders, pointing to things in their books and on their worksheets, and occasionally whispering a bit to the students in their home language so as not to interrupt the teacher or disturb the rest of the class. The asymmetry of power between a qualified monolingual teacher and a lower-paid bilingual assistant, and allowances for only short, discreet and quiet uses of the home language, may also send the wrong message about language status to students.

Scaffolding Language

Many bilingual children are required to attend mainstream schools and learn to operate as quickly as possible in a second language (e.g. ELL students in the United States). They are expected to learn a new language, engage in subject learning and develop thinking skills at the same time. Content instruction will be in that new language and will increasingly become more complex and abstract, and require a different register from informal conversation. Within a short period, such students are expected to have developed a second language so that they can operate in the subject curriculum and show success (e.g. on tests, grade transfer).

Taking the United States as an example, it is unlikely that such students will learn English solely through unmodified content instruction. Their level of understanding of English may be insufficient for them to fully comprehend mathematics or social studies as it normally taught to proficient English-speakers. Irrespective of whether a 'transmission of knowledge' (pouring nuggets of knowledge into empty heads) approach or a progressive 'discovery learning' approach is taken by the teacher, the language level of the child may be insufficient for them to assimilate content and engage in the process of learning in mainstream (submersion) classrooms.

Hence, such students need two types of language support if they are to succeed in the classroom (Wright, 2025). First, they need direct and systematic instruction in the new language. In the United States this may be called **English as a second language (ESL)**, English for speakers of other languages (ESOL), English as an additional language (EAL), English as a new language (ENL) or **English language development (ELD)**. Second, students need content-area instruction in the second language that is made comprehensible and which supports their English language development. In the United States this is typically called **sheltered content instruction** or **specially designed academic instruction in English (SDAIE)** (see Box 13.2). Within these classrooms, teacher–student cooperation appears to be very important for students. In such a social collaboration, the teacher supports the student by a careful pitching of comprehensible language. This is an example of 'scaffolding' (Gibbons, 2015) and originates from the Russian psychologist Lev Vygotsky (1986) and American psychologist Jerome Bruner (1983).

During the decade 1924–1934, Vygotsky outlined the ways that teachers can intervene and arrange effective learning by challenging and extending the child's current level of understanding. This 'stretching' of the child is by locating the **zone of proximal development (ZPD)**. Vygotsky (1986) saw this ZPD as the distance between a student's level of current understanding as revealed when problem solving without

> **Box 13.2** The Sheltered Instruction Observation Protocol (SIOP) model
>
> A challenge in both bilingual and non-bilingual forms of education is making language and content-area instruction in the second language comprehensible and effective. Sheltered instruction, or specially designed academic instruction in English (SDAIE), has long been used to address this challenge. In the early 1990s, out of concern that the field lacked a clear model for providing effective sheltered instruction, Echevarría et al. (2023) developed the Sheltered Instruction Observation Protocol (SIOP) model. That model has been widely adopted by schools in the United States and is beginning to gain an international footing. The SIOP consists of 30 observable strategies and techniques organized into three major sections (preparation, instruction and assessment) and six subsections under 'instruction'. These items are used to plan, deliver and evaluate sheltered instruction. When used for evaluation purposes, each of the 30 items are scored on a scale of 0 (not evident) to 4 (highly evident). Thus, the higher the total SIOP score, the more effective the lesson is for second language learners. For example, in an effective lesson, the following features would be 'highly evident' during instruction:
>
> - **Building background**. Concepts are linked to students' background experiences and previous lessons. Key vocabulary is emphasized.
> - **Comprehensible input**. Teachers modify their speech as appropriate to their students' levels, provide clear explanations of academic tasks and use a variety of techniques to make content concepts clear (e.g. modeling, visuals, hands-on activities).
> - **Strategies**. Students are given opportunities to learn and use strategies; teachers use scaffolding techniques consistently throughout the lesson and use a variety of question types to promote higher-order thinking skills.
> - **Interaction**. Teachers provide frequent opportunities for student interaction, use a variety of grouping configurations (e.g. whole class, small groups, pairs), allow for wait time and clarify key concepts in the home language.
> - **Practice/application**. Teachers engage students in hands-on activities and tasks that enable them to integrate the four language domains (listening, speaking, reading and writing) and apply content and language knowledge.
> - **Lesson delivery**. Language and content objectives are fully supported by the lesson delivery, the pacing of the lesson is appropriate to the students' levels and students are engaged 90–100% of the time.
>
> The model has been criticized by some as behavioristic and representing an eclectic set of strategies that lack a strong unifying theoretical grounding (Crawford & Reyes, 2015). Another concern is that teachers are often given a few days of SIOP training without developing a sufficient understanding of foundational knowledge about language, second language development and bilingualism (Wright, 2025). Nonetheless, many of the individual items in the SIOP represent tried and true strategies. In practice, the SIOP is used for lesson planning and instruction in flexible ways and SIOP scores are used more as a starting point for self-reflection and professional constructive feedback and dialogue. Also, the SIOP is often a gateway for teachers into ELL teaching and can lead to teachers pursuing additional training and certification. Some research evidence demonstrates higher academic achievement among second language learners in SIOP classes than in non-SIOP classrooms (Guarino et al., 2001).

adult help, and the level of potential development as determined by a student problem solving in collaboration with peers or teachers. The ZPD is where new understandings are possible through collaborative interaction and inquiry. Scaffolding can occur only within the ZPD.

Lessons learned from the United States (August, 2002) and the United Kingdom (Breen, 2002) suggest that when bilingual children are in monolingual or weak forms of bilingual education (e.g. transitional, **sheltered English immersion**, mainstream), the following school attributes are important:

- Teachers build on the prior knowledge and experience of children that have often been built through the minoritized language, and not just concentrate on developing the majority language.

> **Box 13.3 The transition of refugee and immigrant children into a new classroom**
>
> Coelho (2012) provides advice regarding the transition of immigrant and refugee children into the classroom. A few suggestions from her wealth of ideas are listed below:
>
> - Create welcome signs in the children's languages.
> - Use an interpreter where possible, to facilitate transition. Interview parents with the interpreter present, to provide basic information and begin a relationship with parents in a friendly and facilitative manner.
> - Provide children with a welcome booklet of basic school information, in their own language. Include the day-to-day life, special events and role of parents.
> - Encourage the home use of the first language and explain to the parents that first language development will help the child in acquisition of the majority language.
> - Appoint friendly and sensitive children as official student ambassadors or student friends, to nurture newcomers and help them adjust.
> - Introduce newcomers positively, showing the country of origin with the aid of a world map, ensuring that all children learn to pronounce and spell new names. Make it clear the new child speaks a different language at home and is learning the majority language, avoiding the negative 'So-and-so doesn't speak English'.
> - Display photographs of all the children to show they all belong equally to the classroom.
> - Provide a resource corner for newcomers and ensure they understand via translation or paralinguistic language the daily activities and announcements.
> - Communicate positive attitudes about the linguistic and cultural diversity of the classroom.
> - A second (host) language program for adult learners that encourages immigrant parents to attend helps both parents and children. Such a program in the school can also provide information about the area and about survival and success in the new culture and employment system.
> - Announce events in the different school languages, to spread information and raise the status of heritage languages.
> - Select classroom and library materials with a multicultural and multiracial approach, as well as books in heritage languages.

- Peer support systems are used in the classroom for language shepherding and support.
- Student linguistic and cultural diversity is valued and elaborated.
- High expectations are communicated to language minoritized students.
- The curriculum is carefully paced so that children comprehend, but is ever challenging and enriching.
- Linguistic competence and conceptual understanding are not confused. For example, a student's proficiency in second language English is not a measure of the quality of their thinking.
- Language and content are comprehensible to the student.
- Literacy and oral language development are integrated.
- Translanguaging enables meaning-making when instruction is not in the language of the child.
- Higher-order thinking skills are developed.
- Assessment needs to be fair and valid, especially when it is not conducted in a child's stronger language, and monolinguals should not be used for unfavorable comparisons.
- Local language minoritized communities and parents are seen as partners.
- Teachers are carefully selected, trained and consistently developed to teach language minoritized students.
- Schools are advocates of children and their families.

One danger faced by some bilingual students is that teachers present less challenging content to them than to monolinguals. This is because those teachers perceive that bilingual children, especially emergent bilinguals, do not have the appropriate levels of language proficiency to cope with complex material. Rather than oversimplifying a task, the teacher can provide 'scaffolding' so that the student is working within their 'zone of proximal development'. Scaffolding is thus a temporary device to enable understanding of content. When learning is successful, that support is removed as the child can then complete the same task independently.

Gibbons (2015) provides a wealth of illustrations for the scaffolding of listening, speaking, reading and writing. This includes use of gestures, visual aids, repeating something in a different way, recasting what a child has said, using concrete examples, and summaries. The provision of **home language support** and use of translanguaging strategies is also a form of scaffolding (Wright, 2025). Scaffolding can be designed before a lesson or more spontaneous, to fit a child's immediate need and the occasion. Thus scaffolding is both a supportive structure and also social collaboration between teacher and student. It is not just support around the building, but building work as well; not just about structure but also about the process by which learning is handed over to a more independent student.

As an example, consider the scaffolding that may be provided as students are learning to write in their second language. Scaffolding occurs when a teacher ensures: (1) that a student has enough prior experience or prior knowledge to make a task understandable and personally relevant; (2) that the student is made familiar with the purpose, structure and linguistic features of the kind of text that they will write; (3) that the teacher and the student write the text together, with advice on the process, content and form; and (4) that students are then be able to write their own text with the scaffold being removed, often gradually. They have moved from the familiar to being stretched, from guidance to independence. Such scaffolding can be provided by strategies other than teacher-mediated support. For example, task scaffolds may give directions (e.g. on cue cards) as to steps through a task. Materials scaffolds are 'advance organizers' or prompts for students (e.g. story maps) regarding content.

Language Teaching and Learning in Bilingual Immersion Classrooms

In this section we shift our attention to language majority students in bilingual immersion classrooms. Bilingual immersion is a strong form of bilingual education (see Chapter 11) and begins with the formidable task of teaching **language majority students** through the minoritized language. Bilingual immersion classrooms typically target language majority students who begin as monolingual speakers of the majority language (e.g. English monolinguals in a French–English immersion program). They may also target heritage students with little to no proficiency in their heritage language (e.g. programs for languages such as Irish, Māori or Diné bizaad (Navajo)). Some students in bilingual immersion classrooms may already be bilingual or multilingual, but not in the target minoritized language (e.g. an English–Vietnamese bilingual in a Chinese–English immersion program). Students in bilingual immersion programs may also be speakers of a dialect of one of the target languages (e.g. African-American Vernacular English, or varieties of Spanish or Chinese that differ from the standard variety taught in the classroom). This section considers this linguistic diversity and the approach to language learning often taken in bilingual immersion education programs, and recently in CLIL.

Main Classroom Features of Bilingual Immersion Classrooms

What are the main classroom features of successful **bilingual immersion programs** in Canada, Finland, Australia, New Zealand, the Basque Country, Catalonia, Ireland, Wales, the United States and elsewhere? The following are eight general features, challenges and issues in providing successful immersion programs (Ballinger *et al.*, 2024; Fortune & Tedick, 2008; Genesee, 2013; Ó Duibhir, 2018; Sung & Tsai, 2019).

(1) The minimum time the second language needs to be used as a medium to ensure customary achievement levels is four to six years. Around the end of elementary schooling, immersion students show equal or higher performance in the curriculum compared with their mainstream peers.
(2) The curriculum tends to be the same for immersion children as for their mainstream peers. While immersion attempts to cultivate empathy for a student's second language culture, the immersion curriculum has hitherto tended not to have major distinctive components to develop such empathy and participation. For example, in Canada a known challenge is that French becomes the language of school and English the language of the playground, street and vocational success. The Anglophone North American cultural influence is often so strong and pervasive that French immersion children are in danger of becoming passive rather than active bilinguals outside the school gates. The same occurs in immersion schools in many other countries, where the minoritized language is a language of the classroom, but the majority language is the peer 'prestige' language in the schoolyard and on the streets. Ó Duibhir (2018: 145), for example, found that 70.2% of post-primary school students from an Irish immersion program agreed with the statement 'I speak more English than Irish in the school playground'. Engineering formal language use inside an immersion classroom is possible; what happens outside the classroom walls is very difficult to influence.
(3) It has often been thought preferable to separate languages in instruction rather than to mix them arbitrarily during a single lesson. Sustained periods of monolingual instruction will require students to attend to the language of instruction; they will thereby simultaneously improve both their language competence and confidence, and acquire subject matter. However, if mathematics, science, technology and computing are taught in English, will the hidden message be that English is of more value for scientific communication, for industrial and scientific vocations? Will English latently receive a special, reserved status? If the minoritized or second language is used for humanities, social studies, sport and art, is the hidden message that minoritized languages are of value only in such human and aesthetic pursuits? The choice of language medium for particular subjects may relegate or promote both the use and the status of minoritized languages. Also, translanguaging may initially be used by the student as scaffolding. As languages develop, it becomes a way the bilingual student thinks and works in the classroom. This can operate through a teacher's strategic use of two or more languages or, much more frequently, latently and spontaneously in thinking and collaborating.

(4) How much time should be devoted to the two languages? Typically, a minimum of 50% of instruction is in the second language. Thus, in French immersion in Canada, French-medium instruction may occur from 50% to 100% of the school week. The amount of instruction in English may increase as children become older. One factor in such a decision can be the amount of exposure to English a child receives outside school. Where a child's environment, home and street, media and community are English medium, for example, such saturation may imply that a smaller proportion of time needs to be spent on English in the school. At the same time, the public will usually require bilingual schools to show that children's majority language competences, particularly literacy, are monitored and promoted.

(5) Immersion education has historically enjoyed the synergy of teacher enthusiasm and strong parental commitment. Immersion parents have tended to be middle class, involved in teacher–parent committees, and taken a sustained interest in their children's progress. Immersion teachers tend to have native or native-like proficiency in both languages, are fully able to understand children speaking their home language, but speak to the children almost entirely in the immersion language. Teachers are thus important language models through their status and power role, identifying the immersion language with something of value and importance. Immersion teachers are typically enthusiastic about bilingualism in society and also provide the child with a model of pronunciation and style in the immersion language. The enthusiasm and commitment of teachers, administrators and staff in an immersion education school is an important and often underestimated factor in success.

(6) The immersion approach implies a relatively homogeneous language classroom. For example, in the early total immersion programs of Canada or Finland, all children are beginners, without second language proficiency. This makes the task of the teacher less complex than in other types of bilingual classes, where there is a mixture of first and second language speakers. However, an increasing number of French immersion students are immigrant children who have some degree of bilingualism in their home language and English, and are adding French as a third language. In immersion programs in other countries (e.g. Ireland), there is sometimes a wide range of proficiency in the classroom language. The Irish and Welsh experiences tend to suggest that most children whose home language is English will cope successfully in minoritized language immersion classrooms (Hickey *et al.*, 2013). The danger is that the majority language of English, being the common denominator, will be the language used between students in the classroom, on the playground and certainly out of school (Ó Duibhir, 2018). It is unclear as to what may be the optimal classroom composition of majority and minoritized language students in successful bilingual education. A balance toward a greater proportion of minoritized language speakers may help to ensure that the 'common denominator' majority language does not always dominate in informal classroom and playground talk.

(7) Immersion provides an additive bilingual environment. Students acquire a second language at no cost to their home language and culture. Such enrichment may be contrasted to subtractive bilingual environments, where the home language is replaced by the second language. For example, where the home language is Spanish and the submersion approach is to replace Spanish with English, negative rather than positive effects may occur in school performance and self-esteem. French must not develop at the expense of the home language, irrespective of that home

language, otherwise the school becomes a subtractive environment. This underlines that the term 'immersion education' is best reserved for additive rather than subtractive environments.
(8) Finally, most immersion teachers have to 'wear two hats': promoting achievement throughout the curriculum and ensuring second language proficiency. Such a dual task requires immersion teacher training at the pre-service and in-service levels. This has tended to be a weakness in some countries. Immersion teaching (and teacher training) methods are still evolving.

Language Strategies in Bilingual Immersion Classrooms

Bilingual immersion education is based on the idea that the first (home) language is acquired relatively subconsciously. Children are unaware that they are learning a language in the home. Immersion attempts to replicate this process in the early years of schooling. The focus is on the content and not the form of the language. It is the task at hand that is central, not conscious language learning. In the early stages, there are no formal language-learning classes, although simple elements of grammar such as verb endings may be taught informally.

In the latter years of elementary schooling, formal consideration may be given to the rules of the language (e.g. grammar and syntax). The early stages of immersion tend to mirror the subconscious acquisition of learning of the first language. Later, a child will be made conscious of language as a system, to reinforce and promote communication. Children will initially speak their first language to each other and to their teacher without any objection or reprimand. Immersion teachers do not force children to use the immersion language until they are naturally willing to do so. Early insistence on the immersion language may inhibit children and develop negative attitudes to that language and to education in general. Over the first two years, immersion children gradually develop an understanding of the immersion language and begin to speak that language, particularly to the teacher.

In Canada, English becomes part of the formal curriculum in early total French immersion most frequently at grade 3. Other practices include introducing English at an earlier grade (or kindergarten) or at grade 4. While initially students will lag behind mainstream students in English **language achievement**, by grade 5 or 6 early-immersion students catch up and perform as well as L1 English mainstream students.

In these beginning stages of early immersion, it is crucial that the teacher is comprehensible to the children. The teacher needs to be sympathetically aware of the level of a child's vocabulary and grammar, to deliver in the immersion language at a level the child can understand, and simultaneously be constantly pushing forward a child's competence in that language. The teacher will aim to push back the frontiers of a child's immersion language by ensuring that messages are both comprehensible and are slightly ahead of the learner's current level of language competence.

The language used to communicate with the child at these early stages is sometimes called **caretaker speech**. For the first year or two in immersion education, the vocabulary will be deliberately limited and there will be a simplified presentation of grammar and syntax. The teacher may be repetitive in the words used and the ideas presented, with the same idea presented in two or more different ways. The teacher will deliberately speak slowly, giving the child more time to process the language input and understand the meaning. This tends to parallel the talk of mother to young child (**motherese**) and foreigner talk (a person deliberately simplifying and slowing down so a foreigner can understand). During this caretaker stage, the teacher may be constantly questioning the child to ensure understanding.

A teacher may also advise students on the language to be used before a lesson topic is presented. When new words and new concepts are being introduced into a lesson, the teacher may spend some time in introducing the words and clarifying the concepts so that the language learner is prepared. Such teachers may also be sensitive to non-verbal feedback from students, such as questioning looks, losing concentration and glazed attention. Students will be encouraged to question the teacher for clarification and simplification when a misunderstanding (or no understanding) has occurred.

Such teaching strategies thus cover two different areas: the importance of **comprehensible input** and the importance of negotiating meaning. The worst case is when neither the teacher nor the student is aware that misunderstanding (or no understanding) has taken place. In more effective classrooms, students and teachers are negotiating meaning, ensuring that mutual understanding has occurred. Not only is the negotiation of meaning important in language development and in maximizing achievement throughout the curriculum, it is also important in aiding motivation of children within the classroom. Patronizing such children and oversimplifying are two of the dangers in this process. Therefore, constantly presenting students with ever-challenging and advancing learning situations is important in fostering classroom achievement.

Bilingual immersion classrooms need to have a particular view about language errors. Language errors are a usual and frequent part of the language-learning process. Errors are not a symptom of failure. Errors are not permanent. They are a natural part of learning. With time and practice, they disappear. Therefore, immersion teachers are often encouraged to avoid over-correcting children's attempts to speak the immersion language. Constant error correction may be self-defeating, even penalizing second language acquisition. Language accuracy tends to develop over time and with experience. Constant correction of error disrupts communication and content learning in the classroom. When a child or several children constantly make the same errors, then appropriate but positive intervention may be of value.

In the early stages of immersion, there will be a natural language use among children, including using features of their home language(s) that help them communicate meaning. A child may change the correct order in a sentence yet produce a perfectly comprehensible message. For example, different syntax may occur due to the influence of the first language on the second language. A child may put the pronoun or a preposition in the wrong order, as in 'go you and get it'. Traditionally, the term **interlanguage** was used to describe such language use, suggesting a halfway stage between monolingualism and proficiency in a second language. However, this term is now questioned, given the way it suggests that language learners are somehow fragmented. Regardless of the label used, such use of home language features at the beginning of the language-learning process should not be seen as an 'error'. Rather, it indicates the linguistic creativity of students who are using their latent understanding of their home language(s) to construct meaningful communication in the new language. Such use is intermediate, approximate and temporary. It is a worthwhile attempt to communicate and therefore needs acceptance rather than condemnation. Furthermore, students' attempts to produce **comprehensible output** in the new language facilitates language learning (Swain, 2005).

However, a danger of bilingual immersion is that students reach high levels in reading and listening but not in writing and speaking. Once students are able to communicate their meaning to teachers and peers, there can be a lack of incentive to achieve native-like accuracy. Therefore, at later stages, intervention in error correction and more focus on form and not just content may be valuable. Encouraging students to be more analytical of the accuracy of their speech may be important if native-like performance is targeted.

Proficiency in the first language will contribute to proficiency in the second language. Concepts already attached to words in the first language will easily be transferred into the second. The acquisition of literacy skills in the first language tends to facilitate the acquisition of literacy skills in the second. However, not all aspects of a language will transfer. Rules of syntax and spelling may not lend themselves to transfer. The closer a language structure is to the second language structure, the greater the transfer there is likely to be between the two languages. For example, the transferability between English and Spanish is likely to be greater than from Arabic to English owing to differences in syntax, orthography (alphabets) and direction of writing. However, the system of meanings, the conceptual map and the skills that a person owns may be readily transferable between languages.

The focus of bilingual immersion classrooms is typically on real, authentic communication, tasks, curriculum content and creative processes. Willingness to communicate is particularly aided when there are authentic uses for the language. There is also a place for an analytical approach to the second and the first language in the classroom. A bilingual immersion classroom will not just enable children to acquire the second language in a subconscious, almost incidental manner. Toward the end of elementary education, the experiential approach may be joined by a meaning-based focus on the form of language. A child may at this point be encouraged to analyze their vocabulary and grammar. At this later stage, some lessons may have progress in the second language as their major aim. After early sheltering with language, the development of vocabulary and grammar may be dealt with in a direct and systematic manner. However, there is value in 'counterbalanced instruction', where students are encouraged to consider language form but in a meaning-oriented context (Lyster & Mori, 2008). That is, highlighting the nature of the language, including both giving corrections and allowing translanguaging, can be achieved within a context where meaning, understanding and content are important.

Key Topics in Effective Bilingual Schools

As this and previous chapters have shown, there is a wide variety of program types and variations for bilingual students. Wright (2025) argues that regardless of program type, all effective bilingual programs contain three essential components (Table 13.1): (1) second language instruction for non-native speakers, (2) content-area instruction provided in the home language and through sheltered instruction, and (3) **home language support/translanguaging** pedagogies.

Bilingual schools must deliver highly effective education for students, not just on language dimensions but also on other areas where various stakeholders want success (Mehisto, 2012). Even if the school is excellent at **language maintenance** and **language revitalization**, its justification for students, parents, public and politicians ultimately derives from it being a form of holistically effective education. While social justice and equity can be a colorful flag to wave for bilingual schools, their success in developing each child academically as well as linguistically, cognitively and as citizens, as contributors to the economy as well as to a community, requires a bilingual school

Table 13.1 Essential components of effective bilingual programs

Second language instruction for non-native speakers		Content-area instruction		Home language support/ translanguaging pedagogies
Pull-out instruction	In-class instruction	Home language instruction	Sheltered instruction	
A trained specialist teacher pulls students out of regular classroom for second language instruction	The classroom teacher is trained and certified to provide second language instruction within the classroom. Alternatively, a trained specialist will 'push in' to the classroom to provide instruction or co-teach	One or more content areas are taught in students' home languages	One or more content areas are taught in the second language using sheltered instruction strategies and techniques	The classroom teacher employs a variety of strategies and techniques involving the effective use of students' home languages and translanguaging pedagogies to increase their comprehension of the second language and sheltered content instruction

Note: Modified from Wright (2025: 104)

to deliver the multiple and complex agenda of education and schooling. While this section concentrates on language issues, all the attributes of effective schooling are relevant to bilingual schools.

There are elements that make all types and models of bilingual education more or less effective (Mehisto & Genesee, 2015). While dual language policies, provision and practices are a keystone of such schools, effectiveness reaches far beyond language. For a bilingual school to become a shining success, the following themes may need addressing, albeit not in separation but as an entity, and as part of a process of continuous enhancement and school development.

Intake of Students and Language Balance

The ingredients of bilingual schooling commence with the students. Their life history (e.g. as immigrants or refugees), identity, community background (e.g. isolation or saturation in their community of their home language), proficiency in languages on entry to the school, cultural knowledge, language aptitude, motivation and self-esteem all affect classroom interaction and learning outcomes. A key issue has been the balance of majority and minoritized language students in a school so that the majority language does not increasingly dominate. This has been an issue both in US dual language bilingual schools and in Irish heritage language schools called Gaelscoileanna (Hickey, 2007). Where the balance is weighted too much to majority language speakers, informal classroom language may turn to the majority language. What is officially about minoritized language development can become unofficial immersion in the majority language.

Particularly in rural language minoritized areas, bilingual classrooms may have a mixture of majority language speakers who are learning through the minoritized language (e.g. Irish) and native speakers of that minoritized language. This can mean two different language agendas: minoritized language children speedily acquiring the majority language; majority language children being applauded for acquiring the minoritized language.

In Ireland, Hickey (2001) found that in pre-school mixed language classes, Irish first language speakers may not be achieving sufficient enrichment in their language development as the emphasis is on second language learners of Irish. Teachers tend to tailor their language to accommodate second language learners of Irish, asking fewer questions, giving less feedback and more repetition for understanding by such L2 children. Even at the pre-school level, children appear aware of the different status, power and inter-group relationship between the two languages. Language preference can thus be affected by the saturation of majority language speakers and also newcomer immigrants in a mixed language classroom (Little et al., 2014).

The language of teachers is likely to be affected by the balance of native speakers and learners in mixed language classrooms. One concern is that teachers may ask fewer questions in mixed language groups compared with more homogeneous language groups. Teachers may also use more simplified language to accommodate the second language learners. Native speakers may thus not be receiving the native language enrichment they need. What is a language opportunity is also a language challenge for the teacher. Conversely, the teacher may tend to gear instruction to the more proficient and native speakers of the target language and thus deprive the lower-level second language learners of the modified linguistic input they need to comprehend and succeed. Consequently, a major challenge in such mixed language classrooms is striking an acceptable balance, and learning to differentiate instruction appropriate to students' level of language proficiency and academic understanding.

While native speakers of a minoritized language provide a language role model for second language speakers in speaking that minoritized language, the danger is that second language speakers overly influence minoritized language speakers. Hickey (2001) aptly asked, when beginners and native speakers are mixed in minoritized language immersion, 'who is immersing whom?' Researching in Ireland, she found that in such mixed home language classrooms, children from Irish language homes tended to switch to English. Such children had less language effect on majority language speakers than those English-only speakers had on Irish-speakers. Even at pre-school level, the majority language (English) was pervasive and was eroding the minoritized language. Majority language students immerse native speakers in the majority language. Similar concerns arise about such 'gentrification' in US dual immersion classrooms (Delavan et al., 2024; Henderson & Palmer, 2015; Hinton, 2015).

This suggests that the numerical balance of native speakers and learners of a minoritized language is important, preferably tilted to a predominance of minoritized language speakers. Also, supporting and enriching the first language competences of native speakers of a minoritized language is crucial in such schools. This implies the possible separation of children of different language abilities for 'language lesson' sessions while avoiding language group separation and discrimination. Small-group composition of students needs care and consideration by teachers. Such teachers need training to become aware of cross-language influence, and of the need to raise the status and increase the use of the minoritized language in the classroom by well designed activities and reward systems. It is important that language minoritized students are empowered by having positions of responsibility in the class and school, and are actively involved in school activities (e.g. sports teams, societies).

Muller and Baetens Beardsmore (2004) provide illustrations of teacher accommodation from the 'European school' experience of mixed language students in 'European hours' sessions (see Chapter 11). Discrimination, exclusion, ghettoization and separation of languages are avoided by rewarding the plurality of (majority) languages and language use. Translanguaging is used strategically by the teacher, and accepted, so as to integrate languages and their native speakers. Bilingualism is celebrated.

Shared Vision, Mission and Goals Among Staff

A consensus in the goals of the school is needed among staff, with consistency across staff in the treatment of language minoritized students, and effective collaboration across staff. Value and status should be given to the language minoritized students' language and culture. Native language skills need to be celebrated and encouraged inside and outside the formal curriculum and flagged as an advantage rather than a liability. While clear and agreed aims, goals and mission are important, an effective bilingual school will have a system for constant improvement and development, and will be always seeking to increase its effectiveness.

Staffing

Without teachers, administrators and other staff members, no bilingual school can commence, continue or succeed. With untrained or poor-quality staff, the best bilingual program will fail, whatever the model. Highly skilled teachers, excellent teacher training and constantly developing teacher effectiveness are a foundation of the sustainability and success of any bilingual program (Howard et al., 2018). Thus foundational ingredients for a bilingual school are the characteristics and language proficiency of the teachers and other support staff, their own biculturalism or multiculturalism, attitudes to minoritized languages and minoritized students, and their professional and personal identity (Alfaro & Hernández, 2024; de Mejia & Hélot, 2015; Muñoz-Muñoz & Briceño, 2024). Mehisto (2012) suggests that the attributes of effective teachers in bilingual education include: high levels of language proficiency, knowledge of students' languages, cooperation with other teachers in delivering the language curriculum, and dedication to student learning.

Teachers must be highly biliterate in order to provide strong literacy instruction in both languages. Finding such teachers, however, can be a challenge. In the United States, for example, bilingual teachers are typically more dominant in English because admission into university teacher education programs and passing state teacher licensure examinations require a high level of English proficiency. In contrast, the bar is relatively low for the level of oral proficiency and literacy required in the other language (e.g. Spanish, Chinese, Arabic). This makes it easier for English-dominant heritage speakers and native English-speakers with some proficiency in the minoritized language to become bilingual teachers, and more difficult for many well qualified immigrants and other native speakers of these languages.

It is important that teachers are positive toward students' language and cultural backgrounds, are sensitive to their home and community contexts, respond to their language and cultural needs, celebrate diversity and recognize their talents (Téllez & Varghese, 2013). Teachers in bilingual classrooms may sometimes find barriers to success in the form of large and overcrowded classes of undernourished students, inadequate teacher training, a lack of teaching resources, poor pay, few promotion prospects, the stigma of working with lowly regarded bilinguals and limited funding.

As Benson (2004) reminds us in the context of developing countries, bilingual teaching is often more challenging than monolingual teaching, frequently occurring in contexts with inequality between urban and rural areas, between elite and subordinate power and status divisions, between language/ethnic groups, and between genders. Teachers are expected to address such inequalities, including racism, provide cultural and linguistic capital, meet high-stakes test standards of student achievement in literacy and numeracy, bridge the home–school gap, become respected members of the community, and advocate for educational reform and innovation. The roles include: 'pedagogue, linguist, innovator, intercultural communicator, community member, and even advocate of bilingual programmes' (Benson, 2004: 207–208).

Teaching in such bilingual contexts therefore requires much professionalism, enthusiasm, commitment and support. School staff need to be committed to the empowerment of language minoritized students through education. Such commitment is realized not just in the classroom but also in staff involvement in extracurricular activities, liaison with parents, participation in community events, interest in developing their pedagogic skills and even cooperation in the political process of improving the lot of language minoritized students.

Teacher Professional Development and Training

Teacher professional development can be designed to help all staff members effectively serve all students. For example, professional development programs can sensitize teachers to students' language, cultural and racial backgrounds, increase their knowledge of second language acquisition and help develop effective curriculum approaches in teaching language minoritized students (de Mejia & Hélot, 2015). All teachers can be trained to recognize themselves as teachers of language, irrespective of their subject area. The mentoring of new teachers by more expert and experienced teachers can be valuable.

Such initial and in-service staff development may include student, community and wider societal awareness programs; models and curriculum approaches to bilingual education; cultural diversity; and the politics that surround local and regional implementation of education for bilinguals (Cabellero, 2014; Dominguez Hills Colectivo Plurilingüe, 2024). Fillmore and Snow (2018) indicate particular teacher competences that bilingual (and all) teachers need, based on their multiple roles as classroom communicators, educators, evaluators, citizens and socializers. They suggest that teachers need to know the basics of language form (e.g. phonemes, morphemes, regularity, **lexicon**, structure, dialects, academic English, spelling) and not just language functions and uses.

Flores *et al.* (2011: xiv) note that despite a strong theoretical knowledge base, 'there is minimal empirical evidence regarding the nature of bilingual education teacher preparation models and their impact on teacher quality and effectiveness'. They argue that it is thus important to understand bilingual teacher preparation as a whole and to examine its various components. Taking a sociocultural perspective, Flores *et al.* (2011: xiv) propose their own model of bilingual teacher preparation – Educar Para Transformar (Educate for Transformation) – with two overarching interdependent, complementary frameworks directing programmatic content: *transformación* (transformation) and *revolución* (revolution), with three interconnecting dimensions – *iluminación* (illumination), praxis and *concientización* (awareness). Téllez and Varghese (2013: 129) argue that it is also essential to provide professional development for bilingual teachers, to build their 'capacity to promote policies and practices to empower language minorities and help bilingual education survive in a hostile political climate'.

Leadership

The leadership of the school is a crucial factor, and ideally the principal, for example, should have an excellent knowledge of curriculum approaches to language minoritized children and communicate this to all the staff (Scanlan & López, 2015). Strong leadership, the willingness to hire bilingual teachers and high expectations of bilingual students tend to be part of the repertoire of effective leaders (Hamayan & Field, 2012). Effectiveness research tends to suggest that such leaders should demonstrate a strength of purpose and proactive management while engaging the professionalism of teachers and empowering all staff in decision-making processes (Mehisto, 2012). Not only do they inspire, motivate, support and communicate well with staff, they also identify, secure and mobilize human, financial and material resources. Open to change and innovation, they are not only politically informed but also developing themselves as educationalists and leaders. Excellent leaders also project their leadership beyond the school into the neighborhood, and liaise with homes and families. Such leaders are likely to be well known, highly respected and easily accessible in their communities. They are likely to work in partnership with community leaders. The crucial nature and influence of leadership is well illustrated in studies by Potowski (2007) of a dual immersion school in Chicago, by Menken and Solarza (2015) of principals in New York City and by Morita-Mullaney (2019) of district-level administrators in Indiana.

Curriculum

The curriculum of a bilingual program needs to provide intellectually challenging, active and meaningful lessons that have coherence, balance, breadth, relevance, progression and continuity (de Jong & Coulter, 2024; Martinez & Fillmore, 2024). This entails a focus on bilingualism and biliteracy development, sociocultural competence and basic skills, but crucially also on developing higher-order thinking skills (Hopewell *et al.*, 2024). Effective planning also tends to include: language and literacy development across the curriculum; smooth language transitions between grades; systematic, equitable and authentic assessment integrated with learning goals; a bilingual and bi-/multicultural curriculum and ethos throughout the school; a safe and orderly school environment; and a supportive, constructive classroom atmosphere.

Supportive Ethos and Environment

Students may experience prejudice and discrimination, racism and intolerance. They may also learn about the subordinate status of their language minoritized group and **assimilation** influences. Such external influences may affect internal psychological workings such as self-esteem, anxiety, integration with peers and achievement in school. A socioculturally supportive environment for language minoritized students is therefore important. What is also vital is a safe and orderly school and classroom environment where students feel they belong, are cared for as well as educated, and that values linguistic, cultural, ethnic and racial diversity.

UNICEF (2012) has developed a framework for promoting such educational environments, called 'Child Friendly Schools'. Within this framework (UNICEF, 2012: 1):

- The school is a significant personal and social environment in the lives of its students. A child-friendly school ensures every child an environment that is physically safe, emotionally secure and psychologically enabling.

- Teachers are the single most important factor in creating an effective and inclusive classroom.
- Children are natural learners, but this capacity to learn can be undermined and sometimes destroyed. A child-friendly school recognizes, encourages and supports children's growing capacities as learners by providing a school culture, teaching behaviors and curriculum content that are focused on learning and the learner.
- The ability of a school to be and to call itself child-friendly is directly linked to the support, participation and collaboration it receives from families and the community.
- Child-friendly schools aim to develop a learning environment in which children are motivated and able to learn. Staff members are friendly and welcoming to children and attend to all their health and safety needs.

Anti-racist Education

It is not enough for bilingual schools to be child-friendly and socioculturally supportive. Bilingual education must also be anti-racist. The need for anti-racist bilingual education became ever more apparent on May 25, 2020, when a Black man named George Floyd was murdered on the streets of Minneapolis, MN, at the hands of police officers. This incident, along with many other senseless killings of unarmed Black men and women, led to massive protests across cities large and small in all 50 states, in addition to other cities around the world, reminding all that 'Black Lives Matter'. The protests were not simply about Mr Floyd and other recent killings, but about the larger underlying issue of systemic racism that deeply impacts the lives of African-Americans and other people of color.

Schools are inherently political institutions designed to reproduce ideal citizens envisioned by the dominant society and its leaders, very often driven by monolingual, **assimilationist** and **raciolinguistic** ideologies (Bale *et al.*, 2023; Cushing, 2022; Flores, 2024; Flores & McAuliffe, 2020). As discussed throughout book, the struggle for bilingual education programs requires changes to the policies and practices that have limited the access of language minoritized students to high-quality education. Most language minoritized students are people of color, and thus must confront racism, systemic racist policies and institutional racist practices that impact their education.

Ibram Kendi (2019) in his book *How To Be an Antiracist* provides the following succinct definitions:

- *Racist*: 'One who is supporting a racist policy through their actions or inactions or expressing a racist idea' (2019: 13).
- *Antiracist*: 'One who is supporting an antiracist policy through their actions or expressing an antiracist idea' (2019: 13). 'One who is expressing the idea that racial groups are equals and none needs developing, and is supporting policy that reduces racial inequity' (2019: 24).
- *Ethnic antiracism*: 'A powerful collection of antiracist policies that lead to equity between racialized ethnic groups and are substantiated by antiracist ideas about racialized ethnic groups' (2019: 56).

Thus, beyond the common bilingual education goal of helping students develop cross-cultural competence, bilingual programs must help students become anti-racist. But this alone is insufficient. Anti-racist education requires educational leaders and teachers to carefully examine and change the ways their own districts, schools, programs, classrooms, words, actions and inactions are racist, and how they may favor some racialized ethnic groups over others. This is consistent with the call by Cervantes-Soon *et al.* (2017) for critical consciousness to be added as a goal for dual language education, to address issues of inequality. Just one example is examining the ways dual language programs are talked about and how – and to whom – they are promoted. Cervantes-Soon *et al.* (2020) examined the media discourse surrounding the promotion of dual language programs in Georgia and North Carolina, and found that these discourses mainly perpetuated notions that dual language programs primarily serve the needs and neoliberal interests of White parents and their children.

Important research has been conducted on racial inequalities in dual language and other bilingual programs, but has mostly focused on **Latinx** and White students (see Chapter 11). More attention to racial inequalities is needed on the increasing number of Black students in bilingual education programs, including African-Americans, Black-Latinx and African immigrant students (Bauer & Sánchez, 2024; Bauer *et al.*, 2018; Dobbs & Bauer, 2024; Wall *et al.*, 2022). The Office of English Language Acquisition (2020b) reports that in 2016, 57% of the foreign-born Black youth in the United States originated from Latin America, and that Black students made up 3.9% of the ELL population, with over 200,000 students. In one Minnesota school district, over half of Black students were classified as ELLs. Spanish, Haitian Creole, French, Somali and Arabic are among the most commonly spoken languages among Black ELLs. The top countries of origin for foreign-born Black ELLs include Haiti, the Dominican Republic, Kenya, Ethiopia, Somalia, Mexico and the Democratic Republic of Congo.

On his blog 'The Educational Linguist – examining language and race in education' Flores asked an important question, 'Do Black Lives Matter in bilingual education?' In this post, he shares his observations of the following five ways that anti-Blackness may be reproduced within bilingual education (Flores, 2016: 1–2). While his observations are from Spanish–English bilingual programs, Flores suggests these are also applicable to non-Black people of color in bilingual programs of other languages as well.

(1) *Assuming native English-speakers are White*. The reality in many programs is that the 'native' English-speakers are Black students, English-dominant Latinx students, or other students of color. Flores argues for the need to be explicit in naming the racial backgrounds of the 'English'-speakers and 'to clearly distinguish those coming from positions of privilege (White native English speakers) and those who are coming from positions of oppression (Black native English speakers)' (Flores, 2016: 1).
(2) *Erasing the experiences of Afro-Latinxs*. Flores notes that curricular materials used in bilingual programs, including those developed in Latin America or Spain, often give the false impression that 'Black people cannot be Native Spanish speakers'. He stresses the need for instructional materials that are inclusive of Afro-Latinx representation.
(3) *Ignoring English language variation*. Some bilingual programs are sensitive to different varieties of Spanish represented by students in the classroom (see e.g. Freire & Feinauer, 2020) but few are sensitive to the non-standard varieties of English spoken by students, including African-American Vernacular English, which may be spoken by Black students (see Bauer & Sánchez, 2024), or varieties of English spoken by recent African immigrants (see Chapter 3). Flores (2016: 2) argues 'it is important to bring attention to and legitimize these linguistic variations by helping students to understand the historical context that allowed for their development'.

(4) ***Fetishizing two-way immersion programs as the gold standard of bilingual education.*** Flores (2016) argues that due to the hyper-segregation of US society, students in Black-majority schools are unlikely to have access to bilingual education if school districts insist on implementing only two-way programs, given the lack of sufficient numbers of native speakers of the target language. Thus, other high-quality models of bilingual education also need to be made available 'so that low-income Black communities have as much access to these programs as affluent White communities' (Flores, 2016: 2).
(5) ***Positioning bilingual education as a panacea for racial inequalities.*** While bilingual education is touted as effective in closing achievement gaps and providing students with potential economic advantages that may come from being bilingual, Flores (2016: 2) argues that 'Being able to speak Spanish will not prevent a police officer from shooting an unarmed Black person'; nor is bilingualism alone sufficient to close the persistent wage gap between Black and White workers.

Flores (2016: 2) concludes that 'the only way to ensure that bilingual education is a tool for social change is to ensure that it is situated within a broader project that seeks to dismantle anti-Blackness. Anything less than this is tantamount to treating Black lives as if they don't matter'.

High Expectations

High expectations among teachers and peers are important for all students, but no more so than for 'at risk' minoritized students (Gold, 2006). When bilingual students come from materially impoverished homes, with low aspirations in the family and community, then low expectations may too easily and implicitly be embedded in a school's ethos. Instead, a positive 'can do' atmosphere for the 'have-nots' will attempt to reverse a self-perpetuating pattern of low expectation and consequent failure. High expectations need to be clearly communicated to such students, with the school responsive to a student's individual needs and to varying community profiles (e.g. culture, newcomers). High expectations are conveyed, for example, by providing opportunities for student-directed activities, involving students in decisions and building their competences, trust and self-esteem, with positive and regular feedback based on careful monitoring.

Individualization

Apart from strategies to motivate students and recognize their achievement, individualized support for language minoritized students is often needed. The provision of counseling, cooperation with parents and the hiring of language minoritized staff in leadership positions to act as role models are some of the ways to raise expectations of success at school.

Parents

Plenty of parental engagement, with home–school collaboration that is reciprocal, is typically a major dimension of school effectiveness (Arias, 2015). Bilingual programs recognize that parental engagement may vary, as it is driven by cultural factors and parents' prior experiences (or lack thereof) with schooling, and that parents may be actively involved in their children's education in ways that are less visible. Nonetheless, bilingual education opens the doors for active minoritized language parent involvement simply by overcoming traditional language and cultural barriers between families and the school (Sarmiento-Quezada, 2024). Parents of language minoritized children can be encouraged to become actively engaged in their children's education, including in governance. This includes participation in parent meetings, contact with teachers and counselors, telephone contact and neighborhood meetings. Parents and their children can be perceived as stakeholders, customers and partners whose satisfaction levels are valued and with whom there is regular two-way communication (see Chapter 14).

Conclusion

In schools and classrooms, there are a myriad of decisions to make, daily, hourly, second by second. Bilingual classrooms and schools add a language dimension to such decision-making. The allocation of languages and linguistic support mixes with decisions about grouping, curriculum materials, styles of learning and use of support assistants and parents. The relationship between language, culture and literacies interacts with overall curriculum decisions about intake, ethos and expectations.

In such a complex situation, teacher training and continuous professional development of the teachers, administrators and other staff is crucial. Without teachers there can be no bilingual school or classroom provision. With effective leadership and well trained staff, the effectiveness of any bilingual school is greatly enhanced.

Key Points in This Chapter

- Heritage language classrooms integrate minoritized language maintenance, majority language development, biliteracy and cultural awareness.
- Minoritized language bilinguals in mainstream classrooms often take seven or more years to reach the language proficiency in the majority language.
- Mainstream classrooms sometimes use bilingual support assistants to help the teacher with minoritized language students in a transition phase.
- Language scaffolding is often needed to support minoritized language students in the early stages of using the majority language in a mainstream classroom.
- Pedagogical translanguaging involves using both languages to maximize learning, for example by varying the language of input and output in a lesson.
- Bilingual school effectiveness requires attention to: intake of students, staffing and professional development, vision, aims and goals, leadership, a challenging curriculum, supportive ethos, high expectations and home–school collaboration.
- Bilingual education needs to be anti-racist and include an anti-racist curriculum component, as many of its students may be people of color, and as bilingual education can be a tool for social change and reducing inequalities.

> - Immersion methodology attempts to ensure high levels of academic proficient language development in both languages, empathy for two or more cultures, and thus an additive experience.
> - Teacher enthusiasm and parental commitment are important ingredients in effective immersion approaches.
> - Policies for when to introduce formal attention to the home language, comprehensible communication in the immersion language, plentiful feedback, attitude to language errors and interlanguage are needed in effective immersion classrooms.

Suggested Further Reading

- Ballinger, S., Fielding, R. and Tedick, D.J. (eds) (2024) *Teacher Development for Content-Based Language Education: International Perspectives.* Multilingual Matters.
- Cenoz, J. and Gorter, D. (2021) *Pedagogical Translanguaging.* Cambridge University Press.
- Paulsrud, B., Tian, Z. and Toth, J. (eds) (2021) *English-Medium Instruction and Translanguaging.* Multilingual Matters.
- Perez, W. and Vásquez, R. (2024) *Culturally Responsive Schooling for Indigenous Mexican Students.* Multilingual Matters.
- Tian, Z., Aghai, L., Sayer, P. and Schissel, J.L. (eds) (2020) *Envisioning TESOL Through a Translanguaging Lens: Global Perspectives.* Springer.

On the Web

- Languages matter! (video produced by UNESCO for International Mother Tongue Day)
  https://youtu.be/Q-XozG0RSCo
- UNESCO: Advocacy kit for promoting multilingual education: Including the excluded
  https://unesdoc.unesco.org/ark:/48223/pf0000152198
- Do Black Lives Matter in bilingual education? (Nelson Flores' blog – The Educational Linguist: Examining language and race in education)
  https://educationallinguist.wordpress.com/2016/09/11/do-black-lives-matter-in-bilingual-education
- English-learners who are black (NCELA infographic)
  https://ncela.ed.gov/resources/infographic-english-learners-who-are-black-april-2021
- What is translanguaging? An interview with Ofelia García (Francois Grosjean's 'Life as a bilingual' blog on *Psychology Today*)
  https://www.psychologytoday.com/blog/life-bilingual/201603/what-is-translanguaging

Discussion Questions

(1) Many bilingual education programs insist on the strict separation of the languages. Why is this strict separation difficult to maintain? What is more recent research suggesting?

(2) The effectiveness of bilingual education inevitably goes far beyond language of instruction and language outcomes. What other factors are essential to consider?

(3) How can bilingual education be anti-racist in terms of its students, curriculum content and structure to reduce inequalities, and obtain social, economic and political change?

Study Activities

(1) Make a list of 'classroom effectiveness factors' from your reading. Following observation in one or more bilingual classrooms, consider the effectiveness of these classrooms against this list. What factors seem, as the result of your classroom observation, to be more and less important?
(2) Observe a bilingual education classroom. Pay attention to the nature of language use by the students, teacher and any bilingual support assistants. Is there an attempt at strict separation of languages? When the focus is on one of the languages, do students or teachers ever use the other language, or engage in translanguaging? Does such language use appear to hinder or support the learning objectives of the lesson or activity?
(3) Conduct an interview with a current bilingual teacher focused on the key topics in effective bilingual schools as outlined in this chapter. How does the teacher view each of these factors, and how much importance is placed on each?

CHAPTER 14

Literacy, Biliteracy and Multiliteracies for Bilingual and Multilingual Students

Introduction

Differing Viewpoints on Literacy for Bilingual and Multilingual Students
The Skills Approach
The 'Construction of Meaning' Approach
The Sociocultural Literacy Approach
The Critical Literacy Approach

Biliteracy
The Development of Biliteracy
Classroom Contexts
Literacy Squared
The Continua of Biliteracy

Multiliteracies in the Classroom
Translingual Literacy
School Resources

Community Relationships

Home–School Relationships

Conclusion

CHAPTER 14

Literacy, Biliteracy and Multiliteracies for Bilingual and Multilingual Students

Introduction

Different bilingual classrooms and schools, different languages and cultures, tend to have different views about the purposes of reading and writing for **bilingual** and multilingual children. Politicians and parents often vary in their viewpoints; educationalists passionately debate methods and strategies. Some think that, for immigrant bilinguals and multilinguals, literacy should be about **enculturation** and **assimilation** into a new language and **culture**. For indigenous and minoritized language bilinguals, literacy may be aimed at reading and writing fluently in two or more languages. In some 'prestigious bilingual' contexts, biliteracy is about promoting a wider rationality, critical thinking, balanced and detached awareness, empathy and sensitivity to varied cultures. In comparison, some academics and politicians narrowly focus on children learning basic reading skills such as phonemic awareness, phonics, fluency, vocabulary and comprehension (National Reading Panel, 2000). Other academics, such as those from the New Literacy Studies camp (Street, 2017), talk about multilingual literacies and multiliteracies among bilingual and multilingual children.

Thus, the nature of being a bilingual (e.g. immigrant, indigenous, elite) interacts with the type of literacy that is offered and experienced. It is not just the school that delivers this. For some **language minoritized** parents, literacy is about memorization, transmission of life stories revealing their heritage, values and morality. In some religions, literacy concerns the transmission of rules of religious and moral behavior. A Muslim, for example, will be expected to read aloud from the Qur'an but will not necessarily be expected to understand what they read, this being provided in their **mother tongue**. In some cultures, the mother is expected to read to her children and help them develop literacy skills, but she is not expected to read national newspapers or complete bureaucratic forms herself. Older siblings may also be expected to help develop the skills of reading and writing in younger siblings. While school is important in developing literacy, a bilingual also develops literacies in the family, community and religion, for example.

Where language minoritized members are labeled as immigrants, as underachievers or as a potentially dissident minority, literacy can be variously regarded as a key to economic self-advancement, as personal **empowerment** or as social control. Such literacy may be encouraged at school only in the majority language and not in two or more languages (e.g. English language literacy in the United States; English in parts of Africa as an 'official' or international language). In the United States, access to English literacy is essential for higher education, employment and vocational mobility.

> The pinnacle of young children's educational development is the acquisition of literacy. Literacy is the ticket of entry into our society, it is the currency by which social and economic positions are waged, and it is the central purpose of schooling. (Bialystok, 2001a: 152)

While US students need English language literacy, many have tended to exit school with 'survival' levels of English literacy that channels them into low-paid jobs. However, strong language and literacy skills are just one factor, and many other factors can impact the success of bilingual and multilingual individuals when seeking employment (see Chapter 19).

With all US states now offering the Seal of Biliteracy (see Chapter 9 and Box 14.1), it may be possible to begin to track the percentage of students who graduate from high school with well developed literacy in more than one language. There are concerns, however, about equity in terms of which students are able to earn the Seal (Davin, 2020; Heineke et al., 2024). While tens of thousands of graduating seniors have earned the Seal, each year the number represents only about 1% of high school graduates (Mitchell, 2015). Subtirelu et al. (2019: 371) found that 'schools with high percentages of students of color and students from low-income families are less likely to participate in the program, suggesting that students privileged along lines of race and class have greater access to the program'.

Box 14.1 The Seal of Biliteracy

In 2011, California became the first state in the United States to pass legislation creating a 'Seal of Biliteracy'. The concept was originally developed by Californians Together and is now promoted nationally in collaboration with the National Association for Bilingual Education, the American Council of Foreign Language Teachers and Velásquez Press (Olsen, 2020). By 2024, all 50 states and Washington, DC, had adopted the Seal. The official website (https://sealofbiliteracy.org/) describes the Seal as follows:

> The Seal of Biliteracy is an award given by a school, district, or county office of education in recognition of students who have studied and attained proficiency in two or more languages by high school graduation. The Seal of Biliteracy encourages students to pursue biliteracy, honors the skills our students attain, and can be evidence of skills that are attractive to future employers and college admission officers.

The Seal is typically awarded to graduating seniors affixed to their high school diplomas or awarded as a separate certificate or medal. This recognition marks a significant turn after many years of policies that have devalued bilingual education. However, a state's adoption of the Seal is no guarantee the schools will adopt the types of strong bilingual programs that will enable students to develop biliteracy skills and properly earn the Seal (Heineke, 2020; Heineke et al., 2024). Some have expressed concerns about how this proficiency is to be demonstrated, and fear that the Seal may lead to greater recognition and benefits for proficient English-speakers who attain a modicum of proficiency in a second language (e.g. native English-speakers in advanced-placement world language classes), and fewer benefits and less recognition for emergent bilinguals who enter school as English language learners (ELLs) and attain a high degree of proficiency in their second language – English (Valdés, 2020). Criteria and implementation vary across states, and in some cases the requirements are more stringent for ELLs and other bilingual students than for English-dominant world language students (Heineke & Davin, 2020; Subtirelu et al., 2019).

In contrast, where bilingual children have access to strong forms of bilingual education, literacy may be introduced in the home language. Whether bilingual children should first become literate in the majority language or in their home language will be discussed later. Before engaging in such discussions, it is important to explore the kind of literacy instruction that bilingual and multilingual students may be given. We start by considering contrasting viewpoints about the nature and value of different kinds of literacy (Street, 2002, 2013; Wiley, 2005).

Differing Viewpoints on Literacy for Bilingual and Multilingual Students

Literacy is often a highly contested subject area in the school curriculum, with debates over the best approach for instruction. These debates are grounded in different views of not only how children learn to read but also different views on the very nature of literacy itself. Below we review the skills approach, the 'construction of meaning' approach, the sociocultural literacy approach and the critical literacy approach.

The Skills Approach

The US No Child Left Behind Act (NCLB) of 2001 mandated that literacy in English from kindergarten to third grade should contain explicit instruction in phonemic awareness, phonics, vocabulary development, reading fluency (including oral reading skills) and reading comprehension strategies (Section 1208 (3) of Title I). NCLB has been replaced by the Every Student Succeeds Act (ESSA) of 2015, but these foundational reading skills remain a key part of 'comprehensive literacy instruction' for all students (Subpart 2, Section 2221(b)(1)(B)). In the 2020s there has been an increasing focus on the implicit instruction in these foundational skills, resulting in legislation and mandates in several states under the name of the '**science of reading**'. In the most basic definition, science of reading (SOR) is simply a reference to the large body of international scientifically based research about reading. Unfortunately the SOR term has 'become a buzzword and a lightning rod in the greater field of education' (Reading League, 2023). The SOR term has been ambiguous, misunderstood, miscommunicated and misused (Wright, 2025), leading to much confusion among teachers and continuing debate among policymakers, researchers and educators.

A narrow focus on these foundational skills alone represents a skills or 'bottom-up' approach to literacy. It assumes that literacy is simply the ability to decode symbols on a page into sounds, followed by making meaning from those sounds. Reading is about decoding, that is, correctly saying the words on the page. Writing is about encoding, that is, being able to spell correctly and to use grammatically correct sentences. National literacy policies in the United Kingdom have placed an emphasis on 'systematic synthetic phonics instruction', and recent policies in Canada, Australia and New Zealand are beginning to push an SOR skills-based approaches under the name of **structured literacy**. Smith (2024), an applied linguistics scholar in New Zealand, has warned that structured literacy approaches focused solely on English reading are a threat to bilingual education and the development of students' mother tongues. Thus, policies and programs supportive of multiliteracy development are needed.

The US research backing for the skills-based approach derives from the National Reading Panel (2000) with its evidence-based assessment of the scientific research literature on reading and its implications for reading instruction. Its 2000 report declares that the key to literacy is developing skills in phonemic awareness, phonics, fluency, vocabulary, text comprehension and oracy. There is general agreement that these skills are an essential foundation for learning to read and write, and do not preclude the other approaches considered below.

Such foundations are needed, but bilingual and multilingual students also need approaches to literacy that are much more than just skill acquisition. Indeed, several comprehensive reviews of the scientifically based academic literature on the literacy development of second language learners has made clear that typical literacy instruction for English-proficient students is not sufficient for multilingual learners classified as **English language learners** (ELLs), that modified instruction in foundational skills is needed, depending on wide variety of factors (e.g. home language literacy, English language proficiency, prior education, etc.) and that instruction requires more than just foundational skills (August & Shanahan, 2006, 2008; August *et al.*, 2014; Genesee *et al.*, 2005, 2006; Takanishi & Le MeMenestrel, 2017). It is essential that second language learners receive **English language development**, including a focus on oral language skills, and also that literacy instruction is differentiated, sheltered and scaffolded as needed, commensurate with students' current language and literacy levels. Strategic use of the home language is also found to be beneficial for English literacy development (August & Shanahan, 2006; Genesee *et al.*, 2005, 2006; Takanishi & Le MeMenestrel, 2017).

There is growing concern among educators and researchers that SOR policies may drive literacy instruction that narrowly focuses on just two of the five foundational reading skills – phonemic awareness and phonics – and that these skills will be taught through a one-size-fits-all approach that is inappropriate for ELL-classified students. These concerns resulted in a summit in March 2023 which brought together literacy scholars from the Reading League – a major advocacy group for the science of reading – and ELL/bilingual education scholars from the National Committee for Effective Literacy for Emergent Bilingual Students (NCEL). Together they found many points of agreement and shared concerns, resulting in the publication of a Joint Statement (Reading League, 2023). This statement has important implications for both policy and practice surrounding SOR implementation. Part of the statement includes a list of reported practices that both group of experts agree are *not* supported by the 'science of reading', including, for example: (1) one-size-fits-all curricular programs; (2) lengthy (~90 minutes) daily phonics instruction that does not include instruction in other subcomponents of language; (3) forsaking English language development, oral language development, home language instruction and support, and writing instruction; (4) failure to use linguistically and culturally appropriate language and literacy assessments to inform instruction; and (5) little to no attention to biliteracy development.

The **assessment** of success in a skills approach is measured by standardized tests of reading and writing. Such tests tend to assess decomposed and decontextualized language skills, eliciting skills comprehension rather than deeper language thinking and understanding. These tests tend to be used as templates for instruction. Measurement-led instruction promotes 'teaching to the test' and possibly decreases the importance of developing higher-order language and thinking skills. Others in the United States argue that, for ELLs, an overemphasis on a bottom-up literacy skills approach in the early grades will fail to incorporate students' language and cultural backgrounds. This will limit their ability to construct meaning.

While there is unlikely to be a simple formula or universal 'best bet' to acquiring reading and writing skills, a review by Genesee *et al.* (2006) of literacy approaches for ELLs in the United States suggests that explicit instruction in reading and writing skills and interactive instruction (e.g. interaction with teachers and competent readers and writers) are both effective, as is a combination of the two. In contrast, solely using process approaches that emphasize authentic uses and de-emphasize skills is less effective. It appears insufficient just to expose students to literacy-rich environments for reading and writing skills to evolve. An appropriate balance is needed. However, there are differences in defining 'effectiveness' and 'balance', as the remainder of this chapter demonstrates.

The 'Construction of Meaning' Approach

In contrast to the skills approach, there is a 'constructivist' view of literacy that is particularly relevant to classrooms where there are bilinguals and multilinguals. It emphasizes that readers bring their own meanings to text, and therefore that reading and writing are essentially a construction and reconstruction of meaning. This implies that the meaning individuals give to a text depends on their language(s), culture, personal experiences and histories, personal understandings of the themes and tone of text, and the particular social context where reading occurs.

Within Vygotskian theory, students are viewed as active constructors of meaning from text. Learning is mediated by the social interaction between the child and an experienced teacher or parent, for example, or peer modeling and coaching, **scaffolding** and instruction that is directed toward the child's **zone of proximal development** (Vygotsky, 1986; see Chapter 13).

Teachers using a 'construction of meaning' approach will typically attempt to help language learners bridge any cultural mismatch by explicitly teaching them the culture, understandings and values of the dominant culture, as well as by providing them with the vocabulary and strategies needed to construct meaning. For bilingual and multilingual students, initial understandings will partly or mainly derive from their home cultures. Different students of varying backgrounds will make different interpretations of the text. When there is a mismatch between the reader's knowledge and that which is assumed by the school, the construction of meaning will be affected. Bilingual and multilingual children, in particular, can be trapped in this situation. Trying to make sense out of texts from a different culture, with different cultural assumptions, makes predicting the storyline and understanding the text more difficult. One role for teachers therefore is to mediate in the construction of meaning, helping students to construct meaning from text. Lavadenz and Armas (2024) developed the Observation Protocol for Academic Literacies (OPAL) as a tool to help build the expertise of teachers in providing effective literacy instruction for students classified as ELLs.

The Sociocultural Literacy Approach

A related view to that of 'construction of meaning' is found in the ideas of sociocultural literacy. This allows for the possibility that different language minoritized communities attach a different value to different types of literacies or multiliteracies. The use of the plural 'literacies' and 'multiliteracies' emphasizes the social nature of literacy, and suggests that reading and writing are not autonomous or independent. As Martin-Jones and Jones (2000: 4–5) explain:

Literacies are social practices: ways of reading and writing and using written texts that are bound up in social processes which locate individual action within social and cultural processes.... Focusing on the plurality of literacies means recognizing the diversity of reading and writing practices and the different genres, styles and types of texts associated with various activities, domains or social identities.

Sociocultural literacy approaches use the idea of **discourses** that do not just include reading and writing but also different ways of talking, listening, interacting, believing, valuing and feeling, and which cannot be explicitly taught (Gee, 2012). Many bilingual and multilingual children enter school with discourses that differ from the dominant school discourse, leading to difficulties in students achieving well. Sociocultural literacy is the ability to construct appropriate cultural meaning when reading. In theory, a person can be functionally literate but culturally illiterate (e.g. reading without meaning). In reading and writing, we bring not only previous experience but also our values and beliefs, enabling us to create cultural meaning from what we read and insert cultural understanding into what we write.

For some people, such cultural literacy may lead to the assimilation of language minoritized immigrants (e.g. accepting the values and norms embedded in English language classics). **Assimilationists** may argue for a common literacy, transmitting the majority language culture to ensure assimilation of language minoritized groups within the wider society. In contrast, a cultural pluralist viewpoint will argue that national unity is not sacrificed by cultural literacy in the minoritized language or by **multicultural** literacy. Multicultural literacy is likely to give a wider view of the world, a less ethnocentric view of human history and customs, and a less narrow view of science and society.

Where there is much variety of language and cultures within a region, issues about 'local literacies' arise (Lin, 2015). Street (2002) regards local literacies as literacy practices identified with local and regional cultures (as different from national culture). Such local literacies may be forgotten by international and national literacy campaigns or there may be tensions between local and national/international literacy practice. Local literacies avoid the impoverishment of uniformity in literacy that is created by the dominance of English, for example. They make literacy relevant to people's lives, their local culture and local community relationships (Hornberger, 2006).

The Critical Literacy Approach

The critical literacy approach is 'a sociocultural orientation to literacy that takes seriously the relationship between meaning making and power' (Janks, 2013: 1). Literacy can work to maintain the status quo, to ensure that those with power and dominance in society influence, even control, what people read and think. Propaganda, political pamphlets, newspapers, books and social media can all be used to attempt to control the thinking and minds of the masses.

Literacy can be conceived as an attempt through schooling and other formal and informal means of education to socialize citizens and produce hegemony in society. Thus, those in power maintain control over those who might subvert the social order or democratically challenge their power base. Literacy can be used to instill centrally preferred attitudes, beliefs and thoughts. Similarly, some religious traditions have used literacy to ensure that their members are, at the least, influenced by writings or, at the worst, brainwashed. Careful selection by religious leaders and parents of what their children read is an attempt to use literacy to control and contain the mind.

Those with power and dominance in society also maintain their position by their view of what is 'correct language'. Language minorities with little political and economic power are often taught that their patterns of speech and writing are inferior and deficient, and such language varieties are connected with their economic, social and cultural deprivation. Such groups are expected to adopt standard majority language use (e.g. to speak 'proper' or 'correct' or 'standard' English).

A philosophical basis of critical literacy is that all cultures are attempts to discover meanings and understandings. No one culture (including the umbrella idea of Western culture) has the monopoly of understanding, knowledge or wisdom. The postmodernist view is that there is little or no transcendent truth, no ultimate reality or wisdom outside of culture, no unalterable or fundamental qualities of women, ethnic groups or language minorities. All meaning is socially constructed. In postmodernism, all meanings are unstable and none is neutral; all change through continuous negotiation and reconstruction. There is value in the meanings of people in a subordinate position (e.g. language minorities) just as there is in those of language majorities. The voices of the poor are as meaningful as those of the privileged; the understandings of the oppressed become as valid as those of the oppressor.

Literacy can be a tool of oppression. Alternatively, it can also be a liberator for language minorities; it can be a door to opportunity or a means of empowerment. One

---

Box 14.2 Alma Flor Ada's creative reading or creative dialogue methodology

Alma Flor Ada presents a critical literacy approach for bilingual students based on Paulo Freire's work. She describes four phases in the creative reading or creative dialogue act, which can facilitate the critical literacy process in any subject matter:

1. Descriptive phase
Recognize or investigate the existing knowledge. The teacher is mainly responsible for presenting this information, but students can also participate in researching information, according to their age and preparation.

2. Personal/interpretive phase
Students are encouraged to express:
- Their personal feelings and emotions as related to the information presented. It is important that the teacher also shares, although always mindful of not supplanting the students' voices.
- Their previous knowledge about the topic. Does the new information support (enrich, contradict) what they knew or had experienced? How can their experiences and the new knowledge be reconciled? This personal interaction with the information is essential for true learning to take place.

3. Critical/reflective/multicultural/anti-bias phase
Students and teachers should address the important questions: How has this knowledge been generated? Who supports it? Whose interests does it serve? Who benefits from it? Is this information inclusive? Who has not been included, considered or respected? Were all possible alternatives considered? Which other alternatives are possible? What would be the consequences of each of the alternatives?

4. Transformative action phase
Learning should provide the possibility to act better in the future, not only to be well informed but to consider the consequences of our choices.

Source: Interview with Alma Flor Ada by Ramirez (2013: 126)

way of attempting to empower people is through critical literacy. Freire (1993) argued for an approach to literacy instruction that aims to develop oppressed communities' political and social consciousness. The argument is that literacy must go well beyond the skills of reading and writing: it must make people aware of their sociocultural context and their political environment (Wink, 2010). This may occur through mother-tongue literacy and local/national/international multiliteracies (discussed later).

For language minoritized speakers, literacy for empowerment can be about stimulating language activism, the demand for language rights, self-determination and an equitable share of power. Freire's literacy education in Brazil's peasant communities (and with other oppressed groups around the world) assumes that when people become conscious of their subordinate role and inferior position in their community and society, they then become empowered to change their own lives, situations and communities (Freire, 1993).

What alternative is posed by the critical literacy movement? At the school level, the critical literacy approach is that bilingual and multilingual students should not just be invited to retell a story. They should be encouraged to offer their own interpretation and evaluation of a text. Who is the writer? What is their perspective and bias? What kind of moral interpretation is made? What alternative interpretations and viewpoints are possible? Children will be encouraged not just to seek answers to such questions but also to look critically and take on multiple viewpoints (see Box 14.2).

Bilingual and multilingual children may be given diverse pieces of writing that reflect different cultural knowledge and attitudes. Differences in interpretation and differences in the experiences and knowledge children bring to the text can be contrasted and compared. Diversity of understanding can be celebrated.

To conclude this section, Table 14.1 lists some of the practical contrasting characteristics of the skills approach and the critical literacy approach.

Table 14.1 The skills approach versus the critical literacy approach

Skills approach	Construction of meaning, sociocultural and critical literacy approaches
Literacy is …	Literacy is …
• decoding words, sometimes without understanding their meaning • spelling words correctly and writing in correct grammar • getting the correct answers on worksheets, filling in blanks, circling appropriate answers • answering closed reading comprehension questions • reading aloud to the teacher and the rest of the class, being perfect in pronunciation, intonation and accent • mechanically going through exercises, practicing skills and giving correct answers on tests • learning to do but not necessarily to think	• seeing oneself as an active reader and writer • enjoying reading, developing independent thoughts and judgments about reading and writing • sharing ideas, reflections, experiences and reactions with others in the classroom, both peers and teachers • gaining insights into oneself, one's life in the family and the community, into social and political control, the use of print and other mass media to inform, persuade and influence so as to maintain the status quo • understanding the power relationships that lie behind reading and writing • constructing and reconstructing meaning, critically examining the range of meanings in the story and outside the story • active writing for various purposes and audiences, often to influence and assert • developing consciousness, increased self-reflection, increased reflection about status, power, wealth and privilege in society • developing critical thinking habits and creative imagination, and posing alternatives, some of which may be radical • learning and interpreting the world, explaining, analyzing, arguing about and acting upon the world in which a person lives

Biliteracy

This section examines biliteracy and strategies that promote biliteracy in the home and classroom. The notion of biliteracy adopted in this chapter is that of 'any or all instances in which communication occurs in two (or more) languages in or around writing, where these instances may be events, actors, interactions, practices, activities, classrooms, programs, situations, societies, sites, or worlds' (Hornberger, 2013: 1). Literacy in two or more languages is advantageous at the individual and societal levels. For individuals, biliteracy reinforces and develops both oral languages in terms of, for example, vocabulary, automatic decoding, fluency and positive attitudes. Strong approaches to bilingual education that aim for biliteracy (see Chapters 10 and 11) are preferable to weak approaches that stress literacy only in the majority language (e.g. English in the United States).

Biliteracy is societally important. In **language revitalization**, for example (see Chapters 3 and 4), an endangered language has higher status and a greater chance of survival when bureaucracy and books, newspapers and magazines, adverts and signposts, and webpages and social media are in that language. Literacy in the minoritized language enables the attendant traditions and the culture to be accessed, reproduced and renewed. Reading in the minoritized language may be for education and for recreation, for instruction and for enjoyment. Whether minoritized language literature is regarded as aiding moral or religious teaching, of value as an art form, or as a form of vicarious experience, literacy is both an emancipator and an educator. Literacy in the minoritized language is of value because it recreates the past in the present. It may both reinforce and extend the oral transmission of a minoritized culture. Literacy facilitates the development of oral language proficiency. Being denied the chance to develop literacy in the minoritized languages they speak can deprive bilingual and multilingual students of rich opportunities and resources. Literacy in the minoritized language not only provides a greater chance of survival at an individual and group level for that language: it also may encourage rootedness, self-esteem, the vision and worldview of one's heritage culture, self-identity and intellectual empathy.

Literacy enables access to language minoritized practices that help make sense of the world and hence affect the structure of human cognition. Biliteracy gives access to different and varied social and cultural worlds and is a strong source of cognitive and curriculum advantage for bilinguals (see Chapter 7). In the United States, research has found that children's reading proficiency in their home language is a strong predictor of their English reading performance (Slavin & Cheung, 2005), as is their oral proficiency in English (August & Shanahan, 2006; Bialystok, 2007). That is, children who have gained more reading proficiency in their home language are more likely to learn to read in English with success. The National Academies of Sciences, Engineering, and Medicine drew the same conclusion in a comprehensive synthesis of the academic literature:

> Evidence reveals significant positive correlations between literacy skills in English learners (ELs') L1 and the development of literacy skills in English-L2. Educational programs that provide systematic support for the development of ELs' L1 often facilitate and enhance their development of skills in English, especially literacy. (Takanishi & Le Menestrel, 2017: 245)

The International Literacy Association (2019) affirms this research in its position statement on the role of **bilingualism** in improving literacy achievement.

In their extensive synthesis of the academic research literature on literacy development for second language learners in the United States, August and Shanahan (2006: 5) conclude:

> Research indicates that instructional programs work when they provide opportunities for students to develop proficiency in their first language. Studies that compare bilingual instruction with English-only instruction demonstrate that language-minority students instructed in their native language as well as in English perform better, on average, on measures of English reading proficiency than language-minority students instructed only in English. This is the case at both the elementary and secondary levels.

Mother-tongue literacy, while often culturally advantageous, is sometimes not without practical problems nor protests. Some languages lack a writing system, have few educational materials for teaching purposes and/or have a shortage of bilingual teachers and teacher training. Political objections include native language literacy being an impediment to national unity and immigrant assimilation, and the cost of maintaining a variety of indigenous and immigrant languages in a region. The supply of well trained teachers who can support mother-tongue literacy is problematic in many regions.

These issues, however, are not insurmountable. For example, Cambodia, with support from UNICEF and CARE International, has developed mother-tongue multilingual education programs in six indigenous languages that previously had no writing system. Orthographies were developed based on the national Khmer script – a political move that was specifically designed to facilitate rapid transition to literacy in the national language (Gregerson, 2009). Books and other curricular materials were then developed in those languages, which made it possible to recruit local speakers and provide intensive bilingual teacher training (Wright & Boun, 2015, 2016; Wright *et al.*, 2022). As a result, thousands of ethnic minoritized indigenous students previously excluded from public education now have access to schooling and are developing their biliteracy skills through effective bilingual education programs (Benson & Wong, 2019; Lee *et al.*, 2015).

The Development of Biliteracy

Given that literacy empowers, emancipates, enculturates and educates, and can be an inherently enjoyable activity, there seems to be a strong argument for biliteracy. Pragmatically, most bilingual students need to function in the minority and majority language society. This requires biliteracy rather than literacy only in the home language. Beeman and Urow (2012: 1) explain that 'biliteracy instruction includes the broad range of teaching and learning activities involving reading and writing that occurs in Spanish and English across the curriculum'. This applies to other majority and minoritized language biliteracy instruction as well. Those authors argue that biliteracy instruction allows students to 'use all of the languages in their linguistic repertoire to develop literacy' (Beeman & Urow, 2012: 5) and embraces a holistic, multilingual perspective on teaching, learning and assessment that is embraced by **translanguaging** (see Chapter 13). They use the metaphor of a bridge to emphasize the benefits of teaching for biliteracy:

> The Bridge occurs once students have learned new concepts in one language. It is the instructional moment when teachers bring the two languages together to encourage students to explore the similarities and differences in the phonology (sound system),

> morphology (word formation), syntax and grammar, and **pragmatics** (language use) between the two languages, that is, to undertake contrastive analysis and transfer what they have learned from one language to the other. The Bridge is also the instructional moment when teachers help students connect the content-area knowledge and skills they have learned in one language to the other language. The Bridge is a simple but powerful concept: with strategic planning, the Bridge allows students who are learning in two languages to strengthen their knowledge of both languages. The Bridge is a tool for developing metalinguistic awareness, the understanding of how language works and how it changes and adapts in different circumstances. An important aspect of the Bridge is that it is two-way.... It recognizes that because bilinguals transfer what they have learned in one language to the other, they do not have to learn content in both languages. (Beeman & Urow, 2012: 4)

While the bridge is a helpful metaphor, translanguaging suggests there is integration and merging rather than a separation of languages beneath the surface.

Key reviews of the research in biliteracy provide strong evidence of positive linguistic **transfer** (Bialystok, 2007, 2013; Cummins, 2017b; Edwards, 2015; Krashen, 2002, 2004b; Takanishi & Le Menestrel, 2017). Bialystok (2013) has shown that children who learn to read in two languages early on have an initial advantage over their **monolingual** peers. A commonly used test in her studies is the 'moving word' task. She showed four- to five-year-old monolingual and bilingual children two pictures: one of a dog and one of a tree. She then showed children a card with the word 'tree' written on it. She first placed the word 'tree' under the picture of the tree. This was seen to be correct. Then, when the children were distracted, she moved the word 'tree' to underneath the picture of the dog. The children were asked what the card said with the word on it. She consistently found that most of the bilingual children knew the word still referred to the tree, while most monolingual children said that the word 'tree' referred to the picture of the dog.

Bialystok (2001b) suggests that children who are familiar with print and story books in two languages (e.g. French and English, or English and Chinese) more quickly develop an understanding that words are symbols that correspond to specific meanings. When bilingual children are shown a picture accompanied by a word, they understand early on that the word contains the meaning as well as the picture.

> Across all the studies, the bilingual children outperformed the monolingual children by a large margin, often revealing more than a year advantage in understanding this principle. On average, the monolinguals were correct about 40% of the time and the bilinguals, about 80%.... Just being exposed to two writing systems, or two kinds of storybooks, enabled bilingual children to appreciate that the written forms are the symbolic system from which the story emerges. (Bialystok, 2001b: 22)

Research has also suggested that many academic and linguistic skills in a minoritized language transfer relatively easily to the second language. For example, a child in the United States who learns to read in Spanish at home or in school does not have to start from the beginning when learning to read in English (August, 2012; August & Shanahan, 2008; Beeman & Urow, 2012; Cummins, 2017b; Relyea & Amendum, 2019). An example is that, once a student has learnt that there is a correspondence between letters and sounds in the first language, they use this understanding immediately when learning to read in the second language. While some of the sounds and letters may be different in the second language, the children do not have to be retaught that such a relationship exists. Such **metalinguistic awareness** of the relationship between sound and meaning is important in learning to read, and bilinguals gain advantages in understanding such insights.

Thus, when biliteracy is encouraged for bilingual children, many literacy skills and strategies from the first language appear to transfer to the second language. The degree to which there is transfer may depend somewhat on the similarity of the writing systems (Bialystok, 2013). For example, we may expect more transfer between languages such as English, French, German and Spanish, which share a common alphabet, and less transfer between English and languages such as Chinese, Khmer, Korean, Russian and Arabic, which have different writing systems. Nonetheless, despite differences in orthography, vocabulary and grammar, generalizable skills in decoding and reading strategies are still found to transfer from first language literacy to second language literacy (Bialystok, 2013; Koda & Zehler, 2008). Pae (2019), for example, found that first language Korean literacy skills are a significant independent predictor of second language (English) ability in both reading and writing. Concepts and strategies easily transfer from first to second language literacy such as scanning, skimming, contextual guessing of words, skipping unknown words, tolerating ambiguity, reading for meaning, making inferences, monitoring, recognizing the structure of text, using previous learning and using background knowledge about the text. For example, Pu (2008) followed the reading development of a group of Chinese-American students in both their regular mainstream English classrooms in the public schools and in their Chinese **heritage language** classes on the weekend. She found that despite the significant differences in the Chinese and English writing systems, there was positive transfer from their Chinese literacy skills to their English literacy skills, and vice versa.

Having self-confidence as a reader of one language tends to lead to being confident in reading in two languages. Bilinguals will use both of their languages to make sense of meaning when reading in a second language, for example by translating and looking for **cognates**. They will compensate for gaps when reading in a second language by drawing on the corresponding skills and knowledge from their first language. Higher cognitive abilities and strategies required in making meaning from text are common to both languages. Overall, reading competence in two languages does not operate separately (Bialystok, 2013).

Transfer from first language to second language literacy is not unconditional, however, but is likely to be contingent on the context of learning and the characteristics of the learner (Sparks, 2024). The following factors may play an intervening role: (1) differences in the facilitating nature of the school, home and community environment; (2) individual differences in **language ability**, language aptitude and language learning strategies; (3) individual differences in the analysis of their language (i.e. metalinguistic abilities); and (4) the inter-relationship between pairs of languages (e.g. Portuguese and Spanish compared with English and Chinese). Reading ability in a second language is also strongly related to the degree of proficiency in that second language (August & Shanahan, 2008). Children literate in their first language still need to acquire the differences found in the second language (e.g. different sounds, vocabulary, grammatical structures) and these may need explicit instruction.

In contrast, Kenner (2004) proposes that some bilingual children successfully acquire literacy in two languages (biliteracy) simultaneously and not as the separate entities that a 'transfer' idea may suggest. Kenner and Gregory (2012) provide evidence that young children are able to differentiate two or more script systems and are able to begin to distinguish the principles on which these are based. Kenner (2004) found in her study that six-year-olds in London learning to write in Chinese, Arabic or Spanish as well as English sought connections between different writing systems. In drawing on experiences from different social and linguistic worlds, these children combined, integrated creatively and synthesized imaginatively. Such children may learn to understand the diverse perspectives of people from different cultures and languages, including beyond their own, in a synchronized manner.

The 'transfer' rather than 'separation' viewpoint has implications for the teaching of reading among bilingual and multilingual students. A 'separation' view is that reading in the second language (e.g. English in the United States) depends on the level of proficiency in the second language and not on home language reading ability. According to this view, students should be swiftly moved to education through the second language to ensure maximal exposure to literacy in that language. The belief is that time spent reading in the home language is time lost in learning to read in the majority language. In contrast, a 'transfer' view argues for an initial mastery of literacy in the home language so that the cognitive skills and strategies needed for reading can be fully developed. Once well developed, these literacy skills and strategies transfer easily and readily to the second language. It is this latter view that receives research support (August & Shanahan, 2006; Cummins, 2017b, 2021; Takanishi & Le Menestrel, 2017). Alternatively, literacy may be developed simultaneously in both languages (see below).

Classroom Contexts

An important intermediate factor is the classroom context in which such language and literacy acquisition occurs. Strategies and advice for developing biliteracy are not universal, but context bound. In Canadian immersion programs, for example, the context is additive. That is, the child's home language of English is not being replaced but is being added to by the acquisition of French. Literacy in French is acquired at no cost to literacy in English. In contrast, in a subtractive environment (e.g. US English-only programs such as sheltered English immersion for ELL-classified students) the transfer of literacy skills between the two languages may be impeded. In such subtractive situations, literacy tends to be developed only in and through the second language (e.g. English in the United States).

However, research shows that literacy may more efficiently be acquired through the primary (home) language (August & Shanahan, 2006; Genesee *et al.*, 2006; Goldenberg, 2008; Takanishi & Le Menestrel, 2017). When literacy is attempted through the second, majority language in the United States, the child's oracy skills in English may be insufficiently developed for such literacy acquisition to occur effectively. Goldenberg (2008: 42) argues:

> If feasible, children should be taught reading in their primary language. Primary language reading instruction a) develops first language skills, and b) promotes reading in English, and c) can be carried out as children are also learning to read, and learning other academic content, in English.

For teachers, this leaves the question of when to encourage biliteracy, given that there is some degree of literacy in one language. One model will be the simultaneous acquisition of biliteracy as well as **bilingualism**. This tends to be the approach in the two-way 50:50 dual language model (see Chapter 11), where both minoritized and majority language children remain integrated all day. A second approach is when children learn to read in a second language before they learn to read in their first (majority) language. Examples of the latter is immersion education in Canada, where English-speaking children learn to read in French before learning to read in English, and one-way dual language models where English-speaking children learn to first read in the target second language (e.g. Spanish, Chinese, Korean, Arabic). This approach tends to result in successful biliteracy, but note that it takes place in an additive language context. The first language, a majority language, is not threatened, and literacy in both languages will follow. A third approach is where children acquire literacy in their home language and then later develop literacy skills in the majority language. In the 90:10 dual language model and in other bilingual education models (e.g. transitional, developmental), all ELL-classified students typically receive literacy instruction in their home language first (see Chapter 11 for an overview of program models).

Krashen (2002: 143) neatly sums up the argument for bilingual children developing literacy in their first language early in order to facilitate strong literacy development in English:

> There is very good reason to believe that learning to read in the primary language is a shortcut to reading in the second language. The argument in favor of this consists of three stages:
>
> 1. We learn to read by reading, by understanding what is on the page.
> 2. It is easier to understand text in a language you already know.
> 3. Once you can read, you can read; reading ability transfers across languages.

Simple answers about when to promote literacy in the second language are made difficult by other factors, such as the educational and societal context, but also the age and ability of the child. Contexts will vary. When a bilingual child is constantly bombarded with majority language written material, from adverts to comics, computers to supermarkets, basic biliteracy may occur relatively easily. The emphasis in school can be on home language literacy, but not exclusively. The preference with younger children may be to ensure home language literacy is relatively well established before introducing literacy in a second language.

Literacy Squared

Kathy Escamilla and her colleagues have developed a comprehensive model called Literacy Squared that emphasizes the development of biliteracy from the start of **emergent bilingual** children's education in kindergarten (Hopewell *et al.*, 2024; Escamilla *et al.*, 2013). In other words, rather than in some traditional bilingual approaches where students are first taught to read in their home language and then transitioned into English literacy, 'paired literacy' provides simultaneous development of literacy in both languages. Also, rather than aiming for eventual transition to all English instruction, Literacy Squared calls for home language literacy and literacy-based English language development instruction through the fifth grade. Other key features include the explicit teaching of cross-language connections, and assessments that account for biliteracy development. For example, the Literacy Squared writing rubric provides a single tool to evaluate students' writing development in both languages. The rubric includes quantitative measures of the content, structural elements and spelling in each language, and also enables qualitative analysis of students' bilingual strategies at the discourse, sentence/phrase, word and phonics levels. This enables teachers to evaluate student writing for such features as literal translations, **codeswitching**, use of loan words and approximate spellings using phonics rules from one language in the other.

Escamilla *et al.* (2013) have developed templates to help teachers create holistic biliteracy lesson plans and units, as well as a comprehensive Literacy Squared observation protocol. These include space for planning and observing literacy instruction in both languages on the same lesson plan template and protocol, including sections for planning and evaluating cross-language connections. On the observation protocol, these cross-language connections include (Escamilla *et al.*, 2013: 187–188):

(1) connections between literacy environments (e.g. theme, genre, standards);
(2) visual side-by-side analysis of languages (e.g. cognates, anchor posters);
(3) metalanguage;
(4) strategic translations;
(5) teachers use languages strategically to enhance student learning;
(6) teachers flexibly respond to students' language alternations.

Note that this Literacy Squared protocol is an effective tool for teachers to engage in pedagogical translanguaging (García *et al.*, 2016), with translanguaging design guided by items 1–5 above and translanguaging shifts by item 6. Escamilla *et al.* (2013: 4) argue: first, that Literacy Squared 'shifts the debate in the field from a narrow focus on the language of instruction to include the qualities of instruction'; second, that their instructional framework 'provides guidance to teachers, in the form of pedagogical methods, about how to maximize the bidirectional transfer of students' knowledge and skills'; and third, that their assessment procedures 'foster the development of biliteracy' and enable 'teachers and schools to monitor student progress via the interpretation of trajectories towards biliteracy'.

The Continua of Biliteracy

The literacy that is developed in classrooms often varies considerably, and often escapes neat classification into transmission, construction of meaning, sociocultural and critical literacy orientations. Such classification is best achieved by reference to Hornberger (2008), who provides a comprehensive set of dimensions to understand, elaborate and situate the nature of biliteracy in the contexts of research, classroom practice and language policy in multilingual settings. Hornberger's 'continua of biliteracy' (Figure 14.1) are four nested and intersecting components (each of which has three sub-dimensions). From this framework, Hornberger (2013: 1) argues that, for multilingual learners:

> the development of biliteracy occurs along intersecting first language–second language, receptive–productive, and oral–written language skills continua; through the medium of two (or more) languages and literacies whose linguistic structures vary from similar to dissimilar, whose scripts range from convergent to divergent, and to which the developing biliterate individual's exposure varies from simultaneous to successive; in contexts that encompass micro to macro levels and are characterized by varying mixes along the monolingual–bilingual and oral–literate continua; and with content that ranges from majority to minority perspectives and experiences, literary to vernacular styles and genres, and decontextualized to contextualized language texts.

Contexts of biliteracy

Micro	◄──────►	Macro
Oral	◄──────►	Literate
Bilingual	◄──────►	Monolingual

Development of biliteracy

Reception	◄──────►	Production
Oral	◄──────►	Written
First language	◄──────►	Second language

Content of biliteracy

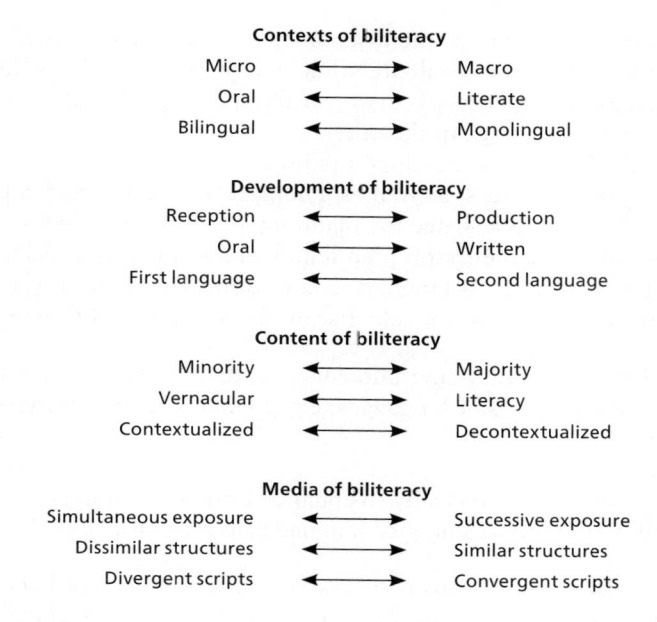

Minority	◄──────►	Majority
Vernacular	◄──────►	Literacy
Contextualized	◄──────►	Decontextualized

Media of biliteracy

Simultaneous exposure	◄──────►	Successive exposure
Dissimilar structures	◄──────►	Similar structures
Divergent scripts	◄──────►	Convergent scripts

Figure 14.1 Continua of biliteracy (Hornberger, 2008)

Hornberger (2013: 6) further explains: 'the continua model posits that what (content) biliterate learners and users read and write is as important as how (development), where and when (context), or by what means (media) they do so'.

The 'continua of biliteracy' framework suggests the need to challenge traditional monolingual, written and decontextualized language and literacy practices, by 'intentionally opening up implementational and ideological spaces for fluid, multilingual, oral, contextualized practices and voices at the local level' (Hornberger, 2013: 1). Thus, schools in the United States providing monolingual English literacy instruction should consider opening up 'implementational space' for instruction and approaches that recognize and value bilingualism and biliteracy. Small shifts along the continua might include reading texts by minority authors from a minority perspective, reading and writing bilingual books, or learning chants, poems and songs in home languages and vernaculars. Finding implementational space might entail starting a heritage language program after school or incorporating heritage language instruction for an hour or more a week during the school day. These can lead to further shifts along the continua to open up more implementational and ideological spaces at the school, such as starting a bilingual education program which aims to fully develop students' bilingualism and biliteracy.

Multiliteracies in the Classroom

In 1994, an international group of 10 outstanding scholars formed the New London Group (1996) having met at New London, New Hampshire, in the United States. They proposed a pedagogy of multiliteracies to broaden literacy to include visual, audio, gestural and spatial modes of literacy, plus the importance of cultural and linguistic diversity evidenced in migration and globalization. Recently, information literacy, disciplinary literacy, civic literacy, social-emotional literacy, math literacy, scientific literacy, financial literacy, media literacy, and technology and digital literacy have all been added to a much-expanded view of literacy. From this 1990s movement derive the contemporary concepts of multilingual literacies and multiliteracies. Two original members of the New London Group, Kalantzis and Cope (2013: 1), explain that multiliteracies refers to two major aspects of communication and representation:

> The first is the variability of conventions of meaning in different cultural, social or domain-specific situations.... The sociolinguistic conditions of our everyday lives increasingly require that we develop a capacity to move between one social setting and another where the conventions of communication may be very different. Such differences are the consequence of any number of factors, including, for instance, culture, gender, life experience, subject matter, discipline domain, area of employment, or specialist expertise.
>
> The second aspect ... is multimodality ... a significant issue today in part as a result of the characteristics of the new information and communications media. The asynchronous meanings across distance that were once the main preserve of the written word are now made in conditions where written linguistic modes of meaning interface with recordings and transmissions of oral, visual, audio, gestural, tactile, and spatial patterns of meaning.

Multiliteracies also refers to different languages, different varieties of a particular language and different regional uses of a language. Since literacy is formed in varied social, cultural and religious **contexts**, there are diverse reading and writing practices. For example, a person in London may speak Sylheti (a regional language of Bangladesh), read and write in Bengali (the standard language of Bangladesh) as well as in English, be fluent in English but also use a local variety of East London English. Such a person may exhibit multiple literacies that have varied and different uses, levels of expertise and degrees of prestige, each of which contains different symbols of social and linguistic **identity**, have different opportunities for use (e.g. according to the speaker's gender), which change over time with experience and opportunity, and are often not used separately but in combinations with innovative blending (syncretism).

Morita-Mullaney *et al.* (2019) document the multiliteracy practices of emergent bilingual Spanish, Karen, Chuj and Mam families in small rural towns in the US Midwest. For example, a family from Guatemala described attending two church services each Sunday, one in Spanish and one in their native Chuj language. In addition to reading the Bible in Spanish and Chuj at home, they engaged with their children's homework in English as well as read letters sent home by the school in English and Spanish. Children from such multilingual homes do not remain in separate language and literacy worlds but acquire their **multilingualism** and multiliteracies simultaneously (Kenner & Gregory, 2012).

This is not just an academic point, as it has implications for literacy in the classroom. Kalantzis and Cope (2013: 1) argue that 'it is no longer sufficient for literacy teaching to focus, as it did in the past, primarily on the formal rules and literary canon of a single, standard form of the national language'. They also note the need to supplement traditional reading and writing with multimodal representations, particularly those typical of digital media. Teachers have choices about what to develop and how. For example, should a classroom concentrate on literacy in 'standard English' or should it include local regional varieties of English? Is only majority language literacy developed or are multilingual literacies developed as well? Are students taught only traditional school-based genres, like the five-paragraph essay? Or do teachers also recognize the multiliteracies students engage in via multimodal emails, text messages, social media postings and in digital storytelling? What value does the teacher give to literacy practices outside the school, including in the early stages of reading and writing? Are such home and community multiliteracies incorporated in the school and classroom, for example with help from parents, grandparents and siblings? Research suggests that teachers may not always be aware of home and community literacies, resulting in much potential loss of a valuable resource for classroom learning (Kim, 2022; Pu, 2008).

Translingual Literacy

Multiliteracies also open up possibilities for what some scholars call translingual literacy or practices (Arregúin-Anderson & Alanís, 2019; Canagarajah, 2013, 2020; Silva & Wang 2021). Canagarajah (2013: 2) explains: 'the term translingual enables a consideration of **communicative competence** not restricted to predefined meanings of individual languages, but the ability to merge different language resources in situated interactions for new meaning constructions'. This goes beyond simple codeswitching in writing; bilingual and multilingual writers are often able to 'mesh their resources for creating new forms and meanings' (Canagarajah, 2013: 2). The term **codemeshing** is also used to describe such translingual literacy practices (Milson-Whyte, 2013). For example, a bilingual writer could include a few words or phrases from their other language, especially when there are no exact equivalents in the main language of the text, or when the translation would not carry the same emotional or conceptual weight. Translingual writing could include reported speech in its original language, or realistic natural dialogue between bilingual characters engaged in translanguaging. Even without using specific words or phrases in the other language, a translingual writer could still draw on unique grammatical constructions or styles of writing in one language while writing in the other. For example, consider how a bilingual writer might compose a poem in English but follow a unique poetic style of their native language.

Kiramba (2017: 115) describes the translingual writing practices of fourth-grade emergent multilingual students in Kenya and argues that such writing 'disrupts unequal voices and language hierarchies by transgressing standard ideologies in academic writing'. Arregúin-Anderson and Alanís (2019) provide evidence of young students developing their translingual practices in early childhood education. Canagarajah (2020) provides examples of translingual writing in autobiographies produced by transnational students reflecting on their biliteracy development. Shin *et al.* (2021) highlight multilingual learners across age levels and educational contexts engaging in multimodal composing.

In the literary world, Kellman (2020: vii) explains that literary translingualism refers more broadly to 'the practice of writing in more than one language or in a language other than one's native tongue'. Kellman (2020) highlights published works by translingual authors and argues that the authors' linguistic choices are fundamental to their identity and how they present themselves. Kiramba (2017) calls upon teachers to take multilingualism as a resource and allow students to use their full range of repertoires in writing – a process she describes as transformative for multilingual students.

School Resources

Where multilingual classes exist, then learning, motivation and self-esteem may be raised by celebrating multiliteracies. Classroom displays can celebrate the different languages of the children in the class, and their scripts. At whole-class or school events, having children read in their heritage language may give them both recognition and pride, and also be educative for other children.

Culturally and linguistically relevant books for children are valuable to engage and excite them. Such books will be more understandable (and supportively predictable) if they connect with the children's personal histories, cultural backgrounds and communities. Motivation to read, and to read independently and enjoyably, will be enhanced when the student meets text that has a friendly cultural meaning. This can be achieved by (1) characterizations that are similar to the student's family and language community, (2) themes and contexts that are comprehensible within their life experiences, and (3) language and discourse that are familiar to the student (Freeman et al., 2003).

As computers, smartphones and other mobile internet devices are increasingly becoming a part of children's lives, representing their varied language worlds and multiliteracies on screen builds status and use for multilingualism. Devices are no longer limited to English or other languages using the Latin alphabet, but are now capable of displaying and receiving input in a wide variety of orthographies. Such electronic literacies build international (e.g. with a 'heritage' country) as well as local networks of multilinguals. Such literacies then become more multimodal: scripts, pictures, moving images and sounds. Stories told by children (and parents) about their homes and family lives which value their home and community culture can be stored and relayed to other children beyond the classroom via the internet.

As far as possible, the language resources of the classroom need to be multilingual, partly to reflect the mother tongues of the children in the classroom, but also for the multilingual awareness of all children. Sometimes it is difficult to find the quantity, quality and variety of reading materials in the mother tongues of children in bilingual classrooms. There are sometimes challenges importing books from other countries and in purchasing expensive books. Some creative bilingual teachers have found they can cheaply convert majority language books into home language books by printing out translated text with a computer and pasting the translations over the original text, or pasting it underneath to create a bilingual book (Wright, 2003; see also Box 14.3). Thus, schools can manage to collect or create excellent libraries of books in different languages (and multicultural books) via the internet and with help from language communities, parents and minoritized language organizations. Partnership with parents in literacy events is important, especially in multilingual classrooms.

Resources include not just materials and literacy strategies but also people. Apart from parents, teacher support staff may be able to help literacy development in another language. Similarly, peer teaching and peer support can be utilized to introduce different scripts, to allow the class to listen to someone reading in a language the teacher does not understand, to compare the script that is used predominantly in the classroom (e.g. directionality, accents) and sometimes to provide a model to emulate.

Literacy strategies typically include combinations of whole-class work, individual tasks, partner activity, small-group discussion, use of technology and individual self-directed learning (Wright, 2025). Cooperative learning can increase inter-group friendships and increase the achievement of bilingual students, raising their motivation, self-esteem and empathy (see Chapter 12). Multiliteracy strategies and activities utilize the child's experience in both private and interactive social activity: for example, discussing experiences of the home as well as the 'home country', of trips and television, religion and family rituals, anecdotes and achievements, imaginations and shared

> **Box 14.3** Dual language books
>
> **Dual language books** are fiction and non-fiction books written in two languages. Such languages may have a similar script (as with French and English, or Spanish and English) or different scripts (as with Chinese and English, Urdu and English, Bengali and English). The two languages may be on the same page or on opposite sides of the page, sharing the same pictures. Multilingual books may have three or more languages.
>
> Some dual language books are professionally produced and published. However, teachers may work with students (and their parents) to produce their own bilingual and multilingual books. Cummins (2019), for example, describes how students from the Thornwood Public Schools near Toronto, Canada, have produced bilingual books in 28 languages with help from their families. Kim and Song (2019) describe the Multilingual Family Storybook Project at a bilingual immersion charter school in the Midwest of the United States, where parents and children produced bilingual (English–Spanish) and trilingual (English–Spanish–Japanese/Mandarin) books.
>
> Such books help both multilingual and monolingual children become aware that other languages have value and functions. Blackledge (2000: 86) suggests that 'The best dual-text books are often written from the perspective of the home culture and translated into English, rather than vice-versa, making them more culturally relevant than books written from an Anglo-centric perspective and translated into the community language'.
>
> For children whose first language is not the majority language of the country, dual language books may serve as a bridge to literacy in English. Such children will read the story in Greek or Korean, Russian or Spanish first. Subsequently, they may read the other language (e.g. the English version) and, having already understood the storyline, be able to make sense of the English words.
>
> Dual language books act as an important bridge between parents and children, and between the home and the school. Parents and other members of the extended family may be able to read to their children in their home language (Wright, 2025). Such books can enable small groups or pairs of students to work collaboratively on the book. If one child can read in Arabic and the other in English, they can work together, discuss the story and complete activities set by the teacher around that story.
>
> Dual language books are not without controversy. First, some teachers and parents argue that children only read one language in the book and ignore the other. Having understood the story in one language, it may be tiresome and pointless reading the story in another language. Children may thus concentrate on just one half of the book. Secondly, teachers and children sometimes observe that the presence of the majority language such as English tends to remove the desire to read in the home language. The different status of the two languages may mean that the child will wish to read only in the higher-status language. The positioning and quality of the minority text can also send subtle messages. For example, a clear bold English text in a large font on top followed by a Vietnamese translation written in a plain, smaller and harder-to-read font underneath makes clear which is the privileged language.

incidents. Teachers, older siblings, grandparents, aunts and uncles and parents can help provide multilingual classroom displays (and video-recordings of multiliteracies, for example in community or religious language classes) celebrating a diversity of scripts (e.g. Arabic, Chinese, Cyrillic, Devanagari, Greek, Hebrew, Japanese, Khmer, Korean, Lao, Latin, Thai, Urdu).

Such a multilingual approach also means avoiding assessment solely by narrow standardized tests that only reflect a skills approach to **dominant language** literacy (Helman *et al.*, 2020). Classroom-based assessment needs to go much further than tests of inauthentic, decontextualized language skills (see Chapter 2). For example, student portfolios – whether in hard copy or digital e-portfolios – are one important way that a teacher may gather information about the performance of their bilingual children in a classroom; they may give a much fuller understanding of the strengths and weaknesses of, and therefore the diagnostic attention needed to improve and develop, a child's literacies (see Chapters 2 and 15).

Community Relationships

The social and cultural context of literacy importantly includes the relationship between an ethnic community and literacy acquisition (García *et al.*, 2013). What constitutes 'reading' differs between cultures, sub-cultures and ethnic groups. The purposes of reading, the resources provided by the home and the process of parents helping their children to read may differ from the purposes, resources and processes for literacy in the school (Ma & Li, 2016). The school may teach reading for recreation and enjoyment; a language minoritized group may want literacy primarily for utilitarian purposes (e.g. avoiding unemployment and poverty, for trading and business transactions). The school literacy policy may aim for a child-centered, individualized approach, with the teacher as facilitator, partner and guide, and a wide choice of colorful, attractive books. An ethnic group may, in contrast, provide heritage language literacy classes in Saturday schools, at the mosque or temple, sometimes with large numbers being tutored in the same class.

In such out-of-school classes, the teacher may act as an authority and director. Learning the will of Allah, for example, may be the valued outcome. A treasured Bible, the Qur'an or another holy or highly valued book may be the focus of reading.

In the best scenario, the biliterate child comes to appreciate and understand different cultures, differing traditions and viewpoints, leading to greater cultural sensitivity and inter-group tolerance. However, the difference between school and ethnic group literacy expectations and practices may be challenging for the child. The child is exposed to two literacy worlds, two versions of appropriate literacy behavior. The school, in particular, has a responsibility to defuse tension and to create a fusion and a harmony between the differences, such that both approaches are respected, prized and celebrated. If this is achieved, the bilingual student becomes not just biliterate but more deeply **bicultural**, with an expanded vision of literacy practices, even more tolerant of difference and variety. Too often, schools take little or no account of the community literacies that children bring to school. This will be discussed in the next section.

Alternatively, some schools disparage or ignore such ethnic group literacies, infer that parents and their children are illiterate if they do not function in English, and exclude parents as literacy partners. When children come from economically poor, minoritized language culture homes, there is a tendency for teachers to assume they derive from less effective language and literacy environments than those from middle-class majority language backgrounds. Literacy is not a separate cultural event but mirrors in its form and function general socialization practices. For particular cultural and ethnic groups, this may make the transition from home to school a more challenging and strange experience.

Home–School Relationships

Many multilingual children often move seamlessly between different literacies. For example, Arabic may be used for reading the Qur'an, Urdu for family talk and English for classroom activities. Such multiliteracy practices facilitate the creation of deep links with the extended family and local networks, the child's heritage and cultural identity, and a broadening of the curriculum of the school. Parents and siblings are typically important in a student's multiliteracy development. They often provide a literacy 'ecosystem' where there is mutual support (e.g. the children help with the parents'

English writing), adaptability and linguistic survival and spread. Different languages may mean differing roles. For example, older siblings may help with school homework, father may help with a religious literacy, with mother listening to her younger children reading story books in one or more languages.

The literacy practices of the school are often different from that of the home. Parents may be educated by the school about 'good reading habits' in their children, mirroring school literacy practices and school culture. This assumes a deficit in family literacy practices that may be unwarranted. Parents are seen as failing to provide school-style literacy experiences and therefore contributing to underachievement in their children. In reality, no home is without literacy, yet multilingual literacy knowledge tends to be invisible in English-dominant neighborhoods. Teachers visiting such homes may find no classroom-type storybooks, but miss the newspapers, religious texts, shopping lists, calendars, flashcards, videos and internet use that provide a different but rich literacy background. Children themselves engage in much hidden self-initiated literacy activity. When children commence elementary school, their literacy worlds may be ignored, with an accent on one literacy only (e.g. school English).

Arias (2015) traces 50 years of the US history of parental involvement from culturally and linguistically diverse families. She observes that traditional models of parental involvement focused on activities such as (1) assisting parents with childrearing skills and creating home environments conducive to learning, (2) communicating with families about schools programs and student progress, (3) recruiting parent volunteers for classrooms and school activities, (4) getting parents to assist with homework and other curricular activities, and (5) getting parents to participate in parent councils and organizations to assist with school decision-making. However, she argues this represents an 'Anglo-centric model' that serves as 'a vehicle for getting parental support for school activities and for getting parents to be teachers of children in the home with little recognition of the meaning that these activities held for immigrant parents' (Arias, 2015: 295). She also argues these traditional models cast parents and their culture in a deficit mode, questioning their support for their children's education.

As an alternative, Arias (2015: 289) argues for non-traditional models of parental and family engagement that include the following features:

(1) develops reciprocal understanding of schools and families;
(2) situates cultural strengths of family and community within the school curriculum;
(3) provides parental education that includes family literacy and understanding school community;
(4) promotes parental advocacy that informs and teaches parents how to advocate for their children;
(5) instills parental empowerment through parent-initiated efforts at the school and community level;
(6) implements culturally and linguistically appropriate practices in all aspects of communication.

Arias (2015) describes a successful non-traditional parental engagement model originally developed in San Diego, California, called Parents Involved in Quality Education (PIQE). The PIQE model seeks to create a full partnership between parents and schools and to develop networks of communication and coordination between parents, administrators and teachers to benefit children, and to respond to issues of change and empowerment. PIQE had reached over 400,000 parents, demonstrating that 'most immigrant and minority parents not only want to be involved, but they will make significant sacrifices for their children' (Arias, 2015: 290). Evaluation studies credit PIQE with substantially increasing levels of parent engagement, and with high graduation rates and college attendance among participating **Latinx** students (Vidano & Sahafi, 2004). Arias also describes the Padres Comprometidos (Committed Parents) program developed by the National Council of La Raza. In this community-based program with schools, local chapters of La Raza work to develop the parental involvement skills of Latinx parents to effectively engage with schools and help their children prepare for college. Arias (2015: 295) notes: 'An important aspect of this program is that it addresses language and culture as assets – rather than obstacles – upon which skills, confidence, and empowerment are built'.

Olivos and Ochoa (2024) note specific challenges of parental engagement in two-way dual language bilingual education programs, where there are often competing interests between the parents of language majority (English-dominant) children and the parents of the linguistically minoritized children with disparate treatment and outcomes. This can lead to preferential treatment for the language majority parents and children, as noted above, in a phenomenon described as the 'gentrification' of dual language bilingual education (Delavan et al., 2024). Olivos and Ochoa (2024) identify four broad models of parental involvement: (1) the Family Influence Paradigm, (2) the Alternative School Reform Paradigm, (3) the Cooperative School Paradigm and (4) the Transformative Education Context Paradigm. Olivos and Ochoa (2024: 558) advocate for the last of these, arguing that:

> [The Transformative Education Context Paradigm] is based on the notion that knowledge and power are socially constructed between participants and as such, all are equally responsible and capable of contributing to transforming the educational process. A philosophy within this paradigm is that 'through analysis and critique all people are capable of engaging in actions that may transform their present realities' (McCaleb, 1997: 26). Parent involvement is a process of transformation in which critical consciousness is achieved by all the participants for the benefit of student literacy, academic achievement, and school and community transformation.

An important explication of processes in teacher–parent relationships is given by Moll (2001) and his colleagues (González et al., 2005). They used ethnographic studies to identify skills, knowledge, expertise and interests that Mexican households possess that can be used for the benefit of all in the classroom. Moll shows how Latinx parents and other community members have much to offer children in classrooms through their **funds of knowledge**. 'Funds of knowledge' broadly means any knowledge that derives from outside of school, not just in the home, and concerns how such knowledge is constructed, revised, maintained and shared (Moje, 2017). Funds of knowledge provides another avenue for non-traditional parental engagement. For example, schools may tap into the knowledge of parents who have experience and expertise with things such as flowers, plants and trees, seeds, agriculture, water distribution and management, animal care and veterinary medicine, ranch economy, car and bike mechanics, carpentry, masonry, electrical wiring and appliances, fencing, folk remedies, herbal cures and natural medicines, midwifery, archaeology, biology and mathematics. The literacy skills and practices in the home and community are also an important knowledge source that may be drawn upon. The concept of funds of knowledge also serves 'to debunk the prevalent idea of working-class households as devoid of intellect or of worthwhile resources' (Moll, 2001). The 'funds of knowledge' framework is equally applicable to other linguistic minorities communities around the world (see e.g. Martin-Jones & Saxena, 2003).

Barriers to active parental engagement for linguistic minoritized parents include language barriers, low levels of education, lack of familiarity with the school system, cultural and religious differences in views on appropriate parent–school relationships, feelings of intimidation by the high status of the school, fear of showing disrespect, the lack of transportation and childcare, lack of time due to work schedules and often the need to work multiple low-wage jobs, and negative experiences with the school, including condescending attitudes from administrators, teachers and/or other staff members (Arias, 2015; Olivos & Ochoa, 2024; Zhou & Logan, 2003). However, many of these barriers are most easily overcome in schools with strong bilingual education programs. Simply having teachers and other school personnel who are bilingual, who are familiar with the home cultures, who recognize and know how to tap into the funds of knowledge available in the homes and who understand the challenges faced by families can go a long way in breaking down communication barriers and opening opportunities for mutual dialogue to find solutions (e.g. holding parent meetings at convenient times, providing interpreters and childcare for parent meetings and teacher conferences, sending home notes, books and instructional materials in the home languages, etc.).

It is also important to remember that many bilingual programs are the direct result of parent grassroots efforts. In some cases, parents have turned to the courts to ensure their local schools adequately fund and deliver high-quality programs that meet their children's language and academic needs. The landmark *Lau v. Nichols* case was brought by Chinese parents in the San Francisco area; that led to the 1974 ruling by the US Supreme Court that schools must address the unique language and academic needs of students classified as ELLs (Morita-Mullaney, 2024b; see Chapter 9). In New York, a group of Puerto Rican parents filed a suit against the New York City Board of Education, leading to the 1974 ASPIRA Consent Decree that subsequently guided policy for providing bilingual education for over 30 years. A group of Latinx parents in Los Angeles under the name of Comité Padres de Familia brought a suit against the state of California in 1987 for failing to monitor district bilingual, English as a second language and other ELL programs for compliance with state and federal laws to ensure students were receiving appropriate language and academic programs (Olsen, 2015). These are just a few of many examples of the power of highly engaged linguistic minority parents in effecting positive school changes.

Conclusion

This chapter has revealed that different approaches to literacy have different expectations about bilingual children that pervade national and school literacy policies, curriculum provision and classroom practices. One recent contrast is literacy only in a majority language (e.g. English) compared with an emphasis on local, regional literacies, perhaps leading to 'multiple literacies' with different uses of literacy in different contexts.

Schools are a powerful provider of literacy and help dictate what counts as proper language, correct ideas and appropriate knowledge to be transmitted through literacy practices. Superior forms of literacy, and the kinds of literacy required for success in education, are school transmitted; other literacies are often devalued (except religious literacies). Therefore, the self-esteem and identity of bilingual and multilingual children may be affected by which literacies are legitimated by the school and which are ignored or despised.

One expectation of education is that children acquire literacy skills so they can function as 'good citizens' in a stable society. A contrasting expectation is that children should become empowered, even politically activated, by becoming literate. Language minoritized children should be able to read, for example, to understand propaganda, and write to defend their community's interests or protest about injustice, discrimination and racism. They need to read the world and not just the word (Freire, 1993).

The importance of different literacy and multiliteracy approaches lies in their varying proposals for the role, status and self-enhancement of bilingual children and adults. Does literacy produce cogs who aid the smooth running of a well oiled wheel? Does literacy produce bilingual students who are activated into asserting their rights to equality of power, purse and opportunity?

A fundamental issue of literacy, biliteracy and multiliteracy is thus political. When clarity is achieved in defining the intended uses of literacy for bilingual students, educational considerations such as approaches, methods and strategies become more rational.

This chapter has suggested the importance of literacy and biliteracy in the empowerment of bilingual and multilingual students and their communities. Classroom practicalities are not divorced from educational and political policies; education provision cannot be separated from issues of power that affect the lives of bilinguals.

Key Points in This Chapter

- Literacy has many uses in bilingual, multicultural societies – for learning, citizenship, pleasure and employment, for example.
- Cultures, sub-cultures and localities differ in their uses of literacy (e.g. religious groups, transmission of heritage values and beliefs).
- Approaches to literacy include: the skills approach, construction of meaning, sociocultural literacy and critical literacy.
- The science of reading (SOR) broadly refers a large and growing body of international scientific research on reading development. In practice, SOR policies at national and state levels (including 'structured literacy') drive skills-based approaches focused on the development of foundational reading skills – phonemic awareness, phonics, vocabulary, fluency, and reading comprehension.
- A skills approach to literacy is contrasted to a critical approach where issues of power, status, equity and justice are addressed from a minoritized language perspective.
- Strategies in the classroom to promote biliteracy require cross-curriculum, collaborative and personalized approaches.
- When biliteracy is encouraged in bilingual children, specific skills and strategies from the first language transfer to the second language.

> Some bilingual children simultaneously learn to read and write in both languages. Other children will learn to read in their home language before they learn to read in the majority language. In immersion education this order is reversed. Both these approaches will tend to result in successful biliteracy. Contexts become important in this decision.
> The concept of multiliteracies broadens literacy to include visual, audio, gestural, spatial and digital modes of literacy, plus the importance of cultural and linguistic diversity, including different languages, different varieties of a particular language and different regional uses of languages.
> Translingual literacy practices refer to the abilities of bilinguals and multilinguals to draw upon and mesh together their linguistic resources in creative ways to generate new forms and meanings in their writing.
> The involvement of parents as partners in biliteracy development is important, including when local and family 'funds of knowledge' are utilized.

Suggested Further Reading

Canagarajah, A.S. (ed.) (2020) *Transnational Literacy Autobiographies as Translingual Writing*. Routledge.

Lavadenz, M. and Armas, E.G. (2024) *The Observation Protocol for Academic Literacies: A Tool for Building Expertise for Teachers of English Learners*. Multilingual Matters.

Silva, T. and Wang, Z. (eds) (2021) *Reconciling Translingualism and Second Language Writing*. Routledge.

Shin, D.S., Cimasko, T. and Yi, Y. (eds) (2021) *Multimodal Composing in K-12 ESL and EFL Education: Multilingual Perspectives*. Springer.

Sparks, R.L. (2024) *Exploring L1–L2 Relationships: The Impact of Individual Differences*. Multilingual Matters.

On the Web

Center for Teaching for Biliteracy
https://www.teachingforbiliteracy.com

Funds of Knowledge Toolkit (Washington Office of the Superintendent of Public Instruction)
https://ospi.k12.wa.us/sites/default/files/2023-10/funds_of_knowledge_toolkit.pdf

Seal of Biliteracy
https://sealofbiliteracy.org/

ChalkBeat: We asked a Denver student what graduating with a Seal of Biliteracy means to her. Here's what she said (web article and video)
https://tinyurl.com/z6m77at

Literacy Squared®: Valuing bilingualism (YouTube video of a presentation by authors Kathy Escamilla, Lucinda Soltero-González and Susan Hopewell)
https://youtu.be/c_511EXuv_s

Discussion Questions

(1) In biliteracy development, what are the various views on when and in what order literacy in each language should be introduced? Which approach do you feel would be most successful in your context?
(2) Discuss the meanings of the terms critical literacy, multiliteracies, translingual literacy and codemeshing. Give examples of what these may look like in the classroom and describe how these differ from traditional views of functional literacy in transmission classrooms.
(3) Examine some commercial and/or student-made dual language books. How can the reading and creation of such books support biliteracy development? What are some of the pros and cons of such books? Analyze the positioning and quality of the texts in the two languages and what messages these may send to readers.

Study Activities

(1) Observe a classroom teacher providing biliteracy instruction. Discuss with the teacher the aims of such biliteracy. Report on the reading materials and instruction in the classroom and discuss how effective these practices appear to be in facilitating students' biliteracy development.
(2) Work with bilingual and multilingual students and their families from a particular classroom to create bilingual and multilingual books in their home languages and the dominant societal language.
(3) Choose two or three states in the United States that have adopted the Seal of Biliteracy. Compare the criteria for earning the Seal, the processes for evaluating students' biliteracy skills, and how and in what forms the Seals are awarded. Analyze these policies and procedures in terms of the extent to which the biliteracy skills of both language minoritized and language majority students may be recognized and awarded.

CHAPTER 15

Support and Assessment of Special Needs and Exceptional Bilingual Students

Introduction

Gifted and Talented Bilingual Children

The Frequency of Special Needs in Bilingual Children

Language Delay

Alternative Causes of Special Needs and
Learning Difficulties in Children

Bilingual Special Education

Appropriate Placement of Exceptional Bilingual Children
The Example of the United States

The Assessment and Testing of Exceptional Bilingual Children

Testing Accommodations for Bilingual Students with Disabilities

Assessment Solutions and Conclusions

CHAPTER 15

Support and Assessment of Special Needs and Exceptional Bilingual Students

Introduction

This chapter considers those bilingual and multilingual children who need special educational support, as well as those who, in the United States, qualify for **gifted-and-talented education**. We will consider the value of bilingual **special education** or inclusive education and of bilingual gifted-and-talented education programs. We will take a close look at the role of **assessment** in the identification and placement – and the misidentification and misplacement – of bilingual students in such programs. Finally, we will discuss the challenges of assessing and accommodating such bilingual students on tests of English language proficiency and academic achievement.

Special or additional needs have many different acceptable and less acceptable terms: disability, handicap, impairment, difficulties and disorders, for example. Such terms refer to problems that are individual and suggest a deficit rather than problems lying outside the individual, for example in an unjust society or deprived community. These terms center on the person rather than on sociocultural factors; on the person rather than their context; on disabilities rather than potential capabilities. The term (dis)ability is used to emphasize that those classified as 'disabled' actually have much ability. Preferred terms vary across time. What is acceptable in one decade typically becomes unacceptable in the next, as undesirable or negative associations develop.

Also, such terms vary across countries. For example, in the United States, the current term is 'exceptional children', used to refer to both students with disabilities and gifted and talented students. Some US schools use the term 'twice exceptional' to refer to gifted students with disabilities. In Wales, the preferred term is currently children with 'additional learning needs'. In contrast, Scotland uses the term 'children and young people with additional support needs', while England has preferred 'children with special educational needs and disability'.

Special needs that are perceived to affect language vary in definition from country to country but are likely to include the following areas: communication, learning (e.g. dyslexia and developmental aphasia), illiteracy, a low level of cognitive development, and behavioral and emotional problems. There is a distinction between special needs that can be assessed by objective criteria (e.g. visual impairment and deafness) and those where a more subjective, value judgment is required (e.g. emotional and behavioral difficulties). The risk of an assessment bias against those who are refugees or immigrants, or those who live in material poverty and speak a minoritized language at home tends to be greater in the latter category (emotional and behavioral difficulties). The placement of immigrants into special education may increase where there is a subjective judgment about their perceived language deficit.

Certainly, some bilingual and multilingual children do have special needs. However, none of these special needs are caused by bilingualism. **Bilingualism** does not cause speech or language impairment, autism, dyslexia, developmental aphasia, severe subnormality in cognitive development, serious emotional disturbance or behavioral problems (on dyslexia in bilinguals, see Peer & Reid, 2016). However, a bilingual child with special needs may have an increased need for support (e.g. if working in school in their second language).

Gifted and Talented Bilingual Children

Exceptional students include those with gifted abilities (e.g. high IQ, very creative, outstanding musical or mathematical talent, artistic and students who excel in leadership or in specific performance areas such as sports). The National Association for Gifted Children (2019: 1) defines such students as those who 'perform – or have the capability to perform – at higher levels compared to others of the same age, experience, and environment in one or more domains'. Such gifted bilinguals and multilinguals are rarely discussed in the literature and are much under-represented in acceleration programs for the gifted (Beam-Conroy & McHatton, 2015; Gentry et al., 2019). According to the National Association for Gifted Children (2020), about 6% of US students are enrolled in gifted-and-talented programs. However, less than 3% of US students are identified as both an **English language learner** (ELL) and gifted; in fact, only about a dozen states report the number of ELL students in gifted programs (Takanishi & Le Menestrel, 2017). States and individual school districts vary widely in their inclusion policies for ELLs in gifted programs (Gentry et al., 2019; National Association for Gifted Children, 2015). It is valuable to recognize that many bilinguals are high achievers, and research on immersion students (see Chapter 11) suggests that bilingualism has been linked with enhanced achievement. Chapters 7 and 8 have portrayed the cognitive giftedness that many bilinguals share (e.g. metalinguistic abilities, creative thinking). Such examples suggest a distinction between those who share language gifts due to their bilingualism or **multilingualism**, and those whose academic, artistic, scientific or musical gifts are less related to their bilingualism, although not necessarily irrelevant to their success.

Gentry et al. (2015) developed the HOPE Teacher Rating Scale as a more equitable tool for identifying gifted and talented students as an alternative to identifying students through the use of problematic standardized IQ tests and high-stakes large-scale achievement tests typically administered only in the majority language (Gentry et al., 2021). For example, the HOPE Scale recognizes 'outstanding talent in a specific content area', including 'foreign language', and thus is inclusive of bilingual students learning English as an additional language. Seward and Gentry (2022) advocate an approach to gifted-and-talented education that recognizes a wide range of gifts and talents that students may have (which may be identified by the HOPE Scale). They push back against ideas that giftedness is an innate trait and argue that all students can develop talents through proper education, training and support.

Research by Valdés (2003) portrays a particular language giftedness of many bilingual students who act as interpreters, especially in immigrant families (see Chapter 5).

A review by Beam-Conroy and McHatton (2015) examines the identification, assessment and classroom education of gifted bilinguals in the United States. Kharkhurin (2015) proposes a bilingual creative education program that fully taps into the creative talents of bilingual students. Such attention to gifted multilinguals and bilinguals helps to refute the negative 'remedial' and 'deficit' labels that have surrounded bilinguals in past decades. Suh *et al.* (2019: 22) argue that there is overlap in the 'toolboxes of differentiation and scaffolding strategies' used by teachers of high-ability students and teachers of emergent multilingual students, and note the need for collaboration between them.

Asperger's syndrome and other disorders at the higher end of the autism spectrum typically involve a combination of giftedness and challenges. It is believed that Albert Einstein, composers Wolfgang Amadeus Mozart and Béla Bartók and pianist Glenn Gould all had Asperger's syndrome. Temple Grandin is a well known biologist and animal behavioral expert who has autism. These individuals and many others exemplify the fact that people on the spectrum are often highly intelligent and artistically gifted. However, such people often lack an understanding of expected appropriate social behavior and of how to interpret emotions. Bilingualism is sometimes blamed by teachers and other professionals for the early signs of Asperger's syndrome or autism, and a move to **monolingualism** has been frequently regarded as a solution. This is unlikely to be helpful and will have minimal or no effect on Asperger's syndrome or autism.

There is very little research on autism or Asperger's syndrome and bilingualism. Marinova-Todd and Mirenda (2016) and Lund *et al.* (2017) provide comprehensive reviews of the limited research that has been done. Their reviews suggest that bilingual families should continue to use both languages at home with their children, and also that language specialists should provide interventions in both languages. One recent study supports this suggestion. Beauchamp *et al.* (2023: 4577) conducted an experimental study comparing bilingual and non-bilingual children with autism on narrative, social and pragmatic abilities. They found that 'bilinguals performed similarly to monolinguals on measures of narrative, social, and pragmatic language skills' but 'bilinguals performed better on a nonliteral language task'. They conclude 'bilingual children on the Autism spectrum can become as proficient in using language as monolinguals and may enjoy a bilingual advantage'.

A book-length study by Rubinyi (2006) of her son who has Asperger's syndrome also provides initial insights. Her son, Ben, became bilingual in English and French using the one-parent one-language approach (OPOL). Rubinyi sees definite advantages for a child who has such challenges, with bilingualism increasing flexibility in thinking and understanding different perspectives. That there are two different ways to describe the same object or concept when using two languages enlarges the perception of the possible. Using two languages encourages the child to view alternative ways of approaching multiple areas of life (food, sports, transport). Rubinyi suggests that, because of bilingualism, Ben's brain had a chance to partly rewire itself even before Asperger's syndrome became obvious. Also, the intense focus of Asperger's syndrome meant that Ben absorbed vocabulary at a very fast rate and acquired almost perfect native-speaker intonation. Thus, 'bilingual students', 'special education students' and 'gifted and talented students' are not mutually exclusive categories. Indeed, a student may be in all three categories.

Another book-length study, by Cioè-Peña (2021), captured the stories and experiences of Latinx mothers in the United States raising bilingual children who are labeled as 'dis/abled'. Cioè-Peña frames the mothers as the real experts on their children's abilities, disabilities and bilingualism, and shows the mothers' commitments to and successes in raising their children bilingually. Her in-depth view of the families also reveals the emotional, physical and financial toll on the mothers as they advocate for their children's academic and socioemotional needs.

Some states and school districts in the United States recognize this and follow procedures to ensure that bilingual ELL students are considered for gifted-and-talented (GT) programs. For example, the Northside School District in San Antonio and other districts throughout Texas use Spanish language tests as part of the identification process for potential Spanish-speaking ELL students in GT programs. Texas is one of just a few states that require students to be assessed for GT programs either in their home language or tested non-verbally (Beam-Conroy & McHatton, 2015). Even rarer are GT programs targeting bilingual students. For example, the Milwaukee Public Schools has a dedicated bilingual GT program at one of its elementary schools – the only one of its kind in Wisconsin. However, such designations do not need to be official. For example, one fourth-grade bilingual Spanish teacher at an inner-city elementary school in southern California simply self-declared her ELL-classified students to be gifted and talented, and provided a rich curriculum for her students that paralleled if not exceeded the curriculum provided for English-proficient students in the school's official GT classrooms.

The Frequency of Special Needs in Bilingual Children

In the United States, 15% of students are in programs serving students with disabilities (National Center for Education Statistics, 2024c). Of these, 19% are identified as having a speech or language impairment and 13% as students with autism. Within the English language learner (ELL) population, 11.9% were identified as students with disabilities in the 2020–2021 school year, when ELLs made only made up 10.1% of the school population (Office of English Language Acquisition, 2023b). ELLs were also found more likely to be identified with specific learning disabilities, speech or language impairments, intellectual disabilities, developmental delay and hearing impairment (Office of English Language Acquisition, 2023b). There is evidence that bilingual children in the United States have historically been both over-represented and under-represented in special education (Counts *et al.*, 2018). For example, Mercer's (1973) pioneering study found that in the early 1970s, Mexican-Americans were 10 times more likely to be in special education than White Americans. However, as shown in Figure 15.1, in the 2022–2023 school year only 15% of Hispanic students were in special education compared with 16% of White students. Black (17%) and American Indian/Alaska native students (19%) had the highest percentages in special education, suggesting possible over-representation. Asian students had the lowest, at 8%, suggesting possible under-representation.

Nonetheless, there have been great variations across and within US states (Office of English Language Acquisition, 2023b). In 2020–2021 school year, for example, in 35 states ELLs are more likely to be identified for special education than non-ELLs, 13 states where they were 1–4% less likely to be identified, two states where they were 7–11% less likely to be identified, and only 12 states where the rate of identification was roughly the same (within less than 1%) of the non-ELL population. This reveals that both over-representation and under-representation continue to be a problem.

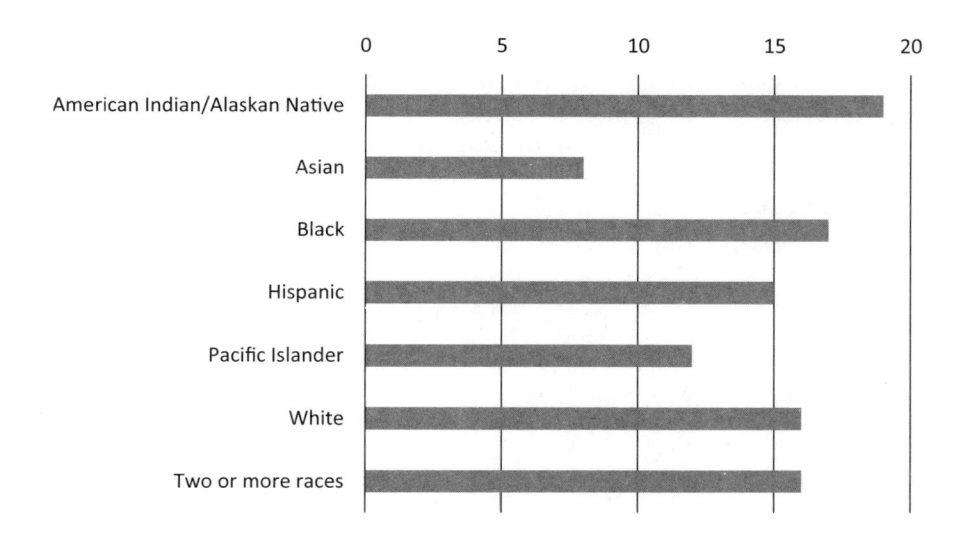

Figure 15.1 Percentage of US students receiving special education services (ages 3–21) by race/ethnicity, 2022–2023

Source: National Center for Education Statistics (2024c). https://nces.ed.gov/programs/coe/indicator/cgg/students-with-disabilities?tid=4

Under-representation may occur over fears of misdiagnosis, particularly in states and districts where **language minoritized students** are a relatively small percentage of the population. Under-representation appears to be especially acute in early childhood education, thus preventing many ELLs with special needs from receiving much-needed early interventions (Takanishi & Le Menestrel, 2017). In the United Kingdom, Cline and Frederickson (1999) reported that the identification of dyslexics who are also bilingual is often overlooked. If bilinguals are ignored or unobserved by teachers, for example, then they may not be allocated the usual assessment or treatment process.

This raises questions as to why **language minoritized** children may need special education. Does bilingualism in some students lead to language and communication disorders? One incorrect assumption is that bilingualism leads to language delay. Research does not attribute such challenges to bilingualism (Takanishi & Le Menestrel, 2017), as will be discussed below. The communicative differences of bilingual children must be distinguished from communicative disorders. The failure to make this important distinction partly occurs because basic mistakes in assessment and categorization are sometimes made. For example, a bilingual child is often assessed in their weaker, second language. Hence, both language development and general cognitive development are measured inaccurately. In the United States and the United Kingdom, immigrant children are often assessed through the medium of English and on their English proficiency. Their level of language and cognitive competence in Spanish, Vietnamese, Hmong, Korean, Cantonese, Mandarin, Turkish, Tagalog, Bengali or Punjabi, for example, is ignored. As a result, such children can be classed as having a 'language disability' and perhaps, by an unfair implication, as having a 'learning disability'. Instead of being seen as developing or **emergent bilinguals**, they may be falsely viewed as having general difficulties with learning. Their below-average test scores in the second language (e.g. English) are wrongly defined as a 'deficit' or 'disability' that can be remedied by some quick intervention or other form of special education. Multi-tiered systems of support for ELL-classified students must recognize such support needs to include bilingual instruction and support, high-quality language instruction, sheltering and scaffolding of academic-content instruction and recognition that students need time – not quick interventions – to develop proficiency in a new language (Wright, 2025).

Language Delay

A particular pathology in children – language delay – is often erroneously attributed to bilingualism. Language delay occurs when a child is very late in beginning to talk or lags well behind peers in language development. Healthline estimates that 5–10% of pre-school children experience language delay (https://www.healthline.com/health/language-delay). Some delays are brief and hardly noticeable, while others are longer lasting.

Language delay has a variety of causes (e.g. autism, severe subnormality, cerebral palsy, physical problems such as cleft palate, psychological disturbance and emotional difficulties). However, the precise reason for language delay is not always known (Li Wei *et al.*, 1997). Children who are medically fit, with no hearing loss, of normal IQ and memory, who are not socially deprived or emotionally disturbed, can be delayed in starting to speak, slow in development or have problems in expressing themselves well. In such cases, specialist, professional help is best sought. Speech therapists, clinical psychologists, educational psychologists, counselors or doctors may be able to give an expert diagnosis and suggest a treatment for the problem. It is vital that such professionals have an understanding of the nature of bilingualism in the clients they advise and treat.

For the teacher, psychologist, speech therapist, counselor and parent, a decision needs to be made in respect of severely language-delayed bilingual children. Will the removal of one language improve, worsen or have no effect on their language development? Given that the cause of the problem may be uncertain, intuition and guesswork rather than 'science' are often relied upon. Research in this area is ongoing.

Let us assume the professional advice is to move from bilingualism to monolingualism. One issue immediately becomes which language to concentrate on if major language delay is diagnosed. The danger is that parents, teachers and other professionals will want to emphasize the perceived importance of the majority language. In the United States, the advice is often that the child should have a solid diet of English (at home and particularly at school). The perceived language of school and success, employment and opportunity is the majority language. The advice often given is that the home, minoritized language should be replaced by the majority language. Even when professionals accept that bilingualism is not the cause of a child's problem, moving from bilingualism to monolingualism is seen by some as a way to help improve the problem. The reasoning is usually that the 'extra demands' of bilingualism, if removed, will lighten the burden for the child. For example, if the child has an emotional problem or a language delay, of whatever cause, simplifying the language demands on the child may be seen as one way of solving or reducing the problem. The apparent complexity of a two-language life is relieved by monolingualism. Is this a rational and suitable solution?

There are many occasions when changing from bilingualism to monolingualism will have no effect on language delay. For example, if the child seems slow to speak without an obvious cause, or seems low in self-esteem, dropping one language is unlikely to have any effect. On the contrary, the sudden change in schooling or family life may exacerbate the problem. The child may be further confused, even upset, if there is a dramatic change in the language of the school or family. If someone who has loved, cared for or educated the child in one language (e.g. a minoritized language) suddenly uses only another language (e.g. the majority language), the emotional well-being of the child may be negatively affected. Simultaneously, and by association, the child may feel that love and care have changed. Such an overnight switch may well have painful outcomes for the language-delayed child. The mother tongue is denied, the language of the family is implicitly derided and the communicative medium of the community is disparaged. The solution in itself may exacerbate the problem.

An alternative is that the home language is retained if pragmatically possible. Even if the child is slow in developing in that language, with progress delayed, it is the vehicle best known to the child. Being forced to switch to the majority language will not make the journey faster or less problematic. Thus, in most cases, it is inappropriate to move from bilingualism to monolingualism. However, it is dangerous to make this suggestion absolute and unequivocal. When there is language delay, there may be a few situations where maximal experience in one language is preferable. For example, where one language of a child is much more secure and more well developed than another, it may be sensible to concentrate on developing the stronger language.

This does not mean that the chance of bilingualism is lost forever. If, or when, language delay disappears, the other language can be reintroduced. If a child with language delay really dislikes using (or even being spoken to) in a particular language, then as part of a solution the family may sensibly decide to accede to the child's preference. Again, once behavioral and language problems have been resolved, the 'dropped' language can be reintroduced, so long as it is immediately and consistently associated with pleasurable experiences.

Any temporary move from bilingualism to monolingualism need not be seen as the only solution needed. A focus on such a language change as the sole remedy to the child's problem is naive and dangerous. For example, emotional problems causing language delay may require other rearrangements in the school or the family's pattern of behavior. Language delay may require visits to a speech therapist for advice about language interaction between the child and significant adults. Temporary monolingualism is one component in a package of attempted changes to solve the child's language problem. However, it is important to reiterate that, in the majority of cases, language delay will not be affected by retaining a bilingual approach.

A systematic review of the academic literature on the language and literacy development of ELLs by the National Academies of Sciences, Medicine, and Engineering includes a focus on ELLs with disabilities. The report has the following conclusions (Takanishi & Le Menestrel, 2017: 385):

Conclusion 10-2. Growing up with two languages does not place dual language learners/ English learners at greater risk for having a language impairment or other disability or when they have a disability, for compromising their language or cognitive development.

Conclusion 10-3. Compared with English-only interventions for language impairment, dual language interventions result in equal or even faster growth of English skills, with the additional benefit that they lead to continuing growth in the home language.

Martin (2009: 69–70) notes, 'Although there are early publications that link multilingualism with speech pathology, more recent research shows that dual language development is a positive experience for bilingual children with language learning difficulties'. Bilingual speech therapy may be more effective than traditional monolingual therapy in the majority language (Marinova-Todd & Mirenda, 2016).

Alternative Causes of Special Needs and Learning Difficulties in Children

Six examples of causes of special needs and learning difficulties outside the child and their bilingualism follow. This list, though not comprehensive, will indicate that bilingualism has nothing directly to do with many learning problems, either as a secondary or as a primary cause.

(1) Poverty and deprivation, child neglect and abuse, feelings of pessimism, helplessness and desperation in the home may create personality, attitudinal and learning conditions that make the assessment of learning difficulties more probable. Sometimes, such assessment will reflect prejudice, misjudgments and misperceptions about the child's home experiences. The learning problem may thus be in a mismatch between the **culture**, attitudes, expectations about education and values of the home and school. Different beliefs, culture, knowledge and cognitive approaches may be devalued, with the child immediately labeled as of inferior intelligence, academically incompetent and of low potential.

(2) The problem may be in the standard of education. A child may be struggling in the classroom because of poor instruction methods, a non-motivating, culturally alien classroom environment, a dearth of suitable teaching materials, or relationship issues with the teacher.

(3) The school may be inhibiting or obstructing learning. If a child is being taught in a second language and the home language is ignored, then failure and perceived learning difficulties may result (e.g. Spanish-speaking ELL-classified students placed in mainstream English-only classes and left to 'sink or swim'). By being assessed in their weaker second language (e.g. English) rather than in their stronger home language (e.g. Spanish), such children are labeled as in need of special or remedial education. Thus, the monolingual school system may itself be responsible for learning failure. A school that promoted bilingualism would more probably ensure learning success for the same child.

(4) Emotional causes of learning difficulties include a lack of self-confidence, low self-esteem, a fear of failure and high anxiety in the classroom.

(5) Failure may be caused partly by interactions among children in the classroom. For example, where a group of children encourage each other to misbehave, have a low motivation to succeed, or where there is bullying, prejudice, hostility, racism or social division rather than cohesion among children in a classroom, the learning ethos may hinder the child's development.

(6) There may be a mismatch between the gradient of learning expected and the ability level of the child. Some children learn to read more slowly than others, though they still learn to read well over a longer period. Less able children can learn two languages within the (unknowable) limits of their ability.

Bilingual Special Education

Special-education bilingual children can be served by a variety of institutional arrangements. These include: special education schools (resident and non-resident), special education units attached to mainstream schools, specially resourced classes in mainstream schools, withdrawal and pull-out programs (e.g. for extra speech and language help, behavioral management) and special help given by teachers, paraprofessionals or support staff in 'regular' classes. A common preference is to integrate such children into mainstream or 'inclusive' education. In the United States this is called **full inclusion**. The guiding principle is to place students in the **least restrictive environment**. That is, students with disabilities should be given the opportunity to learn alongside non-disabled students in a regular classroom as much as possible. The extent to which such provision will be bilingual or monolingual will vary within and across countries, regions and institutions. Such bilingual or monolingual provision will depend on the availability of provision (material, human and financial), the type and degree of special education need or condition, the degree of proficiency in both languages, learning capacity, age, social and emotional maturity, degree of success in any previous education placements, and the wishes of the parents and child.

When ELLs and other bilingual children have been assessed as having special needs, some educators argue that education is needed solely in the dominant, majority language. In the United States, the advice given is sometimes that **Latinx** and other language minoritized children with special needs should be educated in monolingual English language special schools. The argument is that such children are going to live in an English-speaking society.

Many special-needs bilingual children will benefit from bilingual provision rather than monolingual education, where this is practicable. One example is the recently arrived (immigrant) special-needs child. Placing such a child in a class where they do not speak the language of the classroom (e.g. English in the US, UK, Australia or Canada) may only increase failure and lower self-esteem. The child would benefit from initial instruction mostly in the first language, with the chance of becoming as bilingual as possible.

Many children with special needs are capable of developing in two languages, including children with Down's syndrome (see Kay-Raining Bird, 2007; Kay-Raining Bird *et al.*, 2005, 2016), autism (Genesee & Fortune, 2014; Lund *et al.*, 2017; Marinova-Todd & Mirenda, 2016) or Asperger's syndrome (Rubinyi, 2006). Such children may not reach levels of proficiency in either language compared with their peers in mainstream classrooms. Nevertheless, they can reach functional levels of proficiency in two languages according to their abilities. As the above authors testify, becoming bilingual does not detract from achievement in the curriculum (e.g. mathematics and the creative arts).

Early Canadian research showed that less able bilingual children share some of the cognitive and curriculum advantages of bilingualism (Bruck, 1978, 1982). Paradis *et al.* (2003) found that eight French–English bilingual children with specific language impairment (SLI) were successful in learning two languages, at least in terms of grammatical **morphology**. 'Instead of demonstrating that bilingualism impedes language acquisition under conditions of impairment, the children in this study showed that they had the ability to learn two languages despite their impairment' (Paradis *et al.*, 2003: 125).

Just as their mathematical ability, literacy and scientific development may occur at a slower pace, so the two languages will develop with less speed. The size of vocabulary and accuracy of syntax may be less in both languages than for the average bilingual child. Nevertheless, when such children acquire two languages early, they typically communicate in both languages as well as a comparable monolingual communicates in one language. This suggests that bilingualism and multilingualism are possible despite children with language and cognitive challenges often being recommended by well meaning professionals to become monolingual. When such children live in a bilingual or multilingual environment, such a recommendation can isolate children from social and cultural activities in the community. If their parents naturally use two or more languages, then natural patterns of communication in the home may not occur. As Kay-Raining Bird *et al.* (2005: 197) conclude: 'rather than restricting input to one language, it seems important for speech-language pathologists to provide appropriate supports in both languages to bilingual children so as to ensure that they acquire each language to the best of their ability'.

The school or class placement of a bilingual student often occurs after a professional assessment has suggested that the child's needs cannot be met by inclusion in a regular classroom. If children are placed in special education classes, it is important that they gain the advantages of those in other forms of bilingual education: dual language competence, increased achievement and thinking benefits, and other educational, cultural, self-identity and self-esteem benefits. These benefits have been discussed previously in this book.

However, full inclusion has increasingly been regarded as preferable to the stigmatization of segregation (Frederickson & Cline, 2015). Segregation can restrict access to educational opportunities. In the United Kingdom, children who failed an English language screening test were sometimes cut off from a mainstream school environment, with a restricted subject curriculum and subsequent stereotyping as failures and outcasts. Inclusion tries to combat any intolerance of language and cultural difference and the perpetuation of inequalities by severance from mainstream education.

UNESCO has adopted the 'principle of inclusive education, enrolling all children in regular schools unless there are compelling reasons for doing otherwise' (UNESCO, 1994: 44). Such inclusion means special-needs bilingual children attending a mainstream classroom and fully participating in the curriculum. Special-needs teachers, paraprofessionals and teacher assistants will typically work with such children in that school, surrounded by an inclusive education philosophy. Apart from locational integration of bilingual special-needs students, inclusion attempts social (peer) integration and curriculum integration. Social inclusion and matching the mainstream curriculum to the special needs of the child require well trained teachers, high-quality material support, parental involvement and constant monitoring (Frederickson & Cline, 2015).

The concept of inclusion is an important contrast to the historical view of bilingual special-needs children. The belief has historically been that such students have a 'problem' that needs to be 'cured' by 'treatment'. The inclusion movement holds that all children can learn successfully within integrated education that is adapted to their particular needs. Inclusive education may increase positive expectations of special-needs students by their teachers, peers and themselves. In contrast, the current accountability **ideology** and high-stakes testing systems tend to exclude or negatively label culturally and linguistically diverse students in a mainstream system. Menken (2008) argues that it is often automatically assumed with high-stakes testing that Spanish-speakers will underachieve, and that their language and cultural difference is the major explanation.

One example not discussed so far is when children fail in a mainstream school due to their language proficiency not being sufficient to operate in the curriculum. For example, in the United States, most Spanish-speaking children are in mainstream schools (a **'submersion'** experience) and, although of normal ability, fail in the system (e.g. drop out of school, repeat grades) because their English proficiency is insufficiently developed for them to comprehend the increasingly complex curriculum.

This situation creates an apparent dilemma. By being placed in some form of special-education class, the child is possibly stigmatized as having a 'deficiency' and a 'language deficit'. Such classes may not foster bilingualism. Often, they will emphasize children becoming competent in the majority language (e.g. English in the US, UK, Australia or Canada). Such segregation may allow more attention to the second language but result in the ghettoization of language minorities. While giving some sanctuary from sinking in second language submersion in a mainstream school, special-education classes can be a retreat, marginalizing the child. Will such children in special education realize their potential across the curriculum? Will they have increased access to employment? Will the perception of failure be increased because they are associated with a remedial institution? Will there be decreased opportunities for success in school achievement, employment and self-enhancement?

The ideal for children in this dilemma may be education that allows them to start and continue learning in their first language. The second language (e.g. English) is nurtured as well, so as to ensure the development of bilinguals who can operate in mainstream society. In such schools, both languages are developed and used in the curriculum. Such schools avoid the 'remedial' or 'compensatory' or deficit associations of special education. Such schools celebrate the cultural and linguistic diversity of their students.

Yet such mainstream bilingual education is sometimes in danger of being seen as a form of special education. Even when the 'second language delayed' are separated from those who are in the early stages of learning the majority language (e.g. English in the United States), the danger is that the latter will still be assessed as in need of compensatory, remedial special education.

It is also the case that bilingual students with special needs are most often placed in monolingual special-education classes owing to no bilingual special-education provision being viable. Where particular language minoritized special-needs students are geographically isolated or unique, then pragmatism is needed.

Appropriate Placement of Exceptional Bilingual Children

When bilingual children are over-represented in special-needs education, this is frequently due to assessment practices. This over-representation can result from both cultural and linguistic bias in the testing and the tester, in referral practices, poorly trained school psychologists and other professionals, or use of untrained interpreters. When bilingual children are assessed, it is important to keep distinct three different aspects of their development: (1) first language proficiency; (2) second language proficiency; and (3) the existence (or not) of a physical, learning or behavioral difficulty. This threefold distinction enables a more accurate and fair assessment to be made with regard to special education.

The student's level of functioning in a second language must not be seen as representing the child's level of language development. The child's development in the first language needs to be assessed (e.g. by observations, interviews, tests) so as to paint a picture of proficiency rather than deficiency, of potential rather than deficit. The child's **language proficiency** is different from potential problems in an individual's capacities that require specialist treatment (e.g. hearing impairment). Neither the language and culture of the home nor socioeconomic and ethnic differences should be considered as handicapping conditions in themselves. Social, cultural, family, educational and personal information needs to be collected to make a valid and reliable assessment and to make an accurate placement of the child in mainstream or special education (Burr et al., 2015). This is considered separately in the following section on the assessment of exceptional bilingual children.

Hamayan et al. (2023) provide a helpful framework with a wide variety of factors that need to be considered when attempting to determine if a multilingual learner has a learning disability and qualifies for special education services. Their framework requires a collaborative team of ESL/bilingual teachers and special-education teachers with the appropriate expertise to evaluate the factors that may influence the degree of the student's response to interventions and instruction (e.g. learning environment, personal and family factors, physical and psychological factors, previous schooling, oral language and literacy development, academic performance and cross-cultural factors). Castro-Villarreal et al. (2022) also call for multidisciplinary 'individual education plan' (IEP) committees and provide best practices and recommendations when assessing bilingual students. Flores et al. (2022) provide additional guidance for determining if challenges in bilingual students' language development is truly a disorder or simply a difference from monolingual student language development.

A key element of assessment with language minoritized children is that there needs to be early identification, assessment and intervention (Doran & Noggle, 2019). Yet assessment systems often wait until the child fails before there is assessment and intervention. The 'wait to fail before action' approach means that effective early interventions are missing, and later support may have decreased effectiveness. This problem is exacerbated when students come from disadvantaged communities and attend poorly resourced schools. Early screening and interventions are therefore important for disadvantaged language minoritized children.

The Example of the United States

The frequent misdiagnosis of bilingual students and placement in special education in the United States led to court cases that revealed how bilingual students were wrongly assessed as needing special education. For example, the 1970 case of *Diana v. The California State Board of Education* was based on nine Mexican-American parents who protested that their children (who were dominant in Spanish) were given an English language IQ test. That test revealed 'normal' non-verbal IQ scores but very low verbal IQ scores. As a result of using this linguistically and culturally inappropriate IQ test, the Mexican-American children were placed in classes for the 'mentally retarded'. In a preliminary settlement, it was established that testing should be conducted in a child's native language (and in English) and that non-verbal IQ tests were usually a fairer measure of IQ than verbal tests. As a result of this case, the collection of broader data on language minoritized children was required (rather than simple test data) to justify placement of such children in special education.

In 1975, Public Law 94–142, the Education for All Handicapped Children Act, guaranteed a 'free appropriate public education' for all children with disabilities. This law was replaced in 1990 with the Individuals with Disabilities Education Act (IDEA), which added the requirement for eligible students to have their education planned and monitored with an individualized education program (IEP). IDEA was re-authorized in 2004 with an emphasis on IEPs containing measurable annual goals and plans for meeting those goals. The 2004 re-authorization acknowledges problems of misdiagnosis and over-representation of students from non-English-language backgrounds in special education, and thus calls for students to be assessed in the 'language and form most likely to yield accurate information on what the child knows and can do academically, developmentally, and functionally, unless it is not feasible to so provide or administer' (Section 614[a](e)[ii]). All testing and assessment procedures should also be non-discriminatory, by using tests that are culturally and linguistically appropriate. Such testing procedures are to be carried out by trained members of a multidisciplinary team (see below). Apart from tests, factors such as teacher recommendations, observations of the child and other relevant information should create a multi-source file (portfolio) of evidence. IDEA was amended through the Every Student Succeeds Act (ESSA) in December 2015, in order to address specific ESSA requirements for students with disabilities.

Multidisciplinary teams are the most effective practice for making appropriate placements. These teams may comprise a school/educational psychologist, a school nurse, a speech pathologist/therapist, a social worker, a school counselor, a school administrator, a bilingual or ESL specialist, the student's teacher(s) and the parents (Castro-Villarreal *et al.*, 2022; Hamayan *et al.*, 2023). The involvement of parents in the team process is essential, as is collecting evidence other than test scores, such as information on the student's family and home, learning history and community/cultural lifestyle.

Such US litigation and law have shown the importance of separating bilinguals with real learning difficulties from those bilinguals whose English proficiency is below 'native' average. The latter group should not be assessed as having learning difficulties and therefore being in need of special education. The litigation also showed the potential injustices to bilingual students: misidentification, misplacement, misuse of tests and resulting failure when allocated to special education.

The fear of litigation by school districts can lead to both over-referral and under-referral of bilingual students with a real need of special education. In the early 1980s, the trend in California, for example, was to assume that too many language minoritized students were in need of special education. When students did not appear to be benefiting from instruction in 'regular' classrooms, special-education classes became the answer. Or, if teachers were unsure how to deal with a bilingual with a behavioral or learning problem, a transfer to special-education provision became a favored solution. Toward the end of the 1980s, this was reversed. The tendency moved to under-estimating the special needs of language minoritized children. Wrongful placement of children in special education (over-referral) made various administrators cautious of special-education placement. A fear of legal action by parents, and a realization that assessment devices often had low validity, led administrators to be hesitant to place bilingual children in special education.

The seesaw between over- and under-referral to special education makes accurate assessment a key focus, and schools in the United States are thus in need of expert guidance (see Box 15.1). However, accurate assessment and placement in different schools are not enough. The development of effective instruction strategies and an appropriate curriculum for such students is crucial. So is the need to train teachers

> **Box 15.1 Identifying and supporting ELLs with disabilities**
>
> A report by researchers from WestEd (Burr et al., 2015) prepared for the Institute of Educational Sciences of the US Department of Education provides guidance for US schools in identifying and supporting ELL students with disabilities, drawing on academic research and their own study of practices in 20 states. The report notes that 'no single method has proven effective in differentiating between English learner students who have difficulty acquiring language skills and those who have learning disabilities' (Burr et al., 2015: i). However, it recommends asking the following questions to help distinguish when academic challenges are caused by learning disabilities, and when they are natural occurrences of English language development (Burr et al., 2015: i):
>
> - Is the student receiving instruction of sufficient quality to enable him or her to make the accepted levels of academic progress?
> - How does the student's progress in hearing, speaking, reading and writing English as a second language compare with the expected rate of progress for his or her age and initial level of English proficiency?
> - To what extent are behaviors that might otherwise indicate a learning disability considered to be normal for the child's cultural background or to be part of the process of US acculturation?
> - How might additional factors – including socioeconomic status, previous education experience, fluency in his or her first language, attitude toward school, attitude toward learning English, and personality attributes – impact the student's academic progress?
>
> The report also offers five guiding principles for effective policy and practice (Burr et al., 2015: ii):
>
> 1. Having a clear policy statement that additional considerations will be used in placing English learner students in special-education programs.
> 2. Providing test accommodations for English learner students.
> 3. Having exit criteria for English language support programs for English learner students in special education.
> 4. Assessing English learner students' language and disability needs using a 'response to intervention' approach.
> 5. Publishing extensive, publicly available manuals to aid educators in identifying and supporting English learner students who have learning disabilities.

for bilingual students in special education (Burr et al., 2015). Educating the parents of special-needs bilingual children is also a high priority (Takanishi & Le Menestrel, 2017).

Many US schools use a 'response to intervention' (RTI) model focused on a close monitoring of student progress and providing interventions in three tiers (Echevarría & Vogt, 2011). RTI is alternatively referred to as 'multitiered systems of support' (MTSS) (Doran & Turner, 2019). The three tiers of interventions or supports are as follows:

- tier 1 – universal screening and research-based instruction (all students);
- tier 2 – more intensive, targeted, short-term support and supplemental instruction through small-group instruction (20–30% of students);
- tier 3 – intensive individualized instruction and interventions (5–10% of students).

The RTI model originated in special education and is used to identify students in need of special-education services or placement (tier 3). In other words, students who do not respond to 'good' instruction (tier 1) or to more intensive targeted small-group instruction (tier 2) are referred to special education (tier 3). However, as RTI has gone mainstream and school-wide, there are concerns about its appropriateness for bilingual students, especially those classified as English language learners (Echevarría & Vogt, 2011). First, as noted above, many of the screening and monitoring assessments used in tier 1 and tier 2 are inappropriate for bilingual students. Second, RTI makes the assumption that tier 1 and tier 2 represent high-quality effective instruction. However, this is often not the case, due to lack of materials, lack of trained teachers and lack of a supportive policy environment for effective ELL and bilingual program models (Takanishi & Le Menestrel, 2017). Third, bilingual students are blamed for not responding to (ineffective) tier 1 instruction and tier 2 interventions, thus reinforcing a deficit view of students and inappropriate placement into special education (tier 3). If more students were placed in strong bilingual education programs (tier 1), far fewer would likely be deemed in need of tier 2 interventions. And if tier 2 supports were provided by qualified bilingual specialists, with intensive instruction that is linguistically and culturally appropriate, far fewer bilingual students would be placed in tier 3. In addition, a major problem with the RTI model is the whole notion of 'interventions'. As Wright (2025: 21) has argued:

> ELLs don't need intervention. They need instruction. No temporary 'intervention' is going to quickly make them proficient in English. Rather, ELLs need consistent, high-quality language and content-area instruction appropriate to their educational background and level of English proficiency over a period of several years across grade levels.

In recognition of the shortcomings of RTI, Beam-Conroy and McHatton have proposed an RTI model for exceptional ELLs. Unlike traditional RTI models, their model is 'predicated on linguistically and culturally responsive practice whether ELLs need special education and/or gifted services' (Beam-Conroy & McHatton, 2015: 384).

The Assessment and Testing of Exceptional Bilingual Children

The allocation of bilinguals to special education or to gifted-and-talented education programs usually depends on some form of assessment. It is essential for any psychological and educational assessment of bilingual children to be fair, accurate and broad (Mahoney, 2024). Assessment can include tests, observation, interviews, portfolios of work and professional judgment (Noggle & Doran, 2019). Thus, tests are just one component of assessment. Tests are frequently predetermined and highly structured, obtain a very small sample of behavior under standardized conditions, have rules of scoring and result in a numerical outcome. They are a small snapshot in time.

Tests given to bilingual children often serve to suggest their 'disabilities', supposed 'deficits' or lack of proficiency in a second language. Such students may come to be stigmatized by such tests, for example because tests locate apparent weaknesses in the majority language and use monolingual scores (norms) as points of comparison. Such practices tend to lead to over-identification of bilingual students for special education and under-identification of bilingual students for gifted-and-talented education. The **reliability**, **validity** and risks of **bias** in educational and psychological testing of ELLs and other bilingual and multilingual students is recognized in the joint testing standards established by the American Education Research Association, the American Psychological Association and the National Council on Measurement in Education (2014). The joint standards provide guidelines to reduce linguistic and cultural biases and increase the consistency (reliability) and accuracy (validity) of such tests, but there are no accountability measures in place to hold testing companies, states and schools to these standards (Wright, 2025).

Despite advice in the joint standards, in legislation, discussions in academic literature and findings from research, bilinguals tend in many countries to be discriminated against in testing and assessment (Gottlieb & Ernst-Slavit, 2019). Chapter 2 provides a detailed discussion of the general challenges of the assessment of bilingual students. Below, we review several important overlapping and interacting issues that must be considered in the assessment of exceptional bilingual children, as identified by research (Castro & Artiles, 2021; Castro-Villarreal *et al.*, 2022; Goldstein, 2022; Kormos & Smith, 2024; Machado-Casas *et al.*, 2022; Mahoney, 2024; Maldonado, 2024; Paradis *et al.*, 2021; Shohamy & Menken, 2015).

- *Language(s) of assessment*. Children should be assessed in their strongest language. Bilingual assessments may also be appropriate, as they allow students to draw more broadly from their linguistic repertoire to demonstrate what they know and can do. To be valid, testing instruments in other languages must be developed in parallel and cannot simply be translations (e.g. from English into Spanish). Such translation may produce inappropriate, stilted language; differences in vocabulary and grammar may affect the item difficulty. Also, consideration must be given to when bilingual students speak a different variety of the native language to the standard variety used on the test (e.g. Puerto Rican Spanish, Chicano Spanish, Castilian Spanish). The language used must be authentic, capturing the quality of a child's communication abilities across school and home contexts.
- *Normal second language development versus learning disabilities.* The temporary difficulties faced by bilinguals in the natural development of a second language must be distinguished from actual learning disabilities.
- *Teacher observations*. It is important to use the understanding of a child's teachers who have observed that child in a variety of learning environments over time. What do the child's teachers think is the root problem? What solutions and interventions do teachers suggest?
- *Multidisciplinary assessment teams.* It is valuable to have a multidisciplinary team of teachers and specialists (e.g. classroom teacher, ESL/bilingual teachers, special-education teachers, counselors, administrators, school nurses, psychologists, speech therapists) as well as parents meeting regularly to assess the child's developmental and academic strengths and challenges and to develop an instructional or interventional plan. Such a team should be the school decision-maker for referral to special education, gifted-and-talented education or other services.
- *Qualified assessors*. Assessors must be trained and qualified to administer the assessments, and be proficient in the languages used in the assessments. The degree to which the assessors are perceived to be from the same ethnic or language group as the child (or not) may affect the child's performance (and possibly the diagnosis).
- *Qualified interpreters*. If a valid version of a test or assessment device is not available in the child's stronger language, interpreters are sometimes necessary and have a valuable function. If trained in the linguistic, professional and rapport-making competences needed, they can make assessment more fair and accurate. Interpreters, however, can also bring a possible bias ('noise') into the assessment (i.e. 'heightening' or 'lowering' the assessment results through the interpretation they provide) or provide unintended (or intended) hints that invalidate test results.
- *Multiple measures*. Important diagnostic, identification or placement decisions should not be based on the results of a single test. Multiple measures including both formal and informal assessment instruments and procedures, given over an

extended period of time, will provide a more valid language, academic and behavior profile of bilingual students.
- *Test scores*. The scores on educational and psychometric tests tend to be like latitude and longitude: they provide points of reference on a map of human characteristics. As a standard measurement usable on all maps, they provide initial, rapid and instantly comparable information. But imagine the most beautiful place you know (e.g. a flower-enfolded, azure-colored lake set amid tall, green-sloped, ice-capped mountains). Does the expression of the latitude and longitude of that scene do justice to characterizing the beauty and distinctiveness of that location? The attempted precision of the sextant needs to be joined by the full exploration and evaluation of the character and qualities of the exceptional student.
- *Sociocultural context*. Assessment typically focuses solely on the child. The assumption is that the 'problem' lies within the child. A sociocultural focus is needed to consider causes outside the child. Is the problem in the school? Is the school failing the child by denying abilities in the first language and focusing on failure in the second (school) language? Is the school system denying a child's culture and ethnic character, thereby affecting the child's academic success and self-esteem? Is the curriculum delivered at a level that is beyond the child's comprehension or that is culturally foreign to the child? The remedy may be in a change in the school and not to the child.
- *Student's best interest*. Assessment should work in the best, long-term interests of the bilingual child. 'Best interests' does not only mean short-term educational remedies, but also long-term educational and employment opportunities. Assessments that separate children from powerful, dominant, mainstream groups in society may lead to children becoming disempowered. The assessment may lead to categorization in an inferior group of society and to marginalization.

Testing Accommodations for Bilingual Students with Disabilities

In the United States, the No Child Left Behind Act (NCLB) of 2001 halted the exclusion of English language learners (ELLs) and students with disabilities from large-scale assessments and mandated their inclusion in statewide testing. This policy and practice continue with the Every Student Succeeds Act (ESSA) of 2015, though with some leeway in terms of how and when ELL test scores are reported and used in school-wide achievement calculations (see Chapter 9). As before with NCLB, under ESSA the performance of different subgroups must be tracked separately, including ELLs and students with disabilities. However, ESSA includes an important new requirement to separately track and report the progress of ELLs with disabilities. Such data has been seriously lacking. Just prior to ESSA, 'Only 4 states reported both participation and performance for ELLs with disabilities for the general [state] assessment' (Lazarus *et al.*, 2016: iii).

ESSA requires that ELL students be 'assessed in a valid and reliable manner' and 'provided with appropriate accommodations [i.e. modifications]' on assessments. Accommodations are also required for students with disabilities, who include bilingual and ELL students with disabilities, and accommodations must be provided on both state-level language and content-area academic achievement tests. The aim of accommodations is to produce fairness (a level playing field) for ELLs and students with disabilities (Abedi & Sanchez, 2022). Accommodations originally derived from testing children with additional learning needs. For example, Braille is used for blind children, computerized assessment is an option for students with physical difficulties, extended time is often given to dyslexic students, and longer or multiple test time breaks are given for various reasons. Examples of accommodations are: simpler English in the instructions without changing the content; use of a bilingual dictionary and glossary; small-group or individual administration; extra time to complete the test; oral administration (reading items aloud); oral response; and directions in the student's language. The test may be explained to students in an easier form of language and students may be given longer to complete it, so that use of a second language becomes less of an influence and performance is more accurate. Ideally, this produces a more level playing field for ELLs. A translation into the student's home language may not always help, as the instruction and hence 'curriculum language' will have been in English.

The use of accommodations is a much-debated topic (Abedi, 2017, 2021). How can we be sure that accommodations, or which accommodations, have the desired outcome? Research on testing accommodations is still emerging and remains inconclusive while accommodation policies and practices vary widely across US states and schools (Abedi & Sanchez, 2022; Wright, 2025; Yang, 2020). A comprehensive report commissioned by the US Department of Education designed to provide guidance to states and schools on the use of accommodations acknowledges that research is thin and that 'None of the accommodations examined has leveled the playing field for ELLs' (Francis *et al.*, 2006: 29).

One accommodation that shows some potential for reducing the performance gap between ELLs and non-ELLs is linguistic simplification of test directions and test items (Abedi, 2017, 2021). When such linguistic complexity is reduced, then the student is assessed more on content than on a lack of English. Measurement error or 'noise' is then reduced. For example, changes can be made to: unfamiliar words; long and complex questions with many relative clauses; an abstract rather than concrete presentation; use of the passive voice; and confusing negatives. Of course, such linguistic simplification is not appropriate when the assessment construct is ability to process and comprehend complex texts, such as on an English language proficiency test or an English language arts reading comprehension exam. There is also some evidence that providing time extensions may benefit students on reading tests in their second language (Kormos & Ratajczak, 2019) and that read-aloud assistance may benefit the text comprehension of ELLs with dyslexia (Košak-Babuder *et al.*, 2019).

On the **ACCESS** 2.0 English language proficiency exam – in use in over half the states in the United States belonging to the WIDA Consortium – some accommodations are built into the computer-based exam. For example, students can use a highlighter tool to emphasize parts of a question, can use a line guide to focus their reading line by line and use a magnifying glass to zoom in on text or images. The English Language Proficiency Assessment for the 21st Century (ELPA21) includes comprehensive guidelines, procedures, alternative forms (e.g. paper-and-pencil forms, enlarged text and Braille) and supplemental materials (e.g. real objects [*realia*], manipulatives and other hands-on items) for assessing ELLs with hearing and vision loss, speech and language disorders, physical disabilities and cognitive impairments.

For bilingual and other students with severe cognitive disabilities, an alternative form or procedure may be used in lieu of a state's regular English language arts (ELA) or mathematics exams. ESSA caps the allowance for alternative forms to 1% of all students, which roughly equals about 10% of special-education students. This number is arbitrary; it is not grounded in any research suggesting the number or percentage of students who would benefit from the alternative form.

In the United States, the Dynamic Learning Maps (DLM) Alternative Assessment System Consortium, which has 22 member states, has developed shared alternative assessments (as of 2024 – see https://dynamiclearningmaps.org/about/state-member-representatives). Rather than a single summative selected-response assessment form, the DLM Alternative Assessment System integrates assessment with instruction throughout the school year. As described on the Consortium's website:

> Think of the learning map model as a common road map. The learning map model illustrates the connections among the knowledge, skills, and understandings necessary to meet academic content standards. Although students may share a common destination, they often begin their journeys from different points on the map. The learning map model helps parents and educators guide students to success by showing them where a student is now, where the student has been, and where the student is going.
>
> The learning map model shows individual concepts and skills in points called *nodes*. Good instruction, however, requires far more than simply teaching individual facts or skills. Effective teachers need to understand how knowledge and skills are connected. That is why the learning map model also includes many connections, or relationships among its nodes – to show different ways students reach the same goals. (https://dynamiclearningmaps.org/model)

The DLM model in particular seems to have the potential for opening up new ways for accommodating ELLs. However, it is unclear how the specific and unique needs of ELLs with disabilities are currently being addressed.

There are many remaining questions about the influence of accommodations on the validity of the test result, which students are eligible for accommodations and on what criteria, plus the amount of advantage (even unfair advantage) resulting from different accommodations (Abedi, 2017, 2021; Abedi & Sanchez, 2022; Wright, 2025).

Assessment Solutions and Conclusions

An alternative approach to testing exceptional bilingual children is more authentic curriculum-based assessment and portfolio-type assessment, and greater cultural and linguistic awareness (Hamayan *et al.*, 2023). Authentic assessment that is developmental and which has width – linguistically and contextually – is particularly important (Noggle & Doran, 2019). Such assessment is a collection over time of a portfolio of a bilingual child's unique growth in both their languages. A pivotal portfolio can follow a student through their entire bilingual program (Maldonado, 2024). A student's portfolio will reveal advancing accomplishments in the form of authentic activities (possibly with staff observations included). A sense of ownership of the portfolio by the student is important to raise awareness of evolving accomplishments and a personal possession of progress. Frederickson and Cline (2015) argue for the child's perspective to be part of this assessment (e.g. self-perceptions of the school, special needs, friends, home, feelings and the future). Parents' and family collaboration and viewpoints add a further important dimension to assessment and to solutions (Takanishi & Le Menestrel, 2017). An extension of this is the gathering of information not just about the student but also about teaching, program design, family dynamics, parental involvement, previous schooling, cross-cultural expectations and available human and material resources (Castro-Villarreal et al., 2022; Hamayan et al., 2023).

An ecological approach to assessment assumes that an exceptional bilingual student is part of a complex social system and that their behavior cannot be understood except within its context. Thus assessment has to sample students' communication in a variety of contexts and environments, including outside the classroom. Maldonado (2024) argues that students' motivations and self-efficacy beliefs and attitudes are also essential to consider as part of this ecology. This also means collecting information about the expectations of family, friends and teachers for a child's communication. This is exemplified in the RIOT assessment (Martin, 2009):

- Review all available information.
- Interview teachers, friends and family.
- Observe a student in multiple contexts.
- Test school and home languages.

Another approach to assessment of exceptional children is dynamic assessment. 'Dynamic' means that assessment is a process rather than an outcome. It explores mediation between a teacher and student by examining their co-construction of learning and mutual understanding of what is occurring (Kushki & Nassaji, 2024). The emphasis is not just on a student's current level of functioning but also on assessing the best means to facilitate further learning. It goes beyond assessing how much language the child has already learnt to examining what new language is needed. It assesses how scaffolding can best take place, thus informing planning by teachers and their interventions with individual students. It works best with expert teachers who have sufficient professional knowledge both to prevent bias in assessment and to have the insights to inform future lessons.

A radical solution to testing places change in assessment within (and not separate from) a change in expectations about the nature and behavior of exceptional bilingual students. This entails a shift in the politics and policy dimensions of the assessment of bilinguals (Gottlieb, 2024; Gottlieb & Ernst-Slavit, 2019). Merely changing tests may alleviate the symptoms of a problem but not change the root cause. The root cause tends to be a bias against language minorities that is endemic in many societies and is substantiated by unfair tests (Mahoney, 2024; Shohamy et al., 2017). By being biased against bilinguals in a cultural and linguistic form, and by a failure to incorporate an understanding of the cognitive constitution of bilinguals, assessment confirms and perpetuates various discriminatory perceptions about language minoritized children. Machado-Casas et al. (2022: 3) call for a 'decolonial approach' to assessment in bilingual education:

> A decolonial approach encourages bilingual educators and dual language program evaluators to analyze if existing measures of achievement and accountability are aligned with the 'why' as well as the 'how' of 'la lucha' (the collective struggle). Informed by sociopolitical dimensions of power and purpose, culturally responsive evaluation methodological processes are essential to bilingual education programs. Situated within a continuum of power, evaluation processes are either reinforcing or dismantling structural barriers for bilingual learners.

Assessment thus sometimes serves by its nature and purpose, its form, use and outcomes to provide the evidence for discrimination and prejudice against language minorities to be perpetuated. Assessment results can serve to marginalize and demotivate, to reveal underachievement and lower performance in language minoritized children. Hence, there is both the over- and under-representation of exceptional bilingual children in special education and in gifted-and-talented education programs.

Assessment must not in itself be blamed. It is a conveyor and not a root cause of language minority discrimination and bias. Until there is authentic and genuine acceptance of language pluralism in a region, and a minimizing of racism and prejudice against ethnic minorities, assessments will likely continue to confirm the 'lower status' and perceived 'deficiencies' of exceptional bilingual and multilingual children.

Key Points in This Chapter

- Bilingual children are often over-represented in special education, being seen as having a language deficit. Paradoxically, they can also be under-represented, particularly in early childhood education, when there is a fear of legal action for wrongful placement.
- Bilingual children are under-represented in gifted-and-talented education programs.
- Bilingualism has been associated with language and communication disorders (e.g. language delay). This is not supported by research.
- Special-education bilingual children are served by a variety of institutional arrangements, including special-education schools, special-education units attached to mainstream schools, specially resourced classes in mainstream schools, withdrawal and pull-out programs and special help given by teachers, para-professionals or support staff in 'regular' classes.
- Most bilingual special-needs children will benefit from bilingual special education rather than monolingual special education.
- Response to intervention (RTI) and multi-tiered systems of support (MTSS) for bilingual students must ensure high-quality and linguistically appropriate tier 1 instruction and tier 2 interventions/supports provided by qualified bilingual teachers and specialists before placement in tier 3 (special education).
- Assessment of exceptional bilingual children is enhanced when there is not just testing but also observation (in and out of the classroom), curriculum-based assessment, a cultural and linguistic awareness of bilinguals, the use of appropriately trained assessors who seek to empower such children, and the use of multidisciplinary teams of teachers and specialists, and parents.
- Research on testing accommodations for ELLs and other bilingual students with special needs is still emerging and remains inconclusive.

Suggested Further Reading

- Castro, D.C. and Artiles, A.J. (eds) (2021) *Language, Learning, and Disability in the Education of Young Bilingual Children*. Multilingual Matters.
- Cioè-Peña, M. (2021) *(M)othering Labeled Children: Bilingualism and Disability in the Lives of Latinx Mothers*. Multilingual Matters.
- Hamayan, E., Marler, B., Sánchez-López, C. and Damico, J. (2023) *Special Education Considerations for Multilingual Learners* (3rd edn). Brookes.
- Kormos, J. and Smith, A.M. (2024) *Teaching Languages to Students with Specific Learning Differences* (2nd edn). Multilingual Matters.
- Paradis, J., Genesee, F. and Crago, M. (2021) *Dual Language Development and Disorders: A Handbook on Bilingualism and Second Language Learning* (3rd edn). Brookes Publishing.

On the Web

- ¡Colorín colorado! – Special education and English language learners
  https://www.colorincolorado.org/school-support/special-education-and-english-language-learners
- English learners with disabilities
  https://ncela.ed.gov/resources/infographic-english-learners-with-disabilities-october-2023
- Celebrating bilingual special education – P.S. 112 Jose Celso Barbosa Elementary School (YouTube video)
  https://youtu.be/UqOOgAHrAWs
- Bilingual Gifted and Talented Education program at Hollinger Elementary School in Tucson Unified School District (YouTube video)
  https://youtu.be/AcnnxWclFAU?t=1m13s
- Gifted, but still learning English, many bright students get overlooked (National Public Radio)
  https://www.npr.org/sections/ed/2016/04/11/467653193/gifted-but-still-learning-english-overlooked-underserved

Discussion Questions

(1) Is it possible for a student to be bilingual/multilingual, disabled and gifted and talented? Give some examples and discuss how schools could best serve these students.
(2) Why are exceptional bilingual students often over- or under-represented in special education and in gifted-and-talented programs?
(3) How can multidisciplinary teams of teachers, specialists and parents help make more appropriate placement decisions for exceptional bilingual students in special-education and gifted-and-talented education programs? Who should be members of such teams? What information, assessment data and other issues should be considered to guide their decisions?

Study Activities

(1) Conduct interviews with parents or teachers of a bilingual student who has special needs. Define the exact nature of those special needs. Document the history of that student's education. Ask the parents or teachers what their preferences are

for the use of languages in school and if they want their children to be bilingual as a result of schooling. Inquire about the value and use they see in languages for special-needs children.
(2) Conduct a case study of an exceptional bilingual student in a special-education and/or gifted-and-talented education program. How was the student identified and placed in the program? How does the program address, ignore, build upon or suppress the student's home language(s)?
(3) Conduct an analysis of the identification and assessment process used in a local school or district for special-education and gifted-and-talented programs. How are the needs of exceptional bilingual students addressed in this process? Analyze the assessment instruments used to identify students to determine the degree to which they are appropriate to different populations of bilingual students.

CHAPTER 16
Deaf-Signing People, Bilingualism/Multilingualism and Bilingual Education

By Jean F. Andrews and Stephen M. Nover

Introduction

Part I: Preliminaries
Deaf-Signing People and Signed Languages
The Significance of Deaf Epistemology
Deaf Culture
Community Membership and Exclusion
Language Access and Use
Language Contact and Sign Multilingualism
Multimodalities

Part II: How It Began and Where It's Going
Phase 1: The Uniqueness of Deaf-Signing Bilingualism (1817–1867)
Phase 2: Introduction of the Combined System (1867–1930)
Phase 3: Weakening of Deaf-Signing Bilingualism with Oralism (1930–1979)
Phase 4: Revival of Bilingualism (1980 to present)

Part III: Contemporary Supports and Practices
Neuroscience: The Benefits of Signed Language and Early Deaf-Signing Bilingualism
Intelligence, Visual Learning and Signed Language
School Settings: Two Different Media of Instruction (SL–WL and Sp–WL)
Framework for Deaf Bilingual Education
Deaf Bilingual Theories, Methodologies and Strategies
Translanguaging and Sign-Mediated Strategies within a Deaf Sign/Bi/Multilingual Framework
Outcomes
Achievement and Assessment
Teacher Preparation
Families
Conclusions

CHAPTER 16

Deaf-Signing People, Bilingualism/Multilingualism and Bilingual Education

By Jean F. Andrews and Stephen M. Nover

Introduction

In this chapter we cover Deaf bilingualism and Deaf bilingual/multilingual education, Deaf epistemologies and bilingual teaching strategies, including the use of multimodalities and visual technologies to enhance Deaf-signing people's learning. We also present historical and contemporary views of Deaf-signing bilingualism and bilingual education in the United States.

This chapter focuses primarily on Deaf-signing persons who do not use auditory pathways to process spoken language, but utilize their Deaf authentic knowledge and lived experiences. For them, communication does not always include auditory production and reception. Moreover, they do not see themselves as inferior human beings, a stereotype held by a Hearing-speaking society that misunderstands their vibrant Deaf culture and **signed languages**. While we recognize there are Deaf-signing communities with diverse communication, language and sensory strengths and differences,[1] here we focus on the visual and tactile sensory pathways. We show how vision combined with touch as developed by Deaf-signing people has emerged into what Bahan (2014: 247) states are 'culturally developed sensory ways of being in the world, an embodiment in the ways of using the eyes, moving the body, engaging in dialogues, and touching and belonging … and are naturally drawn to drawn to others sharing the same orientation and instantly connect with them'.

In Part I, we provide preliminary key concepts for the reader by describing our own story (i.e. our positionality), then define Deaf-signing persons, Deaf epistemologies,

---

[1] Those from non-English speaking and non-signing homes, Hard of Hearing, DeafBlind (tactile or protactile signers) (Edwards, 2024), DeafDisabled (Singleton *et al.*, 2024), Late Deafened and oral/non-signers (Leigh *et al.*, 2022a), underserved and those from impoverished backgrounds, minority (immigrants and refugees) (Lyngbäck & Andersson, 2024), or those who are LGBTQIA (lesbian, gay, bisexual, transgender, queer, intersex and asexual) (Christensen, 2017) are considered more fully elsewhere (see Cannon & Guardino, 2022; Musyoka, 2022).

Deaf culture, group membership, language use, access and contact, and multimodalities. Part II presents a brief historical snapshot of four phases of deaf bilingual education, showing that **Deaf-signing bilingual education** is not a novel concept but has existed for centuries. Then, Part III shows how contemporary cognition, learning and signed language linguistics research supports Deaf bilingual education. Nonetheless, social barriers still obstruct Deaf bilingual practices, so we conclude by calling for change.

Part I: Preliminaries

Two vignettes establish the positionality of the authors – Nover and Andrews.

I (Nover) was born deaf to Hearing-speaking parents. Professionals recommended that my parents not use signed language as they said it would prevent me from learning to talk. Later, my parents enrolled me in the Boston School for the Deaf, which used a strictly oral-only method (now called the monolingual approach) of communication. As a teen, I was enrolled in a Hearing-speaking vocational technical high school which used spoken language as the language of communication and instruction. I felt socially isolated. But one teacher thought I was misplaced and that I should have been enrolled in an academic program. So, I was then transferred to an out-of-state residential school for the deaf for the last three years of high school in an academic tract with a signed language and written language as the medium of communication and instruction. As a teen, my social world opened up. I was a 'new signer' and joined an all-Deaf basketball team. When I entered Gallaudet University, I continued to learn American Sign Language (ASL) as a 'signer' and English as a 'writer', and become heavily immersed in many Deaf-signing community recreational and intellectual activities. Fast forward to adulthood (age 47), I earned my doctorate in Language, Reading, and Culture at the University of Arizona in 2000. Since then I have been involved working in social agencies and in multiple schools for the deaf and at universities preparing educators, administrators and staff in Deaf-signing bilingual education and professional development (see Nover, 1993; Nover & Moll, 1997).

I (Andrews) was born Hearing and attended Hearing-speaking schools until graduate school, where I enrolled in a teacher-preparation program with a 30% Deaf enrollment. At age 25 I became a new 'signer', immersed in the Deaf-signing community where I learned about Deaf culture from my Deaf classmates. During my first year of teaching at the Maryland School for the Deaf, I taught alongside a Deaf teacher-aide (Alice) who demonstrated CHAMP bilingual practices. I ate lunch with other Deaf-signing teachers and joined after-school Deaf social activities. Later, I earned my doctorate in Speech and Hearing Sciences with a minor in Reading and Linguistics at the University of Illinois–Champaign-Urbana. Upon graduation, I prepared teachers and educational leaders using ASL and English bilingual methodologies, focusing on enrolling and graduating Deaf graduate students, particularly Deaf students of color at the masters and doctoral levels. In 1997, I joined Nover on the bilingual CAEBER project where I joined Deaf professionals focused on exploring the goal of ASL and English bilingualism and bilingual education (CAEBER is discussed below). I continued to conduct literacy research in schools for Deaf-signing students (Andrews, 2012) and joined other Deaf-Hearing collaborative writing teams to address psychosocial and educational issues by textbook writing and literacy research in international venues (Leigh *et al.*, 2022a, 2022b; Wang & Andrews, 2020).

Both Nover and Andrews have been collaborating since 1997 on ASL and English bilingual education projects. Their two vignettes are not unique. Many Deaf-signing persons have similar experiences, such as delayed access to signing as Nover did and then enter the deaf education field to make changes. Moreover, many Hearing-speaking persons like Andrews enter the Deaf-signing community, learn ASL as a second language and about Deaf culture in early adulthood as educators and join Deaf-hearing collaborative teaching and research teams.

With our positionality vignettes in mind, we describe Deaf-signing people, the significance of Deaf epistemology and the parameters of the Deaf-signing community and Deaf culture. These concepts underlie the Deaf-signing bilingual framework which we detail in the remainder of the chapter.

Deaf-Signing People and Signed Languages

In natural communication, the medium through which language is transmitted plays an important role, in our case, signed languages, which have been recognized since at least the fourth century BC (Ruben, 2005). As mentioned above, we focus on the role of signed languages and how Deaf-signing people have not experienced 'hearing' in the same way as persons with typical Hearing (i.e. Hearing-speaking persons). Moreover, they do not actually rely on the sensory path of hearing as a hearer-speaker does for communication as well as for learning. Instead, they primarily rely on the sense of seeing or vision (receptive) to be able to understand the world's visually based information based on the whole human body (see Sandler, 2018). Visual perception is at the center of their lived experiences and epistemological knowledge, which we detail later in the chapter.

As eloquently stated by Thoutenhoofd (1997: 25), 'Their signed language interrelates directly with the dominance of the sense of sight [or seeing] over that of hearing.... Sign[ed] languages are constitutive because they are what united Deaf[-signing] people's awareness of being-in-the-world'. Ruben (2005: 467) has similar insights. He claims that 'Vision alone is able to establish language.... It is no surprise that these techniques reflect the observation of Socrates ("of the deaf and dumb who have words without sound...")'. And as an Italian polymath of the High Renaissance, Leonardo da Vinci (1452–1519) acknowledged the following: 'if he sees two people talking, a deaf-mute understands the substance of their conversation by their expressions and gestures, although he himself can catch no sound' (Werner, 1932: 163). These provide historical examples of philosophers, artists and writers who note the importance of vision, gesture and body movement for Deaf-signing people.

We delve deeper into Deaf-signing modes of expression by contrasting how Hearing-speaking individuals learn. Hearing-speaking persons acquire, use and learn with their expressive *speaking* and receptive *hearing* abilities. With ample exposure, effortlessly, these abilities unfold on a predictable psycholinguistic timetable as Hearing-speaking learners acquire and use spoken languages (oracy) for daily communication. Then, they learn and use written language (literacy) for communication and instruction. In sum, all educational institutions emphasize the national standardization of these four language abilities: *hearing* (or *listening*), *speaking*, *reading* and *writing* (see Table 1.2, 'The four basic language skills', p. 7).

Into the 21st century, it is acknowledged that hearing-speakers use spoken language naturally, which 'involves other modalities, too, such as the visual channel (e.g., through bodily gestures and facial expressions) and the tactitle channel (i.e. physical touch)' (Börstell, 2024: 2). In comparison, 'Sign[ed] languages make use of the gestural-visual modality, being articulated by the signer with the hands, face, and body and perceived visually (or, alternatively, tactilely) by the addressee (also known as the "signee")' (Börstell, 2024: 2).

As articulated by Börstell (2024), Deaf-signing people learn by utilizing their expressive **signing** and receptive viewing of signed language (ASL). With ample signed language exposure, Deaf-signing learners effortlessly acquire and use a **signed language**, which we call **signacy** (Nover *et al.*, 1998) for daily communication and they use written language (literacy) for communication and instruction.

How does this relate to Deaf-signing bilingualism? Deaf-signing people have always embraced the daily use of two different visually based modalities – signing and writing – as part of their natural bilingualism. In fact, as early as 1816, Deaf-signing people used a signed **vernacular** language, referring to everyday social and academic communication, along with a written language (also used in social and academic environments) as their second or foreign language. Written language (WL) becomes a second (or foreign) language of instruction along with signed language (SL) or **signacy**. In short, two visually-based different languages (ASL and written English) become standardized as a **medium of instruction** (MOI) model in deaf education (there is more on this topic later in the chapter).

Another important concept underlying the Deaf-signing bilingual education framework is the notion of **Deaf epistemology**.

The Significance of Deaf Epistemology

Deaf epistemology, or 'deaf ways of knowing and acquiring knowledge', is based on Deaf-signing people's lived experiences of learning through vision rather than audition (Hauser *et al.*, 2010). Relative to classroom instruction, visually based bilingual practices have deep historical roots – in France in the 19th century. While the contemporary term 'epistemologist' was not used in the 19th century, in theory and practice we see that the first Deaf Epistemologist was Laurent Clerc (1795–1869), an early French professor of Deaf-signing students. He 'opened the eyes' of his Hearing-speaking collaborator and ally, Thomas H. Gallaudet (1787–1851), who became a new signer of ASL as a second language. This Hearing-speaking ally embraced and adopted learning 'deaf ways of knowing' and language learning based on the Deaf-signing lived experience with the four languages: Langue Des Signes Française or LSF (French signed language), French written language, American Sign Language (ASL) and English written language. Moreover, these four languages represent two modalities: *signing* and *writing*.

Clerc's Deaf epistemological (learning and teaching) experiences, which consist of signed language (SL) and a written language (WL) (his bilingual methodology), flourished at the American Asylum at Hartford for the Education and Instruction of the Deaf People (now the American School for the Deaf, or ASD). Clerc explicitly demonstrated his bilingual teaching methods at presentations and testimonials to legislatures, schools, conferences and organizations, and even published his findings in journals and conference proceedings (Clerc, 1851, cited in Foster, 1818). Hearing-speaking teachers, who also became new signers of ASL as a second language, enthusiastically embraced

Clerc's early ideas about how natural signs can be used to develop intelligence and emotional expression and express abstract ideas. He linked signs to objects, pictures, alphabet letters and writing to teach reading, as described in his lecture 'Some Hints to the Teacher of the Deaf and Dumb' at the Second Convention of American Instructors of the Deaf and Dumb, a national professional organization for educators of deaf students in the 19th century (Clerc, 1851). Clerc's ideas spread to the many other schools for the deaf set up in the early American 19th century. Although innovative at this time, these insights and strategies look remarkably similar to today's ASL/English bilingual approaches!

In contemporary literature, the concept of epistemology has been applied to experiential and authentic knowledge bases of minority groups as feminists and other minority groups, such as Blacks, Latinos and Asians (see Banks, 1998). In modern times, this concept has been carried in Deaf education as *Deaf-centric ways* of communication and language (Holcomb, 2010), which brings into the classroom Deaf culture, signed language and Deaf 'ways of knowing' based on Deaf lived experiences (Humphries, 2013).

Next we discuss how Deaf *epistemologies* are embedded in the culture of Deaf-signing peoples.

Deaf Culture

We now know that '[l]anguage arise[s] through natural interaction between humans, wherever and whenever needed, and in whatever modality is available' (Börstell, 2024: 2) and Deaf-signing people are no different in this respect. Deaf 'ways of knowing' (e.g. Deaf epistemologies) and their signed languages are embedded in Deaf culture, which consists of a 'multifaceted history of a unique minority group with a distinctive visual culture' (Garrettson, 1981: xix). It includes learning signing and writing behaviors, history, values, traditions, arts and literature (Holcomb, 2013; Padden & Humphries, 2005). The Deaf-signing individual has 'a set of uniquely patterned life experiences that he [or she] shares with others like himself', wrote Carl Croneberg, a Swedish multilingual Deaf-signing person (i.e. Swedish, German, American Sign Language) and co-author of the well known *Dictionary of American Sign Language on Linguistic Principles* (Stokoe *et al.*, 1965).

In sum, Deaf culture reflects a community that is peer-based and interdependent and whose goals are aimed at supporting each other while confronting oppression. Such sentiments of shared group inclusiveness are exemplified by the World Federation of the Deaf (WFD), an international organization established in 1951 that continues to advocate for the human and language rights of Deaf-signing people internationally.

Box 16.1 What's in a label?

Society often uses labels such as auditory-impaired, hearing impaired, deaf-mute, deaf and dumb, or multiply handicapped (those with additional disabilities) and schooled in an 'asylum'. Such antiquated terms imply Deaf-signing people are 'defective', 'broken' or 'inferior' rather than culturally and linguistically different. Some prefer the capital 'D' Deaf, signifying culturally Deaf, but not all Deaf community members agree on its use (Pudans-Smith *et al.*, 2019). Those with additional disabilities are now called DeafPlus, DeafDisabled or neurodivergent (Singleton *et al.*, 2024). See also the American Psychological Association (2024) for guidelines in bias-free terminology for deaf and hard-of-hearing persons.

Deaf-signing people maintain their cultural traditions at Deaf school reunions, athletic events, Deaf clubs, churches, senior citizens gatherings, Deaf-led travel tours, DeafNation Expo (a touring trade show), international conferences and organizations, and through social media, as exhibited in books such as *People of the Eye: Stories from the Deaf World* (McKee, 2001). A distinguished example of Deaf self-determination was shown in the March 1988 Deaf President Now (DPN) protests at Gallaudet University, followed by multiple mini-DPN protests at Deaf schools across the country, as told by Jack Gannon (1989), Deaf-signing author, in *The Week the World Heard Gallaudet* and also in a book by Christensen and Barnett (1995). There are also increasing numbers of Deaf-signing individuals with doctoral degrees researching the lived experience of Deaf-signing individuals, particularly in the field of English language literacy, an area where Deaf scholars have significant input (Andrews *et al*., 2015). On the international front, there are new Deaf postsecondary programs and the increasing recognition of signed languages, both academically as in signed language linguistics, as well as in practice, as in teaching signing to Hearing-speaking students as a second or foreign language (Adamou *et al*., 2020; Mathur & Napoli, 2011; Rosen, 2020). These are just some of the many examples worldwide of the powerful influence of vibrant Deaf-signing communities.

Even though non-signing, oral deaf people (see Nover above in his youth) do not consider themselves part of the Deaf-signing community, they still use visual technologies and collaborate with Deaf-signing people on projects such as captioning, universal newborn hearing screening and a national campaign to address the language foundation of deaf and hard-of-hearing children, ensuring they are kindergarten-ready (LEAD-K). They also enjoy the protections of the Americans with Disabilities Act (ADA) (see Leigh *et al*., 2022b).

Membership and exclusion in Deaf-signing communities varies, depending on many factors, some of which we describe here.

Community Membership and Exclusion

Most Deaf-signing persons are born into Hearing-speaking families (see Nover's vignette above). However, about 10% are born into families with at least one Deaf-signing caregiver (Mitchell & Karchmer, 2004). Deaf-signing persons born into Deaf-signing families enter the community at birth. Others may enter during childhood or adolescence, when enrolled in a school for the deaf (for Nover's story, see Nover & Moll, 1997), a Deaf-signing college or even later into adulthood, at the workplace (Holcomb, 2013).

Deaf-signing people may also identify with the culture of their own locality, region and country, integrating to a greater or lesser extent with Hearing-speaking family members or friends (Leigh, 2009). Within these communities, Deaf-signing adults promote bilingualism, since literacy (reading and writing) provides them with access to communication, education, employment and civic integration (Chen Pichler *et al*., 2019). However, their sign bilingualism has not always been recognized or accepted in the mainstream. Instead, Deaf-signing people have been marginalized and have often faced bigotry and discrimination based on their mode of communication and Hearing-speaking society's attitudes about it (i.e. **audism** – Humphries, 1977) and their suppression of Deaf-signing persons' form of expression (i.e. **linguistic imperialism** or **linguistic hegemony**) (see Branson & Miller, 1998; Rose & Conama, 2018).

More recently, studies of Deaf identities have incorporated the lens of intersectionality, meaning the interconnectedness of an individual's background, such as gender, race, ethnicity, disability, religion and migration, and its resulting relationships of power (Emery & Sanchayeeta, 2022; Leigh *et al.*, 2022a, 2022b). One noteworthy example in the United States came from leaders in the National Black Deaf Advocates, who wrote about the impact of encountering both racism and racism:

> Members of the Black Deaf community must deal with racism and audism compounded. We are first judged on the color of our skin; and then we are judged based on our ability to navigate in a hearing person's world. We face both racism and audism in our everyday lives. (National Black Deaf Advocates, 2020: 1)

This is but one example of how such intersectionality compounds racial disparities among Black Deaf-signing communities. To address issues confronting minority Deaf-signing individuals, Gallaudet University established the Center for Black Deaf Studies in 2020, with Dr Joseph C. Hill named as director in 2024. Moreover, the *Nuestra Casa*, the Center for Latine Deaf Studies, was set up in 2023 to address advocacy and academic research efforts; it is now headed by Dr Carla Garcia-Fernandez. To promote, maintain and develop its ASL and English bilingual mission, Gallaudet University appointed Dr Laurene Simms as the Chief Bilingual Officer (CBO); she directs projects establishing bilingualism, bilingual education and ASL teaching to ensure overall bilingual access and equity on campus in addition to other nationwide bilingual projects.

Membership in the Deaf community is primarily based on access to and use of a signed language, which is the topic of the next section.

Language Access and Use

There are about 70 million Deaf-signing people from 133 countries represented by the World Federation of the Deaf. Chen Pichler *et al.* (2019) have identified the following groups based on language learning:

- *Deaf heritage signers*. Deaf with Deaf-signing parents who learn a signed language in the home (about 5% in the US) (de Quadros, 2018).
- *Deaf immigrants*. Those who migrate from one country to a new country, bringing their indigenous signed and spoken languages (Allard & Wedin, 2017).
- *Deaf children of Hearing parents*. Those who learn some signed language from their non-native hearing-signing parents or learn it after enrolling in school as late language learners (Mayberry, 2002). Such delayed acquisition affects language proficiency levels as compared with heritage signers and may put Deaf-signing learners at risk of mental health issues (Glickman *et al.*, 2020). While they struggle, many late Deaf-signers still can function adequately with their late signed language as their primary language, as Nover demonstrated in his vignette. Andrews, too (see vignette), found in her teaching of Deaf university students that many became 'new signers' in late childhood or teenage years and were successful at the university level with support.

Deaf-signing people are also multilingual and may know and use one or more spoken languages, signed languages, or both (Cannon & Guardino, 2022). The following vignettes illustrate Deaf-signing people's diverse languages and cultures.

- Rosalina is a Deaf girl born into a Hearing-speaking family in Italy. Her family speaks Italian. She learned Lingua dei Segni Italiana (LIS or Italian Sign Language) at school and can read and write Italian. At age 13, she and her family immigrated to Canada. Her family speaks Italian, supported by LIS. Rosalina attends a Deaf school in Canada where she learned ASL and English. She is multilingual. Rosalina speaks, reads and writes Italian, uses two signed languages (LIS and ASL) and is learning English literacy (Cannon *et al.*, 2016).
- Maria became deaf from a childhood illness. Her family immigrated from Mexico to the United States when she was five. Her large extended family primarily communicates in spoken Spanish. Maria communicates with them using written Spanish with the aid of Google Translate. When she entered school in the United States, she learned ASL and written English. She is trilingual, using ASL, written English and written Spanish (Baker & Scott, 2016).
- Jay was born Deaf in a Hearing-speaking family that spoke Mandarin Chinese at home in Singapore. When he attended a school for the Deaf at age six, he learned Chinese Sign Language (CSL), written Chinese and some English. In high school, a Deaf-signing friend taught him ASL. Jay learned more English and ASL when he immigrated to the United States for college. Jay is a multimodal multilingual who utilizes written Chinese, CSL, ASL and English (Wang *et al.*, 2016).

Language contact is another characteristic of signed languages that impacts Deaf community inclusion as well as Deaf bilingual education in the United States today. For example, recall that, as evidenced throughout this volume, languages are not static entities but cultural systems that have evolved over time due to language contact. Related to Deaf-signging communities, the expressive power of sign multilingualism adds to the evolution and development of signed languages.

Language Contact and Sign Multilingualism

As mentioned above, ASL developed from language contact with the French language of signs (called Langue Des Signes Française or LSF) in 1815–1817 (Aicardi, 2009; Shaw & Delaporte, 2011; Stokoe *et al.*, 1965; Woodward, 1978). Clerc provided a bilingual model to his ally and collaborator, T.H. Gallaudet, resulting in a novel design for (ASL) and a written language (English) as a medium of instruction (MOI) at the American Asylum at Hartford for the Education and Instruction of the Deaf (now ASD) (Nover, 2000). Subsequently, ASD became the first school site of language contact – see Baker (2003b) for further discussion of education as a site for language contact.

Another example of language contact with ASL and other signed languages emerged when Clerc, on his international presentation tours, often used and brought back signed languages from other countries to the ASD campus (Nover, 2000; Clerc, 1816/1952). These signed languages, primarily LSF, evolved into the modern-day ASL (Fischer, 2014; Woodward, 1976, 1978, 1979).

This phenomenon of language contact with the Deaf-signing community's use of ASL and English has been described as a bilingual-diglossic continuum between ASL and English (Woodward, 1973). Variations along this continuum are rule-governed and regular, representing 'pure ASL' at one end to a system of coding English into stringing together individual sign words at the other end (Markowicz & Woodward, 1982).

Another type of contact signing is called PSE or Pidgin Signed English, a mixture of ASL and English used by Deaf and hearing people alike, depending on the situation and participants (Berent, 2004; Lucas & Valli, 1989).

Another example of a language contact situation also emerges when Deaf-signing people worldwide communicate with each other and the Hearing-speaking community. Some examples include finger-spelled words, lexicalized finger-spelling and initialized signs borrowed from the languages in contact with each other (see Chen Pichler *et al.*, 2019). This occurs at international gatherings of Deaf-signing people such as the Deaflympics, the International Conference on Education of the Deaf (ICED), the International Conference on Sign Language Acquisition (ICSLA) and the International Deaf Academics and Researchers Conference (among many other conferences). At these gatherings, when Deaf signers do not share signed language, they incorporate features found in all signed language grammars: pointing conventions, use of space, non-manual markings to include topicalization, focus and contrast, filling in vocabulary and using visually oriented strategies. These sign multilingual behaviors have been termed 'cross-signing' (the rapid use of an improvised inner-language), 'sign-speaking' (sign and talk at the same time) and 'sign switching' (between sign languages) (see Adamou *et al.*, 2020; Chen Pichler *et al.*, 2019).

Another language contact variety is the International Sign Language (ISL). However, ISL has no native users but is used by Deaf-signing people and signed language interpreters at international gatherings. While its linguistic status has been contested (Supalla & Webb, 1995), it incorporates unique sociolinguistic characteristics as a visual modality (Zeshan & Panda, 2018).

Examples of language contact among Deaf-signing communities occur throughout the Eastern world as well. Taiwanese Sign Language (TSL) has been influenced by the languages of those who controlled the schools over time – the Chinese, Japanese, Taiwanese – through migration, colonization, occupation, administrative jurisdiction and local advocacy. And due to language contact, modern-day TSL exhibits features of Japanese Sign Language (JSL, 日本手話, nihon-shuwa), with some signs resembling Chinese written characters (Liu *et al.*, 2024). Liu *et al.* (2014: 6) consider TSL signs representing the Chinese characters for 北 *north* and 田 *farmland*). Matsuoka *et al.* (2023) give examples of language contact among other East Asian signed languages.

Such examples of language contact shape the evolution of signed languages which invariably impacts how Deaf-signing bilingual education is delivered. The use of multi-modalities also shapes signed languages.

Multimodalities

According to Sandler *et al.* (2022: 1), multimodal refers to the coexistence of linguistic and gestural modes, regardless of the physical transmission channel – straightforwardly encompassing the two natural language systems, spoken and signed. We extend this definition to include written language, including visual graphemes such as emojis integrated into printed text (see also Grosjean, 2010b; Perniss, 2018).

As noted at the start of this chapter, we focus on Deaf-signing persons who use the visual and tactile modalities (e.g. signed language, written language, tactile communication) for communication and learning. We are not opposed to the teaching of the spoken modality of English as we believe that Deaf-signing children should be taught spoken language. However, we recommend that a signed language be introduced as early as possible, as having a language foundation will facilitate the Deaf-signing child in learning to speak (Pontecorvo et al., 2023).

In our teaching and years of consulting at schools for the deaf, we have seen that Deaf families members often use multimodalities with their young Deaf-signing children. For example, they may use spoken language and speak intelligibly, which they have acquired upon a strong signed language foundation, providing them with a conceptual base. We have also observed that for Deaf-signing children, spoken language is acquired only after years of tedious, explicit and direct instruction, in contrast to how hearing children effortlessly are 'like sponges who soak up spoken language' around them. Put in another way, Humphries et al. (2024: 1) note the harms done to Deaf-signing children with a wide range of hearing losses (including hard of hearing) who are raised by parents who oppose a signed language and have 'zero tolerance to the use of other evidence-based approaches'. (See Nover's vignette above for an example of how delaying a signed language can be socially isolating for the young child struggling to learn to communicate.)

A unique form of multimodality has been studied in the communication modes of hearing children of Deaf-signing parents (referred to as CODAs/KODAs – Child/Kid of Deaf Adults) who are born into culturally Deaf-signing families and who use a type of **codeblending** where they acquire and use both a signed and a spoken language and achieve fluency in both. Some Deaf-signing parents also codeblend, speaking and signing with their deaf children. Codeblending in signed languages provides linguists with unique opportunities to study language production and comprehension mechanisms when two languages are produced simultaneously. This can happen with a sign and spoken language but not with two spoken languages (Emmorey et al., 2012).

Codeblending is *not* to be confused with Simultaneous Communication, which refers to 'intentionally created educational methods for "English on the hands" ("SimCom" or "Signing Exact English") ... to strictly follow strictly English grammar, and are not naturally produced by children before instruction' (Petroj et al., 2014: 2). Even with today's cochlear implant and digital hearing aid technology, spoken English is still not accessible to all deaf children. When teachers over-rely on English-based signing, many Deaf-signing children who are still struggling with learning English may be isolated and marginalized in the classroom. For many of these visually oriented Deaf-signing children, SimCom does not allow them full and complete access to the grammar of ASL and severely curtails their bilingual development (Gárate-Estes et al., 2022).

In sum, when Deaf-signing people, their signed languages, Deaf epistemologies, Deaf culture and multimodalities come together in a school, a Deaf-signing bilingual curriculum can be implemented. However, as history tells us, this is not a new idea, but bilingual practices (SL and WL) have existed in deaf education since the 19th century (Nover, 2000) and have evolved over time in their various forms – strong, weakened and revived. This ushers in the second theme of the chapter – that deaf bilingual education is not a novel idea and has much to teach us if we look back into its history.

Part II: How It Began and Where It's Going

'Study the past if you would define the future', said the ancient Chinese philosopher Confucius (551–479 BC). To this end, we provide a brief four-phase historical overview, highlighting the beginnings, development and implementation of signed language–written language (SL-WL) bilingual education. Then we carry its tenets into the 21st century, when scientific paradigms are viewed as supporting bilingual education through studies in cognition, intelligence, neuroscience, linguistics and education, among others.

Similar to regular bilingual education for *Hearing-speaking* learners (see Chapter 9), *Deaf-signing* bilingual education has a history that extends back hundreds of years. Initially, it was profoundly influenced by French Deaf-signing culture through Deaf schools, Deaf associations, networks, publishers and the arts – all of which made their way to America in 1816 by way of the Deaf-signing Frenchman Clerc and his Hearing-speaking ally-collaborator, T.H. Gallaudet, both of whom we introduced earlier in the chapter. Thus, we see the origins of deaf bilingual programming, as seemingly historically distant yet more recent than we think. Even though Deaf-signing bilingual programming officially began in France, its modern version (which we will see in Phase 4) continues to owe its debt to early French concerns on how to educate its Deaf-signing learners.

Phase 1: The Uniqueness of Deaf-Signing Bilingualism (1817–1867)

Mason Fitch Cogswell (1761–1830) was an American physician (eye doctor) who initially founded education for deaf students. Cogwell's daughter, Alice Cogswell, became deaf after the age of two, from 'spotted fever' (cerebral-spinal meningitis). This propelled her concerned father to collaborate with seven business partners to found, finance and establish the first public school for the deaf in Hartford, Connecticut, called the American Asylum at Hartford for the Education and Instruction of the Deaf (now called the American School for the Deaf or ASD) on April 15, 1817.

Clerc, a well prepared and seasoned educator of French Deaf-signing pupils, was contracted as a consultant for three years to provide 'language planning' to T.H. Gallaudet, who was appointed as the new principal, starting in August 1816, and serving to August 1819 (Fay, 1879: 117). Basically, he was trained (for eight years) as a new professor in the long tradition of signed languages (SLs) and written languages (WLs), a teaching methodology which originated in 1755 at the National Institution for Deaf-Mutes in Paris, the world's first private deaf school. Established by a Hearing-speaking French priest, Abbe Charles-Michel de l'Épeé (1712–1789), this school provided the first private free school for deaf children in 1755. Thirty years later, after l'Épeé died, the school became public. At this time, the government of France, under the title of the Royal Institution of Paris, took over the responsibility for and renamed the school the Institut National de Jeunes Sourds de Paris. It adopted the use of both Langue des Signes Française (LSF, French Sign Language) and French Written Language (FWL) as the medium of instruction (MOI). L'Épeé's successor was Roch-Ambroise Cucurron Sicard (1742–1822), who took over the administration of the school (Aicardi, 2009; Barnard, 1837: 524–527). During his time, Clerc had been a student for eight years (1800–1808); he subsequently became a professional teacher for the next eight years (1808–1816). The important point here is to emphasize the historical roots of early bilingualism in deaf education by using a signed language and a written language as the MOI.

When Clerc entered the American scene, he was today's version of an expert as a language planning consultant and a 'walking dictionary', who was fluent in LSF, international signed language and French Deaf culture. Notably, in America (as well in the world), he was the only and first non-American Deaf-signing professional who served as a living signing and bilingual teaching model for Hearing-speaking teachers and administrators. Subsequently, Gallaudet, with his clear language planning priority, created a new category of 'new signers' of ASL as a second language as well as new professional bilingual teachers (Nover, 2000).

An early and significant description of ASL was provided by a Hearing-speaking man, Charles Dillingham (1799–1834), who taught alongside his two older Deaf-signing sisters, Abigail (1783–1824) and Nancy (1802–1826). Both ladies were former graduates of ASD (Armstrong, 1878: 513). Not only did Dillingham grow up with Deaf-siging sisters but he received formal, intensive bilingual training from Clerc at ASD (1817–1820). Dillingham went on to teach at the Pennsylvania School for the Deaf (PSD) from 1820 to 1821 under the acting PSD superintendent, who was Clerc during a period of seven months (Mayer et al., 1822: 4–5). The point of this historical detail is to underscore the practical and intellectual training in Deaf-signing bilingual education that former teachers like Dillingham, who was trained by Clerc, had prior to their working with Deaf-signing students.

Dillingham went on to be a firm advocate for Deaf-signing bilingual education. As a lecturer and writer, he commented on the complex of learning of ASL as a second language for Hearing-speakers. He eloquently commented that ASL was 'a drop in the ocean, when compared with the countless numbers and ceaseless variations of the movements of the body, hands, hear, eyes, countenance (facial expression) – all of which are required in the language of signs' (Dillingham, 1828: 408–409). Moverover, as a former Hearing-speaking teacher at PSD (1820–1824), he often published his insights about new signers. He said, '[t]he mere learning of signs is not sufficient. To learn signs is one thing; to learn the principles and practice of the system of instruction, is another' (Dillingham, 1828: 409). Therefore, Dillingham stressed that it is not enough to learn signs but teachers must learn about the strategic use of both languages – signed and written – for effective instruction as modeled and executed by his mentor, Clerc.

Interestingly, Clerc referred to written language as a *foreign language* for Deaf-signing children (Clerc cited in Foster, 1818: 173; Clerc, 1851). He explicitly acknowledged the fact that Deaf-born children cannot simply acquire a spoken or written language – they must be taught it, 'as the Greek or Latin is taught, in the colleges, to the young Americans who attend the classes of this kind' (Clerc, 1851: 173). He believed both languages – signed and written – provided the best visual accessibility for all Deaf-signing children who otherwise would be left out of instruction that is presented in oral or spoken language.

This bilingual instructional activity in various schools for the deaf on the east coast effectively taught Deaf-signing students the two languages. Clerc's innovative adaptation of the French method of using SL–WL bilingual instruction was then approved into school-wide language policy in 1819 by the Board of Directors of the Connecticut Asylum for the Education and Instruction of Deaf and Dumb Persons in Hartford, Connecticut. To our knowledge, this is the earliest evidence of a public educational policy supporting the utilization of two visual-based modalities, SL (signed language) and WL (written language), as part of language policy and practice, as explicitly documented in the Asylum's *Third Annual Report* (Terry, 1819; Nover, 2000).

Early educators also stressed the importance of interaction with Deaf-signing students as paramount to effective bilingual instruction and this is evident as early as 1819. As Terry (1819: 5) documented, teachers were expected to be 'masters of their profession' by constant communication with Deaf-signing students, attending daily lectures in a signed language delivered by Clerc, as well as living 'under the same roof' with Deaf-signing students.

Subsequently, at ASD, PSD and throughout America at other schools for the deaf, a signed language (SL) became the primary *language for communication*. Accordingly, signed language was to play a critical role in the socialization, learning and empowerment of Deaf-signing students. These efforts launched *a new SL–WL bilingual model* to serve as the educational framework for all grade levels in the United States.

Guided by this groundbreaking school language policy (i.e. school policy written in the *Third Annual Report*), Deaf bilingual education secured a firm footing in American deaf education. Subsequently, this policy spread and flourished throughout the United States in more than 22 schools.

This SL–WL policy was not without its detractors, however. A vociferous opponent of the bilingual approach was Gardiner Green Hubbard (1822–1897), an oral advocate, a well known millionaire, American patent lawyer, financier and community leader. Hubbard's daughter Mabel became deaf at age five (Hubbard, 1871: 7). Like Cogswell, Hubbard was thus a concerned father of a deaf daughter and wanted the best education for her. But Mabel was different from Alice, who was born deaf. Because Mabel had already acquired a foundation of spoken language prior to becoming deaf (post-lingually deaf), her education consisted of retrieving the language she had lost due to her illness. This etiology and age of onset differed significantly from Deaf-signing children who are born deaf and who have never heard a spoken language or have become deaf before the age of two or three (like Alice), and so do not have the advantage of the first five years of their lives bathed in spoken language as Mabel enjoyed.

To meet his daughter's needs, Hubbard, who had previously founded and financed a small experimental oral school for the deaf in northern Massachusetts, later convinced the legislature to pass a bill to establish a larger oral school, the Clarke School for the Deaf (De Land, 1906). It is important to note that children who are born Hearing-speaking, like Mabel Hubbard, and who become deaf after language already has been acquired are the more successful recipients of oral education because neurologically the spoken language pathways have already been established. In the early days of Deaf education and even into the present times, these children who are post-lingually deaf often become success stories or 'trophies' for oral education. Mabel was later to become Alexander Graham Bell's wife and her oralist success was used as a model for other deaf-speaking children. The importance of the first five years of life for language acquisition was a psycholinguistic fact that had not yet been 'discovered', so Mabel's language history was not comparable to that of the many congenitally Deaf-signing children who have never heard speech. Mabel's schooling consisted of recovering what language she had lost; for those born deaf, learning language is significantly different, hence the need for the visually based SL–WL approach.

So we can see, in the early 19th century of American deaf education, two fathers of deaf daughters made significant contributions. Both were wealthy, professional men with political contacts. Cogswell was impacted by Clerc's work and supported the establishment of a school following a SL–WL instructional methodology (now termed bilingual). In contrast, Hubbard created a different kind of schooling, one that focused on the value of teaching English speech and writing only (now termed monolingual). However, with today's knowledge of psycholinguistics and language acquisition theory, we can see that Alice, with only two years of exposure to spoken/hearing language, had a more difficult challenge to learning language than Mabel, who had a full five years. Clearly, a different kind of language teaching focused on different learners' needs.

Despite these beginning rumblings of oralism infiltrating deaf education schooling that attempted to dramatically alter the landscape of Deaf-signing bilingual education, Clerc's proteges did not merely accept these 'new' ways of 'doing deaf education'. Instead, many were teachers, such as William C. Woodbridge (1817–1822), who continued to write about SL–WL bilingual methods in educational journals, notably the *American Annals of Education and Instruction* (Woodbridge was its editor, 1830–1837) and the *American Annals of the Deaf* (formerly *American Annals of the Deaf and Dumb*). These articles addressed the needs of Deaf-signing children who needed a visually based curriculum and special language instruction that utilized Clerc's successful SL–WL approach.

By 1866, at least 22 schools for the deaf were in agreement with the SL–WL instructional paradigm (Hubbard, 1871: 7). Despite this solid bilingual foundation, as phases 2 and 3 show, a series of unfortunate events cascaded into circumstances that led to the gradual weakening of the SL–WL bilingual model.

Phase 2: Introduction of the Combined System (1867–1930)

Based on our critical reading and observations of what was happening in the schools for the deaf, as we leave the 'golden age' and enter Phase 2, we note that Clerc's 'spirit' for the SL–WL bilingual approach for Deaf-signing children began to dissipate as oralism and the Combined System approach entered the schools, which considerably weakened Deaf-signing bilingual education as put forth by Clerc and his collaborators.

In early 1867, for example, two years after the American Civil War ended, the Massachusetts legislature chartered a new school for Deaf students, the Clark School for the Deaf in Northampton. This school emphasized English only, via the oral method (now termed the monolingual approach). This event marked the birth of oralism or the oralist philosophy in America. This state legislative activity supported by Hearing-speaking progressive educators Horace Mann (1796–1859) and Samuel Gridely Howe (1801–1876) gave a new status to oral education, which resulted in a dramatic shift in instructional methodologies across American schools for the deaf (Nover, 2000).

The news of the Massachusetts legislature's actions to charter a new oral school shook up the deaf education establishment and moved them into a 'protective' mode of advocacy. From 1857, Edward Miner (E.M.) Gallaudet (1837–1917), eighth child of T.H. Gallaudet, was the Superintendent of the Columbia School for the Deaf. As a compromise, he responded to the oralists by recommending that articulation be introduced at the Columbia Institution and that an articulation (spoken language) component be added to the existing SL–WL MOI so that every deaf child had the opportunity to learn to speak and sign. This activity marked the birth of the Combined System, a term which he coined, to be implemented at the Columbia School for the Deaf in fall of 1868 with the approval of his board (Nover, 2000).

In 1864, President Abraham Lincoln (1809–1865) granted the Columbia Institution a charter to offer college degrees and installed E.M. Gallaudet, who became the first President of Gallaudet College (now Gallaudet University), which is still the only liberal arts university in the world for Deaf-signing students. Due to outside political pressures and attempting to compromise, while many aspects of the SL–WL framework were kept intact, E.M. Gallaudet significantly modified it by adding the Combined System approach, which included articulation and lipreading for hard-of-hearing and late-deafened students (Nover, 2000).

But still the debate, inaccurately labeled as manualism versus oralism, raged across the globe in schools for the deaf. Manualism denotes only one language, and in our view this is inaccurate, because the SL–WL approach utilizes two languages – a signed language and a written one, signaling a new kind of bilingualism, a term that would have to wait until contemporary times to emerge in deaf education.

International policies, for example as presented at the International Congress on Education of the Deaf of 1880 held in Milan propelled schools to abandon the SL–WL (with the Combined System utilized with some Deaf-signing students who benefited from articulation and lipreading instruction). For example, a resolution was reached at the 1880 Milan Congress to officially reject signed language in deaf education worldwide, thus rejecting Deaf-signing bilingual education programming. This policy was revoked in 2010, when the International Congress on Education of the Deaf (ICED) issued a public apology (Moores, 2011). Another calamitous circumstance occurred in 1926, when the Conference of Educational Administrators of Schools and Programs for the Deaf (CEASD) issued a policy banning signed language and hiring deaf teachers for the deaf (Nover, 2000). Both of these events considerably censured and woefully weakened Deaf-signing bilingual education for years to come.

Subsequently, from the 1890s onward, the SL–WL bilingual approach (with and without the Combined System) continued to be rejected, with the emphasis placed on the teaching of only speech. This doctrine shackled the hands of Deaf-signing children with its narrow and repressive methodology spreading throughout schools for the deaf.

The Deaf-signing community leaders rebelled. In 1886, for example, a public and vigorous debate ensued between E.M. Gallaudet and Alexander Graham Bell (1847–1922) in which they argued for each of the methods (Greenwald, 2016; Winefield, 1987). Bell's oralist ideas were undoubtedly influenced by his father-in-law, Gardiner Green Hubbard, the wealthy financier of the oral school in Massachusetts, and his deaf wife, Mabel, who supposedly abhorred signed language (see above). These debates (dubbed the oral versus manual controversy) were similar to debates held a century earlier with an exchange of letters between Samuel Heinicke (1727–1790) from Leipez, Germany, who advocated the 'German method', that is, using spoken language only for instruction, and Abbe Charles de l'Epee from Paris, France, who supported the 'French method', which included natural signs, methodical signs and finger spelling (see Garnett, 1968).

Still another instance of the rejection of the bilingual SL–WL methodology was when, in 1911, the Nebraska legislature passed a law requiring the Nebraska School for the Deaf (NSD) to adopt the oral-only methodology and to ban the use of signing in the classroom. This was a political decision without input from the Nebraska Deaf-signing community or from NSD faculty and administrators. In 1869, established by William DeCoursey French (n.d.), who was Deaf, the NSD had a long history of using signed language and written language for students and the Combined System for those Deaf-signing students who benefited from speech and lipreading. However, the new law required the NSD to use the 'oral, aural, and lipreading method' instead of the 'deaf alphabet and sign language' to educate its students (Fay, 1911, cited in Van Cleve, 1984: 195).

While oralism swirled around schools for the deaf during this era, this draconian law banned the use of signing at the NSD. Van Cleve (1984) provides a historical perspective on how this law came to be. One source was the 'intellectual ferment of

Enlightenment Europe when new theories of pedagogy abounded' (1984: 196) and where signing was deprecated in favor of oralism in deaf education. Another source was the financial support and political leverage of Alexander Graham Bell, husband of Mabel, a post-lingually deafened non-signer. Together, they led a movement that advocated for speech and lipreading over signing. A third source, and the most powerful, was two parents who had deaf children (A.N. Dafoe, n.d.) and E.J. Babcock (1913 and 1920). They organized other parent organizations, then led the bill in the legislature to the governor's signature (Van Cleve, 1984).

The Nebraska Deaf-signing community vehemently opposed the law. It disrupted the successful methods of instruction already used at the school: the Combined System for those students who benefited from articulation and lipreading, and the signed language and written language method (SL–WL) for those who cannot benefit from speech (Van Cleve, 1984). They also opposed the law because it would mean many Deaf-signing teachers would lose their positions, Deaf-signing children would be denied role models, and the traditions, culture and language of the Deaf-signing community would not be passed on (Van Cleve, 1984). Upon learning of this law, the National Association of the Deaf (NAD) and other associations began a letter-writing campaign to protest against the law, although it was eventually passed despite their efforts (Van Cleve, 1984). While Deaf-signing students used signed language during after-school activities, in church and among themselves and other Deaf-signing adults, it was banned in the classroom. Therefore, the law considerably weakened Deaf-signing SL–WL bilingual education. According to the legislators' beliefs, the law's purpose was that 'Nebraska's deaf people would be brought into the mainstream of American society' – assimilated – through their use of spoken English (Van Cleve, 1984: 195). This discriminatory and oppressive treatment was similar to the treatment of America's minorities being forced to assimilate (see Chapter 18).

The NSD joined the 40% of schools for the deaf in the United States at the time that taught only oralism; by 1918, the portion had risen to 80%. Instead of its intended assimilation, the detrimental law resulted in massive underachievement for generations of Deaf-signing students (see Babbidge, 1965, and other reports cited below). By 1970, the NSD had brought back signed language into its classrooms and in 1977 the Nebraska legislature repealed the law (see https://www.traillink.com/historic-places/nebraska-school-for-the-deaf/) (for an early oral history see Jones, 1918).

Despite these oralist mandates, the Combined System, which added spoken language to the curriculum but included a signed language, dominated deaf education throughout the early 1900s. So during this era, schools for the deaf began exploring ideas to use oral-only methods. The Combined System at least provided them with an avenue to keep signs in the schools. Schools began exploring how to allocate the signed language, spoken language and written language in the classroom (Nover, 2000).

Phase 3: Weakening of Deaf-Signing Bilingualism with Oralism (1930–1979)

Both oralism and in some ways the Combined System considerably weakened Deaf-signing bilingual education as spoken and written English became the dominant instructional methodology. At its worst, we see an elimination of signed language from the schools and the firing of Deaf teachers. Granted the Combined System was better than oralism alone, as it allowed some signing in the classroom. But it was typically operationalized by Hearing-speaking teachers who mixed signs with English grammar, which did not provide Deaf-signing students with accurate models of both grammars. Despite all the efforts of Hearing-speaking educators and administrators, still the natural signed language could not be totally removed or altered, because where there are Deaf-signing people, there are Deaf-signers. Deaf-signing children and youth and Deaf-signing adults continued to sign in the dormitories, on the playgrounds and during extracurricular activities. In the classroom, however, oralism (known now as monolingualism) became the dominant teaching methodology, and natural signed languages were rejected and replaced with spoken languages.

These events upset the Deaf-signing community and galvanized them into action. From the 1930s to the 1970s, the Deaf-signing community used their second language, English, and they began a writing campaign. They established the Deaf Press, known as the 'Little Paper Family', a network of school journals throughout the US led by Deaf-signing writers who argued vociferously for returning signed language to schools (Buchanan, 1993).

But still, oralism persisted.

However, time has a way of shifting public sentiments and as the 1950s to 1960s unfolded, it became clear that the oral methods were not succeeding. Numerous reports by blue-ribbon committees documented the tragic failure of deaf education to address students' communication, language and learning needs (see Babbidge, 1965; Commission on Education of the Deaf Report, 1988; Johnson *et al*., 1989). Moreover, an epidemic in the 1960s infected more Americans with rubella, a viral disease that can cause newborns to be born deaf if their mothers are infected during pregnancy. 'One of the worst epidemics swept the United States in 1963–1965, leaving in its wake many stillborn infants, spontaneous abortions, and 20,000 to 40,000 deaf infants' (Vernon & Andrews, 1990: 41). This epidemic galvanized the opening of many schools and programs to meet the needs of Deaf-signing children, many of whom were born deaf with additional disabilities such as blindness, cerebral palsy, intellectual, learning disabilities and mental health issues (Vernon & Andrews, 1990: 146–158). These events led educators to look for changes in delivery of instruction as the population of deaf children had different etiological backgrounds.

Confronted with these learning differences and all the challenges they brought to the classroom, educators explored changes to the oral-only communication and teaching methodologies. When signed language was recognized as a natural language in the 1960s, it was brought back into schools, not by using the natural signed language of the Deaf-signing community, but by implementing a philosophy called Total Communication (TC) (Holcomb, 2013). While its founder, Ray Holcomb, who was Deaf-signing teacher and administrator, included ASL in TC, when it was implemented in the classroom it was operationalized as Sign Supported Speech (SSS) or Simultaneous Communication (SC), where signs were simply put in English word order (Leigh *et al*., 2022a, 2022b). Moreover, Deaf-signing teachers were excluded from teaching in early childhood and primary grades and were relegated to teaching older Deaf-signing students or Deaf-signing students with additional disabilities.

Phase 4: Revival of Bilingualism (1980 to present)

From the 1980s to the 1990s, a revival of bilingual education occurred worldwide with a call to bring back to schools signed language and sign bilingual teaching methodologies. This movement began in progressive countries in Scandinavia (Mahshie, 1995), shifted into France (Bouvet, 1990) and even into China (Calloway, 2000), the United Kingdom (Pickersgill & Gregory, 1998) and the United States (Humphries, 2013; Humphries & Allen, 2008). In the last, for example, throughout the 1970s to 1990s, early proponents of the bilingual bicultural approach to Deaf education articulated their position. These include McCay Vernon, who wrote about the significant role of Deaf-signing teachers in the classroom (Vernon, 1970). An in 1972, in an unpublished paper titled 'An untried experiment: Bicultural and bilingual education of deaf children', William Stokoe wrote, 'The time has come to try the experiment suggested here: Let the deaf community itself plan and operate the program of education for deaf children' (see Maher, 1996: 127–128).

Other early proponents of bilingual-bicultural education include the following: Barbara Kannappel (1980), Tom Humphries (1977), James Woodward (1979, 1982), Robert E. Johnson, Scott Liddell, Carol Erting (Johnson et al., 1989), Marie Philip (Philip & Small, 1991) and Eric Drasgow (1993). These scholar-writers wrote a raft of journal articles that had a contemporary resonance with the historical bilingual education originally created by Clerc and his collaborators in the 19th century, as outlined above (Nover, 2000).

A progressive development in contemporary SL–WL bilingual development occurred in 1997 with Nover, who established a rigorous two-year preparation program for teachers and administrators. The aim was to examine the current research in regular Hearing-speaking bilingual education and literacy and see how this research and its practices could apply to the language learning and language teaching of Deaf-signing students. Subsequently, rooted in contemporary notions of bilingual–bicultural education, second language learning and literacy education, Nover led a federally funded Star Schools Project (later to become the Center for ASL and English Bilingual Education and Research or CAEBER). He and his collaborators established the only center in the United States devoted to supporting ASL and English Bilingual Professional Development (now termed AEBPD), which consisted of training for K-12 teachers/mentors and universities' teacher-education program instructors. After the success of its initial five-year project, with continued funding from 2002 to 2004 CAEBER developed online courses. Subsequently, in 2007, CAEBER moved to Gallaudet University to join the Gallaudet Leadership Institute (GLI), where it continued from 2007 to 2010 to host summer institutes preparing administrators and mentors with the theory and practice of ASL and English bilingualism. CAEBER also developed a teacher-preparation curriculum for universities (see Andrews, 2003; Andrews & Covell, 2006; Simms & Thumann, 2007; see also five Star reports – Nover & Andrews, 1998, 1999, 2000; Nover et al., 2001, 2002).

Into the 21st century, researchers and teachers in countries across Asia, Europe, Australia, Africa, South America and North America continue to document their own histories of teachers using signed and written/spoken languages to teach Deaf-signing children (see Christensen, 2017; Gerner de Garcia & Karnopp, 2016; Knoors et al., 2019; Tang et al., 2020).

Another form of scholarly advocacy surfaced on the academic front, where Deaf-signing writers and their Hearing-speaking allies flooded the journals with research summaries providing information for teachers, families, linguists and professionals on the importance of early signed language exposure to offset language deprivation and of support for bilingual instruction starting in early childhood forward (see Humphries et al., 2012, 2014a, 2014b, 2016a, 2016b, 2019, 2020, 2022, 2024).

It is important to reiterate that Deaf-signing bilingual deaf education is not a new concept but has existed since 1817 (Nover, 2000). What is new are novel research paradigms, terminology, use of technology and advocacy pursued in contemporary times that support Deaf-signing bilingual schooling. In the forefront are studies and developments in intelligence testing, visual learning and use of technology for newborn infant hearing screening and intervention during the 20th and 21st centuries, which we view as supporting Deaf-signing bilingual education programming. Therefore, in Part III, we provide a selective survey of contemporary supports and practices of Deaf-signing bilingual education. Interested readers are also encouraged to sample a robust and growing literature in the *American Annals of the Deaf*, the *Journal of Deaf Studies and Deaf Education*, *Deafness and Education International*, *Sign Language Studies* and the *Bilingual Research Journal*, among many others, to read about current developments in Deaf-signing bilingual education.

Part III: Contemporary Supports and Practices

In this final part of the chapter, we present a selection of studies that show support for the Deaf-signnng bilingual education approach in the current research on the numerous benefits of early exposure to a signed language, and the value of bilingualism and bilingual education for the young Deaf-signing child.

Neuroscience: The Benefits of Signed Language and Early Deaf-Signing Bilingualism

A generally accepted finding in neuroscience is that language, whether it comes in through the ears by way of spoken language or in through the eyes via a signed language, is acquired and processed using the same brain mechanisms. Much of this research has emerged from labs worldwide (e.g. Germany, Greece, the UK, Canada, Sweden, the US) among Deaf-signing communities utilizing different signed languages. Neuroscientists are exploring how the brain processes spoken and signed languages using brain imaging tools (e.g. fMRI, structural MRI, ERPs, fTCD).

A currently accepted finding is that both signed languages and spoken languages have significant procession similarities; for example, both are processed in the left hemisphere (Emmorey, 2021; Mayberry *et al.*, 2011; Payne *et al.*, 2019). However, recent neuroscience evidence points to some processing differences. For instance, studies reviewed by Caldwell (2022) show that signed language processing differs from that of spoken language in that it uses the right hemisphere for complex syntax comprehension, has context-dependent timing of expectancy effects on the brain's electrophysiological response to words, and involves earlier semantic and lexical access in comprehension and production. Emmorey (2021) also reviews aspects of language that are unique to signed languages, such as lexical iconicity, finger spelling, linguistic facial expressions, and depictive classifier constructions, referring to signs used to describe the size, shape, texture or pattern of a noun.

Of particular interest to Deaf-signing bilingual educators is the finding that all languages – spoken and signed – if the proper exposure is provided, can occur on the same timetable. This idea has led neuroscientists to explore questions about the

19th-century concept known as the critical period. Petitto *et al.* (2012) posited the 'perceptual wedge hypothesis', which suggests that exposure to more than one language between the ages of 6 and 12 months changes perceptual and neural processing, thus making the brain more receptive to both languages. She argues that exposure to multiple languages acts as a wedge and holds open the closing 'doors' of the baby's typical developmental perceptual processes. In other words, the baby's 'sensitive period' stays open longer to facilitate language acquisition in both languages. Therefore, it is recommended that caregivers provide their Deaf infants with access to a signed language as soon as possible to take advantage of this optimum perceptual window for language development in both spoken and signed languages.

More often than not, Deaf-signing children have delayed exposure to a signed language (see Nover vignette above). Using brain imaging tools, Mayberry *et al.* (2011) found that the dearth of language exposure in early life negatively affects language processing in the adult brain. Moreover, this can lead to language deprivation syndrome, a condition that results from a lack of language exposure during the critical period and early childhood, leading to health risks (Hall *et al.*, 2019; Humphries *et al.*, 2019; Meek, 2020). In contrast, the signed language processing of individuals born deaf and whose age at onset of language acquisition was in early life showed normal neural activation in the brain's classic language regions.

These and many more questions regarding signed languages and the brain are being studied in neuroscience labs at universities worldwide. An example is presented in Box 16.2 (see also the 'On the Web' resources given at the end of the chapter).

Box 16.2 Deaf signers, the brain and reading

The brain functions during reading for Deaf-signing people who are bilingual in English and American Sign Language are being researched using both fMRI and EEG/ERPs (Emmorey 2021; Emmorey *et al.*, 2016b). This research team from San Diego State University is investigating neural systems that support reading, finger spelling and signing in Deaf-signing individuals, asking questions such as:

- What is the neural-behavioral signature for highly skilled Deaf-signing readers?
- Does being Deaf impact the neural responses to visually presented words?
- Does finger spelling engage the Visual Word Form Area?
- How does knowledge of ASL impact word reading?

Intelligence, Visual Learning and Signed Language

Understanding the learning potential of Deaf-signing students provides support for the Deaf-signing bilingual programming approach. Into the mid-20th century, psychologists provided new insight about the learning potential of Deaf-signing people. Before the 1950s, grossly inappropriate IQ tests, many of which were verbal or based on knowledge of English, and behavioral checklists were unfairly given to Deaf-signing persons as well as Hearing-speaking language minority persons on Ellis Island (Andrews *et al.*, 2004). These tests were not valid measures of the cognitive functioning and abilities of Deaf-signing people. Subsequently, results were interpreted as caused by mental pathologies in Deaf-signing adults. Sometimes, this led to incarceration in mental asylums or criminal wards. For example, Junius Wilson (1908–2001) a Black Deaf-signing man in the Jim Crow South, spent 76 years in a state mental hospital in

Goldsboro, North Carolina, including six in the criminal ward, yet was never declared insane by medical authorities or found guilty of any criminal charges (Burch & Joyner, 2007). Many Deaf-signing children were misdiagnosed with 'mental retardation' (known now as cognitive disabilities). This resulted in their placement in classes for 'mentally retarded' children. However, from the 1960s onwards, psychologists realized that when appropriate tests of nonverbal intelligence were administered, then the scores of Deaf-signing people do not differ significantly from those of Hearing-speaking people (Vernon, 1968/2005). These outcomes demonstrated Deaf-signing individuals' potential for language and academic learning similar to Hearing-speaking persons, that is, if they are provided with language access.

Into the 21st century, cognitive scientists' research demonstrated the numerous benefits of using a signed language for learning. For example, compared with Hearing-speaking children, Deaf-signing children do better on tasks involving peripheral vision (Dye, 2016; Hirshorn, 2011), forming pictures in their mind (visual imagery), remembering pictures or objects in a room (visuospatial memory), remembering moving objects (Hamilton, 2011), quickly changing their visual attention, scanning visual material, detecting motion and recognizing faces (Dye & Bavelier, 2010). These enhanced visual learning skills can be harnessed for bilingual learning.

With increased access to newborn infant hearing screening and early identification worldwide, more Deaf children are being identified earlier. Traditionally, these children who are identified at birth or shortly afterward are advised to be raised orally without the introduction of a signed language. This 'zero tolerance' approach (monolingualism) to signing (Humphries *et al.*, 2024) has the risk of language deprivation, a condition that results from lack of linguistic stimuli to the brain that are necessary for language acquisition to occur, with mental health consequences in severe cases (Hall *et al.*, 2019). Deaf children with additional disabilities are now termed DeafPlus, DeafDisabled or neurodivergent; they are particularly at risk. These children have experienced language deprivation in both ASL and English and require special techniques of bilingual instruction (Singleton *et al.*, 2024).

Yet even though current research supports bilingualism and bilingual deaf education, obstacles and challenges remain. One such obstacle is related to types of school settings and use of speaking as the means of communication. The current architecture of school settings is built around concepts of 'inclusion', which, more often than not, fails to provide equal access to both languages for Deaf-signing students. In other words, speaking and hearing are used as the medium of instruction.

School Settings: Two Different Media of Instruction (SL–WL and Sp–WL)

A school setting with a critical mass of Deaf-signing students is necessary for bilingual programming for Deaf-signing students – either large day programs or at boarding schools. Here, Deaf-signing students have language models from other Deaf-signing adults as administrators, teachers, aids, coaches and dormitory parents and from same-age and cross-age peers. Unfortunately, most Deaf-signing students are channeled into the special education system in programs that focus primarily on access to spoken language (monolingualism). Placements can be differentiated on their level of integration with Hearing-speaking students, ranging from full-inclusion settings with or without support (e.g. sign language interpreters) to mainstreaming programs, resource rooms, self-contained classes, special schools (day and residential), charter and home schools (Leigh et al., 2022a, 2022b). In Hong Kong, Spain, the Netherlands and the United States, bilingual co-enrollment programs have classrooms with a critical mass of Deaf-signing students learning alongside Hearing-speaking peers (Marschark & Lee, 2014). However, due to inclusion policies in deaf education in most countries, the majority of Deaf-signing children are educated in inclusive or mainstream settings, for example, in the United Kingdom, 80% of Deaf-signing children spend at least part of the school day in regular schools, as do about 88% in the United States (Tang et al., 2020). These kinds of settings may isolate Deaf-signing students and more often than not do not provide full exposure and a high quality and quantity of language access to a signed language, which is vital for bilingual development to unfold.

Bilingual language access is ranked from full to least in special schools (residential or day), co-enrollment programs (which follow bilingual bicultural programming), mainstream (public school) with support, and full inclusion, including public schools with no support (Gárate-Estes et al., 2022: 231) (see Box 16.3).

Box 16.3 School programs for Deaf students

- **Bilingual/bicultural programs** provide access to two or more languages using a signed and written/spoken language, both equally valued. These bilingual programs can also incorporate lessons using spoken language and signed language techniques, typically called bilingual bimodal programs.

- **Comprehensive programs** provide visual support. They range from a signed language and a written language to a spoken/written language; however, the signed language component is not treated with equal status but is considered as a 'bridge' to English, the dominant language of instruction. These programs utilize Total Communication (TC), Simultaneous Communication (SC) or Signed Supported Speech (SSS).

- **Monolingual programs**, also known as oral/aural or the listening and spoken language method, do not use a signed language.

In some special schools or large day programs, bilingual–bicultural programs provide the full use of signed languages. School settings, called comprehensive programs, provide some sign support via a signing teacher or signed language interpreter and can be found in some special schools but mainly in public schools with self-contained classrooms or in mainstreaming or full-inclusion settings. While signed language interpreters can be an effective accommodation for some Deaf-signing students, it is not for those who are language-deprived, such as those entering school without a full language system, either with a signed or spoken language (Caselli et al., 2020; Meek, 2020). There are also school programs with no sign support, for example with the oral/aural (monolingual) approach (Leigh et al., 2022a, 2022b). Each setting differs in dimensions of language planning (Nover, 1995; Regan, 2022), language allocation (Jacobson, 1995) and teacher training (Humphries & Allen, 2008).

The bilingual–bicultural approach (known as ASL/English bilingual approach in the US and signed bilingualism internationally) follows the tenets of **additive bilingualism** resembling a **developmental maintenance** model (see Chapter 4). Its goal is to strengthen the Deaf-signing child's linguistic and cultural identity by developing a signed and a written language, with the two having equal status. There are strong bilingual programs (see Chapter 10) where all teachers, administrators and dorm staff undergo a two-year professional development program (Nover et al., 2002). Signed language skills are also evaluated. These are also weak bilingual programs (see

Chapter 10) where teachers have not received professional development and schools do not require teacher proficiency in a signed language.

Bilingual–bicultural programs are found in special schools, most of which are boarding schools. Atlanta School for the Deaf is an example of a day school which has a developmental bilingual program. Special schools provide comprehensive programming with a plethora of academic, social, athletics, dormitory and after-school activities. They also provide the maximum access to a signed language and a written language, 'round the clock, 24/7'. Here Deaf-signing teachers are employed who function as cultural and language role models (O'Brien & Placier, 2015). The National Association of the Deaf supports schools for the deaf as providing the 'least restrictive environment' for many Deaf-signing children because of its full language and communication access.

Another type of educational programming – comprehensive programs (mainstreaming, inclusion) – supports the development of written/spoken language. These programs resemble the transitional bilingual model, where the aim is to achieve fluency in the majority language without regard for developing the minority language and ultimately with students being mainstreamed into classes with Hearing-speaking students (Gárate, 2014). These approaches can use a Total Communication (TC) philosophy, a Simultaneous Communication (SC) also known as Sign-Supported Speech (SSS).

As mentioned above, TC came about in the 1970s, when Roy Holcomb, a school administrator who was Deaf, developed the TC philosophy, which encourages the teachers to use *all* forms of communication modalities, including ASL, speech, gestures, amplification and finger spelling with Deaf-signing students, depending on the needs of the children (Holcomb, 2013). When implemented, TC has shifted to what has become Simultaneous Communication (SC) or Sign Supported Speech (SSS) (Lane *et al.*, 1996). But even within mainstream programs (and sometimes special schools that use TC/SC), teachers still utilize bilingual strategies such as linking meaning with ASL signs, words and finger spelling (Andrews & Rusher, 2010). Many school programs are not limited to these three approaches but offer multilingual programming for Deaf-signing multilingual students (Christensen, 2017; Gárate-Estes *et al.*, 2022).

> **Box 16.4** What does a Deaf ESL classroom look like?
>
> In one school in the southwest United States, Deaf multilingual Latinx students spend the school day with on-grade Deaf peers. However, once a day they go to a Deaf ESL (English as a second language) class. Different from a typical ESL class, it focuses on English with resources such as having a teacher fluent in Spanish, ASL, English and Lengua de Senas Mexicana (LSM, or Mexican Sign Language). The goal is to support students' transition into regular deaf education classes (Gárate-Estes *et al.*, 2022).

To promote the revival of deaf bilingual education, there are frameworks that provide support for teachers and administrators that have been promoted in the literature, such as the Nover *et al.* (1998) framework.

Framework for Deaf Bilingual Education

During the the late 1990s and into the 2000s, a Deaf-signing bilingual framework (SL–WL) originally developed by Nover *et al.*, (1998) became widely used in the training of teachers with different signed and written languages in the United States,

Mexico, Venezuela, Argentina, Thailand, Japan, Taiwan, Morocco, Brazil, the Gaza Strip, Jordan and Brazil (Andrews, 2017). This framework emphasizes visual language and visual learning, includes Deaf-signing epistemologies (Cue *et al.*, 2019; Holcomb, 2010), notions of dynamic bilingualism, translanguaging (Gárate-Estes *et al.*, 2022) and sign-mediated strategies (Gárate, 2014; Nussbaum *et al.*, 2012; Wolsely *et al.*, 2018). This language planning framework can be used by teachers across countries with diverse scripts as a handy reference point to conceptualize Deaf-signing bilingual students' language resources. Nover *et al.* (1998) coined the term *signacy* (a signed language) and utilized the more familiar terms of *oracy* (a spoken language) and *literacy* (reading and writing). While the guide displays bilingual abilities as these three silos – signacy, literacy and oracy – when operationalized, Deaf-signing students' languages converge in dynamic ways (García & Cole, 2014). For example, the visually oriented Deaf-signing bilingual child uses signacy, finger spelling and literacy often and interchangeably depending on conversation or lesson. Those with more auditory access may integrate oracy into their literacy communication through codeblending, codeswitching (Gárate, 2011; Nussbaum *et al.*, 2012) and codemixing (Swanwick *et al.*, 2016).

The term **signacy** refers to the student's ability to attend to (i.e. watch/view) and understand as well as produce face-to-face messages (live conversations) and recorded signed messages (film). It also includes creating academic signed videos (face-to-face and recorded) and viewing and analyzing signed videos. It can also include the use of ASL signacy and ASL literature. ASL signacy refers to the ability to understand the linguistic structure of ASL by watching/viewing, comprehending and analyzing signs. It also entails organizing, and communicating information, ideas and thoughts effectively and eloquently in a variety of contexts. ASL literature can include poetry, drama and prose (e.g. narratives, folklore, science fiction, humor, allegories, riddles), some of which has been preserved on film, video-tape and digital media. For emerging Deaf-signing bilinguals, sign handshape lessons, stories, and rhymes can be used to build sign-print vocabularies as reported in the US (Andrews & Baker, 2019; Gietz *et al.*, 2020; Holcomb, 2023) and in Taiwan as well (Lin & Ku, 2020).

Literacy has been traditionally defined as restricted to the reading and writing of print. UNESCO (2024) redefines literacy as 'a means of identification, understanding, interpretation, creation, and communication in an increasingly digital, text-mediated, information-rich and fast-changing world'. A connecting idea came from the New London Group (1996), who proposed use of the term *multiliteracies* to reflect the different forms of literacy and communication in different contexts. Today, we have diverse forms of multiliteracy and multimodal approaches, such as multilingual e-books with different signed, spoken and written languages, picture books with sign graphic illustrations, AI, signing avatars, social media with smartphones and smart tablets, internet-based and creative TikTok video-sharing, drones and robotics, among others. From the late 1990s to the present, scholars worldwide have been writing about the benefits of multilingual, multimodal texts that incorporate multimedia with print and sign languages (see Andrews & Jordan, 1998; Cao *et al.*, 2024; Herzig & Allen, 2023; Herzig & Malzkuhn, 2015; Mirus & Napoli, 2018; Zheng, 2023). As a result, bilingual Deaf-signing adults and students are supported in their literacy learning with various bi/multilingual and multimodal texts.

The framework also utilizes the finger alphabet or commonly known as finger spelling. Clerc used the finger alphabet as a student and teacher in France and brought it to America with his SL–WL methodologies. Historically, the Spanish finger alphabet was used by Ponce de Leon (1520–1584), was later published by Juan Pablo Bonet (1573–1633) in *Reducción de las letras y arte para enseñar a hablar a los mudos* (Simplification of the Letters of the Alphabet and Method of Teaching Deaf-Mutes to Speak) and used in the early French schools for the deaf.

Current researchers have repeatedly documented its efficacy for early communication and literacy (Allen, 2015; Baker, 2010b; Hile, 2009; Lederberg *et al.*, 2019). Research on Deaf-signing mothers shows that it is used very early in the home for communication and to introduce emergent English literacy, highly valued in the Deaf-signing community (MacGlaughlin, 2018). Although not extensively researched, finger spelling is widely used in countries that use either alphabetic or non-alphabetic scripts. Wang and Andrews (2020) give examples of Chinese, Japanese, Korean, Arabic and Latin scripts and their finger alphabet counterparts.

Oracy skills refer to developing speaking and listening skills in a natural context (Nussbaum *et al.*, 2012). Deaf-signing bilingual children's access to auditory language with or without auditory technology is highly variable, depending on many factors (Harris *et al.*, 2017). For some Deaf-signing students, oracy skills may consist of some conversational skills. For others, however, it may include speech-reading and the recognition of environmental sound (Gárate-Estes *et al.*, 2022). As mentioned above, it is our belief that signacy and literacy should be taught first; oracy skills can follow, so that signing and writing can provide a foundation upon which to build oracy skills.

Deaf Bilingual Theories, Methodologies and Strategies

Recent understandings of bilingualism and bilingual education theory have shifted from attention to the additive nature and separation of an L1 (first language) and a L2 (second language) (see Chapter 8). Instead, it focuses on the students' cognitive, social, cultural and social resources, which comprise 'a unitary linguistic repertoire' (García & Cole, 2014). In our case, we see Deaf-signing families integrating signing, finger spelling and writing in their daily communication. Thus, the distinction between the stages of the development of an L1 and L2 is not as clear-cut for them (Humphries, 2016).

From regular bilingual education, García's (2009a) concept of **dynamic bilingualism** has been applied to Deaf-signing students using a 'Deaf lens'. Put somewhat differently, Deaf-signing bilingual learners' unitary linguistic repertoire includes signing, gesturing, mouthing, finger spelling, reading, writing and sometimes speaking, among the other cognitive, linguistic, metacognitive, metalinguistic and social skills (García & Cole, 2014). Central to García and Cole's notion of dynamic bilingualism with Deaf-signing bi/multilinguals is the pedagogical practice of translanguaging with sign-mediated strategies.

Translanguaging and Sign-Mediated Strategies within a Deaf Sign/Bi/Multilingual Framework

As noted throughout this chapter, the Deaf-signing community uses bi/multilingual and multimodal communication strategies when interacting with other Deaf-signing and Hearing-speaking persons (García & Cole, 2014). Using their whole body while signing, they express meanings, ideas and feelings by combining their signed languages, facial expressions, head tilts, eye gazes, eyebrow raises, body shifts and movement, mouthing, finger spelling, reading, writing, visual images and sometimes speaking (Chevrels *et al.*, 2021; Kusters, 2019; Nover *et al.*, 1998; Sandler, 2018, 2022).

In regular bilingual theory and practice, sociolinguists and educators use the term **translanguaging** when discussing bilingual multimodal practices. By way of history, Zhang (2022) notes that the term translanguaging was coined by Colin Baker by placing the 'trans' prefix before the term 'languaging' when he was introduced to the work of Cen Williams (2000), leader of Welsh language revitalization programs (see Chapter 13). Subsequently, the notion of translanguaging has developed as a sociolinguistic theory (Otheguy *et al.*, 2015) and an innovative teaching practice (Canagarajah, 2022).

Translanguaging concepts have extended our understanding of language learners to have an underlying 'unitary linguistic repertoire' rather than simply knowledge of individual languages with distinct boundaries (García, 2009a). Conteh (2018) noted that translanguaging echoes Cummins's (2000a) notion of 'common underlying proficiency' (CUP) and the linguistic interdependence model, underscoring the importance of meaning transfer during language learning. As related to our chapter, this meaning transfer can occur with a signed language such as ASL and the learning of English (Cummins, 2006).

Recently, capturing the interest translanguaging has created within regular bi/multilingual education, educators in deaf education have characterized it as an 'asset-oriented perspective' that validates the linguistic resources Deaf-signing students bring to the classroom, as it encourages the use of all their linguistic resources to increase their communication and language learning (Wolbers *et al.*, 2023: 1). We believe translanguaging is essentially part of Deaf epistemologies used by Deaf-signing people since Clerc's time. It is how Deaf-signing peoples have always communicated with each other and the Hearing-speaking world, not always sensitive to their signed languages and Deaf culture. So, of course, it belongs back in the classroom, as it has always been in Deaf-signing classrooms since 19th-century America.

Multiple examples of translanguaging are found in deaf sign bi/multilingual education classrooms worldwide. For example, McLeister (2019) documents translanguaging in Mainland China, where teachers provide instruction using a combination of Chinese Sign Language (CSL), other sign dialects, sign idiolects and signed Chinese. In Europe, with the influx of immigration in Sweden and the United Kingdom, teachers use translanguaging to leverage newly arrived Deaf students' diverse levels of home languages (e.g. spoken and signed), including English and local spoken languages (Chen Pichler *et al.*, 2019).

In northern Europe, Holmström and Schönström (2018) examined the use of different languages and modalities by three Deaf-signing lecturers who integrated Swedish Sign Language (SSL), English, Swedish mouthing, finger spelling of English and Swedish sign words, and printed English and Swedish texts within a single lecture. In the United States, Hoffman *et al.* (2017) report on five Deaf-signing balanced bilingual adults who used translanguaging to read English texts using their background knowledge, prior experiences, knowledge and experiences with Deaf culture, metacognitive and metalinguistic skills, linguistic knowledge of ASL and English as well as their reading comprehension skills. With younger Deaf-signing learners, Wolsey *et al.* (2018) document how teachers used translanguaging techniques to develop both ASL and English skills using a shared reading instructional approach. Gárate-Estes *et al.* (2022) applied the translanguaging methodology to multilingual Latinx Deaf-signing students who brought their LSM (Mexican Sign Language), Spanish, ASL, English, gestures, home signs to the classroom as well as their Latinx Deaf and Hearing cultures.

Translanguaging also supports the teaching of writing (Nicolarakis & Mitchell, 2023; Wolbers *et al.*, 2023), including learning to write multiple scripts (Wang *et al.*, 2016) and academic learning in the content areas (Scott & Cohen, 2023). With the increase in the numbers of immigrant Deaf signing students (see cases of Rosalina, Maria and Jay presented above) and the increase in Deaf sign multilingualism, there is a need to expand the theory and practice of translanguaging as a pedagogical tool that incorporates both bi/multilingualism and multimodalities, thus providing a more global inclusive view (see Kusters *et al.*, 2024).

Box 16.5 Is translanguaging the same as total communication?

No.

Translanguaging is a theory and a teaching methodology. As a methodology, it involves signing, facial expressions, body tilts, eye gazes, gesturing, body shifts, body language and movement, finger spelling, reading and writing, background knowledge, cultural knowledge, family experiences and personal experiences, as well as metacognitive, metalinguistic and linguistic abilities in all the individual's languages. It can, but does not always, include a spoken language, particularly with those Deaf signing students with auditory access.

Total communication is a teaching philosophy consisting of all communication approaches, including the natural signed languages of Deaf people, body language, gestures, reading and writing and use of auditory technologies depending on the students' language learning needs (Holcomb, 2013). Total communication in practice has shifted to the use of Simultaneous Communication (SimCom) or the use of speaking and signing while using the grammar of English.

Box 16.6 Is translanguaging the same as codeswitching?

No.

Translanguaging is different from codeswitching. Translanguaging refers to a unitary or 'holistic' collection of language features that bilinguals will use. Bilinguals, then, will select features of this collection of features from their multiple languages and multimodalities to communicate or to use as a teaching strategy with students. So, bilinguals are not viewed as 'switching' grammars from one to the other but are using their full linguistic repertoire to communicate in a meaningful way (Otheguy *et al.*, 2015).

Sign-mediated strategies are explicitly planned and utilized within the translanguaging methodology to make meaningful connections between the two languages. Many of these strategies are part of Deaf-signing epistemologies as they mirror indigenous practices of Deaf-signing people who use them daily (Humphries, 2004, 2013). Some of these are described here. Readers can search online (e.g. on Google and YouTube) for examples provided by teachers.

Deaf-signing people also use technologies for communication (i.e. social media) and as visual tools if they are teachers. Recent developments in smart-internet based applications, e-learning platforms, TikTok video-sharing, signing avatars, drones and robotics allow teachers not only to increase access to the languages of their students but also to create innovative and fun materials for students to enjoy and learn from (Kose & Uluer, 2020). There are platforms such as Moodle, Edmodo, Canvas and Blackboard to share and receive written and video-based content. Video-based applications, including iMovie, Glide and Marco Polo, allow teachers and students to video messages or summaries of lessons to share information so that students can

> **Box 16.7** Sign-mediated strategies used in the bilingual bicultural classroom
>
> - **Facial expressions, touch, eye contact**. Deaf mothers use these actions to communicate with Deaf babies (Blumenthal-Kelly, 1995).
> - **Eye-gaze strategies**. Caregivers and teachers use eye gazes to regulate Deaf children's attention and turn-taking (Brooks *et al.*, 2020).
> - **Translation** of a printed text using ASL, either literally, following the exact ideas, or free translation, providing an expanded translation filling in ideas and concepts (Livingston, 1997).
> - **Spelling**. The teacher finger spells a word, then the child writes the word using letters on paper or types on an e-tablet (Humphries, 2013).
> - **Manual/tactile rhyming**. The child finger spells letters in sequence to provide a tactile pattern to remember ABCs (Wolsey *et al.*, 2018).
> - **ASL expansion** where the teacher uses one or more signs to explain the meaning of a sign or word.
> - **Chaining** is a codeswitching strategy that links signs, finger spelling, facial expressions, writing, pictures and gestures (Bailes, 2002; Humphries & MacDougall, 1999).
> - **Sandwiching**. This is similar to chaining; however, it purposefully sequences equivalent meaning concepts by making a 'sandwich' (sign–word–sign; or sign–finger spelling–sign).
> - **Chunking/bridging** is when the teacher identifies words or groups of words that represent one unit of meaning or one sign in ASL. Then, the teacher discusses an appropriate translation. This strategy is useful in the teaching of figurative language and idioms in texts (Ausbrooks-Rusher *et al.*, 2012).
> - **Preview–view–review** (PVR) is an overview of a lesson that is presented in the students' dominant language (preview). The lesson is conducted in the students' other language (view), followed by a summary of lesson highlights, discussions and question-and-answer sessions conducted in the dominant language (review). This strategy helps provide comprehensible input in the students' dominant language. Applied to Deaf-signing students, the teacher provides a summary of the lesson in ASL, has the students read the text silently, then follows up with a summary of key points, discussions and questions and answers using both of the languages (Andrews *et al.*, 1994; Li, 2005).
> - **Reading aloud** gives children opportunities to enjoy stories, books, videos and multimedia presented in different languages and multimodalities (Gietz *et al.*, 2020; Herzig & Allen, 2023; Wolsey *et al.*, 2018).
> - **Purposeful concurrent usage** is when a teacher uses multiple signed and spoken modalities to support the development of ASL and English (Andrews *et al.*, 2016).

access, view, save and review content through their most accessible language. Social media through texting and videoconferences, social, e-books, signing avatars, closed captioning and other forms of technology can be used by teachers to create classroom activities that demonstrate the two languages. Dual language apps with ASL/English programs combined with touch-screen hardware, for example, allow students to tap on printed words to get an instant signed language translation.

In deaf education classrooms worldwide during the 2020 Covid-19 pandemic, teachers faced the challenges of setting up distance or remote learning sites due to social distancing. This accelerated the development of innovative technology tools to provide ASL and English bilingual access and support. Schools, then, established distance learning, distributed technology to students and teachers, prepared online modules, furnished captioning for movies and videos, recorded asynchronous and synchronous signed language video lectures and study materials, provided signed translations of written literature and textbook entries, and opened opportunities for interacting with students and families through instant and/or delayed signed language messaging and/or written text messaging and chat boxes (Aljedaani *et al.*, 2023; Fransciso *et al.*, 2024). To manage these tools, US schools with Deaf-signing students have adopted learning management systems (LMSs) such as Schoology, PowerSchool and Canvas to create and deliver instruction, to assess and to provide interaction with students and families through blended and remote conferencing and learning.

The CORDIS–EU research consortium reports on emerging technologies that are enhancing the development of SL–WL displays through the use of artificial intelligence (AI), machine learning (ML) and augmented reality – all of which are improving how Deaf-signing people communicate and learn. Researchers are using these innovative technologies to develop new algorithms and techniques to enable real-time translation of signed-language videos to text or speech or signed-language avatars who generate speech to text in augmented reality environments. These translations are available through mobile devices such as smartphones and tablets and can be used for communication, particularly for intelligent relay services during emergency services, as well as for classroom instruction. These technologies can foster a more inclusive society and linguistic equity by recognizing and utilizing both languages of Deaf-signing peoples – that is, their signed languages and written languages. These tools continue to evolve and improve, thereby expanding opportunities for teachers and students to communicate and learn together (CORDIS–EU, 2024) and have the potential to impact student achievement outcomes through increased accessible exposure to both languages.

Outcomes

Being held accountable for students' academic achievement as expressed through standardized test scores is a pressure that all educators face, including those in Deaf-igning bilingual programming. Therefore, evaluating the efficacy of bilingual–bicultural education programs based on standardized test scores normed on Speaking-hearing populations is fraught with challenges. Moreover, outside political forces present their own challenges, some of which we highlight here.

In the United States, federal laws and state policies dictate where children are educated, leaving school choice in the margins. For example, well intended, but often unfair, accountability initiatives such as teacher certification tests are administered solely in English. Consequently, these tests are barriers to Deaf-signing candidates who are fluent ASL signers but have difficulty with English-based teacher certification tests. Hearing-speaking teacher candidates, on the other hand, with limited signed language proficiency can easily pass the tests and become teachers because of their English language competency (Simms *et al.*, 2008). Given that teachers' signed language fluency has a considerable impact on Deaf-signing students' achievement, these aspects cannot be ignored when evaluating the efficacy of a particular educational program.

Another challenge in conducting valid evaluation research is controlling the background variables of participants and teachers. For example, Marschark (2011, as cited in Knoors & Marschark, 2012) compared standardized reading achievement scores from a deaf school that used SC and SSS to those scores of a group of deaf schools that utilized the ASL/English bilingual approach (Nover *et al.*, 2002). Deaf students in Marschark's study were 5 to 40 points above the national medians across the same age range and in the same years and also scored at or above the children in the Nover *et al.* study at all ages except one year old. However, the Marschark study neglected to report the background variables of the Deaf-signing children (e.g. how ethnicities, family poverty rates, years enrolled in school, or years using a signed language differed among participants within the schools) nor did they clearly describe how the SC/SSS teaching methodology was implemented. Andrews and Rusher (2010) reported that many TC/SC programs that do not have a bilingual programming policy per se still use sign-to-print mediated strategies, as found in ASL/English bilingual programs. This indicates that researchers should include experts on their team who understand the fundamentals of school language planning. Moreover, they must report more than just standardized test scores but control other student background language learning variables as well as teacher background variables to ensure fidelity in evaluating Deaf-signing education programming.

A contemporary trend we have observed is the dramatic increase in the number of Deaf-signing scholars who could be easily included on language and educational research teams as they are not only professionally trained in research methodologies but are 'Indigenous insiders' who have grown up in educational programs for Deaf-signing students. Such inclusion can counteract the often well intended actions of Hearing-speaking researchers who may nevertheless bring oppressive values and beliefs and function as external outsiders. Banks (1989: 8) eloquently writes, 'The external outsider is criticized by members of the studied community but is often praised and highly rewarded by the outside community, which is more powerful and influential than the studied community'. The inclusion of Deaf-signing researchers captures the authentic voice of Deaf-signing people.

Much of the international research on Deaf-signing bilingual programming has focused on relationships between signing fluency and reading (see reviews in Simms & Andrews, 2020). Others have focused on psychosocial development and language development in co-enrollment programs (see Marschark *et al.*, 2014). Marschark and Lee (2014) have noted that many studies have neglected to address the Deaf cultural awareness component, a vital part of bilingual–bicultural programming (see Box 16.8).

Box 16.8 Deaf cultural/multicultural awareness

Signed language, Deaf culture/Deaf multicultural awareness can be integrated in the school curriculum. Deaf Studies can also be taught as a separate course where students learn about Deaf history, art, performing arts and literature. Visiting Deaf schools with their museums, attending Deaf art festivals, sports events and Deaf expos provide additional opportunities (Leigh *et al.*, 2022a, 2022b).

Still others have examined academic achievement on standardized tests designed for Hearing-speaking monolingual students, linking the positive impact of signed language to learning language and literacy (Hrastinski & Wilbur, 2016; Scott, 2021; Scott & Hoffmeister, 2016; Scott *et al.*, 2022). Others have examined the effects of early signed language on measures of emergent literacy (Allen, 2015; Allen *et al.*, 2014). A recent development is incorporating signed language assessments into language evaluations to get a more comprehensive picture of signed language components of Deaf-signing students' bilingualism language functioning (Clark *et al.*, 2020, 2023).

Achievement and Assessment

Evidence for bilingual academic achievement among Deaf-signing high school students can be found in the Academic Bowl Program at Gallaudet University. Established in 1997, teams from US schools for the deaf compete in regional competitions with 20 teams, advancing to the national competition held at Gallaudet to answer challenging questions in various categories: mathematics, science, social studies, current events, literature, popular culture and Deaf culture. Video-clips of the 2024 competition (https://www.youtube.com/watch?v=h9GCo-caIvI) provide a holistic perspective on how Deaf-signing bilingual youth use their cognitive and language skills, including visual attention, memory, executive functioning (e.g. planning and goal setting), thinking before answering, self-correction, critical and analytic skills (metacognition) and 'theory of mind' (e.g. understanding the perspective of the other team and the announcer). Moreover, the youths show speed in the recall of facts, math calculations, problem-solving skills, collaborative learning and motivation (Leigh *et al.*, 2022a, 2022b). While such evidence provides intriguing findings on Deaf-signing students using their academic skills, more rigorous research studies are needed (Marschark *et al.*, 2014).

Within school systems, Deaf-signing bilinguals are typically assessed in only the majority spoken/written languages. Their scores are then compared with those of Hearing-speaking monolingual students. These types of measures, including those that are standardized and norm-referenced on Hearing-speaking populations, indicate that Deaf students score lower than Hearing-speaking students on measures of academic achievement, including literacy and mathematics (Qi & Mitchell, 2012). This finding is consistent in deaf education programs around the globe (see e.g. Knoors *et al.*, 2019). This test inequity is seldom discussed in educational settings or in the research literature as it is commonly assumed that Deaf-signing students must achieve the same standards in academic achievement and on the same grade level as Hearing-speaking monolingual students. It is important to recognize that Deaf-signing students do not have the same daily **accessible** exposure to English as Hearing-speaking students do, thus their academic learning may be a steeper hill to climb.

One practical reason for the lack of signed language assessments in schools is the fact that there are so few of them. Rosen (2020) aptly points out that compared with spoken language and written language assessments, commercially available signed language assessments are scarce because many signed languages used worldwide have not been fully described in terms of their structure and acquisition patterns. Consequently, educators must resort to more naturalistic measures of observations, rating scales and portfolio assessments. Issues of test validity and reliability come into play as well for both constructed signed language tests and informal measures used by teachers. Haug *et al.* (2020) provide a comprehensive review of signed language tests for children and youth learning a signed language as an L1 across many countries.

Even today, with newborn infant screening and hearing technology and bilingual programs, still many Deaf-signing children arrive at school with severe language delays in both spoken and signed language (Hall *et al.*, 2019). However, there is a tool to evaluate these early sign skills. The Visual Communication and Sign Language Checklist (VSLC) is the only standardized measure of ASL acquisition for young children in the United States for use by teachers, early interventionists and Deaf-signing mentors who work with signing children from birth through five years old (Simms *et al.*, 2013).

Assessments that measure the learning of signed language as a second language (L2) for Hearing-speaking children and adults are needed due to the growing interest in public schools and universities and for the training of signed language interpreters and other Hearing-speaking professionals working with Deaf-signing people. Existing evaluation approaches range from informal observations to more formal evaluations (receptive and expressive) found in the United States, the Netherlands and Germany (Smith *et al.*, 2020).

Given multilingual and multicultural Deaf-signing students and their unique cultures, languages and learning needs, the assessment task may at first appear overwhelming. Pizzo and Chilvers (2016) provide guidelines, resources and recommendations. They suggest that all of the student's languages (both signed and spoken languages) be systematically assessed. Multiple data sources are also recommended to rule out issues of culture, language and socioeconomic status. They also recommend teacher preparation programs include assessment protocols for this population and establish psychometric properties of the assessments.

A final consideration in testing relates to how to assess how Deaf-signing multilingual learners use all of their languages rather than testing them on each individual language. For this, sociolinguistic descriptions, language histories, portfolio assessments and qualitative assessment procedures may be more helpful for teachers to get a true indication of how Deaf-signing students are using both languages (or multiple languages) (Cannon & Guardino, 2022; Musyoka, 2022).

Teacher Preparation

In a few universities, there has been a shift from traditional deaf education approaches to the bilingual–bicultural approach (Andrews & Covell, 2006; Humphries, 2013; Musyoka, 2022; Simms & Thumann, 2007). Still, as Gárate-Estes *et al*. (2022) report, only 9 out of 58 programs in the United States specifically prepare teachers to work in bilingual education settings.

Traditional programs in teacher training are housed in departments of special education and focus on pathological models, deficit pedagogies and social integration. In contrast, the curriculum in bilingual teacher-preparation programs focuses on Deaf 'wellness models'. Teachers in training take courses in Deaf studies, Deaf epistemologies, the linguistics of ASL and English, and bilingual theories, methodologies and strategies. While traditional programs may teach one or two courses in ASL or signed systems, it is taught to support Deaf-signing children's learning of English rather than a language in itself to be developed. Language and literacy curricula in traditional programs are based on phonological approaches rather than on visually based alternative literacy frameworks (Andrews *et al*., 2016; Francisco *et al*., 2024; for an international perspective, see Wang & Andrews, 2020).

We cannot overemphasize the important role that Deaf-signing teachers and Deaf-signing researchers play in outcomes in bilingual educational programming. Historically, Deaf-signing teachers have faced multiple barriers in getting degrees and certifications to teach Deaf-signing children (Andrews, 1992, 2003; Andrews & Covell, 2006; Andrews & Franklin, 1997; Andrews *et al*., 2015; Vernon, 1970). As Vernon (1970: 18) cogently points out, 'Deaf teachers can usually understand what the child is signing and can help him develop the language he needs to express it understandably in writing'. Thus, it is not a matter of how much English Deaf-signing teachers know but how skilled they are in translating the gestures of the Deaf-signing child into writing. Deaf-signing teachers of color face even more barriers. Simms *et al*. (2008) note these Deaf-signing teachers from diverse ethnic/racial backgrounds are under-represented in the field and often get 'caught in the bottleneck of opportunity' due to poverty, lack of early language access, poor K-12 preparation and difficulties in entering universities and passing state certification tests. Consequently, few become certified to work in classrooms with more than 40% of students from ethnic minority backgrounds (Simms *et al*., 2008).

Even when Deaf-signing teachers earn advanced degrees and teach at the college level, they face discrimination and lack of access to interpreters for faculty meetings (Smith & Andrews, 2015). Historically, Deaf-signing professionals at all levels of education have been discriminated against and barred from participating in the education of Deaf-signing children, particularly teachers of color and Deaf-signing teachers of color, who face both racism and audism (Simms *et al.*, 2008). Audism, a term coined by Humphries (1977), refers to prejudice and discrimination against Deaf-Signing people and favoring the sensory avenue of hearing-speaking over signing. It even took more than a century for Gallaudet University to appoint its first Deaf President (Christiansen & Barnartt, 1995). Today, Roberta Cordano is Gallaudet's first female Deaf-signing President.

As introduced above, Nover and his colleagues through the CAEBER institute provided bilingual education programming in-service teacher training for more than 500 teachers, staff and administrators. Deaf-signing school faculty enrolled in a two-year program and followed a curriculum focused on ASL and English bilingual theories and practices for Deaf children in K-12 deaf school and mainstream programs (Gárate, 2012; Nover *et al.*, 2002). An outgrowth of this training led to the establishment of bilingual teacher-preparation programs in many states across the United States (Andrews & Covell, 2006; Simms & Thumann, 2007). Many CAEBER graduates now teach and lead in bilingual K-12 and university teacher-preparation programs in the United States and worldwide, so it functioned as a leadership training ground.

Families

In 2010, an outgrowth of CAEBER's K-12 training was the setting up of an early-childhood education program serving Deaf-signing children from multilinguistic and multicultural families from infancy to eight years old. Led by Laurene Simms, Professor of Education at Gallaudet University and Chief Bilingual Officer (CBO), the National American Sign Language and English Bilingual Consortium for Early Childhood Education (NASL-ECE) is a proactive, Deaf-led non-profit organization that furnishes professional development for more than 175 early-childhood educators annually. NASL-ECE has hosted 12 annual summits, where ECE professionals meet and attend lectures delivered by scholars in early childhood, ASL and English bilingualism, psycholinguistics and other relevant topics, as well as form work groups to share ideas and bilingual strategies for teaching.

Bilingual–bicultural education provides families with tools to combat the risks of linguistic deprivation, which often leads to cognitive, emotional and language delays if Deaf-signing children are not provided with early access to language (Humphries *et al.*, 2016b; Hall, 2017). Today, when a child is first identified as deaf, medical and audiology professionals often advise against signed language as they believe it hinders spoken language development, despite the research showing that this is not so (for a review of these studies see Pontecorvo *et al.*, 2023). Contrary to this advice, ample studies show that using signed language does not require that spoken language be excluded, as the development of both signed language and spoken language can occur in parallel with signing being introduced as soon as the child is diagnosed so that a language foundation can quickly be developed (see Humphries *et al.*, 2016a, 2024; Murray *et al.*, 2020; Pontecorvo *et al.*, 2013).

Another support for families is Deaf-signing mentors who work with medical and audiological professionals during the early intervention to ensure that families are fully informed about the advantages of bilingual–bicultural education. This includes much more than simply adding signed language. Learning about Deaf epistemologies, visual ways of learning and Deaf culture is also vital. These mentor programs connect Hearing families with a Deaf-signing adult who is trained in how to effectively help parents develop high expectations for their Deaf-signing child, introduce Deaf culture as a family resource and support system, learn visual learning strategies (e.g. eye-gaze regulation, visual attention, joint attention), engage in shared storybook reading and the recitation of signed language nursery rhymes to develop age-appropriate language and emergent literacy milestones (Hamilton & Clark, 2020). Moreover, caregivers can obtain support from the Deaf-signing community, which provides 'cultural capital', including resources on how to raise a Deaf-signing child within a Hearing-speaking society (Holcomb, 2013). Parents continue involvement during the school years, and their relationships with teachers and the community can support their Deaf-signing child in developing a positive self-identity as they learn how to navigate the Deaf and Hearing world with access to both languages and cultures.

Conclusions

In 1834, William C. Woodbridge, a pioneering Hearing-speaking teacher of Deaf-signing students (1817–1821), wrote about the complexity of signed language and its 'power of expression' (Woodbridge, 1834: 55). Moreover, his daily interaction and work with Clerc profoundly influenced his thinking and teaching. However, historically and even in contemporary times, rather than building on signed languages' expressive power and Clerc's early SL–WL bilingual teaching practices, deaf education has emphasized spoken languages through technology and inclusion policies. More often than not, this direction not only further isolates Deaf-signing children but curtails their development in neurocognitive, linguistic and social development.

Even with the number of Deaf-signing bilinguals, Deaf bilingual programs are shrinking due to the international inclusion movement and advances in Hearing-speaking technology. We cannot, though, ignore the fact that bilingualism/multilingualism is used in and by Deaf-signing communities every day worldwide. Moreover, bilingualism has decreased health risks and language deprivation (Hall *et al.*, 2019; Wilkinson & Morford, 2020). Clearly, more studies are needed that utilize the Deaf-signing community as a 'special linguistic demographic variable', focusing on diversity rather than the disability framework (Allen, 2014) to learn more about Deaf-signing people and how they use their signed languages for learning. This direction not only benefits Deaf-signing people but society in general, as it leads to new insights into thinking, learning and reading. With this knowledge, we can construct better bilingual–bicultural deaf education programs, with Deaf-signing adults leading this change.

Key Points in This Chapter

➢ Deaf-signing bilinguals have their own language and culture.
➢ Deaf-signing persons do not see themselves as individuals 'lacking in hearing' but persons who utilize a visual approach to social, cultural and linguistic development.
➢ Deaf-signing bilinguals share attributes (and differences) with Hearing-speaking bilinguals
➢ Bilingualism and Deaf bilingual education among Deaf-signing people have existed for centuries and, in their revived form, contemporary research supports them.
➢ Contemporary writings and research show the many benefits of signed languages.
➢ A Deaf bilingual–bicultural education framework, translanguaging methodologies, and sign-mediated strategies can support teachers' use of translanguaging in the classroom.
➢ Issues surrounding assessment, student outcomes, teacher preparation and family services require specific considerations for the Deaf-signing bilingual learner.
➢ Innovative developments in AI, machine learning (ML) and augmented reality (AR) technology for communication and learning access use signed and written languages on mobile devices.
➢ It is important to have Deaf-signing teachers in K-12 schools, in university teacher-preparation classrooms and on research teams.

Suggested Further Reading

- Chen Pichler, D., Kuntze, M., Martin, D., de Quadros, R. and Stump, M. (2023) *Sign Language Acquisition by Deaf and Hearing Children: A Bilingual Introduction*. Gallaudet University Press.
- Golos, D., Kuntze, M., Wolbers, K. and Kurz, C. (2024) *58-IN-MIND: Multilingual Teaching Strategies for Diverse Deaf Students*. Gallaudet University Press.
- Kurz, C., Golos, D., Kuntze, M., Henner, J. and Scott, J. (2021) *Guidelines for Multilingual Deaf Education Teacher Preparation Programs*. Gallaudet University Press.
- Kusters, A., Moriarty, E., le Maire, A., Iver, S. and Emery, S. (2024) *Deaf Mobility Studies: Exploring International Networks, Tourism, and Migration*. Gallaudet University Press.
- Ladd, P. (2022) *The Unrecognized Curriculum: Seeing Through New Eyes, Deaf Culture and Deaf Pedagogies*. Dawn Sign Press.
- Leigh, I.W., Andrews, J.F., Miller, C. and Wolsey, J.A. (2022) *Deaf People and Society: Psychological, Sociological, and Educational Perspectives* (3rd edn). Routledge.

On the Web

- CORDIS–EU, Artificial intelligence for the deaf
  https://cordis.europa.eu/project/id/872139
- Laurent Clerc National Deaf Education Center (Gallaudet University)
  https://clerccenter.gallaudet.edu/
- Language diversity in deaf education (University of Leeds, UK)
  https://deafed.leeds.ac.uk/
- V2L Storybook Apps – Bilingual ASL and English storybooks
  https://vl2storybookapps.com/
- Video – Signing Happy Mother's Day in 71 Sign Languages
  https://www.facebook.com/seektheworld2015/videos/319209118774803/
- Video – 'No more silence'. Deaf people in China urged to speak out
  https://youtu.be/PxD1xl01tbk
- The Society for American Sign Language
  https://societyforasl.org/

Discussion Questions

(1) Much of the linguistic research on ASL has focused on the use of the hands. Discuss how the whole body is involved in ASL, including facial expressions, eyebrow lifts, cheek puffs, head tilts, gestures, hand/arm movements and body position and movement.

(2) Explore UNESCO's expanded definition of literacy. How do Deaf-signing multilinguals use their multiliteracies and multimodalities to communicate in their everyday life that go beyond print literacies alone?

(3) Explore the website of the World Federation of the Deaf (https://wfdeaf.org/who-we-are/). What is its mission? What kinds of projects is it involved in? What other international organizations does it work with?

Study Activities

(1) The best way to get to know Deaf-signing people is to learn signed language, read books by Deaf-signing authors and view videos about Deaf art exhibits and Deaf theater. Check out https://gallaudet.edu/asl/ for ASL online classes, books by Deaf-signing authors at Gallaudet University Press, and search online for videos of Deaf art exhibits and Deaf theater performances.

(2) Deaf and hard of hearing children experience unique communication and social barriers, which can increase their overall risk for trauma exposure, including language deprivation, a hot topic in deaf bilingual education today. See website of Gallaudet University's Deaf and Hard of Hearing Resilience Center to learn more about trauma resources, language justice, human trafficking, and other language-related topics – https://gallaudet.edu/deaf-hard-hearing-child-resilience-center/.

(3) ASL poets and actors create their own poetry and dramatic art forms that utilize hand shape and movement patterns to create artistic expressions, just as spoken language poets and actors create poems with rhyme and meter. Explore online

videos (e.g. on YouTube) for examples of ASL poetry, including Visual Vernacular (VV) by Bernard Bragg from the United States and Yu-Shan Ku from Taiwan, to see how they use VV in their dramatic performances. How is VV different from conversational signing?

CHAPTER 17

Bilingualism and Bilingual Education as a Problem, Right and Resource

Introduction

Three Perspectives on Languages
Language as a Problem
Language as a Right
Language as a Resource

US Language Orientations
The Advance of English in the United States

Conclusion

CHAPTER 17

Bilingualism and Bilingual Education as a Problem, Right and Resource

Introduction

Bilingualism is not only studied linguistically, psychologically and sociologically, it is also studied in relationship to power and political systems in society. The basis of this and the next chapter is that bilingualism and **bilingual education**, whatever form they take, cannot be properly understood unless connected to ideologies and politics in society. The activity of a bilingual classroom, and decisions about how to teach minoritized language children, are not based purely on educational preferences. Rather, calls for and against bilingual and multilingual education are surrounded and underpinned by basic beliefs about minoritized languages and **cultures**, linguistic and cultural diversity, immigration and immigrants, equality of opportunity and equality of outcomes, **empowerment**, affirmative action, the rights of individuals and the rights of **language minoritized groups**, **assimilation** and integration, desegregation and discrimination, pluralism and multiculturalism, diversity and discord, equality of recognition for minoritized groups, social division and social cohesion.

In the view of some people, bilingual and multilingual education will facilitate national cohesion and cultural integration, and enable different language communities inside a country to communicate with each other (e.g. in Singapore). In the view of other people, bilingual and multilingual education will create language factions, national disunity and cultural, economic and political disintegration. Education has thus been conceived as both part of the solution and part of the problem of achieving national unity, achieving diversity, or unity in diversity.

Teachers and education administrators are not only affected by political decisions and processes, they also deliver and implement those decisions and processes. Teachers are language planners and policymakers (Menken & García, 2010). As such, they are part of language paradoxes that are daily enacted and temporarily resolved in the classroom: ensuring equality of opportunity for all while celebrating distinctiveness and difference; ensuring that diversity does not become discord; encouraging students to share a common purpose while encouraging colorful variety; developing the dignity of ethnicity while aiding national stability. In multilingual schools and classrooms, teachers have overt and covert beliefs about languages, ranging from prohibition to tolerance, limited permission to promotion. The same is true in colleges and universities in multilingual contexts, particularly when decisions must be made about which language or languages to use as the medium of instruction (Kuteeva, 2023). Teachers and students are often unwitting actors in the tensions and drama of language and politics.

Three Perspectives on Languages

We begin by considering different assumptions and varying perspectives that are at the root of the politics of bilingualism and bilingual education. In a classic article, Richard Ruiz (1984) proposed three basic orientations or perspectives in relation to language, around which governments, groups and individuals vary: language as a *problem*, language as a *right* and language as a *resource*. These three different orientations may be conscious but they are also embedded in the subconscious assumptions of teachers, planners and politicians. Such orientations are regarded as fundamental and related to a basic philosophy or **ideology** held by an individual or group. Ruiz's framework has been widely adopted, expanded upon (Lo Bianco, 2001, 2016), critiqued (Ricento, 2009) and defended (Ruiz, 2010) and continues to have great influence (Bale, 2016; de Jong *et al.*, 2016; Hornberger, 2017; Wiley, 2022; Wright, 2019; Wright & Boun, 2016), as will be evident in the discussion below.

Language as a Problem

Public discussions of bilingual and multilingual education and languages in society often commence with the idea of language as causing complications and difficulties. This is well illustrated in the historical debates about the supposed cognitive problems of operating in two languages (see Chapters 7 and 8). Perceived problems are not limited to thinking. Personality and social problems such as split-identity, cultural dislocation, a poor self-image, low self-esteem, alienation, emotional vulnerability and anomie (break down in societal moral values) have also sometimes been attributed to bilinguals (Pavlenko, 2014). Bilinguals sometimes have a language anxiety ('schizoglossia') because they feel their language does not compare well with the supposed **monolingual** standard, and in extreme cases this has led to psychoanalysis and therapy (Pavlenko, 2005).

In some multilingual contexts, the positioning of bilingual women may be posed as more connected to their minoritized language and less bilingual than men, and thus be connected to a deficit framework (Mills, 2006). For example, Pavelenko (2001: 128) notes that 'in many language contact communities, the **dominant language**, perceived as a power code, is associated with masculinity, and the minoritized language with domestic values and femininity'. This serves as an important reminder that gender and languages interact in ways that make bilingualism have different meanings to different groups, including more of a problem for one, more of a benefit for another (Langman & Shi, 2020). For example, in some communities, women may be given less access to a second, prestigious language (e.g. English), restricting their bilingualism, access to education, employment or economic advancement. The opposite can also occur. 'Where bilingualism is associated with inequality and social disadvantage, ideologies of language and gender may conspire to put more pressure to be bilingual on the less powerful group, often women' (Pavlenko, 2001: 131). Langman and Shi note a recent shift in studies on gender, language and **identity** from a feminist post-structural perspective:

Recent work urges the perspective that gender is 'performed' in locally situated and socially constructed contexts. Such work further introduces the concept of identity as socially constructed in discourse and urges researchers to think in terms of how individuals use language to construct identity rather than how members of gendered groups enact their gender by using scripts and codes of that group. As such the question of access to communities in which new language forms are used becomes of primary importance. (Langman & Shi, 2020: 221)

At a group rather than an individual level, bilingualism is sometimes connected with the potential for national or regional disunity and inter-group conflict (Davies & Dubinsky, 2018). Language is thus viewed by some people as a political problem. Part of the **language-as-problem orientation** is that perpetuating language minorities and language diversity may cause less integration, less cohesiveness, more antagonism and more conflict in society. It is sometimes claimed that immigrant language minorities threaten national unity and political stability by building self-segregated enclaves and establishing regular connections back to their country of origin, called 'immigrant transnationalism' (Patten & Kymlicka, 2003). This is to be solved by **assimilation** into the majority language (see Chapter 18). Such an argument holds that the majority language (e.g. English) unifies the diversity. The ability of every citizen to communicate with ease in the nation's majority language is regarded as the common leveler. Unity within a nation is seen as synonymous with uniformity and similarity. The opposing argument is that it is possible to have national unity without uniformity. Diversity of languages and national unity can coexist (e.g. in Singapore, Malaysia, Luxembourg, Switzerland, Wales, Ireland, South Africa).

The coexistence of two or more languages is rarely a cause in itself of tension, disunity, conflict or strife. Rather, the history of war suggests that economic, political and religious differences are typically the causes. Language, in and by itself, is seldom the cause of conflict. Religious crusades and jihads, rivalries between different religions, rivalries between different political parties and economic aggression tend to be the instigators of conflict. Underlying many of these conflicts are racism and ethnic discrimination. Where there is language conflict, language is often the symbol but not the underlying issue. The underlying issues are often more economic advantage and disadvantage, contests of power and status, religion and nationalism, military power and imperialism, of which language can be an outward marker but not the inner issue. Research by Sallabank (2013) in Europe suggests that minoritized language policy sometimes serves ends other than language, and includes the desire for political autonomy, economic equality or advantage, and group empowerment (see also Faingold, 2020).

In a classic internationally comparative research study on causes of civil strife, Fishman (1989) found that language was not a cause of such civil discord. His analysis involved 130 countries and just one outcome (dependent) variable, namely civil strife (defined as the frequency, duration and intensity of conspiracy, internal war and turmoil). Predictor variables concerned measures of linguistic homogeneity/heterogeneity as well as sociocultural, economic, demographic, geographic, historical and political measures. 'The widespread journalistic and popular political wisdom that linguistic heterogeneity per se is necessarily conducive to civil strife, has been shown, by our analysis, to be more myth than reality' (Fishman, 1989: 622). Rather, the causes of strife were found to be deprivation, authoritarian regimes and modernization. Romaine (2000: 14) thus concludes:

Because languages and dialects are often potent symbols of class, gender, ethnic and other kinds of differentiation, it is easy to think that language underlies conflict. Yet disputes involving language are really not about language, but instead about fundamental inequalities between groups who happen to speak different languages.

However, in his on-the-ground work with peace-building efforts in Southeast Asia, Lo Bianco (2016: 2) concludes that 'some aspect of language is present in many conflicts, some kinds of conflicts involve many aspects of language, and some conflicts are only about language'. He gives the example of Thailand's deep south, where linguistic grievance over the struggle for official recognition of the Patani Malay language has led to a decade of political violence (Lo Bianco, 2019). Nevertheless, he argues that it is possible to address language in non-reductive ways to reduce conflict: 'disputes around language problems often represent a positive opening as well, sometimes the means whereby entry to solutions can be explored using an engaged and democratic **language planning** practice' (Lo Bianco, 2016: 3).

In the United States, 'becoming American' has historically been symbolized by being English-speaking. This idea of what it means to be an American – monolingual English-speaking – continues and has become increasingly racialized as more recent immigrants tend to be people of color from Latin America, Asia and Africa. Bilingualism is seen as a characteristic of the poor, the disadvantaged, the foreigner and the unassimilated immigrant. Speaking English is valued for its perceived link with liberty, freedom, status, justice and wealth. In consequence, other languages in the United States are sometimes seen as linked to poverty, crime, terror and other societal problems. American ideals and dreams are learnt through English. A belief of some is that other languages teach non-American ideas and therefore must be discouraged in schools. Bilingualism, in this US 'problem' viewpoint, will lower the GNP, increase civil and racial strife, foster political and social unrest, and endanger US stability.

A minoritized language – particularly when spoken by racialized minorities – is often connected with the problems of poverty, economic disadvantage, underachievement in school, political marginalization, less social and vocational mobility and a lack of integration into the majority culture. The term '(dis)citizenship' is used by some scholars to denote 'citizenship minus' or 'disabling citizenship', to highlight how many immigrant students are implicitly restricted by the dominant monolingual majority language ideologies of citizenship, such as the 'English only' idea of citizenship in the United States (Menken, 2013; Ramanathan, 2013). This is especially due to schools where the curriculum is delivered only through English, but also to high-stakes testing and ideologies of school accountability. (Dis)citizenship disables students from fully accessing and participating in society, limiting their future economic opportunities. Thus, such students are often seen as having a language problem.

In this 'language as a problem' perspective, the minoritized language is perceived as a partial cause of social, economic and educational problems rather than an effect of such problems. This 'language is an obstacle' attitude is illustrated in the phrase 'If only they would speak English, their problems would be solved'. The minoritized language is thus seen as a handicap to be overcome by the school system.

One resolution of the problem is regarded to be the increased teaching of a majority language (e.g. English) at the expense of the home language. Thus, mainstreaming, **English as a second language, sheltered English immersion** and **transitional bilingual education** aim to develop competent English **language skills** in minoritized language children as quickly as possible so that they will be on a par with first language English-speakers in the mainstream classroom.

In the United States, the rise of **high-stakes testing** has suggested that language is a problem, since Spanish-speakers have lower test scores. The group label (e.g. **Latinxs**, Hispanics, Spanish-speakers) becomes the named cause such that, for example, Latinx students are immediately associated with lower test performance. The home language is wrongly attributed as the origin of underachievement rather than, for example, the relatively poor economic conditions that surround many such bilinguals and the poor quality of instruction.

A language problem is sometimes perceived as being caused by strong forms of bilingual education. Such education, it is sometimes argued, will cause social unrest or disintegration in society. Fostering the minoritized language and racial and ethnic differences might provoke conflict and disharmony, political and social unrest. The response is generally that strong forms of bilingual education do not create a language problem but, rather, lead to better integration, harmony and social peace. The evidence suggests that developing bilingualism and biliteracy within strong bilingual education leads to higher achievement across the curriculum and therefore a better usage of human resources in a country's economy and less wastage of talent. Fostering self-esteem, self-identity and a more positive attitude to schooling through such bilingual education may also relate to increased social harmony and contentment (see Chapter 12).

Within this 'problem' orientation, there not only exists the desire to remove differences between groups to achieve a common culture. There can be the positive desire for intervention to improve the position of language minorities. Ruiz (1984: 21) observes that 'Whether the orientation is represented by malicious attitudes resolving to eradicate, invalidate, quarantine or inoculate, or comparatively benign ones concerned with remediation and "improvement," the central activity remains that of problem-solving'. Nevertheless, a language-as-a-problem orientation often contributes to racism and inequality, as in the cases of linguistic profiling documented by Baugh (2017), where speaking English with a 'foreign' accent or non-standard dialect can lead to challenges in seeking employment, housing and other opportunities. Even 'solutions' to language 'problems' that appear to be well intentioned (e.g. English-only language education programs) may have a discriminatory impact (e.g. devaluing of and restrictions on the use of home languages) (Flores & Rosa, 2015; Leeman, 2013; Zentella, 2014). The impact of dominant ideologies on bilingualism are explored in Chapters 18 and 19.

Language as a Right

A different orientation from that of 'language as a problem' is thinking of language as a basic human right. Just as there are often individual rights in choice of religion, so, it is argued, there should be an individual rights to choice of language and to bilingual education. Just as there are attempts to eradicate discrimination based on color and creed, so people within this orientation will argue that language prejudice and discrimination need to be eradicated in a democratic society by establishing language rights (May, 2017a; Skutnabb-Kangas, 2000, 2015).

At one level, language rights concern protection from discrimination. Many indigenous peoples (e.g. Māori, Native Americans, First Nations in Canada) and other language minorities have suffered considerable discrimination. Skutnabb-Kangas (2000) vividly portrays the oppression of the Kurdish language by torture, imprisonment, confiscation of books, dismissal from jobs, even execution. Ngugi wa Thiong'o (2005) depicts the discrimination that African people have suffered economically, politically, culturally and linguistically from a European colonialist attitude and Americanization. For Ngugi wa Thiong'o, African language rights concern self-regulation and self-determination, and not just non-discrimination. Ngugi wa Thiong'o spoke Gĩkũyũ as a child, in the fields, in the home and in the community. However, he was sent to a colonial school that taught solely through the medium of English. The language of education was at variance with the language of his culture. Gĩkũyũ was suppressed, as he vividly recalls:

> In Kenya, English became much more than a language: it was the language, and all others had to bow before it in deference. Thus one of the most humiliating experiences was to be caught speaking Gĩkũyũ in the vicinity of the school. The culprit was given corporal punishment – three to five strokes of the cane on bare buttocks – or was made to carry a metal plate around the neck with the inscription: I AM STUPID or I AM A DONKEY. Sometimes the culprits were fined money they could hardly afford. (Thiong'o, 2005: 149)

Such discrimination remains. In Arizona, in the **context** of the state's enforcement of **Proposition 203** to restrict bilingual education (see Chapter 9), some educators believed (and were led to believe) that the Proposition prohibited any use of Spanish or other minoritized languages in the classroom. Soon after its passage, one school principal attempted to ban the use of Spanish school-wide, even in the cafeteria and out on the playground. At another Arizona school, a teacher was fired for hitting students speaking Spanish in her classroom. When asked to comment on the case, the state's superintendent of public instruction essentially praised the teacher for enforcing English-only rules in her classroom but noted it was wrong for her to hit the students (Wright, 2005b).

Videos on social media abound of bilinguals in the United States being publicly attacked – verbally and sometimes physically – for speaking languages other than English in classrooms, at the park, in restaurants, at the mall, at gas stations, in stores, at the airport, on airplanes, on buses, on the subway and on the street, just to give just a few examples. Often profanity-laced tirades directed at the bilinguals include phrases such as 'Speak English!', 'Speak American!' and 'Go back to your country!' In 2016, during the campaign for the Republican presidential nomination, Donald Trump chided opponent Jeb Bush for speaking Spanish on the campaign trail, declaring 'We speak English here, not Spanish', and made other comments disparaging Spanish language use (see below). While such public attacks on bilingual speakers have long been seen in the United States, an impression is that they were increased and emboldened during Trump's first presidency due to his anti-immigration rhetoric and policies, as well as during his campaign for the presidency in 2024, when his anti-immigration rhetoric was prominent at his rallies and during the presidential debates. Trump's name is invoked in some of the tirades posted on social media. These racist acts seek to deny the rights of bilinguals and multilinguals to use their languages in their daily lives in spaces where no official linguistic restrictions exist.

Kloss (1998) makes a distinction between tolerance-oriented rights and promotion-oriented rights (see also Wiley, 2015). At a promotion-oriented level, language rights are more positive and constructive, and include the right to use a minoritized language freely, including in all official contexts (May, 2017a). Such rights flourish particularly where there is greater individual and group self-determination. However, language rights can sometimes be idealistic rather than realistic. For example, if all 200-plus majority and minoritized European languages were used in the European Parliament, translation and interpretation would be prohibitively expensive. Instead, there are 24 official languages in the European Parliament and three procedural languages (English, French and German). In South Africa, it is costly to produce the full range of educational resources (for different ages, curriculum areas and ability levels) for all 11 official languages. Yet to privilege one or more languages over the others will be at a cost to the speakers (e.g. less educational success) and the languages themselves (e.g. **language shift**).

A 'non-rights', laissez-faire approach to minoritized languages serves to strengthen the already powerful and prestigious languages. Therefore, some form of intervention on linguistic rights becomes important for the protection and preservation of minoritized languages, particularly in public domains. Governments typically have less power in economic activities, making rights in government-controlled areas (e.g. law, local government, education) more possible.

Such language rights may be derived from personal, human, legal and constitutional rights. Personal language rights will draw on individual liberties and the right to freedom of individual expression (May, 2018, 2024). It has also been argued that there may be language rights in group rather than individual terms. Languages are rarely spoken in solitude but in pairs, groups and networks. The rights of language groups may be expressed in terms of the importance of the preservation of **heritage languages** and heritage culture communities and expressed as 'rights to protection' and 'rights to participation'. This includes rights to some form of self-determination and social justice. May (2011) argues the case for greater ethnocultural and ethnolinguistic self-determination and democracy as nation states fragment.

Group rights are likely to be contested. What constitutes a group (or **identity** with a group) for collective linguistic human rights, and defining who is, or is not, a member of a language community, is problematic. Also, nation states and liberalism as a political ideology are more built on the notion of individual citizenship rights than on group rights (May, 2017b). Such collective rights may at times clash with individual rights and freedoms (e.g. local employment when a person has the professional qualifications but not bilingual competence). Hoffmann (2000: 435) cites the case of Catalonia (Spain), where 'access to white-collar jobs has become increasingly restricted to those with fluency in Catalan … amid claims that this situation pushes disproportionately high numbers of non-Catalan speakers into low-status occupations'.

Language rights are inclusive of users of non-standard dialects. In the United States, the Conference on College Composition and Communication (CCCC) – the predecessor and now a component of the National Council of Teachers of English (NCTE) – passed the 'Students' Right to Their Own Language' (SRTOL) resolution in 1974. The resolution was reaffirmed and broadened by the NCTE in 2003 (Scott *et al.*, 2008) and reaffirmed again in 2014. The resolution primarily addressed the debates among composition teachers about requiring students to adhere to the norms of standard American English in their writing. The resolution begins, 'We affirm the students' right to their own patterns of varieties of language – the dialects of their nurture or whatever dialects in which they find their own identity and style'. A detailed statement providing background on SRTOL also affirms the importance of students learning to write in standard American English (called 'edited American English' in the document) (Perryman-Clark *et al.*, 2014). A driving force behind SRTOL was a number of African-American scholars, educators and instructors of composition, many of whom worked in programs with a predominance of African-American students.

However, SRTOL applies as well to minoritized language speakers and writers (Scott *et al.*, 2008). Reflection, application and debate over the SRTOL continue (Baker-Bell, 2020a; Dance, 2023; Perryman-Clark *et al.*, 2014).

A further level of language rights is international, deriving mostly from the United Nations, UNESCO, the Council of Europe and the European Union (Faingold, 2020; May, 2024). For example, the 2007 United Nations Declaration on the Rights of Indigenous Peoples states in Article 3 that 'Indigenous peoples have the right to self-determination. By virtue of that right they freely determine their political status and freely pursue their economic, social and cultural development'. Such peoples are also accorded the 'right to establish and control their educational systems and institutions providing education in their own languages' (Article 14.1).

Language rights are also affirmed for children (see Box 17.1). The European Charter for Regional or Minority Languages (Council of Europe, 1992) tends to be more about standards than rights, but it has options (e.g. use of a minoritized language in pre-school education) from which states can choose (Grin *et al.*, 2003). Education is one of the domains in which the contracting states undertake to protect and promote minoritized languages in their territories. Such education can range from being exclusively in the minoritized language (**heritage language education**) to dual language education and to other forms of bilingual education where there is a demand and sufficient numbers. However, individual countries have often ignored such international declarations or violated the agreements (May, 2024; Skutnabb-Kangas, 2015). Nevertheless, a struggle over language rights is important. Non-recognition of language human rights (as often occurs among immigrant language minorities) is in itself a form of oppression, **domination** and injustice.

The kind of rights, apart from language rights, that ethnic groups may claim include: protection, membership of their ethnic group and separate existence, non-discrimination and equal treatment, education and information in their ethnic language, the preferred script of the language, freedom to worship, freedom of belief, freedom of movement, employment, peaceful assembly and association, political representation and involvement, and administrative autonomy. Thus language rights are one component of a wider constellation of rights for minorities.

In the United States, discrimination on the basis of race, color or national origin is clearly prohibited under Title VI of the Civil Rights Act of 1964. Language is not

---

Box 17.1 The United Nations Convention on the Rights of the Child

Tove Skutnabb-Kangas (2015) provides an analysis of where linguistic human rights may be found in various international and regional human rights documents. She notes that, at the international level, the 1989 United Nations Convention on the Rights of the Child (CRC) provides the best protections. The CRC addresses a wide range of basic rights associated with child welfare, and includes brief mention of language. Skutnabb-Kangas explains:

> Article 29, subparagraph (d) stipulates that education should be directed to the development of *respect for the child's parents, his or her own cultural identity, language, and values*. Article 30 provides: *In those States in which ethnic, religious or linguistic minorities or persons of indigenous origin exist, a child belonging to such a minority or who is indigenous shall not be denied the right, in community with other members of his or her own group, to enjoy his or her own culture, to profess and practice his or her own religion,* **or to use his or her own language**. (Skutnabb-Kangas, 2015: 194, bold emphasis added)

As of 2024, the United States is the only UN member country that has not ratified the CRC (see https://www.unicef.org/child-rights-convention/frequently-asked-questions).

specifically mentioned, leaving an unclear picture of what language rights individuals may have. However, civil rights investigations and lawsuits related to cases of linguistic discrimination have been argued on the basis that language is representative of national origin (Leeman, 2018). From the expert perspective of a civil rights lawyer, Del Valle (2003) analyzes how advocates of language rights in the United States can take much heart from an early history of tolerance, from the absence of a history of **monolingualism** in the United States, to the growth and uses of the 14th Amendment of the US Constitution (e.g. the equal protection clause) and supportive court cases (e.g. *Meyer v. Nebraska*). Del Valle shows that English-only laws tend to be 'more symbolic than restrictive' (Del Valle, 2003: 79) but that there has been a 'proliferation of English-only workplace rules enforced by employers of bilingual employees. Unlike state-wide or public English-only laws, these rules can be easily passed, explicitly, consciously, and in writing by an employer without company-wide discussion ... that may be challenged in court' (Del Valle, 2003: 118). Del Valle's wide-ranging examination of language rights in the United States includes interrogation, searches, interpreters, document translation, unfairly removing bilingual jurors and commercial labeling, and serves to demonstrate that the issue of linguistic human rights goes much deeper than national and international laws and charters, as such rights are enacted at a local level, in courts, workplaces and, not least, classrooms.

In the United States, language rights have a history of being tested in court (Faingold, 2018). This is significantly different from the European experience, where language rights have rarely been tried in law. From the early 1920s to the present, there has been a continuous debate in US courts of law regarding the legal status of language minority rights (Wright, 2019). To gain short-term protection and a medium-term guarantee for minoritized languages, legal challenges have become an important part of the language rights movement in the United States. The legal battles are not just minoritized language versus majority language contests. The test cases also concern children versus schools, parents versus school boards, state versus the federal authority (Del Valle, 2003). Whereas minoritized language activists among the Basques in Spain and the Welsh in Britain have been taken to court by the central government for their actions (Williams, 2007), US minoritized language parents and activists have taken the central and regional government to court. Two connected examples will illustrate.

A crucial Supreme Court case in the United States was *Brown v. Board of Education* in 1954. African-American children were deliberately segregated in southern schools. The Supreme Court ruled that equality in the US educational system was denied to such African-American children owing to segregation from their peers. Segregation denied equal educational opportunity through a crucial element in classroom learning: peer interaction. The Court decided that education must be made available to all children on equal terms, as guaranteed by the 14th Amendment. A segregationist doctrine of separate but 'equal' education was in fact inherently unequal.

A landmark in US bilingual education was a lawsuit (discussed in Chapter 9) brought on behalf of Chinese students against the San Francisco School District in 1970 (Morita-Mullaney, 2024a). The case concerned whether or not non-English-speaking students received equal educational opportunity when instructed in a language they could not understand. The failure to address the linguistic needs of the students was alleged to violate both the equal protection clause of the 14th Amendment and Title VI of the Civil Rights Act of 1964. The case, known as *Lau v. Nichols*, was rejected by the federal district court and a court of appeal but was accepted by the Supreme Court in 1974. The verdict prohibited English **submersion** programs and required school districts to offer programs that address the unique linguistic and academic needs of students not yet proficient in English. Soon after the ruling, the US Department of Education issued the **Lau remedies**. These strongly encouraged districts to adopt bilingual education programs as a means of complying with the Supreme Court's ruling in *Lau*. The remedies also helped to broaden the goals of bilingual education to include the possible maintenance of minoritized language and culture. The Lau remedies somewhat expanded the use of minoritized languages in schools, although they rarely resulted in strong forms of bilingual education designed to help students develop and maintain their home languages. As time passed, the Lau remedies were challenged, given that the Court did not mandate bilingual education or any other specific program. Nonetheless, for the purposes of this chapter, the *Lau* case is symbolic of the dynamic and continuing contest to establish language rights in the United States, particularly through testing the law in court.

Language rights are expressed not only in lawsuits. They are often expressed at the grassroots level, by protests and pressure groups, by local action, assertiveness and argument. For example, by such means the Kohanga Reo (language nests) movement in New Zealand provides a grassroots-instituted immersion pre-school experience for the Māori people (May, 2011, 2024). Another example of grassroots expression of 'language as a right' is the Celtic experience in Ireland, Scotland and Wales. In these countries, it is bottom-up (rather than top-down) grassroots movements that created pre-school playgroups, mother-and-toddler groups and adult language learning classes for heritage language preservation (I.W. Williams, 2003). Strong activism and non-violent but insistent demands led to the establishment of Welsh heritage language elementary schools, particularly in urban areas (C.H. Williams, 2014; Özerk & Williams, 2023). Not without struggle, opposition and antagonistic bureaucracy, parents obtained the right for education in the indigenous tongue. Such pressure groups have contained parents who speak the **indigenous language** and those who speak only English yet wish their children to be taught in the heritage language of the area and become thoroughly bilingual (Sallabank, 2013). In the Twin Cities area of Minnesota, the Hmong community formed its own charter schools when local school districts refused to offer Hmong language and culture classes or to take other measures to address the unique academic needs of Hmong students (C. Williams, 2018). The public school districts later began offering Hmong enrichment programs over fear of losing more Hmong students to charter schools.

In North American and British society, no formal recognition is usually made in politics or the legal system of categories or groups of people based on their culture, language or race. Rather, the focus is on individual rights. The accent is on individual equality of opportunity, individual rewards based on individual merit. Policies of non-discrimination, for example, tend to be based on individual rather than group rights (Patten & Kymlicka, 2003).

Language minoritized groups will nevertheless argue for rewards and justice based on their existence as a definable group in society. Sometimes based on territorial rights, often based on ethnic identity, such language group rights have been regarded as a way of redressing injustices to language minorities. This may be a temporary step on the way to full individual citizenship rights, as participative democracy tends to favor the equality of each individual rather than group privilege. Alternatively, language minorities may claim the right to some independent power, some measure of decision-making and some guarantee of self-determination. This is typically seen by the majority language group as a step on the road to self-determination.

May (2018: 249) argues that 'the recognition of language rights can and does support, rather than undermine, wider social and political stability in modern nation-states'. He warns that ignoring demands for language rights is more likely to escalate them. However, when language group rights are obtained, 'even very little autonomy granted to indigenous peoples is usually viewed with a great deal of suspicion, and often with outright opposition, because it may infringe on the individual rights of majority group members' (May, 2011: 288–289). An example is when English monolinguals cannot obtain teaching or local government posts in a bilingual community and feel their rights to employment have been infringed.

Two notes of caution about language rights need sounding. First, Bruthiaux (2009) argues that the financial implications of language rights need considering, so that any implementation is reasonable and not idealistic. For example, when the number of official languages within the European Union rose from 11 in 1995 to 24 in 2013, the costs of interpretation and translation potentially became large. In any cost–benefit analysis, the options for linguistic diversity are neither none nor infinite (Grin, 2005). Toward the 'zero' end of the dimension, much power is transferred to dominant languages; toward the 'infinite' end, costs become prohibitive. Also, the costs of interpretation and translation can be calculated, whereas the benefits may be less measurable but nevertheless valuable to the status of a language. Second, lofty rhetoric about individual rights can hide coercion, conformity and empty promises. When some school administrators express a **language-as-a-right orientation**, they tend

---

Box 17.2 Guidelines for communicating rights to non-native speakers of English

An international group of linguists, psychologists, lawyers and interpreters drafted *Guidelines for Communicating Rights to Non-Native Speakers of English in Australia, England and Wales, and the USA*. In 2016 these Guidelines were endorsed by several national and international language and linguistic professional organizations (see https://www.aaal.org/guidelines-for-communication-rights). The Preamble states, in part:

> Suspects' interview rights, referred to as Miranda Rights in the United States and as police cautions in Australia, England and Wales, are country-specific mechanisms for protecting due process in criminal investigations and trials. These rights include the right not to incriminate oneself.... The purpose of the requirement to communicate these rights/cautions to suspects is to ensure that those in criminal proceedings know their fundamental rights under the law. A failure to protect the rights of individuals during interviews risks the integrity of any investigation.
>
> ...
>
> People who have learned another language later in life process information differently in this second language than in their native language. This processing difference compounds their linguistic and cultural difficulties in communicating in English. Even speakers who can maintain a conversation in English may not have sufficient proficiency to understand complex sentences used to communicate rights/cautions, legal terms, or English spoken at fast conversational rates. They also may not be familiar with assumptions made in the adversarial legal system. Yet, like other vulnerable populations, non-native speakers of English have the right to equal treatment. Therefore, if they do not have mastery of English, it is crucial that their rights be delivered to them in the language they can understand.

The *Guidelines* make the following recommendations to law-enforcement agencies on the wording and communication of rights/cautions:

- Use standardized version in plain English (clear English).
- Develop standardized statements in other languages.
- Inform suspects about access to an interpreter at the beginning of the interview.
- Present each right individually.
- Do not determine understanding by using yes or no questions.
- Adopt an in-your-own-words requirement.
- Video-record the interview.

to provide the legal minimum in support services for language minoritized students. Words do not often relate to action.

A more recent development has been what Wiley (2022) describes as a retreat from language rights in postmodern academic research toward challenging traditional linguistic constructs such as codeswitching, bilingualism, multilingualism and the existence of separate distinct languages (see Chapter 1). Simply put, taken to its extreme, if different languages do not exist, then there is no basis for language rights. Wiley contends that such postmodern academic attempts to disinvent languages, bilingualism and, by extension, language rights do little to assist and defend actual victims of linguistic discrimination. Especially in the current environment of anti-immigrant rhetoric and racist policies and practices, Wiley argues that there is an ongoing need for advocacy of language rights and civil rights more broadly:

> In this environment, there remains an urgent need for linguists, applied linguists, language professionals, and critical theorists to be concerned about the persistent structural social and economic inequities, actual legal restrictions by the state, policy failures to accommodate linguist minorities, linguistic rights in general as well as freedom from linguistic discrimination in social practice, and how these concerns relate to human rights more broadly. (Wiley, 2022: 285)

Language as a Resource

An alternative perspective to 'language as a problem' and 'language as a right' is the idea of language as a personal, community, regional and national resource. Bilingualism can provide an intellectual (see Chapter 7), cultural, economic (see Chapter 19), social, communication (see Chapter 19) and citizenship resource. Bilingualism is seen as an asset, both for communities and for individuals. Languages aid individual participation in public, leisure and private lives. For example, public participation is aided when a person can operate in the different languages of varying groups, fostering inclusion by being able to debate and persuade in the language of a particular group.

The movement in mainland Europe for increased **multilingualism** (e.g. in Spain, Scandinavia, Slovenia) fits into this orientation. Under the general heading of 'language as a resource' also come minoritized and lesser-used languages as a cultural and social resource. While languages may be viewed in terms of their economic bridge-building potential (e.g. foreign trade), languages may also be supported for their ability to build social bridges across different groups (e.g. where there is religious conflict) and bridges for increasing intercultural understanding.

The recent trend in mainland Europe, for example, has been to attempt to expand world language education. In many regions of the world, English as an international language has been added to the school curriculum (Rose *et al.*, 2020). The study of second and third languages is increasingly viewed as an important resource to promote foreign trade, world influence, even peace. However, there is some scholarly concern about the ways languages can be treated in neoliberal marketplaces as simply commodified resources for purposes of personal financial gain and profits for private companies (Codó, 2017; Flubacher & Del Percio, 2017; Phyak & De Costa, 2021) (see Chapter 19).

The paradox is that bilingual education to support minoritized languages has tended to be undervalued in the United States, but English-speakers who learn these same languages are greatly valued and viewed as important to ensure a continued major role for the United States in world politics and the world economy (Wright, 2010). There is a tendency to value the acquisition of languages while devaluing the language minorities who own them (e.g. speakers of Spanish, Arabic, Chinese Mandarin, Hindi and Korean in the United States). While integration and assimilation are still the dominant ideologies in US internal politics, external politics increasingly demands bilingual citizens. Dual language bilingual education programs, many of which were created by Latinx activists since the 1960s, have been of increasing interest to some middle-class parents who see, for example, possible employment and economic gains for their children (Delavan, 2024) (see Chapter 11). Ovando and Combs (2018) observe the irony of English monolinguals being encouraged to study a world language at great cost and with little efficiency while at the same time the linguistic gifts that children from non-English language backgrounds bring to schools are being destroyed. It is thus ironic that many US and UK students spend time in school learning some of the very languages that children of immigrants are pressured to forget (Ricento, 2009). The politics of immigration and institutionalized racial discrimination serve to deny bilingualism; yet the politics of global trade serve increasingly to demand bilingualism and multilingualism. One result is that, along with the United Kingdom, the United States is a 'graveyard for languages because of its historical ability to absorb immigrants by the millions and extinguish their **mother tongues** within a few generations' (Rumbaut, 2009: 64).

In the United States, the idea of language as a resource not only refers to the development of a second language in monolingual speakers; it also refers to the preservation of languages other than English. For example, children whose home language is Spanish or German, Italian or Mandarin, Greek or Japanese, Hmong or French have a home language that can be utilized as a resource (see Chapter 5). One case is Spanish-speakers who together make the United States the fifth largest Spanish-speaking country in the world. Just as water in the reservoir and oil in the oil field are preserved as basic resources and commodities, so a language such as Spanish, despite being difficult to measure and define as a resource, may be preserved for the common economic, social and cultural good. Suppression of language minorities, particularly by the school system, may be seen as economic, social and cultural wastage. Instead, such languages are a natural resource that can be exploited for cultural, spiritual and educational growth as well as for economic, commercial and political gain.

Within the **language-as-a-resource orientation**, there tends to be the assumption that linguistic diversity does not cause separation nor less integration in society. Rather, it is possible that national unity and linguistic diversity can coexist. Unity and diversity are not necessarily incompatible. Tolerance and cooperation between groups may be as possible with linguistic diversity as they would be unlikely when such linguistic diversity is repressed.

A frequent debate concerns which languages are a resource. The favored languages tend to be those that are both international and particularly valuable in international trade. A lower place is given in the status rankings to minoritized languages that are small, regional and of less perceived value in the international marketplace. For example, in England, French was traditionally placed in schools in the first division. German, Spanish, Danish, Dutch, Modern Greek, Italian and Portuguese were the major European languages placed in the second division. Despite large numbers of mother-tongue Bengali-, Panjabi-, Urdu-, Gujarati-, Hindi- and Turkish-speakers, the politics of English education relegates these languages, and many others, to a lowly position in the school curriculum. Thus, a caste system of languages can be created.

At a minimal level, a language-as-a-resource orientation can open space for the use of students' home languages in schools, even in non-bilingual classrooms. Teachers who adopt this orientation recognize that students' home languages are a strength they bring into the classroom and a valuable resource upon which they can build. Providing brief explanations, previews and reviews in the home languages and allowing students to use their home languages to help each other in the classroom can enable students to comprehend and complete academic tasks in the majority language (Wright, 2025). A language-as-a-resource orientation opens space for **translanguaging** pedagogy and practice, which may lead to greater academic success (Cenoz & Gorter, 2021; Cummins, 2019; García *et al.*, 2016). Language-as-a-resource views can eventually lead to stronger forms of bilingual education.

To conclude, while the three language orientations have differences, they also share certain common aims: of national unity, of individual rights and of fluency in the majority language (e.g. English) being important to economic opportunities. The basic difference tends to be whether monolingualism in the majority language or bilingualism should be encouraged as a means to achieving those ends. All three orientations connect language with politics, economics, society and culture. Each orientation recognizes that language is not simply a means of communication but is also connected with socialization into the local and wider society, as well as a powerful symbol of heritage and identity. Each uses liberal values such as individual freedom and equality of opportunity to advance its cause (Schmidt, 2009). The differences between the three orientations lie in the socialization and identity to be fostered: assimilation or pluralism, integration or separatism, monoculturalism or multiculturalism.

US Language Orientations

That the three orientations have common aims as well as differences is illustrated in the case of the United States. The United States has long been a willing receptacle of peoples of many languages: German, French, Yiddish, Polish, Italian, Irish, Greek, Russian, Welsh, Arabic, Cantonese and Mandarin Chinese, Korean, Japanese and particularly Spanish, to name just a few examples. 'A melting pot' ideology aimed to assimilate and unify immigrants, especially via English language hegemony (Schmidt, 2009). The dream became an integrated United States with shared social, political and economic ideals. Quotes from US Presidents and presidential candidates illustrate this 'melting pot' attitude. In 1917 Theodore Roosevelt declared:

> We must have but one flag. We must have but one language. That must be the language of the Declaration of Independence, of Washington's Farewell Address, of Lincoln's Gettysburg Speech and Second Inaugural. We cannot tolerate any attempt to oppose or supplant the language and culture that has come down to us from the builders of the republic with the language and culture of any European country. The greatness of this nation depends on the swift assimilation of the aliens she welcomes to her shores. Any force which attempts to retard that assimilative process is a force hostile to the highest interests of our country. (Quoted in Wagner, 1981: 32)

The same year, Roosevelt urged (or warned) all immigrants to adopt the English language:

> It would be not merely a misfortune but a crime to perpetuate differences of language in this country.... We should provide for every immigrant by day schools for the young, and night schools for the adult, the chance to learn English; and if after say five years he has not learned English, he should be sent back to the land from whence he came. (Quoted in González, 1979)

President Ronald Reagan's view in the late 1980s was that it is:

> absolutely wrong and against American concepts to have a bilingual education program that is now openly, admittedly dedicated to preserving their native language and never getting them adequate in English so they can go out into the job market and participate. (Quoted in Crawford, 2000: 120)

President George W. Bush had some proficiency in Spanish and used it on occasion in speeches and interviews, yet his signature education bill, No Child Left Behind, ended the **Bilingual Education Act** and represented a strong **assimilationist** perspective (see Chapter 9). President Barack Obama made positive comments about linguistic diversity and occasionally expressed concerns about immigrant students losing their native languages. Yet education priorities and policies during his administration did little to promote bilingual education or reverse the assimilationist focus of federal education policies.

During the 2016 presidential campaign, three of the major Republican primary candidates were Spanish-speakers – Jeb Bush, Marco Rubio and Ted Cruz; both Rubio and Cruz were the children of immigrants from Cuba, and Bush's wife was an immigrant from Mexico. None spoke openly in favor of bilingual education, though all were defensive of their own bilingual skills and of language diversity in general when attacked by fellow candidate Donald Trump (whose wife Melania is an immigrant from Slovenia and is reputed to speak Slovene, English, French, German, Italian and Serbo-Croatian). Trump had declared:

> Well, I think that when you get right down to it, we're a nation that speaks English. I think that, while we're in this nation, we should be speaking English.... Whether people like it or not, that's how we assimilate. (*Hollywood Reporter*, 2015: 1)

Trump even chastised Jeb Bush for using Spanish on the campaign trail, saying 'he should really set the example by speaking English while in the United States' (*The Hollywood Reporter*, 2015: 1). On the Democrat side of the 2016 election, vice-presidential candidate Tim Kaine readily utilized the Spanish-speaking skills he picked up as a Catholic missionary in Honduras. Reactions to Kaine's Spanish ranged from praise, to ridicule, to charges of pandering to Latinx voters (Flegenhiemer, 2016). Donald Trump defeated Hillary Clinton in the general election on November 8, 2016. The result was the paradox of a monolingual President who has been critical of immigrants and bilingualism, and an immigrant First Lady, only the second to have been born outside of the United States (following Louisa Catherine Johnson Adams, wife of sixth President John Quincy Adams, born in England), the first non-native English-speaker and first truly multilingual First Lady in US history. However, Melania was never held up as a multilingual role model, was mocked on late-night television with imitations of her foreign-sounding accent, and rarely used her status as First Lady to counter her husband's anti-immigrant rhetoric or to advocate for language minoritized students and communities. Instead, she chose to maintain a very low profile during the four tumultuous years of the first Trump administration.

During the Biden administration there was a shift to a more positive national rhetoric on diversity from the White House. While neither President Joe Biden nor Vice President Kamala Harris appears to be bilingual, both come from strong civil rights backgrounds. Harris has the distinction of being the first woman, first African-American, and first South Asian American to serve as Vice President – and carried many of these firsts as the Democratic nominee for President in the 2024 election. Biden's Department of Education in particular launched an initiative declaring 'bilingualism is a superpower'. Nonetheless, the assimilationist, melting-pot attitude among many in the United States continues and, as noted above, anti-immigrant rhetoric was particularly harsh from the Trump–Vance campaign leading up to the 2024 presidential election, and which may have played a role in Trump's success in regaining the presidency.

The Advance of English in the United States

Within the United States, basic differences in 'language orientation' are especially exemplified in the movement to make English the official rather than the *de facto* national language. The political debate over the place of English in the United States illustrates how languages can be alternatively seen as a problem, right or resource. At the federal level, there is no reference to language in either the 1776 Declaration of Independence or the 1789 United States Constitution, the two founding documents of the United States. However, over the past few decades there have been proposals to add amendments to the Constitution that would name English as the official language. Considerable debate about 'official English' or English-only legislation has occurred.

In April 1981, Senator S.I. Hayakawa, a Californian Republican, proposed an English Language Amendment to the US Constitution. This aimed at making English the official language of the United States so as, he said, to develop further participative democracy and unification. The Amendment failed but it helped spawn the 'English-only' or 'official English' movement. The 'US English' organization was founded in 1983 by Senator Hayakawa and John Tanton, who was particularly interested in restrictions on immigration and population control. While failing to pass federal legislation declaring English as the official language of the United States, the movement has been more successful lobbying at the state level. Currently 32 states have some form of legislation declaring English to be the official language of the state, the most recent being West Virginia, which passed such legislation in 2016. The influence of the US English organization, however, may be on the decline (Box 17.3).

Box 17.3 The case of US English

The US English organization failed in its mission to have English declared as the official language of the United States. As of 2024, it appears that US English may no longer be active. Its website was last updated in 2021 and it no longer appears to have active social media accounts. In 2021 its Twitter account had only 185 followers, and its last tweet was in February 2018. Its last few posts on Facebook were in March and April of 2018, with 7 to 45 likes and just a handful of comments and shares.

However, US English was just part of a larger highly interconnected anti-immigration effort. Wiley (2022) has documented the close connections between US English and 11 other pro-English and anti-immigration organizations that were all founded by John Tanton beginning in the 1970s. Tanton's organizations were mainly funded by one philanthropist, Cordelia May, heiress of the Mellon-Scaife family fortune, and one of the wealthiest women in the United States before her death in 2005. Wiley further documents the close connections of these May–Tanton organizations with five individuals who held top positions within the Trump administrations, including Steven Miller, the architect of Trump's harshest immigration policies.

The English-only movement argues that English is the social glue that bonds diverse Americans and overcomes differences. English is therefore best learnt early (e.g. by mainstreaming) to counteract the tendency for immigrants to refuse to learn English. If heritage languages are allowed to flourish, there will be conflict, separatism and inter-group hostility.

As Barker and Giles (2002) found in one of the few empirical studies of the English-only movement, Anglo-Americans supporting the English-only position believe that Latinx vitality (e.g. economic and political power and status) is growing in the United States as Anglo vitality is decreasing. In this research, attachment to a traditional conceptualization of 'good Americans' was connected to an English-only position. Less contact with the Spanish language was associated with greater support for the English-only position. Those with lower levels of education were more likely to support that position, as were those who were in blue-collar employment or unemployed. Such groups may perceive Latinxs as more of a threat to their chances of enhancement and improvement. This suggests that the roots of English-only may lie not only in personal insecurity and intolerance of difference but also in perceived threats to power, position and privilege, plus a fear of difference and competition for perceived scarce resources (Barker *et al.*, 2001).

For English-only advocates, bilingual education is seen as promoting separatist language communities, a division in US society, an indifference to English, and making English-speakers strangers in their own localities (Crawford, 2003). Instead, they argue, the English language should unite and harmonize. Learning English early in school, and learning curriculum content through English, would produce, it is claimed, integrated neighborhoods. The preferred immigrant is someone who learns English quickly as well as acquiring US customs and culture, acquires skills that are useful to the economic prosperity of the country, works hard and achieves the US dream. For critics of bilingual education in the United States, such education serves to destroy rather than to deliver that dream.

The movement for English as the proclaimed US national language has not been purely about English and national unity. Anti-immigration, racism, bigotry, paranoia, xenophobia, white supremacy and dominance have also been present (Crawford, 2004; Flores, 2024). A memorandum by Dr John Tanton, when chairman of US English, revealed the darker side: 'As Whites see their power and control over their lives declining, will they simply go quietly into the night? Or will there be an explosion?' (quoted in Crawford, 2004: 136). This memorandum went on to pose perceived threats from Latinxs: bribery as an accepted culture, Roman Catholicism as cultivating Church authority rather than national authority, the non-use of birth control and fast population growth, high drop-out rates in school and low educability. This suggests scapegoating, the displacement of fears about social, political and economic positioning onto language, and using English as a means of asserting cultural and economic superiority (Dicker, 2003). US English is deeply connected to anti-immigration organizations (see Box 17.3).

Schmidt (2009) argues that Latinxs are surrounded by English language hegemony in the United States. Such hegemony refers to the apparent consent of oppressed Latinxs to their own domination by the most powerful class in society, who are monolingual English language speakers. 'This hegemonic status of the English language is supported as well by the frequent conflation of race, class and language in US society' (Schmidt, 2009: 142). To some, Latinx can mean a different race, an underclass of 'maids, leaf blowers, gardeners … and a foreign identity' (García, 2009b: 153), with an inherent perceived explanation for failure by being a Latinx. Spanish can then be stigmatized as a barrier to social and economic mobility. A Spanish accent or Spanglish becomes associated with low achievement and illiteracy. Bilingual neighborhoods become equated with slum areas. As Schmidt observes:

> The hegemonic status of the English language, not only in the US itself but increasingly throughout the world, renders English dominance so powerful that living one's public life through it exclusively is experienced as 'common sense' for any rational person trying to advance her interests in the 'real' world. (Schmidt, 2009: 147)

While the debate about integration and pluralism will be examined in the next chapter, there is agreement about certain desirable outcomes between the positions of the English-only group and the 'English-plus' pro-bilingual response in the United States (e.g. both agree about children becoming fluent in English). The difference is in the route to its achievement. For the English-only group, English language skills are best acquired through English monolingual education. For the English-plus group, skills in the English language can be successfully fostered through 'strong' forms of bilingual education. Both groups appear to acknowledge that full English proficiency is important in opening doors to higher education, the economy and the occupational market. Full proficiency in the majority language is usually equated with a route to equality of educational and vocational opportunity. The goal of bilingualism must be strongly identified as meaning high competence in English and not just in a home language. Strong forms of bilingual education can deliver that agenda.

As Chapter 12 shows, there is considerable evidence to support strong versions of bilingual education. Such evidence supports the use of the home minoritized language in the classroom at no cost to majority language competence. Achievement across the curriculum, achievement in subjects as diverse as science and social studies, mathematics and world language learning would not seem to suffer but to be enhanced by strong forms of bilingual education. As Chapter 7 shows, research on the cognitive effects of bilingualism supports the idea that ownership of two languages enhances rather than impoverishes intellectual functioning.

There is a continuing need to counter misleading dominant majority views of bilingual education with strong arguments for linguistic and cultural pluralism. As shown in Chapter 9, there is evidence of hope in the United States. Anti-bilingual education laws have been overturned in California and Massachusetts and loosened in Arizona, dual language programs are growing in popularity and the Seal of Biliteracy has been adopted in all states. The Black Lives Matter and anti-racism protests of 2020 raised awareness for anti-racist education and institutional scrutiny of discriminatory policies and procedures that function in ways that limit opportunities for racialized minorities. Despite recent political backlash on these developments, there will likely be future opportunities for consciousness-raising and gaining even stronger public and institutional support for bilingual forms of education.

Conclusion

Whether the surrounding community and society see language as a problem, right or resource affects the role of languages in a school. When a 'language as a problem' attitude is dominant, bilingual education is likely to be discouraged. Language rights may give bilingual education a protected entitlement to exist. The 'language as a resource' orientation may allow bilingual education to flourish. Thus these three orientations have different outcomes for bilinguals and bilingual education.

But political debates about bilingual education go deeper into politics and personal arguments. Does bilingual education lead to greater or lesser tolerance, a common or a separate identity, or an ability to belong to two cultures simultaneously? Are language minoritized children taught (rightly or wrongly) to be in conflict or at peace with the majority? Is bilingual education the arena for a power struggle between majority and minority? These questions are examined in the next chapter through the central debate on assimilation and pluralism.

Key Points in This Chapter

- Three perspectives on languages depict variations among individuals and institutions: language as a problem, right or resource.
- The 'language as a problem' orientation is currently prevalent in the political and mass media in the United States, where the cultural assimilation of immigrants is sought, but not necessarily their economic assimilation.
- Language rights can be individual, group and international. In the United States, rights are tested in law courts.
- 'Language as a resource' includes languages as a personal, community and societal resource.
- Bilingualism can provide a communication, intellectual, cultural, economic, social and citizenship resource.
- The place of English in the United States is frequently contested, with attempts by English-only groups to have English declared as the sole official US language.

Suggested Further Reading

- Björklund, S. and Björklund, M. (eds) (2023) *Policy and Practice for Multilingual Educational Settings: Comparisons across Contexts*. Multilingual Matters.
- Faingold, E.D. (2020) *Language Rights and the Law in the European Union*. Palgrave Macmillan.
- Kuteeva, M. (2023) *Tension-Filled English at the Multilingual University: A Bakhtinian Perspective*. Multilingual Matters.
- Ndhlovu, F. and Makalela, L. (2021) *Decolonising Multilingualism in Africa: Recentering Silenced Voices from the Global South*. Multilingual Matters.
- Rose, H., Syrbe, M., Montakantiwong, A. and Funada, N. (2020) *Global TESOL for the 21st Century: Teaching English in a Changing World*. Multilingual Matters.
- Rolstad, K., Wright, W.E., Liu, N. and MacSwan, J. (eds) (2025) *Language Diversity, Policy and Social Justice: In Honor of Terrence G. Wiley*. Multilingual Matters.

On the Web

- ABC – What would you do? Waitress berates Latino couple for speaking Spanish (video)
  https://youtu.be/SR0H-TvW9O0
- English Plus vs. English Only (League of United Latin American Citizens)
  https://lulac.org/advocacy/issues/english_vs_spansih/
- Language Rights – Interview with Colin Williams (video)
  https://youtu.be/3x81y0yg13Y
- Students' Rights to Their Own Languages (SRTOL) – Statement by CCCC
  https://cccc.ncte.org/cccc/resources/positions/srtolsummary
- Suzanne Talhouk: Don't kill your language (TedTalk video)
  https://www.ted.com/talks/suzanne_talhouk_don_t_kill_your_language

Discussion Questions

(1) What policies, programs or leaders in your local area appear to take a language-as-problem orientation? What impact does this orientation have on bilingual students and communities? How do such local language issues connect to topics such as immigration, racism, politics, employment and religion in your community?

(2) How can viewing language as a resource help mitigate debates between those viewing language as a problem and those viewing language as a right?

(3) How are debates over language and language policy in the United States or other nations linked to larger issues of immigration and immigrants? Are the debates about language, or more about the people who happen to speak those languages? Organize a group presentation or debate in class where each of three groups takes one of the three orientations.

Study Activities

(1) Visit a local school to learn more about the programs and services for bilingual students. Determine if these programs take the orientation of a language as problem, right or resource. If language as problem, what changes could be made to shift it toward a right or resource orientation?

(2) Conduct an internet search for speeches, comments and position statements of local or national politicians or candidates running for public office as related to language. Analyze these to determine the orientation this individual takes toward language (i.e. problem, right, resource). How might you respond either to challenge or to support this individual's views?

(3) Conduct an online search of local, national or international mass media and/or popular social media to find examples of individuals, schools or government institutions that represent each of the three orientations toward language (as a problem, right or resource).

CHAPTER 18
Bilingualism and Bilingual Education: Ideology, Identity and Empowerment

Introduction

Ideology and Bilingualism
Assimilation
Pluralism
Alternatives

Identity

Empowerment

Conclusion

CHAPTER 18

Bilingualism and Bilingual Education: Ideology, Identity and Empowerment

Introduction

Politicians, policymakers and the public have varying agendas about languages. Some wish to assimilate different language groups into a homogeneous society of **monolinguals** while others are keen to retain linguistic diversity. Some language minorities dream of self-sustainability and self-determination. Others aspire to internationalism (e.g. Europeanization) and globalism. Education for bilingual students is impacted by a range of language ideologies, which in turn may impact students' **identity**. Valdés (2017: 323) synthesizes various definitions of **language ideologies**, as 'feelings, ideas, conceptions, and cultural models of language that may appear to be commonsensical but are, in fact, constructed from specific political economic perspectives and frequently result in evaluative views about speakers and their language use'. Research on language ideologies seeks to 'examine the ways in which our common-sense notions about language are always situated, biased, and the result of historical and contemporary processes' (Rosa & Burdick, 2017: 108). As Archey (2024: 294) notes, 'in bilingual settings, language ideologies are intertwined with the notions of power'. **Empowerment** and the healing of past racial and linguistic discrimination can enable bilingual students to develop positive bilingual identities and higher levels of academic success. We explore these issues below.

Ideology and Bilingualism

Valdés (2017) notes that ideologies are plural and thus need to be regarded as a cluster of different concepts in order to account for a number of convergent dimensions. Drawing on the analytic strands of language ideologies identified by Kroskrity (2010), Valdés highlights some of these different concepts. First, language ideologies 'protect and legitimate the interests of particular social groups'. Second, 'language ideologies are multiple and include divergent and contradictory perspectives' (Valdés, 2017: 324). Third, members of particular communities may be aware of but unable to articulate existing ideologies. And fourth, when users construct language ideologies, they use different semiotic processes as they attempt to differentiate their own language and social practices from those of 'others' from different social groups.

Language ideologies drive language policies in society. Bourhis (2001) proposes four ideologies related to language minorities and **bilingualism** – pluralist, civic, assimilationist and ethnist – and describes how these ideologies influence formal and informal public policies and practices.

(1) *Pluralist ideology* tends to assert an individual's liberty to own, learn and use two or more languages (e.g. at school or in the workplace). This right is then supported by those in power by promotion-oriented language policies (Wiley, 2015). Given that a **language minority** pays taxes, 'it is equitable that state funds be distributed to support the cultural and linguistic activities of both the majority and the minority group' (Bourhis, 2001: 11). Schools, the judiciary and civil administration are expected to operate bilingually, where reasonable, and not in opposition to national coherence and unity. Canada's Official Languages Act (1969, 1988) and Multiculturalism Act (1988) reflect such a pluralist ideology.

(2) *Civic ideology* expects language minorities to adopt the public values of the politically dominant majority while allowing freedom in the private values of individuals (e.g. in relation to a minoritized language and **culture**). No public funding of the language minority is expected. Instead, civic ideology 'is characterized by an official state policy of non-intervention and non-support of the minoritized languages and cultures' (Bourhis, 2001: 12). This is considered as a tolerance-oriented language policy (Wiley, 2015).

(3) *Assimilation ideology* tends to argue that there may be some areas of private values where the state has a right to intervene. Language is such an area. Immigrants are expected to abandon their **heritage language**. This may be voluntarily and gradually, across generations, or speedily, by state regulation in public domains (e.g. exclusion of minoritized languages in schools). The politically and economically dominant group often has a vested interest in preserving its privileged position by asserting that its majority language is a symbol and creator of a unified and integrated nation. In contrast, minoritized languages and cultures are seen as potentially divisive and conflictive, working against national loyalty and allegiance by producing factions. Many forms of restriction-oriented language policies facilitate this ideology (Wiley, 2015).

(4) *Ethnist ideology* encourages or forces language minorities to give up their language and culture and adopt those of the dominant group. It also attempts to prevent or exclude such minorities from assimilating legally or socially, even when such individuals seek cultural, linguistic and economic assimilation. The ideology is exclusive and defines who can be a rightful member of the dominant group or a legitimate citizen. For example, only certain racial groups are given full legal status as determined by 'blood', birth and kinship. Political, economic and social marginalization may result. Wiley (2015) terms this a repression-oriented language policy. At an extreme, ethnist ideology results in a policy of exclusion, expulsion, apartheid, ethnic cleansing and even genocide.

The social and political questions surrounding bilingual education in many countries tend to revolve around two contrasting ideological positions – assimilation and pluralism. Assimilation is a belief that cultural groups should give up their heritage cultures and take on the host society's way of life. In contrast, pluralism believes that these groups should maintain their heritage cultures in combination with the host culture. In the United States, for example, pluralists favor the state recognizing, supporting and promoting minoritized languages, while **assimilationists** push for national and state policies making English the sole official language. In the context of schools, de Jong (2011) distinguishes between those beliefs that reflect **assimilationist discourses** and those that reflect **pluralist discourses**. In schools that uphold assimilationist discourses, the home languages and cultures of bilingual students are devalued and seen as a problem. In contrast, schools sustaining pluralist discourses recognize the home languages and cultures of students as rich resources for helping students learn academic content, and strive to help students develop high levels of proficiency and literacy in both languages (Wright, 2025).

We now consider assimilation and pluralism in more depth, along with potential policy alternatives.

Assimilation

Assimilation has been a favored response to the considerable immigration in the United States and many other countries. Historically, the US deal with immigrants has been: 'Come to this economically prosperous land, start a new and better life, but assimilate and become "American"'. As early as the 1890s, assimilationists (including Presidents such as Theodore Roosevelt and Woodrow Wilson) attacked 'hyphenated Americans' (e.g. German-Americans, Irish-Americans), accusing them of maintaining allegiance to a foreign country. The assimilationist expectation is that immigrants will give up their native tongue and not take on such 'hyphenated' dual identities. Thus, cultural unity and national solidarity are seen as being achieved through assimilation. The pattern of a three-generation shift from a native language to English (see Chapter 4) among immigrant families delivers this assimilationist expectation, with about 80% of the third generation speaking only English in the United States (Salaberry, 2009). The transition to English **monolingualism** and loss of bilingualism can be swift and successful; a recent trend is for some minoritized groups to show a shift to English by the **1.5 generation** (Rumbaut, 2009; Wright, 2014a).

The assimilationist viewpoint is pictured in the idea of a melting pot. Zangwill's (1909) play *The Melting Pot*, first performed in 1908 at the Columbia Theater in Washington, introduced the idea of diverse immigrant elements being merged to make a new homogenized whole. 'Into the Crucible with you all! God is making the American' (Act I). The idea of the melting pot immediately offers two different perspectives. First, there is the idealized notion that the final product, for example the 'American', is made up from contributions from all the cultural groups that enter the pot. The cultural groups melt together until the final product is a unique combination. No one ingredient dominates. Each cultural group makes its own contribution to the final product. However, the second perspective is the usual view associated with the melting pot, where cultural groups give up their heritage culture and adopt that of the host culture. They have been melted into just one substance. The problem with this view is that white-skinned immigrants may 'melt' more easily than immigrants of color. For example, many **Latinx** and Asian Americans born and raised in the United States and who grew up speaking only English frequently face questions from fellow US Americans such as 'What country are you from?' and 'How did you learn to speak English so well?' Such questions may appear as friendly conversation starters, harmless curiosities, or ignorance at best, yet to the recipient they can be 'microaggressions' that send subtle yet hurtful messages such as 'you're not a real American', 'you don't really belong here' and 'you will forever be a foreigner'.

An assimilationist perspective is partly based on equality of opportunity and a meritocracy that enables each individual to have a fair chance of economic prosperity.

Such a view argues that the separate existence of different racial and cultural groups prevents such equality. When the emphasis is on individuality in terms of rights, freedom, effort and affluence, the argument for assimilation is that language groups should not have separate privileges and rights from the rest of society. The advantage and disadvantage associated with language minoritized groups must be avoided so that individual equality of opportunity can prevail.

Assimilationists also argue that bilingual education produces segregation, because language minoritized children are isolated from mainstream society, thereby depriving them of economic, political and social opportunities. Such segregation is claimed both to impede their learning of English and to produce physical segregation from mainstream students. Another element claimed by assimilationists is that bilingual education teaches children to have a separate sense of ethnic and national identity, for example to be Latinx rather than 'American'.

Measuring the extent to which assimilation has occurred is difficult for assimilationists. Is assimilation measured by segregation and integration in terms of housing of immigrants, by their positions within the economic order, by the extent of intermarriage between different cultural groups or by the attitudes they exhibit? Assimilation is thus multidimensional and complex. Assimilation is neither easily defined nor easily quantified. Assimilationists may also have differing views. One example will illustrate. Some assimilationists may accept the idea of students maintaining their home languages and cultures. However, they would argue that this is the responsibility of the home or the local language community and not the school. This tolerance-oriented view (Wiley, 2015) opens up space for **acculturation**; that is, immigrants may adopt the host society's language and culture without sacrificing their own. Other assimilationists, however, want the abandonment of the minoritized languages and cultures.

In a decade-long longitudinal study on the assimilation of children of immigrants, Rumbaut (2009) followed over 3,000 adolescent students in the 1.5 and later generations from age 14 (1992) to age 24 (2002) in South Florida and Southern California. Rumbaut found that for the 2.0 generation, preference for English increased from 81% in 1992 to 98% by 2002. By 2002, less than 45% of the 2.0 generation and less than 29% of the 1.5 generation considered themselves to be fluent bilinguals. The move to English as the dominant or only language was thus apparent. Drawing from the same data, Portes and Rumbaut (2006) used measures of family solidarity, intergenerational conflict, ambition and self-esteem to identify different profiles of students. Their statistical analyses show that fluent bilingual students had the most positive profiles. For example, those fluent in English and their home language were 8% more likely to hold higher educational aspirations. Those children who retained their home language without learning English showed high family solidarity but had much lower self-esteem and ambition. Portes and Rumbaut concluded that such second-generation immigrants who do not become fluent bilinguals are deprived of key social resources at a critical time in their lives. Indeed, a complete transition to English monolingualism in the United States is not the most desirable outcome. Assimilationist ideologies that produce English language monolingualism have hidden costs for family relationships, personality development and adaptation.

Pluralism

With an increased emphasis on ethnicity since the 1960s, the assumptions of assimilation have been challenged (see Fishman, 2010). Assimilationist ideologies in North

America and Europe were challenged by the emergence of concepts like 'integration', 'ethnic diversity', 'pluralism', 'superdiversity' and 'multiculturalism'. The picture of the melting pot has been contrasted with alternative images to represent languages and cultures in society: the patchwork quilt, the tossed salad, the linguistic mosaic and the language garden. One popular metaphor is the salad bowl, with each ingredient separate and distinguishable, but contributing in a valuable and unique way to the whole. A different 'integration' metaphor, favored in Canada, is the linguistic mosaic, with different pieces joined together in one holistic arrangement. But such pictures are essentially simplistic.

A pluralist approach assumes that different language groups can live together in the same territory in relative harmony and without the unjust **domination** of one group by another. An atmosphere of mutual understanding and tolerance is the ideal. As Schmidt explains:

> Pluralists also argue that individual bilingualism is not only possible but desirable in that it facilitates cultural enrichment and cross-cultural understanding. By combating distrust and intolerance toward linguistic diversity, pluralists hope to create a climate of acceptance that will promote greater status equality between ethnolinguistic groups and therefore a higher level of national unity. (Schmidt, 2000: 62–63)

Assimilationists suggest that linguistic pluralism leads to ethnic enclaves that cause inequalities between groups and ethnic conflict, rather than promoting harmony. For such people, linguistic assimilation provides the social, political and economic integration necessary for equality of opportunity and political harmony. In reality, there are often large status differences and hierarchies between languages in a society. Where one language is associated with power, wealth and prestige, the tendency of individuals is to choose the language of economic and social mobility.

Alternatives

The assimilationist argument ignores the legacy of racialized ethnic injustice in the United States and misconstrues the nature of relationships between individual identity, culture, the state and equality of opportunity. But there are also obstacles to complete acceptance of the pluralist position. Schmidt (2000) argues that the kind of social integration envisioned by pluralism may actually perpetuate the very social inequalities between language groups that it seeks to overcome. Similarly, as discussed in Chapter 17, the denial of language rights can lead to the very kinds of conflict such denial seeks to prevent (Davies & Dubinsky, 2018; Lo Bianco, 2019). Pluralists argue for individual choice in language and culture, but there is no equal choice if there is no equal starting point or level playing field. The context of choice for individuals is constrained by numerous unequal circumstances for which language minorities bear no responsibility. The language of power in the United States is English, so individuals will typically choose English in pursuit of their own social and economic advantage. Social mobility and economic advance are pragmatically unlikely from a pluralist position, however strong the intellectual arguments. As Schmidt (2000) concludes, both views are unrealistic:

> Assimilationists are unrealistic because their ideology posits a monocultural and monolingual country that does not exist in the real world; more importantly, a consequence of its unrealistic assumptions is the continued unjust subordination of language

minority groups by the privileged Anglo, European-origin majority. Pluralists too are unrealistic in that they assume that an egalitarian society of multiple cultural communities can be achieved through a combination of individualistic rights-based free choice measures and moral exhortations to Anglos to respect linguistic and cultural diversity. (Schmidt, 2000: 209)

In Québec, one political answer has been to seek to establish a separate French language community. Historically, the establishment of separate linguistic territories was common in the United States as different linguistic minoritized groups immigrated and established isolated small towns in rural areas across the country (e.g. Germans in the Midwest). Tribal lands and Native American reservations also technically provided linguistic territories free from pressures to shift to English (Wiley & Wright, 2004). However, with the advent of infrastructure (e.g. railways, roads, bridges), increased trade, the growth and draw of large cities, and easy access to English language mass media (radio, television, newspapers, movies, the internet and social media), maintaining such linguistic isolation and avoiding contact with English-speakers became increasingly difficult and impractical. In Puerto Rico, English is an official language alongside Spanish, even though Spanish continues to be the **dominant language** of most residents. Another alternative is an enhanced pluralist language policy in the United States that aims for pluralistic integration. This alternative is supported by May (2011, 2018), who argues for language minoritized group rights that retain within them the protection of individual liberties.

The two positions of assimilation and pluralism differ in such fundamental ideological ways that simple compromises and resolutions are virtually impossible. When evidence for the maintenance of minoritized languages and cultures is produced, assimilationists are likely to argue that attitudes and behavior are still in the process of change. That is, assimilationists will argue that, over time, people will move away from minority cultural maintenance and prefer the majority language and culture. Assimilationists tend to believe that bilingualism and biculturalism are temporary and transient, and lead eventually to a preferable, unifying monolingualism. When evidence favors assimilation having taken place in society (e.g. by the second or third generation), pluralists will tend to argue in two different ways: first, that the change towards assimilation has occurred only on certain dimensions (e.g. language rather than economic assimilation); second, that sometimes the wheel turns full circle – revival and resurrection in future generations may occur in response to repression and renouncement by previous generations.

Any such resolution of the assimilation versus pluralism debate is strongly affected by economics. Both assimilation and pluralism can be promoted and defended by the need to earn a living and the desire to acquire or increase affluence. Assimilation may be chosen to secure a job, to be vocationally successful and to achieve prosperity. The minoritized language and culture may be left behind in order to prosper in the majority language community. At the same time, knowledge of the minoritized language and culture may provide access to further economic opportunities, especially when **language planning** is used to ensure that there are jobs and promotion within the minoritized language community (see Chapters 3 and 19).

Resolution of assimilation versus pluralism is sometimes avoided. The dominant group in society may, at times, not prefer the assimilation of minoritized groups. Such minoritized groups may not be permitted to assimilate, thus keeping their members in poorly paid employment. Such a minoritized group is then exploited by the dominant group. The economic interests of the majority group can be served by 'internal colonialism' rather than assimilation (e.g. economically isolating or manipulating an indigenous minoritized language group for majority group advantage).

Despite popular tales of rags to riches and 'living the American dream', proficiency in the majority language is no guarantee of economic improvement (see Chapter 19). According to 2020 data from the US Census Bureau (2021), English-speaking non-Hispanic Whites by far make up the greatest numbers of Americans living in poverty, at 15,942 million (8.2%). In comparison, about 8.5 million African-Americans live below the poverty line, though the percentage is higher (19.5%). Even with high and increasing levels of English language proficiency and English language dominance, poverty rates remain high among individuals of Hispanic origin (17.0%), and individuals of Asian origin also have a poverty rate (8.1%) nearly equal to non-Hispanic Whites.

Two opposing views – assimilation and pluralism – have so far been discussed. Other positions are possible. It is possible to participate in mainstream society and maintain one's minoritized language and culture (i.e. acculturation). For many individuals, there will be both a degree of assimilation and a degree of preservation of one's heritage. Total assimilation and total isolation may be less likely than some accommodation of the majority ideology within an overall ideology of pluralism; this is cultural maintenance within partial assimilation. Within multiculturalism and pluralism, an aggressive, militant pluralism may be seen as a threat to the social harmony of society. Instead, a more liberal pluralistic viewpoint may allow both membership of the wider community and an identification with the heritage cultural community.

The political debate over assimilation and pluralism is fundamental to understanding language minorities and is ever present in language debates, including about bilingual schooling. But such debates need to be placed in their historical context, particularly where immigrants are concerned. The expectation was that refugees and immigrants to the United States, Australia, Canada, Germany and the United Kingdom, for example, would be pleased to have escaped political oppression or economic disadvantage and would be jubilant in embracing equality of opportunity and personal freedom. The expectation was that an individual would be pleased to give up their past identity and make a commitment to a new national identity. Yet heritage culture and cultural identity have persisted, resisted and insisted. Assimilation has not always occurred among immigrants. Is this deliberate or unintended, desired or unwelcome?

Assimilation may be sought by immigrants. Many do wish to assimilate but come to reside in segregated neighborhoods and segregated schools. Thus desired assimilation can be prevented by racism, discrimination and other social and economic factors outside the wishes of the immigrants. Some groups of immigrants may wish to be recognized as US citizens but are categorized and discriminated against by mainstream society as different, separate and as 'foreigners' or 'legal aliens'. The conditions under which immigrants live may create the negative labels and social barriers that enforce non-integration. The result may be the prevention of assimilation and integration, with a consequent need to embrace some form of pluralism for survival, security, status and self-enhancement.

The fact that the United States is a 'language graveyard' with rapid shifts to English dominance among the 1.5 and second generation (Rumbaut, 2009) makes it clear that language minoritized immigrants want to learn English and do learn English. Thus, strong measures to assimilate immigrants or initiatives to promote English assimilation in schools are not necessarily needed. Many immigrants have a motive to learn

English rapidly and well (Salaberry, 2009). Immigration does not pose a threat to the dominance of English in the United States or the United Kingdom.

If the linguistic assimilation of immigrants occurs so easily, what happens to their identity? What is won and lost by an immigrant when assimilating? Why is pluralism not easily accepted by some language minorities and by many language majorities? To begin to answer this, the nature of identity needs exploring.

Identity

The reciprocal relationship between language and identity is complex (Rudolph *et al.*, 2020) (see Chapter 6). For someone who expresses their identity as being Basque or Catalan, speaking in the Basque or Catalan language is typically an important boundary marker. In contrast, ask Celtic people if it is essential to speak Gaelic or Irish to feel Scottish or Irish and the answer is usually 'no'. There are other ways of establishing a Scottish or Irish identity than through language. Otherwise, for example, according to the 2011 national Census, 98.3% of Scottish people might not identify as being Scottish as they do not speak Gaelic (National Records of Scotland, 2018).

Nevertheless, language is, in general, one of the strongest symbols and boundary markers of group, regional, cultural or national identity (Kraus, 2024). Language is a highly influential but not an essential element in a collective identity such as Welsh or Māori or Latinx. Moreover, languages change in individuals across time in terms of competence, usage and attitude. Someone may not retain their Spanish language yet still express their identity as Latinx (Flores & Brown, 2023).

Views about the relationship between language and identity are contested and conflicted (Alfaro & Hernández, 2024; Boun & Duran, 2024; Block, 2014; Newcomer, 2020; Seals, 2020; Shin, 2018; Toohey, 2018; Trofimovich & Turuševa, 2020). Our individual identity is not fixed, given or unitary. Identity is socially created and developed through language, through an intentional negotiation of meanings and understandings. We speak a language or languages and it or they often identify our origins, history, membership and culture. But that identity is daily rewritten, reimagined, reconstructed, renegotiated and displayed as we interpret sociocultural experiences and take on multiple roles and identities (Norton, 2013; Wang & Lamb, 2024). Bilingual education provides an important context for students' identity construction (García-Mateus *et al.*, 2024). Our identity is conveyed in our language, in our expressions and engagements, predilections and preferences. Language is a symbol of our identity, conveying our preferred distinctiveness and allegiance. However, language does not by itself define us. It is one feature or marker among many that make up our constructed, shifting and hybrid identity.

We do not own an identity so much as hybrid and multiple identities. The sociocultural constructions of our gender, age, ethnicity, race, dress, nationality, region (e.g. county, state), locality, group membership (e.g. religion, politics), status, socioeconomic class, for example, provide us with a host of complementary, diverse, interacting, ever-changing, negotiated identities. A girl can speak English and Spanish, be a Muslim, Democrat, see herself as American, San Francisco Californian and Mexican, with identity as a teenager and trombonist, a gifted student and lesbian. As contexts change, our identities are reframed, developed, sometimes challenged, sometimes in conflict. We do not establish our identities by ourselves but through social comparison, labeling by others, dialogue within ourselves and with others, and through the experience of ever-varying dramas and arenas, plays and stages.

No one is purely their labels. To share identity as a woman, White and Welsh-speaking is just a temporary starter and is left behind as further distinctiveness, connections and complexity become apparent. Labels are sometimes fleeting as situations and contexts change. This is particularly the case with ethnic labels (or national identities), which are too general and reductionist. Being a Jew or Arab does not immediately correspond with other fixed religious, economic or personality attributes. Young people in particular reconstruct their 'language' and 'culture' with new mixtures that vary across situations (Ngo, 2010; Poza, 2019). Rampton (2014) noted the 'language crossing' of teenagers in London who shared expressions in each other's languages, a multi-ethnic form of talking. Such a friendly crossing of languages created a new set of multilingual identities. But multiple identities may involve a challenge to establishing a coherent sense of Self, which is not always achieved, as inherent tensions and conflicts may remain (Block, 2014).

A context that affects how language and identity interact is immigration. Eva Hoffman (1989: 107) recalls herself as a 13-year-old Polish immigrant to Canada:

> I wait for the spontaneous flow of inner language which used to be my night-time talk with myself.... Nothing comes. Polish, in a short time, has atrophied, shriveled from sheer uselessness. Its words don't apply to my new experiences.... In English, words have not penetrated to those layers of my psyche from which a private conversation could proceed.

When writing in her teenage diary, Hoffman found that her Polish was now connected with the past, so she wrote in impersonal, school English, the language of the present, but not the language of the Self. However, immigrants often produce vibrant, volatile, commodified, new ethnic identities and are not easily classified into existing cultural, ethnic or linguistic groups (Westerlund, 2019). Young people growing up in multilingual urban settings (e.g. Utrecht, London, New York) are simplistically considered as Turkish-Dutch, Somali-British or Cuban-American. They may be seen by others as Dutch, British or American, but the self-perception of identity may be of a new, dynamic, multiple, overlapping and situationally changing nature. Language and ethnic dimensions of identity interact with other attributes such that we have simultaneous, fluid and complex multiple classifications. Stereotyping, prejudice and distance may be reduced when we see others across multiple classifications rather than just by, for example, ethnicity or language. Reyes (2011), in her study of language, identity and stereotyping among Southeast Asian American youth, found that students often reappropriate stereotypes to reposition their own identities and others in meaningful ways. Deaf people are much more than being deaf, and vary not only among themselves in identity but also on different occasions in seeing themselves as Deaf people or not (see Chapter 16).

Identity is imposed, assumed and negotiated (Evans & Liu, 2018). For some, being called a member of a language minority is imposed and negative since 'minority' suggests a stigma of being marginal, non-mainstream and unusual. They are 'minoritized' by the dominant group. The alternative term 'language minoritized students' highlights the agency of marginalization by the dominant group. However, labels such as 'linguistically diverse' try to create an identity that is more positive.

Such labels can be ascribed rather than chosen. For example, an individual may not describe themselves as a 'Bengali-speaker' or 'Cantonese bilingual' or a 'Deaf-signing person', as these may hint at negative, unwanted differences in a homogeneous society. Instead of 'native speaker' and 'heritage language' to describe the language of a child, 'language expertise' and 'language affiliation' may be more positive. Similarly, the label 'Hispanic' for some is a derogatory term. 'Negro' became 'Black person' to signal an identity based on freedom rather than slavery, and became 'African-American' to signal an identity connected to geographical space instead of a skin color. So too language-based identity labels are sometimes renewed to attempt more positive associations and expectations. Hence, some have a preference for 'Latina' and 'Latino', or the gender-neutral **Latinx** (or Latine), instead of Hispanic. Chhuon and Hudley (2010) describe the contradictory perceptions of Cambodian-American students by educators and how students must negotiate between their identities as Cambodian versus the pan-ethnic Asian identity that is often imposed upon them by others. While identities are frequently negotiated (e.g. being American, Sudanese and bilingual), at other times they are not (e.g. Jews in Nazi Germany and middle-class 'enemies of the people' in Stalinist Russia).

Such group labels are never static. In Europe, ethnic and linguistic identity is dynamic as mass immigration, technology (e.g. air travel, satellite TV, streaming video programming, social media), religion, post-colonialism, mythologizing the past, the enlargement of the European Union, the United Kingdom's exit from the EU (Brexit), feminism and intercultural and interracial marriage are just some of the many interacting modern trends that create ever-changing, hybrid language identities. This is witnessed in the adaptation of English in Europe. Germans in Germany want to sound like Germans when they speak English, not like North Americans or the British. Speaking Indian English in India is the accepted norm. Native speakers of English are outnumbered by second language speakers of English around the globe. The existence of multiple varieties of 'World Englishes' reveals that no single nation or ethnic group can claim sole ownership of English. New varieties of English emerge in multilingual communities, especially in the context of multiple identities found in popular youth culture both off- and online (Dovchin *et al.*, 2017). These multiple identities differ from their family identities and allow different strengths of membership of different networks, plus shared (not divided) loyalties.

Another debate accenting the negative, sometimes voiced by politicians and members of the public, is whether **multilingualism** leads to being caught between two or more languages, with a resulting conflict of identity, social disorientation, even isolation and split personality. This narrow monolingual view is out of touch with the reality that most people in the world are bilingual or multilingual. However, if there are anxieties and struggles in identity, bilingualism is unlikely to be the cause: 'it is not language *per se* that causes the identity crisis; rather, it is often the social, economic and political conditions surrounding the development of bilingualism' (Li Wei *et al.*, 2002: 4). Such conditions tend to relate to economic disadvantage (e.g. material poverty), political oppression, racism, social exclusion, discrimination, hostility and powerlessness.

Pavlenko and Lantolf (2000) suggest that there is a process of reconstruction of identity (e.g. in children and adults following immigration). Examples include thousands of refugees entering Europe from Syria, Iraq, Afghanistan and Ukraine following conflict, war, widespread terror or mass killings. Mango (2012) portrays the difficulties of identity for Arab-American women born in the United States. They are often misrepresented in the mass media (e.g. as belly-dancers) and stereotyped (e.g. as anti-American following 9/11). This can lead internally to frustration and annoyance, yet externally (in interactions) from remaining silent to speaking up and challenging the very negative associations often ascribed to Arab-American women. Song (2019) describes the experience of a Saudi Arabian female student's gendered experiences in the United States, and considers the ways gender intersected with cultural, religious and national discourses both within and beyond the minoritized community as the student continuously reconstructed her new identity.

Pavlenko and Lantolf (2000) suggest that after an initial loss of linguistic identity comes a period of recovery and transformation that goes through stages of: appropriation of others' voices, emergence of a new voice (e.g. in writing), and reconstructing one's past and continuous growth into new understandings and subjectivities. In terms of language, there is transformation or 're-narrativization' (reconstruction) rather than replacement, with an outcome that represents an identity in motion that is not exclusively anchored in one language or another (see e.g. M. Kim, 2016). Data from Rumbaut's (2009) study suggests that even with the rapid shift to English, there is a slight increase in reported bilingualism once adolescents leave high school and enter adulthood. This may be due to less political and social pressure to 'fit in' (assimilate) in high school and the greater freedom and acceptance of diversity in college and in adult life. The growing number of world language courses tailored to heritage language speakers at colleges and universities demonstrates some desire on the part of some students to reclaim the language a K-12 school system attempted to eradicate (Wiley *et al.*, 2014).

Empowerment

This chapter has suggested that bilingualism and bilingual education can be properly understood only through the lens of power, identity, ideology and politics (Ricento, 2022). Relations of power are at the heart of bilingual schooling (Delavan, 2024; Faltis, 2024; Pai *et al.*, 2015). This is no more so than for minoritized language children who often suffer devaluation of identity, subordination, racism and disempowerment in their schooling experience. For example, in history lessons that celebrate majority languages and cultures while devaluing minoritized language groups, a student's identity may be challenged and changed. When such minoritized languages and cultures are celebrated, the student's identity may be affirmed and accepted. Learning about local geography, reading minoritized language set books (including novels) and many writing assignments can influence a student's identity and empowerment or disempowerment.

Cummins (2013) developed a theoretical framework that directly relates to politics, policy, provision and practice with bilingual and multilingual students. He argues that language of instruction is just one of many pedagogical factors leading to empowerment and affirmation of students' identities. Thus, 'bilingual education, by itself, is not a panacea for reversing underachievement if other aspects of students' experience are not focused on empowerment' (Cummins, 2013: 2). In his framework, Cummins makes an important distinction between *coercive* and *collaborative* relations of power:

> Within a societal context of unequal power relations, classroom interactions are never neutral – they are always located on a continuum ranging between the reinforcement of coercive relations of power and the promotion of collaborative relations of power. Coercive relations of power refer to the exercise of power by a dominant individual,

group or country.... Collaborative relations of power, by contrast, reflect the sense of the term power that refers to 'being enabled,' or 'empowered' to achieve more. (Cummins, 2013: 4)

An example of *coercive* relations of power would be the assimilationist approaches described above where schools view the home language and culture of students as a problem to overcome and aim to replace them with the dominant language and culture.

While coercive power moves in one direction from the top downwards, collaborative relations of power are generated through interactions with others. Thus, power is not a fixed quantity. Cummins (2013: 4) explains:

> The more empowered one individual or group becomes, the more is generated for others to share.... Within this context *empowerment* can be defined as the *collaborative creation of power*. Students whose schooling experiences reflect collaborative relations of power know that their voices will be heard and respected within the classroom. Schooling opens up identity options and amplifies rather than silences their power of *self*-expression. [Original emphasis]

In strong forms of bilingual education – where the aim is to develop and maintain high levels of proficiency and literacy in both languages – the incorporation of the home language contributes to the collaborative creation of power. Nonetheless, even in two-way immersion programs, the balance of power is often shifted toward the interests and needs of the language majority students and their parents through the process of gentrification (Cervantes-Soon *et al.*, 2020; Delavan *et al.*, 2024; see Chapter 11). Monolingual programs in the dominant language and weak forms of bilingual education are even less likely to create contexts of empowerment for bilingual students given the aim is to move students as quickly as possible into mainstream instruction. Education and the spread of literacy are primary mechanisms for cultural and linguistic homogenization, even disempowerment of language minorities.

However, even in cases where the majority language is the predominant language of instruction, empowerment can still be generated through the adoption of bilingual strategies and translanguaging pedagogies such as encouraging writing and group discussions in the home language or other opportunities for students to showcase their multilingual talents. Empowerment also comes from developing students' higher-order thinking skills, allowing them to demonstrate their talents, and other activities that reinforce students' sense of pride in their identities. Effective programs leading to empowerment – whether labeled bilingual or not – 'will enable bilingual students to carry out powerful intellectual work using both of their languages as cognitive and creative tools' (Cummins, 2013: 4).

Cummins (2000a) identifies four school characteristics for building bilingual and multilingual student empowerment (see Box 18.1). While the discussion focuses on students, these characteristics also empower or 'disable' teachers and other educators in schools, and affect their professional identity (Wu *et al.*, 2011). The four characteristics can inspire teachers to take ownership of classroom language policy, provision and practices, for the benefit of bilingual and multilingual students (Johnson, 2010).

Empowerment thus becomes an important concept in transforming the situations of many language minorities. Empowerment means movement for bilingual and multilingual students from coercive, superior–inferior (subordinate) relationships, to collaborative relationships, power sharing and power creating, where the identities of minorities are affirmed and voiced. Such empowerment is often part of a healing

> **Box 18.1** School characteristics for bilingual and multilingual student empowerment
>
> Cummins (2000a) suggests that minority language students are 'empowered' or 'disabled' by four major characteristics of schools:
>
> - *The extent to which minority language students' home language and culture are incorporated into the school curriculum.* If a minority language child's home language and culture are excluded, minimized or quickly reduced in school, there is the likelihood that the child may become academically 'disabled'. Where the school incorporates, encourages and gives status to the minority language, the chances of empowerment are increased. This inclusion may also have effects on personality (e.g. self-esteem), attitudes and social and emotional well-being.
> - *The extent to which minority communities are encouraged to participate in their children's education.* Where parents are given power and status in the partial determination of their children's schooling, the empowerment of minority communities and children may result. When such communities and parents are kept relatively powerless, inferiority and lack of school progress may result. Empowerment is encouraged through home reading programs involving bilingual books, family literacy projects that value home language and literacy practices, and collaborative decision-making with parents.
> - *The extent to which education promotes the inner desire of children to become active seekers of knowledge and not just passive receptacles.* A transmission or 'banking' model of teaching views children as buckets into which knowledge is poured or deposited. It is disabling. In contrast, a transformative model is empowering. It requires reciprocal interaction involving genuine dialogue between student and teacher in both oral and written modalities, guidance and facilitation rather than control of student learning by the teacher, and the encouragement of student–student talk in a collaborative learning context. This model emphasizes the development of higher-level cognitive skills rather than just factual recall, and meaningful language use by students rather than the correction of surface forms. Language use and development are consciously integrated with all curricular content rather than taught as isolated subjects, and tasks are presented to students in ways that generate intrinsic rather than extrinsic motivation.
> - *The extent to which the assessment of minority language students avoids locating problems in the student and seeks to find the root of the problem in the social and educational system or curriculum wherever possible.* Psychological and educational tests tend by their very nature to locate problems in the individual student (e.g. low IQ, low motivation, poor reading skills). Assessment needs to be advocacy-oriented, by critically inspecting the social and educational context in which the child operates to locate the root of the problem (e.g. devaluing of home languages and cultures, a transmission model of instruction, exclusions of parents and the community from participation in the school and in the education of their children, etc.). This may involve comments about the power and status relationships between the dominant and dominated groups, at national, community, school and classroom level.

process for students who have historically been marginalized, discriminated against and disempowered. Empowerment can be furthered by strong forms of bilingual education but also needs to be realized in legal, social, cultural and, particularly, economic and political spheres.

Conclusion

Underneath weak and strong forms of bilingual education lie different views about language communities, ethnic minorities and language itself. When language is viewed as a problem, there is often a call for assimilation and integration. Such a view most often leads to monolingual education or weak forms of bilingual education with a focus on moving students to mainstream instruction in the dominant language as quickly as possible. Pluralists view language as a right and/or resource. This view will often lead to stronger forms of bilingual education with high levels of bilingualism and biliteracy as the aim. The relationship between language and identity, and the identity development of bilingual students is complex, constantly negotiated and ever changing. Coercive relations of power are at play when assimilationist policymakers impose education solely in the medium of the dominant language and instigate other policies and programs designed to encourage students to abandon their home languages and cultures. Collaborative relations of power can lead to empowerment of bilingual students and communities. Such empowerment is facilitated through strong forms of bilingual education, as well as education programs that value and allow students to use and showcase their talents and bilingual skills.

Key Points in This Chapter

- Language ideologies are feelings, ideas or conceptions of language that may seem commonsensical but are actually constructed from specific political and economic perspectives. They frequently result in value judgments about languages and their speakers.
- Four ideologies underpin discussions about languages in society and in schools: pluralist and assimilationist are the main 'opposites', but civic and ethnist ideologies are also present.
- Assimilation is a belief that linguistic minoritized groups should give up their home languages and cultures and adopt those of the dominant group in the host society.
- Pluralism is a belief that linguistic minoritized groups should maintain their home languages and cultures in combination with those of the dominant group in the host society.
- The identity or hybrid identities of immigrants is a key topic of debate, with contemporary views of identity suggesting social construction, constant change, negotiation and complexity.
- The term 'coercive relations of power' refers to the exercise of power by a dominant individual, group or country.
- The term 'collaborative relations of power' refers to the empowerment of individuals or groups by enabling them to achieve more. Through collaboration, power is generated and shared.

Suggested Further Reading

- Bale, J., Rajendram, S., Brubacher, K., Owoo, M.A.N., Burton, J., Wong, W., Zhang, Y., Larson, E.J., Gagné, A. and Kerekes, J. (2023) *Centering Multilingual Learners and Countering Raciolinguistic Ideologies in Teacher Education: Principles, Policies and Practices*. Multilingual Matters.
- Rheindorf, M. and Wodak, R. (eds) (2020) *Sociolinguistic Perspectives on Migration Control: Language Policy, Identity and Belonging*. Multilingual Matters.
- Rudolph, N., Selvi, A.F. and Yazan, B. (eds) (2020) *The Complexity of Identity and Interaction in Language Education*. Multilingual Matters.

Seals, C.A. (2020) *Choosing a Mother Tongue: The Politics of Language and Identity in Ukraine*. Multilingual Matters.

Wang, C. and Lamb, T. (eds) (2024) *Negotiating Identities, Language and Migration in Global London: Bridging Borders, Creating Spaces*. Multilingual Matters.

On the Web

Bilingual family night for ELL families
https://www.colorincolorado.org/article/bilingual-family-night-ell-families

Guide for engaging ELL families: 20 strategies for school leaders
https://www.colorincolorado.org/article/introduction-strategies-engaging-ell-families

Journal of Language, Identity and Education
https://www.tandfonline.com/toc/hlie20/current

Things bilingual people do (video)
https://youtu.be/ReHdQsB5rI8

Lost in translation: An interview with Eva Hoffman
https://www.psychologytoday.com/blog/life-bilingual/201511/lost-in-translation

Discussion Questions

(1) What are the differences between assimilationist and pluralist ideologies? What are the limitations of each and what alternatives are there to these views?

(2) How would you describe your identity or identities, especially in terms of your languages and bilingual/multilingual abilities? How have you negotiated your identities and how have they changed over time?

(3) How can schools and teachers promote the empowerment of bilingual students in a context where coercive relations of power often dictate standards, curriculum and program models from an assimilationist point of view?

Study Activities

(1) Follow a political debate concerning languages in school or bilingual education or language minorities in the local or national media. Portray in words the varying political dimensions of the controversy. Identify and analyze the ideologies present in the debate. Does the controversy fit neatly into a two-way split (e.g. assimilationist versus pluralists)? Or does the controversy have a number of overlapping or conflicting ideologies, even among those who appear to be on the same side?

(2) Conduct an interview with one or more bilingual or multilingual immigrant adults who completed at least part of their schooling in the local education system. Ask about their struggles with identity, if any, how they negotiated their identities and how their identities have changed over time.

(3) Using a school you are familiar with, ask teachers and parents about school–home relationships. What forms of collaboration exist? What power relationships exist between teachers and parents? What part do parents play in the language and literacy development of their children?

CHAPTER 19

Bilingualism in the Modern World

Introduction

Occupational Bilingualism

Bilingualism and Tourism

Bilingualism and the Mass Media

Technology, the Internet, Artificial Intelligence and Bilingualism

Bilingualism and the Economy
Bilingualism as an Economic Advantage
The Economic Usefulness of Different Languages
Minoritized Languages and the Economy
Is There an Economic Advantage in Being Bilingual?
Bilingualism and Economic Inequality

Conclusion

CHAPTER 19

Bilingualism in the Modern World

Introduction

This chapter takes a contemporary and future-oriented look at bilingualism and bilinguals. In the modern world, is a heritage (minority) language going to be an asset and/or a hindrance? Will bilinguals and multilinguals with two or more majority languages have a competitive advantage in developing global economies? Are **bilingualism** and **multilingualism** valuable for employment? Does tourism help sustain or dilute minoritized languages and their related cultures? Do the internet, social networking and mass media ensure that English increasingly becomes the international language for global communication, or is there an increasing place for bilingualism and multilingualism?

Forecasting the future is hazardous. The future of majority and minoritized languages in the world is unpredictable. Current economic, political, religious, social and cultural change is rapid (e.g. globalization), affecting all languages of the world. Shin (2018) suggests four flows that contribute to bilingualism and multilingualism in our globalized world: (1) transnational migration, (2) popular music, (3) advertising and (4) the internet. Indeed, the flow of people (e.g. migrants, refugees, tourism), the international movement of money and fast changes in technology, the global spread of information, images, music and pop culture, and the flow of ideas and ideologies are more rapid than ever before. In this chapter, five key modern themes are highlighted – employment, tourism, mass media, information technology and the economy – to demonstrate how languages at the individual and societal level are likely to be subject to fast-moving tides of local and global development.

Occupational Bilingualism

Proficiency in two or more languages is increasingly seen as an asset as the 'communication world' gets smaller. Globalization increases the demand for multilinguals in the workplace (Angouri *et al.*, 2023; Moyer, 2017). With immediate communication by phone, videoconferencing, email and text messaging, distant communications and negotiations across the world have become a reality, favoring bilinguals and multilinguals. As air travel has brought peoples and countries closer together, so the importance of those who can operate in two or more languages has been highlighted. As the amount of information available has dramatically increased, and the ease and speed of delivering information around the world have increased, many bilinguals, particularly those with English bilingualism and multilingualism, have become more important in the employment market. Duchêne and Heller (2012) observe an increasing global trend to invest languages with value as a source for profit-making, driven by the neoliberal ideologies of late capitalism.

In tourism, marketing, call centers, retailing, airlines, public relations, banking, performing arts, media, information and communications technology, accountancy, business consultancy, secretarial work, hotels, law and teaching, for example, bilingual and multilingual employees may often have the competitive edge when applying for a post or for advancement. At the least, a bilingual has 'value added' by offering language competence in employment. In the growing prevalence of screen-based and information-based labor, bilinguals are often very marketable and seen as more multi-skilled. Where there is a customer interface, then interacting in the language of the customer is typically excellent for business. Porras *et al.* (2014: 251) quote a banker in their interview research who revealed how his bilingualism and cultural competence evoked trust in his clients:

> I am not paid more for being multilingual, but as a banker, I make more money than the monolinguals because I have more clients that come to me and have faith in me. They want to invest their money with me.

However, as discussed below, bilingualism in and of itself does not necessarily ensure occupational advantages, and employers' views and treatment of their employees' bilingual skills can be complicated (Alarcón & Heyman, 2013; Gonçalves & Schluter, 2024; Lorente, 2018).

Ever since the September 11, 2011 (9/11) terrorist attacks by al-Qaeda targeting symbolic US landmarks, intelligence-gathering, diplomacy and national security have led to an even greater need for those fluent in languages other than English. The US Defense Language Institute Foreign Language Center (DLIFLC) in Monterey, California, supplies the US military, Department of Defense, CIA and FBI with employees whose language and cultural skills are vital to their post. On its website, its mission statement reads as follows:

> DLIFLC provides exquisite, culturally based foreign language education, training, evaluation, and degrees for the Department of Defense, globally, to afford a comprehensive understanding of the joint operational environment, a competitive edge to our warfighters, and safeguard the national security of the United States.

In addition to values of commitment, adaptability and integrity, the DLCFLC declares its value of respect as follows:

> We honor our cultural and social diversity by treating others with dignity and respect. (https://www.dliflc.edu/about/mission-vision)

The languages taught include: French, Spanish, Indonesian, Hebrew, Persian Farsi, Russian, Tagalog, Urdu, Modern Standard Arabic, Egyptian Arabic, Iraqi Arabic, Levantine Arabic, Chinese (Mandarin), Japanese, Korean and Pashto. Such languages are regarded as important not only in national security but also for encouraging reform in other countries, promoting understanding, and communicating with other countries, especially for economic purposes. However, Charalambous *et al.* (2018) warn that in the context of national security, contradictory language policies may be driven mainly by the principles of 'fear' and 'enemy', which threaten to displace democratic principles of 'freedom' and 'justice'.

A report from the British Council (2013) warns of the diplomatic and trading isolation of the United Kingdom and argues that bilingual skills are needed in the United Kingdom to increase employability. Such bilingual skills have, though, been decreasing in availability in the United Kingdom as students opt not to take second language courses at school and university. Language skills within the UK government have traditionally been regarded as essential for diplomacy, national security and defense. However, the report warns that the decline in graduate language capacity endangers the United Kingdom's future capabilities and influence. The report argues that unless the current decline in language skills is reversed, the United Kingdom will become 'lost for words', with negative consequences for diplomacy and national security. This has been heightened by the United Kingdom leaving the European Union in January 2020 (called Brexit: a combination of 'British' and 'exit'). There is concern that Brexit will make language learning in UK schools even less appealing, with students and parents believing that European language skills (e.g. French, German and Spanish) will become less needed (e.g. for worldwide trade and for employment).

There is a marked contrast between bilingual professions that carry a high prestige and professions where bilinguals are in jobs that symbolize a lower status (Gonçalves & Schluter, 2024; Zhu, 2014). Barakos and Selleck (2019) note the distinction between elite and non-elite multilingualism. In the latter case, language minorities may speak two or more languages yet be in low-paid jobs, even unemployed, and be marginalized in their employment prospects and chances of sharing wealth. For example, Lorente (2018) documents the case of transnational Filipino domestic workers, often marketed as 'supermaids' for their education and skills in English (and/or other languages), yet who are highly marginalized in the households they serve and in the larger communities and societies where they reside. Gonçalves and Schluter (2024) also document the experiences of Spanish- and Portuguese-speaking transnational blue-collar domestic workers who work for a multilingual cleaning company owned and operated by a Brazilian-American woman. The owner and workers draw on a range of multilingual and multimodal embodied practices as they service the homes of primarily Anglophone customers in a very affluent New York City suburb.

We will first consider bilingual professions that are prestigious. In the tourism and travel industries, there are bilingual and multilingual professions that are often prestigious and prosperous: international flight attendants, instructors on ski slopes, tour guides, those who conduct safaris in Africa and those who cater for sun-seekers around the world. To communicate with clients, to inform those being instructed, to satisfy those seeking rest or excitement, the use of two or more languages enhances job performance. While prestigious, these professions are not necessarily well paid. And as the Covid-19 global pandemic revealed, these jobs can also be fairly precarious.

For bilinguals and multilinguals who are skilled in two or more languages, being an interpreter or translator is often a prestigious post. When politicians meet (e.g. at the United Nations, within the European Union, on foreign visits), interpreters form the essential bridge, provide a smooth connection and maintain communication. Interpreting is also done in **language minoritized** regions. In the Highlands and Islands of Scotland, translating facilities are available for those English-only speakers who need a translation when local government officials or elected community representatives are speaking Gaelic. Translating can also be done as a large-scale enterprise (e.g. in the United Nations, NATO and the European Union) where many documents have to be translated into official languages. In the United Nations, the Translation Services department translates all official UN documents, meeting records and correspondence from and into Arabic, Chinese, English, French, Russian and Spanish. Some official documents are also translated into German. UN translators must have a 'perfect command' of their first language and an excellent knowledge of at least two other official languages. Translation may also occur in language minoritized communities where, for example, a book or an article may be translated to or from the minoritized language.

Another example of a relatively prestigious bilingual profession is that of local government officials. When inquiries are made about education, health, social benefit or local taxes, it is often necessary to have people who can use the language(s) of the local people. In many language minority situations, bilinguals in local government may have to work with their superiors and official documents in the majority language but deal orally and in letters in the minoritized language(s) with some or many of the local population. Another example is when a local government official in Canada or India visits an indigenous ethnic group in a relatively remote part of the country. That local government official may need to talk in the dialect or local language of the people as well as talk to colleagues back in the town or city in a more widely used language.

In many developing nations, there is a need for government officials and staff to speak international languages to communicate effectively with visiting delegations, international assistance providers and neighboring countries. In Cambodia, for example, there is a concerted effort to develop the English language proficiency of key personnel from the Ministry of Education, Youth, and Sport so they can represent Cambodia at regional and international education meetings. These skills are also needed internally in Cambodia to work with international aid agencies and international consultants. Those with proficient English (and in some cases French) language skills are also in high demand among local and international non-governmental organizations (NGOs). It is often difficult for government ministries to recruit and retain highly bilingual staff as they are frequently attracted to the higher-paying NGO and private-sector jobs that need their language skills.

In the caring professions (e.g. counselors, therapists, psychologists, doctors, midwives, doulas, nurses, hospice care workers, social workers, religious leaders, etc.), one key performance factor can be bilingual or multilingual abilities. Take, for example, midwives and doulas. They are present at that critical moment of a mother's experience. Communication with the midwife or doula is not only important, it is also very emotional. Can they assist at the moment of pain and joy in the preferred language of the mother? If not, the mother will need to switch to her second language, or may not be able to communicate with the midwife or doula at all.

When people visit a psychiatrist or counselor, it may be important for them to discuss and reveal the innermost depths of their being in the language of their choice. To switch to a second or third language because the professional is **monolingual** may be unsatisfactory for both the client and the professional. In a religious service, it can be important for a religious leader to conduct prayers, worship meetings and funeral services in the language of the people. People may find praying in a second or third language unnatural, even awkward.

There are many times when the more prestigious professional (e.g. the consultant surgeon) speaks only the majority language, while the less prestigious professional (e.g. the medical assistant) is bilingual. This raises the occasional dilemma about whether it is more important to hire a monolingual who is more skilled in a profession or a bilingual who is less skilled. There will be many cases when a bilingual applicant is as skilled as or more skilled than a monolingual applicant, yet will be passed over due to racism, xenophobia or other forms of discrimination.

This leads to the second part of this discussion about bilingual professions. In many situations, those who are bilingual may be unemployed or in lower-status jobs. Some immigrants in the United States and Europe do not have – or are perceived not to have – the majority language skills for the most prestigious positions, or are simply lower graded in the employment market because they are immigrants and/or from racialized minoritized groups. Vigouroux (2017) describes this as **raciolinguistic** stereotyping and provides an account of how Africans in France have long been constructed as incapable of speaking French competently. The more prestigious jobs are sometimes filled by monolinguals and less prestigious posts by bilinguals. The managers may be majority language speakers with high status, while the lower-paid workers are from the local language minority. This may send a signal. **Monolingualism** symbolically connects with higher-status employment and bilingualism with lower-status employment. Racism is often a factor, as employers may prefer to hire a White manager from the dominant societal group with negligible bilingual skills over a more qualified bilingual from a racialized minority. In some cases where bilingualism is needed among the employees, employers elect to try to train their existing monolingual employees from the majority group to a basic level of the target language, rather than hire and train actual bilinguals from the target language and racial minoritized communities. For example, some local police departments in the United States will provide beginning-level Spanish classes or even send officers to short-term language immersion programs in Spanish-speaking countries rather than make an effort to recruit and train bilingual **Latinxs** from the local community – officers who would not only be more capable linguistically but who would also likely bring needed greater cultural understanding and sensitivity. Another challenge is when employers try to hire heritage speakers of needed languages who are proficient in English, only to discover that their proficiency in the **heritage language** is limited due to the monolingual English or weak forms of bilingual education they received in school.

There have been cases in the United States where businesses and institutions hire native bilinguals out of necessity to be able to sell products and provide services to customers from the local community or to compete in global markets, but attempt to place restrictions on when and where their bilingual employees are permitted to speak in a non-English language. For example, they may be expected to speak in Spanish when providing a service to customers, but required to speak English at all other times, even when informally interacting with fellow bilingual employees. Note how this commodifies the language for its economic profit value (Codó, 2017) while simultaneously devaluing the bilingual employees who speak the language. Such workplace policies have been contested as discriminatory and have led to court challenges. The US Equal Employment Opportunity Commission (2014: 2) has concluded that 'a rule requiring employees to speak only English in the workplace at all times, including breaks and lunch time, rarely will be justified'.

There is sometimes a vicious cycle of disempowerment, lower expectations, underfunding, racism and discrimination for linguistic and racialized minoritized students leading to underachievement at school, with unemployment and lower-status jobs becoming part of this cycle. For example, in cities in the United States where there are large proportions of language and racialized minoritized students, most teachers and administrators are White English language monolinguals. The cooks, cafeteria and playground monitors, custodians, secretaries, teacher assistants and other paraprofessionals in the school may often be bilingual and people of color. For students in the school, such a differentiation between races, monolinguals and bilinguals in the roles they play may send out signals and messages to the students and parents (Wright & Boun, 2011). There is a hidden agenda in employment patterns within the school. The students may acquire the idea subconsciously that White monolingual English-speakers are prestigious, relatively well paid and in relatively secure jobs. Those who are minorities and speak other languages as their home language tend to be allocated the lower-status, more menial jobs. The role models in the school convey the message that to be bilingual is to be associated with less status and more poverty and disadvantage, less power and more subservience. Contrast this scenario with a school-wide bilingual program where all or nearly all school personnel are bilinguals and people of color, such as the Dos Puentes Dual Language Elementary School in New York City (Kleyn *et al.*, 2024). What different messages about the value of bilingualism might such a school send?

This discussion of bilingual professions has revealed the paradoxical nature of the link between bilingualism and employment. On the one hand, there are those who can use their bilingualism as an advantage: to sell, to satisfy clients' needs, to succeed in providing a service. Bilingualism has an economic potential; it is an asset used by an individual for advancement. Bilingualism can become a marketable ability to bridge languages and cultures, securing trade and delivery of services. On the other hand, there are those people, for example many immigrants, whose race and bilingual nature tend to lead them being marked for lower-status, more marginalized and precarious employment, or unemployment. Such bilinguals and multilinguals may be less proficient – or be perceived as less proficient – in the majority language and/or may lack the needed professional native language skills. They may be subject to **linguistic racism**, meaning they are 'deprived of both socioeconomic and sociocultural opportunities as a result of their use of language' (Dovchin, 2020: 773). For example, they may be allocated the poorest-paid jobs in schools and shops. Thus bilingualism may be attached to low-status work that symbolizes the least powerful, the least affluent and the least prestigious sections in a society.

Bilingualism and Tourism

In recent decades, tourism has been a major growth industry. There are hundreds of millions of international travelers and most are 'visitors from a non-English-speaking country traveling to a non-English-speaking destination', thus highlighting 'the need for face-to-face international communication' (Graddol, 2006: 29). The ease of international travel and communications, the opening of national boundaries, more leisure time, earlier retirement, longer life and a greater disposable income have meant that vacations in other countries are part of the lifestyle of an increasing proportion of the affluent population of many developed countries. When people go on vacation, some are seemingly indifferent to the local languages and cultures of the region they are visiting, especially if they are minoritized languages and cultures. Others are curious, charmed, even captivated by different tongues and traditions, by varied communication and cultures.

Travel and tourism involve the contact of cultures and languages (Ghosh *et al.*, 2024). This can be enlightening and enriching. 'Cultural tourism' may lead local tourist providers to commodify their culture in a manner that makes it attractive to tourists (Kelly-Holmes & Pietikäinen, 2014). However, tourism is sometimes seen as the enemy of multiculturalism and multilingualism and especially of minoritized languages and cultures. Language minority activists may argue that tourism ruins unspoiled areas of great beauty with large hotels, even larger blocks of flats and marinas. Tourism can negatively affect the linguistic environment as those on vacation expect services to be in their majority language. Tourists can be unaware of and insensitive to cultural and linguistic diversity by expecting the language, food and other customs to be the same as at home. Over-tourism in areas of Spain such as Barcelona led to organized street protests by locals in 2024 over concerns of the disrespect and bad behavior of many tourists, the impact of tourism on local prices at restaurants and other businesses, and crowding out of locals in many areas taken over by the tourists.

If use is made of minoritized languages and cultures in tourist enterprises, this tends to follow an 'ethnic approach', focusing on history, traditions, customs and cultural artifacts in a way that may portray them as 'quaint', 'archaic' or 'strange' (Comaroff & Comaroff, 2009; Ghosh et al., 2024; Jaworski & Thurlow, 2010). Whether we are talking about Breton embroidered costumes, Scottish tartan, Welsh harp music, Amish traditional dress, Hawaiian grass skirts and hula dances, Native American rituals or Māori war dances, they may be presented as spectacles for gawking tourists rather than as part of real-life, contemporary living cultures. However, alongside such difficulties, 'ethnic' tourism can also bring money into the community, educate tourists about minorities and enable empathy with their current language and cultural concerns (Heller et al., 2014). There is danger, though, in relying too heavily on tourism for economic survival. Many ethnic minoritized communities around the world suffered greatly from the loss of tourist dollars due to the Covid-19 global pandemic in 2020–2021.

Mass tourism has contributed to the spread of the English language and Anglo culture throughout the world. English is often the expected means of communication when tourists from different continents are abroad. However, multilingualism may also grow, with those working in the tourist trade becoming proficient in a majority language such as English, French or Chinese, while still retaining their heritage language. In Slovenia, for example, tourism appears to have led to some Slovenians becoming multilingual in German, Italian and English as well as Slovene. Many of the child merchants around Angkor Wat in Cambodia have learned enough words and phrases to hawk their souvenirs in multiple languages such as English, Japanese, Korean, Chinese, Thai, Vietnamese and French. Mass tourism can also weaken the cultural, linguistic and economic structure of a region by its tendency to provide casual, seasonal employment and also a mass influx of temporary workers from other regions. Because of all these negative implications, tourism is sometimes viewed with suspicion and concern by language minoritized groups.

Tourism that promotes the host language and culture has been called 'cultural tourism' (or 'heritage tourism' or 'ethnic tourism'). With the growth of tourism throughout the world, more sophisticated and diverse strategies for boosting the tourist market have been devised. Tourism that includes different cultures and their languages have been part of this growth. For example, different languages and their attendant cultures may be present in visits to archaeological and architectural sites, museums and cultural/sporting events, crafts and festivals, music and theatre, dance and drama, and religious festivals, as well as on pilgrimages. The importance of cultural tourism has been increasingly recognized, and language minorities can raise their profile, create employment and find a niche economy in such tourism (Pietikäinen et al., 2016).

Bilingualism and the Mass Media

Radio, television, newspapers, magazines, smartphones and other mobile internet devices have become important vehicles of mass communication, in the form of news, information, entertainment and social media. Mass media play a major role in defining and constructing social, political, economic and linguistic visions of society and in communicating these visions to the public (Gao & Shao, 2018). The majority of households in Western countries possess at least one television and to own a television is the ambition of many families in less economically advanced countries. Television (especially satellite television) contributed to the creation of the global village, with worldwide diffusion of important and immediate news, sport and culture. Television enables viewers to engage with varied cultures and countries. The development of satellite, cable and internet streaming technology has facilitated the transmission of television program, movies and other content worldwide. Such programming can contribute to an empathy and insight into other cultures, languages and lifestyles.

However, there is another side to television programming. The largest television and movie industry in the world is in North America. It provides a mass of programs and films, light entertainment and news. These often transmit Anglo-American culture to other parts of the world. Anglo-American news broadcasts, music, cultural practices and lifestyles may be seen as prestigious and important and, by implication, the indigenous cultures of other countries may seem outmoded and outdated. As Van Hout and Burger (2017: 489) assert:

> As a driving force in the political economy of language, news media shape cultural values and naturalize specific language codes and ideologies. Indeed, rather than offering value-free representations of the world, news language invariably reflects particular worldviews, interests, and ideas about society, including ideas about language. Understanding whose values, beliefs, and worldviews are foregrounded and what counts as legitimate language use remain central concerns in media linguistics.

The English language is diffused throughout the world by the mass media. The use of subtitling (cheaper than dubbing) means that the English language is experienced by audiences in many worldwide countries, though in some cases subtitles are inaccurate, even misleading. Since the advent of satellite television and the internet streaming of movies, television and original programming, even more viewers have access to English language programs. However, as will be discussed later, these same technologies are increasing global access to programming in other languages as well.

The widespread mass media diffusion of the English language has had some beneficial effects. It has contributed to the development of bilingualism. It has provided a means for speakers of other languages to develop competence in English as a useful language of international communication. In Scandinavian countries, for instance, many English language films and other programs have traditionally been broadcast with subtitles. Only children's programs are dubbed. Motivation to learn English is usually high in Scandinavian countries and television is one aid to competence in English. This is an additive bilingual situation, where the second language does not displace the first.

However, the English language has entered, via television and online streaming, into many majority languages. For example, an influx of borrowings from English into other languages via the mass media has provoked anxiety among language purists in countries such as Japan and France. The French government has therefore taken steps to reduce the quantity of non-French language broadcasting on radio and television. The Cambodian government likewise placed limitations on the amount of English, Thai and other foreign language programming that may be broadcast on local television channels. One result of this policy has been a revitalization of the Cambodian television and film industry, with a substantial increase in the quantity, quality and variety of local programming in the national Khmer language. However, there has also been an increase in the number of English language channels via satellite. More recent developments such as the availability of Netflix make thousands of English language television shows and movies instantly available in Cambodia.

One positive development caused by the proliferation of international satellite, cable and streaming video-channels is that there is an increasing international market for television programs, movies and other content. This, and the increasing use of subtitling, 'voice-overs' and dubbing, means that popular programs and films can be made available in various less-used languages. The minimal costs can then be recouped by selling them on the international market.

In some rare instances such dubbing may simply be a goodwill gesture. For example, in an initiative with the Navajo National Museum to help with Diné bizaad (Navajo) language revitalization and maintenance, Walt Disney Studios recruited native speakers of Diné bizaad to professionally dub *Star Wars Episode IV: A New Hope*. The efforts were so well received that the studio dubbed a second popular film: *Finding Nemo*. This version features an original song in Diné bizaad performed by (non-native) Fall Out Boy front man Patrick Stump. The dubbed version was shown free of charge in selected theaters in Arizona, New Mexico and Utah. Navajo leaders see these efforts as important for connecting the younger generation to their language, and call it 'a huge leap forward in getting the awareness out there and getting kids interested' (Grinberg & Watts, 2016). The popular Marvel movie *The Avengers* was dubbed in Lakota in 2024. Among the voice actors were original stars of the film including Mark Ruffalo, Robert Downey Jr, Scarlett Johansson and Chris Evans, who re-recorded their dialogue in the Lakota language, alongside native Lakota actors voicing the other characters. The addition of these famous original actors speaking in Lakota is something the tribe hopes will draw more young people into the language revitalization efforts of this endangered Native American language. A grassroots effort by two Diné (Navajo) educators – Shawna Begay and Charmaine Jackson – established a successful GoFundMe campaign to support the creation of a *Sesame Street*-like program featuring Diné bizaad-speaking puppets, animals and children, called *Navajo Highways*. Despite delays in production due to the Covid-19 pandemic, they successfully completed production in 2024 and were on track to release the series in 2025.

This is not to suggest that English language channels (and internet use) are always dominant in English-speaking countries. In the United Kingdom, the United States and Australia, there are Arabic, Asian and many other language television channels on satellite watched by speakers of those languages. Non-English movies and television programs are often dubbed or subtitled into English and other languages. Korean soap operas (or K-dramas) are particularly popular throughout Asia and among the Asian diaspora around the world; availability on Netflix with English subtitles has broadened their reach and popularity throughout the world. Netflix and other video streaming services are adding and even producing their own non-English content with English subtitles. The Spanish language crime drama series *La casa de papel* ('House of Paper' but called *Money Heist* in English) was a worldwide hit and one of the most viewed

Netflix series in 2018. Given its popularity, the show was extended for five seasons through 2021.

In the United States, the Spanish television network Univision has grown from small beginnings in the early 1960s to a major provider with a large Spanish-speaking audience across North America and the Caribbean, and has now achieved parity in terms of viewership with the major English language broadcasting networks. Spanish language television is recognized for its influence on Latinx voters, such that many politicians – including those who support strict immigration controls and the dismantling of bilingual education – are enthusiastic to reach and attempt to persuade voters in the Spanish language. Univision co-sponsored (with the *Washington Post*) one of the Democratic primary debates during the 2016 presidential election, and did so again with ABC in the 2020 presidential primary. During the 2024 presidential election campaign, Univision conducted exclusive television interviews with Joe Biden (before he withdrew his candidacy for re-election), Kamala Harris and Donald Trump.

However, when majority language mass media (e.g. English) enter minoritized language homes, the effect may be a subtractive bilingual situation. Language minoritized children can be exposed to the English language and Anglo-American culture on television and via online media from an early age. Minoritized language groups tend to be concerned about a daily diet of majority language and culture having a harmful effect on speakers of their language, especially teenagers and younger children. They are concerned that it weakens the prestige and status of their own language and culture, widening the gap between English (or another majority language) as the language of power, prestige, modern technology, fashion and entertainment and their own language as unfashionable, outmoded and diminishing. There is thus concern that watching majority language television may affect children's acquisition of their native language and hasten **language shift** to the majority language.

During recent decades there has been a concerted effort by many minoritized language groups to gain access to radio and particularly television. As demonstrated in the above examples of *Star Wars* and *Finding Nemo* in Diné bizaad (Navajo), and *The Avengers* in Lakota, language activists have seen minoritized language radio, podcasting, television and film as vitally important to the maintenance of their language, for the following reasons:

(1) minoritized language media add to the prestige and status of a language in the eyes of its speakers;
(2) minoritized language media can add to a sense of unity and **identity** among its speakers;
(3) minoritized language media help to keep minoritized language speakers, especially children and young people, from being overwhelmed by the influence of majority language and culture, and acquaint them with their own heritage and culture and give them pride in them;
(4) minoritized language media can help disseminate a standard form of the language and also promote new and technical vocabulary, while mass media can help the standardization of a minoritized language across a variety of **registers**;
(5) minoritized language media can help the fluency of minoritized language speakers and can also help learners acquire the language;
(6) minoritized language media create well paid, high-prestige jobs for minoritized language speakers, and the radio and television industry can help boost the economy of minoritized language regions.

The value of minoritized language media in the maintenance of minoritized languages and the reversal of language shift was disputed by Joshua Fishman. Fishman (1991) argued that radio and television should not be hailed as the rescuers of a minoritized language. He maintained that many minoritized language groups spend valuable resources in the lengthy and expensive task of establishing and maintaining minoritized language media, at the cost of more basic and fundamental issues such as the **intergenerational transmission** of the minoritized language. Fishman suggested that the impact of majority language television, particularly English language television in the United Kingdom and North America, is so immense that it cannot be countered by the much lesser influence of a minoritized language.

Intergenerational transmission of the minoritized language may be key but needs to be supported with bilingual education and opportunities to use the language outside the home and school in ways that are meaningful and interesting to children and youth. Thus, attempting to do something to counteract majority language mass media by minoritized language ventures is much better than doing nothing. In such ventures there can be added prestige for a minoritized language, leading to the maintenance and promotion of minoritized languages, cultures and economies (e.g. Irish language comedy and other media – see Moriarty, 2011, 2015a). In Wales, the establishment of a Welsh language television channel (S4C) in 1982 led to the creation of various independent television companies in Wales, which have boosted the economy of the country (as has recently occurred in Scotland with the Gaelic language). Such minoritized language television is regarded as important in standardizing the language in a wide range of registers across a region or country. Welsh language television has also been viewed as a major force in the creation and maintenance of a sense of identity and unity among Welsh-speakers. YouTube, TikTok, Facebook and other social media video sites have eliminated much of the cost of producing and disseminating content in non-English languages. YouTube has generated a revenue stream for popular YouTubers with channels appealing to speakers of their languages around the world.

Technology, the Internet, Artificial Intelligence and Bilingualism

On buses and trains, in lecture theaters and playgrounds, shopping malls and busy streets, smartphones, tablets and other mobile internet devices are ever present. Some people are texting, video chatting, using translators (e.g. Google Translate) in live chat rooms or on discussion boards. Many surf the internet for news, information and entertainment. Others are on email, Facebook, YouTube, TikTok, X (formerly Twitter), Tumblr, LinkedIn, Instagram, Reddit, Snapchat, posting and commenting, tweeting and retweeting, blogging and influencing, buying and selling, and social networking via technology. Many are now interacting with chatbots and other artificial intelligence (AI) apps and features built into their smart devices. The global Covid-19 pandemic in 2020–2021 gave prominence to Zoom, Microsoft Teams and other videoconferencing platforms that could just as easily connect families, friends and colleagues scattered across the globe as it could a local classroom of students quarantining at home.

Communication for the old and young, for students and staff, for workers and their bosses, for the hearing and Deaf people has increasingly become electronic. What language is dominant? What languages are used on social media for social networking?

Does such a rapid change lead to extra functions, status and use of majority languages like English? Do the value and use of minoritized languages suffer? Has the use of minoritized languages been valuably extended to electronic communication? Are bilingualism and multilingualism central or peripheral on the web? While the internet has become a central means of communication in the daily lives of bilingual and multilingual individuals, research on 'language and the internet' is just beginning to scratch the surface of the roles and ways the internet functions within the broader context of language and society (Varis & Van Nuenen, 2017).

With the rapid spread of technology and networked information has gone the rapid spread of English. The inherent danger is that minoritized languages, cultural diversity and therefore bilingualism come under threat. As shown in Table 19.1, over 1.2 billion English-speakers in the world are estimated to access the internet, followed by speakers of Chinese (889 million), Spanish (364 million) and Arabic (237 million). However, irrespective of the language(s) of the user, information that transfers across the internet tends often to be in English, albeit increasingly in other languages. Note that 1.1 billion speakers of other languages are users of the internet, with 1114% growth since 2000. Statista (2024) reported that in January 2024, a little more than half (52.1%) of websites most frequently used English, distantly followed by Spanish (5.5%), German (4.8%), Russian (4.5%), Japanese (4.3%) and French (4.3%), with all other languages representing less than 3.2% of web content by share of websites.

Table 19.1 Top 10 languages used in the web (number of internet users by language) (at March 31, 2020)

Language	Estimated number of users	Internet penetration (% of population)	Growth since 2000
English	1.2 billion	78	743%
Chinese	889 million	60	2650%
Spanish	364 million	70	1511%
Arabic	237 million	53	9348%
Portuguese	172 million	59	2167%
Indonesian/Malaysian	198 million	65	3356%
French	152 million	35	1165%
Japanese	119 million	94	152%
Russian	116 million	80	3653%
German	93 million	94	236%
Other languages	1.1 billion	42	1114%

Data retrieved from https://www.statista.com/markets/424/internet/ on March 30, 2020

The language of digitized encyclopedias and the multiplicity of software tends also to be English, as does the language of gaming software. Wikipedia articles per language shows English (6.9 million) at the top, followed by German (2.9 million), French (2.6 million), Russian (2.0 million), Spanish (2.0 million), Italian (1.9 million), Portuguese (1.1 million), Japanese (1.4 million) and Chinese (1.4 million). This diverse virtual linguistic landscape continues to grow, and there are now articles in over 315 other languages. There are 20 languages with over 1 million articles, 54 languages with over 100,000 articles, 101 languages with over 10,000 articles and dozens of other languages with over 1000 articles as of September 2024 (https://wikipedia.org). While English continues to dominate, the cyber-world is becoming increasingly multilingual in content and usage (Kelly-Holmes, 2019). AI translation tools built into computer software, mobile apps, social media sites and web browsers can instantly translate individual posts, articles or entire web pages between a select but growing number of languages with imperfect but increasing accuracy.

The linguistic diversity of the world is not represented on the internet in numbers or status. What is uncertain is whether minoritized languages are at risk as the status of larger languages is consolidated on the internet, or whether the online presence of smaller languages may strengthen them in terms of visibility, status, opportunities and usage. Minoritized languages may seem in comparison to cyber languages to be part of heritage and history, and may fail to attain the status of modern, high-prestige and high-profile international languages used by information technology. The danger lies in the identification of advanced technological society particularly, but not exclusively, with the English language, and consequently minoritized languages being identified with home and history, ritual and religion. The danger is of a tiered information society: those who have the linguistic abilities to access information; and those who cannot access new forms of communication and information as they do not own a language often used in the information society.

Yet it is possible to harness technology to aid minoritized language education. For example, software can be displayed in or translated into the heritage language. Email, texting and tweeting and information exchange can be in that minoritized language. Text messaging apps also allow the quick exchange of short voice recordings, thus making it possible to communicate in any language – even in languages without a writing system. As more businesses begin to advertise using websites, regional networks have developed using local languages on the internet. As schools, colleges, universities, local government, libraries, record offices and local information agencies go online, some of their web pages are bilingual or multilingual.

What is also important in preserving minoritized languages in a technological age is to ensure that there is appropriate **terminology** in the minoritized language. Languages other than English have to extend their vocabulary to embrace technological and computer terms. Such modernization aids the symbolic status of the language, particularly among the impressionable young; it also attempts to move that language into modern domains and to ensure that information technology is a supporter and not a destroyer of bilingualism in children.

It is also possible to harness technology to aid minoritized language employment. The increasing speed of connections to the internet makes residence in language minoritized rural areas more possible. This can also enable home-based or locally based employment through high-speed computer links, as well as the ability to receive and deliver services and products. Thus minoritized languages and bi- or multilingualism can potentially benefit from the current and future growth of the internet.

The internet is ever changing and developing. It has the potential to increase bilingual and multilingual communication, providing new possibilities for social networking among bilinguals: conversations across countries and continents, playing out multiple identities, a vicarious sense of belonging to other speakers of the heritage language, and a private space to be different, distinct and linguistically diverse. This includes Deaf people, who can use new technologies to join Deaf communities across the world and not just in the locality. The rise of messaging (e.g. texting on phones) and videoconferencing services (Zoom, Teams, FaceTime, Messenger, Facebook Live, etc.) makes communication in any language possible across a few blocks, meadows or wide oceans.

When students use communication technology, bilingual and multilingual proficiency can be enhanced. Through the internet, for example, authentic language practice is possible via purposeful and genuine activities (e.g. the use of social networking sites). There may be increased motivation to acquire a language via contact with students in other countries. Authentic language sources may be accessed to complete curriculum activities (e.g. a project on another country). Email, chat rooms, messaging and videoconferencing are a few of the well established internet activities for language students, using both text and video, giving the feeling of the global village where barriers to communication (such as cost and the time of travel) are removed.

By its interactive nature, the internet brings people speaking different languages into closer contact. By exchanging information with those in other countries, students can build increasing independence in language use, vary their language according to audience and use language for real purposes. For example, the site ePals (https://www.epals.com) is a global community that pairs educators and students around the world in project-based learning activities for language learning, language practice and cultural exchange. In one project, partner classrooms from different parts of the world discuss the games they like to play, while another project involves students in partner classrooms exchanging information about the causes and effects of poverty, and students collaborate to develop a plan to address one aspect of global poverty.

Students can take part in conversations over the internet with native speakers, using not only written text but increasingly audio- and videoconferencing as well. Exchange visits can be reinforced with preparatory and follow-up internet links, and there are possibilities of virtual exchanges.

Internet technology and AI enable conversations between speakers of different tongues, minority and majority, in real time. It is now possible to combine (1) speech recognition (turning spoken words into text) followed by (2) a machine translation (converting text into other languages) and then a speech synthesizer that (3) turns translated text back into audible words in the language of the listener's choosing. This will enable conversations in two (or more) languages and help protect minoritized language use and users. However, this feature may be limited to certain major world languages, and accuracy of the translation can vary greatly depending on a number of factors, including clarity of the speakers, ability to recognize variations in accents and speech patterns, background noise interference, topic of conversation, overlapping speech, ambiguity, and limitations in the large datasets used for training the AI model.

The internet provides teachers and learners with ready-to-use banks of multimedia language resources: a wealth of video- and audio-recordings from all over the world, aural, pictorial and written information, and activities generated by many different language centers in various countries. Providers of information and training for language teachers can use the internet to publicize events, courses, materials, services and to provide subscription-based remote training, advice and information service.

Artificial intelligence is also opening up many new possibilities for the teaching, learning and preservation of languages. Language teachers are harnessing the power of AI to generate lesson plans and teaching materials, and to differentiate instruction. Learners are using AI tools to simplify and summarize complex texts, to engage in written or oral exchanges with chatbots, to get assistance with writing and homework, to get feedback on their oral and written language. Intelligent tutoring systems are able to customize instruction based on students' language performance and can provide detailed reports for teachers with suggestions for instruction. These examples are only scratching the surface of what AI is making possible.

Of course, there is also great concern about the use of AI for unethical uses, such as student cheating. Uncritical use of AI by teachers and students will not lead to more effective teaching and learning. Lazy teachers and unmotivated students can simply use AI to take shortcuts without critically evaluating the output, or fail to leverage AI in ways that ensure students meet language learning goals. There are deep concerns about 'hallucinations' leading to AI generating inaccurate information, or providing inappropriate responses to students. In all uses of AI, there needs to be a 'human in the loop' to ensure such uses are appropriate and effective.

While there is hope that AI tools can be utilized for language preservation and revitalization efforts, there is also the reality that generative AI is grounded in large language models that are predominantly trained in English, simply because, as noted above, English dominates the information technology and media worlds from which data are drawn to train the AI models. Thus, there is concern that generative AI, like the internet before it, will dominate in English at the expense of other languages.

Bilingualism and the Economy

Bilingualism as an Economic Advantage

Research on language and the political economy shows that language indeed 'plays a central role in regulating an individual's access to the production, distribution, and consumption of resources' (Del Percio *et al.*, 2017: 69). In most of the great cities of the world, there is a multilingual economy. In such cities, international political organizations (e.g. embassies) and financial institutions (e.g. banks), multinational businesses and education establishments often employ many bilinguals and multilinguals. In cities such as New York, London, Tokyo and Seoul, many bilinguals and multilinguals can wield rich linguistic capital. For example, Baker and Kim (2003) portrayed multilingual London (one of the world's leading financial centers for international business and commerce and one of the 'command centers' for the global economy) as having over 10,000 language facilities and services in 444 different languages.

Bilinguals and especially multilinguals frequently have marketable language skills and intercultural knowledge. However, some minoritized language bilinguals are economically impoverished yet linguistically accomplished. Can such dual or triple **language competence** be an economic asset? Is there an earning bonus or differential for bilinguals? The world language skills of employees are sometimes rewarded by employers, showing that employers find these skills valuable.

In an increasingly bilingual and multilingual world, with trade barriers falling, with new international markets growing and with economic competition rapidly developing on a global scale, competence in languages may be increasingly important. An example is Southern Florida, which has become a main center for South American business, and where Spanish language skills have become a bridge between the business cultures of the United States and Latin America. The growth of legal, financial and banking services in Miami is another example where bilinguals (Spanish and English) have distinct economic and employment advantages. Thus, Spanish language skills are in high demand in Florida's labor force to meet the needs of international business, tourism and Spanish language media enterprises, yet demand can outstrip supply.

Heller (2006) suggests that, to gain advantage in the new global economy, bilinguals will need to adopt a different concept of their identity. The old politics of identity concern maintaining a heritage language and culture, conserving and protecting traditions and perpetuating a minority cultural identity. In contrast, Heller talks about a new pragmatic identity for language minorities, one which allows them to take advantage of their multiple linguistic and cultural resources to participate in a global economy. Heller suggests that it is not multilingualism or a hybrid dual language system that is valued in the new economy, but parallel monolingualism. In such a context, language minorities can act as brokers between different monolingual economic and political zones. However, this requires bilinguals to have appropriate linguistic resources that are sufficiently well developed to operate in either language group. In a Canadian context, Heller argues that 'minorities are now in a good position to market their linguistic capital' (Heller, 2006: 26). To do so, they have to move away from the politics of ethnicity and tradition toward a politics based on capital, globalization and a new international political and economic order. However, language minorities are often politically and economically marginalized, with little chance of escape.

The Economic Usefulness of Different Languages

This raises the question about which languages may be useful for economic advancement. In many countries of the world, it is English as an additional language that has the most visible economic value. An observation by Coulmas in the early 1990s remains true today:

> No Japanese businessman ever tries to operate on the American market without a sufficient command of English, whereas the reverse case, of American business people who expect to be able to do business in Japan without being proficient in Japanese, is not at all rare. On the one hand, this is a reflection of the arrogance of power, but on the other hand, it testifies to the fact that the opportunities for realizing the functional potential of English on the Japanese market are far better than those of realizing the functional potential of Japanese on the American market. (Coulmas, 1992: 66–67)

However, Willy Brandt, a former Chancellor of the old Federal Republic of Germany, once said: 'If I'm selling to you, I speak your language. If I'm buying, dann müssen Sie Deutsch sprechen [then you must speak German]'.

Alongside the English language, French, German, Arabic, Japanese, Chinese Mandarin, Russian, Portuguese and Spanish have historically been regarded as important trading languages. However, this list of modern languages for marketing and trading purposes is growing significantly. For example, Bahasa Melayu and Korean, Vietnamese and Cantonese, Swahili and Hausa, Bengali, Hindi and Urdu may each become increasingly valuable. Although the world is getting economically richer, the wealth created and spent by Eastern countries may proportionally increase in relation to the West, and therefore positively affect the economic attractiveness of major Eastern languages, and therefore the employability of bilinguals and multilinguals. The predicted growth of newer economic superpowers in the BRICS group (Brazil, Russia, India, China and South Africa) may mean the end of five centuries of domination by Europeans and recently North Americans and thus could change the face of **dominant languages**. The rise of Mandarin Chinese is making it a crucial international language for marketing and trade, politics and power. However, the future of individual economies in the world is not predictable, nor is the future of the global economy.

The above scenario of the growth of other modern languages in international trade contains the idea of 'language skills as determinants of the economic variables such as productivity, costs and profits' (Grin *et al.*, 2010: 6). A workplace may need to take into account the language expectations of its target markets as well as the language profile of its suppliers, and ensure that its workforce has the multilingual skills to meet such expectations and preferences. Profitability may be enhanced by such considerations, whether the business is in goods or services, and increasingly whether it is about sharing knowledge (conceptual, procedural, strategic and situational) such as information on high technology.

In the context of Ireland, Ó Riagáin (2001) argues that profit margins lead language life. With the growth of economic prosperity in Ireland from the 1960s to 2009 came ever-widening international trade contacts, export markets, foreign investment, incorporation into international capitalism and an economic marriage with mainland Europe. English and other major European languages gained importance. However, this neoliberal reality 'created severe problems for policies designed to maintain Irish as a minority language' (Ó Riagáin, 2001: 206). The lower economic value of the Irish language has made it difficult to preserve it.

In both the United States and the United Kingdom, English is not enough. English is a global trading language but, in an export-wise and economically competitive world, exclusive reliance on English leaves the United States and the United Kingdom vulnerable and dependent on the linguistic competence and the goodwill of others.

Minoritized Languages and the Economy

In suggesting that bilingualism can have economic advantages for individuals and organizations, the languages highlighted so far have mostly been majority languages. What is the place of local minoritized languages in the economy? Will bilinguals from language minoritized communities have any economic advantage, any valuable trading language in their minoritized language, and any chance of getting out of the poverty trap that some bilinguals experience? Compared with a mainstream language majority, a marginalized language minority may experience higher unemployment, or lower pay, or even poverty and powerlessness. Where language minorities live in remote rural areas or in downtown inner-city areas, then often there is material deprivation.

The economy of many countries has recently moved from material resources and goods partly under the control of a government to an economy based on services and information under the control of multinational corporations and more global enterprises. In this new worldwide knowledge economy, can language minorities use their linguistic resources and social networks for economic and personal gain? The new knowledge economy requires the crossing of linguistic boundaries, and bilinguals and multilinguals are ahead of monolinguals in having this potential. They can become the pivotal bridge makers and go-betweens in global economic operations. Crossing borders can be geographical and linguistic for bilinguals and multilinguals. However, this may be restricted to bilinguals whose languages cross frontiers and are not used only locally or regionally.

The harsh reality for many of the world's bilinguals is that their minoritized language typically has minimal economic value. The pressure is on them to move into a majority language. Where there is economic value associated with an immigrant or heritage minoritized language, it is frequently in sweatshops, factories or fast-food restaurants and is not connected with wealth, affluence or influence. A language is supported by businesses where factory workers, shop workers and managers work partly or mainly through their heritage language. On occasion, the migrant language is a trade language with another trading country (e.g. Spanish, Urdu, Panjabi, Hindi), with resulting profitability and local niche economies.

Where and when there is some small economic value associated with an indigenous minoritized language, it is often associated with non-sustainable developments in rural areas. Such bilinguals may work in barely profitable industries in remote language heartland areas. In Europe, for example, the move from regional and state economies to a single European market policy (with interlocking business structures in different European countries encouraging mobility in businesses across European countries) may leave a distinction between core and periphery, between those in important urban business areas and those in rural peripheries (e.g. rural areas and scattered communities in Ireland). Since many indigenous minoritized languages in Europe are found in regions that are sparsely populated, economically underdeveloped, with poorer rural road and transport systems, there is a danger that there will be growing inequality between core and periphery.

In the economic restructuring that has occurred in recent decades, increased competition has led to the need for greater efficiency to maintain profit. Industries and services have frequently had to 'automate, emigrate or evaporate'. Emigration of industries has been to countries such as India, Taiwan, Mexico, Brazil, China and Singapore, where wages, and therefore production costs, are low. Such outside investment may sometimes offer work and wages to language minoritized members but may also have negative wealth (low-pay) consequences for language minorities. Another negative consequence is that economic investment may not reach a language minority. For example, where such minorities live in remote rural areas, economic growth may be in the urban 'core' rather than the rural periphery. Alternatively, the higher-grade jobs may be in affluent city areas and the lower-grade, poorly paid work in the more remote areas.

A different scenario is when a peripheral area attracts inward investment (e.g. in the form of a factory). The tendency is for the local language minorities to provide relatively cheap workers, while the better-paid (language majority) managers either operate from their far-away city headquarters or move into the peripheral language community. In either case, each language is identified with greater or lesser affluence, higher or lower status, more or less power.

The absence of community-based, ethnically based businesses increases the risk of the emigration of more able, more skilled and more entrepreneurial people away from the area, hence leaving the language itself in peril. Also, a language community without economic activity is in danger of starving the language of one essential support mechanism. An economically wealthy language has a higher probability of being a healthy language. An economically impoverished language is at great risk.

There are success stories. For example, the development of the Cuban enclave economy in Miami shows the possibility of a minoritized language economy developing in a region. Following the influx of Cubans into Miami in the 1960s, a Cuban-focused economy developed. Based on sufficient capital, a capable labor force, a ready market for products and a sufficient Cuban population to support Cuban-owned businesses, economic success of the enclave soon resulted.

Is There an Economic Advantage in Being Bilingual?

The potential advantages of bilingualism, particularly for an individual, have hitherto been summarized as communication, cognitive, cultural, curriculum and character (Baker, 2014). It has also been suggested in recent decades that bilinguals have a potential economic advantage. For example, Alarcón *et al.* suggest that:

> Workers who deal with the public in a multilingual society are helped in their jobs by being able to use diverse languages. Doctors, nurses and medical assistants can understand and communicate more clearly with patients, improving health outcomes; lawyers, police officers, fire officers and government leaders gain similar benefits for public safety. (Alarcón *et al.*, 2014: 132)

The economic advantage could be in having a competitive advantage against monolinguals in finding employment, in opening up more job opportunities, in initial salary, with a salary premium, in promotion and/or in lifetime earnings. Such an advantage may be within a city (e.g. London, Brussels, Washington), a particular state or region (e.g. Catalonia) or in some countries (e.g. Switzerland, Canada, Finland, Sweden) but not others. It may also be an transnational asset in times of the growth of multinational companies, a global economy and increasing international trade.

However, research on the potential economic advantage of being bilingual or multilingual shows varied outcomes, some positive, some negative (Del Percio *et al.*, 2017). This is well illustrated in a book edited by Callahan and Gándara (2014) entitled *The Bilingual Advantage: Language, Literacy and the US Labor Market*. The research in the United States reported in it leads to different, even conflicting, conclusions. For example:

- When bilingual and monolingual workers' earnings are analyzed without controlling for age or gender, there is no apparent advantage for bilinguals in the labor market.
- Spanish-speakers with competence in English show a 6% decrease in wages in comparison with monolingual English speakers.
- A more developed language competence of immigrants in English is related to higher wages in some research.
- There is evidence for the benefits of fluent bilingualism – and even of moderate or **balanced bilingualism** – in the labor markets and local economy of Southern California.
- Balanced bilinguals are more likely to be employed full time compared with English-dominant individuals and to earn significantly more than the monolingual English-speakers (between $2000 and $3200 more annually).
- A Forbes Insights survey showed that managers of businesses operating internationally are increasingly multilingual. More businesses are seeing bilingualism and multilingualism as a significant advantage.
- The economic benefit to a bilingual applicant for a job may not be through increased salary but rather in the hiring process and winning the job competition.
- Bilingual women are more likely to be employed than their monolingual peers.

The problem of these mixed conclusions lies with a too simple 'black box' question: 'Do bilinguals have an economic advantage'? The answer is never going to be straightforward, as there are so many factors that can be influential (by themselves but also in interactions and combinations) (Clifton-Sprigg & Papps, 2020). It is almost impossible to isolate bilingualism as a factor when there are so many other factors causing variations. For example, it also depends on these kinds of other factors:

- What job?
  - Are there different results with different types of employment (e.g. professional, managerial, skilled, semi-skilled and unskilled)?

- Does the job have a customer interface that requires bilingualism (e.g. doctor, nurse, teacher, salesperson) or is the role less customer oriented, with less in the way of language requirements (e.g. software developer, chef, builder)?
- Do males and females show different results?
- Do younger workers show a different trend compared with older workers?
- What socioeconomic class and ethnic group are the workers?
- What are the social class attributes and expectations of the employment?
- In which district, county, state, region, country, continent is the employment?
- In which decade (e.g. 1980s or current decade) was the research done (the statistics change with time)?
- Which international/regional languages does the bilingual/multilingual speak?
- How fluent and biliterate, advanced and balanced in two or more languages is the person?
- How scarce or multitudinous are the speakers of the languages (e.g. English, Chinese, Frisian, Fijian) and hence what is the size of the population requiring bilingual services?
- How scarce or abundant are the applicants for the job with relevant language competences?
- How well educated (drop-out, high school, college, university) is the person?
- How competent is the person in the skills needed for the job (e.g. medical, legal)?
- At which stage is the person in their career (e.g. early, middle, late)?

Furthermore, the answer to the apparently simple question 'Do bilinguals have an economic advantage?' also depends on what is used as the measure of economic success or advantage. That measure may be:

- winning a job – getting hired;
- salary size;
- salary premium for multilingual skills;
- early or later advancement/promotion;
- final position/status/role as an employee;
- lifetime earnings;
- unemployment/employment rates;
- longer-term effects (e.g. on second- and third-generation immigrants);
- amount of local or international trade.

So, with any piece of research, we have to ask: (1) Can any of the factors listed above explain the findings other than (or as well as) bilingualism? (2) If the outcome (success/advantage) measure were different, would different results have been obtained? Over time, with the accumulation of many pieces of research, patterns in the findings will emerge allowing stronger conclusions. Callahan and Gándara (2014) conclude that a unifying sociopolitical linguistic theory is also something to work toward – a theory that can encapsulate the variations and factors above.

Bilingualism and Economic Inequality

Historically, antagonism toward immigrants (particularly in times of economic recession) has typically been directed at newcomers, who are blamed for taking away jobs from long-standing citizens. Immigrants are blamed for economic and social ills in society. However, immigrants can have a stimulating effect on the economy by (1) opening many new businesses, and (2) keeping businesses from relocating outside the country by providing inexpensive labor, which (3) keeps down the costs of goods and services.

While there are ethnic group differences in diverse societies, the overall picture is of low-wage employment among language minoritized members, relatively fewer opportunities for promotion and upward mobility, low vocational expectations and motivation, more economically disenfranchised communities and hence a possible poverty trap. However, it is not an inevitable condition of language minorities that they are economically deprived or impoverished. In the United States, poverty and inequality are not equally shared by all Latinx, Asian, African and other immigrant groups: there is a difference between and within individual ethnic groups. With the Spanish-speaking population of the United States increasing, and with Spanish an important trading language in Latin America and elsewhere, Spanish is of increasing economic value. The growing popularity of Chinese in dual language immersion programs in the United States is also tied to neoliberal views of the future economic value of Chinese language skills (Sung & Tsai, 2019).

Some scholars of language policy have turned their attention to how the forces of the political economy and neoliberalism contribute to class differences and inequality among immigrant and other language minoritized communities, including in post-colonial contexts (Bale, 2015; Flubacher & Del Percio, 2017; Ricento, 2015b; Spolsky, 2021). The political economy considers social power relations 'that mutually constitute the production, distribution, and consumption of resources' (Mosco, 2009: 24). Block (2017) argues for the need to study language practices, language ideology and language management within the context of the political economy. Block describes neoliberalism as 'the generally accepted label for the latest incarnation of capitalism, in more intensively and extensively globalized and technologically advanced circumstances' (Block, 2017: 571). Essentially, neoliberalism is the ideological force behind government efforts to reduce or eliminate government financing of public services (housing, utilities, health care, education, after-school programs, transportation, postal services, etc.) and to deregulate financial markets, leading to what Block (2017: 572) calls 'capitalism without borders'. Neoliberalism also leads to the use of the market metaphor to frame daily activities, which Block (2017: 574) notes reinforces the view 'that human beings only look after their own immediate and long-term self-interest, showing no concern for the collective good'. This is counter to the belief of neoliberalists that if individuals are free to pursue their individual interests without restrictions, the collective good will take care of itself. Block (2017: 574) argues that 'unfortunately, we now have ample proof that this optimistic assumption is misplaced, even if the ideology and its application persist'. Thus, understanding of issues of language as intertwined with identity, education, migration, employment and societal discourses, and of bilingual and multilingual education, require deep considerations of social class and inequality within the political economy.

Conclusion

For many but not all bilinguals and multilinguals, it seems increasingly economically valuable to be able to work in two, three or more languages. For some individuals, this is to gain employment and try to avoid poverty. For others, bilingualism and multilingualism may be of value in working locally or abroad for international and multinational corporations. For yet others who wish to go abroad to trade or translate, teach or travel, two or more languages become important.

The concept that speaking English is all one needs, whether in Europe or the United States, is naive and outdated. While English is often at the leading edge of economic modernization and technological development, selling, marketing and tailoring products and services to suit local markets require other languages.

Moving from a minoritized language to a majority language for perceived economic purposes does not guarantee the expected rewards. There is no assurance that those who become linguistically assimilated (e.g. speak English only) in countries like the United States will gain employment. The ability to speak English does not give equal or automatic access to jobs and wealth. Linguistic **assimilation** does not mean incorporation into the economic structure of the country. If there is a growth of ethnic businesses (e.g. in urban areas) and a development of language minority businesses in peripheral, rural areas, then bilingualism and multilingualism rather than English monolingualism may become more economically valuable.

The economic importance of languages, and the path to self-perpetuating change, is neatly summed up by Strubell (2001) in terms of a positive 'Catherine wheel' cycle (see Figure 19.1).

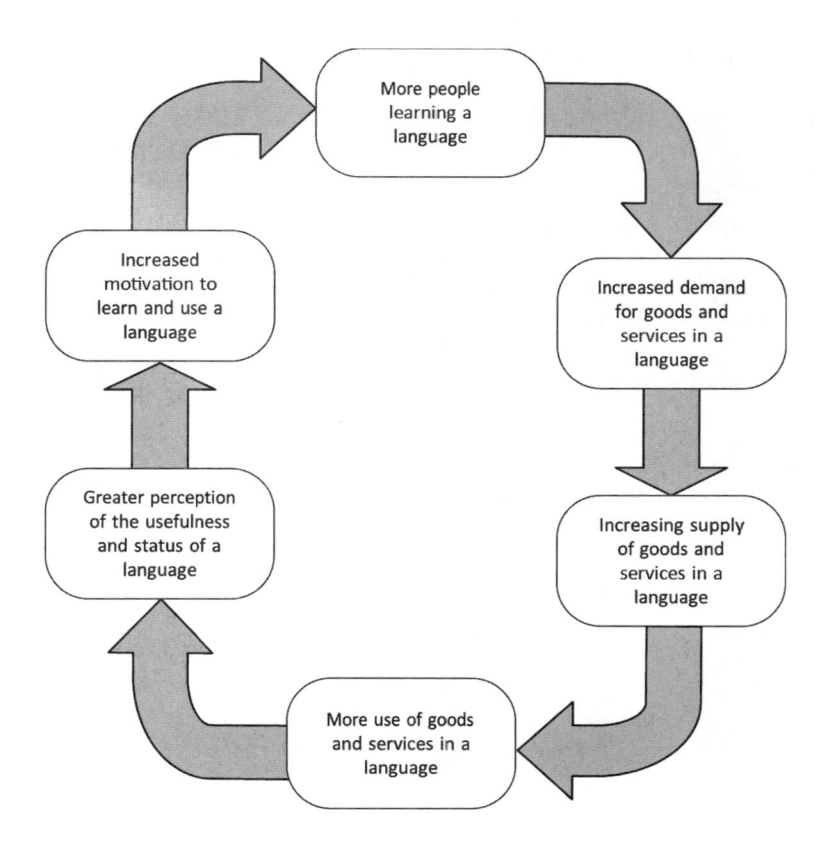

Figure 19.1 Catherine wheel cycle. Adapted from Strubell (2001)

Key Points in This Chapter

- In a global economy and with the ease of international communications, bilinguals and multilinguals are increasingly required in many occupations.
- The growth of tourism has potential economic benefits for many minority languages, but is allied to the rapid spread of English and preference for historical culture rather than contemporary living culture.
- Minority language mass media and use in technology and artificial intelligence contribute to the status of a language but are often in competition with the dominant English language mass media, and the use of English on the internet and with AI tools.
- Minoritized language groups are often identified with relatively high unemployment, low pay, poverty and powerlessness. However, local niche economies, working from home, and community initiatives can support and sustain a language minority.
- Bilingualism and multilingualism can be more valuable than majority language monolingualism, giving a competitive edge for an increasing number of vocations.
- Research on whether bilinguals and multilinguals have an economic advantage is at an early stage of evolution. There are no easy answers as there are so many other contributing factors (e.g. age, gender, different regions and countries).
- What is considered as an economic advantage for bilinguals and multilinguals is varied and multiple.
- It is important to consider the forces of the political economy and neoliberalism to understand the policies and practices surrounding bilingual and multilingual education and other aspects of language issues, policies and practices in society.

Suggested Further Reading

- Angouri, J., Kerekes, J. and Suni, M. (eds) (2023) *Language, Migration and In/Exclusion in the Workplace*. Multilingual Matters.
- Arendt, B. and Reershemius, G. (eds) (2024) *Heritage Languages in the Digital Age: The Case of Autochthonous Minority Languages in Western Europe*. Multilingual Matters.
- Dovchin, S. (ed.) (2020) *Digital Communication, Linguistic Diversity and Education*. Peter Lang.
- Gonçalves, K. and Schluter, A.A. (2024) *Domestic Workers Talk: Language Use and Social Practices in a Multilingual Workplace*. Multilingual Matters.
- Monsen, M. and Steien, G.B. (eds) (2022) *Language Learning and Forced Migration*. Multilingual Matters.

On the Web

- ePals: Connect, communicate and collaborate with educators around the world
  https://www.epals.com
- Wikipedia (explore the offerings in other languages for this online multilingual encyclopedia)
  https://www.wikipedia.org
- Yann Martel – How travel opens your mind and your language defines who you are (video)
  https://bigthink.com/videos/yann-martel-breaking-down-language
- Assembling the Lakota – Marvel Studios' *The Avengers*
  https://youtu.be/r_pPfp7lnIM?si=Q5prSmpaR0h2c970
- TED Talk – Daniel Bogre: How to save a language from extinction
  https://www.ted.com/talks/daniel_bogre_udell_how_to_save_a_language_from_extinction?utm_campaign=tedspread&utm_medium=referral&utm_source=tedcomshare

Discussion Questions

(1) Is there an economic advantage to bilingualism and multilingualism? What factors may or may not contribute to economic advantages for bilingual and multilingual individuals in your local area?

(2) Consider your own use of the internet, social media and AI tools. If you are bilingual or multilingual, what language(s) do you regularly use online, and for what purposes? If you are not bilingual, do you ever encounter other languages online in your routine internet use? Have you used any translation tools or other AI tools for language learning, teaching or communication purposes?

(3) Examine and discuss a selection of the dualisms or dimensions presented below. These sum up some of the debates and important dimensions of thinking in this book. Please regard this as a 'summative' question that requires other chapters of the book to be considered and integrated:
- linguistic compared with the sociocultural/sociolinguistic views of bilinguals;
- individual compared with societal analysis of bilingualism;
- language skills compared with language competences;
- fractional compared with a holistic view of bilinguals;
- subtractive compared with an additive view of bilinguals;
- the rights (individual and group) view compared with the empowerment view;
- the assimilationist compared with the pluralist view;
- the deprivation, remedial, problem, disabled view of bilinguals compared with the resource, beneficial, talent, diversity view of bilinguals.

(a) Briefly state what are the different viewpoints alluded to in those dualisms/dimensions you have selected.

(b) Indicate how these dualisms/dimensions relate to different views of bilingualism, bilingual education and multicultural education. What are the implications for the kind of language and cultural approach adopted in a school?

Study Activities

(1) Carry out a survey of newspapers, radio stations, television stations, markets, restaurants, service providers and other businesses in your local area that cater to linguistic minoritized communities and/or tourists. What languages are used in these businesses? What does the presence (or absence) of these media and businesses indicate about bilingualism and multilingualism in your local area? How important is it for the employees to be bilingual or multilingual?

(2) Conduct a job search via an online job board such as Monster.com. Enter 'bilingual' into the search box and choose a country, state, city of interest. What kinds of jobs are in this area requiring bilingual skills?

(3) View the video 'Top 5 benefits of bilingualism in the workplace', which is essentially a promotional infomercial for a company providing Spanish language courses (Spanish Academy) (https://youtu.be/SxogP-5_YMw). How consistent is the information in this video with the research highlighted in this chapter and other chapters in this book? How would you interpret this video from a framework of political economy and neoliberalism? Who appears to be the target audience for this video.

Glossary

Note: Many of the terms in this glossary represent highly complex social phenomena and some terms and their definitions are the topic of debate. Simple and basic definitions are provided here, but fuller treatment of these terms may be found in this and other texts.

1.5 generation. First-generation immigrants who migrate to a new country at a young age but grow up that country.
academic language proficiency. There are many definitions but generally refers to the level of language proficiency students need to comprehend and perform grade-level academic tasks. However, the level of proficiency needed varies widely depending on the tasks and the language demands of the tasks.
ACCESS. ACCESS for English language learners is a suite of large-scale English proficiency assessments use by most US states that are part of the WIDA Consortium (*see* WIDA).
acculturation. The process by which an individual or group adapts to a new culture.
acquisition planning. Part of formal language planning where interventions are made to encourage families to pass on their minoritized language, and to encourage schools to produce more minoritized language speakers.
additive bilingualism. A situation in which a second language is eventually added to a student's native language without replacing it.
anti-racist. The view that racial groups are equals and none needs developing; the support of policy that reduces racial inequity.
ascendant bilingualism. When a second language is developing.
assessment. The process of collecting and analyzing a wide variety of data from students that provides evidence of their learning and growth over an extended period.
assimilation. The process by which a person or language group loses their own language and culture, which are replaced by a different language and culture.
assimilationist. An individual who maintains the belief that cultural groups should give up their heritage languages and cultures and take on the host society's language, culture and way of life.
assimilationist discourses. Discourses that devalue language minoritized students' home languages and cultures, seeing them as problems to overcome (also called monolingual discourses).
audism. The belief that the ability to hear makes one superior to those who cannot hear.

balanced bilingualism. Approximately equal competence in two languages.
bias. In testing, refers to the unfair advantages or disadvantages that may be given to certain students that can impact their performance. For example, a test given in English will be biased in favor of proficient English-speakers and biased against students who are not yet proficient in English.
bicultural. Identifying with the culture of two different language groups.
bilingual. A term to describe an individual with some command of two languages.
bilingual education. A simplistic label for a complex phenomenon, but in general may refer to where some, most or all the education is through two languages.
Bilingual Education Act. Title VII of the Elementary and Secondary Education Act of 1968, which established US federal policy for bilingual education for language minoritized students. It was re-authorized in 1994 as part of the Improving America's Schools Act, and was replaced in 2002 by Title III under No Child Left Behind. *See also* Title III.
bilingual immersion programs. This model typically involves the immersion of a language majority student in a classroom where the target non-dominant language is taught 90–100% of the time for the first couple of years, which gradually shifts to 50% (and 50% the dominant language). Examples include French immersion programs in Canada and Spanish and Chinese (Mandarin) immersion programs in the US for English-speakers.
bilingualism. The ability of an individual to use two languages, or the use of two languages within a community.
biliteracy. The uses of two or more languages to communicate in or around written text.
caretaker speech. A simplified language used by parents with children to ensure understanding, also called motherese. Caretaker speech usually has short sentences, is grammatically simple and has few difficult words, much repetition and clear pronunciation.
circumstantial bilinguals. Groups of individuals who must become bilingual to operate in the majority language society that surrounds them.
codeblending. The use of both a signed and spoken language. *See also* signed languages.
codemeshing. *See* translingual literacy.
codemixing. The mixing of two languages within a sentence or across sentences. Sometimes used interchangeably with codeswitching.
codeswitching. When a bilingual speaker uses more than one language inside a sentence or across sentences. Sometimes used interchangeably with codemixing.
cognates. Words that are similar in structure and meaning in two languages because they come from the same root (e.g. *education* in English and *educación* in Spanish).
cognition. The internal processing involved in language, memory, perception and thought.
Common European Framework of Reference (CEFR). A framework developed by the Council of Europe for discussing and assessing language proficiency and to guide the development of language assessments and curricular materials.
common underlying proficiency (CUP). Two languages working integratively in the thinking system. Each language serves one underlying, central thinking system.
communicative competence. The ability to use a language to communicate effectively and appropriately with other speakers of the language. Includes grammatical, discourse, sociolinguistic and strategic competence.

communicative language teaching (CLT). Language teaching approaches, methods, strategies and techniques that focus on helping students develop communicative competence.

communicative sensitivity. Sensitivity to the social nature and communicative functions of language.

comprehensible input. Oral or written language that is slightly above a second language learner's current level of proficiency in the second language and thus provides linguistic input that leads to second language acquisition.

comprehensible output. Oral or written language produced by a second language speaker that is comprehensible to the individual or individuals with whom he or she is communicating.

content and language integrated learning (CLIL). An inclusive term, particularly used in Europe, for bilingual or multilingual education in which a second or later language is used for learning subject content, and where both language learning and content learning occur simultaneously, with an emphasis on their integration.

content-based English as a second language (ESL). Using content areas (mathematics, language arts, science, social studies, etc.) as the basis for teaching English as a second language. In contrast to sheltered instruction (*see below*), the emphasis is on learning English more than learning the content area.

content-based instruction (CBI). An approach to second language instruction in which content area subjects and topics are used as the basis of instruction.

context. The setting in which communication occurs and which places possibilities and constraints on what is said and how it is said. The context can refer to the physical setting or to the language context in which a word or utterance occurs.

corpus planning. The selection, codification and expansion of norms of language.

criterion-referenced tests. Tests designed to measure the degree to which students have mastered tested content.

critical period hypothesis. States that younger learners have certain cognitive advantages in learning a new language that end around a certain age. The exact age and the degree to which a critical period or cognitive advantages exist have been the subject of much debate.

cultural pluralism. The ownership of two or more sets of cultural beliefs, values and attitudes. Multicultural education is often designed to encourage cultural pluralism in children.

culture. The set of shared meanings, beliefs, attitudes, customs, everyday behavior and social understandings of a particular group, community or society.

Deaf epistemology. Deaf ways of knowing and acquiring knowledge.

Deaf-signing bilingual education. Education for deaf students that includes instruction in both a signed language (e.g. American Sign Language) and a written language (e.g. standard American English).

developmental (maintenance) bilingual education. A form of bilingual education where students initially receive about 90% of content area instruction in their native language (L1) and 10% of content area instruction through sheltered instruction in the target dominant language (L2). L1 instruction decreases slowly as sheltered L2 instruction increases as students move up in grade level. Instruction continues in both languages until the end of the program, even after students attain proficiency in the L2, to ensure that students attain strong bilingual and biliteracy skills. Also referred to as maintenance late-exit bilingual education.

diglossia. Two languages or language varieties existing together in a society in a stable arrangement through different uses attached to each language.

discourse/Discourse. As defined and distinguished by Gee (2012), discourse (with a lowercase d) refers to language in use or connected stretches of language that make sense, such as conversations, stories, reports, arguments, essays and so forth. Discourse (with a capital D) is made up of distinctive ways of speaking/listening and often, too, writing/reading coupled with distinctive ways of acting, interacting, valuing, feeling, dressing, thinking and believing with other people and with various objects, tools and technologies in order to enact specific socially recognizable identities engaged in specific socially recognizable activities.

divergent (or creative) thinking. Thinking that is original, imaginative and creative. A preference for open-ended, multiple answers to questions.

domains. Particular contexts where a certain language is used. For example, there is the family domain, where a minoritized language may be used. In the work domain, the majority language may be used.

dominant language. The language in which a person has greater proficiency, or uses more often.

domination. The ascendance of one group over another. The dominant group expects compliance and subservience from the subordinate group.

dual language (or two-way) bilingual education. *See* dual language programs.

dual language books. Books printed in two languages in which one language appears above the other or the two languages are written side by side on one page or on opposite pages.

dual language programs. A variety of bilingual program models for English language learners (ELLs) and English- proficient students designed to help them become bilingual and biliterate. In a 50/50 two-way model, half of the students are fluent English-speakers and half are ELLs, and 50% of instruction is English and 50% in the native language of the ELLs. In the 90/10 model, for the first few years, 90% of instruction is in the non-English language and 10% is in English. Instruction gradually reaches 50% in each language. Other variations exist.

Duolingo English Test. An English language proficiency test developed by Duolingo, used as an entrance examination for international students in a growing number of English-medium colleges and universities around the world.

dynamic assessment. A form of assessment that incorporates interactive teaching into the assessment process when students face difficulties in the performance of an academic task.

dynamic bilingualism. A view of bilingualism that focuses on the ways bilinguals draw on the range of features associated with socially constructed languages within their linguistic repertoire in complex and dynamic ways as they communicate with others and engage in collaborative tasks.

ecology of language(s). The study of interactions between one or more languages and a social environment.

elective bilingualism. Becoming bilingualism by conscious choice, rather than due to forced circumstances.

elite/prestigious bilingualism. Typically refers to bilingualism by choice in two (or more) elite or prestigious national and/or international languages, among the highly privileged members of a dominant society.

ELPA21. A small multi-state consortium in the United States to develop and share a

common K-12 English proficiency assessment called the English Language Proficiency Assessment for the 21st Century.
emergent bilingual. An alternative label for students classified as English language learners (ELLs) that draws attention to the other language or languages in the learners' linguistic repertoires, situates these learners in a continuum of bilingual development and emphasizes that a fundamental goal of programs for these learners should be to help them attain high levels of proficiency in both their first language and English.
empowerment. The means by which those of low status, low influence and power are given the means to increase their chances of prosperity, power and prestige. Literacy and biliteracy are major means of empowering such individuals and groups.
enculturation. The process of adapting to a new culture.
endogenous communities. Communities that use more than one language on an everyday basis.
English as a second language (ESL). An academic subject, course or program designed to teach English to students who are not yet proficient in the language. Commonly used even with multilingual students for whom English is their third or later language. Alternative names include English for speakers of other languages (ESOL), English as a foreign language (EFL), English as an additional language (EAL) and English as a new language (ENL). *See also* English language development.
'English for the Children' initiatives. Referendums in four US states to place restrictions on bilingual education programs. In 1998 voters in California approved Proposition 227, in 2000 voters in Arizona approved Proposition 203 and in 2002 those in Massachusetts approved Question 2. An attempt to pass a similar initiative in Colorado (Amendment 31) failed. *See also* LOOK Act and Proposition 58 for reversals.
English language development (ELD). An alternative label for English as a second language (ESL) programs and instruction, commonly used at the elementary school level.
English language learners (ELLs). A formal classification commonly used in federal and state policy in the United States to label students who are non-native speakers of English and are in the process of attaining proficiency in English. Frequently shortened to English learner (EL).
enrichment bilingual education. A form of bilingual education that seeks to develop bilingualism, thus enriching a person's cultural, social and personal education.
European Language Portfolio. A tool developed by the Council of Europe based on the Common European Framework of Reference (CEFR) for students to demonstrate their proficiency in one or more languages. The portfolio consists of a language passport (linguistic profile), a language biography and a dossier of sample work.
Every Student Succeeds Act (ESSA). The current re-authorization in the United States of the Elementary and Secondary Act (ESEA), which establishes federal education policy for state and local education agencies that accept federal education funding. *See also* Title I and Title III.
executive function. A set of inter-related processes in the brain, particularly the frontal lobe. The executive function system is generally believed to consist of three components: inhibition, updating (a.k.a. working memory) and shifting (a.k.a. cognitive flexibility).

fixed mindset. A belief that one's intelligence cannot be changed.

fluent English proficient (FEP). The official designation in the United States for former English language learners who have attained sufficient English proficiency to meet their state's criteria for redesignation.

formative assessment. The use of ongoing assessments that help to identify a student's strengths and needs and thus inform subsequent instruction, building on these strengths while addressing these needs.

full inclusion. In special education, refers to placement of students with disabilities into a regular classroom as the least restrictive environment.

functional bilingualism. The ability to use bilingual skills to accomplish basic functions.

funds of knowledge. Knowledge that exists in communities and individuals outside of school that is valuable to share. Such knowledge particularly derives from heritage language and cultural minorities and is not transmitted in a majority language school curriculum.

gifted-and-talented education. Educational programs and classes designed for exceptional children considered to have, or potentially to have, superior intellectual and/or creative abilities.

global language proficiency. Refers to an individual's overall proficiency in a second language, inclusive of listening, speaking, reading and writing.

growth mindset. A belief that one's intelligence can increase with effort and persistence.

heritage language. The language a person regards as their native, home or ancestral language. This covers indigenous languages (e.g. Welsh in Wales) and immigrant languages (e.g. Spanish in the United States).

heritage language education. Education programs for language minoritized students to develop or maintain their heritage language; includes bilingual programs for students classified as English language learners, world language classes targeting heritage speakers in K-12 and post-secondary education, and community-based after-school or weekend programs.

heteroglossic perspective. Views bilingualism as the norm and treats the languages of bilinguals as coexisting.

high-stakes testing. The use of tests to make important decisions about students (e.g. entrance or exit from special programs, grade promotion, high school graduation) and/or to hold teachers, schools, districts or states accountable.

home language support. Using a student's native language during English as a second language (ESL) or sheltered English content area instruction to make the English instruction more comprehensible.

identity. The combinations and interactions between an individual's values, beliefs, views, experiences, cultures, languages and so on that make the individual a unique person.

ideology. A set of views, beliefs and values that influence the way an individual or group views and interprets the world.

IELTS. International English Language Testing System. Produced by the British Council and Cambridge University Press & Assessments, and used as an entrance examination for international students in many English-medium colleges and universities around the world.

immersion bilingual education. Schooling where some or most subject content is taught through a second language. Pupils in immersion are usually native speakers of a majority language and the teaching is carefully structured to their needs.

incipient bilingualism (bilinguals). The early stages of bilingualism where one language is not strongly developed. The person is beginning to acquire a second language.

indigenous language. A language spoken by an ethnic minoritized group considered to be original inhabitants of a given land or area.

individual bilingualism. The bilingual language competences of an individual language user.

instrumental motivation. Wanting to learn a language for utilitarian reasons (e.g. to get a better job).

integrative motivation. Wanting to learn a language to belong to a social group (e.g. make friends).

intelligence. There are many different definitions of intelligence. In general, it refers to individuals' intellectual capacity to deal with cognitive complexity, learn from experience, act purposefully, adapt effectively to the environment and achieve goals across different environments.

intelligence quotient (IQ). A score derived from standardized tests that claims to measure human intelligence.

intergenerational transmission. The passing on of a home language from the parents to their children.

interlanguage. An intermediate form of language used by second language learners in the process of learning a language. Interlanguage contains some transfer or borrowing from the first language and is an approximate system with regard to grammar and communicating meaning.

language ability. An umbrella term and therefore used ambiguously to describe the outcome of language learning, providing an indication of current language level.

language achievement. Normally seen as the outcome of formal language instruction. Proficiency in a language due to what has been taught or learnt in a language classroom.

language across the curriculum. A curriculum approach to language learning that focuses on language development across all subjects of the curriculum. Language should be developed in all content areas of the curriculum and not just as a subject in its own right.

language-as-a-problem orientation. A point of view in which the home languages of bilinguals are viewed as a problem to be overcome as students learn the dominant societal language and academic content through that language.

language-as-a-resource orientation. A point of view in which the home languages of bilinguals are viewed as a strength to be developed and built on to help the students learn the dominant societal language and academic content.

language-as-a-right orientation. A point of view in which the use of home languages, including in education, is a basic human right. Also recognizes the right of students to learn the dominant societal language without sacrificing their home language.

language attrition. The gradual loss (over time) of a language within a person or a language group.

language borrowing. A word or a phrase from one language that has become established in use in another language. When borrowing is a single word, it is often called a loan word.

language brokers. Any individual who interprets or translates between speakers or writers of two different languages. Children of immigrants often become language brokers between their parents and members of the dominant society.

language competence. A broad and general term, used particularly to describe an inner, mental representation of language, something latent rather than overt. Such competence refers usually to an underlying system inferred from language performance.

language death. When a declining language loses its last remaining speakers through their death or their shift to using another language. This language then no longer exists as a medium of communication in any language domains. Recent scholarship prefers to view a language as dormant (or sleeping) rather than 'dead', with potential for being revitalized or 'reawakened'.

language ideologies. Feelings, ideas or conceptions of language that may seem commonsensical but are actually constructed from specific political and economic perspectives that frequently result in value judgments about languages and their speakers.

language interference. Interference in second language learning is said to occur when vocabulary or syntax patterns transfer from a learner's first language to the second language, causing errors in second language performance. The term 'interference' is decreasing in use because of its negative and derogatory connotations. *See also* transfer.

language loss. The process of losing the ability or use of a language within an individual or group. Language loss is particularly studied among immigrants to a country where their mother tongue has little or no status, little economic value or use in education.

language maintenance. The continued use of a language, particularly among language minorities (e.g. through bilingual education). The term is often used with reference to policies that protect and promote minoritized languages.

language majority students. Students who are native speakers of the standard language variety spoken by the dominant group of a given society.

language minoritized groups/students. Those who are not native speakers of the language spoken by the dominant group of a given society.

language minority. A language community (or person) whose first language is different from the dominant language of the country.

language performance. A person's production of language, particularly within a classroom or test situation. It is the outward evidence of language competence but is not necessarily an accurate measure of language competence.

language planning. The development of a deliberate policy to engineer the use of language varieties within a region or country on linguistic, political or social grounds. Language planning often involves corpus planning (the selection, codification and expansion of norms of language) and status planning (the choice of language varieties for different functions and purposes).

language proficiency. An umbrella term, sometimes used synonymously with language competence, at other times as a specific, measurable outcome from language testing. Language proficiency is viewed as the product of a variety of mechanisms: formal learning, informal uncontrived language acquisition (e.g. on the street) and of individual characteristics such as 'intelligence'.

language revitalization. The process of restoring language vitality by promoting the use of a language and its range of functions within the community.

language shift. A change from the use of one language to another language within an individual or a language community. This often involves a shift from the minoritized language to the dominant language of the country. Usually the term means 'downward' shift (i.e. loss of a language).

language skills. Language skills are usually said to comprise listening, speaking, reading and writing. Each of these can be divided into sub-skills. Language skills refer to highly specific, observable, clearly definable components such as writing.

language socialization. The process by which individuals acquire the knowledge and practices that enable them to participate effectively in a language community.

language spread. An increase in the number of speakers and/or use of a language in or across geographical areas and societies.

language vitality. The extent to which a language minority vigorously maintains and extends its everyday use and range of functions. Language vitality is said to be enhanced by factors such as language status, institutional support, economic value and the number and distribution of its speakers.

Latinx. A gender-neutral term for Latinas and Latinos. *Latine* is growing in acceptance as an alternative.

Lau remedies. A set of guidelines issued to schools by the US Office of Civil Rights following the 1974 US Supreme Court ruling in *Lau v. Nichols*, outlining the procedures and instructional approaches schools need to follow to be in compliance with the ruling.

least restrictive environment. In special education, the principle that students with disabilities should be given the opportunity to learn alongside non-disabled students in a regular classroom as much as possible.

lexicon. The vocabulary of a language.

limited English proficient (LEP). An outdated label once used in the United States to refer to a student who is in the process of developing English language proficiency. This term has been criticized for taking a deficit view of students. 'English language learners', 'emergent bilinguals', 'multilingual learners' and other terms are typically preferred.

linguistic hegemony. When dominant (majority) groups create a consensus by convincing others to accept their language variety (dialect, system) and usage (e.g. enunciation, syntax) as the model or exemplar.

linguistic imperialism. Typically refers to situations where an imperial, colonial or other dominant power imposes its language on speakers of other languages.

linguistic racism. Depriving racialized minorities of educational, socioeconomic or sociocultural opportunities because of the way they use their language(s).

LOOK Act. The Language Opportunity for Our Kids (LOOK) Act passed by the Massachusetts state legislature in 2017 to repeal Question 2 and provide school districts with the flexibility to provide bilingual education programs. *See also* Question 2.

medium of instruction. The predominant language or languages used for classroom instruction. Also referred to as 'language of instruction'.

metalinguistic competence (or awareness). May loosely be defined as thinking about and reflecting upon the nature and functions of language. Metalinguistic awareness includes a collection of abilities, such as print awareness, morphological awareness, grammatical awareness and phonological awareness. They are distinct from language proficiency but are crucial to academic achievement and the acquisition of literacy.

monocultural. Following the cultural practices associated with a single cultural or ethnic group.

monoglossic perspective. Views monolingualism as the norm and treats the languages of bilinguals as two separate distinct systems, as if students are two monolinguals in one (double monolingualism).

monolingual. A person who knows and/or uses one language.

monolingualism. An inability to use more than one language, or the use of only one language within a community.

morphological awareness. Awareness of the structure of words, including the meaning of individual morphemes.

morphology. The study of the structure of words. The central unit of study is the morpheme, the smallest unit of meaning or grammatical function.

mother tongue. The term is used ambiguously. It variously means (1) the language learnt from the mother, (2) the first language learnt, irrespective of 'from whom', (3) the stronger language at any time of life, (4) the 'mother tongue' of the area or country (e.g. Irish in Ireland), (5) the language most used by a person, or (6) the language to which a person has the more positive attitude and affection.

motherese. A simplified language used by parents to young children to ensure understanding. *See also* caretaker speech.

multicultural. Adopting the cultural practices associated with more than one cultural or ethnic group.

multilingual learners. A broad term for any students who are already proficient in two more languages or who are in the process of developing one or more new languages.

multilingualism. The use of more than one language, but typically used to describe the use of three or more languages by an individual or within a society.

multiliteracies. A broadening of the term literacy beyond written text to include other important types of literacy (e.g. digital literacy, visual literacy, mathematical literacy, scientific literacy, financial literacy, civic literacy, socio-emotional literacy).

multiple intelligences. A theory which includes eight types of intelligences: logical-mathematical, verbal-linguistic, visual-spatial, musical-rhythmical, bodily-kinesthetic, naturalist, interpersonal and intrapersonal.

norm-referenced tests. Tests designed to compare a student's score with those of other students. Test results are usually reported as percentile rankings (e.g. a student at the 71st percentile rank scored higher than 71% of the students in the test's norming population, that is, a group of students who have already taken the test).

Office of English Language Acquisition (OELA). An Office of the US Department of Education that is responsible for the implementation of the policies and funding programs of Title III of the Every Student Succeeds Act (ESSA) and for providing support to K-12 schools in implementing federal education policy with students classified as English language learners (ELLs).

passive bilinguals (bilingualism). Being able to understand (and sometimes read) in a second language without speaking or writing in that second language.

phonology. The study of the sound systems of languages.

pluralist discourses. Discourses that recognize English language learners' home languages and cultures as rich resources for helping them learn English and academic content and that strive to help them develop high levels of proficiency and literacy in both languages (also called multilingual discourses).

plurilingual. Often used interchangeably with multilingual, though some use plurilingualism to refer to multilingualism at the individual level (versus at the societal level).

plurilingual education. Increasingly used in Europe to refer to various forms of bilingual, multilingual and world language education programs.
pragmatics. The study of the use of language in communication, with a particular emphasis on the contexts in which language is used.
productive bilingualism. Ability to produce speech and written text in two languages.
productive language. Speaking and writing.
Proposition 58. A voter initiative in California passed in 2016 that repealed Proposition 227 (1998) and thus removed restrictions on bilingual education programs.
Proposition 203. An 'English for the Children' voter initiative passed in Arizona in 2000 that placed restrictions on bilingual education. State legislation has loosened some of the restrictions.
Proposition 227. An 'English for the Children' voter initiative passed in California in 1998 that placed restrictions on bilingual education. It was repealed by Proposition 58 in 2016.
pull-out ESL. A program model for English language learners in which students are placed in mainstream or sheltered English immersion classrooms but are regularly pulled out of class for English as a second language (ESL) lessons taught by an ESL teacher.
Question 2. An 'English for the Children' voter initiative passed in Massachusetts in 2002 that placed restrictions on bilingual education. It was repealed by the LOOK Act in 2017.
raciolinguistics. Considers the relations of ideologies at the intersection of language, race and power.
receptive bilingualism. Ability to comprehend speech and written text in two languages.
receptive language. Listening/understanding and reading.
recessive bilingualism. When proficiency in one of a bilingual's languages is decreasing due to lack of use or development.
recursive bilingualism. A view of bilingualism, especially as related to revitalization of endangered languages, to describe the ways bilinguals reach back to the bits and pieces of their ancestral language as they reconstitute it for new functions and move the language towards the future.
register. Variation in the use of language based on the context in which the language is used.
reliability. The consistency with which a test or assessment measures what it is measuring.
scaffolding. Providing support to build on a student's existing repertoire of knowledge and understanding. As the student progresses and becomes more of an independent learner, the help given by teachers can be gradually removed.
science of reading (SOR). In the most basic terms, a reference to a large body of international scientifically based research about reading. From a policy standpoint, SOR typically refers to mandated skills-based reading instruction programs, typically at the primary school level, that focus on explicit instruction in five foundational reading skills: phonemic awareness, phonics, fluency, vocabulary and reading comprehension. *See also* structured literacy.
Seal of Biliteracy. A formal recognition of bilingualism and biliteracy skills bestowed on graduating high school students in the United States who have met their state's criteria to demonstrate proficiency in a language in addition to English.
second language instructional competence (SLIC). The amount of second language

proficiency needed to complete an academic task based on the linguistic demand of that task.

semantics. The study of the meaning of words, phrases and sentences.

semilingual. A controversial term used to describe people whose two languages appear to be at a low level of development in comparison with the standardized varieties of those languages.

separate storage hypothesis. This hypothesis states that bilinguals have independent language storage and retrieval systems in their brain.

separate underlying proficiency (SUP). The largely discredited idea that two languages exist separately and work independently in the thinking system.

sequential/consecutive bilingualism. Bilingualism achieved via learning a second language later than the first language. When a second language is learnt after the age of three, sequential bilingualism is said to occur.

shared storage hypothesis. This hypothesis states that two languages are kept in a single memory store in the brain with two different language input channels and two different language output channels.

sheltered content instruction. *See* sheltered instruction.

sheltered English. *See* sheltered instruction.

sheltered English immersion (SEI). A program model for English language learners that combines English as a second language (ESL), sheltered content area instruction and home language support. Sometimes called structured English immersion.

sheltered instruction. Grade-level content-area instruction provided in English in a manner that makes it comprehensible to English language learners while supporting their English language development.

Sheltered Instruction Observation Protocol (SIOP). A tool for planning, implementing and evaluating sheltered English content-area instruction.

signacy. Ability to acquire and use a signed language. *See also* signed languages.

signed languages. Languages that use visual and manual signs instead of spoken words to communicate and convey meaning, particular among and with members of a Deaf community.

signing. Communicating through a signed language. *See also* signed languages.

simultaneous bilingualism. Bilingualism achieved via acquiring a first and a second language concurrently. When a second language is learnt before the age of three, simultaneous bilingualism is said to occur.

societal bilingualism. A broad term used to refer to the use of two (or more) languages within a given society.

sociolinguistics. The study of language in relation to social groups, social class, ethnicity and other interpersonal factors in communication.

special education. Specially designed instruction to meet the unique needs of a child with a disability, guided in the United States by regulations in the Individuals with Disabilities Education Act (IDEA).

specially designed academic instruction in English (SDAIE). Another term for sheltered instruction, preferred in California and other states because it places emphasis on the fact that such instruction is academically rigorous but specially designed to match the linguistic needs of the student.

speech community. A group of people who share a common language(s) and norms and expectations for its use.

status planning. Language planning which centers on language use and prestige within a region and within particular language domains. *See also* language planning.

strategic competence. A speaker's ability to adapt their use of a second language to compensate for gaps in their proficiency.

structured immersion. The curriculum is taught in English in such programs in the United States at a level comprehensible to minoritized language students. The goal is to help minoritized language students acquire proficiency in English while at the same time achieving well in content areas of the curriculum.

structured literacy. Refers to skill-based reading instruction programs aligned with science of reading (SOR) policies. The term is commonly used in Canada, Australia and New Zealand.

submersion. The teaching of minoritized language pupils solely through the medium of a majority language, often alongside native speakers of the majority language. Minoritized language pupils are left to sink or swim in the mainstream curriculum.

subtractive bilingualism. A situation in which a second language eventually replaces a student's native language.

summative assessment. Assessments that provide a summary of what students know and can do. Typically given at the end of a unit or at the end of a school year.

superdiversity. Refers to diverse populations made up of many different racial, ethnic, immigrant, refugee and other minority or indigenous groups. Also refers to diversity within individual ethnic and minoritized groups.

syntax. The study of the rules governing the relationships between words and the ways they are combined to form phrases and sentences.

terminology. The creation, selection and standardization of terms for use in specific (e.g. school curriculum) or technical (e.g. science, medicine, computing) contexts. *See also* corpus planning; language planning.

testing. The administration of tests, single instruments designed to systematically measure a sample of a student's ability at one particular time.

testing accommodations. In testing English language learners, refers to modifications in the testing environment or testing procedures, or modifications to the test instrument itself, that are intended to make up for a student's lack of proficiency in the language of the test (e.g. providing extra time, oral interpretation of test directions or items, native-language versions of the test).

threshold theory. A contested theory which suggests that certain cognitive advantages of bilingualism may be available only after a certain level of bilingualism has been attained.

Title I (of ESSA). 'Improving Basic Programs Operated by State and Local Educational Agencies.' The section of the US federal Every Student Succeeds Act (ESSA) that includes requirements for the testing and assessment of K-12 students, with specific regulations for the inclusion and accommodation of students classified as English language learners (ELLs) and regulations on how ELL test scores are included in school accountability determinations.

Title III (of ESSA). 'Language Instruction for English Learners and Immigrant Students.' The section of the US federal Every Student Succeeds Act (ESSA) that specifically addresses mandates for instruction and other federal requirement for students classified as English language learners (ELLs) and the appropriate uses of Title III funds to support ELL programs. Title III replaced the Bilingual Education Act.

TOEFL. Test of English as a Foreign Language (TOEFL). Produced by Education Testing Service and used as an entrance examination for international students in many English-medium colleges and universities around the world.

transfer. The effect of one language on the learning of another. There can be both negative transfer, sometimes called interference, and more often positive transfer, particularly in understandings and meanings of concepts.

transglossia. In contrast to models of diglossia, which typically see majority and minoritized languages relegated to specific domains, functions and use, transglossia considers the ways in which multiple languages are used across multiple domains and functions within a society, or the ways in which multiple languages may be used within a single domain or function.

transitional bilingual education (TBE). A program model for bilingual students. As commonly used in the United States, native language content-area instruction is provided for the first few years of the program, in addition to sheltered content-area instruction and English as a second language (ESL). The amount of native language instruction decreases as sheltered English immersion increases. Students are transitioned to mainstream classrooms after just a few years in the program.

translanguaging. In its original conceptualization, refers to the practice in which bilinguals receive information in one language and then use or apply it in the other language. In its expanded sense, it refers to the natural and normal ways bilinguals mix and use their languages in their everyday lives without adherence to the boundaries of 'named' languages to make sense of their bilingual worlds. In teaching, the term refers to pedagogical practices that use bilingualism as a resource rather than ignore it or perceive it as a problem.

translanguaging pedagogy. Specific pedagogical practices in which teachers and students engage in translanguaging to communicate, affirm bilingual identities and facilitate teaching and learning in the classroom. Practices are grounded in a teacher's translanguaging stance, can be explicitly designed and can take place through natural and spontaneous shifts between languages throughout the day. *See* translanguaging.

translingual literacy. Ability to merge resources from different languages, often to create new forms and meanings, typically in writing. Also referred to as codemeshing. *See also* translanguaging.

trilingual education. The teaching and use of three or more languages for instruction in the classroom. Typically, these would include the home language, a regional and/or national dominant language and/or a major international language.

validity. The accuracy of a test or assessment in measuring what it purports to measure.

vernacular. An indigenous or heritage language of an individual or community. A vernacular language is used to define a native language as opposed to (1) a classical language such as Latin and Greek, (2) an internationally used language such as English and French, (3) the official or national language of a country.

WIDA. A large multi-state consortium consisting of the majority of states in the United States to develop and share common English language proficiency standards and assessments for PK-12 education.

World Englishes. A term that emphasizes that English is more than a single standardized language, and that there are a large number of standard and non-standard varieties of English around the world.

zone of proximal development (ZPD). Refers to a metaphorical space between what an individual can do on his or her own, and what she or he can do with support from a teacher or other more knowledgeable person.

Bibliography

Abedi, J. (2017) Utilizing accommodations in assessment. In E. Shohamy and S. May (eds) *Encyclopedia of Language Education* (3rd edn, vol. 7). Springer.

Abedi, J. (2021) Accommodation and universal design. In G. Fulcher and L. Harding (eds) *The Routledge Handbook of Language Testing* (pp. 306–321). Routledge. https://doi.org/10.4324/9781003220756-24.

Abedi, J. and Sanchez, M.T. (2022) Historical milestones in the assessment of English learners. In B.E. Clauser and M.B. Bunch (eds) *The History of Educational Measurement: Key Advancements in Theory, Policy, and Practice* (pp. 87–110). Routledge.

Abley, M. (2005) *Spoken Here: Travels Among Threatened Languages*. Houghton Mifflin.

Adamou, E. (2024) *Endangered Languages*. MIT Press.

Adamou, E., Crasborn, O., Webster, J. and Zeshan, U. (2020) Forces shaping sign multilingualism. In U. Zeshan and J. Webster (eds) *Sign Multilingualism* (pp. 1–22). Walter De Gruyter.

Adams, R. (2012) Language contact and borrowing. In R. Pfau, M. Steinbach and B. Woll (eds) *Sign Language: An International Handbook* (pp. 841–861). De Gruyter Mouton.

Adesope, O.O., Lavin, T., Thompson, T. and Ungerleider, C. (2010) A systematic review and meta-analysis of the cognitive correlates of bilingualism. *Review of Educational Research* 80 (2), 207–245.

Aicardi, C. (2009) The analytic spirit and the Paris institution for the deaf-mutes, 1760–1830. *History of Science* 47 (2), 175–221.

Alarcón, A. and Heyman, J. (2013) Bilingual call centers at the US–Mexico border: Location and linguistic markers of exploitability. *Language in Society* 42 (1), 1–21.

Alarcón, A., Di Paolo, A., Heyman, J. and Morales, M.C. (2014) The occupational location of Spanish–English bilinguals in the new information economy: The health and criminal justice sectors in the US borderlands with Mexico. In R.M. Callahan and P.C. Gándara (eds) *The Bilingual Advantage: Language, Literacy and the US Labor Market* (pp. 110–137). Multilingual Matters.

Alfaro, C. and Hernández, A. M. (2024) Dual language bilingual teacher preparation: The braided relationship of ideology, identity, language and culture. In J.A. Freire, C. Alfaro and E. de Jong (eds) *The Handbook of Dual Language Bilingual Education* (pp. 597–610). Routledge. https://doi.org/10.4324/9781003269076-50.

Al-Gasem, N.S. (2015) 'A nerdy adrenaline': The influence of ethnomathematics on female mathematical identity. PhD dissertation, University of Texas at San Antonio.

Al-Hoorie, A.H. and MacIntyre, P.D. (eds) (2020) *Contemporary Language Motivation Theory: 60 Years Since Gardner and Lambert (1959)*. Multilingual Matters.

Alim, H.S., Rickford, J.R. and Ball, A.F. (eds) (2016) *Raciolinguistics: How Language Shapes Our Ideas About Race*. Oxford University Press.

Aljedaani, W., Krasniqi, R., Aljedaani, S., Mkaouer, M.W., Ludi, S. and Al-Raddah, K. (2023) If online learning works for you, what about deaf students? Emerging challenges of online learning for deaf and hearing-impaired students during COVID-19: A literature review. *Universal Access in the Information Society* 22 (3), 1027–1046.

Alladi, S., Arshad Sr, F., Kenchaih, R. et al. (2021) Neural correlates of cognitive resilience differ between experiences of bilingualism and education: A cortical surface-based morphometry study in dementia. *Alzheimer's and Dementia* 17, e051875.

Allard, K. and Wedin, Å. (2017) Translanguaging and social justice: The case of education for immigrants who are deaf or hard of hearing. In B. Paulsrud, J. Rosén, B. Straszer and Å. Wedin (eds) *New Perspectives on Translanguaging and Education* (pp. 90–107). Multilingual Matters.

Allen, T.E. (2014) The Deaf community as a 'special linguistic demographic': Diversity rather than disability as a framework for conducting research with individuals who are Deaf. In E. Orfanidou and G. Morgan (eds) *Research Methods in Sign Language Studies: A Practical Guide* (pp. 21–40). Wiley-Blackwell.

Allen, T.E. (2015) ASL skills, fingerspelling ability, home communication context and early alphabetic knowledge of preschool-aged deaf children. *Sign Language Studies* 15 (3), 233–265.

Allen, T.E. and Morere, D.A. (2020) Early visual language skills affect the trajectory of literacy gains over a three-year period of time for preschool aged deaf children who experience signing in the home. *Plos One* 15 (2), e0229591.

Allen, T.E., Letteri, A., Cho, S.H. and Dang, D. (2014) Early visual language exposure and emergent literacy in preschool deaf children: Findings from a national longitudinal study. *American Annals of the Deaf* 159 (4), 346–358.

Alsaadi, H.M.A. (2021) Dynamic assessment in language learning: An overview and the impact of using social media. *English Language Teaching* 14 (8), 73–82. https://doi.org/10.5539/elt.v14n8p73.

Alvear, S.A. (2019) The additive advantage and bilingual programs in a large urban school district. *American Educational Research Journal* 56 (2), 477–513. https://doi.org/10.3102/0002831218800986.

Amara, M., Azaiza, F., Hertz-Lazarowitz, R. and Mor-Sommerfeld, A. (2009) A new bilingual education in the conflict-ridden Israeli reality: Language practices. *Language and Education* 23 (1), 15–35.

American Council on the Teaching of Foreign Languages (2015) *Foreign Language Enrollments in K-12 Public Schools: Are Students Prepared for a Global Society?* https://www.actfl.org/news/reports/foreign-language-enrollments-k-12-public-schools-are-students-ready-global-society.

American Education Research Association, American Psychological Association and National Council on Measurement in Education (2014) *Standards for Educational and Psychological Testing* (2nd edn). American Education Research Association.

American Institutes for Research and WestEd (2006) *Effects of the Implementation of Proposition 227 on the Education of English Learners, K-12: Findings from a Five-Year Evaluation.* http://www.wested.org/online_pubs/227Reportb.pdf.

American Psychological Association (1982) Review of Department of Education report entitled 'Effectiveness of bilingual education: A review of the literature'. *Letter to Congressional Hispanic Caucus*, 22 April.

American Psychological Association (2024) *Guidelines in Terminology. Disability*. APA.

Anderson, J.A., Saleemi, S. and Bialystok, E. (2017) Neuropsychological assessments of cognitive aging in monolingual and bilingual older adults. *Journal of Neurolinguistics* 43, 17–27.

Andrews, J. (1992) Equal access for Deaf teachers in Texas. *Deaf American Monographs* 42, 13–18.

Andrews, J. and Franklin, T.C. (1997) Why hire deaf teachers? *Texas Journal of Speech and Hearing (TEJAS)* 22 (1), 12013. ERIC document:ED 425 600.

Andrews, J., Winograd, P. and DeVille, G. (1994) Deaf children reading fables: Using ASL summaries to improve reading comprehension. *American Annals of the Deaf* 139 (3), 378–386.

Andrews, J.F. (2003) Benefits of an Ed.D. program in deaf education: A survey. *American Annals of the Deaf* 148 (3), 259–266.

Andrews, J.F. (2012) Reading to deaf children who sign: A response to Williams (2012) and suggestions for future research. *American Annals of the Deaf* 157 (3), 307–319.

Andrews, J.F. (2017) Teaching science to Deaf students: Language and literacy considerations. Invited presentation at Universidade Federal Fluminense, Rio de Janerio, Brazil, 18 August.

Andrews, J.F. and Baker, S. (2019) ASL nursery rhymes: Exploring a support for early language and emergent literacy skills for signing Deaf children. *Sign Language Studies* 20 (1), 5–40.

Andrews, J.F. and Covell, J.A. (2006) Preparing future teachers and doctoral-level leaders in Deaf education: Meeting the challenge. *American Annals of the Deaf* 151 (5), 464–475.

Andrews, J.F. and Jordan, D.L. (1998) Multimedia stories for deaf children. *Teaching Exceptional Children* 30 (5), 28–33.

Andrews, J.F. and Rusher, M. (2010) Codeswitching techniques: Evidence-based instructional practices for the ASL/English bilingual classroom. *American Annals of the Deaf* 155 (4), 407–424.

Andrews, J.F., Winograd, P. and DeVille, G. (1994) Deaf children reading fables: Using ASL summaries to improve reading comprehension. *American Annals of the Deaf* 139 (3), 378–386.

Andrews, J.F., Ferguson, C., Roberts, S. and Hodges, P. (1997) What's up, Billy Jo? Deaf children and bilingual-bicultural instruction in East-Central Texas. *American Annals of the Deaf* 142 (1), 16–25.

Andrews, J.F., Leigh, I.W. and Weiner, M.T. (2004) *Deaf People: Evolving Perspectives from Psychology, Education, and Sociology*. Allyn and Bacon.

Andrews, J.F., Byrne, A. and Clark, M.D. (2015) Deaf scholars on reading: A historical review of 40 years of dissertation research (1973–2013): Implications for research and practice. *American Annals of the Deaf* 159 (5), 393–418.

Andrews, J.F., Hamilton, B., Dunn, K.M. and Clark, M.D. (2016) Early reading for young Deaf and hard of hearing children: Alternative frameworks. *Psychology* 7 (4), 510–522.

Angouri, J., Kerekes, J. and Suni, M. (eds) (2023) *Language, Migration and In/Exclusion in the Workplace*. Multilingual Matters.

Archey, X. (2024) Language ideology: The driver of inclusive education. In J.A. Freire, C. Alfaro and E. de Jong (eds) *The Handbook of Dual Language Bilingual Education* (pp. 290–304). Routledge. https://doi.org/10.4324/9781003269076-24.

Arendt, B. and Reershemius, G. (eds) (2024) *Heritage Languages in the Digital Age: The Case of Autochthonous Minority Languages in Western Europe*. Multilingual Matters.

Arias, M.B. (2015) Parent and community involvement in bilingual and multilingual education. In W.E. Wright, S. Boun and O. García (eds) *Handbook of Bilingual and Multilingual Education* (pp. 282–298). Wiley-Blackwell.

Arias, M.B. and Markos, A. (2018) Recent research on the three goals of dual language education. In M.B. Arias and M. Fee (eds) *Profiles of Dual Language Education in the 21st Century* (pp. 3–19). Multilingual Matters.

Armstrong, J.M. (1878) *The Biographical Encyclopedia of Kentucky of the Deaf and Living Men of the Nineteenth Century*. J.M. Armstrong and Company.

Arnau, J. (1997) Immersion education in Catalonia. In J. Cummins and D. Corson (eds) *Bilingual Education* (pp. 297–303). Kluwer.

Arnaut, K., Karrebæk, M.S., Spotti, M. and Blommaert, J. (eds) (2017) *Engaging Superdiversity: Recombining Spaces, Times and Language Practices*. Multilingual Matters.

Arreguín-Anderson, M.G. and Alanís, I. (2019) *Translingual Partners in Early Childhood Elementary-Education: Pedagogies on Linguistic and Cognitive Engagement*. Peter Lang.

Artigal, J.M. (1993) Catalan and Basque immersion programs. In H. Baetens Beardsmore (ed.) *European Models of Bilingual Education* (pp. 30–53). Multilingual Matters.

Arviso, M. and Holm, W. (2001) Tséhootsooídi Olta'gi Diné Bizaad Bíhoo'aah: A Navajo immersion program at Fort Defiance, Arizona. In L. Hinton and K. Hale (eds) *The Green Book of Language Revitalization in Practice* (pp. 203–215). Academic Press.

Athanasopoulos, P. (2007) Interaction between grammatical categories and cognition in bilinguals: The role of proficiency, cultural immersion, and language of instruction. *Language and Cognitive Processes* 22 (5), 689–699.

Atkins, J.D.C. (1887) *Annual Report to the Commissioner of Indian Affairs to United States Bureau of Indian Affairs*. Government Printing Office.

Atkinson, D. (ed.) (2011) *Alternative Approaches to Second Language Acquisition*. Routledge.

Aucamp, A.J. (1926) *Bilingual Education and Nationalism with Special Reference to South Africa*. Van Schaik.

Auer, P. (2022) 'Translanguaging' or 'doing languages'? Multilingual practices and the notion of 'codes'. In J. MacSwan (ed.) *Multilingual Perspectives on Translanguaging* (pp. 126–153). Multilingual Matters.

August, D. (2002) *Transitional Programs for English Language Learners: An Examination of the Impact of English-Only Versus Bilingual Instruction*. CRESPAR Publications Department, Johns Hopkins University.

August, D. (2012) How does first language literacy development relate to second language literacy development? In E. Hamayan and R. Freeman (eds) *English Language Learners at School: A Guide for Administrators* (2nd edn, pp. 56–57). Caslon Publishing.

August, D. and Hakuta, K. (1997) *Improving Schooling for Language-Minority Children: A Research Agenda*. National Academy Press.

August, D. and Shanahan, T. (2006) *Developing Literacy in Second-Language Learners: Report of the National Literacy Panel on Language-Minority Children and Youth*. Lawrence Erlbaum Associates.

August, D. and Shanahan, T. (2008) *Developing Reading and Writing in Second-Language Learners: Lessons from the Report of the National Literacy Panel on Language-Minority Children and Youth*. Taylor and Francis.

August, D., McCardle, P. and Shanahan, T. (2014) Developing literacy in English language learners: Findings from a review of the experimental research. *School Psychology Review* 43 (4), 490–498.

Ausbrooks-Rusher, M., Schimmel, C. and Edwards, S. (2012) Utilizing Fairview as a bilingual response to intervention (RTI): Comprehensive curriculum review with supporting data. *Theory and Practice in Language Studies* 2 (7), 1317–1329.

Avni, S. and Menken, K. (2013) Educating for Jewishness: The teaching and learning of Hebrew in day school education. In O. García, Z. Zakharia and B. Otcu (eds) *Bilingual Community Education and Multilingualism: Beyond Heritage Languages in a Global City* (pp. 190–203). Multilingual Matters.

Babbidge, H.D. (1965) *Education of the Deaf: A Report to the Secretary of Health, Education, and Welfare by His Advisory Committee on the Education of the Deaf* (ED014188). https://files.eric.ed.gov/fulltext/ED014188.pdf.

Babcock, E.J. (1913) Letter from Nebraska Parents' Association. In *Proceedings of the Tenth Convention of National Association of the Deaf, held in Cleveland, Ohio, August 20–27, 1913* (pp. 93–95). Independent Publishing Company.

Babcock, E.J. (1920) How Nebraska adopted the oral method. *Volta Review* 22 (2), 10–12.

Bachi, R. (1955) A statistical analysis of the revival of Hebrew in Israel. *Scripta Hierosolymitana* 3, 179–247.

Bahan, B. (2014) Senses and culture: Exploring sensory orientation. In H.-D.L. Bauman and J.J. Murray (eds) *Deaf Gain: Raising the Stakes for Human Diversity* (pp. 233–254). University of Minnesota Press.

Bailes, C. (2002) Integrative ASL-English language arts: Bridging paths to literacy. *Sign Language Studies* 1 (2), 147–174.

Baker, C. (1992) *Attitudes and Languages*. Multilingual Matters.

Baker, C. (2001) *Foundations of Bilingual Education and Bilingualism* (3rd edn). Multilingual Matters.

Baker, C. (2003a) Biliteracy and transliteracy in Wales: Language planning and the Welsh national curriculum. In N.H. Hornberger (ed.) *Continua of Biliteracy: An Ecological Framework for Educational Policy, Research, and Practice in Multilingual Settings* (pp. 71–90). Multilingual Matters.

Baker, C. (2003b) 6. Education as a site of language contact. *Annual Review of Applied Linguistics* 23, 95–112.

Baker, C. (2008) Postlude. Multilingualism and minority languages: Achievements and challenges in education. *AILA Review* 21, 69–86.

Baker, C. (2010a) Bilingual education. In R.B. Kaplan (ed.) *The Oxford Handbook of Applied Linguistics* (2nd edn, pp. 294–304). Oxford University Press.

Baker, C. (2010b) Increasing bilingualism in bilingual education. In D. Morris (ed.) *Welsh in the 21st Century* (pp. 61–79). University of Wales Press.

Baker, C. (2014) *A Parents' and Teachers' Guide to Bilingualism* (4th edn). Multilingual Matters.

Baker, C. (2019) A tribute to Ofelia García. *Journal of Multilingual Education Research* 9, 175–182. https://fordham.bepress.com/jmer/vol9/iss1/8.

Baker, C. and Jones, S.P. (1998) *Encyclopedia of Bilingualism and Bilingual Education*. Multilingual Matters.

Baker, C. and Jones, M.P. (2000) Welsh language education: A strategy for revitalization. In C.H. Williams (ed.) *Language Revitalization: Policy and Planning in Wales* (pp. 116–137). University of Wales Press.

Baker, C. and Lewis, G. (2015) A synthesis of research on bilingual and multilingual education. In W.E. Wright, S. Boun and O. García (eds) *Handbook of Bilingual and Multilingual Education* (pp. 109–126). Wiley-Blackwell.

Baker, F.S. (2012) The role of the bilingual teaching assistant: Alternative visions for bilingual support in the primary years. *International Journal of Bilingual Education and Bilingualism* 17 (3), 255–271. https://doi.org/10.1080/13670050.2012.748013.

Baker, K.A. (1987) Comment on Willig's 'A meta-analysis of selected studies in the effectiveness of bilingual education'. *Review of Educational Research* 57 (3), 351–362.

Baker, K.A. (1992) Ramirez *et al.*: Misled by bad theory. *Bilingual Research Journal* 16 (1–2), 63–90.

Baker, K.A. and de Kanter, A. (1983) *Bilingual Education: A Reappraisal of Federal Policy*. Lexington Books.

Baker, P. and Kim, J. (2003) *Global London: Where to Find Almost Everything Ethnic and Cultural in the Multilingual Capital*. Battlebridge.

Baker, S. (2010) *The Importance of Fingerspelling for Reading (Research Brief #1)*. Gallaudet University, Visual Language and Visual Learning Science of Learning Center.

Baker, S. and Scott, J. (2016) Sociocultural and academic considerations for school-age d/Deaf and hard of hearing multilingual learners: A case study of a Deaf Latina. *American Annals of the Deaf* 161 (1), 43–55.

Baker-Bell, A. (2020a) *Linguistic Justice: Black Language, Literacy, Identity, and Pedagogy*. Routledge.

Baker-Bell, A. (2020b) Dismantling anti-black linguistic racism in English language arts classrooms: Toward an anti-racist black language pedagogy. *Theory into Practice* 59 (1), 8–21. https://doi.org/10.1080/00405841.2019.1665415.

Bale, J. (2015) Language policy and global political economy. In T. Ricento (ed.) *Language Policy and Political Economy: English in a Global Context* (pp. 72–95). Oxford University Press.

Bale, J. (2016) In defense of language rights: Rethinking the rights orientation from a political economy perspective. *Bilingual Research Journal* 39 (3–4), 231–247. https://doi.org/10.1080/15235882.2016.1224208.

Bale, J., Rajendram, S., Brubacher, K., Owoo, M.A.N., Burton, J., Wong, W., Zhang, Y., Larson, E.J., Gagné, A. and Kerekes, J. (2023) *Centering Multilingual Learners and Countering Raciolinguistic Ideologies in Teacher Education: Principles, Policies and Practices*. Multilingual Matters.

Bali, V.A. (2001) Sink or swim: What happened to California's bilingual students after Proposition 227? *State Politics and Policy Quarterly* 1 (3), 295–311.

Ball, P., Kelly, K. and Clegg, J. (2016) *Putting CLIL into Practice*. Oxford University Press.

Ballinger, S., Fielding, R. and Tedick, D.J. (eds) (2024) *Teacher Development for Content-Based Language Education: International Perspectives*. Multilingual Matters.

Banks, J.A. (1998) The lives and values of researchers: Implications for educating citizens in a multicultural society. *Educational Researcher* 27 (7), 4–17.

Barakos, E. and Selleck, C. (2019) Elite multilingualism: Discourses, practices, and debates. *Journal of Multilingual and Multicultural Development* 40 (5), 361–374. https://doi.org/10.1080/01434632.2018.1543691.

Barker, V. and Giles, H. (2002) Who supports the English-only movement? Evidence for misconceptions about Latino group vitality. *Journal of Multilingual and Multicultural Development* 23 (5), 353–370.

Barker, V., Giles, H., Noels, K., Duck, J., Hecht, M.L. and Clement, R. (2001) The English-only movement: A communication analysis of changing perceptions of language vitality. *Journal of Communication* 51 (1), 3–37.

Barnard, F.A.P. (1837) Art I instruction of the deaf and dumb. *Quarterly Christian Spectator* 9 (4), 521–553.

Barnard, R. and McLellan, J. (eds) (2014) *Codeswitching in University English-Medium Classes: Asian Perspectives*. Multilingual Matters.

Barron-Hauwaert, S. (2004) *Language Strategies for Bilingual Families: The One-Parent-One-Language Approach*. Multilingual Matters.

Barron-Hauwaert, S. (2011) *Bilingual Siblings: Language Use in Families*. Multilingual Matters.

Bartlett, L. and García, O. (2011) *Additive Schooling in Subtractive Times: Dominican Immigrant Youth in the Heights*. Vanderbilt University Press.

Batibo, H.M. (2005) *Language Decline and Death in Africa: Causes, Consequences and Challenges*. Multilingual Matters.

Bauer, E. and Sánchez, L. (2024) 'I Have Magic in My Mouf!' Embodied languaging enactments of African American multilingual students in a Spanish-English immersion program. *Linguistics and Education* 83, 101339. https://doi.org/10.1016/j.linged.2024.101339.

Bauer, E.D., Colomer, S.E. and Wiemelt, J. (2018) Biliteracy of African American and Latinx kindergarten students in a dual-language program: Understanding students' translanguaging practices across informal assessments. *Urban Education* [online first]. https://doi.org/10.1177/0042085918789743.

Baugh, J. (2017) Linguistic profiling and discrimination. In O. García, N. Flores and M. Spotti (eds) *The Oxford Handbook of Language and Society* (pp. 1–23). Oxford University Press.

Bauman, H.D.L. and Murray, J.J. (eds) (2014) *Deaf Gain: Raising the Stakes for Human Diversity*. University of Minnesota Press.

Bayley, R. and Langman, J. (2011) Language socialization in multilingual and second language contexts. In E. Hinkel (ed.) *Handbook of Second Language Learning and Teaching* (Vol. 2, pp. 291–302). Routledge.

Bayton, D.C. (1996) *Forbidden Signs: American Culture and the Campaign Against Sign Language*. University of Chicago Press.

Beam-Conroy, T. and McHatton, P.A. (2015) Bilingual education and students with dis/abilities and exceptionalities. In W.E. Wright, S. Boun and O. García (eds) *Handbook of Bilingual and Multilingual Education* (pp. 370–383). Wiley-Blackwell.

Beauchamp, M.L.H., Rezzonico, S., Bennett, T., Duku, E., Georgiades, S., Kerns, C., Mirenda, P., Richard, A., Smith, I.M., Szatmari, P., Vaillancourt, T., Waddell, C., Zaidman-Zait, A., Zwaigenbaum, L. and Elsabbagh, M. (2023) The influence of bilingual language exposure on the narrative, social and pragmatic abilities of school-aged children on the autism spectrum. *Journal of Autism and Developmental Disorders* 53 (12), 4577–4590. https://doi.org/10.1007/s10803-022-05678-w.

Beeman, K. and Urow, C. (2012) *Teaching for Biliteracy: Strengthening Bridges Between Languages*. Caslon Publishing.

Bekerman, Z. (2016) *The Promise of Integrated Multicultural and Bilingual Education: Inclusive Palestinian-Arab and Jewish Schools in Israel*. Oxford University Press.

Benson, C. (2004) Do we expect too much of bilingual teachers? Bilingual teaching in developing countries. *International Journal of Bilingual Education and Bilingualism* 7 (2–3), 204–221.

Benson, C. (2009) Designing effective schooling in multilingual contexts: The strengths and limitations of

bilingual 'models'. In A.K. Mohanty, M. Panda, R. Phillipson and T. Skutnabb-Kangas (eds) *Multilingual Education for Social Justice Globalising the Local* (pp. 63–99). Orient Blackswan.
Benson, C. (2014) Adopting a multilingual habitus: What North and South can learn from each other about the essential role of non-dominant languages in education. In D. Gorter, V. Zenotz and J. Cenoz (eds) *Minority Languages and Multilingual Education: Bridging the Local and the Global* (pp. 11–28). Springer.
Benson, C. (2019a) Learner's own languages as key to achieving Sustainable Development Goal Four and beyond. In I. Idiazabal and M. Pêrez-Caurel (eds) *Linguistic Diversity, Minority Languages, and Sustainable Development* (pp. 116–132). Servicio de Publicaciones de la Universidad del País Vasco.
Benson, C. (2019b) L1-based multilingual education in the Asia and Pacific region and beyond: Where are we, and where do we need to go? In A. Kirkpatrick and T. Liddicoat (eds) *The Routledge International Handbook of Language Education Policy in Asia* (pp. 29–41). Routledge.
Benson, C. and Wong, K. (2019) Effectiveness of policy development and implementation of L1-based multilingual education in Cambodia. *International Journal of Bilingual Education and Bilingualism* 22 (2), 250–265.
Ben-Zeev, S. (1977a) *The Effect of Bilingualism in Children from Spanish–English Low Economic Neighborhoods on Cognitive Development and Cognitive Strategy* (pp. 83–122). Working Papers on Bilingualism 14. Ontario Institute for Studies in Education.
Ben-Zeev, S. (1977b) The influence of bilingualism on cognitive strategy and cognitive development. *Child Development* 48 (3), 1009–1018.
Berent, G.P. (2004) Sign language-spoken language bilingualism: Code mixing and mode mixing by ASL-English bilinguals. In T.K. Bhatia and W.C. Ritchie (eds) *The Handbook of Bilingualism* (pp. 312–335). Blackwell.
Berlin, D.C. (2013) Death of a language: Last ever speaker of Livonian passes away aged 103. *The Times*, June 5. http://www.thetimes.co.uk/tto/news/world/europe/article3782596.ece.
Bérubé, D., Uchikoshi, Y. and Marinova-Todd, S.H. (2022) A longitudinal examination of French and English reading comprehension in French immersion programs in Canada. *Applied Psycholinguistics* 43 (3), 607–640. https://doi.org/10.1017/s0142716422000030.
Bhabha, H.K. (2004) *The Location of Culture*. Routledge.
Bhalla, S., Liu, N. and Wiley, T.G. (2021) Asian heritage languages in the United States: Chinese and Hindi language communities. In S. Montrul and M. Polinsky (eds) *The Cambridge Handbook of Heritage Languages and Linguistics*. Cambridge University Press.
Bhatia, T.K. (2020) World Englishes and global advertising. In C.L. Nelson, Z.G. Proshina and D.R. Davis (eds) *The Handbook of World Englishes* (2nd edn, pp. 616–634). Wiley Blackwell.
Bhatia, T.K. and Ritchie, W.C. (2013) Bilingualism and multilingualism in South Asia. In T.K. Bhatia and W.C. Ritchie (eds) *Handbook of Bilingualism and Multilingualism* (2nd edn, pp. 843–870). Wiley-Blackwell.
Bhatt, R.M. and Bolonyai, A. (2022) Codeswitching and its terminological other – translanguaging. In J. MacSwan (ed.) *Multilingual Perspectives on Translanguaging* (pp. 154–180). Multilingual Matters.
Bialystok, E. (1987) Influences of bilingualism on metalinguistic development. *Second Language Research* 3 (2), 154–166.
Bialystok, E. (2001a) *Bilingualism in Development: Language, Literacy, and Cognition*. Cambridge University Press.
Bialystok, E. (2001b) Literacy: The extension of languages through other means. In R.L. Cooper, E. Shohamy and J. Walters (eds) *New Perspectives and Issues in Educational Language Policy: In Honour of Bernard Dov Spolsky* (pp. 19–33). John Benjamins.
Bialystok, E. (2007) Acquisition of literacy in bilingual children: A framework for research. *Language Learning* 57 (1), 45–77. https://doi.org/10.1111/j.1467–9922.2007.00412.x.
Bialystok, E. (2013) The impact of bilingualism on language and literacy development. In T.K. Bhatia and W.C. Ritchie (eds) *The Handbook of Bilingualism and Multilingualism* (2nd edn, pp. 624–648). Wiley-Blackwell.
Bialystok, E. (2017) The bilingual adaptation: How minds accommodate experience. *Psychological Bulletin* 43, 17–27.
Bialystok, E. (2018) Bilingualism and executive function: What's the connection? In D. Miller, F. Bayram, J. Rothman and L. Serratrice (eds) *Bilingual Cognition and Language: The State of the Science Across Its Subfields* (pp. 283–306). John Benjamins.
Bialystok, E. and Kroll, J.F. (2018) Can the critical period be saved? A bilingual perspective. *Bilingualism: Language and Cognition* 21 (5), 908–910.

Bialystok, E. and Martin, M.M. (2004) Attention and inhibition in bilingual children: Evidence from the dimensional change card sort task. *Developmental Science* 7 (3), 325–339.
Bialystok, E., Craik, F.I., Klein, R. and Viswanathan, M. (2004) Bilingualism, aging, and cognitive control: Evidence from the Simon task. *Psychology and Aging* 19 (2), 290–303.
Bialystok, E., Luk, G. and Kwan, E. (2005) Bilingualism, biliteracy, and learning to read: Interactions among languages and writing systems. *Scientific Studies of Reading* 9 (1), 43–61.
Bialystok, E., Craik, F.I. and Freedman, M. (2007) Bilingualism as a protection against the onset of symptoms of dementia. *Neuropsychologia* 45 (2), 459–464.
Bialystok, E., Craik, F.I. and Luk, G. (2008) Cognitive control and lexical access in younger and older bilinguals. *Journal of Experimental Psychology: Learning, Memory, and Cognition* 34 (4), 859–873.
Bialystok, E., Craik, F.I. and Luk, G. (2012) Bilingualism: Consequences for mind and brain. *Trends in Cognitive Sciences* 16 (4), 240–250.
Bialystok, E., Craik, F.I., Binns, M.A., Ossher, L. and Freedman, M. (2014a) Effects of bilingualism on the age of onset and progression of MCI and AD: Evidence from executive function tests. *Neuropsychology* 28, 290–304.
Bialystok, E., Poarch, G., Luo, L. and Craik, F.I.M. (2014b) Effects of bilingualism and aging on executive function and working memory. *Psychology and Aging* 29, 696–705.
Bialystok, E., Anderson, J.A. and Grundy, J.G. (2018) Interpreting cognitive decline in the face of cognitive reserve: Does bilingualism affect cognitive aging? *Linguistic Approaches to Bilingualism* 11 (4), 484–504. https://doi.org/10.1075/lab.18040.bia.
Bialystok, E., Hawrylewicz, K., Grundy, J.G. and Chung-Fat-Yim, A. (2022) The swerve: How childhood bilingualism changed from liability to benefit. *Developmental Psychology* 58 (8), 1429–1440. https://doi.org/10.1037/dev0001376.
Birdsong, D. (2006) Age and second language acquisition and processing: A selective overview. *Language Learning* 56 (1), 9–49.
Birdsong, D. (2018) Plasticity, variability and age in second language acquisition and bilingualism. *Frontiers in Psychology* 9, 81.
Björklund, S. and Björklund, M. (eds) (2023) *Policy and Practice for Multilingual Educational Settings: Comparisons across Contexts*. Multilingual Matters.
Björklund, S. and Suni, I. (2000) The role of English as L3 in a Swedish immersion programme in Finland. In J. Cenoz and U. Jessner (eds) *English in Europe: The Acquisition of a Third Language* (pp. 198–221). Multilingual Matters.
Blackledge, A. (2000) *Literacy, Power and Social Justice*. Trentham.
Block, D. (2014) *Second Language Identities*. Bloomsbury Academic.
Block, D. (2017) Inequality and class in language policy and planning. In J.W. Tollefson and M. Pérez-Milans (eds) *The Oxford Handbook of Language Policy and Planning* (pp. 568–588). Oxford University Press.
Blommaert, J. (2013) *Ethnography, Superdiversity and Linguistic Landscape: Chronicles of Complexity*. Multilingual Matters.
Bloomfield, L. (1933) *Language*. Holt.
Blumenthal-Kelly, A. (1995) Fingerspelling interaction: A set of deaf parents and their deaf daughter. In C. Lucas (ed.) *Sociolinguistics in Deaf Communities* (pp. 62–73). Gallaudet University Press.
Boals, T., Kenyon, D.M., Blair, A., Cranley, M.E., Wilmes, C. and Wright, L.J. (2015) Transformation in K-12 English language proficiency assessment: Changing contexts, changing constructs. *Review of Research in Education* 39, 122–164.
Bolander, B. and Sultana, S. (2019) Ordinary English amongst Muslim communities in South and Central Asia. *International Journal of Multilingualism* 16 (2), 162–174. https://doi.org/10.1080/14790718.2019.1575835.
Bolton, K. (2020) World Englishes: Current debates and future directions. In C.L. Nelson, Z.G. Proshina and D.R. Davis (eds) *The Handbook of World Englishes* (2nd edn, pp. 743–760). Wiley Blackwell.
Booton, S.A., Hoicka, E., O'Grady, A.M., Chan, H.Y.N. and Murphy, V.A. (2021) Children's divergent thinking and bilingualism. *Thinking Skills and Creativity* 41, 100918.
Boroditsky, L. (2001) Does language shape thought? Mandarin and English speakers' conceptions of time. *Cognitive Psychology* 43 (1), 1–22.
Boroditsky, L., Ham, W. and Ramscar, M. (2002) What is universal in event perception? Comparing English and Indonesian speakers. Paper presented at the 24th Annual Meeting of the Cognitive Science Society.
Börstell, C. (2024) Finding continuers in Swedish Sign Language. *Linguistics Vanguard*. https://doi.org/https://doi.org/10.1515/lingvan-2024-0025.
Boun, S. and Duran, C.S. (eds) (2024) *English Education in Southeast Asian Contexts: Policy, Practice, and Identity*. Lexington Books/Rowman and Littlefield.

Boun, S. and Wright, W.E. (2021) Translanguaging in a graduate education program at a Cambodian university. In B. Paulsrud, Z. Tian and J. Toth (eds) *English-Medium Instruction and Translanguaging* (pp. 108–123). Multilingual Matters.

Bourdieu, P. (1991) *Language and Symbolic Power* (G. Raymond and M. Adamson, trans.). Harvard University Press.

Bourgoin, R. and Dicks, J. (2019) Learning to read in multiple languages: A study exploring allophone students' reading development in French immersion. *Language and Literacy* 21 (2), 10–28. https://doi.org/10.20360/langandlit29466.

Bourhis, R.Y. (2001) Acculturation, language maintenance, and language shift. In J. Klatter-Folmer and P. Vanavermaet (eds) *Theories on Maintenance and Loss of Minority Languages* (pp. 5–37). Waxmann.

Bouvet, D. (1990) *The Path to Language: Bilingual Education for Deaf Children*. Multilingual Matters.

Boyle, A., August, D., Tabaku, L., Cole, S. and Simpson-Baird, A. (2015) *Dual Language Education Programs: Current State Policies and Practices*. American Institutes for Research.

Branson, J. and Miller, D. (1998) Nationalism and the linguistic rights of Deaf communities: Linguistic imperialism and the recognition and development of sign languages. *Journal of Sociolinguistics* 2 (1), 3–34.

Bravo, M.A., Mosqueda, E. and Solís, J.L. (2022) A classroom observation tool for assessing mathematics in two languages. In M. Machado-Casas, S.I. Maldonado and B.B. Flores (eds) *Assessment and Evaluation in Bilingual Education* (pp. 167–188). Peter Lang.

Brecht, R.D. and Ingold, C.W. (2002) *Tapping a National Resource: Heritage Languages in the United States* (ERIC Digest, EDO-FL-98-12). ERIC Clearinghouse on Languages and Linguistics.

Breen, M.P. (2002) Principles for the teaching of EAL/ESL children in the mainstream: Lessons from experience and professional development. In C. Leung (ed.) *Language and Additional/Second Language Issues for School Education*. NADLIC.

Brennan, J.R. (2022) *Language and the Brain: A Slim Guide to Neurolinguistics*. Oxford University Press.

Brentnall, J., Cann, J. and Williams, C. (2009) *Language in Multilingual Wales*. Bangor University, College of Education and Lifelong Education.

Brinton, D. (ed.) (2008) *Heritage Language Education: A New Field Emerging*. Routledge.

British Council (2013) *Lost for Words: The Need for Languages in UK Diplomacy and Security*. British Council. https://www.thebritishacademy.ac.uk/publications/lost-words-need-languages-uk-diplomacy-and-security/.

Brohy, C. (2005) Trilingual education in Switzerland. *International Journal of the Sociology of Language* 171, 133–148.

Brooks, R., Singleton, J.L. and Meltzoff, A.N. (2020) Enhanced gaze-following behavior in deaf infants of deaf parents. *Developmental Science* 23 (2), e12900.

Brown, T. and Brown, J. (2015) *To Advanced Proficiency and Beyond: Theory and Method for Developing Superior Second Language Ability*. Georgetown University Press.

Bruck, M. (1978) The suitability of early French immersion programs for the language-disabled child. *Canadian Journal of Education/Revue Canadienne de L'education* 3 (4), 51–72.

Bruck, M. (1982) Language impaired children's performance in an additive bilingual education program. *Applied Psycholinguistics* 3 (1), 45–60.

Bruner, J. (1983) *Child Talk*. Norton.

Bruthiaux, P. (2009) Language rights in historical and contemporary perspective. *Journal of Multilingual and Multicultural Development* 30 (1), 73–85.

Buchanan, R.M. (1993) *Illusions of Equality: Deaf Americans in School and Factory 1850–1950*. Gallaudet University Press.

Bunch, G.C. (2014) The language of ideas and the language of display: Reconceptualizing 'academic language' in linguistically diverse classrooms. *International Multilingual Research Journal* 8, 70–86.

Burch, S. and Joyner, H. (2007) *Unspeakable: The Story of Junius Wilson*. University of North Carolina Press.

Burke, G. and Sainz, A. (2016) Migrant children kept from enrolling in school. *The Big Story*. Associated Press. http://bigstory.ap.org/article/b7f933ef6e054c2ca8e32bd9b477e9ab/ap-exclusive-migrant-children-kept-enrolling-school.

Burr, E., Haas, E. and Ferriere, K. (2015) *Identifying and Supporting English Learner Students with Learning Disabilities: Key Issues in the Literature and State Practice*. Institute for Educational Sciences, US Department of Education.

Buttitta, I. (1972) *Lo Faccio il Poeta*. Feltrinelli.

Byers-Heinlein, K., Burns, T. and Werker, J. (2010) The roots of bilingualism in newborns. *Psychological Science* 21, 343–348.

Bylund, E. and Athanasopoulos, P. (2014a) Language and thought in a multilingual context: The case of isiXhosa. *Bilingualism: Language and Cognition* 17, 431–443.

Bylund, E. and Athanasopoulos, P. (2014b) Linguistic relativity in SLA: Toward a new research program. *Language Learning* 64, 952–985. https://doi.org/10.1111/lang.12080.

Bylund, E. and Athanasopoulos, P. (2015) Introduction: Cognition, motion events, and SLA. *Modern Language Journal* 99 (1), 1–13.

Bylund, E. and Athanasopoulos, P. (2017) The Whorfian time warp: Representing duration through the language hourglass. *Journal of Experimental Psychology: General* 146 (7), 911.

Byram, M., Fleming, M. and Sheils, J. (eds) (2023) *Quality and Equity in Education: A Practical Guide to the Council of Europe Vision of Education for Plurilingual, Intercultural and Democratic Citizenship.* Multilingual Matters.

Byrne, A.P.J. (2013) American Sign Language (ASL) literacy and ASL literature: A critical appraisal. Unpublished doctoral dissertation, University of Toronto.

Cabellero, A.M.S. (2014) Preparing teachers to work with heritage language learners. In T.G. Wiley, J.K. Peyton, D. Christian, S.C.K. Moore and N. Liu (eds) *Handbook of Heritage, Community, and Native American Languages in the United States: Research, Policy, and Educational Practice* (pp. 359–369). Routledge and Center for Applied Linguistics.

Cahill, M. (2018) Orthography design and implementation for endangered languages. In K.L. Rehg and L. Campbell (eds) *The Oxford Handbook of Endangered Languages* (pp. 327–346). Oxford University Press.

Caldwell, H.B. (2022) Sign and spoken language processing differences in the brain: A brief review of recent research. *Annals of Neurosciences* 29 (1), 62–70.

California State Department of Education (1984) *Studies on Immersion Education: A Collection for United States Educators.* California State Department of Education.

California State Department of Education (2018) *Global California 2030: Speak, Learn, Lead.* California State Department of Education.

Callahan, R.M. and Gándara, P.C. (eds) (2014) *The Bilingual Advantage: Language, Literacy and the US Labor Market.* Multilingual Matters.

Calloway, A. (2000) *Deaf Children in China.* Gallaudet University Press.

Calvo, N., Anderson, J.A., Berkes, M., Freedman, M., Craik, F.I. and Bialystok, E. (2023) Gray matter volume as evidence for cognitive reserve in bilinguals with mild cognitive impairment. *Alzheimer Disease and Associated Disorders* 37 (1), 7–12.

Canadian Education Association (1991) *Heritage Language Programs in Canadian School Boards.* Canadian Education Association.

Canagarajah, A.S. (2013) Introduction. In A.S. Canagarajah (ed.) *Literacy as Translingual Practice: Between Communities and Classrooms* (pp. 1–10). Routledge.

Canagarajah, A.S. (ed.) (2020) *Transnational Literacy Autobiographies as Translingual Writing.* Routledge.

Canagarajah, S. (ed.) (2017) *The Routledge Handbook of Migration and Language.* Routledge.

Canagarajah, S. (2022) Challenges in decolonizing linguistics: The politics of enregisterment and the divergent uptakes of translingualism. *Educational Linguistics* 1 (1), 25–55.

Canale, M. and Swain, M. (1980) Theoretical bases of communicative approaches to second language teaching and testing. *Applied Linguistics* 1, 1–47.

Cannon, J.E. and Guardino, C. (2022) Learners who are D/deaf or hard of hearing and multilingual perspectives, approaches, and considerations. In J. Cannon, C. Guardino and P. Paul (eds) *Deaf and Hard of Hearing Learners: Foundations, Strategies and Resources* (pp. 1–29). Routledge.

Cannon, J.E., Guardino, C. and Gallimore, E. (2016) A new kind of heterogeneity: What we can learn from d/Deaf and hard of hearing multilingual learners. *American Annals of the Deaf* 161 (1), 8–16.

Cao, J., Peng, X., Liang, F., and Tong, X. (2024) Voices help correlate signs and words: Analyzing Deaf and Hard-of-Hearing (DHH) TikTokers' content, practices, and pitfalls. In *Proceedings of the CHI Conference on Human Factors in Computing Systems* (pp. 1–18). https://doi.org/10.1145/3613904.3642413.

Carder, M. (2013) International school students: Developing their bilingual potential. In C. Abello-Contesse, P.M. Chandler, M.D. López-Jiménez and R. Chacón-Beltrán (eds) *Bilingual and Multilingual Education in the 21st Century: Building on Experience* (pp. 275–298). Multilingual Matters.

Carder, M., Mertin, P. and Porter, S. (2018) *Second Language Learners in International Schools.* Trentham Books.

Cardwell, R., Naismith, B., LaFlair, G.T. and Nydick, S. (2024) *Duolingo English Test: Technical Manual.* https://go.duolingo.com/dettechnicalmanual.

Carlisle, J.F., Beeman, M., Davis, L.H. and Spharim, G. (1999) Relationship of metalinguistic capabilities

and reading achievement for children who are becoming bilingual. *Applied Psycholinguistics* 20 (4), 459–478.
Carmel, S.J. (ed.) (1982) *International Hand Alphabet Charts*. National Association of the Deaf.
Carreira, M.M. (2021) The vitality of Spanish as a heritage language in the United States. In S. Montrul and M. Polinsky (eds) *The Cambridge Handbook of Heritage Languages and Linguistics* (pp. 230–251). Cambridge University Press.
Carroll, L. (1872) *Through the Looking Glass: And What Alice Found There*. Macmillan.
Carter, N., Angelo, D. and Hudson, C. (2020) Translanguaging the curriculum: A critical language awareness curriculum for silenced indigenous voices. In P. Mickan and I. Wallace (eds) *The Routledge Handbook of Language Education Curriculum Design* (pp. 144–174). Routledge.
Carthery-Goulart, M.T., Privitera, A.J. and Weekes, B.S. (2023) Does language distance modulate the contribution of bilingualism to cognitive reserve in seniors? A systematic review. *American Journal of Alzheimer's Disease and Other Dementias* 38, 1–17.
Casasanto, D. and Boroditsky, L. (2008) Time in the mind: Using space to think about time. *Cognition* 106 (2), 579–593.
Caselli, N.K., Hall, W.C. and Henner, J. (2020) American sign language interpreters in public schools: An illusion of inclusion that perpetuates language deprivation. *Maternal and Child Health Journal* 1 (1), 1–7.
Casey, N. (2017) Thousands once spoke his language in the Amazon. Now, he's the only one. *New York Times*, 27 December, p. A1. https://www.nytimes.com/2017/12/26/world/americas/peru-amazon-the-end.html.
Castro, D.C. and Artiles, A.J. (eds) (2021) *Language, Learning, and Disability in the Education of Young Bilingual Children*. Multilingual Matters.
Castro-Villarreal, F., Villarreal, V. and Umaña, I. (2022) Assessment of bilingual students: Best practices and recommendations for members of the multidisciplinary IEP committee. In M. Machado-Casas, S.I. Maldonado and B.B. Flores (eds) *Assessment and Evaluation in Bilingual Education* (pp. 87–105). Peter Lang.
Cazabon, M., Lambert, W.E. and Hall, G. (1993) *Two-Way Bilingual Education: A Progress Report on the Amigos Program*. National Center for Research on Cultural Diversity and Second Language Learning.
Cazden, C.B. (1992) *Language Minority Education in the United States: Implications of the Ramirez Report*. National Center for Research on Cultural Diversity and Second Language Learning.
CCSSO (Chief Council of State School Officers) (2014) *English Language Proficiency (ELP) Standards*. http://www.elpa21.org/sites/default/files/Final%204_30%20ELPA21%20Standards_1.pdf.
Cenoz, J. (2003) The additive effect of bilingualism on third language acquisition: A review. *International Journal of Bilingualism* 7 (1), 71–87.
Cenoz, J. (2009) *Towards Multilingual Education: Basque Educational Research from an International Perspective*. Multilingual Matters.
Cenoz, J. and Etxague, X. (2013) From bilingualism to multilingualism: Basque, Spanish and English in higher education. In C. Abello-Contesse, P.M. Chandler, M.D. López-Jiménez and R. Chacón-Beltrán (eds) *Bilingual and Multilingual Education in the 21st Century: Building on Experience* (pp. 85–106). Multilingual Matters.
Cenoz, J. and Genesee, F. (1998) Psycholinguistic perspectives on multilingualism and multilingual education. In J. Cenoz and F. Genesee (eds) *Beyond Bilingualism: Multilingualism and Multilingual Education*. Multilingual Matters.
Cenoz, J. and Gorter, D. (2015) Minority languages, state languages, and English in European education. In W.E. Wright, S. Boun and O. García (eds) *Handbook of Bilingual and Multilingual Education* (pp. 471–483). Wiley-Blackwell.
Cenoz, J. and Gorter, D. (2021) *Pedagogical Translanguaging*. Cambridge University Press.
Cenoz, J., Genesee, F. and Gorter, D. (2014) Critical analysis of CLIL: Taking stock and looking forward. *Applied Linguistics* 35 (3), 243–262.
Cenoz, J., Gorter, D. and May, S. (eds) (2017) Language awareness and multilingualism. In *Encyclopedia of Language and Education* (3rd edn). Springer.
Cervantes-Soon, C., Dorner, L., Palmer, D., Heiman, D., Schwerdtfeger, R. and Choi, J. (2017) Combating inequalities in two-way language immersion programs: Toward critical consciousness in bilingual education spaces. *Review of Research in Education* 41, 403–427.
Cervantes-Soon, C., Gambrell, J., Kasun, G.S., Sung, W., Freire, J.A. and Dorner, L.M. (2020) 'Everybody wants a choice' in dual language education of El Nuevo Sur: Whiteness as the gloss for everybody in media discourses of multilingual education. *Journal of Language, Identity, and Education* (online first). https://doi.org/10.1080/15348458.2020.1753201.

Chan, V. (2016) Medium of instruction policies in higher education in Cambodia. PhD dissertation, University of Texas at San Antonio.
Chang, J. (2004) Ideologies of English teaching and learning in Taiwan. PhD dissertation, University of Sydney.
Chang-Bacon, C.K. (2021) Generation interrupted: Rethinking 'Students with Interrupted Formal Education' (SIFE) in the wake of a pandemic. *Educational Researcher* 50 (3), 187–196. https://doi.org/10.3102/0013189x21992368.
Chap, V. and Wright, W.E. (2025) Content and language integrated learning in Cambodia's higher education: A study of an introduction to ASEAN course. *TESOL Journal* (in press).
Charalambous, C., Charalambous, P., Khan, K. and Rampton, B. (2018) Security and language policy. In J.W. Tollefson and M. Pêrez-Milans (eds) *The Oxford Handbook of Language Policy and Planning* (pp. 633–653). Oxford University Press.
Cheatham, G.A., Santos, R.M. and Kerkutluoglu, A. (2012) Review of comparison studies investigating bilingualism and bilingual instruction for students with disabilities. *Focus on Exceptional Children* 45 (3), 1–12.
Chen Pichler, D., Reynolds, W. and Palmer, J. (2019) Multilingualism in signing communities. In S. Montanari and S. Quay (eds) *Multidisciplinary Perspectives on Multilingualism: The Fundamentals* (pp. 175–204). Walter De Gruyter.
Chestnut, C.E. and Dimitrieska, V. (2018) *Implementing Indiana's New Dual Language Immersion Programs: Educator's Perspectives*. Center for Evaluation and Education Policy. https://files.eric.ed.gov/fulltext/ED586233.pdf.
Chevrefils, L., Danet, C., Doan, P. et al. (2021) The body between meaning and form: Kinesiological analysis and typographical representation of movement in sign languages. *Languages and Modalities* 1 (1), 49–63.
Chhuon, V. and Hudley, C. (2010) Asian American ethnic options: How Cambodian students negotiate ethnic identities in a U.S. urban school. *Anthropology and Education Quarterly* 41 (4), 341–359. https://doi.org/10.1111/j.1548-1492.2010.01096.x.
Chhuon, V. and Hudley, C. (2011) Ethnic and panethnic Asian American identities: Contradictory perceptions of Cambodian students in urban schools. *Urban Review* 43 (5), 681–701. https://doi.org/10.1007/s11256-010-0172-8.
Chik, C.H. and Wright, W.E. (2017) Overcoming the obstacles: Vietnamese and Khmer heritage language programs in California. In O. Kagan, M. Carreira and C.H. Chik (eds) *A Handbook of Heritage Language Education: From Innovation to Program Building* (pp. 222–236). Routledge.
Chimbutane, F. (2011) *Rethinking Bilingual Education in Postcolonial Contexts*. Multilingual Matters.
Chiswick, B.R. and Miller, P.W. (2008) A test of the critical period hypothesis for language learning. *Journal of Multilingual and Multicultural Development* 29 (1), 16–29.
Chitera, N. (2009) Code-switching in a college mathematics classroom. *International Journal of Multilingualism* 6 (4), 426–442.
Christensen, K. (2017) *Educating Deaf Students in a Multicultural World*. Dawn Sign Press.
Christiansen, J.B. and Barnartt, S.M. (1995) *Deaf President Now! The 1988 Revolution at Gallaudet University*. Gallaudet University Press.
Cioè-Peña, M. (2021) *(M)othering Labeled Children: Bilingualism and Disability in the Lives of Latinx Mothers*. Multilingual Matters.
Clark, M.D., Galloza-Carrero, A., Keith, C.L., Tibbitt, J.S., Wolsey, J. and Zimmerman, H.G. (2015) Eye-gaze development in infants: Learning to look – and looking to learn. *Advance for Speech and Hearing*. http://www.redefiningacademiccollaboration.com/uploads/9/4/9/8/94981482/clark_et_al_2015_eye_gaze_development.pdf.
Clark, M.D., Baker, S. and Simms, L. (2020) A culture of assessment: A bioecological systems approach for early and continuous assessment of deaf infants and children. *Psychology in the Schools* 57 (3), 443–458.
Clark, M.D., Wimberly, M.B., Goyette, D., Metcalf, H.V., Willman, E.C., Greene, A. and Norman, N.J. (2023) How well are young deaf children in early intervention doing on their language acquisition? An assessment view. *Advances in Social Sciences Research Journal* 10 (2), 105–117.
Clerc, L. (1816/1952) *The Diary of Laurent Clerc's Voyage from France to America in 1816*, Laurent Clerc Papers no. 68 (Hartfort, CN: American School for the Deaf, 1952). Manuscripts and Archives. Yale University Library.
Clerc, L. (1851) Some hints to teachers of the deaf and dumb. Proceedings of the Second Convention of American Instructors of the Deaf and Dumb. *American Annals of the Deaf and Dumb* 4 (1), 63–75.

Clifton-Sprigg, J. and Papps, K.L. (2020) Bilingualism in the labour market. In W. Cochrane, M.P. Cameron and O. Alimi (eds) *Labor Markets, Migration, and Mobility – Essays in Honor of Jacques Poot* (pp. 1–24). Springer.

Cline, T. and Frederickson, N. (1999) Identification and assessment of dyslexia in bi/multilingual children. *International Journal of Bilingual Education and Bilingualism* 2 (2), 81–93.

Clyne, M., Hunt, C.R. and Isaakidis, T. (2004) Learning a community language as a third language. *International Journal of Multilingualism* 1 (1), 33–52.

Coady, M. (2020) *The Coral Way Bilingual Program*. Multilingual Matters.

Codó, E. (2017) Language policy and planning, institutions, and neoliberalisation. In J.W. Tollefson and M. Pérez-Milans (eds) *The Oxford Handbook of Language Policy and Planning* (pp. 467–484). Oxford University Press.

Coelho, E. (2012) *Language and Learning in Multilingual Classrooms: A Practical Approach*. Multilingual Matters.

Cohan, A. and Honigsfeld, A. (2017) Students with interrupted formal education (SIFEs): Actionable practices. *NABE Journal of Research and Practice* 8 (1), 166–175.

Collier, V.P. (1995) Acquiring a second language for school. *Directions in Language and Education* 1 (4), 1–12.

Collier, V.P. and Thomas, W.P. (2009) *Education English Learners for a Transformed World*. Fuente Press.

Collier, V.P. and Thomas, W.P. (2017) Validating the power of bilingual schooling: Thirty-two years of large-scale, longitudinal research. *Annual Review of Applied Linguistics* 37, 203–217. https://doi.org/10.1017/S0267190517000034.

Collier, V.P. and Thomas, W.P. (2020) Why dual language works for everyone, PK-12. *Multilingual Educator* (April), 2–4. http://gocabe.org/wp-content/uploads/2020/07/Online-Version-ME-2020-v2.pdf.

Comaroff, J.L. and Comaroff, J. (2009) *Ethnicity, Inc.* University of Chicago Press.

Comeau, L., Genesee, F. and Lapaquette, L. (2003) The modeling hypothesis and child bilingual codemixing. *International Journal of Bilingualism* 7 (2), 113–126.

Commission on Language Learning (2017) *America's Languages: Investing in Language Education for the 21st Century*. American Academy of Arts and Sciences. https://www.amacad.org/publication/americas-languages.

Commission on the Education of the Deaf (1988) *Toward Equality: Education of the Deaf*. US Government Printing Office.

Conklin, N. and Lourie, M. (1983) *A Host of Tongues*. Free Press.

Conteh, J. (2018) Translanguaging. *ELT Journal* 72m (4), 445–447.

Cook, V. (2001) Using the first language in the classroom. *Canadian Modern Language Review/La Revue canadienne des langues vivantes* 57 (3), 402–423.

Cooper, R.L. (1989) *Language Planning and Social Change*. Cambridge University Press.

CORDIS–EU (2024) AI solutions for the deaf and hard of hearing. https://cordis.europa.eu/article/id/450232-ai-solutions-for-the-deaf-and-hard-of-hearing.

Coronel-Molina, S.M. and McCarty, T.L. (eds) (2016) *Indigenous Language Revitalization in the Americas*. Routledge.

Corral, M.A. and Sayer, P. (2024) Transgressive translanguaging: Theorizing la corriente. *International Multilingual Research Journal* 18 (2), 158–172. https://doi.org/10.1080/19313152.2023.2288727.

Costa, A. (2005) Lexical access in bilingual production. In J.F. Kroll and A. De Groot (eds) *Handbook of Bilingualism: Psycholinguistic Approaches* (pp. 289–307). Oxford University Press.

Costa, J. (2016) *Revitalising Language in Provence: A Critical Approach*. Wiley Blackwell.

Costa, A. (2020) *The Bilingual Brain: And What It Tells Us About the Science of Language*. Penguin Books.

Coulmas, F. (1992) *Language and Economy*. Blackwell.

Council of Europe (1992) *European Charter for Regional or Minority Languages: Charte Europeene des Langues Regionales ou Minoritaires*. Council of Europe.

Council of Europe (2001) *Common European Framework of Reference for Languages: Learning, Teaching, Assessment*. Cambridge University Press.

Council of Europe (2020a) *Common European Framework of Reference for Languages: Learning, Teaching, Assessment – Companion Volume*. Council of Europe Publishing. https://www.coe.int/lang-cefr.

Council of Europe (2020b) *European Language Portfolio*. https://www.coe.int/en/web/lang-migrants/european-language-portfolio-elp.

Counts, J., Katsiyannis, A. and Whitford, D.K. (2018) Culturally and linguistically diverse learners in special education: English learners. *NASSP Bulletin* 102 (1), 5–21. https://doi.org/10.1177/0192636518755945.

Coyle, D. (2007) Content and language integrated learning: Towards a connected research agenda for CLIL pedagogies. *International Journal of Bilingual Education and Bilingualism* 10 (5), 543–562.

Coyle, D. and Meyer, O. (2021) *Beyond CLIL: Pluriliteracies Teaching for Deeper Learning*. Cambridge University Press.
Coyle, D., Hood, P. and Marsh, D. (2010) *Content and Language Integrated Learning*. Cambridge University Press.
Coyle, D., Meyer, O., and Staschen-Dielman, S. (eds) (2023) *A Deeper Learning Companion for CLIL: Putting Pluraliteracies into Practice*. Cambridge University Press.
Crawford, J. (2000) *At War with Diversity: US Language Policy in an Age of Anxiety*. Multilingual Matters.
Crawford, J. (2003) *Hard Sell: Why Is Bilingual Education so Unpopular with the American Public?* Language Policy Research Unit, Education Policy Studies Laboratory, Arizona State University.
Crawford, J. (2004) *Educating English Learners: Language Diversity in the Classroom* (5th edn). Bilingual Education Services.
Crawford, J. and Krashen, S.D. (2007) *English Learners in American Classrooms: 101 Questions, 101 Answers*. Scholastic.
Crawford, J. and Reyes, S.A. (2015) *The Trouble with SIOP*. Institute for Language and Education Policy.
Creese, A. and Blackledge, A. (2010a) Towards a sociolinguistics of superdiversity. *Zeitschrift für Erziehungswissenschaft* 13, 549–572. https://doi.org/10.1007/s11618-010-0159-y.
Creese, A. and Blackledge, A. (2010b) Translanguaging in the bilingual classroom: A pedagogy for learning and teaching? *Modern Language Journal* 94 (1), 103–115. https://doi.org/10.1111/j.1540-4781.2009.00986.x.
Creese, A. and Blackledge, A. (eds) (2018) *The Routledge Handbook of Language and Superdiversity*. Routledge.
Croneberg, C.G. (1965) Appendix C: The linguistic community. In W.C. Stokoe, D. Casterline and C. Croneberg (eds) *A Dictionary of American Sign Language on Linguistic Principles* (pp. 297–311). Gallaudet College Press.
Crume, P. K. (2013) Teachers' perceptions of promoting sign language phonological awareness in an ASL/English bilingual program. *Journal of Deaf Studies and Deaf Education* 18 (4), 464–488.
Crystal, D. (2006) *Language and the Internet* (2nd edn). Cambridge University Press.
Crystal, D. (2012) *English as a Global Language* (2nd edn) (Canto Classics). Cambridge University Press.
Crystal, D. (2014) *Language Death* (Canto Classics). Cambridge University Press.
Crystal, D. (2018) *The Cambridge Encyclopaedia of the English Language*. Cambridge University Press. https://doi.org/10.1017/9781108528931.
Cue, K.R., Pudans-Smith, K.K., Wolsey, J.L.A., Wright, S.J. and Clark, M.D. (2019) The odyssey of Deaf epistemology: A search for meaning-making. *American Annals of the Deaf* 164 (3), 395–422.
Cummins, J. (1976) *The Influence of Bilingualism on Cognitive Growth: A Synthesis of Research Findings and Explanatory Hypotheses*. Working Papers on Bilingualism 9. Ontario Institute for Studies in Education.
Cummins, J. (1977) Cognitive factors associated with the attainment of intermediate levels of bilingual skills. *Modern Language Journal* 61 (1–2), 3–12.
Cummins, J. (1979) *Cognitive/Academic Language Proficiency, Linguistic Interdependence, the Optimum Age Question and Some Other Matters* (pp. 121–129). Working Papers on Bilingualism 19, Ontario Institute for Studies in Education.
Cummins, J. (1981a) *Bilingualism and Minority-Children* (Language and Literacy Series). Ontario Institute for Studies in Education.
Cummins, J. (1981b) The role of primary language development in promoting educational success for language minority students. In California State Department of Education Office of Bilingual Education (ed.) *Schooling and Language Minority Students: A Theoretical Framework* (pp. 3–49). Evaluation, Dissemination and Assessment Center, California State University.
Cummins, J. (1983) *Heritage Language Education: A Literature Review*. Ministry of Education.
Cummins, J. (1984) *Bilingualism and Special Education: Issues in Assessment and Pedagogy*. Multilingual Matters.
Cummins, J. (1993) The research base for heritage language promotion. In M. Danesi, K.A. McLeod and S.V. Morris (eds) *Heritage Languages and Education: The Canadian Experience* (pp. 1–22). Mosaic Press.
Cummins, J. (2000a) *Language, Power and Pedagogy: Bilingual Children in the Crossfire*. Multilingual Matters.
Cummins, J. (2000b) Putting language proficiency in its place: Responding to critiques of the conversational/academic language distinction. In J. Cenoz and U. Jessner (eds) *English in Europe: The Acquisition of a Third Language* (pp. 54–83). Multilingual Matters.

Cummins, J. (2003) BICS and CALP: Origins and rationale for the distinction. In C.B. Paulston and R. Tucker (eds) *Sociolinguistics: Essential Reading* (pp. 322–328). Blackwell.
Cummins, J. (2006) The relationship between American Sign Language proficiency and English academic development: A review of the research. *Language* 1 (2), 110–114.
Cummins, J. (2013) Empowerment and bilingual education. In C.A. Chapelle (ed.) *Encyclopedia of Applied Linguistics*. Blackwell.
Cummins, J. (2017a) BICS and CALP: Empirical and theoretical status of the distinction. In S. May (ed.) *Encyclopedia of Language and Education, Vol. 2: Literacy* (3rd edn) (pp. 71–82). Springer.
Cummins, J. (2017b) Teaching for transfer: Challenging the two solitudes assumption in bilingual education. In S. May (ed.) *Encyclopedia of Language and Education, Vol. 5: Bilingual Education* (3rd edn) (pp. 1528–1538). Springer.
Cummins, J. (2019) The emergence of translanguaging pedagogy: A dialogue between theory and practice. *Journal of Multilingual Education Research* 9, 19–36.
Cummins, J. (2021) *Rethinking the Education of Multilingual Learners: A Critical Analysis of Theoretical Concepts*. Multilingual Matters.
Cummins, J. (2022) Pedagogical translanguaging: Examining the credibility of unitary versus crosslinguistic translanguaging theory. *OLBI Journal* 12, 33–55. https://doi.org/10.18192/olbij.v12i1.6073.
Cummins, J. and Danesi, M. (1990) *Heritage Languages: The Development and Denial of Canada's Linguistic Resources*. James Lorimer and Company.
Curdt-Christiansen, X.L. (2018) Family language policy. In J.W. Tollefson and M. Pêrez-Milans (eds) *The Oxford Handbook of Language Policy and Planning* (pp. 420–441). Oxford University Press.
Cushing, I. (2022) *Standards, Stigma, Surveillance: Raciolinguistic Ideologies and England's Schools*. Palgrave Macmillan.
Cushing-Leubner, J. (2020) Heritage language education: A global view. In S. Laviosa and M. González-Davies (eds) *The Routledge Handbook of Translation and Education* (pp. 303–322). Routledge.
Dagenais, D. (2003) Accessing imagined communities through multilingualism and immersion education. *Journal of Language, Identity, and Education* 2 (4), 269–283.
Dance, D.L. (2023) 'Students' right to their own language' and the importance of code-meshing. *Teaching American Speech* 98 (3), 343–355. https://doi.org/10.1215/00031283-10887774
Dannoff, M.N., Coles, G.J., McLaughlin, D.H. and Reynolds, D.J. (1978) *Evaluation of the Impact of ESEA Title VII Spanish/English Bilingual Education Programs*. American Institute for Research.
Dautel, J.B. and Kinzler, K.D. (2018) Once a French speaker, always a French speaker? Bilingual children's thinking about the stability of language. *Cognitive Science* 42, 287–302.
David, L. and Sundberg, B. (2019) Revitalizing Denaakk'e: Learning from the development and implementation of a dual language program in a Head Start classroom in Fairbanks, Alaska. Poster presentation, Office of English Language Acquisition National Professional Development Director's Meeting, Washington, DC, 13–14 November.
Davies, W.D. and Dubinsky, S. (2018) *Language Conflicts and Language Rights: Ethnolinguistic Perspectives on Human Conflict*. Cambridge University Press.
Davin, K.J. (2020) The Seal of Biliteracy across the United States: Considerations for policy implementation. In A.J. Heineke and K.J. Davin (eds) *The Seal of Biliteracy: Case Studies and Considerations for Policy Implementation* (pp. 3–16). Information Age Publishing.
Davis, J.L. (2017) Resisting rhetorics of language endangerment: Reclamation through Indigenous language survivance. *Language Documentation and Description* 14, 37–58. https://doi.org/10.25894/ldd147.
Davis, S., Ballinger, S. and Sarkar, M. (2019) The suitability of French immersion for allophone students in Saskatchewan: Exploring diverse perspectives on language learning and inclusion. *Canadian Journal of Applied Linguistics* 22 (2), 27–63. https://doi.org/10.7202/1063773ar.
De Angelis, G. (2021) *Multilingual Testing and Assessment*. Multilingual Matters.
De Bot, K. (2008) Review article: The imaging of what in the multilingual mind? *Second Language Research* 24 (1), 111–133.
De Bot, K. and Houtzager, N. (2018) Multilingualism processing and aging. In R.R. Heredia and J. Altarriba (eds) *An Introduction to Bilingualism: Principles and Processes* (pp. 93–106). Routledge.
De Bruin, A., Treccani, B. and Della Sala, S. (2015) Cognitive advantage in bilingualism an example of publication bias? *Psychological Science* 26 (1), 99–107.
De Courcy, M. (2002) *Learners' Experiences of Immersion Education: Case Studies of French and Chinese*. Multilingual Matters.
De Courcy, M., Warren, J. and Burston, M. (2002) Children from diverse backgrounds in an immersion programme. *Language and Education* 16 (2), 112–127.

De Graff, R. and van Wilgenburg, O. (2015) The Netherlands: Quality control as a driving force in bilingual education. In P. Mehisto and F. Genesee (eds) *Building Bilingual Education Systems: Forces, Mechanisms and Counterweights* (pp. 167–179). Cambridge University Press.

De Houwer, A. (1999) Environmental factors in early bilingual development: The role of parental beliefs and attitudes. In G. Extra and L. Verhoeven (eds) *Bilingualism and Migration* (pp. 75–96). De Gruyter Mouton.

De Houwer, A. (2003) Home languages spoken in officially monolingual Flanders: A survey. *Plurilingua* 24, 79–96.

De Houwer, A. (2004) Trilingual input and children's language use in trilingual families in Flanders. In C. Hoffmann and J. Ytsma (eds) *Trilingualism in Family, School and Community* (pp. 118–136). Multilingual Matters.

De Houwer, A. (2007) Parental language input patterns and children's bilingual use. *Applied Psycholinguistics* 28 (3), 411–424.

De Houwer, A. (2009) *Bilingual First Language Acquisition*. Multilingual Matters.

De Houwer, A. (2015) Harmonious bilingual development: Young families' well-being in language contact situations. *International Journal of Bilingualism* 19 (2), 169–184. https://doi.org/10.1177/1367006913489202.

De Houwer, A. (2017a) Bilingual language acquisition. In P. Fletcher and B. MacWhinney (eds) *The Handbook of Child Language* (pp. 219–250). Blackwell Publishing. https://doi.org/10.1111/b.9780631203124.1996.00009.x.

De Houwer, A. (2017b) Minority language parenting in Europe and children's well-being in language contact situations. In N. Cabrera and B. Leyendecker (eds) *Handbook on Positive Development of Minority Children and Youth* (pp. 231–246). Springer.

De Houwer, A. (2019) Language choice in bilingual interaction. In A. De Houwer and L. Ortega (eds) *The Cambridge Handbook of Bilingualism* (pp. 324–348). Cambridge University Press.

De Houwer, A. (2021) *Bilingual Development in Childhood*. Cambridge University Press.

DeJesus, J.M., Hwang, H.G., Dautel, J.B. and Kinzler, K.D. (2018) 'American = English speaker' before 'American = White': The development of children's reasoning about nationality. *Child Development* 89 (5), 1752–1767.

de Jong, E.J. (2011) *Foundations for Multilingualism in Education: From Principles to Practice*. Caslon Publishing.

de Jong, E.J. and Coulter, Z. (2024) Curriculum issues in DLBE. In J.A. Freire, C. Alfaro and E. de Jong (eds) *The Handbook of Dual Language Bilingual Education* (pp. 461–472). Routledge. https://doi.org/10.4324/9781003269076-39.

de Jong, E.J. and Harper, C.A. (2005) Preparing mainstream teachers for English-language learners: Is being a good teacher enough? *Teacher Education Quarterly* 32 (2), 101–124.

de Jong, E.J., Gort, M. and Cobb, C.D. (2005) Bilingual education within the context of English-only policies: Three districts' response to Question 2 in Massachusetts. *Educational Policy* 19 (4), 595–620.

de Jong, E.J., Li, Z., Zafar, A. and Wu, C.-H. (2016) Language policy in multilingual contexts: Revisiting Ruiz's language-as-resource orientation. *Bilingual Research Journal* 40 (3,4), 200–212. https://doi.org/10.1080/15235882.2016.1224988.

DeLana, M., Gentry, A.M. and Andrews, J. (2007) The efficacy of ASL/English bilingual education: Considering public schools. *American Annals of the Deaf* 152 (1), 73–87.

De Land, F. (1906) *Dumb No Longer: Romance of the Telephone*. Volta Bureau.

Delaporte, Y. (2020) Foreword. In U. Hedberg and H. Lane (eds) *Elements of French and Deaf Heritage*. Gallaudet University Press.

Delavan, M.G. (2024) Gentrification of dual language bilingual education: Defining types, historical evidence, and alternatives. In J.A. Freire, C. Alfaro and E. de Jong (eds) *The Handbook of Dual Language Bilingual Education* (pp. 235–253). Routledge. https://doi.org/10.4324/9781003269076-19.

Delavan, M.G., Freire, J.A. and Menken, K. (eds) (2024) *Overcoming the Gentrification of Dual Language, Bilingual and Immersion Education: Solution-Oriented Research and Stakeholder Resources for Real Integration*. Multilingual Matters.

Del Percio, A., Flubacher, M.-C. and Duchêne, A. (2017) Language and political economy. In O. García, N. Flores and M. Spotti (eds) *The Oxford Handbook of Language and Society* (pp. 55–76). Oxford University Press.

Del Valle, S. (2003) *Language Rights and the Law in the United States: Finding Our Voices*. Multilingual Matters.

de Mejía, A.-M. (2002) *Power, Prestige and Bilingualism: International Perspectives on Elite Bilingual Education*. Multilingual Matters.

de Mejía, A.-M. and Hélot, C. (2015) Teacher education and support. In W.E. Wright, S. Boun and O. García (eds) *Handbook of Bilingual and Multilingual Education* (pp. 270–281). Wiley-Blackwell.

De Meulder, M., Krausneker, V., Turner, G. and Conama, J.B. (2019a) Sign language communities. In *The Palgrave Handbook of Minority Languages and Communities* (pp. 207–232). Palgrave Macmillan.

De Meulder, M., Kusters, A., Moriarty, E. and Murray, J.J. (2019b) Describe, don't prescribe. The practice and politics of translanguaging in the context of deaf signers. *Journal of Multilingual and Multicultural Development* 40 (10), 892–906.

De Meulder, M., Murray, J.J. and McKee, R.L. (2019c) Epilogue: Claiming multiple positionalities: Lessons from the first two decades of sign language recognition. In M. De Meulder, J.J. Murray and R.L. McKee (eds) *The Legal Recognition of Sign Languages: Advocacy and Outcomes Around the World* (pp. 301–312). Multilingual Matters.

De Meulder, M., Murray, J.J. and McKee, R.L. (2019d) Introduction: The legal recognition of sign languages: Advocacy and outcomes around the world. In M. De Meulder, J.J. Murray and R.L. McKee (eds) *The Legal Recognition of Sign Languages: Advocacy and Outcomes Around the World* (pp. 1–15). Multilingual Matters.

Demmert, W.G. (2001) *Improving Academic Performance Among Native American Students: A Review of the Research Literature.* ERIC Clearinghouse on Rural Education and Small Schools.

De Quadros, R. M. (2018) Bimodal bilingual heritage signers: A balancing act of languages and modalities. *Sign Language Studies* 18 (3), 355–384.

Derhemi, E. and Moseley, C. (eds) (2023) *Endangered Languages in the 21st Century.* Routledge.

Deuchar, M. and Quay, S. (2000) *Bilingual Acquisition: Theoretical Implications of a Case Study* (Vol. 2). Oxford University Press.

Dewaele, J.-M. (2000) Three years old and three first languages. *Bilingual Family Newsletter* 17 (2), 4–5.

Dewaele, J.-M. (2002) Review of M. Yamamoto (2001) Language use in interlingual families: A Japanese–English sociolinguistic study. *Applied Linguistics* 23 (4), 546–548.

Dewaele, J.-M. (2007) Still trilingual at ten: Livia's multilingual journey. *Multilingual Living Magazine*, March/April, 68–71.

Diaz, R.M. (1985) Bilingual cognitive development: Addressing three gaps in current research. *Child Development* 56, 1376–1388.

Dicker, S.J. (2003) *Languages in America: A Pluralist View* (2nd edn). Multilingual Matters.

Dickerson, C. (2019) 'There is a stench': Soiled clothes and no baths for migrant children at a Texas center. *New York Times*, 21 June. https://www.nytimes.com/2019/06/21/us/migrant-children-border-soap.html.

Diebold, A.R. (1964) Incipient bilingualism. In D. Hymes (ed.) *Language in Culture and Society* (pp. 495–510). Harper and Row.

Dillingham, C. (1828) *Education of the Deaf and Dumb.* Report of the Secretary of State in Albany, NY, made to the Senate, 14 April.

Dobbs, C.L. and Bauer, E.D. (2024) Toward a critical multidimensional pedagogy for multilingual Black learners. In J.A. Freire, C. Alfaro and E. de Jong (eds) *The Handbook of Dual Language Bilingual Education* (pp. 360–369). Routledge.

Dolson, D.P. and Mayer, J. (1992) Longitudinal study of three program models for language-minority students: A critical examination of reported findings. *Bilingual Research Journal* 16 (1–2), 105–158.

Dominguez Hills Colectivo Plurilingüe (2024) Professional development for in-service dual language teachers. In J.A. Freire, C. Alfaro and E. de Jong (eds) *The Handbook of Dual Language Bilingual Education* (pp. 624–637). Routledge. https://doi.org/10.4324/9781003269076-52.

Doran, P.R. and Noggle, A.K. (eds) (2019) *Supporting English Learners with Exceptional Needs.* TESOL Press.

Doran, P.R. and Turner, D. (2019) Ecological approaches and multitiered systems of support: Holistic approaches to serving English learners. In P.R. Doran and A.K. Noggle (eds) *Supporting English Learners with Exceptional Needs* (pp. 49–64). TESOL Press.

Dorian, N.C. (1981) *Language Death: The Life Cycle of a Scottish Gaelic Dialect.* University of Pennsylvania Press

Dörnyei, Z. (2001) *Motivational Strategies in the Language Classroom.* Cambridge University Press.

Dörnyei, Z. (2019) From integrative motivation to directed motivational currents: The evolution of the understanding of L2 motivation over three decades. In M. Lamb, K. Csizér, A. Henry and S. Ryan (eds) *The Palgrave Handbook of Motivation for Language Learning* (pp. 39–69). Palgrave Macmillan.

Dörnyei, Z. (2020) *Innovations and Challenges in Language Learning Motivation.* Routledge.

Dörnyei, Z., Csizér, K. and Németh, N. (2006) *Motivation, Language Attitudes and Globalisation: A Hungarian Perspective.* Multilingual Matters.

Douglas Fir Group (2016) A transdisciplinary framework for SLA in a multilingual world. *Modern Language Journal* 100 (S1), 19–47.
Dovchin, S. (ed.) (2020a) *Digital Communication, Linguistic Diversity and Education*. Peter Lang.
Dovchin, S. (2020b) Introduction to special issue: Linguistic racism. *International Journal of Bilingual Education and Bilingualism* 23 (7), 773–777. https://doi.org/10.1080/13670050.2020.1778630.
Dovchin, S., Sultana, S. and Pennycook, A. (2017) *Popular Culture, Voice and Linguistic Diversity: Young Adults On- and Off-line*. Palgrave Macmillan.
Dove, M.G. and Honigsfeld, A. (2018) *Co-teaching for English Learners: A Guide to Collaborative Planning, Interaction, Assessment and Reflection*. Corwin.
Drasgow, E. (1993) Bilingual/bicultural deaf education: An overview. *Sign Language Studies*, 80 (1), 243–266.
Duchêne, A. and Heller, M. (2012) *Language in Late Capitalism: Pride and Profit*. Routledge.
Duff, P.A. (2008) Heritage language education in Canada. In D. Brinton (ed.) *Heritage Language Education: A New Field Emerging* (pp. 71–90). Routledge.
Duff, P.A. (2010) Language socialization. In N.H. Hornberger and S.L. McKay (eds) *Sociolinguistics and Language Education* (pp. 427–455). Multilingual Matters.
Duff, P.A. (2014) Communicative language teaching. In M. Celce-Murcia, D.M. Brinton and M.A. Snow (eds) *Teaching English as a Second or Foreign Language* (4th edn, pp. 2–14). Cengage Learning.
Dulay, H.C. and Burt, M.K. (1978) *Why Bilingual Education? A Summary of Research Findings*. Bloomsbury West.
Dulay, H.C. and Burt, M.K. (1979) *Bilingual Education: A Close Look At Its Effects*. Focus 1. National Clearinghouse for Bilingual Education.
Dunabeitia, J.A., Hernandez, J.A., Anton, E., Macizo, P., Estevez, A., Fuentes, L.J. and Carreiras, M. (2014) The inhibitory advantage in bilingual children revisited. *Experimental Psychology* 61, 234–251. https://doi.org/10.1027/1618-3169/a000243.
Dutcher, N. (2004) *Expanding Educational Opportunity in Linguistically Diverse Societies*. Center for Applied Linguistics.
Dutcher, N. and Tucker, G.R. (1996) *The Use of First and Second Languages in Education: A Review of International Experience*. East Asia and Pacific Country Department III, World Bank.
Dweck, C.S. (2006) *Mindset: The New Psychology of Success*. Random House.
Dye, M.W. (2016) Foveal processing under concurrent peripheral load in profoundly deaf adults. *Journal of Deaf Studies and Deaf Education* 21 (2), 122–128.
Dye, M.W. and Bavelier, D. (2010) Attentional enhancements and deficits in Deaf populations: An integrative review. *Restorative Neurology and Neuroscience* 28 (2), 181–192.
Eberhard, D.M., Simons, G.F. and Fennig, C.D. (eds) (2019) *Ethnologue: Languages of the World* (online version) (22nd edn). SIL International.
Eberhard, D.M., Simons, G.F., and Fennig, C.D. (2023) *Ethnologue: Languages of the World* (26th edn). SIL International. Online version https://www. Ethnologue.com.
Eberhard, D.M., Simons, G.F. and Fennig, C.D. (eds) (2024) *Ethnologue: Languages of the World* (27th edn). SIL International. Online version https://www.ethnologue.com (update current reference).
Echevarría, J. and Graves, A.W. (2011) *Sheltered Content Instruction: Teaching English Language Learners with Diverse Abilities* (4th edn). Pearson Allyn and Bacon.
Echevarría, J. and Vogt, M. (2011) *Response to Intervention (RTI) and English Learners: Making It Happen*. Pearson.
Echevarria, J., Vogt, M., Short, D. and Toppel, K. (2023) *Making Content Comprehensible for Multilingual Learners: The SIOP Model* (6th edn). Pearson.
Economic Affairs Division (2012) *Isle of Man Census Report 2011*. https:// www.gov.im/ media/207882/census2011reportfinalresized_1_.pdf.
Edelsky, C. (2006) *With Literacy and Justice For All: Rethinking the Social in Language and Education* (3rd edn). Lawrence Erlbaum Associates.
Edelsky, C., Hudelson, S., Flores, B., Barkin, F., Altwerger, B. and Jilbert, K. (1983) Semilingualism and language deficit. *Applied Linguistics* 4 (1), 1–22.
Edwards, J. (2012) *Multilingualism: Understanding Linguistic Diversity*. Bloomsbury Publishing.
Edwards, J. (2013) Bilingualism and multilingualism: Some central concepts. In T.K. Bhatia and W.C. Ritchie (eds) *The Handbook of Bilingualism and Multilingualism* (2nd edn, pp. 5–25). Blackwell.
Edwards, T. (2024) *Going Tactile: Life at the Limits of Language*. Oxford University Press.
Edwards, V. (2015) Literacy in bilingual and multilingual education. In W.E. Wright, S. Boun and O. García (eds) *Handbook of Bilingual and Multilingual Education* (p. 75). Wiley-Blackwell.
Ehl, B., Bruns, G. and Grosche, M. (2019) Differentiated bilingual vocabulary assessment reveals similarities

and differences compared to monolinguals: Conceptual versus single-language scoring and the relation with home language and literacy activities. *International Journal of Bilingualism* 24 (4), 715–728. https://doi.org/10.1177/1367006919876994.

Emery, S.D. and Sanchayeeta, S. (2022) Deaf migration through an intersectionality lens. *Disability and Society* 37 (1), 89–110.

Emmorey, K. (2021) New perspectives on the neurobiology of sign languages. *Frontiers in Communication* 6, 748430.

Emmorey, K., Kosslyn, S.M. and Bellugi, U. (1993) Visual imagery and visual-spatial language: Enhanced imagery abilities in deaf and hearing ASL signers. *Cognition* 46 (2), 139–181.

Emmorey, K., Klima, E. and Hickok, G. (1998) Mental rotation within linguistic and non-linguistic domains in users of American sign language. *Cognition* 68 (3), 221–246.

Emmorey, K., Petrich, J.A. and Gollan, T.H. (2012) Bilingual processing of ASL–English code-blends: The consequences of accessing two lexical representations simultaneously. *Journal of Memory and Language* 67 (1), 199–210.

Emmorey, K., Giezen, M.R. and Gollan, T.H. (2016a) Psycholinguistic, cognitive, and neural implications of bimodal bilingualism. *Bilingualism: Language and Cognition* 19 (2), 223–242.

Emmorey, K., McCullough, S. and Weisberg, J. (2016b) The neural underpinnings of reading skill in deaf adults. *Brain and Language* 160, 11–20.

EngageNY (2014) *New York State Bilingual Common Core Initiative*. https://www.engageny.org/resource/new-york-state-bilingual-common-core-initiative.

England, L., Kamhi-Stein, L. and Kormpas, G. (eds) (2023) *English Language Teacher Education in Changing Times: Perspectives, Strategies, and New Ways of Teaching and Learning*. Routledge.

Engman, M.M. and King, K.A. (2017) Language shift and sustainability: Critical discourses and beyond. In O. García, N. Flores and M. Spotti (eds) *The Oxford Handbook of Language and Society* (pp. 197–219). Oxford University Press.

Escamilla, K., Shannon, S., Carlos, S. and García, J. (2003) Breaking the code: Colorado's defeat of the anti-bilingual education initiative (Amendment 31). *Bilingual Research Journal* 27 (3), 357–382.

Escamilla, K., Hopewell, S., Butvilofsky, S., Sparrow, W., Soltero-González, L., Ruiz-Figueroa, O. and Escamilla, M. (2013) *Biliteracy from the Start: Literacy Squared in Action*. Caslon.

Escamilla, K., Hopewell, S. and Butvilofsky, S. (2018) Exacerbating inequalities for bilingual teachers and students through the enactment of the CCSS. In P.C. Ramírez, C.J. Faltis and E.J. de Jong (eds) *Learning from Emergent Bilinguals Latinx Learners in K-12* (pp. 41–60). Routledge.

ESTYN (2001) Cwricwlwm Cymreig. *The Welsh Dimension of the Curriculum of Wales: Good Practice in Teaching and Learning*. ESTYN.

European Commission (2012a) *Euromosaic III: Presence of Regional and Minority Language Groups in the New Member States*. European Commission.

European Commission (2012b) *Europeans and Their Languages*. Special Eurobarometer 386. European Commission.

European Commission (2015) *Language Teaching and Learning in Multilingual Classrooms*. European Union.

European Commission (2024) *Europeans and Their Languages*. Eurobarometer. https://europa.eu/eurobarometer/surveys/detail/2979.

Evans, M. and Liu, Y. (2018) The unfamiliar and the indeterminate: Language, identity and social integration in the school experience of newly-arrived migrant children in England. *Journal of Language, Identity, and Education* 17 (3), 152–167. https://doi.org/10.1080/15348458.2018.1433043.

Eviatar, Z., Taha, H. and Shwartz, M. (2018) Metalinguistic awareness and literacy among semitic-bilingual learners: A cross-language perspective. *Reading and Writing* 31 (8), 1869–1891.

Eysenck, M.W., Ellis, A.W., Hunt, E.B. and Johnson-Laird, P.N.E. (1994) *The Blackwell Dictionary of Cognitive Psychology*. Blackwell.

Faingold, E.D. (2020) *Language Rights and the Law in the European Union*. Palgrave Macmillan.

Fairclough, N. (ed.) (2013) *Critical Language Awareness*. Routledge.

Faltis, C. (1993) Critical issues in the use of sheltered content teaching in high school bilingual programs. *Peabody Journal of Education* 69 (1), 136–151.

Faltis, C. (2020) Pedagogical codeswitching and translanguaging in bilingual schooling contexts: Critical practices for bilingual teacher education. In J. MacSwan and C.J. Faltis (eds) *Codeswitching in the Classroom: Critical Perspectives on Teaching, Learning, Policy, and Ideology* (pp. 39–62). Center for Applied Linguistics and Routledge.

Faltis, C.J. (2022) Understanding and resisting perfect language and eugenics-based language ideologies in bilingual teacher education. In J. MacSwan (ed.) *Multilingual Perspectives on Translanguaging* (pp. 321–342). Multilingual Matters.

Faltis, C. (2024) The hegemonic power of English (and Spanish of elsewhere) and its impact in dual language education. In J.A. Freire, C. Alfaro and E. de Jong (eds) *The Handbook of Dual Language Bilingual Education* (pp. 495–513). Routledge.

Fan, S., Liberman, Z., Keysar, B. and Kinzler, K.D. (2015) The exposure advantage: Early exposure to a multilingual environment promotes effective communication. *Psychological Science* (online first).

Fay, E.A. (ed.) (1879) Contract between Gallaudet and Clerc (1816). *American Annals of the Deaf and Dumb* 24 (2), 115–117.

Fee, M., Liu, N., Duggan, J., Arias, B. and Wiley, T.G. (2014) *Investigating Language Policies in IB World Schools: Final Report*. Center for Applied Linguistics.

Feinauer, E., Freire, J.A., Willardson, K. and Earl, M. (2024) Sociocultural competence in dual language bilingual education: A literature review of student outcomes. In J.A. Freire, C. Alfaro and E. de Jong (eds) *The Handbook of Dual Language Bilingual Education* (pp. 194–212). Routledge. https://doi.org/10.4324/9781003269076-15.

Feng, A. and Adamson, B. (2015) Contested notions of bilingualism and trilingualism in the People's Republic of China. In W.E. Wright, S. Boun and O. García (eds) *Handbook of Bilingual and Multilingual Education* (pp. 484–494). John Wiley and Sons.

Ferguson, C.A. (1959) Diglossia. *Word* 15, 325–340.

Festman, J., Poarch, G.J. and Dewaele, J.-M. (2017) *Raising Multilingual Children*. Multilingual Matters.

Filipino Deaf Students in Multilingual Classrooms Amid a Pandemic. *American Annals of the Deaf* 168 (5), 296–310.

Fillmore, L.W. (1991) When learning a second language means losing the first. *Early Childhood Research Quarterly* 6 (3), 323–346.

Fillmore, L.W. (2013) English learners and the Common Core: A fighting chance to learn. Paper presented at the Common Core State State Standards and English Learners (Webinar), National Clearinghouse of English Language Acquisition, Washington, DC.

Fillmore, L.W. and Snow, C.E. (2018) What teachers need to know about language. In C.T. Adger, C.E. Snow and D. Christian (eds) *What Teachers Need to Know About Language* (2nd edn, pp. 8–51). Multilingual Matters and Center for Applied Linguistics.

Fischer, H. (2024) Arizona schools chief Horne ordered to pay $120k over failed attempt at 'English-only' instruction. KAWC (Radio). https://www.kawc.org/news/2024-05-30/arizona-schools-chief-horne-ordered-to-pay-120k-over-failed-attempt-at-english-only-instruction.

Fischer, S.D. (2014) Sign languages in their historical context. In C. Bowern and B. Evans (eds) *The Routledge Handbook of Historical Linguistics* (pp. 442–464). Routledge.

Fishman, J.A. (1980) Bilingualism and biculturalism as individual and as societal phenomena. *Journal of Multilingual and Multicultural Development* 1 (1), 3–15.

Fishman, J.A. (1989) *Language and Ethnicity in Minority Sociolinguistic Perspective*. Multilingual Matters.

Fishman, J.A. (1991) *Reversing Language Shift: Theoretical and Empirical Foundations of Assistance to Threatened Languages*. Multilingual Matters.

Fishman, J.A. (2001) *Can Threatened Languages Be Saved? Reversing Language Shift, Revisited: A 21st Century Perspective*. Multilingual Matters.

Fishman, J.A. (2006) 300-plus years of heritage language education in the United States. In G. Valdés, J. Fishman, R. Chávez and W. Pérez (eds) *Towards the Developing Minority Language Resources*. Multilingual Matters.

Fishman, J.A. (2010) *Handbook of Language and Ethnic Identity* (Vol. 1). Oxford University Press.

Fishman, J.A. (2013) Language maintenance, language shift, and reversing language shift. In T.K. Bhatia and W.C. Ritchie (eds) *Handbook of Bilingualism and Multilingualism* (pp. 466–494). Blackwell Publishing.

Fishman, J.A. (2014) Three hundred-plus years of heritage language education in the United States. In T.G. Wiley, J.K. Peyton, D. Christian, S.C.K. Moore and N. Liu (eds) *Handbook of Heritage, Community, and Native American Languages in the United States: Research, Policy, and Educational Practice* (pp. 36–44). Center for Applied Linguistics and Routledge.

Fitzgerald, K. (2010) *Deafness of the Mind: The Forgotten Children of Boston Spa*. Kevin Fitzgerald.

Flegenhimer, M. (2016) Habla Español? Tim Kaine is latest candidate to use Spanish to court voters. *New York Times*, 29 July, p. A13.

Flores, B.B., Sheets, R.H. and Clark, E.R. (eds) (2011) *Teacher Preparation for Bilingual Student Populations: Educar Para Transformar*. Routledge.

Flores, E. and Brown, M. (2023) The 'no sabo kids' are pushing back on Spanish-language shaming. NBC News, 16 September. https://www.nbcnews.com/news/latino/latino-no-sabo-kids-push-back-spanish-language-shaming-rcna105170.

Flores, J.B., Garza, K.C., Rochester, T.B., Vera, Y. and Flores, B.B. (2022) Assessing bicultural-bilinguals' language development: Difference or disorder? In M. Machado-Casas, S.I. Maldonado and B.B. Flores (eds) *Assessment and Evaluation in Bilingual Education* (pp. 105–129). Peter Lang.

Flores, N. (2016) Do Black Lives Matter in bilingual education? https://educationallinguist.wordpress.com/2016/09/11/do-black-lives-matter-in-bilingual-education.

Flores, N. (2019) From academic language to language architecture: Challenging raciolinguistic ideologies in research and practice. *Theory Into Practice* (online first). https://doi.org/10.1080/00405841.2019.1665411.

Flores, N. (2020a) From academic language to language architecture: Challenging raciolinguistic ideologies in research and practice. *Theory into Practice* 59 (1), 22–31.https://doi.org/10.1080/00405841.2019.1665411.

Flores, N. (2020b) Are people who support the concept of academic language racist? An FAQ. *The Educational Linguist* (blog). https://educationallinguist.wordpress.com/2020/02/01/are-people-who-support-the-concept-of-academic-language-racist-an-faq.

Flores, N. (2024) *Becoming the System: A Raciolinguistic Genealogy of Bilingual Education in the Post-Civil Rights Era*. Oxford University Press.

Flores, N. and Baetens Beardsmore, H. (2015) Programs and structures in bilingual and multilingual education. In W.E. Wright, S. Boun and O. García (eds) *Handbook of Bilingual and Multilingual Education* (pp. 206–222). Wiley-Blackwell.

Flores, N. and McAuliffe, L. (2020) 'In other schools you can plan it that way': A raciolinguistic perspective on dual language education. *International Journal of Bilingual Education and Bilingualism* (online first). https://doi.org/10.1080/13670050.2020.1760200.

Flores, N. and Rosa, J. (2015) Undoing appropriateness: Raciolinguistic ideologies and language diversity in education. *Harvard Educational Review* 85 (2), 149–171.

Flores, N. and Rosa, J. (2023) Undoing raciolinguistics. *Journal of Sociolinguistics* 27 (5), 421–427. https://doi.org/10.1111/josl.12643.

Flores, N., Kleyn, T. and Menken, K. (2015) Looking holistically in a climate of partiality: Identities of students labeled long-term English language learners. *Journal of Language, Identity and Education* 14 (2), 113–132.

Flubacher, M.-C. and Del Percio, A. (eds) (2017) *Language, Education and Neoliberalism: Critical Studies in Sociolinguistics*. Multilingual Matters.

Fogle, L.W. (2013) Family language policy from the children's point of view: Bilingualism in time and place. In M. Schwartz and A. Verschik (eds) *Successful Family Language Policy: Parents, Children and Educators in Interaction* (pp. 177–200). Springer.

Fortune, T.W. and Tedick, D.J. (2008) *Pathways to Multilingualism: Evolving Perspectives on Immersion Education*. Multilingual Matters.

Fortune, T.W. and Tedick, D.J. (2019) Context matters: Translanguaging and language immersion education in the US and Canada. In M. Haneda and H. Nassaji (eds) *Perspectives on Language as Action* (pp. 27–44). Multilingual Matters.

Foster, R. (ed.) (1818) Laurent Clerc's paper about Deaf and Dumb Asylum at Hartford. *Christian Herald* 5 (1 June), 167–178.

Foucault, M. (1978) *The History of Sexuality, Vol. I: An Introduction* (R. Hurley, trans.). Pantheon Books.

Foucault, M. (1980) *Power/Knowledge: Selected Interviews and Other Writings, 1972–1977*. Pantheon.

Francis, D.J., Rivera, M., Lesaux, N., Kieffer, M. and Rivera, H. (2006) *Practical Guidelines for the Education of English Language Learners: Researched-Based Recommendations for the Use of Accommodations in Large-Scale Assessments*. Center on Instruction.

Francisco, M.P.B.U., Perez, M.V.T. and Reyes, B.R.E.C. (2024) *Teaching Literacy to Freeman, R.D. (1998) Bilingual Education and Social Change*. Multilingual Matters.

Frederickson, N. and Cline, T. (2015) *Special Educational Needs, Inclusion, and Diversity* (3rd edn). Open University Press.

Freeman, R.D. (1998) *Bilingual Education and Social Change*. Multilingual Matters.

Freeman, R.D. (2004) *Building on Community Bilingualism: Promoting Multiculturalism Through Schooling*. Caslon Publishing.

Freeman, Y.S., Freeman, A. and Freeman, D.E. (2003) Home run books: Connecting students to culturally relevant texts. *NABE News* 26 (3), 5–12, 28.

Freire, J.A. and Feinauer, E. (2020) Vernacular Spanish as a promoter of critical consciousness in dual language bilingual education classrooms. *International Journal of Bilingual Education and Bilingualism* 25 (4), 1516–1529. https://doi.org/10.1080/13670050.2020.1775778.

Freire, J.A., Valdez, V.E. and Delavan, M.G. (2017) The (dis)inclusion of Latina/o interests from Utah's dual language education boom. *Journal of Latinos and Education* 16 (4), 276–289.

Freire, J.A., Alfaro, C. and de Jong, E. (2024) *The Handbook of Dual Language Bilingual Education*. Routledge.

Freire, P. (1993) *Pedagogy of the Oppressed* (20th anniversary edn). Seabury Press/Continuum.

Fricke, M., Zirnstein, M., Navarro-Torres, C. and Kroll, J.F. (2019) Bilingualism reveals fundamental variation in language processing. *Brain and Language* 175, 123–129.

Friedner, M. and Kusters, A. (2020) Deaf anthropology. *Annual Review of Anthropology* 49 (1), 16–25.

Frost, K. and McNamara, T. (2018) Language tests, language policy, and citizenship. In J.W. Tollefson and M. Pêrez-Milans (eds) *The Oxford Handbook of Language Policy and Planning* (pp. 280–298). Oxford University Press.

Fu, Y., Lu, D., Kang, C., Wu, J., Ma, F., Ding, G. and Guo, T. (2017) Neural correlates for naming disadvantage of the dominant language in bilingual word production. *Brain and Language* 175, 123–129.

Fukuda, M. (2017) Language use in the context of double minority: The case of Japanese-Catalan/Spanish families in Catalonia. *International Journal of Multilingualism* 14 (4), 401–418.

Fuller, J.M. (2013) *Spanish Speakers in the USA*. Multilingual Matters.

Gal, S. (1979) *Language Shift: Social Determinants of Linguistic Change in Bilingual Austria*. Academic Press.

Gallagher-Brett, A. (2005) *Seven Hundred Reasons for Studying Languages*. Higher Education Academy, Subject Centre for Languages, Linguistics and Area Studies, University of Southampton. https://www.idiomas.idph.com.br/textos/700_reasons.pdf.

Gambino, C.P. (2018) *American Community Survey Redesign of Language-Spoken-at-Home Data, 2016*. SEHSD Working Paper Number 2018–31. US Census Bureau.

Gándara, P. and Hopkins, M. (eds) (2010) *Forbidden Language: English Learners and Restrictive Language Policies*. Teachers College Press.

Gándara, P., Maxwell-Jolly, J., Garcia, E., Asato, J., Gutierrez, K., Stritikus, T. and Curry, J. (2000) *The Initial Impact of Proposition 227 on the Instruction of English Learners*. UC Linguistic Minority Research Institute, Education Policy Center, University of California, Davis.

Gandhi, M. (1927) *Autobiography: The Story of My Experiments with Truth* (1949 English translation). Cape.

Gannon, J.R. (1981) *Deaf Heritage: A Narrative History of Deaf America*. National Association of the Deaf.

Gannon, J.R. (1989) *The Week the World Heard Gallaudet*. Gallaudet University Press.

Gannon, J.R. (2020) *Get Your Elbow Off the Horn: Stories Through the Years*. Gallaudet University Press.

Gao, X.A. and Shao, Q. (2018) Language policy and mass media. In J.W. Tollefson and M. Pêrez-Milans (eds) *The Oxford Handbook of Language Policy and Planning* (pp. 299–317). Oxford University Press.

Gárate, M. (2011) Educating children with cochlear implants in an ASL/English bilingual classroom In R. Paludnevicience and I.W. Leigh (eds) *Cochlear Implants: Evolving Perspectives* (pp. 206–228). Gallaudet University Press.

Gárate, M. (2012) *ASL/English Bilingual Education*. Research Brief No. 8, June. Visual Language and Visual Learning Science of Learning Center. https://vl2.gallaudet.edu/research/research-briefs/english/aslenglish-bilingual-education.

Gárate, M. (2014) Developing bilingual literacy in deaf children. In M. Sasaki (ed.) *Mainoritei no Shakai-sanka: Shogaisha to Tayona Riterashi* [*Literacies of the Minorities: Constructing a Truly Inclusive Society*] (pp. 180–196). Kurosio Publishers.

Gárate-Estes, M., Lawyer, G.L. and García-Fernández, C. (2022) The US Latinx Deaf communities: Situating and envisioning the transformative potential of translanguaging. In M.T. Sánchez and O. García (eds) *Transformative Translanguaging Espacios: Latinx Students and their Teachers Rompiendo Fronteras sin Miedo* (pp. 223–251). Multilingual Matters.

Garberoglio, C.L., Stapleton, L.D., Palmer, J.L., Simms, L., Cawthon, S. and Sales, A. (2019) *Postsecondary Achievement of Black Deaf People in the United States*. US Department of Education, Office of Special Education Programs, National Deaf Center on Postsecondary Outcomes.

García, O. (2008) Teaching Spanish and Spanish in teaching in the USA: Integrating bilingual perspectives. In C. Hélot and A.-M. de Mejía (eds) *Forging Multilingual Spaces: Integrated Perspectives on Majority and Minority Bilingual Education* (p. 31). Multilingual Matters.

García, O. (2009a) *Bilingual Education in the 21st Century: A Global Perspective*. Wiley-Blackwell.

García, O. (2009b) Education, multilingualism and translanguaging in the 21st century. In A.K. Mohanty, M. Panda, R. Phillipson and T. Skutnabb-Kangas (eds) *Multilingual Education for Social Justice: Globalising the Local* (pp. 140–158). Orient BlackSwan.

García, O. (2017a) Translanguaging in schools: Subiendo y bajando, bajano y subiendo as afterward. *Journal of Language, Identity, and Education* 16 (4), 256–263. https://doi.org/10.1080/15348458.2017.1329657.

García, O. (2017b) Critical multilingual language awareness and teacher education. In J. Cenoz, D. Gorter, and S. May (eds) *Language Awareness and Multilingualism. Encyclopedia of Language and Education* (pp. 263–280). Springer. https://doi.org/10.1007/978-3-319-02240-6_30.

García, O. (2020) Translanguaging and Latinx bilingual readers. *Reading Teacher* 73 (5), 557–562. https://doi.org/10.1002/trtr.1883.

García, O. and Cole, D. (2014) Deaf gains in the study of bilingualism and bilingual education. In H.-D.L. Bauman and J.J. Murray (eds) *Deaf Gain: Raising the Stakes for Human Diversity* (pp. 95–111). University of Minnesota Press.

García, O. and Kleifgen, J.A. (2018) *Educating Emergent Bilinguals: Policies, Programs and Practices for English Learners*. Teachers College Press.

García, O. and Kleyn, T. (2016) *Translanguaging with Multilingual Students: Learning from Classroom Moments*. Routledge.

García, O. and Li Wei (2014) *Translanguaging: Language, Bilingualism, and Education*. Palgrave Macmillan.

García, O. and Li Wei (2015) Translanguaging, bilingualism, and bilingual education. In W.E. Wright, S. Boun and O. García (eds) *Handbook of Bilingual and Multilingual Education* (pp. 223–240). John Wiley and Sons.

García, O., Peltz, R. and Schiffman, H. (eds) (2006) *Language Loyalty, Continuity and Change: Joshua A. Fishman's Contributions to International Sociolinguistics*. Multilingual Matters.

García, O., Zakharia, Z. and Otcu, B. (eds) (2013) *Bilingual Community Education and Multilingualism: Beyond Heritage Languages in a Global City*. Multilingual Matters.

García, O., Johnson, S.I. and Seltzer, K. (2016) *Translanguaging Classrooms: Leveraging Student Bilingualism for Learning*. Caslon Publishing.

García, O., Flores, N. and Spotti, M. (2017a) Introduction – Language and society: A critical poststructural perspective. In O. García, N. Flores and M. Spotti (eds) *The Oxford Handbook of Language and Society* (pp. 1–16). Oxford University Press.

García, O., Flores, N. and Spotti, M. (2017b) Conclusion: Moving the study of language and society into the future. In O. García, N. Flores and M. Spotti (eds) *The Oxford Handbook of Language and Society* (pp. 545–552). Oxford University Press.

García, O., Flores, N., Seltzer, K., Wei, L., Otheguy, R. and Rosa, J. (2021) Rejecting abyssal thinking in the language and education of racialized bilinguals: A manifesto. *Critical Inquiry in Language Studies* 18 (3), 203–228. https://doi.org/10.1080/15427587.2021.1935957.

García, O., Flores, N., Seltzer, K., Wei, L., Otheguy, R. and Rosa, J. (2022) Rejecting abyssal thinking in the language and education of racialized bilinguals. In J. Scott and M. Bajaj (eds) *World Yearbook of Education 2023: Racialization and Educational Inequality in Global Perspective* (pp. 81–99). Routledge. https://doi.org/10.4324/9781003241393-7.

García-Mateus, S., Nuñez, I. and Urrieta, L. (2024) Identity construction and students in DLBE classrooms. In J.A. Freire, C. Alfaro and E. de Jong (eds) *The Handbook of Dual Language Bilingual Education* (pp. 373–392). Routledge. https://doi.org/10.4324/9781003269076-34.

Garcia-Sierra, A., Rivera-Gaxiola, M., Percaccio, C.R., Conboy, B.T., Romo, H., Klarman, L. and Kuhl, P.K. (2011) Bilingual language learning: An ERP study relating early brain responses to speech, language input, and later word production. *Journal of Phonetics* 39, 546–557.

Gardner, H. (2011) *Frames of Mind: The Theory of Multiple Intelligences*. Basic Books.

Gardner, R.C. (2010) *Motivation and Second Language Acquisition: The Socio-educational Model*. Peter Lang.

Gardner, R.C. (2019) The socio-educational model of second language acquisition. In M. Lamb, K. Csizér, A. Henry and S. Ryan (eds) *The Palgrave Handbook of Motivation for Language Learning* (pp. 21–37). Palgrave Macmillan.

Gardner, R.C. and Lambert, W.E. (1972) *Attitudes and Motivation in Second Language Learning*. Newbury House.

Garnett, Jr, C. (1968) *The Exchange of Letters Between Samuel Heinicke and Abbe Charles Michel de l'Epee*. Vantage Press.

Garretson, M. (1981) Introduction. In J.R. Gannon, *Deaf Heritage: A Narrative History of Deaf America*. National Association for the Deaf.

Gathercole, V.C.M., Thomas, E.M., Kennedy, I., Prys, C., Young, N., Vinas Guasch, N. and Jones, L. (2014) Does language dominance affect cognitive performance in bilinguals? Lifespan evidence from preschoolers through older adults on card sorting, Simon, and meta-linguistic tasks. *Frontiers in Psychology* 5, 1–14. https://doi.org/10.3389/fpsyg.2014.00011.

Gazzola, M., Gobbo, F., Johnson, D.C. and de León, J.A. (2023) *Epistemological and Theoretical Foundations in Language Policy and Planning*. Palgrave Macmillan.

Gee, J.P. (2012) *Social Linguistics and Literacies: Ideology in Discourses* (4th edn). Routledge.

General Accounting Office (1987) *Bilingual Education. A New Look at the Research Evidence*. General Accounting Office.

Genesee, F. (1983) Bilingual education of majority-language children: The immersion experiments in review. *Applied Psycholinguistics* 4 (1), 1–46.

Genesee, F. (1984) *Historical and Theoretical Foundations of Immersion Education*. California State Department of Education.

Genesee, F. (1987) *Learning Through Two Languages: Studies of Immersion and Bilingual Education*. Newbury House.

Genesee, F. (1992) Second/foreign language immersion and at-risk English-speaking children. *Foreign Language Annals* 25 (3), 199–213.

Genesee, F. (2006) Bilingual first language acquisition in perspective. In P. McCardle and E. Hoff (eds) *Childhood Bilingualism: Research on Infancy through School Age* (pp. 45–67). Multilingual Matters.

Genesee, F. (2013) Insights into bilingual education from research on immersion programs in Canada. In C. Abello-Contesse, P.M. Chandler, M.D. López-Jiménez and R. Chacón-Beltrán (eds) *Bilingual and Multilingual Education in the 21st Century: Building on Experience* (pp. 24–41). Multilingual Matters.

Genesee, F. (2015) Factors that shaped the creation and development of immersion education. In P. Mehisto and F. Genesee (eds) *Building Bilingual Education Systems: Forces, Mechanisms and Counterweights* (pp. 43–57). Cambridge University Press.

Genesee, F. and Fortune, T.W. (2014) Bilingual education and at-risk students. *Journal of Immersion and Content-Based Language Education* 2 (2), 165–180.

Genesee, F., Lindholm-Leary, K., Saunders, W.M. and Christian, D. (2005) English language learners in U.S. schools: An overview of research findings. *Journal of Education for Students Placed at Risk* 10 (4), 363–385.

Genesee, F., Lindholm-Leary, K., Saunders, W.M. and Christian, D. (2006) *Educating English Language Learners: A Synthesis of Research Evidence*. Cambridge University Press.

Gentry, M., Pereira, N., Peters, S., McIntosh, J. and Fugate, M. (2015) *The HOPE Teacher Rating Scale: Involving Teachers in Equitable Identification of Gifted and Talented Students in K-12*. Prufrock Press.

Gentry, M., Gray, A., Whiting, G.W., Maeda, Y. and Pereira, N. (2019) *Gifted Education in the United States: Laws, Access, Equity, and Missingness Across the Country by Locale, Title I School Status, and Race*. Purdue University. https://www.dropbox.com/s/0lxzznnyh5u0jj1/Access%20Denied.pdf.

Gentry, M., Desmet, O.A., Karami, S., Lee, H., Green, C., Cress, A., Chowkase, A. and Gray, A. (2021) Gifted education's legacy of high stakes ability testing: Using measures for identification that perpetuate inequity. *Roeper Review* 43 (4), 242–255.

Gerner de Garcia, B. and Karnopp, L.B. (eds) (2016) *Change and Promise: Bilingual Deaf Education and Deaf Culture in Latin America*. Gallaudet University Press.

Gessner, S., Herbert, T. and Parker, A. (2022) *Report on the Status of B.C. First Nation languages*. First Peoples' Cultural Council. https://fpcc.ca/wp-content/uploads/2023/02/FPCC-LanguageReport-23.02.14-FINAL.pdf.

Ghosh, S.S., Roy, D., Putatunda, T. and Ray, N. (eds) (2024) *Language and Cross-cultural Communication in Travel and Tourism: Strategic Adaptations*. CRC Press/Apple Academic Press.

Giannini, S. (2024) Multilingual education: A key to quality and inclusive learning. *UN Chronicle*, 20 February. https://www.un.org/en/un-chronicle/multilingual-education-key-quality-and-inclusive-learning.

Gibbons, P. (2015) *Scaffolding Language, Scaffolding Learning: Teaching English Language Learners in the Mainstream Classroom* (2nd edn). Heinemann.

Gietz, M.R., Andrews, J.F. and Clark, M.D. (2020) ASL stories with handshape rhyme: An exploratory intervention to support English vocabulary with signing deaf readers. *Archives of Psychology* 4 (2), 1–24.

Glickman, N.S., Crump, C. and Hamerdinger, S. (2020) Language deprivation is a game changer for the clinical specialty of Deaf mental health. *JADARA* 54 (1), 54.

Gold, B.T., Kim, C., Johnson, N.F., Kryscio, R.J. and Smith, C.D. (2013) Lifelong bilingualism maintains neural efficiency for cognitive control in aging. *Journal of Neuroscience* 33 (2), 387–396.

Gold, N. (2006) *Successful Bilingual Schools: Six Effective Programs in California*. San Diego County Office of Education.

Goldenberg, C. (2008) Teaching English language learners: What the research does – and does not – say. *American Educator*, summer, 8–44.

Goldsmith, S.F., El-Baba, M., He, X., Lewis, D.J., Dirani, L.A., Liu, J. and Morton, J.B. (2023) No bilingual advantage in children's attentional disengagement: Congruency and sequential congruency effects in a large sample of monolingual and bilingual children. *Journal of Experimental Child Psychology* 233, 105692.

Goldstein, B.A. (2022) *Bilingual Language Development and Disorders in Spanish–English Speakers* (3rd edn). Brooks Publishing.

Goleman, D. (2006) *Emotional Intelligence: Why It Can Matter More Than IQ* (10th anniversary edn). Bantam Books.

Gollan, T.H. and Acenas, L.-A.R. (2004) What is a TOT? Cognate and translation effects on tip-of-the-tongue states in Spanish–English and Tagalog–English bilinguals. *Journal of Experimental Psychology: Learning, Memory, and Cognition* 30 (1), 246–269.

Gollan, T.H., Montoya, R.I., Cera, C. and Sandoval, T.C. (2008) More use almost always means a smaller frequency effect: Aging, bilingualism, and the weaker links hypothesis. *Journal of Memory and Language* 58 (3), 787–814.

Chen Pichler, D., Kuntze, M., Martin, D., de Quadros, R. and Stump, M. (2023) *Sign Language Acquisition by Deaf and Hearing Children: A Bilingual Introduction*. Gallaudet University Press.

Gomez, G. R. (2024) Judge dismisses State Superintendent's English language learner lawsuit. *AZ Mirror*, March 8. https://azmirror.com/2024/03/08/judge-dismisses-state-superintendents-english-language-learner-suit.

Gómez, L., Freeman, D.E. and Freeman, Y.S. (2005) Dual language education: A promising 50–50 model. *Bilingual Research Journal* 29 (1), 145–164.

Gonçalves, K. and Schluter, A.A. (2024) *Domestic Workers Talk: Language Use and Social Practices in a Multilingual Workplace*. Multilingual Matters.

González, J.M. (1979) Coming of age in bilingual/bicultural education: A historical perspective. In H.T. Trueba and C. Barnett-Mizrahi (eds) *Bilingual Multicultural Education and the Professional: From Theory to Practice*. Newbury House.

González, N., Moll, L.C. and Amanti, C. (eds) (2005) *Funds of Knowledge: Theorizing Practices in Households, Communities, and Classrooms*. Erlbaum.

González, V., Soto-Peña, M., Barton, R. and Palmieri, A. (2024) Theoretical foundations: Conceptualizing sociocultural competence for transformation in dual language and bilingual education. In J.A. Freire, C. Alfaro and E. de Jong (eds) *The Handbook of Dual Language Bilingual Education* (pp. 33–50). Routledge. https://doi.org/10.4324/9781003269076-5.

Gordon, R.A. (1997) Everyday life as an intelligence test: Effects of intelligence and intelligence context. *Intelligence* 24 (1), 203–320.

Gort, M. (2020) Young emergent bilinguals' literate and languaging practices in story retelling. In J. MacSwan and C.J. Faltis (eds) *Codeswitching in the Classroom: Critical Perspectives on Teaching, Learning, Policy, and Ideology* (pp. 162–184). Center for Applied Linguistics and Routledge.

Gorter, D. and Cenoz, J. (2024) *A Panorama of Linguistic Landscape Studies*. Multilingual Matters.

Gottlieb, M. (2024) *Assessing Multilingual Learners: Bridges to Empowerment* (3rd edn). Corwin.

Gottlieb, M. and Ernst-Slavit, G. (2019) Promoting educational equity in assessment practices. In L.C. de Oliveira (ed.) *The Handbook of TESOL in K-12* (pp. 129–148). John Wiley and Sons.

Graddol, D. (2006) *English Next*. British Council.

Graddol, D. (2013) *Profiling English in China: The Pearl River Delta*. Cambridge: Cambridge English Language Assessment. https://www.cambridgeenglish.org/Images/151564-profiling- english-in-china-dg.pdf.

Gramling, D. (2016) *The Invention of Monolingualism*. Bloomsbury Publishing.

Green, D.W., Crinion, J. and Price, C.J. (2007) Exploring cross-linguistic vocabulary effects on brain structures using voxel-based morphometry. *Bilingualism: Language and Cognition* 10 (2), 189–199.

Greene, J. (1998) *A Meta-analysis of the Effectiveness of Bilingual Education*. Thomas Rivera Policy Institute.

Greenwald, B. (2016) Revisiting the memoir: Contesting deaf autonomy and the REAL TRAGEDY of Alexander Graham Bell. In B.H. Greenwald and J. J. Murray (eds) *In Our Own Hands: Essay in Deaf History 1780–1970* (pp. 149–170). Gallaudet University.

Gregerson, M. (2009) Learning to read in Ratanakiri: A case study from northeastern Cambodia. *International Journal of Bilingual Education and Bilingualism* 12 (4), 429–447.

Grin, F. (2005) Linguistic human rights as a source of policy guidelines: A critical assessment. *Journal of Sociolinguistics* 9 (3), 448–460.
Grin, F., Hexel, D. and Schwob, I. (2003) Language diversity and language education: An introduction to the Swiss model. In P. Cuvelier, L.T. Du Plessis and L. Teck (eds) *Multilingualism, Education and Social Integration*. Van Schaik.
Grin, F., Sfreddo, C. and Vaillancourt, F. (2010) *The Economics of the Multilingual Workplace*. Routledge.
Grinberg, E. and Watts, A. (2016) 'Finding Nemo' second film to get Navajo translation, opens in theaters. *CNN*, 18 March.
Grosjean, F. (1997) Processing mixed language: Issues, findings, and models. In A.M. de Groot and J.F. Kroll (eds) *Tutorials in Bilingualism* (pp. 225–254). Lawrence Erlbaum.
Grosjean, F. (2000) Processing mixed languages: Issues, findings, and models. In L. Wei (ed.) *The Bilingualism Reader* (pp. 408–426) Routledge.
Grosjean, F. (2008) *Studying Bilinguals*. Oxford University Press.
Grosjean F. (2010a) *Bilingual: Life and Reality*. Harvard University Press.
Grosjean, F. (2010b) Bilingualism, biculturalism, and deafness. *International Journal of Bilingual Education and Bilingualism* 13 (2), 133–145.
Grosjean, F. (2012) *Bilingual: Life and Reality* (reprint edn). Harvard University Press.
Grosjean, F. (2014) Chasing down those 65%: What percentage of bilinguals in the world today? https://www.psychologytoday.com/us/blog/life-bilingual/201411/chasing-down-those-65.
Grosjean, F. (2016) What is translanguaging? An interview with Ofelia García. https://www.psychologytoday.com/blog/life-bilingual/201603/what-is-translanguaging.
Grosjean, F. (2019) *A Journey in Languages and Cultures: The Life of a Bicultural Bilingual*. Oxford University Press.
Grosjean, F. (2021) *Life as a Bilingual: Knowing and Using Two or More Languages*. Cambridge University Press.
Grosjean, F. and Li, P. (2013) *The Psycholinguistics of Bilingualism*. Wiley-Blackwell.
Guarino, A.J., Echevarría, J., Short, D., Schick, J.E., Forbes, S. and Rueda, R. (2001) The sheltered instruction observation protocol. *Journal of Research in Education* 11 (1), 138–140.
Guilamo, A.S. (2022) Advancing the achievement of dual language learners through program evaluation: A framework for assessing the effectiveness and impact of dual language programs. In M. Machado-Casas, S.I. Maldonado and B.B. Flores (eds) *Assessment and Evaluation in Bilingual Education* (pp. 45–68). Peter Lang.
Gullifer, J.W., Chai, X.J., Whitford, V., Pivneva, I., Baum, S., Klein, D. and Titone, D. (2018) Bilingual experience and resting-state brain connectivity: Impacts of L2 age of acquisition and social diversity of language use on control networks. *Neuropsychologia* 117, 123–134.
Guo, Z. (2014) *Young Children as Intercultural Mediators: Mandarin-Speaking Chinese Families in Britain*. Multilingual Matters.
Guzman, J. (2002) English: New evidence on the effectiveness of bilingual education. *Education Next* 2 (3), 58–65.
Guzman-Orth, D.A., Lopez, A.A. and Tolentino, F. (2019) Exploring the use of a dual language assessment task to assess young English learners. *Language Assessment Quarterly* 16 (4–5), 447–463.
Haas, E., Tran, L., Huang, M. and Yu, A. (2015) *The Achievement Progress of English Learner Students in Arizona*. US Department of Education, Institute of Education Sciences, and National Center for Education Evaluation and Regional Assistance.
Hajar, A. and Manan, S.A. (eds) (2024) *Multilingual Selves and Motivations for Learning Languages other than English in Asian Contexts*. Multilingual Matters.
Haji-Othman, N.A. (2024) English, bilingualism, and national development: The case of Brunei Darussalam. In S. Boun and C.S. Duran (eds) *English Education in Southeast Asian Contexts: Policy, Practice, and Identity* (pp. 25–41). Lexington Books/Rowman and Littlefield.
Hakuta, K. (1986) *The Mirror of Language: The Debate on Bilingualism*. Basic Books.
Hakuta, K. (2001) A critical period for second language acquisition? In D.B. Bailey Jr, J.T. Bruer, F.J. Symons and J.W. Lichtman (eds) *Critical Thinking About Critical Periods*. A Series from the National Center for Early Development and Learning. Paul Brookes Publishing.
Hakuta, K. and d'Andrea, D. (1992) Some properties of bilingual maintenance and loss in Mexican background high-school students. *Applied Linguistics* 13 (1), 72–99.
Hall, M.L., Hall, W.C. and Caselli, N.K. (2019) Deaf children need language, not (just) speech. *First Language* 39 (4), 367–395.
Hall, W.C. (2017) What you don't know can hurt you: The risk of language deprivation by impairing sign language development in deaf children. *Maternal and Child Health Journal* 21 (5), 961–965.

Hamayan, E. and Field, R.F. (eds) (2012) *English Learners at School: A Guide for Administrators*. Caslon.
Hamayan, E.V., Marler, B., Lopez, C.S. and Damico, J. (2013) *Special Education Considerations for English Language Learners: Delivering a Continuum of Services* (2nd edn). Caslon.
Hamayan, E., Marler, B., Lopez, C.S. and Damico, J (2023) *Special Education Considerations for Multilingual Learners* (3rd edn). Brookes.
Hamilton, B. and Clark, M.D.M. (2020) The Deaf mentor program: Benefit to families. *Psychology* 11 (5), 713–736.
Hammerly, H. (1988) French immersion (does it work?) and the 'Development of Bilingual Proficiency' report. *Canadian Modern Language Review* 45 (3), 567–578.
Hamilton, H. (2011) Memory-skills of deaf learners: Implications and applications. *American Annals of the Deaf* 156 (4), 402–423.
Hantzopoulos, M. (2013) Going to Greek school: The politics of religion, identity and culture in community-based Greek language schools. In O. García, Z. Zakharia and B. Otcu (eds) *Bilingual Community Education and Multilingualism: Beyond Heritage Languages in a Global City* (pp. 128–140). Multilingual Matters.
Harris, J. and Cummins, J. (2013) Issues in all-Irish education: Strengthening the case for comparative immersion. In D.M. Singleton, J.A. Fishman, L. Aronin and M. Ó Laoire (eds) *Current Multilingualism: A New Linguistic Dispensation* (pp. 69–98). De Gruyter Mouton.
Harris, M., Terlektsi, E. and Kyle, F.E. (2017) Concurrent and longitudinal predictors of reading for deaf and hearing children in primary school. *Journal of Deaf Studies and Deaf Education* 22 (2), 233–242.
Hartanto, A., Yang, H. and Yang, S. (2018) Bilingualism positively predicts mathematical competence: Evidence from two large-scale studies. *Learning and Individual Differences* 61, 216–227.
Hartshorne, J.K., Tenenbaum, J.B. and Pinker, S. (2018) A critical period for second language acquisition: Evidence from 2/3 million English speakers. *Cognition* 177, 263–277. https://doi.org/10.1016/j.cognition.2018.04.007.
Haug, T., Mann, W., Hoskin, J. and Dumbrill, H. (2020) L1 sign language tests and assessment procedures. In R. Rosen (ed.) *The Routledge Handbook of Sign Language Pedagogy* (pp. 114–128). Routledge.
Hauser, P.C., O'Hearn, A., McKee, M., Steider, A. and Thew, D. (2010) Deaf epistemology: Deafhood and deafness. *American Annals of the Deaf* 154 (5), 486–492.
Hayes, D. (2022) *Early Language Learning in Context: A Critical Socioeducational Perspective*. Multilingual Matters.
Hederberg, U. and Lane, H. (2020) *Elements of French and Deaf Heritage*. Gallaudet University Press.
Heineke, A.J. (2020) Language policy in practice: Implementing the Seal of Biliteracy in state and local contexts. In A.J. Heineke and K.J. Davin (eds) *The Seal of Biliteracy: Case Studies and Considerations for Policy Implementation* (pp. 35–48). Information Age Publishing.
Heineke, A.J. and Davin, K.J. (eds) (2020) *The Seal of Biliteracy: Case Studies and Considerations for Policy Implementation*. Information Age Publishing.
Heineke, A.J., Davin, K.J. and Elliott, J. (2024) The Seal of Biliteracy and dual language bilingual education. In J.A. Freire, C. Alfaro and E. de Jong (eds) *The Handbook of Dual Language Bilingual Education* (pp. 337–346). Routledge.
Heller, M. (2003) *Crosswords: Language, Education and Ethnicity in French Ontario*. Walter de Gruyter.
Heller, M. (2006) *Linguistic Minorities and Modernity: A Sociolinguistic Ethnography* (2nd edn). Longman.
Heller, M., Pujolar, J. and Duchéne, A. (2014) Linguistic commodification in tourism. *Journal of Sociolinguistics* 18 (4), 539–566.
Helman, L., Ittner, A.C. and McMaster, K.L. (2020) *Assessing Language and Literacy with Bilingual Students: Practices to Support English Learners*. Guilford Press.
Henderson, K.I. and Palmer, D.K. (2015) Teacher and student language practices and ideologies in a third-grade two-way dual language program implementation. *International Multilingual Research Journal* 9 (2), 75–92. https://doi.org/10.1080/19313152.2015.1016827.
Henderson, K.I. and Palmer, D.K. (2020) *Dual Language Bilingual Education: Teacher Cases and Perspectives on Large-Scale Implementation*. Multilingual Matters.
Henderson, K.I. and Sayer, P. (2020) Translanguaging in the classroom: Implications for effective pedagogy for bilingual youth in Texas. In J. McSwan and C.J. Faltis (eds) *Codeswitching in the Classroom: Critical Perspectives on Teaching, Learning, Policy, and Ideology* (pp. 207–224). Routledge.
Henrich, J., Heine, S.J. and Norenzayan, A. (2010) Most people are not WEIRD. *Nature* 466 (7302), 29.
Henry, A. and Lamb, M. (2019) L2 motivation and digital technologies. In M. Lamb, K. Csizér, A. Henry and S. Ryan (eds) *The Palgrave Handbook of Motivation for Language Learning* (pp. 21–37). Palgrave Macmillan.

Heredia, R.R. and Brown, J.M. (2013) Bilingual memory. In T.K. Bhatia and W.C. Ritchie (eds) *The Handbook of Bilingualism and Multilingualism* (2nd edn, pp. 269–291). John Wiley and Sons.

Hernandez, B., Allen, T.E., and Morere, D.A. (2023) ASL developmental trends among deaf children, ages birth to five. *Journal of Deaf Studies and Deaf Education* 28 (1), 7–20.

Herrera, L.J.P. (ed.) (2022) *English and Students with Limited or Interrupted Formal Education: Global Perspectives on Teacher Preparation and Classroom Practices*. Springer.

Herzig, M. and Allen, T.E. (2023) Deaf children's engagement with American Sign Language-English bilingual storybook apps. *Journal of Deaf Studies and Deaf Education* 28 (1), 53–67.

Herzig, M. and Malzkuhn, M. (2015) Bilingual storybook apps: An interactive reading experience for children. *Odyssey: New Directions in Deaf Education* 16, 40–44.

Heugh, K. and Skutnabb-Kangas, T. (2010) *Multilingual Education Works: From the Periphery to the Centre*. Orient BlackSwan.

Heugh, K., Benson, C., Bogale, B. and Yohannes, M.A.G. (2007) *Final Report: Study on Medium of Instruction in Primary Schools in Ethiopia*. Commissioned by the Ministry of Education, Ethiopia.

Hibbert, L. and van der Walt, C. (eds) (2014) *Multilingual Universities in South Africa: Reflecting Society in Higher Education*. Multilingual Matters.

Hickey, T. (1997) *Early Immersion Education in Ireland: Na Naionrai*. Institiuid Tean-geolaiochta Eireann.

Hickey, T. (2001) Mixing beginners and native speakers in minority language immersion: Who is immersing whom? *Canadian Modern Language Review/La Revue Canadienne des Langues Vivantes* 57 (3), 443–474.

Hickey, T. (2007) Children's language networks in minority language immersion: What goes in may not come out. *Language and Education* 21 (1), 46–65.

Hickey, T., Lewis, G. and Baker, C. (2013) How deep is your immersion? Policy and practice in Welsh-medium preschools with children from different language backgrounds. *International Journal of Bilingual Education and Bilingualism* 17 (2), 1–20.

Hile, A.E. (2009) Deaf children's acquisition of novel fingerspelled words. Unpublished doctoral dissertation, University of Colorado.

Hill, R. and May, S. (2014) Balancing the language in Māori-Medium education in Aotearoa/New Zealand. In D. Gorter, V. Zenotz and J. Cenoz (eds) *Minority Languages and Multilingual Education* (pp. 159–176). Springer.

Hinton, K.A. (2015) 'We only teach in English': An examination of bilingual-in-name-only classrooms. *Research on Preparing Inservice Teachers to Work Effectively with Emergent Bilinguals* 24, 265–289. https://doi.org/10.1108/S1479-368720150000024012.

Hinton, L. (2017) Learning and teaching endangered indigenous languages. In S. May (ed.) *Encyclopedia of Language and Education, Vol. 4: Second and Foreign Language Education* (3rd edn, pp. 213–223). Springer.

Hinton, L. (2018) Approaches to and strategies for language revitalization. In K.L. Rehg and L. Campbell (eds) *The Oxford Handbook of Endangered Languages* (pp. 443–465). Oxford University Press.

Hinton, L., Huss, L. and Roche, G. (eds) (2022) *The Routledge Handbook of Language Revitalization*. Routledge.

Hirshorn, E. (2011) *Visual Selective Attention and Deafness*. NSF Science of Learning Center on Visual Language and Visual Learning Research Brief No. 3. Gallaudet University.

Hiver, P. and Papi, M. (2019) Complexity theory and L2 motivation. In M. Lamb, K. Csizér, A. Henry and S. Ryan (eds) *The Palgrave Handbook of Motivation for Language Learning* (pp. 117–137). Palgrave Macmillan.

Hoffman, D.L., Wolsey, J.L.A., Andrews, J.F. and Clark, M.D. (2017) Translanguaging supports reading with deaf adult bilinguals: A qualitative approach. *Qualitative Report* 22 (7), 1925–1944.

Hoffman, E. (1989) *Lost in Translation: A Life in a New Language*. Dutton.

Hoffmann, C. (2000) Balancing language planning and language rights: Catalonia's uneasy juggling act. *Journal of Multilingual and Multicultural Development* 21 (5), 425–441.

Holcomb, L. (2023) ASL rhyme, rhythm, and phonological awareness for deaf children. *Perspectives on Early Childhood Psychology and Education* 5 (2), article 3. https://doi.org/10.58948/2834-8257.1058.

Holcomb, T.K. (2010) Deaf epistemology: The deaf way of knowing. *American Annals of the Deaf* 154 (5), 471–478.

Holcomb, T.K. (2013) *Introduction to American Deaf Culture*. Oxford University Press.

Hollywood Reporter (2015) Donald Trump: 'While we're in this nation, we should be speaking English'. https://www.hollywoodreporter.com/news/donald-trump-speak-english-spanish-820215.

Holm, A. and Holm, W. (1990) Rock Point, a Navajo way to go to school: A valediction. *Annals of the American Academy of Political and Social Science* 508 (1), 170–184.

Holmström, I. and Schönström, K. (2018) Deaf lecturers' translanguaging in a higher education setting. A multimodal multilingual perspective. *Applied Linguistics Review* 9 (1), 90–111.

Hong, P. and Pawan, F. (2014) *The Pedagogy and Practice of Western-Trained Chinese English Language Teachers*. Routledge.

Hopewell, S. and Escamilla, K. (2015) How does a holistic perspective on (bi/multi)literacy help educators to address the demands of the Common Core State Standards for English language learners/emergent bilinguals? In G. Valdés, K. Menken and M. Castro (eds) *Common Core Bilingual and English Language Learners: A Resource for Educators* (pp. 39–40). Caslon Publishing.

Hopewell, S., Slavick, J. and Escamilla, K. (2024) Toward a biliterate pedagogy. In J.A. Freire, C. Alfaro and E. de Jong (eds) *The Handbook of Dual Language Bilingual Education* (pp. 473–493). Routledge. https://doi.org/10.4324/9781003269076-40.

Hornberger, N.H. (2006) Voice and biliteracy in indigenous language revitalization: Contentious educational practices in Quechua, Guarani, and Māori contexts. *Journal of Language, Identity, and Education* 5 (4), 277–292.

Hornberger, N.H. (2008) Continua of biliteracy. In A. Creese, M.M. Martin and N.H. Hornberger (eds) *Encyclopedia of Language and Education, Vol. 9: Ecology of Language* (pp. 275–290). Springer.

Hornberger, N.H. (2009) Multilingual education policy and practice: Ten certainties (grounded in Indigenous experience). *Language Teaching* 42 (2), 197–211.

Hornberger, N.H. (2013) Bilingual literacy. In C.A. Chapelle (ed.) *The Encyclopedia of Applied Linguistics*. Blackwell. https://doi.org/10.1002/9781405198431.wbeal0095.

Hornberger, N.H. (ed.) (2017) *Honoring Richard Ruiz and His Work on Language Planning and Bilingual Education*. Multilingual Matters

Hornberger, N.H. and De Korne, H. (2018) Is revitalization through education possible? In L. Hinton, L. Huss and G. Roche (eds) *The Routledge Handbook of Language Revitalization* (pp. 94–104). Routledge.

Hornberger, N.H. and King, K.A. (2001) Reversing Quechua language shift in South America. In J. Fishman (ed.) *Can Threatened Languages Be Saved?* (pp. 166–194). Multilingual Matters.

Hornberger, N.H. and Pütz, M. (eds) (2006) *Language Loyalty, Language Planning, and Language Revitalization: Recent Writings and Reflections from Joshua A. Fishman*. Multilingual Matters.

Horner, K. and Dailey-O'Cain, J. (eds) (2020) *Multilingualism, (Im)mobilities and Spaces of Belonging*. Multilingual Matters.

Horup, B., Lessof, C. and Boyd, J. (2021) *Numbers of Jewish Children in Jewish Schools, 2018/19 to 2020/21*. Institute for Jewish Policy Research. https://www.jpr.org.uk/reports/numbers-jewish-children-jewish-schools-201819-202021.

Housen, A. (2002) Processes and outcomes in the European Schools model of multilingual education. *Bilingual Research Journal* 26 (1), 45–64.

Howard, E.R., Christian, D. and Genesee, F. (2004) *The Development of Bilingualism and Biliteracy from Grade 3 to 5: A Summary of Findings from the CAL/CREDE Study of Two-Way Immersion Education*. University of California at Santa Cruz: CREDA (Center for Research on Education, Diversity and Excellence).

Howard, E.R., Sugarman, J. and Coburn, C. (2006) *Adapting the Sheltered Instruction Observation Protocol (SIOP) for Two-Way Immersion Education: An Introduction to the TWIOP*. Center for Applied Linguistics.

Howard, E.R., Lindholm-Leary, K., Rogers, D., Olague, N., Medina, J., Kennedy, B., Sugarman, J. and Christian, D. (2018) *Guiding Principles for Dual Language Education* (3rd edn). Center for Applied Linguistics.

Hrastinski, I. and Wilbur, R.B. (2016) Academic achievement of deaf and hard-of-hearing students in an ASL/English bilingual program. *Journal of Deaf Studies and Deaf Education* 21 (2), 156–170.

Huang, B.H. (2014) The effects of age on second language grammar and speech production. *Journal of Psycholinguistic Research* 43 (4), 397–420.

Huang, B.H. (2015) A synthesis of empirical research on the linguistic outcomes of early foreign language instruction. *International Journal of Multilingualism* (online first) 13 (3), 257–273. https://doi.org/10.1080/14790718.2015.1066792.

Huang, B.H. (2019) The relationship between oral language and reading in English-only, proficient bilingual, and emergent bilingual adolescents. In S. Keengwe and G. Onchwari (eds) *Handbook of Research on Engaging Immigrant Families and Promoting Academic Success for English Language Learners* (pp. 112–132). IGI Global. https://psycnet.apa.org/doi/10.4018/978-1-5225-8283-0.ch006.

Huang, K.J. (2018) On bilinguals' development of metalinguistic awareness and its transfer to L3 learning: The role of language characteristics. *International Journal of Bilingualism* 22 (3), 330–349.

Hubbard, G.G. (1871) *Thirty-Fourth Annual Report of the Clarke Institution for Deaf-Mutes*. In the *Thirty-Fourth Annual Report of the Board of [Massachusetts] Board of Education, with the Thirty-Fourth Annual Report of the Secretary of the Board*. Wright and Potter, State Printers.

Hull, R. and Vaid, J. (2007) Bilingual language lateralization: A meta-analytic tale of two hemispheres. *Neuropsychologia* 45 (9), 1987–2008.

Hult, F. (2013) Ecology and multilingual education. In C.A. Chapelle (ed.) *The Encyclopedia of Applied Linguistics*. Blackwell. https://doi.org/10.1002/9781405198431.wbeal0354.

Hult, F. and Johnson, D.C. (eds) (2015) *Research Methods in Language Policy and Planning: A Practical Guide*. Wiley-Blackwell.

Humphries, T. (1977) Communicating across cultures (deaf-hearing) and language learning. Unpublished doctoral dissertation, Union Institute and University, Cincinnati, OH.

Humphries, T. (2004) The modern Deaf self: Indigenous practices and educational imperatives. In B. Brueg-Gemann (ed.) *Literacy and Deaf People: Cultural and Contextual Contexts* (pp. 29–40). Gallaudet University Press.

Humphries, T. (2013) Schooling in American Sign Language: A paradigm shift from a deficit model to a bilingual model in deaf education. *Berkeley Review of Education* 4 (1), 7–33.

Humphries, T. (2016) Beyond bilingual education: Transformational deaf education. Paper presented at the 42nd Annual ACE-DHH Conference, New York, NY.

Humphries, T. and Allen, B.M. (2008) Reorganizing teacher preparation in deaf education. *Sign Language Studies* 8 (2), 160–180.

Humphries, T. and MacDougall, F. (1999) 'Chaining' and other links: Making connections between American Sign Language and English in two types of school settings. *Visual Anthropology Review* 15 (2), 84–94.

Humphries, T., Kushalnagar, P., Mathur, G., Napoli, D.J., Padden, C., Rathmann, C. and Smith, S.R. (2012) Language acquisition for deaf children: Reducing the harms of zero tolerance to the use of alternative approaches. *Harm Reduction Journal* 9, 1–9.

Humphries, T., Kushalnagar, P., Mathur, G., Napoli, D.J., Padden, C. and Rathmann, C. (2014a) Ensuring language acquisition for deaf children: What linguists can do. *Language* 90 (2), e31–e52.

Humphries, T., Kushalnagar, P., Mathur, G. et al. (2014b) What medical education can do to ensure robust language development in deaf children. *Medical Science Educator* 24, 409–419.

Humphries, T., Kushalnagar, P., Mathur, G., Napoli, D.J., Padden, C., Rathmann, C. and Smith, S. (2016a) Language choices for deaf infants: Advice for parents regarding sign languages. *Clinical Pediatrics* 55 (6), 513–517.

Humphries, T., Kushalnagar, P., Mathur, G. and Smith, S. (2016b) Avoiding linguistic neglect of deaf children. *Social Service Review* 90 (4), 589–619.

Humphries, T., Kushalnagar, P., Mathur, G., Napoli, D.J., Padden, C., Rathmann, C. and Smith, S. (2017) Discourses of prejudice in the professions: The case of sign languages. *Journal of Medical Ethics* 43 (9), 648–652.

Humphries, T., Kushalnagar, P., Mathur, G., Napoli, D.J., Rathmann, C. and Smith, S. (2019) Support for parents of deaf children: Common questions and informed, evidence-based answers. *International Journal of Pediatric Otorhinolaryngology* 118, 134–142.

Humphries, T., Kushalnagar, P., Mathur, G., Napoli, D.J. and Rathmann, C. (2020) Global regulatory review needed for cochlear implants: A call for FDA leadership. *Maternal and Child Health Journal* 24, 1345–1359.

Humphries, T., Mathur, G., Napoli, D.J., Padden, C. and Rathmann, C. (2022) Deaf children need rich language input from the start: Support in advising parents. *Children* 9 (11), 1609.

Humphries, T., Mathur, G., Napoli, D.J. and Rathmann, C. (2024) An approach designed to fail deaf children and their parents and how to change it. *Harm Reduction Journal* 21 (1), 1–8.

Hymes, D. (1972) On communicative competence. In J.B. Pride and J. Holmes (eds) *Sociolinguistics* (pp. 269–293). Penguin Books.

Ianco-Worrall, A.D. (1972) Bilingualism and cognitive development. *Child Development* 43, 1390–1400.

Iatcu, T. (2000) Teaching English as a third language to Hungarian–Romanian bilinguals. In J. Cenoz and U. Jessner (eds) *English in Europe: The Acquisition of a Third Language* (pp. 236–247). Multilingual Matters. https://doi.org/10.21832/9781800417991-014.

Igboanusi, H. and Peter, L. (2015) The language-in-education politics in Nigeria. *International Journal of Bilingual Education and Bilingualism* 19 (5), 563–578. https://doi.org/10.1080/13670050.2015.1031633.

International Baccalaureate Organization (2014) *Language Policy: Information on the International Baccalaureate's Support for Languages, Language Courses and Languages of Instruction*. International Baccalaureate Organization.

International Literacy Association (2019) *Literacy Leadership Brief: The Role of Bilingualism in Improving Literacy Achievement*. https://literacyworldwide.org/docs/default-source/where-we- stand/ila-role-bilingualism-improving-literacy-achievement.pdf.

Isola, R.R. and Cummins, J. (2020) *Transforming Sanchez School: Shared Leadership, Equity, and Excellence*. Caslon Publishing.

Jacobson, R. (1995) Allocating two languages as a key factor in a bilingual methodology. In R. Jacobson and C. Faltis (eds) *Language Distribution Issues in Bilingual Schooling* (pp. 3–17). Multilingual Matters.

Jaffe, A. (2007) Codeswitching and stance: Issues in interpretation. *Journal of Language, Identity, and Education* 6 (1), 53–77.

Janks, H. (2013) Critical literacy. In C.A. Chapelle (ed.) *The Encyclopedia of Applied Linguistics*. Blackwell. https://doi.org/10.1002/9781405198431.wbeal0281.

Jaspers, J. (2017) Diglossia and beyond. In O. García, N. Flores and M. Spotti (eds) *The Oxford Handbook of Language and Society* (pp. 179–196). Oxford University Press.

Jaworski, A. and Thurlow, C. (2010) Language and globalizing habitus of tourism: Toward a sociolinguistics of fleeting relationships. In N. Coupland (ed.) *Handbook of Language and Globalization* (pp. 255–286). Wiley-Blackwell.

Jensen, B. and Thompson, G.A. (2020) Equity in teaching academic language – An interdisciplinary approach. *Theory into Practice* 59 (1), 1–7. https://doi.org/10.1080/00405841.2019.1665417.

Jessner, U. (2008) Teaching third languages: Findings, trends and challenges. *Language Teaching* 41 (1), 15–56.

Jiang, N. (2023) *The Study of Bilingual Language Processing*. Oxford University Press.

Johnson, D.C. (2010) Implementational and ideological spaces in bilingual education language policy. *International Journal of Bilingual Education and Bilingualism* 13 (1), 61–79.

Johnson, R.K. and Swain, M. (1994) From core to content: Bridging the L2 proficiency gap in late immersion. *Language and Education* 8 (4), 211–229.

Johnson, R.K. and Swain, M. (1997) *Immersion Education: International Perspectives*. Cambridge University Press.

Johnson, R.K., Liddell, S. and Erting, C. (1989) *Unlocking the Curriculum: Principles for Achieving Access in Deaf Education*. Working Paper 89–3. Gallaudet University.

Johnstone, R. (2002) *Immersion in a Second or Additional Language at School: A Review of the International Research*. Scottish CILT (Centre for Information on Language Teaching).

Jones, D.V. and Martin-Jones, M. (2004) Bilingual education and language revitalization in Wales: Past achievements and current issues. In J.W. Tollefson and A.B.M. Tsui (eds) *Medium of Instruction Policies. Which Agenda? Whose Agenda?* (pp. 43–70). Erlbaum.

Jones, G. (2012) Language planning in its historical context in Brunei Darussalam. In E. Ling and A. Hashim (eds) *English in Southeast Asia* (pp. 175–188). John Benjamins.

Jones, G. (2013) A cross-cultural and cross-linguistic analysis of deaf reading practices in China: Case studies using teacher interviews and classroom observations. Dissertation, University of Illinois at Urbana-Champaign.

Jones, G.M. (2015) Bilingual and multilingual education in Brunei and Malaysia: Policies and practices. In W.E. Wright, S. Boun and O. García (eds) *Handbook of Bilingual and Multilingual Education* (pp. 529–539). Wiley-Blackwell.

Jones, J.J. (1918) One hundred years of history in the education of the deaf in America and its present status. *American Annals of the Deaf* 63 (1), 1–47.

Jones, W.R. (1959) *Bilingualism and Intelligence*. University of Wales Press.

Jones, W.R. (1966) *Bilingualism in Welsh Education*. University of Wales Press.

Jurjevich, J. (2019) *Race/Ethnicity and the 2020 Census*. https://www.census2020now.org/faces-blog/same-sex-households-2020-census-r3976.

Juvonen, P. and Källkvist, M. (eds) (2021a) *Pedagogical Translanguaging: Theoretical, Methodological and Empirical Perspectives*. Multilingual Matters.

Juvonen, P. and Källkvist, M. (2021b) Pedagogical translanguaging: Theoretical, methodological and empirical perspectives – An introduction. In P. Juvonen and M. Källkvist (eds) *Pedagogical Translanguaging: Theoretical, Methodological and Empirical Perspectives* (pp. 1–6). Multilingual Matters.

Kachru, B.B. (2005) *Asian Englishes: Beyond the Canon*. Oxford University Press.

Kachru, B.B. (2020) World Englishes and cultural wars. In C.L. Nelson, Z.G. Proshina and D.R. Davis (eds) *The Handbook of World Englishes* (2nd edn, pp. 447–472). Wiley Blackwell.

Kagan, O., Carreira, M. and Chik, C.H. (eds) (2017) *The Routledge Handbook of Heritage Language Education: From Innovation to Program Building*. Routledge.

Kalaja, P. and Melo-Pfeifer, S. (2019) Introduction. In P. Kalaja and S. Melo-Pfeifer (eds) *Visualising Multilingual Lives: More Than Words* (pp. 1–14). Multilingual Matters.

Kalaja, P. and Melo-Pfeifer, S. (eds) (2025) *Visualising Language Students and Teachers as Multilinguals: Advancing Social Justice in Education*. Multilingual Matters.

Kalantzis, M. and Cope, B. (2013) Multiliteracies in education. In C.A. Chapelle (ed.) *Encyclopedia of Applied Linguistics*. Blackwell Publishing.

Kaminksy, J. (2014) Last native speaker of Klallam language dies in Washington state. Reuters, 6 February. https://www.reuters.com/article/us-usa-klallam-death/last-native-speaker-of-klallam-language-dies-in-washington-state-idUSBREA1605W20140207/.

Kannapell, B. (1980) Personal awareness and advocacy in the deaf community. In C. Baker and R. Battison (eds) *Sign Language and the Deaf Community: Essays in Honor of William C. Stokoe* (pp. 105–116). National Association of the Deaf.

Kanno, Y. (2003) Imagined communities, school visions, and the education of bilingual students in Japan. *Journal of Language, Identity, and Education* 2 (4), 285–300.

Kanno, Y. and Norton, B. (2003) Imagined communities and educational possibilities: Introduction. *Journal of Language, Identity and Education* 2 (4), 241–249. https://doi.org/10.1207/S15327701JLIE0204_1.

Kanno, Y., Rios-Aguilar, C. and Bunch, G.C. (2024) English learners? Emergent bilinguals? Multilingual learners? Goals, contexts, and consequences in labeling students. *TESOL Journal* 15 (3), e797. https://doi.org/10.1002/tesj.797.

Karmani, S. and Pennycook, A. (2005) Islam, English, and 9/11. *Journal of Language, Identity, and Education* 4 (2), 157–172.

Kayi-Aydar, H. (2024) *Critical Applied Linguistics: An Intersectional Introduction*. Routledge.

Kay-Raining Bird, E. (2007) The case for bilingualism in children with Down syndrome. In R. Paul and R.S. Chapman (eds) *Language Disorders from a Developmental Perspective: Essays in Honor of Robin S. Chapman*. Lawrence Erlbaum.

Kay-Raining Bird, E., Cleave, P., Trudeau, N., Thordardottir, E., Sutton, A. and Thorpe, A. (2005) The language abilities of bilingual children with Down syndrome. *American Journal of Speech-Language Pathology* 14 (3), 187–199.

Kay-Raining Bird, E., Genesee, F. and Verhoeven, L. (2016) Bilingualism in children with developmental disorders. *Journal of Communication Disorders* 63, 1–14.

Keijzer, M.C. and Schmid, M.S. (2016) Individual differences in cognitive control advantages of elderly late Dutch-English bilinguals. *Linguistic Approaches to Bilingualism* 6 (1–2), 64–85.

Kellman, S.G. (2020) *Nimble Tongues: Studies in Literary Translingualism*. Purdue University Press.

Kelly-Holmes, H. (2019) Multilingualism and technology: A review of developments in digital communication from monolingualism to idiolingualism. *Annual Review of Applied Linguistics* 39, 24–39. https://doi.org/10.1017/S0267190519000102.

Kelly-Holmes, H. and Pietikäinen, S. (2014) Commodifying Sámi culture in an indigenous tourism site. *Journal of Sociolinguistics* 18 (4), 518–538. https://doi.org/10.1111/josl.12092.

Kendi, I.X. (2019) *How To Be an Antiracist*. One Word/Random House.

Kenfield, Y.H. (2021) *Enacting and Envisioning Decolonial Forces while Sustaining Indigenous Language: Bilingual College Students in the Andes*. Multilingual Matters.

Kenner, C. (2004) *Becoming Literate: Young Children Learning Different Writing Systems*. Trentham.

Kenner, C. and Gregory, E. (2012) Becoming biliterate. In J. Larson and J. Marsh (eds) *The SAGE Handbook of Early Childhood Literacy* (pp. 364–378). Sage.

Kharkhurin, A.V. (2009) The role of bilingualism in creative performance on divergent thinking and Invented Alien Creatures tests. *Journal of Creative Behavior* 43 (1), 59–71.

Kharkhurin, A.V. (2015) Bilingualism and creativity: An educational perspective. In W.E. Wright, S. Boun and O. García (eds) *Handbook of Bilingual and Multilingual Education* (pp. 38–55). Wiley-Blackwell.

Kharkhurin, A.V. (2018) Bilingualism and creativity. In R.R. Heredia and J. Altarriba (eds) *An Introduction to Bilingualism: Principles and Processes* (pp. 159–189). Routledge.

Kiaer, J. (2023) *Multimodal Communication in Young Multilingual Children: Learning Beyond Words*. Multilingual Matters.

Kibler, A.K., Walqui, A., Bunch, G.C. and Faltis, C.J. (eds) (2024) *Equity in Multilingual Schools and Communities: Celebrating the Contributions of Guadalupe Valdés*. Multilingual Matters.

Kim, M. (2016) A North Korean defector's journey through the identity-transformation process. *Journal of Language, Identity and Education* 16 (1), 3–16. https://doi.org/10.1080/15348458.2015.1090764.

Kim, S. (2022) Emergent bilinguals' literacy and language use across different contexts. Dissertation, Purdue University Graduate School. https://doi.org/10.25394/PGS.19674402.v1.

Kim, S. and Song, K.H. (2019) Designing a community translanguaging space within a family literacy project. *The Reading Teacher* 73 (3), 267–279. https://doi.org/10.1002/trtr.1820.

Kim, T.K. (2022) *Understanding Success and Failure in Adult ESL: Superación vs Dropout of Adult English Learners in the US*. Multilingual Matters.

King, K.A., Fogle, L.W. and Logan-Terry, A. (2008) Family language policy. *Language and Linguistics Compass* 2 (5), 907–922. https://doi.org/10.1111/j.1749-818X.2008.00076.x.

Kiramba, L.K. (2017) Translanguaging in the writing of emergent multilinguals. *International Multilingual Research Journal* 11 (2), 115–130. https://doi.org/10.1080/19313152.2016.1239457.

Kirkpatrick, A. (ed.) (2010) *The Routledge Handbook of World Englishes*. Routledge.

Kirsch, C. and Mortini, S. (2023) Engaging in and creatively reproducing translanguaging practices with peers: A longitudinal study with three-year-olds in Luxembourg. *International Journal of Bilingual Education and Bilingualism* 26 (8), 943–959. https://doi.org/10.1080/13670050.2021.1999387.

Kleyn, T. and Hunt, V. (2024) Dos Puentes Elementary: An introduction. In T. Kleyn, V. Hunt, A. Jaar, R. Madrigal and C. Villegas (eds) *Lessons from a Dual Language Bilingual School: Celebrando una década de Dos Puentes Elementary* (pp. 1–16). Multilingual Matters.

Kleyn, T., Hunt, V., Jaar, A., Madrigal, R. and Villegas, C. (eds) (2024) *Lessons from a Dual Language Bilingual School: Celebrando una década de Dos Puentes Elementary*. Multilingual Matters.

Kloss, H. (1998) *The American Bilingual Tradition*. Center for Applied Linguistics and Delta Systems (original publication, 1977).

Knoors, H. and Marschark, M. (2012) Language planning for the 21st century: Revisiting bilingual language policy for deaf children. *Journal of Deaf Studies and Deaf Education* 17 (3), 291–305.

Knoors, H., Brons, M. and Marschark, M. (eds) (2019) *Deaf Education Beyond the Western World: Context, Challenges, and Prospects*. Oxford University Press.

Koda, K. and Zehler, A.M. (2008) *Learning to Read Across Languages: Cross-linguistic Relationships in First- and Second-Language Literacy Development*. Routledge.

Kolers, P.A. (1963) Interlingual word associations. *Journal of Verbal Learning and Verbal Behavior* 2 (4), 291–300.

Komesaroff, L.R. (2003) Deaf education and underlying structures of power in communication. *Australian Journal of Communication* 30 (3), 43–59.

Koran, M. (2020) Anxiety looms for thousands of migrant teachers as Trump administration pushes 'zero tolerance' enforcement of Visa program. https://www.the74million.org/article/anxiety-looms-for-thousands-of-migrant-teachers-as-trump-administration-pushes-zero-tolerance-enforcement-of-visa-program.

Kormos, J. and Ratajczak, M. (2019) *Time Extension and the Second Language Reading Performance of Children with Different First Language Literacy Profiles*. ARAGs Research Reports. British Council. https://www.britishcouncil.org/time-extension-and-second-language-reading-performance-children-different-first-language-literacy.

Kormos, J. and Smith, A.M. (2024) *Teaching Languages to Students with Specific Learning Differences* (2nd edn). Multilingual Matters.

Košak-Babuder, M., Kormos, J., Ratajczak, M. and Pižorn, K. (2019) The effect of read-aloud assistance on the text comprehension of dyslexic and non-dyslexic English language learners. *Language Testing* 36 (1), 51–75. https://doi.org/10.1177/0265532218756946.

Kose, H. and Uluer, P. (2020) The uses of technology in L1 and L2/Ln sign language pedagogy. In R. Rosen (ed.) *The Routledge Handbook of Sign Language Pedagogy* (pp. 232–338). Routledge.

Kostromitina, M. (2024) From 2020 to 2024: A look at the evolution of the DET. Duolingo. https://duolingo-testcenter.s3.amazonaws.com/media/resources/Evolution-of-DET-2024.pdf.

Kousaie, S., Chai, X.J., Sander, K.M. and Klein, D. (2017) Simultaneous learning of two languages from birth positively impacts intrinsic functional connectivity and cognitive control. *Brain and Cognition* 117, 49–56.

Kowalski, K. and Lo, Y.F. (2001) The influence of perceptual features, ethnic labels, and sociocultural information on the development of ethnic/racial bias in young children. *Journal of Cross-Cultural Psychology* 32 (4), 444–455.

Krashen, S.D. (1999) *Condemned Without a Trial: Bogus Arguments Against Bilingual Education*. Heinemann.

Krashen, S.D. (2002) Developing academic language: Early L1 reading and later L2 reading. *International Journal of the Sociology of Language* 155 (156), 143–151.

Krashen, S.D. (2004a) The acquisition of academic English by children in two-way programs: What does the research say? Paper presented at the NABE Review of Research and Practice, Albuquerque, NM.

Krashen, S.D. (2004b) *Power of Reading: Insights from the Research* (2nd edn). Heinemann.
Kraus, P.A. (2024) Language, belonging, and citizenship. In M. Gazzola, F. Grin, L. Cardinal and K. Heugh (eds) *The Routledge Handbook of Language Policy and Planning*. Routledge. https://doi.org/10.4324/9780429448843-8.
Kroll, J.F. and De Groot, A.M. (eds) (2009) *Handbook of Bilingualism: Psycholinguistic Approaches*. Oxford University Press.
Kroskrity, P.V. (2010) Language ideologies: Evolving perspectives. In J. Jaspers, J.-O. Ostman, and J. Verschueren (eds) *Society and Language Use* (pp. 192–211). John Benjamins.
Kuo, L.J., Ramirez, G., de Marin, S., Kim, T.J. and Unal-Gezer, M. (2017) Bilingualism and morphological awareness: A study with children from general education and Spanish–English dual language programs. *Educational Psychology* 37 (2), 94–111.
Kurz, C., Golos, D., Kuntze, M., Henner, J. and Scott, J. (2021) *Guidelines for Multilingual Deaf Education Teacher Preparation Programs*. Gallaudet University Press.
Kushki, A. and Nassaji, H. (2024) L2 reading assessment from a sociocultural theory perspective: The contributions of dynamic assessment. *Education Sciences* 14 (4), 342. https://doi.org/10.3390/educsci14040342.
Kusters, A. (2019) Deaf and hearing signers' multimodal and translingual practices. *Applied Linguistics Review* 10 (1), 1–8.
Kusters, A., De Meulder, M. and O'Brien, D. (2017) *Innovations in Deaf Studies: The Role of Deaf Scholars*. Oxford University Press.
Kusters, A., Moriarty, E., le Maire, A., Iver, S. and Emery, S. (2024) *Deaf Mobility Studies: Exploring International Networks, Tourism, and Migration*. Gallaudet University Press.
Kuteeva, M. (2023) *Tension-Filled English at the Multilingual University: A Bakhtinian Perspective*. Multilingual Matters.
Kwon, J. (2022) *Understanding the Transnational Lives and Literacies of Immigrant Children*. Teachers College Press.
Lachance, J.R. and Honigsfeld, A. (2023) *Collaboration and Co-Teaching for Dual Language Learners: Transforming Programs for Multilingualism and Equity*. Corwin.
Ladd, P. (2003) *Understanding Deaf Culture: In Search of Deafhood*. Multilingual Matters.
Ladd, P. (2005) Deafhood: A concept stressing possibilities, not deficits. *Scandinavian Journal of Public Health* 33 (Suppl. 66), 12–17.
Ladd, P. (2022) *The Unrecognized Curriculum: Seeing Through New Eyes, Deaf Culture and Deaf Pedagogies*. Dawn Sign Press.
Laine, M. and Lehtonen, M. (2018) Cognitive consequences of bilingualism: Where to go from here? *Language, Cognition and Neuroscience* 33 (9), 1205–1212.
Lamb, M., Csizér, K., Henry, A. and Ryan, S. (eds) (2019) *The Palgrave Handbook of Motivation for Language Learning*. Palgrave Macmillan.
Lambert, W.E. (1974) Culture and language as factors in learning and education. In F.E. Aboud and R.D. Meade (eds) *Cultural Factors in Learning and Education*. 5th Western Washington Symposium on Learning, Bellingham, WA.
Lambert, W.E. and Tucker, G.R. (1972) *Bilingual Education of Children: The St Lambert Experiment*. Newbury House.
Lane, H.L., Hoffmeister, R. and Bahan, B.J. (1996) *A Journey into the Deaf-World*. Dawn Sign Press.
Langman, J. and Shi, X. (2020) Gender, language, identity, and intercultural communication. In J. Jackson (ed.) *The Routledge Handbook of Language and Intercultural Communication* (2nd edn, pp. 219–232). Routledge.
Language Magazine (2020) Arizona moves to repeal English-only education. *Language Magazine*, February, p. 10.
Lantolf, J.P. (2011) The sociocultural approach to second language acquisition: Sociocultural theory, second language acquisition, and artificial L2 development. In D. Atkinson (ed.) *Alternative Approaches to Second Language Acquisition* (pp. 24–47). Routledge.
Lanza, E. and Lexander, K.V. (2019) Family language practices in multilingual transcultural families. In S. Montanari and S. Quay (eds) *Multidisciplinary Perspectives on Multilingualism: The Fundamentals* (pp. 230–251). De Gruyter Mouton.
Laurén, C. (1994) Swedish immersion programs in Finland. In J. Cummins and D. Corson (eds) *Encyclopedia of Language and Education, Vol. 5: Bilingual Education* (pp 291–296). Springer.
Laurén, U. (1991) A creativity index for studying the free written production of bilinguals. *International Journal of Applied Linguistics* 1 (2), 198–208.

Laurie, S.S. (1890) *Lectures on Language and Linguistic Method in the School.* Cambridge University Press.
Lavadenz, M. and Armas, E.G. (2024) *The Observation Protocol for Academic Literacies: A Tool for Building Expertise for Teachers of English Learners.* Multilingual Matters.
Lazarus, S.S., Albus, D. and Thurlow, M.L. (2016) *2013–2014 Publicly Reported Assessment Results for Students with Disabilities and ELLs with Disabilities.* NCEO Report 401. University of Minnesota, National Center on Educational Outcomes.
Leaton, G.S., Scott, D. and Mehisto, P. (2018) Educated side by side: The role of language in the European schools. In G.S. Leaton, D. Scott and P. Mehisto (eds) *Curriculum Reform in the European Schools* (pp. 49–73). Palgrave Macmillan.
Lederberg, A.R., Branum-Martin, L., Webb, M.Y., Schick, B., Antia, S., Easterbrooks, S.R. and Connor, C.M. (2019) Modality and interrelations among language, reading, spoken phonological awareness, and fingerspelling. *Journal of Deaf Studies and Deaf Education* 24 (4), 408–423.
Lee, J.S. (2014) Community support for Korean as a heritage language. In T.G. Wiley, J.K. Peyton, D. Christian, S.C.K. Moore and N. Liu (eds) *Handbook of Heritage, Community, and Native American Languages in the United States: Research, Policy, and Educational Practice* (pp. 253–262). Center for Applied Linguistics and Routledge.
Lee, J.S. and Chen-Wu, H. (2021) Community-organized heritage language programs. In S. Montrul and M. Polinsky (eds) *The Cambridge Handbook of Heritage Languages and Linguistics* (pp. 777–802). Cambridge University Press.
Lee, J.S. and Wright, W.E. (2014) The rediscovery of heritage and community language education in the United States. *Review of Research in Education* 38, 137–165. https://doi.org/10.3102/0091732X13507546.
Lee, K.C. and Wu, W.M. (2024) Disciplinary academic literacy in Singapore's higher education: Rethinking ELT. In S. Boun and C.S. Duran (eds) *English Education in Southeast Asian Contexts: Policy, Practice, and Identity* (pp. 123–138). Lexington Books/Rowman and Littlefield.
Lee, S., Watt, R. and Frawley, J. (2015) Effectiveness of bilingual education in Cambodia: A longitudinal comparative case study of ethnic minority children in bilingual and monolingual schools. *Compare: A Journal of Comparative and International Education* 45 (4), 526–544.
Lee, T.S. and McCarty, T.L. (2015) Bilingual-multilingual education and indigenous peoples. In W.E. Wright, S. Boun and O. García (eds) *Handbook of Bilingual and Multilingual Education* (pp. 407–425). Wiley-Blackwell.
Lee-James, R. and Washington, J.A. (2018) Language skills of bidialectal and bilingual children: Considering a strengths-based perspective. *Top Language Disorders* 38 (1), 5–26. https://psycnet.apa.org/doi/10.1097/TLD.0000000000000142.
Leeman, J. (2013) Categorizing Latinos in the history of the US Census: The official racialization of Spanish. In J.D. Valle (ed.) *A Political History of Spanish: The Making of a Language* (pp. 305–323). Cambridge University Press.
Leeman, J. (2018) It's all about English: The interplay of monolingual ideologies, language policies and the U.S. Census Bureau's statistics on multilingualism. *International Journal of the Sociology of Language* 252, 21–43. https://doi.org/10.1515/ijsl-2018-0013.
Leeman, J. (2019) Measured multilingualism: Census language questions in Canada and the United States. In T. Ricento (ed.) *Language Policies and Politics: Perspectives from Canada and the United States* (pp. 114–134). Cambridge University Press.
Leider, C.M., Colombo, M.W. and Nerlino, E. (2021) Decentralization, teacher quality, and the education of English learners: Do state education agencies effectively prepare teachers of ELs? *Education Policy Analysis Archives* 29 (100), 1–44. https://epaa.asu.edu/index.php/epaa/article/view/5279/2672.
Leigh, I.W. (2009) *A Lens on Deaf Identities.* Oxford University Press.
Leigh, I.W. and Andrews, J.F. (2017) *Psychological, Sociological, and Educational Perspectives* (2nd edn). Routledge.
Leigh, I.W., Andrews, J.F., Harris, R. and Gonzales, T. (2022a) *Deaf Culture: Exploring Deaf Communities in the United States.* Plural Publishing.
Leigh, I.W., Andrews, J.F., Miller, C. and Wolsey, J.L. (2022b) *Deaf People in Society: Psychological, Sociological, and Educational Perspectives* (3rd edn). Routledge.
Leivada E. (2023) A classification bias and an exclusion bias jointly overinflated the estimation of publication biases in bilingualism research. *Behavioral Sciences* 13 (10), 812. https://doi.org/10.3390/bs13100812.
Leonard, W.Y. (2008) When is an 'extinct language' not extinct? Miami, a formerly sleeping language. In K.A. King, N. Schilling-Estes, J.J. Lou, L. Fogle and B. Soukup (eds) *Sustaining Linguistic Diversity: Endangered and Minority Languages and Language Varieties* (pp. 23–34). Georgetown University Press.

Leonard, W.Y. (2017) Producing language reclamation by decolonising 'language'. In W.Y. Leonard and H. De Korne (eds) *Language Documentation and Description* (vol. 14, pp. 15–36). EL Publishing.

Leopold, W.F. (1970/1939–49) *Speech Development of a Bilingual Child: A Linguist's Record*. AMS Press.

Leung, C. (2022) Language proficiency: From description to prescription and back? *Educational Linguistics* 1 (1), 56–81. https://doi.org/10.1515/eduling-2021-0006.

Leung, C., Evans, M. and Liu, Y. (2021) English as an Additional Language Assessment Framework: Filling a void in policy and provision in school education in England. *Language Assessment Quarterly* 18 (3), 296–315. https://doi.org/10.1080/15434303.2020.1869745.

Levi, S.V. (2018) Another bilingual advantage? Perception of talker-voice information. *Language, Cognition and Neuroscience* 33 (9), 1205–1212.

Lewis, E.G. (1977) Bilingualism and bilingual education: The ancient world to the renaissance. In B. Spolsky and R.L. Cooper (eds) *Frontiers of Bilingual Education* (pp. 22–93). Newbury House.

Lewis, M.P. and Simons, G.F. (2010) Assessing endangerment: Expanding Fishman's GIDS. *Revue Roumaine de Linguistique* 55 (2), 103–120.

Lewis, W.G., Jones, B.M. and Baker, C. (2012) Translanguaging: Developing its conceptualization and contextualisation. *Educational Research and Evaluation* 18 (7), 655–670.

Lewis, W.G., Jones, B.M. and Baker, C. (2013) 100 bilingual lessons: Distributing two languages in classrooms. In C. Abello-Contesse, P.M. Chandler, M.D. López-Jiménez and R. Chacón-Beltrán (eds) *Bilingual and Multilingual Education in the 21st Century: Building on Experience* (pp. 107–135). Multilingual Matters.

Li, C., Goldrick, M. and Gollan, T.H. (2017) Bilinguals' twisted tongues: Frequency lag or interference? *Memory and Cognition* 45 (4), 600–610.

Li, H., Wright, W. E. and Morita-Mullaney, T. (2023) Literacy instruction for English language learners before and during the Covid-19 pandemic. https://edarxiv.org/bnymh.

Li, H., Wright, W.E. and Morita-Mullaney, T. (2023) Literacy instruction for English language learners in Indiana elementary schools before and during the COVID-19 pandemic. https://doi.org/10.35542/osf.io/bnymh.

Li, P. (2013) Cognition and the bilingual brain. In F. Grosjean and P. Li (eds) *The Psycholinguistics of Bilingualism* (pp. 214–228). John Wiley and Sons.

Li, P. and Abarbanell, L. (2018) Competing perspectives on frames of reference in language and thought. *Cognition* 170, 9–24.

Li, Y. (2005) The effects of the bilingual strategy – preview–view–review – on the comprehension of science concepts by deaf ASL/English and hearing Mexican-American Spanish/English bilingual students. Unpublished dissertation, Lamar University, Beaumont, TX.

Lillie, K.E. (2016) 'The ELD classes are … too much and we need to take other classes to graduate': Arizona's restrictive language policy and the dis-citizenship of ELs. In A. Loring and V. Ramanathan (eds) *Language, Immigration and Naturalization: Legal and Linguistic Issues* (pp. 79–100). Multilingual Matters.

Lillie, K.E. and Markos, A. (2014) The four-hour block: SEI in classrooms. In S.C.K. Moore (ed.) *Language Policy Processes and Consequences: Arizona Case Studies* (pp. 133–155). Multilingual Matters.

Lillie, K.E. and Moore, S.C.K. (2014) SEI in Arizona: Bastion for state's rights. In S.C.K. Moore (ed.) *Language Policy Processes and Consequences: Arizona Case Studies* (pp. 1–27). Multilingual Matters.

Lillo-Martin, D., de Quadros, R.M., Chen Pichler, D. and Fieldsteel, Z. (2014) Language choice in bimodal bilingual development. *Frontiers in Psychology* 5, 1163.

Lin, A. (2006) Beyond linguistic purism in language-in-education policy and practice: Exploring bilingual pedagogies in a Hong Kong science classroom. *Language and Education* 20 (4), 287–305.

Lin, A. (2015) Egalitarian bi/multilingualism and trans-semiotizing in a global world. In W.E. Wright, S. Boun and O. García (eds) *Handbook of Bilingual and Multilingual Education* (pp. 19–37). John Wiley and Sons.

Lin, A.M.Y. and He, P. (2017) Translanguaging as dynamic activity flows in CLIL classrooms. *Journal of Language, Identity, and Education* 16 (4), 228–244. https://doi.org/10.1080/15348458.2017.1328283.

Lin, L. and Ku, F. (2020) Reading and writing instruction for young Deaf children using Taiwan sign language. In Q. Wang and J. Andrews (eds) *Literacy and Deaf Education: Toward a Global Understanding* (pp. 305–327). Gallaudet University Press.

Lindholm, K.J. (1991) Theoretical assumptions and empirical evidence for academic achievement in two languages. *Hispanic Journal of Behavioral Sciences* 13 (1), 3–17.

Lindholm, K.J. and Aclan, Z. (1991) Bilingual proficiency as a bridge to academic achievement: Results from bilingual/immersion programs. *Journal of Education* 173 (2), 99–113.

Lindholm-Leary, K.J. (1994) Promoting positive cross-cultural attitudes and perceived competence in culturally and linguistically diverse classrooms. In R.A. DeVillar, C.J. Faltis and J.P. Cummins (eds) *Cultural Diversity in Schools: From Rhetoric to Practice* (pp. 189–206). State University of New York Press.
Lindholm-Leary, K.J. (2001) *Dual Language Education*. Multilingual Matters.
Lindholm-Leary, K.J. and Borsato, G. (2006) Academic achievement. In F. Genesee, K. Lindholm-Leary, W.M. Saunders and D. Christian (eds) *Educating English Learners: A Synthesis of Empirical Evidence* (pp. 157–179). Cambridge University Press.
Lindholm-Leary, K.J. and Genesee, F. (2010) Alternative educational programs for English learners. In California State Department of Education (ed.) *Improving Education for English Learners: Research-Based Approaches* (pp. 323–382). CDE Press.
Lindholm-Leary, K.J. and Genesee, F. (2014) Student outcomes in one-way, two-way, and indigenous language immersion education. *Journal of Immersion and Content-Based Language Education* 2 (2), 165–180. https://doi.org/10.1075/jicb.2.2.01lin.
Linn, M.S. and Dayán-Fernández, A. (eds) (2024) *Agency in the Peripheries of Language Revitalisation: Examining European Practices on the Ground*. Multilingual Matters.
Lippi-Green, R. (2012) *English with an Accent: Language, Ideology, and Discrimination in the United States* (2nd edn). Routledge.
Lipski, J.M. (2021) Heritage languages in South America. In S. Montrul and M. Polinsky (eds) *The Cambridge Handbook of Heritage Languages and Linguistics* (pp. 305–350). Cambridge University Press.
Little, D. and Figueras, N. (eds) (2022) *Reflecting on the Common European Framework of Reference for Languages and Its Companion Volume*. Multilingual Matters.
Little, D., Leung, C. and Van Avermaet, P. (eds) (2014) *Managing Diversity in Education: Language, Policies, Pedagogies*. Multilingual Matters.
Littlebear, R.E. (1996) Preface. In G. Cantoni (ed.) *Stabilizing Indigenous Languages*. Northern Arizona University Press.
Littlebear, R.E. (1999) Some rare and radical ideas for keeping indigenous languages alive. In J.A. Reyhner, G. Cantoni, R.S. Claire and E. Pearsons Yazzie (eds) *Revitalizing Indigenous Languages* (pp. 1–5). Northern Arizona University Press.
Liu, H.T. (2019) Taiwanese sign language receptive skill test for children as an evaluation for elementary level students at Deaf schools. *Bulletin of Special Education* 44 (1), 90–116.
Liu, H.T. and Liu, C.J. (2020) Chinese literacy: Factors, outcomes, and practices for deaf students in Taiwan. In Q. Wang and J.F. Andrews (eds) *Literacy and Deaf Education: Toward a Global Understanding* (pp. 328–351). Gallaudet University Press.
Liu, H.T., Liu, C.J. and Andrews, J.F. (2014) Literacy and deaf students in Taiwan: Issues, practices, and directions for future research: Part I. *Deafness and Education International*, 16 (1), 2–22.
Liu, H.T., Liu, C.J., Tseng, C.H. and Chang, J.H. (2015) Development of a standardized Taiwanese Sign Language comprehension test. *Bulletin of Special Education* 40 (3), 27–57.
Liu, H.T., Hsieh, H.H., Lin, W.Y., Andrews, J.F. and Liu, C.J. (2024) Sign language support in an inclusive environment: Educational sign language interpreting services in Taiwan. *Deafness and Education International* 26 (1), 37–57.
Livingston, S. (1997) *Rethinking the Education of Deaf Students: Theory and Practice from a Teacher's Perspective*. Heinemann.
Li Wei and Moyer, M. (2008) *Blackwell Guide to Research Methods in Bilingualism and Multilingualism*. John Wiley and Sons.
Li Wei, Miller, N. and Dodd, B. (1997) Distinguishing communicative difference from language disorder in bilingual children. *Bilingual Family Newsletter* 14 (1), 3–4.
Li Wei, Dewaele, J.M. and Housen, A. (2002) Introduction: Opportunities and challenges of bilingualism. In L. Wei, J.M. Dewaele and A. Housen (eds) *Opportunities and Challenges of Bilingualism* (pp. 1–14). Mouton de Gruyter.
Lo Bianco, J. (2001) *Language and Literacy Policy in Scotland*. Scottish CILT.
Lo Bianco, J. (2015) Multilingual education across Oceania. In W.E. Wright, S. Boun and O. García (eds) *Handbook of Bilingual and Multilingual Education* (pp. 604–617). Wiley-Blackwell.
Lo Bianco, J. (2016) Conflict, language rights, and education: Building peace by solving language problems in Southeast Asia. *Language Policy Research Network Brief*, April, 1–8.
Lo Bianco, J. (2019) Uncompromising talk, linguistic grievance, and language policy: Thailand's deep South conflict zone. In M. Kelly, H. Footitt and M. Salama-Carr (eds) *The Palgrave Handbook of Languages and Conflict* (pp. 295–330). Palgrave Macmillan.

Lopez, A.A. (2024) Vignette. Using flexible bilingual academic content assessments in the United States: Lessons learned. In C. Reilly, F. Chimbutane, J. Clegg, C. Rubagumya and E.J. Erling (eds) *Multilingual Learning: Assessment, Ideologies and Policies in Sub-Saharan Africa*. Routledge. https://doi.org/10.4324/9781003311553-4.

Lopez, A.A., Turkan, S. and Guzman-Orth, D. (2017) Assessing multilingual competence. In E. Shohamy, I. Or and S. May (eds) *Encyclopedia of Language and Education, Vol. 7: Language Testing and Assessment* (3rd edn, pp. 91–102). Springer.

Lorente, B.P. (2018) *Scripts of Servitude: Language, Labor Migration and Transnational Domestic Work*. Multilingual Matters.

Lortie-Forgues, H. and Inglis, M. (2019) Rigorous large-scale educational RCTs are often uninformative: Should we be concerned? *Educational Researcher* 48 (3), 158–166. https://doi.org/10.3102/0013189X19832850.

Lowe, C.J., Cho, I., Goldsmith, S.F. and Morton, J.B. (2021) The bilingual advantage in children's executive functioning is not related to language status: A meta-analytic review. *Psychological Science* 32 (7), 1115–1146.

Lucas, C. and Valli, C. (1989) Language contact in the American deaf community. In *The Sociolinguistics of the Deaf Community* (pp. 11–40). Academic Press.

Lucy, J.A. and Gaskins, S. (2001) Grammatical categories and the development of classification preferences: A comparative approach. In M. Bowerman and S. Levinson (eds) *Language Acquisition and Conceptual Development* (pp. 257–283). Cambridge University Press.

Luk, G., Anderson, J. and Grundy, J.G. (eds) (2023) *Understanding Language and Cognition Through Bilingualism: In Honor of Ellen Bialystok*. John Benjamins.

Lukes, M. (2015) *Latino Immigrant Youth and Interrupted Schooling: Dropouts, Dreamers and Alternative Pathways to College*. Multilingual Matters.

Lund, E.M., Kohlmeier, T.L. and Durán, L.K. (2017) Comparative language development in bilingual and monolingual children with autism spectrum disorder: A systematic review. *Journal of Early Intervention* 39 (2), 106–124. https://doi.org/10.1177/1053815117690871.

Lyngbäck, L.A. and Andersson, S. (2024) Deaf, Diverse and Denied: Insights and challenges in responding to the educational and linguistic human rights of deaf immigrant students. In N.B. Hanssen, H. Harju-Luukkainen and C. Sundqvist (eds) *Inclusion and Special Needs Education for Immigrant Students in the Nordic Countries* (pp. 216–232). Routledge.

Lyster, R. and Mori, H. (2008) Instructional counterbalance in immersion pedagogy. In T.W. Fortune and D.J. Tedick (eds) *Pathways to Multilingualism: Evolving Perspectives on Immersion Education*. Multilingual Matters.

Ma, W. and Li, G. (eds) (2016) *Chinese-Heritage Students in North American Schools: Understanding Hearts and Minds Beyond Test Scores*. Routledge.

Macalister, J. and Mirvahedi, S.H. (eds) (2017) *Family Language Policies in a Multilingual World: Opportunities, Challenges, and Consequences*. Routledge.

MacDonald, R., Boals, T., Castro, M., Cook, H.G., Lundberg, T. and White, P.A. (2015) *Formative Language Assessment for English Learners: A Four-Step Process*. Heinemann.

MacGlaughlin, H.M. (2018) The role of fingerspelling in early communication, language, and literacy acquisition of deaf children. Unpublished doctoral dissertation, Lamar University-Beaumont.

Machado-Casas, M., Maldonado, S.I. and Flores, B.B. (eds) (2022) *Assessment and Evaluation in Bilingual Education*. Peter Lang.

Machowska-Kosciak, M. (2020) *The Multilingual Adolescent Experience: Small Stories of Integration and Socialization by Polish Families in Ireland*. Multilingual Matters.

Macías, R.F. (2000) The flowering of America: Linguistic diversity in the United States. In S.L. McKay and S.C. Wong (eds) *New Immigrants in the United States* (pp. 11–57). Cambridge University Press.

Mackey, W.F. (1970) A typology of bilingual education. *Foreign Language Annals* 3 (4), 596–606.

Mackey, W.F. (1978) The importation of bilingual education models. In J.E. Alatis (ed.) *Georgetown University Roundtable: International Dimensions of Education* (pp. 1–18). Georgetown University Press.

MacNab, G.L. (1979) Cognition and bilingualism: A reanalysis of studies. *Linguistics* 17 (3–4), 231–256.

Macnamara, B.N. and Burgoyne, A.P. (2023) Do growth mindset interventions impact students' academic achievement? A systematic review and meta-analysis with recommendations for best practices. *Psychological bulletin* 149 (3–4), 133.

MacSwan, J. (2000) The threshold hypothesis, semilingualism, and other contributions to a deficit view of linguistic minorities. *Hispanic Journal of Behavioral Science* 22 (1), 3–45.

MacSwan, J. (2013) Codeswitching and grammatical theory. In W.C. Ritchie and T.K. Bhatia (eds) *Handbook of Bilingualism and Multilingualism* (pp. 321–250). Wiley-Blackwell.

MacSwan, J. (ed.) (2014) *Grammatical Theory and Bilingual Codeswitching*. MIT Press.
MacSwan, J. (2017) A multilingual perspective on translanguaging. *American Educational Research Journal* 54, 167–201. https://doi.org/10.3102/0002831216683935.
MacSwan, J. (2020) Sociolinguistic and linguistic foundations of codeswitching research. In J. MacSwan and C.J. Faltis (eds) *Codeswitching in the Classroom: Critical Perspectives on Teaching, Learning, Policy, and Ideology* (pp. 3–38). Center for Applied Linguistics and Routledge.
MacSwan, J. (ed.) (2022a) *Multilingual Perspectives on Translanguaging*. Multilingual Matters.
MacSwan, J. (2022b) Codeswitching, translanguaging and bilingual grammar. In J. MacSwan (ed.) *Multilingual Perspectives on Translanguaging* (pp. 83–125). Multilingual Matters.
MacSwan, J. and Faltis, C.J. (eds) (2020) *Codeswitching in the Classroom: Critical Perspectives on Teaching, Learning, Policy, and Ideology*. Center for Applied Linguistics and Routledge.
MacSwan, J. and Rolstad, K. (2003) Linguistic diversity, schooling, and social class: Rethinking our conception of language proficiency in language minority education. In C.B. Paulston and R. Tucker (eds) *Sociolinguistics: Essential Reading* (pp. 329–341). Blackwell.
MacSwan, J. and Rolstad, K. (2024) (Un)grounded language ideologies: A brief history of translanguaging theory. *International Journal of Bilingualism* 28 (4), 719–743. https://doi.org/10.1177/13670069241236703.
MacSwan, J., Rolstad, K. and Glass, G.V. (2002) Do some school-age children have no language? Some problems of construct validity in the Pre-Las Español. *Bilingual Research Journal* 26 (2), 213–238.
Maher, J. (1996) *Seeing Language in Sign: The Work of William C. Stokoe*. Gallaudet University Press.
Mahoney, K. (2024) *The Assessment of Multilingual Learners: Supporting English Language Learners* (2nd edn). Multilingual Matters.
Mahoney, K., Thompson, M. and MacSwan, J. (2005) The condition of English language learners in Arizona: 2005. https://www.terpconnect.umd.edu/~macswan/EPSL-0509-110-AEPI.pdf.
Mahshie, S. (1995) *Educating Deaf Children Bilingually*. Gallaudet University Press.
Makoni, S. and Makoni, B. (2015) Too many cooks spoil the broth: Tension and conflict between language institutions in South Africa. In W.E. Wright, S. Boun and O. García (eds) *Handbook of Bilingual and Multilingual Education* (pp. 552–563). Wiley-Blackwell.
Makoni, S. and Pennycook, A. (2007) *Disinventing and Reconstituting Languages*. Multilingual Matters.
Maldonada, S.I. (2024) Assessment, accountability and culture: Key trends in dual language bilingual education. In J.A. Freire, C. Alfaro and E. de Jong (eds) *The Handbook of Dual Language Bilingual Education* (pp. 27–289). Routledge. https://doi.org/10.4324/9781003269076-23.
Malherbe, E.C. (1946) *The Bilingual School*. Longman.
Malinowski, D. and Tufi, S. (eds) (2020) *Reterritorializing Linguistic Landscapes: Questioning Boundaries and Opening Spaces*. Bloomsbury Academic.
Maneva, B. and Genesee, F. (2002) Bilingual babbling: Evidence for language differentiation in dual language acquisition. In B. Skarabela, S. Fish and A. Do (eds) *BUCLD 26: Proceedings of the 26 Annual Boston University Conference on Language Development* (vol. 1, pp. 383–392). Cascadilla Press.
Mango, O. (2012) Arab American women negotiating identities. *International Multilingual Research Journal* 6 (2), 83–103.
Marian, V. (2023) *The Power of Language: How the Codes We Use to Think, Speak, and Live Transform Our Minds*. Dutton/Penguin Random House.
Marian, V. and Spivey, M. (2003) Competing activation in bilingual language processing: Within-and between-language competition. *Bilingualism: Language and Cognition* 6 (2), 97–115. https://doi.org/10.1017/S1366728903001068.
Marinova-Todd, S.H., Marshall, D.B. and Snow, C.E. (2000) Three misconceptions about age and L2 learning. *TESOL Quarterly* 34 (1), 9–34.
Marinova-Todd, S.H. and Mirenda, P. (2016) Language and communication abilities of bilingual children with autism spectrum disorders. In J.L. Patterson and B.L. Rodríguez (eds) *Multilingual Perspectives on Child Language Disorders* (pp. 31–48). Multilingual Matters.
Markowicz, H. and Woodward, J. (1982) *How You Gonna Get To Heaven If You Can't Talk With Jesus?* National Association of the Deaf.
Marschark, M. and Lee, C. (2014) Navigating two languages in the classroom: Goals, evidence, and outcomes. In M. Marschark, G. Tang and H. Knoors (eds) *Bilingualism and Bilingual Deaf Education* (pp. 213–241). Oxford University Press.
Marschark, M., Tang, G. and Knoors, H. (2014) *Bilingualism and Bilingual Deaf Education*. Oxford University Press.
Marschark, M., Antia, S. and Knoors, H. (2019) *Co-enrollment in Deaf Education*. Oxford University Press.

Marsh, D. (2008) Language awareness and CLIL. In J. Cenoz and N.H. Hornberger (eds) *Encyclopedia of Language and Education, Vol. 6: Knowledge About Language* (2nd edn, pp. 1986–1999). Springer.

Martin, D. (2009) *Language Disabilities in Cultural and Linguistic Diversity*. Multilingual Matters.

Martínez, R.A. and Mejía, A.F. (2020) Looking closely and listening carefully: A sociocultural approach to understanding the complexity of Latina/o/x students' everyday language. *Theory into Practice* 59 (1), 53–63. https://doi.org/10.1080/00405841.2019.1665414.

Martínez, R.A., Durán, L. and Hikida, M. (2017) Becoming 'Spanish learners': Identity and interaction among multilingual children in a Spanish-English dual language classroom. *International Multilingual Research Journal* 11 (3), 167–183. https://doi.org/10.1080/19313152.2017.1330065.

Martinez, R.B. and Fillmore, L.W. (2024) On curriculum and pedagogy in dual language bilingual education. In J.A. Freire, C. Alfaro and E. de Jong (eds) *The Handbook of Dual Language Bilingual Education* (pp. 444–460). Routledge. https://doi.org/10.4324/9781003269076-38.

Martin-Jones, M. (2000) Bilingual classroom interaction: A review of recent research. *Language Teaching* 33 (1), 1–9.

Martin-Jones, M. and Jones, K.E. (2000) Introduction: Multilingual literacies. In M. Martin-Jones and K. Jones (eds) *Multilingual Literacies: Reading and Writing Different Worlds* (pp. 1–36). John Benjamins.

Martin-Jones, M. and Romaine, S. (1986) Semilingualism: A half-baked theory of communicative competence. *Applied Linguistics* 7 (1), 26–38.

Martin-Jones, M. and Saxena, M. (2003) Bilingual resources and 'funds of knowledge' for teaching and learning in multi-ethnic classrooms in Britain. *International Journal of Bilingual Education and Bilingualism* 6 (3–4), 267–282.

Martinovic, I. and Altarriba, J. (2013) Bilingualism and emotion: Implications for mental health. In T.K. Bhatia and W.C. Ritchie (eds) *The Handbook of Bilingualism and Multilingualism* (pp. 292–320). Wiley-Blackwell.

Mashie, S. (1995) *Educating Deaf Children Bilingually*. Gallaudet University Press.

Massachusetts Department of Elementary and Secondary Education (2018) LOOK Act: Overview of new law supporting English learners. https://www.doe.mass.edu/ele/look-act.html.

Massachusetts Language Opportunity Coalition (2017) LOOK Act. https://languageopportunity.org/look-act.

Mathur, G. and Napoli, D.J. (eds) (2011) *Deaf Around the World: The Impact of Language*. Oxford University Press.

Matsuoka, K, Crasborn, O. and Coppola, M. (eds) (2023) *East Asian Sign Linguistics*. Ishara Press.

Matthews, T. (1979) *An Investigation into the Effects of Background Characteristics and Special Language Services on the Reading Achievement and English Fluency of Bilingual Students*. Seattle Public Schools, Department of Planning.

Maxwell, M. and Doyle, J. (1996) Language codes and sense-making among Deaf schoolchildren. *Journal of Deaf Studies and Deaf Education* 1 (2), 122–136.

May, S. (2011) *Language and Minority Rights: Ethnicity, Nationalism and the Politics of Language* (2nd edn). Routledge.

May, S. (2017a) Language, imperialism, and the modern nation-state system: Implications for language rights. In O. García, N. Flores and M. Spotti (eds) *The Oxford Handbook of Language and Society* (pp. 35–54). Oxford University Press.

May, S. (2017b) National and ethnic minorities: Language rights and recognitions. In A.S. Canagarajah (ed.) *The Routledge Handbook of Migration and Language* (pp. 149–167). Routledge.

May, S. (2018) Language rights and language repression. In J.W. Tollefson and M. Pêrez-Milans (eds) *The Oxford Handbook of Language Policy and Planning* (pp. 236–253). Oxford University Press.

May, S. (2022) Afterword: The multilingual turn, superdiversity and translanguaging – The rush from heterodoxy to orthodoxy. In J. MacSwan (ed.) *Multilingual Perspectives on Translanguaging* (pp. 343–355). Multilingual Matters.

May, S. (2024) Indigenous language and education rights. In C. McKinney, P. Makoe and V. Zavala (eds) *The Routledge Handbook of Multilingualism* (pp. 127–143). Routledge. https://doi.org/10.4324/9781003214908-11.

Mayberry, R. (2002) Cognitive development of deaf children: The interface of language and perception in neuropsychology. In S.J. Segaolwitz and I. Rapin (eds) *Handbook of Neuropsychology* (2nd edn, vol. 8, part II, pp. 71–107). Elsevier.

Mayberry, R.I. and Kluender, R. (2018) Rethinking the critical period for language: New insights into an old question from American Sign Language. *Bilingualism: Language and Cognition* 21 (5), 886–905.

Mayberry, R.I., Del Giudice, A.A. and Lieberman, A.M. (2011) Reading achievement in relation to phonological coding and awareness in deaf readers: A meta-analysis. *Journal of Deaf Studies and Deaf Education* 16 (2), 164–188.

Mayberry, R.I., Davenport, T., Roth, A. and Halgren, E. (2018) Neurolinguistic processing when the brain matures without language. *Cortex* 99, 390–403.

Mayer, P.F., M'Ilvaine, W. and Bache, F. (1822) *Documents in relation to the dismissal of David G. Seixas from the Pennsylvania Institution for the deaf and dumb.* PSD Board of Directors.

Mazak, C. and Carroll, K.S. (eds) (2017) *Translanguaging in Higher Education: Beyond Monolingual Ideologies*. Multilingual Matters.

McBurney, S. (2012) History of sign languages and sign language linguistics. In R. Pfau, M. Steinbach and B. Woll (eds) *Sign Language: An International Handbook* (pp. 909–948). De Gruyter Mouton.

McCaleb, S.P. (1997) *Building Communities of Learners: A Collaboration Among Teachers, Students, Families, and Community*. Routledge.

McCarty, T.L. (2002) *A Place to be Navajo: Rough Rock and the Struggle for Self-determination in Indigenous Schooling*. Lawrence Erlbaum.

McCarty, T.L. (2004) Dangerous difference: A critical-historical analysis of language education policies in the United States. In J.W. Tollefson and A.B.M. Tsui (eds) *Medium of Instruction Policies. Which Agenda? Whose Agenda?* (pp. 71–93). Erlbaum.

McCarty, T.L. (2013) *Language Planning and Policy in Native America: History, Theory, Praxis*. Multilingual Matters.

McCarty, T.L. (2014) Native American languages: Introduction. In T.G. Wiley, J.K. Peyton, D. Christian, S.C.K. Moore and N. Liu (eds) *Handbook of Heritage, Community, and Native American Languages in the United States: Research, Policy, and Educational Practice* (pp. 189–191). Center for Applied Linguistics and Routledge.

McCarty, T.L. (2017) Bilingual education in the indigenous languages of North America. In S. May (ed.) *Encyclopedia of Language and Education, Vol. 5: Bilingual Education* (3rd edn). Springer.

McCarty, T.L. (2018) Revitalizing and sustaining endangered languages. In J.W. Tollefson and M. Pêrez- Milans (eds) *The Oxford Handbook of Language Policy and Planning* (pp. 356–378). Oxford University Press.

McCarty, T.L. (2019) Indigenous language movements in a settler state. In T. Ricento (ed.) *Language Politics and Policies: Perspectives from Canada and the United States* (pp. 173–191). Cambridge University Press.

McCarty, T.L. and Baker, S. (2024) Indigenous revitalization-immersion education in Native-American settings. In J.A. Freire, C. Alfaro and E.J. de Jong (eds) *The Handbook of Dual Language Bilingual Education* (pp. 348–359). Routledge.

McCarty, T.L., Nicholas, S.E. and Wigglesworth, G. (2019) *A World of Indigenous Languages: Politics, Pedagogies and Prospects for Language Reclamation*. Multilingual Matters.

McConnell, B. (1980) Effectiveness of individualized bilingual instruction for migrant students. Unpublished PhD dissertation, Washington State University.

McField, G.P. and McField, D.R. (2014) The consistent outcome of bilingual education programs: A meta-analysis of meta-analyses. In G. McField (ed.) *The Miseducation of English Learners: A Tale of Three States and Lessons to be Learned* (pp. 267–297). Information Age Publishing.

McKee, R.L. (2001) *People of the Eye: Stories from the Deaf World*. Bridget Williams Books

McKee, R.L. (2008) The construction of deaf children as marginal bilinguals in the mainstream. *International Journal of Bilingual Education and Bilingualism* 11 (5), 519–540.

McLeister, M. (2019) Worship, technology, and identity: A deaf protestant congregation in urban China. *Studies in World Christianity* 25 (2), 220–237.

McQuillan, J. and Tse, L. (1996) Does research matter? An analysis of media opinion on bilingual education, 1984–1994. *Bilingual Research Journal* 20 (1), 1–27.

Mechelli, A., Chinion, J.T., Noppeney, U., O'Doherty, J., Ashburner, J., Frackowiak, R.S. and Price, C.J. (2004) Neurolinguistics: Structural plasticity in the bilingual brain. *Nature* 431, 757.

Meek, D.R. (2020) Dinner table syndrome: A phenomenological study of Deaf individuals' experiences with inaccessible communication. *Qualitative Report* 25 (6), 1676A–1694.

Mehisto, P. (2012) *Excellence in Bilingual Education: A Guide for School Principals*. Cambridge University Press.

Mehisto, P. and Genesee, F. (eds) (2015) *Building Bilingual Education Systems: Forces, Mechanisms and Counterweights*. Cambridge University Press.

Mendoza, A. (2023) *Translanguaging and English as a Lingua Franca in the Plurilingual Classroom*. Multilingual Matters.

Menken, K. (2008) *English Learners Left Behind: Standardized Testing as Language Policy*. Multilingual Matters

Menken, K. (2013) (Dis)citizenship or opportunity? The importance of language education policy for access and full participation of emergent bilinguals in the US. In V. Ramanathan (ed.) *Language Policies and (Dis)citizenship: Rights, Access, Pedagogies* (pp. 209–230). Multilingual Matters.

Menken, K. (2017) High-stakes tests as de facto language education policies. In E. Shohamy, I. Or and S. May (eds) *Encyclopedia of Language and Education, Vol. 7: Language Testing and Assessment* (3rd edn, pp. 385–396). Springer.

Menken, K. and Barron, V. (2002) What Are the Characteristics of the Bilingual Education and ESL Shortage. *Ask NCELA* 14. http://www.ncela.gwu.edu/expert/faq/14shortage.htm.

Menken, K. and García, O. (2010) *Negotiating Language Policies in Schools: Educators as Policymakers*. Routledge.

Menken, K. and Kleyn, T. (2010) The long-term impact of subtractive schooling in the educational experiences of secondary English language learners. *International Journal of Bilingual Education and Bilingualism* 13 (4), 399–417. https://doi.org/10.1080/13670050903370143.

Menken, K. and Sánchez, M.T. (2019) Translanguaging in English-only schools: From pedagogy to stance in the disruption of monolingual policies and practice. *TESOL Quarterly* 53 (9), 741–767. https://doi.org/10.1002/tesq.513.

Menken, K. and Solarza, C. (2015) Principals as linchpins in bilingual education: The need for prepared school leaders. *International Journal of Bilingualism* 18 (6), 676–697.

Mercer, J.R. (1973) *Labeling the Mentally Retarded*. University of California Press.

Meyer, M.M. and Fienberg, S.E. (1992) *Assessing Evaluation Studies: The Case of Bilingual Education Strategies*. National Academies Press.

Mills, J. (2006) Talking about silence: Gender and the construction of multilingual identities. *International Journal of Bilingualism* 10 (1), 1–16.

Milson-Whyte, V. (2013) Pedagogical and socio-political implications of code-meshing in classrooms: Some considerations for a translingual orientation to writing. In A.S. Canagarajah (ed.) *Literacy as Translingual Practice: Between Communities and Classrooms* (pp. 115–127). Routledge.

Mirus, G. and Napoli, D. (2018) Developing language and (pre)literacy skills in deaf preschoolers through shared reading activities with bimodal-bilingual ebooks. *Journal of Multilingual Education Research* 8 (10), 75–110.

Mitchell, C. (2015) Momentum building for biliteracy. *Education Week* 35 (7), 1–12.

Mitchell, C. (2016) Arizona, Federal government settle dispute over English-language learners. https://blogs.edweek.org/edweek/learning-the-language/2016/05/arizona_federal_government_ set.html.

Mitchell, C. (2018) The national shortage of ELL teachers has caught the eye of Congress. https://blogs.edweek.org/edweek/learning-the-language/2018/01/solve_ell_teacher_shortage.html.

Mitchell, C. (2020) Schools failed English-learners during the shutdown. How can they do better? https://blogs.edweek.org/edweek/learning-the-language/2020/08/schools_english_learners_coronavirus_covid.html.

Mitchell, R.E. and Karchmer, M. (2004) Chasing the mythical ten percent: Parental hearing status of deaf and hard of hearing students in the United States. *Sign Language Studies* 4 (2), 138–163.

Miyagawa, S. (2024) Ainu–Japanese bi-directional neural machine translation: A step towards linguistic preservation of ainu, an under-resourced indigenous language in Japan. *Journal of Data Mining and Digital Humanities*, NLP4DH. https://doi.org/10.46298/jdmdh.13151.

Mohanty, A.K. (2019) *The Multilingual Reality: Living with Languages*. Multilingual Matters.

Mohanty, A.K., Panda, M., Phillipson, R. and Skutnabb-Kangas, T. (2009) *Multilingual Education for Social Justice Globalising the Local*. Orient Blackswan.

Mohd-Asraf, R. (2005) English and Islam: A clash of civilizations? *Journal of Language, Identity, and Education* 4 (2), 103–118.

Moje, E.B. (2017) Theory and research on literacy as a tool for navigating everyday and school discourses. In S. May (ed.) *Encyclopedia of Language and Education, Vol. 3: Discourse and Education* (3rd edn, pp. 239–252). Springer.

Moll, L.C. (2001) The diversity of schooling: A cultural-historical approach. In M. Reyes and J.J. Halcón (eds) *The Best for Our Children: Critical Perspectives on Literacy for Latino Students*. Teachers College Press.

Monsen, M. and Steien, G.B. (eds) (2022) *Language Learning and Forced Migration*. Multilingual Matters.

Montanari, E.G., Abel, R., Graßer, B. and Tschudinovski, L. (2018) Do bilinguals create two different sets of vocabulary for two domains? Vocabulary development and overlap in the first years of schooling. *Linguistic Approaches to Bilingualism* 8 (4), 502–522.

Montrul, S. and Polinsky, M. (eds) (2021) *The Cambridge Handbook of Heritage Languages and Linguistics*. Cambridge University Press.

Moon, C., Lagercrantz, H. and Kuhl, P.K. (2013) Language experienced in utero affects vowel perception after birth: A two country study. *Acta Pædiatrica* 102 (2), 156–160. https://doi.org/10.1111/apa.12098.

Moore, E., Bradley, J. and Simpson, J. (eds) (2020) *Translanguaging as Transformation: The Collaborative Construction of New Linguistic Realities*. Multilingual Matters.

Moore, J. and Schleppegrell, M. (2020) A focus on disciplinary language: Bringing critical perspectives to reading and writing in science. *Theory into Practice* 59 (1), 99–108.

Moore, R.E. (2017) Discourses of endangerment from mother tongues to machine readability. In O. García, N. Flores and M. Spotti (eds) *The Oxford Handbook of Language and Society* (pp. 221–242). Oxford University Press.

Moore, S.C.K. (2014) *Language Policy Processes and Consequences: Arizona Case Studies*. Multilingual Matters.

Moore, S.C.K. (2021) *A History of Bilingual Education in the US: Examining the Politics of Language Policymaking*. Multilingual Matters.

Moores, D. (ed.) (2011) *Partners in Education: Issues and Trends from the 21st International Congress on the Education of the Deaf*. Gallaudet University Press.

Morgan, M.H. (2014) *Speech Communities*. Cambridge University Press.

Moriarty, M. (2011) Minority languages and performative genres: The case of Irish language stand-up comedy. *Journal of Multilingual and Multicultural Development* 32 (6), 547–559.

Moriarty, M. (2015a) New roles for endangered languages. In P.K. Austin and J. Sallabank (eds) *The Cambridge Handbook of Endangered Languages* (pp. 446–458). Cambridge University Press.

Moriarty, M. (2015b) *Globalizing Language Policy and Planning*. Palgrave Macmillan.

Morita-Mullaney, T. (2016) Borrowing legitimacy as English learner (EL) leaders: Indiana's 14-year history with English language proficiency standards. *Language Testing* 34 (2), 241–270. https://doi.org/10.1177/0265532216653430.

Morita-Mullaney, T. (2019) At the intersection of bilingual specialty and leadership: A collective case study of district leadership for emergent bilinguals. *Bilingual Research Journal* 42 (1), 31–53. https://doi.org/10.1080/15235882.2018.1563005.

Morita-Mullaney, T. (2024a) Recentering multiple minoritized languages in dual language bilingual education. In J.A. Freire, C. Alfaro and E. de Jong (eds) *The Handbook of Dual Language Bilingual Education* (pp. 154–172). Routledge.

Morita-Mullaney, T. (2024b) *Lau v. Nichols and Chinese American Language Rights: The Sunrise and Sunset of Bilingual Education*. Multilingual Matters.

Morita-Mullaney, T. and Singh, M. (2019) Obscuring English learners from state accountability: The case of Indiana's language blind policies. *Educational Policy* 35 (4), 621–645. https://doi.org/10.1177/0895904818823751.

Morita-Mullaney, T., Li, H. and Renn, J. (2019) Multiliteracies in rural communities: The 'revuelto y mezclado' of home and community literacy practices of midwestern emergent bilingual families. *Rural Educator* 40 (3), 35–48.

Morita-Mullaney, T., Renn, J. and Chiu, M.M. (2021) Contesting math as the universal language: A longitudinal study of dual language bilingual education language allocation. *International Multilingual Research Journal* 15 (1), 43–60. https://doi.org/10.1080/19313152.2020.1753930.

Morita-Mullaney, T., Renn, J. and Chiu, M.M. (2022) Spanish language proficiency in dual language and English as a second language models: The impact of model, time, teacher, and student on Spanish language development. *International Journal of Bilingual Education and Bilingualism* 25 (10), 3888–3906. https://doi.org/10.1080/13670050.2022.2089012.

Morris, D. and Jones, K. (2008) Language socialization in the home and minority language revitalization in Europe. In P.A. Duff and N.H. Hornberger (eds) *Encyclopedia of Language and Education, Vol. 8: Socialization* (2nd edn, pp. 2699–2715). Springer.

Morrison, S. and Voight-Campbell, R. (2017) What is ProTactile and what are its benefits? *TX Sense–Abilities*, fall. https://www.tsbvi.edu/fall-winter-2017-issue/573-tx-senseabilities/ fall-2017/5651-what-is-protactile-and-what-are-its-benefits.

Moschkovich, J. (2020) Codeswitching and mathematics learners: How hybrid language practices provide resources for student participation in mathematical practices. In J. MacSwan and C.J. Faltis (eds) *Codeswitching in the Classroom: Critical Perspectives on Teaching, Learning, Policy, and Ideology* (pp. 88–113). Center for Applied Linguistics and Routledge.

Mosco, V. (2009) *The Political Economy of Communication*. Sage.

Moseley, C. (2010) *Atlas of the World's Languages in Danger* (3rd edn). UNESCO.

Mosqueda, E., Bravo, M.A., Solís, J.L. and Maldonada, S.I. (2022) Assessing emergent bilingual learners' mathematical biliteracy: Authentic mathematics writing assessment system. In M. Machado-Casas, S. I. Maldonado and B.B. Flores (eds) *Assessment and Evaluation in Bilingual Education* (pp. 223–244). Peter Lang.

Moyer, M.G. (2017) Work. In O. García, N. Flores and M. Spotti (eds) *The Oxford Handbook of Language and Society* (pp. 505–524). Oxford University Press.

Muller, A. and Baetens Beardsmore, H. (2004) Multilingual interaction in plurilingual classes – European school practice. *International Journal of Bilingual Education and Bilingualism* 7 (1), 24–42.

Muñoz, C. (2000) Bilingualism and trilingualism in school students in Catalonia. In J. Cenoz and U. Jessner (eds) *English in Europe: The Acquisition of a Third Language* (pp. 157–178). Multilingual Matters.

Muñoz-Muñoz, E.R. and Briceño, A. (2024) Reconsidering language assets: A critical and integrative examination of language proficiency and biliteracy in dual language teacher education. In J.A. Freire, C. Alfaro and E. de Jong (eds) *The Handbook of Dual Language Bilingual Education* (pp. 611–623). Routledge. https://doi.org/10.4324/9781003269076-51.

Murray, J.J., Hall, W.C. and Snoddon, K. (2019) Education and health of children with hearing loss: The necessity of signed languages. *Bulletin of the World Health Organization* 97 (10), 711–716. https://doi.org/10.2471/BLT.19.229427.

Murray, J.J., Hall, W.C. and Snodden, K. (2020) The importance of signed languages for deaf children and their families. *Hearing Journal* 73 (3), 30. https://doi.org/10.1097/01.HJ.0000657988.24659.f3.

Murray, J.J., Snoddon, K., De Meulder, M. and Underwood, K. (2020) Intersectional inclusion for deaf learners: Moving beyond General Comment No. 4 on Article 24 of the United Nations Convention on the Rights of Persons with Disabilities. *International Journal of Inclusive Education* 24 (7), 691–705.

Musyoka, M. (2022) *Deaf Education and Challenges for Bilingual/Multilingual Students*. IGI Global.

Muysken, P. (2000) *Bilingual Speech: A Typology of Code-Mixing*. Cambridge University Press.

Myers-Scotton, C. (1997) Code-switching. In F. Coulmas (ed.) *The Handbook of Sociolinguistics* (pp. 217–237). Blackwell.

Myers-Scotton, C. (2002) *Contact Linguistics*. Cambridge University Press.

Naeem, K., Filippi, R., Periche-Tomas, E., Papageorgiou, A. and Bright, P. (2018) The importance of socio-economic status as a modulator of the bilingual advantage in cognitive ability. *Frontiers in Psychology* 9, 1818.

Nagy, N. (2021) Heritage languages in Canada. In S. Montrul and M. Polinsky (eds) *The Cambridge Handbook of Heritage Languages and Linguistics* (pp. 178–204). Cambridge University Press. https://doi.org/10.1017/9781108766340.010.

National Association for Gifted Children (2015) *2014–2015 State of the States in Gifted Education: Policy and Practice Data*. https://www.nagc.org/sites/default/files/ key%20reports/2014-2015%20State%20 of%20the%20States%20%28final%29.pdf.

National Association for Gifted Children (2019) *Position Statement: A Definition of Giftedness that Guides Best Practice*. https://nagc.org/resource/resmgr/knowledge-center/position-statements/a_definition_of_ giftedness_t.pdf.

National Association for Gifted Children (2020) Frequently asked questions about gifted education. https://www.nagc.org/resources-publications/resources/frequently-asked-questions-about-gifted-education#:~:text=How%20many%20gifted%20children%20are,Gifted%20 Education%20in%20 the%20U.S.

National Black Deaf Advocates (2020) NBDA open letter to Gallaudet University Board of Trustees. https://www.nbda.org/news/nbda-open-letter-to-gallaudet-university-board-of-trust-ees-june-2020.

National Center for Education Statistics (2020a) Students with disabilities. https://nces.ed.gov/programs/coe/indicator_cgg.asp.

National Center for Education Statistics (2020b) English language learners in public schools. https://nces.ed.gov/programs/coe/indicator_cgf.asp.

National Center for Education Statistics (2024a) English learners enrolled in public elementary and secondary schools, by home language, grade, and selected student characteristics: Selected school years, 2011-12 through fall 2021 (Table 204.27). Institute for Education Sciences, US Department of Education. https://nces.ed.gov/programs/digest/d23/tables/dt23_204.27.asp.

National Center for Education Statistics (2024b) English learners (ELs) enrolled in public elementary and secondary schools, by state or jurisdiction: Fall 2011 through fall 2021 (Table 204.20). Institute for Education Sciences, US Department of Education. https://nces.ed.gov/programs/digest/d23/tables/dt23_204.20.asp.

National Center for Education Statistics (2024c) Students with disabilities. Condition of education. US Department of Education, Institute of Education Sciences. https://nces.ed.gov/programs/coe/indicator/cgg.

National Education Association (1966) *The Invisible Minority … pero no vencibles. Report of the NEA–Tucson Survey on the Teaching of Spanish to the Spanish-Speaking*. Department of Rural Education, National Education Association.

National Education Goals Panel (1999) *The National Education Goals Report: Building a Nation of Learners*. National Education Goals Panel.

National Reading Panel (2000) *Teaching Children to Read: An Evidenced-Based Assessment of the Scientific Research Literature on Reading and Its Implications for Reading Instruction. Summary Report*. National Institute of Child Health and Human Development.

National Records of Scotland (2018) *Gaelic Analytic Report (Part 1)*. https://www.scotlandscensus.gov.uk/news/gaelic-analytical-report-part-1.

Ndhlovu, F. and Makalela, L. (2021) *Decolonising Multilingualism in Africa: Recentering Silenced Voices from the Global South*. Multilingual Matters.

Nelson, C.L., Proshina, Z.G. and Davis, D.R. (eds) (2020) *The Handbook of World Englishes* (2nd edn). Wiley Blackwell.

Netten, J. and Germain, C. (2004) Theoretical and research foundations of intensive French. *Canadian Modern Language Review/La Revue canadienne des langues vivantes* 60 (3), 275–294.

Nettle, D. and Romaine, S. (2000) *Vanishing Voices: The Extinction of the World's Languages*. Oxford University Press.

Newcombe, L.P. (2007) *Social Context and Fluency in L2 Learners: The Case of Wales*. Multilingual Matters.

Newcomer, S. (2020) 'Who are we today?' Latinx youth perspectives on the possibilities of being bilingual and bicultural. *Journal of Language, Identity, and Education* 19 (3), 193–207. https://doi.org/10.1080/15348458.2019.1655426.

New London Group (1996) A pedagogy of multiliteracies: Designing social futures. *Harvard Educational Review* 66 (1), 60–92.

Ng, S. and Wicha, N.Y.Y. (2013) Meaning first: A case for language-independent access to word meaning in the bilingual brain. *Neuropsychologia* 51 (5), 850–863. https://doi.org/doi:10.1016/j.neuropsychologia.2013.01.017.

Ngo, B. (2010) *Unresolved Identities: Discourse, Ambivalence, and Urban Immigrant Students*. State University of New York Press.

Nguyen, T.T.T. (2022) *Individual Language Policy: Bilingual Youth in Vietnam*. Multilingual Matters.

Nicholls, C. (2005) Death by a thousand cuts: Indigenous language bilingual education programmes in the Northern Territory of Australia, 1972–1998. *International Journal of Bilingual Education and Bilingualism* 8 (2–3), 160–177.

Nichols, E.S., Wild, C.J., Stojanoski, B., Battista, M.E. and Owen, A.M. (2020) Bilingualism affords no general cognitive advantages: A population study of executive function in 11,000 people. *Psychological Science* 31 (5), 548–567.

Nicoladis, E. and Smithson, L. (2018) Bilingual linguistic and cognitive development. In R.R. Heredia and J. Altarriba (eds) *An Introduction to Bilingualism: Principles and Processes* (pp. 225–241). Taylor and Francis.

Nicolarakis, O.D. and Mitchell, T. (2023) Dynamic bilingualism to dynamic writing: Using translanguaging strategies and tools. *Languages* 8 (2), 141.

Nicolay, A.-C. and Poncelet, M. (2015) Cognitive benefits in children enrolled in an early bilingual immersion school: A follow-up study. *Bilingualism: Language and Cognition* 18 (4), 789–795.

Nikula, T., Dafouz, E., Moore, P. and Smit, U. (eds) (2016) *Conceptualising Integration in CLIL and Multilingual Education*. Multilingual Matters.

Noggle, A.K. and Doran, P.R. (2019) Assessment and identification for English/culturally and linguistically diverse learners: High-incidence disabilities. In P.R. Doran and A.K. Noggle (eds) *Supporting English Learners with Exceptional Needs* (pp. 111–134). TESOL Press.

Norton, B. (2013) *Identity and Language Learning: Extending the Conversation* (2nd edn). Multilingual Matters.

Norton, B. (2020) Motivation, identity and investment: A journey with Robert Gardner. In A.H. Al-Hoorie and P.D. MacIntyre (eds) *Contemporary Language Motivation Theory: 60 Years Since Gardner and Lambert (1959)* (pp. 153–168). Multilingual Matters.

Norton, B. and Pavlenko, A. (2019) Imagined communities, identity, and English language learning in a multilingual world. In X. Gao (ed.) *Second Handbook of English Language Teaching* (pp. 703–718). Springer.

Nover, S.M. (1993) Who will shape the future of deaf education? In M.D. Garretson (ed.) *Deafness 1993–2013: A Deaf American Monograph* (pp. 117–123). National Association of the Deaf.

Nover, S.M. (1995) Language and English in deaf education. In C. Lucas (ed.) *Sociolinguistics in Deaf Communities* (pp. 109–163). Gallaudet University Press.

Nover, S.M. (2000) History of language planning in deaf education: The 19th century. Dissertation, University of Arizona.

Nover, S.M. (2010) What parents and early childhood professionals need to know about language acquisition planning: A new lens for the whole child. Paper presented at the National American Sign Language and Bilingual Early Childhood Education, Washington, DC.

Nover, S.M. and Andrews, J.F. (1998) *Critical Pedagogy in Deaf Education: Bilingual Methodology and Staff Development.* USDLC Star Schools Project Report 1. New Mexico School for the Deaf.

Nover, S. M. and Andrews, J.F. (1999) *Critical Pedagogy in Deaf Education: Bilingual Methodology and Staff Development. Year 2; 1998–1999. USDLC Star Schools Project.* Office of Educational Research and Improvement.

Nover, S.M. and Andrews, J.F. (2000) *Critical Pedagogy in Deaf Education: Bilingual Methodology and Staff Development. Year 3; 1999–2000.* USDLC Star Schools Project. Office of Educational Research and Improvement.

Nover, S.M. and Andrews, J.F. (2002) *Critical Pedagogy in Deaf Education: Bilingual Methodology and Staff Development, USDLC Star Schools Project Report 1.* New Mexico School for the Deaf.

Nover, S.M. and Moll, L. (1997) Cultural mediation of deaf cognition. In M.P. Moeller and B. Schick (eds) *Deafness and Diversity: Sociolinguistic Issues* (pp. 30–50). Boys Town National Research Hospital.

Nover, S.M., Christensen, K.M. and Cheng, L.L. (1998) Development of ASL and English competence for learners who are deaf. *Topics in Language Disorders* 18 (4), 61–72.

Nover, S.M., Andrews, J.F. and Everhart, V.S. (2001) *Critical Pedagogy in Deaf Education: Teachers' Reflections on Implementing ASL/English Bilingual Methodology and Language Assessment for Deaf Learners. Year 4: 2000–2001.* USDLC Star Schools Project. Office of Educational Research and Improvement.

Nover, S.M., Andrews, J.F., Baker, S., Everhart, V.S. and Bradford, M. (2002) *Star Schools' USDLC Engaged Learning Project No. 5 ASL/English Bilingual Staff Development Project in Deaf Education Staff Development in ASL/English Bilingual Instruction for Deaf Students: Evaluation and Impact Study.* New Mexico School for the Deaf.

Nussbaum, D.B., Scott, S. and Simms, L.E. (2012) The 'why' and 'how' of an ASL/English bimodal bilingual program. *Odyssey: New Directions in Deaf Education* 13, 14–19.

O'Brien, C.A. and Placier, P. (2015) Deaf culture and competing discourses in a residential school for the deaf: 'Can do' versus 'can't do'. *Equity and Excellence in Education* 48 (2), 320–338.

O'Brien, D. (2020) Mapping deaf academic spaces. *Higher Education* 80, 739–755.

Ó Duibhir, P. (2018) *Immersion Education: Lessons from a Minority Language Context.* Multilingual Matters.

Office of English Language Acquisition (2017) *Students with Disabilities Who Are English Learners (OELA Fast Facts).* https://ncela.ed.gov/files/fast_facts/05-19-2017/ELStudentsWithDisabilities_ FastFacts_4p.pdf.

Office of English Language Acquisition (2018a) *English Learner (EL) Trends from the Nation's Report Card.* US Department of Education. https://www.ncela.ed.gov/files/fast_facts/ELs-NAEP_Card.pdf.

Office of English Language Acquisition (2018b) *National and State-Level High School Graduation Rates for English Learners.* US Department of Education. https://www. ncela.ed.gov/files/fast_facts/GraduationRatesFactSheet.pdf.

Office of English Language Acquisition (2019a) *The Top Languages Spoken by English Learners (ELs) in the United States.* US Department of Education. https://www.ncela. ed.gov/files/fast_facts/olea-top-languages-fact-sheet-20191021-508.pdf.

Office of English Language Acquisition (2019b) *Dual Language Learning Programs and English Learners.* US Department of Education. https://ncela.ed.gov/files/fast_facts/19-0389_Del4.4_DualLanguagePrograms_122319_508.pdf.

Office of English Language Acquisition (2020a) *English Learners: Demographic Trends.* US Department of Education. https://www.ncela.ed.gov/files/fast_facts/19-0193_Del4.4_ELDemographicTrends_021220_508.pdf.

Office of English Language Acquisition (2020b) *English Learners Who Are Black.* Department of Education. https:// ncela.ed.gov/files/fast_facts/FactSheet_ELsWhoAreBlack_032620_508.pdf.

Office of English Language Acquisition (2023a) *High School Graduation Rates for English Learners*. Department of Education. https://ncela.ed.gov/resources/fact-sheet-high-school-graduation-rates-for-english-learners-june-2023.

Office of English Language Acquisition (2023b) *English Learners with Disabilities*. Department of Education. https://ncela.ed.gov/resources/infographic-english-learners-with-disabilities-october-2023.

Office of English Language Acquisition (2023c) *The Biennial Report to Congress on the Implementation of the Title III State Formula Grant Program: School Years 2018–2020*. Department of Education.

Ó Gliasáin, M. (1996) *The Language Question in the Census of the Population*. Linguistics Institute of Ireland.

Ó hlfearnáin, T. (2015) Sociolinguistic vitality of Manx after extreme language shift: Authenticity without traditional native speakers. *International Journal of the Sociology of Language* 231, 45–62. https://doi.org/10.1515/ijsl-2014-0031.

Olivos, E.M. and Ochoa, A.M. (2024) Families, communities, and activism in dual language bilingual education: Paradigms of parental engagement. In J.A. Freire, C. Alfaro and E. de Jong (eds) *The Handbook of Dual Language Bilingual Education* (pp. 577–594). Routledge. https://doi.org/10.4324/9781003269076-47.

Olko, J. and Sallabank, J. (eds) (2021) *Revitalizing Endangered Languages: A Practical Guide*. Cambridge University Press.

Oller, D.K. and Eilers, R.E. (2002) *Language and Literacy in Bilingual Children*. Multilingual Matters.

Oller, J.W. and Perkins, K. (1980) *Research in Language Testing*. Newbury House.

Olsen, L. (2010) *Reparable Harm: Fulfilling the Unkept Promise of Educational Opportunity for California's Long Term English Learners*. https://californianstogether.org/product/reparable-harm-fulfilling-the-unkept-promise-of-educational-opportunity-for-californias-long-term-english-learner/.

Olsen, L. (2015) *Bilingualism and Education in California and the United States: A Timeline*. https://www.bilingualeducation.org/cabe2015/TimelineForCABE.pdf.

Olsen, L. (2020) The history of the movement: Enacting the State Seal of Biliteracy in the state of California. In A.J. Heineke and K.J. Davin (eds) *The Seal of Biliteracy: Case Studies and Considerations for Policy Implementation* (pp. 3–16). Information Age Publishing.

Orellana, M. (2009) *Translating Childhoods: Immigrant Youth, Language, and Culture*. Rutgers University Press.

Ó Riagáin, P. (2001) Irish language production and reproduction 1981–1996. In J. Fishman (ed.) *Can Threatened Languages Be Saved?* (pp. 195–214). Multilingual Matters.

O'Rourke, B. and Walsh, J. (eds) (2018) Special issue – Comparing 'new speakers' across language contexts: Mobility and motivations. *Journal of Multilingual and Multicultural Development* 39 (5), 377–474.

Ortega, L. (2019) SLA and the study of equitable multilingualism. *Modern Language Journal* 103, 23–38.

Ostler, N. (2005) *Empires of the Word: A Language History of the World*. HarperCollins.

Otcu-Grillman, B. and Borjian, M. (eds) (2022) *Remaking Multilingualism: A Translanguaging Approach*. Multilingual Matters.

Otheguy, R., García, O. and Reid, W. (2015) Clarifying translanguaging and deconstructing named languages: A perspective from linguistics. *Applied Linguistics Review* 6 (3), 281–307. https://doi.org/10.1515/applirev-2015-0014.

Otheguy, R., García, O. and Reid, W. (2019) A translanguaging view of the linguistic system of bilinguals. *Applied Linguistics Review* 10 (4), 625–651. https://doi.org/10.1515/applirev-2018-0020.

Ovando, C.J. (2003) Bilingual education in the United States: Historical development and current issues. *Bilingual Research Journal* 27 (1), 1–24.

Ovando, C.J. and Combs, M.C. (2018) *Bilingual and ESL Classrooms: Teaching in Multicultural Contexts* (6th edn). Rowman and Littlefield.

Özerk, K. and Williams, C.H. (2023) National curriculum reforms and their impact on indigenous and minority languages: The Sami in Norway and the Welsh in Wales in comparative perspective. In S. Björklund and M. Björklund (eds) *Policy and Practice for Multilingual Educational Settings: Comparisons across Contexts* (pp. 39–67). Multilingual Matters.

Ożóg, C. and Marsh, D. (2009) CLIL: An interview with Professor David Marsh. *International House Journal of Education and Development*, spring, 26. https://ihjournal.com/content-and-language-integrated-learning.

Pae, T.-I. (2019) A simultaneous analysis of relations between L1 and L2 skills in reading and writing. *Reading Research Quarterly* 54 (1), 109–124. https://doi.org/10.1002/rrq.216.

Paap, K.R. (2023) *The Bilingual Advantage in Executive Functioning Hypothesis: How the Debate Provides Insight into Psychology's Replication Crisis*. Routledge.

Paap, K.R., Johnson, H.A. and Sawi, O. (2015) Bilingual advantages in executive functioning either do not exist or are restricted to very specific and undetermined circumstances. *Cortex* 69, 265–278.

Paap, K.R., Johnson, H.A. and Sawi, O. (2016) Should the search for bilingual advantages in executive functioning continue? *Cortex* 74, 305–314. https://doi.org/10.1016/j.cortex.2015.09.010.

Padden, C. and Humphries, T. (2005) *Inside Deaf Culture*. Harvard University Press.

Pai, M., Cummins, J., Nocus, I., Salaün, M. and Vernaudon, J. (2015) Intersections of language ideology, power, and identity: Bilingual education and indigenous language revitalization in French Polynesia. In W.E. Wright, S. Boun and O. García (eds) *Handbook of Bilingual and Multilingual Education* (pp. 145–163). John Wiley and Sons.

Paing, C.M. (2018) To know a Bāthā: Family language socialization among Buddhist immigrants from Myanmar in New York City. *Journal of Southeast Asian American Education and Advancement* 13 (1), 1–25. https://doi.org/10.7771/2153-8999.1169.

Palfreyman, D.M. and van der Walt, C. (eds) (2017) *Academic Biliteracies: Multilingual Repertoires in Higher Education*. Multilingual Matters.

Palmer, D.K. (2020) 'You're not a Spanish-speaker!' – 'We are all bilingual': The purple kids on being and becoming bilingual in a dual-language kindergarten classroom. In J. MacSwan and C.J. Faltis (eds) *Codeswitching in the Classroom: Critical Perspectives on Teaching, Learning, Policy, and Ideology* (pp. 247–267). Center for Applied Linguistics and Routledge.

Palmer, D.K., Zuñiga, C.E. and Henderson, K.I. (2015) A dual language revolution in the United States? On the bumpy road from compensatory to enrichment education for bilingual children in the United States. In W.E. Wright, S. Boun and O. García (eds) *Handbook of Bilingual and Multilingual Education* (pp. 449–460). Wiley-Blackwell.

Palmer, D.K., Henderson, K.I., Wall, D., Zúñiga, C.E. and Berthelsen, S. (2016) Team teaching among mixed messages: Implementing two-way dual language bilingual education at third grade in Texas. *Language Policy* 15, 393–413. https://doi.org/10.1007/s10993-015-9361-3.

Panayiotou, A. (2006) Translating guilt: An endeavor of shame in the Mediterranean? In A. Pavlenko (ed.) *Bilingual Minds: Emotional Experience, Expression, and Representation* (pp. 183–208). Multilingual Matters.

Panayiotou, A. (2007) Bilingual emotions: The untranslatable self. *Sociolinguistic Studies* 5 (1), 1–19.

Panda, M. and Mohanty, A.K. (2015) Multilingual education in South Asia. In W.E. Wright, S. Boun and O. García (eds) *Handbook of Bilingual and Multilingual Education* (pp. 542–553). Wiley-Blackwell.

Papafragou, A. (2017) Relations between language and thought: Individuation and the count/mass distinction. In H. Cohen and C. Lefebvre (eds) *Handbook of Categorization in Cognitive Science* (2nd edn, pp. 353–376). Elsevier.

Paradis, J., Crago, M., Genesee, F. and Rice, M. (2003) French-English bilingual children with SLI: How do they compare with their monolingual peers? *Journal of Speech, Language, and Hearing Research* 46 (1), 113–127.

Paradis, J., Genesee, F. and Crago, M. (2021) *Dual Language Development and Disorders: A Handbook on Bilingualism and Second Language Learning* (3rd edn). Brookes Publishing.

Park, K. (2024) Youth counter-storytelling: The educational experiences of refugee-background K'nyaw youth in Korean dual language bilingual education. Dissertation, University of Utah.

Park-Johnson, S.K. (2024) *Korean–English Bilingualism in Early Childhood: A Longitudinal Investigation of Development*. Multilingual Matters.

Parrish, T.B., Linquanti, R., Merickel, A., Quick, H.E. and Esra, P. (2002) *Effects of the Implementation of Proposition 227 on the Education of English Learners, K-12: Year 2 Report*. American Institutes for Research; WestEd.

Patel, M., Solly, M. and Copeland, S. (2023) *The Future of English: Global Perspectives* (B. O'Sullivan and Y. Jin, eds). British Council. https://futureofenglish.britishcouncil.org.

Patten, A. and Kymlicka, W. (2003) Introduction. Language rights and political theory: Context, issues, and approaches. In A. Kymlicka and A. Patten (eds) *Language Rights and Political Theory* (pp. 1–51). Oxford University Press.

Paulsrud, B., Tian, Z. and Toth, J. (eds) (2021) *English-Medium Instruction and Translanguaging*. Multilingual Matters.

Pavlenko, A. (2000) What's in a concept? *Bilingualism: Language and Cognition* 3 (1), 31–36.

Pavlenko, A. (2001) Bilingualism, gender, and ideology. *International Journal of Bilingualism* 5 (2), 117–151.

Pavlenko, A. (2002) Poststructuralist approaches to the study of social factors in second language learning and use. In V. Cook (ed.) *Portraits of the L2 User* (pp. 275–302). Multilingual Matters.

Pavlenko, A. (2003) 'I never knew I was a bilingual': Reimagining teacher identities in TESOL. *Journal of Language, Identity, and Education* 2 (4), 251–268.

Pavlenko, A. (2004) 'Stop doing that, Ia komu skazala!' Language choice and emotions in parent–child communication. *Journal of Multilingual and Multicultural Development* 25 (2–3), 179–203.

Pavlenko, A. (2005) Bilingualism and thought. In J.F. Kroll and A. De Groot (eds) *Handbook of Bilingualism: Psycholinguistic Approaches* (pp. 433–453). Oxford University Press.

Pavlenko, A. (ed.) (2011) *Thinking and Speaking in Two Languages*. Multilingual Matters.

Pavlenko, A. (2014) *The Bilingual Mind and What It Tells Us About Language and Thought*. Cambridge University Press.

Pavlenko, A. and Driagina, V. (2007) Russian emotion vocabulary in American learners' narratives. *Modern Language Journal* 91 (2), 213–234.

Pavlenko, A. and Lantolf, J.P. (2000) Second language learning as participation and the (re)construction of selves. In J.P. Lantolf (ed.) *Sociocultural Theory and Second Language Learning* (pp. 155–178). Oxford University Press.

Pavlenko, A. and Malt, B.C. (2011) Kitchen Russian: Cross-linguistic differences and first-language object naming by Russian–English bilinguals. *Bilingualism: Language and Cognition* 14, 19–45.

Payne, H., Gutierrez-Sigut, E., Woll, B. and MacSweeney, M. (2019) Cerebral lateralisation during signed and spoken language production in children born deaf. *Developmental Cognitive Neuroscience* 36, 100619.

Peal, E. and Lambert, W.E. (1962) The relation of bilingualism to intelligence. *Psychological Monographs: General and Applied* 76 (27), 1–23.

Peer, L. and Reid, G. (eds) (2016) *Multilingualism, Literacy and Dyslexia: Breaking Down Barriers for Education* (2nd edn). Routledge.

Peltz, R. and Kliger, H. (2013) Becoming Yiddish speakers in New York: Burgeoning communities of bilingual children. In O. García, Z. Zakharia and B. Otcu (eds) *Bilingual Community Education and Multilingualism: Beyond Heritage Languages in a Global City* (pp. 190–203). Multilingual Matters.

Pennycook, A. (2013) *The Cultural Politics of English as an International Language*. Routledge.

Perez, W. and Vásquez, R. (2024) *Culturally Responsive Schooling for Indigenous Mexican Students*. Multilingual Matters.

Peristeri, E., Baldimtsi, E., Vogelzang, M., Tsimpli, I.M. and Durrleman, S. (2021) The cognitive benefits of bilingualism in autism spectrum disorder: Is theory of mind boosted and by which underlying factors? *Autism Research* 14 (8), 1695–1709.

Perley, B.C. (2012) Zombie linguistics: Experts, endangered languages and the curse of undead voices. *Anthropological Forum* 22 (2), 133–149.

Perniss, P. (2018) Why we should study multimodal language. *Frontiers in Psychology* 9, 1109.

Perryman-Clark, S., Kirkland, D.E. and Jackson, A. (eds) (2014) *Students' Rights to Their Own Language: A Critical Sourcebook*. Bedford/St Martin's.

Petitto, L.A., Berens, M.S., Kovelman, I., Dubins, M.H., Jasinska, K. and Shalinsky, M. (2012) The 'perceptual wedge hypothesis' as the basis for bilingual babies' phonetic processing advantage: New insights from fNIRS brain imaging. *Brain and Language* 121 (2), 130–143.

Petroj, V., Guerrera, K. and Davidson, K. (2014) ASL dominant code-blending in the whispering of bimodal bilingual children. In *36th Annual Boston University Conference on Language Development*. Cascadilla Press.

Peyton, J.K., Ranard, D.A. and McGinnis, S. (2001) Charting a new course: Heritage language education in the United States. In J.K. Peyton, D.A. Ranard and S. McGinnis (eds) *Heritage Languages in America: Blueprint for the Future* (pp. 3–28). Center for Applied Linguistics; Delta Systems.

Pfau, R. and Zeshan, U. (2016) Positive signs. How sign language typology benefits deaf communities and linguistic theory. *Linguistic Typology* 20 (3), 547–559.

Phakiti, A. and Leung, C. (2024) *Assessment for Language Teaching*. Cambridge University Press.

Philip, M.J. and Small, A. (1991) *Bilingual Bicultural Program Development at the Learning Center for Deaf Children*. Learning Center for Deaf Children.

Phillipson, R. (2018) Linguistic imperialism an NNESTs. In J.I. Liontas (ed.) *The TESOL Encyclopedia of English Language Teaching*. John Wiley and Sons. https://doi.org/10.1002/9781118784235.eelt0023.

Phillipson, R. and Skutnabb-Kangas, T. (2013) Linguistic imperialism and endangered languages. In T.K. Bhatia and W.C. Ritchie (eds) *Handbook of Bilingualism and Multilingualism* (pp. 495–516). Blackwell Publishing.

Phyak, P. and De Costa, P.I. (2021) Decolonial struggles in Indigenous language education in neoliberal times: Identities, ideologies, and activism. *Journal of Language, Identity and Education* 20 (5), 291–295. https://doi.org/10.1080/15348458.2021.1957683.

Pickersgill, M. and Gregory, S. (1998) Bilingualism, current policy and practice. In S. Gregory, P. Knight, W. McCracken and L. Watson (eds) *Issues in Deaf Education* (pp. 88–97). David Fulton Publishers.

Pietikäinen, S., Kelly-Holmes, H., Jaffe, A. and Coupland, N. (2016) *Sociolinguistics from the Periphery: Small Languages in New Circumstances*. Cambridge University Press.

Piller, I. (2001) Private language planning: The best of both worlds. *Estudios de Sociolingüística* 2 (1), 61–80.

Piller, I. (2002) *Bilingual Couples Talk: The Discursive Construction of Hybridity*. John Benjamins.

Pimienta, D., Prado, D. and Blanco, Á. (2009) *Twelve Years of Measuring Linguistic Diversity in the Internet: Balance and Perspectives*. https://unesdoc.unesco.org/ images/0018/001870/187016e.pdf.

Pintner, R. and Arsenian, S. (1937) The relation of bilingualism to verbal intelligence and school adjustment. *Journal of Educational Research* 31 (4), 255–263.

Pizzo, L. (2016) d/Deaf and hard of hearing multilingual learners: The development of communication and language. *American Annals of the Deaf* 161 (1), 17–32.

Pizzo, L. and Chilvers, A. (2016) Assessment and d/deaf and hard of hearing multilingual learners: Considerations and promising practices. *American Annals of the Deaf* 161 (1), 56–66.

Poarch, G.J. (2018) Multilingual language control and executive function: A replication study. *Frontiers in Communication* 3, 46.

Poarch, G.J. and Bialystok, E. (2015) Bilingualism as a model for multitasking. *Developmental Review* 35, 113–124.

Poarch, G.J. and Krott, A. (2019) A bilingual advantage? An appeal for a change in perspective and recommendations for future research. *Behavioral Sciences* 9 (9), 95. https://doi.org/10.3390/bs9090095.

Poarch, G.J. and Van Hell, J.G. (2012) Cross-language activation in children's speech production: Evidence from second language learners, bilinguals, and trilinguals. *Journal of Experimental Child Psychology* 11 (3), 419–438.

Poehner, M.E., Davin, K.J. and Lantolf, J.P. (2017) Dynamic assessment. In E.G. Shohamy, I. Or and S. May (eds) *Language Testing and Assessment: Encyclopedia of Language and Education* (3rd edn, pp. 243–256). Springer International Publishing. https://doi.org/DOI 10.1007/978-3-319-02261-1_18.

Pompeo, M.R. (2020) Designation of the Confucius Institute U.S. Center as a foreign mission of the PRC. https://www.state.gov/designation-of-the-confucius-institute-u-s-center-as-a-foreign-mission-of-the-prc.

Pons, F., Bosch, L. and Lewkowicz, D.J. (2015) Bilingualism modulates infants' selective attention to the mouth of a talking face. *Psychological Science* 26 (4), 490–498.

Pontecorvo, E., Higgins, M., Mora, J., Lieberman, A.M., Pyers, J. and Caselli, N.K. (2023) Learning a sign language does not hinder acquisition of a spoken language. *Journal of Speech, Language, and Hearing Research* 66 (4), 1291–1308.

Popham, W.J. (2025) *Classroom Assessment: What Teachers Need to Know* (10th edn). Pearson.

Poplack, S. and Meechan, M. (1998) Introduction: How languages fit together in codeswitching. *International Journal of Bilingualism* 2 (2), 127–138.

Porras, D.A., Ee, J. and Gándara, P.C. (2014) Employer preferences: Do bilingual applicants and employees experience an advantage? In R. Callahan and P. Gándara (eds) *The Bilingual Advantage: Language, Literacy and the US Labor Market* (pp. 234–260). Multilingual Matters.

Porter, L., Cano, M.V. and Umansky, I.M. (2023) *Bilingual Education and America's Future: Evidence and Pathways. Civil Rights Project*. https://escholarship.org/uc/item/7t494794.

Portes, A. and Rumbaut, R.G. (2006) *Immigrant America: A Portrait* (3rd edn). University of California Press.

Potowski, K. (2007) *Language and Identity in a Dual Immersion School*. Multilingual Matters.

Potowski, K. (2019) When should teachers be cautious about translanguaging? https://docs.google.com/document/d/1frbjr6nOWqsekC98eMuGq9gpjHP93utap5qfkda5rWw/edit?fbclid=IwAR3MNxK4pZRIFZwW8Tc2UCZymxnGiQPGG7ToyuyPnsFb3Nz1laWh9vqeYwg.

Potowski, K. and Rothman, J. (eds) (2011) *Bilingual Youth: Spanish in English-Speaking Societies*. John Benjamins.

Poza, L. (2019) 'Los dos son mi idioma': Translanguaging, identity, and social relationships among bilingual youth. *Journal of Language, Identity, and Education* 18 (2), 92–109. https://doi.org/10.1080/15348458.2018.1504682.

Pu, C. (2008) Learning your heritage language while learning English: Chinese American children's bilingual and biliteracy development in heritage language and public schools. Doctoral dissertation, University of Texas, San Antonio.

Pu, C. and Wright, W.E. (eds) (2022) *Innovating the Practicum in TESOL Teacher Education: Design, Implementation, and Pedagogy in an Era of Change*. Routledge.

Pudans-Smith, K.K., Cue, K.R., Wolsey, J.L.A. and Clark, M.D. (2019) To Deaf or not to Deaf: That is the question. *Psychology* 10 (15), 2091–2114.

Purić, D., Vuksanović, J. and Chondrogianni, V. (2017) Cognitive advantages of immersion education after 1 year: Effects of amount of exposure. *Journal of Experimental Child Psychology* 159, 296–309. https://doi.org/10.1016/j.jecp.2017.02.011.

Purpura, J.E. (2017) Assessing communicative language ability: Models and their components. In S. May, I. Or and E. Shohamy (eds) *Encyclopedia of Language and Education, Vol. 7: Language Testing and Assessment* (3rd edn, pp. 2198–2213). New York: Springer.

Qi, S. and Mitchell, R.E. (2012) Large-scale academic achievement testing of deaf and hard-of-hearing students: Past, present, and future. *Journal of Deaf Studies and Deaf Education* 17 (1), 1–18.

Quay, S. (2001) Managing linguistic boundaries in early trilingual development. In J. Cenoz and F. Genesee (eds) *Trends in Bilingual Acquisition* (pp. 149–199). John Benjamins.

Quay, S. and Chevalier, S. (2019) Fostering multilingualism in childhood. In S. Montanari and S. Quay (eds) *Multidisciplinary Perspectives on Multilingualism: The Fundamentals* (pp. 205–228). De Gruyter Mouton.

Quezada, M.S., Wiley, T.G. and Ramirez, D.J. (1999/2000) How the reform agenda shortchanges English learners. *Educational Leadership* 57 (4), 57–61.

Rahman, T. (2005) The Muslim response to English in South Asia: With special reference to inequality, intolerance, and militancy in Pakistan. *Journal of Language, Identity, and Education* 4 (2), 119–135.

Raijman, R. (2012) Linguistic assimilation of first-generation Jewish South African immigrants in Israel. *Journal of International Migration and Integration* 14 (4), 615–636.

Ramanathan, V. (ed.) (2013) *Language Policies and (Dis)citizenship: Rights, Access, Pedagogies*. Multilingual Matters.

Ramirez, J.D. (1992) Executive summary. *Bilingual Research Journal* 16, 1–62.

Ramirez, J.D., Yuen, S.D., Ramey, D.R., Pasta, D.J. and Billings, D.K. (1991) *Final Report: Longitudinal Study of Structured English Immersion Strategy, Early Exit and Late-Exit Bilingual Education Programs for Language Minority Children, Vol. 1*. Publication No. 300-87-0156. US Department of Education.

Ramirez, J.D., Wiley, T.G., de Klerk, G., Lee, E. and Wright, W.E. (2005) *Ebonics: The Urban Educational Debate* (2nd edn). Multilingual Matters.

Ramirez, P.C. (2013) An interview with Alma Flor Ada. *Journal of Latinos and Education* 12 (2), 121–130. https://doi.org/10.1080/15348431.2012.745406.

Rampton, B. (2014) *Crossing: Language and Ethnicity Among Adolescents* (2nd edn). Routledge.

Rampton, B. and Charalambous, C. (2012) Crossing. In M. Martin-Jones, A. Blackledge and A. Creese (eds) *Routledge Handbook of Multilingualism* (pp. 482–498). Routledge.

Ramsey, C. and Padden, C. (1998) Reading ability in signing deaf children. *Topics in Language Disorders* 18 (4), 30-46.

Ramsey, C. and Padden, C. (1998) Natives and newcomers: Gaining access to literacy in a classroom for deaf children. *Anthropology and Education Quarterly* 29 (1), 5–24.

Reading League (2023) Joint Statement of the Reading League and NCEL – Understanding the difference: The science of reading and implementation for English learners/emergent bilinguals (ELs/EBs). Reading League and National Center for Effective Literacy Instruction for English Learner/Emergent Bilingual Students. https://multilingualliteracy.org/wp-content/uploads/2023/10/Joint-Statement_SOR-EL_EB.pdf.

Reagan, T. (2022) Language planning and language policies for sign languages: An emerging civil rights movement. *Sociolinguistica* 36 (1–2), 169–182.

Rebuffot, J. (1993) *Le Point sur L'immersion au Canada* [The Argument for Immersion in Canada]. Centre éducatif et Culturel.

Rehg, K.L. and Campbell, L. (eds) (2018) *The Oxford Handbook of Endangered Languages*. Oxford University Press.

REL Midwest (2019) ESSA tiers of evidence: What you need to know. https://ies.ed.gov/ncee/edlabs/regions/midwest/pdf/blogs/RELMW-ESSA-Tiers-Video-Handout-508.pdf.

Relyea, J.E. and Amendum, S.J. (2019) English reading growth in Spanish-speaking bilingual students: Moderating effect of English proficiency on cross-linguistic influence. *Child Development* 91 (4), 1150-1165. https://doi.org/10.1111/cdev.13288.

Renn, J., Choi, W., Li, H., Wright, W. and Morita-Mullaney, T. (2024) Supporting bilingualism during the COVID-19 pandemic: dual language bilingual education teachers' experiences and challenges. *International Journal of Bilingual Education and Bilingualism*, 1–14. https://doi.org/10.1080/13670050.2024.2432509.

Reyes, A. (2011) *Language, Identity, and Stereotype Among Southeast Asian American Youth*. Routledge.

Reyhner, J.A. and Eder, J.M.O. (2004) *American Indian Education: A History*. University of Oklahoma Press.

Rheindorf, M. and Wodak, R. (eds) (2020) *Sociolinguistic Perspectives on Migration Control: Language Policy, Identity, and Belonging.* Multilingual Matters.

Ricciardelli, L.A. (1992) Creativity and bilingualism. *Journal of Creative Behavior* 26 (4), 242–254.

Ricento, T. (2009) Problems with the 'language-as-resource' discourse in the promotion of heritage languages in the US. In M.R. Salaberry (ed.) *Language Allegiances and Bilingualism in the US* (pp. 110–131). Multilingual Matters.

Ricento, T. (2015a) Bi/multilingual education in Canada. In W.E. Wright, S. Boun and O. García (eds) *Handbook of Bilingual and Multilingual Education* (pp. 461–472). Wiley-Blackwell.

Ricento, T. (ed.) (2015b) *Language Policy and Political Economy: English in a Global Context.* Oxford University Press.

Ricento, T. (ed.) (2022) *Language Policies and Politics: Perspectives from Canada and the United States.* Cambridge University Press.

Richards, J.C. and Rodgers, T.S. (2014) *Approaches and Methods in Language Teaching* (3rd edn). Cambridge University Press.

Rivera, C. (1984) *Language Proficiency and Academic Achievement.* Multilingual Matters.

Rivera, C. and Collum, E. (eds) (2006) *State Assessment Policy and Practice for English Language Learners.* Lawrence Erlbaum Associates.

Roche, G. (2022) The necropolitics of language oppression. *Annual Review of Anthropology* 51 (1), 31–47. https://doi.org/10.1146/annurev-anthro-041420-102158.

Rogers, C.L., Lister, J.J., Febo, D.M., Besing, J.M. and Abrams, H.B. (2006) Effects of bilingualism, noise, and reverberation on speech perception by listeners with normal hearing. *Applied Psycholinguistics* 27 (3), 465–485.

Roibeaird, F.N. (2024) Community discourses of language reclamation through Irish medium youth work. *Journal of Language, Identity, and Education* (online first), 1–15. https://doi.org/10.1080/15348458.2024.2365233.

Rojo, L.M. (2017) Language and power. In O. García, N. Flores and M. Spotti (eds) *The Oxford Handbook of Language and Society* (pp. 77–102). Oxford University Press.

Rolstad, K., Mahoney, K. and Glass, G. (2005a) The big picture: A meta-analysis of program effectiveness research on English language learners. *Educational Policy* 19 (4), 572–594.

Rolstad, K., Mahoney, K. and Glass, G. (2005b) Weighing the evidence: A meta-analysis of bilingual education in Arizona. *Bilingual Research Journal* 29 (1), 43–67.

Romaine, S. (2000) *Language in Society: An Introduction to Sociolinguistics* (2nd edn). Oxford University Press.

Romaine, S. (2013) The bilingual and multilingual community. In T.K. Bhatia and W.C. Ritchie (eds) *Handbook of Bilingualism and Multilingualism* (pp. 445–465). Blackwell Publishing.

Ronjat, J. (1913) *Le Développement du Langage Observé Chez un Enfant Bilingue.* Champion.

Rosa, J. (2019) *Looking Like a Language, Sounding Like a Race: Raciolinguistic Ideologies and the Learning of Latinidad.* Oxford University Press.

Rosa, J. and Burdick, C. (2017) Language ideologies. In O. García, N. Flores and M. Spotti (eds) *The Oxford Handbook of Language and Society* (pp. 103–124). Oxford University Press.

Rose, H. and Conama, J.B. (2018) Linguistic imperialism: still a valid construct in relation to language policy for Irish Sign Language. *Language Policy* 17 (3), 385–404.

Rose, H., Syrbe, M., Montakantiwong, A. and Funada, N. (2020) *Global TESOL for the 21st Century: Teaching English in a Changing World.* Multilingual Matters.

Rosen, R. (ed.) (2020) *The Routledge Handbook of Sign Language Pedagogy.* Routledge.

Rosenbaum, A. (2022) Inside Jewish day schools: How should North American Jews be educated? *Jerusalem Post*, 27 August. https://www.jpost.com/diaspora/article-715557.

Rosenstock, R. and Napier, J. (2016) *International Sign. Linguistic, Usage, and Status Issues.* Gallaudet University Press.

Rossell, C.H. (1992) Nothing matters? A critique of the Ramírez, et al. Longitudinal study of instructional programs for language-minority children. *Bilingual Research Journal* 16 (1–2), 159–186.

Rossell, C.H. and Baker, K.A. (1996) The educational effectiveness of bilingual education. *Research in the Teaching of English* 30 (1), 7–74.

Ruben, R. J. (2005) Sign language: Its history and contribution to the understanding of the biological nature of language. *Acta Oto-Laryngologica* 125, 464–467.

Rubin, H., Estrada, L. and Honigsfeld, A. (2022) *Digital-Age Teaching for English Learners: A Guide to Equitable learning for all Students* (2nd edn). Corwin.

Rubinyi, S. (2006) *Natural Genius: The Gifts of Asperger's Syndrome.* Jessica Kingsley.

Rubio-Alcalá, F.D. and Coyle, D. (eds) (2021) *Developing and Evaluating Quality Bilingual Practices in Higher Education*. Multilingual Matters.

Rudolph, N., Selvi, A.F. and Yazan, B. (eds) (2020) *The Complexity of Identity and Interaction in Language Education*. Multilingual Matters.

Ruiz, R. (1984) Orientations in language planning. *NABE Journal* 8 (2), 15–34.

Ruiz, R. (2010) Reorienting language-as-resource. In J.E. Petrovic (ed.) *International Perspectives on Bilingual Education: Policy, Practice, and Controversy* (pp. 155–172). Information Age Publishing.

Rumbaut, R.G. (2009) A language graveyard? The evolution of language competencies, preferences and use among young adult children of immigrants. In T.G. Wiley, J.S. Lee and R.W. Rumberger (eds) *The Education of Language Minority Immigrants in the United States* (pp. 35–71). Multilingual Matters.

Rumberger, R.W., Callahan, R. and Gándara, P.C. (2003) Has Proposition 227 reduced the English learner achievement gap? *UC LMRI Newsletter* 13 (1), 1–2.

Saer, D.J. (1923) The effect of bilingualism on intelligence. *British Journal of Psychology* 14 (1), 25–38.

Saer, D.J. (1924) *Bilingual Problem*. Hughes and Son.

Saiegh-Haddad, E., Laks, L. and McBride, C. (eds) (2022) *Handbook of Literacy in Diglossia and in Dialectal Contexts: Psycholinguistic, Neurolinguistic, and Educational Perspectives*. Springer.

Salaberry, M.R. (2009) Bilingual education: Assimilation, segregation and integration. In M.R. Salaberry (ed.) *Language Allegiances and Bilingualism in the US* (pp. 172–195). Multilingual Matters.

Salgado, A.K. and Olague, N. (2020) Getting the most out of GLAD strategies: Addressing integrated and designated English language development. Soleado, Spring. https://intranet.dlenm.org/wp-content/uploads/sites/2/2021/03/Getting-the-Most-out-of-GLAD%C2%AE-Strategies-Addressing-Integrated-and-Designated-ELD.pdf.

Sallabank, J. (2013) *Endangered Languages: Attitudes, Identities and Policies*. Cambridge University Press.

Salomone, R. (2024) *The Rise of English: Global Politics and the Power of Language*. Oxford University Press.

Samuel, S., Cole, G. and Eacott, M.J. (2019) Grammatical gender and linguistic relativity: A systematic review. *Psychonomic Bulletin and Review* 26 (6), 1767–1786.

Sánchez, M.T. (2024) Translanguaging in dual language bilingual education in the United States: Framings, research, and possibilities. In J.A. Freire, C. Alfaro and E. de Jong (eds) *The Handbook of Dual Language Bilingual Education* (pp. 414–443). Routledge.

Sánchez, M.T. and García, O. (eds) (2022) *Transformative Translanguaging Espacios: Latinx Students and their Teachers Rompiendo Fronteras sin Miedo*. Multilingual Matters.

Sandler, W. (2018) The body as evidence for the nature of language. *Frontiers in Psychology* 9, 1782.

Sandler, W., Padden, C. and Aronoff, M. (2022) Emerging sign languages. *Languages* 7 (4), 284.

San Miguel, G. (2004) *Contested Policy: The Rise and Fall of Federal Bilingual Education in the United States, 1960–2001*. University of North Texas Press.

Sargent, B. (2017) As the world turns: The changing fortunes of online languages [blog post]. https://csa-research.com/Insights/ArticleID/121/As-the-World-Turns-The-Changing-Fortuntes-of-Online-Languages-in-2017.

Sarmiento-Quezada, B. (2024) 'To keep nuestra cultura': Math, language, and the importance of bilingual spaces for bilingual and Latinx parents. In M.A. Bravo and K. Téllez (eds) *Mathematics Instruction in Dual Language Classrooms: Theory and Research that Informs Practice*. Information Age Publishing.

Savignon, S.J. (2001) Communicative language teaching for the twenty-first century. In M. Celce-Murcia (ed.) *Teaching English as a Second or Foreign Language* (3rd edn, pp. 13–28). Heinle and Heinle.

Sayer, P. (2012) *Ambiguities and Tensions in English Language Teaching: Portraits of EFL Teachers as Legitimate Speakers*. Routledge.

Sayer, P. and Braun, D. (2020) The disparate impact of Covid-19 remote learning on English learners in the United States. *TESOL Journal* 11 (3), e546. https://doi.org/10.1002/tesj.546.

Scanlan, M. and López, F.A. (2015) *Leadership for Culturally and Linguistically Responsive Schools*. Routledge.

Schepers, O., Brennan, M. and Bernhardt, P.E. (eds) (2022) *Developing Trauma-Informed Teachers: Creating Classrooms that Foster Equity, Resilience, and Asset-Based Approaches: Reflections on Curricular and Program Implementation*. Information Age Publishing.

Schepers, O., Brennan, M. and Bernhardt, P.E. (eds) (2023) *Developing Trauma-Informed Teachers: Creating Classrooms that Foster Equity, Resilience, and Asset-Based Approaches: Reflections on Curricular and Program Implementation*. Information Age Publishing.

Schick, B., De Villiers, P., De Villiers, J. and Hoffmeister, R. (2007) Language and theory of mind: A study of deaf children. *Child Development* 78 (2), 376–396.

Schmidt, R.S. (2000) *Language Policy and Identity Politics in the United States*. Temple University Press.
Schmidt, R.S. (2009) English hegemony and the politics of ethno-linguistic justice in the US. In M.R. Salaberry (ed.) *Language Allegiances and Bilingualism in the United States*. Multilingual Matters.
Schwieter, J.W. (ed.) (2015) *The Cambridge Handbook of Bilingual Processing*. Cambridge University Press.
Schwieter, J.W. and Festman, J. (2023) *The Cognitive Neuroscience of Bilingualism*. Cambridge University Press.
Scott, J. (2021) The relationship between ASL fluency and English literacy. In C. Enns, J. Henner and L. McQuarrie (eds) *Discussing Bilingualism in Deaf Children: Essays in Honor of Robert Hoffmeister* (pp. 171–186). Routledge/Taylor & Francis Group. https://doi.org/10.4324/9780367808686-11-13.
Scott, J. and Cohen, S. (2023) Multilingual, multimodal, and multidisciplinary: Deaf students and translanguaging in content area classes. *Languages* 8 (1), 55.
Scott, J., Amadi, C. and Butts, T. (2022) d/Deaf and hard-of-hearing multilingual learners and literacy instruction. In J.E. Cannon, C. Guardino and P.V. Paul (eds) *Deaf and Hard of Hearing Multilingual Learners: Foundations, Strategies, and Resources* (pp. 142–174). Routledge.
Scott, J.A. and Henner, J. (2021) Second verse, same as the first: On the use of signing systems in modern interventions for deaf and hard of hearing children in the USA. *Deafness and Education International* 23 (2), 123–141. https://doi.org/10.1080/14643154.2020.1792071.
Scott, J.A. and Hoffmeister, R.J. (2016) American Sign Language and academic English: Factors influencing the reading of bilingual secondary school deaf and hard of hearing students. *Journal of Deaf Studies and Deaf Education* 22 (1), 59–71.
Scott, J.C., Straker, D.Y. and Katz, L. (eds) (2008) *Affirming Students' Right to Their Own Language: Bridging Language Policies and Pedagogical Practices*. Routledge.
Seals, C.A. (2020) *Choosing a Mother Tongue: The Politics of Language and Identity in Ukraine*. Multilingual Matters.
Sebastián-Gallés, N., Albareda-Castellot, B., Weikum, W.M. and Werker, J.F. (2012) A bilingual advantage in visual language discrimination in infancy. *Psychological Science* 23 (9), 994–999.
Seilstad, B.D. (2021) *Educating Adolescent Newcomers in the Superdiverse Midwest: Multilingual Students in English-centric Contexts*. Multilingual Matters.
Seltzer, K. (2019) Reconceptualizing 'home' and 'school' language: Taking a critical translingual approach in the English classroom. *TESOL Quarterly* 53 (4), 986–1007
Serratrice, L. (2013) The bilingual child. In T.K. Bhatia and W.C. Ritchie (eds) *The Handbook of Bilingualism and Multilingualism* (2nd edn, pp. 87–108). Wiley-Blackwell.
Seward, K. and Gentry, M. (2022) Students with gifts, creativity, and talents from low-income families. In J.L. Roberts, T.F. Inman and J.H. Robins (eds) *Introduction to Gifted Education* (2nd edn, pp. 343–366). Prufrock Press.
Shaw, E. and Delaporte, Y. (2011) New perspectives on the history of American Sign Language. *Sign Language Studies* 11 (2), 158–204.
Shin, S. (2018) *Bilingualism in Schools and Society* (2nd edn). Routledge.
Shin, D.S., Cimasko, T. and Yi, Y. (eds) (2021) *Multimodal Composing in K-12 ESL and EFL Education: Multilingual Perspectives*. Springer.
Shohamy, E. (2008) At what cost? Methods of language revival and protection. In K.A. King, L. Schilling-Estes, L. Fogle, J.J. Lou and B. Soukup (eds) *Sustaining Linguistic Diversity* (pp. 205–218). Georgetown University Press.
Shohamy, E. (2011) Assessing multilingual competencies: Adopting construct valid assessment policies. *Modern Language Journal* 9 (3), 418–429.
Shohamy, E. (2017) Critical language testing. In E. Shohamy, I. Or and S. May (eds) *Encyclopedia of Language and Education, Vol. 7: Language Testing and Assessment* (3rd edn, pp. 441–454). Springer.
Shohamy, E. and Menken, K. (2015) Language assessment: Past to present misuses and future possibilities. In W.E. Wright, S. Boun and O. García (eds) *Handbook of Bilingual and Multilingual Education* (pp. 253–269). John Wiley and Sons.
Shohamy, E., Or, I. and May, S. (eds) (2017) *Encyclopedia of Language and Education, Vol. 7: Language Testing and Assessment*. Springer.
Short, D. and Boyson, B. (2012) *Helping Newcomer Students Succeed in Secondary Schools and Beyond*. Center for Applied Linguistics.
Silva, T. and Wang, Z. (eds) (2021) *Reconciling Translingualism and Second Language Writing*. Routledge.
Silver, R.E. and Bokhorst-Heng, W.D. (eds) (2016) *Quadrilingual Education in Singapore: Pedagogical Innovation in Language Education*. Springer.

Simms, L. and Andrews, J.F. (2020) Using L1 sign language to teach reading. In R. Rosen (ed.) *The Routledge Handbook of Sign Language Pedagogy* (pp. 59–72). Routledge.

Simms, L. and Thumann, H. (2007) In search of a new, linguistically and culturally sensitive paradigm in deaf education. *American Annals of the Deaf* 152 (3), 302–311.

Simms, L., Rusher, M., Andrews, J.F. and Coryell, J. (2008) Apartheid in deaf education: Examining workforce diversity. *American Annals of the Deaf* 153 (4), 384–395.

Simms, L., Baker, S. and Clark, M.D. (2013) The standardized Visual Communication and Sign Language Checklist for signing children. *Sign Language Studies* 14 (1), 101–124.

Simonton, D.K. (2008) Bilingualism and creativity. In J. Altarriba and R.R. Heredia (eds) *An Introduction to Bilingualism: Principles and Processes* (pp. 147–166). Erlbaum.

Singleton, D.M. and Muñoz, C. (2011) Around and beyond the critical period hypothesis. In E. Hinkel (ed.) *Handbook of Research in Second Language Teaching and Learning* (vol. 2, pp. 407–425). Routledge.

Singleton, D.M. and Ryan, L. (2004) *Language Acquisition: The Age Factor* (2nd edn). Multilingual Matters.

Singleton, J.L., Jones, G. and Hanumantha, S. (2014) Toward ethical research practice with deaf participants. *Journal of Empirical Research on Human Research Ethics* 9 (3), 59–66.

Singleton, J.L., Walker, K., Quinto-Pozos, D. and Decker-Wright, P.D. (2024) Bilingual languaging patterns among deaf ASL-signing students with developmental disabilities: Implications for classroom and interventionist practice. Paper presented at ACEDHH, 2 February, Las Vegas, NV.

Sissons, C.B. (1917) *Bilingual Schools in Canada*. J.M. Dent.

Skutnabb-Kangas, T. (2000) *Linguistic Genocide in Education – Or Worldwide Diversity and Human Rights?* Lawrence Erlbaum Associates.

Skutnabb-Kangas, T. (2015) Language rights. In W.E. Wright, S. Boun and O. García (eds) *Handbook of Bilingual and Multilingual Education* (pp. 186–202). Wiley-Blackwell.

Skutnabb-Kangas, T. and Heugh, K. (eds) (2013) *Multilingual Education and Sustainable Diversity Work: From Periphery to Center*. Routledge.

Skyer, M. (2022) Multimodal transduction in deaf pedagogy. Paper presented at the 2022 Annual Meeting of the Society for Text and Discourse (STandD), 19 July.

Slavin, R.E. and Cheung, A. (2005) A synthesis of research on language of reading instruction for English-language learners. *Review of Educational Research* 75 (2), 247–284.

Slavkov, N. (2017) Family language policy and school language choice: Pathways to bilingualism and multilingualism in a Canadian context. *International Journal of Multilingualism* 14 (4), 378–400.

Smith, D., Davis, J. and Hoffman, D. (2020) L2/Ln sign language tests and assessment procedures. In R. Rosen (ed.) *The Routledge Handbook of Sign Language Pedagogy* (pp. 247–261). Routledge.

Smith, D.H. and Andrews, J.F. (2015) Deaf and hard of hearing faculty in higher education: Enhancing access, equity, policy, and practice. *Disability and Society* 30 (10), 1521–1536.

Smith, H.A. (2024) Bilingualism under threat: Structured literacy will make it harder for children to hold on to their mother tongue. *The Conversation*. https://theconversation.com/bilingualism-under-threat-structured-literacy-will-make-it-harder-for-children-to-hold-on-to-their-mother-tongue-236140.

Smith, N.R. (2021) *The End of the Village: Planning the Urbanization of China*. University of Minnesota Press.

Smith, S.L. and de Oliveira, L.C. (2019) Teaching English language arts to emergent to advanced bilinguals. In L.C. de Oliveira (ed.) *The Handbook of TESOL in K-12* (pp. 291–306). Wiley-Blackwell.

Solís, J.L., Sarmiento-Quezada, B., and Lina Martin Corredor. (2024) 'Ahora ya se que hacer': How translanguaging mediates bilingual teacher candidate reflections and teaching of mathematics. In M.A. Bravo and K. Téllez (eds) *Mathematics Instruction in Dual Language Classrooms: Theory and Research that Informs Practice*. Information Age Publishing.

Song, J. (2019) Contesting and negotiating othering from within: A Saudi Arabian female student's gendered experiences in the US. *Journal of Language, Identity, and Education* 19 (3), 149–162. https://doi.org/10.1080/15348458.2019.1654386.

Sparks, R.L. (2024) *Exploring L1–L2 Relationships: The Impact of Individual Differences*. Multilingual Matters.

Spolsky, B. (1989) Review of 'Key Issues in Bilingualism and Bilingual Education'. *Applied Linguistics* 10 (4), 449–451.

Spolsky, B. (2004) *Language Policy*. Cambridge University Press.

Spolsky, B. (2021) *Rethinking Language Policy*. Edinburgh University Press.

Spotti, M. and Blommaert, J. (2017) Bilingualism, multilingualism, globalization, and superdiversity: Towards sociolinguistic repertoires. In O. García, N. Flores and M. Spotti (eds) *The Oxford Handbook of Language and Society* (pp. 161–178). Oxford University Press.

Spring, J. (2021) *Deculturalization and the Struggle for Equality: A Brief History of the Education of Dominated Cultures in the United States* (10th edn). Routledge.

Stæhr, A. (2017) Languaging and normativity on Facebook. In K. Arnaut, M.S. Karrebæk, M. Spotti and J. Blommaert (eds) *Engaging Superdiversity: Recombining Spaces, Times and Language Practices* (pp. 170–195). Multilingual Matters.

Stanford Center for Assessment, Learning, and Equity (2016) *edTPA: English as an Additional Language Assessment Handbook*. Board of Trustees of the Leland Stanford Junior University.

Stangor, C., Lynch, L., Duan, C. and Glas, B. (1992) Categorization of individuals on the basis of multiple social features. *Journal of Personality and Social Psychology* 62 (2), 207.

Statista (2024) Languages most frequently used for web content as of January 2024, by share of websites. https://www.statista.com/statistics/262946/most-common-languages-on-the-internet.

Statistics Canada (2019) An increasingly diverse linguistic profile: Corrected data from the 2016 Census. https://www150.statcan.gc.ca/n1/daily-quotidien/170817/dq170817a-eng.htm.

Statistics Canada (2020) Table 37-10-0009-01: Number of students in official languages programs, public elementary and secondary schools, by program type, grade and sex. https://www150.statcan.gc.ca/t1/tbl1/en/tv.action?pid=3710000901.

Statistics Canada (2024) Participation in French immersion, bilingualism and the use of French in adulthood, 2021. https://www12.statcan.gc.ca/census-recensement/2021/as-sa/98-200-X/2021018/98-200-X2021018-eng.cfm.

Statistics Isle of Man Cabinet Office (2022) *2021 Isle of Man Census Report*. Isle of Man Government. https://www.gov.im/media/1375604/2021-01-27-census-report-part-i-final-2.pdf.

Stavans, A. and Porat, R. (2019) Codeswitching in multilingual communities. In S. Montanari and S. Quay (eds) *Multidisciplinary Perspectives on Multilingualism: The Fundamentals* (pp. 123–148). De Gruyter Mouton.

Stavans, I. (2003) *Spanglish: The Making of a New American Language*. HarperCollins.

Stavans, I. (2014) In defense of Spanglish. *The Common Reader: A Journal of the Essay*, October 1. https://commonreader.wustl.edu/c/cervantes-spanglish.

Steele, J.L., Slater, R.O., Zamarro, G., Miller, T., Li, J., Burkhauser, S. and Bacon, M. (2017) Effects of dual-language immersion programs on student achievement: Evidence from lottery data. *American Educational Research Journal* 54 (1S), 282s–306s. https://doi.org/10.3102/0002831216634463.

Stein-Smith, K. (2019) Foreign language classes becoming more scarce. *The Conversation*, February 6. https://theconversation.com/foreign-language-classes-becoming-more-scarce-102235.

Stepanova Sachs, O. and Coley, J. (2006) Envy and jealousy in Russian and English: Labeling and conceptualization of emotions by monolinguals and bilinguals. In A. Pavlenko (ed.) *Bilingual Minds: Emotional Experience, Expression, and Representation* (pp. 209–231). Multilingual Matters.

Sternberg, R.J. (ed.) (2002) *Why Smart People Can Be So Stupid*. Yale University Press.

Sterzuk, A. and Sarkar, M. (2024) Belonging, conflict and loss: Learning Ukrainian online during COVID-19. *Journal of Language, Identity and Education*, 1–13. https://doi.org/10.1080/15348458.2024.2306923.

Stokoe, W., Casterline, D. and Croneberg, C. (1965) *A Dictionary of American Sign Language on Linguistic Principles*. Gallaudet University Press.

Stollhans, S. (2024) GCSE results: More young people are studying languages – but the overall picture for language learning remains bleak. *The Conversation*, 22 August. https://theconversation.com/gcse-results-more-young-people-are-studying-languages-but-the-overall-picture-for-language-learning-remains-bleak-237252.

Stone, A. (2014) New directions in ASL-English bilingual ebooks. *Critical Inquiry in Language Studies* 11 (3), 186–206.

Stone, A., Kartheiser, G., Hauser, P.C., Petitto, L.A. and Allen, T.E. (2015) Fingerspelling as a novel gateway into reading fluency in deaf bilinguals. *PLoS One* 10 (10), 1–12.

Street, B.V. (2002) Understanding literacy issues in contemporary multiethnic schooling contexts, with particular reference to EAL pupils. In C. Leung (ed.) *Language and Additional/Second Language Issues for School Education* (pp. 49–58). NADLIC.

Street, B.V. (2013) *Social Literacies: Critical Approaches to Literacy in Development, Ethnography and Education*. Routledge.

Street, B.V. (2017) New literacies, new times: Developments in literacy studies. In S. May (ed.) *Encyclopedia of Language and Education, Vol. 2: Literacy* (3rd edn). Springer. https://doi.org/10.1007/978-3-319-02252-9_1.

Strubell, M. (2001) Catalan a decade later. In J. Fishman (ed.) *Can Threatened Languages Be Saved?* (pp. 260–283). Multilingual Matters.

Su, C.M. (ed.) (2021) *Voices of a New Generation: Cambodian Americans in the Creative Arts*. Southeast Asian Research and Cultural Heritage Center.

Subtirelu, N.C., Borowczyk, M., Hernández, R.T. and Venezia, F. (2019) Recognizing whose bilingualism? A critical policy analysis of the Seal of Biliteracy. *Modern Language Journal* 103 (2), 371–390. https://doi.org/10.1111/modl.12556.

Suh, E., Hoffman, L., Albrecht, D. and Wade, S. (2019) Promoting student voice and choice: Examples from a secondary EL classroom project. *INTESOL Journal* 16 (1), 1–33. https://doi.org/10.18060/23598.

Sullivan, M.D., Poarch, G.J. and Bialystok, E. (2018) Why is lexical retrieval slower for bilinguals? Evidence from picture naming. *Bilingualism: Language and Cognition* 21 (3), 479–488.

Sung, K.-Y. (ed.) (2024) *Chinese-English Dual Language Immersion Programs: Content-Area Instruction, Learners, and Evaluations*. Lexington Books.

Sung, K-Y. and Tsai, H.-M. (2019) *Mandarin Chinese Dual Language Immersion Programs*. Multilingual Matters.

Supalla, T. and Webb, R. (1995) The grammar of International Sign: A new look at pidgin languages. In K. Emmorey and J. Reilly (eds) *Language, Gesture, and Space* (pp. 333–352). Lawrence Erlbaum.

Svitek, P. (2024) U.S. updates how it classifies people by race, ethnicity for first time in decades. *Washington Post*, 28 March. https://www.washingtonpost.com/politics/2024/03/28/census-update-race-ethnicity.

Swain, M. (1997) French immersion programs in Canada. In J. Cummins and D. Corson (eds) *Encyclopedia of Language and Education, Vol. 5: Bilingual Education* (pp. 261–269). Kluwer.

Swain, M. (2005) The output hypothesis: Theory and research. In E. Hinkel (ed.) *Handbook of Research in Second Language Teaching and Learning* (pp. 471–483). Erlbaum.

Swain, M. and Johnson, R.K. (1997) Immersion education: A category within bilingual education. In R.K. Johnson and M. Swain (eds) *Immersion Education: International Perspectives* (pp. 1–16). Cambridge University Press.

Swain, M. and Lapkin, S. (1982) *Evaluating Bilingual Education: A Canadian Case Study*. Multilingual Matters.

Swain, M. and Lapkin, S. (1991) Additive bilingualism and French immersion education: The roles of language proficiency and literacy. In A.G. Reynolds (ed.) *Bilingualism, Multiculturalism and Second Language Learning* (pp. 203–216). Lawrence Erlbaum.

Swain, M. and Lapkin, S. (2005) The evolving sociopolitical context of immersion education in Canada: Some implications for program development. *International Journal of Applied Linguistics* 15 (2), 169–186.

Swain, M. and Lapkin, S. (2008) Oh, I get it now! From production to comprehension in second language learning. In D. Brinton, O. Kagan and S. Bauckus (eds) *Heritage Language Education: A New Field Emerging* (pp. 301–320). Routledge.

Swain, M., Kinnear, P. and Steinman, L. (2015) *Sociocultural Theory in Second Language Education: An Introduction through Narratives* (2nd edn). Multilingual Matters.

Swanwick, R. (2017) *Languages and Languaging in Deaf Education*. Oxford University Press.

Swanwick, R., Wright, S. and Salter, J. (2016) Investigating deaf children's plural and diverse use of sign and spoken languages in a super diverse context. *Applied Linguistics Review* 7 (2), 117–147.

Sylvén, L.K. (2019) *Investigating Content and Language Integrated Learning: Insights from Swedish High Schools*. Multilingual Matters.

Takahashi, C. (2023) *Motivation to Learn Multiple Languages in Japan: A Longitudinal Perspective*. Multilingual Matters.

Takanishi, R. and Le Menestrel, S. (eds) (2017) *Promoting the Educational Success of Children and Youth Learning English: Promising Futures. Report of the National Academies of Sciences, Engineering, and Medicine*. National Academies Press.

Talbot, K.R., Gruber, M.-T. and Nishida, R. (eds) (2021) *The Psychological Experience of Integrating Content and Language*. Multilingual Matters.

Tang, G., Adam, R. and Simpson, K. (2020) Educating bilingual and multicultural deaf children in the 21st century. In G. Morgan (ed.) *Understanding Deafness, Language and Cognitive Development* (pp. 183–204). John Benjamins Publishing.

Tankersley, D. (2001) Bombs or bilingual programmes? Dual-language immersion, transformative education and community building in Macedonia. *International Journal of Bilingual Education and Bilingualism* 4 (2), 107–124.

Tannenbaum, M. and Howie, P. (2002) The association between language maintenance and family relations: Chinese immigrant children in Australia. *Journal of Multilingual and Multicultural Development* 23 (5), 408–424.

Taura, H. and Taura, A. (2012) Linguistic and narrative development in a Japanese–English bilingual's first language acquisition: A 14-year longitudinal case study. *International Journal of Bilingual Education and Bilingualism* 15 (4), 475–508.

Tedick, D.J. (2014) Language immersion education: A research agenda for 2015 and beyond. *Journal of Immersion and Content-Based Language Education* (special issue) 2 (2).

Tedick, D.J., Christian, D. and Fortune, T.W. (2011) *Immersion Education: Activities, Policies, Possibilities*. Multilingual Matters.

Téllez, K. and Varghese, M. (2013) Teachers as intellectuals and advocates: Professional development for bilingual education teachers. *Theory into Practice* 52 (2), 128–135. https://doi.org/10.1080/00405841.2013.770330.

Terry, S. (1819) *Third Annual Report of the Directors of the Connecticut Asylum for the Education and Instruction of Deaf and Dumb Persons*. Hudson and Co.

TESOL (Teachers of English to Speakers of Other Languages) (2006) *PreK–12 English Language Proficiency Standards*. TESOL.

Thiong'o, N.W. (2005) The language of African literature. In G. Desai and S. Nair (eds) *Postcolonialisms: An Anthology of Cultural Theory and Criticism* (pp. 132–142). Rutgers State University Press.

Thomas, W.P. (1992) An analysis of the research methodology of the Ramirez study. *Bilingual Research Journal* 16 (1–2), 213–246.

Thomas, W.P. and Collier, V.P. (1995) *Language Minority Student Achievement and Program Effectiveness. Research Summary*. George Mason University.

Thomas, W.P. and Collier, V.P. (1997) *School Effectiveness for Language Minority Students*. Resource Collection Series 9. National Clearinghouse on Bilingual Education (NCBE).

Thomas, W.P. and Collier, V.P. (2002a) Accelerated schooling for all students: Research findings on education in multilingual communities. In P. Shaw (ed.) *Intercultural Education in European Classrooms: Intercultural Education Partnership* (pp. 15–35). Trentham.

Thomas, W.P. and Collier, V.P. (2002b) *A National Study of School Effectiveness for Language Minority Students' Long-Term Academic Achievement*. Center for Research on Education, Diversity, and Excellence.

Thomas, W.P. and Collier, V.P. (2012) *Dual Language Education for a Transformed World*. Dual Language Education of New Mexico – Fuente Press.

Thomas, W.P. and Collier, V.P. (2015) *English Learners in North Carolina Dual Language Programs: Year 3 of This Study: School year 2009–10*. George Mason University. https://dcimmersion.org/wp-content/uploads/2014/11/north-carolina-longitudinal-study.pdf.

Thomas, W.P., Collier, V.P. and Abbott, M. (1993) Academic achievement through Japanese, Spanish, or French: The first two years of partial immersion. *Modern Language Journal* 77 (2), 170–179.

Thomason, S.G. (2015) *Endangered Languages: An Introduction*. Cambridge University Press.

Thomas-Sunesson, D., Hakuta, K. and Bialystok, E. (2018) Degree of bilingualism modifies executive control in Hispanic children in the USA. *International Journal of Bilingual Education and Bilingualism* 21 (2), 197–206.

Thompson, M., DiCerbo, K., Mahoney, K. and MacSwan, J. (2002) Exito en California? A validity critique of language program evaluations and analysis of English learner test scores. *Education Policy Analysis Archives* 10 (7). https://epaa.asu.edu/ojs/article/view/286.

Thoutenhoofd, E. (1997) Vision/Deaf vision: Vision as a constitutive element of deaf communities. *Deaf Worlds* 13 (1), 19–28.

Tian, Z. and King, N. (eds) (2023) *Developing Translanguaging Repertoires in Critical Teacher Education*. De Gruyter Mouton.

Tian, Z. and Lau, S.M.C. (2023) Translanguaging pedagogies in a Mandarin–English dual language bilingual education classroom: Contextualised learning from teacher–researcher collaboration. *International Journal of Bilingual Education and Bilingualism* 26 (8), 960–974. https://doi.org/10.1080/13670050.2022.2161815.

Tian, Z., Aghai, L., Sayer, P. and Schissel, J.L. (eds) (2020) *Envisioning TESOL Through a Translanguaging Lens: Global Perspectives*. Springer.

Tigert, J., Groff, J., Martin-Beltrán, M., Peercy, M.M. and Silverman, R. (2020) Exploring the pedagogical potential of translanguaging in peer reading interactions. In J. MacSwan and C.J. Faltis (eds) *Code-Switching in the Classroom: Critical Perspectives on Teaching, Learning, Policy, and Ideology* (pp. 65–87). Center for Applied Linguistics and Routledge.

Tollefson, J.W. and Tsui, A.B.M. (2018) Medium of instruction policy. In J.W. Tollefson and M. Pêrez-Milans (eds) *The Oxford Handbook of Language Policy and Planning* (pp. 257–279). Oxford University Press.

Tomozawa, A. and Majima, J. (2015) Bilingual education in Japan: Slow but steady progress. In W.E. Wright, S. Boun and O. García (eds) *Handbook of Bilingual and Multilingual Education* (pp. 493–503). John Wiley and Sons.

Toohey, K. (2018) *Learning English at School: Identity, Socio-material Relations and Classroom Practice* (2nd edn). Multilingual Matters.

Toribio, A.J. (2004) Spanish/English speech practices: Bringing chaos to order. *International Journal of Bilingual Education and Bilingualism* 7 (2–3), 133–154.

Torrance, E.P. (1974) *Torrance Tests of Creative Thinking: Directions Manual and Scoring Guide*. Ginn.

Toukomaa, P. and Skutnabb-Kangas, T. (1977) *The Intensive Teaching of the Mother Tongue to Migrant Children at Pre-school Age*. Research report no. 26. Department of Sociology and Social Psychology, University of Tampere.

Trofimovich, P. and Turuševa, L. (2020) Language attitudes and ethnic identity: Examining listener perceptions of Latvian–Russian bilingual speakers. *Journal of Language, Identity, and Education* 19 (1), 9–24. https://doi.org/10.1080/15348458.2019.1696682.

Troike, R.C. (1978) Research evidence for the effectiveness of bilingual education. *NABE Journal* 3 (1), 13–24.

Truth and Reconciliation Commission of Canada (2015) *Honoring the Truth, Reconciling for the Future: Summary of the Final Report of the Truth and Reconciliation Commission of Canada*. https://nctr.ca/reports2.php.

Tsushima, R. and Guardado, M. (2019) 'Rules ... I want someone to make them clear': Japanese mothers in Montreal talk about multilingual parenting. *Journal of Language, Identity, and Education* 18 (5), 311–328. https://doi.org/10.1080.15348458.2019.1645017.

Tucker, G.R. and d'Anglejan, A. (1972) An approach to bilingual education: The St Lambert experiment. Paper presented at Bilingual Schooling: Some Experiences in Canada and the United States, Ontario Institute for Studies in Education Symposium Series, Canada.

Tupas, R. (2015) *Unequal Englishes: The Politics of English Today*. Palgrave Macmillan.

Tupas, R. and Rani, R. (2015) Introduction: From world Englishes to unequal Englishes. In R. Tupas (ed.) *Unequal Englishes: The Politics of English Today* (pp. 1–17). Palgrave Macmillan.

Umansky, I.M. and Reardon, S.F. (2014) Reclassification patterns among Latino English learner students in bilingual, dual immersion, and English immersion classrooms. *American Educational Research Journal* 51 (5), 879–912. https://doi.org/10.3102/0002831214545110.

Umansky, I.M., Valentino, R.A. and Reardon, S.F. (2016) The promise of two-language education. *Educational Leadership* 73 (5), 10–17.

Ünal, E. and Papafragou, A. (2020) Relations between language and cognition: Evidentiality and sources of knowledge. *Topics in Cognitive Science* 12, 115–135.

UNESCO (1953) *The Use of Vernacular Languages in Education*. UNESCO.

UNESCO (1994) *The Salamanca Statement and Framework for Action on Special Needs Education*. UNESCO.

UNESCO (2007) *Advocacy Kit for Promoting Multilingual Education: Including the Excluded*. UNESCO Asia and Pacific Region Bureau for Education.

UNESCO (2016) *If You Don't Understand, How Can You Learn?* Global Education Monitoring Report, Policy Paper 24. UNESCO.

UNESCO (2024) What you need to know about literacy. https://www.unesco.org/en/literacy/need-know#:~:text=Beyond%20its%20conventional%20concept%20as,rich%20and%20fast%2Dchanging%20world.

UNICEF (2012) *Child Friendly Schools*. http://www.unicef.org/lifeskills/index_7260.html.

US Census Bureau (2015a) American Community Survey (ACS) – Why we ask: Languages spoken at home. https://www2.census.gov/programs-surveys/acs/about/qbyqfact/Language.pdf.

US Census Bureau (2015b) How the American Community Survey works for your community (infographic). https://www.census.gov/content/dam/Census/library/infographics/how_acs_works.pdf.

US Census Bureau (2019) Table B-2. People in poverty by selected characteristics: 2017 and 2018. https://www.census.gov/data/tables/2019/demo/income-poverty/p60-266.html.

US Census Bureau (2021) Income and poverty in the United States: 2020. https://www.census.gov/library/publications/2021/demo/p60-273.html.

US Census Bureau (2024) U.S. and world population clock. https://www.census.gov/popclock/world.

US Department of Education (1992) *The Condition of Bilingual Education in the Nation: A Report to the Congress and the President*. Department of Education.

US Department of Education (2012) *ESEA Flexibility*. https://www.ed.gov/esea/flexibility/documents/esea-flexibility-acc.doc.

US Department of Education (2020) IDEA Section 618 Data Products: Static Tables. Number and percent of students ages 6 through 21 served under IDEA, Part B, by English Learner status and state: 2018–19. https://www2.ed.gov/programs/osepidea/618-data/static-tables/index.html.

US Department of Education, National Center for Education Statistics (2019) *Digest of Education Statistics, 2018* (NCES 2020–009). https://nces.ed.gov/fastfacts/display.asp?id=59

US Department of State (2020) 'Confucius Institute US Center' designation as a foreign mission, fact sheet. https://2017-2021.state.gov/confucius-institute-u-s-center-designation-as-a-foreign-mission.

US Equal Employment Opportunity Commission (2014) *Employment Rights of Immigrants Under Federal Anti-discrimination Laws*. https://www.eeoc.gov/laws/guidance/employment-rights-immigrants-under-federal-anti-discrimination-laws-brochure.

US Government Accountability Office (2023) China: With nearly all U.S. Confucius Institutes closed, some schools sought alternative language support (GAO-24-105981). https://www.gao.gov/products/gao-24-105981.

Utah Senate (2016) Dual language immersion: Origin story. http://senatesite.com/ utahsenate/dual-language-immersion.

Vaid, J. (2018) The bilingual brain revisited: What is right and what is left? In R.R. Heredia and J. Altarriba (eds) *An Introduction to Bilingualism: Principles and Processes* (pp. 139–155). Taylor and Francis.

Valdés, G. (1997) Dual-language immersion programs: A cautionary note concerning the education of language-minority students. *Harvard Educational Review* 67 (3), 391–429.

Valdés, G. (2001) *Learning and Not Learning English: Latino Students in American Schools*. Teachers College Press.

Valdés, G. (2003) *Expanding Definitions of Giftedness: The Case of Young Interpreters from Immigrant Communities*. Lawrence Erlbaum.

Valdés, G. (2004) Between support and marginalization: The development of academic language in linguistic minority children. *International Journal of Bilingual Education and Bilingualism* 7 (2–3), 102–132.

Valdés, G. (2006) *Developing Minority Language Resources: The Case of Spanish in California*. Multilingual Matters.

Valdés, G. (2014) Heritage language students: Profiles and possibilities. In T.G. Wiley, J.K. Peyton, D. Christian, S.C.K. Moore and N. Liu (eds) *Handbook of Heritage, Community, and Native American Languages in the United States: Research, Policy, and Educational Practice* (pp. 19–26). Center for Applied Linguistics and Routledge.

Valdés, G. (2015) What is bilingualism/multilingualism? In G. Valdés, K. Menken and M. Castro (eds) *Common Core Bilingual and English Language Learners: A Resource for Educators* (pp. 38–39). Caslon Publishing.

Valdés, G. (2017) Entry visa denied: The construction of symbolic language borders in educational settings. In O. García, N. Flores and M. Spotti (eds) *The Oxford Handbook of Language and Society* (pp. 321–348). Oxford University Press.

Valdés, G. (2018) Analyzing the curricularization of language in two-way immersion education: Restating two cautionary notes. *Bilingual Research Journal* 41 (4), 388–412. https://doi.org/10.1080/15235882.2018.1539886.

Valdés, G. (2020) The future of the Seal of Biliteracy: Issues of equity and inclusion. In A.J. Heineke and K.J. Davin (eds) *The Seal of Biliteracy: Case Studies and Considerations for Policy Implementation* (pp. 177–204). Information Age Publishing.

Valdés, G. and Figueroa, R.A. (1994) *Bilingualism and Testing: A Special Case of Bias*. Ablex Publishing.

Valdés, G., Fishman, J.A., Chavez, R.M. and Perez, W. (2006) *Towards the Development of Minority Language Resources: Lessons from the Case of California*. Multilingual Matters.

Valdés, G., Poza, L. and Brooks, M.D. (2015) Language acquisition in bilingual education. In W.E. Wright, S. Boun and O. García (eds) *Handbook of Bilingual and Multilingual Education* (pp. 56–74). Wiley-Blackwell.

Valdiviezo, L.A. and Nieto, S. (2015) Culture in bilingual and multilingual education: Conflict, struggle, and power. In W.E. Wright, S. Boun and O. García (eds) *Handbook of Bilingual and Multilingual Education* (pp. 92–108). Wiley-Blackwell.

Valentino, R.A. and Reardon, S.F. (2015) Effectiveness of four instructional programs designed to serve English learners: Variations by ethnicity and initial English proficiency. *Educational Evaluation and Policy Analysis* 37 (4), 612–637. https://doi.org/10.3102/0162373715573310.

Valian, V. (2015) Bilingualism and cognition. *Bilingualism: Language and Cognition* 18, 3–24.

Valli, C., Lucas, C., Mulrooney, K.J. and Villanueva, M. (2011) *Linguistics of American Sign Languages*. Gallaudet University Press.

Van Cleve, J.V. (1984) Nebraska's Oral Law of 1911 and the deaf community. *Nebraska History* 65 (2), 195–220.
Van Cleve, J.V. (1989) *Gallaudet Encyclopedia of Deaf People and Deafness*. McGraw Hill.
van der Walt, C. (2013) *Multilingual Higher Education: Beyond English Medium Orientations*. Multilingual Matters.
van der Walt, C. (2015) Bi/multilingual higher education: Perspectives and practices. In W.E. Wright, S. Boun and O. García (eds) *Handbook of Bilingual and Multilingual Education* (pp. 353–369). Wiley-Blackwell.
Van Horn, S. (2020) World Englishes and global commerce. In C.L. Nelson, Z.G. Proshina and D.R. Davis (eds) *The Handbook of World Englishes* (2nd edn, pp. 635–656). Wiley Blackwell.
Van Hout, T. and Burger, P. (2017) Mediatization and the language of journalism. In O. García, N. Flores and M. Spotti (eds) *The Oxford Handbook of Language and Society* (pp. 489–504). Oxford University Press.
Varis, P. and Van Nuenen, T. (2017) The internet, language, and virtual interactions. In O. García, N. Flores and M. Spotti (eds) *The Oxford Handbook of Language and Society* (pp. 473–488). Oxford University Press.
Velázquez, I. (2019) *Household Perspectives on Minority Language Maintenance and Loss: Language in the Small Spaces*. Multilingual Matters.
Verhoeven, L. (2017) Learning to read in a second language. In K. Cain, D. Compton and R. K. Parrila (eds) *Theories of Reading Development* (pp. 215–234). John Benjamins.
Verhoeven, L., Perfetti, C. and Pugh, K. (2019) Cross-linguistic perspectives on second language reading. *Journal of Neurolinguistics* 50, 1–6.
Vernon, M. (1968/2005) Fifty years of research on the intelligence of deaf and hard of hearing children: A review of literature and discussion of implications. *Journal of Deaf Studies and Deaf Education* 10, 225–231.
Vernon, M. (1970) The role of deaf teachers in the education of the deaf. *Deaf American* 22 (11), 17–20.
Vernon, M. and Andrews, J.F. (1990) *The Psychology of Deafness: Understanding Deaf and Hard of Hearing People*. Longman.
Vertovec, S. (2007) Super-diversity and its implications. *Ethnic and Racial Studies* 30 (6), 1024–1054.
Vertovec, S. (2017) Mooring, migration milieus and complex explanations. *Ethnic and Racial Studies* 40 (9), 1574–1581. https://doi.org/10.1080/01419870.2017.1308534.
Vidano, G. and Sahafi, M. (2004) *Parent Institute for Quality Education: Organizational Special Report on PIQE's Performance Evaluation*. San Diego State University, College of Business Administration, Marketing Department.
Vigouroux, C. (2017) The discursive pathway of two centuries of raciolinguistic stereotyping: 'Africans as incapable of speaking French'. *Language in Society* 46, 5–21. https://doi.org/10.1017/S0047404516000804.
Villegas, L. and Pompa, D. (2020) *The Patchy Landscape of State English Learner Policies Under ESSA*. Migration Policy Institute.
Vivas, A.B., Ladas, A.I., Salvari, V. and Chrysochoou, E. (2017) Revisiting the bilingual advantage in attention in low SES Greek-Albanians: Does the level of bilingual experience matter? *Language, Cognition and Neuroscience* 32 (6), 743–756.
Vygotsky, L.S. (1986) *Thought and language* (revised edn, A. Kozulin, trans.). MIT Press.
Wagner, E. (2020) Duolingo English Test, revised version July 2019. *Language Assessment Quarterly* 17 (3), 300–315. https://doi.org/10.1080/15434303.2020.1771343.
Wagner, S.T. (1981) The historical background of bilingualism and biculturalism in the United States. In M. Ridge (ed.) *The New Bilingualism* (pp. 29–52). University of Southern California Press.
Wall, D.J., Greer, E. and Palmer, D.K. (2022) Exploring institutional processes in a district-wide dual language program: Who is it for? Who is left out? *Journal of Latinos and Education* 21 (1), 87–102. https://doi.org/10.1080/15348431.2019.1613996.
Wang, C. and Lamb, T. (eds) (2024) *Negotiating Identities, Language and Migration in Global London: Bridging Borders, Creating Spaces*. Multilingual Matters.
Wang, H.L. (2020) With no final say, Trump wants to change who counts for dividing up Congress' seats. National Public Radio. https://www.npr.org/2020/07/21/892340508/with-no-final-say-trump-wants-to-change-who-counts-for-dividing-up-congress-seat.
Wang, L. (2024) Artificial intelligence's role in the realm of endangered languages: Documentation and teaching. *Applied and Computational Engineering* 48 (1), 123–129. https://doi.org/10.54254/2755-2721/48/20241249.

Wang, L. and Kirkpatrick, A. (2019) *Trilingual Education in Hong Kong Primary Schools*. Springer.
Wang, Q. and Andrews, J.F. (eds) (2020) *Literacy and Deaf Education: Toward a Global Understanding*. Gallaudet University Press.
Wang, Q., Andrews, J., Liu, H.T. and Liu, C.J. (2016) Case studies of multilingual/multicultural Asian Deaf adults: Strategies for success. *American Annals of the Deaf* 161 (1), 67–88.
Wang, X.-L. (2008) *Growing Up With Three Languages: Birth To Eleven*. Multilingual Matters.
Wang, X.-L. (2011) *Learning to Read and Write in the Multilingual Family*. Multilingual Matters.
Wang, X.-L. (2015) *Maintaining Three Languages: The Teenage Years*. Multilingual Matters.
Wang, X.-L. (2019) Multilingualism through schooling. In S. Montanari and S. Quay (eds) *Multidisciplinary Perspectives on Multilingualism: The Fundamentals* (pp. 253–274). De Gruyter Mouton.
Wang, Y. and Wei, L. (2021) Two languages, one mind: The effects of language learning on motion event processing in early Cantonese–English bilinguals. In *Proceedings of the Annual Meeting of the Cognitive Science Society* (Vol. 43, No. 43). Cognitive Science Society.
Warmington, M.A., Kandru-Pothineni, S. and Hitch, G.J. (2019) Novel-word learning, executive control and working memory: A bilingual advantage. *Bilingualism: Language and Cognition* 22 (4), 763–782.
Weber, J.-J. (2014) *Flexible Multilingual Education: Putting Children's Needs First*. Multilingual Matters.
Weber, J.-J. and Horner, K. (2018) *Introducing Multilingualism: A Social Approach* (2nd edn). Routledge.
Wedin, Å. (2021) (Trans)languaging mathematics as a source of meaning in upper-secondary schools in Sweden. In P. Juvonen and M. Källkvist (eds) *Pedagogical Translanguaging: Theoretical, Methodological and Empirical Perspectives* (pp. 146–166). Multilingual Matters.
Welsh Language Board (2001) *A Guide to Bilingual Design*. Welsh Language Board.
Wermelinger, S., Gampe, A. and Daum, M.M. (2017) Bilingual toddlers have advanced abilities to repair communication failure. *Journal of Experimental Child Psychology* 155, 84–94.
Werner, H. (1932) *History of the Problem of Deaf Mutism from the 17th Century* (trans. C.K. Bonning). Verlag Von Gustav Fisher.
Wernicke, M., Hammer, S., Hansen, A. and Schroedler, T. (eds) (2021) *Preparing Teachers to Work with Multilingual Learners*. Multilingual Matters.
Westerlund, R.A. (2019) *From Borsch to Burgers: A Cross-cultural Memoir*. Self-published.
Whitehead, S. (2015) How the Manx language came back from the dead. *Guardian*, 2 April. https://www.theguardian.com/education/2015/apr/02/how-manx-language-came-back-from-dead-isle-of-man.
Whorf, B.L. (1956) *Language, Thought and Reality*. Wiley.
Whynot, L.A. (2016) *Understanding International Sign: A Sociolinguistic Study*. Gallaudet University Press.
WIDA Consortium (2012) 2012 amplification of the English language development standards: Kindergarten – grade 12. https://www.wida.us/get.aspx?id=540.
WIDA Consortium (2020) *WIDA English Language Development Standards Framework, 2020 Edition, Kindergarten – Grade 12*. Board of Regents of the University of Wisconsin System.
Wiese, A.-M. and Garcia, E.E. (2001) The bilingual education act: Language minority students and US federal educational policy. *International Journal of Bilingual Education and Bilingualism* 4 (4), 229–248.
Wiley, T.G. (1998) The imposition of World War I era English-only policies and the fate of German in North America. In T. Ricento and B. Burnaby (eds) *Language and Politics in the United States and Canada: Myths and Realities* (pp. 211–241). Lawrence Erlbaum Associates.
Wiley, T.G. (2005) *Literacy and Language Diversity in the United States* (2nd edn). Center for Applied Linguistics.
Wiley, T.G. (2013a) A brief history and assessment of language rights in the United States. In J.W. Tollefson (ed.) *Language Policies in Education: Critical Issues* (pp. 61–90). Routledge.
Wiley, T.G. (2013b) Constructing and deconstructing 'illegal' children. *Journal of Language, Identity and Education* 12 (3), 173–178.
Wiley, T.G. (2014a) Policy considerations for promoting heritage, community, and Native American languages. In T.G. Wiley, J.K. Peyton, D. Christian, S.C.K. Moore and N. Liu (eds) *Handbook of Heritage, Community, and Native American Languages in the United States: Research, Policy, and Educational Practice* (pp. 45–53). Center for Applied Linguistics and Routledge.
Wiley, T.G. (2014b) The problems of defining heritage and community languages and their speakers: On the utility and limitations of definitional constructs. In T.G. Wiley, J.K. Peyton, D. Christian, S.C.K. Moore and N. Liu (eds) *Handbook of Heritage, Community, and Native American Languages in the United States: Research, Policy, and Educational Practice* (pp. 19–26). Center for Applied Linguistics and Routledge.
Wiley, T.G. (2015) Language policy and planning in education. In W.E. Wright, S. Boun and O. García (eds) *Handbook of Bilingual and Multilingual Education* (pp. 164–184). Wiley-Blackwell.

Wiley, T.G. (2020) Afterword: On contested theories and the value and limitations of pure critique. In J. MacSwan and C.J. Faltis (eds) *Codeswitching in the Classroom: Critical Perspectives on Teaching, Learning, Policy, and Ideology* (pp. 268–281). Center for Applied Linguistics and Routledge.

Wiley, T.G. (2021) Heritage language planning and policy. In S. Montrul and M. Polinsky (eds) *The Cambridge Handbook of Heritage Languages and Linguistics* (pp. 934–957). Cambridge University Press.

Wiley, T.G. (2022) The grand erasure: Whatever happened to bilingual education and language minority rights? In J. MacSwan (ed.) *Multilingual Perspectives on Translanguaging* (pp. 248–292). Multilingual Matters.

Wiley, T.G. and Rolstad, K. (2014) The Common Core State Standards and the great divide. *International Multilingual Research Journal* 8 (1), 38–55. https://doi.org/10.1080/19313152.2014.852428.

Wiley, T.G. and Wright, W.E. (2004) Against the undertow: The politics of language instruction in the United States. *Educational Policy* 18 (1), 142–168.

Wiley, T.G., Peyton, J.K., Christian, D., Moore, S.C.K. and Liu, N. (eds) (2014) *Handbook of Heritage, Community, and Native American Languages in the United States: Research, Policy, and Educational Practice*. Center for Applied Linguistics and Routledge.

Wilkinson, E. and Morford, J. (2020) How bilingualism contributes to health development in Deaf children: A public health perspective. *Maternal and Child Health Journal* 24 (11), 1330–1338.

Williams, C. (1994) Arfarniad o Ddulliau Dysgu ac Addysgu yng Nghyd-destun Addysg Uwchradd Ddwyieithog [An evaluation of teaching and learning methods in the context of bilingual secondary education]. Unpublished doctoral thesis, University of Wales, Bangor.

Williams, C. (1996) Secondary education: Teaching in the bilingual situation. In C.H. Williams, E.G. Lewis and C. Baker (eds) *The Language Policy: Taking Stock* (pp. 193–211). CAI.

Williams, C. (2000) Bilingual teaching and language distribution at 16+. *International Journal of Bilingual Education and Bilingualism* 3 (2), 129–148.

Williams, C. (2018) Minnesota is preserving student culture, raising test scores and attracting non-Hmong students. *The 74*. https://www.the74million.org/article/williams-how-one-hmong-charter-school-in-minnesota-is-preserving-student-culture-raising-test-scores-and-attracting-non-hmong-students.

Williams, C.H. (2000) Restoring the language. In G.H. Jenkins and M.A. Williams (eds) *'Let's Do Our Best for the Ancient Tongue': The Welsh Language in the Twentieth Century* (pp. 657–681). Cardiff University Press.

Williams, C.H. (2007) *Language and Governance*. University of Wales Press.

Williams, C.H. (2013) Multilingualism and minority languages. In C.A. Chapelle (ed.) *Encyclopedia of Applied Linguistics*. Blackwell Publishing.

Williams, C.H. (2014) The lightening veil: Language revitalization in Wales. *Review of Research in Education* 38 (1), 242–272. https://doi.org/10.3102/0091732X13512983.

Williams, C.P. (2023) What's the best way for Arizona schools to help English learners succeed? *The Century Foundation*. https://tcf.org/content/commentary/whats-the-best-way-for-arizona-schools-to-help-english-learners-succeed/

Williams, I.W. (2003) *Our Children's Language: The Welsh-Medium Schools of Wales, 1939–2000*. Y Lolfa.

Willig, A.C. (1981) The effectiveness of bilingual education: Review of a report. *NABE Journal* 6 (2–3), 1–19.

Willig, A.C. (1985) A meta-analysis of selected studies on the effectiveness of bilingual education. *Review of Educational Research* 55, 269–317. https://doi.org/10.3102/00346543055003269.

Willig, A.C. and Ramirez, D.J. (1993) The evaluation of bilingual education. In B. Arias and U. Casanova (eds) *Bilingual Education: Politics, Research and Practice*. McCutchan.

Wilson, W.H. (2014) Hawaiian: A Native American language official for a state. In T.G. Wiley, J.K. Peyton, D. Christian, S.C.K. Moore and N. Liu (eds) *Handbook of Heritage, Community, and Native American Languages in the United States: Research, Policy, and Educational Practice* (pp. 219–229). Center for Applied Linguistics and Routledge.

Windle, J.A., de Jesus, D. and Bartlett, L. (eds) (2020) *The Dynamics of Language and Inequality in Education: Social and Symbolic Boundaries in the Global South*. Multilingual Matters.

Winefield, R. (1987) *Never the Twain Shall Meet: Bell, Gallaudet, and the Communications Debate*. Gallaudet University Press.

Wines, M. (2019) Census won't ask citizen question as Trump yields. *New York Times*, July 3, p. 1. https://www.nytimes.com/2019/07/02/us/trump-census-citizenship-question.html.

Wink, J. (2010) *Critical Pedagogy: Notes from the Real World* (4th edn). Pearson.

Winke, P. and Brunfaut, T. (eds) (2021) *The Routledge Handbook of Second Language Acquisition and Language Testing*. Routledge.

Wolbers, K., Dostal, H. and Holcomb, L. (2023) Teacher reports of secondary writing instructionwith deaf students. *Journal of Literacy Research* 55 (1), 28–50.
Wölck, W. (1988) Types of natural bilingual behavior: A review and revision. *Bilingual Review* 14 (3), 3–16.
Wolfram, W. (2020) African American English. In C.L. Nelson, Z.G. Proshina and D.R. Davis (eds) *The Handbook of World Englishes* (2nd edn, pp. 314–330). Wiley-Blackwell.
Woll, B. (2019) Applied linguistics from the perspective of sign language and deaf studies. In C. Wright, L. Harvey and J. Simpson (eds) *Voices and Practices in Applied Linguistics: Diversifying a Discipline* (pp. 51–70). White Rose University.
Woll, N. (2018) Investigating dimensions of metalinguistic awareness: What think-aloud protocols revealed about the cognitive processes involved in positive transfer from L2 to L3. *Language Awareness* 27 (1–2), 167–185.
Wolsey, J.L.A., Clark, M.D. and Andrews, J.F. (2018) ASL and English bilingual shared book reading: An exploratory intervention for signing deaf children. *Bilingual Research Journal* 41 (3), 1–17.
Wood, J. (2015) Top languages of the internet, today and tomorrow [blog post]. https://unbabel.com/blog/top-languages-of-the-internet.
Woodbridge, W.C. (1834) Education of the deaf and dumb. *American Annals of Education and Instruction* 4 (2), 55–58.
Woodward, J. and Allen, T. (1987) Classroom use of ASL by teachers. *Sign Language Studies* 54, 1–10.
Woodward Jr, J.C. (1973) Implicational lects on the deaf diglossic continuum. Unpublished doctoral dissertation, Georgetown University.
Woodward Jr, J.C. (1976) Signs of change: historical variation in American Sign Language. *Sign Language Studies* 10, 81–94.
Woodward Jr, J.C. (1978) Historical bases of American Sign Language. In P. Siple (ed.) *Understanding language through sign language research* (pp. 333–348). Academic Press.
Woodward Jr, J.C. (1979) Sociolinguistic aspects of French and American Sign Language. *Languages* 13 (56), 78–91.
Woodward Jr, J.C. (1982) Some sociolinguistic problems in the implementation of bilingual education for deaf students. In *How You Gonna Get to Heaven if You Can't Talk With Jesus: On Depathologizing Deafness* (pp. 21–50). T. J. Publishers.
World Bank (1997) *Project Appraisal Document, Guatemala, Basic Education Reform Project*. World Bank.
World Federation of the Deaf (2016) https://wfdeaf.org.
Wright, L. and Higgins, C. (eds) (2022) *Diversifying Family Language Policy*. Bloomsbury Academic.
Wright, W.E. (2003) The success and demise of a Khmer (Cambodian) bilingual education program: A case study. In C.C. Park, A.L. Goodwin and S.J. Lee (eds) *Asian American Identities, Families, and Schooling* (pp. 225–252). Information Age Publishing.
Wright, W.E. (2004) What English-only really means: A study of the implementation of California language policy with Cambodian American students. *International Journal of Bilingual Education and Bilingualism* 7 (1), 1–23.
Wright, W.E. (2005a) *Evolution of Federal Policy and Implications of No Child Left Behind for Language Minority Students* (EPSL-0501–101-LPRU). http://files.eric.ed.gov/fulltext/ED508474.pdf.
Wright, W.E. (2005b) The political spectacle of Arizona's Proposition 203. *Educational Policy* 19 (5), 662–700. https://doi.org/10.1177/0895904805278066.
Wright, W.E. (2008) Pull-out ESL instruction. In J.M. Gonzalez (ed.) *Encyclopedia of Bilingual Education* (pp. 704–707). Sage.
Wright, W.E. (2010) The great divide between federal education policy and our national need for bilingual citizens. http://www.academia.edu/3459981/Wright_W._E._2010_._The_Great_Divide_Between_Federal_Education_Policy_and_Our_National_Need_for_Bilingual_Citizens.
Wright, W.E. (2014a) Khmer. In T.G. Wiley, J.K. Peyton, D. Christian, S.C.K. Moore and N. Liu (eds) *Handbook of Heritage, Community, and Native American Languages in the United States: Research, Policy, and Educational Practice* (pp. 284–296). Center for Applied Linguistics and Routledge.
Wright, W.E. (2014b) Teaching English language learners in post-Proposition 203 Arizona: Structured English immersion or sink-or-swim submersion? In G.P. McField (ed.) *The Miseducation of English Learners: A Tale of Three States and Lessons To Be Learned* (pp. 151–182). Information Age Publishing.
Wright, W.E. (2019) Language rights and policy in K-12 TESOL. In L.C. de Oliveira (ed.) *The Handbook of TESOL in K-12* (pp. 55–68). Wiley-Blackwell.
Wright, W.E. (2025) *Foundations for Teaching English Language Learners: Research, Theory, Policy, and Practice* (4th edn). Brookes Publishing.

Wright, W.E. and Baker, C. (2017) Key concepts in bilingual education. In O. García and A.M.Y. Lin (eds) *Encyclopedia of Language and Education, Vol. 5: Bilingual Education* (3rd edn, pp. 1–15). Springer.

Wright, W.E. and Boun, S. (2011) Southeast Asian American education 35 years after initial resettlement: Research report and policy recommendations. Conference Report of the National Association for the Education and Advancement of Cambodian, Laotian, and Vietnamese Americans. *Journal of Southeast Asian American Education and Advancement* 6, 1–120.

Wright, W.E. and Boun, S. (2015) Striving for education for all through bilingual education in Cambodia. In W.E. Wright, S. Boun and O. García (eds) *Handbook of Bilingual and Multilingual Education* (pp. 517–530). Wiley-Blackwell.

Wright, W.E. and Boun, S. (2016) The development and expansion of multilingual education in Cambodia: An application of Ruiz's orientations in language planning. *Bilingual Review/Revista Bilingüe* 33 (3), 1–17.

Wright, W.E. and Chan, V. (2019) Multilingualism in North America. In S. Montanari and S. Quay (eds) *Multidisciplinary Perspectives on Multilingualism: The Fundamentals* (pp. 77–100). De Gruyter Mouton.

Wright, W.E. and Chan, V. (2021) Khmer language use and presence in the linguistic landscape of 'Greater Los Angeles' Cambodia Town. In C.H. Chik (ed.) *Multilingualism in La La Land*. Routledge.

Wright, W.E. and Chan, V. (2022) Khmer language use and presence in the linguistic landscape of Greater Los Angeles' Cambodia Town. In C.H. Chik (ed.) *Multilingual La La Land* (pp. 170–189). Routledge.

Wright, W.E. and Choi, D. (2006) The impact of language and high-stakes testing policies on elementary school English language learners in Arizona. *Education Policy Analysis Archives*, 14(13), 1–56. https://epaa.asu.edu/index.php/epaa/article/view/84.

Wright, W.E. and Choi, W. (2024) DLBE program types for different target populations. In J.A. Freire, C. Alfaro and E. de Jong (eds) *The Handbook of Dual Language Bilingual Education* (pp. 94–114). Routledge. https://doi.org/10.4324/9781003269076-9.

Wright, W.E. and Pu, C. (2005) Academic achievement of English language learners in post Proposition 203 Arizona. https://nepc.colorado.edu/publication/academic-achievement-english-language-learners-post-proposition-203-arizona.

Wright, W.E. and Ricento, T. (2017) Language policy and education in the United States. In T.L. McCarty (ed.) *Encyclopedia of Language and Education, Vol. 1: Language Policy and Political Issues in Education* (3rd edn, pp. 383–400). Springer.

Wright, W.E., Boun, S. and García, O. (eds) (2015) *Handbook of Bilingual and Multilingual Education*. John Wiley and Sons.

Wright, W.E., Boun, S. and Chan, V. (2022) Implementation of multilingual mother tongue education in Cambodian public schools for indigenous ethnic minority students. *Educational Linguistics* 1 (1), 196–217. https://doi.org/10.1515/eduling-2022-0002.

Wright, W.E., Morita-Mullaney, T., Choi, W. and Li, H. (2023) Building bilingual teachers' translanguaging repertoires in a new immigrant destination state. In Z. Tian and N. King (eds) *Developing Translanguaging Repertoires in Critical Teacher Education* (pp. 123–144). De Gruyter Mouton. https://doi.org/10.1515/9783110735604-007.

Wu, H.P., Palmer, D.K. and Field, S.L. (2011) Understanding teachers' professional identity and beliefs in the Chinese heritage language school in the USA. *Language, Culture and Curriculum* 24 (1), 47–60.

Yamamoto, M. (2002) Language use in families with parents of different native languages: An investigation of Japanese-non-English and Japanese-English families. *Journal of Multilingual and Multicultural Development* 23 (6), 531–554.

Yang, J.H. (2008) Sign language and oral/written language in deaf education in China. In C. Plaza-Pust and E. Morales-Lopez (eds) *Sign Bilingualism: Language Development, Interaction, and Maintenance in Sign Language Contact Situations* (pp. 297–331). John Benjamins.

Yang, W., Gu, Y., Fang, Y. and Sun, Y. (2022) Mental representations of time in English monolinguals, Mandarin monolinguals, and Mandarin–English bilinguals. *Frontiers in Psychology* 13, 791197.

Yang, X. (2020) Assessment accommodations for emergent bilinguals in mainstream classroom assessments: A targeted literature review. *International Multilingual Research Journal* 14 (3), 217–232. https://doi.org/10.1080/19313152.2019.1681615.

Yosso, T.J. (2005) Whose culture has capital? A critical race theory discussion of community cultural wealth. *Race Ethnicity and Education* 8 (1), 69–91.

Yow, W.Q. and Markman, E.M. (2011) Young bilingual children's heightened sensitivity to referential cues. *Journal of Cognition and Development* 12, 12–31.

Yow, W.Q. and Markman, E.M. (2015) A bilingual advantage in how children integrate multiple cues to understand a speaker's referential intent. *Bilingualism: Language and Cognition* 18 (3), 391–399.

Ytsma, J. (2000) Trilingual primary education in Friesland. In J. Cenoz and U. Jessner (eds) *English in Europe: The Acquisition of a Third Language* (pp. 222–235). Multilingual Matters.

Yurtsever, A., Anderson, J.A.E. and Grundy, J.G. (2023) Bilingual children outperform monolingual children on executive function tasks far more often than chance: An updated quantitative analysis. *Developmental Review* 69, 1–20. https://doi.org/10.1016/j.dr.2023.101084.

Zalbide, M. and Cenoz, J. (2008) Bilingual education in the Basque Autonomous Community: Achievements and challenges. *Language, Culture and Curriculum* 21 (1), 5–20.

Zangwill, I. (1909) *The Melting Pot: Drama in Four Acts*. Macmillan.

Zappert, L.T. and Cruz, B.R. (1977) *Bilingual Education: An Appraisal of Empirical Research*. Bay Area Bilingual Education League.

Zentella, A.C. (2014) TWB (talking while bilingual): Linguistic profiling of Latina/os, and other linguistic torquemadas. *Latino Studies* 12 (4), 620–635. https://doi.org/10.1057/lst.2014.63.

Zeshan, U. and Panda, S. (2018) Sign-speaking: The structure of simultaneous bimodal utterances. *Applied Linguistics* Review 9 (1), 1–34.

Zhang, L. J. (2022) Deepening the understanding of translanguaging as a practical theory of language: A conversation with Professor Li Wei. *RELC Journal* 53 (3), 739–746.

郑璇 (Zheng, Xuan) (2023) *Big Hands, Small Hands: My First CSL Book*.|大手拉小手：我的第一套手语书.

Zhou, M. and Logan, J.R. (2003) Increasing diversity and persistent segregation: Challenges of educating minority and immigrant children in urban America. In S.J. Caldas and C.L. Bankston (eds) *The End of Desegregation?* (pp. 177–194). Nova Science Publishers.

Zhu, H. (2014) Piecing together the 'workplace multilingualism' jigsaw puzzle. *Multilingua* 33 (1–2), 233–242.

Zuckerman, G.A. and Monaghan, P. (2012) Revival linguistics and the new media: Talknology in the service of the Barngarla language reclamation. In T. Ka'ai, M. Ó Laoire, N. Ostler, R. Ka'ai-Mahuta, D. Mahuta and T. Smith (eds) *Language Endangerment in the 21st Century: Globalisation, Technology, and New Media* (pp. 119–126). Te Ipukarea and Printsprint, AUT University and Foundation for Endangered Languages.

Index

Abedi, J. 384, 385
Aboriginal languages 249 *see also* indigenous languages
Abutalebi, J. 163
academic language proficiency 14, 180, 181, 182
Académie Française 133
accent 64, 136, 433, 446
ACCESS 2.0 384
acculturation 4, 456
acquisition planning 86
ACTFL (American Council on the Teaching of Foreign Languages) 16
active learning 307
activism, language 59, 198, 346, 438, 441
Ada, A.F. 345
Adamson, B. 63, 70, 110, 249
additional needs, students with 366–389 *see also* special educational needs
additive bilingualism
  bilingual education 214, 223
  biliteracy 258, 351
  Deaf-signing people 412
  definitions 13, 53
  early development of bilingualism 107
  elite/prestigious bilingualism 4
  immersion programs 323
  later development of bilinguals 129
  United States 213
additive effects period 157–159
Adesope, O.O. 161, 163, 168, 171, 172
adult language learning 134–139, 438
Advocates for Indigenous California Language Survival (AICLS) 254–255
affect *see* emotions
affiliation/group belonging 7, 120, 140, 141, 142–143
African languages 59, 63, 83, 110, 433
African-American Vernacular English 65, 246, 250, 306, 333
African-Americans 246, 435, 437
Afro-Latinx 333
age 6, 134–139, 167
agency 104, 240
AI (Artificial Intelligence) 97, 134, 419, 476–480

Ainu people 51, 97
Alanís, I. 356
Alarcón, A. 484
Alaska 78, 86, 253
Alaskan Eyak 78
Al-Gasem, N.S. 315
Alim, H.S. 12
Alvear, S.A. 285
ambilingual people 10
American Association for Applied Linguistics 147
American Community Survey 40–41
American Council of Teachers of Foreign Languages (ACTFL) 204, 231
American Education Research Association 296, 381
American Indian languages 253 *see also* indigenous languages; Native American languages
American Psychological Association 154, 273, 296, 381
American Recovery and Reinvestment Act (ARRA) 2009 (US) 202
American School for the Deaf (ASD) 394, 398, 401, 403
American Sign Language (ASL) 390–427
Americanization 39, 193
Americans with Disabilities Act (ADA) 396
Andrews, J. 392, 407, 419
anti-bilingualism 152
anti-immigrationism 207, 209, 434, 445
anti-racism 332, 446
anti-racist education 65
anti-tourist protests 472
apps 134
Arabic
  dual language programs 248
  economic/employment benefits 70
  and the internet 477
  mass media 474
  powerful majority languages 59, 73
  United States 212
  varieties of 65
Archey, X. 450

Arias, M.B. 214, 241, 334, 360–361
Arizona 198–200, 211, 228, 233, 239, 254, 276, 316, 434, 446
Armas, E.G. 343
Arregúin-Anderson, M.G. 356
Arsenian, S. 157
ascendant bilingualism, definitions 3
ASL and English Bilingual Professional Development (AEBPD) 408
Asperger's syndrome 369, 375
ASPIRA Consent Decree 362
assessment
    accommodations 296, 383–385
    ambiguity of language assessment terminology 22–23
    authentic assessment 385–386
    bilingual education 38, 201, 202
    bilingual teaching assistants 317
    Common Core State Standards 203
    communicative competence 17
    communicative language testing 26–32
    critical language testing 37–38
    Deaf-signing people 420–422
    dynamic assessment 24–25, 386
    ecological approaches to assessment 386
    Every Student Succeeds Act 2015 (US) 205–206
    gifted and talented bilingual children 370, 381–383
    high-stakes language testing 37, 202, 205, 241, 245, 330, 432
    holistic view of bilingualism 14
    interconnected 24
    language-as-a-problem orientation 431
    literacy 341–342, 357–358
    monolingualism 13
    multiliteracies 357–358
    norm- and criterion-referenced language tests 25–26
    political view of language testing 37–38
    sign languages 422
    sociocultural contexts 383
    special educational needs 372, 374, 378, 379
    in strongest language 382
    summative and formative 24
    teacher evaluations 206
    testing standards 381
assessment for learning (AfL) 24
asset-oriented perspectives 416
assimilationism
    and bilingual education 191, 221, 228–229
    cultural literacies 344
    Deaf-signing people 406
    dual language programs antithesis to 246
    as goal of bilingual education 224
    ideologies 128, 441, 451, 452–453, 456
    indigenous languages 253
    partial assimilation 456
    political ideologies 273
    second language instruction 128
    United States 130, 193, 213, 441, 442–446, 451–454
    and World War I 193
asymmetrical bilingualism 52
Atkins, John D.C. 253
audism 396, 423
August, D. 273, 274, 277, 316, 318, 342, 347, 348, 349, 350, 351
Australia
    assessment 14, 37
    communicative language testing 27
    heritage language education 249
    immersion programs 288
    immigrant languages 53, 139
    non-English films/TV 474–475
    science of reading (SOR) 341
    world language teaching 231
Austria 58
authentic assessment 385–386
authentic language situations 143, 241, 262, 326, 479
autism spectrum 172, 281, 369, 375
Avengers, The 474

Babbel 134
Bachi, R. 137
Baetens Beardsmore, H. 222, 262, 328
Bahan, B. 391
Bahasa Melayu 481
Baker, C. 33, 88, 114, 134, 213, 220, 222, 252, 275, 293, 294, 309, 311, 415–416, 484
Baker, F.S. 227
Baker, K.A. 273, 274, 275
Baker, P. 480
Baker-Bell, A. 65
balanced bilingualism 10, 35, 104, 105, 164, 171, 238
Balkans 248
Ballinger, S. 262
Banks, J.A. 420
Barakos, E. 468
Barcelona 472
Barker, V. 445
Bartlett, L. 222
basic interpersonal communicative skills (BICS) 180–181, 186
basic reading skills 339
Basque
    bilingual education 110, 216
    dual language programs 265
    identity 63, 457
    immersion programs 260
    intensive language learning 134
    language maintenance 52
    language rights 437
    status planning 87

Batibo, H. 83
Baugh, J. 433
Beam-Conroy, T. 369, 370, 381
Beauchamp, M.L.H. 369
Beeman, K. 348–349
Begay, Shawna 474
'Being Bilingual is a Superpower' 208–209
Bekerman, Z. 248
Belgium 39, 42, 52, 106, 108
Bengali 481
Benson, C. 222, 329–330, 348
Ben-Zeev, S. 160, 169
Bhabha, H. 4
Bhatia, T.K. 70, 72
Bialystok, E. 152, 156, 157, 159, 161, 162, 163, 166, 167, 168, 173, 179, 347, 349, 350
biculturalism 3–4, 71, 171, 256, 413, 418
Biden, Joe 39, 208, 443, 444, 475
bilingual bicultural programs 413, 418
bilingual books 357, 358
Bilingual Common Core Initiative 186
Bilingual Education Act 1967 (US) 195, 196–198, 201, 210, 443
bilingual special education 375–377
bilingual support assistants 317–318 *see also* teaching assistants
bilingualism
    abilities 8–10
    definitions 2, 8
    degrees of 8–10
    dimensions 3–4
    holistic view of 13–14
    measurement of 21–46
    monolingual view of bilingualism 11–13
biliteracy 204–205, 220, 221, 238, 242, 263, 330, 338–365
Biliteracy Education Seal Teaching (BEST) Act 209
Birdsong, D. 135, 138
'black box' research 297–298
Black English 16
Black Lives Matter 332, 446
Blackledge, A. 64, 310, 358
Block, D. 457, 458, 486
Blommaert, J. 64, 73
Bloomfield, L. 8, 17, 36
body language 16, 171, 180
Bolander, B. 71
Booton, S.A. 164
borderlands 62–63
Boroditsky, L. 171
borrowing 117, 473
Börstell, C. 394, 395
Boun, S. 205, 230, 232, 308, 348, 430, 471
Bourdieu, P. 132, 142–143
Bourhis, R.Y. 450–451
brain development 103, 113, 164–167, 179, 181, 409–410

brain imaging techniques 165–167, 409, 410
Brandt, Willy 481
Bravo, M.A. 38
Brecht, R.D. 129, 130
Breton 6, 87
Brexit 459, 468
BRICS group (Brazil, Russia, India, China and South Africa) 481
bridging programs 288
British Council 68, 70, 468
Brohy, C. 265
brokering roles 121–123, 481
Brown v. Board of Education 1958 210, 437
Bruck, M. 288
Brunei 261
Bruner, J. 318
Bruthiaux, P. 439
building a bilingual education system 299
Bunch, G.C. 186
Burger, P. 473
Burgoyne, A.P. 154
Burr, E. 378, 379, 380
Burt, M.K. 273, 274
Bush, George H.W. 197
Bush, George W. 201, 443
Bush, Jeb 434, 443
business purposes, language for 67, 68, 70, 72, 129, 481–486 *see also* economic/employment benefits; trade
Busuu 134
Buttitta, Ignazio 83
Byram, M. 31

CAEBER project 392, 408, 423
Caldwell, H.B. 409
California 198–199, 204–205, 211, 227, 239, 251, 340, 360, 379, 446
Callahan, R. 484–486
Cambodia
    bilingual education 230, 232
    codeswitching 308
    dynamic bilingualism 54
    English 264, 308
    indigenous languages 52, 87, 230, 264, 348
    international languages 469
    multilingualism for tourism 472
    translanguaging 313
    TV/film 474
Cambodian-Americans 459
Cameroon 78
Canada
    assessment 14, 37
    biliteracy development 351
    communicative language testing 27
    cues to language choices 5–6
    elementary schools 324
    First Nations Languages 91–92

French 6, 50, 52, 58, 63, 128, 232, 250, 255–256, 289–290, 322, 323
heritage language education 132, 250, 251, 290–292
history of bilingual education 191
ideologies 451
immersion programs 146, 255–258, 288, 289–290, 322, 324
immigrant languages 53
indigenous languages 253
language censuses 42
language rights 52
linguistic capital 481
nationalism 63
Québec 6, 52, 63, 257–258, 455
science of reading (SOR) 341
special educational needs 375
studies into bilingualism and cognition 158
Truth and Reconciliation Commission of Canada 59, 254
world language teaching 231, 232
Canadian Language Benchmarks 16
Canagarajah, A.S. 63, 356
Canale, M. 16
Cantonese 481
Carder, M. 263
Cardona, Miguel 208–209
CARE International 348
caretaker speech 324
caring professions 469
Carlisle, J.F. 168
Carthery-Goulart, M.T. 168
Castro-Villarreal, F. 378, 379
Catalan 87, 260, 435, 457
Catalonia 110, 259, 435
Catherine wheel cycle 487
Catholic Church 192, 193
Celtic languages 60–61, 438, 457
Cenoz, J. 113, 135, 222–223, 260, 261, 262, 264, 265, 308, 310
censuses 23, 39–44, 60
Center for Applied Linguistics (CAL) 238–239, 243, 263
Center for Black Deaf Studies 397
Center for Research on Education, Diversity, and Excellence (CREDE) 277
Cervantes-Soon, C. 241, 245, 333
CHAMP bilingual practices 392
Chan, V. 110, 138, 250, 291, 308
Chang, J. 109
Chang-Bacon, C.K. 215
Charalambous, C. 105, 467
Cheatham, G.A. 172–173
Chen Pichler, D. 397, 399
Cheung, A. 276, 347
Chevalier, S. 102, 103, 104, 108, 109, 111, 115
Cheyenne 78
Chhuon, V. 459

Chichewa 308
'Child Friendly Schools' 331–332
childhood *see also* elementary schools; pre-school
children as interpreters/brokers 121–123
Deaf-signing people 410, 411
early development of bilingualism 100–125
language loss 138
Chilvers, A. 422
China
Confucius Institutes 70, 133
English in 63, 71
heritage language education 249
indigenous languages 52, 63
promotion of Chinese abroad 70
sign languages 416
trilingualism 110
urbanization 60
Chinese 68, 168, 194, 195, 212, 246, 261, 312–313, 416, 486
Chiswick, B.R. 136
Chuj 355
Cioé-Peña, M. 369–370
circumstantial bilingualism 4, 31, 132
citizenship 39, 233, 326–327, 332, 432, 435, 438
civic ideologies 451
civil rights 194, 316, 436, 440
Civil Rights Act 1964 (US) 194, 436
Civil Rights Project, University of California 278
Clarke School for the Deaf 403
classifier languages 171
classrooms
versus authentic language situations 143
bilingual classroom talk 308–309
biliteracy development 351–352
classroom language 180, 258, 308–309
effective classrooms for bilingual students 303–337
language strategies 324–326
multiliteracies 354–358
resources for biliteracy 356–357
Clerc, Laurent 394, 395, 398, 401, 402, 404
CLIL (content and language integrated learning) 261–263, 304
Cline, T. 371, 376, 385
Clinton, Bill 197
Clyne, M. 113
Coalition of Community-Based Heritage Language Schools 249
CODAs/KODAs – (Child/Kid of Deaf Adults) 400
codeblending 400, 414
codemeshing 356
codemixing 6, 114, 160
codeswitching 7, 112, 114–121, 171, 307–309, 399, 414, 417 *see also* translanguaging
Coelho, E. 321

cognates 156, 350
cognition 102, 113, 130, 151–176, 179, 181, 311, 368, 411, 430
cognitive academic language proficiency (CALP) 180–181, 182
cognitive continuum quadrant model 180
cognitive overload 157
Cogswell, Mason Fitch 401
Cohan, A. 215
Cole, D. 415
Coley, J. 171
collective rights 435
Collier, V.P. 281–282, 309, 316
colonialism 50, 65, 70, 71, 72, 192, 250, 434
Combs, M.C. 226, 230, 307, 441
Comité Padres de Familia 362
Commission on Language Learning 231
commodification of languages 440–441, 470, 482
Common Core State Standards 182, 203, 206–207, 211
Common European Framework of Reference (CEFR) 16, 29–32
common underlying proficiency (CUP) 178–179, 416
communicative competence 15–17, 26, 27, 31, 133, 170, 241, 262, 356, 446
communicative disorder 372 see also speech/language impairments
communicative language teaching (CLT) 16
communicative language testing 26
communicative sensitivity 169–170
community heritage language classes 196, 249, 251, 438
community relationships 359
compartmentalization of languages in dual language education 243, 244–245
complementary schools 132
complex dynamic systems 140
comprehensible output 325
computer adaptive testing (CAT) 28–29
Conference of Educational Administrators of Schools and Programs for the Deaf (CEASD) 405
Conference on College Composition and Communication (CCCC) 435
conflict 61–62, 247, 431–432
Confucius Institutes 70, 133
Congressional Caucus on America's Languages 209, 211
Connell, B. 78
consecutive bilingualism see sequential bilingualism
Consortium for Language Teaching and Learning 249
constructivism 343
Conteh, J. 416
content instruction 231
content-based ESL 225

content-based instruction (CBI) 254, 262, 304, 318
contexts see also sociocultural contexts
  contextual support 180
  early development of bilingualism 109
  functional bilingualism 5, 9–10
  and IQ testing 155–156
  measurement of bilingualism 36
  motivations to learn 140
continua of multilingual education 222–223
continuum of bilingual language proficiency 9–10, 313
continuum of biliteracy 353–354
conversational skills 14, 180
Cooper, R.L. 85, 89
cooperative learning 307, 357
Cope, B. 355
Coral Way Elementary School, Dade County, Florida 194–195, 238, 246
CORDIS–European Union consortium 419
corpus planning 85, 87
Corsica 309
Corsican 309
cosmopolitanism 62, 246
cost–benefit analysis 291–292, 439
co-teaching 226, 242, 243
Coulmas, F. 481
Council of Chief State School Officers (CCSSO) 184
Council of Europe 29, 30–31, 436
counterbalanced instruction 326
count/mass nouns 171
Covid-19 28, 39, 207–208, 215, 418, 468, 472, 474, 476
Coyle, D. 191, 261
Crawford, J. 192, 197, 198, 199, 272, 277, 316, 319, 445
creative thinking 163–164
Creese, A. 64, 310
criminal proceedings and language rights 439
criterion-referenced testing 25–26
critical consciousness 241, 333
critical language awareness 65, 186
critical language testing 37–38
critical literacy 307, 344–346
critical period hypothesis 134, 136, 165, 410
critical post-structuralist sociolinguistics 73–74
critical translinguistics 183
Croneberg, Carl 395
cross-cultural competence 314–315, 332–333
cross-curricular benefits of dual language programs 287–288, 315
cross-signing 399
Cruz, B.R. 273, 274
Cruz, Ted 443
Crystal, D. 68, 78, 82–83, 84
CSA Research 68
Cuba 50

Cuban-Americans 194–195, 238, 246, 443, 483
cues to language choices 5–6, 169–170, 308
cultural assimilation 62, 196 *see also* assimilationism
cultural awareness 129, 130, 143, 227, 343
cultural capital 143, 289, 330, 424
cultural genocide 59
cultural mediation 121
cultural pluralism 221, 260–261, 263, 344, 446, 451, 477
cultural tourism 471–472
Cummins, J. 14, 116, 164, 178, 179, 180, 182, 248, 249, 307, 351, 358, 416, 460–461, 462
curriculum
　access to 287–288
　bilingual education 331
　cross-cultural competence 314–315
　cross-curricular benefits of dual language programs 287–288, 315
　language across the curriculum 304–305
　mathematical achievement 168, 282, 285, 288, 296
　theories of 177–189
Cushing, I. 11, 12, 65
Cushing-Leubner, J. 248

Dade County 194–195, 238, 246
Dagenais, D. 146
Danaakk'e 86
d'Anglejan, A. 256
Dannoff, M.N. 271
Davis, J.L. 59
De Bot, K. 161, 166
de Bruin, A. 173
de Courcy, M. 288
De Houwer, A. 102, 103, 104, 105, 106, 108, 110, 114
de Jong, E.J. 129, 198, 223, 228, 430, 452
de Kanter, A. 273, 274
De Korne, H. 86
de l'Épeé, Charles-Michel 401, 405
Deaf epistemology 394–395
Deaf Press 'Little Paper Family' 407
Deaf-signing bilingual education 400–409
Deaf-signing people 314, 390–427, 458, 478
death, language 51, 55–60, 78–97
decolonial approaches 386
Defence Language Institute Foreign Language Center (DLIFLC) 468
deficit-oriented perspectives
　to codeswitching 118
　cognition 152, 178, 181
　heritage languages 133
　limited English proficient (LEP) label 13
　monolingualism 114
　No Child Left Behind (NCLB) 201
　raciolinguistics 15
　special educational needs 372, 377, 381
　standardized proficiency testing 11
　women 430
definitions 2–18
Del Perico, A. 479, 484, 486
Del Valle, S. 194, 437
Delavan, M.G. 215, 240, 245, 361
democratic citizenship 65
detrimental effects, period of 153–157
Deuchar, M. 109
developmental bilingual education 238, 275, 279, 283
developmental interdependence hypothesis 179–180
developmental maintenance bilingual education 196
DeVos, Betsy 207
Dewaele, J.-M. 112
dialects 13, 31–32, 64 *see also* non-standard varieties
Diana v. The California State Board of Education 378
Diaz, R.M. 158
digital divide 96
digital literacy 354, 355, 357
digital technologies 134, 141, 358, 414, 417–419, 476–480 *see also* internet; social media
diglossia 49–53, 309
Dillingham, Charles 402
Diné bizaad (Navajo) 54, 59, 60, 118, 251, 254, 259, 474
diplomacy, languages of 130, 133, 467
direct instruction 102
disabilities, bilinguals with 172–173, 215–216, 259, 367, 370–371, 375, 380, 383–385, 395, 411 *see also* Deaf-signing people; special educational needs
(dis)citizenship 233, 432
discourse 144, 344
discovery learning approaches 318
discrimination 52, 215, 241, 246, 328, 331, 423, 433, 438, 440
Disney films, dubbed 474
distance learning 134
divergent/creative thinking 163–164
diversity 63–64, 82–83, 92, 192, 221, 291, 346, 431, 439, 441 *see also* cultural pluralism
domains
　and age of learner 136
　communicative language testing 28
　degrees of bilingualism 8–10
　differing 3
　diglossia 51
　infant bilingual development 103
　interpreting 122
　language revitalization 91
　spread of English 68
　status planning 87, 88
　translanguaging 118–119

domestic workers 107, 468
dominant languages *see also* power; prestige
   definitions of bilingualism 3, 6
   diglossia 51
   and gender 430
   identity and second languages 144
   language dominance measures 33–34
   language policies 84–85
   linguistic imperialism 71
   political view of language testing 37–38
   shifting in children 107–108
   subtractive bilingualism 53
Dominican Republic 50
Dong 52
Dorian, N.C. 58
dormant languages 56, 91
Dörnyei, Z. 72, 140, 141
Dos Puentes Elementary School, New York 247, 471
Douglas Fir Group 147–148
Douglass, Justice William 225
Dove, M.G. 226
Down's syndrome 375
Driagina, V. 171
'drip-feed' language programs 231, 286–287
dual language bilingual education (DLBE) 238–248
dual language programs
   effectiveness of bilingual education 179, 278–286, 352
   federal support 209
   gentrification of bilingual education 215, 240, 361
   history of bilingual education 191, 194–195, 197
   refugees 111
   Senate Bill 1014 200
   as 'strong' bilingual education 221
   Title VII Bilingual Education Act 196
   United States 193, 199
   university-level bilingual education 223
dual language resources 317, 349, 357, 358
Dual Language Training Institute 239, 243
dubbing 474
Duchêne, A. 441, 467
Dulay, H.C. 273, 274
Duolingo 134
Duolingo English Test (DET) 28–29
Dutch 261
Dutcher, N. 291, 306
Dweck, C.S. 154
Dwibahasa (two-language) school system in Brunei 261
dynamic assessment 24–25, 386
dynamic bilingualism
   in the 21st century 54
   bilingual assessment and testing 38
   Deaf-signing people 415
   early development of bilingualism 102, 106
   holistic view of bilingualism 8, 13, 17
   language balance measures 35
   translanguaging 115, 310
dynamic identities 459
Dynamic Learning Maps (DLM) Alternative Assessment System Consortium 385
dyslexia 371, 384

early development of bilingualism 100–125, 139, 169–170, 181
Eberhard, D.M. 68, 69, 80, 81
Ebonics 65
Echevarría, J. 227, 307, 319, 380
ecological approaches to assessment 386
ecology of language 85, 92
economic/employment benefits 129, 131, 140, 245, 455–456, 466–471, 480–486
Educar Para Transformar (Educate for Transformation) 330
Education Endowment Foundation 293–294
Education for All Handicapped Children Act 1975 (US) 378
Edwards, J. 7
EEG (electroencephalography) 165
effectiveness of bilingual education 270–302, 326–335
Eilers, R.E. 309
elective bilingualism 4, 31
Elementary and Secondary Education Act (ESEA) 1965 (US) 195, 196, 197, 201, 202–204, 210
elementary schools
   dual language programs 242, 243
   effectiveness of bilingual education 280, 282
   formal grammar tuition 324
   heritage language education 251, 252
   home language development 305
   immersion programs 256
   indigenous languages 254
   literacy development 349
   second language learning 136
   special educational needs 371
embedded second language instruction 231
emergent bilinguals 3, 12, 13, 186, 192, 321, 352
emergent trilingualism 112
Emmorey, K. 409
emojis 54
emotions
   affective goals 131
   barriers to learning 374
   emotional intelligence 154
   emotional literacy 354
   grammatical encoding of 171
   and language choice 105
   and language loss 110
employment, languages for 6, 129, 131, 140, 245, 435, 455–456, 466–471, 481–486

empowerment 460–462
enculturation 70, 339
endangered languages 58–60, 80–84, 91, 258
endogenous communities 4
England 11, 24, 42, 132, 231 *see also* United Kingdom
English
   academic English 182
   for business 67, 68, 70, 72, 129, 481–486
   in China 63, 71
   colonialism 50, 434
   count/mass nouns 171
   dynamic identities 459
   economic/employment benefits 481–482
   English as a Foreign Language (EFL) 67, 68, 70
   English as a Global Language 66–73
   English as a new language (ENL) 318
   English as a Second Language (ESL) 128, 129, 195–196, 214, 318
   English as an Additional Language (EAL) 225, 227, 317, 318
   English as an international language (EIL) 70, 110, 129, 140, 261, 440
   English for speakers of other languages (ESOL) 318
   European Schools movement 264
   figures of speech 16
   as a first language 68
   future of 68–69
   global mass media 474–475
   in India 6, 71
   and the internet 68, 477
   and Islam 71
   as language of IQ tests 154–155
   as language of the playground 322
   as a lingua franca (ELF) 31, 70, 71, 72
   literacy 340
   as medium of instruction 54, 193, 194, 263–264, 398
   for multinational communication 71
   nationalism 62
   non-standard varieties 65
   and pluralist ideologies 454–455
   and power 59, 454–455
   prestige 51, 309
   proficiency standards 183–186
   Puerto Rico 59
   South Korea 145
   spread of 67–68
   standard varieties 435
   statistics on speakers 68
   three-generation shift to 58
   and tourism 471–472
   transglossia 52
   United States 137, 442, 445–446, 456–457
   for work purposes 6
   World Englishes 66
   world language teaching 232

English as an Additional Language (EAL) Assessment Framework 24
English First 196
'English for the Children' 198
English language development (ELD) 318, 342
English language learner (ELL) label 13
English Language Proficiency (ELP) 184–185
English Language Proficiency Assessment for the 21st Century (ELPA21) 24, 184, 384
English-only mandates 192, 193, 195, 199, 404, 432, 444, 445, 470
English-plus viewpoints 446
Engman, M.M. 60
enrichment bilingual education 220–221, 239, 243–244, 261, 328
ePals 479
Equal Employment Opportunity Commission 470
equal opportunities in education 195–196
equilingual people 10
equity 326–327
ERPs (event-related potentials) 165, 409
errors in the classroom 325
Escamilla, K. 13, 186, 198, 352–253
ESEA Flexibility 203–204, 211
Esther Martinez Native American Languages Preservation Act (HR 4766) 209, 211, 253
ethnic community mother-tongue schools 196
ethnicity
   in censuses 39
   communicative sensitivity 169–170
   ethnic tourism 471–472
   and exclusion from education 233
   identity 457–458
   immersion programs 259
   and language conflict 61
   language rights 436, 438
   language-as-a-problem orientation 431
   and languages 63
   multiple identities 145
   nationalism 62
ethnist ideology 451
ethnography of communication 15
Ethnologue 23, 68, 69, 80, 81, 93
Eurobarometer 131
European Charter for Regional or Minoritized languages 436
European Commission 90, 131, 265
European Language Portfolio 31
European Parliament 435
European Schools movement 264–265, 328
European Union 53, 63, 436, 439, 459, 468
evening classes 133
Every Student Succeeds Act 2015 (US) 205–209, 293, 341, 379, 383
evidence-based policy making 341–342
exceptional children 367, 368–369, 381–383
executive control system 161

executive function skills 161, 173
Expanded GIDS (EGIDS) 93
expanding circle English 67
experimental studies 285, 293, 294, 297–298
expert panels 277–278
Eyak 78

Facebook 54
Faingold, E.D. 431, 435, 437
Fairbanks Native Association 86
Faltis, C.J. 114, 117, 228
family *see also* parental engagement
    acquisition planning 85
    Deaf-signing people 423–424
    diglossia 49
    domains 5–6
    early development of bilingualism 104–105
    intergenerational transmission 51, 81, 86, 88, 95–96, 104–105, 253, 476
    in the language classroom 358, 361
    language policies 104
    reversing language shift 92, 95
Farrington v. Tokushige 194
feminist scholarship 430–431
Feng, A. 63, 70, 110, 249
Ferguson, C. 49
Festman, J. 105, 112, 113
Figueroa, R.A. 38
figures of speech 16
Filipino domestic workers 468
Fillmore, L.W. 138, 139, 182, 330
fingerspelling 399, 414–415
Finland 39, 110, 256, 259
Finnish 259
first language *see also* home languages; subtractive bilingualism
    displacement of 36, 53, 105, 129, 138, 152, 155, 178
    early development of bilingualism 3, 102
    formal schooling in 317
    literacy 307, 316, 347, 348, 351–352
    sociocultural theory of learning 311
    special educational needs 373, 377, 378
    as support in second language classroom 313–314
    supported by translanguaging 312
    supporting in immersion programs 328
First Nations Languages 91–92 *see also* Native American languages
Fishman, J. 49, 50, 51, 58, 92–93, 95, 196, 249, 253, 431, 453, 476
fixed mindsets 154
Flemish 52
Flores, N. 11, 12, 14, 15, 31, 138, 183, 330, 333–334, 378, 433
Florida 194–195, 238, 246, 453, 480
Floyd, George 332
fluency 8, 22, 91–92, 156

fMRI (functional magnetic resonance imaging) 165, 409
Fogle, L.W. 104, 201
formality/informality 49 *see also* register
formative assessment 24
Foucault, M. 73, 144
four basic language skills 7–8
four-quadrants model 180
France 87–88, 133, 474
Francis, D.J. 384
Franklin, Benjamin 192
Frederickson, N. 180, 371, 376, 385
Freeman, R.D. 246
Freire, P. 205, 293, 345, 346
French
    in Belgium 52
    Canada 6, 50, 52, 58, 63, 128, 232, 250, 255–256, 289–290, 322, 323
    in Corsica 309
    European Schools movement 264
    on the internet 68
    language-as-a-resource 441
    Luxembourg 265
    status planning 87–88
    Switzerland 265
    United States 58
    world language teaching 232
French Sign Language 394, 398, 401
Friesland 110
Fukuda, M. 107
full inclusion 375
functional bilingualism 5, 9–10, 33, 155, 287
funds of knowledge 214, 361

Gaelic 58, 60–61, 249, 457, 476
Gaelscoileanna 328
Gal, S. 58
Gallagher-Brett, A. 130
Gallaudet University 392, 396, 397, 401, 404–405, 408
Gándara, P. 130, 484–486
Gandhi, M. 71
Garcia, E.E. 195, 196, 197
García, O. 8, 11, 13, 51, 52, 54, 55, 65, 73, 74, 102, 106, 115, 116, 121, 186, 221, 222, 223, 230, 231, 244, 310, 311, 353, 415, 442, 445
García García, Amadeo 78
Garcia-Sierra, A. 103
Gardner, H. 154
Gardner, R.C. 140, 141
Garrettson, M. 395
GCSEs (UK) 231
gender 41, 143, 146, 169–170, 330, 430
generalizability of research 155, 158, 273, 274, 289, 290, 295
Genesee, F. 113, 119, 277, 279, 288, 299, 316, 327, 343, 351, 375

gentrification of bilingual education 215, 240, 361
Gentry, M. 368
geographical boundaries 52–53, 62–63
geographical mapping 23
German
   in Austria 58
   in Belgium 52
   European Schools movement 264
   as heritage US language 250
   on the internet 68
   Luxembourg 265
   Switzerland 265
   United States 192
   world language teaching 232
Germany 133, 459
Gessner, S. 91–92
gesture 394, 399–400, 415–416
Giannini, S. 48
Gibbons, P. 311, 318, 321
gifted and talented bilingual children 368–369, 381–383
Gĩkũyũ 434
Giles, H. 445
'glass box' research 297–298
Global California 2030 199
Global South 222
globalization 48, 52, 54, 63, 66–73, 129, 130, 147, 262, 466, 484
Goals 2000: Educate America Act 197
Goethe-Institut 133
Goldenberg, C. 351
Goldsmith, S.F. 161
Gollan, T.H. 156, 157
Gómez and Gómez dual language enrichment model 239, 243–244
Gonçalves, K. 468
Google Translate 96, 476
Gorter, D. 264, 265, 308, 310
Gottlieb, M. 24
Government Accountability Office (GAO) 276–277
Graddol, D. 68, 70, 80, 471
Graded Intergenerational Dislocation Scale (GIDS) 93
Gramling, D. 11, 191
grammar
   bilingual grammar 115, 162
   codeswitching 114
   cognition 171
   communicative competence 11, 15, 128, 130
   critical period hypothesis 136
   explicit teaching of 326
   formal grammar tuition 324
   language arts instruction 242
   non-standard varieties 16, 64
   structured English immersion 228
   transfer 325, 350

grassroots movement 88, 91, 249, 299, 362, 438
Greek 250
Greene, J. 275
Gregorio Luperón High School in New York 222
Gregory, E. 350, 355
Grijalva, Raúl 209
Grosjean, F. 4, 9, 10, 14, 33, 48, 102, 114, 117, 155, 179
group belonging/affiliation 8, 120, 140, 141, 143
group work 310, 357
growth mindsets 154
Guaraní 50
Guardado, M. 108
Guatemala 291–292
Guided Language Acquisition Design (GLAD) 227
Guidelines for Communicating Rights to Non-Native Speakers of English in Australia, England and Wales, and the USA 439
Gullifer, J.W. 163, 166
Guzman, J. 201

Hakuta, K. 136, 138, 155, 273, 274, 277
Hamayan, E. 378
Hantzopoulos, M. 250
Harris, Kamala 444, 475
Hartanto, A. 168
Haug, T. 421
Hausa 481
Hawaiian 54, 252, 253, 259
Hayakawa, S.I. 444
He, P. 115
Hebrew 38, 89, 92, 132, 133, 137, 248, 250
Heineke, A.J. 339, 340
Heller, M. 289, 441, 467, 472, 480
Henderson, K.I. 186, 240, 244, 313
heritage languages
   biliteracy 350
   in censuses 40
   community heritage language classes 196, 249, 251, 438
   Deaf-signing people 397
   early development of bilingualism 105
   economic costs of education 291
   education in 132, 196, 231, 249, 251, 438
   effectiveness of 290–292
   grassroots movement 438
   heritage language education 248–255
   hiring practices 470
   history of bilingual education 194
   language rights 435
   one-parent families 110
   tourism 471–472
   translators 130
   use of term 250–251
heteroglossic perspectives 13–14, 222

Heugh, K. 221, 222
Hickey, T. 289, 323, 328
high expectations 334
high schools *see* secondary schools
higher-order thinking 181
high-stakes language testing 37, 201, 205, 241, 245, 330, 432
Hindi 6, 59, 72, 481
Hinton, K.A. 245, 328
Hinton, L. 86, 91, 245, 254, 255
hip hop 67
historical repositories, languages as 83
H-languages 49–53
Hmong 251, 438
Hoffman, D.L. 416
Hoffman, E. 458
Hoffmann, C. 435
Holcomb, Ray 407
holistic view of bilingualism 13–14, 308, 309
Holmström, I. 416
home languages *see also* first language; heritage languages; indigenous languages
    developing proficiency in 54
    early development of bilingualism 100–125
    encouraging 86
    immersion programs 323
    language-as-a-problem orientation 433
    language-as-a-resource 442
    literacy 351–352
    loss in children 138–139
    scaffolding 321
    in schools 196, 259, 305–315
    sociocultural theory of learning 311
    and submersion bilingual education 224–225
    as support in second language classroom 313–314
    supporting in immersion programs 258
    supporting literacy instruction 342
home–school relationships 359–362 *see also* parental engagement
Hong Kong 261, 308
Honigsfeld, A. 215, 226
HOPE Teacher Rating Scale 368
Hopewell, S. 13, 352
Hornberger, N.H. 85, 86, 95–96, 223, 251, 344, 347, 353–354, 430
Horne, Tom 200
Horner, J.-J. 265
Horner, K. 65, 87, 89, 92
Housen, A. 264
Howe, Samel Gridely 404
Howie, P. 139
Huang, B.H. 136, 161, 162
Hubbard, Gardiner Green 403, 404, 405
Hudley, C. 459
Hull, R. 165
Hult, F. 85, 296
human rights 84

Humphries, T. 400
Hungarian 58
Hunt, V. 247
Hymes, D. 15
hyphenated identities 452, 458

Ianco-Worrall, A.D. 160
ideal self-concept 141
identity
    affiliation/group belonging 8, 120, 140, 141, 143
    assimilationist ideologies 452–453
    bilingual education 222, 223
    codeswitching and translanguaging 120
    cross-cultural competence 314–315
    Deaf-signing people 397
    in diglossic situations 50
    employment and languages 132
    hyphenated identities 452, 458
    immersion programs 259
    indigenous languages 255
    labels 458–459
    language and 6, 83, 457–460
    and language conflict 61
    and language revitalization 58, 60
    language rights 435
    Latinx identity 138
    maintenance bilingual education programs 220
    measurement of bilingualism 36
    motivations to learn languages 140
    multiple identities 146
    nationalism 63
    parental choices of language 104
    pragmatic identities 481
    and second language acquisition 142–148
    self 458
    social construction of 430–431
    social identity and second languages 142–143
    and submersion bilingual education 224–225
ideologies 449–464
    about heritage languages 130
    anti-racist education 332
    assimilationism 128, 441, 451, 452–453, 456
    civic ideologies 451
    critical post-structuralist sociolinguistics 73–74
    definitions 450–451
    endangered languages 81
    English superiority 240
    ethnist ideology 451
    inclusion 376
    language attitudes 141
    language ideologies and social varieties 65–66
    macro level of ideological structures 147
    monolingualism 11, 118, 135, 138, 152, 196, 277, 432
    neoliberalism 486

pluralist 451, 453–454
political view of language testing 37–38
researcher bias 173
shared vision 329
idioms 8
imagined communities 146
immersion programs
  bilingual education 255–260
  classroom teaching and learning 321–326
  community heritage language classes 133
  effective classrooms for bilingual students 321–326, 328
  effectiveness of bilingual education 273, 283, 286–290
  federal support 209
  and imagined communities 146
  indigenous languages 254–255
  international schools 263
  limitations 288–290
  teacher commitment 323
  in third languages 323
  types of bilingual education 221
  United States 199, 256
immigrant languages
  acculturation 456
  assimilationist ideologies 452–453
  bilingual education 191, 192–216
  children as interpreters/brokers 121–123
  Deaf-signing people 417
  diglossia 53
  dynamic bilingualism 54
  early development of bilingualism 105
  effects on family language patterns 139
  and exclusion from education 233
  exogenous communities 4
  heritage language education 249
  identity 458
  identity and second languages 143
  interrupted schooling 215
  language shift 56
  multiple identities 145
  nationalism 63–64
  second language learning 137
  United States 192–193
imperialism 213
Improving America's Schools Act (IASA) 1994 (US) 197, 210
incipient bilingualism 3, 9, 131
India 6, 50, 71, 72, 459
Indian Education Act 1972 (US) 253
Indian Self-Determination and Educational Assistance Act 1975 (US) 253
Indiana 284, 292–293, 313, 317
'Indigenous insiders' 420
indigenous languages *see also* heritage languages
  Canada 254
  categories of bilingual 10
  China 63
  decline of 72
  in dual language classrooms 246
  economic/employment benefits 482–483
  education 253–255
  endangered languages 78–79
  grassroots movement 438
  heritage language education 248
  Japan 51
  language revitalization 91
  language rights 52
  linguistic oppression 59, 192
  literacy 348
  maintenance/revitalization 52–53
  nationalism 63
  No Child Left Behind (NCLB) 201
  statistics 42
  and submersion bilingual education 224
  United States 192, 201, 253–255
  writing systems 348
Indigenous Languages Act 2019 (Canada) 253
individual bilingualism 2, 4–7, 50
individual language policies 104
individualized education programs (IEP) 378, 379
individualized support 334
Individuals with Disabilities Education Act (IDEA) 1990 (US) 379
industrialization 56, 58
inequality 131, 241, 330, 333, 334, 433, 438, 454, 486
infant bilingual development 103
informal language acquisition 102
Inglis, M. 293–294
Ingold, C.W. 129, 130
inhibitory control 167
inner circle English 66
inner language 112
Institute of Education Sciences (IES) 294
instrumental motivations for learning languages 140
integrative motivations for learning 140–141
intelligence/intelligence quotient (IQ) 153–159, 173, 378
intensive language learning 133
intercultural understanding 48, 69–70, 129–130, 314–315, 467
interdependence between languages 159, 179–180
interference 114, 156, 160, 166, 169
intergenerational transmission 51, 81, 86, 88, 95–96, 104–105, 253, 476
interlanguage 325
internalization processes 171
International Baccalaureate (IB) 263
International Conference on Sign Language Acquisition (ICSLA) 399
International Congress on Education of the Deaf (ICED) 405

International English Language Testing System (IELTS) 26–28
international languages 8, 68, 261, 469 *see also* English, English as an international language (EIL)
International Literacy Association 347
international schools 263–264
International Sign Language (ISL) 399
internationalism 48, 72
internet *see also* social media
   and bilingualism 476–480
   biliteracy resources 357
   early development of bilingualism 104, 107
   and language shift 96
   mass media and bilingualism 473–476
   spread of English 68
   and superdiversity 64
   translanguaging 310
interpreting 121–123, 321, 361, 382, 412, 439, 468
interrupted schooling 215, 233
intersectionality 397
'interventions' 381
intonation 103
investment in second language learning 143
Ireland/Irish
   bilingual education 191, 259, 322, 323, 328, 482
   grassroots movement 438
   heritage language education 249
   identity 457
   immersion programs 259, 322
   language censuses 42
   status planning 87
Islam 71, 132, 339
Isle of Man 60–61
Israel 89, 92, 128, 133, 137, 247–248
Italian 58, 265

Jackson, Charmaine 474
Jaffe, A. 309
James F. Oyster Bilingual Elementary School in Washington, DC 246–247
Janks, H. 344
Japanese
   bilingualism 108
   classifier languages 171
   imagined communities 146
   indigenous languages 51, 97
   on the internet 68
   subtractive bilingualism 53
   for trade 129
   translation from Ainu 97
   United States 194
Johnson, D.C. 296
Johnson, R.K. 260, 287, 288
Joint National Committee for Languages (JNCL) 209

Jones, K. 86
Jones, K.E. 343–344
Jones, M.P. 134
Jones, W.R. 155, 157
Juvonen, P. 308, 310

Kachru, B. 66
Kaine, Tim 443
Kalaja, P. 4–5
Kalantzis, M. 355
Källkvist, M. 308, 310
Kanno, Y. 13, 146
Kasabe/Luo 78
Kay-Raining Bird, E. 375, 376
Kellman, S.G. 356
Kendi, I. 332
Kenner, C. 350–351
Kenya 72, 434
Keres Children's Learning Center 255
Keyes v. School District No. 1, Denver, Colorado 210
Kharkhurin, A.V. 163, 164, 369
Khmer 54, 119, 225, 264, 313, 348
Kiaer, J. 108
Kim, J. 480
Kim, M. 145
Kim, S. 143, 356, 358
kindergarten
   bilingual education 191, 230, 240, 243, 256, 265
   cognition 168
   effectiveness of bilingual education 280, 282, 283
   home language development 305
   immersion programs 256
   Literacy Squared 352
   mainstreaming programs 316
King, K.A. 60, 95–96
Kiramba, L.K. 356
Kirsch, C. 310
Klallam 56, 78–79
Kleifgen, J.A. 230
Kleyn, T. 240, 247
Kloss, H. 434
knowledge
   endangered languages 83
   fluidity of knowledge 307
   funds of knowledge 361
   prior knowledge 311, 318
Kohanga Reo 248, 249, 438
Kolers, P.A. 159
Korea 145
Korean 108, 474, 481
Krashen, S.D. 272, 276, 279, 349, 352
Kristina, Grizelda 78
Kroskrity, P.V. 450
Kui 6
Kuo, L.J. 162

INDEX 583

Kurdish 433
Kushki, A. 25
Kwon, J. 215

L2 motivational self-system 141
La Raza 360
Ladino 92
Laine, M. 156
Lakota 474
Lamb, M. 140, 141
Lambert, W.E. 53, 140, 141, 157–158, 159
Langman, J. 143, 430–431
language acquisition 102
language across the curriculum 304–305
language architecture 183
language arts instruction 242
language as a resource 197, 440–442
language background scales 33, 34
language balance measures 33–35
language brokering 121–123, 481
language communities 48, 49–53
language contact 398–399
language crossing 458
language delay 372–374
language deprivation 411
language documentation 97
language equality 246–247
language learning skills 113
language nest immersion programs 255, 438
language of ideas versus language of display 186
language socialization 86
language use surveys 43
language vitality 81
language-as-a-problem orientation 11, 430–433
language-as-a-resource 440–442
language-as-right *see* rights
languaging 74
Langue Des Signes Française or LSF 394, 398, 401
Lantolf, J.P. 311, 459–460
Lanza, E. 104
Lapkin, S. 260, 286
Lara, Ricardo 199
Latinx identity 138
Latvia 78
Lau, S.M.C. 312
Lau remedies 196, 197, 210, 438
Lau v. Nichols 195, 210, 225, 246, 362, 437–438
Laurén, C. 259
Laurén, U. 164
Laurie, S.S. 152
Lavadenz, M. 343
Le Menestrel, S. 278, 316, 347, 351, 368, 371, 373, 379, 381, 385
leadership 330
LEAD-K (Language Equality and Acquisition for Deaf Kids) 396
leaky diglossia 51

learning difficulties 215–216, 272, 281
Leaton, G.S. 264
Lee, J.S. 133, 249, 251
Lee, T.S. 253, 254, 255
Leeman, J. 39, 40, 41
left brain hemisphere 165
Lehtonen, M. 156
Leider, C.M. 317
Leigh, I.W. 421
Leivada, E. 173
Leopold, W.F. 107–108, 160
letter–sound correspondence 349–350
Leung, C. 24, 31–32
Lewis, G. 213, 293, 294
Lewis, M.P. 93
Lexander, K.V. 104
lexical access 157, 161
Li, P. 9, 10, 14, 33, 114, 179
Li Wei 13, 52, 54, 116, 186, 222, 310, 372, 459
liberalism 435, 442, 456
lifelong learning 223
Lillie, K.E. 228, 233
limited English proficient (LEP) label 13, 197, 201
Lin, A.M.Y. 115
Lindholm-Leary, K. 241, 279
lingua francas 72
linguistic capital 132, 289, 330, 480, 481
linguistic cleansing 61
linguistic developmental interdependence hypothesis 179–180
linguistic differentiation 73–74
linguistic distance between languages 168
linguistic imperialism 62, 65, 71, 396
linguistic mosaic 454
linguistic profiling 433
linguistic repertoires 12, 31–32, 38, 115, 117, 356, 422
lipreading 405–406
literacies 344
literacy 168, 326, 344, 410, 414 *see also* biliteracy
Literacy Squared 186, 352–353
literacy standards 341
Littlebear, Richard 78
Livonian 78
L-languages 49–53
Lo Bianco, J. 247, 430, 432
loan words 117
local government officials 468–4469
local literacies 344
London 62, 480
longitudinal studies 107–108, 112, 163, 271, 274, 281, 283, 285, 310, 316
long-term English language learners (LTELL) 11
LOOK Act (Language Opportunity for Our Kids, Massachusetts) 199, 211, 276

Lorente, B.P. 468
Lortie-Forgues, H. 293–294
lower-ability learners 288, 375
low-status bilingual professionals 470
Lukes, M. 233
Lund, E.M. 369
Luxembourg 128, 191, 261, 265, 310, 431
Luxembourgish (Lëtzebuergesch) 265, 310

MacDonald, R. 24
Macedonia 247–248
machine translation 97, 479
Mackey, W.F. 191, 221
MacNab, G.L. 171, 172
Macnamara, B.N. 154
MacSwan, J. 11, 114, 115, 116, 179, 183, 288, 307
Maddrell, Edward 60
Mahoney, K. 23, 25, 199, 381, 386
mainstream education with world language teaching 221, 231–232
mainstreaming (special educational needs) 375, 376
mainstreaming programs 197, 221, 315–321, 412
maintenance, language 51, 55–58, 252, 255
maintenance bilingual education programs 196, 220, 222, 224–226, 282
majority language dual education 260–266
majority languages and bilingual education 260–266
Makoni, K. 89
Malawi 308
Malay 261
Maldonado, S.I. 386
Malherbe, E.C. 271
Mandarin 59, 63, 70, 73, 312–313
Mann, Horace 404
Manx Gaelic 48, 60–61
Māori 54, 79, 248, 249, 438, 457
mapping 23
Marinova-Todd, S.H. 135, 136, 369, 374, 375
marriage 56
Marschark, M. 419, 420
Martin, D. 374, 386
Martin, M.M. 161
Martin-Jones, M. 118, 259, 308, 343–344
mass media 473–476
Massachusetts 198–199, 211, 239, 404, 446
master–apprentice language learning programs 254–255
mathematical achievement 168, 282, 285, 288, 296
matrix language 114
Matsuoka, K. 399
Matthews, T. 271
May, S. 85, 433, 434, 435, 439, 455
Mayan languages 246
McCarty, T.L. 61, 88, 90, 91, 192, 249, 253, 254, 255

McConnell, B. 271
McField, G.P. 276
McHatton, P.A. 369, 370, 381
McLeister, M. 416
meaning
    construction of meaning approaches to literacy 343
    construction of meaning in a second language 143–144
    cultural meaning 344, 345
    negotiation of 310
    semantic fluency 156
    socially constructed 345
    spatial semantics 136
    transferability 326
measurement of bilingualism 21–46
Mechelli, A. 165–166
media discourse 333
medical professions 469
MEG (magnetoencephalography) 165
Mehisto, P. 299, 327, 329
Melo-Pfeifer, S. 4–5
'melting pot' ideologies 452
memory 138, 159, 167, 171
Menken, K. 38, 376, 432
Mercer, J.R. 370
meta-analysis 154, 165, 172, 173, 274, 275, 276
metalinguistic awareness 16, 111, 112, 113, 122–123, 159–163, 168, 310, 350
Mexican-Americans 194–195
Meyer v. Nebraska 194, 210, 437
Miami 309, 480, 483
Miami/Myaamia 91
migration *see* immigrant languages
Migration Policy Institute (MPI) 207
migration/displacement 60
Miller, P.W. 136
mindsets 154
Miniwats Marketing Group 68
Minnesota 251
minoritized languages *see also* heritage languages; indigenous languages
    bilingual education in the US 190–218
    in censuses 39–44
    corpus planning 87
    cross-cultural competence 315
    in diglossic situations 49–53
    economic/employment benefits 480, 482–483
    empowerment 462–463
    exclusion from schooling 233
    home language development at school 305–306
    identity 458
    intergenerational transmission 51
    and the internet 476–478
    language as a right 433–440
    language choice 6
    language conflict 61

language dominance measures 33–35
language planning 85–90
language shift and maintenance 55–58
language-as-a-problem orientation 431, 432
language-as-a-resource 441–442
literacy 347
loss in children 138–139
multiple identities 145
nationalism 62–63
in schools 53
separatist bilingual education 232
subtractive bilingualism 53–54
theory of language reversal 92–97
translators/interpreters 130
TV/film 474–476
two-way dual language programs 238–240
Mirenda, P. 369, 374, 375
missionaries 192
mixed-methods studies 297
Miyagawa, S. 97
Mohanty, A.K. 4, 6
Mohd-Asraf, R. 71
Moll, L.C. 361
monoculturalism 4, 232
monoglossic perspectives 11, 222
monolingualism
 assimilationist ideologies 452
 and bilinguals' language anxiety 430
 cognitive perspectives 152–153
 Deaf-signing people 411
 as goal of bilingual education 221, 222, 223–229
 and high-status professions 470
 ideologies 11–13, 118, 135, 138, 152, 196, 277, 432
 intelligence/intelligence quotient (IQ) 153–159
 language policies 84–85
 maintenance bilingual education programs 315–321
 monolingual forms of bilingual education 220, 221, 223–229
 monolingual view of bilingualism 11–13, 114
 oralism for Deaf people 410, 411
 parallel monolingualism 481
 as point of reference 36
 in previously diglossic societies 51
 seen as stable and ordered 61
 as a sociopolitical invention 191
 teaching staff 230
 temporary periods of 373
 United States 192–193, 432
MOOCs (massive online organized courses) 134
Moore, J. 115, 183, 186, 288
Moore, R.E. 80, 81
Morgan, M.H. 48
Morita-Mullaney, T. 195, 204, 246, 284, 317, 355
morphological awareness 162

Morris, D. 86
Mortini, S. 310
Moschkovich, J. 309
Moseley, C. 81
Mother Tongue Day 306
mother tongue plus two 265
mother tongues 40, 65, 192, 348 *see also* heritage languages; home languages
motivations to learn 72, 128–132, 135, 140–142
Muller, A. 328
multicompetencies 14
Multicultural Education Act 1988 (Canada) 250
multiculturalism
 bilingual education 264
 and bilingualism 3–4
 Canada 291
 cultural pluralism 221, 261, 263, 344, 446, 451–454, 477
 in the curriculum 307
 emotional intelligence 154
 literacy 344
 multicultural competence 314–315
 social varieties of language 67
 sociocultural competence 241
 two-way dual language programs 242
multidisciplinary individual education plan committees 378–379, 382
multi-ethnic communication 458
multilingual cities 62, 106, 112, 458, 480
multilingual education 222–223, 251, 259
Multilingual Family Storybook Project 358
multilingual learners label 13
multilingualism
 definitions 2
 early development of 110–113
 elite versus non-elite 468
 identity 458
 and the internet 477–478
 language-as-a-resource 440–442
 for tourism 471–472
multiliteracies 354–358, 414
multimodality 8, 36, 54, 68, 74, 357, 394, 399–400, 479
multiple intelligences 154
multitiered systems of support (MTSS) 380
Muñoz, C. 136
Myaamia (Miami) 79

narrative integration 274
Nassaji, H. 25
National Academies of Sciences, Engineering, and Medicine 278, 316, 347, 373
National Assessment of Educational Progress (NAEP) 213
National Association for Bilingual Education (NABE) 204
National Association for Gifted Children 368
National Association for the Deaf (NAD) 406

National Black Deaf Advocates 397
National Center for Education Statistics 212, 370–371
National Center for Educational Evaluation and Regional Assistance 293–294
National Committee for Effective Literacy for Emergent Bilingual Students (NCEL) 342
National Council of Teachers of English (NCTE) 435
National Council on Measurement in Education 296, 381
National Defense Education Act 1958 (US) 194, 210
National Education Association (NEA) 195
National Education Goals Panel 197
national languages 53
National Literacy Panel (NLP) 277
National Literacy Strategy UK 341
National Reading Panel 339, 341–342
National Research Council 277
national security 467
nationalism 62–63, 72
Nationality Act 1906 (US) 193, 210
Native American languages
    bilingual education 253–255, 455
    endangered languages 78–79
    federal support 209
    heritage language education 248, 249
    identity 255
    language revitalization 91–92
    language shift 56, 59
    linguistic oppression 192
    media 474
    reversing language shift 91, 96
Native American Languages Act (US) 253
Native American Languages Preservation Act (US) 253
Native American Languages Resource Center Act 2022 253
'native speakers' 31–32, 70
"native-like" ability 8
Nazis 62
Nebraska ruling 194
Nebraska School for the Deaf 405–406
neoliberalism 262, 293, 333, 408, 435, 440, 467, 486
Netflix 134, 474
Netherlands 261, 262
neuroimaging 165–167, 168
neurolinguistics 164–167, 168
neuroscience 409–410
neutral effects period 157
New Literacy Studies 339
New London Group 354–355, 414
New Mexico 255
'new speaker movement' 91
New York 12, 52, 62, 108, 183, 222, 247, 471
New Zealand 27, 54, 79, 248, 249, 341, 438

Newcomer, S. 109, 457
newcomers 224, 228, 321, 328, 375
Nguyen, T.T.T. 104
Nigeria 261
'9/11' 71, 129–130, 467
No Child Left Behind (NCLB) 201–202, 211, 293, 341, 383, 443
'no sabo kids' 138
'non-nons' 11
non-standard varieties 16, 65, 246, 250, 306, 333, 355, 382, 433, 435
non-verbal communication 324, 354
non-verbal executive functioning 161
norm-referenced tests 25–26
North Carolina Department of Education 281–282
Northern Pomo 96
Norton, B. 132, 143, 146, 457
noun class languages 171
Nover, S.M. 392, 396, 398, 400, 404, 405, 408, 414, 423
Nuestra Casa 397
nursery 102, 107 *see also* kindergarten

Ó Duibhir, P. 322, 323
Ó Riagáin, P. 482
Oaxaca, Mexico 6
Obama, Barack 202, 203, 205, 443
Observation Protocol for Academic Literacies (OPAL) 343
occupational bilingualism 466–471
Ochoa, A.M. 361, 362
Odia 6
Office of English Language Acquisition (OELA) 208, 213, 239, 333, 370
official language status 66, 72, 79, 87, 253, 434, 444, 455
Official Languages Act (1969, 1988) Canada 451
Olague, N. 227
older learners 167
Olivos, E.M. 361, 362
Oller, D.K. 309
Oller, J.W. 14
1.5 generation 6, 58
one-parent families 110
one-parent one-language (OPOL) approaches 102, 104, 106, 107, 112, 309, 369
one-way dual language bilingual education 238, 352
online learning 134
oppression, linguistic 59, 61, 213, 253–254, 445
oral proficiency 316, 325, 341, 342, 347, 405
oralism for Deaf people 404, 405, 406–407
Orellana, M. 122
Ortega, L. 12
orthography 87, 230, 326, 348, 350, 417
Otheguy, R. 115, 179, 308
outer circle English 66

Ovando, C. 230, 441
Oyster-Adams Bilingual School 246–247
Özerk, K. 216

Pacific Islanders 253
Padres Comprometidos (Committed Parents) 360
Pae, T.-I. 350
Paing, C.M. 108
pair work 316
Pakistan 63
Palmer, D.K. 239, 240, 244, 245, 246, 309, 313
Panayiotou, A. 171
Panjabi 58
Papua New Guinea 249
Paradis, J. 375
Paraguay 50
parallel monolingualism 481
paraprofessionals 223, 225, 227, 242, 317–318, 357, 376, 471
parental choices of language 104–105
parental engagement 242, 272, 274, 295, 321, 322, 334–335, 358, 359–362, 379, 386, 462
Parents Involved in Quality Education (PIQE) 360
Park, K. 111
Park-Johnson, S.K. 108
parliaments, multilingual 87
Partnership for Assessment of Readiness for College and Careers (PARCC) 203
passive bilinguals 3, 8, 105, 107–108
passive trilingualism 112
Patani Malay 247, 432
Patel, M. 68, 70
Pavlenko, A. 105, 141, 145, 146, 154, 161, 171, 173, 430, 459–460
peace 129, 248, 433, 440
Peal, E. 157–158, 159
pedagogical translanguaging 308, 309–314, 353
peer support 357
Pennsylvania Dutch (Amish) 58
Pennycook, A. 67
Peristeri, E. 172
Perkins, K. 14
Perley, B.C. 91
personality principle 52
PET (positron emission tomography) 165
Petitto, L.A. 410
Petroj, V. 400
Phakiti, A. 24
phonics 341, 342
phonology 136 *see also* accent
Phulbani District, India 6
picture books 349
Piller, I. 103, 104, 107
Pimsleur 134
Pintner, R. 157
Pizzo, L. 422

planning, language 10, 81, 85–90, 139, 220
playground, languages of the 14, 180, 181, 183, 259, 322, 323
plurilingualism 31–32, 65
Poehner, M.E. 24
policies, language 10, 59, 62, 78–79, 84–85, 292–298
policing language 52
politeness 16
political ideologies *see also* assimilationism; monolingualism
  codeswitching 309
  content and language integrated learning (CLIL) 262
  economics of bilingualism 486
  effectiveness of bilingual education 272
  English in US 277
  mainstreaming programs 316
  problem/resource/rights views 428–448
  United States 442–446
  US bilingual education 273
Popham, W.J. 23, 37
population-based measurement of bilingualism 23
Porras, D.A. 467
Porter, L. 278
Portes, A. 453
portfolios 26, 31, 357–358, 385
post-colonialism 62, 486
postmodernism 116, 345, 440
post-structuralism 73–74, 141, 144, 430–431
Potowski, K. 312
power
  balancing languages 328
  and choice of content in dual language provision 245
  codeswitching and translanguaging 117–121
  coercive versus collaborative 460–461
  conflicts 431
  cost–benefit analysis 439
  critical literacy 344–346
  critical post-structuralist sociolinguistics 73–74
  dual language programs 248
  empowerment 460–462
  and English 444–446, 454–455
  and gender 430
  and language 144–145
  and language conflict 61
  language rights 433–440
  and language shift 33, 93, 96
  linguistic capital 132
  majority languages 51, 59
  and minoritized languages 49–50
  political view of language testing 37–38
  problem/resource/rights views 428–448
  teachers and bilingual teaching assistants 317
  and teaching staff 230

pragmatic competence 15, 16, 369
pre-school 248, 255, 310, 328, 372, 438 *see also* kindergarten
prestige 4, 51, 67, 68, 107, 144, 313, 434
Price, David 209
primary schools *see* elementary schools
principals (school) 330
prior knowledge 311, 318
private language planning 104
problem, language as a 430–433
productive bilingualism 3
proficiency
    ability and bilingualism 8–10
    academic language proficiency 14, 180, 181, 182
    and the age of learner 134–139
    ambiguity of language assessment terminology 22–23
    communicative language testing 26
    cross-curricular benefits of dual language programs 241
    in different domains 9–10
    early development of bilingualism 107–108
    effectiveness of bilingual education 273, 279, 282, 283, 286–287
    global language proficiency 14–17
    in home languages 54
    measurement issues 295–296
    monolingualism 11–12, 31
    proficiency standards 183–186
    raciolinguistics 31
    self-rating 35
    special educational needs 375, 378
    teachers' 329–330
    threshold theory 179
    time taken to achieve English proficiency 316
    trilingualism 111
'Proposition 203' 198, 199, 211, 228, 275–276, 434
'Proposition 227' 198, 199, 211, 275–276
'Proposition 58' 199, 211, 276
prosody 136
psycholinguistics 161, 165, 393, 403
Pu, C. 350, 356
public opinion polls 276
Pueblo communities 255
Puerto Ricans in New York 52, 362
Puerto Rico 59, 65, 455
pull-out/push-in classes 225–226, 280, 327, 328, 375
PUMI – Purpose, Use, Method, Instrument 25

qualitative research methods 296–297
quantitative research methods 296–297
Quay, S. 102, 103, 104, 108, 109, 111, 115
Québec 6, 52, 63, 257–258, 455
Quechua 52
Question 2 198, 199, 211, 275–276

race
    and bilingual education 194
    in censuses 39
    communicative sensitivity 169–170
    and minoritized languages 12
    multiple identities 145
    racism 62, 194, 330, 332, 433, 434, 445, 454, 470
    and submersion bilingual education 225
race categories in US Census 39
Race to the Top (RTTT) 202, 211
raciolinguistics 12, 15, 31, 65, 181, 183, 240, 332, 470
racism 215, 423
Rahman, T. 71
Ramanathan, V. 233, 432
Ramirez, J.D. 65, 250, 274, 275
Ramirez, P.C. 345
Rampton, B. 458
randomized control trials 285, 293–294, 297–298
Rani, R. 67
reading 339, 349–350, 358 *see also* biliteracy; literacy
Reading League 341, 342
Reagan, Ronald 197, 443
Reardon, S.F. 282, 283, 284–285
Rebuffot, J. 255
receptive bilingualism 3, 8, 112
recessive bilingualism 3
recursive bilingualism 54
refugees 111, 215, 224, 228, 233, 321, 459
register 16, 49, 186
relationship-building 120, 171, 291
religion 49, 62, 72, 132, 192, 339, 345, 359, 431, 469
reported speech 120
representing (as mode of communication) 8
research ethics 295, 297–298
research methods 292–298
researcher bias 297, 298
resource, language as a 440–442
response to intervention (RTI) 380
reversal, theory of language 92–97
revitalization, language 54–58, 60–51, 80, 84–85, 91, 254, 347, 474
revival, language 60–61
Reyes, A. 458
Ricento, T. 231, 250, 430, 441, 486
Richards, J.C. 15
rights
    bilingual education 197
    heritage language education 248
    indigenous languages 253, 255
    language-as-a-right 433–440
    literacy for empowerment 346
    Native American languages 253
    status planning 87
    territorial principle 52
    United States 196

RIOT assessment 386
Ritchie, C. 72
Rock Point Community School 254
Rodgers, T.S. 15
Roibeaird, F.N. 249
Rojo, L.M. 144–145
Rolstad, K. 116, 182–183, 276, 288
Romaine, S. 48, 431
Romania 110
Romansh 265
Ronjat, J. 107
Roosevelt, Theodore 442, 452
Rosa, J. 12, 15, 31, 141
Rosen, R. 421
Rosetta Stone 134
Rossell, C.A. 275
RSFC (resting-state functional connectivity) 166
Ruben, R.J. 393
Rubin, H. 8
Rubinyi, S. 369, 375
Rubio, Marco 443
Ruiz, R. 430, 433
Rumbaut, R.G. 108, 441, 452, 453, 456, 460
rural areas 328, 468, 483
Rusher, M. 419
Russian 68, 146, 171, 212
Ryan, L. 135
Ryukyu people 51

Saer, D.J. 153, 271
Salaberry, M.R. 246, 452, 457
salad bowl metaphor 454
Salgado, A.K. 227
Sallabank, J. 431, 438
sampling 295
Sampson, Hazel M. 78
Sanchez, M.T. 244–245, 384, 385
Sandler, W. 399
Savignon, S.J. 16
Sayer, P. 6
scaffolding 115, 139, 311, 312, 318–321, 342, 343, 369
Scandinavia 232, 267, 441, 473
Schleppegrell, M. 183, 186, 288
Schluter, A.A. 468
Schmidt, R.S. 442, 445–446, 454–455
Schönström, K. 416
school leadership 330
schooling *see also* classrooms; elementary schools; secondary schools; teachers
  assimilationism 193–194
  community heritage language classes 132–133
  Deaf-signing people 411–413
  diglossia and transglossia 53
  early development of bilingualism 102
  effective classrooms for bilingual students 303–337
  language planning 86
  and language shift 60, 95
  shift towards English 72
  trilingual 110–113
science of reading (SOR) 341, 342
Scotland 58, 438, 468, 476
Seal of Biliteracy 204–205, 209, 211, 242, 340, 446
Seals, C.A. 146
second generation migrants 6, 56
second language as medium of instruction 231, 242, 261, 264, 321–326 *see also* immersion programs
second language instructional competence (SLIC) 183
second language learning 126–150
secondary schools 136, 241, 242, 252, 254, 261
segregated learning 228, 437, 453
self-assessment 30–31, 35
self-awareness 36
self-confidence 131, 225, 350
'self-contained ESL' classrooms 227
self-determination 62–63, 92, 267, 346, 434, 438, 450
self-esteem 36, 122, 131, 154, 225, 291, 306, 323, 331, 374, 375, 433
Selleck, C. 468
Seltzer, K. 183
semilinguals 11
semi-speakers 91–92
Senate Bill 1014 200, 229
separate shortage hypothesis 159
separate underlying proficiency (SUP) model 178
separation of languages 118, 244, 309, 313, 322, 328, 351, 455
separatist bilingual education 221, 232
sequential bilingualism 3, 102, 126–150
Seward, K. 368
Shanahan, T. 277, 316, 342, 347, 348, 349, 350, 351
shared storage hypothesis 159
sheltered content instruction 23, 214, 221, 225, 227–229, 262, 318–319
sheltered English immersion (SEI) 227–229, 258, 351
Sheltered Instruction Observation Protocol (SIOP) 227, 319
Shi, X. 430–431
shift, language 33, 51, 55–58, 72, 92–97, 118
Shin, S. 457, 466
Shohamy, E. 37, 38, 92, 386
siblings 104, 107, 339
sign languages 390–427
Sign Supported Speech 407
signacy 394, 414
sign-mediated strategies 417, 418
Simms, L. 419, 422, 434
Simons, G.F. 93

simultaneous bilingualism 3, 102–105, 126–150, 355 *see also* early development of bilingualism
simultaneous biliteracy development 352–353
Simultaneous Communication 400, 407
Singapore 72, 261, 431
Singh, M. 204
Singleton, D.M. 135, 136
skills approach to biliteracy 341–342, 346
Skutnabb-Kangas, T. 179, 221, 222, 233, 433, 436
Slavin, R.E. 276, 347
Slavkov, N. 107
sleeping languages 56, 91
Slovenia 232, 443, 472
Smarter Balanced Assessment Consortium 203
Smith, H.A. 341
Smith, N.R. 60
Smith Jones, Chief Marie 78
Snow, C.E. 330
social class
   dual language programs 245
   early development of bilingualism 107
   European Schools movement 265
   funds of knowledge 361
   heritage language education 249
   immersion programs 259, 322
   occupational bilingualism 468–470
   US bilingual education 213, 441
social competence 8
social desirability measurement of bilingualism 36
social engineering 246
social justice 326–327, 435
social media
   and bilingual education 476–480
   Deaf-signing people 414, 417
   language rights 434
   multilingualism 68
   multiliteracies 355
   reversing language shift 96
   social competence 8
   and superdiversity 64
   translanguaging 54
social networks 34, 48, 95, 96
social varieties of language 65–66
socialization 143
societal bilingualism 2, 47–76
sociocultural competence 15, 16, 241, 259, 330
sociocultural contexts 147, 158–159, 181, 314–315, 331–332, 346, 383
sociocultural literacy approach 343–344
sociocultural theory of learning 311
socioculturally supportive environments 331
socioeconomic factors
   bilingual education 196, 281
   cognition 157, 158, 172
   effectiveness of bilingual education 272

high expectations 334
language-as-a-problem orientation 432
and learning difficulties 374
occupational bilingualism 468
US bilingual education 213
sociolinguistics 2, 14–17, 47–76
Solís, J.L. 38
Song, K.H. 358
South Africa 62, 89, 271, 435
South Korea 145
Southeast Asia 110, 133, 432, 458, 474
Spanglish 118, 446
Spanish
   bilingual education 194–195, 222, 231
   in Catalonia 260
   dual language programs 246
   economic value of 70, 486
   fingerspelling 414–415
   as a global language 231
   as heritage US language 251
   hiring practices 470
   and the internet 68, 477
   language as a resource 440–442
   language as a right 434
   language background scales 33
   Latinx identity 457
   Paraguay 50
   powerful majority languages 59, 73
   proficiency measures 284
   Puerto Rico 59
   Race to the Top (RTTT) 203
   statistics on speakers 68
   teaching staff 230
   transglossia 52
   translanguaging 312
   TV/film 474–475
   United States 33, 58, 108, 110, 138, 186, 192, 195, 198, 203, 212, 230, 307, 309, 313, 333–334, 355, 370, 377, 433, 434, 441, 443, 445–446, 475, 480, 486
   varieties of 65
   world language teaching 232
Sparks, R.L. 350
spatial semantics 136
special education 23, 375–377
special educational needs 215–216, 272, 281, 366–389
specially designed academic instruction in English (SDAIE) 227, 318–319
specific language impairment (SLI) 375
speech acts 15
speech communities 15, 48, 222
speech/language impairments 368–372
Spolsky, B. 59, 95
Spotti, M. 64, 73
spread, language 56, 67–68
St Lambert, Canada 255–256
standard varieties 65, 345, 435

standardization 81, 87, 96, 242, 261
standardized, named varieties 12
standardized language proficiency tests 11
Stanford Center for Assessment, Learning, and Equity 16
Statistics Canada 257
statistics on bilingualism 48, 68, 102
status planning 85, 87
Stavans, I. 118
Steele, J.L. 285–286, 293
Stein-Smith, K. 127
Stepanova Sachs, O. 171
Stephenson, Howard 292–293
Sternberg, R.J. 154
stigmatization 65, 226, 228, 255
Stokoe, William 408
strategic competence 15, 16
Street, B.V. 339, 344
'strong' forms of bilingual education
   effective classrooms for bilingual students 314
   effectiveness of bilingual education 237–269, 275, 291–292
   empowerment 462
   gentrification of 215
   language-as-a-problem orientation 433
   types of bilingual education 220, 221
   United States 213, 214
Strubell, M. 487
structured English immersion (SEI) 200, 256, 258
structured literacy 341
'Students' Right to Their Own Language' (SRTOL) 435
'students with interrupted formal education' (SIFE) 215
subjective experience of multilingualism 4–5, 36
submersion programs 195, 197, 214, 221, 224–226, 377, 437
subtitling 473, 474
subtractive bilingualism 4, 13, 53, 129, 138, 155, 205, 323, 351, 475
Suh, E. 369
Sultana, S. 71
summative assessment 24
superación (self-actualization) 143
superdiversity 63–64, 81, 454
Supporting Young Language Learners' Access to Bilingual Education' (SYLLABLE) Act 2020 (US) 209
supra-ethnic nation states 62
supranationalism 63, 64, 264
Supreme Court (US) 194, 225, 362, 437
Swahili 481
Swain, M. 16, 260, 286, 288, 311, 325
Sweden 110, 310, 416
Switzerland 222, 265, 431
syncretism 355
synthetic phones 341

Taiwanese Sign Language 399
Takanishi, R. 278, 316, 347, 351, 368, 371, 373, 379, 381, 385
Talbot, K.R. 262
Tampuen 87
Tankersley, D. 247–248
Tannenbaum, M. 139
Tanton, John 444, 445
Taura, H. 108
Taushiro 78
Te Kohanga Reo 248, 249, 438
te reo Māori 54, 79, 248, 249, 438, 457
teacher auxiliaries 242 *see also* teaching assistants
teacher observations 382
teachers
   anti-racist education 332–333
   bilingual 227, 230, 242, 258, 317, 322, 329
   biliteracy 330
   caretaker speech 324
   credentials 317
   Deaf-signing people 402, 412, 422–423
   diverse backgrounds 470
   dual language programs 242
   Education Teacher Preparation Assessment (EdTPA) 182
   effectiveness of bilingual education 329–330
   encouraging bilingualism 129
   language attitudes 213
   language planning 90
   language policies 429
   language strategies 324–326
   mainstreaming programs 317–318
   monolingual bilingual education 223
   mother tongue literacy support 348
   No Child Left Behind (NCLB) 201
   pre-service training 323
   professional development 330–331
   quality of education 214
   sheltered content instruction 227
   sign languages 394–395, 408, 422–423
   sociocultural competence 330
   special educational needs 376
   strategies for motivating learners 141
   training 259, 317, 323, 330–331, 379–380, 408
   training in ESL 227
   translanguaging 38, 310, 312
teaching assistants 317, 357, 376
'teaching to the test' 37, 342
Teams, Microsoft 476, 478
Tedick, D.J. 259
Telegu 6
Téllez, K. 329, 330
territorial principle 52
terrorism 129
Terry, S. 402–403
TESOL (Teachers of English to Speakers of Other Languages) 146, 183

standardization 81, 87, 96, 242, 261
standardized, named varieties 12
standardized language proficiency tests 11
Stanford Center for Assessment, Learning, and Equity 16
Statistics Canada 257
statistics on bilingualism 48, 68, 102
status planning 85, 87
Stavans, I. 118
Steele, J.L. 285–286, 293
Stein-Smith, K. 127
Stepanova Sachs, O. 171
Stephenson, Howard 292–293
Sternberg, R.J. 154
stigmatization 65, 226, 228, 255
Stokoe, William 408
strategic competence 15, 16
Street, B.V. 339, 344
'strong' forms of bilingual education
　effective classrooms for bilingual students 314
　effectiveness of bilingual education 237–269, 275, 291–292
　empowerment 462
　gentrification of 215
　language-as-a-problem orientation 433
　types of bilingual education 220, 221
　United States 213, 214
Strubell, M. 487
structured English immersion (SEI) 200, 256, 258
structured literacy 341
'Students' Right to Their Own Language' (SRTOL) 435
'students with interrupted formal education' (SIFE) 215
subjective experience of multilingualism 4–5, 36
submersion programs 195, 197, 214, 221, 224–226, 377, 437
subtitling 473, 474
subtractive bilingualism 4, 13, 53, 129, 138, 155, 205, 323, 351, 475
Suh, E. 369
Sultana, S. 71
summative assessment 24
superación (self-actualization) 143
superdiversity 63–64, 81, 454
Supporting Young Language Learners' Access to Bilingual Education' (SYLLABLE) Act 2020 (US) 209
supra-ethnic nation states 62
supranationalism 63, 64, 264
Supreme Court (US) 194, 225, 362, 437
Swahili 481
Swain, M. 16, 260, 286, 288, 311, 325
Sweden 110, 310, 416
Switzerland 222, 265, 431
syncretism 355
synthetic phones 341

Taiwanese Sign Language 399
Takanishi, R. 278, 316, 347, 351, 368, 371, 373, 379, 381, 385
Talbot, K.R. 262
Tampuen 87
Tankersley, D. 247–248
Tannenbaum, M. 139
Tanton, John 444, 445
Taura, H. 108
Taushiro 78
Te Kohanga Reo 248, 249, 438
te reo Māori 54, 79, 248, 249, 438, 457
teacher auxiliaries 242 *see also* teaching assistants
teacher observations 382
teachers
　anti-racist education 332–333
　bilingual 227, 230, 242, 258, 317, 322, 329
　biliteracy 330
　caretaker speech 324
　credentials 317
　Deaf-signing people 402, 412, 422–423
　diverse backgrounds 470
　dual language programs 242
　Education Teacher Preparation Assessment (EdTPA) 182
　effectiveness of bilingual education 329–330
　encouraging bilingualism 129
　language attitudes 213
　language planning 90
　language policies 429
　language strategies 324–326
　mainstreaming programs 317–318
　monolingual bilingual education 223
　mother tongue literacy support 348
　No Child Left Behind (NCLB) 201
　pre-service training 323
　professional development 330–331
　quality of education 214
　sheltered content instruction 227
　sign languages 394–395, 408, 422–423
　sociocultural competence 330
　special educational needs 376
　strategies for motivating learners 141
　training 259, 317, 323, 330–331, 379–380, 408
　training in ESL 227
　translanguaging 38, 310, 312
teaching assistants 317, 357, 376
'teaching to the test' 37, 342
Teams, Microsoft 476, 478
Tedick, D.J. 259
Telegu 6
Téllez, K. 329, 330
territorial principle 52
terrorism 129
Terry, S. 402–403
TESOL (Teachers of English to Speakers of Other Languages) 146, 183

testing accommodations 296, 383–385
Texas 370
text messages 8
Thai 49, 247
Thailand 247, 432
thinking abilities 171, 317, 318, 343
Thiong'o, Ngugi wa 433–434
third-generation migrants 56
'third spaces' 4
Thomas, W.P. 281–282, 309, 316
Thomason, S.G. 59, 81, 96
Thomas-Sunesson, D. 172
Thornwood Public Schools 358
Thoutenhoofd, E. 393
threshold theory 164, 179
Tian, Z. 312
Tigert, J. 310
Title VII Bilingual Education Act 195, 196–198, 201, 210, 229–330
TOEFL (Test of English as a Foreign Language) 26–27
To'Hajiilee Community school 254
Torrance, E.P. 163
Total Communication (TC) 407, 417
total immersion programs 255–256
Toukomaa, P. 179
tourism 9, 129, 467, 468, 471–472
trade 129, 440, 441, 467–468, 480, 481, 482 *see also* business purposes, language for
transdisciplinary framework for second language acquisition 146–148
transfer 162, 171, 325, 349–350
Transformative Education Context Paradigm 361
transformative pedagogy 307, 462
transglossia 52
transitional bilingual education (TBE) 196, 220, 221, 222, 229–231, 275, 282, 283
translanguaging
  in academic settings 186
  in a bilingual classroom 53, 244–245, 309–314, 327
  bilingual education 222
  biliteracy development 348
  in the classroom 307–309
  Common European Framework of Reference (CEFR) 31
  communicative competence 31
  critical post-structuralist sociolinguistics 74
  Deaf-signing people 415–416
  debates 116
  dual language programs 244
  dynamic bilingualism 13, 54
  early development of bilingualism 106, 115–121
  language-as-a-resource 442
  in monolingual classrooms 223
  multiliteracies 356
  postmodernism 116
  scaffolding 321, 322
  and self-assessment 35–36
  in sheltered instruction 227
  stance, design and shifts 311, 313
  teachers 38
  by teachers 329
  transglossia 52
translanguaging pedagogy 308, 309–314, 353
translation 121–123, 129, 130, 245, 350, 382, 418, 439, 468, 478, 479
translingual literacy 356
tribal languages 6 *see also* indigenous languages
trilingual education 191, 265
trilingualism 110–113
Troike, R.C. 273, 274
Trump, Donald 39, 70, 207, 209, 233, 434, 443, 445, 475
Trump, Melania 443
Truth and Reconciliation Commission of Canada 59, 253
Tsilhqot'in 92
Tsushima, R. 108
Tucker, G.R. 256
Tupas, R. 66, 67, 70
TV/film 134, 473–476
Twin Cities, Minnesota 438
two-way dual language programs 238–239, 252, 278–280, 285, 334
Two-Way Immersion Observation Protocol (TWIOP) 227
types of bilingual education 219–236
typology of program models 221–223

Ukraine 146
Ukrainian 146, 251
Ulpan courses 133
Umansky, I.M. 282, 284, 316
underachievement 213–216
unequal Englishes 66
UNESCO 48, 68, 80, 81, 84, 93, 305–306, 376, 436
UNICEF 331, 348
United Kingdom
  assessment 14, 37
  communicative language testing 27
  community heritage language classes 132, 133
  European Schools movement 264
  immigrant languages 53
  literacy standards 341
  non-English films/TV 474–475
  pull-out/push-in EAL support 225
  special educational needs 376
  teaching assistants 317
  world language deficit 128
  world language teaching 231, 441–442
United Nations 468

United Nations Convention on the Rights of the Child 436
United Nations Declaration on the Rights of Indigenous Peoples 436
United States
  African-American English 65
  assessment 14, 37
  assimilationism 130, 193, 213–214, 441, 442–446, 451–452
  bilingual education 219–236, 271, 328
  bilingual teachers 317, 329–330
  bilingualism 108
  bilingualism without diglossia 50
  Chinese 70, 194, 195, 213
  classroom support for bilinguals 318
  Common Core State Standards 182
  communicative language testing 27
  community heritage language classes 132, 133
  content-based instruction (CBI) 262
  cues to language choices 6
  Deaf bilingual education 411–413
  Deaf-signing people 392–394, 419
  effectiveness of bilingual education 272–278
  ELLs in mainstream classrooms 316
  English 137, 442, 444–446, 456–457
  English as medium of instruction 54
  English literacy levels 340
  evidence-based policy making 293–294, 297, 341–342
  exclusion from schooling 233
  heritage languages 130, 249, 250–251
  high-stakes language testing 37
  history of bilingual education 190–218
  immersion programs 256, 328
  immigrant languages 52, 53
  indigenous languages 42, 192, 201, 253–255
  inequality 485–486
  language censuses 39–44
  language conflict 61
  'language graveyard' 456
  language loss in children 138
  language policies 84
  language revitalization 54
  language rights 436–438
  language shift and maintenance 58
  language-as-a-problem orientation 432
  literacy instruction 341–342
  long-term English language learners (LTELL) 11
  mainstreaming programs 225–226, 318
  monolingual ideologies 11, 135, 138, 354
  nationalism 62
  non-English films/TV 474–475
  non-standard varieties 435
  occupational bilingualism 467–468
  pluralist ideologies 451–452, 455
  problem/resource/rights views 442–446
  proficiency standards 184
  second language learning 137
  sign languages 401–402
  Spanish 33, 58, 108, 110, 138, 186, 192, 195, 198, 203, 213, 230, 307, 309, 313, 333–334, 355, 370, 377, 433, 434, 441, 443–444, 445–446, 475, 480, 486
  special educational needs 372–373, 375, 378–381
  statistics on languages 209, 212–213, 239
  testing accommodations 384–385
  transglossia 52
  trilingual education 110
  United States 475
  WIDA Consortium 7–8, 24
  world language deficit 128, 130
  world language teaching 231, 441–442
Universal Declaration of Linguistic Rights 84
university-level bilingual education 223
Univision 475
untranslatable concepts 119
Unz, Ron 198
urbanization 56, 58, 60, 455, 458
Urdu 59, 481
Urow, C. 348–349
US Committee on Education and Labor 276–277
US English (organization) 445
US Native American Languages Act 1990 84
Utah 292–293

Vaid, J. 165
Valázquez, I. 108
Valdés, G. 4, 9, 11, 38, 61, 121–122, 138, 182, 205, 229, 241, 245, 250, 368–369, 450
Valentino, R.A. 283–284
Van Cleve, J.V. 405–406
Van Hout, T. 473
Varghese, M. 329, 330
Vernon, McCay 407, 408, 422
Vertovec, S. 63
videoconferencing 476–477, 478
Vietnamese 481
viewing (as mode of communication) 8
Vigouroux, C. 470
Visual Communication Sign Language Checklist (VCSL) 421
visual perception 393, 410–411, 414, 415–416
vocabulary
  domain-specific 122
  explicit teaching of 326
  immersion programs 324
  infant bilingual development 103
  and the internet 478
  learning 161
  lexical access 157, 161
  monolinguals' versus bilinguals' 156–157
  status planning 87

Vogt, M. 380
voice recordings 478
Vygotsky, L. 318, 343

W3Techs 68
Wagner, E. 28, 29
Wales
    assessment 14
    bilingual education 191, 222, 271
    cross-cultural competence 314–315
    diglossia 51
    grassroots movement 438
    heritage language education 251, 252
    immersion programs 259
    language rights 437
    status planning 88
    translanguaging 309
    world language teaching 231
Wang, X.-L. 111
'weak' forms of bilingual education
    Deaf-signing people 412–413
    effective classrooms for bilingual students 315–321
    effectiveness of bilingual education 275, 291–292
    theories of bilingualism 179
    types of bilingual education 220, 221, 229–232
    United States 197, 214
Weber, J.-J. 87, 89, 92, 265–266
Wedin, A 310
Welsh
    anti-bilingualism 152
    bilingual education 191, 216, 323
    domains 51
    English cognates 156
    figures of speech 16
    heritage language education 251
    identity 457
    intensive language learning 134
    newcomers 228
    revitalization 58, 90
    status planning 87, 88
    translanguaging 115
    TV/film 476
Wermelinger, S. 169–170
Werner, H. 393
WestEd 316, 380
Western, educated, industrialized, rich and democratic (WEIRD) bias 154, 155

What Works Clearinghouse (WWC) 294
white gaze 12
Whorf hypothesis 171, 173
WIDA Consortium 7–8, 24, 184–185, 186, 204, 384
Wiese, A.-M. 195, 196, 197
Wikipedia 477
Wiley, T.G. 11, 14, 59, 85, 117, 132, 182–183, 194, 195, 201, 233, 248, 249, 250, 251, 430, 440, 445, 451, 453, 455, 460
Williams, C. 13, 114, 115, 309, 310, 312, 415–416, 438
Williams, C.H. 90, 216
Williams, C.P. 200
Willig, A.C. 273, 274, 275
Wilson, Junius 410–411
withdrawal lessons 225–226
Wolsey, J.L.A. 416
women 430 *see also* gender
Woodbridge, W.C. 404, 424
Wôpanâak 91
World Bank 291
World Englishes 66, 73, 459
World Federation of the Deaf 395, 397
world languages teaching 231, 238, 440
worldviews, influence of languages on 171
Wright, W.E. 13, 26, 58, 59, 110, 129, 130, 133, 138, 139, 201, 221, 223, 224, 225, 226, 227, 228, 230, 231, 232, 250, 308, 312–313, 321, 326, 341, 348, 357, 372, 381, 385, 430, 434, 437, 441, 442, 452, 455, 471
writing proficiency 326, 417
writing systems 168, 348, 350, 357
written forms, development 87, 96

Yarborough, Ralph 195
Yiddish 58, 92, 250
Young, Don 209
YouTube 476
Yurtsever, A. 173

Zaire 110
Zangwill, I. 452
Zappert, L.T. 273, 274
Zeshan, U. 399
Zhang, L.J. 415–416
zone of proximal development (ZPD) 318–319, 343
Zoom 476, 478
Zuckerman, G. 91